# The Variety Almanac 1999

## The Editors of *Variety*

*Variety Inc.*
Peter Bart, Vice President, Editor-in-Chief
Gerry Byrne, Group Vice President, Publisher

*The Variety Almanac*
Book Editor: Peter Cowie
Managing Editors: Leonard Klady (U.S.), Damjana Finci (U.K.)
Copy Editor: John Adair

BXTREE

# MACMILLAN

First published 1999 by Boxtree
an imprint of Macmillan Publishers Ltd
25 Eccleston Place London SW1W 9NF,
Basingstoke and Oxford

Associated companies throughout the world

ISBN 0 7522 2454 9

Copyright © 1999 *Variety, Inc.*

Picture credits for plate section: Braveworld: page 16
*bottom*; Dream Works Pictures: page 4 *bottom*;
FSP/Gamma: page 16; Henry Deas III: pages 9, 10 *top*;
Joan Marcus: pages 12 *bottom*, 13 *top*; Mathew
Photographic Services: page 11; Meridian Broadcasting:
page 14; Michael Le Poer Trench: page 13 *bottom left*;
Miramax Films: pages 4, 6; Miramax International: page
2 *bottom*; MTV Europe: page 15; October Films: page 5
*bottom*; Performing Arts Library: page 13 *bottom right*;
Sundance Channel: page 1 *top*; Twentieth Century Fox:
pages 3, 7 *bottom*; United Artists: page 1 *bottom*;
Warner Bros.: pages 7 *top*, 8 *top left*.

9 8 7 6 5 4 3 2 1

A CIP catalogue record for this book is available from
the British Library.

Designed by: Dan Newman
Printed by: Mackays of Chatham plc, Chatham, Kent

# Acknowledgements

The editors would like to thank the following individuals and organisations
for their kind co-operation during the preparation of this book:

Bruce Apar, *Video Business*
Peter Bart
Michael Billington
British Video Association
Gerry Byrne
Nick Burfitt
Gennaro Castaldo, HMV
Derek Elley
Liza Foreman
Beatriz Goyoaga
Alex Hamilton
Doug Hopper
Clare Hulton
Charles Isherwood
Keith Sherman & Associates Inc
Anthony Knight, Blockbuster
Nicole Kyriacou, MTV Networks Europe
Geoffrey Macnab
Peter Matcham, CIN
Mediametrie
Tim Murray, Timecode
Thomas O'Neil
Jack Pitman
Nora Rawlinson, *Publishers Weekly*
David Rooney
Adam Sandler
Adrian Sington
Michael Speier
Mary Sutter
Michelle Todman
Howard Watson, Society of London Theatre
Cecilia Zecchinelli

# Contents

# Introduction

It's an axiom of show business that resilience and adaptability are the keys to survival. Those entertainers with "staying power" have managed to make the shift from vaudeville to radio or from radio to television to film and then, inevitably, into the great playground of cyberspace.

In its nearly century-long history, *Variety*, too, has demonstrated its talent for shifting gears. Started as a repository for vaudeville news and reviews, it responded to the winds of change not only in its ever-expanding coverage, but also in its traditionally quirky headlines. *Variety* banners have run the gamut from "Sticks Nix Hick Pix" (1935) and "Wall St. Lays an Egg" (1929) to "Lizards Eat Arnold's Lunch" (1993) and "Pic Biz Freaked by Cybergeek's Leaks" (1997).

People often ask me why *Variety* has maintained its "attitude," not only in headlines, but also in its style of reporting, even to the point of building its own arcane vocabulary. People don't quit their jobs in *Variety*, they "ankle" them. A show doesn't open to good business in the pages of *Variety*; unless it's "boffo" it's downright disappointing.

From the outset, *Variety*'s reporters and editors realized they were covering show business, not issues of national security, hence the insistence on bringing a bit of levity to the table. Then, too, *Variety* was founded as the voice of the working entertainer, not the corporate "suit." Its lexicon thus reflected Shubert Alley, not the Harvard Business School.

And the "attitude" worked. Over the years, *Variety* has not only continually regenerated itself, but has also spun off new ventures. The Weekly gave birth in 1933 to *Daily Variety*, published in Los Angeles. That publication last year spawned a sister newspaper, *Daily Variety Gotham*, published each day in New York City. Also born last year was Variety.com, which firmly planted *Variety* onto the web.

All these publications were created in the knowledge that what was once the entertainment industry has been transformed into the global media and entertainment industry. Show business has become inextricably linked with information and technology. And if there's one single trait that defines the practitioners of this industry, it's that they are news junkies – they have an insatiable need for information that they can digest and act upon. Surely there are few sectors of the global economy that are as volatile as this industry, or as open to innovation and change. As the millennium draws to an end, it is *Variety*'s mission not only to meet these information needs, but to serve where possible as the connective tissue between the world's media communities.

In accomplishing this, to be sure, there is a primary need for objectivity and integrity. No newspaper can maintain its viability if it appears to play favorites or to propagate disinformation. This responsibility weighs heavily on *Variety*'s editors and reporters, all of whom want to "get it first," but also, and more importantly, to get it right. The qualifications of *Variety*'s writers have changed markedly in recent years as their jobs have become more demanding. Not only are higher educational credentials de rigueur, but substantial experience on other respected journals also is required. It takes sharp minds to penetrate the blizzard of information and misinformation that confronts the typical *Variety* reporter on a daily basis. It is a demanding job because, in writing their pieces, they know full well that any errors they may make will be replicated over and over again by the general press, who look upon *Variety* as a primary information source.

There have been many occasions when *Variety* has been under pressure to "cooperate" with a major industry power player or advertiser, going back to the days a couple of generations ago when some major producers would open a play, get it reviewed and then promptly cut back the size of the orchestra, cast, and even the chorus line. *Variety*'s reviewers would revisit the shows a week or so after the opening and re-review it until they were banned from the theaters. They kept sneaking in and filing their stories anyway.

*Variety* has fought its battles and still maintains its legacy as the "bible of show business," and this scenario will doubtless continue well into the new millennium. After another hundred years or so, the continuing adventures of this "bible" may become downright biblical.

**Peter Bart, Editor-in-Chief**

# Film

Our five personalities of the year illustrate the all-pervasive power of film and the public's awareness of its icons. Had *Beloved* achieved more, we would certainly have included Oprah Winfrey. Instead, we plump for one of Hollywood's least ostentatious individuals, Peter Schneider, for so long the creative engine for Disney's flow of animated features, and for the glory of *The Lion King* on Broadway. Spielberg qualifies by dint not just of his own accomplishment with *Saving Private Ryan*, but also of his part in the rise and rise of DreamWorks. Di Caprio represents one kind of star, a soaring talent so associated with the triumph of *Titanic*. Cage, on the other hand, has had to claw his way up the ladder over the past fifteen years, to become one of Hollywood's most versatile actors. Finally, Roberto Benigni, who has swept all before him with the controversial *Life is Beautiful*, could now make almost any film he wished – and still be a European!

## Personalities of the Year

### Roberto Benigni

Chaplin managed it with *The Great Dictator*, Lubitsch followed suit with *To Be Or Not To Be*, Mel Brooks attempted it with the *Springtime For Hitler* routine in *The Producers*, but squeezing laughs out of the Nazi genocide remains a perilous business. When Italian actor-director-comedian Roberto Benigni embarked on *Life is Beautiful* (*La vita è bella*), a romantic comedy set against the backcloth of the Holocaust, the potential for embarrassment was immense. Benigni readily admits that many of his friends and associates warned him "Don't do it please!"

By the end of 1998, when *Life is Beautiful* had been feted at festivals everywhere from Cannes to Jerusalem, from Toronto to Vancouver, and had already grossed around $10 million in the U.S., $40 million in Italy and $20 million in France, Benigni could finally feel vindicated. Not only had the film consolidated his position as one of Italy's top box-office draws. It had at last enabled him to make an international breakthrough.

Not that Benigni was exactly unknown. A former magician's assistant and singer who first caught the public's eye with monologues and underground theater performances in the mid-1970s, he has long been a household name in his native Italy. His earlier movies, notably *Johnny Stecchino* and *The Little Devil*, were big hits in Italy. Thanks to his

appearances in Jim Jarmusch films, he also had a cult following in the U.S.. You may remember him behind the wheel in *Night On Earth* (he played a fast-talking Roman taxi driver with an unholy passion for sheep) or as the oddball convict in Jarmusch's *Down By Law*. You might also have seen him as the hapless detective in the Blake Edwards comedy, *The Son of the Pink Panther* (1993), a film in which he shone in Peter Sellers' shoes, but which had far too threadbare a script to make much impact. (It grossed less than $3 million in the U.S.)

In *Life is Beautiful*, his usual effervescence is only slightly dampened by the grim nature of the material. He stars as a Jewish-Italian waiter thrown into a Nazi death camp along with his young son Giosue (played with doe-eyed charm by the Jackie Coogan-like newcomer, Giorgio Cantarini). That's in the second half of the movie. The first half unfolds like a conventional romantic comedy, complete with Mack Sennett-style slapstick, as we see Benigni wooing the beautiful Dora (played by his real-life wife Nicoletta Braschi) away from a jackbooted local fascist.

The film was released in Italy just before Christmas 1997. Not long afterwards, Miramax picked up the international rights from Cecchi Gori for a reported $7 million. Benigni acknowledges that without Harvey Weinstein's enthusiastic championing, the movie would have struggled to crack the U.S. When it was unveiled in Cannes in a cut eight minutes shorter than the one seen in Italian cinemas, sceptics tutted that Weinstein must have been meddling. Benigni denies that he was bullied into making changes by the Miramax supremo. The re-editing was intended to improve the rhythm of the storytelling in the first half of the film. The second half, he insists, remains exactly the same.

Although Benigni was born in 1952, there is a strong autobiographical undertow to *Life is Beautiful*. His father, a Tuscan farmer sent off to fight with the Italian army in Albania during the Second World War, was imprisoned by the Nazis in a labour camp after the Italian Armistice of 1943. "When he came back two years later, he was a skeleton – only 35 kilos. He was like a crazy man, like a dead man."

Benigni remembers that his father was haunted by his experiences. "But when he started – unconsciously maybe because I and my sister were terrified by his stories – to talk about it in a lighter way, he was able to smile, and he stopped having nightmares."

Benigni has been accused of trivializing the Holocaust and of lapsing into extreme sentimentality. He argues that what happened during the Nazi genocide was a tragedy so inexpressible that it belongs to everybody. His humour, he points out, is seldom cruel. "When you think about St. Francis – he was laughing in front of somebody who was dying, but in a very light and wonderful way. He was trying to make the man happy before he died."

He cites the film's reception at the Jerusalem Film Festival, where it won four awards, as the strongest endorsement of what he was trying to do. "I don't know if silence can have a quality, but the quality of the silence during that screening was unbearable for me," he says. "I remember there was one minute of silence at the end of the screening, which seems like an infinitely long time, and then they started applauding in rhythm."

As 1998 drew to an end, Benigni added both Best Actor and Best Picture prizes at the European Film Awards to the Grand Jury prize he had already won at Cannes. It was also announced that Martin Scorsese and Italian producer Vittorio Cecchi Gori were joining forces to present a season of his films in LA, another sign of his new-found popularity in the U.S. Whatever else, he was a publicist's dream. He conducted press conferences and interviews as if they were improvisational comedy slots and seemed capable of charming any audience. There is

certainly nobody who enjoys winning prizes quite as much as he does. As he puts it, "I explode with joy, I radiate gladness. There are people who throw roses. I throw myself – yes – as a rose – in front of whoever loves me!"

Benigni has appeared in only one other feature since *Life is Beautiful* – the expensive new French production of *Asterix et Obelix*, in which he co-stars opposite Gérard Depardieu and Christian Clavier. He hopes to work with Jarmusch again and acknowledges that "the English language is becoming the language of the movies." Whether or not he'll defect to Hollywood remains to be seen. His own English is as idiosyncratic as ever. He also remains fiercely patriotic. "Italian," he proclaims, "is my language, my soul, my culture, my roots, my life." **Geoffrey Macnab**

## Nicolas Cage

At the world premiere of Paramount's *Snake Eyes*, studio topper Sherry Lansing gave a heady compliment to the pic's star.

"It's quite simple," Lansing told the audience upon his introduction. "I wish all of our movies could star Nicolas Cage."

It's a good bet that the majority of Hollywood's heavy hitters feel the same way. For in the past few years, the 35-year-old, Oscar-winning thesp has transformed himself from an awkward eccentric who was far more respectable than bankable into a commercial draw whose involvement virtually guarantees a producer or director will get his project made.

From Oscar glory for *Leaving Las Vegas* in 1996 to box-office A list with the 1997 duo of *Con Air* and *Face/Off*, Cage proved himself at the top of his game in craft and business acumen. It just got better in '98 and shows no signs of abating.

This year, Warner Bros.' *City of Angels* opened with $15 million in April '98 and ended up with a $78 million domestic take and a $210 million international haul. Co-starring Meg Ryan, the Brad Silberling pic was Cage's first non-pyro dramatic film in almost two years, and it reminded the community that he cannot be pigeonholed or second guessed. Just when audiences and critics may have tired of his bang-up, Rambo-esque heroics, he carried a solemn tale about lost love and missed opportunities.

Then, in August, came *Snake Eyes*, Brian De Palma's kinetic look at mistaken identity. And while the helmer's Hitchcock-style comeback wasn't the blockbuster many had anticipated, it underscored once again Cage's affinity toward showy roles.

As hyperactive cop Rick Santoro, Cage brought his offbeat brand of seriocomic passion to a fairly standard character. Corrupt detectives in the movies may not be portraits of originality, but Cage's approach was full of buoyant sizzle. In particular, the opening scene (which De Palma shot in one, unedited take) showcases a charming, cocky and frenzied police officer who can't sit still and lives for attention.

Cage's '98 double play was clearly a snapshot of his career. In both films he plays a free spirit who takes risks and jeopardizes normalcy. That's a familiar position for the actor, who has combined that rebelliousness with a brooding intimacy. Sometimes a dark knight, sometimes a goofy paramour, there emerges from Cage's methods an unorthodox complexity. Even when people in the film business probably still thought of him as Francis Ford Coppola's nephew, Cage eschewed the ordinary for the unconventional: As a dopey husband in the Coen Bros.' *Raising Arizona* (1987), a lovesick baker in Norman Jewison's *Moonstruck* (1987), or a small time pseudo-Elvis in David Lynch's *Wild at Heart* (1990), Cage cornered the market in oddball personalities and kooky romantics.

It was unquestionably an odd path to that rarefied strata of $20 million players. But unlike such fellow members as Tom Cruise, Mel Gibson, and Jim Carrey, Cage is more apt to roll the dice and rarely comes up with snake eyes. With Cage, there is a "not-knowingness" about his processes and the steps he'll take to develop them. It's a guess as to what he will bring to the job, even if the part seems otherwise predictable.

There's more to him than just box-office muscle, however; he's got real ones, too, and his uninterrupted trio of high-octane actioners (*The Rock, Con Air* and *Face/Off*) in '96 and '97 added to an already enigmatic path. Since 1983's *Valley Girl*, the Long Beach, Calif.-born actor has conquered every genre, from drama (*Birdy*, 1984) to comedy (*Honeymoon in Vegas*, 1992) to romance (*It Could Happen To You*, 1994). That diversity spotlights his allure: His next script can be a big-budget spectacle, a light confection, or an ensemble-led melodrama, and such wide-ranging versatility is surely the key to his success with filmmakers and ticket-buyers. Cage is the rarest of Hollywood players — an outright movie star with a penchant for a challenge who hasn't alienated his audience.

It wasn't always so perfect. His early pics were indeed odd and quirky. He was often the best and most watchable thing in such otherwise misfires as *Amos and Andrew* (1993), *Guarding Tess* (1994), and *Trapped in Paradise* (1994). But even when some of his movies didn't click with auds, something about Cage often did: He played a sweet failure in his uncle Francis' *Peggy Sue Got Married* (1986), he feasted on a live cockroach in Robert Bierman's *Vampire's Kiss* (1989), and he was the perfect fish out of water in John Dahl's noirish *Red Rock West* (1992).

Cage's hits and misses, however erratic the outcomes, certainly readied him for what would become his most celebrated performance. His star turn in Mike Figgis' *Leaving Las Vegas* pushed him to another level in more ways than one. His portrayal of a determined-to-die drunk won him a Golden Globe, an Academy Award and an unobstructed path onto motion-picture power lists. Anyone, as critics pointed out, could have played a boozer, but Cage elevated the character of Ben Sanderson from a down-on-his-luck gutter-dweller to a sympathetic Everyman. Hollywood took notice: Since his trip to "Vegas," Cage's paycheck has steadily increased, and those willing to pay up have multiplied like rabbits.

There will be no cooling down period in 1999. Though his plans to play the lead in Tim Burton's *Superman* have been indefinitely grounded, he continues to find top projects with the town's most distinctive talent. Earlier this year brought *8mm*, directed by Joel Schumacher and written by *Seven* scribe Andrew Kevin Walker. In the murder mystery, Cage played Frank Welles, a man obsessed with the truth behind a snuff film, and the pic's somber tone was tailor-made for the actor's intensity. His next film, *Bringing Out The Dead*, co-starring wife Patricia Arquette, puts him under the helm of Martin Scorsese (for the first time) in the pressured world of paramedics, and he's signed on to portray Howard Hughes in a biopic that will reteam him with De Palma. **Michael Speier**

## Leonardo DiCaprio

1998 was supposed to be Leonardo DiCaprio's year off. Somehow, though, his attempts at keeping a low profile didn't quite work out. As *Titanic* chugged inexorably toward the billion-dollar mark at the box office, he was revealed in its wake as probably the biggest Hollywood phenomenon this side of Rudolph Valentino.

Not only was DiCaprio given much of the credit for *Titanic's* success (all those teenage girls who went to see the movie twice or more weren't coming back for the special effects), he was also named *Entertainment Weekly's* Personality of The Year. *Premiere* ranked him at 25 on its "Top 100" power list. *Playgirl* published naked photographs of him. (He reacted by suing.) He was chosen by *People Magazine* as one of "the 50 most beautiful people in the world."

It was recently calculated that there were close to 500 websites devoted to him. DiCaprio fan clubs mushroomed all over the world. DiCaprio biographies sold by the barrowload. There were angry protests when he failed to earn an Oscar nomination. Academics tried to work out just what he stood for, a sure sign of his growing celebrity. (One, Camille Paglia, noticing his k.d. lang-like fringe, decided his appeal lay in the fact that he looked like a teenage lesbian.)

Even his most obscure films suddenly became marketable. *Total Eclipse* (1995), a low-budget arthouse pic about the French symbolist poet Arthur Rimbaud, enjoyed an extraordinary new lease of life on video, mainly, it seemed, because DiCaprio (who plays Rimbaud) cited it as one of his most important films and took his clothes off to prove the point. "All the girls wanted to see Leonardo naked... their reaction to the film has been a little strange," confessed the movie's Polish director, Agnieszka Holland.

The hysteria surrounding DiCaprio was at its most heightened during the Cannes Film Festival, when Lions Gate Films announced that he had agreed to play the lead in *American Psycho*. He wasn't even in Cannes, but the very notion of America's favourite teen idol as a yuppie psychopath sent the international press into convulsions of excitement.

The fact that his role had previously been earmarked for Christian Bale (the young British star of *Velvet Goldmine*) was overlooked. What had been conceived as a low-budget adaptation of Bret Easton Ellis' controversial novel suddenly swelled up into a $40 million blockbuster. Oliver Stone was lined up as a possible director. This particular bubble soon burst when DiCaprio withdrew from the production, but the furore only served to underline how powerful he had become.

DiCaprio's fee for *Titanic* was said to be $2.5 million. Now, his going rate is reported to be ten times that much. Throughout 1998, his name was linked with dozens of new projects, everything from James Cameron's mooted *Spiderman* film to adaptations of two bestselling novels, *All The Pretty Horses* and *Snow Falling On Cedars*. Thanks to Kubrick's long-gestating *Eyes Wide Shut*, Tom Cruise was out of circulation all year long. DiCaprio was the only other name which seemed to carry the same weight. Even Matt Damon, the year's other golden boy, seemed puny by comparison. As one sardonic journalist noted, "Leonardo has merely to indicate the slightest interest in a film role and the Hollywood executives will sell their own mothers to secure him."

As everybody waited to see which part DiCaprio would choose next, he was busy acting up like a junior member of the Rat Pack. There were accounts of him and his entourage on the town, invariably causing mischief wherever they went. He was behaving with a recklessness which suggested just why why his cameo as the pampered, hotel-wrecking movie star in Woody Allen's *Celebrity* came so easily to him. "He seldom sleeps, so intense is his partying," gossip columnist Liz Smith wrote of him.

The DiCaprio backlash wasn't long in coming. Pointing out that, apart from *Celebrity*, his only other new film of the year was the swashbuckler, *The Man In The Iron Mask*, even *Entertainment Weekly* seemed vexed by the scale of his success. "DiCaprio – or rather, the phenomenon of DiCaprio – is much greater than the sum of his accomplishments," the magazine argued. This wasn't entirely fair. Whether as the lead in *William Shakespeare's Romeo and Juliet*, the junky in *Basketball Diaries*, the mentally disabled Arnie in *What's Eating Gilbert Grape?*, or the son estranged from his brutal stepfather in *This Boy's Life*, DiCaprio has consistently tackled challenging parts in offbeat movies. "I have always been nervous of big-budget studio films," he once told journalists, as if to underline that his role as Jack Dawson in *Titanic* was one of his least characteristic.

It was hardly a surprise when DiCaprio signed up to appear as the backpacker in *The Beach*, Danny Boyle's adaptation of Alex Garland's cult novel set in Thailand. (At $20 million, his paycheck is around half the overall cost of the movie.) Nor should anyone have been startled when Miramax bought the rights to a biopic of Chet Baker, the self-destructive jazz trumpeter, as a vehicle for the young star. Both projects suggest a return to the territory he had explored earlier in his career. Perhaps perversely (given his own success), he still seems to have an affinity with outsiders, losers and dreamers.

---

**...January 4...**
**The Phantom of the Opera** breaks the house record at New York's Majestic Theater two weeks in a row, taking $879,864.

DiCaprio was born in 1974 and grew up in Echo Park, Los Angeles. His parents, who divorced when he was one, were 1960s radicals with close links to the counter-culture. His father, who sold comic books, was friendly with Bukowski and Hubert Selby (author of *Last Exit To Brooklyn*). His acting career began when he was still a kid in an educational show called *Romper Room*, but he left school at 16 and his upbringing can hardly be described as privileged. His background is closer to that of a River Phoenix than to that of the typical Hollywood bratpack star.

What happens to Leonardo now? If he strays too far from the type of romantic hero he played in *Titanic*, he may alienate the millions of teen fans who worship him, but if he doesn't tackle awkward, offbeat roles, he risks seeming bland anyway. Whatever the case, in 1998, he was unassailable as the world's most popular movie star – a singular achievement for somebody who hardly set foot in front of the film cameras all year long. **Geoffrey Macnab**

## Peter Schneider

As Disney heads into the next millennium with competitors snapping at its heels, it's no surprise that a strong management structure remains its highest priority. And that's where Peter Schneider comes in.

Formerly president of Walt Disney Feature Animation and its live-production division, Schneider, 48, was upped in January 1999 to prexy of the studio. With the appointment, Disney gets a veteran creator, producer, and artist, and someone who has been a Mouse House resident for 14 years.

By restructuring its corporate staff, Disney CEO Michael Eisner has placed Schneider among the power elite. In his new position, Schneider will oversee creative development, production, marketing, and distribution of all Disney's entertainment products, including live-action pics, animation, and theater. He will also consult on issues related to all of its theme parks.

The move ushers in a new era at Disney, one in which crossover appeal, multimedia prospects, and emerging international territories are essential parts of its plans. The Magic Kingdom may have been built on fairy tales, but industry insiders and savvy consumers know there's more to Disney's solid foundation than just singing birds.

It also illustrates Eisner's reluctance to sit still while rival studios try to knock Disney from atop

the animation world. While Fox's *Anastasia* (1997) and Warner Bros.' *The Quest for Camelot* (1998) struggled to draw viewers, both raised the threat of serious competition. However, last year's decided challenger was DreamWorks with *Antz* and *The Prince of Egypt* (and *Small Soldiers* to some degree) taking on Disney's supremacy. While nobody would contend that Disney is on the verge of a creative collapse, it's apparent that other runners have joined the race.

Why Schneider? Since he joined Disney in 1985, the studio has undergone a toon rebirth. He came on board after *The Black Cauldron*, and has since developed and shepherded projects that have become aesthetic and financial standards. *Who Framed Roger Rabbit?*, *The Little Mermaid*, *Aladdin*, *Pocahontas* and *Mulan* were all produced during Schneider's tenure to domestic and overseas B.O. success. And artistically, Schneider helped to alert the world that animation is a viable artform: *Beauty and the Beast* was the first animated motion picture ever to be nominated for a best pic Oscar. There have also been technological advancements: Disney was the first to champion the CAPS computer animation system, and its partnership with Pixar has led to blockbusters like *Toy Story* and *A Bug's Life*.

And this could be just the beginning: Some have already suggested that Schneider is the logical replacement should Disney chairman Joe Roth decide not to reup when his contract expires at the end of this year.

Despite all of the coin Schneider's pics have reaped, it's his legit theatrical ties that have separated him from other execs. As the company begins to invade the live-performance arena, someone who is well versed in that world's dynamics and procedural strategies must gather the troops. Earlier in his career, Schneider directed and produced plays and musicals in Chicago, New York, and in London's West End, and he helmed the Olympic Arts Festival in 1984.

But no achievement has symbolized his crossover success as much as *The Lion King*. Under his guidance, the 1994 toon became the studio's most successful release ever and the sixth-highest-grossing domestic title of all time. The pic also scored on the retail front: Tie-in coin reached new highs and product sales related to the film hit levels unparalleled since *Star Wars*.

What symbolized the future of Disney, however, was what happened to the film after its B.O. and homevid shelf-life. Partnered with exec veepee

Thomas Schumacher, who has since been upped to prexy of feature animation and co-prexy of its theatrical productions arm, Schneider guided the film's transition onto the stage: The Broadway production won six 1998 Tony Awards, including Best New Musical, and continues to be a hot draw.

It is this "King"-sized accomplishment that Eisner and Co. hope to reproduce in the next century. If the goal is to stay one step ahead of the competition, then Disney has already made an important first move. By expanding onto Broadway and beyond, Disney can conquer a new medium that is experiencing a fiscal renaissance, is relatively untouched by other studios, and contains endless, lucrative possibilities. Since other studios are waging war on the toon battlefield, then Disney has decided it must extend its reach.

The plan is already paying off: Under the banner of Walt Disney Theatrical Productions, Schneider has overseen an ambitious line-up, including the Elton John–Tim Rice musical *Elaborate Lives: The Legend of Aida* and a Harlem Globetrotters project, *Hoopz.*

As Disney tackles The Boards, it is also prepping a full slate of animated and live-action films which Schneider will navigate. With *Tarzan* and *Toy Story 2* to be released in '99 along with *Bicentennial Man* and *Inspector Gadget*, it will continue to protect its turf. As the '98 box-office leader, its pics nabbed $1.1 billion at home and $1.2 billion overseas; *Armageddon* claimed the title of year's biggest grosser; and *A Bug's Life* outdueled DreamWorks' *Antz* by a hefty take. There were also a Mouse House record-tying five $100 million dollar releases.

But as rosy a financial picture as '98 painted, and though the studio is already well-stocked with high-profile undertakings, Eisner has professed his disappointment with Disney's returns on more than one occasion. In a Jan. letter to shareholders, Eisner wrote, "in too many instances, profits did not mat-erialize from the revenues achieved by our films."

That's Eisner's way of saying '98 may have been a lucrative year, but it *should* have been better. And Peter Schneider is apparently the man to lead the way. **Michael Speier**

## Steven Spielberg

During the press conference for *Saving Private Ryan* at the 1998 Venice Film Festival, Tom Hanks paid his director an unlikely compliment, calling him a "great artist and industrialist." Spielberg looked a little bemused, as if he had just been compared to a Victorian factory owner.

In hindsight, though, the remark seems apt. Spielberg is indeed an *industrialist* – any director who has directed, produced or executive-produced seven of the top-grossing films of all time and is already worth $1 billion (the figure which *Business Week* put on his holdings and investments in a 1998 survey) can hardly be described as anything else.

The year didn't get off to a particularly auspicious start for Spielberg. By his standards, his most recent feature had been a flop. Whether because the storytelling lacked spark or because cinemagoers simply weren't interested in an historical epic about slavery, *Amistad* just didn't register. Spielberg was even accused of plagiarism – more attention was paid to the lawsuit brought against him by novelist Barbara Chase-Riboud than to the film itself. Nobody was suggesting he had lost his grip, but there were murmurings that DreamWorks – the company he, Jeffrey Katzenberg, and David Geffen had formed amid such fanfare in 1994 – was underperforming. And his state of mind can't have been much helped by the discovery that a psychopathic bodybuilder was stalking him.

By the end of 1998, the picture looked very different. The stalker was safely behind bars, DreamWorks was slowly beginning to function like a proper studio, and *Saving Private Ryan* had generated worldwide sales of well over $220 million while also garnering reviews at least as flattering as those lavished on *Schindler's List.*

*Ryan* is a special case, a movie which revealed just what a consummate showman Spielberg was. In the summer, the director embarked on a five-city promotional tour during which he warned potential viewers that they might find the violence in the film hard to stomach. (Hitchcock and William Castle, let's not forget, employed roughly similar tactics to lure cinemagoers to their horror pics.)

Spielberg also rallied historians and D-Day veterans to testify to just how realistic his depiction of the Omaha Beach landings was. He claimed he had shot the sequence as graphically as the veterans had told him they had experienced it. Even before the film's release, *Saving Private Ryan* was being talked about as "the greatest war movie ever made." It was certainly one of the most cleverly marketed. This may have been a gruelling, three-hour epic, but it still earned more than $30 million on its opening weekend.

As Spielberg acknowledged, the wheel had come full circle. For the first 25 years of his career, he was invariably asked when he was going to make a serious film. Now, after *Amistad, Schindler's List*, and *Saving Private Ryan*, the question was, "When are you going to go back to entertainment?"

At one stage, it looked as if he was going to try to trump the sweaty machismo of *Saving Private Ryan* with a film about Japanese women in beautiful dresses. His next feature, he announced, would be *Memoirs Of A Geisha*, an adaptation of the Arthur Golden novel about a young girl sold into slavery in the late 1920s who goes on to become one of Japan's most celebrated geishas. That has since been put on the back-burner. (Reportedly, Spielberg decided it would be a bad idea to release "a little Asian film" when the world was busy celebrating the millennium.)

In late December 1998, the news slipped out that DreamWorks and 20th Century Fox were co-producing *Minority Report*, a sci-fi thriller which he would direct and Tom Cruise star in.

Meanwhile, Spielberg remained as busy as ever, supervising the building of DreamWorks' studio headquarters, and developing a myriad new projects, among them Ridley Scott's *Gladiator* movie, *The Flintstones 2*, a 13-part HBO series *The Band Of Brothers*, and a wartime romance, *The Betty Schimmel Story*, which Kenneth Branagh is set to direct. There was talk of *Jurassic Park 3* (which Spielberg would produce rather than direct) and even speculation that Indiana Jones may be brought out of mothballs.

Spielberg's protégés continued to flourish. Brad Silberling, a young TV director he hired to helm *Casper* in 1995, enjoyed a major hit with *City Of Angels*. Silberling is now due to work for Spielberg again: his next mooted project, the romance *Baby in Black*, will be made at DreamWorks.

"He is arguably the most influential artist of the twentieth century. And arguably the least understood," Michael Crichton observed of Spielberg. It is Spielberg's "industrialist" side which fazes critics. They can't get their head around the idea of a filmmaker capable of directing *Schindler's List* by day and editing *Jurassic Park* by night.

Pauline Kael once famously accused him of "infantilizing" the movies.

Spielberg is now 51. In an interview he gave to the *LA Times* in late 1998, he suggested that he wasn't entirely content in present-day Hollywood. In the old days, he said, the studio system was "a sweeter place to exist within. When I first got started, there didn't seem to be this kind of hysteria and true nail-biting anxiety before a film opened. Films opened quietly, there weren't full-page ads touting the three-day box office in the trades. It just didn't seem as frantic as today... I would love it if studios stopped boasting about how much money their movies made. It would be so wonderful if it didn't become the Olympics every Monday of every holiday weekend."

The irony is that Spielberg helped make Hollywood what it is now. Even if he wanted to direct a small-scale, independent movie away from the studio glare, he probably wouldn't be able to – the audience wouldn't stand for it.

Was 1998 really an exceptional year for Spielberg? The very question shows how inflated our expectations of him have become. *Saving Private Ryan* would mark the high point in any other filmmaker's career. For Spielberg, who already had five features in the American Film Institute's list of the 100 greatest movies of all time, it seemed like just another staging post. We take it for granted he'll astound us again soon. **Geoffrey Macnab**

> *Making movies is a game played by a few thousand toy-minded folk. (Ben Hecht)*

# The Oscars

The Academy Awards in March mark the highpoint of the Hollywood calendar. Watched by billions around the world, the long, sprawling TV show crowns the great and the good for the prior calendar year. *Variety* estimates that an Oscar win can add tens of millions of dollars to a film's eventual gross, and quite a few million dollars to the asking salary of any actor nabbing a statuette.

The awards ceremony is only the climax to a long campaign season, starting for *Variety* in early December (when submissions for the Best Foreign Film Oscars are announced) and the studios begin jockeying for position in the race to win nominations in February. Cassettes pile up outside the front doors of Academy members, ads swell the pages of *Variety*, while special screenings are laid on all over Los Angeles, in New York, London, and elsewhere. On the night itself, anything can happen, from Marlon Brando sending a Native American princess to pick up his award for *The Godfather*, to a dying John Wayne saying, "Let's get the wagons in a circle" as he presented an Oscar, or to James Cameron declaring himself "King of the World" as he triumphed with *Titanic*.

The Academy Awards have been bestowed since the 1927-28 season. The coveted Best Picture Oscar has been won by many a remarkable film, yet it's ironic that neither *Citizen Kane* nor *Casablanca* (voted the two best films of all time in an American Film Institute poll in 1998) took home that honor.

## Academy Awards: 1927-98

### 1927-28

Picture: *Wings* (Paramount, Lucien Hubbard)
Most artistic quality of production: *Sunrise*
Actor: Emil Jannings, *The Last Command, The Way of the Flesh*
Actress: Janet Gaynor, *Sunrise*
Dramatic direction: Frank Borzage, *Seventh Heaven*
Comedy direction: Lewis Milestone, *Two Arabian Knights*
Writing/adaptation: Benjamin Glazer, *Seventh Heaven*
Writing/Original story: Ben Hecht, *Underworld*
Title writing: Joseph Farnham, *Telling the World, The Fair Coed, Laugh, Clown, Laugh*
Cinematography: Charles Rosher, Karl Struss, *Sunrise*
Interior decoration: William Cameron Menzies, *The Dove, The Tempest*
Engineering effects: Roy Pomeroy, *Wings*
Special awards: Charles Chaplin for *The Circus*; Warner Bros. for *The Jazz Singer*

### 1928-29

Picture: *The Broadway Melody* (MGM)
Actor: Warner Baxter, *In Old Arizona*
Actress: Mary Pickford, *Coquette*
Director: Frank Lloyd, *The Divine Lady, Weary River, Drag*
Writing achievement: Hans Kraly, *The Patriot*

Cinematography: Clyde De Vinna, *White Shadows in the South Seas*
Interior decoration: Cedric Gibbons, *The Bridge of San Luis Rey, The Hollywood Revue*

### 1930

Film: *All Quiet on the Western Front* (Universal, Carl Laemmle, Jr.)
Actor: George Arliss, *Disraeli*
Actress: Norma Shearer, *The Divorcée*
Director: Lewis Milestone, *All Quiet on the Western Front*
Writing achievement: Frances Marion, *The Big House*
Cinematography: Joseph T. Rucker, Willard Van Der Veer, *With Byrd at the South Pole*
Interior decoration: Herman Rosse, *King of Jazz*
Sound recording: *The Big House*

### 1931

Picture: *Cimarron* (RKO Radio, William LeBaron)
Actor: Lionel Barrymore, *A Free Soul*
Actress: Marie Dressler, *Min and Bill*
Director: Norman Taurog, *Skippy*
Screenplay: Howard Estabrook, *Cimarron*
Original story: John Monk Saunders, *The Dawn Patrol*
Cinematography: Floyd Crosby, *Tabu*

Interior decoration: Max Ree, *Cimarron*
Sound recording: Paramount Sound Dept

## 1932

Picture: *Grand Hotel* (MGM, Irving G. Thalberg)
Actor: Wallace Beary (*The Champ*) and Fredric March
(*Dr Jekyll and Mr Hyde*)
Actress: Helen Hayes, *The Sin of Madelon Claudet*
Director: Frank Borzage, *Bad Girl*
Screenplay: Edwin Burke, *Bad Girl*
Original story: Frances Marion, *The Champ*
Cinematography: Lee Garmes, *Shanghai Express*
Interior decoration: Gordon Wiles, *Transatlantic*
Sound recording: Paramount Sound Dept
Short/cartoon: *Flowers and Trees* (Walt Disney/Silly
Symphonies)
Short/comedy: *The Music Box* (Laurel and Hardy)
Short/novelty: *Wrestling Swordfish* (Mack
Sennett/Cannibals of the Deep)
Special awards: Walt Disney for creating Mickey Mouse

## 1933

Film: *Cavalcade* (Fox, Winfield Sheehan)
Actor: Charles Laughton, *The Private Life of Henry VIII*
Actress: Katharine Hepburn, *Morning Glory*
Director: Frank Lloyd, *Cavalcade*
Screenplay: Victor Heerman, Sarah Y. Mason, *Little Women*
Original story: Robert Lord, *One Way Passage*
Cinematography: Charles Lang, *A Farewell to Arms*
Interior decoration: William S. Darling, *Cavalcade*
Assistant director (given to one from each studio):
Charles Burton (Paramount), Scott Beal (Universal),
Charles Dorian (MGM), Fred Fox (United Artists),
Gordon Hollingshead (Warner Bros), Dewey Starkey
(RKO Radio), William Tummel (Fox)
Sound recording: *A Farewell to Arms*
Short/cartoon: *The Three Little Pigs* (Walt Disney/Silly
Symphonies)
Short/comedy: *So This Is Harris* (RKO Radio Special/
Phil Harris)
Short/novelty: *Krakatoa* (Educational Studio)

## 1934

Picture: *It Happened One Night* (Columbia, Harry Cohn)
Actor: Clark Gable, *It Happened One Night*
Actress: Claudette Colbert, *It Happened One Night*
Director: Frank Capra, *It Happened One Night*
Screenplay: Robert Riskin, *It Happened One Night*
Original story: Arthur Caesar, *Manhattan Melodrama*
Cinematography: Victor Milner, *Cleopatra*
Score: *One Night of Love*, Victor Schertzinger
Song: "The Continental" from *The Gay Divorcée*, music:
Con Conrad, lyrics: Herb Magidson

Editing: *Eskimo*
Interior decoration: Cedric Gibbons, *The Merry Widow*
Assistant director: John Waters, *Viva Villa!*
Sound recording: *One Night of Love*
Short/cartoon: *The Tortoise and the Hare* (Walt
Disney/Silly Symphonies)
Short/comedy: *La Cucaracha* (RKO Radio Special)
Short/novelty: *City of Wax* (Educational/Battle for Life)
Special award: Shirley Temple

## 1935

Picture: *Mutiny on the Bounty* (MGM, Irving G. Thalberg)
Actor: Victor McLaglen, *The Informer*
Actress: Bette Davis, *Dangerous*
Director: John Ford, *The Informer*
Screenplay: Dudley Nichols, *The Informer*
Original story: Ben Hecht, Charles MacArthur, *The
Scoundrel*
Cinematography: Hal Mohr, *A Midsummer Night's Dream*
Score: *The Informer*, Max Steiner
Song: "Lullaby of Broadway" from *Gold Diggers of 1935*,
music: Harry Warren, lyrics: Al Dubin
Editing: *A Midsummer Night's Dream*
Interior decoration: Richard Day, *The Dark Angel*
Dance direction: David Gould, "I've Got a Feeling You
Are Fooling" from *Broadway Melody of 1936*, "Straw
Hat" from *Folies Bergère*
Assistant director: Clem Beauchamp, Paul Wing, *The
Lives of a Bengal Dancer*
Sound recording: *Naughty Marietta*
Short/cartoon: *Three Orphan Kittens* (Walt Disney/Silly
Symphonies)
Short/comedy: *How to Sleep* (MGM/Robert Benchley)
Short/novelty: *Wings over Mt. Everest* (Educational)
Special award: David Wark Griffith

## 1936

Picture: *The Great Ziegfeld* (MGM, Hunt Stromberg)
Actor: Paul Muni, *The Story of Louis Pasteur*
Actress: Luise Rainer, *The Great Ziegfeld*
Supporting actor: Walter Brennan, *Come and Get It*
Supporting actress: Gale Sondergaard, *Anthony Adverse*
Director: Frank Capra, *Mr. Deeds Goes to Town*
Screenplay: Pierre Collings, Sheridan Gibney, *The Story
of Louis Pasteur*
Original story: Pierre Collings, Sheridan Gibney, *The
Story of Louis Pasteur*
Cinematography: Gaetano (Tony) Gaudio, *Anthony
Adverse*
Score: Erich Wolfgang Korngold, *Anthony Adverse*
Song: "The Way You Look Tonight" from *Swing Time*,
music: Jerome Kern, lyrics: Dorothy Fields
Editing: *Anthony Adverse*

---

Interior decoration: Richard Day, *Dodsworth*
Dance direction: Seymour Felix, "A Pretty Girl Is Like a Melody" from *The Great Ziegfeld*
Assistant director: Jack Sullivan, *The Charge of the Light Brigade*
Sound recording: *San Francisco*
Short/cartoon: *Country Cousin* (Walt Disney/ Silly Symphonies)
Short/one-reel: *Bored of Education* (Hal Roach/Our Gang)
Short/two-reel: *The Public Pays* (MGM/Crime Doesn't Pay)
Short/colour: *Give Me Liberty* (Warner/Broadway Brevities)
Special awards: *The March of Time* for having revolutionised the newsreel; W. Howard Green; Harold Rosson for colour cinematography, *The Garden of Allah*

## 1937

Picture: *The Life of Emile Zola* (Warner Bros., Henry Blanke)
Actor: Spencer Tracy, *Captains Courageous*
Actress: Louise Rainer, *The Good Earth*
Supporting actor: Joseph Schildkraut, *The Life of Emile Zola*
Supporting actress: Alice Brady, *In Old Chicago*
Director: Leo McCarey, *The Awful Truth*
Screenplay: Heinz Herald, Geza Herczeg, Norman Reilly Raine, *The Life of Emile Zola*
Original story: William A Wellman, Rober Carson, *A Star Is Born*
Cinematography: Karl Freund, *The Good Earth*
Score: *100 Men and a Girl*, Universal Studio Music Dept., Charles Previn, head
Song: "Sweet Leilani" from *Waikiki Wedding* , music and lyrics: Harry Owens
Editing: *Lost Horizon*
Interior decoration: Stephen Goosson, *Lost Horizon*
Dance direction: Hermes Pan, "Fun House" from *A Damsel in Distress*
Assistant director: Robert Webb, *In Old Chicago*
Sound recording: *The Hurricane*
Short/cartoon: *The Old Mill* (Walt Disney/Silly Symphonies)
Short/one-reel: *Private Life of the Gannets* (Educational)
Short/two-reel: *Torture Money* (MGM/Crime Doesn't Pay)
Short/colour: *Penny Wisdom* (MGM/Pete Smith Specialities)
Irving G. Thalberg award: Darryl F. Zanuck
Special awards: Mack Sennett; Edgar Bergen; The Museum of Modern Art Film Library; W. Howard Green for colour photography, *A Star Is Born*

## 1938

Picture: *You Can't Take It With You* (Columbia, Frank Capra)

Actor: Spencer Tracy, *Boys Town*
Actress: Bette Davis, *Jezebel*
Supporting actor: Walter Brennan, *Kentucky*
Supporting actress: Fay Bainter, *Jezebel*
Director: Frank Capra, *You Can't Take It With You*
Screenplay: Ian Dalrymple, Cecil Lewis, W.P. Lipscomb for adaptation of George Bernard Shaw's *Pygmalion*
Original story: Eleanore Griffin, Dore Schary, *Boys Town*
Cinematography: Joseph Ruttenberg, *The Great Waltz*
Original score: Erich Wolfgang Korngold, *The Adventures of Robin Hood*
Score: Alfred Newman, *Alexander's Ragtime Band*
Song: "Thanks for the Memory" from *Big Broadcast of 1938*, music: Ralph Rainger, lyrics: Leo Rubin
Interior decoration: Carl J Weyl, *The Adventures of Robin Hood*
Editing: *The Adventures of Robin Hood*
Sound recording: *The Cowboy and the Lady*
Short/cartoon: *Ferdinand the Bull* (Walt Disney)
Short/one-reel: *That Mothers Might Live* (MGM miniatures, directed by Fred Zinnemann)
Short/two-reel: *Declaration of Independence* (Warners Historical Featurette)
Irving G. Thalberg award: Hal B. Wallis
Special awards: Deanna Durbin and Mickey Rooney, youth actors; Harry M. Warner for the production of historical short subjects; Walt Disney for *Snow White and the Seven Dwarfs*; Oliver Marsh, Allen Davey, colour cinematography; *Sweethearts* for special photographic and sound effects; *Spawn of the North*; J. Arthur Ball for the advancement of colour photography

## 1939

Picture: *Gone With the Wind* (MGM, David O. Selznick)
Actor: Robert Donat, *Goodbye Mr. Chips*
Actress: Vivien Leigh, *Gone With the Wind*
Supporting actor: Thomas Mitchell, *Stagecoach*
Supporting actress: Hattie McDaniel, *Gone With the Wind*
Director: Victor Fleming, *Gone With the Wind*
Screenplay: Sidney Howard, *Gone With the Wind*
Original story: Lewis R. Foster, *Mr. Smith Goes to Washington*
Cinematography/B&W: Greg Toland, *Wuthering Heights*
Cinematography/colour: Ernest Haller, Ray Rennahan, *Gone With the Wind*
Original score: Herbert Stothart, *The Wizard of Oz*
Score: Richard Hageman, Frank Harling, John Leipold, Leo Shiken, *Stagecoach*
Song: "Over the Rainbow" from *The Wizard of Oz*, music: Harold Arlen, lyrics: E.Y. Harburg
Interior decoration: Lyle Wheeler, *Gone With the Wind*
Editing: *Gone With the Wind*
Sound recording: *When Tomorrow Comes*

---

**... January 10 ...**
CBS announces development of a one-hour drama, **Bronx County**, with Sydney Pollack.

Special effects: *The Rains Came*
Short/cartoon: *The Ugly Duckling* (Walt Disney/Silly Symphonies)
Short/one-reel: *Busy Little Bears* (Paramount Paragraphics)
Short/two-reel: *Sons of Liberty* (Warner Historical Featurette, directed by Michael Curtiz)
Irving G. Thalberg award: David O. Selznick
Special awards: Douglas Fairbanks, first president of the Academy; The Motion Picture Relief Fund presented to Jean Hersholt, president; Judy Garland, screen juvenile; William Cameron Menzies for the use of colour for the enhancement of dramatic mood in *Gone With the Wind*; The Technicolor Company for three-colour feature production

## 1940
Picture: *Rebecca* (UA, David O. Selznick)
Actor: James Stewart, *The Philadelphia Story*
Actress: Ginger Rogers, *Kitty Foyle*
Supporting actor: Walter Brennan, *The Westerner*
Supporting actress: Jane Darwell, *The Grapes of Wrath*
Director: John Ford, *The Grapes of Wrath*
Original screenplay: Preston Sturges, *The Great McGinty*
Adapted screenplay: Donald Ogden Stewart, *The Philadelphia Story*
Original story: Benjamin Glazer, John S. Toldy, *Arise My Love*
Cinematography/B&W: George Barnes, *Rebecca*
Cinematography/colour: Georges Perinal, *The Thief of Bagdad*
Original score: Leigh Harline, Paul J. Smith, Ned Washington, *Pinocchio*
Score: Alfred Newman, *Tin Pan Alley*
Song: "When You Wish upon a Star" from *Pinocchio*, music: Leigh Harline, lyrics: Ned Washington
Interior decoration/B&W: Cedric Gibbons, *Pride and Prejudice*
Interior decoration/colour: Vincent Korda, *The Thief of Bagdad*
Editing: *Northwest Mounted Police*
Sound recording: *Strike up the Band*
Special effects: *The Thief of Bagdad*
Short/cartoon: *The Milky Way* (MGM/Rudolph Ising)
Short/one-reel: *Quicker 'N a Wink* (MGM/Pete Smith Specialities)
Short/two-reel: *Teddy the Rough Rider* (Warner Historical Featurette)
Special awards: Bob Hope; Colonel Nathan Levinson for making possible the mobilisation of industry facilities for Army training films

## 1941
Picture: *How Green Was My Valley* (20th Century-Fox, Darryl F. Zanuck)

Actor: Gary Cooper, *Sergeant York*
Actress: Joan Fontaine, *Suspicion*
Supporting actor: Donald Crisp, *How Green Was My Valley*
Supporting actress: Mary Astor, *The Great Lie*
Director: John Ford, *How Green Was My Valley*
Original screenplay: Herman J. Mankiewicz, Orson Welles, *Citizen Kane*
Adapted screenplay: Sidney Buchman, Seton I. Miller, *Here Comes Mr. Jordan*
Original story: Harry Segall, *Here Comes Mr. Jordan*
Cinematography/B&W: Arthur Miller, *How Green Was My Valley*
Cinematography/colour: Ernest Palmer, Ray Rennahan, *Blood and Sand*
Dramatic score: Bernard Hermann, "All That Money Can Buy" from *The Devil and Daniel Webster*
Music score: Frank Churchill, Oliver Wallace, *Dumbo*
Song: "The Last Time I Saw Paris" from *Lady be Good*, music: Jerome Kern, lyrics: Oscar Hammerstein II
Interior decoration/B&W: Richard Day, Nathan Juran, *How Green Was My Valley*
Interior decoration/colour: Cedric Gibbons, Urie McCleary, *Blossoms in the Dust*
Editing: *Sergeant York*
Sound recording: *That Hamilton Woman*
Special effects: *I Wanted Wings*
Short/cartoon: *Lend a Paw* (Walt Disney/Pluto)
Short/one-reel: *Of Pups and Puzzles* (MGM Passing Parade Series)
Short/two-reel: *Main Street on the March* (MGM)
Documentary: *Churchill's Island* (National Film Board of Canada)
Irwing G. Thalberg award: Walt Disney
Special awards: Rey Scott for producing *Kukan*, documentary on war in China; The British Ministry of Information, *Target for Tonight*; Leopold Stokowski and his associates for their unique achievement in the creation of a new form of visualized music in *Fantasia*

## 1942
Picture: *Mrs. Miniver* (MGM, Sidney Franklin)
Actor: James Cagney, *Yankee Doodle Dandy*
Actress: Greer Garson, *Mrs. Miniver*
Supporting actor: Van Heflin, *Johnny Eager*
Supporting actress: Teresa Wright, *Mrs. Miniver*
Director: William Wyler, *Mrs. Miniver*
Original screenplay: Michael Kanin, Ring Lardner, Jr., *Woman of the Year*
Adapted screenplay: George Froeschel, James Hilton, Claudine West, Arthur Wimperis, *Mrs. Miniver*
Original story: Emeric Pressburger, *The Invaders (49th Parallel)*

---

Cinematography/B & W: Joseph Ruttenberg, *Mrs. Miniver*
Cinematography/colour: Leon Shamroy, *The Black Swan*
Dramatic or comedy score: Max Steiner, *Now, Voyager*
Musical score: Ray Heindorf, Heinz Roemheld, *Yankee Doodle Dandy*
Song: "White Christmas" from *Holiday Inn*, music and lyrics: Irving Berlin
Interior decoration/B&W: Richard Day, *This Above All*
Interior decoration/colour: Richard Day, *My Gal Sal*
Editing: *The Pride of the Yankees*
Sound recording: *Yankee Doodle Dandy*
Special effects: *Reap the Wild Wind*
Short/cartoon: *Der Fuehrer's Face* (Walt Disney/Donald Duck)
Short/one-reel: *Speaking of Animals and Their Families* (Paramount/Speaking of Animals)
Short/two-reel: *Beyond the Line of Duty* (Warner Broadway Brevities)
Documentary: *Battle of Midway* (U.S. Navy); *Kokoda Front Line* (Australian News Information Bureau); *Moscow Strikes Back* (Artkino), *Prelude to War* (U.S. Army Special Services/Why We Fight series)
Irving G. Thalberg award: Sidney Franklin
Special awards: Charles Boyer for establishing French Research Foundation in Los Angeles as a source of reference for the industry; Noël Coward for *In Which We Serve*; MGM for representing the American way of life in the Andy Hardy series

## 1943

Picture: *Casablanca* (Warner Bros., Hal B. Wallis)
Actor: Paul Lukas, *Watch on the Rhine*
Actress: Jennifer Jones, *Song of Bernadette*
Supporting actor: Charles Coburn, *The More the Merrier*
Supporting actress: Katina Paxinou, *For Whom the Bell Tolls*
Director: Michael Curtiz, *Casablanca*
Original screenplay: Norman Krasna, *Princess O'Rourke*
Adapted screenplay: Julius J. Epstein, Philip G. Epstein, Howard Koch, *Casablanca*
Original story: William Saroyan, *The Human Comedy*
Cinematography/B&W: Arthur Miller, *The Song of Bernadette*
Cinematography/colour: Hal Mohr, W. Howard Greene, *The Phantom of the Opera*
Dramatic or comedy score: Alfred Newman, *The Song of Bernadette*
Musical score: Ray Heindorf, *This is the Army*
Song: "You'll Never Know" from *Hello Frisco, Hello*, music: Hary Warren, lyrics: Mack Gordon
Interior decoration/B&W: James Basevi, William Darling, *The Song of Bernadette*
Interior decoration/colour: Alexander Golitzen, *The Phantom of the Opera*

Editing: *Air Force*
Sound recording: *This Land is Mine*
Special effects: *Crash Drive*
Short/cartoon: *Yankee Doodle Mouse* (MGM/Hanna-Barbera/Tom & Jerry)
Short/one-reel: *Amphibious Fighters* (Paramount)
Short/two-reel: *Heavenly Music* (MGM)
Documentary/feature: *Desert Victory* (British Ministry of Information)
Documentary/short: *December 7th* (U.S. Navy, directed by John Ford, Gregg Toland)
Irwing G. Thalberg award: Hal B. Wallis
Special award: George Pal for Puppetoons (stop-motion animation)

## 1944

Picture: *Going My Way* (Paramount, Leo McCarey)
Actor: Bing Crosby, *Going My Way*
Actress: Ingrid Bergman, *Gaslight*
Supporting actor: Barry Fitzgerald, *Going My Way*
Supporting actress: Ethel Barrymore, *None but the Lonely Heart*
Director: Leo McCarey, *Going My Way*
Original screenplay: Lamar Trotti, *Wilson*
Adapted screenplay: Frank Butler, Frank Cavett, *Going My Way*
Original story: Leo McCarey, *Going My Way*
Cinematography/B&W: Joseph LaShelle, *Laura*
Cinematography/colour: Leon Shamroy, *Wilson*
Dramatic or comedy score: Max Steiner, *Since You Went Away*
Musical score: Carmen Dragon, Morris Stoloff, *Cover Girl*
Song: "Swinging on a Star" from *Going My Way*, music: James Van Heusen, lyrics: Johnny Burke
Interior decoration/B&W: Cedric Gibbons, *Gaslight*
Interior decoration/colour: Wiard Ihnen, *Wilson*
Editing: *Wilson*
Sound recording: *Wilson*
Special effects: *Thirty Seconds over Tokyo*
Short/cartoon: *Mouse Trouble* (MGM/Hanna-Barbera/Tom & Jerry)
Short/one-reel: *Who's Who in Animal Land* (Paramount/Speaking of Animals)
Short/two-reel: *I Won't Play* (Warner Bros. Featurette)
Documentary/feature: *The Fighting Lady* (20th Century-Fox, U.S. Navy)
Documentary/short: *With the Marines at Tarawa* (U.S. Marine Corps)
Irwing G. Thalberg award: Darryl F. Zanuck
Special awards: Margaret O'Brien, outstanding child actress of 1944; Bob Hope for his many services to the Academy

---

**...January 12...**
Tim Allen returns to ABC's **Home Improvement** for $1.25 million per episode.

## 1945

Picture: *The Lost Weekend* (Paramount, Charles Brackett)
Actor: Ray Milland, *The Lost Weekend*
Actress: Joan Crawford, *Mildred Pierce*
Supporting actor: James Dunn, *A Tree Grows in Brooklyn*
Supporting actress: Anne Revere, *National Velvet*
Director: Billy Wilder, *The Lost Weekend*
Original screenplay: Richard Schweizer, *Marie-Louise* (Switzerland)
Adapted screenplay: Charles Brackett, Billy Wilder, *The Lost Weekend*
Original story: Charles G. Booth, *The House on 92nd Street*
Cinematography/B&W: Harry Stradling, *The Picture of Dorian Gray*
Cinematography/colour: Leon Shamroy, *Leave Her to Heaven*
Dramatic or comedy score: Miklos Rozsa, *Spellbound*
Musical score: Georgie Stoll, *Anchors Aweigh*
Song: "It Might As Well Be Spring" from *State Fair*, music: Richard Rodgers, lyrics: Oscar Hammerstein II
Interior decoration/B&W: Wiard Ihnen, *Blood on the Sun*
Interior decoration/colour: Hans Dreier, Ernst Fegte, *Frenchman's Creek*
Editing: *National Velvet*
Sound recording: *The Bells of St. Mary's*
Special effects: *Wonder Man*
Short/cartoon: *Quiet Please* (MGM/Hanna-Barbera/Tom & Jerry)
Short/one-reel: *Stairway to Light* (MGM/Passing Parade)
Short/two-reel: *A Star in the Night* (Warner Bros. Broadway Brevities, directed by Don Siegel)
Documentary/feature: *The True Glory* (Governments of U.S. & Britain, directed by Carol Reed, Garson Kanin)
Documentary/short: *Hitler Lives?* (Warner Bros., directed by Don Siegel)
Special awards: Walter Wanger; Peggy Ann Garner; *The House I Live In*; Republic Studio

## 1946

Picture: *The Best Years of Our Lives* (RKO Radio, Samuel Goldwyn)
Actor: Fredric March, *The Best Years of Our Lives*
Actress: Olivia de Havilland, *To Each His Own*
Supporting actor: Harold Russell, *The Best Years of Our Lives*
Supporting actress: Anne Baxter, *The Razor's Edge*
Director: William Wyler, *The Best Years of Our Lives*
Original screenplay: Muriel Box, Sydney Box, *The Seventh Veil*
Adapted screenplay: Robert E. Sherwood, *The Best Years of Our Lives*
Original story: Clemence Dane, *Vacation from Marriage*
Cinematography/B&W: Arthur Miller, *Anna and the King of Siam*
Cinematography/colour: Charles Rosher, Leonard Smith, Arthur Arling, *The Yearling*
Dramatic or comedy score: Hugo Friedhofer, *The Best Years of Our Lives*
Musical score: Morris Stoloff, *The Jolson Story*
Song: "On the Atchison Topeka and Santa Fe" from *The Harvey Girls*, music: Harry Warren, lyrics: Johnny Mercer
Interior decoration/B&W: Lyle Wheeler, William Darling, *Anna and the King of Siam*
Interior decoration/colour: Cedric Gibbons, Paul Groesse, *The Yearling*
Editing: *The Best Years of Our Lives*
Sound recording: *The Jolson Story*
Special effects: *Blithe Spirit*
Short/cartoon: *The Cat Concerto* (MGM/Hanna-Barbera/Tom & Jerry)
Short/one-reel: *Facing Your Danger* (Warner Bros. Sports Parade)
Short/two-reel: *A Boy and His Dog* (Warner Bros. Featurettes)
Documentary/short: *Seeds of Destiny* (U.S. War Dept)
Irving G. Thalberg award: Samuel Goldwyn
Special awards: Laurence Olivier; Harold Russell; Ernst Lubitsch; Claude Jarman, Jr.

## 1947

Picture: *Gentleman's Agreement* (20th Century-Fox, Darryl F. Zanuck)
Actor: Ronald Colman, *A Double Life*
Actress: Loretta Young, *The Farmer's Daughter*
Supporting actor: Edmund Gwenn, *Miracle on 34th Street*
Supporting actress: Celeste Holm, *Gentleman's Agreement*
Director: Elia Kazan, *Gentleman's Agreement*
Original screenplay: Sidney Sheldon, *The Bachelor and the Bobby-Soxer*
Adapted screenplay: George Seaton, *Miracle on 34th Street*
Original story: Valentine Davies, *Miracle on 34th Street*
Cinematography/B&W: Guy Greene, *Great Expectations*
Cinematography/colour: Jack Cardiff, *Black Narcissus*
Song: "Zip-A-Dee-Doo-Dah" from *Song of the South*, music: Allie Wrubel, lyrics: Ray Gilbert
Dramatic or comedy score: Miklos Rozsa, *A Double Life*
Musical score: Alfred Newman, *Mother Wore Tights*
Art direction/B&W: John Bryan, *Great Expectations*
Art direction/colour: Alfred Junge, *Black Narcissus*
Editing: *Body and Soul*
Sound recording: *The Bishop's Wife*
Special effects: *Green Dolphin Street*
Short/cartoon: *Tweetie Pie* (Warner/Friz Freleng, Tweety & Sylvester)
Short/one-reel: *Goodbye Miss Turlock* (MGM/Passing Parade)

Short/two-reel: *Climbing the Matterhorn* (Monogram Color, Irving Allen)
Documentary/feature: *Design for Death* (RKO Radio)
Documentary/short: First Steps (United Nations Division of Films and Visual Education)
Special awards: James Baskette; *Bill and Coo* (live-action animal film); *Shoeshine* (Italy), outstanding foreign-language film; Colonel William N. Selig and George K. Spoor (early film pioneers)

## 1948

Picture: *Hamlet* (Universal, Rank/Two Cities, Laurence Olivier)
Actor: Laurence Olivier, *Hamlet*
Actress: Jane Wyman, *Johnny Belinda*
Supporting actor: Walter Huston, *The Treasure of the Sierra Madre*
Supporting actress: Claire Trevor, *Key Largo*
Director: John Huston, *The Treasure of the Sierra Madre*
Screenplay: John Huston, *The Treasure of the Sierra Madre*
Original story: Richard Schweizer, David Wechsler, *The Search*
Cinematography/B&W: William Daniels, *The Naked City*
Cinematography/colour: Joseph Valentine, William V. Skall, Winton Hoch, *Joan of Arc*
Dramatic or comedy score: Brian Easdale, *The Red Shoes*
Musical score: Johnny Green, Roger Edens, *Easter Parade*
Song: "Buttons and Bows" from *The Paleface*, music and lyrics: Jay Livingstone
Art direction/B&W: Roger K. Furse, *Hamlet*
Art direction/colour: Hein Heckroth, *The Red Shoes*
Costumes/B&W: Roger K. Furse, *Hamlet*
Costumes/colour: Dorothy Jeakins, Karinska, *Joan of Arc*
Editing: *The Naked City*
Sound recording: *The Snake Pit*
Special effects: *Portrait of Jennie*
Short/cartoon: *The Little Orphan*
Short/one-reel: *Symphony of a City* (Movietone Specialty)
Short/two-reel: *Seal Island* (Walt Disney's True Life Adventures)
Documentary/feature: *The Secret Land* (U.S. Navy, MGM)
Documentary/short: *Toward Independence* (U.S. Army)
Irving G. Thalberg award: Jerry Wald
Special awards: *Monsieur Vincent* (France), outstanding foreign-language film; Ivan Jandl, outstanding juvenile performance, *The Search*; Sid Grauman, master showman; Adolph Zukor, for his services to the industry; Walter Wanger, for distinguished services to the industry

## 1949

Picture: *All the King's Men* (Columbia, Robert Rossen)
Actor: Broderick Crawford, *All the King's Men*

Actress: Olivia de Havilland, *The Heiress*
Supporting actor: Dean Jagger, *Twelve O'Clock High*
Supporting actress: Mercedes McCambridge, *All the King's Men*
Director: Joseph L. Mankiewicz, *A Letter to Three Wives*
Screenplay: Joseph L. Mankiewicz, *A Letter to Three Wives*
Story and screenplay: Robert Pirosh, *Battleground*
Original story: Douglas Morrow, *The Stratton Story*
Cinematography/B&W: Paul C. Vogel, *Battleground*
Cinematography/colour: Winton C. Hoch, *She Wore a Yellow Ribbon*
Dramatic or comedy score: Aaron Copland, *The Heiress*
Musical score: Roger Edens, Lennie Hayton, *On the Town*
Song: "Baby, It's Cold Outside" from *Neptune's Daughter*, music and lyrics: Frank Loesser
Art direction/B&W: John Meehan, Harry Horner, *The Heiress*
Art direction/colour: Cedric Gibbons, Paul Groesse, *Little Women*
Costumes/B&W: Edith Head, *The Heiress*
Costumes/colour: *Adventures of Don Juan*
Editing: *Champion*
Sound recording: *Twelve O'Clock High*
Special effects: *Mighty Joe Young* (Willis O'Brien, Ray Harryhausen)
Short/cartoon: *For Scentimental Reasons* (Warner/Chuck Jones/Pepe LePew)
Short/one-reel: *Aquatic House-Party* (Grantland Rice Sportlights)
Short/two-reel: *Van Gogh*
Documentary/feature: *Daybreak in Udi* (British Information Service)
Documentary/short: *A Chance to Live* (March of Time); *So Much for so Little* (Public Health Service and Warner Bros. cartoon unit)
Special awards: *The Bicycle Thief* (Italy), outstanding foreign-language film; Bobby Driscoll, outstanding juvenile actor; Fred Astaire; Cecil B. DeMille; Jean Hersholt, for service to the industry

## 1950

Picture: *All about Eve* (20th Century-Fox, Darryl F. Zanuck)
Actor: José Ferrer, *Cyrano de Bergerac*
Actress: Judy Holliday, *Born Yesterday*
Supporting actor: George Sanders, *All about Eve*
Supporting actress: Josephine Hull, *Harvey*
Director: Joseph Mankiewicz, *All about Eve*
Screenplay: Joseph Mankiewicz, *All about Eve*
Story and screenplay: Charles Brackett, Billy Wilder, D.M. Marshman, Jr., *Sunset Boulevard*
Original story: Edna Anhalt, Edward Anhalt, *Panic in the Streets*
Cinematography/B&W: Robert Krasker, *The Third Man*

Cinematography/colour: Robert Surtees, *King Solomon's Mines*

Dramatic or comedy score: Franz Waxman, *Sunset Boulevard*

Musical score: Adolph Deutsch, Roger Edens, *Annie Get Your Gun*

Song: "Mona Lisa" from *Captain Carey*, music and lyrics: Ray Evans, Jay Livingstone

Art direction/B&W: Hans Dreier, John Meehan, *Sunset Boulevard*

Art direction/colour: Hans Dreier, *Samson and Delilah*

Costumes/B&W: Edith Head, *All about Eve*

Costumes/colour: Edith Head, *Samson and Delilah*

Editing: *King Solomon's Mines*

Sound recording: *All about Eve*

Special effects: *Destination Moon*

Short/cartoon: Gerald McBoing-Boing (UPA/Robert Cannon)

Short/one-reel: *Granddad of Races* (Warner Bros. Sports Parade)

Short/two-reel: *In Beaver Valley* (Disney True-Life Adventures)

Documentary/feature: *The Titan – The Story of Michaelangelo* (Robert Snyder)

Documentary/short: *Why Korea?* (Fox Movietone)

Irving G. Thalberg award: Darryl F. Zanuck

Special awards: George Murphy; Louis B. Mayer; *The Walls of Malapaga* (France/Italy), outstanding foreign-language film

## 1951

Picture: *An American in Paris* (MGM, Arthur Freed)

Actor: Humphrey Bogart, *The African Queen*

Actress: Vivien Leigh, *A Streetcar Named Desire*

Supporting actor: Karl Malden, *A Streetcar Named Desire*

Supporting actress: Kim Hunter, *A Streetcar Named Desire*

Director: George Stevens, *A Place in the Sun*

Screenplay: Michael Wilson, Harry Brown, *A Place in the Sun*

Story and screenplay: Alan Jay Lerner, *An American in Paris*

Original story: Paul Dehn, James Bernard, *Seven Days to Noon*

Cinematography/B&W: William C. Mellor, *A Place in the Sun*

Cinematography/colour: Alfred Gilks, John Alton, *An American in Paris*

Dramatic or comedy score: Franz Waxman, *A Place in the Sun*

Musical score: Johnny Green, Saul Chaplin, *An American in Paris*

Song: "In the Cool, Cool, Cool, of the Evening" from *Here Comes the Groom*, music: Hoagy Carmichael, lyrics: Johnny Mercer

Art direction/B&W: Richard Day, *A Streetcar Named Desire*

Art direction/colour: Cedric Gibbons, Preston Ames, *An American in Paris*

Costumes/B&W: Edith Head, *A Place in the Sun*

Costumes/colour: Walter Plunkett, Irene Sharaff, *An American in Paris*

Editing: *A Place in the Sun*

Sound recording: *The Great Caruso*

Special effects: *When Worlds Collide*

Short/cartoon: *Two Mouseketeers* (MGM/Hanna-Barbera/Tom & Jerry)

Short/one-reel: *World of Kids* (Vitaphone, Novelties, Robert Youngson)

Short/two-reel: *Nature's Half Acre* (Disney True-Life Adventures)

Documentary/feature: *Kon-Tiki* (Norway)

Documentary/short: *Benjy* (Fred Zinnemann, Los Angeles Orthopædic Hospital)

Irving G. Thalberg award: Arthur Freed

Special awards: Gene Kelly; *Rashomon* (Japan), outstanding foreign-language film

## 1952

Picture: *The Greatest Show on Earth* (Paramount, Cecil B. DeMille)

Actor: Gary Cooper, *High Noon*

Actress: Shirley Booth, *Come Back, Little Sheba*

Supporting actor: Anthony Quinn, *Viva Zapata!*

Supporting actress: Gloria Grahame, *The Bad and the Beautiful*

Director: John Ford, *The Quiet Man*

Screenplay: Charles Schnee, *The Bad and the Beautiful*

Story and screenplay: TEB Clarke, *The Lavender Hill Mob*

Original story: Frederic M. Frank, Theodore St. John, Frank Cavett, *The Greatest Show on Earth*

Cinematography/B&W: Robert Surtees, *The Bad and the Beautiful*

Cinematography/colour: Winton C. Hoch, Archie Stout, *The Quiet Man*

Dramatic or comedy score: Dimitri Tiomkin, *High Noon*

Musical score: Alfred Newman, *With a Song in My Heart*

Song: "High Noon (Do Not Forsake Me, Oh My Darlin')" from *High Noon*, music: Dimitri Tiomkin, lyrics: Ned Washington

Art direction/B&W: Cedric Gibbons, *The Bad and the Beautiful*

Art direction/colour: Paul Sheriff, Marcel Vertes, *Moulin Rouge*

Costumes/B&W: Helen Rose, *The Bad and the Beautiful*

Costumes/colour: Marcel Vertes, *Moulin Rouge*

Editing: *High Noon*

Sound recording: *Breaking the Sound Barrier*

Special effects: *Plymouth Adventure*, MGM

---

Short/cartoon: *Johann Mouse* (MGM/Hanna-Barbera/Tom & Jerry)

Short/one-reel: *Light in the Window*

Short/two-reel: Water Birds (Disney True-Life Adventures)

Documentary/feature: *The Sea Around Us* (RKO Radio, Irwin Allen)

Documentary/short: *Neighbours* (National Film Board of Canada, Norman McLaren)

Irving G. Thalberg award: Cecil B. DeMille

Special awards: George Alfred Mitchell; Joseph M. Schenck; Merian C. Cooper; Harold Lloyd; Bob Hope; *Forbidden Games* (France), outstanding foreign-language film

## 1953

Picture: *From Here to Eternity* (Columbia, Buddy Adler)

Actor: William Holden, *Stalag 17*

Actress: Audrey Hepburn, *Roman Holiday*

Supporting actor: Frank Sinatra, *From Here to Eternity*

Supporting actress: Donna Reed, *From Here to Eternity*

Director: Fred Zinnemann, *From Here to Eternity*

Screenplay: Daniel Taradash, *From Here to Eternity*

Story and screenplay: Charles Brackett, Walter Reisch, Richard Breen, *Titanic*

Original story: Ian McLellan Hunter, *Roman Holiday*

Cinematography/B&W: Burnett Guffey, *From Here to Eternity*

Cinematography/colour: Loyal Griggs, *Shane*

Dramatic or comedy score: Bronislau Kaper, *Lili*

Musical score: Alfred Newman, *Call Me Madam*

Song: "Secret Love" from *Calamity Jane*, music: Sammy Fain, lyrics: Paul Francis Webster

Art direction/B&W: Cedric Gibbons, *Julius Caesar*

Art direction/colour: Lyle Wheeler, George W. Davis, *The Robe*

Costumes/B&W: Edith Head, *Roman Holiday*

Costumes/colour: Charles LeMaire, Emile Santiago, *The Robe*

Editing: *From Here to Eternity*

Sound recording: *From Here to Eternity*

Special effects: *War of the Worlds*

Short/cartoon: *Toot, Whistle, Plunk and Boom* (Walt Disney)

Short/one-reel: *The Merry Wives of Windsor Overture* (MGM Overture Series)

Short/two-reel: *Bear Country* (Disney True-Life Adventures)

Documentary/feature: *The Living Desert* (Disney True-Life Adventures)

Documentary/short: *The Alaskan Eskimo* (Disney True-Life Adventures)

Irving G. Thalberg award: George Stevens

Special awards: Pete Smith; 20th Century-Fox; Joseph I. Breen

## 1954

Picture: *On the Waterfront* (Columbia, Sam Spiegel)

Actor: Marlon Brando, *On the Waterfront*

Actress: Grace Kelly, *The Country Girl*

Supporting actor: Edmond O'Brien *The Barefoot Contessa*

Supporting actress: Eva Marie Saint, *On the Waterfront*

Director: Elia Kazan, *On the Waterfront*

Screenplay: George Seaton, *The Country Girl*

Story and screenplay: Budd Schulberg, *On the Waterfront*

Original story: Philip Yordan, *Broken Lance*

Cinematography/B&W: Boris Kaufman, *On the Waterfront*

Cinematography/colour: Milton Krasner, *Three Coins in the Fountain*

Dramatic or comedy score: Dimitri Tiomkin, *The High and the Mighty*

Musical score: Adolph Deutsch, Saul Chaplin, *Seven Brides for Seven Sisters*

Song: "Three Coins in the Fountain" from *Three Coins in the Fountain*, music: Jule Styne, lyrics: Sammy Cahn

Art direction/B&W: Richard Day, *On the Waterfront*

Art direction/colour: John Meehan, *20,000 Leagues under the Sea*

Costumes/B&W: Edith Head, *Sabrina*

Costumes/colour: Sanzo Wada, *Gate of Hell*

Editing: *On the Waterfront*

Sound recording: *The Glenn Miller Story*

Special effects: *20,000 Leagues under the Sea*

Short/cartoon: *When Magoo Flew* (UPA. Mr. Magoo/Pete Burness)

Short/one-reel: *This Mechanical Age* (Warner Bros., Robert Youngson)

Short/two-reel: *A Time out of War* (Carnival Prods.)

Documentary/feature: *The Vanishing Prairie* (Disney True-Life Adventures)

Documentary/short: *Thursday's Children* (British Information Service)

Special awards: Bausch & Lomb Optical Company; Kemp R. Niver; Greta Garbo; Danny Kaye; Jon Whiteley, Vincent Winter (outstanding juvenile performances, *The Little Kidnappers*); *Gate of Hell* (Japan), best foreign-language film

## 1955

Picture: *Marty* (UA, Hecht-Hill-Lancaster)

Actor: Ernest Borgnine, *Marty*

Actress: Anna Magnani, *The Rose Tattoo*

Supporting actor: Jack Lemmon, *Mister Roberts*

Supporting actress: Jo Van Fleet, *East of Eden*

Director: Delbert Mann, *Marty*

Screenplay: Paddy Chayefsky, *Marty*

Story and screenplay: William Ludwig, Sonya Levien, *Interrupted Melody*

Original story: Daniel Fuchs, *Love Me or Leave Me*

Cinematography/B&W: James Wong Howe, *The Rose Tattoo*
Cinematography/colour: Robert Burks, *To Catch a Thief*
Dramatic or comedy score: Alfred Newman, *Love Is a Many-Splendored Thing*
Musical score: Robert Russell Bennett, Hay Blackton, Adolph Deutsch, *Oklahoma!*
Song: "Love Is a Many-Splendored Thing" from *Love Is a Many-Splendored Thing*, music: Sammy Fain, lyrics: Paul Francis Webster
Art direction/B&W: Hal Perira, Tambi Larsen, *The Rose Tattoo*
Art direction/colour: William Flannery, *Picnic*
Costumes/B&W: Helen Rose, *I'll Cry Tomorrow*
Costumes/colour: Charles LeMaire, *Love Is a Many-Splendored Thing*
Editing: *Picnic*
Sound recording: *Oklahoma!*
Special effects: *The Bridges at Toko-Ri*
Short/cartoon: *Speedy Gonzales* (Warner Bros./Friz Freleng)
Short/one-reel: *Survival City*
Short/two-reel: *The Face of Lincoln* (University of Southern California)
Documentary/feature: *Helen Keller in Her Story*
Documentary/short: *Men against the Arctic* (Walt Disney)
Special award: *Samurai, the Legend of Musashi* (Japan), outstanding foreign-language film

## 1956

Picture: *Around the World in 80 Days* (UA, Michael Todd)
Actor: Yul Brynner, *The King and I*
Actress: Ingrid Bergman, *Anastasia*
Supporting actor: Anthony Quinn, *Lust for Life*
Supporting actress: Dorothy Malone, *Written on the Wind*
Director: George Stevens, *Giant*
Original screenplay: Albert Lamorisse, *The Red Balloon*
Adapted screenplay: James Poe, John Farrow, S.J. Perelman, *Around the World in 80 Days*
Original story: Robert Rich, *The Brave One* (note: pseudonym for blacklisted Dalton Trumbo)
Cinematography/B&W: Joseph Ruttenberg, *Somebody up There Likes Me*
Cinematography/colour: Lionel Lindon, *Around the World in 80 Days*
Dramatic or comedy score: Victor Young, *Around the World in 80 Days*
Musical score: Alfred Newman, Ken Darby, *The King and I*
Song: "Whatever Will Be, Will Be" from *The Man Who Knew Too Much*, music and lyrics: Jay Livingstone, Ray Evans
Art direction/B&W: Cedric Gibbons, *Somebody Up There Likes Me*
Art direction/colour: Lyle Wheeler, *The King and I*
Costumes/B&W: Jean Louis, *The Solid Gold Cadillac*

Costumes/colour: Irene Sharaff, *The King and I*
Editing: *Around the World in 80 Days*
Sound recording: *The King and I*
Special effects: *The Ten Commandments*
Short/cartoon: *Mister Magoo's Puddle Jumper* (UPA/ Pete Burness)
Short/one-reel: *Crashing the Water Barrier* (Warner Bros.)
Short/two-reel: *The Bespoke Overcoat* (Romulus Films, directed by Jack Clayton)
Documentary/feature: *The Silent World* (Jacques-Yves Cousteau)
Documentary/short: *The True Story of the Civil War*
Foreign-language film: *La Strada* (Italy)
Irving G. Thalberg award: Buddy Adler
Jean Hersholt Humanitarian Award: Y. Frank Freeman
Special award: Eddie Cantor

## 1957

Picture: *The Bridge on the River Kwai* (Columbia, Sam Spiegel)
Actor: Alec Guinness, *The Bridge on the River Kwai*
Actress: Joanne Woodward, *The Three Faces of Eve*
Supporting actor: Red Buttons, *Sayonara*
Supporting actress: Miyoshi Umeki, *Sayonara*
Director: David Lean, *The Bridge on the River Kwai*
Original screenplay: George Wells, *Designing Woman*
Adapted screenplay: Pierre Boulle, *The Bridge on the River Kwai*
Cinematography: Jack Hildyard, *The Bridge on the River Kwai*
Score: Malcolm Arnold, *The Bridge on the River Kwai*
Song: "All the Way" from *The Joker Is Wild*, music: James Van Heusen, lyrics: Sammy Cahn
Art direction: Ted Haworth, *Sayonara*
Costume design: Orry-Kelly, *Les Girls*
Editing: *The Bridge on the River Kwai*
Sound: *Sayonara*
Special effects: *The Enemy Below*
Short/cartoon: *Birds Anonymous* (Warner Bros./Friz Freleng/Sylvester & Tweety)
Short/live action: *The Wetback Hound* (Walt Disney)
Documentary/feature: *Albert Schweitzer*
Foreign-language film: *Nights of Cabiria* (Italy)
Jean Hersholt Humanitarian award: Samuel Goldwyn
Special awards: Charles Brackett; B.B. Kahane, Gilbert M. (Bronco Billy) Anderson; The Society of Motion Picture and Television Engineers

## 1958

Picture: *Gigi* (MGM, Arthur Freed)
Actor: David Niven, *Separate Tables*
Actress: Susan Hayward, *I Want to Live*
Supporting actor: Burl Ives, *The Big Country*

---

**...January 17 ...**
Cher, Richard Dreyfuss, and Quincy Jones ink to produce docudrama projects for NBC, skedded to air during the 1998-99 season.

Supporting actress: Wendy Hiller, *Separate Tables*
Director: Vincente Minnelli, *Gigi*
Original screenplay: Nathan E. Douglas, Harold Jacob Smith, *The Defiant Ones*
Adapted screenplay: Alan Jay Lerner, *Gigi*
Cinematography/B&W: Sam Leavitt, *The Defiant Ones*
Cinematography/colour: Joseph Ruttenberg, *Gigi*
Dramatic or comedy score: Dimitri Tiomkin, *The Old Man and the Sea*
Musical score: André Previn, *Gigi*
Song: "Gigi" from *Gigi*, music: Frederick Loewe, lyrics: Alan Jay Lerner
Art direction: William A. Horning, Preston Ames, *Gigi*
Costume design: Cecil Beaton, *Gigi*
Editing: *Gigi*
Sound: *South Pacific*
Special effects: *Tom Thumb*
Short/cartoon: *Knighty Knight Bugs* (Warner Bros./Friz Freleng/Bugs Bunny)
Short/live action: *Grand Canyon* (Walt Disney)
Documentary/feature: *White Wilderness* (Walt Disney)
Documentary/short: *AMA Girls* (Walt Disney)
Foreign-language film: *My Uncle (Mon Oncle)* (France)
Irving G. Thalberg award: Jack L. Warner
Special award: Maurice Chevalier

## 1959

Picture: *Ben-Hur* (MGM, Sam Zimbalist)
Actor: Charlton Heston, *Ben-Hur*
Actress: Simone Signoret, *Room at the Top*
Supporting actor: Hugh Griffith, *Ben-Hur*
Supporting actress: Shelley Winters, *The Diary of Anne Frank*
Director: William Wyler, *Ben-Hur*
Original screenplay: Russell Rouse, Clarence Green, Stanley Shapiro, Maurice Richlin, *Pillow Talk*
Adapted screenplay: Neil Paterson, *Room at the Top*
Cinematography/B&W: William C. Mellor, *The Diary of Anne Frank*
Cinematography/colour: Robert L. Surtees, *Ben-Hur*
Dramatic or comedy score: Miklos Rozsa, *Ben-Hur*
Musical score: André Previn, Ken Darby, *Porgy and Bess*
Song: "High Hopes" from *A Hole in the Head*, music: James Van Heusen, lyrics: Sammy Cahn
Art direction/B&W: Lyle R. Wheeler, George W. Davis, *The Diary of Anne Frank*
Art direction/colour: William A. Horning, *Ben-Hur*
Costumes/B&W: Orry-Kelly, *Some Like It Hot*
Costumes/colour: Elizabeth Haffenden, *Ben-Hur*
Editing: *Ben-Hur*
Sound: *Ben-Hur*
Special effects: *Ben-Hur*
Short/cartoon: *Moonbird* (John Hubley)

Short/live action: *The Golden Fish* (Jacques-Yves Cousteau)
Documentary/feature: *Serengeti Shall Not Die* (Germany)
Documentary/short: *Glass* (Bert Haanstra, Holland)
Foreign-language film: *Black Orpheus* (France)
Jean Hersholt Humanitarian award: Bob Hope
Special awards: Lee de Forest; Buster Keaton

## 1960

Picture: *The Apartment* (UA, Mirisch, Billy Wilder)
Actor: Burt Lancaster, *Elmer Gantry*
Actress: Elizabeth Taylor, *Butterfield 8*
Supporting actor: Peter Ustinov, *Spartacus*
Supporting actress: Shirley Jones, *Elmer Gantry*
Director: Billy Wilder, *The Apartment*
Original screenplay: Billy Wilder, I.A.L. Diamond, *The Apartment*
Adapted screenplay: Richard Brooks, *Elmer Gantry*
Cinematography/B&W: Freddie Francis, *Sons and Lovers*
Cinematography/colour: Russell Metty, *Spartacus*
Dramatic or comedy score: Ernest Gold, *Exodus*
Musical score: Morris Stoloff, Harry Sukman, *Song Without End*
Song: "Never on Sunday" from *Never on Sunday*, music and lyrics: Manos Hadjidakis
Art direction/B&W: Alexander Trauner, *The Apartment*
Art direction/colour: Alexander Golitzen, *Spartacus*
Costume design/B&W: Edith Head, *The Facts of Life*
Costume design/colour: Valles and Bill Thomas, *Spartacus*
Editing: *The Apartment*
Sound: *The Alamo*
Special effects: *The Time Machine*
Short/cartoon: *Munro* (William L Snyder)
Short/live action: *Day of the Painter* (Little Movies, Ezra R. Baker)
Documentary/feature: *The Horse with the Flying Tail* (Walt Disney)
Documentary/short: *Giuseppina* (James Hill)
Foreign-language film: *The Virgin Spring* (Sweden)
Jean Hersholt humanitarian award: Sol Lesser
Special awards: Gary Cooper; Stan Laurel; Hayley Mills (outstanding juvenile performance)

## 1961

Picture: *West Side Story* (UA, Mirisch-B&P Enterprises)
Actor: Maximilian Schell, *Judgment in Nuremberg*
Actress: Sophia Loren, *Two Women*
Supporting actor: George Chakiris, *West Side Story*
Supporting actress: Rita Moreno, *West Side Story*
Director: Robert Wise, Jerome Robbins, *West Side Story*
Original screenplay: William Inge, *Splendor in the Grass*
Adapted screenplay: Abby Mann, *Judgment in Nuremberg*

---

**...January 18...**
**Titanic** wins Best Pic honors at the Golden Globes... Miramax acquires indie **Next Stop Wonderland** for eyebrow-raising $6 million at Sundance.

Cinematography/B&W: Eugene Shuftan, *The Hustler*
Cinematography/colour: Daniel L. Fapp, *West Side Story*
Dramatic or comedy score: Henry Mancini, *Breakfast at Tiffany's*
Musical score: Saul Chaplin, Johnny Green, Sid Ramin, Irwin Kostal, *West Side Story*
Song: "Moon River" from *Breakfast at Tiffany's*, music: Henry Mancini, lyrics: Johnny Mercer
Art direction/B&W: Harry Horner, *The Hustler*
Art direction/colour: Boris Leven, *West Side Story*
Costume design/B&W: Piero Gherardi, *La Dolce Vita*
Costume design/colour: Irene Sharaff, *West Side Story*
Editing: *West Side Story*
Sound: *West Side Story*
Special effects: *The Guns of Navarone*
Short/cartoon: *Ersatz (The Substitute)* (Zagreb Film, Dusan Vukotic, Yugoslavia)
Short/live action: *Seawards the Great Ships*
Documentary/feature: *Le ciel et la boue* (*The Sky above, the Mud below*) Pierre-Dominique Gaisseau (France)
Documentary/short: *Project Hope*
Foreign-language film: *Through a Glass Darkly* (Sweden)
Irving G. Thalberg award: Stanley Kramer
Jean Hersholt humanitarian award: George Seaton
Special awards: William Hendricks; Fred L. Metzler; Jerome Robbins

## 1962

Picture: *Lawrence of Arabia* (Columbia, Sam Spiegel)
Actor: Gregory Peck, *To Kill a Mockingbird*
Actress: Anne Bancroft, *The Miracle Worker*
Supporting actor: Ed Begley, *Sweet Bird of Youth*
Supporting actress: Patty Duke, *The Miracle Worker*
Director: David Lean, *Lawrence of Arabia*
Original screenplay: Enio de Concini, Alfredo Giannetti, Pietro Germi, *Divorce Italian Style*
Adapted screenplay: Horton Foote, *To Kill a Mockingbird*
Cinematography/B&W: Jean Bourgoin, Walter Wottitz, *The Longest Day*
Cinematography/colour: Freddie Young, *Lawrence of Arabia*
Original score: Maurice Jarre, *Lawrence of Arabia*
Adapted score: Ray Heindorf, *The Music Man*
Song: "Days of Wine and Roses" from *Days of Wine and Roses*, music: Henry Mancini, lyrics: Johnny Mercer
Art direction/B&W: Alexander Golitzen, Henry Bumstead, *To Kill a Mockingbird*
Art direction/colour: John Box, *Lawrence of Arabia*
Costume design/B&W: Norma Koch, *What Ever Happened to Baby Jane?*
Costume design/colour: Mary Wills, *The Wonderful World of the Brothers Grimm*
Editing: *Lawrence of Arabia*
Sound: *Lawrence of Arabia*

Special effects: *The Longest Day*
Short/cartoon: *The Hole* (John and Faith Hubley)
Short/live action: *Heureux anniversaire* (*Happy Anniversary*) (Pierre Etaix)
Documentary/feature: *Black Fox*
Documentary/short: *Dylan Thomas*
Foreign-language film: *Sundays and Cybèle* (France)
Jean Hersholt humanitarian award: Steve Broidy

## 1963

Picture: *Tom Jones* (UA-Lopert, Woodfall)
Actor: Sidney Poitier, *Lillies of the Field*
Actress: Patricia Neal, *Hud*
Supporting actor: Melvyn Douglas, *Hud*
Supporting actress: Margaret Rutherford, *The V.I.P.s*
Director: Tony Richardson, *Tom Jones*
Original screenplay: James R. Webb, *How the West Was Won*
Adapted screenplay: John Osborne, *Tom Jones*
Cinematography/B&W: James Wong Howe, *Hud*
Cinematography/colour: Leon Shamroy, *Cleopatra*
Original score: John Addison, *Tom Jones*
Adapted score: André Previn, *Irma La Douce*
Song: "Call Me Irresponsible" from *Papa's Delicate Condition*, music: James Van Heusen, lyrics: Sammy Cahn
Art direction/B&W: Gene Callahan, *America, America*
Art direction/colour: John DeCuir (and nine others), *Cleopatra*
Costume design/B&W: Piero Gherardi, *Federico Fellini's 8½*
Costume design/colour: Irene Sharaff, Vittorio Nino Novarese, Renie, *Cleopatra*
Editing: *How the West Was Won*
Sound: *How the West Was Won*
Special visual effects: *Cleopatra*
Sound effects: *It's a Mad, Mad, Mad, Mad World*
Short/cartoon: *The Critic* (Ernest Pintoff/Mel Brooks)
Short/live action: *An Occurence at Owl Creek Bridge* (Robert Enrico)
Documentary/feature: Robert Frost: *A Lover's Quarrel with the World* (WGBH Educational Foundation)
Documentary/short: *Chagall*
Foreign-language film: *Federico Fellini's 8½* (Italy)
Irving G. Thalberg award: Sam Spiegel

## 1964

Picture: *My Fair Lady* (Warner Bros., Jack L. Warner)
Actor: Rex Harrison, *My Fair Lady*
Actress: Julie Andrews, *Mary Poppins*
Supporting actor: Peter Ustinov, *Topkapi*
Supporting actress: Lila Kedrova, *Zorba the Greek*
Director: George Cukor, *My Fair Lady*
Original screenplay: S.H. Barnett, Peter Stone, Frank Tarlogg, *Father Goose*
Adapted screenplay: Edward Anhalt, *Becket*

---

Cinematography/B&W: Walter Lassally, *Zorba the Greek*
Cinematography/colour: Hary Stradling, *My Fair Lady*
Original score: Richard M. Sherman, Robert B. Sherman, *Mary Poppins*
Adapted score: André Previn, *My Fair Lady*
Song: "Chim Chim Cher-ee" from *Mary Poppins*, music and lyrics: Richard M. Sherman, Robert B. Sherman
Art direction/B&W: Vassilis Fotopoulos, *Zorba the Greek*
Art direction/colour: Gene Allen, Cecil Beaton, *My Fair Lady*
Costume design/B&W: Dorothy Jeakins, *The Night of the Iguana*
Costume design/colour: Cecil Beaton, *My Fair Lady*
Editing: *Mary Poppins*
Sound: *My Fair Lady*
Special visual effects: *Mary Poppins*
Sound effects: *Goldfinger*
Short/cartoon: *The Pink Phink* (Friz Freleng/Pink Panther)
Short/live action: *Casals Conducts: 1964*
Documentary/feature: *Jacques-Yves Cousteau's World Without Sun*
Documentary/short: *Nine from Little Rock* (U.S. Information Agency)
Foreign-language film: *Yesterday, Today and Tomorrow* (Italy)
Special awards: William Tutle, make-up; *The 7 Faces of Dr Lao*

## 1965

Picture: *The Sound of Music* (20th Century-Fox, Argyle, Robert Wise)
Actor: Lee Marvin, *Cat Ballou*
Actress: Julie Christie, *Darling*
Supporting actor: Martin Balsam, *A Thousand Clowns*
Supporting actress: Shelley Winters, *A Patch of Blue*
Director: Robert Wise, *The Sound of Music*
Original screenplay: Frederic Raphael, *Darling*
Adapted screenplay: Robert Bolt, *Doctor Zhivago*
Cinematography/B&W: Ernest Laszlo, *Ship of Fools*
Cinematography/colour: Freddie Young, *Doctor Zhivago*
Original score: Maurice Jarre, *Doctor Zhivago*
Adapted score: Irwin Kostal, *The Sound of Music*
Song: "The Shadow of Your Smile" from *The Sandpiper*, music: Johnny Mendel, lyrics: Paul Francis Webster
Art direction/B&W: Robert Clatworthy, *Ship of Fools*
Art direction/colour: John Box, Terry Marsh, *Doctor Zhivago*
Costume design/B&W: Julie Harris, *Darling*
Costume design/colour: Phyllis Dalton, *Doctor Zhivago*
Editing: William Reynolds, *The Sound of Music*
Sound: *The Sound of Music*
Special visual effects: *Thunderball*
Sound effects: *The Great Race*

Short/cartoon: *The Dot and the Line* (MGM/Chuck Jones)
Short/live action: *The Chicken (Le Poulet)*, Claude Berri (France)
Documentary/feature:*The Eleanor Roosevelt Story*
Documentary/short: *To Be Alive!* (Johnson Wax Co., for New York World's Fair)
Foreign-language film: *The Shop on Main Street* (Czechoslovakia)
Irving G. Thalberg award: William Wyler
Jean Hersholt humanitarian award: Edmond L. DePatie
Special award: Bob Hope

## 1966

Picture: *A Man for All Seasons* (Columbia, Fred Zinnemann)
Actor: Paul Scofield, *A Man for All Seasons*
Actress: Elizabeth Taylor, *Who's Afraid of Virginia Woolf?*
Supporting actor: Walter Matthau, *The Fortune Cookie*
Supporting actress: Sandy Dennis, *Who's Afraid of Virginia Woolf?*
Director: Fred Zinnemann, *A Man for All Seasons*
Original screenplay: Claude Lelouch, Pierre Uytterhoeven, *A Man and a Woman*
Adapted screenplay: Robert Bolt, *A Man for All Seasons*
Cinematography/B&W: Haskell Wexler, *Who's Afraid of Virginia Woolf?*
Cinematography/colour: Ted Moore, *A Man for All Seasons*
Original score: John Barry, *Born Free*
Adapted score: Ken Thorne, *A Funny Thing Happened on the Way to the Forum*
Song: "Born Free" from *Born Free*, music: John Barry, lyrics: Don Black
Art direction/B&W: Richard Sylbert, *Who's Afraid of Virginia Woolf?*
Art direction/colour: Jack Martin Smith, Dale Hennesy, *Fantastic Voyage*
Costume design/B&W: Irene Sharaff, *Who's Afraid of Virginia Woolf?*
Costume design/colour: Elizabeth Haffenden, Joan Bridge, *A Man for All Seasons*
Editing: *Grand Prix*
Sound: *Grand Prix*
Sound effects: *Grand Prix*
Special visual effects: *Fantastic Voyage*
Short/cartoon: *Herb Alpert and the Tijuana Brass Double Feature* (John and Faith Hubley)
Short/live action: *Wild Wings* (British Transport Films, Edgar Anstey)
Documentary/feature: *The War Game* (BBC Production for the British Film Institute, Peter Watkins)
Documentary/short: *A Year Toward Tomorrow* (Office of Economic Opportunity)
Foreign-language film: *A Man and a Woman* (France)

**. . . January 20 . . .**
The Broadcast Film Critics Assn. chooses **L.A. Confidential** as Best Pic.

Irving G. Thalberg award: Robert Wise
Jean Hersholt humanitarian award: George Bagnall
Special awards: Y. Frank Freeman; Yakima Canutt

## 1967

Picture: *In the Heat of the Night* (UA, Walter Mirisch)
Actor: Rod Steiger, *In the Heat of the Night*
Actress: Katharine Hepburn, *Guess Who's Coming to Dinner*
Supporting actor: George Kennedy, *Cool Hand Luke*
Supporting actress: Estelle Parsons, *Bonnie and Clyde*
Director: Mike Nichols, *The Graduate*
Original screenplay: William Rose, *Guess Who's Coming to Dinner*
Adapted screenplay: Stirling Silliphant, *In the Heat of the Night*
Cinematography: Burnett Guffey, *Bonnie and Clyde*
Original score: Elmer Bernstein, *Thoroughly Modern Millie*
Adapted score: Alfred Newman, Ken Darby, *Camelot*
Song: "Talk to the Animals" from *Doctor Dolittle*, music and lyrics: Leslie Bricusse
Art direction: John Truscott, Edward Carrere, *Camelot*
Costume design: John Truscott, *Camelot*
Editing: Hal Ashby, *In the Heat of the Night*
Sound: *In the Heat of the Night*
Sound effects: *The Dirty Dozen*
Special visual effects: *Doctor Dolittle*
Short/cartoon: *The Box* (Brandon Films, Fred Wolf)
Short/live action: *A Place to Stand* (Ontario Dept. of Economics and Development, made for Expo '67)
Documentary/feature: *The Anderson Platoon* (French Broadcasting System, Pierre Schöndörffer)
Documentary/short: *The Redwoods*
Foreign-language film: *Closely Watched Trains* (Czechoslovakia)
Irving G. Thalberg award: Alfred Hitchcock
Jean Hersholt humanitarian award: Gregory Peck
Special award: Arthur Freed

## 1968

Picture: *Oliver!* (Columbia, Romulus, John Woolf)
Actor: Cliff Robertson, *Charly*
Actress: Katharine Hepburn, *The Lion in Winter*; Barbra Streisand, *Funny Girl* (tie)
Supporting actor: Jack Albertson, *The Subject Was Roses*
Supporting actress: Ruth Gordon, *Rosemary's Baby*
Director: Carol Reed, *Oliver!*
Original screenplay: Mel Brooks, *The Producers*
Adapted screenplay: James Goldman, *The Lion in Winter*
Cinematography: Pasqualino De Santis, *Romeo and Juliet*
Original score: John Barry, *The Lion in Winter*
Adapted score: John Green, *Oliver!*

Song: "The Windmills of Your Mind" from *The Thomas Crown Affair*, music: Michel Legrand, lyrics: Alan and Marilyn Bergman
Art direction: John Box, Terry Marsh, *Oliver!*
Costume design: Danilo Donati, *Romeo and Juliet*
Editing: *Bullitt*
Sound: *Oliver!*
Special visual effects: Stanley Kubrick, *2001: A Space Odyssey*
Short/cartoon: *Winnie the Pooh and the Blustery Day* (Walt Disney)
Short/live action: *Robert Kennedy Remembered*
Documentary/feature: *Journey into Self* (Western Behavioral Sciences Institute)
Documentary/short: *Why Man Creates* (Saul Bass)
Foreign-language film: *War and Peace* (USSR)
Jean Hersholt Humanitarian Award: Martha Raye
Special awards: John Chambers, make-up, *Planet of the Apes*; Onna White, choreography, *Oliver!*

## 1969

Picture: *Midnight Cowboy* (UA, Jerome Hellman)
Actor: John Wayne, *True Grit*
Actress: Maggie Smith, *The Prime of Miss Jean Brodie*
Supporting actor: Gig Young, *They Shoot Horses Don't They?*
Supporting actress: Goldie Hawn, *Cactus Flower*
Director: John Schlesinger, *Midnight Cowboy*
Original screenplay: William Goldman, *Butch Cassidy and the Sundance Kid*
Adapted screenplay: Waldo Salt, *Midnight Cowboy*
Cinematography: Conrad Hall, *Butch Cassidy and the Sundance Kid*
Dramatic score: Burt Bacharach, *Butch Cassidy and the Sundance Kid*
Musical score: Lennie Hayton, Lionel Newman, *Hello Dolly!*
Song: "Raindrops Keep Fallin' on My Head" from *Butch Cassidy and the Sundance Kid*, music: Burt Bacharach, lyrics: Hal David
Art direction: John DeCuir, Jack Martin Smith, *Hello, Dolly!*
Costume design: Margaret Furse, *Anne of the Thousand Days*
Editing: *Z*
Sound: *Hello, Dolly!*
Special visual effects: *Marooned*
Short/cartoon: *It's Tough to Be a Bird* (Walt Disney, Ward Kimball)
Short/live action: *The Magic Machines* (Fly-by-Night Prods., Joan Keller Stern)
Documentary/feature: *Arthur Rubinstein – The Love of Life*
Documentary/short: *Czechoslovakia 1968* (U.S. Information Agency)
Foreign-language film: *Z* (France-Algeria)
Jean Hersholt humanitarian award: George Jessel
Special award: Cary Grant

---

## 1970

Picture: *Patton* (20th Century-Fox, Frank McCarthy)
Actor: George C. Scott, *Patton*
Actress: Glenda Jackson, *Women in Love*
Supporting actor: John Mills, *Ryan's Daughter*
Supporting actress: Helen Hayes, *Airport*
Director: Franklin J. Schaffner, *Patton*
Original screenplay: Francis Ford Coppola, Edmund H. North, *Patton*
Adapted screenplay: Ring Lardner, Jr., *M*A*S*H*
Cinematography: Freddie Young, *Ryan's Daughter*
Score: Francis Lai, *Love Story*
Song score: The Beatles, *Let It Be*
Song: "For All We Know" from *Lovers and Other Strangers*, music: Fred Karlin, lyrics: Robb Royer, James Griffin
Art direction: Urie McCleary, *Patton*
Costume design: Nino Novares, *Cromwell*
Editing: *Patton*
Sound: *Patton*
Special visual effects: *Tora! Tora! Tora!*
Short/cartoon: *Is It Always Right to Be Right?* (Stephen and Nick Bosustow)
Short/live action: *The Resurrection of Broncho Billy* (University of Southern California, directed by John Carpenter)
Documentary/feature: *Woodstock* (Michael Wadleigh)
Documentary/short: *Interviews with My Lai Veterans* (Joseph Strick)
Foreign-language film: *Investigation of a Citizen Above Suspicion* (Italy)
Irving G. Thalberg award: Ingmar Bergman
Jean Hersholt humanitarian award: Frank Sinatra
Special awards: Lillian Gish; Orson Welles

## 1971

Picture: *The French Connection* (20th Century-Fox, D'Antoni-Schine-Moore)
Actor: Gene Hackman, *The French Connection*
Actress: Jane Fonda, *Klute*
Supporting actor: Ben Johnson, *The Last Picture Show*
Supporting actress: Cloris Leachman, *The Last Picture Show*
Director: William Friedkin, *The French Connection*
Original screenplay: Paddy Chayefsky, *The Hospital*
Adapted screenplay: Ernest Tidyman, *The French Connection*
Cinematography: Oswald Morris, *Fiddler on the Roof*
Art direction: John Box, *Nicholas and Alexandra*
Costume design: Yvonne Blake, Antonio Castillo, *Nicholas and Alexandra*
Original score: Michel Legrand, *Summer of '42*
Scoring adaptation: John Williams, *Fiddler on the Roof*
Song: "Theme from Shaft", *Shaft*, music and lyrics: Isaac Hayes

Editing: *The French Connection*
Special visual effects: *Bedknobs and Broomsticks*
Short/animated: *The Crunch Bird*
Short/live action: *Sentinels of Silence*
Documentary/feature: *The Hellstrom Chronicle* (David L. Wolper, Walon Green)
Documentary/short: *Sentinels of Silence*
Foreign-language film: *The Garden of the Finzi-Continis* (Italy)
Special award: Charles Chaplin

## 1972

Picture: *The Godfather* (Paramount, Albert S. Ruddy)
Actor: Marlon Brando, *The Godfather*
Actress: Liza Minnelli, *Cabaret*
Supporting actor: Joel Gray, *Cabaret*
Supporting actress: Eileen Heckart, *Butterflies Are Free*
Director: Bob Fosse, *Cabaret*
Original screenplay: Jeremy Larner, *The Candidate*
Adapted screenplay: Mario Puzo, Francis Ford Coppola, *The Godfather*
Cinematography: Geoffrey Unsworth, *Cabaret*
Original score: Charles Chaplin, Raymond Rasch, Larry Russell, *Limelight*
Scoring adaptation: Ralph Burns, *Cabaret*
Song: "The Morning After" from *The Poseidon Adventure*, music and lyrics: Al Kasha, Joel Hirschhorn
Art direction: Rolf Zehetbauer, *Cabaret*
Costume design: Anthony Powell, *Travels with My Aunt*
Editing: *Cabaret*
Sound: *Cabaret*
Visual effects: *The Poseidon Adventure*
Short/animated: *A Christmas Carol* (ABC, Richard Williams)
Short/live action: *Norman Rockwell's World... An American Dream*
Documentary/feature: *Marjoe* (Howard Smith, Sarah Kernochan)
Documentary/short: *This Tiny World*
Foreign-language film: *The Discreet Charm of the Bourgeoisie* (France)
Jean Hersholt humanitarian award: Rosalind Russell
Special awards: Edward Robinson; Charles S. Boren

## 1973

Picture: *The Sting* (Universal, Tony Bill, Michael and Julia Phillips)
Actor: Jack Lemmon, *Save the Tiger*
Actress: Glenda Jackson, *A Touch of Class*
Supporting actor: John Houseman, *The Paper Chase*
Supporting actress: Tatum O'Neal, *Paper Moon*
Director: George Roy Hill, *The Sting*
Original screenplay: David S. Ward, *The Sting*

---

**...January 22...**

Paul Brickman (**Risky Business**) zeroes in on comedy drama **Providence** as his first directorial project in eight years.

Adapted screenplay: William Peter Blatty, *The Exorcist*
Cinematography: Sven Nykvist, *Cries and Whispers*
Original score: Marvin Hamlisch, *The Way We Were*
Scoring adaptation: Marvin Hamlisch, *The Sting*
Song: "The Way We Were" from *The Way We Were*, music:
Marvin Hamlisch, lyrics: Alan and Marilyn Bergman
Art direction: Henry Bumstead, *The Sting*
Costume design: Edith Head, *The Sting*
Editing: *The Sting*
Sound: *The Exorcist*
Short/animated: *Frank Film* (Frank Mouris)
Short/live action: *The Bolero*
Documentary/feature: *The Great American Cowboy*
(Keith Merrill)
Documentary/short: *Princeton: A Search for Answers*
Foreign-language film: *Day for Night* (France)
Irving G. Thalberg award: Lawrence Weingarten
Jean Hersholt humanitarian award: Lew Wasserman
Special awards: Henri Langlois; Groucho Marx

## 1974

Picture: *The Godfather, Part II* (Paramount, Francis Ford
Coppola, Gray Frederickson, Fred Roos)
Actor: Art Carney, *Harry and Tonto*
Actress: Ellen Burstyn, *Alice Doesn't Live Here Anymore*
Supporting actor: Robert De Niro, *The Godfather, Part II*
Supporting actress: Ingrid Bergman, *Murder on the
Orient Express*
Director: Francis Ford Coppola, *The Godfather, Part II*
Original screenplay: Robert Towne, *Chinatown*
Adapted screenplay: Francis Ford Coppola, Mario
Puzo, *The Godfather, Part II*
Cinematography: Fred Koenenkamp, Joseph Biroc, *The
Towering Inferno*
Original score: Nino Rota, Carmine Coppola, *The
Godfather, Part II*
Scoring adaptation: Nelson Riddle, *The Great Gatsby*
Song: "We May Never Love Like This Again" from *The
Towering Inferno*, music and lyrics: Al Kasha, Joel
Hirschhorn
Art direction: Dean Tavoularis, *The Godfather, Part II*
Costume design: Theoni V. Aldredge, *The Great Gatsby*
Editing: *The Towering Inferno*
Sound: *Earthquake*
Visual effects: *Earthquake*
Short/animated: *Closed Mondays* (Will Vinton)
Short/live action: *One-Eyed Men Are Kings*
Documentary/feature: *Hearts and Minds* (Peter Davis,
Bert Schneider)
Documentary/short: *Don't*
Foreign-language film: *Amarcord* (Italy)
Jean Hersholt humanitarian award: Arthur B. Krim
Special awards: Howard Hawks; Jean Renoir

## 1975

Picture: *One Flew over the Cuckoo's Nest* (UA Fantasy
Films, Saul Zaentz, Michael Douglas)
Actor: Jack Nicholson, *One Flew over the Cuckoo's Nest*
Actress: Louise Fletcher, *One Flew over the Cuckoo's Nest*
Supporting actor: George Burns, *The Sunshine Boys*
Supporting actress: Lee Grant, *Shampoo*
Director: Milos Forman, *One Flew over the Cuckoo's Nest*
Original screenplay: Frank Pierson, *Dog Day Afternoon*
Adapted screenplay: Lawrence Hauben, Bo Goldman,
*One Flew over the Cuckoo's Nest*
Cinematography: John Alcott, *Barry Lyndon*
Original score: John Williams, *Jaws*
Scoring adaptation: Leonard Rosenman, *Barry Lyndon*
Song: "I'm Easy" from *Nashville*, music and lyrics: Keith
Carradine
Art direction: Ken Adam, *Barry Lyndon*
Costume design: Ulla-Brit Soderlund, Milena Canonero,
*Barry Lyndon*
Editing: Verna Fields, *Jaws*
Sound: *Jaws*
Sound effects: *The Hindenburg*
Visual effects: *The Hindenburg*
Short/animated: *Great* (Bob Godfrey)
Short/live action: *Angel and Big Joe*
Documentary/feature: *The Man Who Skied Down Everest*
Documentary/short: *The End of the Game*
Foreign-language film: *Dersu Uzala* (USSR)
Irving G. Thalberg memorial award: Mervyn LeRoy
Jean Hersholt humanitarian award: Jules C. Stein
Special award: Mary Pickford

## 1976

Picture: *Rocky* (UA, Irwin Winkler, Robert Chartoff)
Actor: Peter Finch, *Network*
Actress: Faye Dunaway, *Network*
Supporting actor: Jason Robards, *All the President's Men*
Supporting actress: Beatrice Straight, *Network*
Director: John G. Avildson, *Rocky*
Original screenplay: Paddy Chayefsky, *Network*
Adapted screenplay: William Goldman, *All the
President's Men*
Cinematography: Haskell Wexler, *Bound for Glory*
Original score: Jerry Goldsmith, *The Omen*
Scoring adaptation: Leonard Rosenman, *Bound for Glory*
Song: "Evergreen" from *A Star Is Born*, music: Barbra
Streisand, lyrics: Paul Williams
Art direction: George Jenkins, *All the President's Men*
Costume design: Danilo Donati, *Fellini's Casanova*
Editing: *Rocky*
Sound: *All the President's Men*
Visual effects: Carlo Rambaldi, *King Kong, Logan's Run*
(special award – not a tie)

Short/animated: *Leisure* (Film Australia)

Short/live action: *In the Region of Ice* (American Film Institute)

Documentary/feature: *Harlan County, USA* (Barbara Kopple)

Documentary/short: *Number Our Days* (Lynne Littman)

Foreign-language film: *Black and White in Colour* (Ivory Coast)

Irving G. Thalberg award: Pandro S. Berman

## 1977

Picture: *Annie Hall* (UA, Rollins-Joffe)

Actor: Richard Dreyfuss, *The Goodbye Girl*

Actress: Diane Keaton, *Annie Hall*

Supporting actor: Jason Robards, *Julia*

Supporting actress: Vanessa Redgrave, *Julia*

Director: Woody Allen, *Annie Hall*

Original screenplay: Woody Allen, Marshal Brickman, *Annie Hall*

Adapted screenplay: Alvin Sargent, *Julia*

Cinematography: Vilmos Zsigmond, *Close Encounters of the Third Kind*

Original score: John Williams, *Star Wars*

Scoring adaptation: Jonathan Tunick, *A Little Night Music*

Song: "You Light up My Life" from *You Light up My Life*, music and lyrics: Joseph Brooks

Art direction: John Barry, *Star Wars*

Costume design: John Mollo, *Star Wars*

Editing: *Star Wars*

Sound: *Star Wars*

Sound effects: Benjamin Burtt, Jr., *Star Wars*

Visual effects: John Dykstra, Richard Edlund, *Star Wars*

Short/animated: *Sand Castle* (National Film Board of Canada, Co Hoedeman)

Short/live action: *I'll Find a Way* (National Film Board of Canada)

Documentary/feature: *Who Are the DeBolts? And Where Did They Get 19 Kids?* (John Korty)

Documentary/short: *Gravity Is My Enemy*

Foreign-language film: *Madame Rosa* (France)

Irving G. Thalberg award: Walter Mirisch

Jean Hersholt humanitarian award: Charlton Heston

Special awards: Margaret Booth (editing); Gordon E. Sawyer and Sidney P. Solow (service and dedication to the Academy)

## 1978

Picture: *The Deer Hunter* (Universal, EMI Films, Michael Cimino)

Actor: John Voight, *Coming Home*

Actress: Jane Fonda, *Coming Home*

Supporting actor: Christopher Walken, *The Deer Hunter*

Supporting actress: Maggie Smith, *California Suite*

Director: Michael Cimino, *The Deer Hunter*

Original screenplay: Nancy Dowd, Waldo Salt, Robert C. Jones, *Coming Home*

Adapted screenplay: Oliver Stone, *Midnight Express*

Cinematography: Nestor Almendros, *Days of Heaven*

Original score: Giorgio Moroder, *Midnight Express*

Scoring adaptation: Joe Renzetti, *The Buddy Holly Story*

Song: "Last Dance" from *Thank God It's Friday*, music and lyrics: Paul Jabara

Art direction: Paul Sylbert, *Heaven Can Wait*

Costume design: Anthony Powell, *Death on the Nile*

Editing: *The Deer Hunter*

Sound: *The Deer Hunter*

Visual effects: *Superman*

Short/animated: *Special Delivery* (National Film Board of Canada)

Short/live action: *Teenage Father* (New Visions Inc. for the Children's Home Society)

Documentary/feature: *Scared Straight!*

Documentary/short: *The Flight of the Gossamer Condor*

Foreign-language film: *Préparez vos mouchoirs (Get out Your Handkerchiefs)* (France)

Jean Hersholt humanitarian award: Leo Jaffe

Special awards: Walter Lantz; Laurence Olivier; King Vidor; The Museum of Modern Art Department of Film

## 1979

Picture: *Kramer vs. Kramer* (Columbia, Stanley R. Jaffe)

Actor: Dustin Hoffman, *Kramer vs. Kramer*

Actress: Sally Field, *Norma Rae*

Supporting actor: Melvyn Douglas, *Being There*

Supporting actress: Meryl Streep, *Kramer vs. Kramer*

Director: Robert Benton, *Kramer vs. Kramer*

Original screenplay: Steve Tesic, *Breaking Away*

Adapted screenplay: Robert Benton, *Kramer vs. Kramer*

Cinematography: Vittorio Storaro, *Apocalypse Now*

Original score: Georges Delerue, *A Little Romance*

Scoring adaptation: Ralph Burns, *All That Jazz*

Song: "It Goes Like It Goes" from *Norma Rae*, music: David Shire, lyrics: Norman Gimbel

Art direction: Philip Rosenberg, Tony Walton, *All That Jazz*

Costume design: Albert Wolsky, *All That Jazz*

Editing: *All That Jazz*

Sound: Walter Murch, *Apocalypse Now*

Sound editing: Alan Splet, *The Black Stallion*

Visual effects: HR Giger, Carlo Rambaldi, *Alien*

Short/animated: *Every Child* (National Film Board of Canada, Derek Lamb)

Short/live action: *Board and Care*

Documentary/feature: *Best Boy* (Ira Wohl)

Documentary/short: *Paul Robeson: Tribute to an Artist*

Foreign-language film: *The Tin Drum* (West Germany)

Irving G. Thalberg award: Ray Stark

---

### . . . January 24 . . .

Urban drama **Slam** wins top prize with Sundance jury; Native American **Smoke Signals** nabs audience award.

Jean Hersholt humanitarian award: Robert Benjamin
Special awards: Alec Guinness; Hal Elias, for service to
the Academy

## 1980

Picture: *Ordinary People* (Paramount, Wildwood, Ronald
L. Schwary)
Actor: Robert De Niro, *Raging Bull*
Actress: Sissy Spacek, *Coal Miner's Daughter*
Supporting actor: Timothy Hutton, *Ordinary People*
Supporting actress: Mary Steenburgen, *Melvin and
Howard*
Director: Robert Redford, *Ordinary People*
Original screenplay: Bo Goldman, *Melvin and Howard*
Adapted screenplay: Alvin Sargent, *Ordinary People*
Cinematography: Geoffrey Unsworth, Ghislain
Cloquet, *Tess*
Score: Michael Gore, *Fame*
Song: "Fame" from *Fame*, music: Michael Gore, lyrics:
Dean Pitchford
Art direction: Pierre Guffroy, Jack Stevens, *Tess*
Costume design: Anthony Powell, *Tess*
Editing: Thelma Schoonmaker, *Raging Bull*
Sound: *The Empire Strikes Back*
Visual effects: Richard Edlund, Denis Muren, *The Empire
Strikes Back*
Short/animated: *The Fly* (Ferenc Rofusz, Hungary)
Short/live action: *The Dollar Bottom*
Documentary/feature: *From Mao to Mozart: Isaac Stern
in China*
Documentary/short: *Karl Hess: Toward Liberty*
Foreign-language film: *Moscow Does Not Believe in Tears*
(USSR)
Special award: Henry Fonda

## 1981

Picture: *Chariots of Fire* (The Ladd Company, Warner
Bros., Enigma, David Puttnam)
Actor: Henry Fonda, *On Golden Pond*
Actress: Katharine Hepburn, *On Golden Pond*
Supporting actor: John Gielgud, *Arthur*
Supporting actress: Maureen Stapleton, *Reds*
Director: Warren Beatty, *Reds*
Original screenplay: Colin Welland, *Chariots of Fire*
Adapted screenplay: Ernest Thompson, *On Golden Pond*
Cinematography: Vittorio Storaro, *Reds*
Score: Vangelis, *Chariots of Fire*
Song: "Arthur's theme" from *Arthur*, music and lyrics:
Burt Bacharach, Carole Bayer Sager, Christopher Cross,
Peter Allen
Art direction: Norman Reynolds, *Raiders of the Lost Ark*
Costume design: Milena Canonero, *Chariots of Fire*
Editing: *Raiders of the Lost Ark*

Sound: *Raiders of the Lost Ark*
Sound-effects editing: *Raiders of the Lost Ark*
Make-up: Rick Baker, *An American Werewolf in London*
Visual effects: Richard Edlund, Joe Johnston, *Raiders of
the Lost Ark*
Short/animated: *Crac* (Canada)
Short/live action: *Violet*
Documentary/feature: *Genocide*
Documentary/short: *Close Harmony*
Foreign-language film: *Mephisto* (Hungary)
Irving G. Thalberg award: Albert R. "Cubby" Broccoli
Jean Hersholt humanitarian award: Danny Kaye
Special award: Barbara Stanwyck

## 1982

Picture: *Gandhi* (Columbia, Indo-British Films, Richard
Attenborough)
Actor: Ben Kingsley, *Gandhi*
Actress: Meryl Streep, *Sophie's Choice*
Supporting actor: Louis Gossett, Jr., *An Officer and a
Gentleman*
Supporting actress: Jessica Lange, *Tootsie*
Director: Richard Attenborough, *Gandhi*
Original screenplay: John Briley, *Gandhi*
Adapted screenplay: Costa-Gavras, Donald Stewart, *Missing*
Cinematography: Billy Williams, Ronnie Taylor, *Gandhi*
Original score: John Williams, *E.T.*
Song score: Leslie Bricusse, Henry Mancini,
*Victor/Victoria*
Song: "Up Where We Belong" from *An Officer and a
Gentleman*, music: Jack Nitzsche, Buffy Saint-Marie,
lyrics: Will Jennings
Art direction: Stuart Craig, Bob Laing, *Gandhi*
Costume design: John Mollo, Bhanu Athaiya, *Gandhi*
Editing: *Gandhi*
Sound: *Gandhi*
Sound-effects editing: *E.T.*
Visual effects: Carlo Rimbaldi, Dennis Muren, *E.T.*
Short/animated: *Tango* (Film Polski, Zbigniew
Rybczynski)
Short/live action: *A Shocking Accident*
Documentary/feature: *Just Another Missing Kid* (Canada)
Documentary/short: *If You Love This Planet* (National
Film Board of Canada)
Foreign-language film: *Volver a empezar (To Begin Again)*
(Spain)
Jean Hersholt humanitarian award: Walter Mirisch
Special award: Mickey Rooney

## 1983

Picture: *Terms of Endearment* (Paramount, James L.
Brooks)
Actor: Robert Duvall, *Tender Mercies*

---

**. . . January 25 . . .**
**Titanic** passes $200 million overseas.

Actress: Shirley MacLaine, *Terms of Endearment*
Supporting actor: Jack Nicholson, *Terms of Endearment*
Supporting actress: Linda Hunt, *The Year of Living Dangerously*
Director: James L. Brooks, *Terms of Endearment*
Original screenplay: Horton Foote, *Tender Mercies*
Adapted screenplay: James L. Brooks, *Terms of Endearment*
Cinematography: Sven Nykvist, *Fanny and Alexander*
Original score: Bill Conti, *The Right Stuff*
Song score: Michel Legrand, Alan and Marilyn Bergman, *Yentl*
Song: "Flashdance… What a Feeling" from *Flashdance*, music: Giorgio Moroder, lyrics: Keith Forsey, Irene Cara
Art direction: Anna Asp, *Fanny and Alexander*
Costume design: Marik Vos, *Fanny and Alexander*
Editing: *The Right Stuff*
Sound: *The Right Stuff*
Sound-effects editing: *The Right Stuff*
Visual effects: Richard Edlund, Dennis Muren, Ken Ralston, Phil Tippett, *Return of the Jedi*
Short/animated: *Sundae in New York* (Jimmy Picker)
Short/live action: *Boys and Girls*
Documentary/feature: *He Makes Me Feel Like Dancin'* (Emile Ardonlino)
Documentary/short: *Flamenco at 5:15* (National Film Board of Canada)
Foreign-language film: *Fanny and Alexander* (Sweden)
Jean Hersholt humanitarian award: M.J. "Mike" Frankovich
Special award: Hal Roach

## 1984

Picture: *Amadeus* (Orion, Saul Zaentz)
Actor: F. Murray Abraham, *Amadeus*
Actress: Sally Field, *Places in the Heart*
Supporting actor: Haing S. Ngor, *The Killing Fields*
Supporting actress: Peggy Ashcroft, *A Passage to India*
Director: Milos Forman, *Amadeus*
Original screenplay: Robert Benton, *Places in the Heart*
Adapted screenplay: Peter Shaffer, *Amadeus*
Cinematography: Chris Menges, *The Killing Fields*
Original score: Maurice Jarre, *A Passage to India*
Song score: Prince, *Purple Rain*
Song: "I Just Called to Say I Love You" from *The Woman in Red*, music and lyrics: Stevie Wonder
Art direction: Patrizia Von Brandenstein, *Amadeus*
Costume design: Theodor Pistek, *Amadeus*
Editing: *The Killing Fields*
Sound: *Amadeus*
Sound-effects editing: *The River*
Makeup: Paul LeBlanc, Dick Smith, *Amadeus*
Visual effects: Dennis Muren, et al, *Indiana Jones and the Temple of Doom*

Short/animated: *Charade*
Short/live action: *Up* (Pyramid Films, Mike Hoover)
Documentary/feature: *The Times of Harvey Milk*
Documentary/short: *The Stone Carvers*
Foreign-language film: *Dangerous Moves* (Switzerland)
Jean Hersholt humanitarian award: David L. Wolper
Special awards: National Endowment for the Arts; James Stewart

## 1985

Picture: *Out of Africa* (Universal, Sydney Pollack)
Actor: William Hurt, *Kiss of the Spider Woman*
Actress: Geraldine Page, *The Trip to Bountiful*
Supporting actor: Don Ameche, *Cocoon*
Supporting actress: Anjelica Huston, *Prizzi's Honor*
Director: Sydney Pollack, *Out of Africa*
Original screenplay: Earl W. Wallace, William Kelley; story by William Kelley, Pamela Wallace, Earl W. Wallace, *Witness*
Adapted screenplay: Kurt Luedtke, *Out of Africa*
Cinematography: David Watkin, *Out of Africa*
Score: John Barry, *Out of Africa*
Song: "Say You, Say Me" from *White Nights*, music and lyrics: Lionel Richie
Art direction: Stephen Grimes, *Out of Africa*
Costume design: Emi Wada, *Ran*
Editing: *Witness*
Sound: *Out of Africa*
Sound-effects editing: *Back to the Future*
Makeup: *Mask*
Visual effects: *Cocoon*
Short/animated: *Anna & Bella* (Cilia Van Dijk)
Short/live action: *Molly's Pilgrim*
Documentary/feature: *Broken Rainbow*
Documentary/short: *Witness to War: Dr Charlie Clements*
Foreign-language film: *The Official Story* (Argentina)
Jean Hersholt humanitarian award: Charles "Buddy" Rogers
Special awards: Paul Newman; Alex North; John H. Whitney

## 1986

Picture: *Platoon* (Orion, Hemdale, Arnold Kopelson)
Actor: Paul Newman, *The Color of Money*
Actress: Marlee Matlin, *Children of a Lesser God*
Supporting actor: Michael Caine, *Hannah and Her Sisters*
Supporting actress: Dianne Wiest, *Hannah and Her Sisters*
Director: Oliver Stone, *Platoon*
Original screenplay: Woody Allen, *Hannah and Her Sisters*
Adapted screenplay: Ruth Prawer Jhabvala, *A Room with a View*
Cinematography: Chris Menges, *The Mission*
Score: Herbie Hancock, *'Round Midnight*

---

### … January 26 …

James Brooks, Jim Cameron, Curtis Hanson, Steven Spielberg, and Gus Van Sant announced as Directors Guild feature finalists… Madonna inks to star in the indie pic, **The Red Door.**

Song: "Take My Breath Away" from *Top Gun*, music: Giorgio Moroder, lyrics: Tom Whitlock
Art direction: Gianni Quaranta, Brian Ackland-Snow, *A Room with a View*
Costume design: Jenny Beavan, John Bright, *A Room with a View*
Editing: *Platoon*
Sound: *Platoon*
Sound-effects editing: *Aliens*
Makeup: Chris Walas, Stephan Dupuis, *The Fly*
Visual effects: Stan Winston, *Aliens*
Short/animated: *A Greek Tragedy*
Short/live action: *Precious Images* (Chuck Workman)
Documentary/feature: *Artie Shaw: Time is All You've Got; Down and Out in America* (tie)
Documentary/short: *Women-For America, for the World*
Foreign-language film: *The Assault* (The Netherlands)
Irving G. Thalberg award: Steven Spielberg
Special award: Ralph Bellamy

## 1987

Picture: *The Last Emperor* (Columbia, Hemdale, Jeremy Thomas)
Actor: Michael Douglas, *Wall Street*
Actress: Cher, *Moonstruck*
Supporting actor: Sean Connery, *The Untouchables*
Supporting actress: Olympia Dukakis, *Moonstruck*
Director: Bernardo Bertolucci, *The Last Emperor*
Original screenplay: John Patrick Shanley, *Moonstruck*
Adapted screenplay: Mark Peploe, Bernardo Bertolucci, *The Last Emperor*
Cinematography: Vittorio Storaro, *The Last Emperor*
Score: Ryuichi Sakamoti, David Byrne, Cong Su, *The Last Emperor*
Song: "(I've Had) the Time of My Life" from *Dirty Dancing*, music: Franke Previte, John DeNicola, Donald Markowitz, lyrics: Franke Previte
Art direction: Ferdinando Scarfiotti, *The Last Emperor*
Costume design: James Acheson, *The Last Emperor*
Editing: *The Last Emperor*
Sound: *The Last Emperor*
Sound-effects editing: *Robocop*
Makeup: Rick Baker, *Harry and the Hendersons*
Visual effects: Dennis Muren, *Innerspace*
Short/animated: *The Man Who Planted Trees* (Société Radio-Canada/Canadian Broadcasting Corporation, Frederic Back)
Short/live action: *Ray's Male Heterosexual Dance Hall*
Documentary/feature: *The Ten-Year Lunch: The Wit and Legend of the Algonquin Round Table*
Documentary/short subject: *Young at Heart*
Foreign-language film: *Babette's Feast* (Denmark)
Irving G. Thalberg award: Billy Wilder

## 1988

Picture: *Rain Man* (United Artists, Guber-Peters Co., Mark Johnson)
Actor: Dustin Hoffman, *Rain Man*
Actress: Jodie Foster, *The Accused*
Supporting actor: Kevin Kline, *A Fish Called Wanda*
Supporting actress: Geena Davis, *The Accidental Tourist*
Director: Barry Levinson, *Rain Man*
Original screenplay: Ronald Bass, Barry Morrow, story by Barry Morrow, *Rain Man*
Adapted screenplay: Christopher Hampton, *Dangerous Liaisons*
Cinematography: Peter Biziou, *Mississippi Burning*
Score: Dave Grusin, *The Milagro Beanfield War*
Song: "Let the River Run" from *Working Girl*, music and lyrics: Carly Simon
Art direction: Stuart Craig, *Dangerous Liaisons*
Costume design: James Acheson, *Dangerous Liaisons*
Editing: *Who Framed Roger Rabbit?*
Sound: *Bird*
Sound-effects editing: *Who Framed Roger Rabbit?*
Makeup: *Beetlejuice*
Visual effects: *Who Framed Roger Rabbit?*
Short/animated: *Tin Toy* (Pixar, John Lasseter)
Short/live action: *The Appointment of Dennis Jennings* (Dean Parisot, Seten Wright)
Documentary/feature: *Hotel Terminus: The Life and Time of Klaus Barbie* (Marcel Ophüls)
Documentary/short: *You Don't Have to Die*
Foreign-language film: *Pelle the Conqueror* (Denmark)
Special awards: Eastman Kodak; National Film Board of Canada
Special award/animation direction: Richard Williams, *Who Framed Roger Rabbit?*

## 1989

Picture: *Driving Miss Daisy* (Warner Bros., Richard Zanuck, Lili Fini Zanuck)
Actor: Daniel Day-Lewis, *My Left Foot*
Actress: Jessica Tandy, *Driving Miss Daisy*
Supporting actor: Denzel Washington, *Glory*
Supporting actress: Brenda Fricker, *My Left Foot*
Director: Oliver Stone, *Born on the Fourth of July*
Original screenplay: Tom Schulman, *Dead Poets Society*
Adapted screenplay: Alfred Uhry, *Driving Miss Daisy*
Cinematography: Freddie Francis, *Glory*
Score: Alan Menken, *The Little Mermaid*
Song: "Under the Sea" from *The Little Mermaid*, music: Alan Menken, lyrics: Howard Ashman
Art direction: Anton Frust, *Batman*
Costume design: Phyllis Dalton, *Henry V*
Editing: *Born on the Fourth of July*
Sound: *Glory*

---

### ... January 27 ...

**ER** crew shares in $850 million license-fee windfall... Clint Eastwood honored by Producers Guild with Selznick prize for career achievement.

Sound-effects editing: *Indiana Jones and the Last Crusade*
Makeup: *Driving Miss Daisy*
Visual effects: Dennis Muren, et al, *The Abyss*
Short/animated: *Balance*
Short/live action: *Work Experience*
Documentary/feature: *Common Threads: Stories from the Quilt* (Robert Epstein, Bill Couturie)
Documentary/short: *The Johnstown Flood*
Foreign-language film: *Cinema Paradiso* (Italy)
Jean Hersholt humanitarian award: Howard W. Koch
Special award: Akira Kurosawa

## 1990

Picture: *Dances with Wolves* (Orion, Tig Prods, Jim Wilson, Kevin Costner)
Actor: Jeremy Irons, *Reversal of Fortune*
Actress: Kathy Bates, *Misery*
Supporting actor: Joe Pesci, *GoodFellas*
Supporting actress: Whoopi Goldberg, *Ghost*
Director: Kevin Costner, *Dances with Wolves*
Original screenplay: Bruce Joel Rubin, *Ghost*
Adapted screenplay: Michael Blake, *Dances with Wolves*
Cinematography: Dean Semler, *Dances with Wolves*
Score: John Barry, *Dances with Wolves*
Song: "Sooner or Later" from *Dick Tracy*, music and lyrics: Stephen Sondheim
Art direction: Richard Sylbert, *Dick Tracy*
Costume design: Franca Squarciapino, *Cyrano de Bergerac*
Editing: *Dances with Wolves*
Sound: *Dances with Wolves*
Sound-effects editing: *The Hunt for Red October*
Makeup: *Dick Tracy*
Short/animated: *Creature Comforts* (Aardman Animations, Nick Park)
Short/live action: *The Lunch Date* (Adam Davidson)
Documentary/feature: *American Dream* (Barbara Kopple)
Documentary/short: *Days of Waiting*
Foreign-language film: *Journey of Hope* (Switzerland)
Irving G. Thalberg award: Richard D. Zanuck, David Brown
Special awards: Sophia Loren; Myrna Loy

## 1991

Picture: *The Silence of the Lambs* (Orion, Strong Heart, Jonathan Demme)
Actor: Anthony Hopkins, *The Silence of the Lambs*
Actress: Jodie Foster, *The Silence of the Lambs*
Supporting actor: Jack Palance, *City Slickers*
Supporting actress: Mercedes Ruehl, *The Fisher King*
Director: Jonathan Demme, *The Silence of the Lambs*
Original screenplay: Callie Khouri, *Thelma & Louise*
Adapted screenplay: Ted Tally, *The Silence of the Lambs*
Cinematography: Robert Richardson, *JFK*
Score: Alan Menken, *Beauty and the Beast*

Song: "Beauty and the Beast" from *Beauty and the Beast*, music: Alan Menken, lyrics: Howard Ashman
Art direction: Dennis Gassner, *Bugsy*
Costume design: Albert Wolsky, *Bugsy*
Editing: *JFK*
Sound: Gary Rudstrom, et al, *Terminator 2: Judgment Day*
Sound effects editing: *Terminator 2: Judgment Day*
Make-up: Stan Winston, Jeff Dawn, *Terminator 2: Judgment Day*
Visual effects: Dennis Muren, Stan Winston, *Terminator 2: Judgment Day*
Short/animated: *Manipulation*
Short/live action: *Session Man*
Documentary/feature: *In the Shadow of the Stars*
Documentary/short: *Deadly Deception: General Electric, Nuclear Weapons and Our Environment*
Foreign-language film: *Mediterraneo* (Italy)
Irving G. Thalberg award: George Lucas
Special award: Satyajit Ray

## 1992

Picture: *Unforgiven* (Warner Bros., Clint Eastwood)
Actor: Al Pacino, *Scent of a Woman*
Actress: Emma Thompson, *Howards End*
Supporting actor: Gene Hackman, *Unforgiven*
Supporting actress: Marisa Tomei, *My Cousin Vinny*
Director: Clint Eastwood, *Unforgiven*
Original screenplay: Neil Jordan, *The Crying Game*
Adapted screenplay: Ruth Prawer Jhabvala, *Howards End*
Cinematography: Philippe Rousselot, *A River Runs Through It*
Score: Alan Menken, *Aladdin*
Song: "Whole New World" from *Aladdin*, music: Alan Menken, lyrics: Tim Rice
Art direction: Luciana Arrighi, Ian Whittaker, *Howards End*
Costume design: Eiko Ishioka, *Bram Stoker's Dracula*
Editing: *Unforgiven*
Sound: *The Last of the Mohicans*
Sound-effects editing: *Bram Stoker's Dracula*
Makeup: *Bram Stoker's Dracula*
Visual effects: *Death Becomes Her*
Short/animated: *Mona Lisa Descending a Staircase*
Short/live action: *Omnibus*
Documentary/feature: *The Panama Deception* (Barbara Trent)
Documentary/short: *Educating Peter*
Foreign-language film: *Indochine* (France)
Jean Hersholt humanitarian award: Audrey Hepburn, Elizabeth Taylor
Special award: Federico Fellini

## 1993

Picture: *Schindler's List* (Universal, Amblin

---

Entertainment, Steven Spielberg, Gerald R. Molen, Branko Lustig)
Actor: Tom Hanks, *Philadelphia*
Actress: Holly Hunter, *The Piano*
Supporting actor: Tommy Lee Jones, *The Fugitive*
Supporting actress: Anna Paquin, *The Piano*
Director: Steven Spielberg, *Schindler's List*
Original screenplay: Jane Campion, *The Piano*
Adapted screenplay: Steven Zaillian, *Schindler's List*
Cinematography: Janusz Kaminski, *Schindler's List*
Score: John Williams, *Schindler's List*
Song: "Streets of Philadelphia" from *Philadelphia*, music and lyrics: Bruce Springsteen
Art direction: Allan Starski, Ewa Braun, *Schindler's List*
Costume design: Gabriella Pescucci, *The Age of Innocence*
Editing: *Schindler's List*
Sound: Gary Rydstrom, *Jurassic Park*
Sound-effects editing: Gary Rydstrom, *Jurassic Park*
Makeup: *Mrs. Doubtfire*
Visual effects: Dennis Muren, Stan Winston, Phil Tippett, Michael Lantieri, *Jurassic Park*
Short/animated: *The Wrong Trousers* (Aardman Animations, Nick Park)
Short/live action: *Black Rider* (Germany)
Documentary/feature: *I Am a Promise: The Children of Stanton Elementary School*
Documentary/short: *Defending Our Lives*
Foreign-language film: *Belle Epoque* (Spain)
Jean Hersholt humanitarian award: Paul Newman
Special award: Deborah Kerr

## 1994

Picture: *Forrest Gump* (Paramount, Wendy Finerman, Steve Tisch, Steve Starkey)
Actor: Tom Hanks, *Forrest Gump*
Actress: Jessica Lange, *Blue Sky*
Supporting actor: Martin Landau, *Ed Wood*
Supporting actress: Dianne Wiest, *Bullets over Broadway*
Director: Robert Zemeckis, *Forrest Gump*
Original screenplay: Quentin Tarantino, story by Quentin Tarantino, Roger Avary, *Pulp Fiction*
Adapted screenplay: Eric Roth, *Forrest Gump*
Cinematography: John Toll, *Legends of the Fall*
Score: Hans Zimmer, *The Lion King*
Song: "Can You Feel the Love Tonight?" from *The Lion King*, music: Elton John, lyrics: Tim Rice
Art direction: Ken Adams, *The Madness of King George*
Costume design: Lizzy Gardiner, Tim Chappel, *The Adventures of Priscilla, Queen of the Desert*
Editing: *Forrest Gump*
Sound: *Speed*
Sound-effects editing: *Speed*
Makeup: Rick Baker, *Ed Wood*

Visual effects: *Forrest Gump*
Short/animated: *Bob's Birthday* (Channel Four/National Film Board of Canada)
Short/live action: *Franz Kafka's It's a Wonderful Life* (Peter Capaldi, Ruth Kenley-Letts), *Trevor* (Peggy Rajski, Randy Stone) (tie)
Documentary/feature: *Maya Lin: A Strong Clear Vision* (Freida Lee Mock)
Documentary/short: *A Time for Justice* (Southern Poverty Law Center)
Foreign-language film: *Burnt by the Sun* (Russia)
Irving G. Thalberg award: Clint Eastwood
Jean Hersholt humanitarian award: Quincy Jones
Special award: Michelangelo Antonioni

## 1995

Picture: *Braveheart* (Paramount, Icon, Mel Gibson, Alan Ladd, Jr., Bruce Davey)
Actor: Nicolas Cage, *Leaving Las Vegas*
Actress: Susan Sarandon, *Dead Man Walking*
Supporting actor: Kevin Spacey, *The Usual Suspects*
Supporting actress: Mira Sorvino, *Mighty Aphrodite*
Director: Mel Gibson, *Braveheart*
Original screenplay: Christopher McQuarrie, *The Usual Suspects*
Adapted screenplay : Emma Thompson, *Sense and Sensibility*
Cinematography: John Toll, *Braveheart*
Musical or comedy score: Alan Menken and Stephen Schwartz, *Pocahontas*
Dramatic score: Luis Bacalov, *Il Postino*
Song: "Colors of the Wind" from *Pocahontas*, music: Alan Menken, lyrics: Stephen Schwartz
Art direction: Eugenio Zanetti, *Restoration*
Costume design: James Acheson, *Restoration*
Editing: *Apollo 13*
Sound: *Apollo 13*
Sound-effects editing: *Braveheart*
Makeup: Peter Frampton, Paul Pattison, Lois Burwell, *Braveheart*
Visual effects: *Babe*
Short/animated: *A Close Shave* (Aardman Animation, Nick Park)
Short/live action: *Liberman in Love*
Documentary/feature: *Anne Frank Remembered* (BBC/Disney)
Documentary/short: *One Survivor Remembers* (HBO)
Foreign-language film: *Antonia's Line* (The Netherlands)
Special awards: Kirk Douglas; Chuck Jones

## 1996

Picture: *The English Patient* (Miramax, Saul Zaentz)
Actor: Geoffrey Rush, *Shine*

---

Actress: Frances McDormand, *Fargo*
Supporting actor: Cuba Gooding, Jr., *Jerry Maguire*
Supporting actress: Juliette Binoche, *The English Patient*
Director: Anthony Minghella, *The English Patient*
Original screenplay: Ethan and Joel Coen, *Fargo*
Adapted screenplay: Billy Bob Thornton, *Sling Blade*
Cinematography: John Seale, *The English Patient*
Original musical or comedy score: Rachel Portman, *Emma*
Original dramatic score: Gabriel Yared, *The English Patient*
Song: "You Must Love Me" from *Evita*, music: Andrew
Lloyd Webber, lyrics: Tim Rice
Art direction: Brian Morris, *The English Patient*
Set direction: Stephanie McMillan, *The English Patient*
Costume design: Ann Roth, *The English Patient*
Editing: *The English Patient*
Sound: *The English Patient*
Sound-effects editing: *The Ghost and the Darkness*
Makeup: Rick Baker and David Leroy Anderson, *The
Nutty Professor*
Visual effects: *Independence Day*
Short/animated: *Quest*
Short/live action: *Dear Diary*
Documentary/feature: *When We Were Kings* (Leon Gast
and David Sonenberg)
Documentary/short: *Breathing Lessons: The Life and
Work of Mark O'Brien*
Foreign-language film: *Kolya* (Czech Republic)
Special awards: Volker W. Bahnemann, Michael Kidd;
Joe Lombardi; Burton "Bud" Stone

## 1997

Picture: *Titanic* (James Cameron, Jon Landau)
Actor: Jack Nicholson, *As Good As It Gets*
Actress: Helen Hunt, *As Good As It Gets*
Supporting actor: Robin Williams, *Good Will Hunting*
Supporting actress: Kim Basinger, *L.A. Confidential*
Director: James Cameron, *Titanic*
Original screenplay: Ben Affleck and Matt Damon, *Good
Will Hunting*
Adapted screenplay: Brian Helgeland and Curtis Hanson,
*L.A. Confidential*
Cinematography: Russell Carpenter, *Titanic*
Original musical or comedy score: Anne Dudley, *The
Full Monty*
Original dramatic score: James Horner, *Titanic*
Song: "My Heart Will Go On" from *Titanic*
Art direction: Peter Lamont and Michael Ford, *Titanic*
Costume design: Deborah L. Scott, *Titanic*
Editing: *Titanic*
Sound: *Titanic*
Sound-effects editing: *Titanic*
Makeup: Rick Barker and David LeRoy Anderson, *Men
in Black*

Visual effects: *Titanic*
Short/animated: *Geri's Game*
Short/live action: *Visas and Virtue*
Documentary/feature: *The Long Way Home* (Rabbi
Marvin Hier and Richard Tank)
Documentary/short: *A Story of Healing*
Foreign-language film: *Character* (The Netherlands)
Special awards: Pete Clark; Stanley Donen

## 1998

Picture: *Shakespeare in Love* (David Parfitt, Donna
Gigliotti, Harvey Weinstein, Edward Zwick and Marc
Norman)
Actor: Roberto Begnini, *Life Is Beautiful*
Actress: Gwyneth Paltrow, *Shakespeare in Love*
Supporting actor: James Coburn, *Affliction*
Supporting actress: Judy Dench, *Shakespeare in Love*
Director: Steven Spielberg, *Saving Private Ryan*
Original screenplay: Marc Norman and Tom
Stoppard, *Shakespeare in Love*
Adapted screenplay: Bill Condon, *Gods and Monsters*
Cinematography: Janusz Kaminski, *Saving
Private Ryan*
Original musical or comedy score: Stephen Warbeck,
*Shakespeare in Love*
Original dramatic score: Nicola Piovani, *Life
Is Beautiful*
Song: "When You Believe" from *The Prince of Egypt*
Art direction: Martin Childs, Jill Quertier,
*Shakespeare in Love*
Costume design: Sandy Powell, *Shakespeare in Love*
Editing: *Saving Private Ryan*
Sound: *Saving Private Ryan*
Sound effects editing: *Saving Private Ryan*
Make-up: Jenny Shircore, *Elizabeth*
Visual effects: *What Dreams May Come*
Short/animated: *Bunny*
Short/live action: *Election Night (Valgaften)*
Documentary/feature: *The Last Days* (James Moll
and Ken Lipper)
Documentary/short: *The Personals: Improvisations
On Romance In The Golden Years*
Foreign-language film: *Life Is Beautiful* (Italy)
Honorary Oscar: Elia Kazan
Irving G. Thalberg award: Norman Jewison

---

**. . . January 30 . . .**
ER cast members share a reported $7 million bonus.

# Golden Globe nominations: 1998

Motion picture – drama: *Elizabeth, Gods & Monsters, The Horse Whisperer, Saving Private Ryan, The Truman Show*
Motion picture – musical or comedy: *Bulworth, The Mask of Zorro, Patch Adams, Shakespeare in Love, Still Crazy, There's Something About Mary*
Performance by an actress in a motion picture – drama: Cate Blanchett, *Elizabeth*; Fernanda Montenegro, *Central Station*; Susan Sarandon, *Stepmom*; Emily Watson, *Hilary and Jackie*
Performance by an actor in a motion picture – drama: Jim Carrey, *The Truman Show*; Stephen Fry, *Wilde*; Tom Hanks, *Saving Private Ryan*; Ian McKellen, *Gods and Monsters*; Nick Nolte, *Affliction*
Performance by an actress in a motion picture – musical or comedy: Cameron Diaz, *There's Something About Mary*; Jane Horrocks, *Little Voice*; Gwyneth Paltrow, *Shakespeare in Love*; Christina Ricci, *The Opposite of Sex*; Meg Ryan, *You've Got Mail*
Performance by an actor in a motion picture – musical or comedy: Antonio Banderas, *The Mask of Zorro*; Warren Beatty, *Bulworth*; Michael Caine, *Little Voice*; John Travolta, *Primary Colors*; Robin Williams, *Patch Adams*
Foreign-language film: *The Celebration*, Thomas Vinterberg; *Central Station*, Walter Salles; *Hombres Armados (Men With Guns)*, John Sayles; *The Polish Bride*, Karim Traidia; *Tango*, Carlos Saura
Performance by an actress in a supporting role in a motion picture – drama: Kathy Bates, *Primary Colors*; Brenda Blethyn, *Little Voice*; Judi Dench, *Shakespeare in Love*; Lynn Redgrave, *Gods and Monsters*; Sharon Stone, *The Mighty*

Performance by an actor in a supporting role in a motion picture – drama: Robert Duvall, *A Civil Action*; Ed Harris, *The Truman Show*; Bill Murray, *Rushmore*; Geoffrey Rush, *Shakespeare in Love*; Donald Sutherland, *Without Limits*; Billy Bob Thorton, *A Simple Plan*
Director, motion picture – drama: Shekhar Kapur, *Elizabeth*; John Madden, *Shakespeare in Love*; Robert Redford, *The Horse Whisperer*; Steven Spielberg, *Saving Private Ryan*; Peter Weir, *The Truman Show*
Screenplay – motion picture: Warren Beatty and Jeremy Pikser, *Bulworth*; Andrew Niccol, *The Truman Show*; Mark Norman and Tom Stoppard, *Shakespeare in Love*; Robert Rodat, *Saving Private Ryan*; Todd Solondz, *Happiness*
Original score – motion picture: Burkhard Dallwitz, additional music by Philip Glass, *The Truman Show*; Jerry Goldsmith, *Mulan*; Randy Newman, *A Bug's Life*; Stephen Schwartz, Hans Zimmer, *The Prince of Egypt*; John Williams, *Saving Private Ryan*
Original song – motion picture: "The Flame Still Burns" from *Still Crazy*, music and lyrics: Mick Jones, Marti Frederiksen, Chris Difford; "The Mighty" from *The Mighty*, music: Sting, lyrics: Trevor Jones; "The Prayer" from *Quest for Camelot: The Magic Sword*, music and lyrics: David Foster and Carole Bayer Sager; "Reflection" from *Mulan*, music: Matthew Wilder, lyrics: David Zippel; "Uninvited" from *City of Angels*, music and lyrics: Alanis Morissette; "When You Believe" from *The Prince of Egypt*, music and lyrics: Stephen Schwartz

# Golden Globe Film Awards: 1998

Motion picture – drama: *Saving Private Ryan*, DreamWorks & Paramount Pictures
Motion picture – musical or comedy: *Shakespeare in Love*, Miramax Films/Universal Pictures/The Bedford Falls Company
Performance by an actress in a motion picture – drama: Cate Blanchett, *Elizabeth*
Performance by an actor in a motion picture – drama: Jim Carrey, *The Truman Show*
Performance by an actress in a motion picture – musical or comedy; Gwyneth Paltrow, *Shakespeare in Love*

Performance by an actor in a motion picture – musical or comedy : Michael Caine, *Little Voice*
Foreign-language film: *Central Station*, Sony Pictures Classics (Brazil)
Performance by an actress in a supporting role in a motion picture: Lynn Redgrave, *Gods and Monsters*
Performance by an actor in a supporting role in a motion picture: Ed Harris, *The Truman Show*
Director – motion picture: Steven Spielberg, *Saving Private Ryan*
Screenplay – motion picture: Marc Norman and Tom Stoppard, *Shakespeare in Love*

---

**...January 31...**
Sellout London revival of Ionesco's **The Chairs**, which closed tonight, is the latest British production to set its sights on Broadway.

Original score – motion picture: Burkhard Dallwitz/Additional music by Philip Glass, *The Truman Show*
Original song – motion picture: "The Prayer –

*Quest For Camelot: The Magic Sword"*; music and lyrics: David Foster and Carole Bayer Sager (Italian Translation: Alberto Testa and Tony Renis)

# Critics' Awards

## Golden Globes: 1997

Motion picture – Drama: *Titanic*
Performance by an actress – drama: Judi Dench, *Her Majesty Mrs. Brown*
Performance by an actor – drama: Peter Fonda, *Ulee's Gold*
Motion picture – musical or comedy: *As Good As It Gets*
Performance by an actress – musical or comedy: Helen Hunt, *As Good As It Gets*
Performance by an actor – musical or comedy: Jack Nicholson, *As Good As It Gets*
Foreign-language film: *Ma vie en rose* (Belgium)
Performance by an actress in a supporting role: Kim Basinger, *L.A. Confidential*
Performance by an actor in a supporting role: Burt Reynolds, *Boogie Nights*
Director – motion picture: James Cameron, *Titanic*
Screenplay – motion picture: Matt Damon and Ben Affleck, *Good Will Hunting*
Original score – motion picture: James Horner, *Titanic*
Original song – motion picture: "My Heart Will Go On" from *Titanic*

## LA Film Critics: 1998

Picture: *Saving Private Ryan*
Director: Steven Spielberg, *Saving Private Ryan*
Actor: Ian McKellen, *Gods and Monsters*
Actress: Fernanda Montenegro, *Central Station*, and Ally Sheedy, *High Art*
Supporting actor: Billy Bob Thorton, *A Simple Plan*, and Bill Murray, *Rushmore* and *Wild Things*
Supporting actress: Joan Allen, *Pleasantville*
Screenplay: Warren Beatty, Jeremy Pikser, *Bulworth*
Best cinematography: Janusz Kaminski, *Saving Private Ryan*
Best foreign film: *The Celebration* (Denmark)
Best documentary: *The Farm: Angola USA*

## National Board Of Review: 1998

Picture: *Gods and Monsters*
Director: Shekhar Kapur, *Elizabeth*
Actor: Ian McKellen, *Gods & Monsters*

Actress: Fernanda Montenegro, *Central Station*
Supporting actor: Ed Harris, *The Truman Show* and *Stepmom*
Supporting actress: Christina Ricci, *The Opposite of Sex*, *Buffalo 66*, and *Pecker*
Best foreign film: *Central Station* (Brazil)
Best documentary: *Wild Man Blues*
Special awards: Roberto Benigni, *Life is Beautiful*, special achievement in filmmaking; Martin Scorsese, Billy Wilder award; Bernardo Bertolucci, Freedom of Expression honor; Michael Caine, Career Achievement

## New York Film Critics' Awards: 1998

Picture: *Saving Private Ryan*
Director: Terrence Malick, *The Thin Red Line*
Actor: Nick Nolte, *Affliction*
Actress: Cameron Diaz, *There's Something About Mary*
Supporting actor: Bill Murray, *Rushmore*
Supporting actress: Lisa Kudrow, *The Opposite of Sex*
Screenplay: Mark Norman and Tom Stoppard, *Shakespeare in Love*
Cinematography: John Toll, *The Thin Red Line*
Foreign film: *The Celebration* (Denmark)
Documentary: *The Farm: Angola USA*
First film: *Love and Death on Long Island*
Special award: *Touch of Evil*

## Boston Film Critics: 1998

Picture: *Out of Sight*
Director: John Boorman, *The General*
Actor: Brendan Gleeson, *The General* and *I Went Down*
Actress: Samantha Morton, *Under the Skin*
Supporting actor: Billy Bob Thorton, *A Simple Plan*
Supporting actress: Joan Allen, *Pleasantville*
Screenplay: Scott Frank, *Out of Sight*
Cinematography: Janusz Kaminski, *Saving Private Ryan*
Foreign film: *The Taste of Cherry* (Iran)
Documentary: *The Big One*
Special awards: Carine Adler, Best New Filmmaker; William H. Macy, awarded for his body of work

# National Awards

## European Academy Awards 1998

European film: *La vita è bella* (*Life is Beautiful*), Roberto Benigni, Italy

European actor: Roberto Benigni, *La vita è bella*

European actress: Elodie Bouchez and Natacha Régnier, *La vie rêvée des anges* (*The Dreamlife of Angels*), France

European screenwriter: Peter Howitt, *Sliding Doors*, U.K.

European cinematographer: Adrian Biddle, *The Butcher Boy*, Ireland

European achievement in world cinema: Stellan Skarsgard, Sweden, *Amistad, Good Will Hunting*

Screen International award for a non-European film: *The Truman Show*, Peter Weir, U.S.

The people's choice awards: (voted for by movie fans across Europe):

Best European director: Roland Emmerich (Germany) *Godzilla*

Best European actor: Antonio Banderas (Spain) *The Mask of Zorro*

Best European actress: Kate Winslet (U.K.) *Titanic*

European discovery – Fassbinder award: Joint winners: *Festen* (*The Celebration*) Thomas Vinterberg, Denmark and *La vie rêvée des anges* (*The Dreamlife of Angels*) Eric Zonca, France

European documentary award – Prix Arte: Claudio Pazienza, Belgium

European short film: *Un Jour*, Marie Paccou, France

European critics' award – Prix Fipresci: Goran Paskaljevic, *Bure Baruta* (*The Powder Keg*), Yugoslavia

European Film Academy special achievement award: Jeremy Irons (U.K.)

## European Academy Awards 1997

European Film: *The Full Monty*, Peter Cattaneo, U.K.

European actress: Juliette Binoche, *The English Patient*

European actor: Bob Hoskins, *TwentyFourSeven*

European screenwriter: Chris Van Der Stappen and Alain Berliner, *Ma vie en rose*

European cinematographer: John Seale, *The English Patient*

European Film Academy lifetime achievement Award: Jeanne Moreau

European achievement in world cinema: Milos Forman

European Discovery – Fassbinder award: Bruno Dumont, *La vie de Jésus*

European documentary award – Prix Arte: Benoît Dervaux, Jean-Pierre Dardenne, Luc Dardenne

European Fipresci award: Manoel de Oliveira

Screen International Award for a non-European film: *Hana-Bi*, Takeshi Kitano, Japan

## People's Awards:

Film: *The Full Monty*

Actress: Jodie Foster

Actor: Javier Bardem

## AFI Australian Film Awards

Film: *The Interview*, Craig Monahan

Director: Rowan Woods, *The Boys*

Actor: Hugo Weaving, *The Interview*

Actress: Deborah Mailman, *Radiance*

Supporting actor: John Polson, *The Boys*

Supporting actress: Toni Collette, *The Boys*

Original screenplay: Craig Monahan, Gordon Davie, *The Interview*

Adapted screenplay: Stephen Sewell, *The Boys*

Foreign film: *L.A. Confidential*

Cinematogrpahy: Geoffrey Simpson ACS, *Oscar and Lucinda*

Editing: Jill Bilcock, *Head On*

Sound: Andrew Plain, Ben Osmo, Gethin Creagh, *Oscar and Lucinda*

Original music score: Thomas Newman, *Oscar and Lucinda*

Production design: Luciana Arrighi, *Oscar and Lucinda*

Costume design: Janet Patterson, *Oscar and Lucinda*

## British Academy of Film and Television Awards

Film: *The Full Monty*, Peter Cattaneo

British film: *Nil By Mouth*, Gary Oldman

Direction: Baz Luhrmann, *William Shakespeare's Romeo and Juliet*

Actor: Robert Carlyle, *The Full Monty*

Actress: Judi Dench, *Mrs. Brown*

Supporting actor: Tom Wilkinson, *The Full Monty*

Supporting actress: Sigourney Weaver, *The Ice Storm*

Original screenplay: Gary Oldman, *Nil By Mouth*

Adapted screenplay: Baz Luhrmann, Craig Pearce, *William Shakespeare's Romeo and Juliet*

Foreign-language film: *L'Appartement* (France)

Audience award: *The Full Monty*

Fellowship award: Sean Connery

## French César Awards

Director: Luc Besson, *The Fifth Element*

Film: *On connaît la chanson*, Claude Chabrol

Actor: Andre Dussollier, *On connaît la chanson*

**. . . February 2 . . .**
Jim Carrey signs on to star in **The Incredible Mr. Limpet.**

Actress: Ariane Ascaride, *Marius et Jeannette*
Supporting actor: Jean-Pierre Bacri, *On connaît la chanson*
Supporting actress: Agnès Jaoui, *On connaît la chanson*
Young actor: Stanislas Merhar, *Nettoyage à sec*
Young actress: Emma de Caunes, *Un frère*
First film: *Didier*
Foreign film: *Brassed Off* (U.K.)
Original or adapted screenplay: Agnès Jaoui, Jean-Pierre Bacri, *On connaît la chanson*
Music: Bernardo Sandoval, *Western*
Photography: Thierry Arbogast, *The Fifth Element*
Best editing: Hervé de Luze, *On connaît la chanson*
Best sets: Dan Weil, *The Fifth Element*
Costumes: Christian Gasc, *On Guard*
Short film: David Fourier, *Des Majorêtes dans l'Espace*

## Chinese Golden Rooster Awards

Film: *The Opium War,* Xie Jin
Director: Wei Lian, *The Turning Point*
Script: Wang Xingdong, *The Days Without a Hero*
Actor: Liu Peiqi, *The Days Without a Hero*
Actress: Yu Hui, *Happy Lotus*
Supporting actor (shared): Lin Liankun, *The Opium War,* Sun Chun, *Drug-Busting Heroes*
Supporting actress: Ma Xiaoqing, *My Daddy*

## Danish Bodil Film Awards

American film: *L.A. Confidential,* Curtis Hanson
Non-American film: *The Full Monty,* Peter Cattaneo (U.K.)
Danish film: *Let's Get Lost,* Jonas Elmer
Actor: Holger Juul Hansen, *Riget II* (*The Kingdom II*)
Actress: Sidse Babett-Knudsen, *Let's Get Lost*
Supporting actor: Jesper Christensen, *Barbara*
Supporting actress: Birgitte Raaberg, *Riget II* (*The Kingdom II*)
Special Bodil award: Joachim Holbek, composer

## Finnish Jussi Film Awards

Picture: *Freakin' Beautiful World* (*Sairaan kaunis maailma*), Jarmo Lampela
Director: Olli Saarela, *Lunastus*
Actor: Kari Heiskanen, *Lunastus*
Actress: Leea Klemola, *Neitoperho*
Script: Olli Saarela, Heikki Vuento, *Lunastus*

## German Film Awards

Film: *Comedian Harmonists*
Silver Filmband: (shared) *Winterschlaefer* (*Wintersleepers*), Tom Tykwer; *Zugvoegel* (*Train Birds*), Peter Lichtefeld
Director: Wim Wenders, *The End of Violence*

Actor: Ulrich Noethen, *Comedian Harmonists*
Actress: Katja Riemann, *Bandits, Die Apothekerin*
Supporting actor: Peter Lohmeyer, *Zugvoegel* (*Train Birds*)
Supporting actress: Meret Becker, *Comedian Harmonists*
Cinematography: Frank Griebe, *Winterschlaefer* (*Wintersleepers*), *Zugvoegel* (*Train Birds*)
Editing: Peter R. Adam, *Comedian Harmonists*
Foreign film: (shared) *Brassed Off* (U.K.); *The Full Monty* (U.K.)
Production design: Rolf Zehetbauer, *Comedian Harmonists*
Lifetime achievement awards: Heinz Badewitz; Gregory Peck

## Hong Kong Film Awards

Film: *Made in Hong Kong,* Fruit Chan
Director: Fruit Chan, *Made in Hong Kong*
Best script: To Kwok-wai, *The Mad Phoenix*
Actor: Tony Leung Chiu-wai, *Happy Together*
Actress: Maggie Cheung, *The Soong Sisters*
Supporting actor: Jiang Wen, *The Soong Sisters*
Supporting actress: Anita Mui, *Eighteen Spring*

## Italian Donatello Awards

Film: *La vita è bella* (*Life is Beautiful*)
Director: Roberto Benigni, *La vita è bella*
Producer: Elda Ferri, Gianluigi Braschi, *La vita è bella*
Debuting director: Roberta Torre, *Tano da morire*
Actor: Roberto Benigni, *La vita è bella*
Actress: Valeria Bruni Tedeschi, *La parola amore esiste* (*The Word Love Exists*)
Supporting actor: Silvio Orlando, *Aprile*
Supporting actress: Nicoletta Braschi, *Ovosodo*
Screenplay: Vincenzo Cerami, Roberto Benigni, *La vita è bella*
Best cinematography: Tonino Delli Colli, *La vita è bella*
Music: Nino d'Angelo, *Tano da morire*
Art direction: Danilo Donati, *La vita è bella*
Costumes: Danilo Donati, *La vita è bella*
Editing: Jacopo Quadri, *Teatro di guerra* (*Rehearsal for War*)
Sound: Tullio Morgati, *Ovosodo*
Foreign film: *The Full Monty* (U.K.)

## Norwegian Film Awards (Amandas)

Nordic Amanda: *The Celebration,* Thomas Vinterberg, Denmark
Norwegian feature film: *Blessed Are Those Who Thirst,* Carl Jørgen Kionig
The Amanda Committee's Golden Clapperboard

---

**. . . February 3 . . .**
Bette Midler and Nathan Lane commit to star in novelist Jacqueline Susann (**Valley of the Dolls**) bio **Isn't She Great?** for Universal.

(professional award): Make-up artist Siw Jarbyn
Dramatic television production: *Blood Ties*, Leidulv
Risan (NRK)
Supporting role: Nils Ole Oftebro, *Thrane's Method*
Actress: Kjersti Elvik, *Blind Goddess* and *Blessed Are
Those Who Thirst*
Actor: Sverre Anker Ousdal, *Blood Ties*
The Amanda committee's honorary award: Egil
Monn-Iversen, film composer/producer
Screenplay: Bent Hamer, *Water Easy Reach*
Amanda Committee's best debutant award: Gørdil
Mauseth, *Burnt by Frost*
Documentary film: *Living amongst Lions*, Sigve Endersen
Short film: *One Day a Man Bought a House*, by Pjotr
Sapegin
The Amanda Committee's professional award: Inge-
Lise Langfeldt, editor
Foreign film: *Titanic*, James Cameron

## Spanish Goya Awards

Film: *La buena estrella (Lucky Star)*, Ricardo Franco
Director: Ricardo Franco, *Lucky Star*
Actor: Antonio Resines, *Lucky Star*
Actress: Cecilia Roth, *Martin (Hache)*
Supporting actor: Jose Sancho, *Carne tremula (Live Flesh)*
Supporting actress: Charo Lopez, *Secretos del corazon
(Secrets of the Heart)*
Most promising young actor: Andoni Erburu, *Secrets*

*of the Heart*
Most promising young actress: Isabel Ordaz, *Chevrolet*
Original screenplay: Ricardo Franco, Angeles
Gonzales Sinde, *Lucky Star*
Adapted screenplay: Bigas Luna, Cuca Canals, *La
camarera del Titanic (The Chambermaid and the Titanic)*
Cinematography: Jaume Peracaula, *El color de los
nubes (The Color of Clouds)*
Original music: Eva Gancedo, *Lucky Star*
Animated short: *Megasonics*
Live-action short: *Hunters*
European film: *The Full Monty* (U.K.)
Spanish-language foreign film: *Cenizas del paraiso
(Ashes of Paradise)* (Argentina)
Honorary academy award: Rafael Azcona

## Swedish Golden Bug Film Awards

Picture: *Tic Tac*, Daniel Alfredson
Director: Daniel Alfredson, *Tic Tac*
Actor: Göran Stangertz, *Spring för livet*
Actress: Johanna Sällström, *Under ytan*
Script: Annika Thor, *Sanning eller konsekvens*
Photography: Jens Fischer, *Under ytan*
Supporting actor: Emil Forselius, *Adam & Eva*
Supporting actress: Tintin Anderson, *Tic Tac*
Foreign picture: *The Ice Storm*, Ang Lee
Golden Bug for creative achievement: Stefan Nilsson
Short film: *Hem ljuva hem*, Ulla-Carin Grafström

# MTV Movie Awards: 1998

Best movie: *Titanic*
Best male performance: Leonardo DiCaprio, *Titanic*
Best female performance: Neve Campbell, *Scream 2*
Breakthrough performance: Heather Graham, *Boogie
Nights*
Best villain: Mike Myers, *Austin Powers: International
Man of Mystery*
Best song from a movie: *Men in Black* – Will Smith,
from *Men in Black*
Best comedic performance: Jim Carrey, *Liar, Liar*
Best on-screen duo: John Travolta and

Nicolas Cage, *Face/Off*
Best kiss: Adam Sandler and Drew Barrymore, *The
Wedding Singer*
Best action sequence: *Face/Off*; Speedboat chase; John
Woo (director)
Best fight: Will Smith and Cockroach, *Men in Black*
Best dance sequence: Mike Myers and Londoners, *Austin
Powers: International Man of Mystery*
Best new filmmaker: Peter Cattaneo, *The Full Monty*
Lifetime achievement: Clint Howard

# Prizes awarded at major film festivals: 1998

## Berlin

Golden Berlin Bear: *Central do Brasil (Central Station)*
(Walter Salles)
Silver Berlin Bear, Special Jury Prize: *Wag the Dog* (Barry
Levinson)
Silver Berlin Bear for the best director: Neil Jordan,

*The Butcher Boy*
Silver Berlin Bear for the best actress: Fernanda
Montenegro, *Central do Brasil (Central Station)*
Silver Berlin Bear for the best actor: Samuel L. Jackson,
*Jackie Brown*
Silver Berlin Bear on the occasion of the screening of his

film *On Connaît la chanson (The Same Old Song)*: Alain Resnais, for his lifetime contribution to the art of cinema

Silver Berlin Bear for an outstanding single achievement: Matt Damon, as scriptwriter and actor in *Good Will Hunting*

The Blue Angel, the prize of the European Academy of Film and TV: Jeroen Krabbé, *Left Luggage*

## Cannes

Palme d'Or: *Mia eoniotita ke mia mera (Eternity and a Day)*, Theo Angelopoulos

Grand Prix: *La vita è bella (Life is Beautiful)*, Roberto Benigni

Actress: Elodie Bouchez and Natacha Tegnier, *La vie rêvée des anges (The Dreamlife of Angels)*

Actor: Peter Mullan, *My Name is Joe*

Director: John Boorman, *The General*

Scenario: *Henry Fool*

Jury Prizes: *La classe de neige (Class Trip)* and *Festen (The Celebration)*

Prix de la meilleure contribution artistique: *Velvet Goldmine*

Shorts: Palme d'Or: *Interview*

Jury Prizes: *Horseshoe* and *Gasman*

Grand Prix technique de la CST: Vittorio Storaro for *Tango*

Golden camera: *Slam*

## Karlovy Vary

Main Prize (The Crystal Globe): *Le coeur au poing (Streetheart)*, Charles Binamé

Special prize: *Den polnolunija (Full Moon)*, Karen Shkhnazarov

Director: Charles Binamé, *Le coeur au poing (Streetheart)*

Actress: Julia Stiles, *Wicked*

Actor: Olaf Lubaszenko, *Je treba zabit Sekala (Sekal Has to Die)*

Special Prize for directorial debut: Sandra Goldbacher, *The Governess*

Kodak Vision Audience Prize: *The Governess*, Sandra Goldbacher

## San Sebastián

Golden Shell: *El Viento se llevo lo que*, Alejandro Agresti

Special Jury Award: *Gods and Monsters*, Bill Condon, and *A la place du coeur*, Robert Guédiguian

Silver Shell for the best director: Fernando León de Aranoa, *Barrio*

Silver Shell for the best actress: Jeanne Balibar, *Fin août, début septembre*

Silver Shell for the best actor: Ian McKellen, *Gods and Monsters*

Award for the best photography: Rodrigo Prieto, *Un embrujo*

Jury award: *Don*, Abolfazl Jalili

## Sundance

Grand Jury Prize (dramatic): *Slam*, Levin

Grand Jury Prize (documentary): *Frat House*, Phillips & Gurland and *The Farm*, Stack & Garbus

Film-makers Trophy (dramatic): *Smoke Signals*, Eyre

Film-makers Trophy (documentary): *Divine Trash*, Yaeger

## Thessaloniki

Best full-length film award (The Golden Alexander): *Fishes in August*, Yoichiro Takahashi

Special jury award (Silver Alexander): *The Flight of the Bee*, Jamshed Usmanov and Byoung Hun Min, and *Knoflikari (The Buttoners)*, Petr Zelenka

Director award: Constantine Giannaris, *Apo tin akri tis polis (From the Edge of the City)*

Screenplay award: Petr Zelenka, *Knoflikari*

Actress award: Jeanne Balibar, *Dieu seul me voit (God's Got My Number)*

Actor award: Mehmet Kurtulus, *Kurz and schmerzlos (Short Sharp Shock)*

Artistic achievement award: *A rum da woon shee chul (Spring in My Hometown)*

Special mention: *Sib (The Apple)*, Samira Makhmalbaf

## Venice

Golden Lion for best film: *Cosí ridevano*, directed by Gianni Amelio

Special Jury Grand Prix: *Terminus Paradis*, directed by Lucian Pintilie

Silver Lion for best direction: Emir Kusturica, *Black Cat, White Cat*

Coppa Volpi for best actress: Catherine Deneuve, *Place Vendôme*

Coppa Volpi for best actor: Sean Penn, *Hurlyburly*

Marcello Mastroianni award to a young promising actor or actress: Niccoló Senni, *L'albero delle pere*

Osella d'Oro for best original screenplay: Eric Rohmer, *Conte d'automne*

Osella d'Oro for best photography: Luca Bigazzi, *Cosí ridevano* and *L'albero delle pere*

Osella d'Oro for best original film music: Gerardo Gandini, *La nube*

Golden Medal of the Italian Senate: *Le silence*, directed by Mohsen Makhmalbaf

Short-film competition (Silver Lion): *Mashe'hoo Ba'al Erech (Small Change)* by Dorit Hakim

Special Mention: *Tann for Tann*, by Emil Stang Lund

---

# Screen Superstars

*Variety* tends to measure a star by his or her bankability. We've charted the rise and rise in salaries and packages, upfront and backend alike. With several male actors earning north of $20 million an outing, and actresses commanding up to $17 million, the pressures of finding tomorrow's new talent grow more daunting by the day.

Our 1998 list of current superstars reflects the marketplace as much as editorial opinion. A wonderful actress can often fail to set the B.O. tills ringing. A lousy performer can be swept to fame and fortune by the right vehicle at the right moment. Each of the actors below has the ability to get a movie off the ground; behind the scenes, many are producers in their own right. The filmographies list only the most recent work in each star's career, from the most abstinent (Streisand) to the most prolific (arguably Travolta).

## Woody Allen

Real name Allen Stewart Konigsberg; legal name Heywood Allen. Born on December 1, 1935 in Brooklyn, NY. Angst-ridden actor, writer-director, still one of the most inventive and original filmmakers in the U.S. He won Oscar for *Annie Hall*. Married to Soon Yi, Mia Farrow's (his ex-partner's) adopted daughter. Recent films: *Stuck on You* (1999), *Celebrity, Wild Man Blues, Antz* (animated, voice only) (1998), *Deconstructing Harry* (1997), *Everyone Says I Love You* (1996), *Mighty Aphrodite* (1995).

## Antonio Banderas

Born in Malaga, Spain in 1960. Married to Melanie Griffith, daughter Stella. Spanish heart-throb who became international star after his success in Almodóvar's hit films. Recent films: *The 13th Warrior, White River Kid* (1999), *The Mask of Zorro* (1998), *Evita* (1996), *Two Much* (1996), *Never Talk to Strangers* (1995), *Assassins* (1995).

## Warren Beatty

Born in Richmond, VA on March 3, 1937. Married to actress Annette Bening, father of three. Actor, producer, writer, director. His virile good looks brought him popularity in the 1960s while later films secured him critical acclaim, Oscar nominations, and finally the Oscar for best directon for *Reds*. Recent films: *Town and Country* (1999), *Bulworth* (1998), *Love Affair* (1994), *Bugsy* (1991).

## Roberto Benigni

Born in Misericordia, Arezzo, Italy on 27 October 1952. Actor, screenwriter, director, comedian. Elastic-faced, comic actor hit it big in 1998 with his highly acclaimed and box-office success, controversial *La Vita è bella (Life is Beautiful)*. The film was also Italy's entry for the foreign-language Oscar. Recent films: *Asterix et Obelix* (1999), *La Vita è bella* (1997), *Il Mostro* (1994), *Son of the Pink Panther* (1993), *Night on Earth* (1991).

## Sandra Bullock

Born in Arlington, VA on 29 July 1965. Plain-speaking, appealing lead with girl-next-door looks who became a mega-star after the box-office smash *Speed* in 1994. Also producer. Recent films: *Exactly 3:30, Forces of Nature, Gun Shy, Prince of Egypt* (voice), *Practical Magic, Hope Floats* (1998), *Making Sandwiches, Speed 2: Cruise Control* (1997), *In Love and War, Two if by Sea, A Time to Kill* (1996).

## Nicolas Cage

Real name Nicholas Coppola (nephew of Francis Ford Coppola). Born in Long Beach, CA on July 1, 1964. Married to Patricia Arquette, father of one. Aggressive, engaging actor who after years in the wilderness joined the Hollywood A list with an Oscar-winning performance in Mike Figgis' *Leaving Las Vegas*, and showed a gentler side to his talent in *City of Angels*. Recent films: *8 MM, Bringing out the Dead* (1999), *City of Angels, Snake Eyes* (1998), *Face/Off* (1997), *Con Air* (1997), *The Rock* (1996).

## Jim Carrey

Real name James Eugene Carrey. Born in Jackson Point, Canada on January 17, 1962. Divorced twice, father of one. Became a household name with outrageous, offbeat, physical comedies and proved with *The Truman Show* that he could tackle more serious roles. He has joined the ranks of the highest-paid stars in the history of film. Recent films: *Man on the Moon, The Incredible Mr. Limpet, Simon Birch* (1999), *The Truman Show* (1998), *Liar, Liar* (1997), *The Cable Guy* (1996), *Ace Ventura: When Nature Calls*

(1995), *Batman Forever* (1995), *Ace Ventura Pet Detective, The Mask* (1994), *Dumb and Dumber* (1994).

## Jackie Chan

Real name: Chan Kwong-Sang. Born in Hong Kong on April 7, 1954. Agile, intrepid action star who's graduated from Chinese-language chop-socky flicks to Hollywood top billing. Chan does all his own (often terrifying) stunts, rare these days. Recent films: *Mr. Nice Guy, Rush Hour* (1998), *Jackie Chan's First Strike, Operation Condor* (1997), *Rumble in the Bronx* (1996).

## George Clooney

Born in Lexington, KY on May 6, 1961. Relationship: Céline Balitran. The sexy star of *ER* finally made a big-screen impact with the critically acclaimed if modestly performing *Out of Sight*. Recent films: *Designated Survivor, Three Kings* (1999), *The Thin Red Line, Out of Sight, Waiting for Woody* (1998), *The Peacemaker, Batman and Robin* (1997).

## Sean Connery

Real name: Thomas Connery. Born in Edinburgh, Scotland on August 25, 1930. Wife Micheline, son Jason. Enduring star whose post-Bond career has propelled him into production deals and even the launch of a possible Scottish studio. Recent films: *Entrapment* (1999), *Playing by Heart, The Avengers* (1998), *The Rock* (1996), *Dragonheart* (voice) (1996), *First Knight, Just Cause* (1995).

## Kevin Costner

Born in Lynwood, CA on January 18, 1957. Father of three, star on the wane after flops and disappointments in the late 1990s. But cast in the right vehicle he's still capable of recapturing the glory years (when his *Dances with Wolves* earned zillions and swept the Oscars). Runs his own production outfit, Tig. Recent films: *For Love of the Game, Message in a Bottle, Thirteen Days* (1999), *The Postman* (1997), *Tin Cup* (1996), *Waterworld* (1995), *Wyatt Earp* (1994).

## Tom Cruise

Real name: Thomas Cruise Mapother IV. Born in Syracuse, NY on July 3, 1962. Wife Nicole Kidman, father of two adopted children. Matinee idol Tom Cruise soon showed he was not just a pretty face and by the end of the 1980s had become a genuine star and mature actor. Recent films: *Untitled Mission: Impossible Sequel, Magnolia, Eyes Wide Shut* (1999), *Mission: Impossible, Jerry Maguire* (1996), *Interview with the Vampire* (1994), *The Firm* (1993), *A Few Good Men* (1992).

## Matt Damon

Born on October 8, 1970 in Cambridge, MA. A rising star and all-American boy became a household name after *Good Will Hunting* (which he also co-wrote, earning an Oscar in the process). Recent films: *All the Pretty Horses, Dogma, The Talented Mr. Ripley* (1999), *Saving Private Ryan, Rounders* (1998), *Good Will Hunting, John Grisham's The Rainmaker, Chasing Amy* (1997).

## Robert De Niro

Born in New York, NY on August 17, 1943. Father of three. De Niro's accelerated slate finds him popping up in two or three movies a year. Nurtured early on by Scorsese and Coppola, De Niro remains a prestige name for any marquee, but willing to take small, meaty roles with offbeat directors. Recent films: *The Adventures of Rocky and Bullwinkle, Analyze This, Flawless* (1999), *Ronin, Great Expectations* (1998), *Jackie Brown, Wag the Dog, Cop Land* (1997), *The Fan, Marvin's Room* (1996), *Heat, Casino* (1995).

## Gérard Depardieu

Born in Chateauroux, France on 27 December 1948. Partner: French actress Carole Bouquet, father of three. A natural successor to such domineering French stars as Gabin and Montand. Remarkable range of skills, from swashbuckling to crime movies and subtler chamber pieces. Recent films: *Bimboland, Asterix et Obelix, Mirka Passionnement, Vidocq, Wings against the Wind* (1999), *La parola amore esiste, The Man in the Iron Mask* (1998), *XXL* (1997), *Hamlet, Le plus beau métier du monde, Bogus, Unhook the Stars, The Secret Agent* (1996).

## Cameron Diaz

Born in San Diego, CA on August 30, 1972. A superstar thanks to the left-field triumph of *There's Something About Mary*. Her leggy, ingenuous charm makes her a natural heiress to Goldie Hawn. Recent films: *Being John Malkovich, Invisible Circus, Oliver Stone's Untitled Football Project* (1999), *There's Something About Mary, Very Bad Things, Fear and Loathing in Las Vegas* (1998), *My Best Friend's Wedding, A Life Less Ordinary, Keys to Tulsa* (1997), *Head Above Water, Feeling Minnesota, She's the One* (1996).

## Leonardo DiCaprio

Born in Los Angeles on November 11, 1974. Every teenage girl's dream, this handsome young actor is probably the most bankable of contemporary stars after *Titanic*, although he made his mark early in offbeat work like *What's Eating Gilbert Grape?* and *The Quick and the Dead*. Recent films: *The Beach, The Chet Baker Story* (1999), *Don's Plum, The Man in the Iron Mask, Celebrity* (1998), *Titanic* (1997), *Marvin's Room, Romeo & Juliet* (1996).

## Michael Douglas

Born in New Brunswick, NJ on September 25, 1944. Divorced, father of one. Son of the great star of the 1940s and 1950s, Kirk Douglas, Michael Douglas became a marquee name with hits as an actor (and producer, e.g. *One Flew Over the Cuckoo's Nest*). Recent films: *Still Life* (1999), *A Perfect Murder* (1998), *The Game* (1997), *The Ghost and the Darkness* (1996), *The American President* (1995), *Disclosure* (1994).

## Clint Eastwood

Born in San Francisco, CA on May 31, 1930. Married to Dina Ruiz, father of five. Rugged, durable icon who surged via *Rawhide* and spaghetti westerns to being Hollywood's favorite screen enforcer. Still a hybrid, with his directed-only pix grossing less than his starring vehicles. Recent films: *True Crime* (1999), *Absolute Power* (1997), *The Bridges of Madison County* (1995), *A Perfect World, In the Line of Fire* (1993), *Unforgiven* (1992) (Oscars for best director and best film).

## Harrison Ford

Born in Chicago, IL on July 13, 1942. Married to Melissa Mathison, father of four. The rugged, po-faced star of Spielberg films has been on all top lists from the biggest stars ever to the sexiest men, since he was first noted in Coppola's *The Conversation*. Recent films: *Random Hearts* (1999), *Six Days, Seven Nights* (1998), *Air Force One* (1997), *The Devil's Own* (1997), *Sabrina* (1995), *Clear and Present Danger* (1994).

## Jodie Foster

Real name: Alicia Christian Foster. Born in Los Angeles, CA on November 19, 1962. Mother of one; did not want to reveal the name of father or the manner of conception. Brilliantly gifted double Oscar-winner, intent on finding the right roles and setting up cool projects through her own shingle, Egg, at Paramount. Recent films: *Anna and the King, Flora Plum* (1999), *Contact* (1997), *Nell* (1994), *Home for the Holidays* (director), *Maverick* (1994), *Sommersby* (1993).

## Morgan Freeman

Born in Memphis TN, on June 1, 1937. Married to Myrna Colley-Lee, father of four. Late-maturing black star whose engaging gravitas has brought him an Oscar nomination (for *Shawshank*) and increasingly rewarding roles. Recent films: *Along Came a Spider, Desert Blue, Long Way to Freedom, Nurse Betty, Rendezvous with Rama, Under Suspicion* (1999), *Deep Impact, Hard Rain* (1998), *Amistad, Long Way Home, Kiss the Girls* (1997), *Chain Reaction, Moll Flanders* (1996), *Outbreak, Seven* (1995), *The Shawshank Redemption* (1994), *Unforgiven* (1992).

## Richard Gere

Born in Philadelphia, PA on August 31, 1949. Partner: Carey Lowell. Satin-smooth lady-killer who's acquired a fresh lease of life since *Pretty Woman*. Recent films: *Autumn in New York, Runaway Bride* (1999), *The Jackal, Red Corner* (1997), *Primal Fear* (1996).

## Mel Gibson

Born in Peekskill, NY on January 3, 1956. Married to Robyn Moore, father of 6. Handsome, compelling actor and sex symbol, whose breakthrough came with the *Mad Max* movies in Oz. Also a thoughtful director (*The Man without a Face, Braveheart*) and producer (Icon Productions). Recent films: *The Billion Dollar Hotel, Payback* (1999), *Lethal Weapon 4* (1998), *Conspiracy Theory* (1997), *Ransom* (1996), *Braveheart* (1995) (Oscars for best director and best picture), *Maverick* (1994), *The Man Without a Face* (1993).

## Gene Hackman

Born in San Bernardino, CA on January 30, 1930. Married to Betsy Arakawa, father of three. Gruff, often abrasive character actor, Hackman has been one of the busiest, most sought-after screen personalities in Hollywood in the three decades since winning an Oscar for *The French Connection*. Recent films: *Love Boat: The Movie, Under Suspicion* (1999), *Twilight, Enemy of the State, Antz* (voice) (1998), *Absolute Power* (1997), *Extreme Measures, The Chamber, The Birdcage* (1996).

## Tom Hanks

Born in Concord, CA on July 9, 1956. Married to Rita Wilson, father of four. Arguably the most respected Hollywood actor of the 1990s, with back-to-back Oscars for *Philadelphia* and *Forrest Gump*, and nominations for every other award under the sun. At enviable ease in both dramatic and comedy roles. Recent films: *Castaway, The Green Mile* (1999), *You've Got Mail, Saving Private Ryan* (1998), *That Thing You Do!* (1996), *Apollo 13* (1995), *Forrest Gump* (1994), *Philadelphia, Sleepless in Seattle* (1993).

## Dustin Hoffman

Born in Los Angeles, CA on August 8, 1937. Married to Lisa Gottsegen, father of six. One of the most versatile and enduring Hollywood stars (and charismatic stage actor), this two-time Oscar winner (*Kramer vs. Kramer* and *Rain Man*) has also been involved in production. Recipient of the 1999 American Film Institute's Lifetime Achievement Award. Recent films: *Cosm, Joan of Arc* (1999), *Sphere* (1998), *Wag the Dog, Mad City* (1997), *Sleepers, American Buffalo* (1996), *Outbreak* (1995).

---

**... February 8 ...**

Horror writer Stephen King to ink original six-hour mini-series for ABC called **Storm of the Century**, set to air on the Alphabet web next season.

## Sir Anthony Hopkins

Born in Port Talbot, Wales on December 31, 1937. Married to Jennifer Ann Lynton, father of one. Distinguished stage career, but a muted presence on screen until *The Silence of the Lambs* (Oscar, 1991) catapulted him to Hollywood stardom. Now resolved to withdraw from movies. Recent films: *Instinct, Titus* (1999), *Meet Joe Black, The Mask of Zorro* (1998), *Amistad, The Edge* (1997), *Surviving Picasso, August* (directed only) (1996), *Nixon* (1995).

## Jennifer Lopez

Born in the Bronx, New York on July 24, 1970. Twice divorced. After her sizzling performance and on-screen chemistry with co-star George Clooney in *Out of Sight*, Jennifer Lopez became one of the hottest stars of 1998 in Hollywood. Films: *The Hollow Man, Impostor, Pluto Nash, Thieves* (1999), *Out of Sight* (1998), *Antz* (voice) (1998), *Anaconda, Blood and Wine, Selena, U Turn* (1997).

## Demi Moore

Real name: Demetria Guynes. Born in Roswell, NM on November 11, 1962. Separated from husband Bruce Willis, mother of three. Spirited, sexy, strong leading lady, and one of the highest-paid Hollywood female stars. She formed her own production company, Rufglen. Recent films: *Airframe, Passion of Mind* (1999), *G.I. Jane, Deconstructing Harry, Destination Anywhere* (1997), *Striptease, If These Walls Could Talk* (TV film), *The Juror* (1996), *Now and Then, The Scarlet Letter* (1995), *Disclosure* (1994).

## Jack Nicholson

Born in Neptune, NJ on April 22, 1937. Partner: Rebecca Broussard, father of four. Actor, director, erstwhile screenwriter, an enduring star who dominates virtually any movie he appears in. Owns two best actor Oscars, for *As Good as It Gets* and *One Flew over the Cuckoo's Nest* and one best supporting actor statuette (*Terms of Endearment*). Recent films: *As Good as It Gets, Blood and Wine* (1997), *Mars Attacks!, The Evening Star* (1996), *The Crossing Guard* (1995), *Wolf* (1994).

## Al Pacino

Real name Alfredo James Pacino. Born in New York, NY on April 25, 1940. Relationship: Beverly D'Angelo. Star off-Broadway before making debut in *The Panic in Needle Park* and spectacular breakthrough with *The Godfather* movies. Rough patch in the 1980s, but back on track with a slew of rasping, authoritative, and sardonic perfs in recent years. Recent films: *Chinese Coffee, Man of the People, Oliver Stone's Untitled Football Project* (1999), *The Devil's Advocate, Donnie Brasco* (1997), *Looking for Richard* (also directed), *City Hall* (1996), *Heat, Two Bits* (1995).

## Gwyneth Paltrow

Born in Los Angeles, CA on September 28, 1973. Relationship: Ben Affleck. 1998 was a hugely successful year for this fresh, sophisticated, and very talented young actress. Recent films: *The Talented Mr. Ripley, Duets* (1999), *Hush, Shakespeare in Love, A Perfect Murder, Great Expectations, Sliding Doors* (1998), *Emma, Hard Eight, The Pallbearer* (1996), *Jefferson in Paris, Moonlight and Valentino, Seven* (1995).

## Brad Pitt

Real name: William Bradley Pitt. Born in Shawnee, OK on December 18, 1963. Relationship with *Friends* star Jennifer Aniston. All-too-handsome blond star who still looks 20, and, like the young Robert Redford, at his best in the great outdoors. Recent films: *Fight Club, Ambrose Chapel* (1999), *Meet Joe Black* (1998), *Seven Years in Tibet, The Dark Side of the Sun, The Devil's Own* (1997), *Sleepers* (1996), *Twelve Monkeys, Seven* (1995), *Interview with the Vampire, The Favor, Legends of the Fall* (1994).

## Robert Redford

Real name: Charles Robert Redford, Jr. Born in Santa Monica, CA on August 18, 1937. Partner: Kathy O'Rear, father of three. Actor who has moved from pretty-boy parts in the 1960s to Oscar-winning director (*Ordinary People*) and producer, and now flagbearer for the indie movement, with his Sundance Institute, Festival, and TV channel well established. Recent films: *The Legend of Bagger Vance* (1999), *The Horse Whisperer* (also directed, 1998), *Up Close and Personal* (1996), *Quiz Show* (directed only, 1994), *Indecent Proposal* (1993).

## Julia Roberts

Real name: Julie Fiona Roberts. Born on October 28, 1967 in Smyrna, GA. Busy, broad-smiling actress whose forte for screen comedy helped her to stardom with *Pretty Woman* in 1990. Her abiding glamor has remained in tune with a turbulent private life. Recent films: *From Alice to Ocean, Notting Hill, Runaway Bride* (1999), *Stepmom* (1998), *Conspiracy Theory, My Best Friend's Wedding* (1997), *Everyone Says I Love You, Mary Reilly, Michael Collins* (1996).

## Meg Ryan

Real name Margaret Hyra. Born on November 19, 1961 in Fairfield, CT. Married to Dennis Quaid, son Jack Henry. Two copper-bottomed hits in a row have made Ryan probably the hottest female star in the world. At her best in comedy, but *Courage Under Fire* and *City of Angels* revealed a tough, introspective facet of her talent. Recent films: *Hanging up* (1999), *You've Got Mail, Hurlyburly, City of Angels* (1998), *Addicted to Love, Two for the Road, Anastasia* (voice) (1997), *Courage Under Fire* (1996), *French Kiss* (1995).

## Susan Sarandon

Real name Susan Abigail Tomaling. Born in New York, NY on October 4, 1946. Partner: Tim Robbins, mother of three. The thinking man's crumpet for numerous years, the seemingly ageless and radiant Sarandon just gets better and better. Recent films: *Anywhere but Here, The Cradle Will Rock* (1999), *Stepmom, Twilight, Illuminata* (1998), *Dead Man Walking* (best actress Oscar), *Safe Passage* (1995), *The Client* (1994), *Little Women* (1994).

## Arnold Schwarzenegger

Born in Graz, Austria on July 30, 1947. Married to Maria Owings Shriver, father of four. The ultimate bodybuilder turned terminator, Schwarzenegger remains among Hollywood's highest-paid stars, although his career has been on hold recently owing to a heart problem. Recent films: *End of Days* (1999), *Batman and Robin* (1997), *Eraser* (1996), *Jingle All the Way* (1996), *Junior, True Lies* (1994).

## Will Smith

Born in Philadelphia, PA on September 25, 1968. Married to actress Jada Pinkett, father of one. Actor and singer whose insolent, off-the-cuff delivery recalls the young Eddie Murphy. Thus far, all his screen appearances have been in major hits. Recent films: *Anything for Love, Love for Hire, The Wild, Wild West* (1999), *Enemy of the State* (1998), *Men in Black* (1997), *Independence Day* (1996), *Bad Boys* (1995).

## Wesley Snipes

Born in Orlando, FL on July 31, 1962. Father of one. Caught the eye in Michael Jackson's music video, *Bad,* and then appeared in *New Jack City,* and Spike Lee's *Jungle Fever.* Now earmarked as an agile, menacing action star. Recent films: *US Marshals, Blade, Down in the Delta* (1998), *Murder at 1600* (1997), *One Night Stand* (1997), *America's Dream, The Fan* (1996).

## Sylvester Stallone

Born in New York, NY on July 6, 1946. Married to model Jennifer Flavin, father of four. The Italian stallion who for more than a decade ruled as the world's leading action star, although he'd prefer to be remembered as the writer-star of Oscar-winning *Rocky. Cop Land* suggested he could score in more thoughtful roles. Recent films: *Detox* (1999), *Antz* (animated, voice) (1998), *An Alan Smithee Film, The Good Life, Cop Land* (1997), *Daylight* (1996), *Assassins, Judge Dredd* (1995).

## Sharon Stone

Born in Meadville, PA on March 10, 1958. Married to newspaper executive Phil Bronstein. An overnight sensation in *Basic Instinct* after years in the wilderness, Stone became the siren of the 1990s, the cool, dangerous blonde with lotsa sex appeal and an unusually high IQ to match. Recent films: *The Muse, Gloria, Simpatico* (1999), *The Mighty, Sphere* (1998), *Antz* (animated, voice) (1998), *Diabolique, Last Dance* (1996), *The Quick and the Dead, Casino, Catwalk* (1995).

## Meryl Streep

Real name: Mary Louise Streep. Born in Summit, NJ on June 22, 1949. Married to Don Gummer, mother of four. Coming of age in both *Julia* and *The Deer Hunter,* Streep dominated the 1980s as Hollywood's foremost screen actress, a natural heir to Katharine Hepburn, and with a gift for accents that has thus far encompassed Polish, Danish, Irish, Spanish, and Australian. Took Best Actress Oscar for *Sophie's Choice,* the statuette for best supporting role in *Kramer vs. Kramer,* and has received 11 nominations as Actress. Recent films: *50 Violins, Still Life* (1999), *One True Thing, Dancing at Lughnasa* (1998), *Before and After* (1996), *Marvin's Room* (1996), *The Bridges of Madison County* (1995).

## Barbra Streisand

Born in Brooklyn, NY on April 24, 1942. Married to actor James Brolin, mother of one. Singer, actor, director, super-star entertainer of the American stage, TV, recordings, and films; has her own production company Barwood Films. Now rarely tempted by screen roles, but still boasting the clout to get projects greenlighted. Best Actress Oscar for *Funny Girl.* Recent films: *The Mirror Has Two Faces* (1996), *The Prince of Tides* (1991).

## John Travolta

Born in Englewood, NJ on February 18, 1954. Married to Kelly Preston, father of one. After the success of *Saturday Night Fever* and *Grease* in the 1970s, his career sagged, but he made an unexpected comeback in the early 1990s with *Pulp Fiction* and has been among the busiest and highest-paid actors since. Recent films: *The General's Daughter, The Shipping News* (1999), *The Thin Red Line, A Civil Action, Primary Colors* (1998), *Mad City, Face/Off, She's So Lovely* (1997), *Michael, Phenomenon* (1996), *Broken Arrow, Get Shorty, White Man's Burden* (1995).

## Denzel Washington

Born in Mount Vernon, NY on December 28, 1954. Married to Pauletta Pearson. Actor, producer, director whose gaze of integrity has brought him the kind of screen and TV roles once inhabited by Sidney Poitier. Won

---

**...February 10...**

**Amistad** unshackled: Barbara Chase-Riboud abruptly settles plagiarism lawsuit centering on non-fiction tome **Echo of Lions**.

Oscar for best supporting role in *Glory*. Production company is Mundy Lane Entertainment. Recent films: *The Bone Collector, Lazarus and the Hurricane* (1999), *The Siege, He Got Game, Fallen* (1998), *The Preacher's Wife, Courage under Fire* (1996).

## Robin Williams

Born in Chicago, IL on July 21, 1952. Married to Marsha Garces, father of three. Ebullient, irrepressible comic with extraordinary vocal gifts (e.g. *Aladdin*), Williams is among the most prolific and consistent of stars, winning an Oscar at last for *Good Will Hunting* after nominations for *Good Morning Vietnam* and *Dead Poets Society*. Recent films: *Jakob the Liar* (1999), *Patch Adams, What Dreams May Come* (1998), *Good Will Hunting, Flubber, Deconstructing Harry, Father's Day* (1997), *The Birdcage, Hamlet, Jack, The Secret Agent* (1996).

## Bruce Willis

Real name: Walter Bruce Willis. Born in Idar-Oberstein, Germany on March 19, 1955. Married to Demi Moore since 1987, but separated last summer. Father of three daughters. After a huge success with the TV series *Moonlighting*, Willis became equally popular as a big-screen hero with his portrayal of tough, cynical, chain-smoking cops. Teamed with Stallone and Schwarzenegger to launch Planet Hollywood chain. Recent films: *Breakfast of Champions, Die Hard 4, The Russian Militia, The Sixth Sense, The Story of Us* (1999), *Armageddon, Mercury Rising, The Siege, Apocalypse* (1998), *The Jackal, The Fifth Element* (1997), *Last Man Standing* (1996).

## Kate Winslet

Born in Reading, England on October 5, 1975. Married to Jim Threapleton. After a brilliant teenage debut as the New Zealand murderess in *Heavenly Creatures*, this chocolate-box beauty chose her parts well, leading to the arduous role of Rose in *Titanic*. Recent films: *Holy Smoke, Plunge* (1999), *Hideous Kinky* (1998), *Titanic* (1997), *Hamlet* (1996), *Jude* (1996), *Sense and Sensibility* (1995).

# International box office: 1998

## Australia

| Title | Gross ($m) |
|---|---|
| 1. *Titanic* | 30.7** |
| 2. *There's Something About Mary* | 12.5 |
| 3. *As Good As It Gets* | 12.1 |
| 4. *Saving Private Ryan* | 11.7 |
| 5. *The Wedding Singer* | 11.1 |
| 6. *Deep Impact* | 10.9 |
| 7. *Dr. Dolittle* | 10.7 |
| 8. *Good Will Hunting* | 9.5 |
| 9. *Armageddon* | 9.2 |
| 10. *Sliding Doors* | 8.9 |
| 11. *Godzilla* | 8.6 |
| 12. *The Truman Show* | 7.4 |
| 13. *A Bug's Life* | 7.0 |
| 14. *Lethal Weapon 4* | 6.7 |
| 15. *Mouse Hunt* | 6.3 |
| 16. *The Horse Whisperer* | 6.1 |
| 17. *Lost in Space* | 6.0 |
| 18. *The Jackal* | 5.6 |
| 19. *Tomorrow Never Dies* | 5.5** |
| 20. *Six Days, Seven Nights* | 5.0 |
| *The Wiggles* * (top locally produced grosser) | 2.7 |

## Brazil

| | |
|---|---|
| 1. *Titanic* | 70.2 |
| 2. *Armageddon* | 9.7 |

| | |
|---|---|
| 3. *Godzilla* | 8.1 |
| 4. *The Mask of Zorro* | 8.0 |
| 5. *Mulan* | 7.6 |
| 6. *The Devil's Advocate* | 6.9 |
| 7. *As Good As It Gets* | 6.9 |
| 8. *Lethal Weapon 4* | 6.1 |
| 9. *City of Angels* | 5.7 |
| 10. *Saving Private Ryan* | 5.6 |
| 11. *Deep Impact* | 5.5 |
| 12. *There's Something About Mary* | 5.3 |
| 13. *O Novico Rebelde (Rebel Nun)* * | 5.2 |
| 14. *The Man in the Iron Mask* | 5.2 |
| 15. *Central Station* * | 5.1 |
| 16. *George of the Jungle* | 4.7 |
| 17. *Six Days, Seven Nights* | 4.2 |
| 18. *The X-Files* | 3.8 |
| 19. *Dr. Dolittle* | 3.7 |
| 20. *In & Out* | 3.3 |

## Canada

| | |
|---|---|
| 1. *Titanic* | 59.5** |
| 2. *Armageddon* | 22.2 |
| 3. *Saving Private Ryan* | 16.9 |
| 4. *There's Something About Mary* | 16.0 |
| 5. *Good Will Hunting* | 15.9 |
| 6. *As Good As It Gets* | 12.6** |
| 7. *Deep Impact* | 11.7 |

* *Local production*                    ** *Does not include 1997 B.O.*

| | |
|---|---|
| 8. *The Waterboy* | 11.2 |
| 9. *The Truman Show* | 11.1 |
| 10. *Rush Hour* | 9.8 |
| 11. *Lethal Weapon 4* | 9.7 |
| 12. *Godzilla* | 9.5 |
| 13. *A Bug's Life* | 9.1 |
| 14. *Enemy of the State* | 9.0 |
| 15. *Dr. Dolittle* | 8.5 |
| 16. *The X-Files* | 8.5 |
| 17. *Mulan* | 8.4 |
| 18. *Six Days, Seven Nights* | 7.1 |
| 19. *The Man in the Iron Mask* | 6.6 |
| 20. *City of Angels* | 6.4 |
| *Les Boys* * (top locally produced grosser) | 5.8 |

## France

| | |
|---|---|
| 1. *Titanic* | 130.4 |
| 2. *Le Dîner de Cons (Dinner Game)* * | 53.9 |
| 3. *Les Couloirs de Temps (Visitors II)* * | 50.5 |
| 4. *Taxi* * | 39.3 |
| 5. *Armageddon* | 28.9 |
| 6. *Mulan* | 28.2 |
| 7. *Saving Private Ryan* | 27.0 |
| 8. *Lethal Weapon 4* | 20.8 |
| 9. *Life is Beautiful* | 20.7 |
| 10. *The Mask of Zorro* | 20.0 |
| 11. *Godzilla* | 17.7 |
| 12. *Anastasia* | 17.5 |
| 13. *There's Something About Mary* | 16.2 |
| 14. *The Prince of Egypt* | 16.1 |
| 15. *The Horse Whisperer* | 15.9 |
| 16. *The Man in the Iron Mask* | 14.6 |
| 17. *Scream 2* | 13.3 |
| 18. *Truman Show* | 9.4 |
| 19. *The X-Files* | 8.7 |
| 20. *The Avengers* | 8.5 |

## Germany

| | |
|---|---|
| 1. *Titanic* | 138.7 |
| 2. *Armageddon* | 38.0 |
| 3. *Tomorrow Never Dies* | 31.1 |
| 4. *The Horse Whisperer* | 29.4 |
| 5. *Saving Private Ryan* | 27.3 |
| 6. *My Best Friend's Wedding* | 23.2 |
| 7. *Dr. Dolittle* | 22.6 |
| 8. *Deep Impact* | 21.1 |
| 9. *Godzilla* | 20.5 |
| 10. *As Good As It Gets* | 20.0 |
| 11. *Comedian Harmonists* * | 18.2 |
| 12. *There's Something About Mary* | 18.1 |
| 13. *Mulan* | 16.8 |
| 14. *City of Angels* | 16.6 |

| | |
|---|---|
| 15. *The X-Files* | 16.4 |
| 16. *Lethal Weapon 4* | 15.8 |
| 17. *The Truman Show* | 15.8 |
| 18. *Run Lola Run* * | 13.8 |
| 19. *In & Out* | 13.0 |
| 20. *Flubber* | 12.6 |

## Italy

| | |
|---|---|
| 1. *Titanic* | 67.9 |
| 2. *Tre Uomini e una Gambia (Three Men and a Leg)* * | 24.2** |
| 3. *La Vita è Bella (Life is Beautiful)* * | 21.5** |
| 4. *Cosi è la Vita (That's Life)* * | 18.4 |
| 5. *Saving Private Ryan* | 17.7 |
| 6. *There's Something About Mary* | 16.6 |
| 7. *The Truman Show* | 14.5 |
| 8. *Armageddon* | 13.8 |
| 9. *The Full Monty* | 13.5 |
| 10. *Sliding Doors* | 12.9 |
| 11. *The Man in the Iron Mask* | 12.3 |
| 12. *The Rooster (Gallo Cedrone)* * | 11.9 |
| 13. *My Best Friend's Wedding* | 11.6 |
| 14. *The Devil's Advocate* | 9.2** |
| 15. *Mulan* | 9.0 |
| 16. *As Good As It Gets* | 8.6 |
| 17. *Seven Years in Tibet* | 8.4** |
| 18. *Godzilla* | 8.3 |
| 19. *In & Out* | 8.1 |
| 20. *Deep Impact* | 8.0 |

## Japan

| | |
|---|---|
| 1. *Titanic* | 200.8 |
| 2. *Deep Impact* | 56.0 |
| 3. *Pocket Monsters* * | 37.0 |
| 4. *Godzilla* | 34.9 |
| 5. *Saving Private Ryan* | 34.1 |
| 6. *The Big Investigation* * | 31.2 |
| 7. *Armageddon* | 24.5 |
| 8. *Doraemon* * | 18.7 |
| 9. *City of Angels* | 16.4 |
| 10. *The Man in the Iron Mask* | 15.4 |
| 11. *Seven Years in Tibet* | 14.6 |
| 12. *Lethal Weapon 4* | 13.7 |
| 13. *The Truman Show* | 13.3 |
| 14. *Bean* | 12.1 |
| 15. *Face/Off* | 12.0 |
| 16. *The Jackal* | 10.5 |
| 17. *Pride* * | 10.0 |
| 18. *Sleepless Town* * | 9.8 |
| 19. *Young Kindaichi's Cookbook* * | 9.4 |
| 20. *The Horse Whisperer* | 8.8 |

*\* Local production*

*\*\* Does not include 1997 B.O.*

## Mexico

| | |
|---|---|
| 1. *Titanic* | 27.0 |
| 2. *Armegeddon* | 10.8 |
| 3. *Deep Impact* | 10.7 |
| 4. *The Mask of Zorro* | 8.2 |
| 5. *Mulan* | 7.0 |
| 6. *Antz* | 6.8 |
| 7. *The Man in the Iron Mask* | 6.0 |
| 8. *City of Angels* | 5.0 |
| 9. *Dr. Dolittle* | 5.0 |
| 10. *As Good As It Gets* | 4.2 |
| 11. *Lethal Weapon 4* | 4.1 |
| 12. *Saving Private Ryan* | 4.0 |
| 13. *There's Something About Mary* | 3.9 |
| 14. *Mercury Rising* | 3.9 |
| 15. *The X-Files* | 3.7 |
| 16. *Mouse Hunt* | 3.6 |
| 17. *Alien Resurrection* | 3.3 |
| 18. *Snake Eyes* | 3.0 |
| 19. *A Perfect Murder* | 2.6 |
| 20. *Lost in Space* | 2.2 |
| 20. *Good Will Hunting* | 2.2 |
| *La Prima Noche (top locally produced grosser)* | 2.0 |

## Spain

| | |
|---|---|
| 1. *Titanic* | 44.1 |
| 2. *The Mask of Zorro* | 14.3 |
| 3. *Armageddon* | 13.8 |
| 4. *Torrente, the Dumb Arm of the Law* * | 13.7 |
| 5. *As Good As It Gets* | 13.6 |
| 6. *There's Something About Mary* | 13.3 |
| 7. *Six Days, Seven Nights* | 12.8 |
| 8. *Saving Private Ryan* | 10.9 |
| 9. *Mulan* | 9.1 |
| 10. *The Man in the Iron Mask* | 8.9 |

| | |
|---|---|
| 11. *Deep Impact* | 8.2 |
| 12. *Abre Los Ojos (Open Your Eyes)* * | 7.8 |
| 13. *Blade* | 7.7 |
| 14. *The Jackal* | 7.2 |
| 15. *La Nina de Tus Ojos (Girl of Your Dreams)* * | 7.1 |
| 16. *Flubber* | 6.8 |
| 17. *The Truman Show* | 6.7 |
| 18. *Antz* | 6.2 |
| 19. *Anastasia* | 6.0 |
| 20. *A Perfect Murder* | 5.9 |

## U.K.

| | |
|---|---|
| 1. *Titanic* | 116.3 |
| 2. *Dr. Dolittle* | 32.7 |
| 3. *Saving Private Ryan* | 29.3 |
| 4. *Armageddon* | 28.0 |
| 5. *Godzilla* | 27.1 |
| 6. *There's Something About Mary* | 25.7 |
| 7. *Sliding Doors* * | 20.5 |
| 8. *Lock, Stock and Two Smoking Barrels* * | 18.9 |
| 9. *Flubber* | 18.1 |
| 10. *Lost in Space* | 17.6 |
| 11. *Deep Impact* | 17.0 |
| 12. *The Truman Show* | 16.3 |
| 13. *Antz* | 16.0 |
| 14. *As Good As It Gets* | 15.8 |
| 15. *Mulan* | 14.6 |
| 16. *The X-Files* | 14.3 |
| 17. *The Wedding Singer* | 14.2 |
| 18. *The Full Monty* * | 14.1** |
| 19. *Scream 2* | 13.5 |
| 20. *Mouse Hunt* | 13.2 |

*\* Local production*
*\*\* Does not include 1997 B.O.*

> *Look at me: I worked my way up from nothing to a state of extreme poverty.* (Groucho **Marx**, Monkey Business)

# All-time rental champions

When the press reports that a film has grossed $100 million dollars at the U.S. box-office in the first 20 days of its release, that does not of course mean that the producer has received such a sum. Each week, *Variety* charts the box-office gross of each new picture in the U.S. and several other territories around the world because it's a convenient touchstone of achievement. Far more significant, however, is the following list, which shows how much each film has returned to its distributor in North America. Occasionally, the distributor can negotiate with the cinema-owners from a position of strength. In 1974, everyone wanted to screen *The Godfather Part II*, so many theater chains were prepared to pony up irrevocable advances. The film fared disappointingly, but Paramount did well. In 1993, everyone was clamoring for *Jurassic Park*, so the worldwide distributor, UIP, could exact from the exhibitor up to 90% of the B.O. revenue after deduction of house costs. Where the trade anticipates a flop, or poor business, then that division of the spoils becomes much more even.

| Title (Director; Producer; Studio; Year) | Rental ($) |
|---|---|
| *Titanic* (J. Cameron; J. Cameron/J. Landau; Par; 1997) | 324,425,520 |
| *Star Wars* (G. Lucas; G. Kurtz; Fox; 1977) | 270,918,000 |
| *E.T. – The Extra-Terrestrial* (S. Spielberg; S. Spielberg/K. Kennedy; U; 1982) | 228,168,939 |
| *Jurassic Park* (S. Spielberg; K. Kennedy/G. Molen; U; 1993) | 212,953,417 |
| *Return of the Jedi* (R. Marquand; H. Kazanjian/G. Lucas; Fox; 1983) | 191,648,000 |
| *Independence Day* (R. Emmerich; D. Devlin; Fox; 1996) | 177,190,000 |
| *The Empire Strikes Back* (I. Kershner; G. Lucas/G. Kurtz; Fox; 1980) | 173,814,000 |
| *The Lion King* (Anim; R. Allers/R. Minkoff; D. Hahn; BV; 1994) | 173,057,366 |
| *Forrest Gump* (R. Zemeckis; W. Finerman/S. Tisch/S. Starkey; Par; 1994) | 156,000,000 |
| *Batman* (T. Burton; J. Peters/P. Guber; WB; 1989) | 150,500,000 |
| *Home Alone* (C. Columbus; J. Hughes; Fox; 1990) | 140,099,000 |
| *Twister* (J. de Bont; K. Kennedy/I. Bryce/M. Crichton; WB; 1996) | 133,464,330 |
| *Ghostbusters* (I. Reitman; Col; 1984) | 132,720,000 |
| *The Lost World* (S. Spielberg; G. Molen/C. Wilson; U; 1997) | 130,086,760 |
| *Jaws* (S. Spielberg; R. Zanuck/D. Brown; U; 1975) | 129,549,325 |
| *Men in Black* (B. Sonnenfeld; W. Parkes/L. MacDonald; Sony; 1977) | 117,844,613 |
| *Raiders of the Lost Ark* (S. Spielberg; F. Marshall/H. Kazanjian/G. Lucas; Par; 1981) | 115,598,000 |
| *Indiana Jones and the Last Crusade* (S. Spielberg; R. Watts/G. Lucas/F. Marshall; Par; 1989) | 115,500,000 |
| *Terminator 2* (J. Cameron; J. Cameron/G.A. Hurd /M. Kassar; TriStar, 1991) | 112,500,000 |
| *Aladdin* (Anim; J. Musker/R. Clements; BV; 1992) | 111,740,683 |
| *Mrs. Doubtfire* (C. Columbus; M. Williams/R. Williams/M. Radcliffe; Fox; 1993) | 111,000,000 |
| *Indiana Jones and the Temple of Doom* (S. Spielberg; R. Watts/G. Lucas/F. Marshall; Par; 1984) | 109,000,000 |
| *Beverly Hills Cop* (M. Brest; D. Simpson/J. Bruckheimer; Par; 1984) | 108,000,000 |
| *Back to the Future* (R. Zemeckis; B. Gale/N. Canton/S. Spielberg/F. Marshall/K. Kennedy; U; 1985) | 105,496,267 |
| *Batman Forever* (J. Schumacher; T. Burton/P. MacGregor-Scott; WB; 1995) | 105,100,000 |
| *Armageddon* (M. Bay; J. Bruckheimer; BV; 1998) | 104,806,521 |
| *Home Alone 2: Lost in New York* (C. Columbus; J. Hughes; Fox; 1991) | 103,377,614 |
| *Toy Story* (J. Lasseter; R. Guggenheim/B. Arnold; BV; 1995) | 103,200,000 |
| *Batman Returns* (T. Burton; D. DiNovi/T. Burton; WB; 1992) | 100,100,000 |

| | |
|---|---|
| *Saving Private Ryan* (S. Spielberg; S. Spielberg/ I. Bruce/ M. Gordon/G. Levinsohn; DreamWorks; 1998) | 98,642,308 |
| *Ghost* (J. Zucker; L. Weinstein; Par; 1990) | 98,200,000 |
| *The Fugitive* (A. Davis; A. Kopelson; WB; 1993) | 97,000,000 |
| *Grease* (R. Kleiser; R. Stigwood/A. Carr; Par; 1978) | 96,300,000 |
| *Liar Liar* (T. Shadyac; B. Grazer; U; 1997) | 95,931,900 |
| *Tootsie* (S. Pollack; S. Pollack/D. Richards; Col; 1982) | 94,910,000 |
| *Mission: Impossible* (B. DePalma; T. Cruise/P. Wagner; Par; 1996) | 93,067,933 |
| *Apollo 13* (R. Howard; B. Grazer; U; 1995) | 92,642,370 |
| *Air Force One* (W. Petersen; W. Petersen/G. Katz/ A. Bernstein/J. Shestack; Sony; 1997) | 92,214,082 |
| *The Exorcist* (W. Friedkin; W.P. Blatty; WB; 1973) | 89,000,000 |
| *Rain Man* (B. Levinson; M. Johnson/P. Guber/ J. Peters; MGM/UA; 1989) | 86,813,000 |
| *The Godfather* (F. Coppola; A. Ruddy; Par; 1972) | 86,691,000 |
| *Robin Hood: Prince of Thieves* (K. Reynolds; J. Watson/ P. Densham/R.B. Lewis; WB; 1991) | 86,000,000 |
| *Superman* (R. Donner; P. Spengler; WB; 1978) | 82,800,000 |
| *Close Encounters of the Third Kind* (S. Spielberg; J. & M. Phillips; Col; 1977) | 82,750,000 |
| *Pretty Woman* (G.K. Marshall; A. Milchan/S. Reuther; BV; 1990) | 81,905,530 |
| *Dances with Wolves* (K. Costner; J. Wilson/K. Costner; Orion; 1990) | 81,537,971 |
| *Three Men and a Baby* (L. Nimoy; T. Fields/R. Cort; BV; 1987) | 81,356,000 |
| *Who Framed Roger Rabbit?* (R. Zemeckis; R. Watts/F. Marshall/S. Spielberg/K. Kennedy; BV; 1988) | 81,244,000 |
| *Gone With the Wind* (V. Fleming; D. Selznick; MGM; 1939) | 81,148,362 |
| *Snow White and the Seven Dwarfs* (Anim; D. Hand; W. Disney; RKO; BV; 1937) | 80,886,993 |
| *Beverly Hills Cop II* (T. Scott; D. Simpson/ J. Bruckheimer; Par; 1987) | 80,857,776 |
| *Lethal Weapon 3* (R. Donner; J. Silver/ R. Donner; WB; 1992) | 80,000,000 |
| *True Lies* (J. Cameron; J. Cameron/ S. Austin; Fox; 1994) | 80,000,000 |
| *The Sound of Music* (R. Wise; Fox; 1965) | 79,975,000 |
| *Gremlins* (J. Dante; M. Finnell/S. Spielberg/ F. Marshall; K. Kennedy;WB; 1984) | 79,500,000 |
| *Lethal Weapon 2* (R. Donner; R. Donner/ J. Silver; WB; 1989) | 79,500,000 |
| *Top Gun* (T. Scott; D. Simpson/ J. Bruckheimer; Par; 1986) | 79,400,000 |
| *Rambo: First Blood Part II* (G.P. Cosmatos; B. Feitshans/ A. Vajna/M. Kassar; TriStar; 1985) | 78,919,250 |
| *The Sting* (G.R. Hill; T. Bill/J. & M. Phillips; U; 1973) | 78,212,000 |
| *The Firm* (S. Pollack; S. Rudin/J. Davis; Par; 1993) | 77,047,044 |
| *Rocky IV* (S. Stallone; R. Chartoff/ I. Winkler/UA; MGM/UA; 1985) | 76,023,246 |
| *Jerry Maguire* (C. Crowe; J. Brooks/L.Mark/ R. Sakai/C. Crowe; Sony; 1996) | 74,937,042 |
| *There's Something About Mary* (P. Farrelly/ B. Farrelly; F. Beddor/M. Steinberg/C. Wessler/ B. Thomas; Fox; 1998) | 74,537,493 |
| *The Santa Clause* (J. Pasquin; B. Reilly/J. Silver/ R. Newmyer; BV; 1994) | 74,348,689 |
| *Saturday Night Fever* (J. Badham; R. Stigwood; Par; 1977) | 74,100,000 |
| *Back to the Future, Part II* (R. Zemeckis; B. Gale/N. Canton/S. Spielberg/F. Marshall/ K. Kennedy; U; 1989) | 72,319,630 |
| *Honey, I Shrunk the Kids* (J. Johnston; R. Finkelman Cox/T.G. Smith; BV; 1989) | 72,007,000 |
| *A Few Good Men* (R. Reiner; D. Brown/ R. Reiner/A. Scheinman; Col; 1992) | 71,000,000 |
| *Godzilla* (R. Emmerich; D. Devlin; Sony; 1998) | 70,850,116 |
| *National Lampoon's Animal House* (J. Landis; M. Simmons/I. Reitman; U; 1978) | 70,826,000 |
| *The Flintstones* (B. Levant; B. Cohen; U; 1994) | 70,753,383 |
| *The Rock* (M. Bay; J. Bruckheimer/ D. Simpson; BV; 1996) | 70,600,000 |
| *Crocodile Dundee* (P. Faiman; J. Cornell; Par; 1986) | 70,227,000 |
| *Fatal Attraction* (A. Lyne; S; Jaffee/S. Lansing; Par; 1987) | 70,000,000 |
| *Platoon* (O. Stone; A. Kopelson; Orion; 1986) | 69,937,092 |
| *Beauty and the Beast* (Anim; G. Trousdale/ D. Wise; D. Hahn; BV; 1991) | 69,415,000 |
| *Look Who's Talking* (A. Heckerling; J. Krane; TriStar; 1989) | 68,872,000 |
| *101 Dalmatians* (Anim; W. Reitherman; H. Luske; W. Disney; BV; 1961) | 68,648,000 |
| *As Good As It Gets* (J. Brooks; B. Johnson/ K. Zea/J. Brooks; Sony; 1997) | 67,926,368 |
| *Pocahontas* (J. Pentecost; M. Gabriel/ E. Goldberg; BV; 1995) | 67,848,010 |
| *Teenage Mutant Ninja Turtles* (S. Barron; K. Dawson/S. Fields/D. Chan/R. Chow; New Line; 1990) | 67,650,000 |
| *Die Hard 2* (R. Harlin; L. Gordon/J. Silver/ C. Gordon; Fox; 1990) | 67,512,000 |

---

**... February 15 ...**

With crucial elections set for early March, India's beleaguered politicos come up with a gimmick, persuading an impressive gaggle of film stars to run for office.

| | |
|---|---|
| *Deep Impact* (M. Leder; R. Zanuck/ D. Brown; Par; 1998) | 67,422,722 |
| *Mulan* (Anim; B. Cook/T. Bancroft; P. Coats; BV; 1998) | 66,333,297 |
| *Rocky III* (S. Stallone; I. Winkler/ R. Chartoff; MGM/UA; 1982) | 66,262,796 |
| *Superman II* (R. Lester; P. Spengler; WB; 1981) | 65,100,000 |
| *Ransom* (R. Howard; S. Rudin/B. Grazer/ B.K. Hagopian; BV; 1996) | 65,070,443 |
| *Coming to America* (J. Landis; G. Folsey, Jr./ R. Wachs; Par; 1988) | 65,000,000 |
| *Hook* (S. Spielberg; K. Kennedy/F. Marshall/ G. Molen; TriStar; 1991) | 65,000,000 |
| *Sleepless in Seattle* (N. Ephron; G. Foster; TriStar; 1993) | 64,930,137 |
| *Dumb and Dumber* (P. Farrelly; C. Wessler/ B. Krevoy/S. Stabler; New Line; 1994) | 63,600,000 |
| *Total Recall* (P. Verhoeven; B. Feitshans/ R. Shusett/M. Kassar/A. Vajna; TriStar; 1990) | 63,511,048 |
| *Dr. Dolittle* (B. Thomas; J. Davis/J. Singer/ D. Friendly; Fox; 1998) | 63,382,444 |
| *Sister Act* (E. Ardolino; T. Schwartz/ S. Rudin; BV; 1992) | 62,420,000 |
| *101 Dalmatians* (S. Herak; J. Hughes/ R. Mestres; BV; 1996) | 61,585,660 |
| *On Golden Pond* (M. Rydell; B. Gilbert/ ITC/IPC; U/AFD; 1981) | 61,175,028 |
| *Lethal Weapon 4* (R. Donner; J. Silver/ R. Donner; WB; 1998) | 61,025,268 |
| *Jungle Book* (Anim; W. Reitherman; W. Disney; BV; 1967) | 60,964,000 |
| *Doctor Zhivago* (D. Lean; C. Ponti; MGM/UA; 1965) | 60,954,000 |
| *City Slickers* (R. Underwood; I. Smith/ B. Crystal; Col; 1991) | 60,750,000 |
| *Dick Tracy* (W. Beatty; BV; 1990) | 60,611,145 |
| *Ghostbusters II* (I. Reitman; Col; 1981) | 60,490,000 |
| *The Mask* (C. Russell; B. Engelman; New Line; 1994) | 60,000,000 |
| *Kramer vs. Kramer* (R. Benton; S. Jaffe; Col; 1979) | 59,986,335 |
| *One Flew Over the Cuckoo's Nest* (M. Forman; S. Zaentz/M. Douglas; UA; 1975) | 59,939,701 |
| *The Silence of the Lambs* (J. Demme; E. Saxon/K. Utt/R. Bozman; Orion; 1991) | 59,882,870 |
| *9 to 5* (C. Higgins; B. Gilbert; Foz; 1980) | 59,068,000 |
| *Speed* (J. de Bont; M. Gordon; Fox; 1994) | 59,000,000 |
| *Smokey and the Bandit* (H. Needham; M. Engelberg; U; 1977) | 58,949,938 |
| *Tomorrow Never Dies* (R. Spottiswoode; M. Wilson/B. Broccoli; MGM; 1997) | 58,889,122 |
| *My Best Friend's Wedding* (P.J. Hogan; | |

| | |
|---|---|
| J. Zucker/R. Bass; Sony; 1997) | 58,555,396 |
| *The Hunt for Red October* (J. McTiernan; M. Neufeld; Par; 1990) | 58,500,000 |
| *Batman and Robin* (J. Schumacher; P. Macgregor-Scott; WB; 1997) | 58,492,667 |
| *The Karate Kid Part II* (J. Avildsen; J. Weintraub; Col; 1986) | 58,310,000 |
| *Good Morning Vietnam* (B. Levinson; M. Johnson/L. Brezner; BV; 1987) | 58,038,108 |
| *The Waterboy* (F. Coraci; R. Simonds/ J. Giarraputo; BV; 1998) | 58,172,386 |
| *Twins* (I. Reitman; U; 1988) | 57,715,127 |
| *Crocodile Dundee II* (J. Cornell; J. Cornell/ J. Scott; Par; 1988) | 57,300,000 |
| *The Birdcage* (M. Nichols; M. Nichols; MGM/UA; 1996) | 57,187,100 |
| *Star Trek IV: The Voyage Home* (L. Nimoy; H. Bennett; Par; 1986) | 56,820,071 |
| *The Nutty Professor* (T. Shadyac; Grazer/ R. Simmons; U; 1996) | 56,713,400 |
| *Rocky* (J. Avildsen; R. Chartoff/ I. Winkler; UA; 1976) | 56,524,972 |
| *The Truman Show* (P. Weir; S. Rudin/ A. Niccol/E.S. Feldman; A. Schroeder; Par; 1998) | 56,521,344 |
| *The Bodyguard* (M. Jackson; L. Kasdan/ J. Wilson/K. Costner; WB; 1992) | 56,260,000 |
| *The Addams Family* (B. Sonnenfeld; S. Rudin; Par; 1991) | 56,200,000 |
| *Star Trek* (R. Wise; G. Roddenberry; Par; 1979) | 56,000,000 |
| *Porky's* (B. Clark; D. Carmody/B. Clark/ M. Simon/ Astral Bellevue Pathe; Fox; 1982) | 55,559,000 |
| *An Officer and a Gentleman* (T. Hackford; M. Elfand/Lorimar; Par; 1982) | 55,223,000 |
| *American Graffiti* (G. Lucas; F. Coppola; U; 1973) | 55,128,175 |
| *Rush Hour* (B. Ratner; R. Birnbaum; A. Sarkissian; J. Glickman; New Line; 1998) | 54,123,698 |
| *Clear and Present Danger* (P. Noyce; M. Neufeld/R. Rehme; Par; 1994) | 54,100,000 |
| *Wayne's World* (P. Spheeris; L. Michaels; Par; 1992) | 54,000,000 |
| *Good Will Hunting* (G. Van Sant; L. Bender; Miramax; 1997) | 53,988,869 |
| *Big* (P. Marshall; J.L. Brooks/ R. Greenhut; Fox; 1988) | 53,700,000 |
| *A League of Their Own* (P. Marshall; R. Greenhut/E. Abbott; Col; 1992) | 53,500,000 |
| *Basic Instinct* (P. Verhoeven; A. Marshall/ M. Kassar; TriStar; 1992) | 53,000,000 |
| *Jumanji* (J. Johnston; S. Kroopf/ W. Teitler; Sony; 1995) | 52,200,000 |

---

**... February 16 ...**

**Titanic** breaks domestic B.O. record for best initial release as it climbs to $375 million... Producer Leonard Ho, 71, co-founder of Golden Harvest productions and Asia's largest film studio, succumbs.

| | |
|---|---|
| *Every Which Way But Loose* (J. Fargo; R. Daley; WB; 1978) | 51,900,000 |
| *Face/Off* (J. Woo; D. Permut/B. Osborne/ T. Chang/C. Godsick; Par; 1997) | 51,520,300 |
| *Phenomenon* (J. Turteltaub; B. Boyle/ M. Taylor; BV; 1996) | 51,100,000 |
| *Indecent Proposal* (A. Lyne; S. Lansing; Par; 1993) | 50,846,697 |
| *Driving Miss Daisy* (B. Beresford; R. Zanuck/ L.F. Zanuck; WB; 1989) | 50,500,000 |
| *Jaws 2* (J. Szwarc; R. Zanuck/D. Brown; U; 1978) | 50,431,964 |
| *The Rocky Horror Picture Show* (J. Sharman; M. White/L. Adler; Fox; 1975) | 50,420,189 |
| *Terms of Endearment* (J.L. Brooks; M. Jurow/ J.L. Brooks; Par; 1983) | 50,250,000 |
| *Parenthood* (R. Howard; B. Grazer; U; 1989) | 50,004,367 |
| *The Color Purple* (S. Spielberg; S. Spielberg/ K. Kennedy/F. Marshall/Q. Jones/ Guber-Peters; WB; 1985) | 49,800,000 |
| *Michael* (N. Ephron; S. Daniel/N. Ephron/ J. Jacks; New Line; 1996) | 49,542,300 |
| *A Time to Kill* (J. Schumacher; A. Milchan/ M. Nathanson/H. Lowry/J. Grisham; WB; 1996) | 49,502,617 |
| *Maverick* (R. Donner; B. Davey/R. Donner; WB; 1993) | 49,500,000 |
| *Heaven Can Wait* (W. Beatty/B. Henry; W. Beatty; Par; 1978) | 49,400,000 |
| *The Pelican Brief* (A.J. Pakula; A.J. Pakula/ P. Jan Brugge; WB; 1993) | 49,300,000 |
| *Casper* (B. Silberling; C. Wilson; U; 1995) | 49,160,810 |
| *Back to the Future, Part III* (R. Zemeckis; B. Gale/N. Canton/S. Spielberg/F. Marshall/ K. Kennedy; U; 1990) | 49,071,998 |
| *Contact* (R. Zemeckis; R. Zemecki/S. Starkey; WB; 1997) | 49,033,708 |
| *In the Line of Fire* (W. Petersen; J. Apple; Col; 1993) | 49,000,000 |
| *The Towering Inferno* (J. Guillermin; I. Allen; Fox/WB; 1975) | 48,838,000 |
| *Love Story* (A. Hiller; H. Minsky; Par; 1970) | 48,700,000 |
| *Dead Poets Society* (P. Weir; S. Haft/P.J. Witt/ T. Thomas; BV; 1989) | 48,427,506 |
| *Blazing Saddles* (M. Brooks; M. Hertzberg; WB; 1974) | 47,800,000 |
| *Kindergarten Cop* (I. Reitman; I. Reitman/ B. Grazer; U; 1990) | 47,365,485 |
| *The Best Little Whorehouse in Texas* (C. Higgins; T. Miller/E. Milkis/R. Boyett/RKO; U; 1982) | 47,333,927 |
| *Bambi* (Anim; W. Disney; RKO/BV; 1942) | 47,265,000 |
| *Bram Stoker's Dracula* (F. Coppola; F. Coppola/ F. Fuchs/C. Mulvehill; Col; 1992) | 47,200,000 |
| *Die Hard With a Vengeance* (J. McTiernan; J. McTiernan/M. Tadross; Fox; 1995) | 47,005,870 |
| *The Hunchback of Notre Dame* (Anim; G. Trousdale/K. Wise; D. Hahn; BV; 1996) | 46,900,000 |
| *Sleeping With the Enemy* (J. Ruben; L. Goldberg; Fox; 1991) | 46,629,000 |
| *A Bug's Life* (Anim; J. Lasseter; D. Anderson/ K. Reher; BV; 1998) | 46,300,000 |
| *Goldeneye* (M. Campbell; M. Wilson/ B. Broccoli; MGM/UA; 1995) | 46,099,300 |
| *Space Jam* (J. Pytka; I. Reitman/J. Medjuck/ D. Goldberg; WB; 1996) | 46,077,380 |
| *Eraser* (C. Russell; A. Kopelson; A. Kopelson; WB; 1996) | 46,032,666 |
| *Butch Cassidy and the Sundance Kid* (G.R. Hill; J. Foreman; Fox; 1969) | 45,953,000 |
| *Con Air* (S. West; J. Bruckheimer; BV; 1997) | 45,466,108 |
| *Airport* (G. Seaton; R. Hunter; U; 1970) | 45,220,000 |
| *Interview With the Vampire* (N. Jordan; D. Geffen/S. Woolley; WB; 1994) | 45,100,000 |
| *Mary Poppins* (R. Stevenson; W. Disney; BV; 1964) | 45,000,000 |
| *The First Wives Club* (H. Wilson; S. Rudin; Par; 1996) | 44,618,964 |
| *George of the Jungle* (S. Weisman; D. Hoberman/J. Kemer/J. Avnet; BV; 1997) | 44,616,118 |
| *Unforgiven* (C. Eastwood; WB; 1992) | 44,400,000 |
| *Schindler's List* (S. Spielberg, S. Spielberg/ B. Lustig/G. Molen; U; 1993) | 44,164,190 |
| *The Naked Gun 2½ : The Smell of Fear* (D. Zucker; R.K. Weiss; Par; 1991) | 44,200,000 |
| *The Graduate* (M. Nichols; L. Turman; AvcoEmb; 1968) | 44,090,729 |
| *Crimson Tide* (T. Scott; D. Simpson/ J. Bruckheimer; BV; 1995) | 43,865,850 |
| *Presumed Innocent* (A.J. Pakula; S. Pollack/ M. Rosenberg; WB; 1990) | 43,800,000 |
| *Aliens* (J. Cameron; G.A. Hurd; Fox; 1986) | 43,753,000 |
| *Hercules* (Anim; J. Musker; A. Dewey/ J. Musker/R. Clements; BV; 1997) | 43,682,414 |
| *Out of Africa* (S. Pollack; U; 1985) | 43,448,253 |
| *Cliffhanger* (R. Harlin; A. Marshall; TriStar; 1993) | 43,306,664 |
| *The Karate Kid* (J. Avildsen; J. Weintraub; Col; 1984) | 43,120,000 |
| *Seven* (D. Fincher; A. Kopelson; New Line; 1995) | 43,100,000 |
| *Father of the Bride* (C. Shyer; N. Meyers/ C. Baum/H. Rosenman; BV; 1991) | 43,027,000 |
| *The Ten Commandments* (C.B. DeMille; C.B. DeMille; Par; 1956) | 43,000,000 |
| *The Mask of Zorro* (M. Campbell; D. Claybourne/D. Foster; Sony; 1998) | 42,879,818 |

---

**. . . February 17 . . .**
Songwriter Bob Merrill, 74, of **Funny Girl** fame and **How Much Is That Doggie in the Window?** plays last bar... Samuel L. Jackson squares off against Spike Lee over racial epithets in **Jackie Brown** at pic's Berlin fest preem.

| | |
|---|---|
| *Flubber* (L. Mayfield; J. Hughes/ R. Mestres; BV; 1997) | 42,777,244 |
| *Waterworld* (K. Reynolds; C. Gordon/ J. Davis/K. Costner; U; 1995) | 42,358,180 |
| *The Goodbye Girl* (H. Ross; R. Stark; MGM/WB; 1977) | 41,839,170 |
| *The Jerk* (C. Reiner; D. Picker/ W.E. McEuen; U; 1979) | 42,989,656 |
| *Rocky II* (S. Stallone; R. Chartoff/ I. Winker; UA; 1979) | 42,169,387 |
| *The Poseidon Adventure* (R. Neame; I. Allen; Fox; 1972) | 42,000,000 |
| *Arthur* (S. Gordon; R. Greenhut; Orion/WB; 1981) | 42,000,00 |
| *Back to School* (A. Metter; E. Endler/ M. Endler/H. Ramis/C. Russell; Orion; 1986) | 41,948,383 |
| *Teenage Mutant Ninja Turtles II* (M. Pressman; T. Gray/ K. Dawson/D. Chan/R. Chow; New Line; 1991) | 41,900,000 |
| *When Harry Met Sally* (R. Reiner; R. Reiner/ A. Scheinman; Col; 1989) | 41,790,000 |
| *Fantasia* (Anim; W. Disney; RKO/BV; 1940) | 41,660,000 |
| *The War of the Roses* (D. DeVito; J.L. Brooks/ A. Milchan; Fox; 1989) | 41,400,000 |
| *Cinderella* (Anim; W. Jackson; W. Disney; RKO/BV; 1949) | 41,087,000 |
| *Stripes* (I. Reitman; D. Goldberg/ I. Reitman; Col; 1981) | 40,886,589 |
| *Airplane!* (J. Abrahams/D. Zucker/J. Zucker; H.W. Koch/J. Davison; Par; 1980) | 40,610,000 |
| *Trading Places* (J. Landis; A. Russo; Par; 1983) | 40,600,000 |
| *Any Which Way You Can* (B. Van Horn; F. Manes; WB; 1980) | 40,500,000 |
| *Star Trek: First Contact* (J. Frakes; R. Berman; Par; 1996) | 40,491,880 |
| *Pinocchio* (Anim; W. Disney; RKO/BV; 1940) | 40,442,000 |
| *Alien* (R. Scott; G. Carroll/D. Giler/W. Hill; Fox; 1979) | 40,300,000 |
| *The X-Files* (R. Bowman; C. Carter/ D. Sackheim; Fox; 1998) | 40,268,161 |
| *Backdraft* (R. Howard; R.B. Lewis/ P. Densham/J. Watson; U; 1991) | 40,260,678 |
| *Lady and the Tramp* (Anim; W. Disney; BV; 1985) | 40,249,000 |
| *The Little Mermaid* (Anim; R. Clements/ J. Musker; H. Ashman/J. Musker; BV; 1989) | 40,227,000 |
| *Another 48 Hours* (W. Hill; L. Gordon/ R. Wachs; Par; 1990) | 40,100,000 |
| *Star Trek II: The Wrath of Kahn* (N. Meyer; R. Sallin/H. Bennett; Par; 1982) | 40,000,000 |
| *Cocoon* (R. Howard; R. Zanuck/D. Brown/ L.F. Zanuck; Fox; 1985) | 40,000,000 |
| *Steel Magnolias* (H. Ross; R. Stark; TriStar; 1989) | 40,000,000 |
| *Days of Thunder* (T. Scott; D. Simpson/ J. Bruckheimer; Par; 1990) | 40,000,000 |
| *The Golden Child* (M. Ritchie; E. Feldman/ R. Wachs; Par; 1986) | 39,723,089 |
| *Dangerous Minds* (J.N. Smith; D. Simpson/ J. Bruckheimer; BV; 1995) | 39,586,890 |
| *Scream* (W. Craven; C. Woods/C. Konrad; Miramax; 1996) | 39,502,716 |
| *Cape Fear* (M. Scorsese; B. De Fina/ K. Kennedy/F. Marshall; U; 1991) | 39,490,060 |
| *Scream 2* (W. Craven; C. Konrad/ M. Maddelena; Miramax; 1997) | 39,531,561 |
| *The Hand That Rocks the Cradle* (C. Hanson; D. Maden; BV; 1992) | 39,334,000 |
| *Star Trek III: The Search for Spock* (L. Nimoy; H. Bennett; Par; 1984) | 39,000,000 |
| *Disclosure* (B. Levinson; B. Levinson/ M. Crichton; WB; 1994) | 39,000,000 |
| *Smokey and the Bandit II* (H. Needham; H. Moonjean; U; 1980) | 38,911,473 |
| *While You Were Sleeping* (J. Turteltaub; J. Roth/R. Birnbaum; BV; 1995) | 38,907,370 |
| *Young Frankenstein* (M. Brooks; M. Gruskoff; Fox; 1975) | 38,823,000 |
| *Antz* (Anim; E. Damell/Tim Johnson; B. Lewis/A. Warner/P. Wooton; DreamWorks; 1998) | 38,562,749 |
| *WarGames* (J.Badham; H. Schneider/ L. Goldberg; MGM/UA; 1983) | 38,519,833 |
| *Police Academy* (H. Wilson; P. Maslansky; Ladd/WB; 1984) | 38,500,000 |
| *Fiddler on the Roof* (N. Jewison; UA; 1971) | 38,260,954 |
| *Poltergeist* (T. Hooper; S. Spielberg/ F. Marshall; MGM/UA; 1982) | 38,248,762 |
| *Congo* (F. Marshall; K. Kennedy/S. Mercer; Par; 1995) | 38,080,500 |
| *The Godfather, Part III* (F. Coppola; Par; 1990) | 38,000,000 |
| *Apocalypse Now* (F. Coppola; UA; 1979) | 37,980,163 |
| *Three Men and a Little Lady* (E. Ardolino; T. Field/R. Cort; BV; 1990) | 37,757,378 |
| *Peter Pan* (Anim; W. Disney; RKO/BV; 1953) | 37,584,000 |
| *Patriot Games* (P. Noyce; M. Neufeld/ R. Rehme; Par; 1992) | 37,500,000 |
| *Philadelphia* (J. Demme; J. Demme/ E. Saxon; TriStar; 1993) | 37,500,000 |
| *Annie* (J. Huston; R. Stark; Col; 1982) | 37,480,000 |
| *Fried Green Tomatoes* (J. Avnet; J. Avnet/ J. Kerner; U; 1991) | 37,402,827 |
| *Superman III* (R. Lester; P. Spengler/ I. Salkind; WB; 1983) | 37,200,000 |

---

**... February 18 ...**

Filmmaker Ivan Reitman and Universal Pic's topper Tom Pollock form a new production company financed by Polygram.

| | |
|---|---|
| *A Star Is Born* (F. Pierson; J. Peters; WB; 1976) | 37,100,000 |
| *Under Siege* (A. Davis; A. Milchan/S. Seagal/ S. Reuther; WB; 1992) | 37,100,000 |
| *10* (B. Edwards; B. Edwards/T. Adams; Orion/WB; 1979) | 37,000,000 |
| *Ben-Hur* (W. Wyler; S. Zimbalist; MGM; 1959) | 36,992,088 |
| *King Kong* (J. Guillermin; D. De Laurentiis; Par; 1976) | 36,915,000 |
| *The Untouchables* (B. DePalma; A. Linson; Par; 1987) | 36,866,530 |
| *Born on the Fourth of July* (O. Stone; A.K. Ho/O. Stone; U; 1989) | 36,803,148 |
| *The Cannonball Run* (H. Needham; A. Ruddy; Fox; 1981) | 36,800,000 |
| *M\*A\*S\*H* (R. Altman; I. Preminger; Fox; 1970) | 36,720,000 |
| *Mortal Kombat* (P. Anderson; L. Kasanoff; New Line; 1995) | 36,600,000 |
| *Mr. Holland's Opus* (S. Herek; T. Field/ M. Nolin/R. Cort; BV; 1995) | 36,550,000 |
| *The Jewel of the Nile* (L. Teague; M. Douglas; Fox; 1985) | 36,500,000 |
| *The Rugrats Movie* (Anim; N. Virgien/ I. Kovalyov; A. Klasky/G. Csupo; Par; 1998) | 36,500,000 |
| *Cocktail* (R. Donaldson; T. Field/R. Cort; BV; 1988) | 36,474,000 |
| *City of Angels* (B. Silberling; D. Steel/ C. Roven; WB; 1998) | 36,225,048 |
| *Father of the Bride, Part II* (C. Shyer; N. Meyers/C. Baum/H. Rosenman; BV; 1995) | 36,200,000 |
| *Flashdance* (A. Lyne; D. Simpson/ J. Bruckheimer; Par; 1983) | 36,180,000 |
| *The Prince of Tides* (B. Streisand; B. Streisand/A. Karsch; Col; 1991) | 36,100,000 |
| *Romancing the Stone* (R. Zemeckis; M. Douglas; Fox; 1984) | 36,000,000 |
| *Die Hard* (J. McTiernan; L. Gordon/ J. Silver; Fox; 1988) | 36,000,000 |
| *Star Trek IV: The Undiscovered Country* (N. Meyer; R. Winter/S.C. Jaffe; Par; 1991) | 36,000,000 |
| *Free Willy* (S. Wincer; L. Shuler-Donner/ J. Tugend; WB; 1993) | 36,000,000 |
| *Earthquake* (M. Robson; U; 1974) | 35,849,994 |
| *Grumpier Old Men* (H. Deutch; J. Davis/ R. Berman; WB; 1995) | 35,792,663 |
| *Star Trek Generations* (D. Carson; R. Berman; Par; 1994) | 35,700,000 |
| *Pulp Fiction* (Q. Tarantino; L. Bender; Miramax; 1994) | 35,614,180 |
| *Turner & Hooch* (R. Spottiswoode; R. Wagner; BV; 1989) | 35,260,000 |
| *The Last of the Mohicans* (M. Mann; M. Mann/H. Lowry; Fox; 1992) | 35,177,486 |
| *Conspiracy Theory* (R. Donner; J. Silver/ R. Donner; WB; 1997) | 35,108,500 |
| *Grumpy Old Men* (D. Petrie; R. Berman/ J. Davis; WB; 1993) | 35,100,000 |
| *Coal Miner's Daughter* (M. Apted; B. Larson; U; 1980) | 35,030,225 |
| *The Amityville Horror* (S. Rosenberg; R. Saland/E. Geisinger; AIP/FWS) | 35,000,000 |
| *Hooper* (H. Needham; B Reynolds/ L. Gordon; WB; 1978) | 34,900,000 |
| *Sudden Impact* (C. Eastwood; WB; 1983) | 34,800,000 |
| *National Lampoon's Christmas Vacation* (J. Chechik; J. Hughes/T. Jacobson/ M. Simmons; WB; 1989) | 34,800,000 |
| *Enemy of the State* (T. Scott; J. Bruckheimer; BV; 1998) | 34,800,000 |
| *Broken Arrow* (J. Woo; M. Gordon/ B. Badalato; Fox; 1996) | 34,619,070 |
| *The Wedding Singer* (F. Coraci; R. Simonds/ J. Giarraputo; BV; 1998) | 34,505,348 |
| *Private Benjamin* (H. Zieff; N. Meyers/ C. Shyer/H. Miller; WB; 1980) | 34,400,000 |
| *The Naked Gun* (D. Zucker; R.K. Weiss; Par; 1988) | 34,400,000 |
| *Moonstruck* (N. Jewison; P. Palmer/ N. Jewison; MGM/UA; 1987) | 34,393,000 |
| *The Bridges of Madison County* (C. Eastwood; C. Eastwood/K. Kennedy; WB; 1995) | 34,355,230 |
| *Six Days, Seven Nights* (I. Reitman; I. Reitman/W. Nicita/R. Birnbaum; BV; 1998) | 34,195,477 |
| *White Men Can't Jump* (R. Shelton; D. Miller/D. Lester; Fox; 1992) | 34,115,000 |
| *Splash* (R. Howard; B. Grazer; BV; 1984) | 34,103,000 |
| *Octopussy* (J. Glen; A. Broccoli; MGM/UA; 1983) | 34,031,000 |
| *My Fair Lady* (G. Cukor; J. Warner; WB; 1964) | 34,000,000 |
| *Footloose* (H. Ross; L.J. Rachmil/C. Zadan/ D. Melnick; Par; 1984) | 34,000,000 |
| *JFK* (O. Stone; A.K. Ho/O. Stone; WB; 1991) | 34,000,000 |
| *Boomerang* (R. Hudlin; B. Grazer/W. Hudlin; Par; 1992) | 34,000,000 |
| *Ace Ventura: Pet Detective* (T. Shadyac, J. Robinson; WB; 1993) | 34,000,000 |
| *Wolf* (M. Nichols; D. Wick; Col; 1994) | 34,000,000 |
| *Stargate* (R. Emmerich; J. Michaels/ O. Eberle/D. Devlin; MGM/UA; 1994) | 34,000,000 |
| *Moonraker* (L. Gilbert; A. Broccoli; UA; 1979) | 33,924,008 |

---

**... February 19 ...**

For the sixth consecutive week the **Titanic** soundtrack was the bestselling album in the U.S., logging a whopping 848,000 copies sold, a 200,000-unit increase over the previous week.

*The Horse Whisperer* (R. Redford; R. Redford/
P. Markey; BV; 1998)    33,917,384
*Staying Alive* (S. Stallone; R. Stigwood/
S. Stallone; Par; 1983)    33,650,000
*Hot Shots!* (J. Abrahams; B. Badalato;
Fox; 1991)    33,761,000
*The Cable Guy* (B. Stiller; A. Licht/J. Mueller/
J. Apatow; Sony; 1996)    33,600,000
*Rising Sun* (P. Kaufman; P. Kaufman;
Fox; 1993)    33,392,872
*Beetlejuice* (T. Burton; M. Bender/L.Wilson/
R. Hashimoto; Geffen/WB; 1988)    33,200,000
*Oliver & Company* (Anim; G. Scribner;
BV; 1988)    33,199,470
*Waiting to Exhale* (F. Whitaker; E. Swerdlow/
D. Schindler; Fox; 1995)    33,010,822
*Harlem Nights* (E. Murphy; R. Wachs/
M. Lipsky/E. Murphy; Par; 1989)    33,000,000
*The English Patient* (A. Minghella; S. Zaentz;
Miramax; 1996)    32,763,702
*Nine Months* (C. Columbus; A. Francois/
C. Columbus/ M. Radcliffe/M. Barnathan;
Fox; 1995)    32,754,660
*Billy Jack* (T. Laughlin; M. Solti; WB; 1971) 32,500,000
*Groundhog Day* (H. Ramis; T. Albert/
H. Ramis; Col; 1993)    32,500,000
*Legends of the Fall* (E. Zwick; E. Zwick/
B. Wittliff/M. Herskovitz; Sony; 1994)    32,100,000
*The Blues Brothers* (J. Landis; R.K. Weiss;
U; 1980)    32,098,717
*The Muppet Movie* (J. Frawley; J. Henson;
AFD; 1979)    32,000,000
*Braveheart* (M. Gibson; M. Gibson/
A. Ladd, Jr./B. Davey; Par; 1995)    31,818,442
*The Witches of Eastwick* (G. Miller;
N. Canton/P. Guber/J. Peters; WB; 1987)    31,800,000
*Alien³* (D. Fincher; G. Carroll/D. Giler/
W. Hill; Fox; 1992)    31,762,000
*Purple Rain* (A. Magnoli; R. Cavallo/
J. Ruffalo/S. Fargnoli; WB; 1984)    31,700,000
*Dante's Peak* (R. Donaldson; G.A. Hurd/
J.M. Singer; U; 1997)    31,572,690
*Get Shorty* (B. Sonnenfeld; D. DeVito/
M. Shamberg/S. Sher; MGM/UA; 1995)    31,542,110
*Bad Boys* (M. Bay; D. Simpson/
J. Bruckheimer; Col; 1995)    31,531,110
*Oh, God* (C. Reiner; J. Weintraub; WB; 1977) 31,500,000
*Scrooged* (R. Donner; R. Donner/A. Linson;
Par; 1988)    31,500,000
*Outbreak* (W. Petersen; A. Kopelson/
W. Petersen/G. Katz; WB; 1995)    31,500,000
*Ruthless People* (J. Abrahams/D. Zucker/
J. Zucker; M. Peyser; BV; 1986)    31,443,000

*Arachnophobia* (F. Marshall; K. Kennedy/
R. Vane/S. Spielberg/F. Marshall; BV; 1990) 31,366,000
*The Deep* (P. Yates; P. Guber; Col; 1977)    31,266,000
*The Trial of Billy Jack* (F. Laughlin; J. Cramer;
Taylor-Laughlin/WB; 1974)    31,100,000
*Predator* (J. McTiernan; J. Silver/J. David/
L. Gordon; Fox; 1987)    31,000,000
*I Know What You Did Last Summer*
(J. Gillespie; N. Moritz/E. Feig/S. Chaffin;
Sony; 1997)    30,926,393
*The Shining* (S. Kubrick; WB; 1980)    30,900,000
*The Godfather, Part II* (F. Coppola;
F. Coppola/G. Fredrickson/F. Roos;
Par; 1974)    30,673,000
*Chariots of Fire* (H. Hudson; D. Puttnam;
Ladd/WB; 1981)    30,600,000
*Field of Dreams* (P.A. Robinson; L. Gordon/
C.Gordon; U; 1989)    30,531,000
*Spies Like Us* (J. Landis; B. Grazer/G. Folsey Jr.;
WB; 1985)    30,500,000
*A Perfect Murder* (A. Davis; A. Kopelson/
A. Kopelson/C. Mankiewicz/
P. MacGregor-Scott; WB; 1998)    30,446,098
*Death Becomes Her* (R. Zemeckis;
R. Zemeckis/S. Starkey; U; 1992)    30,433,483
*The Parent Trap* (N. Meyers; C. Shyer;
BV; 1998)    30,411,482
*Risky Business* (P. Brickman; J. Avnet/
S. Tisch; Geffen/WB; 1983)    30,400,000
*National Lampoon's Vacation* (H. Ramis/
M. Simmons; WB; 1983)    30,400,000
*HouseSitter* (F. Oz; B. Grazer; U; 1992) 30,390,622
*Uncle Buck* (J. Hughes; J. Hughes/
T. Jacobson; U; 1989)    30,335,176
*48 Hrs.* (W. Will; L. Gordon/J. Silver;
Par; 1982)    30,328,000
*The Electric Horseman* (S. Pollack;
Col; 1979)    30,282,966
*Dragnet* (T. Mankiewicz; D. Permut/
R.K. Weiss; U; 1987)    30,234,468
*Heat* (M. Mann; M. Mann/A. Linson;
WB; 1995)    30,248,117
*Tango & Cash* (A. Konchalovsky; P. Guber/
J. Peters; WB; 1989)    30,100,000
*Dave* (I. Reitman; L. Shuler-Donner/
I. Reitman; WB; 1993)    30,100,000
*The Rescuers* (Anim; W. Reitherman/
J. Lounsbury/A. Stevens; W. Reitherman;
BV; 1977)    30,090,000
*Silver Streak* (A. Hiller; E. Milkis/T. Miller;
Fox; 1976)    30,018,000
*All the President's Men* (A.J. Pakula;
W. Coblenz; WB; 1976)    30,000,000

---

**... February 20 ...**
Robert Wise honored with American Film Institute Life Achievement Award ...
After a banner year that included **In & Out** and **Breakdown**, Spelling Entertainment
shutters its film division.

| | |
|---|---|
| *Hard to Kill* (B. Malmuth; G. Adelson/ J. Simon/B. Todman Jr.; WB; 1990) | 30,000,000 |
| *The American President* (R. Reiner; R. Reiner; Sony; 1995) | 30,000,000 |
| *Cool Runnings* (J. Turteltaub; D. Steel; BV; 1993) | 29,982,934 |
| *Spawn* (M.A.Z. Dippe; C. Goldman; New Line; 1997) | 29,914,700 |
| *The Goonies* (R. Donner; R. Donner; H. Bernhard/S. Spielberg/F. Marshall/ K. Kennedy; WB; 1985) | 29,900,000 |
| *The Secret of My Success* (H. Ross; U; 1987) | 29,855,540 |
| *The Fox and the Hound* (Anim; A. Stevens/ T. Berman/R. Rich; W. Reitherman/ A. Stevens; BV; 1981) | 29,812,000 |
| *A Fish Called Wanda* (C. Crichton; M. Shamberg; MGM/UA; 1988) | 29,766,000 |
| *Jingle All the Way* (B. Levant; C. Columbus/ M. Radcliffe/M. Barnathan; Fox; 1996) | 29,683,200 |
| *Lethal Weapon* (R. Donner; R. Donner/ J. Silver; WB; 1987) | 29,500,000 |
| *The Fifth Element* (L. Besson; P. Ledoux; Sony; 1997) | 29,357,282 |
| *What About Bob?* (F. Oz; L. Ziskin; BV; 1991) | 29,282,227 |
| *Song of the South* (H. Foster/W. Jackson; W. Disney; RKO/BV; 1946) | 29,228,720 |
| *Blade* (S. Norrington; P. Fankfurt/ W. Snipes/R. Engelman; New Line; 1998) | 29,124,479 |
| *Far and Away* (R. Howard; B. Grazer/ R. Howard; U; 1992) | 28,910,698 |
| *The Blue Lagoon* (R. Kleiser; Col; 1980) | 28,838,022 |
| *The Abyss* (J. Cameron; G.A. Hurd; Fox; 1989) | 28,800,000 |
| *Flatliners* (J. Schumacher; M. Douglas; R. Beiber; Col; 1990) | 28,800,000 |
| *Sea of Love* (H. Becker; M. Bregman/ L.A. Stroller; U; 1989) | 28,623,522 |
| *Thunderball* (T. Young; K. McClory; UA; 1965) | 28,621,434 |
| *Ferris Bueller's Day Off* (J. Hughes; J. Hughes/T. Jacobson; Par; 1986) | 28,600,000 |
| *Working Girl* (M. Nichols; D. Wick; Fox; 1988) | 28,600,000 |
| *The Omen* (R. Donner; H. Bernard; Fox; 1976) | 28,544,000 |
| *Rambo III* (P. Macdonald; B. Feitshans/ M. Kassar/A. Vajna; TriStar; 1988) | 28,509,000 |
| *Witness* (P. Weir; E. Feldman; Par; 1985) | 28,500,000 |
| *Scent of a Woman* (M. Brest; M. Brest; U; 1993) | 28,500,000 |
| *Courage Under Fire* (E. Zwick; J. Davis/ J. Singer/D. Friendly; Fox; 1996) | 28,417,322 |
| *Up in Smoke* (L. Adler; L. Adler/L. Lombardo; Par; 1978) | 28,300,000 |
| *Down and Out in Beverly Hills* (P. Mazursky; BV; 1986) | 28,277,000 |
| *The Saint* (P. Noyce; D. Brown/R. Evans/ W.J. Macdonald/M. Neufeld; Par; 1997) | 28,227,120 |
| *Stakeout* (J. Badham; J. Kouf/ C. Summers; BV; 1987) | 28,215,000 |
| *Anaconda* (L. Llosa; V. Harrah/ L. Rabinowitz/C. Little; Sony; 1997) | 28,213,628 |
| *Never Say Never Again* (I. Kershner; J. Schwartzman; WB; 1983) | 28,200,000 |
| *Ever After* (A. Tennant; M. Soria/T. Trench; Fox; 1998) | 28,167,585 |
| *Patton* (F.J. Schaffner; F. McCarthy; Fox; 1970) | 28,100,000 |
| *What's Up Doc?* (P. Bogdanovich; WB; 1972) | 28,000,000 |
| *Cobra* (G.P. Cosmatos; M. Golan/Y. Globus; WB; 1986) | 28,000,000 |
| *The Living Daylights* (J. Glen; A. Broccoli/ M. Wilson; MGM/UA; 1987) | 27,878,804 |
| *Willow* (R. Howard; N. Wooll/G. Lucas; MGM/UA; 1988) | 27,835,000 |
| *My Girl* (H. Zieff; B. Grazer; Col; 1991) | 27,700,000 |
| *Throw Momma From the Train* (D. DeVito; L. Brezner; Orion; 1987) | 27,758,311 |
| *Species* (R. Donaldson; F. Mancuso Jr./ D. Feldman; MGM/UA; 1995) | 27,625,050 |
| *The Last Boy Scout* (T. Scott; J. Silver/ M. Levy; WB; 1991) | 27,600,000 |
| *Foul Play* (C. Higgins; T. Miller/E. Milkis; Par; 1980) | 27,500,000 |
| *Edward Scissorhands* (T. Button; D. DeNovi/ T. Burton; Fox; 1990) | 27,500,000 |
| *The Deer Hunter* (M. Cimino; B. Spikings/ M. Deeley/M. Cimino; U; 1978) | 27,436,325 |
| *Honey, I Blew Up the Kid* (R. Kleiser; D. Steel/E.S. Feldman; BV; 1992) | 27,417,000 |
| *Legal Eagles* (I. Reitman; U; 1986) | 27,244,588 |
| *Police Academy 2 – Their First Assignment* (J. Paris; P. Maslansky; WB; 1985) | 27,200,000 |
| *Beavis and Butt-head Do America* (M. Judge; A. Terkuhle; Par; 1996) | 27,091,100 |
| *The Four Seasons* (A. Alda; M. Bregman; U; 1981) | 27,137,478 |
| *Jaws 3-D* (J. Alves; R. Hitzif; U; 1983) | 27,035,452 |
| *Star Trek V: The Final Frontier* (W. Shatner; H. Bennett/R. Winter; Par; 1989) | 27,035,452 |
| *Misery* (R. Reiner; A. Scheinman/ R. Reiner; Col; 1990) | 26,880,000 |
| *Last Action Hero* (J. McTiernan; S. Roth/ J. McTiernan; Col; 1993) | 26,800,000 |
| *Boyz in the Hood* (J. Singleton; S. Nicolaides; Col; 1991) | 26,700,000 |

---

**... February 21 ...**

Antonio Banderas is set to make his directorial debut with **Crazy in Alabama**, with wife Melanie Griffith to star.

| | |
|---|---|
| The Verdict (S. Lumet; R. Zanuck/D. Brown; Fox; 1982) | 26,650,000 |
| The Crying Game (N. Jordan; S. Woolley; Miramax; 1993) | 26,583,302 |
| For Your Eyes Only (J. Glen; A. Broccoli; MGM/UA; 1981) | 26,577,736 |
| Beethoven (B. Levant; J. Medjuck/M.C. Gross/I. Reitman; U; 1992) | 26,450,910 |
| The Main Event (H. Zieff; J. Peters/B. Streisand; WB; 1979) | 26,400,000 |
| Pet Sematary (M. Lambert; R.P. Rubinstein; Par; 1989) | 26,400,000 |
| Unlawful Entry (J. Kaplan; C. Gordon; Fox; 1992) | 26,357,000 |
| Funny Girl (W. Wyler, R. Stark; Col; 1968) | 26,325,000 |
| The French Connection (W. Friedkin; P. D'Antoni/Scine-Moore; Fox; 1971) | 26,315,000 |
| Kiss the Girls (G. Fleder; D. Brown/J. Wizan; Par; 1997) | 26,261,452 |
| Tombstone (G. Cosmatos; J. Jacks/S. Daniel/B. Misiorowski; BV; 1993) | 26,122,000 |
| Clueless (A. Heckerling; S. Rudin/R. Lawrence; Par; 1995) | 26,121,600 |
| Cleopatra (J.L. Mankewicz; W. Wanger; Fox; 1963) | 26,000,000 |
| Mouse Hunt (G. Verbinski; A. Richel/T. Ludwig/B. Cohen) | 25,998,836 |
| Hope Floats (F. Whitaker/L. Obst; Fox; 1998) | 25,847,311 |
| Twelve Monkeys (T. Gilliam; C. Roven; U; 1995) | 25,621,600 |
| The Devil's Advocate (T. Hackford; A. Kopelson/A. Kopelson; WB; 1997) | 25,603,748 |
| Jack (F. Coppola; R. Mestres/F. Fuchs/F. Coppola; BV; 1996) | 25,602,504 |
| National Lampoon's European Vacation (A. Heckerling; M. Simmons; WB; 1985) | 25,600,000 |
| My Cousin Vinny (J. Lynn; D. Launer/P. Schif; Fox; 1992) | 25,565,000 |
| 2001: A Space Odyssey (S. Kubrick; MGM/UA; 1968) | 25,521,917 |
| Snake Eyes (B. DePalma; B. DePalma; Par; 1998) | 25,513,056 |
| Guess Who's Coming to Dinner (S. Kramer; Col; 1968) | 25,500,000 |
| Demolition Man (M. Brambilla; J. Silver/M. Levy/H. Kazanjian; WB; 1993) | 25,500,000 |
| Beethoven's 2nd (R. Daniel; J. Medjuck/M. Gross; U; 1993) | 25,472,162 |
| U.S. Marshals (S. Baird; A. Kopelson/A. Kopelson; WB; 1998) | 25,446,517 |
| The Black Hole (G. Nelson; R. Miller; BV; 1979) | 25,437,000 |
| Revenge of the Pink Panther (B. Edwards; UA; 1978) | 25,406,182 |
| A View to a Kill (J. Glen; A. Broccoli/M. Wilson; MGM/UA; 1985) | 25,316,185 |
| The China Syndrome (J. Bridges; M. Douglas; Col; 1979) | 25,342,000 |
| Airport 1975 (J. Smight; W. Frye; U; 1974) | 25,305,576 |
| Sister Act 2: Back in the Habit (B. Duke; D. Steel/S. Rudin; BV/WB; 1993) | 25,288,302 |
| Dirty Dancing (E. Ardolino; L. Gottlieb; Vestron; 1987) | 25,218,742 |
| Problem Child (D. Dugan; R. Simonds; U; 1990) | 25,134,781 |
| Anastasia (Anim; D. Bluth/G. Goldman; D. Bluth/G. Goldman; Fox; 1997) | 25,114,852 |
| Rookie of the Year (D. Stern; R. Harper; Fox; 1993) | 25,039,085 |
| Firefox (C. Eastwood; WB; 1982) | 25,000,000 |
| The Natural (B. Levinson; M. Johnson; TriStar; 1984) | 25,000,000 |
| Black Rain (R. Scott; S. Jaffe/S. Lansing/M. Douglas; Par; 1989) | 25,000,000 |
| Little Women (G. Armstrong; D. DiNovi; Sony; 1994) | 25,000,000 |
| Gandhi (R. Attenborough; M. Stanley-Evans/R. Dube; Col; 1982) | 24,970,000 |
| Speed 2: Cruise Control (J. De Bont; J. De Bont; Fox; 1997) | 24,967,110 |
| The Specialist (L. Llosa; J. Weintraub; WB; 1994) | 24,941,930 |
| Broadcast News (J.L. Brooks; Fox; 1987) | 24,900,000 |
| Beaches (G. Marshall; B. Bruckheimer-Martell/B. Midler/M. Jennings South; BV; 1988) | 24,900,000 |
| The Bad News Bears (M. Ritchie; S. Jaffe; Par; 1976) | 24,888,000 |
| Executive Decision (S. Baird; J. Silver; WB, 1996) | 24,888,632 |
| Raw (R. Townsend; R. Wachs/K.I. Wayans; Par; 1987) | 24,800,000 |
| Primal Fear (G. Hoblit; G. Lucchesi; Par; 1996) | 24,587,400 |
| Popeye (R. Altman; R. Evans; Par; 1980) | 24,568,541 |
| Doc Hollywood (M. Caton-Jones; S. Solt/D.D. Johnson; WB; 1991) | 24,500,000 |
| The Man in the Iron Mask (R. Wallace; R.Wallace/R. Smith; MGM; 1998) | 24,496,242 |
| Fletch (M. Ritchie; A. Greisman/P. Douglas; U; 1985) | 24,495,613 |
| The Toy (R. Donner; P. Feldman; Col; 1982) | 24,440,000 |
| The Color of Money (M. Scorsese; I. Axelrad/B. DeFina; BV; 1986) | 24,435,000 |

**... February 22 ...**
Brazil's **Central Station** takes top honors at Berlin Film Fest.

| | |
|---|---|
| Something to Talk About (L. Hallstrom; A. Sylbert/P. Weinstein; WB; 1995) | 24,415,480 |
| Forever Young (S. Miner; B. Davey/ E.S. Feldman/J. Abrams; WB; 1992) | 24,400,000 |
| Starship Troopers (P. Vcrhoeven; J. Davison/A. Marshall; Sony; 1997) | 24,393,721 |
| The Spy Who Loved Me (L. Gilbert; A. Broccoli; UA; 1977) | 24,364,501 |
| La Bamba (L. Valdez; T. Hackford/ B. Borden; Col; 1987) | 24,320,000 |
| Dragonheart (R. Cohen; R. De Laurentiis; U; 1996) | 24,319,200 |
| Austin Powers (J. Roach; S. Todd/D. Moore/ J. Todd/M. Myers; New Line; 1997) | 24,303,600 |
| Sneakers (P.A. Robinson; W. Parkes/ L. Lasker; U; 1992) | 24,300,000 |
| Dennis the Menace (N. Castle; J. Hughes; WB; 1993) | 24,200,000 |
| The Big Chill (L. Kasdan; M. Shamberg; Col; 1983) | 24,060,000 |
| RoboCop (P. Verhoeven; A. Schmidt; Orion; 1987) | 24,036,727 |
| Volcano (M. Jackson; N.H. Moritz/ A.Z. Davis; Fox; 1997) | 24,022,770 |
| The Enforcer (J. Fargo; R. Daley; WB; 1976) | 24,000,000 |
| The Three Musketeers (S. Herek; J. Roth/ R. Birnbaum; BV; 1993) | 23,899,769 |
| The Dark Crystal (J. Henson/F. Oz; J. Henson/G. Kurtz; U/AFD; 1982) | 23,887,846 |
| Shampoo (H. Ashby; W. Beatty; Col; 1975) | 23,822,000 |
| Urban Cowboy (J. Bridges; R. Evans/ I. Azoff; Par; 1980) | 23,810,000 |
| The Net (I. Winkler; I. Winkler/R. Cowan; Col; 1995) | 23,771,600 |
| In Search of Noah's Ark (J.L. Conway; C.E. Sellier Jr; Schick Sunn; 1970) | 23,770,000 |
| A Walk in the Clouds (A. Arau; G. Netter/ D. Zucker/J. Zucker; Fox; 1995) | 23,503,820 |
| Sleepers (B. Levinson; B. Levinson/ S. Golin; WB; 1996) | 23,404,700 |
| Scarface (B. DePalma; M. Bregman; U; 1983) | 23,333,440 |
| Sabrina (S. Pollack; S. Rudin/S. Pollack; Par; 1995) | 23,321,710 |
| Addams Family Values (B. Sonnenfeld; M.A. Page/S. Rudin; Par; 1993) | 23,294,800 |
| Under Siege 2: Dark Territory (G. Murphy; S. Seagal/A. Milchan/S. Perry; WB; 1995) | 23,262,330 |
| Always (S. Spielberg; S. Spielberg/ F. Marshall/K. Kennedy; U; 1989) | 23,256,055 |
| 1941 (S. Spielberg; B. Feitshans; U; 1979) | 23,254,390 |
| Evita (A. Parker; R. Stigwood/A. Parker/ A. G. Vajna; BV; 1996) | 23,251,800 |
| Awakenings (P. Marshall; W. Parkes/ L. Lasker; Col; 1990) | 23,240,000 |
| Greystoke: The Legend of Tarzan, Lord of the Apes (H. Hudson; WB; 1984) | 23,200,000 |
| Four Weddings and a Funeral (M. Newell, D. Kenworthy; Gramercy; 1994) | 23,188,100 |
| The Rocketeer (J. Johnston; L. Gordon/ C. Gordon/L. Levin; BV; 1991) | 23,178,970 |
| Small Soldiers (J. Dante; M. Finnell/ C. Wilson; DreamWorks; 1998) | 23,159,644 |

# All-time foreign language films in North America

| Title (U.S./Canadian distributor) | Gross ($m) | | Title | Gross |
|---|---|---|---|---|
| 1. Il Postino (Miramax/Alliance) | 21.8 | | 17. Marriage Italian Style (Embassy) | 9.1 |
| 2. Like Water For Chocolate (Miramax) | 21.7 | | 18. Dear John (Sigma 3) | 8.8 |
| 3. I Am Curious (Yellow) (Grove Press) | 20.2 | | 19. Cousin, Cousine (Libra) | 8.6 |
| 4. La Dolce Vita (Astor) | 19.5 | | 20. Cyrano de Bergerac (Orion Classics/CFP) | 8.0 |
| 5. La Cage aux Folles (UA) | 17.7 | | 21. Belle de Jour (AA/Miramax) | 8.0 |
| 6. Z (Cinema 5) | 15.8 | | 22. Women on the Verge (Orion Classics) | 7.5 |
| 7. A Man and a Woman (AA) | 14.3 | | 23. Fanny and Alexander (Embassy) | 7.4 |
| 8. Cinema Paradiso (Miramax) | 12.0 | | 24. Ran (Orion Classics) | 7.3 |
| 9. Das Boot (Triumph) | 11.6 | | 25. Eat Drink Man Woman (Goldwyn) | 7.3 |
| 10. Emmanuelle (Col) | 11.5 | | 26. Two Women (Embassy) | 7.2 |
| 11. 8½ (Embassy) | 10.4 | | 27. Life is Beautiful (Miramax)* | 7.1 |
| 12. My Life as a Dog (Skouras/Vivafilm) | 10.1 | | 28. The Wedding Banquet (Goldwyn) | 6.9 |
| 13. Elvira Madigan (Cinema 5) | 10.1 | | 29. Diva (UAC) | 6.5 |
| 14. Story of O (AA) | 10.0 | | 30. Swept Away (Cinema 5) | 6.0 |
| 15. Shall We Dance (Miramax) | 9.7 | | 31. Garden of Finzi-Continis (Cinema 5) | 6.0 |
| 16. Yesterday, Today & Tomorrow (Embassy) | 9.3 | | 32. Belle Epoque (Sony Classics/CFP) | 6.0 |
| | | | 33. Mediterraneo (Miramax/Alliance) | 5.8 |

**... February 23 ...**
Huge ratings racked up by simultaneous **X-Files** reruns in syndication and on FX cable net could translate into gross revenues of $1.5 million an episode, a record for a one-hour off-network series in its first go-round.

| | | | |
|---|---|---|---|
| 34. *La Cage aux Folles II* (UA) | 5.8 | 43. *Babette's Feast* (Orion Classics) | 5.2 |
| 35. *Kolya* (Miramax) | 5.8 | 44. *La Femme Nikita* (Goldwyn) | 5.0 |
| 36. *King of Hearts* (UA/Lopert) | 5.7 | 45. *Wings of Desire* (Orion Class/Alliance) | 4.9 |
| 37. *Indochine* (Sony Classics) | 5.7 | 46. *Les Boys* (CFP) | 4.8 |
| 38. *Europa Europa* (Orion Classics) | 5.6 | 47. *Decline of American Empire* (Cplx/Malo) | 4.7 |
| 39. *Jean de Florette* (Orion Classics) | 5.5 | 48. *Manon of the Spring* (Orion Classic) | 4.7 |
| 40. *Au Revoir les Enfants* (Orion Classics) | 5.3 | 49. *Antonia's Line* (First Look/CFP) | 4.2 |
| 41. *Farewell My Concubine* (Miramax) | 5.2 | 50. *Tie Me Up! Tie Me Down!* (Miramax) | 4.1 |
| 42. *Madame Rosa* (Atlantic) | 5.2 | *\*Gross through December 31, 1998* | |

# North American top grossers: 1998

| Title (U.S./Canadian distributor) | Gross | | |
|---|---|---|---|
| *Titanic* (Par) * | 488,194,015 | *Star Trek: Insurrection* (Par) + | 53,895,383 |
| *Armageddon* (BV) | 201,578,182 | *Tomorrow Never Dies* (MGM) * | 51,989,026 |
| *Saving Private Ryan* (DreamWorks) + | 190,805,259 | *Patch Adams* (U) + | 46,444,325 |
| *There's Something About Mary* (Fox) + | 174,422,745 | *Practical Magic* (WB) + | 46,404,796 |
| *The Waterboy* (BV) + | 147,895,431 | *The Negotiator* (WB) | 44,748,766 |
| *Dr. Dolittle* (Fox) | 144,153,418 | *Meet Joe Black* (U) + | 43,240,705 |
| *Deep Impact* (Par) | 140,464,664 | *Wag the Dog* (NLC) * | 42,869,209 |
| *Godzilla* (Sony) | 136,314,294 | *Ronin* (MGM) | 41,552,061 |
| *Rush Hour* (NLC) | 136,065,335 | *The Siege* (Fox) + | 39,908,508 |
| *Good Will Hunting* (Miramax) * | 134,063,347 | *Primary Colors* (U) | 39,299,835 |
| *Lethal Weapon 4* (WB) | 130,444,603 | *I Still Know What You Did Last* | |
| *A Bug's Life* (BV) + | 127,589,564 | *Summer* (Sony) + | 38,889,884 |
| *The Truman Show* (Par) | 125,618,201 | *Pleasantville* (NLC) + | 38,761,264 |
| *As Good As It Gets* (Sony) * | 124,083,542 | *How Stella Got Her Groove Back* (Fox) | 37,665,439 |
| *Mulan* (BV) | 120,620,254 | *Out of Sight* (U) | 37,562,568 |
| *The Mask of Zorro* (Sony) + | 93,715,262 | *Urban Legend* (Sony) + | 37,506,463 |
| *Enemy of the State* (BV) + | 92,027,903 | *Sphere* (WB) | 37,297,851 |
| *Antz* (DreamWorks) + | 88,668,349 | *Stepmom* (Sony) + | 35,435,611 |
| *The Rugrats Movie* (Par) + | 86,430,992 | *Mouse Hunt* (DreamWorks) * | 33,317,341 |
| *The X-Files* (Fox) | 83,898,313 | *Mercury Rising* (U) | 32,983,332 |
| *The Wedding Singer* (NLC) | 80,245,725 | *Bride of Chucky* (U) + | 32,305,400 |
| *City of Angels* (WB) | 78,892,664 | *A Night at the Roxbury* (Par) | 30,312,145 |
| *The Horse Whisperer* (BV) | 75,373,563 | *Wild Things* (Sony) | 30,147,739 |
| *Six Days, Seven Nights* (BV) | 74,339,294 | *Madeline* (Sony) | 29,967,750 |
| *Blade* (NLC) | 70,095,974 | *Spice World* (Sony) | 29,342,592 |
| *Lost in Space* (NLC) | 69,117,629 | *The Object of My Affection* (Fox) | 29,187,243 |
| *A Perfect Murder* (WB) | 67,658,331 | *Grease* (reissue) (Par) | 28,411,018 |
| *The Parent Trap* (BV) | 66,308,518 | *Jack Frost* (WB) + | 27,986,773 |
| *Ever After* (Fox) | 65,667,434 | *Paulie* (DreamWorks) | 27,084,499 |
| *You've Got Mail* (WB) + | 63,762,374 | *The Big Hit* (Sony) | 27,066,941 |
| *Hope Floats* (Fox) | 60,110,313 | *L.A. Confidential* (WB) * | 27,059,840 |
| *U.S. Marshals* (WB) | 57,833,603 | *Bulworth* (Fox) | 26,528,684 |
| *The Man in the Iron Mask* (MGM) | 56,968,169 | *Great Expectations* (Fox) | 26,420,672 |
| *Everest* (MacGillivray-Freeman) + | 55,742,120 | *Scream 2* (Miramax) * | 25,731,495 |
| *Snake Eyes* (Par) | 55,591,409 | *Can't Hardly Wait* (Sony) | 25,605,015 |
| *What Dreams May Come* (Polygram) | 55,382,891 | *Fallen* (WB) | 25,493,642 |
| *Small Soldiers* (DreamWorks) | 55,143,823 | *Amistad* (DreamWorks) * | 23,582,870 |
| *The Prince of Egypt* (DreamWorks) + | 55,106,631 | *The Avengers* (WB) | 23,523,710 |
| *Halloween: H20* (Miramax) | 55,041,738 | *One True Thing* (U) | 23,337,196 |
| | | *The Players Club* (NLC) | 23,047,939 |

| | | | |
|---|---:|---|---:|
| Quest for Camelot (WB) | 22,931,682 | I Got the Hook-Up (Miramax) | 10,317,779 |
| Rounders (Miramax) | 22,921,898 | The Spanish Prisoner (Sony Classics) | 10,272,230 |
| Beloved (BV) | 22,747,234 | Home Fries (WB) | 10,053,369 |
| The Borrowers (Polygram) | 22,619,589 | Air Bud: Golden Receiver (Miramax/Alliance) | 10,031,536 |
| Jackie Brown (Miramax) * | 22,470,563 | Dirty Work (MGM) | 10,022,221 |
| He Got Game (BV) | 21,567,853 | Very Bad Things (Polygram) + | 9,735,745 |
| The Apostle (October) * | 20,695,276 | Wrongfully Accused (WB) | 9,717,322 |
| Psycho (U) + | 20,363,450 | Belly (Artisan) | 9,449,688 |
| Mighty Joe Young (BV) + | 20,028,356 | Thrill Ride (Sony Classics) + | 8,873,829 |
| John Carpenter's Vampires (Sony) | 19,967,510 | Apt Pupil (Sony) | 8,814,516 |
| Jane Austen's Mafia! (BV) | 19,889,299 | Ringmaster (Artisan) | 8,695,301 |
| Hard Rain (Par) | 19,870,567 | Return to Paradise (Polygram) | 8,352,677 |
| The Replacement Killers (Sony) | 19,204,929 | The Postman (WB) * | 8,276,713 |
| Species II (MGM) | 19,221,174 | Firestorm (Fox) | 8,164,661 |
| The Odd Couple II (Par) | 18,912,328 | Anastasia (Fox) * | 8,152,825 |
| The Faculty (Miramax) + | 18,409,135 | Deconstructing Harry (NLC) * | 8,149,960 |
| Simon Birch (BV) | 18,253,415 | My Giant (Sony) | 8,072,007 |
| Disturbing Behavior (MGM) | 17,509,368 | Woo (NLC) | 8,064,972 |
| The Big Lebowski (Gramercy) | 17,498,804 | Into the Deep (Imax) | 7,997,648 |
| Half Baked (U) | 17,460,020 | Krippendorf's Tribe (BV) | 7,571,115 |
| 54 (Miramax) | 16,757,163 | BASEketball (U) | 7,042,541 |
| Dance With Me (Sony) | 15,923,354 | Star Kid (Trimark) | 6,966,021 |
| Flubber (BV) * | 15,776,601 | Smoke Signals (Miramax) | 6,888,442 |
| Babe: Pig in the City (U) + | 15,768,180 | Caught Up (Artisan) | 6,754,958 |
| Elizabeth (Gramercy) + | 15,472,961 | Gone With the Wind (reissue) (NLC) | 6,750,112 |
| Dead Man on Campus (Par) | 15,064,948 | The Opposite of Sex (Sony Classics) | 6,367,164 |
| Twilight (Par) | 15,055,091 | Shakespeare in Love (Miramax) + | 6,239,569 |
| The Wizard of Oz (reissue) (WB) + | 14,690,446 | Almost Heroes (WB) | 6,175,688 |
| Soldier (WB) | 14,623,082 | American History X (NLC) + | 6,045,176 |
| Dark City (NLC) | 14,435,076 | The Boxer (U) * | 5,960,295 |
| Les Misérables (Sony) | 14,096,321 | Palmetto (Sony) | 5,878,911 |
| Blues Brothers 2000 (U) | 14,089,198 | Phantoms (Miramax) | 5,755,333 |
| Desperate Measures (Sony) | 13,806,137 | The Wings of the Dove (Miramax) * | 5,561,459 |
| Hush (Sony) | 13,587,246 | Kundun (BV) * | 5,543,060 |
| Senseless (Miramax) | 13,109,234 | Ride (Miramax) | 5,503,007 |
| Black Dog (U) | 12,951,088 | L5: First City in Space (Imax) | 5,488,495 |
| Mr. Nice Guy (NLC) | 12,716,953 | Slums of Beverly Hills (Fox Searchlight) | 5,480,868 |
| An American Werewolf in Paris (BV) * | 12,710,987 | Waking Ned Devine (Fox Searchlight) + | 5,335,460 |
| Living Out Loud (NLC) + | 12,626,134 | Celebrity (Miramax) | 5,009,081 |
| Why Do Fools Fall in Love? (WB) | 12,506,676 | Your Friends & Neighbors (Gramercy) | 4,714,658 |
| Barney's Great Adventure (Polygram) | 12,218,638 | Dangerous Beauty (WB) | 4,553,271 |
| Holy Man (BV) | 12,069,719 | Mission to Mir (Imax) | 4,439,877 |
| I'll Be Home for Christmas (BV) + | 12,025,266 | Meet the Deedles (BV) | 4,356,126 |
| Sliding Doors (Miramax) | 11,911,200 | Kissing a Fool (U) | 4,106,388 |
| Home Alone 3 (Fox) * | 11,709,452 | The Governess (Sony Classics) | 4,012,658 |
| For Richer or Poorer (U) * | 11,507,576 | Africa's Elephant Kingdom (Discovery) + | 4,005,624 |
| Mr. Magoo (BV) * | 11,399,184 | Major League: Back to the Minors (WB) | 3,597,284 |
| Deep Rising (BV) | 11,203,026 | Next Stop Wonderland (Miramax) | 3,395,581 |
| The Full Monty (Fox Searchlight) * | 10,935,103 | Mrs. Dalloway (First Look) | 3,309,421 |
| Fear and Loathing in Las Vegas (U) | 10,672,165 | Pi (Artisan) | 3,221,152 |
| The Newton Boys (Fox) | 10,451,854 | The Last Days of Disco (Gramercy) | 3,024,198 |
| Life is Beautiful (Miramax) + | 10,336,425 | The Sweet Hereafter (Alliance/NLC) * | 2,873,716 |
| Knock Off (Sony) | 10,319,915 | Cosmic Voyage (Imax) | 2,819,336 |

---

**... February 25 ...**

Bob Dylan takes three awards at the Grammys; Shawn Colvin's **Sonny Came Home** is
named song of the year.

| | | | |
|---|---|---|---|
| Les Boys (CFP) * | 2,762,200 | Suicide Kings (Artisan) | 1,740,156 |
| Happiness (Good Machine/Behaviour) | 2,756,587 | Titanica (Imax) | 1,729,813 |
| Freeriders (Warren Miller) | 2,750,064 | Live Flesh (MGM) | 1,713,163 |
| Boogie Nights (NLC) * | 2,713,966 | Across the Sea of Time (Sony Classics) * | 1,683,449 |
| The Mighty (Miramax) | 2,652,246 | The Gingerbread Man (Polygram) | 1,677,131 |
| T-Rex: Back to the Cretaceous (Imax) | 2,610,511 | Gods and Monsters (Lions Gate) | 1,667,414 |
| Love & Death on Long Island (Lion Gate) | 2,581,014 | Special Effects (Imax) | 1,660,498 |
| Down in the Delta (Miramax) | 2,497,557 | In God's Hands (Sony) | 1,546,414 |
| Afterglow (Sony Classics) * | 2,455,656 | Eve's Bayou (Trimark) * | 1,485,802 |
| Les Boys II (Lions Gate) + | 2,440,775 | Lolita (Samuel Goldwyn/Lions Gate) | 1,475,951 |
| Wilde (Sony Classics) | 2,412,601 | Mortal Kombat Annihilation (NLC) * | 1,391,352 |
| Buffalo 66 (Lions Gate) | 2,380,606 | Henry Fool (Sony Classics) | 1,385,002 |
| Ma Vie en Rose (Sony Classics/Motion) * | 2,350,087 | One Tough Cop (Stratosphere) | 1,313,607 |
| The Jackal (U) * | 2,344,426 | Cousin Bette (Fox Searchlight) | 1,295,194 |
| Hav Plenty (Miramax) | 2,337,637 | Nightwatch (Miramax) | 1,278,516 |
| Alien Resurrection (Fox) * | 2,303,786 | WB 75th Anni Fest (WB) | 1,234,684 |
| John Grisham's The Rainmaker (Par) * | 2,289,635 | The Celebration (October) + | 1,199,830 |
| Pecker (NLC) | 2,281,761 | Destiny in Space (Imax) | 1,173,240 |
| Chinese Box (Trimark) | 2,272,923 | Permanent Midnight (Artisan) | 1,171,001 |
| Touch of Evil (reissue)(October) | 2,213,147 | Strike (Alliance/Miramax) | 1,153,948 |
| Midnight in the Garden of Good | | The Red Violin (Alliance) | 1,145,646 |
| and Evil (WB) * | 2,209,283 | A Price Above Rubies (Miramax) | 1,130,732 |
| The Imposters (Fox Searchlight) | 2,194,929 | The Thief (Stratosphere) | 1,124,700 |
| Tarzan and the Lost City (WB) | 2,172,941 | Déjà Vu (Rainbow) | 1,085,640 |
| Billy's Hollywood Screen Kiss (Trimark) | 2,100,430 | Velvet Goldmine (Miramax) | 1,053,788 |
| I Know What You Did Last Summer (Sony) | * 2,098,876 | Mark Twain's America (Sony Classics) + | 1,041,630 |
| Zero Effect (Sony) | 2,087,471 | Slam (Trimark) | 1,009,819 |
| The Butcher Boy (WB) | 2,063,722 | Dancing at Lughnasa (Sony Classics) + | 963,184 |
| Two Girls and a Guy (Fox Searchlight) | 2,057,193 | Air Force One (Sony) * | 962,280 |
| The Devil's Advocate (WB) * | 2,012,612 | Men with Guns (Sony Classics) | 956,145 |
| A Simple Plan (Par) + | 2,003,920 | The Ice Storm (Fox Searchlight) * | 952,337 |
| High Art (October) | 1,936,997 | The Tango Lesson (Sony Classics) * | 945,968 |
| Oscar and Lucinda (Fox Searchlight) * | 1,853,445 | The Imax Nutcracker (Imax) * | 922,475 |
| C'a'ton tour Laura Cadieux (Alliance) | 1,851,188 | Le dîner de cons (Lions Gate) + | 860,950 |
| A Soldier's Daughter Never Cries (October) | 1,799,537 | | * Does not include 1997 box office |
| Clay Pigeons (Gramercy) | 1,793,359 | | + Still on release at year end |

## Films grossing $100m-plus in the U.S.

| Title | Gross ($) | | |
|---|---|---|---|
| 1. Titanic | 600,788,188 | 13. Men in Black | 250,690,539 |
| 2. Star Wars | 460,998,007 | 14. Raiders of the Lost Ark | 242,374,454 |
| 3. E.T. - The Extra-Terrestrial | 399,804,539 | 15. Twister | 241,721,524 |
| 4. Jurassic Park | 357,067,947 | 16. Ghostbusters | 238,600,000 |
| 5. Forrest Gump | 329,693,974 | 17. Beverly Hills Cop | 234,760,478 |
| 6. The Lion King | 312,855,561 | 18. The Lost World: Jurassic Park | 229,086,679 |
| 7. Return of the Jedi | 309,205,079 | 19. Mrs. Doubtfire | 219,195,051 |
| 8. Independence Day | 306,169,268 | 20. Ghost | 217,631,306 |
| 9. The Empire Strikes Back | 290,271,960 | 21. Aladdin | 217,350,219 |
| 10. Home Alone | 285,761,243 | 22. Back to the Future | 208,242,016 |
| 11. Jaws | 260,000,000 | 23. Terminator 2 | 204,843,345 |
| 12. Batman | 251,188,924 | 24. Armageddon | 201,578,182 |
| | | 25. Gone With the Wind | 198,674,752 |

**...February 26...**

On this day in 1962, first day's shooting on the first James Bond film, **Dr. No**.

| | | | | |
|---|---|---|---|---|
| 26. *Indiana Jones and the Last Crusade* | 197,171,806 | 78. *Platoon* | 138,530,565 |
| 27. *Toy Story* | 191,796,233 | 79. *Good Will Hunting* | 138,433,935 |
| 28. *Saving Private Ryan* | 190,805,259 | 80. *Ransom* | 136,492,681 |
| 29. *Dances with Wolves* | 184,208,848 | 81. *Godzilla* | 136,314,294 |
| 30. *Batman Forever* | 184,031,112 | 82. *101 Dalmatians* | 136,182,161 |
| 31. *The Fugitive* | 183,875,760 | 83. *Rush Hour* | 136,065,335 |
| 32. *Grease* | 181,513,510 | 84. *Teenage Mutant Ninja Turtles* | 135,265,915 |
| 33. *Liar, Liar* | 181,410,615 | 85. *The Godfather* | 134,966,411 |
| 34. *Mission: Impossible* | 180,981,866 | 86. *Superman* | 134,218,018 |
| 35. *Indiana Jones and the Temple of Doom* | 179,870,271 | 87. *The Rock* | 134,069,511 |
| 36. *Pretty Woman* | 178,406,268 | 88. *Silence of the Lambs* | 130,726,716 |
| 37. *Tootsie* | 177,200,000 | 89. *Honey I Shrunk the Kids* | 130,724,172 |
| 38. *Top Gun* | 176,781,728 | 90. *The Flintstones* | 130,531,208 |
| 39. *Snow White and the Seven Dwarfs* | 175,263,233 | 91. *Lethal Weapon 4* | 129,841,420 |
| 40. *Crocodile Dundee* | 174,803,506 | 92. *An Officer and a Gentleman* | 129,795,549 |
| 41. *There's Something About Mary* | 174,422,745 | 93. *The Nutty Professor* | 128,814,019 |
| 42. *Home Alone 2* | 173,585,516 | 94. *Coming to America* | 128,152,301 |
| 43. *Air Force One* | 172,956,409 | 95. *Rocky IV* | 127,873,414 |
| 44. *Rain Man* | 172,825,435 | 96. *A Bug's Life* | 127,589,564 |
| 45. *Apollo 13* | 172,070,496 | 97. *Dumb and Dumber* | 127,175,374 |
| 46. *Three Men and a Baby* | 167,780,960 | 98. *My Best Friend's Wedding* | 126,813,153 |
| 47. *Robin Hood: Prince of Thieves* | 165,493,908 | 99. *Smokey and the Bandit* | 126,737,428 |
| 48. *The Exorcist* | 165,000,000 | 100. *Sleepless in Seattle* | 126,680,884 |
| 49. *Batman Returns* | 162,831,698 | 101. *The Truman Show* | 125,603,360 |
| 50. *The Sound of Music* | 160,476,331 | 102. *Tomorrow Never Dies* | 125,263,449 |
| 51. *The Firm* | 158,340,292 | 103. *Rocky III* | 125,049,125 |
| 52. *Fatal Attraction* | 156,645,693 | 104. *The Birdcage* (MGM/UA) | 124,060,553 |
| 53. *The Sting* | 156,000,000 | 105. *City Slickers* | 124,033,791 |
| 54. *Close Encounters of the Third Kind* | 155,691,323 | 106. *Good Morning Vietnam* | 123,922,370 |
| 55. *Who Framed Roger Rabbit?* | 154,112,492 | 107. *Clear and Present Danger* | 122,012,656 |
| 56. *Jerry Maguire* | 153,952,592 | 108. *Hunt for Red October* | 122,012,643 |
| 57. *Beverly Hills Cop 2* | 153,665,036 | 109. *The Bodyguard* | 121,945,720 |
| 58. *Gremlins* | 153,083,102 | 110. *Wayne's World* | 121,697,323 |
| 59. *Rambo: First Blood II* | 150,415,432 | 111. *Speed* | 121,248,145 |
| 60. *As Good As It Gets* | 148,478,011 | 112. *Mulan* | 120,620,193 |
| 61. *The Waterboy* | 147,895,431 | 113. *The Mask* | 119,938,730 |
| 62. *Lethal Weapon 2* | 147,253,986 | 114. *Hook* | 119,654,823 |
| 63. *True Lies* | 146,282,411 | 115. *Blazing Saddles* | 119,500,000 |
| 64. *Beauty and the Beast* | 145,863,363 | 116. *Total Recall* | 119,394,839 |
| 65. *The Santa Clause* | 144,833,357 | 117. *On Golden Pond* | 118,710,777 |
| 66. *Lethal Weapon 3* | 144,731,527 | 118. *Back to the Future II* | 118,450,002 |
| 67. *Dr. Dolittle (98)* | 144,153,418 | 119. *Basic Instinct* | 117,727,224 |
| 68. *101 Dalmations* | 143,932,335 | 120. *Die Hard 2* | 117,540,947 |
| 69. *The Jungle Book* | 141,843,612 | 121. *Rocky* | 117,235,247 |
| 70. *Animal House* | 141,600,000 | 122. *The Towering Inferno* | 116,000,000 |
| 71. *Pocahontas* | 141,579,773 | 123. *Karate Kid II* | 115,103,979 |
| 72. *A Few Good Men* | 141,340,178 | 124. *American Graffiti* | 115,000,000 |
| 73. *Deep Impact* | 140,464,664 | 125. *Big* | 114,968,774 |
| 74. *Look Who's Talking* | 140,088,813 | 126. *The Addams Family* | 113,502,246 |
| 75. *Sister Act* | 139,605,150 | 127. *Ghostbusters II* | 112,494,738 |
| 76. *Saturday Night Fever* | 139,486,124 | 128. *Face/Off* | 112,276,146 |
| 77. *The Rocky Horror Picture Show* | 139,189,642 | 129. *One Flew Over the Cuckoo's Nest* | 112,000,000 |
| | | 130. *Twins* | 111,936,388 |

**. . . February 27 . . .**

Oprah Winfrey prevails against Texas cattleman's $11 million damages suit that she besmirched the meat industry. She tells press, "I refuse to be muzzled."

| | | | |
|---|---|---|---|
| 131. Doctor Zhivago | 111,721,913 | 153. Every Which Way But Loose | 104,268,727 |
| 132. Porky's | 111,543,479 | 154. Dick Tracy | 103,738,726 |
| 133. The Little Mermaid | 109,865,128 | 155. 9 to 5 | 103,290,500 |
| 134. Star Trek IV | 109,713,132 | 156. Scream | 103,046,663 |
| 135. Crocodile Dundee II | 109,306,210 | 157. Bambi | 102,797,150 |
| 136. A Time to Kill | 108,766,007 | 158. Mary Poppins | 102,272,727 |
| 137. Terms of Endearment | 108,423,489 | 159. In the Line of Fire | 102,243,874 |
| 138. Ace Ventura: When Nature Calls | 108,385,533 | 160. Maverick | 101,631,272 |
| 139. Superman II | 108,185,706 | 161. Sleeping with the Enemy | 101,599,005 |
| 140. Pulp Fiction | 107,921,755 | 162. Scream 2 | 101,363,301 |
| 141. A League of Their Own | 107,533,925 | 163. Stir Crazy | 101,300,000 |
| 142. Batman and Robin | 107,325,195 | 164. Eraser | 101,295,562 |
| 143. Indecent Proposal | 106,614,059 | 165. Unforgiven | 101,157,447 |
| 144. Driving Miss Daisy | 106,593,296 | 166. Con Air | 101,117,573 |
| 145. Goldeneye (MGM/UA) | 106,429,941 | 167. Contact | 100,920,329 |
| 146. Love Story | 106,397,186 | 168. The Pelican Brief | 100,768,056 |
| 147. Kramer vs. Kramer | 106,260,000 | 169. Jumanji | 100,475,249 |
| 148. The First Wives Club | 105,489,203 | 170. Casper | 100,328,194 |
| 149. Interview With the Vampire | 105,264,608 | 171. The Hunchback of Notre Dame | 100,138,851 |
| 150. George of the Jungle | 105,263,257 | 172. Seven | 100,125,643 |
| 151. The Graduate | 104,642,560 | 173. Parenthood | 100,047,830 |
| 152. Phenomenon | 104,632,573 | 174. Die Hard With a Vengeance | 100,012,499 |

# All-time adjusted domestic B.O. champs
## (in $ millions, based on admissions)

| | |
|---|---|
| 1. Gone With the Wind (MGM, 1939) | 1,306.1 |
| 2. Snow White and the Seven Dwarfs (BV, 1937) | 1,034.3 |
| 3. Star Wars (Fox, 1977) | 812.0 |
| 4. E.T. - The Extra-Terrestrial (U, 1982) | 725.4 |
| 5. 101 Dalmatians (BV, 1961) | 656.6 |
| 6. Bambi (BV, 1942) | 646.1 |
| 7. Titanic (Par, 1997) | 600.8 |
| 8. Jaws (U, 1995) | 590.3 |
| 9. The Sound of Music (Fox, 1965) | 565.8 |
| 10. The Ten Commandments (Par, 1956) | 547.6 |
| 11. Return of the Jedi (Fox, 1983) | 540.5 |
| 12. Mary Poppins (BV, 1964) | 517.4 |
| 13. Cinderella (BV, 1949) | 503.3 |
| 14. The Empire Strikes Back (Fox, 1980) | 451.5 |
| 15. Fantasia (BV, 1940) | 450.7 |
| 16. Raiders of the Lost Ark (Par, 1981) | 442.4 |
| 17. The Exorcist (WB, 1973) | 436.4 |
| 18. Ben-Hur (MGM, 1959) | 434.2 |
| 19. Ghostbusters (Col, 1984) | 427.6 |
| 20. Doctor Zhivago (MGM, 1965) | 423.2 |
| 21. Beverly Hills Cop (Par, 1984) | 420.7 |
| 22. The Sting (U, 1973) | 412.6 |
| 23. The Graduate (Avco, 1967) | 408.7 |
| 24. The Robe (Fox, 1953) | 399.0 |
| 25. Jurassic Park (U, 1993) | 393.4 |

## Champs by decade
### 1990s

| | |
|---|---|
| 1. Titanic (Fox, 97) | 600.8 |
| 2. Jurassic Park (U, 93) | 357.1 |
| 3. Forrest Gump (Par, 94) | 329.7 |
| 4. The Lion King (BV, 94) | 312.8 |
| 5. Independence Day (Fox, 96) | 306.2 |
| 6. Home Alone (Fox, 92) | 285.8 |
| 7. Men in Black (Sony, 97) | 250.1 |
| 8. Twister (WB, 96) | 241.7 |
| 9. The Lost World: Jurassic Park (U, 97) | 229.1 |
| 10. Mrs. Doubtfire (Fox, 93) | 219.2 |

### 1980s

| | |
|---|---|
| 1. E.T. - The Extra-Terrestrial (U, 82) | 399.8 |
| 2. Return of the Jedi (Fox, 83) | 309.2 |
| 3. The Empire Strikes Back (Fox, 80) | 290.3 |
| 4. Batman (WB, 89) | 251.2 |
| 5. Raiders of the Lost Ark (Par, 81) | 242.4 |
| 6. Ghostbusters (Col, 84) | 238.6 |
| 7. Beverly Hills Cop (Par, 84) | 234.8 |
| 8. Back to the Future (U, 85) | 208.2 |
| 9. Indiana Jones and the Last Crusade (Par, 89) | 197.2 |
| 10. Indiana Jones and the Temple of Doom (Par, 84) | 179.9 |

---

**. . . February 28 . . .**

Fox's **The Full Monty** (budget $3.5 million) has now grossed in excess of $200 million.

## 1970s

| | |
|---|---|
| 1. *Star Wars* (Fox, 77) | 461.0 |
| 2. *Jaws* (U, 75) | 260.0 |
| 3. *Grease* (Par, 78) | 181.5 |
| 4. *The Exorcist* (WB. 73) | 165.0 |
| 5. *The Sting* (U, 73) | 156.0 |
| 6. *Close Encounters of the Third Kind* (Col, 77) | 155.7 |
| 7. *Animal House* (U, 78) | 141.6 |
| 8. *Saturday Night Fever* (Par, 77) | 139.5 |
| 9. *The Rocky Horror Picture Show* (Fox, 75) | 139.2 |
| 10. *The Godfather* (Par, 72) | 135.0 |

## 1960s

| | |
|---|---|
| 1. *The Sound of Music* (Fox, 65) | 160.5 |
| 2. *101 Dalmatians* (BV, 61) | 143.9 |
| 3. *The Jungle Book* (BV, 67) | 141.8 |
| 4. *Doctor Zhivago* (MGM, 65) | 111.7 |
| 5. *The Graduate* (Avco, 67) | 104.6 |
| 6. *Mary Poppins* (BV, 64) | 102.3 |
| 7. *Butch Cassidy and the Sundance Kid* (Fox, 69) | 96.7 |
| 8. *Thunderball* (UA, 65) | 63.6 |
| 9. *Cleopatra* (Fox, 63) | 61.8 |
| 10. *Funny Girl* (Col, 68) | 55.3 |

## 1950s

| | |
|---|---|
| 1. *Lady and the Tramp* (BV, 55) | 88.3 |
| 2. *The Ten Commandments* (Par, 56) | 85.4 |
| 3. *Peter Pan* (BV, 53) | 81.6 |
| 4. *Ben-Hur* (MGM, 59) | 73.2 |
| 5. *Around the World in 80 Days* (UA, 56) | 61.1 |
| 6. *Sleeping Beauty* (BV, 59) | 50.4 |
| 7. *The Robe* (Fox, 53) | 45.2 |
| 8. *The Bridge on the River Kwai* (Col, 57) | 41.3 |
| 9. *South Pacific* (Fox, 58) | 38.2 |
| 10. *This is Cinerama* (CRC, 52) | 36.5 |

## 1940s

| | |
|---|---|
| 1. *Bambi* (BV, 42) | 102.8 |
| 2. *Cinderella* (BV, 49) | 81.1 |
| 3. *Fantasia* (BV, 40) | 76.2 |
| 4. *Pinocchio* (BV, 40) | 73.6 |
| 5. *Song of the South* (BV, 46) | 56.4 |
| 6. *Samson and Delilah* (Par, 49) | 29.3 |
| 7. *The Best Years of Our Lives* (RKO, 46) | 28.5 |
| 8. *Duel in the Sun* (Selznick, 46) | 27.8 |
| 9. *The Bells of St. Mary's* (RKO, 45) | 23.7 |
| 10. *The Jolson Story* (Col, 47) | 22.9 |

## 1930s

| | |
|---|---|
| 1. *Gone With the Wind* (MGM, 39) | 198.7 |
| 2. *Snow White and the Seven Dwarfs* (BV, 37) | 175.3 |
| 3. *The Wizard of Oz* (MGM, 39) | 32.3 |
| 4. *Modern Times* (UA, 36) | 27.6 |
| 5. *King Kong* (RKO, 33) | 26.3 |
| 6. *It Happened One Night* (Col, 33) | 24.2 |
| 7. *The Adventures of Robin Hood* (WB, 38) | 22.8 |
| 8. *Mutiny on the Bounty* (MGM, 35) | 21.7 |
| 9. *Jesse James* (Fox, 39) | 19.4 |
| 10. *Tarzan, the Ape Man* (MGM, 32) | 18.8 |

## Pre-Sound *

| | |
|---|---|
| 1. *The Big Parade* (MGM, 25) | |
| 2. *The Birth of a Nation* (Epoch, 15) | |
| 3. *The Gold Rush* (UA, 25) | |
| 4. *Ben-Hur* (MGM, 25) | |
| 5. *The Four Horsemen of the Apocalypse* (MGM, 21) | |
| 6. *The Singing Fool* (WB, 28) | |
| 7. *What Price Glory?* (Fox, 26) | |
| 8. *Robin Hood* (UA, 22) | |
| 9. *The Jazz Singer* (WB, 27) | |
| 10. *The Covered Wagon* (Par, 23) | |

*\* Box-office records in the pre-sound era are sketchy at best, so* Variety *offers its 10 money-winners of that era (including two early sound pics) based on the best available information.*

> *Acting is a masochistic form of exhibitionism. It is not quite the occupation of an adult.*
> *(Laurence Olivier)*

**... March 1 ...**
Polygram Filmed Entertainment hires Filippo Roviglioni to launch its Italian distribution company, which opens for business today.

# Festivals

Film festivals have proliferated during the past two decades to the point at which no town or city worth its salt can afford to be without some kind of movie event. They have gradually replaced the network of arthouse cinemas that flourished during the 1960s and 1970s – although precious few producers glean any compensation for the screening of their films to anything up to 3,000 eager fans.

Film festivals come in all shapes, sizes, and flavors. They range from gargantuan, metropolitan affairs with attendances running into six figures, to tiny specialized gatherings devoted to films on mountaineering or children's issues. There are national festivals, which showcase the entire production of a nation from one year to the next, as well as festivals taking place in political hot-spots of the world like Sarajevo, Jerusalem, and Tehran. Specific genres such as animation, documentaries, thrillers, or even silent movies all have their watering-holes somewhere in the world. Then there are the television markets, where the mood is strictly suits-and-ties and appointments through the day.

Craziest of all is the mother of all festivals, Cannes, where critics and conmen crowd the Croisette in what Robin Williams once described as "Disneyland designed by Dante." The amount of business achieved at film and TV markets around the globe is hard to quantify, but it certainly runs into the hundreds of millions of dollars. Throughout the year, *Variety*'s reporters and reviewers are on the spot to follow developments at such events. We covered the first Cannes Festival in 1946, and we now produce a daily newspaper on site during the Riviera event. Of the approximately 1,100 films reviewed in *Variety* each year, a majority is seen and written about at festivals.

## January

### NorTel Palm Springs International Film Festival
1700 E. Tahquitz #3, Palm Springs, CA 92262, U.S.
Tel: +1-760 322 2930
Fax: +1-760 322 4087
E-mail: filmfest@ix.netcom.com.
Executive director: Craig Prater

### International Film Festival of India (New Delhi)
Directorate of Film Festivals, Ministry of Information and Broadcasting, 4th Floor, Lok Nayak Bavan, Khan Market, New Delhi 110 003, India
Tel: +91-11 461 5953/469 49210/461 7226
Fax: +91-11 462 3430
Festival director: Malti Sahai
Festival programmers: Shankar Mohan and S Santhanam

Market and Competition: Golden Peacock for Best Film by an Asian director (Rs500,000)

### Kid Film Festival (Dallas)
2917 Swiss Ave, Dallas 75204, Texas, U.S.
Tel: +1-214-821 6300
Fax: +1-214-821 6364
Website: http://www.usafilmfestival.com
Festival director: Ann Alexander
Festival programmer: Alonso Duralde

### Travelling – Rennes Film Festival
Université Rennes 2, 6 avenue Gaston Berger, F-35043 Rennes Cédex, France
Tel: +33-299-141143
Fax: +33-299-141145
E-mail: hussam.hindi@uhb.fr
Festival director/programmer:

Hussam Hindi
Competition: The Jury Prize (FFr30,000)

### 12th Stuttgart Filmwinter (short film, experimental film, documentary, etc)
Filmhaus, Friedrichstraße 23/a, D-70174 Stuttgart, Germany
Tel: +49-711 226 9160
Fax: +49-711 226 9161
E-mail: wanda@wand 5.de
Website: www.wand 5.de
Festival director: Ulrich Wegenast
Festival programmers: Ulrich Wegenast and Martin Wolf
Competition: Three awards for three different sections

### Cine Latino (Tübingen)
Osterbergstr. 9, Tübingen, Germany 72074
Tel: +49-7071 56960
Fax: +49-7071 56 96 96

... **March 2** ...

Jim Carrey signs to play comic Andy Kaufman in Milos Forman's **Man on the Moon**.

E-mail: filmtage tuebingen@t-online.de
Festival director: Paolo Robert de Carvalho

## Imagina (Monaco)
4 avenue de l'Europe, Bry-Sur-Marne, 94366, France
Tel: +33-1-4983 2693
Fax: +33-1-4983 3185
E-mail: Imagina@imagina.ina.fr
Festival director: JM Villaret
Competition: Grand Prix Imagina

## FIPA (Festival International de Programmes Audiovisuels) (Biarritz)
14 rue Alexandre Parodi, 75010 Paris, France
Tel: +33-1-44 89 99 99
Fax: +33-1-44 89 99 60
Festival president: Marie-France Pisier
Festival programmer: Pierre-Henri Deleau
Competition: FIPA d'Or

## Max Ophüls Preis Film Festival
Filmfestival Max Ophüls Preis, Mainzer Str 8, 66111 Saarbrücken, Germany
Tel: +49-681-39452
Fax: +49-681-905 1943
E-mail: Filmhaus@aol.com
Festival director: Christel Drawer
Competition: Max Ophüls Preis (DM30,000 award and DM30,000 support for the distributor)

## Brussels International Film Festival
30 Chaussée de Louvain, B-1210 Brussels, Belgium
Tel: +32-2 227 3980
Fax: +32-2 218 1860
E-mail: infoffb@netcity.be
Website: http://ffb.cinebel.com
Festival director and programmer: Christian Thomas
Competition: Crystal Star ($150,000)

## Sundance Film Festival (Park City)
PO Box 16450, Salt Lake City, Utah 84116, U.S.
Tel: +1-801-328 3456
Fax: +1-801-575 5175
Festival director: Nicola Guillemet

Festival programmer: Geoffrey Gilmore
Competition: Grand Jury Prize (Drama/documentary) ($5,000)

## New York Festivals (Non-broadcast Media and TV Programming and Promotion) (NYC)
780 King St, Chappaqua, NY 10514, U.S.
Tel: +1-914-238 4481
Fax: +1-914-238 5040
Festival director: Bilha Goldberg
Competition: Gold, Silver, Bronze World Medals; four Grand Awards
Entry deadline: 15 September 1998

## Premiers Plans (Angers)
54 rue Beaubourg, 75003 Paris, France
Tel: 33-1-42 71 53 70
Fax: 33-1-42 71 47 55
Website: www.anjou.com/premiersplans/
Festival director and programmer: Claude-Eric Poiroux
Competition: Grand Prix (FFr100,000)

## Women in Cinema Film Festival (Seattle)
801 East Pine St, Seattle, 98122 WA, U.S.
Tel: +1-206-324 9996
Fax: +1-206-324 9998
E-mail: mail@seattlefilm.com
Festival director: Darryl Macdonald
Festival programmers: Darryl Macdonald, Kathleen McInnis
Market and Competition

## Slamdance Film Festival (Park City)
6381 Hollywood Blvd #520, Los Angeles, CA 90028, U.S.
Tel: +1-213 466 1786
Fax: +1-213 466 1784
Festival director: Peter Baxter
Competition: Grand Jury Award

## Golden Globe Awards (LA)
292 South La Cienega Blvd, Suite 316, Beverly Hills, CA 90211-3055, U.S.
Tel: +1-310 657 1731
Fax: +1-310 657 5576
Contact: Chantal Dennage

## MIDEM (Cannes)
11 rue du Colonel Avia, 75726, Paris, Cédex 15, France
Tel: +33-1-41 90 44 00
Fax: +33-1-41 90 44 50
Chief executive: Xavier Roy
Market

## NATPE (National Association of TV Programming Executives) (New Orleans)
2425 Olympic Blvd, Suite 550E, Santa Monica, CA 90404, U.S.
Tel: +1-310-453 4440
Fax: +1-310-453 5258
Website: www.natpe.org
Festival director: Nick Orfanopoulos
European Offices: 454 Oakleigh Rd North, London N20 ORZ, U.K.
Tel: +44-81-361 3793
Fax: +44-81-368 3824
Contact: Pam Mackenzie
Market

## Solothurn Film Festival
Unt. Steingrubenstrasse 19, PO Box 1030, CH-4502 Solothurn, Switzerland
Tel: + 41-32-625 8080
Fax: +41-32-623 6410
E-mail: filmtage@cuenet.ch
Festival director and programmer: Ivo Kummer

## Gerardmer Fantastic Arts
36 rue Pierret, 92200 Neuilly, France
Tel: +33-1-46 40 5500
Fax: +33-1-46 40 5539
E-mail: publics@imaginet.fr
Festival director: Lionel Chouchan
Festival programmer: Daniel Benzakein
Competition: Grand Prix Gerardmer Fantastic Arts

## International Film Festival Rotterdam
Kruiskadehof 36b, 3002 EJ Rotterdam, The Netherlands
Tel: +31-10-890 9090
Fax: +31-10-890 9091
E-mail: iffr@luna.nl
Festival director and programmer: Simon Field
Market and Competition: Tiger Awards (3 x $10,000)

---

**... March 3 ...**
**Time** magazine holds star-studded 75th birthday bash at Radio City Music Hall.

## Tromsø – The Arctic Film Festival

PO Box 285, Tromsø, N-9001
Norway
Tel: +47-77 62 0607
Fax: +47-77 62 0616
E-mail: tromsofilmfestival@
lofotnett.no
Website: www.tromsokino.no/
filmfestival
Festival director: Hans Henrik Berg
Festival programmer: Ola Lund
Renolen
Competition: Film Most Worthy of
Import (NKr100,000)

## Cinequest Film Festival (San José)

PO Box 720040, San José, CA 95172-
0040, U.S.
Tel: +1-408-995 5033
Fax: +1-408-995 5713
E-mail: sjfilmfest@aol.com
Festival director: Halfdan Hussie
Festival programmer: Mike Rabehl
Competition: Maverick Spirit Award

## Internale Filmwochenende (Würzburg)

Gostbertsteige 2, D-97082,
Würzburg, Germany
Tel: +49-931-414098
Fax: +49-931-416279
E-mail: ifw24@aol.com
Festival director: Berthold Kremmler
Competition: Audience Award
(DM5,000)

## Clermont-Ferrand Short Film Festival

26, rue des Jacobins, F-63000
Clermont-Ferrand, France
Tel: +33-473 91 65 73
Fax: +33-473 92 11 93
E-mail: festival@gdebussac.fr
Festival programmers: Roger Gonin,
Christian Guinot
Competition: Grand Prix
(FFr20,000)

## Göteborg Film Festival

Box 7079, S-402 32 Göteborg, Sweden
Tel: +46-31-410 546
Fax: +46-31-410 063
E-mail: goteborg@filmfestival.org
Festival director: Gunnar Bergdahl
Festival programmer: Agneta Green

## The International Film Festival (Belgrade)

Sava Centar, Milentija Popovica 9,
11000 Belgrade, Yugoslavia
Tel:+381-11-622 555
Fax: +381 11 622 555/555 015
E-mail: film@scentar.co.yu
Festival director: Nevena Djonlic
Festival programmers: Miroljub
Vuckovic, Dragan Jelicic

## Alpe Adria Cinema Film Festival (Trieste) (Meetings with Central and Eastern European Cinema)

Via S. Rocco 1, 34121 Trieste, Italy
Tel: +39 40 311 153
Fax: +39 40 311 993
E-mail: aac@spin.it
Festival director and programmer:
Annamaria Percavassi
Competition: Prize for the best
feature film (L5 million)

## Networks in the Studio Seminar (Geneva)

Ancienne Route, 17A (European
Broadcasting Union), Grand
Saconnex (Geneva) Switzerland 1218
Tel: +41 22 717 2721/2725
Fax: +41 22 717 2749/10
E-mail: peters@ebu.ch
Festival director: Jean-Jacques Peters

## The Chicago International TV Competition Awards

32 West Randolph St, Suite 600,
Chicago, IL 60610, U.S.
Tel: +1-312 425 9400
Fax: +1-312 425 0944
E-mail: filmfest@wwa.com
web site: www.chicago.ddbn.com/
filmfest
Contact: Jim Healy

# February

## Fajr Film Festival (Tehran)

Farhang Cinema, Dr. Shariati Ave,
Gholhak, Tehran, 19139, Iran
Tel: +98 21 200 2088/89/90
Fax: +98 21 267 082
Festival director and programmer:
Jamal Omid
Competition: Crystal Simorgh
Award ($5,500)

## San Diego International Film Festival

Dept 0078, UCSD, 9500 Gilman Dr,
La Golla, CA, U.S., 92093-0078
Tel: +1-619 534 0497
Fax: +1-619 534 7665
E-mail: rbaily@uesd.edu
Festival director: Ruth Baily
Festival programmers: Ruth Baily,
Elaine Lea-Chou
Competition: Patrons' Award for
best film

## Tokyo Video Festival

1-7-1 Shinbashi, Minato-ku, Tokyo
105-0004 Japan
Tel: +81-33 28 92 815
Fax: +81-33 2 89 28 19
Festival director: Mr Yasumoto
Competition: Video Grand Prize
($5,000)

## Brussels Cartoon and Animated Film Festival

19 rue de la Rhétorique, 1060
Bruxelles, Belgium
Tel: +32-2-534 4125
Fax: +32-2-534 2279
E-mail: folioscope@skynet.be
Festival directors and programmers:
Doris Cleven, Philippe Moins

## Academy Award Nominations

Academy of Motion Picture Arts
and Sciences
8949 Wilshire Blvd, Beverly Hills,
CA 90211, U.S.
Tel: +1-310-247 3000
Fax: +1-310-859 9351
Contact: Bruce Davis

## Berlin International Film Festival

Budapester Strasse 50, D-10787
Berlin, Germany
Tel: +49-30-25 48 92 25/254 890
Fax: +49-30-25 48 92 49
E-mail: info@berlinale.de
Festival director: Moritz de Hadeln
Competition: Golden Bear

## International Forum of New Cinema (Berlin)

Budapester Strasse 50, D-10787
Berlin, Germany
Tel: +49-30-254 89246
Fax: +49-30-261 5025
E-mail: forum@forum-

ifb.b.shuttle.de;
10024.327@compuserve.com
Website: www.b.shuttle.de
/forum-ifb
Festival director: Ulrich Gregor
Festival programmers: Erika and
Ulrich Gregor, Klaus Dermutz, Erika
Richter, Peter B. Schumann,
Christoph Terhechte, Dorothee
Wenner
Non-competitive, but awards are
given. Wolfgang Staudte Preis
(DM20,000)

## European Film Market (Berlin)

Budapester Strasse 50, D-10787
Berlin, Germany
Tel: +49-30-25 48 92 25
Fax: +49-30-25 48 92 49
Contact: Beki Probst

## The Mobius Advertising Awards (Chicago)

841 North Addison Ave, Elmhurst,
60126-1291 Illinois, U.S.
Tel: +1-630-834 7773
Fax: +1-630-834 5565
E-mail: filmfestivalandmobius
awards@compuserve.com
Festival director: J.W. Anderson
Competition: The Mobius Statuette

## Portland International Film Festival

1219 SW Park Ave, Portland 97205,
Oregon, U.S.
Tel: +1-503-221 1156
Fax: +1-503-226 4842
E-mail: info@nwfilm.org
Festival director and programmer:
Bill Foster
Competition: Audience Award

## Transmedia '99 – Video Fest (Berlin)

Klosterstr. 68-70, Berlin, Germany,
10179
Tel: +49-30 2472 1907
Fax: +49-30 2472 1909
E-mail: videofest@mediopolis.de
Festival director: Johannes Lenz
Pavlichek
Artistic director: Micky Kuella
Competition: Four prizes: video,
computer animation, TV,
multimedia (DM2,000 each)

## MILIA (Cannes)

Conference 8 February
BP 572, 11 rue du Colonel Pierre
Avia, 75726 Paris Cédex 15, France
Tel: +33-1-41 90 44 00
Fax: +33-1-41 90 44 70
Website: www.reedmidem.
milia.com
Program manager: Laurine Garaude
Competition and Market: Milia
d'Or

## Kino Festival of American Underground Cinema (Manchester)

Kinofilm, Kino Screen, 48 Princess
St, Manchester M1 6HR, U.K.
Tel: +44-161 288 2494
Fax: +44-161 281 1374
E-mail: john.kino@good.co.uk
Website: www.kinofilm.org.uk
Festival director: John Wojowski
Festival coordinator: Abigail
Christenson

## Miami Film Festival

444 Brickell Ave, #229, Miami, FL
33131, U.S.
Tel: +1-305-377 3456
Fax: +1-305-577 9768
E-mail: mff@gate.net
Festival director: Nat Chediak
Festival programmer: Nat Chediak
Competition: Audience Award

## Monte Carlo Television Festival

4 Blvd de Jardin Exotique, MC-
98000, Monaco, Monaco
Tel: +377-93 10 40 60
Fax: +377-93 50 70 14
Festival director: David Tomatis
Market and Competition: Golden
Nymph Awards (Best TV Film,
Miniseries, News Reports, News
Features)

## Local Heroes

3rd Floor, 10022 103rd St,
Edmonton, Alberta T5J 0X2,
Canada
Tel: +1-403-421 4084
Fax: +1-403-425 9099
E-mail: filmhero@nsi-canada.ca
Festival director: Cheryl Ashton
Festival programmers: Anthony
King
Market

## American Film Market (AFM)

10850 Wilshire Blvd, Los Angeles,
CA 90024, U.S.
Tel: +1-310-446 1000
Fax: +1-310-446 1600
Market director: Brady Craine
Market

## Fantasporto (Oporto International Film Festival)

Rua Da Constituição 311, P-4200
Oporto, Portugal
Tel: +351-2-507 3880
Fax: +351-2-550 8210
E-mail: fantas@caleida.pt
Website:
http://www.caleida.pt/fantasporto
Festival director: Mário Dorminsky
Festival programmer: Beatriz
Pacheco-Pereira
Competition: Best Film Award

## NatFilm Festival (Copenhagen)

Store Kannikestraede 6, 1169
Copenhagen K, Denmark
Tel: +45-33 12 0005
Fax: +45-33 12 7505
E-mail: natfilm@centrum.dk
Festival programmer: Kim Foss

## Green Screen (London)

**Festival tours seven U.K. cities and
foreign capitals**
114 St. Martin's Lane, London
WC2N 4AZ, U.K.
Tel: +44-171-379 7390
Fax: +44-171-379 7197
Festival director: Victoria Cliff
Hodges
The Bill Travers Award (£1,000)

## Hungarian Film Week (Budapest)

c/o Filmunio, Varoslygeti Fasor 38,
1068 Budapest, Hungary
Tel: +36-1 351 7760
Fax: +36-1 351 6734
E-mail: filmunio@elender.hu
Competition for Hungarian films
only

## Mardi Gras Film Festival (Sydney)

94 Oxford St/PO Box 1081,
Darlinghurst, NSW 2010, Australia
Tel: +61-2 9332 4938
Fax: +61-2 9331 2088
E-mail: info@queerscreen.com.au

---

**. . . March 5 . . .**
Columbia Pictures grabs film rights to T. Coraghessan Boyle's comic novel **Budding
Prospects**, with **Full Monty** helmer Peter Cattaneo attached.

Festival director: Tony Grierson
Competition (for Australian and New
Zealand queer shorts)
My Queer Career Award (A$2,000)

**Mumbai International Film
Festival for Documentary,
Short and Animation Films**
Films Division, Ministry of
Information and Broadcasting,
Government of India, 24-Dr. G.
Deshmuks Marg, Mumbai-400 026,
India
Tel: +91-22 386 4633/387 3655/386
1421/386 1461
Fax: +91-22-386 0308
Festival director: Mr D. Gautaman
Competition and Market
Various categories: Golden Conch
(Rs250,000) and Silver Conch
(Rs100,000)

**Oslo Filmdager**
PO Box 1584, Vika, N-0118 Oslo,
Norway
Tel: +47-22 82 44 00
Fax: +47-22 82 43 68/69
Festival director: Ingeborg Moraus
Hanssen

**PanAfrican Film and TV
Festival of Ouagadougou**
Secrétariat Général Permanent du
Fespaco, 01BP – 2505 Ouagadougou
01, Burkina Faso
Tel: +226-30 7538
Fax: +226-31 2509
Festival director: Filippe Sawadogo
Competition: Etalon de Yennega
(CFA5 million)

**Tourism International Film
Festival**
ACTL, via Silvio Pellico 6, 20121
Milano, Italy
Tel: +39-2 86 46 40 80
Fax: +39-2 72 02 25 83
Festival director: Andrea Archidi
Competition: Best Film Award

# March

**Cairo International Film
Festival for Children**
17 Kasr El Nil St, 202 Cairo, Egypt
Tel: +202-392 3562/392 3962
Fax: +202-393 8979

Festival director: Saad Eldin Wahba
Competition: Golden Cairo

**Dublin Film Festival**
1 Suffolk St, Dublin, Ireland
Tel: +353-1 679 2937
Fax: +353-1 679 2939
Festival director and programmer:
Aine O'Halloran

**Viewpoint: Documentary
Now (Ghent)**
Sint-Annaplein 63, Ghent 9000,
Belgium
Tel: +32-9-225 0845
Fax: +32-9-233 7522
Festival director: Walther Vander
Cruysse
Festival programmer: Cis Bierinckx

**Santa Barbara Film Festival**
1216 State St, Suite 710, Santa
Barbara, CA 93101, U.S.
Tel: +1-805-963 0023
Fax: +1-805-962 2524
E-mail: sbiff@west.net
Festival director: Renée Missel
Festival programmer: Colleen
McNichols
Competition: Best of the Fest (plaque)

**Cinéma du Reel (Paris)**
BPI- 19 rue Beaubourg, 75197 Paris,
Cédex 04, France
Tel: +33-1-44 78 44 21/44 78 45 16
Fax: +33-1-44 78 12 24
Festival director and programmer:
Suzette Glenadel
Competition: Prix du cinéma du
réel (FFr50,000)

**Fribourg Film Festival**
Rue de Locarno 8, 1700 Fribourg,
Switzerland
Tel: +41-26 3222 232
Fax: +41-26 3227 950
Festival director and programmer:
Martial Knaebel
Competition: Grand Prix
(SFr25,000)

**ShoWest (Las Vegas)**
Suite 708, 116 N Robertson Blvd,
Los Angeles, CA 90048, U.S.
Tel: +1-310-657 7724
Fax: +1-310-657 4758
Executive director: Herb Burton
Director: Laura Rooney
Tradeshow

**International Festival of
Films on Art (Montreal)**
640 Saint-Paul St West, Suite 406,
Montréal, Québec H3C 1L9, Canada
Tel: +1-514-874 1637
Fax: +1-514-874 9929
Festival director and programmer:
René Rozon
Competition: Grand Prix (honorary
prize)

**San Diego Latino Film
Festival**
c/o Centro Cultural de la Raza, 2125
Park Blvd, San Diego, CA 92101,
U.S.
Tel: +1-619 230 1938
Fax: +1-619-230 1938
E-mail: LatinoFilm@aol.com
Festival director: Ethan van Thilo
Entry deadline: 30 November 1998

**Femme Totale Film Festival
(Dortmund)**
Kleppingstr. 21-23, 44122
Dortmund, Germany
Tel: +49-231-50 25 162
Fax: +49-231-50 22 497
E-mail: 106212.3237@compuserve.com
Festival director: Silke Johanna Räbiger
Market

**The New York Underground
Film Festival**
225 Lafayette St, Ste. 401, New York,
NY 10012, U.S.
Tel: +1-212 925 3440
Fax: +1-212 925 3430
E-mail: festival@nyuff.com
Festival director: Ed Halter
Competition: Festival Choice Award
($750)

**Nordic Film Festival (Rouen)**
22 rue de la Champmesle, Rouen
76000, France
Tel: +33-235 98 28 46
Fax: +33-235 70 92 08
Festival director: Jean Michel
Mongredien
Festival programmers: Jean Michel
Mongredien, Isabelle Duault
Competition: Grand Jury Award

**Tampere Short Film Festival**
Box 305, 33101 Tampere, Finland
Tel: +358-3-213 0034
Fax: +358-3-223 0121
E-mail: film.festival@tt.tampere.fi

---

**... March 6 ...**
Paul Simon's $11 million, critically scorched musical **The Capeman** will close March 28,
reversing its producers' vows to keep running at least until Tony Award noms are
announced in May.

Festival director: Pertti Paltila
Festival programmer: Raimo Silius
Market and Competition: Grand
Prix (FMk25,000) and 'Kiss'
statuette

## The Television Show (London)

33-39 Bowling Green Lane, London,
EC1R 0DA, U.K.
Tel: +44-171-505 8014
Fax: +44-171-505 8020
E-mail: julian-graves@theframe.com
Show director: Tim McPhearson
Conference director: Helen Golden

## San Francisco International Asian-American Film Festival

NAATA, 346 Ninth St, 2nd Floor,
San Francisco, CA 94103, U.S.
Tel: +1-415 957 1205/863 0814
Fax: +1-415 957 1520/863 7428
E-mail: naata@sirius.com
Festival director and programmer:
Corey Tong

## Brussels International Festival of Fantasy Film

144 Ave de la Reine, B-1030,
Brussels, Belgium
Tel: +32-2 201 1713
Fax: +32-2 201 1469
E-mail: peymey@skypro.be
Festival directors: Delmote Georges,
Guy Delmote
Festival programmers: Bozzo Annie,
Freddy Bozzo-Gigli
Competition: Golden Raven Award
(Corbeau d'or) (U.S.$27,000)

## Creteil International Festival of Women's Films

Maison des Arts, Place Salvador
Allende, 94000 Creteil, France
Tel: +33-1-49 80 38 98
Fax: +33-1-43 99 04 10
Festival director: Jackie Buet
Festival programmers: Jackie Buet,
Nicole Fernandez
Competition: Jury Prize (FFr25,000)

## Guadalajara Film Festival

Griegos 120 Col. Altamira, Zapopan,
Halisco Mexico, 45 160
Tel: + 523-812 1523/811 2882
Fax: +523-811 1882
Festival president: Raul Padilla
Festival director: Susana Lopez

## Minimalen Short Film Festival

Box 10830, Innherredsk 73, N-7002
Trondheim, Norway
Tel: +47-73 52 27 57
Fax: +47-73 53 57 40
E-mail: minimalen@mail.link.no
Festival director and programmer:
Per Fikse
National competition: The Minimalen
Festival Award (NKr5,000)

## South by Southwest Film Conference and Festival

PO Box 4999, Austin, TX 78765,
U.S.
Tel: +1-512 467 7979
Fax: +1-512 451 0754
E-mail: sxsw@sxsw.com.
Website: www.sxsw.com

## Bergamo Film Meeting

Via Giovanni Reich 49,
Torreboldone, Bergamo, Italy, 24020
Tel: +39-35-36 30 87
Fax: +39-35-34 12 55
E-mail: bfm@alasca.it
Festival directors and programmers:
Emanuela Martini, Angelo Signorelli
Competition: Rosa Camuna d'Oro

## The Kino Festival of New Irish Cinema (Manchester) and The Irish World Heritage Film Awards

48 Princess St, Manchester M1 6HR,
U.K.
Tel: +44-161 288 2494
Fax: +44-161 237 3423
Festival director: John S. Wojowski
Competition

## Ann Arbor Film Festival

PO Box 8232, Ann Arbor, MI 48107,
U.S.
Tel: +1-734-995 5356
Fax: +1-734-995 5396
E-mail: vicki@honeyman.org
Festival director and programmer:
Vicki Honeyman
Competition: Best of Festival
($2,500)

## Diagonale-Festival of Austrian Films (Graz)

Diagonale, Obere Augerterstrasse 1,
1020 Vienna, Austria
Tel: +43-1-216 1303
Fax: +43-1-216 1303200

E-mail: wioen@diagonale.at
Festival directors: Christine
Dollhofer, Constantin Wulff
Competition: Grosser
Diagonalepreiss (DM30,000)

## Cleveland International Film Festival

1621 Euclid Ave, #428, Cleveland,
Ohio 44115-2107, U.S.
Tel: +1-216-623 0400
Fax: +1-216-623 0103
E-mail: cfs@clevelandfilm.org
Website: www.clevefilmfest.org
Festival director and programmer:
David W. Wittkowsky
Competition: Roxanne T. Mueller
Award

## African Film Festival (Milan)

Via Lazzaroni 8, 20124 Milano, Italy
Tel: +39-2 66 96 258
Fax: +39-2 6671 4338
E-mail: coe@iol.it
Festival directors: Annamaria
Gallone, Alessandra Speciale
Competition: 1st Premio Agip (L15
million)

## Spotlight (Ravensburg)

Location Office Bodensee-
Oberschwaben, Ittenbeuren 5, 88212
Ravensburg, Germany
Tel: +49-751 24 758
Fax: +49-751 24 753
Festival director: Dr. Thomas Knubben
Festival programmers: Dr. Thomas
Knubben, Peter Frey
Competition: Spotlight in Gold
Award

## Academy Awards (Los Angeles)

Academy of Motion Picture Arts
and Sciences, 8949 Wilshire Blvd,
Beverly Hills, CA 90211
Tel: +1-310-247 3000
Fax: +1-310-271-3395
Academy Awards

## Deutsches Kinder-Film and Fernseh-Festival (Gera)

Stiftung Goldener Spatz,
Amthorstrasse 11, D-07545 Gera,
Germany
Tel: +49-365-800 4874
Fax: +49-365-800 1344
E-mail: gold-spa@gera-web.de
Festival director and programmer:

---

**... March 7 ...**
James Cameron wins Directors Guild of America award for **Titanic.**

Margret Albers
Market and Competition: Goldener
Spatz (Golden Sparrow) Award

## International Film Festival For Young People (Laon)

BP 526, 8 rue Cereurier, Laon, Cédex
02001, France
Tel: +33-3 23 79 39 37/26
Fax: +33-3 23 79 39 32
Festival president and programmer:
Raymond Lefevre
Competition: Grand Prix
(FFr50,000)

## SporTel (Miami)

4 Blvd de Jardin Exotique, MC-
98000 Monaco, Monaco
Tel: +377-93-30 20 32
Fax: +377-93-30 20 33
President: Alexandre de Merode
Executive Vice-President: David
Tomatis
Market and Competition: Golden
Podium Trophy

## Action and Adventure Film Festival (Valenciennes)

6 Place Froisart, Valenciennes,
France 59 300
Tel: +33-3 2725 55 40
Fax: +33-3 27 41 67 49
Festival directors and programmers:
Patricia Lasou, Sylvie Lemaire,
Patricia Riquet
Competition: Grand Prize (20,000
FF for the director)

## Celtic Film and Television Festival (Portree, Skye)

1 Bowmont Gardens, Glasgow,
Scotland G12 9LR
Tel: +44-141 342 4947
Fax: +44-141 342 4948
E-mail: mail@celticfilm
Festival director: Mark McLachlan
Competition: Spirit of the Festival

## East Lansing Film Festival

510 Kedzie St, East Lansing, MI
48823, U.S.
Tel: +1-517 336 5802
Fax: +1-517 336 5802
E-mail: swelff@aol.com
Festival director: Susan W. Woods

## Festival of Yugoslav Documentary and Short Film (Belgrade)

Jugoslavia Film, Makedonska 22/VI,
11000 Beograd, Yugoslavia
Tel: +381-11 324 8554/324 8282
Fax: +381-11 324 8659
Contact: Vojislav Vucinic
Competition: Grand Prix

## Newport Beach International Film Festival

4000 MacArthur Blvd, 5th Floor,
Newport Beach, CA 92660, U.S.
Tel: +1-949-851 6555
Fax: +1-949-851 6556
Festival director: Jeff Conner
Festival programmer: Joseph
Mahoney
Competition and Market
The Jury Award

## Midwest Filmmakers Conference

Cleveland Filmmakers, 1621 Euclid
Ave, #428, Cleveland, Ohio 44115-
2107, U.S.
Tel: +1 216 623 0400
Fax: +1 216 623 0103
Website: www.clevelandfilm.org
Festival programmer: Frank O'Grady

## Cape Town International Film Festival

University of Cape Town, Private
Bag, Rondebosch, Cape Town, South
Africa, 8001
Tel: +27 21 4238 257
Fax: +27 21 4242 355
E-mail: filmfest@hiddingh.uct.ac.za
Festival director: James A. Polley
Festival programmers: Mignon
Coetzee

## International Film Festival of Uruguay (Montevideo)

Lorenzo Carnelli 1311, Montevideo
11 200, Uruguay
Tel: +598-2-408 2460/409 5795
Fax: +598-2-409 45 72
E-mail: cinemuy@chasque.apc.org
Festival director: Manuel Martínez
Carril
Festival programmers: Manuel
Martínez Carril, Ricardo Casas
Competition: Gran Premio de
Montevideo

## Hong Kong International Film Festival

Level 7, Administration Bldg, Hong
Kong Cultural Centre, 10 Salisbury
Rd, Tsimshatsui, Kowloon, Hong
Kong
Tel: +852-2734 2903
Fax: +852-2366 5206
Festival director: Lo Tak-Sing
Festival programmers: Li Cheuk-to,
Jacob Wong, Law Kar

## Days of Independent Film (Augsburg)

Schroeckstr. 6, 86152 Augsburg,
Germany, 86152
Tel: +49-821 349 1060
Fax: +49-821-349 5218
E-mail: filmbuero@t-online.de
Festival director: Harald Munding
Festival programmers: Sabine Samm,
Harald Bann, Barbara Mauch

## Bradford Film Festival

National Museum of Photography,
Film and Television, Bradford, BD1
1NQ, U.K.
Tel: +44-1274- 773 399
Fax: +44-1274 770 217
Festival director: Bill Lawrence
Festival programmer: Chris Fell
Audience Award

## Chicago Film Critics Awards

1152 North LaSalle St, Building B,
Chicago, IL 60610-2695, U.S.
Tel: +1-773 509 8155
Fax: +1-773 664 2925

## IVCA Awards 1999 (London)

IVCA, Bolsover House, 5-6 Clipstone
St, London W1P 8LD, U.K.
Tel: +44-171-580 0962
Fax: +44-171 436 2606
Chief executive: Wayne Drew
Competition: Grand Prix

## Jewish and Israeli Film Festival (Montpellier)

500, Blvde d'Antigone, Montpellier
3400, France
Tel: +33-467 15 08 76/72 32 63
Fax: +33-467 15 08 72/72 32 62
Festival director: Janine Gdaia
Competition: Levy Award

## New Directors/New Films (New York City)

The Film Society of Lincoln Center,

70 Lincoln Center Plaza, New York, NY 10023, U.S.
Tel: +1-212-875 5638
Fax: +1-212-875 5636
Website: www.filmlinc.com
Contact: Sara Bensman

### Royal Television Society Awards

Holborn Hall, 100 Gray's Inn Rd, London WC1X 1AL, U.K.
Tel: +44-171 430 1000
Fax: +44-171 430 0924
Contact: Nicky Harlow

### Seoul Cable and Satellite Festival

Korea Exhibition Centre, 159 Samsung-Dong, Kangham-gu, Seoul 135-731, Korea
Tel: +822-551 1147
Fax: +822-551 1259
E-mail: chonsh@star.koex.co.kr
Festival director: Sang Hwi Chon

### !Viva! Spanish Film Festival (Manchester)

70 Oxford St, Manchester, MI 5NH, U.K.
Tel: +44-161 228 7621
Fax: +44-161 200 1506
Festival programmer: Linda Pariser

# April

### Cognac International Thriller Film Festival (Cognac)

36 rue Pierret, 92200 Neuilly, France
Tel: +33-1-46 40 55 00
Fax: +33-1-46 40 55 39
E-mail: publics@imaginet.fr
Festival director: Lionel Chouchan
Festival programmer: Daniel Benzakein
Competition: Grand Prix

### St Barth Film Festival (St Jean, St. Barthelemy)

410 West 24th St, #16K, New York City, NY 10011, U.S.
Tel: +1-212 989 8004
Fax: +1-212 727 1774
E-mail: jpharris@inerative.net
Festival directors and programmers: Ellen Lampert-Greaux, Joshua Harrison
Focus on Caribbean films

### Aspen Shortfest

110 East Hallam, Suite 102, Aspen, CO 81611, U.S.
Tel: +1-970-925 6882
Fax: +1-970-925 1967
E-mail: lthielen@aspenfilm.org
Festival director: Laura Thielen
Competition: Grand Jury Prize ($2,000)

### Festival du Film de Paris

7 rue Brunef, 75017 Paris, France
Tel: +33 1 45 72 96 40
Fax: +33 1 45 72 96 41
Festival director and programmer: Louise Maurin
Competition

### Internationale Grenzland Filmtage (Selb)

Postfach 307, D-95622 Wunsiedel, Germany
Tel:+49-923-2 4770
Fax: +49-923-2 4710
E-mail: grenzland-filmtage@t-online.de
Festival director: Lena Wilfert

### London Lesbian and Gay Film Festival

South Bank, Waterloo, London SE1 8XT, U.K.
Tel: +44-171-815 1323/815 1324
Fax: +44-171-633 0786
E-mail: jane.ivey@bfi.org.uk
Executive director: Adrian Wootton
Festival programmers: Briony Hanson, Robin Baker

### It's All True – International Documentary Film Festival (São Paulo/Rio de Janeiro)

Rua Simáo Alvares 784/2, São Paulo, Brasil 05417 020
Tel/fax: +55-11 852 9601
E-mail: itstrue@ibm.net
Festival director: Amir Labaki
Competition: Best documentary

### Udine Incontri Cinema

Centro Espressioni Cinematografiche, Via Gregorutti-25, 33100 Udine, Italy
Tel: (39 432) 522 717
Fax: (39 432) 601 421
E-mail: cecudine@tin.it
Festival director: Sabrina Baracette
Artistic director: Derek Elley

### Canyonlands Film and Video Festival (Moab)

435 River Sands Rd, Moab, UT 84532, U.S.
Tel: +1-801 259 9135 (435 259 4979)
Website: http://moab-utah.com/film/video/festival.html
E-mail: cvfv@usa.net
Festival director: Nicholas Brown
Competition: 'Best of Festival' ($500)

### Taos Talking Picture Festival

216M North Pueblo Rd, #216, Taos, NM 87571, U.S.
Tel: +1-505 751 0637
Fax: +1-505 751 7385
E-mail: ttpix@taosnet.com
web site: http://www.taosnet.com/ttpix/
Executive director: Mary Lane Lesley
Festival programmer: Kelly Clement
Competition: The Taos Land Grant Award

### Turin International Gay and Lesbian Film Fest 'From Sodom to Hollywood'

Via Tasso 11, Turin, Italy 10122
Tel: +39 11 534 888
Fax: +39 11 535 796
E-mail: ayfilmfest@assioma.com
Festival director: Giovanni Minerba
Festival programmer: Angelo Acerbi
Competition: Three jury awards (feature, short, and documentary) and three audience awards

### Italian Film Festival (Glasgow/Edinburgh)

Italian Institute, 82 Nicolson St, Edinburgh, EH8 9EW, U.K.
Tel: +44-131-668 2232
Fax: +44-131-668 2777
Festival director: Richard Mowe
Festival programmers: Richard Mowe, Luisa Magera

### Los Angeles Independent Film Festival

5455 Wilshire Blvd, # 1500, Los Angeles, CA, 90036 U.S.
Tel: +1-213 937 9155
Fax: +1-213 937 7770
Website: www.laiff.com
Festival director: Robert Faust
Festival programmer: Thomas Ethan Harns

---

### ...March 9...

Granada Film is negotiating with MGM for an output deal to co-finance around eight films a year, split evenly between big-budget U.S. projects and smaller Euro pics.

## Minneapolis International Film Festival

2331 University Ave SE, Suite 130B,
Minneapolis, 55414, U.S.
Tel: +1-612-627 4431
Fax: +1-612-627 4111
E-mail: Filmsoc@gold.tc.umn.edu
Website: www.umn.edu/nlhome/
g023/filmfoc/
Festival director: Albert Milgrom
Festival programmer: Albert
Milgrom, Bob Strong
Competition: Audience Poll

## Singapore International Film Festival

29A Keong Saik Rd, Singapore,
Singapore 089136
Tel: +65-738 7567
Fax: +65-738 7578
E-mail: filmfest@pacific.net.sg
Festival directors: Philip Cheah, Teo
Swee Leng
Festival programmer: Philip Cheah
Competition (for Asian features
only): Silver Screen Award for Best
Asian Feature

## Istanbul International Film Festival

Istiklal Cad: 146 Luvr Apt., 80070,
Istanbul, Turkey
Tel: +90-212-293 3133 (ext. 20, 21)
Fax: +90-212 249 7771
E-mail: film@istfest-tr.org
Festival director: Hülya Uçansu
Competition: Golden Tulip Award

## National Association of Broadcasters – NAB

1771 N Street, NW, Washington, DC
20036-2891, U.S.
Tel: +1-202-429 5350
Fax: +1-202 429 5406
President and CEO of NAB: Eddie
Fritz

## Visions du Réel Festival International du Cinéma Documentaire (Nyon)

18 rue Juste-Olivier, CP 593, CH-
1260 Nyon, Switzerland
Tel: +41-22-361 6060
Fax: +41-22-361 7071
Website: www.webdo.ch/
visions_97.html
Festival director: Jean Perret
Competition: Grand Prix Visions du
Réel

## European Cinema Congress (Wiesbaden)

Forum Film Mediengesellschaft
GmbH, Wiesbaden, Germany 65205
Tel: +49-611-723448
Fax: +49-611-723403
E-mail: hdfev@aol.com.
Managing director: Wolf Virsthuer

## Washington DC International Film Festival (Filmfest DC) (Washington)

Box 21396, Washington DC 20009,
U.S.
Tel:+1-202-724 5613
Fax: +1-202-724 6578
E-mail: FilmfestDC@aol.com
Festival director and programmer:
Anthony Gittens
Competition: Audience Award

## Golden Rose of Montreux

c/o Television Suisse Romande, Quai
Ernest-Ansermet 20/CP, 234/1211
Geneva 8, Switzerland
Tel: +41-22-708 8599
Fax: +41-22-781 5249
E-mail: gabrielle.bucher@tsr.ch
Festival director: Chris Zoebeli
Secretary General: Pierre Grandjean
Competition: Golden Rose Award

## International Short Film Festival Oberhausen

Grillostrasse 34, D-46045
Oberhausen, Germany
Tel: +49-208-825 2652
Fax: +49-208-825 5413
E-mail: kurzfilmtage-oberhausen
@ani-duisburg.de
Festival director: Lars Henrik Guss
Grosser Preis der Stadt Oberhausen
(DM10,000)

## USA Film Festival (Dallas)

2917 Swiss Ave, Dallas, TX 75204,
U.S.
Tel: +1-214-821 6300
Fax: +1-214-821 6364
Website: www.usafilmfestival.com
Festival director: Ann Alexander
Festival programmer: Alonso
Duralde
Competition (only for short films).
National Short Film Video
Competition – Grand Prize ($,1000)

## San Francisco International Film Festival

1521 Eddy St, San Francisco, CA
94115, U.S.
Tel: +1-415-929 5014
Fax: +1-415-921 5032
E-mail: ggwards@stiff.org
Festival director: Peter Scarlett
Festival programmers: Brian
Gordon, Rachel Rosen, Marie-Pierre
Macia
Competition: SKYY Prize ($10,000)

## Vue d'Afrique (Montreal)

Les Journées du Cinema Africain et
Creole, 67 rue Ste. Catherine Ouest,
5Eme étage, Montréal, Québec H2X
1Z7, Canada
Tel: +1-514 284 3322
Fax: +1-514 845 0631
Festival director: Gerard Lechene
Competition: Le Prix

## Trento International Festival of Mountain and Exploration Films

Via S. Croce 67, 38100 Trento, Italy
Tel: +39 461 98 61 20
Fax: +39 461 23 18 32
Festival director: tbc
Competition: Gran Premio

## New England Film and Video Festival

1126 Boylston St, #201, Boston MA
02215, U.S.
Tel: +1-617 536 1540
Fax: +1-617 536 3576
E-mail: devon@bfvf.org
Festival director: Devon Demonte
Competition: Best of Festival
($1,500)

## Györ Media Wave

Mediawave Foundation, H-9028
Györ, Soprani út 45, Hungary
Tel: +36-96-449 444/328 888
Fax: +36-96-415 285
Festival director: Hartyándi Jenö

## Philadelphia Festival of World Cinema

3701 Chestnut St, Philadelphia,
19104-3195 Pennsylvania, U.S.
Tel: +1-215-895 6593
Fax: +1-215-895 6562
E-mail: pfwc@libertynet.org
Festival director: Phyllis Kaufman

---

**... March 10 ...**
Ulrich Schamoni, 58, vanguard filmmaker of German New Wave and Berlin prize winner
with **Every Year Again** in 1967, unspools last reel.

## Ankara International Film Festival

Bülten Sokak 64:2, 06700 Ankara, Turkey
Tel: +90-312 468 7745/3892
Fax: +90-312 467 7830
Festival director: Mahmut Tali Öngören
Festival programmer: Gökhan Erkihç
Competition: Golden Hatti Dear for best Turkish film ($10,000)

## Munich International Documentary Film Festival

Trogerstrasse 46, D-81675, Munich, Germany
Tel: +49-89-470 3237
Fax: +49-89-470 6611
Festival director and programmer: Gudrun Geyer
Competition: Der Dokumentarfilmpreis (DM20,000)

## Arizona State University Art Museum Annual Outdoor Film Festival (Tempe, Arizona)

ASU Art Museum, Tenth St and Mill Ave, Tempe, AZ 85287-2911, U.S.
Tel: +1-602 965 2787
Fax: +1-602 965 5254
E-mail: spiak@asu.edu
Festival director: John D Spiak
Festival programmer: Jurors
Competition: Juror choice award and LeBlanc audience choice

## BAFTA Film Awards

195 Piccadilly, London W1V 0LN, U.K.
Tel: +44-171-734 0022
Fax: +44-171-439 0473
Acting chief executive: John Chambers
Competition: Bafta Awards

## Chicago Latino Film Festival

600 South Michigan Ave, Chicago, Illinois 60605, U.S.
Tel: +1-312-431 1330
Fax: +1-312-360 0629
Festival director: Pepe Vargas
Festival programmer: Michele Johnson
Competition: Kodak Emerging Filmmaker Award ($25,000)

## Gen Art Film Festival (New York City)

145 W 28th St, Suite 116, New York,
NY, U.S. 10001, U.S.
Tel: +1-212 290 0312
Fax: +1-212 290 0254
E-mail: genart@emedia.net
Festival director: Ian Gerard

## INTERCOM 98 Film and Video Festival (Chicago)

32 West Randolph St, Suite 600, Chicago, Illinois, U.S. 60601
Tel: +1-312 425 9400
Fax: +1-312 425 0944
E-mail: filmfest@wwa.com
Festival director: Michael Kutza
Festival programmer: Jim Healy
Competition: Gold Hugo Statues

## International Animation Film Festival (Stuttgart)

Int. Trick film Festival E.V., Tecker 56, Stuttgart, Germany 70 190
Tel: +49-711-925 4610
Fax: +49-711 2624 980
Festival director: Albert Ade
Capital Stuttgart Award/State of Baden-Württenberg Award (DM15,000 each)

## International Electronic Cinema Festival (Montreux)

Rue du Theatre 5, Montreux CH-820, Switzerland
Tel: +41-21-963 3220
Fax: +41-21-963 8851
E-mail:
r.crawford@tvsympo.menet.ch
ph.guillemin@tvsympo.menet.ch
Festival directors: Philippe Guillemin, Renee Crawford
Competition: Astrolabium

## MIP-TV (Cannes)

Reed Midem Organisation, BP 572, 11 rue du Colonel Pierre Abia, Paris Cedex 15, 75726, France
Tel: +33-1-41 90 45 80
Fax: +33-1-41 90 45 70
Program director: André Vaillant
International TV Market

## North West Film Festival Southport

33 Barrington Rd, Altrincham, Cheshire WA14 1HZ, U.K.
Tel: +44-161-929 1423
Fax: +44-161-929 1067
Festival director: Gil Lane-Young
Festival programmer: Harry Nadler
Competition

## Palm Beach International Film Festival

7108 Fairway Drive, Suite 235, Palm Beach Gardens, Florida 33 418, U.S.
Tel: +1-561 233 1044
Fax: +1-561 683 6957

## Schermi d'amore, Sentimental and Mélo Film Festival (Verona)

Comune di Verona, Corso Porta Borsari 17, 37121 Verona, Italy
Tel: +39-45 800 5348
Fax: +39-45 803 6205
Competition

## The Shadow Line (Salerno)

Piazza Umberto 1, 84095 Giffoni Valle Piana (SA), Italy
Tel: +39-89 868 544/866 361
Fax: +39-89 866 111
E-mail: gff@pn.itnet.it
Website: www.starnet.it/gff/giffoni.news.html
Festival director: Peppe D'Antonio
Competition

## Worldfest Houston

PO Box 56566, Houston, TX 77256, U.S.
Tel: +1-713-965 9955
Fax: +1-713-965 9960
E-mail: Worldfest@aol.com
Festival director: J Hunter Todd
Market and Competition: Gold Remi Statuette, Gold Lone Star

## International Television Festival 'Golden Prague'

ITF 'Golden Prague', Kavci Hory, 140 70, Prague 4, Czech Rep.
Tel: +420 2 6113 4028/4405/4153/4133
Fax: +420 2 6121 2891
E-mail: ruzena.jezkova@czech-tv.cz
Website: www.czech-tv.cz
Festival director: Jiri Vejvoda
Competition: Golden Prague (DM10,000)

## FIFREC (International Film and Student Directors Festival) – (Cannes)

FIFREC, BP 7144, 30913, Nîmes Cédex, France
Tel: +33-472 02 20 36
Fax: +33-472 0220 36
Festival director: Jean Sondel
Competition: Crocodil d'or

---

**...March 11...**
Actor Lloyd Bridges, whose career included **High Noon, Airplane!** and TV's **Sea Hunt**, is dead at 85.

# May

**European Media Art Festival (Osnabrück)**
Postfach 1861, 49008 Osnabrück, Germany
Tel: +49-541 216 58
Fax: +49-541 283 27
Festival director: Alfred Rotert

**Toronto Jewish Film Festival**
33 Prince Arthur Ave., 2nd Floor, Toronto, Canada M5R 1B2
Tel: +1-416 324 8226
Fax: +1-416 324 8668
E-mail: tjff@interlog.com
Festival producer: Helen Zukerman
Festival programmer: Shlomo Schwartzberg

**Cannes Film Festival**
99 Blvd Malesherbes, 75008 Paris, France
Tel: +33-1-45 61 66 00
Fax: +33-1-45 61 97 60
E-mail: festival@cannes.bull.net
Festival director: Pierre Viot
Festival programmer: Gilles Jacob
Market and competition: Palme d'Or

**Seattle International Film Festival**
801 East Pine St, Seattle, WA 98122, U.S.
Tel: +1-206-324 9996
Fax: +1-206-324 9998
E-mail: mail@seattlefilm.com
Festival director: Darryl Macdonald
Festival programmers: Darryl Macdonald, Carl Spence
Competition: American Independent Award ($70,000 in goods and services)

**Cable and Satellite (London)**
Oriel House, 26 The Quadrant, Richmond-upon-Thames, Surrey, TW9 1DL, U.K.
Tel: +44-181 910 7918
Fax: +44-181 910 7866
Contact: Sonya Gent

**International Festival of Animation and Computer Graphics "Anigraph" (Moscow)**
3 Budaiskaya St, Moscow 129128 Russia
Tel: +7-095 187 1942/187 3498
Fax: +7-095 187 7560
Festival director: Elena Lavrenkova

**Inside Out Lesbian and Gay Film and Video (Toronto)**
401 Richmond St W, Suite 456, Toronto, Ontario, M5V, 3A8, Canada
Tel: +1-416 977 6847
Fax: +1-416 977 8025
Festival director: Ellen Flanders
Competition: Bulloch Award ($1,500)

**Workshop for Young Filmmakers (Wiesbaden)**
Bundesverband Jugend and Film CV, Kennedyallec 105a, Frankfurt am Main, Germany D-60596
Tel: +49-69 631 2723
Fax: +49-69 631 2922
Festival director: Berndt Güntzel-Linghet

**27th Algarve International Film Festival**
Festival Internacional de Cinema do Algarve, PO Box 8091, 1801 Lisbon, -Codex, Portugal
Tel: +351-1 851 3615
Fax: +351-1 852 1150
E-mail: algarvefilmfest@mail.telepac.pt
Website: www.algarvefilmfest.com
Festival director: Carlos Manuel
Festival programmers: José Barbosa, Miguel Valverde
Competition: The Festival Big Prize "Cidade de Portimão" (Trophy and 500,000 Portuguese escudos)

**Children's World – International Festival of Films for Children and Teenagers (Varna)**
31 Liuben Karavelov Str., Sofia 1000, Bulgaria
Tel: +359-2 665 564
Fax: +359-2 802 391
Festival director and programmer: Alexander Grozev
Competition: Ilko Cat Award

**International Short Film Festival – Kraków**
Ul Pychowicka 7, 30-364 Kraków, Poland
Tel: +48-12-267 2340
Fax: +48-12-267 1552
Festival director: Janusz Solarz
Festival programmer: Tadeusz Lubelsi
Market and Competition: Grand Prix – The Golden Dragon Award (12000PLN)

**Annecy International Animated Film Festival (Biennale)**
6 avenue des Iles, B.P. 399, 74013 Annecy, Cédex, France
Tel: +33-4 50 10 09 00
Fax: +33-4 50 10 09 70
Festival director and programmer: Jean-Luc Xiberraf
Competition: Grand Prix for best animated feature

**Prix Jeunesse International (Munich)**
c/o Bayerischer Rundfunk, D-80300 Munich, Germany
Tel: +49-89 59002058
Fax: +49-89 59003053
E-mail: prixjeunesse@papyrus.de
Contact: Ursula von Zallinger
Competition: Prix Jeunesse International

**Toronto Worldwide Short Film Festival**
60 Atlantic Ave, Suite 110, Toronto, Ontario, M6K 1X9, Canada
Tel: +1-416 535 8506
Fax: +1-416 535 8342
Festival director and programmer: Brenda Sherwood
Market and Competition: Cammy Award

**Docfest (New York International Documentary Festival)**
159 Maiden Lane, New York, NY 10038, U.S.
Tel: +1-212 943 6333
Fax: +1-212 943 6396
E-mail: dockfest@aol.com
Festival director: Gary Pollard

**Hudson Valley Film Festival (Poughkeepsie and Rhinebeck)**
40 Garden St, Poughkeepsie, NY, 12601, U.S.

Tel: +1-914 473 0318
Fax: +1-914 473 0082
E-mail: hvfo@vh.net
Festival director: Nancy Cozean

## International Bochum Videofestival (Bochum)

Bochumer Videofestival, ASTA
Kulturreferat der Ruhr-Universität,
Universitätstr. 150, 44801 Bochum,
Germany
Tel: +49-234 700 6712
Fax: +49-234 70 16 23
Festival director: Joeng-ho Cheung
Competition

## Los Angeles Asian Pacific American Film and Video Festival

Visual Communications, 263 South
LA St, Suite 307, Los Angeles, CA
90012, U.S.
Tel: +1-213 680 4462
Fax: +1-213-687 4848
e-mail: viscom@vc.apanet.org
website:
http://vc.apanet.org~viscom/
Festival director: Abraham Ferrer

## National Media Owl Awards (Chicago)

The Retirement Research
Foundation, 8765 W. Higgins Rd,
Suite 401, Chicago, Illinois 60631-
4170, U.S.
Tel: +1-773 714 8080
Fax: +1-773 714 8089
E-mail: bradford@rrf.org
Project director: Ray Bradford
Wise Old Owl Award (statuette and
$5,000)

## National Educational Media Network (Oakland)

655 13th St, Oakland, CA 94612-
1222, U.S.
Tel: +1-510-465 6885
Fax: +1-510-465 2835
E-mail: nemn@aol.com
Festival director and programmer:
Jean Paul Petraud
Market and Competition: Gold
Apple

## Short Film Weekend (Augsburg)

Schroeckstr. 8, Augsburg, Germany,
86152
Tel: +49-821 349 1060

Fax: +49-821 349 5218
Festival director and programmer:
Erwin Schletterer
Competition

## Silver Images Film Festival (Chicago)

Terra Nova Films, 9848 S Winchester
Ave, Chicago, IL 60643, U.S.
Tel: +1-773 881 6940
Fax: +1-773 881 3368

## Music Film Fest (Sofia)

37 Ekzarch Yossif Str., Sofia 1000,
Bulgaria
Tel: +359-2 980 3911/880 676
Fax: +359-2 529 325
Festival director and programmer:
Stefan Kitanov

## Festival of European Co-productions (Sofia)

2-A Dondukov Blvd, Sofia 1000,
Bulgaria
Tel: +359-2 987 4096
Fax: +359-2 873 626
E-mail: nfc@mail.bol.bg
Festival director: Dimitar Dereliev
Festival programmers: Irina
Kanousheva, Gergana Dakovska

# June

## Emden International Film Festival

Postfach 2343, 26703 Emden,
Germany
Tel: +49-4921 915 533/35
Fax: +49-4921 915 591
Festival directors and programmers:
Rolf Eckard, Thorsten Hecht
Competition for German-language
films and north-west European
feature films: Emden Film Prize
(DM15,000)

## Troia International Film Festival (Setúbal)

Forum Luisa Todi, Av Luisa Todi 65,
2900 Setúbal, Portugal
Tel: +351-65-525 908
Fax: +351-65-525 681
Festival director: Mário Ventura
Festival programmer: Fernanda
Silva
Competition: Golden Dolphin

## Shots in the Dark, Mystery and Thriller Festival (Nottingham)

Broadway Media Centre, 14 Broad
St, Nottingham, NG1 3AL, U.K.
Tel: +44-115-952 6600
Fax: +44-115-952 6622
E-mail: broadway@
bwymedia.demon.co.uk

## Huesca Film Festival

Avda. Parque, 1 piso, 22002 Huesca,
Spain
Tel: +34-974-212582
Fax: +34-974-210065
E-mail: huescafest@fsai.es
Festival director: José María Escriche
Competition: Danzante de oro
(Pta1,000,000)

## Sydney Film Festival

PO Box 950, Glebe, NSW 2037,
Sydney, Australia
Tel: +61-2-9660 3844
Fax: +61-2-9692 8793
E-mail: info@sydfilm-fest.com.au
Festival director and programmer:
Gayle Lake
Competition: Dendy Awards for
Australian Short Films (A$2,500 for
each award)

## Balticum Film and TV Festival (Gudhjem, Rønne, Svaneke)

Skippergade 8, Svaneke, DK- 3940
Denmark
Tel: +45-70 202002
Fax: +45-70202001
E-mail: balticmediacentre@bmc.dk
Festival director: Bent Nørby Bonde
Festival programmer: Tue Steen
Müllern
Competition: Balticum Prize
(DKr10,000)

## The Princes' Award

The Prince's Award Foundation, c/o
European Environment Agency,
Kongens Nytorv 6, DK-1050
Copenhagen K, Denmark
Tel: +45-33 36 7100/7121
Fax: +45-33 36 7199
E-mail: princes.award@eea.dk
Website: www.eea.dk/events/pa97
Director: Tage Mikkelsen
Prize for the producers of the best
CD-ROM, video, and film on the
environment of Europe

---

**...March 13...**

For the first time in the history of the homevideo industry, 13 major studios will team in
a joint marketing effort to herald the release or reissue of the best 100 films of the past
100 years, as selected by a panel of industry professionals.

## Filmfest Ludwigsburg/ Stuttgart 1999
Filmakademie Baden-Württemberg,
Mathildenstr. 20, D-1638
Ludwigsburg, Germany
Tel: +49-7141 969 361/364/360
Fax: +49-7141 969 363
E-mail: filmfest@filmakademie.de
Website: www.filmakademie.de/
filmfest
Competition: Various awards for
various sections

## U.S. International Film and Video Festival (Chicago)
841 North Addison Ave, Elmhurst,
Illinois 60126-1291, U.S.
Tel: +1-630-834 7773
Fax: +1-630-834 5565
Festival director: J.W. Anderson
Competition: Gold Camera and
Silver Screen Awards

## Montreux 1997 International Television Symposium
PO Box 1451, rue du Théâtre 5, CH-
1820 Montreux, Switzerland
Tel: +41-21 963 3220
Fax: +41-21 963 8851
E-mail: message@symposia.ch

## Florida Film Festival (Maitland)
Enzian Theater, 1300 S. Orlando Ave
Maitland, FL 32751, U.S.
Tel: +1-407 629 1088 x 222
Fax: +1-407 629 6870
E-mail address: filmfest@gate.net
President: Sigrid Tiedtke
Executive director: Melanie Gasper
Festival programmer: Matthew Curtis
Competition: Grand Jury Prize

## Banff TV Festival
1516 Railway Ave, Canmore, Alberta
T1W 1P6, Canada
Tel: +1-403-678 9260
Fax: +1-403-678 9269
E-mail: info@banfftvfest.com
Website: www.banfftvfest.com
Festival director: Pat Ferns
Festival programmer: Jerry Ezekiel
Competition: The Banff Rockie

## National Cable TV Association 47th Annual Convention and International Exposition (Chicago)
NCTA Convention/Exposition

Headquarters, c/o Dobson and
Associates Ltd 1225 19th St, NW,
Suite 310, Washington, DC 20036,
U.S.
Tel: +1-202-775 3606
Fax: +1-202 775 1028

## International Hamburg Short Film Festival
Kurtzfilmagentur, D-22765
Hamburg, Germany
Tel: +49-40-398 26 122
Fax: +49-40 398 26 123
Festival director: Astrid Kühl
Competition: Hamburg Short Film
Prize (DM5,000)

## Norwegian Short Film Festival (Grimstad)
Filmens Hus, Dronningens Gate 16,
N-0152 Oslo, Norway
Tel: +47-22 47 46 46
Fax: +47-22 47 46 90
Website: http://www.nfi.no/krtf/
welcome.html
Festival director: Torunn Nyen
Competition (Norwegian films
only)

## Midnight Sun Film Festival (Sodankylä)
Malminkatu 36, 00100 Helsinki,
Finland
Tel: +358-9-685 2242
Fax: +358-9-694 5560
Festival director: Peter von Bagh
Festival programmer: Göran
Michelsson

## San Francisco Lesbian and Gay Film Festival
346 Ninth St, San Francisco, CA
94103, U.S.
Tel: +1-415 703 8650
Fax: +1-415 861 1404
E-mail: info@frameline.org
Festival director: Michael Lumpkin
Festival programmer: Jennifer
Morris
Competition: Audience Award

## Art Film Festival (Trencianske Teplice)
Konventna 8, Bratislava, Slovak
Republic, 81103
Tel: +42-17 531 9479/9480/9481
Fax: +42-17 531 1679/531 9372
E-mail: festival@artfilm.sk
Festival director: Peter Hledik

Festival programmer: Vladimir Stric
Market and Competition
Golden Key Award ($3,000)

## Cinema Expo International (Amsterdam)
244 West 49th St #200, New York
10019, U.S.
Tel: +1-212-246 6460
Fax: +1-212-265 6428
Contact: Jon Margolis

## International Advertising Film Festival (Cannes)
27-35 Mortimer St, London, W1N
7RJ, U.K.
Tel: +44-171-291 8444
Fax: +44-171-291 8400
Website:
http:/www.canneslions.com
Festival president: Roger Hatchuel
Market and Competition: Lions
Award

## Festival of Festivals (St Petersburg)
10 Kamennoostrovsky Ave, St
Petersburg, 197101, Russia
Tel: +7-812-237 0304
Fax: +7-812-237 0304/
394 5870
Festival director: Alexander
Mamontov
Market and Competition: Grand
Prix

## Hong Kong International Film Market
38th Floor, Office Tower Convention
Plaza, 1 Harbour Rd, Wanchai,
Hong Kong
Tel: +852 2584 4333
Fax: +852 2824 0249
E-mail: ernest.chan@tdc.org.hk
Festival director: Jenny Koo
Market

## Showbiz Expo West (Los Angeles)
383 Main Ave, Norwalk, CA 06851,
U.S.
Tel: +1-203 840 5945
Fax: +1-203 840 9945
E-mail: ibogardus@reedexpo.com
Festival director: Dave Bonaparte

## Filmfest München
Internationale München
Filmwochen GmbH, Kaiserstraße

---

**... March 14 ...**
ABC is in talks with actor Malcolm McDowell to star as the lead character in the Columbia
TriStar TV-produced remake of **Fantasy Island**.

39, D-80801 Munich, Germany
Tel: +49-89 38 19 040
Fax: +49-89 38 19 04 27/26
Festival director: Eberhard Hauff
No competition, but special awards
given. Top TV Award, Media Net
Award

## Adriaticocinema (Bellaria, Rimini, Catolica)

Via Gambalunga 27, 47900
Rimini, Italy
Tel: +39-541-226 27/26 399/52 038
Fax: +39-541-24 227
Festival director: Marco Bellocchio
Organising director: Gianfranco
Miro Gori
International competition only for
film schools

## Bradford Animation Festival (BAF!)

National Museum of
Photography, Film and TV,
Pictureville, Bradford BD1 1NQ, U.K.
Tel: +44-1274 725 347
Fax: +44-1274 723 155
E-mail: c.sawhney@nmsei.ac.uk or
c.fell@nmsi.ac.uk
Festival programmer: Chris Fell
Competition

## Charlotte Film and Video Festival

Mint Museum of Art, 2730 Randolph
Rd, Charlotte, NC 28207, U.S.
Tel: +1-704 337 2019
Fax: +1-704 337 2101
Festival director: Robert West
Competition

## Cologne Conference

Adolf Grimme Institut, Im
Mediapark 5b, 50670 Köln, Germany
Tel: +49-221-454 3280
Fax: +49-221-454 3289
E-mail: 100776,2621@
compuserve.com
Festival director: Lutz Hachmeister
Festival programmer: Martina
Richter
Market

## European TV Sports Conference (London)

Kagan Seminars International, 524
Fulham Rd, London SW6 5NR, U.K.
Tel: +44-171 371 8880
Fax: +44-171 371 8715

Contact: Alex Guthrie

## Fantafestival (Rome)

Viale Gioachino Rossini 9, Rome,
00198 Italy
Tel: +39-6 807 6999
Fax: +39-6 807 7199
Festival directors: Adriano Pintaldi,
Alberto Ravagioli

## Festival of European Cinema (La Baule)

97 rue Raumur, F-75002 Paris,
France
Tel: +33-1 40 41 04 54
Fax: +33-1 40 26 54 78
Festival director: Robert Parienti
Festival programmer: Andre Halimi
Competition: Prix Europe/Europa

## Festival of Film Schools (Munich)

Kaiser Str. 39, Munich 80801,
Germany
Tel: +49-89 381 9040
Fax: +49-89 381 90426
Festival director: Prof Wolfgang
Längsfeld
Competition

## French-American Film Workshop (New York/Avignon)

10 montée de la Tour, 30400
Villeneuve-les-Avignon, France
Tel: +33-490 25 93 23
Fax: +33-490 25 93 24
Festival director: Jérôme Henry
Rudes
Tel: +1-212-343 2675
Fax: +1-212-343 1849
Competition: Tournage Awards
($20,000)

## Human Rights Watch International Film Festival (New York City)

350 Fifth Ave, 34th Floor, New York,
NY, 10118 U.S.
Tel: +1-212-216 1264/216 1235
Fax: +1-212-736 1300
E-mail: burres b@hrw.org
Festival director: Bruni Burres
Festival programmers: Bruni Burres,
Heather Harding
Competition: New film dealing with
human rights themes ($5,000)

## International and Open Russian Film Festivals Kinotavr (Sochi)

35 Arbat, Moscow 121835, Russia
Tel: +7-095 248 0911/248 9187
Fax: +7-095 248 0966

## International Animation Festival (Cardiff)

18 Broadwick St, London, W1V
1FG, U.K.
Tel: +44-171-494 0506
Fax: +44-171-494 0807
Festival director: Jane Williams

## International Festival of Animated Film, Zagreb

Koncertna Direkcija Zagreb,
Animafest, 41000 Zagreb, Kneza
Mislava 18, Croatia
Tel: +385-1 461 1709
Fax: +385-1 461 1808/807
E-mail: kdz@zg.tel.hr
Festival director: Margit Antauer
Competition: Grand Prix (18,000
Kunas)

## International Film Fest Cinematograph (Innsbruck)

CineVision, c/o Cinematograph,
Museumstrasse 31, Innsbruck,
Austria 6020
Tel: +43-512-580723
Fax: +43-512-581762
E-mail: cinema@nomad.transit.or.at
Program director: Dr. Helmut
Groschup

## 'Message to Man' International Documentary, Short and Animated Film Festival

Karavannaya 12, Saint Petersburg,
Russia, 191011
Tel: +7-812 235 2660/230 2200
Fax: +7-812 235 2660/235 3995
Festival director: Mikhail Litviakov
Festival programmer: Victor
Semenyuk
Competition: Golden Centaur
Award ($5,000)

## Mostra Internazionale del Cinema Libero/Il Cinema Ritrovato (Festival of film restoration from archives from all over the world)

Via Galliera 8, I-40121 Bologna,
Italy

---

Weekend estimates project a tie between Leonardo DiCaprio in **Titanic** and **Man in the Iron Mask**, each reporting $17.6 million – actuals give boat a $300,000 lead.

Tel: +39-51-237 088
Fax: +39-51-261 680
Festival director: Gianluca Farinelli

### Pesaro Film Festival
Via Villafranca 20, 00185 Rome, Italy
Tel: +39-6-445 66 43/49 11 56
Fax: +39-6-491 163
E-mail: pesarofilmfest@mclink.it
Festival director and programmer:
Adriano Aprà

### La Rochelle International Film Festival
16 rue Saint Sabin, 75011 Paris, France
Tel: +33-1-48 06 16 66
Fax: +33-1-48 06 15 40
E-mail: festival.de.la.rochelle@
wanadoo.fr
Festival director: Jean-Loup Passek
Festival programmer: Sylvie Pras-
Pruneengler
Market

### Potsdam Film Fest
Dianastr. 21, 14482 Potsdam,
Germany
Tel: +49-331 706 0369
Fax: +49-331 706 0339
Festival director: Heidrun Podazus
Festival programmer: festival team

### Vue Sur les Docs – The International Documentary Film Festival
3 Square Stalingrad, 13001,
Marseille, France
Tel: +33-495 04 44 90
Fax: +33-491 84 38 34
E-mail:
100560.1511@compuserve.com
Festival and market director: Olivier
Masson
Competition: Grand Prix
(FFr50,000)

### World Animation Celebration
30101 Agoura Court, Suite 110,
Agoura Hill 91301, California, U.S.
Tel: +1-818-991 2884
Fax: +1-818-991 3773
Festival director: Dan Bolton
Competition: The Grand Prize

# July

### Age d'or Prize/Prizes for the distribution of quality films in

### Belgium (Cinédécouverts) (Brussels)
Royal Film Archive, Ravenstein
St. 23, B-1000 Brussels, Belgium
Tel: +32-2-507 8370
Fax: +32-2-513 1272
Festival director and programmer:
Gabrielle Claes
Competition: The Age d'Or prize
(BFr500,000)

### Karlovy Vary International Film Festival
Panska 1, 110 00 Prague 1, Czech
Republic
Tel: +420-2-24 23 54 48
Fax: +420-2-24 23 3408
E-mail: iffkv@tlp.cz
Festival president: Jiri Bartoska
Festival programmer: Eva Zaoralova
Competition: Grand Prix Crystal
Globe ($20,000)

### International Film Festival for Children and Young People (Montevideo)
Lorenzo Carnelli 1311, 11200
Montevideo, Uruguay
Tel: +598-2 408 2460/409 5795
Fax: +598-2 409 4572
E-mail: cinemuy@chasque.apc.org
Festival director and programmer:
Ricardo Casas
Competition: Guri Award

### Galway Film Fleadh
Cluain Mhuire, Monivea Rd,
Galway, Ireland
Tel: +353-91 751655
Fax: +353-91 770746
E-mail: galfilm@iot.ie
Festival manager: Deborah McVey
Program director: Pat Collins
Market

### Outdoor Short Film Festival (Grenoble)
4 rue Hector Berlioz, Grenoble
38000, France
Tel: +33-476 544 351
Fax: +33-476 5124 43
Festival director and programmer:
Michel Warren
Competition: Grand Prix
(FFr15,000)

### Hometown Video Festival
The Alliance for Community Media,
666 11th St, NW #806, Washington,

DC 20001, U.S.
Tel: (1 202) 393 2650
Fax: (1 202) 393 2653
Festival director: Steve Fortriede

### Auckland International Film Festival
PO Box 9544, Wellington, 6035 New
Zealand
Tel: +64-4 385 0162
Fax: +64-4 801 7304
E-mail: enzedff@actrix.gen.nz
Festival director: Bill Gosden
Festival programmer: Sandra Reid

### Zanzibar International Film Festival
Karume House, PO Box 3032,
Zanzibar, Tanzania
Tel: +255-54 33408
Fax: +255-54 33406/33135
E-mail: ziff@zanzibar.org
Festival director: Mark Leveri
Festival programmer: Yusuf
Mahmoud
Competition: Golden Dhow Award
($5,000)

### 28th Wellington Film Festival
PO Box 9544, Wellington 6035, New
Zealand
Tel: +64-4-385 0162
Fax: +64-4-801 7304
E-mail: enzedff@actrix.gen.nz
Festival director: Bill Gosden
Festival programmer: Sandra Reid

### Giffoni Film Festival
Piazza Umberto 1, 84095 Giffoni
Valle Piana, Salerno Italy
Tel: +39-89-868 544
Fax: +39-89-866 111
E-mail:
gilfonif@mcorrino.peoples.it
Festival director and programmer:
Claudio Gubitosi
Competition: Silver Gryphon Award

### Melbourne International Film Festival
1st Floor, 207 Johnston St, Fitzroy,
Melbourne, Australia 3065
Tel: +61-3-9417 2011
Fax: +61-3-9417 3804
E-mail: miff@netspace.net.au
Festival director: Sandra Sdraulig
Festival programmer: Brett
Woodward
Competition (short films only)

---

### ...March 16
ABC is finalizing negotiations with Drew Carey to host and exec-produce a summer
version of the British improv show **Whose Line Is It Anyway?**... **Variety** launches new
daily Gotham edition.

Grand Prix for best short film (A$5,000)

## Rio Cine International Festival

Mahatma Gandhi 2, gr. 402 Rio De Janeiro, 20018-900 Brazil
Tel: +55-21 262 3902
Fax: +55-21 262 8870
Festival director: Walkiria Barbosa
Festival programmer: Vilma Lustosa
Market and Competition
Golden Sun Award ($50,000)

## Fantasy Film Festival (Munich-Frankfurt-Cologne-Stuttgart-Hamburg-Berlin)

Rosebud Entertainment, Herzog-Wilhelmstr. 27, 80331 Munich, Germany
Tel: +49-89-260 22838
Fax: +49-89-260 22839
E-mail: rosebud-entertainment@t-online.de
Festival directors and programmers: Rainer Stefan, Schorsch Müller

## Dublin Lesbian and Gay Film Festival

6 South William St, Dublin 2, Ireland
Tel: +353-1- 492 0597
Fax: +353-1-670 6377
Festival directors and programmers: Kevin Sexton, Yvonne O'Reilly

## Cairo Exhibition for Electronic Communications

IV Bldg Kornish El Nil, Masparo, Cairo Festival Management, Cairo Egypt, 11515
Tel: +202-760 454
Fax: +202- 578 7010

## Cairo Festival for Radio and TV Programmes

IV Bldg Kornish El Nil, Masparo, Cairo Festival Management, Cairo Egypt, 11515
Tel: +202-578 7010
Fax: +202-574 6989
Festival director: Abdel Rahman-Hafez
Festival programmer: Hamdi Al Konayessy
Competition: Festival Golden Award ($5,900)

## CAMAR TV 98 (Cairo Market for Radio and TV Programmes)

IV Bldg Kornish El Nil, Masparo, Cairo Festival Management, Cairo Egypt, 11515
Tel: +202-760 454/574 6841
Fax: +202-578 7010/773 441
Contact: Maha Darwish
Market

## Cambridge Film Festival

Cambridge Arts Cinema, 8 Market Passage, Cambridge CB2 3PF, U.K.
Tel: +44-1223-578 944
Fax: +44-1223-578 929
E-mail: festival@cambarts.co.uk
Festival co-directors and programmers: Tony Jones, Sorley Macdonald

## Fant-Asia Festival (Montreal, Toronto)

300 Leo Pariseau Street, Suite 1500
Montréal, Québec H2W 2P3, Canada
Tel: +1-514 982 0020
Fax: +1-514 982 0796
E-mail: festival@videotron.ca
Website: www.fantasiafest.com
Festival director: Pierre Corbeil
Festival programmers: Mitch Davis, Julien Fonfrede, Karin Hussain, Martin Sauvageau
Competition and Market

## International Film Festival (Palic)

Otvoreni Univerzitet, Trg Cara Jovana Nenada 15. 24000 Subotica, Yugoslavia
Tel: +381-24 554 726
Fax: +381-24 37116
Festival director: Radoslav Zelenovic
Festival programmer: Dinko Tucakovic
Competition: Alexandar Lifka Award

## International Short Film Festival of Vila do Conde

Auditorio Municipal – Praga da Republica, 4480 Vila do Conde, Portugal
Tel: +351-52-641 644
Fax: +351-52-642871
Festival directors and programmers: M Dias, M Micaelo, R Maia, D Oliveira, J Rodrigues

Market and Competition
Great Prize City of Vila do Conde (Pta500,000)

## Jerusalem Film Festival

PO Box 8561, Derech Hebron, Wolfson Gardens, Jerusalem 91083, Israel
Tel: +972-2-672 4131
Fax: +972-2-673 3076
E-mail: jer-cine@inr.net.il
Festival director: Lia van Leer
Festival programmer: Avinoam Harpak
Competition: Israeli Cinema Awards

## Monitor Awards (New York)

2230 Gallows Rd, Suite 310, Dunn Loring, VA 22027, U.S.
Tel: +1-703 319 0800
Fax: +1-703 641 8776
Contact: Julie Chung

## Moscow International Film Festival

Khokhlovski Pereulok 10/1, Moscow 109028, Russia
Tel: +7-095-917 2486/0944
Fax: +7-095-916 0107
Festival president: Renat Davletiarov
Festival programmer: Kiril Razlogov
Competition: Statuette of Saint George

## PIA Film Festival (Tokyo)

5-19 Sanban-cho, Chiyoda-ku, Tokyo 102-0075, Japan
Tel: +81-3-32 65 14 25
Fax:+81-3-32 65 56 59
Festival director and programmer: Keiko Araki
Competition: Grand Prize (¥1 million)

## Pula Film Festival

Matka Laginje 5, Istarsko Narodno Kazaliste, Pula 52100, Croatia
Tel: +385-52 22380
Fax: +385-52 214 303
Festival director: Ljubo Sikic
Competition: Golden Arena Award

## Sopot Film Festival

Centar za kulturu Sopot, Kosmajski trg 7, 11450 Sopot, Yugoslavia
Tel: +381-11 825 1238/825 1315
Fax: +381-11 825 1315
Contact: Zivorad Milosavljevic

---

**...March 17...**
Alan Parker signs to direct adaptation of Pulitzer Prize-winning book **Angela's Ashes.**

### Taormina International Film Festival
Palazio dei Congressi, 98039
Taormina, 98039, Italy
Tel: +39 942 21142
Fax: +39 942 23348
Festival director: Felice Laudadio
Festival programmer: Carmelo
Marabello
Competition: Cariddi d'oro and
d'argento – Premio Marco Melani
(L75 million in total)

### Wine Country Film Festival
PO Box 303, Glen Ellen, CA 95442,
U.S.
Tel: +1-707-996 2536
Fax: +1-707-996 6964
E-mail: wc.filmfest@aol.com
Festival director and programmer:
Stephen Ashton
Competition
First Feature Award, Blockbusters
Film Competition

# August

### Urbanworld Film Festival (New York)
375 Greenwich St. NY, NY 10013,
U.S.
Tel: +1-212 941 3845
Fax: +1-212 941 3849
E-mail: aphill@aol.com
Festival directors: Angelique
Phillips, Stacy Spikes
Festival programmer: Angelique
Phillips
Market and Competition: Best
Picture

### Hollywood Film Festival
433 N Camden Drive, Suite 600,
Beverly Hills, CA 90210, U.S.
Tel: +1-310 288 1882
Fax: +1-310 475 0193
E-mail:
awards@hollywoodawards.com
Festival director and programmer:
Carlos de Abreu
Competition: Hollywood Discovery
Award ($,20,000)

### Locarno International Film Festival
Via della Posta 6, 6600 Locarno,
Switzerland
Tel: +41-91-751 0232

Fax: +41-91-751 7465
E-mail: pardo@tinet.ch
Festival director and programmer:
Marco Müller
Market and Competition: Golden
Leopard (SFr30,000)

### Hollywood Film Market
433 North Camden Drive, #600,
Beverly Hills, CA 90201, U.S.
Tel: +1-310 288 1882
Fax: +1-310 475 0193
E-mail: awards@
hollywoodfestival.com
Website: www.hollywoodfestival.com
Contact: John Jacobson

### Odense International Film Festival
Vindegade 18, DK-5000 Odense C,
Denmark
Tel: +45-6-613 1372 ext 4044
Fax: +45-6-591 4318
Festival director: Christian Braad
Thomsen
Competition: Grand Prix (DKr35,000)

### Weiterstadt Open Air Filmfest
Bahnhofstrasse 70, D-64331,
Weiterstadt, Germany
Tel: +49-615 012 185
Fax: +49-615 014 073
E-mail: sfk@hrzpub.tu-darmstadt.de
Website: www.home.pages.de/
~sfk/weiterstadt
Festival director: Jochen Pollitt

### Film Screenplay Festival (Vrnjacka Banja)
Vrnjacka 20, 36210 Vrnjacka Banja,
Yugoslavia
Tel: +381-36 662 398
Fax: +381-36 662 398
Festival director and programmer:
Milan Nikodijevic
Competition: Best Screenplay Award

### Edinburgh International Film Festival
88 Lothian Rd, Edinburgh EH3 9BZ,
Scotland, U.K.
Tel: +44-131-228 4051
Fax: +44-131-229 5501
E-mail: info@edfilmfest.org.uk
Festival director and programmer:
Lizzie Francke

### Espoo Ciné
PO Box 95, Espoo 02101 Finland
Tel:+358-9-466 599
Fax: +358-9-466 458
E-mail: espoocine@cultnet.fi
Festival director: Timo Kuismin

### São Paulo International Short Film Festival
Rua Simao Alvares 784/2, 05417-020
São Paulo – SP Brazil
Tel/Fax: +55-11 852 9601
E-mail: spshort@ibm.net
Festival director: Zita Carvalhosa
Festival programmer: Francisco
Cesar Filho

### Norwegian International Film Festival (Haugesund)
PO Box 145, 5501 Haugesund,
Norway
Tel: +47-52 73 44 30
Fax: +47-52 73 44 20
E-mail: haugfest@online.no
Festival director: Gunnar Johan
Loevvik
Festival programmer: Christine Berg
Market

### Sarajevo Film Festival
Obala Kulina Bana 10, 71000
Sarajevo, Bosnia
Tel: +387-71 524 127/668 186
Fax: +387-71 664 547
Festival director: Mirsad Purivatra
Festival programmer: Philippe
Bober
Competition: Sarajevo Best Film
Award

### Montreal World Film Festival
1432 De Bleury, Montreal H3A 2JI,
Canada
Tel: +1-514 848 3883
Fax: +1-514 848 3886
E-mail: ffm@interlink.net
Website: www.ffm-montreal.org
Festival directors and programmers:
Serge Losique, Daniele Cauchard
Market and Competition: Grand
Prix of the Americas

### Edinburgh International Television Festival
2nd Floor, 24 Neal St, London
WC2H 9PS, U.K.
Tel: +44-171 379 4519
Fax: +44-171 836 0702

---

**... March 18 ...**
Universal announces first Hollywood entertainment complex in China, with the Universal
Experience set to open later in the year in Beijing.

E-mail: eitf@festival.demon.co.uk
Festival director: Charlotte Ashton

### International Festival of Tourist, Ecological, and Sport Films – Mefest (Zlatibor)

Mefest c/o Film Danas, Bulevar Crvene Armije 38, 11 000 Beograd, Yugoslavia
Tel/fax: +381-11 430 837/444 5677
Festival director: Gavrilo Azinovic
Festival programmer: Dinko Tucakovic
Competition: Golden Pine

### Love is Folly (Varna)

31 Liuben Karavelov Str., Sofia 1000, Bulgaria
Tel: +359-2 665 564
Fax: +359-2 803 791
Festival director and programmer: Alexander Grozev
Competition: Golden Aphrodita

### Chichester Film Festival

New Park Film Centre, New Park Rd, Chichester, West Sussex, PO19 1XN, U.K.
Tel: +44-1243-786 650/533 081
Fax: +44-1243-533 081
Festival director and programmer: Roger Gibson
Competition: International Shorts Award

### Festival of Actors (Nis)

Pavla Orlovica 28 A, 18000 Nis, Yugoslavia
Tel: +381-18 47 757/42 849
Fax: +381-18 23 197
Festival director and programmer: Predrag Jelenkovic
Grand Prix for the Best Actors

### Gramado Film Festival – Latin and Brazilian Cinema

Rua dos Andradas 736, 3 Andar, Centro, 90 020 004
Porto Alegre, Brazil
Tel: +55-51 226 3932
Fax: +55-51 226 3932
E-mail: festival@via-rs.com.br
Festival director: Esdras Rubinn
Market and Competition: Kikito

### International Festival 'Window into Europe' (Vyborg)

Chistoprudni Blvd. 12 A, Room 601,
Moscow 123242, Russia
Tel: +7-095 924 8508
Fax: +7-095 924 1331/937 7025
Festival director: Sava Koulish
Competition

### Palm Springs International Short Film Festival

1700 E. Tahquitz Cyn Way, Palm Springs, CA 92262, U.S.
Tel: +1-760 322 2930
Fax: +1-760 322 4087
E-mail: filmfest@ix.net.com
Executive director: Craig Prater
Artistic director: Paola Freccero
Market and Competition: Best of Festival ($1,000)

### Yugoslav Film Festival (Herceg-Novi)

JUK Herceg-Fest, Dvorana Park, Njegoseva bb, 85340 Herceg-Novi, Yugoslavia
Tel: +381-88 22 098
Fax: +381-88 22004
Festival president: Dragan Jankovic
Festival programmer: Zoran Zivkovic
Competition: Grand Prix

### Motovun International Film Festival

Imaginary Academy, Zagreb, 10000, Croatia
Tel: +385-1 485 6455
Fax: +385-1 485 6459
Email: boris.matic@radio101.hr
Festival director: Boris T Matic
Competition: Golden Tower of Motovun

### Hiroshima International Animation Festival

4-17 Kako-machi, Naka-ku, Hiroshima 730, Japan
Tel: +81-82-245 0245
Fax: +81-82-245 0246
E-mail: hiroanim@urban.or.jp
Website: www.city.hiroshima.jp
Festival director and programmer: Sayoko Kinoshita
Competition: Grand Prix (¥1,000,000)

### Fantoche International Animation Film Festival (Baden)

Ottikerstrasse 53, 8006 Zürich, Switzerland
Tel: +41-1 361 4151
Fax: +41-1 364 0371
E-mail: fantoche@access.ch
Contact: Otto Alder
Competition

# September

### Festival der 'Neue Heimat Film' (Freistadt, Upper Austria)

Salzgasse 25, 4240 Freistadt, Austria
Tel: +43-79 42 77722
Fax: +43-79 42 77733
Festival director and programmer: Wolfgang Steininger
Competition: Preis der Stadt Freistadt (ASch30,000)

### Festival Internacional de Cinema (Figueira da Foz)

Apartado dos Correios 50407, 1709 Lisboa Codex, Portugal
Tel: +351-1-812 6231
Fax: +351-1-812 6228
Festival director: José Viera Marques
Competition: Grande Premio da Figueira da Foz

### Mostra Internazionale d'arte Cinematografica (Venice)

Ca Giustinian, S Marco 1364A, I-Venice 30124, Italy
Tel: +39-41-521 8878/8711
Fax: +39-41-522 7639
Festival director: Alberto Barbera
Festival programmers: Silvia Menegazzi, Tiziana Finzi, Nadia Zande
Competition: Golden Lion Award

### Sub Fiction – 3. Werkleitz Biennale (Werkleitz and Tornitz)

Straße des Friedens 26, 39249, Torintz, Germany
Tel: +49-39298 6750
Fax: + 49-39298 675 55
Website: www.werkleitz.de/sub-fiction
Festival director: Peter Zorn

### Telluride Film Festival

53 South Main St, Suite 212, Hanover, New Hampshire 03755, U.S.
Tel: +1-603-643 1255
Fax: +1-603-643 5938
E-mail: Tellufilm@aol.com
Festival directors: Bill Pence, Tom Luddy

---

**... March 19 ...**
Rupert Murdoch's Fox Group acquires ownership of the Los Angeles Dodgers baseball team.

**Deauville Festival of American Films**
36 rue Pierret, Neuilly 92 200, France
Tel: +33-1-46 40 5500
Fax: +33-1-46 40 5539
E-mail: publics@imaginet.fr
Festival director: Lionel Chouchan, Andre Halimi
Festival programmer: Daniel Benzakein
Competition: Grand Prix 'Special Deauville'

**Festival of Fantastic Films (Manchester)**
33 Barrington Rd, Altrincham, Cheshire, WA14 1H2, U.K.
Tel: +44-161-929 1423
Fax: +44-161-929 1067
Festival director: Gil Lane Young
Festival programmer: Harry Nadler
Competition: Award for the best film

**Latin American Film Festival (London)**
79 Wardour St, London W1V 3TH, U.K.
Tel: +44-171-434 3357
Fax: +44-171-287 2112
Festival director and programmer: Eva Tarr

**LA Freewaves (Los Angeles)**
120 Judge John Atlo St, Basement Level, Los Angeles, CA 90012, U.S.
Tel: +1-213 617 3950
Fax: +1-213 687 4848
E-mail: info@freewaves.org
Festival director and programmer: Ming-Yuen S Ma (plus 12-member committee)

**Tacoma Tortured Artists Film Festival**
728A Pacific Ave., Tacoma, WA 98402, U.S.
Tel: +1-253 627 5932
Fax: +1-253 627 1525
E-mail: TacomaFilm@aol.com
Festival director: James Hume
Competition: The Barbie Award ($1,500)

**Internationales Filmfest Oldenburg**
Bahnhof str. 15, Oldenburg 26122, Germany

Tel: +49-441 25659
Fax: +49-441 26155
Festival directors: Torsten Neumann, Thorsten Ritter

**Boston Film Festival**
Box 516, Hull, MA 02045, U.S.
Tel: +1-617-925 1373
Fax: +1-617-925 3132
Festival director: Mark Diamond

**Toronto International Film Festival**
2 Carlton St, Suite 1600, Toronto, Ontario M5B 1J3, Canada
Tel: +1-416-967 7371
Fax: +1-416 967 9477
E-mail: tiffg@torfilm fest.ca
Website: www.bell.ca/toronto/filmfest
Contact: Piers Handling
Competition: Audience Award; Air Canada People's Choice Award

**Athens International Film Festival – Opening Nights**
5 Benaki and Ag. Nektariou St., 152-35 Vrilissia, Athens, Greece
Tel: +30-1-606 1363/606 1428
Fax: +30-1-601 4137
Festival director: George Tziotzios
Festival programmer: George Krassakopoulos
Competition: Audience Award (Dr2 million)

**The Mango Film Festival (Black and Asian Film and TV) (Bradford)**
National Museum Photography, Film and TV, Pictureville, Bradford, BD11 NQ, U.K.
Tel: +44-1274 725 347
Fax: +44 1274 723 155
E-mail: c.sawhney@nmsi.ac.uk or fell@nmsi.ac.uk
Festival director: Bill Lawrence
Festival programmer: Irsan Ajeeb
Market (Trade Festival of South Asian and Black Film and TV)

**Focus on Asia Fukuoka International Film Festival**
1-8-1 Tenjin, Chuo-ku, Fukuoka 810, Japan
Tel: +81-92-733 5170
Fax: +81-92-733 5595
Festival director and programmer: Tadao Sato

**Forum of European Cinema (Strasbourg)**
10 rue Alexandre Parodi, Paris, France 75010
Tel: +33-1 44 89 99 99
Fax: +33-1 44 89 99 60
Festival director: Patrice Vivancos
Festival programmer: Pierre-Henri Deleau

**International Broadcasting Convention, Amsterdam**
IBC Office, Savoy Place, London, WC2R 0BL, U.K.
Tel: +44-171 240 3839
Fax: +44-171 240 3724
E-mail: show@ibc.org.uk
Website: www/ibc.org.uk/ibc/
Contact: Joanne Jones

**Yugoslav Feature Film Festival Novi Sad Arena**
Zvezda Film, Trg Slobode 2, 21000 Novi Sad
Tel: +381-21 615 759
Fax: +381-21 613 759
Festival director: Pavle Milivojev
Competition: Zlatna Arena

**Bogota Film Festival**
Calle 26 No. 4-92, Santa Fe de Bogota, Colombia
Tel: (57 1) 282 5196, 243 1901
Fax: (57 1) 342 2872
E-mail: cidc@coll.telecom.com.co.
Festival director: Henry Laguado
Competition: Gold Cycle Award

**SporTel (Monte Carlo)**
4 Blvd de Jardin Exotique, MC-98000 Monaco, Monaco
Tel: +377-93-30 20 32
Fax: +377-93-30 20 33
President: Alexandre de Merode
Market and Competition: Golden Podium Trophy (FFr30,000)

**Breckenridge Festival of Film**
P.O. Box 718, Riverwalk Center, 150 W. Admas, Breckenridge, CO 80424, U.S.
Tel: +1-970 453 6200
Fax: +1-970 453 2692
E-mail: filmfest@brecknet.com
Festival director: Julie Bullock
Festival programmer: Terese Keil
Competition

---

**... March 20 ...**
Sydney Pollack, the director who brought **Dirty Harry** to exec John Calley when he ran Warner Bros. more than 20 years ago, will be reunited with Calley in a new multi-year production deal linking his Mirage Enterprises with Sony Pictures Entertainment.

## Fantasy Film Festival (Lund)

Box 1693, S-22101 Lund, Sweden
Tel: +46-40 122 266
Fax: +46-40 122 264
Festival director: Magnus Paulsson
Competition

## The British Short Film Festival

BBC British Short Film Festival,
BBC Centre House, Room A 214, 56
Wood Lane, London W12 7SB, U.K.
Tel: +44-181-743 8000 ext. 62222
Fax: +44-181-740 8540
Festival director: Amanda Casson
Competition: Awards for Best
British + Best International
productions (£1,000 each)

## Mostra Rio – Rio de Janeiro Film Festival

Rua Voluntários da Pátria 97, 22270-
000 Botafogo, Rio de Janeiro, Brazil
Tel: +55-21 539 1505
Fax: +55-21 539 1247
E-mail: ildasan@ibm.net
Website: www.estacao.com.br
Festival director: Nelson Krumholz
Festival programmers: Marcelo
Mendes, Ilda Santiago

## San Sebastián International Film Festival

Plaza de Oqendo s/n, 20004 San
Sebastián, Spain
Tel: +34-43-48 12 12
Fax: +34-43-48 12 18
Festival director: Diego Galan
Market and Competition: Golden
Shell

## Showbiz Expo East (New York)

383 Main Ave, Norwalk, CT 06951,
U.S.
Tel: +1-203 840 5378
Fax: +1-203 840 9378
Contact: Liz Cassidy

## Atlantic Film Festival (Halifax)

c/o CBC 5600 Sackville St, Halifax,
Nova Scotia B3J 3E9, Canada (PO
Box 36139)
Tel: +1-902-422 3456
Fax: +1-902-422 4006
E-mail: festival@atlanticfilm.com
Festival director: Gordon Whittaker
Festival programmer: Ron Foley
McDonald

Market and Competition: Best film
or video 60 mins or over ($2,500)

## Empire State Exhibitions Film and Video Fest

PO Box 177, Mohawk, NY 13407,
U.S.
Tel: +1-212-802 4679
Fax: +1-518 581 7614
E-mail: Empirefilm@aol.com
Website: members.aol.com/
empirefilm/festival
Festival directors and programmers:
Michael J Zimmerman, Jon Galt
Competition: The 'Essey' Award

## Helsinki Film Festival – Love and Anarchy

Unioninkatu 10, FIN-00130
Helsinki, Finland
Tel: +358-9-629 528
Fax: +358-9-631 450
E-mail: randa@cultnet.fi
Website: loveandanarchy.cultnet.fi
Director of programming: Pekka
Lanerva
Festival programmers: Jari Mäkela,
Eija Niskanen, Matti Pauunio, Mika
Siltala

## Independent Feature Film Market (New York)

104 West 29th St, 12th Floor, New
York, NY 10001-5310, U.S.
Tel: +1-212-465 8200
Fax: +1-212-465 8525
E-mail: IFPNY@ifp.org
Festival director: Valerie Sheppard
Market: Gordon Parks Independent
Film Award ($10,000, sponsored by
MTV Films)

## Umeå International Film Festival

PO Box 43, 90102 Umeå, Sweden
Tel: +46-90-133388
Fax: +46-90-777961
Festival director: Thom Palmen

## Cinec 98 – International Trade Fair for Motion Picture Technology and Postproduction (Munich)

Messe München GmbH,
Messegelände, D-80325 Munich,
Germany
Tel: +49-89 5107 219/220
Fax: +49-89 5107 138
E-mail: info@messe-muenchen.de

## Prix Danube (Bratislava)

Slovenska Televizia, Bratislava,
Slovak Republic, 845 45
Tel: +421-7 6542 8609/6542 6501
Fax: +421-7 6542 8609
Competition: Prix Danube Award in
four categories
Festival director: Jela Kezmanova

## Arsenals International Film Forum (Riga)

PO Box 626, Märstalu 14, Riga,
Latvia LV 1047
Tel: +371-722 1620
Fax: +371-782 0445
E-mail: arsenals@
sisenis.com.latnet.lv.
Festival director: Benita Sarma
Festival programmers: Ileva Pitruka,
Laima Freimane, Liana Boksa

## Drama Short Film Festival (Drama)

Ag. Varvaras 9, Drama, Greece
Tel: +30-521 47575/1-330 0309
Fax: +30-521 33526/1-330 2818
Website: www.hyper.gr/dramaFest/
Contact: Antonis Papandopoulos
Competition and Market
Grand Prix (Dr1 million)

## Cinefest – The Sudbury Film Festival

Suite 218, 40 Elm St, Sudbury,
Ontario, PC3 1S8, Canada
Tel: +1-705-688 1234
Fax: +1-705-688 1351
Executive director: Tammy Frick
Competition: Best
International/Best Canadian

## Festival Cinéma Tout Ecran

Maison des Arts du Grütli, 16 rue du
Général Dufour, Case postale 5305,
CH_1211 Genève 11, Switzerland
Tel: +41 22 328 8554
Fax: +41 22 329 6809
E-mail: info@cinema-tout-ecran.ch
Festival director: Leo Kaneman
Festival programmer: Stéphanie
Billeter
Competition: Grand Prize
(SFr10,000)

---

**... March 21 ...**
Robert Duvall's **The Apostle** wins top honors at Independent Spirit Awards in
Los Angeles.

## Lucas '99 – International Film Festival for Children and Young People (Frankfurt am Main)

Deutsches Filmmuseum,
Schaumainkai 41, D-60596
Frankfurt am Main, Germany
Tel: +49-69-620167
Fax: +49-69-6032185
Festival directors: Petra Diebold,
Petra Eggensperger
Festival programmers: Petra
Diebold, Petra Eggensperger,
Christian Exner, Günther Kinstler
Competition: Lucas Award
(DM1,000)

## ABTA 98 (São Paulo)

Rua Ministro Nelson Ungria 239,
Suite 4, 05690-050 São Paulo, Brazil
Tel: +55-11 844 9111/844 5733
Fax: +55-11 844 9121
Contact: Fabio Murad

## Aspen Film Fest

110 E Hallam, Suite 102, Aspen,
Colorado 81611, U.S.
Tel: +1-970-925 6882
Fax: +1-970-925 1967
E-mail: lthielen@aspenfilm.org
Festival director: Laura Thielen

## Santa Fe de Bogota Festival

Calle 26, No 4-92, Santa Fe de
Bogota, Colombia
Tel: +57-1 282 5196
Fax: +57-1 342 2872
Festival director: Henry Laguado
Festival programmer: Camilla Lobo-
Guerrera

## Film Camera Festival Manaki Brothers (Bitola)

Vardar-Film 8 Mart 4, 91000 Skopje,
Macedonia
Tel: +389-91-117527/116626
Fax: +389-91-132 150/117 038
Festival director: Delco Mihajlov
Festival programmer: Blagoja
Kunevski
Competition: Golden Camera 300

## FilmFest Hamburg

Friedensallee 44, D-22765
Hamburg, Germany
Tel: +49-40-399 19000
Fax: +49-40-399 190010
E-mail: film fest-hamburg @t-
online.de

Festival director: Josef Wutz
Festival programmer: Johannes Wachs

## Netherlands Film Festival (Utrecht)

PO Box 1581, 3500 BN Utrecht, The
Netherlands
Tel: +31-30-232 2684
Fax: +31-30-213 3200
E-mail: nedfilmfest@artnet.xshall.nl
Festival director: Jacques van
Heyningen
Festival programmer: Herman de Wit
Market and competition: Golden
Calf ($10,000)

## European Television and Film Forum (Helsinki)

EIM, Kaistrasse 13, 40221
Düsseldorf, Germany
tel: +49-211 901 0457
Fax: +49-211 901 0456
E-mail: forum@eim.org
Contact: Marjon Agema

## Pusan International Film Festival (PIFF)

Room 208, # 1393 Woo 1 Dong,
Hacuudac-Ku, Pusan, Korea
Tel: +82-51 747 3010/1
Fax: +82-51 747 3012
Contact: Sun Young Lee

## Festival de cinéma Internationale Ste-Thérèse/Ste-Adèle (Ste-Thérèse et Ste-Adèle)

34 rue Blainville Ouest, Sainte-
Thérèse, Québec J7E 1W9, Canada
Tel: +1-514-434 0387
Fax: +1-514-434 7868
E-mail: festival@ odyssee.net
Festival director: André Marion
Festival programmer: Frédéric
Lapierre
Competition: Best Film Award ($1,000)

## Short Cuts Cologne

c/o Kölner Filmhaus, Maybachstr.
111, 50670 Köln, Germany
Tel: +49-221 222 7100
Fax: +49-221 222 71099
Festival director: Stefan Sarasi
Competition

## Black Filmworks Festival of Film and Video (Oakland)

Black Filmmakers Hall of Fame, 405
14th St, Suite 515, Oakland,

CA 94612, U.S.
Tel: +1-510 465 0804
Fax: +1-510 839 9858
Contact: Felix Curtis
Market and Competition: Best Film
($1,000)

## Festival International du Film Francophone (Namur)

175 rue des Brasseurs, B-5000
Namur, Belgium
Tel: +32-81 24 12 36
Fax: +32-81 22 43 84
Festival director: Dany Martin
Festival programmer: Nicole Gillet
Competition: Golden Bayard for
Best Film (BFr50,000)

## Films from the South (Oslo)

Fimens Hus, Dronningens Gate 16,
N-0152, Oslo, Norway
Tel: +47-22 47 45 00
Fax: +47-22 47 46 90
Contact: Brynjar Bjerkem

## Holland Film Meeting (Utrecht)

PO Box 1581, 3500 BN, Utrecht, The
Netherlands
Tel: +31-30-232 2684
Fax: +31-30-213 3200
Festival director: Jacques van
Heijningen
Competition and Market:
Golden Calf Awards

## New York Film Festival

Film Society of Lincoln Center, 70
Lincoln Center Plaza, New York, NY
10023, U.S.
Tel: +1-212-875 5638
Fax: +1-212-875 5636
Website: www.filmlinc.com
Festival director: Richard Peña

## Vancouver International Film Festival

Suite 410, 1008 Homer St.,
Vancouver V6B 2X1, Canada
Tel: +1-604-685 0260
Fax: +1-604-688 8221
E-mail: viff@viff.org
Website: http://viff.org/viff/
Festival director: Alan Franey
Festival programmer: PoChu AuYeung
Audience-generated awards

---

**. . . March 22 . . .**
Despite an unexpected snowstorm, spring was in full bloom on Broadway with receipts
rising 6%.

## Videonale International Video and Media Festival (Bonn)

Hochstadenring 22, 53 119
Bonn, Germany
Tel/fax: +49-228 69 28 18
Contacts: Ute Hörner, Judith Ruzicka
Competition

## Ottawa International Animation Festival

2 Daly Ave, Suite 140, Ottawa, Ontario K1N 6E2, Canada
Tel:+1-613-232 8769
Fax: +1-613-232-6315
E-mail: crobinso@DocuWeb.ca
Festival director: Chris Robinson
Market and Competition: Grand Prize

## Screens on the Bay (Amalfi)

Sacis, Via Teulada 66, Rome 00195, Italy
Tel: +39-6 3749 8269
Fax: +39-6 370 1343
Contact: Carmela Carmarota

## International Festival of Film and Video for Children and Young Adults (Isfahan)

Farhang Cinema, Dr. Shariati Ave., Gholhak, Tehran, Iran 19139
Tel: +98-21 200 2088/89/90
Fax: +98-21 267 082
Festival director: S Daad
Festival programmer: Jamal Omid
Competition: Golden Butterfly ($1,200)

## Yugoslav Animated Film Festival (Cacak)

Dom kulture- Foto kino-klub Cacak, 32000 Cacak, Yugoslavia
Tel: +381-32 23508
Contact: Slobodan Pajic

# October

## Austin Film Festival and Heart of Film Screenwriters

AHFF, Inc, 1600 Nueces, Austin, TX 78701, U.S.
Tel: +1-512 478 4795
Fax: +1-512 478 6205
E-mail: austinfilm@aol.com
Festival directors: Barbara Morgan, Marsha Milam

Festival programmer: Jason White
Competition and Market: Bronze Award ($750 for feature film)

## Feminale Women's Film Festival (Cologne)

Hansaring 86, D-50670 Cologne, Germany
Tel: +49-221 130 0225
Fax: +49-221 130 0281
Festival director: Katja Mildenberger
Festival programmer: Regina Eichen,Verena Mundt

## Festival du Film Britannique (Dinard)

2 Blvd Féart, 35800 Dinard, France
Tel: +33-299-88 19 04
Fax: +33-299-46 67 15
Festival director: Thierry de la Fournière
Competition: Hitchcock Award

## Mill Valley Film Festival

38 Miller Ave, Suite 6, Mill Valley, CA 94941, U.S.
Tel: +1-415 383 5256/0990
Fax: +1-415 383 8606
Festival director: Mark Fishkin
Festival programmer: Zoë Elton

## Warsaw Film Festival

PO Box 816, 00-950 Warsaw 1, Poland
Tel: +48-22-644 11 84
Fax: +48-22-644 11 84
E-mail: festiv@wff.org.pl
Festival director: Stefan Laudyn

## Human Rights Watch International Film Festival (London)

350 Fifth Ave, 34th Floor, New York, NY, 10118 U.S.
Tel: +1-212-216 1264/216 1235
Fax: +1-212-736 1300
E-mail: burres b@ hrw.org
Festival director: Bruni Burres
Festival programmers: Bruni Burres, Heather Harding

## Leeds International Film Festival

The Town Hall, The Headrow, Leeds, LS1 3AD, U.K.
Tel: +44-113-247 8389
Fax: +44-113-247 8397
web site: www.sensei.co.uk/films/
Festival director: Liz Rymer

## UFVA Student Film and Video Festival (Philadelphia)

Department of Film and Media Arts Temple University 011-00, Philadelphia PA 19122, U.S.
Tel: +1-215 923 3532
Fax: +1-215 204 6740
E-mail: ufva@vm.temple.edu
website: thunder.ocis.temple.edu/~ddoyon
Festival director: Juan Carlos Rojas
Competition

## Film in Weimar – Festival of the Eastern European Cinema (Weimar)

Etfuster Str. 40, Jena, Germany 07745
Tel: +49-3641 45 06 30
Fax: +49-3641 61 52 34
E-mail: Klaus.Hattenbach@Jena.Thur.de
Festival director and programmer: Klaus Hattenbach

## MIPCOM JUNIOR (Cannes)

Reed Midem Organisation, BP 572, 11 rue du Colonel Pierre Avia, Paris, France 75726
Tel: +33-1 41 90 45 80
Fax: +33-1 41 90 45 70
Program director: André Vaillant

## Festival Internazionale del cinema di Salerno

Casella Postale 137, I-84100 Salerno, Italy
Tel: +39-89-231 953
Fax: +39-89-223 632
Festival director: Ettore Capuano
Festival programmer: Mario De Cesare
Competition: Gran Trofeo Golfo di Salerno

## International Festival of New Film and Video (Split)

Zagrebacka 35A, PO Box 244, 21000 Split, Croatia
Tel/fax: +385-21 52 59 25
E-mail: split.filmfest@st.tel.hr
Festival director: Branko Karabatic
Competition: Grand Prix

## Israel Film Festival (Haifa)

142, Hanassi Ave, Haifa, Israel 34633
Tel: +972-4838 3424/6246
Fax: +972-4838 4327
Festival director: Pnina Blayer

---

Competition: The "Golden Anchor" award for Mediterranean films ($25,000)

### MIPCOM (Cannes)

BP 572, 11 rue du Colonel Pierre Avia, F- 75726 Paris, France
Tel: +33-1-41 90 45 80
Fax: +33-1-41 90 45 70
Market director: André Vaillant
Market

### Flanders International Film Festival (Ghent)

1104 Kortrijksesteenweg, B-9051 Ghent, Belgium
Tel: +32-9-221 8946
Fax: +32-9-221 9074
E-mail: filmfestival@infoboard.be
website: www.rug.ac.be/
filmfestival/Welcome.html
Contacts: Jacques Dubrulle, Walter Provo, Peter Bouckaert, Marian Ponnet
Competition: Golden Spur Award ($130,000)

### Dokumentart – European Film workshop (Neubrandenburg)

Holm-Henning-Freier, Rasenstrasse 3, D-17033, Neubrandenburg, Germany
Tel: +49-395 566 6610/6109
Fax: +49-395 566 6612
E-mail: latuecht@t-online.de
Festival director: Holm-Henning Freeier
Competition: Latücht-Preis (DM7,000)

### Vevey International Comedy Film Festival

La Grenette CP 421, 1800 Vevey, Switzerland
Tel: +41-21-922 2027
Fax: +41-21-922 2024
Festival director and programmer: Yves Moser
Competition: Golden Cane (SFr6,000)

### Chicago International Film Festival

32 West Randolph St, Suite 600, Chicago, Illinois 60601, U.S.
Tel: +1-312 425 9400
Fax:+1-312 425 0944
E-mail: filmfest@wwa.com

internet sight: http//www. chicago. ddbn. com/filmfest/
Festival director: Michael J Kutza
Festival programmers: Helen Gramates, Colleen Sulliyan, Suzanne McCormick
Competition: The Gold Hugo Award (Grand Prix) ($300)

### Denver International Film Festival

1430 Larimer Square, Suite 201, Denver, CO 80202, U.S.
Tel: +1-303-595 3456
Fax: +1-303-595 0956
E-mail: DenverFilm@csn.net
Festival director: Ron Henderson

### Sitges International Fantasy Film Festival

Rossello 257 3-E, 08008 Barcelona, Spain
Tel:+34-3-415 3938
Fax: +34-3-237 6521
E-mail: cinsit@arrakis.es
Festival director: Alex Gorina
Competition: Best Film Award

### The Golden Rhyton (Plovdiv)

2-A Dondukov Blvd, Sofia 1000, Bulgaria
Tel: +359 2 987 4096/883 831
Fax: +359 2 873 626
E-mail: nfc@mail.bol.bg
Festival director: Dimitar Dereliev
Competition: Grand Prix

### International Film Festival Mannheim-Heidelberg

Collini-Center, Galerie, D-68161 Mannheim, Germany
Tel: +49-621-102943
Fax: +49-621-291564
Festival director: Dr Michael Koetz
Market and Competition: International Independent Award (DM30,000)

### New Orleans Film and Video Festival

PO Box 50819, New Orleans, 70150 LA, U.S.
Tel: +1-504-523 3818
Fax: +1-504-529 2430
Festival director: Carol Gniady
Festival programmer: John Despias
Competition: Lumiere Awards

### Le Giornate del Cinema Muto (Pordenone)

c/o Cineteca del Friuli, Palazzo Gurisatti, Via G. Bini, I-33013 Gemona, Italy
Tel: +39-432-980458
Fax: +39-432-970542
E-mail: gcm@proxima./conecta.it
Festival director: David Robinson
Market

### Wildscreen (Bristol)

Deanery Rd, College Green, Bristol, BS1 5DB, U.K.
Tel: +44-117 909 6300
Fax: +44-117-909 5000
E-mail: wildscreen@gn.apc.org
Website: www.wildscreen.org.uk
Festival director: Jane Krish
Competition: Golden Panda

### The Athens Film Festival (Athens, Georgia)

PO Box 1631, Athens, Georgia, U.S. 30603
Tel: +1-706 613 7669
Fax: +1-706 613 0959
E-mail: gafilm@negia.net
Festival director: Juanita M Giles
Festival programmer: Todd Campbell
Competition: The Kudzu Award

### Cork International Film Festival

Hatfield House, Tobin St, Cork, Ireland
Tel: +353-21-271711
Fax: +353-21-275945
Festival director and programmer: Michael Hannigan
Competition: European Short Film (Ecu7,500)

### The Golden Chest International TV Festival (Plovdiv)

29 San Stefano Str., Sofia, 1000, Bulgaria
Tel: +359-2 946 1034/963 3095
Fax: +359-2 946 1034
Festival director: Valentin Stoyanov
Competition: Grand Prix 'Golden Chest'

### The Hamptons International Film Festival (East Hampton)

3 Newtown Mews, East Hampton, NY 11937, U.S.
Tel: +1-516-324 4600

---

Fax: +1-516-324 5116
E-mail: hiff@peconic.net
Festival director: Denise Kasell
Festival programmers: David Schwartz, Deena Juras, Linda Blackaby, Lynda Hanse
Competition: Golden Starfish Award ($200,000)

## San Juan Cinemafest

PO Box 4543, San Juan, Puerto Rico 00902-4543
Tel: +1-787-721 6125
Fax: +1-787-723 6412
e-mail: JMV333@aol.com
Festival director: Gabriel Suau
Festival programmer: Dominique Borrell
Competition: Pitirre

## World Media Expo (Seattle)

PO Box 3379, Frederick, MD 21705, U.S.
Tel: +1-301 694 5243/(202 429 4194)
Fax: +1-301 694 5124/(202 775 2146)

## Chicago International Children's Film Festival

Facets Multimedia, 1517 West Fullerton Ave, Chicago, Illinois 60614, U.S.
Tel: +1-773 281 9075
Fax: +1-773 929 5437
E-mail: kidsfest@facets.org
Festival director and programmer: Rebekah Cowing
Competition: Grand Prize ($2,500)

## FCMM (Montreal International Festival of Cinema and New Media)

3668 Blvd St-Laurent, Montréal, Québec H2X 2V4, Canada
Tel: +1-514-843 4725
Fax: +1-514-843 4631
E-mail: montrealfest@fcmm.com
Festival director and programmer: Claude Chamberlan

## Mostra de Valencia/Cinema de Mediterrani

Plaza del Arzobispo, 2 Bajo, 46003, Valencia, Spain
Tel: +34-96-392 1506
Fax: +34-96-391 5156
Festival director: Luís Fernández
Festival programmer: Elena Escriba
Competition: Palmera de Oro (Pta3 million)

## São Paolo International Film Festival

Al. Lorena 937 Cj.303, 01424-001 São Paolo, Brazil
Tel: +55-11-883 5137/30645819
Fax: +55-11-853 7936
E-mail: info@mostra.org
Website: http://www.mostra.org.
Festival director: Leon Cakoff
Festival programmers: Leon Cakoff, Renata de Almeida
Market and Competition: Bandeira Paulista Trophy

## Viennale (Vienna)

Stiftgasse 6, A-1070 Vienna, Austria
Tel: +43-1-526 5947
Fax: +43-1-523 4172
E-mail: organisation@viennale.or.at
Festival director and programmer: Alex Horwath
Fipresci prize

## Cinekid (Amsterdam)

Weteringschaus 249, NL-1017 XY Amsterdam, The Netherlands
Tel: +31-20-624 7110
Fax: +31-20-620 9965
Festival director: Sannatte Naeye
Festival programmer: Harry Peters
Competition: Cinekid Award (DFl5,000)

## Mifed (Milan)

EA Fiera Milano, Largo Domodossola 1, I-20145 Milano, Italy
Tel: +39-2-48 01 29 12/48 01 29 20/48 01 29 42
Fax: +39-2-49 97 70 20
E-mail: mifed @fnd.it
Director: Tullio Galleno
Market

## Prix Europa Berlin

SFB, Berlin 14046, Germany
Tel: +49-30-30 31 1610
Fax: +49-30-30 31 1619
Festival director: PL Braun
Festival programmer: Susanne Hoffmann
Competition: Prix Europa TV programme of the year (fiction)

## Sheffield International Documentary Festival

The Workstation, 15 Paternoster Row, Sheffield, S1 2BX, U.K.
Tel: +44-114-276 5141
Fax: +44-114-272 1849

E-mail: shefdoc@fdgroup.co.uk
Festival director: Kathy Loizou

## ShowEast (Atlantic City)

244 West 49th St #200, New York , NY 10019, U.S.
Tel: +1-212-246 6460
Fax: +1-212-265 6428
Festival directors: Robert and Jimmy Sunshine

## Uppsala International Short Film Festival

PO Box 1746, S-751 47 Uppsala, Sweden
Tel: +46-18-12 00 25
Fax: +46-18 12 13 50
E-mail: //www2.passagen.se/opulus/com/film/film.htm
Festival director: Anders Engström
Festival programmers: Anders Engstrom, Åsa Garnert
Market and Competition: six awards for six categories (SKr6000)

## Yamagata International Documentary Film Festival

YIDFF, Tokyo Office, Kitagawa Bldg, 4fl, 6-42 Kagurazaka, Shinjuku-ku, Tokyo 162_0825, Japan
Tel: +81-33266-9704
Fax: +81-33266-9700
E-mail: yidff@bekkoame.ne.jp
Festival director: Yano Kazuyuki
Festival programmers: Ono Seiko, Fujioka Asako
Competition: The Grand Prize (The Robert and Frances Flaherty Prize) (¥3,000,000)

## Nordic Film Festival

Peinsens Gt. 2B, N-7013 Trondheim, Norway
Tel: +47-72 54 73 69
Fax: +47-73 52 25 50
Festival director: Egil Aksilsen
Festival programmer: Eli Gjerde

## European Cable Communications '98 (London)

The Cable Communications Association, The Fifth Floor, Artillery House, Artillery Row, London SW1P 1RT, U.K.
Tel: +44-171-222 2900
Fax: +44-171-799 1471
Contact: Sharon Chapman

---

### ... March 25 ...

DreamWorks reported to have anted up mid-six figures for a pitch by James P. Crow, based on a Philip K. Dick short story about a society of robots.

**Geneva Film Festival 'Stars of Tomorrow'**
35 rue des Bains, CP 5615, CH-1211 Geneve 11, Switzerland
Tel: +41-22 809 9450
Fax: +41-22 809 9444
Festival director and programmer: Gérald Morin
Competition: European Golden Star (SFr10,000 each)

**Premio Saint-Vincent Per Il Cinema Italiano**
Via Giulia 66, Rome 00186, Italy
Tel: +39-6-68 75 330
Fax: +39-6-68 75 333
Festival director: Felice Laudadio
Competition: Grolle d'Oro

**Lesbian and Gay Film Festival (Hamburg)**
Schanzenstr. 45, 20357 Hamburg, Germany
Tel: +49-40 348 0670
Fax: +49-40 34 05 22
Festival director: Joachim Post
Competiton: Short film (only)

**Heartland Film Festivals (Indianapolis)**
613 N East St, Indianapolis, IN 46202, U.S.
Tel: +1-317-464 9405
Fax: +1-317-635 4201
E-mail: hff@inquest.net
Festival director and programmer: Jeffrey L. Sparks
Competition: Crystal Heart Award ($100,000)

**AFI Los Angeles International Film Festival**
2021 N Western Ave, Los Angeles, CA 90027, U.S.
Tel: +1-213-856 7707
Fax: +1-213-462 4049
E-mail: afifest@afionline.org
Festival director: Jon Fitzgerald
Festival programmers: Carla Sanders, Nancy Collet
Grand Jury Prize/The Studio Prize ($20,000)

**Raindance Film Showcase (London)**
81 Berwick St, London W1V 3PF, U.K.
Tel: +44-171-287 3833
Fax: +44-171-439 2243
Website: www: ftech.net/n ind film

Festival director: Elliot Grove
Festival programmer: Suzanne Ballantyne
Market

**Cinéma Meditérranéen Montpellier**
6 rue Vielle Aiguillerie, F-34000 Montpellier, France
Tel: +33-4-67 66 36 36
Fax: +33-4-67 66 36 37
Festival director and programmer: Pierre Pitiot
Competition: Antigone d'Or ($20,000)

**Film and Music Fest (Bielefeld)**
Körnerstr. 3, 33602 Bielefeld, Germany
Tel: +49-521 677 43
Fax: +49-521 677 27
E-mail: eisenstein.filmfestival@t-online-de
Festival director: Johnen Kurt

**Valladolid International Film Festival**
PO Box 646, 47080 Valladolid, Spain
Tel: +34-83-305700/305777
Fax: +34-83-309835
Festival director: Fernando Lara
Festival coordinator: Denise O'Keefe
Competition: Golden Spike (Pta3 million)

**International Film Festival 'Molodist' (Kiev)**
6 Saksagansky str., Kiev, Ukraine, 252033
Tel: +380-44-227 4557/246 6798
Fax: +380-44-227 4557
E-mail: molodist@gu.kiev.ua
Festival director: Andrei Khalpakhtchi
Festival programmer: Alexander Shpilyuk
Competition: Scythian Deer ($10,000)

**Kinofilm '97 (Manchester)**
48 Princess St, Manchester M1 6HR, U.K.
Tel: +44-161-288 2494
Fax: +44-161-237 3423
Festival director and programmer: John Wojowski

**Framed III: Architecture on Film (London)**
66 Portland Place, London W1N 4AD, U.K.
Tel: +44-171 307 3699
Fax: +44-171 307 3703
Festival director: Tamara Horbacka

**London Premiere Screenings**
23-24 George St, Richmond, Surrey TW3 1HY, U.K.
Tel: +44-181 948 5522
Fax: +44-181 332 0495
Festival director: Tim Etchells
Market

**International Leipzig Festival for Documentary and Animated Film**
PO Box 0940, D-04009 Leipzig, Germany
Tel: +49-341-980 3921
Fax: +49-341-980 6141
Festival director and programmer: Fred Gehler
Market and Competition: Golden Dove (DM9,000)

**Fort Lauderdale International Film Festival**
2633 East Sunrise Blvd, Fort Lauderdale, Florida 33304-3205, U.S.
Tel: +1-954-563 0500
Fax: +1-954-564 1206
E-mail: Brofilm@aol.com
Website: www.vcn.net/filmfest
Festival director and programmer: Greg von Hausch
Competition: Best Film Award

**International Hofer Filmtage (Hof)**
Loth Str.28, D-80335 Munich, Germany
Tel: +49-89-129 7422/332003
Fax: +49-89-123 6868
Festival director and programmer: Heinz Badewitz

**Latino Film Festival of Marin (Larkspur)**
3100 Kerner Blvd, Suite G, San Rafael, CA 94901, U.S.
Tel: +1-415 459 3530
Fax: +1-415 456 0560
E-mail: sperel@linex.com
Festival director and programmer: Sylvia Perel
Competition

---

**... March 26 ...**
U.S. Senate passes Bono Bill (named after late pol), extending copyright protection to authors and songwriters by an additional 20 years.

## Golden Knight International Amateur Film and Video Festival (Valletta-Malta)

Malta Amateur Cine Circle, PO Box 450, Valletta CMR 01, Malta
Tel: +356-222345
Fax: +356-225047
Website: www.global/net.mt/amacc
Festival director: Alfred Stagno Navarra
Festival programmer: Vincent Lungaro Mifsud
Competition : Golden Knight

## International Short Film Festival (Tübingen)

Osterbergsytr. 9, Tübingen, Germany 72074
Tel: +49-7071 56960
Fax: +49-7071 56 96 96
E-mail: filmtage tuebingen@t-online.de
Festival directors and programmers: Jean-Michel Sidaine, Dieter Betz

## San Luis Obispo International Film Festival

PO Box 1449, San Luis Obispo, CA 93401, U.S.
Tel: +1-805-546 3456
Fax: +1-805-781 6799
E-mail: slofilmfest@slonet.org
Festival director: Mary A Harris
Festival programmer: Catherine Peacock
Competition: George Sydney Award ($500)

## Saint Louis International Film Festival

55 Maryland Plaza, Suite A, Saint Louis, 63108-1501 Missouri, U.S.
Tel: +1-314-454 0042
Fax: +1-314-454 0540
E-mail: info@sliff.org
Festival director: Delcia Corlew
Festival programmer: Audrey Hutti
Competition: The Mark Twain Banks' Audience Choice Award ($1,000)

## Virginia Film Festival (Charlottesville)

Drama Department, The University of Virginia, Culbreth Rd, Charlottesville, VA 22903, U.S.
Tel: +1-804-982 5277
Fax: +1-804-924 1447
E-mail: rj.h2s@virginia.edu

Festival director: Richard Herskowitz

## Peachtree International Film Festival (Atlanta)

Peachtree International Film Society, 2180 Pleasant Hill Rd, #A-5221, Duluth, Georgia, 30096, U.S.
Tel:+1-770-729 8487
Fax: +1-770-263 0652
E-mail: film@peachtreefilm.org
Festival director and programmer: Michelle Forren

## Festival du Cinéma International en Abitibi-Témiscamingue (Rouyn-Noranda)

215 Mercier Ave, Rouyn-Noranda, Québec J9X 5W8, Canada
Tel: +1-819-762 6212
Fax: +1-819-762 6762
E-mail: fciatt@sac.Telebec.qc.ca
Festival director and programmer: Jacques Matte

## Tokyo International Film Festival

4F Landic Building No. 2, Ginza, Chuo-ku, Tokyo 104, Japan
Tel: +81-3-3563 6305
Fax: +81-3-3563 6310
Festival director: Yasuyoshi Tokuma
Competition: 1.Tokyo Grand Prix – International Competition
2. Tokyo Gold Prize – Young Cinema Competition (¥20 million)

## IBTS – (10th International Audio, Video, Broadcasting, Motion Picture and Telecommunications Show)

Via Domenichino 11, 20149, Milan, Italy
Tel: +39-2 481 5541
Fax: +39-2 498 0330
E-mail: mc1703@mclink.it

## VIPER – International Film, Video, and Multimedia Festival (Lucerne)

PO Box 4929, CH-6002 Lucerne, Switzerland
Tel: +41-1-450 6262
Fax: +41-1-450 6261
E-mail: viper@dial.eunet.ch
Festival director: Conny E Voester
Festival programmers: Conny E. Voester, A. Ensini

Competition: Film Award, Video Award (SF5,000 each)

# November

## Nature Film Festival Valvert (Brussels)

E Facto SA – Rue Masui 45, Brussels, Belgium 1000
Tel: +32-2 203 4363
Fax: +32-2 203 4294
Festival directors: Sebastian Lob, Marc Van Doornick
Festival programmer: Claudine Brasseur
Competition: Aigle de cristal (BFr100,000)

## Kidscreen (Milan)

Rue des Palais 112, B-1030 Brussels, Belgium
Tel: +32-2-242 5409
Fax: +32-2-242 7427
Market director: Felix van Ginderhuysen
Market

## British Film Festival (Cherbourg)

8 Passage Digard, F-50100 Cherbourg, France
Tel: +33-233 93 38 94
Fax: +33-233 01 20 78
Festival director: Jean-Charles Saint
Festival programmer: Jean-François Cornu
Competition: Audience Award (FFr20,000)

## News World International Forum for Broadcast News (Barcelona)

39 St. James's St, London SW1A 1JD
Tel: +44-171 491 0880
Fax: +44-171 491 0990
Managing director: Kerry Innes

## Film Arts Festival (San Francisco)

346 Ninth St, 2nd Floor, San Francisco, CA 94103, U.S.
Tel: +1-415-552 8760
Fax: +1-415-552 0882
Festival director: Mark Taylor

## Northampton Film Festival

351 Pleasant St. Suite 137, Northampton, MA 01060, U.S.

---

**... March 27 ...**
Following Oscar wave, **Titanic** sails past $500 million B.O. in North America.

Tel: +1-413 586 3471
Fax: +1-413 584 4432
E-mail: filmfest@nohofilm.org
Festival directors and programmers:
Howard Polonsky, Dee DeGeiso
Competition: Northern Arts
Entertainment Best of Fest Award
($500)

### The Ohio Independent Film Festival

2258 West 10th St, Cleveland, Ohio
44113, U.S.
Tel: +1-216 781 1755
E-mail: OhioIndieFilmFest@
juno.com
Festival directors and
programmers: Bernadette Gillota,
Annetta Marion

### Ljubljana International Film Festival

Presernova 10, 1000 Ljubljana,
Slovenia
Tel: +386-61-176 7150
Fax:+386-61-22 42 79
Festival director: Jelka Stergel
Kingfisher Prize

### London Film Festival

National Film Theatre, South Bank,
Waterloo, London SE1 8XT, U.K.
Tel: +44-171-815 1323
Fax: +44-171-633 0786
Festival co-directors: Adrian
Wootton and Mark Adams
Festival programmer: Sandra
Hebron

### Nordic Film Days (Lübeck)

Senat der Hansestadt Lübeck,
Schleswig-Holstein, Germany,
D-23539
Tel: +49-451 122 4102
Fax: +49-451 122 4106
Festival director: Andrea
Kunsemüller
Competition: NDR Promotion Prize
(DM25,000)

### Northwest Film and Video Festival (Portland)

1219 SW Park Ave, Portland,
Oregon 97205, U.S.
Tel: +1-503-221-1156
Fax: +1-503-294 0874
E-mail: info@nwfilm.org
Festival director: Meagan Atiyeh
Competition: Best of Festival

($12,000 in production service
awards)

### Amiens International Film Festival

MCA, Place Léon Gontier, F-80000
Amiens, France
Tel: +33-322 71 35 70
Fax: +33-322 92 53 04
E-mail: amiensfilmfestival@
burotec.fr
Festival director and programmer:
Jean-Pierre Garcia
Competition: The Golden Unicorn
(FFr50,000)

### Banff Mountain Film Festival

PO Box 1020, Stn. 38, Banff, Alberta
T0L 0C0, Canada
Tel: +1-403-762 6125
Fax: +1-403-762 6277
E-mail: cmc@banffcentre.ab.ca
Website: www.banffcentre.ab.ca
Festival director and programmer:
Bernadette McDonald
Market and Competition: Grand
Prize (C$12,500)

### Children's Film Festival (Augsburg)

Schroeckstr. 6, D-86152 Augsburg,
Germany
Tel: +49-821 349 1060
Fax: +49-821 349 5218
Festival director and programmer:
Ellen Gratza

### Hawaii International Film Festival (Honolulu and Neighboring Islands)

1001 Bishop St, Pacific Tower, Suite
745, Honolulu, Hawaii 96813, U.S.
Tel: +1-808-528 3456
Fax: +1-808-528 1410
E-mail: hiffinfo@hiff.org
Festival director: Christian Gaines
Festival programmer: Jeannette
Paulson
Competition: Golden Maile Award

### Margaret Mead Film and Video Festival (New York)

American Museum of Natural
History, 79th St at Central Park
West, New York, 10024 NY, U.S.
Tel: +1-212-769 5305
Fax: +1-212-769 5329
E-mail: meadfest@amnh.org
Festival director: Elaine Charnov

### Stockholm International Film Festival

PO Box 3136, Stockholm, 10362
Sweden
Tel: +46-8-677 5000
Fax: +46-8-200590
E-mail: filmfestivalen@cinema.se
internet:
http://www.filmfestivalen.se
Festival director: Git Scheynius
Festival programmer: Jacob
Abrahamson
Competition: The Bronze Horse

### Start Moving Image Festival (Plymouth)

51 Amherst Rd, Plymouth PL3 4HJ,
U.K.
Tel: +44-1752 265 562
Fax: +44-1752 265 562
E-mail: start@sundog.zynet.co.uk
Festival director: Stuart More
Festival programmer: Kayla Parker

### 3rd International Independent Film Festival of Ourense

Apartado 664, Ourense, Spain 32080
Tel: +34-988 224 127
Fax: +34-988 249 561
E-mail: turiour@fegamp.es
Festival director: Eloy Lozano
Festival programmer: Jorge Maroto
Competition: Calpurnia Prize
(Pta1,500,000)

### XX Rassegna Citta di Palermo/International Sport Film Festival

Via Notarbartolo 1/G, 90141
Palermo, Italia
Tel: +39-91 611 4968
Fax: +39-91 611 4968
Festival director: Vito Maggio
Competition: Paladino d'Oro (L5
million)

### Duisburger Filmwoche (Duisburg)

Am König-Heinrich-Platz, D-47049
Duisburg, Germany
Tel: +49-203 283 4171
Fax: +49-203 283 4130
Festival director: Werner Ruzicka
Competition: German-speaking
documentaries only
German Film Critics Prize
(DM10,000)

---

**... March 28 ...**
Maverick producers Andy Vajna and Mario Kassar have pushed their desks together once
again – **Rambo 4** and **Terminator 3** are high on their agenda.

## London Programme Market
23-24 George St, Richmond, Surrey
TW9 1HY, U.K.
Tel: +44-181-948 5522
Fax: +44-181-332 0495
Market director: Jonathan
Bainbridge

## Cinanima – International Animated Film Festival (Espinho)
Apartado 43, 4501 Espinho Codex,
Portugal
Tel: +351-2-734 4611
Fax: +351-2-734 6015
Festival director: Antonio Gaio
Festival programmer: Organizing
Committee Cinanima
Competition: Grand Prize (Esc500)

## Cottbus 8th Festival of Young East European Cinema
Bautzner Straße 91, D-03050
Cottbus, Germany
Tel: +49-355 431070
Fax: +49-355 4310 720
Artistic director: Roland Rust
Competition

## Ökomedia-International Ecology Film Festival (Freiburg)
Ökomedia Institut, Habsburger Str.
9a, 79104 Freiburg, Germany
Tel: +49-761 52024
Fax: +49-761 555 724
Festival director: Werner Kobe
Competition

## Verzaubert, Gay and Lesbian Film Festival (Munich, Cologne, Frankfurt, Stuttgart, Berlin)
Rosebud Entertainment, Herzog
Wilhelm str 27, 80331 Munich,
Germany
Tel: +49-89 260 22 838
Fax: +49-89 260 22 839
E-mail: rosebud-entertainment@t-online.de
Festival directors and programmers:
Schorsch Müller, Rainer Stefan

## Mar del Plata International Film Festival
Lima 219, Piso 10, 1073 Buenos
Aires, Argentina
Tel: +54-1-383 0028 ext. 130
Fax: +54-1-379 0986
E-mail: incaa@microstar.com.ar
Festival director: Sabina Sigler
Festival programmer: Nicolas Sarquis
Market and competition: Golden
Ombú ($625,000)

## Brynmawr Film Festival
Blaenau Gwent Arts Development
Office, Beaufort Theatre, Beaufort,
Ebbw Vale, Gwent NP3 5QQ, South
Wales, U.K.
Tel: +44-1495 308996
Fax: +44-1495 308996
Festival director and programmer:
Geoff Cripps

## European Short Film Festival (London)
11 Holbein House, Holbein Place,
London, SW1 W8NH, U.K.
Tel: +44-171 460 3901
Fax: +44-171 259 9278
Contact: Fritz Kohle

## Festival de Cine de Alcala de Henares
Plaza del Empecinado 1, Alcala de
Henares 28801, Spain
Tel: +34-91-881 3934
Fax: +34-91-881 3906
Festival director: Pedro Medina
Competition
Primer premio nacional
(Pta800,000)

## Festival dei Popoli International Review of Social Documentary Film (Florence)
Borgo Pinti 82R, I-Firenze 50121,
Italy
Tel: +39-55 244 778
Fax: +39-55 241 364
E-mail: fespopol@dada it
Festival director: Mario Simondi
Competition: Award for best
Documentary Film

## International Festival of Authorial Film (Belgrade)
Jugoslavija film, Makedonska 22/VI,
11000 Beograd, Yugoslavia
Tel: +381-11 324 8554/324 8282
Fax: +381-11 324 8659
Festival director: Vojislav Vucinovic
Competition
Aleksandar Petrovic Award

## International Thessaloniki Film Festival
Paparigopoulou 40, 11473 Athens,
Greece
Tel: +30-1 645 3668/644 8194
Fax: +30-1 644 8143
E-mail: info@filmfestival.gr
Festival director and programmer:
Michel Demopoulos
Competition: Golden Alexander
(Dr12,500,000)

## Oslo International Film Festival
Ebbellsgate 1, N-0183 Oslo, Norway
Tel: +47-22 20 07 66
Fax: +47-22 20 18 03
E-mail: filmfestival@login.eunet.no
Website: http://wit.no/filmfestival
Festival director and programmer:
Tommy Lørdahl

## Welsh International Film Festival (Cardiff)
6G Park Gwyddoniaeth, Cefn Llan,
Aberystwyth SY23 3AH, Wales, U.K.
Tel: +44-1222 490 034
Fax: +44-1222 485 728
Festival director: Grant Vidgen
Competition: DM Davies Award (£25)

## Worldfest – Flagstaff
PO Box 56568, Houston, TX, U.S.
Tel: +1-713 965 9955
Fax: +1-713 965 9960
E-mail: worldfest@aol.com
Website: vannevar.com/worldfest
Festival director: J Hunter Todd
Festival programmer: Maribel
Amador
Market and Competition: Golden
Palm

## Encontros Internacionais de Cinema Documental (Odivelas)
Rua Angola, Olival Basto, 2675
Odivelas, Portugal
Tel: +351-1 938 8407
Fax: +351-1 938 9347
E-mail: amascultura@mail.telepc.pl
Festival director and programmer:
Manuel Costa e Silva
Competition: Grand Prix for the
best documentary feature

## Oulu International Children's Film Festival
Torikatu 8, 90100 Oulu, Finland

---

Tel: +358-8 881 1293
Fax: +358-8 881 1290
E-mail: raimo.kinisjarvi@
oufilmcenter.inet.fi
Festival director: Pentti Kejonen
Festival programmer: Eszter Vuojala
Competition: Star Boy Award
(Ecu3,000)

**Action and Adventure Film Festival (Antwerp)**
1104 Kortrijksesteenweg, Ghent,
Belgium, B-9051
Tel: +32-9-221 8946
Fax: +32-9-221 9074
E-mail: filmfestival@infoboard.be
website: www.rug.ac.be/filmfestival
/Welcome.html
Contacts: Jacques Dubrulle, Walter
Provo, Peter Bouckaert, Marian
Ponnet

**Southern African International Film and Television Market (Cape Town)**
PO Box 1176, Oakland Park,
Johannesburg, 2006, South Africa
Tel: +27-11 714 3229
Fax: +27-11 714 3275
Contact: Kim Dearham

**Birmingham International Film and TV Festival**
9 Margaret St, Birmingham B3 3SB,
U.K.
Tel: +44-121 212 0777
Fax: +44-121 212 0666
Festival director: Sarah McKenzie
Festival programmer: Barbara
Chapman
Competition for local filmmakers

**Holland Animation Film Festival (biennial)**
Hoogt 4, 3521 GW Utrecht, The
Netherlands
Tel: +31-30 233 1733
Fax: +31-30 233 1079
E-mail: haff@knoware.nl
Website: www.awn.com/haff
Festival director: Gerben Schermer
Festival programmer: Metter Peters
and Erik van Drunan
Competition

**Brief Encounters (Short Film Festival) (Bristol)**
PO Box 576, Bristol BS99 2BD, U.K.

Tel: +44-117 922 4628
Fax: +44-117 922 2906
E-mail: brief.encounters@
dial.pipex.com
Contact: Louise Jannings
Competition

**Cine Golden Eagle Film and Video Competition (Washington DC)**
1001 Connecticut Ave NW, Suite
638, Washington, DC 20036, U.S.
Tel: +1-202-785 1136
Fax: +1-202-785 4114
Cine Golden Eagle Award (prof)
and Cine Eagle (amateur)

**Mavericks in Manchester, Festival of American Independent Film (Manchester)**
70 Oxford St, Manchester, MI 5NH
Tel: +44-161 228 7621
Fax: +44-161 200 1506
Festival programmer: Linda Pariser

**SMPTE**
Tel: +1 914 761 1100
Fax: +1 914 761 3115

**EuropaCinema (Viareggio)**
Via 20 Settembre 3, 00187 Rome, Italy
Tel: +39-6 420 111 84/42 000 211
Fax: +39-6 4201 0599
Festival director: Monique Veaute
Competition

**French Film Festival (Edinburgh/Glasgow)**
French Institute, 13 Randolph
Crescent, Edinburgh, EH3 8TX, U.K.
Tel: +44-131 225 6191
Fax: +44-131 220 0648
Festival director and programmer:
Richard Mowe
Hennessy Audience Award (non-
monetary)

**Gijon International Film Festival for Young People**
Po. Begoña No 24 entlo, 33205
Gijon, Spain
Tel: +34-98-534 3739
Fax: +34-98-535 4152
E-mail: festcine@airastuz.es
Festival director and programmer:
Jose Luis Cienfuegos
Competition: Principado de
Asturias

**Turin International Film Festival**
Via Monte di Pietá 1, Torino, Italy,
10121
Tel: +39-11-562 3309
Fax: +39-11-562 9796
E-mail: ficg@webcom.com
Festival director and programmer:
Stefano Della Casa
Competition: Best Film ($20,000)

**IberoAmerican Film Festival (Huelva)**
Casa Colon, Plaza del Punto, 21003
Huelva, Spain
Tel: +34-959 21 0170
Fax: +34-959 210173
Festival director and programmer:
Jon Apaolaza
Competition: Colon de oro (Pta3
million)

**Tranny Fest (San Francisco)**
584 Castro St, Suite 273, San
Francisco, CA 94114, U.S.
Tel/fax: +1-415 552 4249
E-mail: trannyfest@aol. com
Festival directors: Christopher Lee
and Alison Austin

**Junior Dublin Film Festival**
c/o Irish Film Centre, Eustache St,
Dublin 2, Ireland
Tel: +353-1 671 4095
Fax: +353 1 677 8755
Festival director and programmer:
Alan Robinson

**International Festival of Documentary and Short Films (Bilbao)**
C/Colón de Larreategui, nº 37-4º
drch, 48009 Bilbao, Spain
Tel: +34-94 424 8698/424 5507
Fax: +34-94 424 5624
Festival director: Jaseba Inchaurraga
Festival programmer: Maria Angeles
Olea
Competition: Grand Premio
(Pta400,000)

**Festival des Trois Continents (Nantes)**
19a Passage Pommeraye, BP 43302,
F-44033, Nantes Cedex 1, France
Tel: +33-240 69 74 14
Fax: +33-240 73 55 22
Festival directors and
programmers: Alain Jalladeau,

---

**...March 30...**

MTV to launch four new primetime music shows Aug. 6, giving the channel its first
consistent schedule in the 8-10p.m. block and marking a shift in strategy.

Philippe Jalladeau
Competition (only for feature films): Montgolfiere d'Or (FFr30,000)

## International Biennale Film+Arc Graz

Hallerschloszstrasse 21, 8010 Graz, Austria
Tel: +43-316-35 6155
Fax: +43-316-356156
Festival director and programmer: Charlotte Pöchhacker
Competition: Grand Prix film+arc.graz (ASch100,000)

## Cairo International Film Festival

17th Kasr El Nil St, Cairo, 202 Egypt
Tel: +202-392 3562
Fax: +202-393 8979
Festival director: Saad Eldin Wahba
Competition: Golden Pyramid

## International Documentary Film Festival Amsterdam (IDFA)

Kleine Gartmanplantsoen 10, 017 RR Amsterdam
Tel: +31-20 627 3329
Fax: +31-20 638 5388
E-mail: idfa@xs4all.nl
Festival director and programmer: Ally Derks
Competition: UPRO Joris Juens Award (Fl25,000)

## Mediterranean Film Festival (Tübingen)

Osterbergstr. 9, Tübingen, Germany, 72074
Tel: +49-7071 56960
Fax: +49-7071 56 96 96
E-mail: filmtage.
tuebingen@t-online.de
Festival director: Dieter Betz

## Canadian International Annual Film/Video Festival (Campbell River, British Columbia)

25 Eugenia St, Barrie, Ontario L4M 1P6, Canada
Tel: +1-705 737 2729
Fax: +1-705 733 8232
E-mail: ciaff@canada.com
Festival director: Ben VW Andrews
Festival programmer: Kevin Harrison

Competition: Best Amateur, Best Student, Best Independent

## Camerimage (Torun)

Rynek Nowomiejski 28, 87-100 Torun, Poland
Tel: +48-56-6522179
Fax: +48-56-27595
Festival director: Marek Zydowicz
Festival programmers: Maciej Kruzewski, Marek Zydowicz
Competition: The Golden Frog Award

## Taipei Golden Horse Film Festival

Floor 7, No 45, Chilin Rd, Taipei, 104 Taiwan ROC
Tel: +886-22 567 5861/523 2195
Fax: +886-22 531 8966/521 6311
E-mail: tghff@email.gen.net.tw
Festival director: You-Ning Lee
Festival programmer: Johnny Yang

## Festival Tous Courts

Cité du Livre – 8-10 rue des Allumettes, 13090 Aix en Provence, France
Tel: +33-4 42 27 08 64
Fax: +33-4 42 38 47 83
E-mail: aixfilms@club-internet.fr
Festival president: Sir Marc Ripoll
Competition for short films

## The Forum (Amsterdam)

Kleine-Gartmanplantsoen 10, 1017 RR Amsterdam, The Netherlands
Tel: +31-20-627 3329
Fax: +31-20-638 5388
E-mail: idfa@xs4all.nl
Market director: Jolanda Klarenbeek Market

## Festival of French Cinema (Acapulco)

Unifrance, 4 Villa Bosquet, 75007 Paris, France
Tel: +33-1 47 53 95 80/47 53 27 48
Fax: +33-1 47 05 96 55
Contact: Stephan Melchiori

## Festival Primer Plano (Dijon)

4 Place Darcy BP 1002, F-21024 Dijon Cedex, France
Tel: +33-3-80 30 59 78
Fax: +33-3-80 50 18 08
Festival director: Laurence Karoibi
Competition

## Foyle Film Weekend (Derry)

2nd Floor, Northern Counties Building, 8 Custom House St, Derry, U.K.
Tel: +44-1504 267 432
Fax: +44-1504 371 738
E-mail:shona@iscm.ulst.ac.uk.
Festival director and programmer: Shona McCarthy
Competition (£1,000)

## International French Film Festival (Tübingen)

Frierichstrasse 11, D-72074 Tübingen, Germany
Tel: +49-70 71 56960
Fax: +49-70 71 59 96 96
E-mail: filmtage.tuebingen@t-online.de
Festival directors and programmers: Dieter Betz, Stefanie Schneider
Competition: Flying Camera (DM10,000)

## Cinewomen (Norwich)

Cinema City, St. Andrews St, Norwich, Norfolk, NR2 4AD, U.K.
Tel: +44-1603 622 047
Fax: +44-1603 767 838

## Cinemania (Sofia)

1 Bulgaria Square, National Palace of Culture, 1414 Sofia, Bulgaria
Tel: +359-2 54 3061/9166 2841
Fax: +359-2 65 7053
Festival director: Christo Droumev

## International Film Festival Bratislava

Mosovkeho 16, 81103 Bratislava, Slovakia
Tel: +421-7 5441 0673
Fax: +421-7 5441 0674
Festival programmer: Peter Nagel
Competition first and second films
Entry deadline for films: 31 September 1999

# December

## International Festival of New Latin American Cinema (Havana)

Calle 23, No 1155, Vedado, Havana 10600, Cuba
Tel: +53-7 552 841/552 849
Fax: +53-7 333 078/334 273
Festival president: Alfredo Guevara

---

**...March 31...**
Columbia and TriStar units retain names but are folded into the single Sony Pictures umbrella.

Festival director: Iván Giroud
Competition and Market: Coral
Prizes

**Black Nights Film Festival (Tallinn, Tarta)**
Nafta St 1, Tallinn, Estonia, 10152
Tel: +372-2 425 939
Fax: +372-6 431 351
E-mail: filmimax@pb.eepinet.ee
Festival director: Jaak Kilmi
Festival programmer: Tlina Rokk

**Forum Festival (Bratislava)**
Groesslingova 32, 81109 Bratislava,
Slovakia
Tel: +421 7 531 0673
Fax: +421-7 532 0647
Festival director: tbc
Competition for first feature film
Main prize (3000m of negative film
stock)

**Cinemagic International Film Festival for Young People (Belfast)**
4th Floor, 38 Dublin Rd, Belfast BT2
7HN, Northern Ireland, U.K.
Tel: +44-1232-311 900
Fax: +44-1232-319 709
Festival director: Shauna McCarthy
Festival programmer: Frances
Cassidy
Competition: Cinemagic Young Jury
Award (£1,000)

**Israel Film Festival (Los Angeles, New York)**
6404 Wilshire Blvd, #1240, Los
Angeles, CA 90048, U.S.
Tel: +1-213 966 4166
Fax: +1-213 658 6346
Festival director: Meir Fenigstein
Competition: Audience Award

**Noir In Festival (Courmayer, Italy)**
Via Tirso 90, I-Rome 00198, Italy
Tel: +39-6 884 8030
Fax: +39-6 884 0450
Festival director: Giorgio Gosetti
Festival programmer: Maria Teresa
Cavina
Competition: Mystery Award

**European Film Academy Awards**
Segitzdam 2, D-10969 Berlin,
Germany
Tel: +49-30 615 3091
Fax: +49-30 614 3131
Chairman of the European Film
Academy: Nik Powell

**Cine Asia (Hong Kong)**
244 West 49th St #200, New York
10019, U.S.
Tel: +1-212-246 6460
Fax: +1-212-265 6428
E-mail: sunshine@maestro.com
CineAsia Conference and
Exhibition Secretariat Pte. Ltd,
103 Sophia Rd, Singapore 228168
Tel: 65-337 3476
Fax: 65-337 0694
E-mail: ces83@singnet.com.sg
Contact: Jimmy Sunshine

**MIP-ASIA (Hong Kong)**
Reed Midem Organisation, 11 rue
du Colonel Pierre Avia, F-75015,
Paris, France
Tel: +33-1-41 90 45 80
Fax: +33-1-41 90 45 70
Program director: André Vaillant
Market

**Rencontres d'Annecy du Cinema Italien**
Bonlieu Scene Nationale, 1 rue Jean
Jaures, BP 294, Annecy 74007,
France
Tel: +33-450 33 44 00
Fax: +33-450 51 82 09
Festival director: Salvador Garcia
Festival programmer: Pierre
Todeschini
Competition: Grand Prix des
Rencontres

**Echo Television and Radio Awards (Vienna)**
Echo Awards Secretariat, 26-34
Emerald St, London WC1N 3QA,
U.K.
Tel: +44-171 253 0880
Fax: +44-171 312 0039
E-mail: medianatura@gn.apc.org
Festival director: Mandy Duncan-
Smith
Entry information: Lydia Cerbelle

**MECLA (Havana)**
Calle 23, No. 1155, Vedado, La
Habana 10600, Cuba
Tel: +53-7 333 862/304 666
Fax: +53-7 333 3032
MECLA director: Francisco Leon
Market

**TV Festival: The Chicago International TV Competition (Chicago)**
32 West Randolph St, Suite 600,
Chicago, Illinois 60601, U.S.
Tel: +1-312 425 9400
Fax: +1-312 425 0944
E-mail: filmfest@suba.com
Festival director: Michael Kutza
The Gold Hugo Statue

---

> *When* Dr No *went to Japan,
> they translated it as* No Need
> for Any Doctors. (*Sean
> Connery*)

---

# Film Reviews

Year in, year out, *Variety*'s film reviews are among the most eagerly scanned and saved items in the paper. They have become longer and more searching during the 1990s, as the significance attached to a notice in *Variety* has increased within the industry. Often *Variety* is one of the very first publications to review a picture, and this carries with it an unenviable responsibility. A bad review, appearing two days prior to opening, can influence the box office in the U.S. and, for a foreign-language film, materially affect its sales potential. An Italian producer once assailed us in the streets of Cannes, claiming that *Variety*'s savage critique of his new film that week had resulted in a call from the U.S. distributor reducing its offer by $750,000! Conversely, a favourable notice may provoke a rash of phone calls and faxes to the happy producer in Finland or New Zealand – sometimes enquiring about remake rights even before seeing the film.

The following is an alphabetical list of more than half the reviews published in the paper in 1998. Each of these films had either a wide release, or in some way traveled beyond their national borders (to leading festivals, for example). We have abridged them for space purposes, added where relevant some box-office information, and refer readers to our website for access to the full version.

*N.B. All numbers are through Dec. 31, 1998. All films are 1998 release unless otherwise indicated. Domestic release refers to pictures that debuted in the U.S., Canada and Puerto Rico.*

## The Acid House (U.K.)

A Picture Palace North/Umbrella Prods. production, with the participation of Channel Four. Produced by David Muir, Alex Usborne. Directed by Paul McGuigan. Screenplay, Irvine Welsh, based on his collection of short stories. Camera, Alasdair Walker; editor, Andrew Hulme; music, Primal Scream, Nick Cave, Barry Adamson, Beth Orton, Marc Bolan, Oasis, The Verve; production designers, Richard Bridgland, Mike Gunn; costumes, Pam Tait, Lynn Aitken. Reviewed at Cannes Festival, May 17. Running time: 118 mins.
**Stephen McCole (Boab), Maurice Roeves (God), Jenny McCrindle (Evelyn), Kevin McKidd (Johnny), Michelle Gomez (Catriona), Gary McCormack (Larry), Ewen Bremner (Coco), Martin Clunes (Rory), Jemma Redgrave (Jenny), Arlene Cockburn (Kirsty).**

*The Acid House* makes *Trainspotting* look like a mild-mannered youth comedy. For better or worse, pic is 100% uncut Irvine Welsh, author of *Trainspotting*. A grim portrait of life in inner-city Edinburgh, the striking film's unrelenting brutality will make it a tough slog for mainstream auds. Stateside chances are further complicated by the heavy Scottish accents. Based on three Welsh stories, these ultra-gritty tales put the spotlight on beer-swilling, drug-taking, lumpen proles. There are obvious thematic connections between the three stories but, with its disorienting jumps between sections, *The Acid House* suffers from the usual problems associated with multipart pics. Final seg, however, is an inspired comic fantasy. Coco desperately fears committing to his relationship with Kirsty and, in a wild but effective leap of narrative logic, changes personalities with close friend's unborn child.

## The Adventures Of Sebastian Cole

A Paramount Classics release of a Culpan Prods production. Produced by Karen Barber, Jasmine Kosovic. Directed, written by Tod Williams. Camera, John Foster; editor, Affonso Goncalves; music supervisor, Amanda Demme; costume designer, Eric Daman. Reviewed at Toronto Festival, Sept. 16. Running time: 104 mins.
**Adrian Grenier (Sebastian), Clark Gregg (Hank/Henrietta), Aleska Palladino (Mary), Margaret Colin (Joan), John Shea (Hartley), Marni Lustig (Jessica).**

*The Adventures of Sebastian Cole* simply isn't special enough to cut it in the theatrical marketplace, and probably won't fare markedly better in video and cable venues. Writer-director Tod Williams' debut feature is yet another tale of a troubled teen who dabbles in sex, drugs, and dangerous pranks during his final months of high school. Sebastian is first seen as a bloody mess after surviving an auto crackup, and the narrative begins with him flashing back to events of the past year. Dysfunctional is too mild a term for his extended family. His parents are divorced, his mother Joan remarried. Mom is just a few shots shy of full-fledged alcoholism. And his stepfather, Hank, announces that he wants to be known as Henrietta, because he's decided to have a sex change. The revelation sends Joan packing back to England, her son in tow. But after a few months, Sebastian returns and moves in with Henrietta, who has taken to wearing women's clothing and makeup while preparing for a future as a transsexual.

### Africa's Elephant Kingdom (Docu)

An Imax Corp. presentation of a Discovery Channel Pictures production. Produced by Michael Caulfield. Directed, written by Caulfield. Camera (Imax), Tim Cowan; editor, Cathleen Korth; music, Roger Mason; scientific consultant, Dr. Iain Douglas-Hamilton. Reviewed at California Science Center, April 26. Running time: 40 mins.
**Narrator: Avery Brooks.**
*Africa's Elephant Kingdom* marks an apt union of the world's largest land mammals and the world's largest screen. Juxtaposing expansive panoramas of African landscapes with astonishingly intimate lensing of an elephant clan, docu is both informative and visually stunning. The first oversize screen effort from Discovery Channel Pictures, pic makes excellent use of Imax format and ought to be a popular family item on that circuit. Beginning with sweeping aerial shots of Mount Kilimanjaro and assorted Kenyan vistas, docu draws viewers into its sumptuous landscape, where colors are so bold and saturated as to seem almost surreal. Over the next 40 minutes, the elephant "Old Bull" (voiced by actor Avery Brooks) recounts a journey replete with revelations about his species.

U.S. release: Apr. 3      U.S. B.O.: $3.8 million
Int'l release: May 1      Int'l B.O.: $2.6 million

### After Life (Japan)

A TV Man Union/Engine Film production. Produced by Shiho Sato, Masayuki Akieda. Directed, written by Hirokazu Kore-eda. Camera, Yutaka Yamazaki; editor, Kore-eda; music, Yasuhiro Kasamatsu; art directors, Toshihiro Isomi, Hideo Gunji. Reviewed at Toronto Festival, Sept. 11. Running time: 118 mins.
**Arata (Mochizuki), Erika Oda (Shiori), Susumu Terajima, Hisako Hara, Taketoshi Naito (Watanabe).**
Following his impressive debut with *Maborosi*, Nipponese helmer Hirokazu Kore-eda jumps to the head of the queue as a major talent with *After Life*, a slyly humorous, utterly original, and generous-hearted tribute to the power of basic human attributes of memory, love, and forgiveness. A sleeper hit at Toronto, it looks certain to gather further attention worldwide as it rolls out to other fests. Pic will require dedicated handling to work commercially, but critical support is unlikely to be wanting. The movie opens with a small group of people clocking in at a gray, somewhat shabby, school-like complex. Their supervisor tells them, this week, there will be 22 people arriving. The newcomers, of all ages and social backgrounds, register at a front desk and go on to interviews. Only then, in a casual aside by a pollster, do we realize that everyone is dead – and that the building is a transit station between life and eternity. The newcomers are told they have only a few days to select a special memory. It will be reconstructed, filmed, screened for their approval, and given to them to carry into their afterlife. All other memories will be erased.

### Air Bud: Golden Receiver (Canada)

A Miramax Films release of a Keystone Pictures presentation, in association with Dimension Films. Produced by Robert Vince. Directed by Richard Martin. Screenplay, Paul Tamasy, Aaron Mendelsohn, based on the character Air Bud created by Kevin DiCicco. Camera, Mike Southon; editors, Bruce Lange, Melinda Seabrook; music, Brahm Wenger; production design, Rex Raglan; costume design, Patricia Hargreaves; dog trainer, Coe's Talent. Reviewed at Aidikoff Screening Room, Beverly Hills, Aug. 6. MPAA Rating: G. Running time: 90 mins.
**Kevin Zegers (Josh Framm), Cynthia Stevenson (Jackie Framm), Gregory Harrison (Dr. Patrick Sullivan), Nora Dunn (Natalya), Perry Anzilotti (Popov), Robert Costanzo (Coach Fanelli), Alyson MacLaren (Andrea Framm).**
As sequels go, *Air Bud: Golden Receiver* is barking up the wrong tree. The continuing saga of a canine with uncanny athletic ability and a boy with growing pains has evolved into a by-the-numbers, wholesome family comedy. There are smart dog tricks, stupid human antics and important moral lessons in the mix. But the humanity of the original has been excised, making the new chapter far too predictable and pedestrian. The film's commercial pedigree promises OK theatrical returns and slightly better results in video sales. New yarn picks up post-basketball season with Josh Framm trying to come to terms with the return of his widowed mother, Jackie, to the dating circuit. It becomes a big problem when things get serious between her and the town's new vet, Patrick Sullivan. Josh simply won't warm to the doc. Meanwhile, golden retriever, Buddy, adapts to football and Josh discovers he has a pretty good throwing arm. Perennially losing coach Fanelli puts the lad on the junior high squad as backup quarterback.

U.S. release: Aug. 14      U.S. B.O.: $10.5 million

### Alice and Martin (Alice et Martin) (France-Spain)

A Les Films Alain Sarde, France 2 Cinema, France 3 Cinema (France)/Vertigo Films (Spain) production, with the participation of Canal Plus, Television Espanola. Produced by Alain Sarde. Directed by Andre Techine. Screenplay, Techine, Gilles Taurand, Olivier Assayas. Camera, Caroline Champetier; editor, Martine Giordano; music, Philippe Sarde; production design, Ze Branco; costume design, Elizabeth Tavernier. Reviewed at Valladolid Festival, Spain, Oct. 23. Running time: 130 mins.
**Juliette Binoche (Alice), Alexis Loret (Martin), Carmen Maura (Jeanine), Mathieu Amalric (Benjamin), Pierre Maguelon (Victor),**
With *Alice and Martin*, an involving love story between two emotionally damaged outsiders, vet auteur Andre Techine returns to the haunting, emotionally intense terrain of such previous pics as 1994's award-winning *Wild Reeds*, though with harder-edged results. Typically daring in its unflinching exploration of psychological extremes, the film also sidesteps any implicit sensationalism. The presence of Juliette Binoche and, briefly, Spanish thesp Carmen Maura, guarantees decent B.O. in France and Spain, while Techine's reputation should lead to arthouse exposure in selected territories.

Early scenes show the young Martin living with his hairdresser mom, Jeanine, and her taxi-driver lover. Jeanine insists that Martin meet his father, Victor, but the boy instinctively senses it will end in trouble. When he goes to live with Victor, his instincts are quickly proved right – his father is a tyrant. In a neat cut, Martin is shown running away from the same house, initially as a boy and then mysteriously, 10 years later, as an adult. After wandering across pastoral landscapes and trying unsuccessfully to drown himself, Martin heads for the Paris house of his half-brother Benjamin, a gay wannabe actor living in garret squalor with violinist Alice who's nervous

**...April 3 ...**
20th Century Fox enters into an agreement with George Lucas to distribute the next three **Star Wars** prequels.

and on edge. Incapable of expressing emotion, Martin stalks Alice for a while before she succumbs to his animal charms.

Int'l release: Oct. 30                    Int'l B.O.: $2 million

### All For One (Chacun Pour Soi) (France-Belgium)

A Quo Vadis Cinema, La Boîte Prods., CRRAV, La Sept Cinema, RTBF, SM Films production. Produced by Jerome Vidal. Directed by Bruno Bontzolakis. Screenplay, Bontzolakis, Melina Jochum. Camera, Miguel Sanchez Martin; editor, Matyas Veress; art directors, Patrick Colpaert, Thomas Peckre. Reviewed at Cannes Festival, May 21. Running time: 105 mins.
**Alexandre Carrière (Nicolas), Nicolas Ducron (Thierry), Florence Masure (Françoise), Dominique Baeyens (Annie).**

While it begins unexceptionally like those melancholy coming-of-age tales that flow like wine from French film schools, Bruno Bontzolakis' *All for One* cranks up an entirely unexpected emotional thrust that signals the director as a highly disciplined young talent. This arresting, beautifully observed account of the problematic path to adulthood may segue from festivals into very select arthouse markets.

Longtime friends Nicolas and Thierry are winding up the compulsory army stint and are faced with carving out an independent life without skills or higher education. They stall the return to their families and to certain unemployment by checking into a seaside camping ground where they strike up a friendship with Françoise and Annie. Depicting his unglamorized characters with directness and honesty, Bontzolakis steers them through a series of subtle shifts.

Int'l release: Oct. 21                    Int'l B.O.: $50,000

### All The Little Animals (U.K.)

A Recorded Pictures Co. presentation, in association with British Screen, J&M Entertainment, Isle of Man Film Commission, BBC Films, Entertainment Film Distributors. Produced, directed by Jeremy Thomas. Screenplay, Eski Thomas, based on the novel by Walker Hamilton. Camera, Mike Molloy; editor, John Victor Smith; music, Richard Hartley; production designer, Andrew Sanders; costume designer, Louise Stjernsward. Reviewed at Sunset Screening Room, L.A., May 5. Running time: 111 mins.
**John Hurt (Mr. Summers), Christian Bale (Bobby), Daniel Benzali (De Winter), James Faulkner (Mr. Whiteside).**

Vet British producer Jeremy Thomas makes a creditable directorial debut with *All the Little Animals*, an eccentric drama about an outcast teen. Boosted by a fine character turn from John Hurt, pic is modest in ambition and accomplishment, and its oddball, unclassifiable nature will make it difficult to market.

Overly melodramatic at its worst, but disarmingly offbeat at its best, this nicely mounted adaptation centers on an emotionally damaged boy's search for a place in the world. Teenager Bobby has the maturity of someone perhaps half his age, the result of a head injury as a child. His stepfather, De Winter, has only one aim: to induce Bobby to sign over ownership in the family department store. Sniffing out this nefarious scheme isn't too tough even for Bobby. So the boy hits the road, encountering Summers, an antisocial extremist, who collects and buries the remains of road kills and other critter casualties. And an unexpected bond begins to form.

### Almost Heroes

A Warner Bros. release of a Turner Pictures presentation of a Di Novi Pictures production. Produced by Denise Di Novi. Directed by Christopher Guest. Screenplay, Mark Nutter, Tom Wolfe, Boyd Hale. Camera, Adam Kimmel, Kenneth MacMillan; editor, Ronald Roose; music, Jeffery CJ Vanston; production designer, Joseph Garrity; costume designer, Durinda Wood. Reviewed at Cinemark Tinseltown 290, Houston, May 29. MPAA Rating: PG-13. Running time: 90 mins.
**Chris Farley (Bartholomew Hunt), Matthew Perry (Leslie Edwards), Eugene Levy (Guy Fontenot), Kevin Dunn (Hidalgo), Lisa Barbuscia (Shaquinna), Bokeem Woodbine (Jonah).**

Neither a pleasant surprise nor a total disaster, *Almost Heroes* is a fitfully funny period comedy that will be remembered as the final screen effort of Chris Farley. As such, pic may generate interest among long-time fans and the morbidly curious. But this long-delayed Warners release isn't likely to attract a wide audience until it reaches home video. Pic plays like an old-fashioned road-movie comedy spiked with broadly played slapstick and bits of Monty Pythonesque zaniness. Farley is Bartholomew Hunt, a hard-drinking and robustly rude tracker who joins an 1804 mission to blaze a trail to the Pacific Northwest.

U.S. release: May 29                    U.S. B.O.: $6.1 million

### Amazing Women by the Sea (Ihanat Naiset Rannalla) (Finland)

A Kinoproduction production, in association with FilmLance Int'l (Sweden) and Pandora Film (Germany). Produced, directed by Claes Olsson. Screenplay, Tove Idstrom, based on the novel by Monika Fagerholm. Camera, Pertti Mutanen; editor, Lena Paersch; music, Yari; production design, Minna Santakari; costume design, Karin Sundvall, Elina Kolehmainen. Reviewed at Haugesund Festival, Norway, Aug. 28. Running time: 104 mins.
**Marika Krook (Bella), Asa Karlin (Rosa), Nicke Lignell (Gabbe), Onni Thulesius (Thomas), Outi Paasivirta (Renee), Micke Rejstrom (Kajus).**

Based on a bestselling novel, *Amazing Women by the Sea* is a highly stylized, often entertaining look at summer life in Finland's archipelago during the 1960s. Combination of colorful locations and offbeat story and characters should help this local B.O. success swim offshore. Set in Paradise, a favored vacation spot for Helsinki's monied class, the film depicts the events of three consecutive summers and is centered on two families, especially the wives. One is Rosa, who, with husband Kajus and son Thomas, is a regular in Paradise. The other is the voluptuous Bella, who arrives one summer with her womanizing, U.S.-crazed husband, Gabbe, and their daughter, Renee. Despite their major differences, the two families start to socialize, and Rosa and Bella become friends. They remain friends even after Rosa has started an affair with Gabbe. Events during the third summer lead to the two women disappearing on a trip to Copenhagen together.

Int'l release: Jan. 4                    Int'l B.O.: $500,000

### American Cuisine (Cuisine Americaine) (France)

A Polygram Film Distribution release of a Les Films Balenciaga, Polygram Audiovisuel, M6 Films production. Produced by Regine Konickier, Jean-Luc Ormières. Directed, written by Jean-Yves Pitoun. Camera, Jean-Marie Dreujou; editor, Monica Coleman; music, Rene-Marc Bini; art director, Valerie Gral; costume design, Edith Vesperini; culinary stylist, Danielle Sommet. Reviewed at UGC Normandie, Paris, Aug. 27. Running time: 92 mins.

---

**...April 4...**
**Life is Beautiful** named top film at 53rd Italian journalists' awards.

Eddy Mitchell (Louis Boyer), Irene Jacob (Gabrielle), Jason Lee (Loren), Thibault de Montalembert (Vincent), Michel Muller (Tax Inspector). (French version)
A pleasant cross-cultural comedy with just the right dose of mutual Franco-American joshing, *American Cuisine* follows the trajectory of a self-taught young cook from New York who apprentices with a crusty four-star legend in Dijon. With suspense, romance, and plenty of mouthwatering examples of the controlled frenzy behind the scenes in a top-flight eatery, pic is recommended as a box-office entrée on international menus. Food enthusiast Loren is kicked out of the U.S. Navy after slugging a superior who bawled him out for serving "sissy food" to an admiral. After two days making pizzas in Brooklyn, he's en route to France to apprentice with his idol, chef Louis Boyer, working in the great man's kitchen for room and board. Loren can't begin to match the pace of the experienced staff, who call him "New York." However, he survives the hazing and manages to win respect from his co-workers. But will the boss give his seal of approval?
Int'l release: Oct. 21 Int'l B.O.: $1.5 million

## American History X

A New Line Cinema release of a Turman-Morrissey Co. production. Produced by John Morrissey. Co-producers, Jon Hess, David McKenna. Directed by Tony Kaye. Screenplay, David McKenna. Camera, Kaye; editors, Jerry Greenberg, Alan Heim; music, Anne Dudley; production design, Jon Gary Steele; costume design, Doug Hall. Reviewed at New Line, L.A., Oct. 20. MPAA Rating: R. Running time: 118 mins.
Edward Norton (Derek Vinyard), Edward Furlong (Danny Vinyard), Fairuza Balk (Stacey), Beverly D'Angelo (Doris Vinyard), Avery Brooks (Bob Sweeney), Stacy Keach (Cameron Alexander), Jennifer Lien (Davina Vinyard), Elliott Gould (Murray), William Russ (Dennis Vinyard), Ethan Suplee (Seth)
A relatively conventional can't-we-all-get-along message is served up in an intense package in *American History X.* Already controversial owing to the neo-Nazi leading characters and the final-cut dispute between New Line and tyro feature director Tony Kaye, resulting film digs to uncommon depths in examining the roots of prejudice and the wages of hate-inspired violence. This jolting, superbly acted film will draw serious-minded upscale viewers. But to attract more general audiences, distrib will have to overcome the sociological, issue-oriented aroma most media coverage of the picture will emit. And while the film has flaws, it is by no means messy, nor does it feel sanitized or airbrushed. Startling black-and-white kickoff has teenager Danny Vinyard bursting into the bedroom of older brother, Derek, with news that two young blacks are breaking into his car. In a fury, Derek, festooned with a swastika and white-power tattoos, pulls out a pistol, walks out and guns them down. Shortly, Danny, who has a shaved head, is upbraided by his black high-school principal, Sweeney, for writing a pro report on *Mein Kampf.* He has the boy take what he calls American History X. For his first assignment, Danny is told to write a paper on his brother, and that account effectively sets the picture on dual tracks. The extensive flashbacks chart Derek's rise as a charismatic leader of previously aimless malcontents. Intercut present-day footage, in color, presents the matured Derek's difficult process of trying to disengage from the neo-Nazis and to convince his astonished brother of the error of their old, hate-filled ways.
U.S. release: Oct. 28 U.S. B.O.: $6 million

## An American Werewolf in Paris (U.K.-Netherlands-Luxembourg)

An Entertainment Film Distributors/Buena Vista Pictures release of a Hollywood Pictures presentation, in association with Cometstone Pictures, J&M Entertainment. Produced by Richard Claus. Directed by Anthony Waller. Screenplay, Tim Burns, Tom Stern, Waller, based on characters created by John Landis in *An American Werewolf In London.* Camera, Egon Werdin; editor, Peter R. Adam; music, Wilbert Hirsch; production design, Matthias Kammermeier; costume design, Maria Schicker; visual-effects supervisors, John Grower, Bruce Walters; werewolf design, Peter Lloyd; animatronics/prosthetics effects supervisors, Joachim Grueninger, Jez Harris. Reviewed at Carlton, London, Oct. 27, 1997. MPAA Rating: R. Running time: 98 mins.
Tom Everett Scott (Andy), Julie Delpy (Serafine), Vince Vieluf (Brad), Phil Buckman (Chris), Julie Bowen (Amy), Pierre Cosso (Claude), Tom Novembre (Insp. LeDuc), Thierry Lhermitte (Dr. Pigot).
Adopting the same mix of shocks and yocks as John Landis' 1981 London-based scare comedy, *An American Werewolf in Paris* starts off as an entertaining ride but loses its compass midway. Though it looks unlikely to become a howling success, energetic pic should accrue red-blooded returns on a worldwide basis, with a long afterlife in ancillaries. Operatic opener features a man escaping from the sewers of Paris and then being dragged back inside by some unseen beastie. Pic then cuts to three young Americans – sensitive Andy and his girl-chasing pals, Brad and Chris. A "dare" to bungee-jump off the Eiffel Tower finds Andy saving Serafine, who jumps into the void sans safety net. The young man loses her in the fog but manages to find her again and invites her out on a date. Her sudden display of superhuman strength in a café and interest in blood-soaked human organs sets Serafine apart from your average French babe.
U.S. release: Dec. 25, 1997 U.S. B.O.: $25.5 million
Int'l release: Oct. 31, 1997 Int'l B.O.: $10 million

## Am I Beautiful? (Bin Ich Schoen?) (Germany)

An Atlas Int'l presentation of a Constantin Film/Fanes Film production. Produced by Bernd Eichinger, Martin Moszkowicz. Directed by Doris Dorrie. Screenplay, Dorrie, Rolf Basedow, Ruth Stadler. Camera, Theo Bierkens; editor, Inez Regnier; music, Roman Bunka; production design, Claus Kottmann; costume design, Yoshi'o Yabara. Reviewed at Venice Festival, Sept. 12. Running time: 115 mins.
Senta Berger (Unna), Gottfried John (Herbert), Otto Sander (David), Franka Potente (Linda), Anica Dobra (Franziska), Maria Schrader (Elke), Elisbaeth Romano (Jessica), Steffen Wink (Klaus), Iris Berben (Rita).
A gallery of characters who are all tormented about the way they look, the onset of old age or the impermanence of relationships feature in Doris Dorrie's intermittently engaging *Am I Beautiful?* Many of the characters and incidents have considerable validity; others seem included for no special reason. Uneven as it is, pic should perform well on its home territory, thanks to a solid cast of fine actors. International theatrical distribution is more iffy, though quality tube programmers will stand in line. Pic starts off in the countryside near Seville, Spain, where just about every character to pass by happens to be from Germany. There's Linda, a hitchhiker who tells tall tales in order to persuade men to give her a bed

for the night. Then there's Klaus, who can't get over the fact that Franziska, the girl who came with him to Spain a year ago, has dumped him. Franziska plans to marry Holger that very weekend – despite nagging doubts. Driving home in blinding rain, Franziska collides with a car driven by Elke who has a sad story to tell about her own fiancé. And so it goes.

Int'l release: Sept. 17                Int'l B.O.: $6.2 million

## Amistad

A DreamWorks Pictures release, in association with HBO Pictures. Produced by Steven Spielberg, Debbie Allen, Colin Wilson. Directed by Spielberg. Screenplay, David Franzoni. Camera, Janusz Kaminski; editor, Michael Kahn; music, John Williams; production design, Rick Carter; costume design, Ruth E. Carter; visual effects, Scott Farrar; casting, Victoria Thomas. Reviewed at Amblin, Universal City, Nov. 28, 1997. MPAA Rating: R. Running time: 152 mins.

**Morgan Freeman (Theodore Joadson), Anthony Hopkins (John Quincy Adams), Matthew McConaughey (Baldwin), Nigel Hawthorne (Martin Van Buren), Djimon Hounsou (Cinque), David Paymer (Forsyth), Pete Postlethwaite (Holabird), Stellan Skarsgard (Tappan).**

The forces of power, racism, and justice momentously clash in Steven Spielberg's *Amistad*, an artistically solid, if not always dramatically exciting, chronicle of the 1839 slave rebellion onboard a Spanish slave ship. True story is presented as an international intrigue, one that involved the governments of the U.S., Great Britain, Spain and, of course, the 53 Africans held captive. Boasting a high-voltage cast, the release should sail safely as a message film that touches on the very fabric of the American social system.

Pre-credit sequence shows how Sengbe Pieh (called Cinque) – a former rice farmer – begins the rebellion by breaking free of his shackles. However, they are unskilled sailors and are picked up by the U.S. Coast Guard and thrown into prison. Abolitionists attempt to enlist a decent attorney, but end up with Baldwin, a lawyer with a shady rep who presents the case as a property, not a human-rights issue. He tries to prove that the Africans were "stolen goods."

U.S. release: Dec. 10, 1997          U.S. B.O.: $44 million
Int'l release: Feb. 19               Int'l B.O.: $27.6 million

## Among Giants (U.K.)

A Capitol Films presentation of a Kudos production, with the participation of British Screen, Arts Council of England, BBC Films, Yorkshire Media Production Agency. Produced by Stephen Garrett. Directed by Sam Miller. Screenplay, Simon Beaufoy. Camera, Witold Stok; editors, Ellen Pierce Lewis, Paul Green; music, Tim Atack; production designer, Luana Hanson; costume designer, Stephanie Collie. Reviewed at Cannes Festival, May 15. Running time: 90 mins.

**Pete Postlethwaite (Ray), Rachel Griffiths (Gerry), James Thornton (Steve), Lennie James (Shovel), Andy Serkis (Bob), Rob Jarvis (Weasel).**

Screenwriter Simon Beaufoy's rep is riding high after his success with last year's *The Full Monty*, but his new effort, *Among Giants*, isn't in the same league. Like the earlier film, it's set in the city of Sheffield and centers on a group of amiable working-class characters, but it lacks the humor and passion that made *Monty* a treat. With less attractive characters, and a rather dull plot, expect this grungy romance to trickle into cinemas worldwide, with modest B.O. results. This time the characters aren't unemployed; led by Ray, they've found work painting a series of electric pylons that straddle the picturesque Yorkshire countryside. The twist is the arrival of a female Aussie hitchhiker looking for work and the improbability of being taken on by Ray for a job and, soon after, romance.

Int'l release: June 24               Int'l B.O.: $250,000

## Amy (Australia)

A Village Roadshow release of a Cascade Films production. Produced by Nadia Tass, David Parker. Directed by Tass. Screenplay, David Parker. Camera, Parker; editor, Bill Murphy; music, Philip Judd; production designer, Jon Dowding; costume designer, Christiana Plitzco. Reviewed at Cannes Festival, May 15. Running time: 103 mins.

**Alana De Roma (Amy Enker), Rachel Griffiths (Tanya Rammus), Ben Mendelsohn (Robert Buchanan), Nick Barker (Will Enker), Kerry Armstrong (Sarah Trendle), Jeremy Trigatti (Zac Trebdle), Willian Zappa (Bill Trendle).**

An emotional drama about grief and healing, *Amy* centers on the fanciful premise of a traumatized child whose elective mutism allows her to hear and speak only through song. Straddling straight drama, comedy, and elements of musical fantasy, the film sits at times uneasily between those genres and makes it a difficult commercial sell. Amy has been a deaf-mute since witnessing the death of her rock-star father in an electrical accident during a concert. Her mother Tanya has taken her to her father's outback farm but is forced back to Melbourne by child-welfare officers attempting to force special treatment and schooling on the young girl.

Int'l release: Sept. 2               Int'l B.O.: $250,000

## Anastasia

A 20th Century Fox release of a Fox Family Films presentation. Produced by Don Bluth, Gary Goldman. Exec producer, Maureen Donley. Directed by Bluth, Goldman. Screenplay, Susan Gauthier, Bruce Graham, Bob Tzudiker, Noni White, based on the play by Marcelle Maurette as adapted by Guy Bolton, and the screenplay by Arthur Laurents. Technicolor, CinemaScope widescreen; editor, Fiona Trayler; original score, David Newman; song lyrics, Lynn Ahrens; music, Stephen Flaherty. Reviewed at 20th Century Fox, L.A., Nov. 3, 1977. MPAA Rating: G. Running time: 94 mins.

**Voices: Meg Ryan (Anastasia), John Cusack (Dimitri), Kelsey Grammer (Vladimir), Christopher Lloyd (Rasputin), Hank Azaria (Bartok), Bernadette Peters (Sophie), Kirsten Dunst (Young Anastasia), Angela Lansbury (Dowager Empress Marie).**

The much-anticipated debut offering of Fox's animation unit, *Anastasia* reps an ambitious, serious but not particularly stimulating musical feature that unconvincingly attempts to graft warm and cuddly family-film motifs onto turbulent aspects of modern history and mythology. Grandly produced, graced by strong-name talent and tirelessly marketed in an effort to crack the lock Disney has enjoyed in animated, this effort seems poised to appeal most to girls between the approximate ages of 7 and 12. Overall, it lacks the special creative spark needed to lift it to an uncommon imaginative level. The heavy promotion will probably generate potent numbers at the outset, followed by a fairly rapid slide and eventual landing in a B.O. middle range that will not be disgraceful for Fox nor threatening to Disney. Prologue effectively establishes Anastasia as the beloved daughter of Czar

Nicholas in 1916, but stumbles as it attributes Russia's social unrest to the sinister sorcerer Rasputin. Little Anastasia and grandmother, the Dowager Empress Marie, manage to escape the curse Rasputin lowers upon the rest of the Romanovs with the aid of a kitchen boy. But while Marie makes it to Paris, Anastasia becomes separated and is next seen, as a young woman named Anya, emerging from a "People's Orphanage" a decade later. At that moment, Dimitri and Vladimir are auditioning candidates for an alleged theatrical piece while actually looking for a young woman to convincingly pass off as the real Anastasia and collect a handsome reward from Marie. Anya, who has no recollections of her early years, just wants to go to Paris.

U.S. release: Nov. 14, 1997     U.S. B.O.: $58 million
Int'l release: Dec. 12, 1997     Int'l B.O.: $80 million

### Angel on my Shoulder (Docu)

A D.D. Prods production. Produced, directed, edited by Donna Deitch. Narration, Deitch, Terri Jentz. Camera, Deitch. Reviewed at Berlin Film Festival, Feb. 15, 1998. Running time: 83 mins.
With: Gwen Welles.

Watching the slow, agonizing death of a vibrant human being is an exceedingly painful experience. So it is with *Angel on My Shoulder*, Donna Deitch's heartrending film about the illness and eventual death of a friend, actress Gwen Welles. A very specialized pic, it should play the fest circuit and could find tube slots. Welles, best known for her knockout role in Robert Altman's *Nashville*, met Deitch when she appeared in the filmmaker's first movie, *Desert Hearts*. They became close friends and neighbors, despite different lifestyles (Welles straight, Deitch gay).Welles was diagnosed with an anal tumor in 1992, but refused conventional treatments of chemotherapy or a colostomy.

### Another Day in Paradise

A Trimark Pictures release of a Chinese Bookie Pictures production. Produced by Stephen Chin, Larry Clark, James Woods. Directed by Larry Clark. Screenplay, Christopher Landon, Stephen Chin, based on the book by Eddie Little. Camera, Eric Edwards; editor, Luis Colina; production design, Aaron Osborne; costume design, Kathryn Morrison. Reviewed at Venice Festival, Sept. 11. Running time: 100 mins.
James Woods (Mel), Melanie Griffith (Sid), Vincent Kartheiser (Bobbie), Natasha Gregson Wagner (Rosie), James Otis (Reverend).

Larry Clark's second feature, *Another Day in Paradise* resembles *Drugstore Cowboy* in its human take on a surrogate family glued together by drugs and crime. More conventional and arguably more satisfying than Clark's provocative debut, *Kids*, this imperfect but compelling outlaw drama may be too raw and unflinching to make a wide splash, but should find an audience ready to respond to its gritty aesthetic.

Teenage junkie Bobbie breaks into a community college to empty its vending machines of cash and gets pulped by a security guard, whom he eventually subdues with a knife. Staggering home to the slummy apartment he shares with his g.f., Rosie, and friend Danny, he shoots some heroin to dull the pain, and his injuries are treated by Danny's slick, drug-dealing uncle, Mel. After nursing him back to health, Mel recruits Bobbie to help steal a major haul of speed from an out-of-town doctor's clinic. Bobbie and Rosie hit the road with Mel and his tough but maternal sidekick, Sid, who broaden the waifs'

horizons, giving them their first taste of good living.

### Antz (Animated)

A DreamWorks release of a DreamWorks Pictures and PDI presentation. Produced by Brad Lewis, Aron Warner, Patty Wooton. Directed by Eric Darnell, Tim Johnson. Screenplay, Todd Alcott, Chris Weitz, Paul Weitz. Editor, Stan Webb; music, Harry Gregson-Williams, John Powell; production design, John Bell; story consultant, Zak Penn; character designer, Raman Hui; visual-effects supervisor, Ken Bielenberg. Reviewed at Amblin, Universal City, Sept. 17. MPAA Rating: PG. Running time: 83 mins.
Voices: Woody Allen (Z), Dan Aykroyd (Chip), Anne Bancroft (Queen), Jane Curtin (Muffy), Danny Glover (Barbatus), Gene Hackman (Mandible), Jennifer Lopez (Azteca), John Mahoney (Drunk Scout), Paul Mazursky (Psychologist), Sylvester Stallone (Weaver), Sharon Stone (Bala), Christopher Walken (Cutter).

*Antz* is a dazzling delight. This initial collaboration between DreamWorks and Pacific Data Images doesn't possess the potential to match the levels of Disney's 1995 CGI blockbuster, *Toy Story*, but its considerable appeal should translate into a long and healthy B.O. The commercial question marks relate to the just slightly sophisticated nature of the bucking-the-system story, non-kid-related characters, and the ability of the Woody Allen-voiced lead character to click with the sort of wide audience the comic auteur has never reached.

Pic is a sort of Metropolis meets Microcosmos with a commoner-princess, lovers-on-the-run romance at its core. It's fresh and inventive, visually stimulating and extremely well-served by a starry voice cast. Mandible convinces his queen that the colony is threatened by termites and that he must launch a pre-emptive strike. On the night before the invasion, the queen's daughter, Princess Bala – unhappily engaged to Mandible – goes slumming in a bar to see what the simple folk do and asks an unsuspecting Z – a hopelessly insecure and neurotic worker ant – to dance. So delirious is Z from his encounter that he convinces a soldier to let him take his place, hoping to glimpse Bala. Instead it places him on the front lines, where termites spew bile and chow down on ants. By a fluke, Z is the sole survivor of the massacre, leaving the battlefield with the final words of a fallen friend ringing in his ears: "Don't follow orders all your life."

U.S. release: Oct. 2     U.S. B.O.: $88 million
Int'l release: Nov. 1     Int'l B.O.: $66 million

### Anxiety (Inquiétude) (Portugal-France-Spain-Switzerland)

A Madragoa Filmes (Portugal)/Gemini Films (France)/Wanda Films (Spain)/Light Night (Switzerland) co-production. International sales, Gemini, Paris. Produced by Paulo Branco. Directed, written by Manoel de Oliveira. Camera, Renato Berta; editor, Valerie Loiseleux; production/costume designer, Isabel Branco. Reviewed at Cannes Festival, May 19. Running time: 110 mins.
Jose Pinto (Father), Luis Miguel Cintra (Son), Lenor Silveira (Suzy), Rita Blanco (Gabi), Diogo Doria (Him), Irene Papas (Mother), Leonor Baldaque (Fisalina), Ricardo Trepa (Fiance).

*Anxiety* marks yet another turning point in the career of Portuguese maestro Manoel de Oliveira – a three-part omnibus of stories vaguely linked together by the theme of death. A work certain to be of interest to Oliveira's arthouse and festival followings, it is probably too quirky and full of longueurs to widen his net. No strong connecting thread winds through this trio of stories, other than an obsession with the encroaching end. *Anxiety* keeps death at a finely literate distance, a good place from which to contemplate it.

Int'l release: Sept. 23                    Int'l B.O.: $150,000

### The Apple (Sib) (Iran)

A Cinema Workshop (Tehran) production. Directed by Samirah Makhmalbaf. Screenplay, Mohsen Makhmalbaf. Camera, Ebrahim Ghafuri; editor, Mohsen Makhmalbaf. Reviewed at Fajr Festival, Feb. 6, 1998. Running time: 85 mins.
With: Zahra Naderi, Masume Naderi, Qorban Ali Naderi, Azize Mohammadi, Zahra Saqari Saz, Amir Hossein Khosrojerdi.

A haunting, reality-based drama about two 11-year-old girls who were locked up from birth by their parents, *The Apple* offers an allegory of Iranian society that's at once poetic and perplexing in more ways than may be intended. Although credited to Samirah Makhmalbaf, who was 17 at the time of its making, pic seems full of the stylistic assurance of her dad, renowned helmer Mohsen Makhmalbaf, who gets script and editing credits. While chances of arthouse crossover appear slight, the Makhmalbaf name and pic's curious subject matter should make it a festival favorite.

Pic starts with news accounts of twin girls discovered by social workers to have lived virtually as prisoners of their poor father and blind mother. Acting within days of the story's unveiling, Makhmalbaf and his daughter persuaded the family members to play themselves in a scripted tale that opens with shot-on-video footage, presumably staged, of the girls, Zahra and Masume, being released from the state's custody and returning home.

### Aprile (Italy-France)

A Tandem Distribuzione release of a Sacher Film presentation of a Sacher Film (Rome)/Bac Films (Paris) production in association with RAI, Canal Plus. Produced by Angelo Barbagallo, Nanni Moretti. Directed, written by Nanni Moretti. Camera, Giuseppe Lanci; editor, Angelo Nicolini; art director, Marta Maffucci; costume designer, Valentina Taviani. Reviewed at Nuovo Sacher Cinema, Rome, March 26. Running time: 78 mins.
With: Nanni Moretti, Silvio Orlando, Silvia Nono, Pietro Moretti, Agata Apicella Moretti, Nuria Schoenberg, Angelo Barbagallo.

More than four years after his international breakthrough, *Caro diario*, Italian moralist-auteur Nanni Moretti continues his idiosyncratic dissection of self, society, and state with *Aprile.* Taking its title from a month marked by two momentous occasions – the birth of his son and the election of Italy's first left-wing government – this fragmentary diary interweaves the personal with the political much more than its predecessor. The director's customary wry humor and biting observations are still out in force, but this is a smaller, more intimate, and introspective essay than *Diario*, and outside Italy looks to be considered a disappointing follow-up.

Int'l release: March 13                    Int'l B.O.: $5.5 million

### Apt Pupil

A Sony Pictures Entertainment release from TriStar Pictures of a Phoenix Pictures presentation of a Bad Hat Harry production.

Produced by Jane Hamsher, Don Murphy, Bryan Singer. Directed by Bryan Singer. Screenplay, Brandon Boyce, based on the novella by Stephen King. Camera, Newton Thomas Sigel; editor, John Ottman; music, Ottman; production design, Richard Hoover; costume design, Louise Mingenbach. Reviewed at Sony, Culver City, Aug. 21. MPAA Rating: R. Running time: 111 mins.
Ian McKellen (Kurt Dussander), Brad Renfro (Todd Bowden), Bruce Davison (Richard Bowden), Elias Koteas (Archie), Joe Morton (Dan Richler), Jan Triska (Isaac Weiskopf), Michael Byrne (Ben Kramer), Heather McComb (Becky Trask), Ann Dowd (Monica Bowden), David Schwimmer (Edward French).

A creepy, well-acted story of contagious evil, *Apt Pupil* has more than enough chilling dramatic scenes to rivet the attention but suffers from some hokey contrivances and ill-conceived motivation. Ian McKellen and Brad Renfro excel as, respectively, a Nazi war criminal and an aggressive small-town high school student who uncovers his past. Director Bryan Singer sustains a compellingly sinister tone until unduly extending the final act. Pic has dual potential audiences – teens drawn by the Stephen King name and more discerning viewers – which should combine for reasonable returns. But pic's claustrophobic nature and relative lack of action will likely prevent it from breaking out to a wider public.

Teen Todd Bowden becomes fascinated by the Holocaust in a school course and, via an old photograph, recognizes a grizzled local resident as one Kurt Dussander, a former officer at the Paten concentration camp, where 90,000 prisoners died. Brazenly, he turns up at the old man's door, announces that he has incontrovertible proof that he is, in fact, Dussander and, under threat of turning him in, commands the Nazi to tell him the brutal truth about what he did during the war. His old self thus revived, Dussander warns Todd that he's playing with fire, then veers over the top into some dramatically ludicrous behavior. For his part, Todd is now so preoccupied by Nazi evil that he's lost all personal perspective.

U.S. release: Oct. 23                    U.S. B.O.: $8.8 million
Int'l release: Nov. 13                   Int'l B.O.: $1.4 million

### Armageddon

A Buena Vista release of a Touchstone Pictures presentation of a Jerry Bruckheimer production, in association with Valhalla Motion Pictures. Produced by Bruckheimer, Gale Anne Hurd, Michael Bay. Directed by Bay. Screenplay, Jonathan Hensleigh, J.J. Abrams, story by Robert Roy Pool, Hensleigh, adaptation by Tony Gilroy, Shane Salerno. Camera, John Schwartzman; editors, Mark Goldblatt, Chris Lebenzon, Glen Scantlebury; music, Trevor Rabin; production designer, Michael White; costume designers, Michael Kaplan, Magali Guidasci; visual-effects supervisors, Pat McClung, Richard Hoover. Reviewed at Crest, L.A., June 22. MPAA Rating: PG-13. Running time: 150 mins.
Bruce Willis (Harry Stamper), Billy Bob Thornton (Dan Truman), Liv Tyler (Grace Stamper), Ben Affleck (A.J. Frost), Will Patton (Charles "Chick" Chapple), Peter Stormare (Lev Andropov), Keith David (Gen. Kimsey), Steve Buscemi (Rockhound), Owen Wilson (Oscar Choi).

Bruce Willis saves the world but can't save *Armageddon.* The second of the season's nuke-the-asteroid-or-bust pre-millennium spectaculars is so effects-obsessed and dramatically benumbed as to make *Deep Impact* look like a humanistic masterpiece. Despite its frequently incoherent staging and an editing style that amounts to a 2½-hour sensory pummeling, $150 million sci-fi actioner nonetheless has the Willis juice, Jerry Bruckheimer–Michael Bay bad-boy ingredients and Disney marketing muscle going for it to launch it into high commercial orbit.

Film begins with fireballs raining down on Gotham, disemboweling Grand Central Station, decapitating the Chrysler Building and generally wrecking the town. Despite the fact that an asteroid the size of Texas is heading straight for the planet, the U.S. administration figures it can keep a lid on the news. Determining, as in *Deep Impact*, that the only thing to do is to implant a nuke or two in the giant hunk of rock to split it apart before it creates a big bang, NASA director Dan Truman recruits the world's top oil-driller, Harry S. Stamper, for the job. A maverick, but responsive to the greater need, he agrees, on condition he can select his team, and it's here that the picture becomes irretrievably ludicrous: The "Dirty 14," which will fly up on two space shuttles, consists mostly of miscreants with bad attitudes.

U.S. release: July 1
Int'l release: July 23

U.S. B.O.: $202 million
Int'l B.O.: $262 million

## As Good As It Gets

A Sony Pictures Entertainment release of a TriStar Pictures presentation of a Gracie Films production. Produced by James L. Brooks, Bridget Johnson, Kristi Zea. Directed by Brooks. Screenplay, Mark Andrus, Brooks, story by Andrus. Camera, John Bailey; editor, Richard Marks; music, Hans Zimmer; production design, Bill Brzeski; costume design, Molly Maginnis. Reviewed at Fine Arts, Beverly Hills, Dec. 4, 1997. MPAA Rating: PG-13. Running time: 138 mins.

Jack Nicholson (Melvin Udall), Helen Hunt (Carol Connelly), Greg Kinnear (Simon Bishop), Cuba Gooding, Jr. (Frank Sachs), Skeet Ulrich (Vincent), Shirley Knight (Beverly), Jesse James (Spencer Connelly).

James L. Brooks' sitcom roots are apparent in *As Good As It Gets*, a sporadically funny romantic comedy with all the dramatic plausibility and tonal consistency of a TV variety show. The filmmaker's ability to deliver crowd-pleasing entertainment remains intact via the outrageous one-liners of Jack Nicholson's hopelessly misanthropic, anti-pc character. But this arch film constantly shifts gears, creating a messy, tiresome, and off-putting ambience. Pic's blatantly accessible humorous and emotional elements should land this in the commercial winner's circle, although the $50 million-plus budget puts recoupment a good way off.

Gotham curmudgeon Melvin Udall is the neighbor from hell. His sarcastic vitriol is so fearlessly extreme as to be outlandishly funny. But his obsessive-compulsive personality has become encrusted and moldy; he lives alone, has no friends or family; and emerges from his shell just once a day to eat at the same restaurant where he's barely tolerated by favorite waitress, Carol Connelly. She has problems enough, the most serious – and cliched – an asthmatic son. From the start, pic is clearly heading toward the humanization of Melvin. Unfortunately, the road is too long and very contrived, with the door to his self-awakening opened by, of all things, a dog. Melvin is obliged to care for it when his painter neighbor is hospitalized after a brutal mugging. To his astonishment, he melts for the mutt, which seemingly opens this Scrooge heart.

U.S. release: Dec. 23, 1997
Int'l release: Jan. 30

U.S. B.O.: $148.5 million
Int'l B.O.: $165.6 million

## At Satchem Farm

An Itasca Pictures production. Produced by Daniel Grodnik, Robert Snukal. Directed, written by John Huddles. Camera, Mark Vicente; editor, Dennis Hill; additional editing, Sean Thompson; music, Jeff Danna; production designer, Rick Walken; costumes, Laura Bauer; Reviewed at Toronto Festival, Sept. 15. Running time: 110 mins.

Rufus Sewell (Ross), Nigel Hawthorne (Cullen), Minnie Driver (Kendal), Amelia Heinie (Laurie), Michael E. Rodgers (Paul), Keone Young (Mr. Tang), Gregory Sporleder (Tom).

The California-shot, Brit-seeming *At Satchem Farm* pours on the New Age malarkey in earnest. Pic, which co-stars Minnie Driver and lists her as an exec producer, couldn't be more out of sync with current indie or commercial themes. At once schizoid in feel and schmaltzy to a fault, this talky, gorgeous-looking indie is suited to specialty audiences predisposed to its look-within message. Owing to the prevailing accents, it's assumed that we're somewhere in the English countryside. Actually, this is Simi Valley and environs, and the farm/arboretum of the title is an enclave of expatriate Brits who never bother to explain what they're doing in the neighborhood. Driver, really a supporting player, appears as a Brit power suit engaged to the hero of the piece but carrying a torch for another. Rufus Sewell is center of interest here, playing a befuddled type who dreams of cornering the market in manganese.

## August 32nd on Earth (Un 32 Aout Sur Terre)

(Canada)

A Max Films production. Produced by Roger Frappier. Directed, written by Denis Villeneuve. Camera, Andre Turpin; editor, Sophie Leblond; music, Pierre Desrochers, Nathalie Boileau, Robert Charlebois, Jean Leloup; art director, Jean Babin; costumes, Suzanne Harel. Reviewed at Cannes Festival, May 21. Running time: 88 mins.

Pascale Bussieres (Simone), Alexis Martin (Philippe), Richard S. Hamilton (Cab Driver).

Denis Villeneuve's feature bow, *August 32nd on Earth*, is an appealing though ultimately slight drama about a young woman thrown into an emotional tizzy after surviving a car crash. Essentially a two-hander, its lead thesps Pascale Bussieres and Alexis Martin lend intriguing charm to their characters, but the thin story doesn't have the goods to keep auds interested over the long haul.

The most striking thing about *August 32nd* is the visual style, and there's no question Villeneuve has real talent in that department. Commercial prospects aren't especially bright. Opening has Simone falling asleep at the wheel on the highway and careening off the road. While she doesn't suffer serious physical damage, there are psychic scars. She immediately quits her job and desperately phones her best friend Philippe, suggesting they have a baby.

U.S. release: Oct. 16

U.S. B.O.: $120,000

## The Avengers

A Warner Bros. release of a Jerry Weintraub production. Produced by Weintraub. Directed by Jeremiah Chechik. Screenplay, Don Macpherson. Camera, Roger Pratt; editor, Mick Audsley; music, Joel McNeely; "Avengers Theme" by Laurie Johnson; production design, Stuart Craig; costume designer, Anthony Powell; visual-effects supervisor, Nick Davis. Reviewed at Loews Village, N.Y., Aug. 14. MPAA Rating: PG-13. Running

---

**...April 9...**

Cannes officials select **Primary Colors** to be the fest's opening pic.

time: 89 mins.
Ralph Fiennes (John Steed), Uma Thurman (Emma Peel), Sean Connery (Sir August de Wynter), Patrick Macnee (Invisible Jones), Jim Broadbent ("Mother"), Fiona Shaw ("Father"), Eddie Izzard (Bailey), Eileen Atkins (Alice), John Wood (Tribshaw).

While not the complete calamity that rumor suggested, *The Avengers* is a pretty thin cuppa Earl Grey. Pic makes a game effort at reviving the popular 1960s British spy serial and boasts plenty of surface sparkle, including a witty look and super-duper special effects. What's missing is chemistry: the right blend of seriousness and whimsy, and charmingly compelling interplay between leads Ralph Fiennes and Uma Thurman. Fast-paced but uninvolving, the result seems unlikely to captivate either series fans or newcomers, making for dim B.O. prospects. *The Avengers*, it seems, assumes incorrectly that the old formulas can simply be replayed without irony or updating.

Steed works for a secret government arm called the Ministry. His controllers, the paradoxically monikered Mother and Father, bring him together with the chic, agile Mrs. Peel to combat the predation of an out-of-control project called Prospero, which threatens to wreak havoc on Britain's weather. The plot's further unfurling, not surprisingly, involves lots of chases, high-tech gimmickry, and heavy weather.

U.S. release: Aug. 14      U.S. B.O.: $23.3 million
Int'l release: Aug. 14      Int'l B.O.: $32 million

## Ayn Rand: A Sense of Life (Docu)

A Strand release of an AG Media Corp. Ltd presentation, in association with Copasetic Inc. Produced, directed, written by Michael Paxton. Camera, Alik Sakharov; editors, Lauren Schaffer, Christopher Earl; music, Jeff Britting. Reviewed on videocassette, Los Angeles, Feb. 11, 1998. Running time: 144 mins.
Narrator: Sharon Gless.

The late author-philosopher Ayn Rand of *The Fountainhead* fame is indisputably a fascinating and worthy documentary subject. Michael Paxton's Oscar-nominated effort – benefiting from first-rate archival, personal, and commercial film material – serves as a solid and appreciative precis of her life and views, but doesn't get down in the trenches to illustrate how and why she stirred up such passions for her stance on the primacy of uncompromising individualism. Pic should ride the nomination to good returns in specialized situations, with a long life all but assured in various TV outlets and video.

U.S. release: Feb. 13      U.S. B.O.: $200,000

## Babyface (Canada)

A Stable Films production. Produced by Barbara Tranter. Directed by Jack Blum. Screenplay, Blum, Sharon Corder. Camera, Harald Bachmann; editor, George Roulston; music, Donald Quan; production design, Ingrid Jurek; costumes, Michael Harris. Reviewed at Cannes Festival, May 19. Running time: 112 mins.
Lenore Zann (Margaret), Elisabeth Rosen (Lisa), James Gallanders (Jim), Shawn Doyle (Brian), Richard McMillan (Leo).

TV writer Jack Blum makes his feature debut with *Babyface*, a pic about a seriously dysfunctional mother-daughter relationship. This explosive yarn, centering on an oversexed single mom, her very confused 13-year-old daughter, and their shared boyfriend, is an uneven take on a difficult subject. As the film lacks the nuance such a story cries out for, it will be a tough sell internationally. *Lolita*-esque tone is set in the first moments, when the blonde, innocent-looking Lisa flirts openly with the school bus-driver. Her mother, Margaret, works in a Laundromat and spends most of her free time boozing, chasing guys, and generally partying like a wild, horny teenager.

U.S. release: Aug. 7      U.S. B.O.: $25,000

## Baby, It's You (Docu)

An ITVS presentation of a Makepeace production. Produced, directed, written by Anne Makepeace. Camera, Uta Briesewitz; editors, Makepeace, Jennifer Chinlund; music, Simon Kendall. Reviewed at Sundance Festival, Jan. 17, 1998. Running time: 56 mins.

With every boomer's biological clock ticking as loudly as Big Ben, Anne Makepeace's autobiographical *Baby, It's You* couldn't be more timely. Incredibly personal doc chronicles Makepeace's attempts to conceive in her late forties. Much-in-the-news topic, plus filmmaker's wry, self-analytical take, make this ITVS project a strong choice for fests and PBS, although sub-60-minute length will make hard-top bookings a longshot.

## The Back Country (L'arrière Pays) (France)

A Mars Films release of a Magouric Prods presentation. Produced by Laurent Benegui. Directed, written by Jacques Nolot. Camera, Agnes Godard; editor, Martine Giordano; art director, Patrick Durand. Reviewed at Videothèque de Paris, Paris, May 4. Running time: 90 mins.
Jacques Nolot (Jacques), Henri Gardey (Yvan), Mathilde Mone (Line). With: Christian Sempe, Henriette Sempe, Raphaeline Goupilleau, Simone Artus.

A modest but scathing portrait of ordinary small-mindedness in a nowhere town in southwestern France, *The Back Country* radiates eerie, piercing authenticity. This first feature directed by and starring scripter Jacques Nolot won the Prix Georges Sadoul and is a shoo-in for fests, especially gay ones. Pic provides an unusually trenchant glimpse of brutish men and women leading lives of quiet desperation, as seen through the eyes of a successful actor, now 50, who left home at age 16. Dapper native son Jacques Pruez returns home after 20 years to see his dying mother. His brief, eventful stay will underline all the reasons he had to leave in the first place.

Int'l release: Sept. 8      Int'l B.O.: $150,000

## The Ballad of the Windshield Washers (La Ballata Dei Lavavetri) (Italy)

A Mikado release of a P.F.A. Films production, in collaboration with RAI Cinemafiction. Produced by Pier Francesco Aiello. Directed by Peter Del Monte. Screenplay, Del Monte, Sergio Bazzini, Dominik Wieczorkowski, loosely based on the novel *The Polish Car Window Cleaner* by E. Albinati. Camera, Pasquale Mari; editor, Roberto Missiroli; music, Dario Lucantoni; production design, Anna Maria Donatella Sciveres; costume design, Paola Marchesin. Reviewed at Venice Festival, Sept. 10, 1998. Running time: 93 mins. (Polish and Italian dialog)
Olek Mincer (Zygmunt), Agata Buzek (Justyna), Kim Rossi Stuart (Rafal), Andrzej Grabowski (Pawel), Grazyna Wolszak (Helena), Eljana Nikolova Popova (Irina), Stefan Burczyk (The Pope), Romuald Andrzej Klos (Janusz).

Realism and fantasy make uneasy bedfellows in this oddity

---

**...April 10...**
Hungarian telecom giant MATAV enters the cable TV industry in a development that could endanger TV interests owned by Time Warner.

about members of a Polish family in Rome in the late 1980s. Peter Del Monte can't engender a great deal of interest in his often unconvincing characters, and the unexpectedly downbeat ending won't help the film find bookings in many territories.

Janusz is the head of an extended family of Polish emigrés who arrive in Rome, find cheap lodgings, and set about finding menial work while they await visas for Canada. Family members include Janusz's slightly deranged brother, Zygmunt; his son, Rafal (Kim Rossi Stuart); his companion, Helena; and Helena's teenage daughter, Justyna. The men find work cleaning the windshields of cars stuck in Rome's notorious traffic jams; Justyna is employed as a nanny to a small, sick child. Not long after their arrival, Janusz disappears. Rafal is certain his father is dead; Zygmunt, now thoroughly disturbed, wanders aimlessly about the city and begins to see visions of the Pope, with whom he has long conversations.

### Barbara (Denmark-Sweden-Norway)

A Per Holst Film (Copenhagen)/Svensk Filmindustri (Stockholm)/Felicia Film, Northern Light Film & TV (Oslo) co-production, with the support of Eurimages, Danish Film Institute, Swedish Film Institute, Norwegian Film Institute. Produced by Per Holst. Directed by Nils Malmros. Screenplay, Malmros, John Mogensen, based on the novel by Jorgen-Franz Jacobsen. Camera, Jan Weincke; editor, Birger Moller Jensen; music, Gunner Moller Pedersen; production design, Soren Krag Sorensen; costume design, Manon Rasmussen. Reviewed at Berlin Festival, Feb. 16, 1998. Running time: 144 mins.
**Anneke von der Lippe (Barbara Christina Salling), Lars Simonsen (Pastor Poul Aggersoe), Helene Egelund (Suzanne), Trond Hovik (Gabriel), Peter Hesse Overgaard (Pastor Wenzel), Jytte Kvinesdal (Anna Sophia), Daniel Ceccaldi (French Admiral).**

Passions run riot on a tiny, windswept island off the coast of Denmark in the mid-18th century in *Barbara*, a too leisurely bodice-ripper that delivers a powerful second half after a slow start. The period piece is a change of pace for vet Danish helmer Nils Malmros; though wonderfully visual it will have difficulty finding theatrical berths outside the Scandi territories.

When shy, inexperienced 25-year-old pastor Poul (Lars Simonsen) is sent to serve the far-flung parishioners in Torshavn, everyone is quick to tell him about the scandalous behavior of beautiful Barbara Christina Salling (Anneke von der Lippe), who, though only in her twenties, has already survived two husbands, both pastors. Pastor Poul is smitten with Barbara's charms and, ignoring all advice, marries her. After performing ceremonies on the outer islands, he returns to find that Barbara has run off with Andreas (Peter Reichardt), a student from Copenhagen, and he's egged on to prosecute the lovers for the crime of fornication.
Int'l release: Oct. 3, 1997          Int'l B.O.: $3 million

### Barrio (Spain)

A Warner Sogefilms release of a Sogetel/Elias Querejeta P.C.S.L./Mact Prods./MGN Filmes production with the participation of TVE Television Espanola, Esicma, Sogepaq, Canal Plus. Produced by Elias Querejeta. Directed, written by Fernando Leon de Aranoa. Camera, Alfredo Mayo; editor, Nacho Ruiz Capillas; music, Hechos Contra el Decoro; art director, Soledad Sesena; costume design, Maiki Marin. Reviewed at San Sebastian Festival, Sept. 23. Running time: 99 mins.
**Crispulo Cabezas (Rai), Timy (Javi), Eloi Yebra (Manu), Marieta Orozco (Susi), Alicia Sanchez (Carmen), Enrique Villen (Ricardo), Francisco Algora (Angel).**

Making good on the promise of his multi-award-winning 1997 debut, *Familia*, Fernando Leon de Aranoa looks beyond the family to survey an entire environment, in this case a tough, lower-working-class quarter of Madrid and the modest, sadly impossible dreams of its youth. In *Barrio*, the Spanish writer-director rejects the common angry, no-future view of life in the 'hood, instead injecting humor, warmth, humanity, and heart. Winningly played by a likeable young cast, this emotionally satisfying slice of life should spring from festivals into select arthouses.

Bored 15-year-old school chums Rai, Manu, and Javi dream of babes and beaches but are all too aware that these dreams are out of reach. Lacking the financial resources to get even as far as the city center let alone the seaside, they hang around the concrete wasteland killing time by reading the sex classifieds.
Int'l release: Oct. 2          Int'l B.O.: $2.6 million

### Barney's Great Adventure

A Polygram Films release of a Polygram Filmed Entertainment presentation, in association with Lyrick Studios. Produced by Sheryl Leach, Dennis DeShazer. Directed by Steve Gomer. Screenplay, Stephen White, story by White, Sheryl Leach, Dennis DeShazer. Camera, Sandi Sissel; editor, Richard Halsey; executive music producer, Jan Rhees; production designer, Vincent Jefferds; special visual effects, Cinemotion Pictures. Reviewed at Polygram, Beverly Hills, March 25. MPAA Rating: G. Running time: 75 mins.
**George Hearn (Grandpa), Shirley Douglas (Grandma), Trevor Morgan (Cody), Kyla Pratt (Marcella), Diana Rice (Abby).**

Arguably the most critic-proof picture of the decade, *Barney's Great Adventure* will delight everyone who can't wait to see it and be a grin-and-bear-it experience for those who must accompany members of the former group. No film could have a higher must-see rating among the 2-to-5-year-old target audience, assuring good B.O. during the Easter holiday season. All the same, pic does present some unusual distribution and exhibition challenges, in that it has zero potential to do evening business. Prolonged theatrical life as a weekend matinee item is probable, but the real goldmine lies ahead in video. No matter how young, small fry will have little trouble identifying with the premise, in which Mom and Dad dump son Cody, daughter Abby, latter's best friend, Marcella, and a perennially pacified baby on the farm with Grandpa and Grandma.
U.S. release: Apr. 3          U.S. B.O.: $12.2 million
Int'l release: June 11          Int'l B.O.: $6.3 million

### BASEketball

A Universal Pictures release of a David Zucker Game. Produced by Zucker, Robert LoCash, Gil Netter. Directed by David Zucker. Screenplay, Zucker, Robert LoCash, Lewis Friedman, Jeff Wright. Camera, Steve Mason; editor, Jeffrey Reiner; music, James Ira Newborn; production design, Steven Jordan; costume design, Catherine Adair. Reviewed at Avco Cinema, L.A., July 28. MPAA Rating: R. Running time: 103 mins.
**Trey Parker (Joe Cooper), Matt Stone (Doug Remer), Yasmine Bleeth (Jenna Reed), Jenny McCarthy (Yvette Denslow), Robert Vaughn (Baxter Cain), Ernest Borgnine (Ted Denslow), Dian Bachar (Squeak Scolari).**

**... April 11 ...**
MTV Networks will launch a 24-hour MTV channel dedicated to the Russian market, the first time a Western web has set up a localized network in Russia.

Sports and movies generally don't add up commercially or artistically, and *BASEketball* has the heightened entertainment challenge of presenting an invented sport, à la *Rollerball* or *Quintet*. But while the likelihood of this game becoming an athletic reality is remote, the broad, bawdy antics onscreen will be a slam-dunk at the box office. The vulgar, obvious humor of Zucker brother David and *South Park* creators Trey Parker and Matt Stone elicits easy, guilty laughs, yet the material has an underlying innocence that's just shy of good clean fun. The film's physical comedy should translate well internationally and chalk up high scores on video.

Finding themselves pitted against two basketball jocks in a game of two-on-two, Coop and Remer quickly change the contest to something "more difficult." They make the rules up as they play, and BASEketball evolves. The game becomes a driveway sensation, and sports entrepreneur Ted Denslow approaches the boys to buy the game and set up a pro league. The story's central conflict concerns Baxter Cain, owner of the Dallas Felons, who wants to make the sport more lucrative through professional endorsements, product placement, and the like.

U.S. release: July 31          U.S. B.O.: $7 million

### Beck 2 (Beck 2: Spar I Morker) (Sweden-Germany-Denmark)

An Egmont Film release of a Victoria Film, FilmLance Int'l, TV4 (Sweden)/Frankfurter Film Produktion (Germany)/TV2 (Denmark) production, in association with Canal Plus, TV2 Norge, Merkur Film. Produced by Lars Blomgren, Thomas Lydholm. Directed by Morten Arnfred. Screenplay, Rolf Borjlind. Camera, Erik Kress; editor, Morten Giese; music, Ulf Dageby; art direction, Lasse Westfelt; costume design, Mona Theresia Forsin. Reviewed at Columbia TriStar screening room, Stockholm, Nov. 18, 1997. Running time: 88 mins.
**Peter Haber (Insp. Martin Beck), Mikael Persbrandt (Gunvald Larsson), Stina Rautelin (Lena Klingstrom), Cecilia Hall (Annika), Carlo Schmidt (Erik Lindgren).**
The second in the new round of Inspector Beck movies looks like a thriller made by Lars von Trier. But despite some good moments, pic is a step backward. The current series is based on new stories set in present-day Stockholm. Scriptwriter Rolf Borjlind has used the characters created by Maj Sjowall and Per Wahloo and tried to make them function in a Sweden that has become much colder and more violent than the one depicted in their bestselling novels of the 1960s and 1970s.

In *Beck 2*, people are being slaughtered on the platforms of Stockholm's subway, and, as the resulting panic threatens the collapse of the city's main transportation artery, Beck & Co. have to solve the murders quickly. Weakness of the pic is that there's no surprise when the killers are discovered.

Int'l release: Oct. 31, 1997          Int'l B.O.: $600,000

### The Bed (Postel) (Czech Republic, B&W)

A Barrandov Biografia/Etamp Film/Ceska Televize/Cinecam GmbH co-production. Directed, written by Oskar Reif. Camera, Igor Luther; editor, Ludek Hudec; costumes, Simona Rybakova. Reviewed at Cannes Festival, May 17. Running time: 88 mins.
**Michael Przebinda (Lubosh Urna), Stanislava Jachnicka (Olga), Jana Hruskova (Vera), Martin Stavel (Young Lubosh), Sylva Langova-Williams (Babicka), Jiri Hasil (Eduard).**
Part homage, part revisionism, *The Bed*, from the Czech Republic, recalls the style and tone of productions from the region that caught the world's attention in the 1960s. A heady, fanciful yarn ironically subtitled "The Czech Pornotragedy," pic grapples with the battle of the sexes in a wry, philosophical manner. Though uneven, this first feature from Oskar Reif demonstrates budding talent that could generate some specialized theatrical play in upscale territories. Title refers to something both literal and figurative: it's the place where life and death occur for the central character, Lubosh. It also provides him with the one place where he feels secure, whether he's alone or with someone else.

### Bedrooms & Hallways (U.K.)

A Pandora Cinema presentation, in association with ARP, Pandora Film, BBC Films, of a Berwin and Dempsey production. Produced by Dorothy Berwin, Ceci Dempsey. Directed by Rose Troche. Screenplay, Robert Farrar. Camera, Ashley Rowe; editor, Chris Blunden; music, Alfredo Troche; production designer, Richard Bridgland; costume designer, Annie Symons. Reviewed at Cannes Festival, May 20. Running time: 96 mins.
**Kevin McKidd (Leo), Hugo Weaving (Jeremy), Jennifer Ehle (Sally), Simon Callow (Keith), Harriet Walter (Sybil), Tom Hollander (Darren), Julie Graham (Angie), Christopher Fulford (Adam).**
A comedy about the mutability of sexual identity in the contemporary relationships arena, *Bedrooms & Hallways* represents a substantial leap forward for U.S. director Rose Troche who made *Go Fish* in 1994. While the pace is not as zippy nor the laugh quota quite as high as could be hoped for, the London-set film's appealingly drawn characters and accomplished cast keep it buoyant and entertaining. Despite being largely centered on gay male characters, the story's sexual inclusiveness should help sell it to hip, urban audiences.

Disconsolately single Leo has surrendered to disillusionment and begun to opt out of a social life, despite the urgings of his flatmate Darren and neighbor Angie. But a beacon appears when his friend Adam convinces him to join a men's therapy group.

### Belleville (Vite In Sospeso) (Italy)

A RAI Cinemafiction production. Produced by M. Flavia Villevielle Bideri for BI.G. Comunicazione. RAI producer, Cecilia Cope. Directed by Marco Turco. Screenplay, Doriana Leondeff, Andrea Porporati, Turco. Camera, Franco Lecca; editor, Simona Paggi; music, Riccardo Fassi; soprano sax solos, Steve Lacy; costume design, Lia Morandini; Tullio Morganti. Reviewed at Venice Festival, Sept. 9. Running time: 96 mins.
**Ennio Fantastichini (Dario), Isabella Ferrari (Eugenia), Massimo Bellinzoni (Jacopo)**
Exile, remorse, guilt, and responsibility are themes of Italian newcomer Marco Turco's uncommonly well-handled debut, *Belleville*, which examines the lives of a close-knit community of former terrorists living as political refugees in Paris. While a number of recent Italian features have dealt with 1970s urban terrorism, this modest production makes the issues in question more immediate than most. Festival and TV exposure should tag this new director as one to watch.

Setting is the late 1980s in the Belleville quarter of Paris, which is home to many Italians avoiding conviction on terrorism charges. Young journalist Jacopo travels from Rome with his father for the wedding of his exiled older brother Dario. When Dario's father leaves after some bitter confrontations, Jacopo decides to stay on and get to know the brother he has always idealized as a heroic free spirit. But Jacopo's presence upsets the fragile equilibrium. The situation worsens when he begins probing into the past, conducting video interviews of Dario's former comrades. As old wounds are reopened, members of the group become suspicious of his motives. Their fear of extradition and imprisonment provokes hostility, which spirals out of control when Jacopo becomes involved with Eugenia, who participated years earlier with Dario in a hit on an Italian industrialist.

## Belly

An Artisan Entertainment release of a Big Dog Films production. Produced by Ron Rotholz, Hype Williams, Robert Salerno, Larry Meistrich. Directed, written by Hype Williams, story by Anthony Bodden, Nas, Williams. Camera, Malik Sayeed; editor, David Leonard; music, Stephen Cullo; production design, Regan Jackson; costume design, June Ambrose. Reviewed at Festival Theater, L. A., Nov. 2. MPAA Rating: R. Running time: 95 mins.
**Nas (Sincere), DMX (Tommy Brown), Taral Hicks (Kisha), Tionne "T-Boz" Watkins (Tionne), Method Man (Shameek), Hassan Johnson (Mark), Power (Knowledge), Louie Rankin (Lennox).**
The "Belly" of this particular beast is a cacophonous, visually aggressive inner-city saga of crime and mayhem. The film is never boring – there's no question that filmmaker Hype Williams has the fancy moves – but the rhythmic, stylistic repetition becomes tedious, and serves to keep the audience removed from the story. Expect no showy B.O. numbers for this cinematic menace, which will quickly hightail it from theaters and might score a few points in ancillaries, where sampling will be quite enough to appreciate the picture.

Set in summer 1999 and leading up to the eve of the new millennium, the film centers on Tommy and Sincere, two young black men who have embraced a violent, outlaw lifestyle. Power, drugs and money have taken them from a poor Queens neighborhood to upscale addresses. But their gunslinger status makes them constant targets for other gangbangers and the feds. Belly isn't much different from countless Warner Bros. gangster melodramas of the 1930s or 1970s blaxploitation pictures. In this formula, crime equals death, and education and contrition are the bad man's only chances for redemption.
U.S. release: Nov. 4                     U.S. B.O.: $9.4 million

## Beloved

A Buena Vista release of a Touchstone Pictures presentation of a Harpo Films/Clinica Estetico production. Produced by Edward Saxon, Jonathan Demme, Gary Goetzman, Oprah Winfrey, Kate Forte. Directed by Demme. Screenplay, Akosua Busia, Richard LaGravenese, Adam Brooks, based on the novel by Toni Morrison. Camera, Tak Fujimoto; editors, Carol Littleton, Andy Keir; music, Rachel Portman; production design, Kristi Zea; costume design, Colleen Atwood. Reviewed at Walt Disney, Burbank, Sept. 30. MPAA Rating: R. Running time: 172 mins.
**Oprah Winfrey (Sethe), Danny Glover (Paul D), Thandie Newton (Beloved), Kimberly Elise (Denver), Beah Richards (Baby Suggs), Lisa Gay Hamilton (Young Sethe), Albert Hall (Stamp Paid), Irma P. Hall (Ella), Jason Robards (Mr. Bodwin).**
A mysterious and sometimes startling journey into the lives of people struggling to cope with the disfiguring effects of slavery and its aftermath, this meticulously mounted adaptation of Toni Morrison's Pulitzer Prize-winning novel *Beloved* has power and impressive artistry to spare. At nearly three hours, however, it rather overstays its welcome, trying the patience even as it sustains intrigue as to what its final revelations will be. Jonathan Demme's picture will surely be warmly embraced in many quarters, but the film is also open to criticism for a sense of self-importance and for the modest emotional catharsis it offers. Generally strong reviews, Morrison's following, Demme's name, and the guarantee of tireless promotional activities on the part of co-producer/star Oprah Winfrey assure the picture success as a class fall entry that will attract major portions of the black, upscale, and general female audiences.

Film begins in 1873, eight years after the end of the Civil War. Sethe, a middle-aged woman is trying to eke out a living near Cincinnati with her teenage daughter, Denver. Turning up unannounced, the disarming, easygoing Paul D, a former fellow slave with Sethe at a plantation called Sweet Home in Kentucky, has been on the move since emancipation and easily insinuates himself into Sethe's life and bed. Matters take a bizarre turn, however, when a strange young woman drags herself out of the primordial muck and, covered with insects, makes her way to Sethe's house. Denver instantly takes charge of nursing this drooling, grunting, stuttering creature to some approximation of health. Called Beloved, she is an untamed challenge to the fragile family that takes her in, and an extreme living testament to the ruinous legacy of slavery. There is also the unspoken suspicion that Beloved, either in literal or figurative form, could be Sethe's older daughter returned from the dead.
U.S. release: Oct. 16               U.S. B.O.: $22.7 million

## Besieged (Italy)

A Fine Line Cinema release of a Fiction/Navert Film production, in association with Mediaset. Produced by Massimo Cortesi. Directed by Bernardo Bertolucci. Screenplay, Clare Peploe, Bertolucci, based on a story by James Lasdun. Camera, Fabio Cianchetti; editor, Jacopo Quadri; music, Alessio Vlad; piano solos, Stefano Arnaldi; production design, Gianni Silvestri; costume design, Metka Kosak. Reviewed at Toronto Festival, Sept. 15. Running time: 94 mins. (English and Italian dialog)
**Thandie Newton (Shandurai), David Thewlis (Jason Kinsky), Claudio Santamaria (Agostino).**
The butter is spread pretty thinly over the bread in Bernardo Bertolucci's *Besieged*, a chamber drama about the relationship between a lonely pianist and his African maid in a Rome apartment. Structured in a rambling manner, often borderline risible in its dialog and featuring a performance by David Thewlis that's eccentric even by his standards, this small-scale entry looks unlikely to steal much B.O. coin outside Bertolucci-loyal territories like Italy.

Shandurai is a young woman in an unnamed, clearly repressive African country, first seen wandering the streets of her village in shellshocked silence. Action abruptly shifts to room where she cleans house for Jason Kinsky, a withdrawn British pianist-composer. She lives in the basement, where she pores over books in pursuit of a medical degree and listens to Kinsky pounding the keyboard. With music (African vs. Western) largely substituting for exposition, and Bertolucci's loose, mobile camerawork teasing the audience, the scene seems set for an unconventional romance between two isolated individuals, one a prisoner of his own artistry, the other afloat in a foreign culture. As soon as the principals directly engage, pic goes awry. Kinsky blurts out his love for Shandurai; she, horrified, demands that he try freeing her husband, a political prisoner back home. Kinsky starts selling off his belongings, presumably to fund the release of Shandurai's husband.

## The Best Man (Il Testimone Dello Sposo) (Italy)

An October Films release of a Luigi and Aurelio De Laurentiis/Antonio Avati presentation of a Filmauro-Duea Film production. Produced by Aurelio De Laurentiis, Antonio Avati. Directed, written by Pupi Avati. Camera, Pasquale Rachini; editor, Amedeo Salfa; music, Riz Ortolani; production design, Alberto Cottignoli, Steno Tonelli; costume design, Vittoria Guaita. Reviewed at the UA Westwood, Jan. 14, 1998. Running time: 100 mins.

**Diego Abantantuono (Angelo Beliossi), Ines Sastre (Francesca Babini), Dario Cantarelli (Edgardo Osti), Cinia Mascoli (Cinia Mascoli), Valeria D'Obici (Olimpia Campeggi Babini).**

A wedding held on the eve of the 20th century propels the action of *The Best Man*. Italy's Oscar submission, Pupi Avati's blend of humor and romance, centering on the collision of past and future, makes for a highly enchanting tale that should translate into more than just local appeal. It shapes up as one of the stronger foreign-language B.O. performers, with U.S. success triggering solid sales and distribution in upscale international territories.

Set in a northern province, the film opens as the townspeople prepare for the arranged union of Francesca (Ines Sastre) to wealthy businessman Edgardo (Dario Cantarelli). The other big event of the day is the arrival of Angelo (Diego Abantantuono), a man who left for America as a youth and has returned with a fortune already being eyed by the groom for a series of land deals.

| | |
|---|---|
| Int'l release: Jan. 23 | Int'l B.O.: $3.5 million |
| U.S. release: Aug. 14 | U.S. B.O.: $100,000 |

## Best Men

A Film Four Distributors release of an Orion Pictures presentation, in association with Rank Film Distributors, of a Brad Krevoy/Steve Stabler production. Produced by Brad Krevoy, Steve Stabler, Brad Jenkel, Deborah Ridpath. Directed by Tamra Davis. Screenplay, Art Edler Brown, Tracy Fraim. Camera, James Glennon; editor, Paul Trejo; music, Mark Mothersbaugh; production designer, Toby Corbett. Reviewed at ABC Shaftesbury Avenue 1, London, March 27. MPAA Rating: R. Running time: 89 mins.

**Dean Cain (Sgt. Buzz Thomas), Andy Dick (Teddy Pollack), Sean Patrick Flanery (Billy Phillips), Mitchell Whitfield (Sol Jacobs), Luke Wilson (Jesse Reilly), Drew Barrymore (Hope), Fred Ward (Sheriff Bud Phillips), Raymond J. Barry (Hoover), Brad Dourif (Lt. John G. "Gonzo" Coleman.**

An offbeat bank robbery picture that sticks to its guns and doesn't shoot for Tarantino-esque hipness in either dialog or action, *Best Men* reps a fine entry in the so-far wobbly feature career of former musicvid director Tamra Davis. Tightly constructed and admirably character-driven, pic manages to improve on the promise shown in her first feature, *Guncrazy*, though its modest scope and lack of marquee names signal this more for ancillary than theatrical action.

Film gets straight into character mode as four tuxedo-clad friends go to a California penitentiary to meet Jesse, who plans to head straight from three years in the stir to marry g.f. Hope.

The group is a mixed bunch of social marginals who don't tow to social norms.

| | |
|---|---|
| Int'l release: March 27 | Int'l B.O.: $100,000 |

## Betty

A Legacy Films release of a Skimmer Films and Upright Pictures production. Produced by Cheryl Pollak, Stephen Gregory, Richard Murphy. Directed, written by Murphy. Camera, Holly Fink; editor, Tricia Cooke; music, Charles Olins; original songs, Alex Desert; art direction, Thunk! Inc. Reviewed at Palm Springs Festival, Jan. 10, 1998. Running time: 88 mins.

**Cheryl Pollak (Betty Monday), Udo Kier (Vincent Lord), Holland Taylor (Crystal Ball), Ron Perlman (Donnie Shank).**

Despite its stylish look, *Betty* is an irritating, one-note picture about a famous actress who flees Hollywood and the pressures of stardom for a retirement community in Palm Springs. Basically a short film extended to feature length, this well-produced pic should enjoy a brief theatrical life on its way to the video bin.

Richard Murphy's feature directorial debut is meant to be a satirical look at the culture of celebrity, but comes across as a laboriously monotonous effort. Cheryl Pollak plays Betty Monday, a glamorous star who, in a moment of crisis, decides to flee her $70 million picture. She drives to Palm Springs and rents an elegant condo from an eccentric real estate agent. Isolated and alone, Betty resolves to live a more meaningful life.

## Beware of my Love (Si Je T'aime... Prends Garde A Toi) (France)

A Rezo Films production. Produced by Jean-Michel Rey, Philippe Liegeois. Directed, written by Jeanne Labrune. Camera, Andre Neau; editor, Guy Lecorne; music, Philip Glass, Richard Strauss; art director, Emile Ghigo; costumes, Anne Schotte. Reviewed at World Film Festival, Montreal, Aug. 29. Running time: 110 mins.

**Nathalie Baye (Muriel), Daniel Duval (Samuel), Hubert Saint Macary (Nicolas). With: Jean-Pierre Darroussin, Philippe Khorsand, Elisabeth Commelin, Michel Danieli, Philippe Cariou.**

With its controversial mix of ultra-steamy action and violence, there is no question that *Beware of My Love* will attract attention; if anything, this sexy psychodrama is precisely what North Americans used to love in Gallic cinema. Helmer Jeanne Labrune has created an emotionally wrenching pic that takes a fresh, far from politically correct look at a woman's near-fatal attraction to a dangerously unbalanced guy. Pic will almost certainly elicit strong response in France and could click with film buffs in the U.S. But it will require an adventurous distrib to take on the racy material about a woman who keeps coming back for more abuse – both physical and psychic – from her lover.

Yarn opens with Samuel staring lasciviously at Muriel, curled up sleeping in her train compartment. When she comes to, he begins pestering her. It looks to be finito when Muriel hops off the train at her stop. But the persistent Samuel calls her up, announcing that he'll be popping round with coffee and croissants. Before you can say "petit déjeuner," they're vigorously having sex on the floor of Muriel's chic Paris apartment. She feels a seemingly irresistible attraction to the brutish, penniless carpet salesman, but is frightened by the more psychotic elements of his unhinged personality.

| | |
|---|---|
| Int'l release: Sept. 8 | Int'l B.O.: $350,000 |

---

### ...April 14...

Michael Ovitz acquires 12% of financially beleaguered legit group Livent, producers of **Ragtime** and **Phantom of the Opera** ... Laurence Fishburne inks to star in Broadway's **The Lion in Winter**.

## The Big Hit

A Sony Pictures Entertainment release of a TriStar Pictures presentation of an Amen Ra Films/Zide-Perry/Lion Rock production. Produced by Warren Zide, Wesley Snipes. Directed by Che-Kirk Wong. Screenplay, Ben Ramsey. Camera, Danny Nowak; editors, Robin Russell, Pietro Scalia; music, Graeme Revell; production designer, Taavo Soodor; costume designer, Margaret Mohr; stunt coordinators, John Stoneham, Jr., Lau Chi-Ho. Reviewed at the UA Westwood, L.A., April 20. MPAA Rating: R. Running time: 91 mins.

**Mark Wahlberg (Melvin Smiley), Lou Diamond Phillips (Cisco), Christina Applegate (Pam Shulman), Avery Brooks (Paris), Bokeem Woodbine (Crunch), China Chow (Keiko Nishi), Antonio Sabato Jr. (Vince), Lela Rochon (Chantel).**

Combine the high-energy pyrotechnic choreography of a Hong Kong actioner with the plight of a banal sitcom schnook and you have *The Big Hit*. A fleet piece of sock-'em entertainment, its kinetic force plows through myriad plot holes and inconsistencies with game abandon. But the melange is apt to be shy of a bull's-eye for either the hard-core thrill crowd or a more rarefied group that's gravitated to off-kilter genre variations. Pic's theatrical results are likely to be disappointing, though it could find a second wind in pay cable rotation and on video.

The piece opens with a take-no-prisoners slam-bang contract job. The conceit of *The Big Hit* is that killer Mel is simply too nice. He's a bighearted lug who wants to be liked and have a normal family life once he arrives home from "the office."

U.S. release: Apr. 24 · U.S. B.O.: $27 million
Int'l release: June 4 · Int'l B.O.: $8.2 million

## The Big Lebowski

A Gramercy release of a Polygram Filmed Entertainment presentation of a Working Title production. Produced by Ethan Coen. Directed by Joel Coen. Screenplay, Joel and Ethan Coen. Camera, Roger Deakins; editors, Roderick Jaynes, Tricia Cooke; original music, Carter Burwell; production design, Rick Heinrichs; costume design, Mary Zophres. Reviewed at Sundance Festival, Jan. 18, 1998. MPAA Rating: R. Running time: 127 mins.

**Jeff Bridges (The Dude), John Goodman (Walter Sobchak), Julianne Moore (Maude Lebowski), Steve Buscemi (Donny), David Huddleston (The Big Lebowski), Philip Seymour Hoffman (Brandt), Sam Elliott (The Stranger).**

Spiked with wonderfully funny sequences and some brilliantly original notions, *The Big Lebowski* – a pseudo-mystery thriller with a keen eye and ear for societal mores and modern figures of speech – nonetheless adds up to considerably less than the sum of its often scintillating parts, simply because the film doesn't seem to be about anything other than its own cleverness. The film appears headed for a mixed critical and lukewarm B.O. reception. Not really a detective story, but taking the form of one, story clicks in when the Dude – real name Jeff Lebowski – is beaten up by two goons looking for a multimillionaire with the same name. That prompts him to track down his namesake, a Pasadena philanthropist, and leads to a hopelessly complex series of odd plot turns.

U.S. release: March 6 · U.S. B.O.: $17.5 million
Int'l release: March 19 · Int'l B.O.: $26 million

## Billy's Hollywood Screen Kiss

A Trimark Pictures release of a Revolutionary Eye LLC production. Produced by David Moseley. Directed, written by Tommy O'Haver. Camera, Mark Mervis; editor, Jeff Betancourt; music, Alan Ari Lazar; production design, Franco-Giacomo Carbone; costumes, Julia Bartholomew. Reviewed at Sundance Festival, Jan. 20, 1998. Running time: 92 mins.

**Sean P. Hayes (Billy), Brad Rowe (Gabriel), Richard Ganoung (Perry), Meredith Scott Lynn (Georgiana), Armando Valdes-Kennedy (Fernando), Paul Bartel (Rex Webster).**

Any helmer who'd label his debut feature "A Tommy O'Haver Trifle" clearly isn't aiming for profundity. Still, you'd think a movie whose sole point is basically "Don't fall head-over-heels on the basis of good looks alone" would avoid being as swell-looking but substance-depleted as *Billy's Hollywood Screen Kiss*. Pleasant but paper-thin romantic comedy lacks the stuff to travel beyond gay fests and very limited theatrical dates. It does, however, demonstrate tyro director Tommy O'Haver's visual flair.

U.S. release: July 24 · U.S. B.O.: $2 million

## The Big Mambo (Das Mambospiel) (Germany)

A Kinowelt release of a Neue Deutsche Filmgesellschaft production, in association with Mitteldeutscher Rundfunk, Sueddeutscher Rundfunk, Arte. Produced by Hermann Florin. Directed, written by Michael Gwisdek. Camera, Roland Dressel; editors, Gwisdek, Andreas Helm, Wolfgang Schuhkrafft; music, Detlef Petersen; production design, Thomas Kappe; costume design, Marion Greiner. Reviewed at Berlin Festival, Feb. 14, 1998. Running time: 106 mins.

**Corinna Harfouch (Maria), Michael Gwisdek (Martin), Juergen Vogel (Gregor), Uwe Kokisch (Winne), Henry Huebchen (Chris), Michael Schweighofer (Peter).**

The central relationship isn't the only dysfunctional thing in *The Big Mambo*, a dramedy that only rarely hits its marks. Shapelessly helmed by actor-director Michael Gwisdek as a showcase for himself and wife Corinna Harfouch, this modern battle-of-the-sexes pic too often plays as an in-joke between its stars with humor that's too local to travel. Things start in breezy fashion as Maria (Harfouch) happens on a stash of stolen money in a garbage bin, hiding it at home from her wimpish partner Gregor (Juergen Vogel), whom she's about to dump.

Int'l release: March 26, 1997 · Int'l B.O.: $50,000

## Birth of a Butterfly (Tavalod-E Parvaneh) (Iran)

A Sima Film (Tehran) production. Directed by Mojtaba Raie. Screenplay, Saeed Shahpoori. Camera, Mohammad Davudi; editor, Hassan Hassandoost; music, Kambiz Rowshan-Ravan; art direction, Raie, Mallak-Jahan Khazai. Reviewed at Fajr Festival, Tehran, Feb. 8, 1998. Running time: 110 mins.

**With: Rahin Jahani, Mahmud Nazar-Alian, Mohammad Mehdi Faqih, Zahra Farhadi, Seyed Saeed Musavi, Hamid Nahrain.**

Filmed amid the spectacular waterfalls and rugged mountain villages of northern Iran and Azerbaijan, *Birth of a Butterfly* proves that gorgeous visuals, attractive thesps, and an assured stylistic sense can override weaknesses associated with poetic and episodic narratives. Pic, one of only three Iranian titles chosen to compete in the Fajr fest (where it picked up the art direction prize), may be too mystical to pass muster with staunch rationalists, but that quality and a ravishing pictorial sense are sure to make it an unqualified fest crowd-pleaser, with selective arthouse playoff a strong likelihood.

## Black Cat, White Cat (France-Germany-Yugoslavia)

An October Films/Goldwyn Films release of a Ciby 2000 (Paris)/Pandora Film (Frankfurt)/Komuna Film (Belgrade) co-production. Produced by Karl Baumgartner. Directed by Emir Kusturica. Screenplay, Gordan Mihic, Kusturica. Camera, Thierry Arbogast; editor, Svetolik Mica Zajc; music, D. Nele Karajlic, Vajislav Aralica, Dejo Sparavalo; production design, Milenko Jeremic; costume design, Nebojsa Lipanovic. Reviewed at Venice Festival, Sept. 10. Running time: 129 mins.

**Bajram Severdzan (Matko Destanov), Florijan Ajdini (Zare Destanov), Salija Ibraimova (Afrodita), Branka Katic (Ida), Srdan Todorovic (Dadan Karambolo), Zabit Memedov (Zarije Destanov), Sabri Sulejman (Grga Pitic).**

(Serbo-Croatian dialog)

*Black Cat, White Cat*, Bosnian-born filmmaker Emir Kusturica's highly anticipated followup to his 1995 Cannes Palme d'Or winner *Underground*, emerges as a colorful, frenetic mixture of slapstick and folklore that stands a good chance of delighting arthouse audiences worldwide.

There's hardly a hint of Balkan politics in this prodigiously well-made, frantically paced comedy, which is filled to the brim with colorful characters involved in sometimes familiar but always engaging situations. The people here are gypsies who live on the banks of the Danube river. These cheerful outcasts make a living via all kinds of skullduggery. Grga Pitic, garbage-dump godfather, and Zarije, cement works czar, are both in their eighties; they're old, dear friends. When Zarije's good-for-nothing son, Matko, becomes involved in the heist of a train carrying valuable fuel, he needs money to finance the hijack; unable to seek help from his father, he goes to Grga for help. But Matko is double-crossed by Dadan Karambolo, the manic, coke-snorting boss of the gypsy gangsters. Dadan demands compensation from the hapless Matko – he orders that Matko's son, Zare, marry Dadan's sister, Afrodita. But Zare is in love with barmaid Ida (Branka Katic).

Int'l release: Aug. 3                    Int'l B.O.: $5.5 million

## Black Dog

A Universal release of a Mutual Film Co. presentation of a Prelude Pictures production. Produced by Raffaella De Laurentiis, Peter Saphier, Mark W. Koch. Directed by Kevin Hooks. Screenplay, William Mickelberry, Dan Vining. Camera, Buzz Feitshans IV; editors, Debra Neil-Fisher, Sabrina Plisco-Morris; music, George S. Clinton; production designer, Victoria Paul; costume designer, Peggy Stamper; stunt coordinators, Vic Armstrong, Gary Hymes. Reviewed at the Cinemark Tinseltown Westchase, Houston, April 30. MPAA Rating: PG-13. Running time: 88 mins.

**Patrick Swayze (Jack Crews), Meat Loaf (Red), Randy Travis (Earl), Brenda Strong (Melanie Crews), Graham Beckel (Cutler), Stephen Tobolowsky (McClaren), Charles Dutton (Ford).**

Patrick Swayze does some dirty driving in *Black Dog*, a stripped-for-speed B movie that redefines the term "road rage." Aptly cast as a soulfully virile ex-convict who's tricked into hauling a truckload of illegal weapons across state lines, Swayze provides some much-needed, femme-skewing marquee allure for an otherwise male-oriented action opus. Overly familiar but fitfully exciting, pic has potential to post respectable B.O. numbers before making a bigger splash in ancillary venues.

Jack Crews is struggling to provide for his family after serving a two-year prison sentence for causing a fatal mishap after falling asleep at the wheel. He's lost his license to operate big rigs, working as a mechanic at a trucking firm, when he's offered an "off the books" drive with a no-questions-asked cargo.

U.S. release: May 1                    U.S. B.O.: $13 million
Int'l release: July 29                  Int'l B.O.: $4 million

## Blade

A New Line Cinema release of an Amen Ra Films production, in association with Imaginary Forces. Produced by Peter Frankfurt, Wesley Snipes, Robert Engleman. Directed by Stephen Norrington. Screenplay, David S. Goyer, based on characters created by Marv Wolfman, Gene Colan. Camera, Theo Van De Sande; editor, Paul Rubell; music, Mark Isham; production design, Kirk M. Petruccelli; costumes, Sanja Mikovic Hays; makeup effects, Greg Cannom; stunt coordinators, Jeff Ward, Henry Kingi, Jr. Reviewed at Variety Club, San Francisco, Aug. 10. MPAA Rating: R. Running time: 121 mins.

**Wesley Snipes (Blade), Stephen Dorff (Deacon Frost), Kris Kristofferson (Whistler), N'Bushe Wright (Karen), Donal Logue (Quinn), Udo Kier (Dragonetti), Arly Jover (Mercury), Traci Lords (Racquel).**

The edge is off *Blade*, with Wesley Snipes as a Marvel Comics-derived vampire slayer. Though slick and diverting, increasingly silly pic has trouble meshing disparate elements – horror, superhero fantasy, straight-up action – into a workable whole. It also problematically lurches between a sort of *Mortal Kombat* appeal and vague attempts at grown-up weirdness, never quite realizing either. Thrown into a marketplace already crowded with waning summer actioners, it's likely to experience a fast dropoff after hale but unspectacular opening numbers. Ancillary life may be brighter. Prolog, set in 1967, sets up title character's origin; child of a woman bitten by a vampire but not fully infected, Blade grows up carrying characteristics of both undead and mortals but his human conscience renders him an ace vampire hunter. He has a tacit agreement with the vampire colony so long as they stay "underground." But Turk vampire Frost wants to rock the boat and instigate a full-fledged "vampire apocalypse."

U.S. release: Aug. 21                  U.S. B.O.: $70 million
Int'l release: Aug. 27                  Int'l B.O.: $47 million

## Blessed Are Those Who Thirst (Salige Er De Som Torster) (Norway)

A Nordic Screen Prod. production, in association with TV2. Produced by Petter J. Borgli, Tomas Backstrom. Directed by Carl Jorgen Kionig. Screenplay, Axel Hellstenius, based on the novel by Anne Holt. Camera, Kjell Vassdal; editor, Inge-Lise Langfeldt; music, Rain 9; production design, Karl Juliusson. Reviewed at Haugesund Festival, Norway, Aug. 29. Running time: 118 mins.

**Kjersti Elvik (Hanne Wilhelmsen), Lasse Kolsrud (Hakon Sand), Anne Ryg (Karen Borg), Bjorn Sundquist (Billy T), Nils Ole Oftebro (Finn Haverstad), Jorgen Langhelle (Olaf Frydenberg).**

Recent winner of a Norwegian Amanda for best film, *Blessed Are Those Who Thirst* is an uneven but at times interesting cop-thriller-with-a-twist that would be a natural for offshore small screens if the sex and nudity were toned down.

Pic is based on the highly successful series of crime novels by Norwegian author Anne Holt, the nation's former justice minister. The twist in Holt's novels, featuring policewoman Hanne Wilhelmsen, is that her heroine is a lesbian with a live-in lover and drives around on a Harley-Davidson. Holt's novels have so far generated a TV series and this feature – both with the same principal cast and directed by Carl Jorgen Kionig. In *Blessed*, several women have mysteriously disappeared without trace, and the police suspect the work of a serial killer. Enormous amounts of blood are found in different locations around the city, but no bodies are discovered. When a young woman is brutally raped in her apartment and one of the missing bodies is found, Wilhelmsen starts putting two and two together in the hunt for the killer.

Int'l release: Oct. 24, 1997        Int'l B.O.: $600,000

### Blood Guts Bullets & Octane

A Short Fuse Films production, in association with Next Wave Films. Produced by Dan Leis, Joe Carnahan, Leon Corcos, Patrick M. Lynn. Directed, written, edited by Joe Carnahan. Camera, John A. Jiminez; music, Mark Priolo. Reviewed at Sundance Festival, Jan. 22, 1998. Running time: 87 mins.

With: Dan Leis, Joe Carnahan, Dan Harlan, Ken Rudulph, Hugh McCord, Mark S. Allen.

Yet another tongue-in-cheek crime meller grasping onto Tarantino coat-tails, *Blood Guts Bullets & Octane* seems to have expended all its energy in the title. Commercial prospects are anemic for this talk-laden snore. Bob (Dan Leis) and Sid (Joe Carnahan) are pushy but hapless used-car-lot owners whose biz is not going well. So, they have little choice when an associate promises $250,000 for mere "valet service" on a '63 Le Mans convertible. They don't know the said auto has already left a trail of dead guys in its wake.

### Blue Moon (Lan Yue) (Taiwan)

A Blue Moon Films production. Produced by Aaton Cheng. Directed by Ko Yi-cheng. Screenplay, Ko, Joe Liu. Camera, Jack Le; editor, Hokka Lin; music, Tseng Szu-ming; production design, Michael Hsu, Hsu Shu-yu; costume design, Sarina Wei, Emily Lin. Reviewed at London Festival, Nov. 17, 1997. Running time: 97 mins.

Tarcy Su (Yi-fang), Leon Dai (Chuen-shu), David Wang (A-gua), Chang Han (A-chuan), Teddy Lo (Luo-an).

(Mandarin dialog)

A potentially pretentious idea manages to skirt disaster and come up trumps in *Blue Moon*, a relationships ensemble set among young Taiwanese urbanites that's made to be shown with the five reels projected in any order. This first movie in six years by '1980s New Waver Ko Yi-cheng is his most mature and substantial work. Gimmick of having the projectionist randomly choose the reels' running order in fact works rather well. The idea was to mirror a "blue moon" – signifying a second chance to those lucky enough to see one.

### Blues Brothers 2000

A Universal release of a Landis/Belzberg production. Produced by John Landis, Dan Aykroyd, Leslie Belzberg. Directed by Landis. Screenplay, Aykroyd, Landis, based on *The Blues Brothers* by Aykroyd, Landis. Camera, David Herrington; editor, Dale Beldin; music, Paul Shaffer; production design, Bill Brodie; costume design, Deborah Nadoolman. Reviewed at AMC Studio 30, Houston, Feb. 3, 1998. MPAA Rating: PG-13. Running time: 123 mins.

Dan Aykroyd (Elwood Blues), John Goodman (Mighty Mack McTeer), Joe Morton (Cabel Chamberlain), J. Evan Bonifant (Buster), Nia Peeples (Lt. Elizondo), Kathleen Freeman (Mother Mary Stigmata) and with Aretha Franklin, James Brown, B.B. King.

Dan Aykroyd and director John Landis take a bumpy trip down memory lane in *Blues Brothers 2000*, a sluggishly paced, fitfully funny follow-up to their 1980 musical-comedy extravaganza. It's always a risky business to make a sequel to any pic that's more than a decade old, even with several members of the original cast. But given the continuing popularity of the original *Blues Brothers* in video and pay TV venues, this wildly uneven sequel might attract enough ticketbuyers to generate decent, though not spectacular, B.O. coin before finding greener pastures in ancillary markets.

New outing begins with Elwood Blue's release from prison after serving 18 years. Despite the fact that his brother has died, he sets out to reassemble the Blues Brothers Band.

U.S. release: Feb. 6        U.S. B.O.: $14 million
Int'l release: Apr. 30      Int'l B.O.: $18 million

### Blues Harp (Japan)

A MAC production. Produced by Narita Naoya. Directed by Takashi Miike. Screenplay, Matsuo Toshihiko, Morioka Toshiyuki. Camera, Yamamoto Hideo; editor, Shimamura Taiji; music, Okuno Atsushi; production design, Ishige Akira. Reviewed at Vancouver Festival, Oct. 11. Running time: 105 mins.

With: Ikeuchi Hiroyuki (Kenji), Tanabe Seichi (Chuji), Sekino Saori, Mickey Curtis.

This latest effort from Nippon helmer Takashi Miike takes him in a new direction. Set in Okinawa's underground youth culture, *Blues Harp* pairs up a struggling musician with a slick, up-and-coming gangster, with volatile and stylish results. It's solid fest fodder, with a special nod to gay events looking for something different.

Helmer goes to the fringes of Nippon life by centering on Chuji, a part-time bartender and occasional pot salesman. The son of a black GI and an Okinawan mother, Chuji appears to be a multiply marginalized no-hoper, but things look up when his talents as a harmonica player are noticed by a hotshot record exec. He's also spotted by a doe-eyed veterinarian's assistant who has enough medical knowledge to help patch up the well-dinged Kenji, a young yakuza who collapses in the alley behind the club where Chuji works. The mob man owes them both his life, but he takes a special interest in the woolly-haired bluesman – something that leads to big, big trouble when his admiring lieutenant gets jealous and sneaks off to undo the interloper's success.

### B. Monkey (U.K.-U.S.)

A Buena Vista Int'l/Miramax release of a Miramax/Scala presentation of a Scala Prods./Syn-chronistic Pictures production. Produced by Colin Vaines, Stephen Woolley. Directed by Michael Radford. Screenplay, Michael Thomas, Radford, Carole King, from the novel by Andrew Davies. Camera, Ashley Rowe; editor, Joelle Hache; music, Jennie Muskett; production design, Sophie Becker; costume design, Valentine Breton des Loys. Reviewed at London Film Festival, Nov. 7. Running time: 90 mins.

Asia Argento (Beatrice), Jared Harris (Alan), Rupert Everett (Paul), Jonathan Rhys Meyers (Bruno), Tim Woodward (Frank), Ian Hart (Steve).

Two years after wrapping principal photography, Michael Radford's *B. Monkey* finally swings down from the trees in surprisingly respectable shape. Though its mixed-to-goodish reception at the London fest is unlikely to translate into a canopy of green when pic hits theaters early next year, this quirky, romantic thriller could scoop up handfuls of nuts here and there before a fast forward to video. Miramax, which bankrolled the movie, pushes it out Stateside Feb. 26.

Yarn is initially told through the eyes of both leading characters: Alan, an average Joe schoolteacher, and Beatrice, an Italian-born punk cat burglar. (Her nickname is "B. Monkey" because "I can get into anything.") Alan, a jazz fan, works nights as a DJ; Beatrice shares an apartment with her partners in crime. When she decides she wants out, Beatrice changes her hairstyle and goes to a bar where she attracts the attention of Alan, who woos her with his seductive combination of normality and a more settled lifestyle.

## Bocage, The Triumph of Love (Bocage, O Triunfo do Amor) (Brazil)

A Cinema do Seculo XXI and Antonio da Cunha Telles production distributed by Prefeitura Rio Filme. Produced by Antonio da Cunha Telles. Directed by Djalma Limongi Batista. Screenplay, Gualter Limongi Batista, Djalma Limongi Batista. Camera, Djalma Limongi Batista, Zeca Abdalla; editor, Jose Carvalho Motta; music, Livio Tragtenberg; production design, Bruno Testore Schmidt; costumes, Lino Villaventura. Reviewed at Sundance Festival, Jan. 17. Running time: 85 mins.
**Victor Wagner (Bocage), Francisco Farinelli (Josino), Vietia Rocha (Manteigui), Majo de Castro (Alzira).**
The most febrile, phantasmagorical Fellini tapestries have nothing on Djalma Limongi Batista's *Bocage, the Triumph of Love*, unspooled to gasps of approval at Sundance's World Cinema program. Brilliantly shot, audaciously designed, and incorrigibly naughty, one-of-a-kind biopic tracks the titular Portuguese poet in exile through stylized tableaux and ironic verse. Baroque, non-narrative structure and obscure subject make this one a tough sell, but discriminating arthouse patrons will be duly impressed by this 1960s-feeling nose-thumb. Pic is the tale of a man arrested for "contempt of the Brazilian government" and forced by church and state to become a New Age martyr.
Int'l release: Jan. 16                    Int'l B.O.: $400,000

## Body Count

A Polygram Filmed Entertainment release of a PFE presentation of an Island Pictures production, in association with Jackson/McHenry Films, Main Line Pictures. Produced by Mark Burg, Doug McHenry, George Jackson. Directed by Robert Patton-Spruill. Screenplay, Theodore Witcher. Camera, Charles Mills; editor, Richard Nord; music, Curt Sobel; production designer, Tim Eckel; costume designer, Pauline White. Reviewed at ABC Piccadilly, London, April 28. MPAA Rating: R. Running time: 85 mins.
**David Caruso (Hobbs), Linda Fiorentino (Natalie), John Leguizamo (Chino), Ving Rhames (Pike), Donnie Wahlberg (Booker), Forest Whitaker (Crane).**
Reservoirs of talent are dogged by a so-so script and styleless direction in *Body Count*, an after-the-heist road movie that sizzles here and there but ends up going no place special. Director Robert Patton-Spruill draws reasonable perfs in this sophomore outing but doesn't bring anything new to the overcrowded post-Tarantino table. Theodore Witcher's expletive-heavy screenplay opens with four no-goods fleeing

a bungled art-museum robbery in Boston. At their hideout, the group's security-systems expert (Ving Rhames), suggests they all lie low while he goes to Miami to sell the stolen paintings. But mutual trust is already in short supply.

## Bongwater

An Alliance Independent Films presentation. Produced by Alessandro Uzielli, Laura Bickford. Directed by Richard Sears. Screenplay, Nora Maccoby, Eric Weiss, based on the book by Michael Hornburg. Camera, Richard Crudo; editor, Lauren Zuckerman; music, Mark Mothersbaugh, Josh Mancell; production designer, Gideon Ponte; costume designer, Nancy Steiner. Reviewed at L.A. Independent Festival, April 19. Running time: 98 mins.
**Luke Wilson (David), Alicia Witt (Serena), Amy Locane (Jennifer), Brittany Murphy (Mary), Jack Black (Devlin), Andy Dick (Tony), Jeremy Sisto (Robert), Jamie Kennedy (Tommy).**
The latest entry in the growing field of indie youth ensemble films, *Bongwater* is an uneven, intermittently likeable movie about a group of Portland residents for whom getting high is a way of life. While its fresh-faced but largely unknown cast members rise above the material, pic isn't distinctive enough to suggest it will yield more than a limited run in specialized markets. Serena and David become friends, roommates and nearly lovers. Introducing him to her well-connected friend Mary, Serena tries to help David gain a foothold in the art scene.

## The Book Of Life (France)

A Collection 2000 Seen By presentation of a La Sept ARTE/Haut & Court/True Fiction Pictures production. Produced by Pierre Chevalier, Carole Scotta, Caroline Benjo, Simon Arnal, Thierry Cajianut, Matthew Myers. Directed, written by Hal Hartley. Camera, Jim Denault; editor, Steve Hamilton; music, P.J. Harvey, P. Comelade, David Byrne, Ben Watt, Yo La Tengo. Reviewed at Cannes Festival, May 18. Running time: 63 mins.
**Martin Donovan (Jesus Christ), P.J. Harvey (Magdalena), Thomas Jay Ryan (Satan), Dave Simonds (Guy in Bar), Miho Nikaido (Edie).**
Hal Hartley is the only American director to contribute to France's Collection 2000 Seen By series, a group of one-hour TV films about the end of the millennium. In *The Book of Life*, he gives a playful, irreverent and quite unorthodox account of the Second Coming of Jesus, who is depicted as a young businessman returning to earth to kick off the Apocalypse. It is one of the hipper items in the Collection 2000 and should be one of its most popular episodes. A feeling of doom pervades the jaded population of New York as they get ready to turn the Big Page on the calendar. In a hotel bar, a young gambler and the waitress who secretly loves him chat with a down-and-outer who is the devil in disguise.

## The Borrowers (U.K.)

A Polygram release of a Polygram Filmed Entertainment presentation of a Working Title production. Produced by Tim Bevan, Eric Fellner, Rachel Talalay. Directed by Peter Hewitt. Screenplay, Gavin Scott, John Camps, based on novels by Mary Norton. Camera, John Fenner, Trevor Brooker; editor, David Freeman; music, Harry Gregson-Williams; production design, Gemma Jackson; costume design, Marie France; visual-effects supervisor, Peter Chiang; stunt coordinator, Jim Dowdall. Reviewed at Empire 1, London, Oct. 19, 1997. Running time: 83 mins.

---

### ... April 18 ...
Vet French producer Anatole Dauman (**Hiroshima, Mon Amour, The Tin Drum**) calls it a wrap.

John Goodman (Ocious P. Potter), Jim Broadbent (Pod Clock), Mark Williams (Exterminator Jeff), Hugh Laurie (Officer Steady), Bradley Pierce (Pete Lender), Flora Newbigin (Arrietty Clock), Tom Felton (Peagreen Clock), Raymond Pickard (Spiller), Celia Imrie (Homily Clock).

Sumptuously decked out but with a poorly conceived script, *The Borrowers* is a top-notch family film that welds English quaintness and eccentricity with high-tech effects. Based on Mary Norton's kidtomes about a family of four-inch-high "little people" who live under the floorboards of a British house, its entry in the effects-driven market looks set for bright biz locally pre-Christmas. The pic's chances Stateside will depend on getting a clear field and tweaking U.S. auds' curiosity with a fresh spin and lots of promo coin.

Titular family – so-called because they "borrow" items from the house under which they live – consists of father Pod, mother Homily and kids Arrietty and Peagreen. Paper-thin plot emerges with the introduction of the bad guy, Ocious P. Potter, an avaricious lawyer-cum-realtor. Discovering the owner of a house has died, Potter decides to evict the tenants and demolish the cottage-like abode to build luxury apartments. The Borrowers unwillingly ally themselves with the tenants' son, Pete. This involves finding and absconding with the will, and getting to City Hall before Potter can register the house for demolition. Majority of the pic is an extended chase, with the little people pursued into the "outside world" with the indestructible Potter always close behind.

U.S. release: Feb. 13      U.S. B.O.: $22.5 million
Int'l release: Dec. 5, 1997      Int'l B.O.: $28 million

## The Boxer (U.K.-Ireland-U.S.)

A Universal release of a Hell's Kitchen production. Produced by Jim Sheridan, Arthur Lappin. Directed by Sheridan. Screenplay, Sheridan, Terry George. Camera, Chris Menges; editor, Gerry Hambling; music, Gavin Friday, Maurice Seezer; production design, Brian Morris; costume design, Joan Bergin; boxing consultant, Barry McGuigan. Reviewed at Universal Studios, Universal City, Dec. 8, 1997. MPAA Rating: R. Running time: 113 mins.

Daniel Day-Lewis (Danny Flynn), Emily Watson (Maggie), Brian Cox (Joe Hamill), Ken Stott (Ike Weir), Gerard McSorley (Harry), Eleanor Methven (Patsy).

The third collaboration between director Jim Sheridan and actor Daniel Day-Lewis, *The Boxer* is an involving but rather prosaic report from the Belfast front with a melancholy undertow of romantic yearning. Intelligently conceived and well acted, this compact, straightforward drama about two ordinary people caught in the ongoing political crossfire packs enough punch to command audience interest, but won't light up critics or the B.O. to the extent achieved by the team's previous outings.

U.S. release: Dec. 31, 1997      U.S. B.O.: $6 million
Int'l release: Feb. 6      Int'l B.O.: $10.2 million

## The Boys (Australia)

A Globe Films release of an Arenafilm production, in association with the Australian Film Commission, Premium Movie Partnership for Showtime, SBS Independent, Axiom, Screen Partners, New South Wales Film & TV Office. Produced by Robert Connolly, John Maynard. Directed by Rowan Woods. Screenplay, Stephen Sewell, based on the play by Gordon Graham. Camera, Tristan Milani; editor, Nick Meyers; music, the

Necks; production design, Luigi Pittorino; costume design, Annie Marshall. Reviewed at Greater Union Pitt Centre, Sydney, Feb. 3, 1998. Running time: 84 mins.

David Wenham (Brett Sprague), Toni Collette (Michelle), Lynette Curran (Sandra Sprague), John Polson (Glenn Sprague), Anthony Hayes (Stevie Sprague), Jeanette Cronin (Jackie), Anna Lise (Nola).

A chilling, corrosive depiction of the banality of evil, Rowan Woods' powerful debut film essentially covers a 24-hour period leading up to a never-seen, but evidently hideous, crime. Boasting extraordinary performances, and an intensity that is at times almost unbearable, although there's little on-screen violence, with strong critical support and agressive distribution, it should find a niche audience. Film is based on an award-winning play, which was in turn inspired by the real-life rape and murder of a young nurse in Sydney.

Int'l release: May 7      Int'l B.O.: $850,000

## The Boys (Les Boys) (Canada)

A Melenny Prods production, with the participation of Telefilm Canada, Super Ecran, the Québec government. Produced by Richard Goudreau. Directed by Louis Saia. Screenplay, Christian Fournier, based on an original idea by Richard Goudreau. Camera, Sylvain Brault; editor, Yvann Thibaudeau; music, Normand Corbeil; production design, Claude Pare; costumes, Suzanne Harel. Reviewed at the Quartier Latin Cinema, Montreal, Dec. 12, 1997. Running time: 107 mins.

Marc Messier (Bob), Remy Girard (Stan), Patrick Huard (Ti-Guy), Serge Theriault (François), Michel Barrette (Roger), Paul Houde (Fernand), Luc Guerin (Marcel), Yvan Ponton (Jean-Charles), Roc Lafortune (Julien).

A hockey tale told with large dollops of broad-appeal comedy, *The Boys* is a sure-fire recipe for scoring big-time as a home-team favorite. The story of a gang of ordinary guys who get their kicks by playing in an amateur hockey league, the French-lingo pic is a highly entertaining effort that delivers the goods by keeping things simple and to the point. It will attract notice wherever hockey is hot, but this type of down-home French-Canadian humor doesn't usually travel well; pic will certainly be a tough sell in non-French-speaking territories.

U.S. release: Dec. 12, 1997      U.S. B.O.: $4.8 million

## The Boys II (Les Boys II) (Canada)

A Lions Gate release of a Melenny Prods production. Produced by Richard Goudreau. Directed by Louis Saia. Screenplay, Saia, Rene Brisebois, François Camirand, based on an idea by Richard Goudreau. Camera, Georges Archambault; editor, Gaetan Huot; music, Normand Corbeil; costume design, Suzanne Harel. Reviewed at Place des Arts, Montreal, Dec. 8. Running time: 120 mins.

Marc Messier (Bob), Remy Girard (Stan), Patrick Huard (Ti-Guy), Serge Theriault (François), Paul Houde (Fernand), Luc Guerin (Marcel), Yvan Ponton (Jean-Charles), Roc Lafortune (Julien).

Les Boys are back in town. The sequel to the all-time top-grossing French-Canadian film doesn't tamper with the magic formula that pulled in some C$6 million in Québec last year. Delivering plenty of down-home laughs and a few nifty on-ice match-ups, it makes for a highly enjoyable slice of light entertainment. Pic opened on more than 80 screens across Québec and its success is all but guaranteed. But it doesn't look to score anywhere near as well in international rinks, given that

---

**...April 19...**
**The Full Monty** wins Best Picture at the BAFTA Awards.

this sort of Québeçois humor rarely travels.

This time around Les Boys are on their way to France to take part in an international amateur hockey competition held in picturesque Alps town Chamonix. Most of the attention is focused on the comic foibles of these ordinary Montrealers who are perplexed by life on the other side of the Atlantic rather than on-ice action. Comic hay is made of the cultural differences between the Québecers and the French, and the writers deserve top marks for avoiding the obvious cliches. In the tournee, the team starts out by losing badly to a squad from the Ivory Coast! Things predictably climax with an emotional match where Les Boys fare better.

U.S. release: Dec. 11      U.S. B.O.: $2.5 million

### The Brandon Teena Story (Docu)

A Bless Bless Prods production. Produced by Susan Muska. Directed, written by Muska, Greta Olafsdottir. Camera, Muska; editors, Muska, Olafsdottir. Reviewed at Berlin Festival, Feb. 21, 1998. Running time: 89 mins.

The background to a triple homicide committed on New Year's Eve 1993 in a small Nebraska town is explored in depth in this probing, powerful documentary. *The Brandon Teena Story* is a study of the banality of evil based on deep-seated prejudices. Only the poor standard of the video-to-film transfer will prevent the pic from securing select theatrical bookings, but it should play successfully on quality TV nets.

Brandon Teena was born a girl, Teena Brandon, in Lincoln, Neb. When Teena decided her sexual orientation was male, she changed her name and underwent surgery to remove her breasts. As Brandon, he started dating girls, some of whom are interviewed. The revelation of the true gender of a man they'd accepted as one of them outraged a couple of macho locals, who attacked Brandon on Christmas Eve, beating and raping him.

U.S. release: Sept. 24      U.S. B.O.: $50,000

### Break Even (Plus-Minus Null) (Germany)

A Deutschen Film and Fernsehakademie Berlin production, with assistance from ZDF/3sat. Produced by Christian Hohoff. Directed, written by Eoin Moore. Camera, Bernd Lohr, Moore; editor, Dirk Grau, Moore; art director, Gudrun Schroter; costume designer, Viola Volk. Reviewed at San Sebastian Film Festival, Sept. 25, 1998. Running time: 83 mins.

**Andreas Schmidt (Alex), Tamara Simunovic (Svetlana), Kathleen Gallego Zapata (Ruth).**

A moody drama centering on an emotionally rootless man's half-hearted attempts to connect with two prostitutes, *Break Even* achieves a natural intimacy with its characters and establishes an authentic feel for the story's grungy Berlin milieu via its unpretentious approach and unconstrained camera style. A prize-winner at this year's Munich Festival that also earned a special jury mention in San Sebastian's New Directors competition, this resourceful, no-budget debut will serve as a quietly impressive calling card for newcomer Eoin Moore.

Posing as a cop to intervene and protect inexperienced Bosnian hooker Svetlana from a pimp attempting to enlist her, construction worker and petty criminal Alex drifts almost casually into the young woman's life. Both are financially burdened: Svetlana is turning tricks to reopen her mother's hair salon in Bosnia, while Alex is paying child support for a daughter his ex-wife would prefer he didn't see.

Things coast along smoothly until Alex is caught stealing tools from a construction site and given a week to reimburse the foreman.

### Bride of Chucky

A Universal release of a David Kirschner production. Produced by Kirschner, David Gilroy. Directed by Ronnie Yu. Screenplay, Don Mancini, based on his original characters. Camera, Peter Pau; editors, David Wu, Randolph K. Bricker; music, Graeme Revell; production design, Alicia Keywan; James McAteer; puppet effects, Kevin Yagher; costume design, Lynne MacKay. Reviewed at Universal City Cineplex, Universal City, Oct. 14. MPAA Rating: R. Running Time: 89 mins.

**Jennifer Tilly (Tiffany), Katherine Heigl (Jade), Nick Stabile (Jesse), John Ritter (Chief Warren Kincaid), Alexis Arquette (Damien Baylock), Gordon Michael Woolvett (David), Lawrence Dane (Lt. Preston), Kathy Najimy (Maid), Brad Dourif (Voice of Chucky).**

Apart from the current vogue for horror films, there appeared to be little foundation for resurrecting the *Child's Play* franchise. But after an eight-year hiatus, *Bride of Chucky* emerges with recharged batteries and a mordantly funny edge that's attuned to the dawning millennium. A relatively straightforward genre piece, it has flair and a dash of wit that should produce very strong opening numbers and could well have better-than-average theatrical stamina in addition to potent ancillary revenue dollars.

Chucky – the former serial killer Charles Lee Ray, whose spirit was mystically transferred into a doll at the moment of his death – is resurrected from the evidence morgue in a heist engineered by his ex-girlfriend Tiffany and a money-hungry cop. Stitching and stapling the remnants of the doll together, Tiffany invokes a voodoo chant and the smart-mouth Chucky is back in the sort of lethal business he engaged in as a flesh-and-blood felon. Combining an overt reference to *The Bride of Frankenstein* with a hipper, sexually slanted appeal to young adults à la *Halloween* and *Scream*, the story proceeds to involve a high-school couple whose relationship is blocked at every turn by the girl's police-chief uncle, Warren.

U.S. release: Oct. 16      U.S. B.O.: $32 million
Int'l release: Dec. 25      Int'l B.O.: $1.1 million

### Bring Me the Head of Mavis Davis (U.K.)

A Goldcrest Films Int'l/BBC Films presentation of a Mission film. Produced by Stephen Colegrave, Joanne Reay. Directed by John Henderson. Screenplay, Craig Strachan, from an original idea by Joanne Reay. Camera, Clive Tickner; editor, Paul Endacott; music, Christopher Tyng; production design, Michael Carlin; costume design, Helen McCabe. Reviewed at Cannes Film Festival, May 10, 1997. Running time: 99 mins.

**Rik Mayall (Marty Starr), Jane Horrocks (Marla Dorland), Danny Aiello (Rathbone), Ronald Pickup (Percy Stone), Jaclyn Mendoza (Cynthia).**

A wannabe waspish black comedy set in the Brit music industry, *Bring Me the Head of Mavis Davis* ends up a TV-style effort decapitated by a lame script and often-clumsy direction. Local tube stars Rik Mayall and Jane Horrocks mug their way through this yarn of a diskery owner who tries to deep-six his fading star, and guesting Danny Aiello looks like he caught the wrong plane. Pic, which opened Jan. 16 in London, looks headed for a fast trip through theaters.

Int'l release: Jan. 18      Int'l B.O.: $100,000

---

**. . . April 20 . . .**

Indie drama **Broken Vessels** wins top honors at L.A. Indie fest.

## Broken Vessels

A Ziehl and Zal presentation. Produced by Roxana Zal, Scott Ziehl. Directed by Scott Ziehl. Screenplay, David Baer, John McMahon, Ziehl. Camera, Antonio Calvache; editors, David Moritz, Chris Figler; production designer, Rodrigo Castillo; costume designer, Roseanne Fiedler; paramedic consultant, Jeff Rogers. Reviewed at L.A. Independent Festival, April, 19. Running time: 90 mins.

Todd Field (Jimmy Warzniak), Jason London (Tom Meyer), Roxana Zal (Elizabeth Capalino), Susan Traylor (Susy), James Hong (Mr. Chen), Patrick Cranshaw (Gramps).

A vivid, embracing tale of life on the edge, *Broken Vessels* is an assured first feature with potent commercial appeal. Focused on a pair of paramedics behind the wheel of an ambulance, the film skillfully careens through the incidental and dark humor of their lives and plows forward into the bleak personal terrain that comes with the job. Winner of the L.A. Indie fest best-picture prize, *Vessels* has sufficient high-octane quality to overcome the noisy, overcrowded specialized scene and carve out a respectable theatrical niche. Ancillary activity should also be better than the current norm for indie fare.

Recently arrived in Los Angeles from Pennsylvania, Tom lands a job with an ambulance company. He's teamed with fleet vet Jimmy, seemingly unflappable but famous for going through a lot of partners.

## Brother Tied (B&W/Color)

A Pope Innocent and Celluloid Studios production, in association with Antiques Made Weekly Films and Morgan 100 Entertainment. Produced by Alexis Howerton, Todd Lubin, Chase Morgan. Directed by Derek M. Cainfrance. Screenplay, Cainfrance, Joey Curtis, Mike Tillmann. Camera, Cainfrance; editor, Curtis; art direction, David Handley. Reviewed at Sundance Festival, Jan. 21, 1998. Running time: 109 mins.

Keith Zimmerman (Cal), Carey Westbrook (Aaron), Jason Hauser (Aaron), Christina Chang (Camille), Jacques Scott (Mika).

A modern meditation, with some allegorical overtones, about the power of blood ties, the stylishly imposing *Brother Tied* concerns the relationship between two brothers who drift apart when a third party comes between them. Derek M. Cainfrance's feature directorial debut shows a striking command of film grammar, but his noirish tale is drowned in style, resulting in a self-conscious work that doesn't engage emotionally. Theatrical prospects are dim, though a small distributor might take a risk and showcase the film.

## Buffalo 66

A Lions Gate Films/Cinepix Film Properties presentation of a Muse production. Produced by Chris Hanley. Directed by Vincent Gallo. Screenplay, Gallo, Alison Bagnall, original story by Gallo. Camera, Lance Acord; editor, Curtiss Clayton; music, Gallo; production design, Gideon Ponte. Reviewed at Sundance Festival, Jan. 21, 1998. Running time: 112 mins.

Vincent Gallo (Billy Brown), Christina Ricci (Layla), Anjelica Huston (Janet Brown), Ben Gazzara (Jimmy Brown), Mickey Rourke (Bookie), Rosanna Arquette (Wendy).

Both an impressive first film and an irritating one, Vincent Gallo's *Buffalo 66* exudes honest emotional expression and overweening ego in equal and continuous measure. Alive to cinematic ideas, generous to its actors and peppered with unexpected humor, this ultimately sweet-natured low-budgeter is nonetheless riddled with enough off-putting and digressive material to create significant obstacles to critical and commercial acceptance.

Gallo is obviously a creative force to be reckoned with. Unfortunately, he dumbs down to an almost ludicrous extreme in the role of Billy Brown, a convict who, upon his release from prison, hatches a preposterous scheme to try to impress his thick parents and then to throw his life away in taking revenge on the man he feels ruined his life.

U.S. release: June 26     U.S. B.O.: $2.4 million
Int'l release: May 29     Int'l B.O.: $800,000

## A Bug's Life (Animated)

A Buena Vista release of a Walt Disney Pictures presentation of a Pixar Animation Studios film. Produced by Darla K. Anderson, Kevin Reher. Directed by John Lasseter. Co-director, Andrew Stanton. Screenplay, Stanton, Donald McEnery, Bob Shaw, original story by Lasseter, Stanton, Joe Ranft. Camera, Sharon Calahan; supervising film editor, Lee Unkrich; music, Randy Newman; production design, William Cone; supervising technical directors, William Reeves, Eben Ostby; supervising animators, Glenn McQueen, Rich Quade. Reviewed at El Capitan, L.A., Oct. 23. MPAA Rating: G. Running time: 96 mins.

VOICES: Dave Foley (Flik), Kevin Spacey (Hopper), Julia Louis-Dreyfus (Princess Atta), Hayden Panettiere (Dot), Phyllis Diller (Queen), Richard Kind (Molt), David Hyde Pierce (Slim), Joe Ranft (Heimlich), Denis Leary (Francis), Jonathan Harris (Manny), Madeline Kahn (Gypsy), Bonnie Hunt (Rosie), Michael McShane (Tuck & Roll), John Ratzenberger (P.T. Flea), Roddy McDowall (Mr. Soil).

Entertaining in a very showbizzy sort of way, *A Bug's Life* reps the second computer-animated ant adventure in as many months. More broad based and kid friendly in its appeal than DreamWorks' more sophisticated *Antz*, John Lasseter's film won't reach the exalted B.O. levels of his 1995 *Toy Story*, which raked in $360 million worldwide. However, its imaginative design and spirited storytelling will make it a must-see for family audiences, and Disney's big holiday bugfest ultimately should enjoy the equivalent commercial relationship with the surprisingly durable *Antz*.

The film centers on an ineffectual misfit character who's out of step with the uniformity of ant society; involves an above-ground odyssey by this character into unknown territory, as well as a struggle with large hostile insects as part of an effort to save the colony. Presented in CinemaScope, *A Bug's Life* bursts upon the screen with beautiful verdant hues as a legion of ants laboriously transports pieces of food up to await the arrival of their terrorizors, a gang of grasshoppers. Unfortunately, the hapless Flik, who fancies himself a brilliant inventor, knocks over the offering, and when the ants' swaggering enemies turn up to find nothing to eat, their big bully-chief, Hopper, gravely threatens the colony's existence unless they double their donation by the end of the season.

U.S. release: Nov. 20     U.S. B.O.: $127 million
Int'l release: Dec. 4     int'l B.O.: $23 million

## Bulworth

A 20th Century Fox release. Produced by Warren Beatty, Pieter Jan Brugge. Directed by Warren Beatty. Screenplay, Beatty, Jeremy Pikser, story by Beatty. Camera, Vittorio Storaro; editors, Robert C. Jones, Billy Weber; music, Ennio Morricone; production designer, Dean Tavoularis; costume designer, Milena

Canonero; Reviewed at the Bruin, L.A., May 5. MPAA Rating: R. Running time: 107 mins.

**Warren Beatty (Jay Bulworth), Halle Berry (Nina), Don Cheadle (L.D.), Oliver Platt (Dennis Murphy), Paul Sorvino (Graham Crockett), Jack Warden (Eddie Davers), Isaiah Washington (Darnell).**

A film with an infectiously giddy sense of risk-taking and droll provocation, *Bulworth* is bitingly black comic. Warren Beatty's disarmingly blunt look at a U.S. senator who suddenly starts speaking the truth about important issues – in rap cadences, no less – is an uncommonly smart, sharp, and irreverent picture, taking liberal broadsides against political sell-outs, corporate deceit, media manipulation, aggravated race relations, and even mediocre, cynical Hollywood filmmaking. However, the roughly $40 million grossed by both *Wag the Dog* and *Primary Colors* would seem to mark the current ceiling for explicitly politically themed pictures, and *Bulworth* will have to have luck on its side to get that far, given the early summer behemoths that will surround it in the marketplace.

On the eve of the 1996 California primary, Sen. Jay Bulworth is despondent, not over his re-election chances, but over the hollow sound of his own voice and campaign slogans. He's taken out a $10 million insurance policy and orders a hit on himself.

U.S. release: May 15                   U.S. B.O.: $25.5 million

## Burn

A Look Ma, We're Moguls presentation. Produced by David Hayter. Directed by Scott Storm. Screenplay, Dylan Kussman. Camera, Peter Blue Rieveschl; editor, Storm; music, Joe Kraemer; production design, Yvette Taylor; wardrobe, Frank Helmer. Reviewed at Slamdance Festival, Park City, Utah, Jan. 20, 1998. Running time: 97 mins.

**Randall Slavin (Ben Sharpe), David Hayter (Tom Rice), Andrea Roth (Amanda Powers).**

As dark tales of Hollywood go, *Burn* is pitch-black. A vivid and unrelenting look at creativity and competition, the first feature by Scott Storm is a scorcher that pulls no punches as it puts a rabid dog-eat-dog environment under the microscope. However skillful, though, pic's ceaselessly grim tone and modest production values limit it to specialized play. *Burn* can expect decent niche theatrical response and gain some foreign sales and ancillary action but will primarily serve as a calling card for future efforts. A kindred spirit to Stephen King's *The Shining*, the story centers on Ben (Randall Slavin), a twentysomething screenwriter who's having problems getting beyond the blank page.

## Bury Me in Kern County

A Krank production. Produced by Hayley Marcus, Rachel Frazin. Directed, written by Julien Nitzberg. Camera, Kelly Evans, Warren Yeager; editor, Charlie Webber; music, Roger Neill; production design, Jill McGraw; costume design, Julie Vogel. Reviewed at World Film Festival, Montreal, Aug. 30. Running time: 90 mins.

**Mary Sheridan (Sandra), Judson Mills (Dean), Mary Lynn Rajskub (Amanda), Johnny Strong (Oldie), Thom Rachford (Sgt. Pollock), Sandra Tucker (Dani).**

Though it hails from the proverbial depths of no-budget 16mm first-featuredom, *Bury Me in Kern County*, a self-described "white-trash black comedy," reps an impressively assured and surprisingly pro debut from writer-director Julien

Nitzberg. It's somehow reassuring that original, fiercely committed indie satires like this one are still emerging to offset the tamer send-ups found on TV. Commendably avoiding predictable gross-out humor, Nitzberg combines a well-developed sardonic sense and some truly inspired casting choices to fashion a redneck mayhem fiesta that could find a welcoming fan base if accurately targeted toward hipper college and young urban auds.

Granted, spoofs of stoners and low-rent criminals aren't new to indie films. What sets Nitzberg's feature apart is the consistent freshness of his comic p.o.v., beginning with pic's focus on two sisters who're the unlikeliest banditas since Thelma met Louise. Timid-as-a-kitten Sandra gets in trouble first. The calamity isn't just that the cops raid her home on Halloween and bust her husband, Dean, for selling homemade speed; it's also that the whole thing is filmed for a *Cops*-style reality TV show. When that's broadcast, Dean's mother dies of a heart attack, which means that Sandra has to raise Dean's bail as well as his mom's funeral costs.

## Campus (Der Campus) (Germany)

A Constantin Film release of a Constantin Filmproduktion production. Produced by Bernd Eichinger, Martin Moszkowicz. Directed by Soenke Wortmann. Screenplay, Dietrich Schwanitz, Wortmann, Stefan Grund, Bettina Salomon, based on the novel by Schwanitz. Camera, Tom Faehrmann; editor, Ueli Christen; music, Nikolaus Glowna; art director, Thomas Freudenthal; costume designer, Katharina von Martius. Reviewed at Berlin Festival, Feb. 15. Running time: 122 mins.

**Heiner Lauterbach (Hanno Hackmann), Axel Milberg (Bernie Weskamp), Sibylle Canonica (Gabrielle Hackmann), Barbara Rudnik (Dr. Wagner), Sandra Speichert (Babsi Claasen), Rudolf Kowalski (Schacht).**

*The Campus* is a quality widescreen dramedy about a university prof facing a sexual-harassment case that in every respect, save language, plays like a well-honed Hollywood pic. Latest by Soenke Wortmann is a step up into the big league, and has attracted warm biz locally. But whether a foreign-lingo movie that's so close to U.S. fare can click offshore, let alone Stateside, remains to be seen.

Based on the novel by Dietrich Schwanitz, story unfolds at an esteemed Hamburg campus where respected sociology professor Hanno Hackmann (Heiner Lauterbach) delights his snooty wife (Sibylle Canonica) by agreeing to run for president of the university against the incumbent, corrupt smoothie Schacht (Rudolf Kowalski). Before sailing into battle, Hackmann has one crease to iron out of his life – his affair with a drama student, Babsi (Sandra Speichert).

Int'l release: Feb. 8                   Int'l B.O.: $4.6 million

## Can't Hardly Wait

A Sony Pictures Entertainment release of a Columbia Pictures presentation of a Tall Trees production. Produced by Jenno Topping, Betty Thomas. Directed, written by Deborah Kaplan, Harry Elfont. Camera, Lloyd Ahern; editor, Michael Jablow; music, David Kitay, Matthew Sweet; production designer, Marcia Hinds-Johnson; costume designer, Mark Bridges. Reviewed at Chinese Theater, L.A., June 2. MPAA Rating: PG-13. Running time: 98 mins.

**Jennifer Love Hewitt (Amanda), Ethan Embry (Preston), Charlie Korsmo (William), Lauren Ambrose (Denise), Peter Facinelli (Mike), Seth Green (Kenny).**

---

**. . . April 22 . . .**

Crossover dreams: Singer Mariah Carey to star with Chris Tucker in **OO-Soul**.

*Can't Hardly Wait* is a mediocre attempt to recapture the exuberance and candid portraiture of such high-school movie classics as *American Graffiti* and *Fast Times at Ridgemont High*. Boisterous comedy's appealing and energetic cast compensates only up to a point for an uneven script and rough direction. Pandering to its target audience by recycling cliches and stereotypes, pic should benefit from its timely release in early summer. Muddled music and comedy is neither authentic in its lingo and concerns, nor universal enough to appeal to a broader audience. As soon as the graduation ceremony is over at Huntington Hills High, preparations begin for the real festivity – a bash at the house of a hysterical hostess, whose sole role is to protest the carpet stains, petty thefts, and lewd graffiti perpetrated by her guests.

U.S. release: June 12      U.S. B.O.: $25.5 million
Int'l release: June 25      Int'l B.O.: $2.7 million

## Caresses (Caricies) (Spain)

A Lauren Films release of an Els Films de la Rambla production, in association with Television Espanola, Televiso de Catalunya. Produced by Ventura Pons. Directed by Pons. Screenplay, Pons, Sergi Belbel, based on the play by Belbel. Camera, Jesus Escosa; editor, Pere Abadal; music, Carles Cases; art direction, Gloria Marti. Reviewed at Cine Imperial, Madrid, Feb. 11. Running time: 92 mins.
David Selvas (Young Man), Laura Conejero (Young Woman), Julieta Serrano (Older Woman), Montserrat Salvador (Old Woman), Agustin Gonzalez (Old Man), Naim Thomas (Kid), Sergi Lopez (Man), Merce Pons (Girl).
Prolific and idiosyncratic producer-helmer Ventura Pons delivers probably his most accomplished pic with the Catalan-language *Caresses*, a darkly intelligent, wordy, and distinctly non-cinematic take on the trials of urban love. Pic is liberatingly daring in both theme and treatment, but the price of such daring is occasional pretentiousness. Though it will consolidate Pons' reputation, mainstream auds do not react kindly to this kind of intensity, and good fest runs and arthouse showings are pic's likeliest offshore fate. Based on a play, pic is structured like a chain: Each of its 11 interlocking scenes involves two characters, one of whom then passes forward into the next until the chain clicks neatly into a circle at the end. There is no plot, and dynamics are built around shifts in perspective and mood. And that perspective is pretty pessimistic, whatever kind of love you're feeling.
Int'l release: Feb. 13      Int'l B.O.: $250,000

## Cascadeur: The Amber Chamber (Cascadeur: Die Jagd Nach Dem Bernsteinzimmer) (Germany)

A Cascadeur Filmproduktion/ProSieben/FIMA production. Produced by Jimmy C. Gerum, Hardy Martins. Directed by Hardy Martins. Co-directors, Sandra Barger, Veronika Bauriedl. Screenplay, Uwe Wilhelm, Uwe Kossmann, based on an idea by Martins. Camera, Markus Fraunholz; editor, Uwe Klimmeck; music, Philipp F. Koelmel; production designers, Silke Buhr, Uwe Stanik, Bettina Glier, Claudia Walter; stunt coordinator, Martins. Reviewed at Cannes Festival, May 17. Running time: 106 mins.
Hardy Martins (Vincent), Regula Grauwiller (Christin), Heiner Lauterbach (The Colonel), Andreas Hop (Bull), Eckhard Preuss (Gonzo), Robert Viktor Minich (Pierre).
Anything Hollywood can wreck, we can wreck better, seems to be the philosophy behind *Cascadeur: The Amber Chamber*, a largely enjoyable widescreen romp. As a demo of current German filmdom's ability to replicate Hollywood's ground rules, this $4 million action-adventure has everything going for it, except charismatic leads. Its theatrical career both within and without Germany will be a litmus test of whether the U.S. can be taken on at its own game. Opening like gangbusters in Caracus with art-history student Christin tracking down an old, dying Nazi and getting hold of a special key that will help her find the Amber Room, a long-lost cultural treasure that was pilfered from Leningrad by Adolf's boys during WWII. Rogue elements from German military intelligence give chase through the streets of the Venezuelan capital.
Int'l release: July 31      Int'l B.O.: $600,000

## Caught Up

A Live Entertainment release of a Heller Highwater production, in association with Live Film and Mediaworks. Produced by Peter Heller. Directed, written by Darin Scott. Camera, Tom Callaway; editor, Charles Bornstein; music, Marc Bonilla; production design, Terrence Foster; costume design, Tracey White. Reviewed at the Sunset Screening Room, L.A., Feb. 25. MPAA Rating: R. Running time: 97 mins.
Bokeem Woodbine (Daryl Allen), Cynda Williams (Vanessa Dietrich/Trish), Joseph Lindsey (Billy Grimm), Clifton Powell (Herbert/Frank Lowden), Basil Wallace (Ahmad), Tony Todd (Jake).
*Caught Up* occupies classic film-noir terrain, with a wicked comic twist and just a sliver of social commentary. An engrossing, skillful yarn that takes its protag on a twisted path of murder, deceit, treachery, and passion, pic is nonetheless apt to get lost in the marketplace as just another Afrocentric thriller. But if it can hold its target audience, the film has good crossover prospects that could spell mid-range success and strong subsequent play on pay cable and videotape. Pic's convoluted structure of flashbacks and flashbacks within flashbacks is an obvious homage to bygone noirs. Daryl Allen (Bokeem Woodbine), who provides de rigueur voiceover narration, is back on the street after serving time for drugs. The experience has sobered him, and he's on the path to opening a nightclub when fate steps in with a curve ball.
U.S. release: Feb. 27      U.S. B.O.: $6.7 million

## The Celebration (Festen) (Denmark)

An October Films release of a Nimbus Film production, in collaboration with DR TV, SVT Drama. Produced by Brigitte Hald. Directed by Thomas Vinterberg. Screenplay, Vinterberg, in collaboration with Mogens Rukov. Camera, Anthony Dod Mantle; editor, Valdis Oskarsdottir. Reviewed at Cannes Festival, May 17. Running time: 105 mins.
Ulrich Thomsen (Christian), Henning Moritzen (Helge), Thomas Bo Larsen (Michael), Paprika Steen (Helene), Birthe Neumann (Else), Trine Dyrholm (Pia), Helle Dolleris (Mette).
Thomas Vinterberg's *The Celebration* arrives in the Cannes competition touting its adherence to the principles of Dogma 95, an artistic manifesto issued three years ago by Danish filmmakers. Seemingly a half-serious update of the French New Wave's brash pronouncements, Dogma 95 urges location shooting, direct sound, hand-held camerawork, and the avoidance of technical trickery. Vinterberg brings an idiosyncratic tone to *The Celebration*, a propulsively inventive but uneven family comedy-cum-melodrama. Though pic should score well in international fests and Euro sites, its

prospects for wider arthouse success appear limited. The celebrants converge on a handsome country estate to commemorate the 60th birthday of patriarch Helge (Henning Moritzen), whose three grown-up children evidence various problems... It quickly becomes apparent that the family gathering about to commence won't be all lighthearted revelry.

Int'l release: June 19     Int'l B.O.: $4.5 million
U.S. release: Oct. 9     U.S. B.O.: $1.2 million

## Celebrity

A Miramax release of a Sweetland Films presentation of a Jean Doumanian production. Produced by Doumanian. Directed, written by Woody Allen. Camera, Sven Nykvist; editor, Susan E. Morse; production design, Santo Loquasto; costume design, Suzy Benzinger. Reviewed at Aidikoff screening room, Beverly Hills, Aug. 28, 1998. MPAA Rating: R. Running time: 113 mins.
**Hank Azaria (David), Kenneth Branagh (Lee Simon), Judy Davis (Robin Simon), Leonardo DiCaprio (Brandon Darrow), Melanie Griffith (Nicole Oliver), Famke Janssen (Bonnie), Michael Lerner (Dr. Lupus), Joe Mantegna (Tony Gardella), Bebe Neuwirth (Hooker), Winona Ryder (Nola), Charlize Theron (Supermodel).**

The spectacle of Kenneth Branagh and Judy Davis doing Woody Allen impersonations creates a neurotic energy meltdown in *Celebrity*, a once-over-lightly rehash of now-stale Allen themes and motifs. Annoyingly mannered in performance as well as tiresomely familiar in the way it trots out its angst-ridden urban characters' problems, pic has a hastily conceived, patchwork feel that is occasionally leavened by some lively supporting turns. But even a 10-minute appearance by the world's hottest star, Leonardo DiCaprio, won't be able to lift this above Allen's usual low-level B.O. flight path.

Shooting in black-and-white for the first time in six years, Allen here deals with such subjects as fame and sexual treachery. A colossally miscast Branagh portrays Lee Simon, a feature and travel writer who, when first glimpsed, is doing a story on screen queen Nicole Oliver. Thus begins Lee's mostly desultory series of sexual escapades in the wake of his split from his wife Robin. Lee energetically throws himself into the social scene. First, with a blonde supermodel who teases Lee with intimations of orgasmic delights, only to drop him. He then becomes serious about Bonnie, who moves in with Lee as he starts to get the itch for Nola, a waitress-actress who has been hovering around the edges of his life for some time.

U.S. release: Nov. 20     U.S. B.O.: $5 million
Int'l release: Dec. 25     Int'l B.O.: $1.1 million

## Central Station (Central do Brasil) (Brazil-France)

A Sony Pictures Classics release of an Arthur Cohn production, in association with Martine and Antoine de Clermont-Tonnerre (MACT Prods., France), Videofilms (Brazil), Riofilme (Brazil), Canal Plus (France). Produced by Cohn, Martine de Clermont-Tonnerre. Directed by Walter Salles. Screenplay, Joao Emanuel Carneiro, Marcos Bernstein, based on the original idea by Salles. Camera, Walter Carvalho; editors, Isabelle Rathery, Felipe Lacerda; music, Antonio Pinto, Jaques Morelembaum; production design, Cassio Amarante, Carla Caffe; costumes, Cristina Camargo. Reviewed at Sundance Festival, Jan. 19, 1998. Running time: 110 mins.
**Fernanda Montenegro (Dora), Marilia Pera (Irene), Vinicius de Oliveira (Josue), Soia Lira (Ana), Othon Bastos (Cesar).**

A sensitive art film of the old school, Walter Salles' *Central*

*Station* is a melancholy Brazilian road movie shot through with gently stressed cultural commentary. Reminiscent of the work of Vittorio De Sica, this handsomely crafted study of a search for family connections and, in a larger sense, personal and national hope, doesn't quite manage the climactic emotional catharsis at which it aims. But it will involve and move most viewers and will be a solid specialized attraction for discerning audiences internationally.

Helmer sets a highly intimate story about the often-troubled journey of a young boy and an ageing woman against the backdrop of a country in transition. While well judged and credibly played, the film drops dollops of meaning that are, if anything, rather too carefully and gingerly planted, leaving nothing to chance.

Int'l release: Apr. 9     Int'l B.O.: $5.5 million
U.S. release: Nov. 20     U.S. B.O.: $550,000

## Cha Cha Cha (Spain)

A Sogepaq release of a Sogetel production, in association with Tele 5 and with the participation of Canal Plus. Produced by Cesar Benitez. Directed by Antonio del Real. Screenplay, Fernando Leon, Carlos Asorey Brey, del Real. Camera, Juan Amoros; editor, Miguel Angel Santamaria; music, Pablo Miyar; art director, Luis Valles, Juan Borrell. Reviewed at Cines Palafox, Madrid, July 11. Running time: 109 mins.
**Eduardo Noriega (Antonio), Ana Alvarez (Lucia), Maria Adanez (Maria), Jorge Sanz (Pablo).**

Swiftly paced but largely routine, comedy helmer Antonio del Real's *Cha Cha Cha* is a by-the-book relationships movie about twentysomething love. Home B.O. is likely to be solid, given its sexy young cast, but offshore prospects look bleak for the mainstream-oriented item. Latin American and tube sales look likeliest. All-work-and-no-play career girl Lucia works in the casting department of an ad agency. Her best friend, Maria, a dance teacher, is going out with terminally sexist Pablo. One night at a party, Lucia gets drunk, ends up sleeping with Pablo, and falls in love

Int'l release: July 10     Int'l B.O.: $3.8 million

## Chairman of the Board

A Trimark Pictures release of a 101st Street Films/Trimark production. Produced by Peter M. Lenkov, Rupert Harvey. Directed by Alex Zamm. Screenplay, Al Septien, Turi Meyer, Zamm, story by Septien, Meyer. Camera, David Lewis; editor, Jim Hill; music, Chris Hajian; production designer, Aaron Osborne; costume designer, Seok H. Yoon. Reviewed at UA Plaza, Sacramento, March 14. MPAA Rating: PG-13. Running time: 95 mins.
**Carrot Top (Edison), Courtney Thorne-Smith (Natalie), Larry Miller (Bradford), Raquel Welch (Grace Kosik), Mystro Clark (Ty), Jack Plotnick (Zack), Jack Warden (Armand McMillan).**

Part Gen-X Gallagher, part face-pulling Jerry Lewis, popular standup comic Carrot Top attempts the crossover to the bigscreen in *Chairman of the Board*. The results, peppered with the comic's signature gag inventions and enough fart jokes to keep your average 11-year-old in hysterics, are silly enough to assure the acquired-taste headliner a second turn in front of the camera. As for the film itself, wherein C.T. plays Melvin to Jack Warden's generous Howard Hughes zillionaire, look for a fast break to discount houses, and then decent word of mouth in ancillary markets. Carrot Top plays a Venice Beach surfer-inventor who resides with a couple of slacker buddies. Down

on their luck and minutes from the street, the roommates elect Edison to raise rent with his Glo Gunk and other inventions.
U.S. release: March 13                    U.S. B.O.: $350,000

## The Chambermaid and the Titanic (La Femme De Chambre Du Titanic) (Spain-France-Italy)

An Alta Films/UFD release of a Mate Prod, Tornasol Films (Spain)/UGC Images, La Sept Cinema, France 2 Cinema (France)/Rodeo Drive (Italy) production, in association with Westdeutscher Rundfunk and with the participation of Sogepaq. Produced by Mate Cantero, Yves Marmion, Daniel Toscan du Plantier. Directed by Bigas Luna. Screenplay, Luna, Cuca Canals, based on the novel by Didier Decoin. Camera, Patrick Blossier; editor, Kenout Peltier; music, Alberto Iglesias; production design, Gualtiero Caprara. Reviewed at Roxy B Cinema, Madrid, Oct. 16, 1997. Running time: 98 mins.
**Olivier Martinez (Horty), Aitana Sanchez-Gijon (Marie), Romane Bohringer (Zoe). With: Didier Bezace, Aldo Maccione.** (French dialog)

Catalan helmer Bigas Luna changes direction with *The Chambermaid and the Titanic*, a stylish and intelligent, though chilly, romance. Much of Luna's offshore appeal has come from his quirky, exuberantly parodic takes on Spanish culture, and this time around, pic's relative sobriety might catch auds unawares. But there is still enough elegance and wit to ensure that *Titanic* should pull safely into foreign arthouse ports.

French foundry worker Horty, who's married to Zoe, wins a trip to see the launch of the *Titanic* in a work contest. At his hotel, he meets Marie, a chambermaid on the *Titanic* who has nowhere to stay. Horty lets her share his bed, but they don't have sex. When he awakens, Marie has gone, though he later sees a cameraman snap her and buys the photo. Back in France, Horty's drinking friends find the photo and prod him into telling them what they want to hear – an imagined erotic adventure. With news of the vessel's sinking, the story increases in intensity and becomes a nightly ritual at the bar.
Int'l release: Oct. 20, 1997          Int'l B.O.: $1.3 million
U.S. release: Aug. 14                    U.S. B.O.: $350,000

## Chicago Cab

A GFT Entertainment presentation of a Child's Will production, in association with New Crime production. Produced by Paul Dillon, Suzanne De Walt. Directed by Mary Cybulski, John Tintori. Screenplay, Will Kern, based on his play *Hellcab*. Camera, Hubert Taczanowski; music, Page Hamilton; production designer, Maria Nay; costume designer, Carolyn Greco. Reviewed at South by Southwest Festival, Austin, March 14. Running time: 95 mins.
**With: Paul Dillon (cabby), Michael Ironside, Laurie Metcalf, John C. Reilly, Gillian Anderson, John Cusack, Julianne Moore, Moira Harris, April Grace, Harry Lennix.**

A compassionate portrait of a lonely cabby is at the center of the seriocomic *Chicago Cab*, co-directed by husband-and-wife team John Tintori and Mary Cybulski. Based on Will Kern's 1992 play *Hellcab*, pic aims to depict the life of a cabby from the inside, centering on the funny, frightening, and curious episodes that occur one long wintry day. Two dozen passengers, played by such topline thesps as John Cusack, Julianne Moore, Laurie Metcalf, and Michael Ironside, highlight the funny, scary and dreary moments in a typical working day of a city cabdriver. Nonetheless, pic's episodic structure, uneven material and dawdling rhythm should restrict its theatrical prospects,

relegating it to appreciative niche auds.

## Children Of Hannibal (Figli Di Annibale) (Italy)

A Medusa Film release of a Colorado Film production, in association with Medusa Film. Produced by Maurizio Totti. Directed by Davide Ferrario. Screenplay, Ferrario, Diego Abatantuono, story by Ferrario, Abatantuono, Sergio Rubini. Camera, Giovanni Cavallini; editors, Claudio Cormio, Luca Gasparini; music, Fabio Piazzalunga, Damiano Rota; art direction, Franca Bertagnolli; costume design, Emanuela Pischedda. Reviewed at Fiamma Cinema, March 6, 1998. Running time: 89 mins.
**Diego Abatantuono (Tommaso), Silvio Orlando (Domenico), Valentina Cervi (Rita), Flavio Insinna (Orfeo), Ugo Conti (Ermes), Elena Giove (Carmela).**

Davide Ferrario hits all the right notes with the delightful comedy *Children of Hannibal*. Enlivened by a soundtrack and visuals that are as punchy and entertaining as its dialog, this warmhearted tale of an odd couple heading south in search of happiness has a spontaneity and wit all too rare in Italian comedies. A seemingly surefire national hit, the pic could also spark some offshore interest and may have potential for a U.S. remake. The loose-limbed road movie is fronted by a winning team of popular thesps in Diego Abatantuono and Silvio Orlando. Deftly playing off their characters' contrasting physicality and personalities – the former towering and expansive, the latter an unimposing, luckless type – the two actors deliver their best work in some time.
Int'l release: March 13          Int'l B.O.: $1.5 million

## Cholera Street (Agir Roman) (Turkey-Hungary-France)

An Ozen Film release (in Turkey) of a Belge Film, Ozen Film, Soz Film (Turkey)/Focus Film (Hungary)/Les Film Singuliers (France) co-production. Directed by Mustafa Altioklar. Screenplay, Metin Kacan, Altioklar, based on a novel by Kacan. Camera, Ertunc Senkay; music, Attila Ozedemiroglu; production designer, Mustafa Ziya Ulkenciler; costume designer, Yudum Yontan. Reviewed at Cannes Film Festival, May 18. Running time: 118 mins.
**Okan Bayulgen (Salih), Mujde Ar (Tina), Savas Dincel (Barber), Burak Sergen (Sado).**

The season's mega-grossing Turkish melodrama, *Cholera Street* is a sprawling, overlong but basically enjoyable Greek tragedy set in an Istanbul slum. With two of the country's most popular stars in the leading roles, and acting to match its shamelessly over-the-top scripting, pic's domestic success is no surprise. Though much of pic is good exotic fun, it's far too corny to be taken seriously outside Mideastern and Mediterranean markets, where too much is never enough. Residents of the rough-and-tumble Cholera Street are awed by the arrival of high-class call girl Tina. With her chauffeured car and buxom allure, she steals the heart of a barber's lionhearted but weakwilled son, Salih.

## The City (La Ciudad)

A North Star Films production. Produced by David Riker, Paul S. Mezey. Executive producers, Doug Mankoff, Robin Alper. Directed, written, edited by David Riker. Camera, Harlan Bosmajian; music, Tony Adzinikolov; production designers, Arianne Burgess, Roshelle Berliner. Reviewed at Toronto Film Festival, Sept. 15. Running time: 88 mins.

Fernando Reyes (José), Marcos Martinez Garcia (Armando), Moises Garcia (Abel), Anthony Rivera (Boy), Cipriano Garcia (Francisco), Leticia Herrera (Maria) Jose Rabelo (Luis), Stephanie Viruet (Dulce).

A heartbreaking look at the abuses heaped on Latino laborers in New York City, David Riker's *The City* can take its place beside such postwar neo-realist classics as Rossellini's *Paisan* and Bunuel's *Los Olvidados*. The film, in B&W and Spanish, poses major marketing challenges, even in urban areas with large Spanish-speaking populations. But inevitable festival kudos and glowing reviews should help get the word out about this plaintive, unremitting call for social change. Arthouse bookings, followed by cable, are a must. Shot piecemeal over a six-year stretch, street-level vignettes unfold as separate episodes, and employ mostly non-actors and ravaged tenements. Omnibus is tied together by a Queens photo studio, a sort of crossroads where immigrants symbolically have their identities affirmed in ID, wedding, and First Communion snaps. The common theme here is abject neglect: These newcomers to our shores are cut off from their culture and their families and, in each scenario, are treated as if they were invisible.

### City at Peace (Docu)

A Cabin John production. Produced by Christopher Koch. Directed by Susan Koch. Camera, Foster Wiley; editor, Jeff Werner; music, Rickey Payton Sr.; story consultant, Robert Ward. Reviewed at Raleigh Studios, L.A., April 2. Running time: 95 mins.

Featuring Rickey Payton, Sr. and the youth performers of "City at Peace."

An energetic, passion-filled docu about a group of Washington, D.C., youths involved in a performing-arts program, *City at Peace* is an affecting, at times inspirational pic, although it wears its earnestness on its sleeve. Still, timing couldn't be less propitious, as it arrives just months after the Oscar-nominated *Colors Straight Up*, whose tone, subject matter, and message it shares. While it lacks the edge of originality, *City* nevertheless comes bearing impressive credentials – Barbra Streisand and Cis Corman exec produced – which could help it earn attention on the festival and possibly arthouse circuit. Like *Colors*, new docu centers on a group of urban teens for whom a local theater project (called "City at Peace") is designed to offer a constructive outlet.

### City of Angels

A Warner Bros. release, in association with Regency Pictures, of an Atlas Entertainment production. Produced by Charles Roven, Dawn Steel. Directed by Brad Silberling. Screenplay, Dana Stevens, based on Wim Wenders' film *Wings of Desire*. Camera, John Seale; editor, Lynzee Klingman; music, Gabriel Yared; production designer, Lilly Kilvert; costume designer, Shay Cunliffe; visual-effects supervisor, John Nelson. Reviewed at Warner Bros., Burbank, March 27. MPAA Rating: PG-13. Running time: 117 mins.

Nicolas Cage (Seth), Meg Ryan (Maggie), Andre Braugher (Cassiel), Dennis Franz (Messinger), Colm Feore (Jordan), Robin Bartlett (Anne).

Loosely based on Wim Wenders' enchanting 1987 *Wings of Desire*, Brad Silberling's *City of Angels* is a superlatively crafted romantic drama that solidly stands on its own merits. Like the German film, new pic offers a haunting, lyrical meditation

on such universal issues as spirit vs. matter, human courage, and the true meaning of love and desire. The endlessly resourceful Nicolas Cage, as a celestial angel, and a terrifically engaging Meg Ryan, as a pragmatic surgeon, create such blissful chemistry that they elevate the drama to a poetic level seldom reached in a mainstream movie. Topline stars – and an exceedingly handsome production – should help position the film as a major spring release. But Warners still faces a challenge in marketing a stylish movie with philosophical overtones that deviates substantially from Hollywood's more conventional romantic fare.

U.S. release: April 10     U.S. B.O.: $78 million
Int'l release: April 23     Int'l B.O.: $110 million

### Claire Dolan (France)

A Marin Karmitz presentation of an MK2 Prods/Serene Films production. Produced by Ann Ruark. Directed, written by Lodge Kerrigan. Camera, Teodoro Maniaci; editor, Kristina Boden; music, Ahrin Mishan, Simon Fisher Turner; production designer, Sharon Lomofsky; costume designer, Laura Jean Shannon. Reviewed at Cannes Festival, May 20. Running time: 95 mins.

Katrin Cartlidge (Claire Dolan), Vincent D'Onofrio (Elton Garrett), Colm Meaney (Roland Cain), John Doman (Cain's friend), Maryanne Plunkett (Mary Egan), Miranda Stuart-Rhyne (Angela), Kate Skinner (Madeline Garrett).

A rarefied, emotionally distant art film, *Claire Dolan* is a rigorously controlled, occasionally arresting study of a New York prostitute's systematic attempt to take control of her life. Much more attentive to aspects of film form, hard stylized surfaces, and its clinical interest in a call girl's work schedule than in illuminating the inner life of its characters, Lodge Kerrigan's new work represents a slightly disappointing sidestep from his edgy, genuinely disturbing debut with *Clean, Shaven* in 1993. Appealing only to the most intellectual critics and viewers, this falls in the watching-paint-dry category even for specialized audiences, spelling dim commercial prospects. Unlike some similar dramas, *Claire Dolan* does not pursue conventional themes. There are no value judgments here, nor is there an emotional catharsis to offer an audience even the slightest assist in warming up to this calculated tale. Claire (Katrin Cartlidge) is a Dublin native who devotes nearly all her waking hours to working off a large debt to presumed mobster Roland Cain (Colm Meaney), who has known her since she was a girl.

Int'l release: Nov. 18     Int'l B.O.: $200,000

### Clandestine Stories in Havana (Historias Clandestinas En La Habana) (Cuba-Argentina)

An Adagio Films production. Produced by Diego Fernandez. Directed, written by Diego Musiak. Camera, Carlos Ferro; editor, Miguel Perez; music, Leonardo Lebas. Reviewed at Cinequest San José Film Festival, Jan. 31, 1998. Running time: 76 mins.

With: Susu Pecoraro, Jorge Perugorria, Ulises Dumont, Luis Alberto Garcia, Veronica Lynn, Humberto Paez, Jorge Martinez, Laura de la Uz.

A breezy, if contrived, confection, *Clandestine Stories in Havana* weaves together four romantic threads to pleasant effect. Limited Latin-market theatrical action and wider-spread tube play are indicated. A co-production with Argentina, film hinges to an extent on two Argentine visitors. It might aptly be re-

**...April 26...**

A bullseye for TriStar's **The Big Hit** as the pyrotechnic comedy shoots to the top of the U.S. B.O.

titled "See Cuba – and Find Love!" Writer-helmer Diego Musiak (*Pictures of the Soul*) maintains a balmy, lighthearted atmosphere, helped by a likeable cast.

### Class Trip (La Classe De Neige) (France)

A Les Films de la Boissière presentation, in co-production with Warner Bros., PECF-FR3 Cinema, Rhone Alpes Cinema, with the participation of Canal Plus. Directed by Claude Miller. Screenplay, Emmanuel Carrere, based on her novel. Camera, Guillaume Schiffman; editor, Anne Lafarge; music, Henri Texier; production designer, Jean-Pierre Kohut-Svelko; costume designers, Jacqueline Bouchard, Catherine Bouchard. Reviewed at Cannes Festival, May 16. Running time: 96 mins.
**Clement Van Den Bergh (Nicolas), Lokman Nalcakan (Hodkann), François Roy (Father), Tina Sportolard (Mother), Yves Verhoeven (Patrick), Emmanuelle Bercot (Ms. Grimm).**
Despite a strong beginning and some powerful moments, the intense, narrowly focused *Class Trip* is only intermittently involving, emotionally or intellectually. Expect just modest response to a film that's likely to divide more discerning critics and viewers, as it depicts (rather than illuminates) the traumatic experience of one boy's winter vacation. The frail and melancholy Nicolas (Clement Van Den Bergh) is about to embark on a school skiing trip. A professional worrier, his insecure father raises numerous questions about the safety of the trip, spurred by a recent bus accident in which 15 children were killed. Refusing to let Nicolas take the bus, he opts to drive him to the camp, a journey that increases the boy's anxieties.
Int'l release: Sept. 23                                     Int'l B.O.: $700,000

### The Cloud (La Nube) (Argentina-France-Italy-Germany)

A Cinesur (Buenos Aires)/Les Films du Sud (Paris)/Bim Distribuzione (Rome)/Continent Film (Munich) co-production. Produced by Fernando E. Solanas. Directed, written by Solanas. Camera, Juan Diego Solanas; editor, Luis Cesar D'Angiolillo; music, Gerardo Gandini; production design, At Hoang; costume design, Horace Lannes. Reviewed at Venice Film Festival, Sept. 7. Running time: 121 mins.
**Eduardo Pavlovsky (Max), Angela Correa (Fulo), Franklin Caicedo (Enrique), Carlos Perez (Cachito), Leonor Manso (Sonia), Christophe Malavoy (Cholo), Bernard Le Coq (Eduardo), Laura Novoa (Paula), Favio Posca (Tito), Luis Cardei (Lucas).**
After a six-year absence, Fernando E. Solanas returns with *The Cloud*, an ambitious, visually impressive pic about an ailing theater company and a bunch of underemployed actors. Evidently meant to be seen as a microcosm for contemporary Argentina, the film seems aimed at a domestic audience, though it's certain to get arthouse distribution in many parts of Europe. Solanas' films have always contained strong political content, but this time his message is puzzling. Buenos Aires is, literally, under a cloud – a great black one that has brought heavy rain for 1,600 days. Max, who runs a theatrical company, is an ageing ham who does impersonations of Laurence Olivier and flirts with the young women in his troupe. He is nevertheless, representative of a noble theatrical tradition. When hard times threaten the survival of the theater, which is facing demolition, Max is forced to take a stand. Point of the film seems to be that the people of Argentina are still paying for a history over which they had little or no control. The burdens of the past, like the cloud, hang heavily over them.
Int'l release: Sept. 17                                     Int'l B.O.: $350,000

### Comedian Harmonists (Germany)

A Senator Film/Miramax release of a Senator Film Produktion production, in association with Perathon Film, IdunaFilm, Bavaria Film, DOR Film (Austria). Produced by Hanno Huth, Reinhard Klooss, Danny Krausz. Directed by Joseph Vilsmaier. Screenplay, Klaus Richter. Camera, Vilsmaier; editor, Peter R. Adam; music, Harald Kloser; production design, Rolf Zehetbauer; costume design, Ute Hofinger; choreography, Regina Weber. Reviewed at Berlin Festival, Feb. 14. Running time: 124 mins.
**Ben Becker (Robert Biberti), Heino Ferch (Roman Cycowski), Ulrich Noethen (Harry Frommermann), Heinrich Schafmeister (Erich A. Collin), Max Tidof (Ari Leschnikoff), Kai Wiesinger (Erwin Bootz), Meret Becker (Ema Eggstein).**
*Comedian Harmonists* is a big, enjoyable musical biopic of the kind Hollywood used to produce in the 1950s. Conventionally structured but high on production values, this true story of a hugely popular German barbershop sextet that fell victim to anti-Semitism and the rise of Nazism in the 1930s has everything going for it except the fact that it's in a foreign language. Pic has been a B.O. winner on home soil, but foreign distribs will have a hard time with the arcane material. Basic story has very commercial elements: Berlin in its wild, decadent heyday; marital and sexual tensions within the group; a trip Stateside at a crucial point in their career; plus a *Sound of Music* last-concert-on-home-soil finale that's a genuine tear-jerker.
Int'l release: Dec. 25, 1997                         Int'l B.O.: $18.5 million

### The Commissioner (Germany-U.K.-Belgium)

A Metropolis Filmproduktion (Berlin)/New Era Vision (London)/Saga Film (Brussels) co-production, with the support of Eurimages, Canal Plus. Produced by Kallas, Luciano Gloor. Directed by George Sluizer. Screenplay, Christina Kallas, Sluizer, based on the novel by Stanley Johnson. Camera, Bruno de Keyzer, Witold Stok; editor, Denise Vindvogel; music, Loek Dikker; production design, Heidi Ludi; costume design, Jany Temime. Reviewed at Berlin Festival, Feb. 21. Running time: 111 mins.
**John Hurt (James Morton), Rosana Pastor (Helena Noguentes), Alice Krige (Isabelle Morton), Armin Mueller-Stahl (Hans Konig), Johan Leysen (Horst Kramer), James Faulkner (Gordon Cartwright).**
Corporate skullduggery involving European chemical companies provides an unenthralling backdrop for this convoluted, languid thriller. There's little here to draw American audiences, suggesting that outside Europe pic will face an uphill struggle, even in ancillaries. Story centers on a jaded British politician (John Hurt) who's in disgrace due to some undefined scandal and agrees to relocate to Belgium to serve as a British commissioner to the Euro parliament. His wife (Alice Krige), already disenchanted with his infidelities, refuses to join him. His problems begin when, just as a merger is announced between two chemical companies, one British, one German, he gets an anonymous tip that the German outfit is producing chemical weapons and is run by a former member of the Nazi Party.

### Conquest (Canada-U.K.)

A Shaftsbury Films/Heartland Motion Pictures/Greenpoint Films production. Produced by Christina Jennings, Stephen Onda. Directed by Piers Haggard. Screenplay, Rob Forsyth. Camera, Gerald Packer; editor, Ralph Brunjes; music, Ron Sures;

production designer, Hayden Griffin; costume designer, Cathy McComb. Reviewed at World Film Festival, Montreal, Sept. 1. Running time: 92 mins.

**Lothar Bluteau (Pincer Bedier), Tara Fitzgerald (Daisy MacDonald), Monique Mercure (Grace Gallagher), David Fox (Carl Gallagher), Eugene Lipinski (Glenn Boychuk), Daniel Macdonald (Erwin Boychuk), Quyen Hua (My Lang).**

A small prairie town weaves a magic spell on all who pass through it in *Conquest*. A tale of forgotten eccentrics given a new lease on life by a visitor stranded in their midst, the film has echoes of *Fried Green Tomatoes* and *The Spitfire Grill*. Commercial prospects for the quirky yarn aren't as vibrant as the earlier movies, but it could find a modest theatrical niche and score decent sales as a direct-to-cable offering.

Conquest, Saskatchewan, Pop. 124, has seen considerably better days. Most of the farmers in the town are too old to make their land work, and their children long ago departed for big cities. But local banker Pincer Bedier remains a dreamer, encouraging the remaining few to try new crops and pursue start-up business ventures. When Daisy MacDonald's Alfa Romeo conks out in the outpost, Pincer attempts to enlist the financially strapped young woman to take charge of the local hardware store in exchange for the cost of the repair. She initially balks at the deal, but reconsiders when other options evaporate. Pincer is an anachronism, a banker with a heart who wants to do right and revive the dying pit stop. But, as one local tells him, propping up the failing farmlands isn't necessarily a good deed.

### The Corridors of Time: The Visitors II (Les Couloirs Du Temps: Les Visiteurs II) (France)

A Gaumont Buena Vista Int'l release of a Gaumont, CinéComic, France 3 Cinéma co-production with the participation of Canal Plus, the CNC, and a helping hand from the Conseil Général de la Dordogne. Produced by Alain Terzian. Directed by Jean-Marie Poire. Screenplay, Christian Clavier, Poire; Camera, Christophe Beaucarne; editors, Catherine Kelber, Jean-Marie Poire; music, Eric Levi; art direction, Hugues Tissandier; costume design, Catherine Leterrier; digital special effects, Mac Guff Ligne. Reviewed at UGC Ciné Cité Cinéma, Paris, Feb. 16. Running time: 116 mins.

**Christian Clavier (Jacquouille/Jacquart), Jean Reno (Godfroy de Montmirail), Muriel Robin (Beatrice/Frenegonde), Marie-Anne Chazel (Ginette).**

The Visitors – a noble time-traveling knight and his scruffy vassal – are back in *The Corridors of Time: The Visitors II*, the sequel, after a five-year hiatus, to the second-most-successful French film (13.6 million tickets sold) of the postwar era. Part II picks up where the open-ended original left off, and sustains non-stop silliness and mayhem for nearly two frenetic hours. Expect boffo local returns. But whether this second adventure in time will journey much beyond French-lingo territories is another story. Original generated an OK $10 million or so outside its native country but barely surfaced in the U.S. The characters here are central to an undeniable pop culture phenomenon, but the culture in question is French to the bone.

| | |
|---|---|
| Int'l release: Feb. 17 | Int'l B.O.: $56 million |
| U.S. release: March 27 | U.S. B.O.: $300,000 |

### Count Me Out (Stikkfri) (Iceland-Norway-Germany-Denmark)

An Icelandic Film Corp. (Reykjavik)/Filmhuset (Oslo)/Peter Rommel Filmproduktion (Berlin)/Zentropa Entertainments (Copenhagen) co-production, in association with the Icelandic Film Fund. Produced by Fridrik Thor Fridriksson, Ari Kristinsson. Directed, written by Ari Kristinsson, based on an idea by Hrafn Gunnlaugsson. Camera, Halldor Gunnarsson; editor, Steingrimur Karlsson; music, Valgeir Gudjonsson; production designer, Gudny Arndis Oskarsdottir. Reviewed at Cannes Festival, May 16. Running time: 78 mins.

**Bergthora Aradottir (Hrefna), Freydis Kristofersdottir (Yrsa).**

This wholly delightful and naturalistic children's film is set in the real world where broken homes and fleeting relationships cause all kinds of emotional problems for the small fry. Funny, emotional and poignant, it should be grabbed by programmers of children's fare everywhere, and remake rights should also be considered. Hrefna's celebrating her 10th birthday but misses the father she's never known. Her mother has told her he's living in Paris, but Hrefna discovers that, in fact, her father is in Reykjavik and living with his new wife in another part of the city.

### The Cousin (Le Cousin) (France)

A Bac Films release of a Les Films Alain Sarde/TF1 Films Prod/Divali Films & Co./Cinéematographique Prima production, with the participation of Canal Plus, Studio Images 3. Produced by Alain Sarde. Directed by Alain Corneau. Screenplay, Corneau, Michel Alexandre, based on a story by Alexandre. Camera, Michel Amathieu; editor, Thierry Derocles; art direction, Dan Weil; costume design, Corinne Jorry. Reviewed at UCG Ciné Cité Cinéma, Paris, Dec. 20, 1997. Running time: 108 mins.

**Alain Chabat (Gérard Delvaux), Patrick Timsit (Nounours), Samuel Le Bihan (Francis), Caroline Proust (Fanny), Marie Trintignant (Judge Lambert).**

In exploring the perverse symbiosis between police detectives and their informants, *The Cousin* provides a sharp look at the blurred edges between the right and wrong sides of the law. Shady system's pitfalls and contradictions come vividly to life in Alain Corneau's tense drama, which parlays solid research into a dense, riveting ride. Although American TV currently has several top-notch series devoted to law enforcement, offshore auds may well enjoy this tightly paced primer on Gallic-style police work, which takes a surprise turn before the jig is up. Cast against type in a script written with them in mind, well-known comedians Alain Chabat and Patrick Timsit give sober, convincing perfs.

Int'l release: Dec. 10, 1997                    $5.5 million

### Cousin Bette

A Fox Searchlight release. Produced by Sarah Radclyffe. Directed by Des McAnuff. Screenplay, Lynn Siefert, Susan Tarr, based on the novel by Honoré de Balzac. Camera, Andrzej Sekula; editors, Tariq Anwar, Barry Alexander Brown; music, Simon Boswell; production designer, Hugo Luczyc-Wyhowksi; costume designer, Gabriella Pescucci; choreography, Jane Gibson; Reviewed at the Sunset Screening Room, L.A., June 1. MPAA Rating: R. Running time: 107 mins.

**Jessica Lange (Bette Fisher), Elisabeth Shue (Jenny Cadine), Bob Hoskins (Cesar Creval), Hugh Laurie (Baron Hector Hulot), Kelly Macdonald (Hortense Hulot), Aden Young (Count Wenceslas Steinbach).**

In his screen-directing debut, theatrical wizard Des McAnuff serves up a handsome, witty but frosty film that contemplates

**. . . April 28 . . .**

Kate Winslet follows **Titanic** with a cameo role in **Plunge**.

behavior both chilling and casual. The decadent Parisian setting of Honoré de Balzac's 1846 novel *Cousin Bette* lends a rich backdrop to a tale of greed, infidelity, and chicanery. Still, the subtlety of the material will limit its commercial appeal to an upscale niche. Despite the presence of marquee performers and some ribald antics, it's far too erudite a yarn to hold out much hope for crossover appeal. With unrest growing in the 1840s, France is wallowing in a moral and social decay in which politesse has been quietly swept under the carpet. In this tale of revenge, Bette is the poor, spinster relative of a noble family headed by the lecherous Hector whose wastrel ways have virtually bankrupted the household. The downturn of family fortunes – coupled with the political schisms in France – provide an ideal climate for Bette to "take care" of her relatives.

U.S. release: June 12      U.S. B.O.: $1.3 million
Int'l release: April 30      Int'l B.O.: $700,000

### The Cream Will Rise (Docu)

A First Fleet Prods presentation. Produced by Brian Bantry, Collen Camp, Gigi Gaston, Oyst Rockafella. Directed by Gaston. Camera, Gaston, William MacCollum, Shawn Owen, John Longenecker; editors, Jeff Sells, Bonnie Hoffenberg. Reviewed at Sydney Gay & Lesbian Festival, Feb. 17. Running time: 90 mins.

A hit at its Sydney world preem, *The Cream Will Rise* starts as a fairly standard music docu but lurches off in an enthrallingly personal direction as long-forgotten secrets about singer-songwriter Sophie B. Hawkins' childhood are uncovered. For the most part, this is a bullseye first helming effort for Gigi Gaston, who sensitively captures moments of personal revelation, desperation, and elation while playing more than 20 of Hawkins' songs. This unexpectedly compelling piece deserves legs beyond fests on music and other webs and, given some deft marketing, in theatrical dates.

### Cremaster 5

An Artangel presentation. Produced by Barbara Gladstone, Matthew Barney. Directed, written by Barney. Camera, Peter Strietmann; music, Jonathan Bepler; set designer, Robert Wogan; sculpture designer, Paul Pisora; prosthetic designer, Gabe Bartalos. Reviewed at Metro Cinema, London, March 23. Running time: 51 mins.

**Ursula Andress (Queen of Chains), Matthew Barney (Diva/Magician/Giant).**

Ursula Andress miming an unsubtitled Hungarian aria for almost an hour may not be everyone's idea of a good time, but N.Y.-born vid/performance artist Matthew Barney's latest work is made with a conviction that triumphs over its preciousness and its meld of Peter Greenaway/Derek Jarman imagery. Casting of the iconic actress will ensure a slightly wider audience than the art-gallery faithful, and anyone with an appreciation of music and exotic visuals won't go away feeling shortchanged. This is the third *Cremaster* to be made in Barney's planned series of five, which, when completed, will be shown as part of an exhibition at Gotham's Guggenheim in 2000. Pic is set in the restored Budapest Opera House, in whose royal box the Queen of Chains (Andress) takes up residence and starts singing – mostly dolefully, always passionately – of her past lover (Barney).

### Crisis (Mexico)

A FilmoImagen, S.A. de C.V. production. Produced by Gilberto Martinez Solares. Directed by G. Martinez Solares, Adolfo Martinez Solares. Screenplay, G. Martinez Solares, A. Martinez Solares, Diana Legarreta. Camera: Arturo de la Rosa; editors, A. Martinez Solares, Jorge Perez Solano; music, Pablo Arellano; production designers, Gabriela Perera, Gabriela Paredes. Reviewed at Guadalajara Festival, March 9. Running time: 95 mins.

**Jose Alonso (Jorge Zepeda), Hector Bonilla (Jose Ramirez), Manuel Ojeda (Ramon Alvarado), Hugo Stieglitz (Marcelo), Rafael Rojas (Julian Ramirez), Lisa Owen (Monica).**

The last film by late vet Mexican helmer Gilberto Martinez Solares, who co-directed with son Adolfo Martinez Solares, *Crisis* is a political thriller overlaid on a domestic meller. While some of the intrigue concerning a feud between a mob kingpin and a noble politician proves riveting, an unnecessarily complicated plot line and weak handling of the domestic angle softens impact. Stateside prospects are slim, though some Spanish-language markets might bite. Jose Ramirez (Hector Bonilla) is a congressman bent on dismantling organized crime. Through his efforts, Ramon Alvarado (Manuel Ojeda) is arrested and jailed. Bent on revenge and forcing Ramirez not to run for re-election, Alvarado arranges for pol's adored brother Julian (Rafael Rojas) to be kidnapped. When Ramirez wavers, Julian's head arrives at the family home in a cardboard box.

### Croupier (U.K.-Germany)

A Channel Four Films presentation, in association with Filmstiftung NRW, WDR, La Sept/Arte, of a Little Bird/Tatfilm production. Produced by Jonathan Cavendish. Directed by Mike Hodges. Screenplay, Paul Mayersberg. Camera, Mike Garfath; editor, Les Healey; music, Simon Fisher Turner; production designer, Jon Bunker; costume designer, Caroline Harris; Reviewed at Berlin Festival, Feb. 14. Running time: 91 mins.

**Clive Owen (Jack Manfred), Kate Hardie (Bella), Alex Kingston (Jani de Villiers), Gina McKee (Marion), Nicholas Ball (Jack's Father).**

Writing and direction both seem out of kilter with the central idea in *Croupier*, a psychological drama-cum-thriller that rarely catches fire and falls short of its slicker, neo-noir aspirations. British director Mike Hodges has an aptitude for tougher, grungier fare that is ill matched with an already underworked script by Paul Mayersberg about a straight-arrow London croupier seduced into compromising his ideals. Pic's lack of dramatic tension and small-scale setting stack the odds against its taking much at the theatrical table. Jack Manfred (Clive Owen) is an emotional-bypass case who's struggled for years to escape from the shadow of his buccaneering father (Nicholas Ball).

### The Cruise (Documentary, B&W)

A Charter Films presentation. Produced, directed by Bennet Miller. Camera, Miller; editor, Michael Levine; music, Marty Beller. Reviewed at Raleigh Studios, L.A., April 7, 1998. Running time: 76 mins.

**With: Timothy (Speed) Levitch.**

This mini-budget docu about an eccentric New York City tour guide has, at the very least, the distinction of a truly unique personality at its center. The appeal of the film rests entirely upon one's reaction to Timothy (Speed) Levitch, a hugely self-absorbed character with a peculiarly intense personal relationship to Gotham, and it's fair to say that feelings about him will run the gamut. Bennett Miller's homemade, video-lensed item is unusual enough to generate further play on the

---

**. . . April 29 . . .**
Steven Spielberg announces **Memoirs of a Geisha** will be his next film.

fest circuit and possible limited theatrical dates in hip specialized urban venues.

U.S. release: Oct. 23 U.S. B.O.: $200,000

## Cure (Japan)

A Daiei Co. production. Produced by Tsutomu Tsuchikawa, Junyuki Shimoba. Directed, written by Kiyoshi Kurosawa. Camera, Noriaki Kikumura; editor, Kan Suzuki; art direction, Tomoyuki Maruo. Reviewed at Rotterdam Festival, Feb. 1. Running time: 110 mins.

Koji Yakusho (Kenichi Takabe), Tsuyoshi Ujiki (Shin Sakuma), Anna Nakagawa (Fumie Takabe), Masato Hagiwara (Kunihiko Mamiya).

Tone and atmosphere mirror subject to perfection in Kiyoshi Kurosawa's hypnotic trip into the lower depths of the human mind, *Cure*. Combining a bleak austerity familiar from many recent Japanese alienation pics with elements of more mainstream serial-killer psycho-thrillers, this unsettling brew is slightly diluted by its unsatisfying ending. But the chilling drama nonetheless should find takers on the fest circuit. Tokyo detective Takabe (Koji Yakusho) is assigned to investigate a bizarre, fast-multiplying series of murders in which the victims are found with a large X carved into their chests. Their killers are apprehended nearby in a trancelike state, with no memory of the crime.

Int'l release: Dec. 30, 1997 Int'l B.O.: $1 million

## The Dance (Dansinn) (Iceland)

An Isfilm/Oxford Film Co./Nordisk/Hamburger Kino Kompanie production. Produced, directed by August Gudmundsson. Co-producers, Andy Patterson, Erik Crone, Dschingis Bowakow. Screenplay, Gudmundsson, Kristin Atladottir, based on the short story *We Must Dance* by William Heinesen. Camera, Ernie Vincze; editors, Elisabet Ronaldsdottir, Valdis Oskarsdottir; music, Kai Dorenkamp, Jurgen Peukert, Rainer Grunebaum; production design, Tonie Jan Zetterstrom, Halldor Thorgeirsson. Reviewed at Toronto Festival, Sept. 14. Running time: 86 mins.

Palina Jonsdottir (Sirsa), Dofri Hermannsson (Harald), Baldur Trausti Hreinsson (Ivar), Gunnar Helgason (Peter), Kristina Sundar Hansen (Anna Linda), Gisli Halldorsson (Nicholas), Arnar Jonsson (Deacon Sigvaldi).

In structure a memory play, *The Dance* is an effective ghost story, handsomely produced and professionally realized. Filmmaker August Gudmundsson brings enough novel twists to the familiar mix to engage upscale crowds and score international dates outside Scandinavia. Pic should also find OK niche response in ancillary exploitation.

Story is set on a sparsely populated island in 1913. Narrator Peter recalls the time when the lonely outpost was invaded by mainlanders attending a wedding celebration. The free-spirited Sirsa is about to be united with Harald, son of the island's most prosperous landowner. It seems an odd match of tempera-ments, with the young, flirtatious woman more obviously suited to the charismatic Ivar. The festivities are interrupted when news arrives that offshore a ship is sinking – not an uncommon occurrence in this grave site of the Atlantic. The men depart on a rescue mission that nets several sailors, including the doomed craft's captain and engineer. After shaking off their oilskins, the men resume their positions in the circle for the next dance. When news reaches the party that the engineer has died, the local clergyman asks the guests to stop

the dance out of respect for the departed seaman. Sirsa protests, but Harald and the old liners cower before the demand. The interruption causes the participants to find other ways of completing the rite of passage – none particularly a testament to human virtue.

## Dancemaker (Docu)

A Walter Scheuer production. Produced by Jerry Kupfer, Matthew Diamond. Directed, written by Diamond. Camera, Tom Hurwitz; editor, Pam Wise. Reviewed at Seattle Festival, June 14. Running time: 98 mins.

With: Paul Taylor, Francie Huber, Patrick Corbin, Caryn Heilman, Andrew Asnes, Heidi Berest, Lisa Viola, Rachel Berman, Kristi Egtvedt, Richard Chen See.

This extraordinary docu puts you in the trenches with young (and not-so-young) dancers of New York's famed Paul Taylor Dance Co., and under the skin of the founder, an elusive genius with more instinctive flair than people skills. Helmed by Matthew Diamond, a former choreographer, pic reps one of the most scrupulous records of the ballet world ever committed. Making fest rounds before inevitable pubcasting berths, *Dancemaker* is worth pitching to same specialized theatrical auds. Taylor has been a legendary figure among balletomanes for more than 40 years, first as an unusually tall and muscular dancer with shockingly modern ideas, and then as a choreographer capable of driving his troupes to dazzling artistic heights, as well as to the brink of insanity.

## Dance Me to My Song (Australia)

A Vertigo production, in association with Fandango Srl, Smile Production Srl, Intra Films, with the assistance of the South Australian Film Corp., the Australian Film Commission. Produced by Rolf de Heer, Giuseppe Pedersoli, Domenico Procacci. Directed by Rolf de Heer. Screenplay, Heather Rose, Frederick Stahl, de Heer. Camera, Tony Clark; editor, Tania Nehme; music, Graham Tardif; production designer/costume designer, Beverley Freeman. Reviewed at Film Australia, Sydney, April 1. Running time: 103 mins.

Heather Rose (Julia), Joey Kennedy (Madelaine), John Brumpton (Eddie), Rena Owen (Rix), Phil Macpherson (Trev).

Aussie auteur Rolf de Heer has established himself as an uncompromising filmmaker with pics like *Bad Boy Bubby* (1993) and *The Quiet Room* (1996). His latest, an unflinching drama that takes the viewer into the incredibly painful world of a young woman confined to a wheelchair and unable to talk, will be an exceedingly hard commercial sell, both at home and abroad, but de Heer's compassion and the amazing performance of his leading actress, Heather Rose, will certainly cause debate and receive admiration.

Rose, who was born with severe cerebral palsy, is a lovely, intelligent personality trapped in a twisted, stunted body. The film is structured around her: although she's portraying a character, in many ways this is clearly a self-portrait, and an immensely brave one at that. Rose and de Heer never flinch from depicting the most intimate aspects of Julia's limited life, and she communicates almost as much with her eyes as she does via the machinery she uses.

Int'l release: Oct. 22 Int'l B.O.: $100,000

## Dancer, Texas Pop. 81

A Sony Pictures Entertainment release of a TriStar Pictures presentation of an HSX Film production, in association with

---

Chase Prods, Caribou Pictures. Produced by Chase Foster, Peter White, Dana Shaffer. Directed, written by Tim McCanlies. Camera, Andrew Dintenfass; editor, Rob Kobrin; music, Steve Dorff; production designer, Dawn Snyder; costume designer, Susan Matheson. Reviewed at South by Southwest Festival, Austin, Texas, March 13. MPAA Rating: PG. Running time: 95 mins.

**Breckin Meyer (Keller), Peter Facinelli (Terrell Lee), Eddie Mills (John), Ethan Embry (Squirrel), Ashley Johnson (Josie), Patricia Wettig (Mrs. Lusk).**

Evoking the spirit of Frank Capra's Depression comedies, *Dancer, Texas Pop. 81*, Tim McCanlies' impressive directorial feature debut, is an immensely charming small-town movie about a pact made by a quartet of high-schoolers and its effects on the remaining 77 residents. With proper handling, TriStar acquisition could score big among teenage and twenty-something viewers. When the four teens announce their resolve to move to L.A. upon graduation, town residents mobilize to stop them from fulfilling that dream.

U.S. release: May 1         U.S. B.O.: $700,000

## Dance With Me

A Sony Pictures release of a Columbia Pictures and Mandalay Entertainment presentation of a Weissman/Egawa production. Produced by Lauren C. Weissman, Shinya Egawa, Randa Haines. Executive producer, Ted Zachary. Directed by Haines. Screenplay, Daryl Matthews. Camera, Fred Murphy; editor, Lisa Fruchtman; music, Michael Convertino; production designer, Waldemar Kalinowski; art director, Barry Kingston; costume designer, Joe I. Tompkins; sound, David Ronne; choreographers, Liz Curtis, Matthews; casting, Lora Kennedy. Reviewed at the Directors Guild, L.A., June 1. MPAA Rating: PG-13. Running time: 126 mins.

**Vanessa L. Williams (Ruby Sinclair), Chayanne (Rafael Infante), Kris Kristofferson (John Burnett) , Joan Plowright (Bea Johnson), Jane Krakowski (Patricia), Beth Grant (Lovejoy).**

*Dance With Me* is *Flashdance* for the 1990s, for good and ill. On the positive side, this romance with a Latin beat has a bouncy charisma that's appealing and infectious. On the downside, the film is unquestionably simple-minded and archly melodramatic; in popular terms, modest production's assets prevail. Item shapes up as a solid mid-range performer with breakout prospects should higher-profile competition stumble, and subsequent ancillary play is a recipe for hot salsa.

Rafael (Chayanne) is a young Cuban who's just buried his mother and is about to go to Houston to meet his father, a dance instructor, for the first time. Unbeknownst to him, his papa is unaware of the biological connection, and Rafael doesn't quite know how to break the news.

U.S. release: Aug. 21       U.S. B.O.: $16 million
Int'l release: Sept. 3       Int'l B.O.: $6 million

## Dancing at Lughnasa (Ireland-U.K.-U.S.)

A Sony Pictures Classics release of a Ferndale Films production for Capitol Films/Sony Pictures Classics/Channel Four Films of a Noel Pearson production. Produced by Pearson. Directed by Pat O'Connor. Screenplay, Frank McGuinness, based on the play by Brian Friel. Camera, Kenneth MacMillan; editor, Humphrey Dixon; music, Bill Whelan; production design, Mark Geraghty; costume design, Joan Bergin. Reviewed at Telluride Festival, Sept. 4. Running time: 92 mins.

**Meryl Streep (Kate Mundy), Michael Gambon (Father Jack Mundy), Catherine McCormack (Christina Mundy), Kathy Burke (Maggie Mundy), Sophie Thompson (Rose Mundy), Brid Brennan (Agnes Mundy), Rhys Ifans (Gerry Evans), Darrell Johnston (Michael Mundy).**

*Dancing at Lughnasa* reps a conventionally elegiac screen adaptation of Brian Friel's outstanding play about the turning point in the lives of five Irish sisters. In opening up Friel's work, and in compressing it to an hour and a half, filmmakers have both suffused it with local period color and diluted much of its cumulative emotional impact. Given the work's cultural pedigree, fine cast led by Meryl Streep and even the current vogue for things Irish, distrib should position this as a solid class offering in the U.S.

Set on a farm in Donegal in 1936, the piercingly melancholy work centers on the Mundy sisters. All unmarried, thanks in part to the man shortage caused by emigration, the religious calling, and wanderlust. The sisters are nominally led by the eldest, Kate, a buttoned-up, middle-aged schoolteacher upset to learn that she is called "the gander." Christina, the youngest, is responsible for the family's one moral embarrassment, "love child" Michael. In a way, however, the 8-year-old is the center of the family, doted on endlessly by his aunts. Changes are set in motion by the return of the sisters' older brother, Jack, a priest who has spent decades as a missionary in Africa and who now seems not only a bit batty but, from the Irish Catholic point of view, suspiciously affected by the ungodly ways of the people he was meant to convert.

U.S. release: Nov. 13       U.S. B.O.: $1 million
Int'l release: Sept. 25       Int'l B.O.: $1.3 million

## Dangerous Beauty

A Warner Bros. release of a Regency Enterprises presentation of an Arnon Milchan/Bedford Falls production. Produced by Milchan, Marshall Herskovitz, Edward Zwick, Sarah Kaplan. Directed by Herskovitz. Screenplay, Jeannine Dominy, based on the book *The Honest Courtesan* by Margaret Rosenthal. Camera, Bojan Bazelli; editors, Steven Rosenblum, Arthur Coburn; music, George Fenton; production design, Norman Garwood; costume design, Gabriella Pescucci. Reviewed at the Aidikoff Screening Room, Beverly Hills, Jan. 14. MPAA Rating: R. Running time: 111 mins.

**Catherine McCormack (Veronica Franco), Rufus Sewell (Marco Venier), Jacqueline Bisset (Paola Franco), Oliver Platt (Maffio Venier), Moira Kelly (Beatrice Venier), Fred Ward (Domenico Venier).**

Imagine Barbara Cartland or Danielle Steel enriched with historical veracity and social conscience and you have the beginnings of *Dangerous Beauty*. The 16th-century yarn of courtly intrigue, affairs of the heart, and sumptuous images is an odd mix of high-toned intentions and cornball romance that works in fits and bursts. Commercially, it's not about to turn many heads on the domestic front but could have some modest theatrical success in upscale international markets. Veronica Franco is a young woman whose circle falls just outside the core of the Venetian court and who aspires to rise above her station.

U.S. release: Feb. 20       U.S. B.O.: $4.5 million

## Dark City

A New Line Cinema release of a Mystery Clock production. Produced by Andrew Mason, Alex Proyas. Directed by Proyas.

**Above:** Steven Spielberg          **Below:** Nicolas Cage

**Above:** Peter Schneider
**Below:** Roberto Benigni

**Above:** Leonardo Dicaprio
**Opposite:** Robert Carlyle in *The Full Monty*

**Above:** *La Vita è Bella* (Life is Beautiful)
**Below:** *Saving Private Ryan*

**Above:** *Il Postino*

**Ab** *...nity and a Day*                    **Below:** *The Celebration*

**Above:** *Shakespeare in Love*          **Below:** *Gone With the Wind*

**Above:** Tom Hanks
**Below:** Brad Pitt

**Below:** Gwyneth Paltrow

**Above:** Meg Ryan
**Below:** Morgan Freeman

**Above:** Rupert Murdoch

Screenplay, Proyas, Lem Dobbs, David S. Goyer, story by Proyas. Camera, Dariusz Wolski; editor, Dov Hoenig; music, Trevor Jones; production design, George Liddle, Patrick Tatopolous; costume design, Liz Keogh; visual-effects supervisors, Mara Bryan, Arthur Windus, Andrew Mason. Reviewed at New Line Cinema, L.A., Feb. 3. MPAA Rating: R. Running time: 101 mins.
**Rufus Sewell (John Murdoch), Kiefer Sutherland (Dr. Daniel Schreber), Jennifer Connelly (Emma Murdoch), William Hurt (Insp. Frank Bumstead), Richard O'Brien (Mr. Hand), Ian Richardson (Mr. Book).**
A fusion of *The Crow* and Kafka, *Dark City* trades in such weighty themes as memory, thought control, human will, and the altering of reality, but is engaging mostly in the degree to which it creates and sustains a visually startling alternate universe. Alex Proyas' second feature repeats notions and motifs from his debut (*Crow*) and aims for grander ideas with a veneer of pretension that proves not all that edifying. New Line should rack up decent coin based on strong support from the hard-core sci-fi/fantasy audience.

This is essentially an old film-noir amnesiac yarn, set in a hostile urban environment defined by late 1940s noir. Appropriately for a picture about a desperate search through a labyrinth of time, memory, and sinister manipulation, it takes a while for viewers to get their bearings.

U.S. release: Feb. 27            U.S. B.O.: $14.5 million
Int'l release: May 29          Int'l B.O.: $12.5 million

## Dark Harbor

A Hart Sharp Enterprises presentation, in association with Killer Films, ACC Enterprises. Produced by John N. Hart, Jr., Jeff Sharp, Justin Lazard. Directed by Adam Coleman Howard. Screenplay, Howard, Justin Lazard. Camera, Walt Lloyd; editor, Annette Davey; music, David Mansfield; production design, Markus Canter; costume design, Kevin Donaldson, Erin Flanagan. Reviewed at Seattle Festival, June 13. Running time: 88 mins.
**Alan Rickman (David Weinberg), Polly Walker (Alexis Chandler Weinberg), Norman Reedus (Young Man).**
The combination of inclement weather and an injured man by the roadside is bound to add up to no good. In *Dark Harbor* – a three-hander thriller – one just knows this tight little group will be reduced in its ranks. But for all its inevitability, the film manages to keep its darkest secrets to the end. Shy of the sort of charismatic star cast that would ensure it a ticket to the mainstream, the slick indie thriller could score a specialized theatrical success with careful handling. Most likely, however, it will toil in pay cable, earning modest rep and coin.

On a night full of rain, David and Alexis Weinberg race to catch the last ferry to their island cottage. Alexis dimly catches sight of something at the side of the road through the sheet of water; when they stop to investigate, they find a young man curled in a ball, bleeding from a severe beating by persons unknown. He accepts their help only after the couple agree that they won't call the cops. The detour lasts just a few minutes, but the delay is long enough to leave the couple waving goodbye to the boat. But unknown to them, the man with no name has stowed away on the very ferry that transports them to their island getaway. Soon their paths will cross again, and circumstances will lead the Weinbergs to invite him to stay in their cottage. Whether he's targeted the couple for some terrible fate or was enlisted into a conspiracy by one against the other gives the picture a cat-and-mouse sensibility that's playful and disturbing.

## Day After Day (Yom Yom) (Israel-France)

An Agav Films/Cinema Factory production. Produced by Eyal Shiray, Laurent Truchot. Directed by Amos Gitai. Screenplay, Jacky Cukier, Gitai. Camera, Renato Berta; editors, Nili Richter, Ruben Kornfeld; music, Philippe Eidel, Josef Bradanashvily; art director, Thierry François; costume design, Hefi Bohem; Reviewed at World Film Festival, Montreal, Sept. 2. Running time: 106 mins.
**Moshe Ivgi (Moshe), Hanna Maron (Hanna), Juliano Merr (Jule), Dalit Kahan (Didi), Yussef Abu Warda (Yussef), Nataly Atiya (Grisha), Anne Petit-LaGrange (Doctor), Keren Mor (Mimi).**
The second part of a trilogy on contemporary Israeli cities, Amos Gitai's *Day After Day* is a moving family drama set in the port of Haifa as seen through the lives of a Jewish-Arab clan. Simply told in a series of vignettes, it packs unexpected emotion. A film with travel potential, it should score OK international sales in top markets once it completes fest engagements.

The unnamed family is the result of a union between Hanna, a Jewish woman, and her Arab husband, Yussef, who runs a bakery. But much of the plot focuses on their son, Moshe, or Mussa, whose marriage is falling apart and who is experiencing some sort of identity crisis. The other thread concerns an Israeli developer who wants to buy the shop for a proposed retail mall. Though the couple plan to retire, for Yussef selling the property would be a political statement, with implications regarding the balance between the two cultures.

## Dead Man on Campus

A Paramount Pictures release, in association with MTV Films of a Pacific Western production. Produced by Gale Ann Hurd. Directed by Alan Cohn. Screenplay, Michael Traeger, Mike White, based on a story by Anthony Abrams, Adam Larson Broder. Camera, John Thomas; editor, Debra Chiate; music, Mark Mothersbaugh; production design, Carol Winstead Wood; costume design, Kathleen Detoro. Reviewed at Cinemark Tinseltown Westchase, Houston, Aug. 18. MPAA Rating: PG-13. Running time: 93 mins.
**Tom Everett Scott (Josh Miller), Mark-Paul Gosselaar (Cooper), Poppy Montgomery (Rachel), Lochlyn Munro (Cliff), Randy Pearlstein (Buckley), Corey Page (Matt), Alyson Hannigan (Lucy).**
Although it falls far short of fulfilling its full potential as a dark comedy of desperation, *Dead Man on Campus* is a modestly amusing trifle that merits a passing grade. A likely box office underachiever, pic's cable and homevid prospects are reasonably bright.

Josh Miller is an Indiana-born honor student with a medical scholarship at prestigious Daleman College. But Cooper, the self-indulgent son of a well-to-do businessman, has plans that don't include studying for his roommate. Before long, Josh is carousing like a natural-born party animal – drinking, smoking pot, and enjoying extracurricular activities with Rachel.

But the long party ends with a sobering wake-up call: Josh flunks his midterm exams and is in danger of losing his scholarship. Cooper is also badly rattled by his grades, knowing that if he flunks, he will working in his father's janitorial business. They discover an obscure loophole in the college's charter: Any student whose roommate commits suicide gets an automatic top-grade average.

U.S. release: Aug. 21            U.S. B.O.: $15 million

---

**. . . May 2 . . .**
French film aficionados in seventh heaven as "City of Lights, City of Angels: a Week of New French Films" unspools at the Directors Guild Theater in Los Angeles.

## Dead Man's Curve

An Alain Siritzky and Hope Street Entertainment presentation, in association with Pierre Kalfon, Michel Chambat, Ian Jessel, of a Mount Royal Entertainment production. Produced by Michael Amato, Theodore Schipper, Jeremy Lew. Directed, written by Dan Rosen. Camera, Joey Forsyte; editor, William Mercer; music, Shark; production design, Robert Harbour; costumes, Shanna Gold. Reviewed at Sundance Festival, Jan. 24. Running time: 90 mins.
**Matthew Lillard (Tim), Michael Vartan (Chris), Randall Batinkoff (Rand), Keri Russell (Emma), Tamara Craig (Natalie), Dana Delany (Dr. Ashley).**
*Rope* meets *Scream* in Dan Rosen's confident yet shallow *Dead Man's Curve*. As surely as *Curve* bends too low for upscale auds, it's also problematic for mainstream ones as a near-horror thriller sans onscreen violence. It will take aggressive marketing to reap quick payoff.

Tim (Matthew Lillard), Rand (Randall Batinkoff), and Chris (Michael Vartan) are senior-class roommates. It's pop folklore that if your roomie commits suicide, you get released from class work with a perfect 4.0 semester report. Having discovered this is actually true at their college, Chris improbably agrees to aid Tim in faking his death.
Int'l release: Aug. 22     Int'l B.O.: $500,000

## The Decline of Western Civilization Part III

(Docu)
A Spheeris Films Inc. production. Produced by Scott Wilder. Directed by Penelope Spheeris. Camera, Jamie Thompson; editor, Ann Trulove; music supervisor, Stephen E. Smith. Reviewed at Sundance Festival, Jan. 19. Running time: 86 mins.
**With: Final Conflict, Litmus Green, Naked Aggression, the Resistance.**
After a mostly disappointing series of recent mainstream films, director Penelope Spheeris gets back to her punk roots in the third *Decline of Western Civilization* docu. Film doesn't try to suggest it's portraying an original or distinctive musical scene – nothing's heard here that the first chapter's weaker bands mightn't have done in 1979. Instead, focus shifts to social observation as a punk aesthetic defines life for myriad homeless L.A. kids. Though at times more stylish than layered, this engaging, sometimes poignant, always energetic docu should echo predecessors' success in initial playoff; more sober theme will lessen its viability as a long-term rep staple.

## Deep Impact

A Paramount release of a Paramount and DreamWorks Pictures presentation of a Zanuck/Brown production. Produced by Richard D. Zanuck, David Brown. Directed by Mimi Leder. Screenplay, Michael Tolkin, Bruce Joel Rubin. Camera, Dietrich Lohmann; editor, David Rosenbloom; music, James Horner; production designer, Leslie Dilley; costume designer, Ruth Myers; visual-effects supervisor, Scott Farrar. Reviewed at Paramount, L.A., May 1. MPAA Rating: PG-13. Running time: 120 mins.
**Robert Duvall (Spurgeon Tanner), Tea Leoni (Jenny Lerner), Elijah Wood (Leo Biederman), Vanessa Redgrave (Robin Lerner), Morgan Freeman (President Beck), Maximilian Schell (Jason Lerner), James Cromwell (Alan Rittenhouse), Jon Favreau (Gus Partenza), Leelee Sobieski (Sarah Hotchner).**
The season's first comet-targets-Earth special effects extravaganza is spectacular enough in its cataclysmic scenes of the planet being devastated by an unstoppable fireball, but proves far from emotionally thrilling. Hitting the market eight weeks before the reputedly more high-tech *Armageddon*, *Deep Impact* will score some powerhouse B.O. as the first event picture of the summer.

An amateur teenage astronomer Leo Biederman and an observatory technician independently identified a new comet that is on a collision course with Earth. With impact looming in a year, U.S. President Beck announces the news to the world and that a giant spaceship will blast off to plant eight nukes on the comet in the hope of blowing it to smithereens. But the mission is a dismal failure, splitting the comet in two unequal pieces one of which will create an Extinction Level Event. The trauma ensues by the who-will-live/who-will-die scenario.
U.S. release: May 8     U.S. B.O.: $140 million
Int'l release: May 14     Int'l B.O.: $210 million

## Deep Rising

A Buena Vista release of a Hollywood Pictures presentation of a Laurence Mark production. Produced by Mark, John Baldecchi. Directed, written by Stephen Sommers. Camera, Howard Atherton; editors, Bob Ducsay, John Wright; music, Jerry Goldsmith; production design, Holger Gross; costume design, Joseph Porro; creature design, Rob Bottin; visual-effects supervisor, Mike Shea. Reviewed at the Avco Cinema, L.A., Jan. 26. MPAA Rating: R. Running time: 106 mins.
**Treat Williams (John Finnegan), Famke Janssen (Trillian), Anthony Heald (Simon Canton), Kevin J. O'Connor (Joey Pantucci), Wes Studi (Hanover).**
*Deep Rising* is an old-fashioned B movie with A-budget effects, but the quality sheen can't disguise the cheap-thrills hokum. As such, the film is better than average at delivering the chills, and after a rocky start, setting the tongue-in-cheek tone for this yarn of sea creatures vs. bandits. Decidedly programmer fare, it will play off quickly to fair B.O., but will have to wade through every revenue stream to return its hefty pricetag. Pic opens with adventurer-for-hire John Finnegan (Treat Williams) and crew buffeting the waves in the South China Sea with a surly lot paying the charter fee.
U.S. release: Jan. 30     U.S. B.O.: $11 million
Int'l release: May 4     Int'l B.O.: $15 million

## Dee Snider's Strangeland

A Raucous Releasing release. Produced by David L. Bushell, Dee Snider. Directed by John Pieplow. Screenplay, Dee Snider. Camera, Goran Pavicevic; editor, Jeff Kushner; music, Anton Sanko; production design, Debbie Devilla; costume design, Jillian Ann Kreiner; special-effects makeup, Michael Burnett. Reviewed at UA Criterion, N.Y., Oct. 2. MPAA Rating: R. Running time: 86 mins.
**Dee Snider (Capt. Howdy/Carleton Hendricks), Kevin Gage (Mike Gage), Brett Harrelson (Steve Christianson), Elizabeth Pena (Toni Gage), Robert Englund (Jackson Roth), Linda Cardellini (Genevieve Gage).**
*Dee Snider's StrangeLand* is a funeral-paced genre item that fails to deliver suspense, shocks or the campy fun that Snider brought to his mid-1980s metal outfit, Twisted Sister. Snider, making his screenwriting and producing debut, should have given his idea, which centers on a psychopath who lures nubiles into his basement via the Internet, to more capable hands. Curiosity factor may provide passable first-weekend B.O., but bad word of mouth will quickly consign pic to video shelves and latenight TV.

---

**... May 3 ...**

Having starred in the TF1 mini-series **The Count of Monte Cristo**, Gérard Depardieu agrees to put his name to three more mini-series: **Balzac, Les Misérables,** and **Notre Dame de Paris.**

Two young girls innocently flirt in an Internet chat-room with someone named Capt. Howdy and make a date. One is later found strung up by her wrists with her lips sewn shut. Shifting into police procedural, despite a bungled investigation, the culprit and his captive are found, resulting in Howdy being hauled off to a loony bin. The child-murdering Howdy, is released from the institution in less than four years. It's left open as to whether Howdy, properly medicated, is truly reformed: Within hours, he's hanged from a tree by an angry mob. The hanging doesn't kill his spirit, and somehow the benign-looking Carleton Hendricks has a serial-killer makeover. Thus reborn, Capt. Howdy quickly extracts revenge on the would-be vigilantes, then re-kidnaps the detective's daughter, leading to another limp face-off.

U.S. release: Oct. 2    U.S. B.O.: $700,000

## Delivered

A Banner Entertainment production. Produced by Brian Swardstrom, Mickey Liddell, Guy Ferland. Directed by Guy Ferland. Screenplay, Andrew Liotta, Lawrence Trilling. Camera, Shane F. Kelly; editor, Deborah Zeitman; music, Nicholas Pike; production designer, James Gelarden; costume designer, Laura Cunningham. Reviewed at Cannes Festival, May 18. Running time: 90 mins.
**David Strickland (Will Sherman), Ron Eldard (Reed), Leslie Stefanson (Claire), Scott Bairstow (Canyon), Nicky Katt (Barry), Jillian Armenante (Danielle).**
One doppelganger with pepperoni and extra cheese is the recipe for *Delivered*, an amiable, comedy-spiced thriller about a pizza delivery guy's worst nightmare come true. Smartly put across by an appealing cast and helmer Guy Ferland, pic serves up a flavorful portrait of life among underachieving Seattle slackers and grungers whose postgrad work tends to smell of dough and tomato sauce. Though it's perhaps too lightweight and genre-bound to clean up in a wide theatrical bow, creative distribution could deliver this polished Gen-X fable to an appreciative following among collegiate and twentysomething auds.

An embittered college dropout and aspiring cartoonist, Will has a particularly bad night delivering pies when he shows up at a run-down house where, unbeknownst to him, the sinister-looking man who receives the pizza has just killed the guy who ordered it.

## Denial

A Kushner-Locke/Tapestry Films presentation of a Brad Wyman production. Produced by Brad Wyman, Louise Rosner. Directed, written by Adam Rifkin. Camera, Francis Kenny; editor, Peter Schink; music supervisor, Christopher Violette; production designer, Steve Hardie; costume designer, Denise Wingate. Reviewed at Seattle Festival, June 13. Running time: 93 mins.
**Jonathan Silverman (Joel), Leah Lail (Sophie), Ryan Alosio (Isaac), Amy Yasbeck (Claudia), Patrick Dempsey (Sam), Christine Taylor (Sammie), Jason Alexander (Art).**
*Denial* could be money in the bank for this sexy, frequently hilarious pic. Thanks to gag-heavy script and frankly adult situations, it initially plays like adult tube fare. But helmer Adam Rifkin adds enough edge and originality to make it a potential click with theater auds. Tale begins at an L.A. dinner party where runty novelist Art Witz claims that couples live in a permanent state of titular you-know-what, their days filled with lies and half-truths, thanks to the basic unworkability of

monogamous relationships. He hits upon the other guests' assorted sore spots.

## Desert Blue

A Samuel Goldwyn Co. release of an Ignite Entertainment production. Produced by Andrea Sperling, Nadia Leonelli, Michael Burns. Directed, written by Morgan J. Freeman. Camera, Enrique Chediak; editor, Sabine Hoffman; music, Vytas Nagisetty; costumes, Trish Summerville. Reviewed at Toronto Festival, Sept. 13. Running time: 90 mins.
**Brendan Sexton III (Blue), Kate Hudson (Skye), Christina Ricci (Ely), John Heard (Father), Lucinda Jenney (Caroline), Casey Affleck (Pete), Sara Gilbert (Sandy), Isidra Vega (Haley), Ethan Suplee (Cale).**
Morgan J. Freeman fails to dodge the sophomore curse. His return, *Desert Blue*, boasts a veritable Who's Who of Hot New Talent in a cloying, mechanically plotted comedy about Mojave water rights, arson, a hazardous-waste spill and the world's largest ice-cream cone. The cast will mean some curiosity, but box office should dry up quickly once word gets out this ain't no Gen-X *Last Picture Show*. Beach, Calif. is a desert town with an abandoned water slide and a kitschy statue of a giant pink ice-cream cone. Brendon Sexton is the anything-but-moody Blue of the title. His goal is to avenge the memory of his father, whose dream of diverting water to the town was thwarted by the Empire Cola Co., which now placates locals with all the free off-brand pop they can consume. Dad's pet project, the water slide, was put on hold when he died mysteriously in an hotel fire. Blue is determined to finish the attraction.

## Desperate Measures

A TriStar release of a Mandalay Entertainment presentation of an Eaglepoint/Schroeder/Hoffman production. Produced by Barbet Schroeder, Susan Hoffman, Gary Foster, Lee Rich. Directed by Schroeder. Screenplay, David Klass. Camera, Luciano Tavoli; editor, Lee Percy; music, Trevor Jones; production design, Geoffrey Kirkland; costume design, Gary Jones. Reviewed at the Sony screening room, New York, Jan. 20. MPAA Rating: R. Running time: 100 mins.
**Michael Keaton (Peter McCabe), Andy Garcia (Frank Conner), Brian Cox (Jeremiah Cassidy), Marcia Gay Harden (Samantha Hawkins), Eric King (Nate Oliver).**
A desperately unthrilling thriller, *Desperate Measures* is hackneyed and instantly forgettable. Lacking the human complexity and dramatic sophistication that's distinguished the recent work of helmer Barbet Schroeder, pic proffers a lifeless compendium of genre cliches. Its one virtue – a solid perf by Michael Keaton as a psycho menace – poses the question of whether the actor's fans will clamor to see him as a leering baddie. Tale opens with cop Frank Conner (Andy Garcia) bending department rules in trying to aid his terminally ill son whose one hope of survival is a bone marrow transplant. The perfect match for the boy's DNA is Peter McCabe (Keaton), a homicidal killer serving a life term in a maximum security prison.

U.S. release: Jan. 30    U.S. B.O.:
Int'l release: March 11    Int'l B.O.: $12 million

## Detention

A Filmsnoir Motion Picture Presentation. Produced by Dana Lynne Comegys, Darryl LeMont Wharton. Directed, written by LeMont Wharton. Camera, Boots Shelton; music, Camara

---

Kambon; production design, Nerenda Eid; costumes, Dale G. Madison. Reviewed at Dances With Films Festival, Santa Monica, July 29. Running time: 83 mins.
**Charisse Brown (Mrs. Deakins), Justin Black (Black), John Hall (Tenspeed), Darryl LeMont Wharton (Langston), Acirfa (Kiatenai), Poochie (Kersha Harvia).**
The socially conscious teen drama *Detention* shows some considerable filmmaking skills in young first-time writer-helmer Darryl LeMont Wharton. Script is a tad too concerned with dramatizing every imaginable inner-city problem, but pic features a rewarding variety of characters and some raw moments of emotion that make it a worthy addition to the genre. That said, cracking the commercial marketplace will be difficult because of shabby production values.

Focus is on a group of black high-school students that gathers after school one afternoon for detention. The kids have myriad difficulties: involvement in the drug trade, sexual promiscuity, abusive parents, pregnancy; there's even an athlete who dreams of making it to the NBA and is trying to keep his homosexuality a secret. Righteous, been-around-the-block teacher Mrs. Deakins is supervising the teens, and uses the detention to urge them to open up about their problems and find a way to communicate with one another.

### Dharma Blues (Avrio Tha Xeroume) (Greece)

An Andreas Thomopoulos/EPT/Greek Television ET-1/Fasma/Cinemagic/Greek Film Centre production. Produced by Andreas Thomopoulos. Directed, written by Thomopoulos. Camera, Aris Stavrou; editors, Menios Ditsas, Iro Vretzaki; music, Giorgos Kalkanis; production/costume design, Tassos Zografos. Reviewed at Thessaloniki Festival, Nov. 26, 1997. Running time: 110 mins.
**Stavros Paravas (Thomas/Raskolnikov), Tamilla Koulieva-Karantinaki (Sonya), Anna Fonsou (Soso), Alberto Eskenazy (Max), Thodoris Prokopiou (Bobas).**
(Greek, Russian and English dialog)
*Dharma Blues* is a superb, loose, highly cinematic update of Dostoyevsky's *Crime and Punishment*. Pic's deft direction, unpredictable plot, and rich textures make it a surefire fest attraction, with arthouse coin outside Greece a good possibility. Helmer Andreas Thomopoulos enhances the novel's spiritual component with the theme of predestination: The two main characters "meet" metaphysically before they actually encounter each other. Conceit may seem a bit highbrow, but Thomopoulos achieves a successful balancing act by placing action on the terra firma of contemporary Athens.

### Digging to China

A Moonstone Entertainment presentation, in association with Davis Entertainment Classics and the Ministry of Film, of an Alan Mruvka/Marilyn Vance/John Davis/J. Todd Harris production. Produced by Mruvka, Vance, Davis, Harris. Directed by Timothy Hutton. Screenplay, Karen Janszen. Camera, Jorgen Persson; editors, Dana Congdon, Alain Jakubowicz; music, Cynthia Miller; production design, Robert De Vico; costumes, Mary Zophres. Reviewed at Sundance Festival, Jan. 23. Running time: 98 mins.
**Kevin Bacon (Ricky Schroth), Mary Stuart Masterson (Gwen Frankovitz), Cathy Moriarty (Mrs. Frankovitz), Evan Rachel Wood (Harriet Frankovitz), Marian Seldes (Leah Schroth).**
In mid-1960s rural New Hampshire, ailing divorcée Mrs. Frankovitz (Cathy Moriarty) has her hands full running a

rustic motel while tending two daughters. Thesp Timothy Hutton's directorial debut, *Digging to China* is a respectably crafted, sentimental nostalgia piece whose thin character motivations and development thwart any genuine emotional engagement. Story of friendship between a troubled young girl and a retarded man will ultimately move only those inclined to cry on cue, making it a better bet for telecast than theatrical play.
U.S. release: Sept. 11                          U.S. B.O.: $35,000

### The Dinner (La Cena) (Italy-France)

A Medusa release of a Massfilm/Medusa Film (Rome)/Les Films Alain Sarde/Filmtel (Paris) co-production. Produced by Franco Committeri. Directed by Ettore Scola. Screenplay, Scola, Furio Scarpelli, Silvia Scola, Giacomo Scarpelli, based on an idea by Scola. Camera, Franco Di Giacomo; editor, Raimondo Crociani; music, Armando Trovajoli; production design, Luciano Ricceri; costume design, Odette Nicoletti. Reviewed at Rivoli Cinema, Rome, Nov. 29. Running time: 127 mins.
**Fanny Ardant (Flora), Vittorio Gassman (Maestro Pezzullo), Stefania Sandrelli (Mother), Lea Gramsdorff (Daughter), Eros Pagni (Chef), Giancarlo Giannini (Professor), Marie Gillain (Cecilia), Rolando Ravello (Ernesto), Antonio Catania (Magician), Francesca D'Aloja (Alessandra).**
A grotesque grab-bag of trattoria diners, repping a cross-section of Italian society, eats its way through Ettore Scola's *The Dinner*, a relaxing, well-oiled comedy with little to digest. Missing the searing social commentary and emotional poignancy of the filmmaker's best work, this meal is strictly Scola-lite. Yet the director's masterly feel for comedy and uncanny ability to keep the ball in the air and dialog flowing around 14 tables with some 40-odd characters suggests that the film will have a small but faithful stream of customers.

Flora, the owner's wife who possesses Zen-like composure, is the calm in the turbulent sea of patrons who include a timid, toupée-wearing loner who invites a party magician to dinner, under the prying eye of gentleman-philosopher Maestro Pezzullo. The all-eros world of a blowzy divorcée caves in when her prim collegiate daughter informs her she's entering a convent. Giancarlo Giannini is allowed an exhilarating star turn as a philandering prof who cynically disillusions his young student/lover to keep her from spilling the beans to his wife.
Int'l release: Nov. 27                       Int'l B.O.: $1.7 million

### The Dinner Game (Le Dîner De Cons) (France)

A Gaumont Buena Vista Int'l release of a Gaumont presentation of a Gaumont/TF1 Films Prod. production, with the participation of TPS Cinema. Produced by Alain Poiré. Directed, written by Francis Veber, based on his play *Le dîner de Cons*. Camera, Luciano Tavoli; editor, Georges Klotz; music, Vladimir Cosma; art director, Hugues Tissandier; costume designer, Jacqueline Bouchard. Reviewed at 14 Juillet Odéon, Paris, April 28. Running time: 78 mins.
**Jacques Villeret (François Pignon), Thierry Lhermitte (Pierre Brochant), Francis Huster (Leblanc), Alexandra Vandernoot (Christine), Daniel Prevost (Cheval), Catherine Frot (Marlene).**
A nasty parlor game backfires with increasingly drastic and comical results in *The Dinner Game*, Francis Veber's efficient and entertaining screen adaptation of his hit play. Abetted by an excellent cast, he weaves a simple premise into comic gold. Tasty local returns are assured and, properly translated, could

nourish patrons in any territory where the well-oiled mechanisms of escalating distress and attendant laughter are welcome. Every Wednesday night, tony Paris publisher Pierre Brochant and his friends try to outdo one another by bringing the most flagrantly idiotic dimbulb they can find to join them for dinner. He who unearths the biggest dope, wins.

Int'l release: April 21      Int'l B.O.: $56 million
U.S. release: Oct. 9      U.S. B.O.: $900,000

## Dirty (Canada)

A Dirty/Stephen Hegyes production, with the participation of Canada TV, Cable Production Fund, Telefilm Canada. Produced by John Dippong, Linda Guns, Bruce Sweeney. Directed, written by Bruce Sweeney. Camera, David Pelletier; editor, Ross Weber; music, Don MacDonald; production design, Tony Devenyi; costume design, Laurel Colins. Reviewed at Sundance Festival, Jan. 19. Running time: 94 mins.

**Tom Scholte (David), Babz Chula (Angie), Benjamin Ratner (Tony), Nancy Sivak (Nancy), Vincent Gale (Ethan).**

A darkly comic psychological exploration of half a dozen urban dwellers, *Dirty* boosts Bruce Sweeney as a filmmaker to watch. Pic additionally sports terrific ensemble acting. Nonetheless, prevalent caustic tone and the emotional intensity with which he dissects his characters – sexual masochism, neurosis, and anomie – restricts pic's theatrical prospects. Central figure Angie is a middle-aged drug dealer who fulfills the masochistic fantasies of a young MBA student who derives pleasure from being spanked. Nancy, who's on the verge of declaring bankruptcy, lives in the basement of Angie's apartment. She, like Angie's son Ethan, is dangerously lonely and desperately eager for some meaningful human communication.

U.S. release: Sept. 25      U.S. B.O.: $50,000

## Dirty Work

A Metro-Goldwyn-Mayer release of a Robert Simonds/Brad Grey production. Produced by Robert Simonds. Directed by Bob Saget. Screenplay, Frank Sebastiano, Norm Macdonald, Fred Wolf. Camera, Arthur Albert; editor, George Folsey Jr.; music, Richard Gibbs; production designer, Gregory Keen; costume designer, Beth Pasternak. Reviewed at Cinemark Tinseltown Westchase, Houston. MPAA Rating: PG-13. Running time: 81 mins.

**Norm Macdonald (Mitch), Jack Warden (Pops), Artie Lange (Sam), Traylor Howard (Kathy), Don Rickles (Hamilton), Christopher McDonald (Travis Cole), Chevy Chase (Dr. Farthing). With: Chris Farley, Gary Coleman, Ken Norton, John Goodman, Adam Sandler.**

Highly reminiscent of *Kingpin* in its willingness to try anything for a laugh, *Dirty Work* is a shameless and sporadically hilarious comedy about two thirtysomething underachievers who start a revenge-for-hire business. Pic lacks sufficient pizzazz and marquee power to be anything more than a midrange B.O. performer, and likely will get lost in the summer shuffle. But if it connects with a large enough segment of its target audience – under-25 males – word of mouth could generate decent ancillary biz down the line. Norm Macdonald plays Mitch Weaver, a chronically unemployable smart aleck more successful at plotting revenge than finding gainful employment. He and buddy Sam open Dirty Work Inc., a business dedicated to providing revenge at reasonable rates.

U.S. release: June 12      U.S. B.O.: $10 million

## Disturbing Behavior

An MGM release, presented in association with Village Roadshow and Hoyts Film Partnership, of a Beacon Communications production. Produced by Armyan Bernstein, Jon Shestack. Directed by David Nutter. Screenplay, Scott Rosenberg. Camera, John S. Bartley; editor, Randy Jon Morgan; music, Mark Snow; production design, Nelson Coates; costume design, Trish Keating. Reviewed at Cinema 21, San Francisco, July 22. MPAA Rating: R. Running time: 83 mins.

**James Marsden (Steve Clark), Katie Holmes (Rachel Wagner), Nick Stahl (Gavin Strick), Steve Railsback (Officer Cox), Bruce Greenwood (Dr. Caldicott), William Sadler (Dorian Newberry).**

The current *Scream*-bred resurgence of teen-horror pics, and the youth aud's eternal identification with conformity resistance, bodes well for *Disturbing Behavior* – a blatant transplant of *Stepford Wives* ideas in adolescent torsos. A savvy high concept, in other filmic categories it scores somewhere just above lobotomized. Brisk, slick, sloppily plotted, cliche-ridden pic won't win many critical allies. But that shouldn't hinder its racking up a couple of weeks' solid theatrical biz.

Gavin witnesses a bizarre peer murder and police coverup in pic's opener. He's considered a "freak" in the too-picture-perfect community of Cradle Bay where high-school society is dominated by the Blue Ribbons – a "club" of study-grouping, cardigan-wearing, ice-cream-soda-drinking athletes and cheerleaders. These "perfect" students are considered "robots" by other classmates. Adults turn a suspiciously blind eye. Gavin suspects some "sinister conspiracy." Natch, he turns up one day spouting Moral Majority-type homilies, with fresh crewcut and mean streak to match. Steve and g.f. Rachel investigate further, finding evidence that points toward school psychiatrist Dr. Caldicott, whose background is in neuropharmacology.

U.S. release: July 24      U.S. B.O.: $17.5 million
Int'l release: Nov. 5      Int'l B.O.: $600,000

## Divine (El Evangelio De Las Maravillas) (Mexico-Argentina-Spain)

A Producciones Amaranta, Gardenia Producciones, Instituto Mexicano de Cinematografia (Mexico)/Aleph Producciones (Argentina)/Wanda Films (Spain)/Fondo de Fomento a la Calidad Cinematografica production. Produced by Jorge Sanchez, Laura Imperiale. Directed by Arturo Ripstein. Screenplay, Paz Alicia Garciadiego. Camera, Guillermo Granillo; editor, Ximena Cuevas; music David Mansfield; production designer, Osami Kawano. Reviewed at Churubusco Studios, April 22. Running time: 112 mins.

**Francisco Rabal (Papa Basilio), Katy Jurado (Mama Dorita), Carolina Papaleo (Nelida), Edwarda Gurrola (Tomasa), Bruno Bichir (Gavilan), Patricia Reyes Spindola (Micaela).**

Renowned Mexican helmer Arturo Ripstein's latest offering is his most ambitious. Loosely based on true events that happened in Mexico during the 1970s, *Divine* is a quirky, fascinating description of a loony religious cult, anticipating with fervor the end of the world. Pic's offbeat sense of humor and visual splendor will make it a must-see on the fest circuit. And by capturing the crazed, self-destructive logic of cults, it is a film very much in tune with the end of the millennium. *Divine* has an anachronistic feel to it, a sense of medieval lunacy that ideally sets the tone for the story of the New Jerusalem, a cult led by Mama Dorita and Papa Basilio. The congregation is a motley crew of zealots, misfits, and losers

...**May 6**...
Showtime Cable acquires U.S. broadcast rights to controversial **Lolita,** which still lacks theatrical distrib.

who have adopted their leaders' weird, Hollywood-style biblical credo.

Int'l release: Sept. 25                    Int'l B.O.: $100,000

### Divine Trash (Docu)

A Stratosphere release of a Divine Trash production. Produced by Cindy Miller, Steve Yeager. Directed by Yeager. Camera, Jeff Atkinson, Jim Harris, Yeager; editors, Terry Campbell, Kahoe, Yeager; music, Dan Barto; historical consultant, Kevin Heffernan. Reviewed at Sundance Festival, Jan. 18. Running time: 105 mins.

With: John Waters, Jeanine Basinger, Steve Buscemi, Patricia Hearst, Jim Jarmusch, George and Mike Kuchar, Herschell Gordon Lewis, Jonas Mekas, Paul Morrissey, Robert Shaye, Mink Stole, John and Patricia Waters.

Part biopic of Baltimore's enfant terrible/shockmeister John Waters, part chronicle of the making of the notorious *Pink Flamingos*, which catapulted drag queen Divine to the limelight, *Divine Trash* is an interesting, informative docu that surveys in its background three decades of non-mainstream and avant-garde cinema. Commercially, Steve Yeager's docu, which won the 1998 Filmmakers Trophy at Sundance, could get a PR boost from the release of Waters' new comedy, *Pecker*, later this year, but main audience still rests with his fans, who might even learn a fact or two about the iconic filmmaker, a maverick artist congenitally devoted to breaking the mold and shattering bourgeois precepts.

### Divorcing Jack (U.K.-France)

A BBC Films/Winchester Films presentation of a Scala Films production. Produced by Robert Cooper. Directed by David Caffrey. Screenplay, Colin Bateman, based on his novel. Camera, James Welland; editor, Nick Moore; music, Adrian Johnston; production designer, Claire Kenny; costume designer, Pamela Selby. Reviewed at Cannes Festival , May 15. Running time: 110 mins.

David Thewlis (Dan Starkey), Rachel Griffiths (Lee Cooper), Robert Lindsay (Michael Brinn), Jason Isaacs (Cow Pat Keegan), Laura Fraser (Margaret), Richard Gant (Charles Parker).

A bold attempt at a comedy-thriller set in the near future in Belfast, this first feature from David Caffrey shows plenty of promise and chutzpah, but veers wildly in tone from sweet romantic comedy to bloody thriller. Given conditions in Northern Ireland, it's to be expected that, in the U.K. the pic will face a mixed reaction. In other territories, including the U.S., *Jack* can probably be enjoyed as a mostly entertaining man-on-the-run adventure, and as a solid vehicle for the talented David Thewlis, who plays an irresponsible journalist out of his depth when he becomes involved in a politically motivated murder. Set in 1999, pic unfolds against a background of a hard-fought political campaign for the new post of prime minister of Northern Ireland.

Int'l release: Aug. 14                    Int'l B.O.: $1.4 million

### Dr. Akagi (Kanzo Sensei) (Japan)

An Imamura Prods/Toei Co./Tohoku Shinsha/Kadokawa Shoten/Comme des Cinemas/Catherine Dussart Prods co-production. Produced by Hisa Ino, Koji Matsuda. Directed by Shohei Imamura. Screenplay, Imamura, Daisuke Tengan, based on the book *Doctor Liver* by Ango Sakaguchi. Camera, Shigeru Komatsubara; editor, Hajime Okayasu; music, Yosuke Yamashita; art director, Hisao Inagaki; costume designers, Keisuke Chiyoda, Ikuko Kozu. Reviewed at Cannes Festival, May 17. Running time: 129 mins.

Akira Emoto (Dr. Akagi), Kumiko Aso (Sonoko), Jyuro Kara (Umemoto), Masanori Sera (Toriumi), Jacques Gamblin (Piet), Keiko Matzuzaka (Tomiko).

Two-time Cannes Palme d'Or winner Shohei Imamura returns with one of his most personal outings in *Dr. Akagi*. But the wartime saga of a country general-practitioner doggedly pursuing a cure for hepatitis is shy on the international appeal of much of the helmer's earlier work. A sturdy piece of classical-style cinema, pic lacks the universality that's made Imamura one of Japan's best-known filmmakers. On the sheer force of his name, the film could snare some foreign sales, but outside its native land it will unspool primarily at fest settings. The title character is a tireless medic. The setting is a coastal island village in 1945. The tide of the war has turned, but the local troops manning a prisoner-of-war camp continue to fight as if victory were still at hand. For Akagi they are merely a nuisance, rationing his supply of glucose needed to fight the virulent spread of hepatitis.

Int'l release: Oct. 17                    Int'l B.O.: $1.2 million

### Doctor Chance (Docteur Chance) (France-Chile)

A Films Sans Frontières release (in France) of a Compagnie des Films, 3 Lumières (France)/Valcine (Chile) production, with the participation of Canal Plus, CNC. Produced by Jacky Ouaknine. Directed, written by F.J. Ossang. Camera, Remi Chevrin; editor, Thierry Rouden; music, Messagero Killer Boy; art direction, Santiago Isidro Pin; costume design, Pierre-Yves Guayraud. Reviewed at Locarno Festival, Aug. 13. Running time: 100 mins.

Elvire (Ancetta), Pedro Hestnes (Angstel), Marisa Paredes (Milady), Joe Strummer (Vince Taylor).

French wild man F.J. Ossang returns after seven years with his third feature, *Doctor Chance*, an all-guns-blazing, acid-head film noir about a bunch of lowlifes on a metaphysical road trip through Chile. Ossang's small fan club will trip out on this dilettantish collection of neo-Godardian shavings, while the rest of the world will gratefully pass. Pic is, however, an advance on Ossang's previous creation, *Land of the Dead*. In *Chance*, souped-up hit man Angstel picks up old class hooker Ancetta (Elvire) in a baroque South American hotel, and the pair, armed and with cash to blow, head into the wide open spaces in an impenetrable farrago about seedy drug-dealers and sensory gratification.

Int'l release: Feb. 25                    Int'l B.O.: $50,000

### Dr. Dolittle

A 20th Century Fox release of a Davis Entertainment Co./Joseph M. Singer Entertainment production. Produced by John Davis, Joseph M. Singer, David T. Friendly. Directed by Betty Thomas. Screenplay, Nat Mauldin, Larry Levin, based on the *Doctor Dolittle* stories by Hugh Lofting. Camera, Russell Boyd; editor, Peter Teschner; music, Richard Gibbs; production designer, William Elliott; costume designer, Sharen Davis; animatronic creatures, Jim Henson's Creature Shop. Reviewed at Mann Plaza, L.A., June 15. MPAA Rating: PG-13. Running time: 85 mins.

Eddie Murphy (Dr. John Dolittle), Ossie Davis (Archer Dolittle), Oliver Platt (Dr. Mark Weller), Peter Boyle (Calloway), Richard Schiff (Dr. Gene Reiss), Kristen Wilson (Lisa Dolittle), Jeffrey Tambor (Dr. Fish). Voices: Norm Macdonald (Lucky), Albert Brooks (Jacob), Chris Rock

---

(Rodney), Reni Santoni (Rat #1), John Leguizamo (Rat #2), Julie Kavner (Female Pigeon), Garry Shandling (Male Pigeon), Gilbert Gottfried (Compulsive Dog).

The concept must have looked great on paper: remake and contemporize Hugh Lofting's *Doctor Dolittle* (lavishly produced by Fox as a kid's musical in 1967, starring Rex Harrison) with Eddie Murphy and state-of-the-art tech wizardry from Jim Henson's Creature Shop. But the resulting *Dr. Dolittle* is a letdown. Slim on story and rife with scatological jokes, the film may strike a chord with pre-teens but misses for an older crowd despite some nifty effects and broad humor. Costly venture will require considerable commercial muscle to recoup the investment, but theatrical biz appears to be no better than OK, with the film's big payday down the line on video.

Thrusting the story into the present robs it of any storybook magic. The updated Dr. John Dolittle was exorcised of his gift of "talking to the animals" as a child, when he began to adopt the social customs of a family pet. His unique ability suddenly returns when, as an adult, he strikes his head on his car's windshield after swerving to avoid a stray dog in the road. When his family and colleagues catch him conversing with dogs, guinea pigs, birds and the like, they strongly urge him to take the rest cure. The dilemma for the noted surgeon is that this rapport enables him to rediscover the sheer joy of the doctor-patient relationship.

| | |
|---|---|
| U.S. release: June 26 | U.S. B.O.: $144 million |
| Int'l release: June 26 | Int'l B.O.: $133 million |

## Dog Park (Canada)

A Lions Gate Films release/Independent Pictures presentation of an Accent Entertainment Corp. production. Produced by Susan Cavan. Directed, written by Bruce McCulloch. Camera, David Makin; editor, Christopher Cooper; music, Craig Northey; production design, Marian Wihak; costumes, Linda Muir. Reviewed at Toronto Festival, Sept. 14. Running time: 91 mins. **Natasha Henstridge (Lorna), Luke Wilson (Andy), Kathleen Robertson (Cheryl), Janeane Garofalo (Jeri), Bruce McCulloch (Jeff), Kristen Lehman (Keiran), Gordon Currie (Trevor).**

The intriguing notion that the dog park is the singles bar of the late 1990s is the starting point for Bruce McCulloch's feature directorial debut, a charming, funny take on modern romance. The former member of the Kids in the Hall troupe stumbles in the final reel, however, when he segues from light comedy to syrupy sentimentality, a move that serves only to highlight the rather shallow development of the characters. If marketed properly, *Dog Park* could attract hip, young auds, but its bark probably won't translate into much theatrical bite. Tale of contemporary dating revolves around the hapless Andy. His g.f., Cheryl, has just walked out and moved in with Trevor; she's also taken their dog. Andy has already fallen for the beautiful but distant Lorna, a kids' TV show host who is also on the rebound and prefers to focus her emotional attention on her dog.

## Don Juan (France-Spain-Germany)

A Bac Films release of a Gerard Jourd'hui presentation of a Blue Dahlia Prod, France 3 Cinema, Mate Prod. (France)/Tornasol Films (Spain)/Road Movies (Germany) production, with the participation of Canal Plus. Produced by Gerard Jourd'hui. Directed, written by Jacques Weber, based on the play by Molière. Camera, Jose Luis Alcaine; editor, Jacques Witta; music,

Bruno Coulais; art director, Claude Lenoir; costume designer, Sylvie de Segonzac. Reviewed at UGC Orient Express, Paris, April 1. Running time: 104 mins. **Jacques Weber (Don Juan), Michel Boujenah (Sganarelle), Emmanuelle Béart (Elvire), Penelope Cruz (Mathurine), Ariadna Gil (Charlotte), Michel Lonsdale (Don Luis).**

Distinguished thesp and first-time helmer Jacques Weber has fashioned an honorable but underwhelming variation on the Don Juan yarn. Set in 17th-century Spain, episodic costumer benefits from gorgeous sun-drenched vistas, a varied, highly appealing score, and an excellent perf from Michel Boujenah as the Don's faithful servant. But overall there's not much depth in this version. Fests and quality tube dates await. With a mane of gray hair and a self-satisfied smirk, Weber plays the character unapologetically older. His ability to attract fetching young women seems anchored in his outlaw status rather than in any genuine charm.

| | |
|---|---|
| Int'l release: March 18 | Int'l B.O.:$700,000 |

## Down in the Delta

A Miramax release of a Showtime presentation of an Amen Ra Films and Chris/Rose production. Produced by Rick Rosenberg, Bob Christiansen, Victor McGauley, Wesley Snipes, Reuben Cannon. Directed by Maya Angelou. Screenplay, Myron Goble. Camera, William Wages; editor, Nancy Richardson; music, Stanley Clarke; production design, Lindsey Hermer-Bell; costume design, Maxyne Baker; Tom Hidderley. Reviewed at Toronto Festival, Sept. 17. Running time: 111 mins. **Alfre Woodard (Loretta), Al Freeman Jr. (Earl), Mary Alice (Rosa Lynn), Esther Rolle (Annie), Loretta Devine (Zenia), Wesley Snipes (Will), Mpho Koaho (Thomas), Kulani Hassen (Tracy).**

Poet Maya Angelou's feature-directing debut is a solid and affecting piece of work that will need careful marketing and strong critical support to attract ticket buyers. Originally produced for Showtime cable, *Down in the Delta* never really transcends the limitations of an intimate, well-crafted, and resolutely old-fashioned TV drama. Still, this emotionally involving story of an African-American family has definite crossover appeal, and could find a receptive audience in wide theatrical release come Christmastime.

Loretta is a chronically unemployed single mother living with her mother and two young children in an inner-city Chicago apartment. She has eased the pain of constant despair with drugs and alcohol, to the point of neglecting her son and autistic daughter. The boy is in danger of becoming a product of his environment, and already talks about getting "strapped" like his gun-toting classmates. Desperate to move out of harm's way, Loretta's mother pawns a prized family heirloom to send the family to the Mississippi Delta to spend the summer with Uncle Earl.

| | |
|---|---|
| U.S. release: Dec. 25 | U.S. B.O.: $2.5 million |

## The Draft (Naja) (Italy)

A Cecchi Gori Distribuzione release of a Cecchi Gori Tiger Cinematografica production. Produced by Vittorio and Rita Cecchi Gori. Directed by Angelo Longoni. Screenplay, Longoni, Massimo Sgorbani, based on their stage play. Camera, Italo Petriccione; editor, Mauro Bonanni; music, Paolo Vivaldi; art direction, Gianni Quaranta; costume design, Ornella Campanale. Reviewed at Quirinale Cinema, Rome, March 1. Running time: 100 mins.

---

**... May 8 ...**
Robin Williams inks to star in Disney's **Bicentennial Man**.

Enrico Lo Verso (Carmelo), Stefano Accorsi (Tonino), Francesco Siciliano (Franco), Lorenzo Amato (Claudio), Adelmo Togliani (Luca), Claudia Pandolfi (Bruna).

With a self-conscious tip of the hat to Robert Altman's 1983 *Streamers*, helmer Angelo Longoni has adapted his successful play *The Draft* to the screen. Lacking a Vietnam war or the equivalent to give it wider resonance, pic remains a well-penned character study offering its excellent thesps a chance to shine. Local box office has been disappointing, but pic could sell in Euro markets where systems like Italy's draft are in force. Five young soldiers doing their mandatory one-year military service find themselves grounded on a hot summer Sunday because vandals have destroyed the barracks bathroom while they were on duty.

Int'l release: Feb. 20                    Int'l B.O.: $100,000

## Dragon Town Story (Long Cheng Zhengyue)

(Hong Kong-China)

A China Star Entertainment Group release (in Hong Kong) of a Win's Entertainment (Hong Kong)/Tianjin Film Studio (China) production. Produced by Han Zhenduo, Charles Heung. Directed by Yang Fengliang. Screenplay, Yang Jiang, Jing Shi. Camera, Zhao Fei; editor, Yuan Fang; music, Zhao Jiping; art director, Wang Biao; costume designer, Ye Gensheng; martial-arts director, Tung Wai. Reviewed on videodisc, London, March 31. Running time: 96 mins.

Wu Chien-lien (Jiang Lanjuan), You Yong (Li Qingyang), Huang Zhongqiu (Xiong Jinbao), Lam Wai (Hu Danlong). (Mandarin dialog)

An artily lensed revenge drama set during the early days of Republican China, *Dragon Town Story* is a quality fest and upscale tube item. Played mostly as a psychological drama rather than an action entry, and exec-produced by Zhang Yimou, this reps a strong solo showing by mainland director Yang Fengliang. Pic opens on the wedding day of Lanjuan (Wu Chien-lien), whose marriage is suddenly aborted when gunmen mow down her entire family. Nine years later, wandering in a harsh, deserted landscape, she hooks up with legendary contract killer Li Qingyang (You Yong), whom she eventually persuades to take on the job of wiping out the assassins and their powerful warlord.

## The Dreamlife of Angels (La Vie Rêvée des Anges) (France)

A Bagheera/Diaphana/France 3 Cinema production, with the participation of Canal Plus, Le Centre National de la Cinématographie, la Région Nord Pas de Calais, la Région Centre, la Fondation GAN, La Procirep. Produced by François Marquis. Directed by Erick Zonca. Screenplay, Zonca, Roger Bohbot. Camera, Agnes Godard; editor, Yannick Kergoat; music, Yann Thiersen; art director, Jimmy Vansteenkiste; costumes, Françoise Clavel. Reviewed at Cannes Festival, May 16. Running time: 113 mins.

Elodie Bouchez (Isa), Natacha Regnier (Marie), Gregoire Colin (Chris), Jo Prestia (Fredo), Patrick Mercado (Charly).

*The Dreamlife of Angels*, the feature debut of Erick Zonca, is the sort of stirring, assured filmmaking normally associated with seasoned auteurs. A deceptively simple yarn about two young women on the fringes of society in Lille, the pic impresses with its original take and because Zonca never resorts to anything resembling standard-issue storytelling. Boosted by critical reaction, *Angels* is almost certain to be a hot upscale item in

Europe and may even get specialized U.S. distribs dreaming of box-office action. This is the story of two very different women whose common bond is a sense of being alienated from mainstream society.

Int'l release: Oct. 14                    Int'l B.O.: $9 million

## Drive, She Said (Canada)

A Malofilm release of a 47 Films presentation of a Drive, She Said Prods production, with the participation of Canada Television & Cable Production Fund, Telefilm Canada. Produced by Stephen Hegyes. Directed, written by Mina Shum. Camera, Peter Wunstorf; editor, Michelle Floyd; music, Dennis Burke; production design, Michael Bjornson; costume design, Barb Nixon; sound, Bill Sheppard. Reviewed at Toronto Festival, Sept. 10, 1997. Running time: 93 mins.

Moira Kelly (Nadine), Sebastian Spence (Jonathan), Josh Hamilton (Tass), Jim Byrnes (Shrink), Mina Shum (Chen).

*Drive, She Said* is a meet-cute road movie that starts in high gear but soon takes too many left turns for its own good. Mina Shum's second feature is too mild a confection to motor on to much theatrical business. On Nadine's first day at work in a bank the place is held up; the upside is that she falls for co-worker Jonathan. Five years later the two are in counseling. Enter Tass, a bank robber, who takes her as a hostage and sends the pic into interesting but unresolved directions.

U.S. release: Sept. 4                    U.S. B.O.: $20,000

## The Duo (Iruvar) (India)

A Madras Talkies production. Produced by Mani Rathnam. Directed, written by Mani Rathnam. Camera, Santosh Sivan; editor, Suresh Urs; music, A.R. Rahman; production design, Sameer Chanda. Reviewed at Toronto Festival, Sept. 5, 1997. Running time: 118 mins.

With: Mohanlal, Prakash Raj, Aishwarya Rai, Gautami, Tabu, Nasser.

A long-limbed tale of male friendship across some 40 years of Indian history, *The Duo* plays like a three-hour movie with an hour cut out. Too many plot bones and not enough emotional meat make this a sometimes entertaining and stylistically interesting cadaver of a much more full-scaled movie. Latest by prolific Tamil director Mani Rathnam is destined for thin Western exposure. Story follows an initially clumsy but driven actor, Anandan, and a writer-turned-politician, Selvam, from Indian independence to more modern times.

## The Dust of Naples (Polvere Di Napoli) (Italy)

A Fulvio Lucisano presentation of an Italian Int'l Film release of an AMA Film/GMF production in association with RAI Cinemafiction. Produced by Gianni Minervini. Directed by Antonio Capuano. Screenplay, Capuano, Paolo Sorrentino. Camera (color), Pasquale Rachini; editor, Giogio Franchini; music, Marco Zurzolo; production/costume designer, Mario Di Pace. Reviewed at Savoy Cinema, Rome, May 10. Running time: 104 mins.

Gigio Morra (Bilancione), Antonio Iuorio (Bibbero), Gianni Ferreri (Sanguetta), Teresa Saponangelo (Teresa), Raffaele Musella (Gino), Francesco Pennasilico (Pasqualo), Silvio Orlando (Ciraco), Lola Pagnani (Rosita), Giovanni Esposito (Mimmo Pezzella), Silvio Orlando (Charlie), Tonino Taiuti (Jerry).

Neapolitan directors have been delivering top efforts recently as evidenced in *The Dust of Naples* by Antonio Capuano.

Designed as a sober update of Vittorio De Sica's 1954 classic *The Gold of Naples*, Capuano's pic refashions the characters of yore in modern incarnations. In this switch to grotesque comedy, Capuano retains a sharply ironic edge in pic's five episodes, showing how Naples' gold has turned to dirt and grime without diminishing the Neapolitans' raw, warmhearted humanity. A genuinely funny film, as well as a sincere one, it is well worth a look for fests and specialized buyers.

In its best moments, pic strikes a deep chord because it avoids pontificating as it unveils the city's lowly, streetwise, terribly human denizens scraping by 40 years after De Sica. Echoes of the original film appear in the excellent *Charlie and Jerry*, where two fine sax players go from a kitschy wedding to a concert performance sans instruments which were stolen from their car.

Int'l release: May 8                    Int'l B.O.: $150,000

## Earth (India-Canada)

A Behaviour/MGM release of a Goldwyn Films presentation of a Cracking the Earth Films production. Produced by Delip Mehta, Anne Masson, Deepa Mehta. Directed, written by Deepa Mehta, based on the autobiography *Cracking India* by Bapsi Sidhwa. Camera, Giles Nuttgens; editor, Barry Farrell; music, A.R. Rahman; art director, Aradhana Seth. Reviewed at Toronto Festival, Sept. 11. Running time: 108 mins.

**Aamir Khan (Ice Candy Man), Nandita Das (Aysh Shanta), Rahul Khanna (Hasan), Maia Sethna (Lenny), Kitu Gidwani (Bunty Sethna), Kulbushan Kharbanda (Imam Din), Arif Zakaria (Rustom Sethna), Gulshan Grover (Mr. Singh), Eric Peterson (Mr. Rogers).**

The second part of a trilogy whose theme is the elements, Deepa Mehta's *Earth* examines the subject of India's partition as a means to deal with land literally and figuratively. Based on an autobiographical tome, the film mixes romance and social drama in an uneasy balance of schmaltz and wrenching emotion. It has a potent denouement that almost makes up for some uninspired early sentimentality but requires some astute trims to tighten the pace and avoid the languorous stretches. Despite the underlying political and historical context, pic has sufficient universal elements to work as an upscale drama theatrically in a slightly abbreviated form.

The story is told from the perspective of 8-year-old Lenny, a girl from an affluent Parsee family. The setting is Lahore in 1947, a city in which Hindu, Muslim, Sikh, and Parsee co-exist peacefully. However, the prospect of independence is looming with the notion of a separate Muslim country, Pakistan, presumably part of the bargain. Initially, the prospect of violent change appears distantly removed from the group of young adults who gravitate around Lenny's Hindu nanny Shanta.

## Edge of Seventeen

A Blue Streak Films/Luna Pictures presentation. Produced by David Moreton, Todd Stephens. Directed by Moreton. Screenplay, Todd Stephens. Camera, Gina DeGirolamo; editor, Tal Ben-David; production designer, Ivor Stilin; costumes, Anne Crabtree; music, Tom Bailey. Reviewed at San Francisco Lesbian & Gay Festival, June 26. Running time: 99 mins.

**Chris Stafford (Eric), Tina Holmes (Maggie), Andersen Gabrych (Rod), Stephanie McVay (Mom), Lea DeLaria (Angie), John Eby (Dad).**

A perceptive, accomplished seriocomedy, *Edge of Seventeen* feels like a gay-p.o.v. version of the deft early-to-mid-1980s John Hughes teen pics, even revisiting their era for trendy nostalgia value. Appealing young players and humorous yet delicately felt adolescent coming-out portrait, pic should score similarly well in urban centers, with bright select-export and vid prospects to follow.

Midwestern 16-year-old Eric (Chris Stafford) is introduced psyched-up for his first real job: – slinging ribs 'n' 'taters in a brown-checkered polyester uniform at an Ohio theme park. Disillusionment is offset by Ohio State hotel-management student Rod, whose flirty, forward attentions push Eric toward a sexual-identity awakening – capped by an idyllic, romantic first sexual experience.

## The Education of Little Tree

A Paramount release of a Jake Eberts production, in association with Allied Films/Lightmotive. Produced by Jake Eberts. Directed, written by Richard Friedenberg, based on the novel by Forrest Carter. Camera, Anastas Michos; editor, Wayne Wahrman; music, Mark Isham; production design, Dan Bishop; costume design, Renee April. Reviewed at Paramount, L.A., Nov. 15, 1997. MPAA Rating: PG. Running time: 112 mins.

**James Cromwell (Granpa), Tantoo Cardinal (Granma), Joseph Ashton (Little Tree), Graham Greene (Willow John).**

Handsomely produced, *The Education of Little Tree*, Richard Friedenberg's directorial debut, offers a tenderly compassionate, highly evocative chronicle of the turbulent childhood of a Cherokee orphan during the Depression. Pic admirably captures the distinctive lifestyle of American Indians and their struggle against racism, but it's too earnest and elegiac by the commercial standards of today's teen and family fare. Paramount will have to take an aggressive approach in marketing this worthy family drama, the message of which is still very much relevant.

Protagonist is 8-year-old Little Tree (Joseph Ashton), who has lost both his father and mother. Resisting his aunt's efforts to raise him, he chooses to go to his grandparents, Indian Granma (Tantoo Cardinal) and white Granpa (James Cromwell).

U.S. release: Dec. 25, 1997          U.S. B.O.: $300,000
Int'l release: Sept. 24               Int'l B.O.: $25,000

## The Elevator

A United Film Distributors presentation of a Hit Entertainment production. Produced by Brian Shuster, Athena Stensland. Directed by Rafael Zelinsky, Arthur Borman, Nigel Dick. Screenplay, Gabriel Bologna. Camera, Jens Sturup; editor, Lawrence Maddox; music, James Covell; production design, Mary Gullickson, Hunter Cressall; costume design, Cathryn Wagner. Reviewed at Seattle Festival, June 7, 1997. Running time: 95 mins.

**Martin Landau (Roy Tilden), Gabriel Bologna (David Brochman), Arye Gross (Moshe), Athena Stensland (Katy), Martin Sheen (Sarge), Bokeem Woodbine (Malcolm).**

A large cast is wasted in *The Elevator*, a silly, ill-conceived pastiche presumably aimed at Hollywood insiders, but unlikely to connect with any auds. An omnibus effort disguised as a single narrative, this multi-helmer project would be better off broken up and sold for scrap. The all-too-literal deus ex machina of the title is where hotshot production exec Roy Tilden (Martin Landau) finds himself stuck on the night of a big testimonial dinner in his honor. His cellmate for the night – thanks to a calculated mechanical failure – is one David Brochman, a young would-be screenwriter who just happens to have a stack o' manuscripts which form the basis of pic's vignettes.

### Elizabeth (U.K.)

A Gramercy/Polygram Filmed Entertainment presentation, in association with Channel Four Films, of a Working Title production. Produced by Alison Owen, Eric Fellner, Tim Bevan. Directed by Shekhar Kapur. Screenplay, Michael Hirst. Camera, Remi Adefarasin; editor, Jill Bilcock; music, David Hirschfelder; production design, John Myhre; costume design, Alexandra Byrne. Reviewed at Venice Festival, Sept. 7. Running time: 121 mins.

Cate Blanchett (Elizabeth I), Geoffrey Rush (Sir Francis Walsingham), Christopher Eccleston (Duke of Norfolk), Joseph Fiennes (Robert Dudley), Richard Attenborough (Sir William Cecil), Fanny Ardant (Mary of Guise), Kathy Burke (Queen Mary Tudor), Eric Cantona (M. de Foix), James Frain (Alvaro de la Quadra), Vincent Cassel (Duc d'Anjou), John Gielgud (The Pope).

Brimming with royal intrigue, court conspiracies, sex, violence, treachery, bloodshed, and even a touch of cross-dressing, *Elizabeth* is superior historical soap opera that shrewdly sidesteps the cliches of British costume drama with its bold, often modern approach. Propelled by Shekhar Kapur's muscular direction, Michael Hirst's witty script, and Cate Blanchett's remarkable performance as the Virgin Queen, this richly entertaining saga is accessible enough to go beyond upscale crowds and find wider appeal.

Story kicks off in 1554, with England financially troubled, under threat from abroad, and fiercely divided along religious lines. The ailing Queen Mary maneuvers to restore Catholicism. Having no heir, she attempts to prevent her Protestant half-sister, Elizabeth, from succeeding her. But the ploy fails, and Elizabeth is crowned, provoking the ire of Mary-loyalist the Duke of Norfolk. Elizabeth's chief adviser, Sir William Cecil, urges her to produce an heir, suggesting marriage to the King of Spain or France's Duc d'Anjou. But the feisty queen rejects both – openly and shockingly entertaining her childhood sweetheart, Robert Dudley. Elizabeth turns increasingly for guidance to Master of Spies Sir Francis Walsingham. As conspiracies within her council threaten to end her reign and the arrival of an unscrupulous Vatican emissary brings the risk of assassination even closer, Elizabeth strikes first.

| U.S. release: Nov. 6 | U.S. B.O.: $15.5 million |
| Int'l release: Oct. 2 | Int'l B.O.: $19 million |

### Elles (Luxembourg)

An Artemis presentation of a Samsa Film production, in association with Canal Plus, Esicma. Produced by Jani Thiltges, Claude Waringo. Directed by Luis Galvao Teles. Screenplay, Teles, Don Bohlinger. Camera, Alfredo Mayo; editor, Regina Bartschi; music, Alejandro Masso; art director, Veronique Scarez. Reviewed at Palm Springs Festival, Jan. 11. Running time: 95 mins.

Miou-Miou (Eva), Carmen Maura (Linda), Marthe Keller (Barbara), Marisa Berenson (Chloe), Guesch Patti (Branca), Joaquim De Almeida (Gigi).

Wavering between cinema and sociology, genuine drama, and schmaltzy soap, the international co-production *Elles* tackles the issue of ageing among fortysomething women. Starring five beautiful actresses, the film begins well but then veers toward soap and sitcom territory, cramming within its short time frame just about any problem concerning middle-aged femmes one can imagine. Still, relevant subject matter and illustrious international cast might persuade a small distributor to release this meller in major American cities, with stronger prospects in European theatrical and ancillary markets. Initial sequences promise something more in the vein of Almodovar's *Women on the Verge of a Nervous Breakdown* than that of *On Golden Pond* or other social-problem melodramas about old age.

### Elvjs & Merilijn (Italy)

An Istituto Luce release of an Alia Film/Istituto Luce production, in association with RAI Radiotelevisione Italiana. Produced by Enzo Porcelli. Directed by Armando Manni. Screenplay, Manni, Massimo Torre. Camera, Renato Tafuri; editor, Ugo De Rossi; music, Pivio, Aldo De Scalzi; art director, Marco Dentici; costume designer, Metella Raboni. Reviewed at Anica, Rome, May 5. Running time: 93 mins.

Edyta Olszowka (Ileana/Merilijn), Goran Navojec (Nicolaj/Elvjs), Giorgio Faletti (Gino), Toni Bertorelli (Colonel), Julietta Koleva (Eva Petrova), Sasa Vulicevic (Goran). (Italian, Romanian, Bulgarian, Serbo-Croatian, and French dialog)

Newcomer Armando Manni weighs in with an original slant on the plight of Central European refugees in the West in *Elvjs & Merilijn*, which chronicles the melancholy journey of two celebrity look-alikes chasing their dream of *la dolce vita* in Italy. While the direction could be more muscular, this plaintive tale of beautiful losers remains intense, involving, and ambitious. This resourcefully made low-budget production's strategic fest launch pad may facilitate some limited sales. Romanian Marilyn Monroe impersonator Ileana (Edyta Olszowka) and Bulgarian Elvis double Nicolaj (Goran Navojec) win a look-alike competition in Bucharest for which the prize is a summer engagement at a nightclub on Italy's Adriatic coast. Seizing the opportunity, the strangers take off together, forced to communicate in the only language they have in common: the broken Italian they've picked up from TV.

| Int'l release: May 1 | Int'l B.O.: $50,000 |

### Endurance (U.S.-U.K.)

A Buena Vista release of a Hollywood Pictures presentation of a La Junta production, in association with Film Four, Helkon Media Film Veritrieb. Produced by Edward R. Pressman, Terrence Malick, Max Palesvky. Directed by Leslie Woodhead. Director, Atlanta Olympic games sequence, Bud Greenspan. Camera, Ivan Strasburg; editors, Saar Klein, Oral Norrie Ottey; music, John Powell. Reviewed at Telluride Festival, Sept. 4. Running time: 83 mins.

Shawananness Gebrselassie (Haile's Mother), Yonas Zergaw (Young Haile), Tedesse Haile (Young Haile's Father), and Haile Gebrselassie, Gebrselassie Bekele (Haile's Father), Alem Tellahun (Haile's Wife) as themselves. (Amharic and English dialog)

A docudrama about the world's foremost long-distance runner that is shot like a full-blown feature, *Endurance* overpowers its plain, appealing subject matter with ultra-elaborate technique. Younger and more impressionable viewers may be swept away by the stunning images of Africa and the insistent East-meets-West score, but the more analytically inclined will be suspicious of the degree of contrivance involved and the stylistic idealization of Third World poverty. Disney marketing will be put to the challenge when pic opens in 1999.

Vet Brit ethnographic documentarian Leslie Woodhead focuses on the diminutive Ethiopian runner Haile Gebrselassie, who won the gold medal in the men's 10,000 meters at the 1996 Atlanta Olympics. Framed by that race, body of the picture impressionistically evokes the Olympian's life, with Yonas Zergaw, a nephew of the runner, playing him as a pre-adolescent, and Gebrselassie himself taking over from adulthood. From the earliest, it seems, he would never walk when running would do; scenes depict him scampering around the farm, where a family of 12 lived in a one-room mud hut. Inspired by the 1980 Olympic victory of fellow Ethiopian Miruts Yifter, Haile decided to become a serious runner.

From the first image of the adult Gebrselassie moving with seemingly effortless grace and speed across a striking rural landscape, *Endurance*, with its exceptionally smooth tracking shots, widescreen framing, complicated setups and, especially, its souped-up soundtrack, has much more the feel of a dramatic feature than of a documentary. The basic story of the runner's life is inspiring, of course, and the man himself, a devoted Coptic Christian, seems exceedingly decent, a true gentleman despite his fierce competitiveness.

### Enemy of the State

A Buena Vista release of a Touchstone Pictures presentation of a Don Simpson/Jerry Bruckheimer production, in association with Scott Free. Produced by Jerry Bruckheimer. Directed by Tony Scott. Screenplay, David Marconi. Camera, Dan Mindel; editor, Chris Lebenzon; music, Trevor Rabin, Harry Gregson-Williams; production design, Benjamin Fernandez; costume design, Narlene Stewart; surveillance advisers, Martin Kaiser, Steve Uhrig. Reviewed at Crest, L.A., Nov. 6. MPAA Rating: R. Running time: 127 mins.
**Will Smith (Robert Clayton Dean), Gene Hackman (Brill), Jon Voight (Thomas Reynolds), Lisa Bonet (Rachel Banks), Regina King (Carla Dean), Stuart Wilson (Congressman Albert), Tom Sizemore (Pintero), Loren Dean (Hicks), Barry Pepper (Pratt), Jason Lee (Zavitz), Gabriel Byrne ("Brill"), Congressman (Jason Robards).**
Tony Scott's political thriller, *Enemy of the State*, aspires to the level of the great 1970's cycle of conspiracy-paranoia pictures: *Three Days of the Condor*, *Chinatown*, *The Conversation*. Scott shrewdly uses the likeable Will Smith in the classic role of an innocent Everyman framed for murder by a corrupt intelligence officer for unwittingly possessing embarrassing information. With Smith and Hackman heading a terrific cast, this briskly paced actioner should enjoy a robust pre-Thanksgiving opening and a solid theatrical run through the holidays.

A vet congressman, who's a vocal opponent of a new surveillance bill, is murdered by Thomas Brian Reynolds, an ambitious National Security Agency official, and his assistants in a public park. Meanwhile, a nature photographer, Zavitz, has unknowingly filmed the incident and now possesses the incriminating video. Enter Robert Clayton Dean, a young hotshot attorney who bumps into old friend Zavitz, on the run from government ops. He secretly drops the tape into Dean's shopping bag. David Marconi's script sees to it that his Everyman is gradually stripped of his job, his money, and his family's trust.

| U.S. release: Nov. 20 | U.S. B.O.: $92 million |
| Int'l release: Nov. 26 | Int'l B.O.: $20 million |

### Espresso (Presszo) (Hungary)

A Magic Media production. Produced by Peter Barbalics, Gergely Z. Horvath, Eva Schulze. Directed by Tamas Sas. Screenplay, Sas, Gabor Nemeth. Camera, editor, Sas; music, Laszlo Melis; production design, Zsolt Buday Juhasz; costume design, Krisztina Berzsenyi. Reviewed at Hungarian Film Week, Budapest, Feb. 7. Running time: 106 mins.
**Andrea Soptei (Anna), Andrea Fullajtar (Bori), Karina Kecskes (Dora), Andras Stohl (Gabor), Gabor Mate (Tulaj), Zoltan Rajkai (Gabika).**
A stylistically bold low-budgeter, *Espresso* unfolds during the course of a year in a Budapest bar where a bunch of regulars meet. Director, cameraman, editor, and co-screenwriter Tamas Sas shoots the entire pic – except for the opening and closing establishing shots of the bar's exterior – from one fixed position, with the static camera focusing on a particular table. The result is undeniably claustrophobic but, thanks to the presence of several characters, one that holds the viewer's attention. The best first film in the Hungarian Film Awards (and best screenplay), it needs expert subtitling for the full flavor of the principal characters to be appreciated internationally.
Int'l release: N/A                    Int'l B.O.: $50,000

### Eternity and a Day (Mia Eoniotita Ke Mia Mera)

(Greece-France-Italy)
A Theo Angelopoulos Films, Greek Film Centre, Greek TV (ERT) (Athens)/Paradis Films, La Sept Cinéma (Paris)/Intermedias (Rome) co-production. Produced by Theo Angelopoulos, Eric Heumann, Giorgio Silvagni, Amedeo Pagani. Directed by Angelopoulos. Screenplay, Angelopoulos, Tonino Guerra, Petros Markaris, Giorgio Silvagni. Camera (color), Giorgos Arvanitis, Andreas Sinani; editor, Yannis Tsitsopoulos; music, Eleni Karaindrou; production designers, Giorgos Patsos, Giorgos Ziakas; sound (Dolby SR), Bernard Leroux. Reviewed at Cannes Festival, May 23, 1998. Running time: 134 mins.
**Bruno Ganz (Alexander), Isabelle Renauld (Anna), Achileas Skevis (The Boy), Despina Bebedeli (Mother), Helene Gerasimidiou (Urania), Fabrizio Bentivoglio (Poet).**
A celebrated author faces the end of his life in Cannes Palme d'Or winner *Eternity and a Day*, the latest offering of Greek maestro Theo Angelopoulos. One of the helmer's most accessible films, pic is assured theatrical bookings in territories where this kind of lyrical, intelligent fare attracts upscale audiences. Bruno Ganz plays Alexander, a celebrated scribe who's seriously ill and setting his house in order. On this particular Sunday he unexpectedly gets involved with a a little boy who's one of thousands of illegal immigrants from Albania. Having rescued him from a gang selling youngsters to wealthy Greeks unable to adopt legally, he sets out to reunite him with his family.
Int'l release: Aug. 25                    Int'l B.O.: $850,000

### Ever After

A 20th Century Fox release of a Mireille Soria production. Produced by Soria and Tracey Trench. Directed by Andy Tennant. Screenplay, Susannah Grant, Tennant, Rick Parks, based on the legend of Cinderella. Camera, Andrew Dunn; editor, Roger Bondelli; music, George Fenton; production design, Michael Howells; costume design, Jenny Beavan; stunt coordinator/sword master, Graeme Crowther; casting, Lucinda Syson. Reviewed at 20th Century Fox, L.A., July 23. MPAA Rating: PG-13. Running time: 122 mins.

---

**...May 12...**

Tune giant Wherehouse offers to buy Blockbuster Music.

Drew Barrymore (Danielle), Anjelica Huston (Rodmilla), Dougray Scott (Prince Henry), Patrick Godfrey (Leonardo da Vinci), Megan Dodds (Marguerite), Melanie Lynskey (Jacqueline), Jeanne Moreau (Grande Dame), Timothy West (King Francis), Judy Parfitt (Queen Marie), Jeroen Krabbe (Auguste).

Fairy tales can come true. The legend of *Cinderella* has apparently inspired more than 500 tales of a young woman, abused by parents and siblings, who gets the guy in the clinch. *Ever After* goes to the same well to tell the saga realistically, without stripping it of its magical qualities.

A lush, romantic reinvention of the story, the new version is a quality outing that may falter less for what's onscreen than for the baggage associated with the story. While the original has long been a staple of children's lit, *Ever After* is primarily aimed at the young adult audience of Baz Luhrmann's *Romeo & Juliet*, and the pic's success will be dependent upon that crowd's picking up on it right away. Given the challenge of succeeding with disparate audiences, pic will likely fall short of its full B.O. potential, and subsequent video life could be marred if it doesn't work for pre-teen auds.

Yarn centers on Danielle, daughter of a wealthy, widowed landowner in 16th-century France. He returns from travels with a new bride, the titled Rodmilla, and her two daughters. In the blink of an eye, he succumbs to a heart attack, and Danielle is relegated to servant status. But fate takes a hand in elevating her from a life of indenture. Henry, the heir to the throne, has taken flight rather than accept an arranged marriage. Mistaking him for a thief when she eyes him plucking a horse from the farm, Danielle knocks him off his perch. Henry discovers she's no ordinary servant.

| U.S. release: July 31 | U.S. B.O.: $65.5 million |
| Int'l release: Oct. 9 | Int'l B.O.: $10 million |

**Everest** (Docu, 70mm Imax)
A MacGillivray Freeman Films production, in association with Arcturus Motion Pictures. Produced by Greg MacGillivray, Alec Lorimore, Stephen Judson. Directed by Greg MacGillivray, David Breashears, Stephen Judson. Screenplay, Tim Cahill, Judson. Camera (15 perf 70mm), Breashears; editor, Judson; original score, Steve Wood, Daniel May; additional camera, MacGillivray, Brad Ohlund. Reviewed at the Sony Lincoln Square, New York, March 8. Running time: 44 mins.
**Narrator: Liam Neeson.**

*Everest* combines real-life tragedy and derring-do with eye-popping scenery for an effect that's as dramatic as it is fascinating and spectacular. Documenting a climb of world's premier rockpile that made global headlines when eight mountaineers died, pic reps a remarkable, indeed historic, use of the Imax format, due in part to the unexpected and unfortunate circumstances that surrounded its making. Somber yet exciting and beautiful, this dazzling doc is sure to be a favorite in all Imax situations where it appears.

Helmer David Breashears, who had climbed and filmed Everest before, assembled for his first Imax attempt a team that included expedition leader Ed Viesturs, an American expert in Himalayan climbs; Araceli Segarra, who hoped to become the first Spanish woman to reach the peak; and Jamling Tensing Norgay, son of the Sherpa guide who first conquered the mountain with Sir Edmund Hillary in 1953.

| U.S. release: March 6 | U.S. B.O.: $55.5 million |
| Int'l release: May 27 | Int'l B.O.: $13.5 million |

**The Eye (Ogat)** (Sweden)
A Sonet Film release of a Cimbria Film production, in association with SVT Drama Malmo, FilmhusAteljeerna, Film pa Osterlen. Produced by Goran Lindstrom. Directed, written by Richard Hobert. Camera, Lars Crepin; editor, Leif Kristiansson; music, Bjorn Hallman; production design, Aida Kalnins; costume design, Kajsa Tosting. Reviewed at Saga Cinema, Stockholm, Aug. 5. Running time: 114 mins.
**Lena Endre (Ingrid), Samuel Froler (Fredrik), Goran Stangertz (Mikael), Camilla Lundin (Catti), Sven Wollter (The Inspector), Fredrik Hammar (Jonas), Thomas Roos (The Preacher).**

Although not as hard-hitting as its predecessor *Run for Your Life*, Richard Hobert's *The Eye* is a clever and entertaining psychological thriller. The fifth installment in the writer-director's series based on the seven deadly sins, it's a well-acted study of an obsession that goes too far. Pic should generate healthy returns in Sweden and not prove an impossible sell to other countries. Nurse Ingrid has met rich businessman Fredrik and moved in with him. Fredrik and Ingrid announce their engagement at a big party. Next morning, Fredrik disappears. The police tell Ingrid that he obviously committed suicide, jumping from one of the ferries between Malmo and Copenhagen. But a friend has reason to believe that Fredrik is alive, and that he staged a fake suicide.

| Int'l release: Oct.2 | Int'l B.O.: $1.5 million |

**The Faculty**
A Dimension Films release of a Hooligans production. Produced by Elizabeth Avellan. Directed by Robert Rodriguez. Screenplay, Kevin Williamson, from a story by David Wechter, Bruce Kimmel. Camera, Enrique Chediak; editor, Rodriguez; music, Marco Beltrami; production design, Cary White; costume design, Michael T. Boyd; visual-effects supervisor, Brian M. Jennings. Reviewed at Bridge Theatre, San Francisco, Dec. 23. MPAA Rating: R. Running Time: 102 mins.
**Jordana Brewster (Delilah), Clea DuVall (Stokely), Laura Harris (Marybeth), Josh Harnett (Zeke), Shawn Hatosy (Stan), Salma Hayek (Nurse Harper), Famke Janssen (Miss Burke), Piper Laurie (Mrs. Olsen), Chris McDonald (Casey's Dad), Bebe Neuwirth (Principal Drake), Robert Patrick (Coach Willis), Usher Raymond (Gabe), Jon Stewart (Mr. Furlong), Elijah Wood (Casey).**

Movies don't come any more review-proof than *The Faculty*, a rip-snorting hunk of giddy, self-aware genre trash. Latest *Invasion of the Body Snatchers* remodel has been cranking up MTV-demographic awareness for months and, with little else to waylay anyone between puberty and college graduation, there's no reason this E-ticket ride shouldn't have 'em lining up well into early 1999.

Gonzo action director Robert Rodriguez and *Scream* scenarist Kevin Williamson together make a complete lack of socially redeeming value seem so much fun. Business as usual at Herrington High is like a *Blackboard Jungle* comic book with 1990s budget cuts making remote any hope of actual education. Brainiac Casey discovers a piece of icky tissue on the playing field that does very odd things when moistened in biology class. In quick order, others witness alarming things in the boys' locker room and the teachers' lounge. Something very wrong is going on at the school.

| U.S. release: Dec. 25 | U.S. B.O.: $18.5 million |

---

**. . . May 13 . . .**
WB to produce first primetime animated drama series — the Steven Spielberg-produced **Invasion America.**

## Fallen

A Warner Bros. release of a Turner Pictures presentation of an Atlas Entertainment production. Produced by Charles Roven, Dawn Steel. Directed by Gregory Hoblit. Screenplay, Nicholas Kazan. Camera, Newton Thomas Sigel; editor, Lawrence Jordan; music, Tan Dun; production design, Terence Marsh; costume design, Colleen Atwood; visual-effects supervisor, Kent Houston. Reviewed at Warner Bros., Burbank, Jan. 8. MPAA Rating: R. Running time: 124 mins.

**Denzel Washington (John Hobbes), John Goodman (Jonesy), Donald Sutherland (Lt. Stanton), Embeth Davidtz (Gretta Milano), James Gandolfini (Lou), Elias Koteas (Edgar Reese).**

Scripter Nicholas Kazan has constructed a hodgepodge of a movie in which an outer-space creature implants himself in the bodies of innocent civilians and causes them to commit violent crimes. As a high-concept mating of two familiar genres – the police story and the supernatural thriller – *Fallen* is a movie that might frustrate aficionados of both genres, despite some strong elements. Playing a bright detective who's tormented by conflicting forces of good and evil, Denzel Washington has the almost impossible task of holding together a convoluted picture that's only intermittently suspenseful and not very engaging emotionally or intellectually. Warner's release should enjoy a reasonably decent opening but, ultimately, B.O. results will fall below expectations.

| U.S. release: Jan. 16 | U.S. B.O.: $25 million |
| Int'l release: Feb. 12 | Int'l B.O.: $10 million |

## Falling Bodies (Corps Plongés) (France-Germany-Haiti)

A JBA production in association with Arte/Le Sept Cinéma, Velvet Films. Produced by Jacques Bidou. Directed, written by Raoul Peck. Camera, Pascal Marti; editor, Jacques Comets; music, Mino Cinelu; production design, Denis Renault. Reviewed at World Film Festival, Montreal, Aug. 31. Running time: 100 mins.

**Geno Lechner (Chase Dellal), Jean-Michel Martial (Dimitri Sanville), Bob Meyer (Ralph Benton), Israel Horovitz (Timothy), Dominic Gould (Bernard)**

(English and French dialog)

An unusual tale of romance and intrigue, *Falling Bodies* is a love story of exiles in Manhattan that touches on personal and institutional politics. An unquestionably ambitious venture, the film is for a specialized crowd and could score niche success in several key territories. But pic's absence of marquee players and its focus on issues that hold interest for a limited audience will make its wider commercial prospects an uphill battle.

The film is slow in revealing its true nature, dangling several false clues before settling into the drama. The central character is Chase Dellal, a Manhattan medical examiner. She's at a point where both her job and personal life are forcing her to question her options. Several of the city's key political-influence blocs want her to soften testimony. At that point Dimitri, a deposed Haitian politician and former classmate, comes back into her life. His wife was murdered and he was ousted from his country. Dimitri's travails and resolute nature allow Chase to get a better perspective on her life.

## Falling into the Evening (Rakka Suru Yugata) (Japan)

A Shochiku Co. release and production, in association with TV Man Union. Produced by Naoe Gozu, Toma Hisashi. Directed, written by Gozu, based on the novel by Kaori Ekuni. Camera, Masao Nakabori; editor, Tomoyo Oshima; music, Yukie Nishimura; production design, Mayumi Tomita; special effects, Yuli Atae. Reviewed at Berlin Festival, Feb. 22. Running time: 106 mins.

**Tomoyo Harada (Rica), Atsuro Watanabe (Kengo), Miho Kanno (Hanako), Midori Kiuchi (Rica's mother), Ren Osugi (Hanako's father), Sayuri Kokusho (Ryoko).**

First feature by femme director Naoe Gozu deals delicately and humorously with the friendship that forms between two women who are involved with the same man. Based on a well-regarded novel by Kaori Ekuni, the film should play the fest circuit and provide fodder for quality tube programmers. Rica (Tomoyo Harada), the film's compliant protagonist, is in love with Kengo (Atsuro Watanabe), with whom she's been living for four years. Her serenity is shattered when she learns he's leaving her for another woman.

| Int'l release: Nov. 7 | Int'l B.O.: $350,000 |

## The Farm: Angola, USA (Docu)

A Gabriel Films production. Produced by Jonathan Stack, Liz Garbus. Directors, Stack, Garbus. Camera (video-to-16mm), Samuel Henriques, Bob Perrin; editors, Mona Davis, Mary Manhardt; music, Curtis Lundy. Reviewed at Sundance Festival, Jan. 17. Running time: 93 mins.

**Narrator: Bernard Addison.**

The much-deserving top-doc co-winner at Sundance, *The Farm: Angola, USA* is an ambitious, appropriately moody peek behind the razor-wire that surrounds Louisiana State Penitentiary – America's largest maximum-security prison. Co-directed by Jonathan Stack and Liz Garbus, with a strong assist from prison-mag editor Wilbert Rideau, doc has terrific narrative drive and dramatic heft. Rave reviews and strong word of mouth could mean *Hoop Dreams*-type bookings for this matter-of-fact – and, therefore, all the more devastating – indictment of the U.S. penal system.

## Fear and Loathing in Las Vegas

A Universal release of a Rhino Films/Laila Nabulsi production. Produced by Nabulsi, Patrick Cassavetti, Stephen Nemeth. Directed by Terry Gilliam. Screenplay, Gilliam, Tony Grisoni, Tod Davies, Alex Cox, based on the book by Hunter S. Thompson. Camera, Nicola Pecorini; editor, Lesley Walker; production designer, Alex McDowell; costume designer, Julie Weiss; visual-effects supervisor, Kent Houston. Reviewed at Universal Studios, Universal City, May 1. MPAA Rating: R. Running time: 119 mins.

**Johnny Depp (Raoul Duke), Benicio Del Toro (Dr. Gonzo), Christina Ricci (Lucy). With: Ellen Barkin, Gary Busey, Cameron Diaz, Flea, Mark Harmon, Michael Jeter, Lyle Lovett, Tobey Maguire, Harry Dean Stanton.**

*Fear and Loathing in Las Vegas* is a bad trip. Long-gestating adaptation of Hunter S. Thompson's hallucinatory 1971 gonzo tome has become an over-elaborate gross-out under Terry Gilliam's direction, a visualization of a flashpoint in the history of trendy pharmaceuticals without a story or detectable point of view. Johnny Depp's impersonation of the Thompson figure is effective up to a point, but it's hard to imagine any segment of the public embracing this off-putting, unrewarding slog through the depths of the drug culture. Beyond whatever draw Depp and Gilliam provide for the opening round, pic's

---

commercial ride will be a bummer.

Some cryptic narration and more than two dozen pop tunes of various vintages provide a fragile frame for the indulgent spree of sportswriter Duke, who drives from L.A. to Vegas with his attorney and partner-in-crime Dr. Gonzo, ostensibly to cover the off-road Mint 400 motorcycle race.

U.S. release: May 22      U.S. B.O.: $10.5 million
Int'l release: July 16      Int'l B.O.: $4.7 million

### Felice Felice (The Netherlands)

An NFM Distributie release of a Pieter van Huystee Film & TV/Ariel Film production in co-production with KRO Television. Produced by Pieter van Huystee, Suzanne van Voorst. Directed, written by Peter Delpeut. Camera, Walther Vanden Ende; editor, Menno Boerema; music, Loek Dikker; art direction, Vincent de Pater; costume design, Jany Temime. Reviewed at Rotterdam Festival, Jan. 31. Running time: 99 mins.
Johan Leysen (Felice Beato), Toshie Ogura (Ume), Rina Yasima (O-Take), Noriko Sasaki (Hana), Kumi Nakamura (O-Kiku), Yoshi Oida (Matsukichi).
(Dutch, Japanese dialog)
Dutch filmmaker Peter Delpeut uses hand-tinted photographs from the late 19th century to evoke a time and place in *Felice Felice*. Shot entirely in an Amsterdam studio, the somber romantic drama's rather cold formalism belies an evolving emotionalism that's worthy of admiration. Delpeut's tragic love story about the cultural chasm between East and West is a *Madame Butterfly* variant; with Dutch protagonist Felice Beato on a seemingly hopeless quest to reconjure a lost love – a bought Japanese bride he abandoned six years earlier.

### 54

A Miramax release of a Redeemable Features/Dollface/Film Colony production. Produced by Richard N. Gladstein, Dolly Hall, Ira Deutchman. Directed, written by Mark Christopher. Camera, Alexander Gruszynski; editor, Lee Percy; music, Marco Beltrami; production design, Kevin Thompson; costume design, Ellen Lutter. Reviewed at Fairfax Cinemas, L.A., Aug. 21. MPAA Rating: R. Running time: 92 mins.
Ryan Phillippe (Shane O' Shea), Salma Hayek (Anita), Neve Campbell (Julie Black), Mike Myers (Steve Rubell), Sela Ward (Billie Auster), Breckin Meyer (Greg Randazzo), Sherry Stringfield (Viv), Ellen Albertini Dow (Disco Dottie), Heather Matarazzo (Grace O'Shea). With: Lauren Hutton, Michael York, Daniel Lapaine, Ron Jeremy.
The second movie this year about the disco era, *54*, a chronicle of the notorious nightclub at its height, is just as disappointing as Whit Stillman's *The Last Days of Disco*, albeit for different reasons. Strong on ambience and vividly capturing the circus-like, celeb-driven spot, this basically plotless movie suffers from a formulaic script that feels like a reworking of *Saturday Night Fever*, a conventional style, and a neat ending that sugarcoats the story. Even so, tyro director Mark Christopher gives the picture a brisk pace and a colorful, party-like mood that makes the experience painless and sporadically enjoyable. The film should enjoy a decent run in major urban centers, where young to middle-age viewers might be motivated by nostalgia, but pic is not likely to play well in the rest of the country.

The misunderstood rebel-hero is Shane O'Shea, a naive, 19-year-old Irish-American whose mother died when he was 12. He arrives at the disco uninvited and "unprepared," wearing the wrong outfit, but his good looks and charm get him into the

club, where he quickly absorbs its distinctive sensibility. The rather thin, cliched tale concerns Shane's fast rise from busboy to the "glamorous" job of a shirtless bartender. The club and its employees become his surrogate family, particularly co-owner and entrepreneurial spirit Steve Rubell, who runs the place in the peculiar style of a stern but understanding father. Shane is essentially an innocent, goodhearted kid who aspires to find his place in the world by hooking with the right crowd, here represented by an attractive soap star, who shows slight romantic interest, and a bunch of Park Avenue types, decadent men, and rich older women. Unfortunately, Christopher ignores the interesting class issue: how blue-collar men could build a career based on their charisma and sex appeal, but at a price.

U.S. release: Aug. 28      U.S. B.O.: $16.5 million
Int'l release: Nov. 12      Int'l B.O.: $3 million

### Finding Graceland

A TCB Prods production. Produced by Cary Brokaw. Directed by David Winkler. Screenplay, Jason Horwitch, based on a story by Horwitch, Winkler. Camera, Elliot Davis; editor, Luis Colina; music, Stephen Endelman; production design, Jeffrey Townsend, Caty Maxey; costume design, Julie Weiss. Reviewed at Toronto Festival, Sept. 11. Running time: 105 mins.
Harvey Keitel (Elvis), Johnathon Schaech (Byron Gruman), Bridget Fonda (Ashley), Gretchen Mol (Beatrice Gruman).
The promise of seeing Harvey Keitel strutting his stuff impersonating Elvis will at the very least attract attention to *Finding Graceland*, but this indie effort never manages to develop into more than a curiosity. Keitel overplays the part, often hamming up the Southern accent, and the film adds little to the already too-crowded field of pop artifacts surrounding the Elvis mythology. Pic is unlikely to find much of an audience, although hardcore fans of the King will turn out, if only because this is the first dramatic feature to include a scene shot inside the Graceland mansion.

Helmer David Winkler has constructed a rather routine road movie about an unlikely couple of guys on their way to Graceland. Byron Gruman is driving through New Mexico in a dilapidated blue 1959 Cadillac convertible when he spots a strange hitchhiker. He's initially reluctant to pick up the dude in shades and pink sports jacket, but he agrees to take him at least part way to Memphis. The hitchhiker introduces himself as Elvis and announces that he's headed back home to mark the anniversary of his death. Byron is not buying any of this. He drops Elvis off as soon as he can, but ultimately finds himself unable to shake off his odd new acquaintance, who turns up late one night at Byron's motel and maneuvers himself back into the young man's road trip.

### Fire-Eater (Tulennielija) (Finland-Sweden)

A Marko Rohr Prods (Helsinki)/Aquavite Film & Media AB, SVT Drama (Stockholm) co-production. International sales: Nordisk Films, Copenhagen. Produced by Marko Rohr. Directed by Pirjo Honkasalo. Screenplay, Pirkko Saisio. Camera (color/B&W), Kjell Lagerroos; editors, Michal Leszczylowski, Bernhard Winkler; music, Richard Einhorn; production designer, Tiina Makkonen; costume designer, Auli Turtiainen-Kinnunen. Reviewed at Cannes Festival, May 21. Running time: 99 mins.
Elina Hurme (Helena), Tiina Weckstrom (Sirkka), Vappu Jurkka (Grandmother), Jordi Borrell (Ramon), Per Ragnar

---

(Circus Director).

Pirjo Honkasalo, one of Finland's most interesting helmers, has come up with an intimate, generation-spanning drama in *Fire-Eater*, which follows the lives and fortunes of three women – a mother and her twin daughters – from the Second World War until the present. Unfolding on the fringes of society, mostly in a rundown circus touring Central Europe, pic is colorful and intriguing but the drama doesn't cut as deep as it should. Quality item is perfect for fest bookings but theatrical chances outside its home territory are decidedly limited.

Pic deals with the ways in which cruelty, repression, and lack of love are handed down from one generation to the other. Born near the end of the war, twin sisters are abandoned when their mother leaves the country with a retreating German soldier. Eventually, the mother returns with a Spanish trapeze artist who picks one girl as ideal for the circus ring. But it's the unchosen one who proves resilient and, in the end, more talented, learning the art of fire-eating.

Int'l release: Nov. 7                    Int'l B.O.: $100,000

### Firestorm

A 20th Century Fox release of a Loeb/Weisman production. Produced by Joseph Loeb III, Matthew Weisman, Thomas M. Hammel. Directed by Dean Semler. Screenplay, Chris Soth. Camera, Stephen F. Windon; editor, Jack Hofstra; music, J. Peter Robinson; production design, Richard Paris, Linda Del Rosario; stunt coordinators, Glenn Wilder, Ken Kirzinger; special effects coordinator, Chris Corbould. Reviewed at Cinemark Tinseltown Westchase, Houston, Jan. 6. MPAA rating: R. Running time: 89 mins.

Howie Long (Jesse Graves), Scott Glenn (Wynt Perkins), William Forsythe (Earl Shaye), Suzy Amis (Jennifer), Christianne Hirt (Monica).

*Firestorm* is a half-baked B movie designed to launch Howie Long – former NFL star and current TV sports commentator – as the next action hero. Despite generic plotting and ho-hum execution, pic might generate a slight B.O. sizzle during its opening weekend, considering the lack of similar product in the marketplace. After that, however, expect a quick flame-out. Ancillary prospects are only slightly brighter. Long tackles his first leading role as a second-generation Wyoming firefighter who heads an elite team of "smokejumpers" – men and women who parachute into forest blazes when all other access is cut off.

U.S. release: Jan. 9                    U.S. B.O.: $8 million
Int'l release: March 12                Int'l B.O.: $3 million

### The First Night (La Primera Noche) (Mexico)

An A Grupo Televisa Film Production Co. presentation of a Televicine S.A. de C.V. production. Produced by Roberto Gomez Bolanos. Directed by Alejandro Gamboa. Screenplay, original story, Benjamin Cann. Camera, Alfredo Kassem; editor, Oscar Figueroa; music, Santiago Ojeda; production designer, Juan Trujillo; costume designer, Monica Neumaier; special effects, Alejandro Vazquez; casting, Manuel Teil. Reviewed at Guadalajara Festival, March 10. Running time: 100 mins.

Osvaldo Benavides (Sergio), Mariana Avila (Mariana), Xavier Massimi (Bruno), Julio Casado (Fatso), Audrey Vera (Monica), Margarita Magana (Rosita).

This potent cocktail from director Alejandro Gamboa and screenwriter Benjamin Cann received top honors at the Guadalajara Film Festival. Pic at first safely seduces with the familiar gambits of horny teen boy, then spectacularly bursts

out of that generic straitjacket to touch poignantly on issues of generational divide, class division, and higher love. Gamboa's classically smooth direction, inflected with very Mexican expressionism of color and texture, makes for a film of definite international potential, and marks the director as an emerging talent. Story pivots around a gaggle of high-school-age buddies whose aspirations segue into wild fantasy.

Int'l release: March 27                Int'l B.O.: $2.2 million

### The First Night of my Life (La Primera Noche De Mi Vida) (Spain-France)

A Lolafilms release of an Alphaville production, in association with Haut & Court, La Sept/Arte. Produced by Mariel Guiot. Directed by Miguel Albaladejo. Screenplay, Albaladejo, Elvira Lindo. Camera, Alfonso Sanz Alduan; editor, Angel Hernandez; music, Lucio Godoy; art director, Angel Sarrion. Reviewed at Cine Palafox, Madrid, June 18. Running time: 85 mins.

Leonor Watling (Paloma), Juanjo Martinez (Manuel), Emilio Gutierrez Caba (Paloma's Father), Carlos Fuentes (Johny), Mariola Fuentes (Jasmina), Roberto Hernandez (Litri), Adriana Ozores (Adri).

*The First Night of My Life* is an assured, skillfully constructed debut that tickles the pleasure buds without forgetting it has a social point. A lively script, witty dialog, and deft playing from a generally young cast give pic plenty of indie/cult appeal for home auds, but whether its plethora of local refs can take it to theatrical release outside Spain and France is doubtful. Another in the series of films commissioned by France's Haut & Court and set at the end of the millennium, pic consists of interlinked vignettes set on New Year's Eve 1999, but far away from any celebratory action.

Int'l release: June 14                  Int'l B.O.: $400,000

### The First Time (Das Erste Mal) (Germany)

A Sudwestfunke (Baden-Baden) production, in association with WDR, MDR, dffb production. Directed by Connie Walther. Screenplay, Walther, Anke Schenkluhn. Camera, Peter Nix; editor, Carola Hulsebus; music, Reinhold Heil; production designer, Monika Nix; costume designer, Simone Simon. Reviewed at New Directors/New Films, N.Y., March 20. Running time: 89 mins.

Lavinia Wilson (Fili), Benno Furmann (Ike), Eva Hassmann (Nina), Hannes Jaenicke (George), Andreas Herder (Johnny).

A crisply textured, moderately insightful account of a teenage girl's initial sexual encounters, *The First Time* gains a double meaning and a certain authenticity from being a feature debut. Like other new German pics, it's stylistically polished and shrewdly poised between prurience and seriousness in its approach to sex. Although ultimately lightweight, pic's sharply observed melodrama and appealing young cast make it a natural for fest slots. Story's main dramatic hook is that its heroine, Fili (Lavinia Wilson), is in love with Johnny Depp and aspires to lose her virginity to none but him. Of course that goal is complicated by the fact that she's a 15-year-old Berliner and he a Hollywood movie star.

### Fishes in August (Mizu No Naka No Hachigatsu) (Japan)

An NHK Drama Programs Division production. Produced by Koji Yoshikawa. Directed by Yoichiro Takahashi. Screenplay, Masato Kato, based on the novel by Natsuo Sekikawa. Camera, Fumio Kodaka; editor, Kiyoko Mizushima; music, Norihiro

---

**. . . May 16 . . .**
Miramax and Universal combine forces to co-produce **Shakespeare in Love**.

Tsuru; art director, Juichi Inaba. Reviewed at San Sebastian Festival, Sept. 21. Running time: 89 mins.

**Kenji Mizuhashi (Kenji), Ayumi Ito (Reiko), Yoshiki Sekino (Arai), Ryuzo Hayashi (Father), Tomoko Mayumi (Sister), Eri Yu (Rie).**

TV director Yoichiro Takahashi contributes a striking, lyrical variation on the recent Japanese mini-genre of emotionally confused teens with his first feature, *Fishes in August*. Winner of San Sebastian's $165,000 New Directors Prize, this seductive drama is a disciplined debut that deserves to make a splash in festival waters and in specialized situations receptive to new Japanese cinema.

Center of the story's triangle is Kenji, an unmotivated member of the high-school swimming team with a secret crush on classmate Reiko. She in turn hankers after Korean-Japanese swim-team star Arai, and ropes Kenji into acting as a go-between. But Kenji's affection for the girl is obvious to Arai, and he steps aside, offering to help bring them together. Arai takes the less worldly Kenji under his wing, even attempting to kickstart his sexual education with local barmaid Rie, who dreams of becoming a fish. But Kenji's illusions are shattered when he turns up for a date with Reiko and finds her with Arai. The fragmented narrative strikes universal chords in its quiet reflection on being an outsider, on individuality, and on the impulse to compete. This latter theme emerges through pep talks from the swim coach, who urges the boys to become one with their watery environment like fish, to swim for themselves and not for the achievement of winning.

### Flames in Paradise (Flammen Im Paradies)

(Switzerland-Germany-France)

A Cini Manufacture presentation of a Flimpa Filmproduktion, Thelma Film, Markus Imhoof Film/Zero Film (Berlin)/Cini Manufacture (Paris) production, in association with Westdeutsches Rundfunk, Schweizer Fernsehen DRS, France 2 Cinema, Tiliclub, with the participation of Canal Plus. Produced by Pierre-Alain Meier. Directed by Markus Imoof. Screenplay, Imhoof, Judith Kennel, Jacques Akchoti. Camera, Lukas Strebel; editor, Jacques Comets; music, Bruno Coulais; production designers, Susanne Jauch, Prakash Moorthy; costume designers, Catherine Caldray, Loveleen Bains. Reviewed at Gothenburg Festival, Sweden, Feb. 3. Running time: 105 mins.

**Elodie Bouchez (Juliette), Laurent Grevill (Gustav Walser), Bruno Todeschini (Philipp Braun), Swetlana Schonfeld (Olga Oppliger), Heinz Buehlmann (Robert Oppliger), Sylvie Testud (Esther), Geeta Nair (Hosannah).**

Although handsomely appointed and visually rich, this new film from Swiss director Markus Imhoof fails to hook the emotions. Despite its title, there's not much passion in this period love story, set in India, about an adventure-seeking young woman who takes another's place. Pic starts in 1912, with a couple, Juliette and Philipp, on their honeymoon, traveling the world. During an argument, she accuses him of having married her for her father's money. A short time later she meets Olga who's en route to an arranged marriage and the women decide, on impulse, to swap identities.

### The Flight of the Bee (Parvaz-E Zanbur)

(Tajikistan)

Produced by Jamshed Usmonov, Min Biong Hun. Directed by Usmonov, Min Biong Hun. Screenplay, Usmonov. Camera, Biong Hun; editors, Igor Bosc, Safar Hakadodov; music, Satyajit

Ray. Reviewed at Turin Festival, Nov. 25. Running time: 87 mins.

**With: Muhammadjon Shodi, Mastura Ortik, Taghoymurod Rozik, Fakhriddin Fakhriddin, Beknazar Kabirov, Mardonkul Kulbobo.**

A simple, humanist fable about the rewards of goodness and generosity in the face of arrogance and injustice, *The Flight of the Bee* acknowledges a debt to the poetic realism of Satyajit Ray. The low-budget, B&W debut feature from Tajikistan, co-directed by Jamshed Usmonov and South Korean Min Biong Hun, dominated the awards at the 16th Turin Festival, winning top honors from the competition jury, the Fipresci critics' nod, and the audience popularity vote. Limited by its modest production values to fests and specialized forums, the film's measured rhythms and basic message of hope nonetheless should travel well.

Set in a small mountain village, it's the chronicle of an obsessive quest for dignity and basic human rights. The wronged party in this fable is a local teacher whose wealthy neighbor constructs an outdoor toilet under his window. Further incensed by the neighbor's relentless ogling of his wife, he goes to a town official but is told the man has violated no laws. Selling his sheep and cattle, the teacher buys property adjoining his neighbor's and begins digging a hole to be used as a latrine by the entire village. Threats from his neighbor, the town official, and the police fail to make him desist, causing his wife to step in for the good of her family. In true parable fashion, the teacher's quest ends not with defeat but with unforeseen rewards when he unearths a natural spring, bringing water to the previously dry village.

Pic also received the Silver Alexander Award at the Thessaloniki fest.

### Flowers of Shanghai (Haishang Hua) (Taiwan-Japan)

A Shochiku Co. presentation of a 3H Films production. Produced by Yang Teng-kuei, Shozo Ichiyama. Directed by Hou Hsiao-hsien. Screenplay, Chu Tien-wen, based on the novel *Biographies of Flowers of Shanghai* by Han Ziyun, as translated by Eileen Chang. Script consultant, Zhong A-cheng. Camera, Lee Ping-bin; editor, Liao Ching-song; music, Yoshihiro Hanno; production designer, Hwarng Wern-ying; costume designer, Sung Ming-huei. Reviewed at Cannes Festival, May 19. Running time: 120 mins. (Shanghainese dialog)

**Tony Leung Chiu-wai (Wang Lingsheng), Michiko Hada (Crimson), Michele Reis (Emerald), Carina Liu (Pearl), Jack Kao (Luo), Rebecca Pan (Auntie Huang), Wei Hsiao-hui (Jasmin), Fang Hsuan (Jade).**

Gorgeously mounted, but butt-numbingly slow, the costume drama *Flowers of Shanghai* represents a subtle change of course for Taiwanese helmer Hou Hsiao-hsien. More fests look likely to take this one than his previous, gratuitously obscure *Goodbye South, Goodbye*, with select sales in territories receptive to his oeuvre.

Set amid the elegant brothels in the British quarter of late 19th-century Shanghai, pic is based on an 1894 novel that was translated in the 1930s. Flowers is a common Chinese euphemism for hookers, but the protagonists here are not the standard-issue prosties; rather, they're closer to Japanese geishas – elegant, idealized women to spend time with in club-like surroundings away from the home. Existing during the final years of Imperial China, this formalized milieu was to vanish for ever with the coming of the Republic. The putative

---

protagonist, civil servant Wang, is in a funk over woman trouble. The film has little real plot to speak of and is more a series of conversation pieces peppered with small emotional squalls and capped by the news that he is returning to Canton province to take up a new post.

Int'l release: Sept. 25        Int'l B.O.: $600,000

## Foolish Heart (Corazon Iluminado)

(Brazil-Argentina-France)
An HB Filmes (Brazil)/Oscar Kramer S.A. (Argentina)/Flach Film (France) co-production, in association with Sony Entertainment, TV Cultura Secretaria de la Cultura de São Paulo. Produced by Hector Babenco, Francisco Ramalho. Directed by Babenco. Screenplay, Babenco, Ricardo Piglia, based on an idea by Babenco. Camera, Lauro Escorel; editor, Mauro Alice; music, Zbigniew Preisner; production designer, Carlos Conti. Reviewed at Cannes Festival, May 23. Running time: 132 mins.
Miguel Angel Sola (Adult Juan), Maria Luisa Mendonca (Ana), Walter Quiroz (Adolescent Juan), Xuxa Lopes (Lilith), Oscar Ferrigno (Martin), Arturo Maly (Jacobo).

*Foolish Heart* is a deeply personal film in which the many presumably autobiographical details haven't been properly shaped or focused to express eloquently matters close to the heart of director Hector Babenco. Story of an Argentine teenager's tragic first love affair and its resonance in later life wears all its sincere intentions on its sleeve, and never generates the hoped-for emotional investment in its reckless, self-absorbed characters. Without a measure of critical support, pic will have tough sledding in the international marketplace.

The script introduces any number of promising topics but can't get them to cohere in a satisfactory way. Opening scene plunges the viewer into bohemian café society. A 17-year-old student Juan meets Ana and becomes immediately intoxicated by her provocative flirtatiousness and quicksilver mood changes.

Int'l release: Nov. 13        Int'l B.O.: $150,000

## Forbidden Encounters (Incontri Proibiti) (Italy)

A Filmauro/Aurelia Cinematografica production. Produced by Aurelio de Laurentiis. Directed by Alberto Sordi. Screenplay, Rodolfo Sonego, Sordi. Camera, Armando Nannuzzi; editor, Tatiana Casini Moriggi; music, Piero Piccioni; production design, Marco Dentici; costume design, Paola Marchesin. Reviewed at Venice Festival, Sept. 6, 1998. Running time: 103 mins.
Alberto Sordi (Armand Andreoli), Valeria Marini (Federica), Franca Faldini (Alessandra Andreoli), Enrico Bertolino (Giorgio), Enzo Robutti (Federica's Father).

At the age of 78, Alberto Sordi, an actor beloved by many Italians, has come up with this delightfully old-fashioned throwback to the kind of comedy that used to be a staple of Italian cinema. Younger audiences may not appreciate the jokes about old age and sexual yearnings, and *Forbidden Encounters* probably won't travel, but this beautifully timed and sustained comedy deserves to click in Italy. It played in Venice as a deserved tribute to Sordi.

Sordi plays Armando Andreoli, an elegant engineering expert traveling by train from Rome to Bologna to attend a conference. His private compartment is invaded by Federica, a statuesque blonde in her late twenties. She seems bright and friendly, but Armando believes she might be a thief or prostitute. His suspicions increase when she follows him to the conference and, when he's unable to find a hotel room for the night, she offers to share her bed in a pensione. The night passes without incident, but when Federica's fiancé bursts into the room the next morning, he breaks off the engagement. Back in Rome, Federica, a nurse devoted to caring for elderly patients, contacts Armando, and before long they're seeing a lot of each other, despite their age difference or the fact that he's married. Still, things remain innocent – until they dance the tango together.

Int'l release: Sept. 25        Int'l B.O.: $500,000

## For Richer or Poorer

A Universal Pictures release of a Universal/Bubble Factory presentation, in association with Yorktown Prods, of a Sheinberg production. Produced by Sid, Bill, and Jon Sheinberg. Directed by Bryan Spicer. Screenplay, Jana Howington, Steve LuKanic. Camera, Buzz Feitshans IV; editor, Russell Denove; music, Randy Edelman; production design, Stephen Hendrickson; costume design, Abigail Murray. Reviewed at Cineplex Odeon Century Plaza, Century City, Dec. 4, 1997. MPAA Rating: PG-13. Running time: 115 mins.
Tim Allen (Brad Sexton), Kirstie Alley (Carol Sexton), Jay O. Sanders (Samuel Yoder), Michael Lerner (Phil Kleinman), Wayne Knight (Bob Lachman), Larry Miller (Derek Lester), Miguel A. Nunez, Jr. (Frank Hall), Megan Cavanagh (Levinia Yoder), John Pyper-Ferguson (Henner Lapp), Carrie Preston (Rebecca Yoder).

Renowned philosopher Sophie Tucker observed, "I have been poor and I have been rich. Rich is better." The makers of the romantic comedy *For Richer or Poorer* try to convince you otherwise, and to a degree this corny tale of a conspicuously profligate couple brought to their knees by the tax man succeeds in making its point that hard work and true friends are better than a Mercedes and limitless spending at Bloomingdale's. But pic makes its case in such an obvious and ham-fisted manner that only the most forgiving of audiences will accept it whole. Its kernel of truth and game cast should ring up OK theatrical response and allow it to eke by when it collects ancillary revenues.

Brad and Caroline Sexton are a lavish-living Manhattan couple who keep up the appearance of bliss and wealth. In truth their ardor is an orchestrated show for friends and associates, and their assets are mortgaged to the hilt. Brad finds out too late that his accountant has deftly siphoned off $5 million and made him look like the guilty party to tax officials. Pursued by a pistol-packing revenue agent, the Sextons steal a cab and bolt, fatefully landing in the lap of an Amish enclave. Seizing a lucky opportunity, they pose as relatives of a local farmer.

The comedy dynamic is pretty straightforward – put two city sophisticates into the simple, 19th-century ways of a religious work order and watch them try to fake their way through the foreign customs. Each faction will learn something from the other and be enriched in small ways.

U.S. release: Dec. 12, 1997     U.S. B.O.: $31.5 million
Int'l release: April 23        Int'l B.O.: $1 million

## For Sale (A Vendre) (France)

A Pyramide release of a François Cuel presentation of a CLP/La Studio Canal Plus/La Sept Cinema co-production, with the participation of Canal Plus, La Sept Arte, CNC. Produced by François Cuel, François Marquis. Directed, written by Laetitia

---

Masson. Camera, Antoine Heberle; editor, Ailo Auguste; music, Siegfried; art director, Arnaud de Moleron; costume designer, Elisabeth Mehu. Reviewed at Cannes Festival, May 16. Running time: 120 mins.

**Sandrine Kiberlain (France Robert), Sergio Castellitto (Luigi Primo), Jean-François Stevenin (Pierre Lindien), Chiara Mastroianni (Mireille).**

When Marseilles health club and nightclub owner Pierre is left standing at the altar by his former employee France, he sends his friend Luigi, a private investigator, to find her and bring her back.

A compelling, nuanced portrait of a ferociously self-reliant young woman told in flashbacks as a private detective attempts to trace her whereabouts, *For Sale* pays off. Sandrine Kiberlain is aces as the enigmatic country girl turned city slicker who longs for something but never stays anywhere long. A solid arthouse contender, pic would be a feather in any festival's cap.
Int'l release: Aug. 26    Int'l B.O.: $2.5 million

## 14 Days To Life (14 Tage Lebenslaenglich)
(Germany)

A Nil Film Art & Entertainment release of a Helkon Media Filmproduktion production, in association with Degeto Film, for ARD and Premiere. Produced by Werner Koenig. Directed by Roland Suso Richter. Screenplay, Holger Karsten Schmidt. Camera (color, widescreen), Martin Langer; editor, Peter R. Adam; music, Ulrich Reuter, Christoph Gracian Schubert; art director, Mathias Kammermeier; costume designer, Solke Sommer. Reviewed at Cannes Festival, May 19. Running time: 113 mins.

**Kai Wiesinger (Konrad von Seidlitz), Michael Mendl (Viktor Czemetzky), Katharina Meinecke (Annika Hofer), Axel Milberg (Axel Haering), Sylvia Leifheit (Cornelia), Marek Wlodarczyk (Ramon).**

A sleazeball lawyer ends up trapped by his own prison stunt in *14 Days to Life*, a smoothly directed, well-scripted prison pic that slips its moorings only in the final reels. Handsome lensing and a well-textured lead perf by star Kai Wiesinger make this a solid item for non-arty German cinema. Konrad is an arrogant careerist with a beautiful fiancee, who's the justice minister's daughter, and a lifestyle fueled by money, sex, and drugs. Considering himself almost above the law, he arranges to serve a prison sentence of 14 days for unpaid parking tickets, casually continuing his business from his prison cell.

## Fragments * Jerusalem (Israel, Docu, 16mm)

A Ron and Jacqueline Havilio production, with support from Israel Film Service, Israel Broadcasting Authority, and the Fund for the Promotion of Israeli Quality Films. Directed, written by Ron Havilio. Camera, Havilio; editors, Tor Ben Mayor, Yael Perkov. Reviewed on videocassette, Vancouver, Sept. 18. Running time: 358 mins. (English, Hebrew, and French dialog)

Mammoth history of the world's most fought-over city is both comprehensive and deeply personal. A phenomenal work of structural ambition and profound emotion, *Fragments * Jerusalem* is likely to stand as a model of acute documaking. Aside from some specialized urban play, expect a long circulation on worldwide pubcasting routes. Six-hour, seven-part dissection of Jerusalem's past (and implied future) weaves helmer Ron Havilio's life into the mix, with satisfying results. Some viewers might expect a family saga to get in the way of the facts, but the helmer happens to have roots that connect with significant movements in the Jewish Diaspora over the past 500 years. Descended from a Sephardic family tossed out of Spain in Columbus' time, Havilio's paternal forebears were intimately involved with the mystical cabala and with the roots of Zionism. His mother's family, the Rosenthals, came to the Holy City in 1812, and were part of a messianic sect. The helmer's father, Shlomo, became a respected diplomat, taking his family to Paris, Istanbul, and Tanzania to live. Consequently, Havilio grew up with an expansive view of Jerusalem's small place in the world. Pic's quality is understandably rough, with Havilio doing his own hand-held lensing. But his sense of rhythm and organization is so astute and his relationship with interview subjects is so effortlessly emotive, tech considerations are swept aside.

## Frank Lloyd Wright (Docu)

A Florentine Films production, produced in association with WETA-TV. Produced by Ken Burns, Lynn Novick, Peter Miller. Directed by Burns, Novick. Written by Geoffrey C. Ward. Camera, Buddy Squires, Burns; editor, Tricia Reidy. Reviewed at Sundance Festival, Jan. 23. Running time: 146 mins.

**Narrator: Edward Herrmann.**

The life of one of the century's towering creative figures, U.S. architect Frank Lloyd Wright, receives appropriately grand and probing treatment in this utterly absorbing study. Ken Burns and Lynn Novick bring the tumultuous life to bear on the career in constantly illuminating ways. Result is a justifiably long film that warrants some specialized theatrical play before skedded PBS airing in November. The film should make clear to any viewer the enormous force of personality Wright possessed and the particular ways his genius was expressed.

## Frat House (Docu)

A Home Box Office presentation of a Todd & Andrew production. Produced, directed by Todd Phillips, Andrew Gurland. Camera (16mm), Anthony Hardwick, W. Mott Hupfel; editor, Salamo Levin; original music, J.F. Coleman. Reviewed at Sundance Festival, Jan. 21. Running time: 60 mins.

Everyone knows college fraternity hazing is "mean," but actually seeing it in practice is a whole different kettle of rancid fish. A gold medalist amidst stranger-than-fiction documentaries, *Frat House* reveals an appalling indulgence of childish cruelty bordering on fascism at said age-old college institution. Results are grotesquely funny – emphasis on the grotesque. Delivered at telecast length for funder HBO, docu could easily have been stretched a bit further toward theatrical-feature viability; it may get some limited rep-house play anyhow. At times, the action here is so over-the-top one suspects it may have been staged. But helmers claim they gained sufficient trust of the frats here to capture straight-up reality.

## Friendly Fire (Acao Entre Amigos) (Brazil)

A Dezenove Som e Imagens production, in association with TV Cultura de São Paolo Prods Produced by Sara Silveira. Directed by Beto Brant. Screenplay, Marcal Aquino, Renato Ciasca, Beto Brant. Camera, Marcelo Durst; editor, Mingo Gattozzi; music, Andre Abujamra; production design, Cassio Amarante; costume design, Cristina Camargo. Reviewed at Venice Festival, Sept. 8. Running time: 75 mins.

**Leonardo Villar (Correia), ZeCarlos Machados (Miguel), Caca Amaral (Eloi), Genesio de Barros (Osvaldo), Carlos Meceni (Paulo).**

The sophomore outing for talented young Brazilian helmer Beto Brant is a terrifically sleek and suspenseful thriller. If anything, it's almost too short; in cutting to the chase, Brant loses an opportunity for a more nuanced exploration of his characters. Nevertheless, *Friendly Fire* delivers in spades, and will likely perform well in Latino territories as well as feature in Latin American sections of festivals. Quality tube programmers should take note, and there could also be international video interest.

When Miguel, Eloi, Osvaldo, and Paolo, four friends who were politically active in the 1970s, meet for their regular fishing trip, Miguel reveals that the cop who arrested and tortured them 25 years earlier is not dead, as they had been informed, but is living in a small country town. Committed to bringing the cop, who was responsible for the death of Miguel's pregnant girlfriend, to justice, he railroads his buddies into joining him on an expedition of revenge. They arrive in the village and, with little difficulty, track down the ex-cop, who now breeds fighting cocks. The friends ambush their quarry on a country road, but, before Miguel kills him, he reveals that one of them had betrayed the other three.

Int'l release: Sept. 25 — Int'l B.O.: $200,000

### Frogs for Snakes

A Shooting Gallery presentation, in association with Rain Film. Produced by Phyllis Freed Kaufman. Directed, written by Amos Poe. Camera, Enrique Chediak; editor, Jeff Kushner; music, Lazy Boy; production designer, Michael Shaw; costume designer, Candice Donnelly. Reviewed at Berlin Festival, Feb. 20. Running time: 115 mins.

**Barbara Hershey (Eva), Robbie Coltrane (Al Santana), Harry Hamlin (Klensch), Ian Hart (Quint), John Leguizamo (Zip), Lisa Marie (Myrna), Debi Mazar (Simone), Ron Perlman (Gascone).**

Billing itself as "a neo-noir comic thriller," indie maverick Amos Poe's latest is more like "Putz Fiction" mainlining David Mamet. Stuffed with iconic casting, and self-consciously smart, *Frogs for Snakes* will turn off as many as it ultimately seduces, though for those who stay the course it coalesces in its final reel. Fests are likely to bite at this jokey, actor-led jeu, but expect a tough theatrical sell. Tales centers on Eva (Barbara Hershey), a struggling actress, who does collections on the side for her ex-husband, loan shark Al (Robbie Coltrane). During the day, she waitresses at a Lower Manhattan diner owned by Quint (Ian Hart).

### Fucking Amal (aka Show Me Love) (Sweden)

A Sonet Film release of a Memfis Film production, in association with Zentropa Prods (Denmark), Film i Vast, SVT Drama Goteborg. Produced by Lars Jonsson. Directed, written by Lukas Moodysson. Camera, Ulf Brantas; editors, Michal Leszcykowski, Bernhard Winkler; music, Robyn, Lars Gullin, Broder Daniel; production design, Lina Strand, Heidi Saikkonen; costume design, Maria Swenson. Reviewed at Astoria, Stockholm, Oct. 9. Running time: 89 mins.

**Alexandra Dahlstrom (Elin), Rebecca Liljeberg (Agnes), Erica Carlson (Jessica), Mathias Rust (Johan), Stefan Horberg (Markus), Josefin Nyberg (Viktoria).**

The feature debut of acclaimed 20-year-old poet Lukas Moodysson, the provocatively titled *Fucking Amal* is a small gem. A sensitive, funny, and bittersweet story about growing up in a small town, pic deals with universal subjects that should certainly strike a chord with buyers and audiences in other countries. Amal, a tiny Swedish burg, is a symbol for the kind of place where youngsters grow up feeling trapped, with life paths predestined by family, job, and contented Saturday nights watching television.

Focus is 15-year-old Elin. She's been going out with lots of guys at school but still hasn't "gone all the way." Both Johan and Agnes are enamored with Elin. At Agnes' 15th birthday party, Elin and Jessica, her sister, decide to pull a prank. Elin kisses the birthday girl passionately and then the two run off. Feeling guilty, Elin later returns to ask forgiveness. The two girls end up kissing again — this time for real. After Elin pretends she's been with Johan and ends up sleeping with him, Agnes feels betrayed and must decide whether she should follow her heart or stick with the traditional way. Pic is not a "gay movie" per se, and the lesbian angle is not over-stressed: Like Amal, lesbianism is a metaphor, in this case for doing something unusual in a conservative setting.

Pic was submitted to AMPAS as Sweden's submission for Foreign-language Oscar under the alternative title, *Show Me Love.*

Int'l release: Oct. 23 — Int'l B.O.: $4.5 million

### Funkytown (Docu)

A Drummer Boy Pictures production of a Steven Greenberg film. Produced by Scott Turk. Directed, written by Steven Greenberg. Camera, Ron Halpern. Reviewed at Santa Barbara Festival, March 14. Running time: 101 mins.

**Featuring music and performances by Greazy Meal, the Delilahs, Iya, the Found, Tina, and the B-Side Movement.**

A surprisingly affecting documentary from writer-director Steven Greenberg, *Funkytown* takes a look at five aspiring bands in the Minneapolis area. With an unflinching, sometimes gently sardonic eye, doc traces the failures, successes, and tragedies that befall the band members in their struggles to hit the big time. Though the bands are unknown, their music is catchy enough that pic could be exploited for its commercial music potential alone. If that tack works and the music in turn works to sell the film, it could become a breakout hit.

### Gangster Film (Gengszter Film) (Hungary)

A Goess Film/Hunnia Film Studio/Hungarian Television production. Produced by Sandor Simo, Miklos Szita. Directed by Gyorgy Szomjas. Screenplay, Zoltan Tabori, Szomjas. Camera, Ferenc Grunwalsky; editor, Anna Kornis; art direction, Tamas Vayer. Reviewed at Hungarian Film Week, Budapest, Feb. 9. Running time: 112 mins.

**With: Zoltan Mucsi, Peter Scherrer, Tunde Bacsko, Annamaria Prokai, Andras Szoke, Roland Tzafetas.**

In his first feature in three years, Gyorgy Szomjas returns with the blackly comic *Gangster Film*, a typical meld of reality and genre elements that will ring harmoniously with devotees of previous pics like *Fast and Loose* and *Kisses and Scratches*. Film would benefit from tightening by about 15 minutes, and is mostly a fest item, but it still showed more youthful vigor and basic craft than most of the movies unspooled at the recent subpar Hungarian Film Week. Closely based on real-life events, but given a spin of mordant, anarchic humor, pic follows the exploits of a bunch of klutzy criminals who couldn't get arrested if they tried.

**...May 20...**

**Titanic** edges out **Princess Mononoke** as Japan's highest-grossing pic of all time.

### The Garden of Eden (I Giardini Dell'Eden) (Italy)

A Medusa Film release of a Marco Valsania/Medusa Film/Rete Italia presentation of a Medusa Film/Rete Italia/Magic Moments production made by Produzioni Corsare. Produced by Marco Valsania. Directed by Alessandro D'Alatri. Screenplay, D'Alatri, Miro Silvera. Camera, Federico Masiero; editor, Cecilia Zanuso; music, Pivio and Aldo De Scalzi; production design, Luca Merlini; costume design, Sergio Ballo. Reviewed at Venice Festival, Sept. 5. Running time: 102 mins.
**Kim Rossi Stuart (Jeoshua), Said Taghmaoui (Aziz), Boris Terral (Jochannan), Kassandra Voyagis (Miriam), Renzo Stacchi (Centurion), Asher Cohen (Young Jeoshua), Omar Chenbod (Josef), Lorenzo Cherubini (David), Mohamed Miftah (Shimon).**

Portraying Jesus Christ in distinctly human terms, *The Garden of Eden* maps the formative 18-year period spanning his childhood, adolescence, and early adulthood, which immediately precedes the Gospels and is interpreted in the Apocrypha. Given the often heatedly divergent views on this unchronicled period, director Alessandro D'Alatri has delivered a surprisingly conventional, peace-and-love vision that seems unlikely to raise temperatures even in the most devout circles. Visually accomplished but rather bland and dramatically naive, the film will struggle to find a theatrical niche outside predominantly Catholic territories like Italy, where it goes out next month.

The screenplay by D'Alatri and Sephardic writer Miro Silvera uses the actual names of the time, rather than those of the Bible. Jeoshua is introduced as an adult recounting the journey that led him into the desert, where he was picked up by the Essenes, baptized, and accepted into their monastery-like community. The film also recaps his Jewish upbringing in Galilee which precipitates the spiritual questioning that becomes Jeoshua's path to enlightenment. Jeoshua begins a dialog with God, asking for a key to understand the ways of man. What religious audiences will perhaps most be taken aback by is the absence of a sense of entitlement and of any acknowledgment that Jeoshua is the son of God.
Int'l release: Sept. 25                    Int'l B.O.: $200,000

### The General (Ireland-U.K., B&W)

A Warner Bros./Sony Classics release of a Merlin Films presentation, in association with J&M Entertainment. Produced by John Boorman. Directed, written by Boorman. Camera, Seamus Deasy; editor, Ron Davis; music, Richie Buckley; production designer, Derek Wallace; costume designer, Maeve Paterson. Reviewed at Warners, London, April 30, 1998. Running time: 123 mins.
**Brendan Gleeson (Martin Cahill), Adrian Dunbar (Noel Curley), Sean McGinley (Gary), Maria Doyle Kennedy (Frances Cahill), Angeline Ball (Tina), Jon Voight (Insp. Ned Kenny).**

Vet filmmaker John Boorman is back in form with *The General*, a fresh-off-the-slab biopic of maverick Irish crime lord Martin Cahill that both challenges and entertains the audience. Still, in commercial terms it's a specialized item for upscale urban auds and movie buffs. Latter, especially, will get an immediate charge out of the pic's bold choice of B&W and widescreen. We meet the adult Cahill as an already boisterous character in Dublin's working-class slum neighborhood where he has a jokey but wary relationship with local cop Ned Kenny. Cahill supports a wife, four kids and sister-in-law through

thieving and burglary.
Int'l release: May 29                    Int'l B.O.: $3 million
U.S. release: Dec. 18                    U.S. B.O.: $150,000

### Get Real (U.K.)

A Distant Horizon presentation of a Graphite Films production, in association with British Screen, the Arts Council of England. Produced by Stephen Taylor. Directed by Simon Shore. Screenplay, Patrick Wilde, from his play *What's Wrong With Angry?* Camera, Alan Almond; editor, Barie Vince; music, John Lunn; production design/costumes, Bernd Lepel. Reviewed at Edinburgh Festival, Aug. 25. Running time: 108 mins.
**Ben Silverstone (Steven Carter), Brad Gorton (John Dixon), Charlotte Brittain (Linda), Stacy A. Hart (Jessica), Kate McEnery (Wendy), Tim Harris (Kevin).**

Fresh, funny, and thoroughly engaging, *Get Real* plays like a British version of John Hughes' teen-angst comedies from the early 1980s. Well-tooled in every department, from its bright widescreen lensing through freshman Simon Shore's direction to the performances by its mostly unknown cast, this drily humorous portrait of a high-school kid (who happens to be gay) and his romantic travails proved a popular choice at the Edinburgh festival, where it won the Audience Award. With the right marketing push and good reviews, pic could catch on locally and internationally in a moderate way among mainstream auds.

Set in the southern English town of Basingstoke – a byword for upper-middle-class respectability – the movie follows a group of teenagers whose lives seem to unfold in a parallel universe to their parents. Chief among them is 16-year-old Steven, whose best friend and confidante is dumpy neighbor Linda. She's the only one who knows his terrible secret – he's gay! – and, even worse, that he has the hots for the school's leading jock, local rich kid Dixon.

### Getting Off

A CineBLAST! production. Produced by Gill Holland, Eilhys England, Nadia Leonelli, Julie A. Lynch. Directed, written by Lynch. Camera, Enrique Chediak; editor, Brian A. Kates; music, Ed Tomney; production design, Petra Barchi; costume design, Daniel Lawson. Reviewed at Toronto Festival, Sept. 18. Running time: 85 mins.
**Christine Harnos (Josie Ray), Brooke Smith (Jennifer Sharp), Bill Sage (Matt Devlin), David Marshall Grant (Michael), Amy Ryan (Elaine Devlin), Garret Dillahunt (Chris Goodman), Tom Gilroy (Ryan).**

Think *Friends* with an acerbic Dorothy Parker aftertaste and you're in the vicinity of *Getting Off*, a complex, sharply observed tale of three female buddies coping with the specter of AIDS in 1992 New York. The anything-but-downbeat production is a coup for first-time helmer Julie A. Lynch; her assured way with large ensemble and difficult locales – plus a refusal to wallow in the situation's implicit melodrama – make this pic a good bet for special-house payday, plus decent ancillary afterlife.

Josie, Jennifer, and Elaine form that proverbial study in contrast. Josie is the tortured artist whose aggressively promiscuous ways hide a basic sense of inferiority; Jennifer is the surface-cynical standup comic whose intimacy problems are manifested in her choice of gay lovers; Elaine is the all-business MBA student who's always sweating the details. When the group's college pal Chris is hospitalized with complications

**...May 21...**
Nicolas Cage inks to star in Martin Scorsese's city drama, **Bringing Out The Dead**.

from HIV, the wildly dissimilar lifestyles are put under the microscope. The inevitable AIDS tests and their outcome may sound like a plot contrivance, but it works here because Lynch concentrates on secrets and recriminations that flow from the pressure-cooker situation.

## The Gingerbread Man

A Polygram Filmed Entertainment release of an Island Pictures and Enchanter Entertainment production. Produced by Jeremy Tannenbaum. Directed by Robert Altman. Screenplay, Al Hayes, based on an original story by John Grisham. Camera, Changwei Gu; editor, Geraldine Peroni; music, Mark Isham; production design, Stephen Altman. Reviewed at Polygram, Beverly Hills, Jan. 6. MPAA Rating: R. Running time: 115 mins.

**Kenneth Branagh (Rick Magruder), Embeth Davidtz (Mallory Doss), Robert Downey, Jr. (Clyde Pell), Daryl Hannah (Lois Harlan), Tom Berenger (Pete Randle), Famke Janssen (Leeanne), Robert Duvall (Dixon Doss).**

The second John Grisham directed by a heavyweight auteur, *The Gingerbread Man* is an adequate thriller that reveals an adventurous filmmaker working obediently within the boundaries of conventional material. Engaging enough initially, this tale of deceit, manipulation, misguided lust, kidnapping, and murder down South goes astray with an excess of melodramatic implausibility as the climax approaches. Soft conclusion and lack of true star names among the colorful cast will spell just-OK B.O. for this nicely mounted programmer.

| | |
|---|---|
| U.S. release: Jan. 23 | U.S. B.O.: $1.7 million |
| Int'l release: May 21 | Int'l B.O.: $6.5 million |

## Girl

A Kushner-Locke presentation of an HSX Films/Muse/Jess Most-Brad Wyman production. Produced by Jeff Most, Brad Wyman, Chris Hanley. Directed by Jonathan Kahn. Screenplay, David E. Tolchinsky, based on the novel by Blake Nelson. Camera, Tami Reiker; editor, Gillian Hutshing; music, Michael Tavera; production designer, Magda Lavandez-Berliner. Reviewed at Cannes Festival, May 16. Running time: 94 mins.

**Dominique Swain (Andrea Marr), Sean Patrick Flanery (Todd Sparrow), Summer Phoenix (Rebecca), Tara Reid (Cybil), Selma Blair (Darcy), Channon Roe (Kevin), Portia Di Rossi (Carla).**

Dominique Swain, gives a bright, intelligent performance as an 18-year-old small-town girl who discovers sex, love, and music the summer before she leaves for an Ivy League college in *Girl*, a well-cast, modestly effective pic aimed squarely at teens. Though no world-beater, pic could do some business, especially after Swain's memorable portrayal of *Lolita*, and it certainly has a long life in vidbins. Andrea Marr (Swain) is the spoiled daughter of well-to-do, late-middle-age parents and lives in an affluent suburb of Seattle. Still a virgin at 18, she's determined to end that condition as soon as possible, preferably with local rocker Todd Sparrow.

## The Girl of Your Dreams (La Nina De Tus Ojos)
(Spain)

A Lola Films Distribucion release of a Cartel/Fernando Trueba/Lola Films production, in association with Antena 3 Television, Via Digital. Produced by Andres Vicente Gomez, Cristina Huete, Eduardo Campoy. Directed by Fernando Trueba. Screenplay, Rafael Azcona, David Trueba. Camera, Javier Aguirresarobe; editor, Carmen Frias; music, Antoine Duhamel; art director, Gerardo Vera. Reviewed at Cine Palafox, Madrid, Nov. 3. Running time: 121 mins.

**Penelope Cruz (Macarena Granada), Antonio Resines (Blas), Neus Asensi (Lucia Gandia), Jesus Bonilla (Bonilla), Loles Leon (Trini), Jorge Sanz (Julia Torralba), Rosa Maria Sarda (Rosa Rosales), Santiago Segura (Castillo), Miroslav Taborsky (Vaclav), Johannes Silberschneider (Josef Goebbels), Karel Dobry (Leo).**

An ambitious, engaging big-budgeter about a Spanish film crew in the middle of Nazi Germany, *The Girl of Your Dreams* is Fernando Trueba's first Spanish feature since 1993's Oscar-winning *Belle Epoque*. Though lacking the warmth of the earlier movie, it works like a dream on most levels. A satisfyingly watertight plot, energetic perfs from a high-profile cast, and gold-plated craftsmanship and production values combine to unite a range of genres under a comic banner. Pic looks set to be the domestic B.O. hit of the year. Offshore, however, the plethora of local refs could prove a stumbling block in *Girl* finding homes.

In 1938, a troupe of Spanish actors under director Blas is in Berlin to shoot *The Girl of Your Dreams*, a cheesy Andalucian musical, as part of a reciprocal agreement between Hitler and Franco. Script nicely characterizes the crew members who include the nervy, golden-hearted singer Macarena Granada; Fascist leading man Julian Torralba; and alcoholic ex-femme fatale Rosa Rosales. Nazi propaganda minister Josef Goebbels falls for Macarena and promises everything at his disposal; this includes supplying a cast of Jewish extras and buying a mansion for her. Blas focuses on his film, sidestepping politics while Macarena is increasingly uneasy about Goebbels' designs and her safety. She falls for hunky Russian Jewish extra Leo. Realizing that, when the shoot ends, Leo will be sent to a concentration camp, she plots his escape. The stage is set for a conclusion which neatly blends traditional farce with the easy-to-swallow moral that saving human lives is more important than making movies.

| | |
|---|---|
| Int'l release: Nov. 13 | Int'l B.O.: $7 million |

## Girls' Night (U.K.)

A Granada presentation, in association with Showtime, of a Granada Film production. Produced by Bill Boyes. Directed by Nick Hurran. Screenplay, Kay Mellor. Camera, David Odd; editor, John Richards; music, Ed Shearmur; production design, Taff Batley. Reviewed at Sundance Festival, Jan. 20. Running time: 111 mins.

**Brenda Blethyn (Dawn), Julie Walters (Jackie), Kris Kristofferson (Cody), James Gaddas (Paul), George Costigan (Steve), Philip Jackson (Dave).**

In the English North Country, best friends and in-laws Dawn and Jackie work together on an electronics assembly line and dream of the sort of escape nurtured by movies.

Two powerhouse Brit actresses expertly work the opportunities at hand in *Girls' Night*, though they can elevate this formulaic tearjerker only so far. Seriocomedy evoked predictable, sentimental enthusiasm at Sundance, but is unlikely to gain the crit support needed at the wickets outside its native turf. Pic is best suited for telecast, with co-presenter Showtime the obvious Stateside vehicle.

| | |
|---|---|
| Int'l release: June 25 | Int'l B.O.: $1.5 million |

**... May 22 ...**
Manhattan Theater Club cancels production of Terrence McNally's controversial religious-themed **Corpus Christi**.

### The Glassblower's Children (Glasblasarens Barn)
(Sweden-Norway-Denmark)
A Sonet Film release of a Birkeland Film Co./Nordic Screen Prod/Zentropa Prods production, in association with Spice Production, TV-1000, Gamla Filmstaden Studios, Mutter Media, Orrefors, Bahrke Malmqvist Thor Produktion. Produced by Anders Birkeland. Directed, written by Anders Gronros, based on the novel by Maria Gripe. Camera, Philip Ogaard; editor, Gronros; music, Johan Soderkvist; production designer, Jan Olof Agren; costume designer, Lotta Pettersson. Reviewed at Gothenburg Festival, Sweden, Feb. 3. Running time: 110 mins.
**Stellan Skarsgard (Albert), Pernilla August (Sofia), Thommy Berggren (The Master), Elin Klinga (The Mistress), Lena Granhagen (Flaxa), Mans Westfelt (The Driver).**
Based on the much-loved children's book by Maria Gripe, *The Glassblower's Children* is a visually impressive but slightly uneven kidpic whose scary scenes may turn off both toddlers and their parents, negatively affecting the movie's box-office prospects. The book, which was published in 1964 and has been translated into more than 20 languages, is regarded as a modern kids' classic. Set at the start of the 19th century, it centers on Albert, a glassblower, whose life turns topsy turvy when royalty kidnap his children and a local witch sends him on a mystical quest.
Int'l release: March 5                Int'l B.O.: $1 million

### God Said, Ha!
An Oh Brother production. Produced by Rana Joy Glickman. Directed, written by Julia Sweeney, based on Greg Kachel's stage production. Camera, John Hora; editor, Fabienne Rawley; music, Anthony Marinelli; production designer, Gail Bennett; costume designer, Mary Zophres. Reviewed at South By Southwest Festival, Austin, Texas, March 14. Running time: 85 mins.
In *God Said, Ha!*, Julia Sweeney delivers an extended monolog so exquisitely written, so emotionally touching – and so entertaining – that she manages the almost impossible task of captivating the audience for 85 minutes with quite demanding material. With no changes in set or costume, and with only minimal alteration of lighting, Sweeney recounts with dark humor a traumatic chapter in her life, when brother Mike struggled and lost a battle with cancer and she herself was diagnosed with a rare form of cervical cancer. Filmed monologs have admittedly limited theatrical appeal with best results in major urban markets, where sophisticated viewers are likely to support and enjoy such challenging fare.

### God's Got My Number (Dieu Seul Me Voit [Versailles – Chantiers]) (France)
A UFD release of a Why Not Prods presentation of a Why Not Prods/Le Studio Canal Plus/France 2 Cinema production, with the participation of Canal Plus, CNC. Produced by Pascal Caucheteux, Gregoire Sorlat. Directed by Bruno Podalydes. Screenplay, Bruno Podalydes, Denis Podalydes. Camera, Pierre Stoeber; editor, Joelle Van Effenterre, Suzanne Koch, Marie-France Cuenot; music, Django Reinhardt, Stephane Grappelli, Serge Gainsbourg; art director, Antoine Platteau; costume design, Bernard Floch, Jane Milon. Reviewed at UCG Danton, Paris, July 20. Running time: 122 mins.
**Denis Podalydes (Albert), Jeanne Balibar (Anna), Isabelle Candelier (Sophie), Cecile Bouillot (Corinne), Jean-Noel Broute (Otto), Michel Vuillermoz (François).**

A critical and popular success that wears its narrative flimsiness with pride, *God's Got My Number (Versailles – Chantier)* follows the romantic entanglements of an indecisive nebbish as he quasi-courts three women. Practically the only French release to win a following post-Cannes, pic is still going strong after two months, but will require extra-special handling to penetrate offshore.
Brothers Bruno and Denis Podalydes deftly construct the central character's endearingly clumsy approach to politics, women, and social gatherings. Balding soundman Albert has a terrible time nailing down his convictions. While working on a spot for a political campaign in Toulouse, Albert and pal Otto donate blood so as to meet cute nurse Sophie.
Int'l release: June 3                Int'l B.O.: $1.8 million

### Gods and Monsters
A Regent Entertainment production, in association with Gregg Fienberg. Produced by Paul Colichman, Fienberg, Mark Harris. Directed, written by Bill Condon, based on the novel *Father of Frankenstein* by Christopher Bram. Camera, Stephen M. Katz; editor, Virginia Katz; music, Carter Burwell; production design, Richard Sherman; costumes, Bruce Finlayson. Reviewed at Sundance Festival, Jan. 21. Running time: 105 mins.
**Ian McKellen (James Whale), Brendan Fraser (Clayton Boone), Lynn Redgrave (Hanna), Lolita Davidovich (Betty), Kevin J. O'Connor (Harry), Jack Plotnick (Edmond Kay).**
Ian McKellen's brilliant performance as 1930s director James Whale electrifies *Gods and Monsters*. This historical Hollywood fiction doesn't always convince, but it's an engrossing, unusual, imaginatively executed bit of psychological gamesmanship. Director-scenarist Bill Condon's first-class production will need good reviews and strong marketing to cross over beyond gay and arthouse auds. Pic is set in final days of Whale, famed for his Universal horror films, painting a portrait of a physically frail, socially isolated has-been who feigns contentment hanging about his tony digs under the watchful eye of his housekeeper Hanna. The arrival of gardener Clayton (Fraser), a muscle-bound, rootless odd-jobber, sets off a psychological cat-and-mouse play.
U.S. release: Nov. 4                U.S. B.O.: $1.7 million

### Godzilla
A Sony release of a TriStar Pictures presentation of a Centropolis Entertainment production in association with Fried Films, Independent Pictures. Produced by Dean Devlin. Directed by Roland Emmerich. Screenplay, Devlin, Emmerich, from a story by Ted Elliott, Terry Rossio, Devlin, Emmerich, based on the character Godzilla, owned/created by Toho Co. Camera, Ueli Steiger; editors, Peter Amundson, David J. Siegel; music, David Arnold; production designer, Oliver Scholl; costume designer, Joseph Porro; Godzilla designer, Patrick Tatopoulos; visual-effects supervisor, Volker Engel. Reviewed at Sony Lincoln Square, New York, May 15. MPAA Rating: PG-13. Running time: 138 mins.
**Matthew Broderick (Dr. Niko Tatopoulos), Jean Reno (Philippe Roache), Maria Pitillo (Audrey Timmonds), Hank Azaria (Victor "Animal" Palotti), Kevin Dunn (Col. Hicks), Michael Lerner (Mayor Ebert).**
No doubt about it: *Godzilla* will be a killer at the box office during the early stages of its release. The slam-bang excitement and state-of-the-art special effects are more than impressive enough to ensure every 12-year-old boy will want to see it early

---

**... May 23 ...**
Theo Angelopoulos' **Eternity and a Day** wins the Palme d'Or at Cannes.

and often. And millions of nostalgic baby-boomers will be drawn by the novelty of a new and improved version of the lizard who repeatedly razed Tokyo in B-movies of yore. But even with all that going for it, *Godzilla* isn't likely to post *Titanic*-size grosses, or even challenge records set by *Independence Day*, the last high-concept sci-fi spectacle devised by director Roland Emmerich and producer Dean Devlin.

In this version, as in the original, the title creature is a side effect of nuclear testing. French nuclear blasts in the South Pacific have turned a lizard into a gigantic mutant monster who lumbers from the Far East to create havoc in Manhattan.

| | |
|---|---|
| U.S. release: May 20 | U.S. B.O.: $136 million |
| Int'l release: May 26 | Int'l B.O.: $240 million |

### Going to Kansas City (Canada-Finland)

A Mandart Entertainment Ltd. production, in association with Telescene Film Group. Produced by Pamela Mandart, Lise Abasto. Directed by Pekka Mandart. Screenplay, Morrie Ruvinsky, story by Pekka Mandart, Tony MacNabb. Camera, Pini Hellstedt; editor, David McLeod; music, Marty Simon; production design, John Meighen; costume design, Paul-Andre Guerin. Reviewed at American Film Institute, L.A., Oct. 6, 1998. Running time: 97 mins.

**Mikko Nousiainen (Mikko Vihavainen), Melissa Galianos (Carly Malone), Michael Ironside (Mike Malone), Susie Almgren (Bonnie Bruckner), Mark Camacho (Jack Bruckner).**

The debut feature *Going to Kansas City*, while not wholly successful, suggests a promising future for Finnish helmer Pekka Mandart. The story of a Finnish exchange student's adventures in the American Midwest, the film has a brisk, energetic pace and an engaging, lighthearted approach to its subject matter. While it has just an outside chance at an arthouse run, pic should be popular on the festival circuit and serve as a cornerstone on which Mandart can build a career.

Leaving Helsinki, Mikko, a musician, dreams of entering the Kansas City blues scene. When he arrives, he finds things are not as he expected. Instead of staying in Kansas City, Mikko finds himself in rural Canaan, living with a farming family. While Mikko's host mother, Bonnie Bruckner, and her sons are welcoming, others in the town are not. Xenophobic locals label the newcomer a Swede. One exception is the waitress Melissa (Carly Malone), whose father is the town's gruff, protective police chief. After Melissa sneaks out to watch Mikko perform during amateur night she's reprimanded by her father. When Mikko is caught in a convenience store robbery that leaves two young people fatally wounded, Malone and others blame the foreigner.

| | |
|---|---|
| Int'l release: July 31 | U.S. release: $300,000 |

### Gone with the Train (Exspress Exspress)

(Slovenia)

An AAC production, in association with TV Slovenia. Produced, directed by Igor Sterk. Screenplay, Matjaz Pograjc, Sterk. Camera, Valentin Perko; editor, Stanko Kostanjevic; music, Mitja Vrhovnik-Smrekar. Reviewed at Kiev Festival, Ukraine, Oct. 24, 1997. Running time: 76 mins.

**Gregor Bakovic (The Boy), Barbara Cerar (The Girl), Lojze Rozman (The Conductor), Andrej Rozman-Roza (The Stowaway).**

The spirits of Buster Keaton, Jacques Tati, and Jiri Menzel preside benignly over *Gone With the Train*, a gentle, surrealist comedy from Slovenian first-time director Igor Sterk. Largely wordless and packed with beguiling sight gags, picture deserves a greater life beyond the fest circuit. Gossamer plot concerns a young man (Gregor Bakovic) who, after his father's death, hops the first available train. En route, he meets a bunch of eccentric characters and a pretty girl (Barbara Cerar).

### Goodbye Lover

A Warner Bros. release of an Arnon Milchan/Gotham Entertainment Group/Lightmotive production. Produced by Alexandra Milchan, Patrick McDarrah, Joel Roodman, Chris Daniel. Directed by Roland Joffe. Screenplay, Ron Peer, Joel Cohen, Alec Sokolow, story by Peer. Camera, Dante Spinotti; editor, William Steinkamp; music, John Ottman; production designer, Stewart Starkin; costume designers, Theadora Van Runkle. Reviewed at Warner Hollywood, L.A., May 7. MPAA Rating: R. Running time: 104 mins.

**Patricia Arquette (Sandra Dunmore), Dermot Mulroney (Jake Dunmore), Ellen DeGeneres (Det. Rita Pompano), Mary-Louise Parker (Peggy Blane), Don Johnson (Ben Dunmore), Alex Rocco (Crowley), John Neville (Bradley).**

A glossy, sexy, twisty comic thriller, *Goodbye Lover* is entertaining for a while on the pulpiest superficial level, thanks in large measure to its lush physical trappings. This amoral tale of multiple murders and betrayals should have been funnier by half and frankly becomes just too silly and convoluted for its own good. Sandra and Ben are edgy, provocative lovers, with Sandra favoring locations where they could easily be caught. She's married to Ben's messed-up younger brother Jake who is barely clinging to his job at a high-powered L.A. ad agency where Ben runs the show.

### Good Will Hunting

A Miramax release of a Lawrence Bender production. Produced by Lawrence Bender. Directed by Gus Van Sant. Screenplay, Ben Affleck, Matt Damon, story by Damon. Camera, Jean Yves Escoffier; editor, Pietro Scalia; music, Danny Elfman; production design, Melissa Stewart; costume design, Beatrix Aruna Pasztor. Reviewed at Culver Studios, Culver City, Nov. 24, 1997. MPAA Rating: R. Running time: 126 mins.

**Matt Damon (Will Hunting), Robin Williams (Sean McGuire), Ben Affleck (Chuckie), Minnie Driver (Skylar), Stellan Skarsgard (Lambeau), Casey Affleck (Morgan), Cole Hauser (Billy).**

A towering performance by Matt Damon, and a superlative ensemble, elevate *Good Will Hunting* a notch or two above the mainstream therapeutic sensibility of its story. Centering on a brilliant working-class youngster who's forced to come to terms with his creative genius and true feelings, this beautifully realized tale is engaging and often quite touching. Distrib could score big with pic whose old-fashioned virtues should play well in cities as well as in Middle America.

Protagonist is Will Hunting, a 20-year-old lad who works as a janitor at MIT. Unschooled, Will has a certain genius, a photographic memory, and mathematical aptitude. He anonymously solves a math challenge offered to students by Professor Lambeau and is taken under his wing. However, he must meet two conditions: Will has to meet with him once a week and begin therapy. A succession of psychologists tries to reach Will but he won't cooperate. Finally, Lambeau summons his old classmate, Sean McGuire, a community college instructor and therapist – and the real drama begins.

| | |
|---|---|
| U.S. release: Dec. 5, 1997 | U.S. B.O.: $138 million |
| Int'l release: March 1 | Int'l B.O.: $88 million |

---

**... May 24 ...**

The enfant terrible of talk TV, Jerry Springer, finds himself the subject of lurid stories in the tabloid media.

**Goreville, U.S.A.** (Docu, B&W)

A Leaning Silo production. Produced by James F. Roberts, James T. Volk. Directed by Seth Henrikson, Dave Sarno, Rob Shields. Camera, Henrikson; editors, Martha Kelly, Chris Segich; music, Jeff Tweedy. Reviewed at Hollywood Festival, L.A., Aug. 10. Running time: 64 mins.

Initially intriguing but ultimately condescending, *Goreville, U.S.A.* seems at first to be about the citizens of an Illinois backwater (the only town in the U.S. to pass an ordinance requiring at least one member of every household to own a firearm). But doc changes gears midway to focus on right-wing militias and the broad issue of gun control. Theatrical distribution is unlikely for this hourlong doc, but public TV and cable play are not out of the question. The very-out-of-the-loop residents explain that Goreville passed the law in response to the growing sentiment across the country to ban weapons. Pic causes guilty laughs because every interviewee comes across as, frankly, an ignorant hick. There may be culturally savvy people in Goreville, but none of them is on display here.

**The Governess** (U.K.)

A Sony Pictures Classics presentation of a Pandora Cinema/Parallax Pictures production. Produced by Sarah Curtis. Directed, written by Sandra Goldbacher. Camera, Ashley Rowe; editor, Isabel Lorente; music, Edward Shearmur; production designer, Sarah Greenwood; costume designer, Caroline Harris. Reviewed at Seattle Festival, June 11. Running time: 114 mins.

**Minnie Driver (Rosina), Tom Wilkinson (Cavendish), Florence Hoath (Clementina), Jonathan Rhys Meyers (Henry), Harriet Walter (Mrs. Cavendish).**

Minnie Driver gets a showy workout in *The Governess*, a beautifully crafted, if ultimately opaque, study of art, sensuality, and outsider status in early Victorian England. The pic, set among the Sephardic community of London, gets high marks for originality and style, but will have a tough time selling to auds, who are likely to find its claustrophobic atmosphere more oppressive than seductive. Privileged Rosina da Silva finds her world shaken by the violent death of her father, a Jewish merchant with a secret craving for the dangerous night life. With the family in debt, she decides to pass herself off as a Gentile and takes employment with a family in faraway Scotland.

U.S. release: July 31      U.S. B.O.: $4 million
Int'l release: Oct. 23      Int'l B.O.: $350,000

**The Grandfather (El Abuelo)** (Spain)

A Columbia TriStar release of a Nickel Odeon Dos production, in association with RTVE. Produced by José Luis Garci. Directed by Garci. Screenplay, Garci, Horacio Valcarcel, based on the novel by Benito Perez Galdos. Camera, Raul Perez Cubero; editor, Miguel Garcia Sinde; music, Manuel Balboa; art director, Gil Parrondo. Reviewed at Multicines Ideal, Madrid, Nov. 1. Running time: 147 mins.

**Fernando Fernan-Gomez (Rodrigo de Arista), Rafael Alonso (Pio Coronado), Cayetana Guillen-Cuervo (Lucrecia Richmond), Agustin Gonzalez (Senen), Cristina Cruz (Doli), Alicia Rozas (Neli).**

Spain's submission for the foreign-language-film Oscar, *The Grandfather* is a gracefully told moral fable about an aristocrat fallen on hard times and anxious to regain some dignity. Pic is dominated by the towering presence of vet actor Fernando

Fernan-Gomez and is typically praiseworthy of director Garci in its earnestness, intensity, and intelligence, but its defiant refusal to bow even slightly to the dictates of film fashion could limit its B.O..

Pic was shot with serialization on local TV in mind. Set amongst the sumptuous green landscapes of northern Spain in the late 19th century, when the aristocracy and the bourgeoisie were exchanging power places, story finds Rodrigo de Arista returning to the town of his birth to find out which of his two young granddaughters, Doli or Neli, is his true heir. Relations between Rodrigo and Lucrecia are strained, but he becomes close friends with Pio Coronado, the gloomy teacher of the two girls. Irritated by the threat Rodrigo represents to her reputation, Lucrecia orders social climber Senen to have him confined to a monastery. Rodrigo escapes and returns to the town with renewed determination.

Int'l release: Oct. 31      Int'l B.O.: $2.5 million

**Great Expectations**

A 20th Century Fox release of an Art Linson production. Produced by Linson. Directed by Alfonso Cuaron. Screenplay, Mitch Glazer, based on the novel by Charles Dickens. Camera, Emmanuel Lubezki; editor, Steven Weisberg; music, Patrick Doyle; production design, Tony Burrough; costume design, Judianna Makovsky. Reviewed at 20th Century Fox, L.A., Jan. 12. MPAA Rating: R. Running time: 111 mins.

**Ethan Hawke (Finnegan Bell), Gwyneth Paltrow (Estella), Hank Azaria (Walter Plane), Chris Cooper (Joe), Anne Bancroft (Ms. Dinsmoor), Robert De Niro (Lustig).**

Eight-year-old orphan Finn Bell is growing up in marginal circumstances in a sleepy fishing village along the Florida coast. This *Great Expectations* is something less than a pip. A fanciful and free modern-day adaptation of Charles Dickens' classic novel about a poor boy's circuitous ascent in the world, beautifully made production lacks the emotional depth and dramatic tension needed to command audience attention beyond the level of a talented curiosity. This picaresque drama describing several characters' peculiar destinies will have trouble raising much interest among the general public.

U.S. release: Jan. 30      U.S. B.O.: $26.5 million
Int'l release: Feb. 28      Int'l B.O.: $29 million

**A Great Shout Of Love (Un Grand Cri D'Amour)** (France)

An AMLF release of a Katharina/Renn, TF1 Films, Josy Films production, in association with Canal Plus. Directed, written by Josiane Balasko, based on her play. Camera, Gerard de Battista; editor, Claudine Merlin; music, Catherine Ringer; costume design, Fabienne Katany. Reviewed at Rive Gauche theater, Perpignan, France, Jan. 18. Running time: 92 mins.

**Josiane Balasko (Gigi Ortega), Richard Berry (Hugo Martial), Daniel Ceccaldi (Sylvestre), Daniel Prevost (Léon).**

Adapting a stage comedy to the screen is always tricky, especially when the subject matter is the stage itself. In *A Great Shout of Love*, helmer-scripter-thesp Josiane Balasko makes a gallant effort to mix the two media, but ends up somewhere in between – with a sitcom shouting match best suited to the tube. On the strength of Balasko's rep as comic iconoclast, pic should get theatrical release in most French-language territories, but its limited, local appeal will soon relegate it to Gallic broadcast limbo.

Setup has vet Paris actor and midlife lothario Hugo Martial

**. . . May 25 . . .**

*Elizabeth* helmer Shekhar Kapur inks to helm **Long Walk to Freedom** on life of Nelson Mandela.

looking for a leading lady for his comeback stage vehicle. Thanks to his unscrupulous agent and director, Martial's former wife and stage partner, Gigi Ortega, now a bloated post-detox prima donna, is prevailed upon to take the part, despite the ex-couple's mutual loathing.

Int'l release: Dec. 27, 1997      Int'l B.O.: $2.8 million

### Half A Chance (1 Chance Sur 2) (France)

A UFD release of a Christian Fechner presentation of a Films Christian Fechner/UGCF/TF1 Films Prod. production. Produced by Fechner. Directed by Patrice Leconte. Screenplay, Patrick Dewolf, Leconte, Serge Frydman; story idea, Bruno Tardo. Camera, Joelle Hache; editor, Joelle Hache; music, Alexandre Desplat; art director, Ivan Maussion; costume designer, Annie Perier-Foulon; stunt coordinator, Remy Julienne. Reviewed at UGC Ciné Cité, Paris, March 31. Running time: 109 mins.

**Jean-Paul Belmondo (Leo Brassac), Alain Delon (Julien Vignal), Vanessa Paradis (Alice Tomaso), Eric Defosse (Carella), Valery Gataev (Anatoli Sharkov), Michel Aumont (Ledoyen).** (French and Russian dialog)

After *Ridicule*, helmer Patrice Leconte goes from the sublime to the ridiculous with *Half a Chance*, a game, if choppy, excuse to reunite Gallic screen icons Jean-Paul Belmondo and Alain Delon. Throw in the Russian mob and lots of stuff that blows up on the Côte d'Azur and you've got a watchable but uninspired programmer that will sell internationally on the strength of its pedigree.

Before expiring, Alice's mother leaves an audiocassette confessing that 20 years earlier she'd fallen madly in love with two men at the same time, never knowing which one was Alice's father. The young woman steals a sports car and heads for the South of France to confront her two possible progenitors. Unfortunately she steals one that happens to have $50 million of Russian Mafia money in the trunk.

Int'l release: March 3      Int'l B.O.: $7.5 million
U.S. release: April 10      U.S. B.O.: $80,000

### Half Baked

A Universal Pictures release of a Robert Simonds production. Produced by Robert Simonds. Directed by Tamra Davis. Screenplay, Dave Chappelle, Neal Brennan. Camera, Steven Bernstein; editor, Don Zimmerman; music, Alf Clausen; production design, Perry Andelin Blake; costume design, Vicki Graef. Reviewed at the Atwater Cinema, Montreal, Jan. 17. MPAA Rating: R. Running time: 84 mins.

**Dave Chappelle (Thurgood), Guillermo Diaz (Scarface), Jim Breuer (Brian), Harland Williams (Kenny), Rachel True (Mary Jane), Clarence Williams III (Samson Simpson). With: Jon Stewart, Snoop Doggy Dogg, Stephen Baldwin, Willie Nelson, Janeane Garofalo, Steven Wright, Tommy Chong.**

*Half Baked* is just that. Life is one big smoky bash for pals and roommates Thurgood, Scarface, Brian, and Kenny. This late-'90s update of the classic stoner comedy is a couple of hash brownies short of a satisfying cinematic picnic, with far too few comic highs during the bigscreen reefer party. Pic may have campus bong enthusiasts and hip-hop pro-pot lobbyists giggling, but most mainstream auds will almost certainly just say no, and *Half Baked* will fade from theaters quickly. The pic may light up some action with couch smokers when it puffs its way to the video shelf.

U.S. release: Jan. 16      U.S. B.O.: $17.5 million

### Halloween: H20 Twenty Years Later

A Dimension Films release of a Nightfall production. Produced by Paul Freeman. Directed by Steve Miner. Screenplay, Robert Zappia, Matt Greenberg, story by Zappia, based on characters created by Debra Hill and John Carpenter. Camera, Daryn Okada; editor, Patrick Lusser; music, John Ottman; original musical theme, Carpenter; production design, John Willet; costume design, Deborah Everton. Reviewed at UA Galaxy, San Francisco, July 30. Running time: 85 mins.

**Jamie Lee Curtis (Laurie Strode/Keri Tate), Adam Arkin (Will), Josh Hartnett (John), Michelle Williams (Molly), Adam Hann-Byrd (Charlie), Jodi Lyn O'Keefe (Sarah), Janet Leigh (Norma), LL Cool J (Ronny)**

*Halloween: H20* – the franchise responsible for 1980s teen slash-'em-ups – proves an exception to banal retreads. While plot mechanics aren't wildly imaginative, pic nonetheless delivers requisite jolts in an above-average package, while giving Jamie Lee Curtis sufficient character meat to justify revisiting her career-making role. Expect solid if medium-legged B.O. performance, followed by a dynamic video shelf life.

Laurie Strode of the original faked her death years ago to "go into hiding"; using a different name, she's now live-in headmistress at a gated, upscale boarding school, with teenage son John duly enrolled. Guess who's coming cross-country to visit – the long-presumed-dead Michael, her demented, demonic brother. It's not coincidentally Halloween and the majority of staff and students are on a camping trip. John has secretly stayed behind for a "romantic dinner" with g.f. Molly, and Laurie is also on campus for the fateful confrontation with her sibling.

U.S. release: Aug. 5      U.S. B.O.: $55 million
Int'l release: Oct. 19      Int'l B.O.: $22 million

### Hamilton (Sweden)

A Buena Vista Int'l release of a Moviola/TV4/Yellow Cottage production. Produced by Hans Lonnerheden. Directed by Harald Zwart. Screenplay, Jonas Cornell, William Aldridge, based on the novels *Ingen mans land* (*No Man's Land*) and *Den enda segern* (*The Only Victory*) by Jan Guillou. Camera, Jerome Robert; editor, Darek Hodor; music, Trond Bjerknaes; production design, Mikael Varhilyi; costume design, Lenamari Wallstrom. Reviewed at Rigoletto Theater, Stockholm, Jan. 23. Running time: 127 mins.

**Peter Stormare (Cmd. Carl Hamilton), Lena Olin (Tessie), Mark Hamill (Mike Hawkins), Mats Langbacka (Ake Stalhandske), Madeleine Elfstrand (Anna), Thomas Hedengran (Gustavsson).**

(Swedish, English, Russian, and Arabic dialog)

The powerful presence of Peter Stormare is the main asset in this fifth entry following the exploits of Swedish super-agent Carl Hamilton. Despite a confused ending, this crisply directed actioner centered on some stolen atomic weapons should generate a fair buzz on foreign soil. Pic opens with the theft of atomic weapons from the former Soviet Union. In this case, the CIA learns that Russian rebels are transporting a stolen missile through the Arctic and are planning to smuggle it through Sweden. Hamilton and his men are ordered to find and execute the rebels and secure the missile.

Int'l release: Feb. 6      Int'l B.O.: $4.5 million

---

**. . . May 26 . . .**

**Godzilla** reports a less-than-expected $55 million take over the Memorial Day weekend.

## Happiness

An October Films release of a Good Machine/Killer Films production. Produced by Ted Hope, Christine Vachon. Directed, written by Todd Solondz. Camera, Maryse Alberti; editor, Alan Oxman; music, Robbie Kondor; production designer, Therese Deprez; costume designer, Kathryn Nixon. Reviewed at Cannes Festival, May 15. Running time: 139 mins.
**Jane Adams (Joy Jordan), Dylan Baker (Bill Maplewood), Lara Flynn Boyle (Helen Jordan), Ben Gazzara (Lenny Jordan), Jared Harris (Vlad), Philip Seymour Hoffman (Allen), Jon Lovitz (Andy Kornbluth), Cynthia Stevenson (Trish Maplewood), Elizabeth Ashley (Diane Freed), Camryn Manheim (Kristina).**
The dark dementia lurking beneath placid everyday life bubbles to the surface in Todd Solondz's *Happiness*, a disturbing black comedy that, at bottom, is about all the trouble sex causes. A skillfully made examination of the problems a host of interconnected characters face even approaching the ideal represented by the title, overlong pic sees the writer-director flexing his ambition and successfully sustaining a tricky tone of low-key morbid humor. But some of the subject matter, including upfront treatment of prepubescent sexual curiosity and pedophilia, will raise hackles, leaving a delicate marketing challenge. Controversy and critical support will create want-see among discerning and adventurous specialty audiences, but a wider breakout will be difficult.

Focus is three New Jersey sisters repping a range of contempo female options with a stylistic emphasis upon the facades that enforce "normalcy." Solondz's picture is unsettling because it explores taboo territory with moral ambiguity, acknowledging its forbidden nature while stressing a common, and undeniable, fascination with it.

U.S. release: Oct. 11            U.S. B.O.: $2.8 million
Int'l release: Oct. 25           Int'l B.O.: $200,000

## Hard Rain

A Paramount release, presented in association with Mutual Film Co. Produced by Mark Gordon, Gary Levinsohn, Ian Bryce. Directed by Mikael Salomon. Screenplay, Graham Yost. Camera, Peter Menzies, Jr.; editor, Paul Hirsch; music, Christopher Young; production design, J. Michael Riva; visual-effects supervisor, Ed Jones; special-effects supervisor, John Frazier. Reviewed at Paramount Studios, L.A., Jan. 5. MPAA Rating: R. Running time: 96 mins.
**Morgan Freeman (Jim), Christian Slater (Tom), Randy Quaid (Sheriff), Minnie Driver (Karen), Ed Asner (Charlie), Richard Dysart (Henry).**
*Hard Rain* is a waterlogged would-be thriller deep-sixed by its misguided notion of high concept. A cat-and-mouse tale centered on a botched heist during a humongous flood, this dark and wet picture is filled with furious action that seems to unfold in slow motion thanks to the simple fact that people and things move with exceedingly retarded speed. An effective campaign and the promise of unusual thrills should produce a solid opening, but lack of credible dramatic ballast will cause it to sink quite quickly. On paper, the idea of an armored-truck robbery pulled during a raging storm, even if far-fetched, might have seemed sufficiently ripe with offbeat promise to be worth a try.

U.S. release: Jan. 16           U.S. B.O.: $20 million
Int'l release: Jan. 27          Int'l B.O.: $22 million

## Head On (Australia)

A Palace Films (Australia) release of a Great Scott production, in association with the Australian Film Finance Corp. and with the assistance of Film Victoria. Produced by Jane Scott. Directed by Ana Kokkinos. Screenplay, Andrew Bovell, Mira Robertson, Kokkinos, based on the book *Loaded* by Christos Tsiolkas. Camera, Jaems Grant; editor, Jill Bilcock; music, Ollie Olsen; production designer, Nikki di Falco; costume designer, Anna Borghesi. Reviewed at Verona 2, Sydney, May 7. Running time: 104 mins. (English and Greek dialog)
**Alex Dimitriades (Ari), Paul Capsis (Johnny), Julian Garner (Sean), Tony Nikolakopoulos (Dimitri), Elena Mandalis (Betty), Eugenia Fragos (Sophia), Damien Fotiou (Joe).**
This bold feature from Greek-Australian director Ana Kokkinos hones in on the confused world of its 19-year-old hero, Ari. Over a 24-hour period, he confronts both his sexuality and his Greek background. Uncompromising and dynamic, compassionate pic, adapted from the book *Loaded* by Christos Tsiolkas, is bound to provoke debate and perhaps censorship problems. *Head On* should find a niche in urban venues and deserves to cross over from a strictly gay audience to a wider arthouse crowd.

Ari is obsessed with sex and has several sexual encounters, most of them gay, though he does make a half-hearted attempt to fulfill the sister of a friend. At the same time, he's facing problems with his traditional Greek parents, who have no clue about his sexual – and drug-taking – activities.

Int'l release: Aug. 13            Int'l B.O.: $1.5 million

## Healing By Killing (Ripui B'hareg) (Docu, Israel)

A New Yorker Films release of a Per Capita (Tel Aviv) production. Produced, directed, written by Nitzan Aviram. Camera, Yorman Millo; editor, Naomi Press-Aviram; music, Oded Zehavi. Reviewed at the Film Forum, N.Y., April 27. Running time: 80 mins.
Showing how the Nazis' mass killings grew out of the German medical establishment's willing implementation of euthanasia and other seemingly legitimate practices, *Healing by Killing* adds a valuable, chilling chapter to the Holocaust, one so devastating in its depiction of collapsed ethical standards that it deserves to be required viewing in medical schools. Israeli director Nitzan Aviram's primary concern is to trace the terrible logic that led doctors, of all people, to lay the operational groundwork for mass murder. Avoiding undue emotionalism or familiar Holocaust photos, pic employs a calm, analytical tone that's powerful. The New Yorker release bids to captivate arthouse and festival auds.

## Heaven (New Zealand)

A Miramax Films release of a Midnight Films production. Produced by Sue Rogers. Directed by Scott Reynolds. Screenplay, Reynolds, based on the novel by Chad Taylor. Camera, Simon Raby; editor, Wayne Cook; music, Victoria Kelly; production design, John Girdlestone; costumes, Emily Carter. Reviewed at World Film Festival, Montreal, Sept. 1. Running time: 102 mins.
**Martin Donovan (Robert Marling), Danny Edwards (Heaven), Richard Schiff (Stanner), Joanna Going (Jennifer), Patrick Malahide (Dr. Melrose), Sean (Michael Langley).**
A gritty, pumped-up thriller with jaw-dropping plot twists to spare, *Heaven* kicks off in strong, stylish fashion but is eventually weakened by a convoluted, contrived plot. The second feature from writer-director Scott Reynolds (*The Ugly*)

---

comes off like *The Crying Game* meets *The Usual Suspects*. Tall tale revolves around a transsexual stripper and includes a dizzying series of narrative kinks that will make viewers work hard to keep track of everything going on. As a hard-edged thriller, pic reps a marketing challenge, but it will stir chat on the fest circuit and could interest hip, young audiences.

Robert Marling is having a bad year. His wife, Jennifer, has dumped him, is trying to extract every last penny from him in alimony payments, and is about to try to gain sole custody of their son. Marling, a less-than-successful architect, also has a big-time gambling problem and tends to drink too much. Things are so bad that the only project he's working on is the redesign of his low-life friend Stanner's strip club, the Paradise. That's where Marling meets Heaven, an imposing transsexual dancer who is tormented by violent visions, most of which accurately predict future events.

### He Got Game
A Buena Vista release of a Touchstone Pictures presentation of a 40 Acres and a Mule Filmworks production. Produced by Jon Kilik, Spike Lee. Directed, written by Lee. Camera, Malik Hassan Sayeed; editor, Barry Alexander Brown; music, Aaron Copland; production designer, Wynn Thomas; costume designer, Sandra Hernandez. Reviewed at the Directors Guild, L.A., April 21. MPAA Rating: R. Running time: 134 mins.

**Denzel Washington (Jake Shuttlesworth), Ray Allen (Jesus Shuttlesworth), Milla Jovovich (Dakota Burns), Rosario Dawson (Lala Bonilla), Hill Harper (Coleman "Bogger" Sykes), Zelda Harris (Mary Shuttlesworth), John Turturro (Coach Billy Sunday).**

After two small-scale, independently made films and a worthy documentary, Spike Lee again plays in the big arena with *He Got Game*, a contemporary basketball drama with comic overtones, centering on the turbulent relationship between a convict-father and his extraordinarily gifted athlete son. Lacking the moral indignation, outrage, and militant politics that marked Lee's earlier work, this vibrantly colorful film is a tad too soft at the center, and arguably the director's most mainstream movie with its broad canvas of family drama, black youth, college life, and, above all, the obsession with basketball. Dramatically, pic centers on the tumultuous father-son interaction, which underscores pic's chief moral concern: the ability truly to forgive someone who has caused harm and injustice.

| | |
|---|---|
| U.S. release: May 1 | U.S. B.O.: $21.5 million |
| Int'l release: Sept 4 | Int'l B.O.: $4 million |

### Hideous Kinky (U.K.-France)
An AMLF release of a The Film Consortium and BBC Films presentation, in association with the Arts Council of England, of a Greenpoint Films (U.K.)/L Films, AMLF (France) production. Produced by Ann Scott. Directed by Gillies MacKinnon. Screenplay, Billy MacKinnon, based on the novel by Esther Freud. Camera, John de Borman; editor, Pia Di Ciaula; music, John Keane; production design, Louise Marzaroli, Pierre Gompertz; costume design, Kate Carin. Reviewed at Dinard Festival, France, Oct. 2. Running time: 97 mins.

**Kate Winslet (Julia), Said Taghmaoui (Bilal), Bella Riza (Bea), Carrie Mullan (Lucy), Pierre Clementi (Santoni), Sira Stampe (Eva). (English, Arabic, and French dialog)**

Kate Winslet continues an uninterrupted line of fine performances with the modest yet affecting *Hideous Kinky*,

an episodic drama set in North Africa in hippie-dippy days but filtered through a sober and intelligent artistic eye. Adapted from Esther Freud's autobiographical novel, pic embraces the heady atmosphere of Marrakesh and its environs c. 1972, as a single mom tries to juggle her own search for self-actualization with what's best for her two young daughters. International arthouse prospects look reasonably good, but mainstream auds may find the somewhat choppy proceedings as jarring as pic's curious title.

In a low-rent residence hotel in Marrakesh, 25-year-old Julia, 6-year-old Lucy and 8-year-old Bea are scraping by on the meager proceeds from hand-sewn dolls and the occasional check from the girls' father. Dad is a poet back in London involved with at least one other woman. When the girls introduce their mom to a streetwise acrobat, Bilal, there's an immediate sexual spark, and the hunky young Moroccan is soon sharing their modest quarters. Bilal is a bit of a con man, but he is also a gentle soul, with a genuine affinity for the two girls.

### High Art
An October Films release. Produced by Dolly Hall, Jeff Levy-Hinte, Susan A. Stov`er. Directed, written by Lisa Cholodenko. Camera, Tami Reiker; editor, Amy E. Duddleston; music, Shudder to Think; production design, Bernhard Blythe; costume design, Victoria Farrell. Reviewed at Sundance Festival, Jan. 21. Running time: 102 mins.

**Ally Sheedy (Lucy Berliner), Radha Mitchell (Syd), Patricia Clarkson (Greta), Tammy Grimes (Lucy's Mother), Gabriel Mann (James), Bill Sage (Arnie).**

Lisa Cholodenko's script revolves around two women whose paths cross – and lives change – as a result of a chance meeting. Protagonist Syd is an ambitious editor-in-training at a photography magazine who discovers her neighbor, Lucy, is a noted lens woman who dropped out several years earlier. *High Art*, set in the contempo art world of New York, and centering on a triangle of fascinating women, depicts with unwavering veracity the breakup of one longtime relationship just as another, unexpected one begins. October release should be wholeheartedly embraced by the lesbian community and, with the right marketing, cross over to a larger sophisticated audience.

| | |
|---|---|
| U.S. release: June 12 | U.S. B.O.: $2 million |

### Hilary And Jackie (U.K.)
An Intermedia Films/Film Four presentation, with the participation of British Screen and the Arts Council of England, of an Oxford Films production. Produced by Andy Paterson, Nicolas Kent. Directed by Anand Tucker. Screenplay, Frank Cottrell-Boyce, based on the book *A Genius in the Family* by Hilary and Piers du Pré. Camera, David Johnson; editor, Martin Walsh; music, Barrington Pheloung; cellist, Caroline Dale; production design, Alice Normington; costume design, Sandy Powell. Reviewed at Venice Festival, Sept. 5. Running time: 124 mins.

**Emily Watson (Jacqueline du Pré), Rachel Griffiths (Hilary du Pré), James Frain (Daniel Barenboim), David Morrissey (Kiffer Finzi), Charles Dance (Derek du Pré), Celia Imrie (Iris du Pré), Rupert Penry-Jones (Piers du Pré).**

Eye-grabbing performances from Emily Watson and Rachel Griffiths as celebrated British cellist Jacqueline du Pré and her older sister, Hilary, distinguish this ambitious but flawed

---

**... May 28 ...**

Phil Hartman killed in murder-suicide by wife at age 49.

biography. Debut feature from Anand Tucker is aimed at the *Shine* audience, and the often powerful and ultimately tragic story of a troubled musical genius who died at 42 of multiple sclerosis provoked mixed reactions in Venice. The film is told mostly from Hilary's perspective and then, without warning, shifts into flashback to reveal the story from Jackie's p.o.v. It's a bold and ambitious structure.

Children of an unworldly father and a fiercely dedicated, musical mother, the women grew up in a house full of music. Hilary learns the flute; Jackie the cello. After a humiliating experience at the BBC, Jackie is told she must be as good as her sister if she's to continue playing duets. Soon she's wowing audiences with her virtuoso, though somewhat eccentric, playing. Hilary fails her flute exam at the Royal Academy and marries ebullient conductor Kiffer Finzi, while Jackie marries Daniel Barenboim, a gifted Jewish-Argentine musician. Some years later, a distraught Jackie turns up at her sister's cottage and asks to stay. At this point, the film shifts to Jackie's perspective – lonely nights on tour in foreign cities, unable to speak the language; her meeting with Daniel; and her increasing unhappiness, to the point at which she hates even her beloved cello.

U.S. release: Dec. 30                    U.S. B.O.: $50,000

### Hi-Life

A Lions Gate Films release of a Silverman production, in association with Gun for Hire Films. Produced by Erica Spellman-Silverman. Directed, written by Roger Hedden. Camera, John Thomas; editor, Tom McArdle; music, David Lawrence; production design, Sharon Lomofsky; costume design, Isis Mussenden. Reviewed at Mill Valley Festival, Oct. 7. Running time: 82 mins.
**Katrin Cartlidge (April), Charles Durning (Fatty), Daryl Hannah (Maggie), Moira Kelly (Susan), Peter Reigert (Miner), Campbell Scott (Ray), Eric Stoltz (Jimmy), Anne DeSalvo (Sherry).**
One night around Christmastime finds various friends and mere passers-by embroiled in a wild-goose chase for money around the Upper West Side, instigated by out-of-work actor Jimmy, whom many of them detest. He owes $900 to local bookie Fatty and might get a limb broken if he doesn't pony up. To get the cash fast, he's told long-suffering girlfriend Susan that he needs it to fund an emergency abortion for gold-digging sis Maggie.

A solid cast of upscale-indie stalwarts makes the time pass painlessly enough in *Hi-Life*, a Manhattan-set ensemble piece. Like writer-turned-helmer Roger Hedden's prior produced screenplays, this relationship comedy is talky, amiable, and no great shakes. Given that this particular genre has long since lost novelty appeal, middling pic looks to eke out just minor arthouse and ancillary returns.

U.S. release: Dec. 4                    U.S. B.O.: $50,000

### The Hitman (Satsau Chi Wong) (Hong Kong)

A Flea Market production, for Win's Entertainment/China Star Entertainment Group. Produced by Charles Heung. Directed by Tung Wai. Screenplay, Chan Hing-kar, Vincent Kuk, Cheng Kam-fu. Camera, Arthur Wong; editor, Cheung Ka-fai; music, T. TWO; art director, Bill Lui; costumes, Shirley Chan; action directors, Tung, Ku Huan-chiu, Ling Chi-wah, Chan Siu-wah. Reviewed on videodisc, London, Aug. 2. Running time: 103 mins.

Jet Li (Fu), Eric Tsang (Ngok Lo), Simon Yam (Kwan), Gigi Leung (Kiki), Keiji Sato (Eiji).
Jet Li is showcased to good effect in *The Hitman*, an above-average blend of comedy and action. Cast in a role he's honed to perfection – the seemingly dumb mainlander manipulated by wiseacre Hongkies – Li plays well against local comic Eric Tsang. After the assassination in Hong Kong of a Japanese businessman, various parties congregate at a meeting held by the overseers of the dead man's Revenge Fund, a $100 million pot set up to find his killer. Fu, a penniless mainlander, stumbles into the session and is taken under the wing of Ngok Lo, a fast-talking agent for hired guns who proposes Fu track down the killer. Fu and Ngok have to stay one step ahead of Eiji, son of the dead businessman, who is also after the assassin. Pic took a reasonable HK$10 million ($1.5 million) locally off its spring release.
Int'l release: April 4                    Int'l B.O.: $3.5 million

### Hold You Tight (Yu Failok Yu Dolok) (Hong Kong)

A Golden Harvest presentation of a Kwan's Creation Workshop production. Produced by Raymond Chow. Directed by Stanley Kwan. Screenplay, Jimmy Ngai, based on a story by Elmond Yeung. Camera, Kwan Pun-leung; editor, Maurice Li; music, Yu Yat-yiu, Keith Leung; production design, Bruce Yu. Reviewed at Berlin Festival, Feb. 15. Running time: 93 mins.
**Chingmy Yau (Moon/Rosa Gao), Sunny Chan (Fung-wai), Eric Tsang (Tong), Ko Yu-lun (Dou-jie), Tony Rayns (Gay Englishman).**
(Cantonese and Mandarin dialog)
Frustratingly diffuse and often perversely contrary, Hong Kong helmer Stanley Kwan's *Hold You Tight* is an interesting idea handicapped by lack of rigor in script and direction. An examination of sexual identity told through the intertwined stories of five people, pic holds a whole lot of promise, but jumps the rails in its second half. Kwan's name is likely to spark some foreign interest, but theatrical sales in major territories look to be on the meager side.

Though purportedly about many shades of sexual orientation, *Tight* is at heart about male homosexuality, and its widest audience will be from that demographic. Best part of the film is the first half, in which Kwan and debuting scripter Jimmy Ngai construct an engrossing, multilayered fresco of sexual desire, both straight and gay.
Int'l release: Feb. 5                    Int'l B.O.: $1 million

### The Hole (Dong) (Taiwan-France)

An Arc Light Films (Taipei)/Haut et Court (Paris) co-production, in association with China Television, Central Motion Picture Corp., La Sept Arte. Produced by Peggy Chiao, Carole Scotta, Caroline Benjo. Directed by Tsai Ming-liang. Screenplay, Yang Ping-ying, Tsai. Camera, Liao Peng-jung; editor, Hsiao Ju-kuan; production designer, Lee Pao-lin; costume designer, Chow Min. Reviewed at Cannes Festival, May 15. Running time: 93 mins.
**Yang Kuei-mei (Woman Downstairs), Lee Kang-sheng (Man Upstairs), Miao Tien (Shopper), Tong Hsiang-chu (The Plumber).**
Tsai Ming-liang, the prodigiously talented Taiwanese filmmaker, has come up with an eerie, dank, claustrophobic mood piece with *The Hole*. This end-of-the-millennium story started out as a contribution to a French TV series of one-hour films about the turn of the century. Although Tsai's bold vision

---

**... May 29 ...**
Kristin Scott Thomas inks to star in Sydney Pollack's romantic drama
**Random Hearts** for Col.

pays off in a sublime conclusion, film's minimalist dramatics make this a marginal commercial entity internationally. Virtually a two-hander, pic concentrates on a man and a woman who live in identical apartments in a run-down building in a quarantined area. Taipei is in the grip of panic. After days of endless rain, some kind of epidemic is afflicting the city, perhaps borne by cockroaches.

Int'l release: June 12     Int'l B.O.: $200,000

## Hollywoodism: Jews, Movies, And The American Dream (Docu, Canada)

An Associated Producers presentation of a Halpern/Jacobovici production, in association with Canadian Broadcasting Corp., A&E Network, Channel 4. Produced by Elliott Halpern, Simcha Jacobovici. Directed, written by Simcha Jacobovici, based on the book *An Empire of Their Own: How the Jews Invented Hollywood* by Neal Gabler. Camera, Mark MacKay; editor, Reid Dennison; music, Aaron Davis, John Lang; creative consultant, Stuart Samuels. Reviewed at Berlin Festival, Feb. 12. Running time: 98 mins.

**Narrator: R.H. Thomson.**

Hold that dream. Though the facts have always been hiding in plain sight, *Hollywoodism: Jews, Movies, and the American Dream* connects the dots in persuasive ways. Using both archival material and clips from classic pics, plus interviews with relatives of long-dead moguls, this fascinating though sometimes oversimplified item by documaker Simcha Jacobovici shows how that dream, as proselytized by Tinseltown, was in fact the creation of a bunch of Jewish immigrants. Pic's argument should score well in both festival and small-screen outings.

The feature-length docu largely focuses on six key moguls from the Golden Age of Hollywood, some of whom came from towns within a few miles of one another: Carl Laemmle (founder of Universal) from Germany, Harry Warner and Sam Goldwyn from Poland, William Fox and Adolph Zukor (Paramount) from Hungary, and Louis B. Mayer from Russia.

## Holy Man

A Buena Vista release of a Touchstone Pictures presentation, in association with Caravan Pictures. Produced by Roger Birnbaum, Stephen Herek. Directed by Herek. Screenplay, Tom Schulman. Camera, Adrian Biddle; editor, Trudy Ship; music, Alan Silvestri; production design, Andrew McAlpine; costume design, Aggie Guerard Rodgers. Reviewed at Beverly Connection, L.A., Oct. 6. MPAA Rating: PG. Running time: 114 mins.

**Eddie Murphy (G.), Jeff Goldblum (Ricky Hayman), Kelly Preston (Kate Newell), Robert Loggia (John McBainbridge), Jon Cryer (Barry), Eric McCormack (Scott Hawkes), and Morgan Fairchild, Nino Cerruti as themselves.**

Eddie Murphy has been called many things in the course of his career but never a "Holy Man." So it's a bit of a surprise to see him cast as a genuine religious guru, albeit one with an appreciation for the humor of life. However, his winning performance cannot salvage a muddled script that descends into 100% pure corn. Pic should score strong opening numbers but is likely to stumble because its marketing campaign runs counter to the film's serious underpinnings and the fact that Murphy actually has the secondary role.

Story's focus is Ricky Hayman (Jeff Goldblum), programmer for Good Buy Shopping Network. As the film opens, the new boss has given Ricky an ultimatum to outfit the station with a distinctive image and boost sales within 14 days. Opportunity takes the form of G. (Murphy), a man on a spiritual pilgrimage who stops to lend a hand when Ricky and the station's new marketing director Kate (Kelly Preston) are side-tracked on the freeway with a flat tire. A deal is struck and G. goes on the air. Ignoring the cue cards, he talks to the audience about things that really matter, which don't include the products for sale. Ratings go up and sales balloon. The combination of getting the straight goods on life and the razzle dazzle of television hucksterism is just the formula to relieve people of their daily worries and cash.

U.S. release: Oct. 9     U.S. B.O.: $12 million
Int'l release: Nov. 5     Int'l B.O.: $2.5 million

## Home Alone 3

A 20th Century Fox release of a John Hughes production. Produced by Hughes, Hilton Green. Directed by Raja Gosnell. Screenplay, John Hughes. Camera, Julio Macat; editors, Bruce Green, Malcolm Campbell, David Rennie; music, Nick Glennie-Smith; production design, Henry Bumstead; costume design, Jodie Tillen; stunt coordinators, R.A. Rondell, Freddie Hice. Reviewed at AMC Studio 30, Houston, Dec. 3, 1997. MPAA Rating: PG. Running time: 102 mins.

**Alex D. Linz (Alex), Olek Krupa (Beaupre), Rya Kihlstedt (Alice), Lenny Von Dohlen (Jernigan), David Thornton (Unger), Haviland Morris (Karen), Kevin Kilner (Jack), Marian Seldes (Mrs. Hess).**

Five years after proving he could make box-office lightning strike twice, John Hughes has revived his popular franchise. This time, however, the law of diminishing returns is evident. *Home Alone 3* essentially is a remake of the first outing, with a new protagonist, slightly craftier villains – and much more brutal comic mayhem. By now the formula is too flat, and the premise too familiar, to have real appeal. The brand name may be enough to generate respectable returns during the holiday season, but pic likely won't find its biggest audience until it reaches vid-store shelves.

Alex D. Linz plays Alex Pruitt, a crafty youngster who defends his suburban Chicago home from unwelcome visitors. Four high-tech industrial spies obtain a top-secret computer chip for missile-guidance systems. They hide it in a remote-control toy car to elude airport security en route to Hong Kong. But a baggage mix-up puts it in the hands of grumpy old Mrs. Hess, who gives it to neighbor Alex just before the spies arrive. The baddies set out to burglarize each home on the street, hoping to find the toy before their North Korean client runs out of patience. Alex manages to rig all manner of cunning booby traps in and around his house, to trip, hobble, pummel, electrocute, and otherwise humiliate the supposedly superior spies.

U.S. release: Dec. 12, 1997     U.S. B.O.: $31 million
Int'l release: Dec. 19, 1997     Int'l B.O.: $36 million

## Home Fries

A Warner Bros. release of a Mark Johnson/Baltimore Pictures/Kasdan Pictures production. Produced by Johnson, Barry Levinson, Lawrence Kasdan, Charles Newirth. Directed by Dean Parisot. Screenplay, Vince Gilligan. Camera, Jerzy Zielinski; editor, Nicholas C. Smith; music, Rachel Portman; production design, Barry Robison; costume design, Jill Ohanneson. Reviewed at Toronto Festival, Sept. 17. Running time: 93 mins.

---

**... May 30 ...**

Walt Disney's daughter and grandchildren are prepping to sell seven TV stations amassed by the late animation king himself for an amount estimated at $200 million.

Drew Barrymore (Sally Jackson), Luke Wilson (Dorian Lever), Catherine O'Hara (Mrs. Lever), Jake Busey (Angus Lever), Shelley Duvall (Mrs. Jackson), Kim Robillard (Billy), Daryl Mitchell (Roy).

You wouldn't know it from the title or ads, but *Home Fries*, starring Drew Barrymore, is a black comedy about a latter-day Ma Barker who cajoles her grown boys into killing their philandering stepdad. Gonzo elements are kept to a minimum in favor of more macabre moments that should leave target audience scratching its collective head. Barrymore's profile will get this one open, but nasty tone and zero chemistry between star and leading man, Luke Wilson, will mean fast-food shelf life.

Setup has weekend warrior helicopter pilots Dorian and Angus strafing the woods at night for a lone man. The guy is literally scared stiff. The fly-by victim was also the father of Barrymore's baby. In this landslide of contrivance and coincidence, it turns out the helicopter frequency was picked up at the hamburger drive-thru where Barrymore works. Angus decides that Dorian should infiltrate the eatery as a new employee and figure out who knows what. As Dorian falls for Sally, Mama Lever and wild-eyed Angus plot further mayhem.

U.S. release: Nov. 25          U.S. B.O.: $10 million

## Homegrown

A Sony Pictures Entertainment release of a TriStar Pictures presentation, in association with Lakeshore Entertainment of a Rollercoaster Films production. Produced by Jason Clark. Directed by Stephen Gyllenhaal. Screenplay, Nicholas Kazan, Gyllenhaal; story by Jonah Raskin, Gyllenhaal. Camera, Greg Gardiner; editor, Michael Jablow; music, Trevor Rabin; production designer, Richard Sherman; costume designer, Joseph Porro. Reviewed at Sony Pictures, Culver City, April 15. MPAA Rating: R. Running time: 101 mins.

Billy Bob Thornton (Jack Madsen), Hank Azaria (Carter), Kelly Lynch (Lucy), Ryan Phillippe (Harlan), Jon Bon Jovi (Danny), John Lithgow (Malcolm/Robert Stockman)

Somewhere in the hinterlands of Northern California, there's a community of marijuana sharecroppers co-existing with local authorities and handsomely propping up the area's economy. With talk of the legalization of marijuana a subject of current debate, *Homegrown* would appear a natural film subject. However, the picture steers clear of overt politics, opting for a droll tone that puts the yarn of illegal growing and selling into the leagues of muted outlawism that characterized such vintage fare as *Beat the Devil* and *The Gang That Couldn't Shoot Straight*. The difficulty with this approach is that it needs to hit a precise tone that's often a result of serendipity rather than design. In this instance, the shaggy-dog tale renders more tin than tune and will result in tepid theatrical prospects. Best potential lies down the line in pay TV and video.

U.S. release: April 17          U.S. B.O.: $300,000

## Hope Floats

A 20th Century Fox release of a Lynda Obst production, in association with Fortis Films. Produced by Obst. Directed by Forest Whitaker. Screenplay, Steven Rogers. Camera, Caleb Deschanel; editor, Richard Chew; music, Dave Grusin; production designer, Larry Fulton; costume designer, Susie DeSanto. Reviewed at 20th Century Fox Studios, L.A., May 1. MPAA Rating: PG-13. Running time: 114 mins.

Sandra Bullock (Birdee Pruitt), Harry Connick, Jr. (Justin Matisse), Gena Rowlands (Ramona Calvert), Mae Whitman (Bernice Pruitt), Michael Pare (Bill Pruitt), Kathy Najimy (Toni Post).

*Hope Floats* doesn't. A dreadfully dull, completely conventional story of a young wife's recuperation from being dumped, this is a by-the-numbers bit of emotional calculation without an original or offbeat idea. Nonetheless, pic could stir up some business with a female audience. Birdee learns her best friend is bedding her husband on a national trash TV show and repairs with her young daughter to her hometown in rural Texas. Pic crawls along in advancing the story towards a new romance.

U.S. release: May 29          U.S. B.O.: $60 million
Int'l release: Sept. 11       Int'l B.O.: $14 million

## The Horse Whisperer

A Buena Vista release of a Touchstone Pictures presentation of a Wildwood Enterprises production. Produced by Robert Redford, Patrick Markey. Directed by Redford. Screenplay, Eric Roth, Richard LaGravenese, based on the novel by Nicholas Evans. Camera, Robert Richardson; editors, Tom Rolf, Freeman Davies, Hank Corwin; music, Thomas Newman; production designer, Jon Hutman; costume designer, Judy L. Ruskin; equine technical adviser, Buck Brannaman. Reviewed at Harmony Gold, L.A., April 29. MPAA Rating: PG-13. Running time: 168 mins.

Robert Redford (Tom Booker), Kristin Scott Thomas (Annie MacLean), Sam Neill (Robert MacLean), Dianne Wiest (Diane Booker), Scarlett Johansson (Grace MacLean), Chris Cooper (Frank Booker), Cherry Jones (Liz Hammond).

In *The Horse Whisperer*, Robert Redford has made an exquisitely crafted, morally, and thematically mature picture out of Nicholas Evans' schematic melodrama about a modern cowboy who brings about the physical and spiritual regeneration of a teenage girl and her horse after they suffer crippling injuries. Audience response to this emotionally powerful work should be strong, particularly among women, spelling excellent mainstream B.O. prospects. However, there are certain clouds on the horizon that could prevent it from realizing its theoretical full commercial potential, most notably its near-three-hour running time and an elimination of the book's sexual element that may perplex and frustrate fans of the novel.

U.S. release: May 15          U.S. B.O.: $75 million
Int'l release: June 4         Int'l B.O.: $109 million

## How Stella Got Her Groove Back

A 20th Century Fox release of a Deborah Schindler production. Produced by Schindler. Directed by Kevin Rodney Sullivan. Screenplay, Terry McMillan, Ron Bass, based on the novel by McMillan. Camera, Jeffrey Jur; editor, George Bowers; music, Michel Colombier; production design, Chester Kaczenski; costume design, Ruth E. Carter. Reviewed at the Avco Cinema, L.A., Aug. 4. MPAA Rating: R. Running time: 124 mins.

Angela Bassett (Stella), Taye Diggs (Winston Shakespeare), Regina King (Vanessa), Whoopi Goldberg (Delilah), Suzzanne Douglas (Angela), Michael J. Pagan (Quincy), Sicily (Chantel), Carl Lumbly (Judge Boyle).

All the complaints about the recent trend of older man–younger woman films can stop now that *How Stella Got Her Groove Back* is upon us. Outrageously glossy and sometimes quite funny, this fantasy-driven romance about a woman who rediscovers her sexual self is choppy, poorly structured, and unconvincing, but still holds strong appeal for precisely the same audience that made Fox's previous Terry McMillan adaptation, Waiting to Exhale, a surprise hit in 1995. This time, though, it won't be such a surprise. Slick production is an ideal girls-night-out attraction, as well as sure-fire date fare.

Stella puts a contempo black spin on the Hollywood "women's picture", featuring an uncommonly attractive character discovering passion. Stella is a stunning, perfectly fit, high-powered 40-year-old San Francisco stockbroker with a well-behaved 11-year-old son. She's totally realized – except, natch, for her love life. Stella goes on a Jamaican vacation with friend Delilah, who encourages her to let go, something she's been considering after meeting a strikingly handsome local man. Winston is 20 years old, but is persistent enough to get his foot in the slight opening in the door of Stella's resolve, and the two beautiful people inevitably end up between the sheets in Stella's fancy bungalow with its resplendent view.

| | |
|---|---|
| U.S. release: Aug. 14 | U.S. B.O.: $37.5 million |
| Int'l release: Nov. 19 | Int'l B.O.: $750,000 |

## How To Make The Cruelest Month

A Fugue State/Magnet Prods presentation. Produced by Alison Dickey, Mark Lipson. Directed, written by Kip Koenig. Camera, Julian Whatley; editor, Chris Figler; music, Jeff Martin; production design, Jodi Ginnever; costume design, Agnes NaDene Baddoo, Dalhia Schuette. Reviewed at Sundance Festival, Jan. 19. Running time: 99 mins.
**Clea DuVall (Bell Bryant), Gabriel Mann (Leonard Crane), John David Souther (Uncle Jerry), Mary Kay Place (Mary Bryant), Marianne Jean-Baptiste (Christina Parks), Dennis Haysbert (Manhattan Parks).**
Though brimming with fresh ideas, zany humor, and offbeat characters, the comic How to Make the Cruelest Month also displays the sheer audacity, messy structure, and lack of discipline that often characterize first features. Writer-director Kip Koenig exhibits a remarkable sensitivity to the raw energy and sexual and moral confusion of American youngsters today. Drastic cuts would improve theatrical prospects for a picture that holds appeal for the twentysomething crowd. Almost a female version of the young Woody Allen screen character, protagonist is Bell (Clea DuVall), a bright, neurotic, fast-talking, sexually confused woman.

## How the War Started on my Island (Kako Je Paceo Rat Na Mom Otuko) (Croatia)

An HRT (Croatian Television) production. Produced by Ivan Mudrinic. Directed by Vinko Bresan. Screenplay, Ivo Bresan. Camera, Zivko Zalar; editor, Sandra Botica Bresan; music, Mate Matisic; production designer; Ivica Trpcic; costume designer, Vanda Ninic. Reviewed at Seattle Festival, June 9. Running time: 97 mins.
**With: Vlatko Dulic (Blaz), Ljubomir Kerekes (Aleksa), Ivan Brkic, Predrag Vuovic-Predjo, Matija Prskalo (Aleksa's wife), Ivica Vidovic.**
Father-son team of Ivo and Vinko Bresan (Dad writes, offspring directs) combines gritty political humor and box-office savvy: How the War Started on My Island is the top-grossing movie in the young Croatian republic, even beating out Independence Day. Depiction of outsize meeting of

wills in early days of Yugoslav breakup also won several top prizes at Croatia's Pula fest in 1996, and looks like a sure winner on fest trail.

Reality-based comic tale concerns a lone Yugoslav army outpost on a small Adriatic island when Croatia suddenly declares independence. Locals want the Serb-led army out – preferably in time for the noon ferry – and to speed things up, they've set up a stage near the compound's perimeter, from which a steady stream of noisy talkers, bad rock bands, and even worse poets attempt to harangue beleaguered camp commander Aleksa into peaceful surrender.

## Hurlyburly

A Fine Line release of a Storm Entertainment production. Produced by Anthony Drazan, Richard Gladstein, David Hamburger. Directed by Drazan. Screenplay, David Rabe, based on his play. Camera, Gu Changwei; editor, Dylan Tichenor; music, David Baerwald, Steve Lindsey; production design, Michael Haller; costume design, Mary Claire Hannan. Reviewed at Venice Festival, Sept. 10. Running time: 122 mins.
**Sean Penn (Eddie), Kevin Spacey (Mickey), Robin Wright-Penn (Darlene), Chazz Palminteri (Phil), Garry Shandling (Artie), Anna Paquin (Donna), Meg Ryan (Bonnie).**
A trio of morally bankrupt men nest in a house in the Hollywood Hills. Eddie and Mickey are casting agents and Phil is an out-of-work actor. Eddie is almost permanently wired on drugs; Mickey dryly disapproves of Eddie's habits and Phil's desperate behavior but is too reptilian really to care. The women are only marginally less irredeemable, but the raw deal they get from the men makes them a little more sympathetic. Hurlyburly is two long hours with three self-absorbed misogynists and the articulate women who allow these guys to treat them like dirt. David Rabe's 1984 play about denizens of heartless Hollywood trying to fathom their relationships and their world may have worked in a stylized stage setting. But up close, it is a punishing talkfest that functions purely as a performance piece. Distrib faces an uphill task in finding more than a niche audience for this dark, cynical film.
U.S. release: Dec. 25          U.S. B.O.: $300,000

## Hush

A Sony Pictures Entertainment release of a TriStar Pictures presentation of a Douglas Wick production. Produced by Wick. Directed by Jonathan Darby. Screenplay, Darby, Jane Rusconi; story by Darby. Camera, Andrew Dunn; editors, Dan Rae, Lynzee Klingman, Robert Leighton; music, Christopher Young; production design, Thomas A. Walsh, Michael Johnston; costume design, Ann Roth; casting, Heidi Levitt. Reviewed at Sony Studios, Culver City, March 3. MPAA Rating: PG-13. Running time: 95 mins.
**Jessica Lange (Martha Baring), Gwyneth Paltrow (Helen), Johnathon Schaech (Jackson Baring), Nina Foch (Alice Baring), Debi Mazar (Lisa), Hal Holbrook (Dr. Hill).**
Jackson Baring brings his live-in girlfriend Helen home for Christmas to meet his mother Martha, a chatty, somewhat overbearing widow who clearly would like nothing more than for her only child to live with her in perennial togetherness at their grand estate.

A trashy melodramatic thriller about an evil mom preying upon her vulnerable pregnant daughter-in-law, Hush is gussied up by its classy distaff cast members, but remains trashy all the same. Grossly implausible, this risible concoction nonetheless manipulates emotions relating to family ties, motherhood, and babies in ways that could induce the vaunted young female audience to overlook its deficiencies and turn out in sizable numbers initially.

U.S. release: March 6 U.S. B.O.: $13.5 million
Int'l release: March 26 Int'l B.O.: $5.5 million

## I.D. (Pièces D'Identités) (Belgium-France-Congo)

A Films Sud, Videocam (Belgium)/Petrouchka Films (France)/Sol'oeil Films (Congo) production. Produced by Mweze Ngangura. Directed, written by Ngangura. Camera, Jacques Besse; editors, France Duez, Ingrid Ralet; music, Jean-Louis Daulne, Papa Wemba; art director, Andre Fonsny; costumes, Agnes Dubois. Reviewed at Toronto Festival, Sept. 13, 1998. Running time: 96 mins.
Gerard Essomba (Mani Kongo), Herbert Flack (Jefke Schengen), Jean-Louis Daulne (Chaka-Jo), Dominique Mesa (Mwana-Mwata), David Steegen (Van Loo), Cecilia Kankonda (Safi). (French and Wolof dialog)
Making a belated but assured return to features since writing and co-helming La vie est belle with Benoît Lamy, Congolese filmer Mweze Ngangura scores big with I.D., a rich multicultural romp involving a Congolese king and diverse denizens of an ethnic enclave in contempo Brussels. Pic has major crossover potential for specialized distribs. Decked out in the regal trappings of his coronation – the "identity pieces" of the movie's original title – Mani Kongo, King of the Bakongo, returns to Brussels in search of the daughter, Mwana-Mwata, he left behind to pursue her studies on a brief visit long ago. Unbeknownst to him, she's been in prison because of some unexplained connection with pimp Viva-Wa-Viva, but is now dating mulatto taxi driver Chaka-Jo, who happened to pick up her dad at the airport and has since befriended him.

## The Idiots (Idioterne) (Denmark)

An October Films release of a Zentropa Entertainments2 ApS/DRTV/Danish Broadcasting Corp. production. Produced by Vibeke Windelov. Directed, written by Lars von Trier. Camera, von Trier; editor, Molly Malene Stensgaard. Reviewed at Cannes Festival, May 20. Running time: 115 mins.
Bodil Jorgensen (Karen), Jens Albinus (Stoffer), Louise Hassing (Susanne), Troels Lyby (Henrik), Nikolaj Lie Kaas (Jeppe), Henrik Prip (Ped), Luis Mesonero (Miguel).
Never one to deal in the commonplace, Lars von Trier cooks up perhaps his most eccentric offering yet, exploring notions of normalcy, constraining behavioral codes, and conditioned emotional responses in The Idiots. This unclassifiable drama with frequent comic overtones centers on a commune whose residents shrug off middle-class apathy by nurturing their "inner idiot."

Somewhat ambling, the film nonetheless is studded with moments of dramatic intensity audiences have come to expect from the Danish iconoclast. But while his name will ensure the release is seen in most territories, the obscure central thesis and raw approach likely will confine it to the extreme high end of the arthouse market. Whether von Trier is a prankster or a visionary is open to debate, but The Idiots – which he wrote in four days – is a disturbing, provocative film that at the very least provides further proof he is a true original playing strictly by his own rules.

Int'l release: July 17 Int'l B.O.: $1.5 million

## I Got The Hook-Up

A Dimension Films release of a No Limit Films and Priority Films presentation of a Shooting Stars Pictures production. Produced by Jonathan Heuer. Directed by Michael Martin. Screenplay, Master P, from a story by Master P, Carrie Mingo, Leroy Douglas. Camera, Antonio Calvache; editor, T. Davis Binns; music, Tommy Coster, Brad Fairman; production designer, Michael Pearce; costume designer, Jhane Isaacs. Reviewed at AMC Meyer Park, Houston, Texas, May 28. MPAA rating: R. Running time: 93 mins.
Master P (Black), A.J. Johnson (Blue), Gretchen Palmer (Sweet Lorraine), Frantz Turner (Dalton), Tommy "Tiny" Lister Jr. (T-Lay), Anthony Boswell (Little Brother), Helen Martin (Grandmother), Ice Cube (Gun Runner).
Rap star and recording mogul Master P gets little comic mileage from his first star vehicle, a raucous but witless farce called I Got the Hook-Up. Little more than a loosely connected string of sketch-comedy episodes, pic will click only with the least demanding of inner-city ticket buyers. Master P, who also served as screenwriter and exec producer, co-stars with stand-up comic A.J. Johnson as a pair of South-Central L.A. scam artists who operate a "shopping center" from a van in a vacant lot. Most of the time they deal in boom boxes and defective TV sets. But when a van driver mistakenly delivers a shipment of cell phones to their marketplace, they become slightly more upscale entrepreneurs.
U.S. release: May 27 U.S. B.O.: $10.5 million

## I'll Be Home For Christmas

A Buena Vista release of a Walt Disney Pictures presentation of a Mandeville Films production. Produced by David Hoberman, Tracey Trench. Directed by Arlene Sanford. Screenplay, Harris Goldberg, Tom Nursall, story by Michael Allin. Camera, Hiro Narita; editor, Anita Brandt-Burgoyne; music, John Debney; production design, Cynthia Charette; costume design, Maya Mani. Reviewed at Avco Cinemas, L.A., Nov. 7. MPAA rating: PG. Running time: 85 mins.
Jonathan Taylor Thomas (Jake), Jessica Biel (Allie), Adam LaVorgna (Eddie), Gary Cole (Jake's Dad), Eve Gordon (Carolyn), Lauren Maltby (Tracey), Andrew Lauer (Nolan).
With I'll Be Home for Christmas, Disney is clearly zeroing in on the same holiday B.O. territory it mined successfully with the Tim Allen starrer The Santa Clause. This time, the studio is stuffing its Christmas stocking with a blandly appealing family comedy. Lacking the high concept and broad-based appeal of the earler blockbuster, new item will do solid-to-middling B.O., but Santa won't break his back hauling in the grosses.

Jake is a California college student with a locker full of schemes and a long-suffering girlfriend, Allie. Though his father had sent him money for a trip home, Jake instead uses it to buy tickets to Mexico. Only when Dad bribes Jake with a long-coveted Porsche does he agree to fly back to New York with Allie at his side. But there's a catch: Jake must make it home by 6 p.m. Christmas Eve or give up the car. However, when one of Jake's money-making schemes goes awry, several disgruntled school bullies beat him up to teach him a lesson. Jake awakens in the desert dazed and disoriented with a Santa Claus suit glued to his body and no ATM or cell phone in sight. And the clock is ticking: He has just over 48 hours in which to get home.
U.S. release: Nov. 13 U.S. B.O.: $12 million
Int'l release: Dec. 17 Int'l B.O.: $1.3 million

## Illuminata

An Overseas Filmgroup presentation of a GreenStreet Films production. Produced by John Penotti, John Turturro. Directed by Turturro. Screenplay, Brandon Cole, Turturro, based on Cole's stage play. Camera, Harris Savides; editor, Michael Berenbaum; music, William Bolcom, Arnold Black; production designer, Robin Standefer; costume designer, Donna Zakowska. Reviewed at Cannes Festival, May 21. Running time: 120 mins.
**John Turturro (Tuccio), Katherine Borowitz (Rachel), Christopher Walken (Bevalaqua), Susan Sarandon (Celimene), Beverly D'Angelo (Astergourd), Bill Irwin (Marco), Rufus Sewell (Dominique), Georgina Cates (Simone), Ben Gazzara (Flavio), Donal McCann (Pallenchio).**

John Turturro's sophomore effort, *Illuminata*, is an audacious, structurally messy film about a tightly knit acting troupe in turn-of-the century New York. This meditation on love – its compromises, imperfections, sacrifices, and rewards – takes on a note as Turturro and his wife, actress Katherine Borowitz, address intimate issues that affect a marriage. A colorful, illustrious cast should help secure theatrical distribution Stateside, though this film, which vacillates quite a bit before finding its emotional center, will sharply divide critics. A rather weak, rambling beginning introduces the large ensemble of players. Turturro plays Tuccio, the ambitious resident playwright anxious to stage his new play, *Illuminata*.
Int'l release: Nov. 6 — Int'l B.O.: $200,000

## I Married a Strange Person

An Italtoons production. Produced by Bill Plympton. Directed, written, animated by Bill Plympton. Camera, John Donnelly; editor, Anthony Arcidi; production design, Signe Baumane; backgrounds, Greg Pair, Graham Blyth; music, Maureen McElheron. Reviewed at Toronto Festival, Sept. 8, 1997. Running time: 73 mins.
**Voices: Charis Michaelson, Tom Larson, Richard Spore, Toni Rossi, J.B. Adams, John Russo.**

Imagine Tex Avery on acid, and you're ready for Bill Plympton's *I Married a Strange Person*, an exuberantly twisted fantasy that could click with hip audiences in urban markets. There is a plot, of sorts, in the surreal lunacy, though Plympton never allows it to impede his proclivity for letting his imagination run riot. Grant develops a small but potent lobe on the back of his neck after being zapped by a strange energy source. Thanks to it, he's able to make any of his fantasies come true..
U.S. release: Aug. 28 — U.S. B.O.: $200,000

## I'm Losing You

A Lions Gate Films presentation of a Killer Films production. Produced by Pamela Koffler, Christine Vachon. Directed, written by Bruce Wagner, based on his novel. Camera, Rob Sweeney; editor, Janice Hampton; music, Daniel Catan; production design, Richard Sherman; costume design, Theadora Van Runkle. Reviewed at Telluride Festival, Sept. 3. Running time: 102 mins.
**Rosanna Arquette (Rachel Krohn), Amanda Donohoe (Mona Deware), Buck Henry (Philip Dragom), Salome Jens (Diantha Krohn), Frank Langella (Perry Needham Krohn), Andrew McCarthy (Bertie Krohn), Elizabeth Perkins (Aubrey), Gina Gershon (Lidia), Ed Begley, Jr. (Zev).**

"I'm death warmed over. You're death warming up," a dying AIDS patient advises a Stage 4 cancer victim in *I'm Losing You*, and the exchange sums up the excessive morbidity that consumes the piece. Well written and displaying a certain visual elegance and tonal control, novelist and professional Hollywood chronicler Bruce Wagner's directorial debut shows some promise, but is too grim by half to stand a chance with anything other than a specialized public.

Wealthy, seemingly fit, TV producer Perry Krohn learns, on the verge of his sixtieth birthday, that he stands a 90% chance of dying of inoperable cancer within the year. His psychiatrist wife takes the news poorly, and Perry decides to postpone telling his son, Bertie, a has-been actor and adopted daughter Rachel. These characters, and seemingly everyone in their orbit, are saddled with extreme sorrows and conflicts of nearly biblical proportions. The accidental death of a character, which occurs shortly, is not only contrived, but irrevocably cloaks the film in an all-pervasive sense of doom. Wagner hasn't sufficiently connected his nearly single-minded concentration on these matters to other aspects of society or, more important, to a broader philosophical/religious view of life and death to make his obsession pay off in any meaningful or resonant way.

## The Impostors

A Fox Searchlight release of a First Cold Press production. Produced by Beth Alexander, Stanley Tucci. Directed, written by Tucci. Camera, Ken Kelsch; editor, Suzy Elmiger; music, Gary DeMichele; production designer, Andrew Jackness; costume designer, Juliet Polcsa. Reviewed at Cannes Festival, May 18. Running time: 101 mins.
**Oliver Platt (Maurice), Stanley Tucci (Arthur), Elizabeth Bracco (Pancetta Leaky), Steve Buscemi (Happy Franks), Billy Connolly (Sparks), Hope Davis (Emily), Dana Ivey (Mrs. Essendine), Alfred Molina (Jeremy Burton), Isabella Rossellini (The Queen), Campbell Scott (Meistrich), Tony Shalhoub (First Mate), Lili Taylor (Lily).**

The farcical *The Impostors* begins on a high of comic giddiness, but the air all too quickly seeps out of its balloon. Acted by a splendid cast with a degree of wit and sophistication that is in unfortunately short supply in the script, Stanley Tucci's solo directorial outing works overtime to replicate the fun of 1930s Hollywood comedies, but serves to demonstrate that the classics are hard to match. Fox Searchlight's release looks like a passable specialized commercial item at best.

Maurice and Arthur are struggling actors in New York during the Depression. A drunken insult to a ham actor results in a chase in which the two men take refuge in a box that is placed on board a luxury liner sailing to France. Disguised as stewards, they spend the cruise avoiding the actor and a series of on-board antic dramas from the large "Ship of Fools" cast of characters.
U.S. release: Oct. 2 — U.S. B.O.: $2.2 million

## In God's Hands

A Sony Pictures Entertainment release of a TriStar Pictures presentation of a Triumph Films production. Produced by Tom Stern. Directed by Zalman King. Screenplay, King, Matt George. Camera, John Aronson; special water photography, Sonny Miller; editors, James Gavin Bedford, Joe Shugart; music, Paradise; production designers, Marc Greville-Mason, Paul Holt; costume designer, Jolie Anna Andreatta. Reviewed at Sony, Culver City, April 21. MPAA rating: PG-13. Running time: 96 mins.
**Patrick Shane Dorian (Shane), Matt George (Mickey), Matty Liu (Keoni), Shaun Thompson (Wyatt), Waylin Pultar**

---

... **June 3** ...
Museum of Modern Art announces a campaign to select 200 pix for preservation as part of film's second century.

(Serena), Bret Michaels (Philips), Brion James (Captain).
An extended surfing video thinly disguised as an action movie, *In God's Hands* is a disjointed blend of technical superiority and narrative and dramatic weakness. In the hands of director Zalman King, whose tendency is to privilege style over substance, pic hits the pulse-pounding high notes that action fans will relish but delivers only a vague facsimile of a story. Pic should score with surfing aficionados and sports-minded audiences, but crossover appeal is unlikely.

The film follows three pro surfers on their quest for the ultimate wave. Along the way, one suffers from malaria, another romances a beautiful girl from Ipanema, and the other falls victim to the surf.

U.S. release: April 24     U.S. B.O.: $1.5 million
Int'l release: July 5     Int'l B.O.: $200,000

### The Inheritors (Die Siebtelbauern) (Austria)

A DOR Film production in association with ORF, Bayerischer Rundfunk, and with the support of the Austrian Film Institute, Land Oberosterreich. Produced by Danny Krausz, Kurt Stocker. Directed, written by Stefan Ruzowitzky. Camera, Peter von Haller; editor, Britta Burkert-Nahler; art direction, Isi Wimmer; costume design, Nicole Fischnaller. Reviewed at Rotterdam Festival, Feb. 2. Running time: 93 mins.
Simon Schwarz (Lukas), Sophie Rois (Emmy), Lars Rudolph (Severin), Julia Gschnitzer (Old Nane), Ulrich Wildgruber (Danninger), Elisabeth Orth (Rosalind), Tilo Pruckner (Grossknecht).
When the heirless, tyrannical owner of a large farm is found with his throat cut, his will sets in motion a series of funny and frightening results. He leaves it and the livestock to his long-exploited peasant workers, hoping that they kill each other fighting over it.

Billed as an Alpine Western, *The Inheritors*, originally known as *The One-Seventh Farmers*, is a smartly mounted ensemble drama about class conflict and oppression set in an Austrian farming village in the early 1930s. Showing considerable command and an arresting visual sense in his sophomore feature, writer-director Stefan Ruzowitzky invests the jaunty folkloric tale with the scope of a small epic as he steers it from its gently humorous beginnings through its violent closing act. Some fringe theatrical exposure looks likely, with quality TV sales a definite. The film won one of the Tiger Awards in the Rotterdam fest's competition devoted to new filmmakers.
Int'l release: June 5     Int'l B.O.: $250,000

### Insomnia (Insomnio) (Spain)

A Columbia TriStar Espana release of a Sogetel/Boca Boca Producciones production, in association with Sogepaq and Canal Plus. Directed by Chus Gutierrez. Screenplay, Gutierrez, Juan Flahn, Fernando Leon. Camera, Arnaldo Catinari; editor, Miguel Angel Santamaria; music, Mateo Alonso; art director, Luis Valles. Reviewed at Columbia TriStar, Madrid, Feb. 4. Running time: 106 mins.
Cristina Marcos (Eva), Candela Pena (Alba), Ernesto Alterio (Juan), Maria Pujalte (Isabel), Gines Garcia Millan (Adrian).
Love 1990s style, from a female point of view, is the underlying theme of *Insomnia*, which like many comedy-dramas by young Spanish helmers, centers on twentysomething angst. Chus Gutierrez consolidates her reputation with a solid young cast, good characterization, a perceptive script, and compassionate

direction. But the film's overly familiar feel and lack of ambition are unlikely to move offshore auds.

Yuppie Eva, who's going out with unemployed Adrian, works for a TV production company and has just had a baby, both of which cause her sleepless nights. Passionate Alba is on a sex-and-alcohol binge after being dumped by her b.f., while henpecked real estate salesman Juan is about to be married to shopping-obsessed Isabel.
Int'l release: Feb. 13     Int'l B.O.: $300,000

### The Insurance (Bulgaria-Italy)

A Ramdas Prods presentation, in association with Film Artists Network. Produced by Momchil Karamitev, Gabriella di Saverio. Directed by Evgeni Mihailov. Screenplay, Alexander Tomov. Camera, Eli Mihailova, Plamen Somov; editor, Paolo Vanghetti; music, Bojidar Petkov; production design, Boris Neshev; costume design, Gabriella di Saverio, Eli Stojanov. Reviewed at Dances With Films Festival, Santa Monica, July 27. Running time: 94 mins. (Italian dialog)
Momchil Karamitev (Stefo Likina), Todor Kolev (Insp. Meranzof), Deljana Hadjiankova (Margot Likina), Ilia Karaivanov (George), Plamena Ghetova (Viviana).
An unusual noirish tale from Bulgaria, *The Insurance* is a period thriller in which deception and power intertwine for a deft, surprising entertainment. The feature by Evgeni Mihailov is a class outing that would benefit from further fest circuit exposure and score some specialized sales in upscale markets. Set in Sofia of the 1930s, story centers on much-feared police inspector Meranzof, who is informed that he has inoperable cancer by his doctor. Taking it in stride, he literally shoots the messenger, erases the record of his illness, and proceeds to secure a bank credit by bribing an official with the promise of sexual favors from a local prostitute. But the perfect plan has a few glitches. The prostie, Margot, has decided to leave the biz after locating her twentysomething brother, Stefo, in an orphanage. They find temporary lodgings in a local movie house, and the young man is hired to sell tickets.

### The Interview (Australia)

A Globe Films release of an Australian Film Finance Corp. presentation of a Pointblank Picture/Interview Films production, with the assistance of the Australian Film Commission. Produced by Bill Hughes. Directed by Craig Monahan. Screenplay, Monahan, Gordon Davie. Camera, Simon Duggan; editor, Suresh Ayyar; music, David Hirschfelder; production design, Richard Bell; costume design, Jeanie Cameron. Reviewed at UIP, Sydney, March 2. Running time: 101 mins.
Hugo Weaving (Eddie Rodney Fleming), Tony Martin (Det. Sgt. John Steele), Aaron Jeffery (Det. Sr. Constable Wayne Prior), Paul Sonkkila (Det. Insp. Jackson), Michael Caton (Barry Walls), Peter McCauley (Det. Insp. George Hudson), Glynis Angel (Det. Sgt. Robran).
First-rate performances distinguish *The Interview*, a taut, consistently intelligent drama about the grilling of a murder suspect by a tenacious, though flawed, law officer. The debut film from Craig Monahan is a rich cinematic experience despite its claustrophobic settings. It should perform solidly in arthouses in Australia and, if carefully handled, in other key territories.

Eddie Fleming is rudely awakened one morning when police smash into his one-room apartment. The unemployed Fleming is a sad case: He's lost his wife, home, and self-respect

---

**... June 4 ...**
Harrison Ford agrees to star in **What Lies Beneath**, a supernatural murder mystery for director Robert Zemeckis and DreamWorks.

and lives in near poverty. Carted off to the police station, he's quized about a stolen car by wily, tenacious detective Steele and his assistant detective, Prior.

It's gradually revealed that the car owner is missing and the police are looking for a serial killer. As the interview proceeds, we become aware that the investigators themselves are under investigation, being secretly videotaped by a police internal-affairs unit. Steele, it seems, has a bad reputation, and there are those in his department out to get him. It's a Kafkaesque atmosphere in which authorities may be persecuting an innocent man. Or, these cops may simply be doing their best to extract a confession from a cunning and dangerous killer.

Int'l release: Aug. 20                    Int'l B.O.: $350,000

### In That Land (V Toi Stranje) (Russia)

A LenFilm Studios and Narodny Film-Video Studio production. Produced by Alexander Golutva. Directed, written by Lidia Bobrova. Camera, Sergei Astakhov, Valeri Revich; editors, Tatiana Bistrova, Raisa Lisova; set designer, Gennadi Popow. Reviewed at San Francisco Festival, May 1. Running time: 87 mins.

With: Dmitri Clopov, Vladimir Barchaninov, Anna Ovsiannikova, Alexander Stakheev, Andrei Dunaek, Svetlana Gaytan.

Depressing everyday realities – most notably alcoholism – in contemporary rural Russia are given largely comic yet uncaricatured treatment in Lidia Bobrova's flavorful second feature. Slice-of-lifer's willful lack of polish won't inspire much offshore commercial exposure, but it's solid fest fare. Set in a snowbound village, story roams freely around its inhabitants, whose agricultural workforce leader Chapurin tries to hold things together despite scant government support. His personal campaign is to end the male population's tendency toward layabout boozing. But the eternally put-upon villagers resent being told any problem exists.

### In the Navel of the Sea (Sa Pusod Ng Dagat)

(Philippines)

A GMA Films/Neptune Films production. Produced by Marilou Diaz-Abaya, Butch Jiminez, Jimmy Duavit. Directed by Diaz-Abaya. Screenplay, Jun Lana. Camera, Romy Vitug; editor, Jess Navarro; music, Nonong Buencamino; production designer, Len Santos; costume designer, Manny Santos. Reviewed at Berlin Festival, Feb. 16. Running time: 113 mins.

Jomari Yllana (Pepito), Elizabeth Oropesa (Rosa), Chin Chin Gutierrez (Mrs. Santiago), Rolando Tinio (Apo), Pen Medina (Gusting), Mia Gutierrez (Ta-le).

The ebb and flow of life among fisherfolk on a peaceful, beautiful Philippine island is the backdrop for this simple tale of a young man coming to terms with life. Director Marilou Diaz-Abaya avoids the melodrama and though the film is decidedly lightweight, *In the Navel of the Sea* could find berth in fests with Asian sections.

Pepito, looking back over the years, recalls his fisherman father and Rosa, his mother, the island's only midwife. Because Rosa has no daughter, Pepito is expected to follow her profession, a prospect the youngster finds embarrassing.

### In the Presence of a Clown (Larmar Och Gor Sig Till) (Sweden)

An SVT production, in collaboration with DR (Denmark), NRK (Norway), RAI (Italy), YLE 1 (Finland), ZDF (Germany).

Produced by Pia Ehrnvall. Directed, written by Ingmar Bergman. Camera, Per Sundin; editor, Sylvia Ingmarsson; set decorator, Goran Wassberg; costume designer, Mette Moller. Reviewed at Cannes Festival, May 16. Running time: 120 mins.

Borje Ahlstedt (Carl Akerblom), Marie Richardson (Pauline Thibault), Erland Josephson (Osvald Voogler), Pernilla August (Karin Bergmann), Anita Bjork (Anna Akerblom), Agneta Ekmanner (Rigmor), Anna Bjork (Mia Falk).

*In the Presence of a Clown,* Ingmar Bergman's latest telepic, isn't in the filmmaker's pantheon, but it reps a solid piece of work that will delight aficionados. Inspired by episodes and figures from Bergman's family, this sharply observed, well-acted chamber piece centers on Uncle Carl, a charismatic, middle-aged inventor who was a mental patient in an asylum.

Best chances for this film, which has already been shown on Euro TV, lie with premium cable channels. Roughly divided into four parts, the film is set in an Uppsala psychiatric hospital in 1925. In due course, Bergman offers the kind of wry commentary that only an accomplished artist can on the art of acting, the difference between movies and theater, and the meaning of role-playing onstage and off.

### In The Winter Dark (Australia)

A Globe Films release of an Australian Film Finance Corp. presentation of an R.B. Films production, in association with the Australian Film Commission, NSW Film & TV Office, Premium Movie Partnership. Produced by Rosemary Blight. Directed by James Bogle. Screenplay, Peter Rasmussen, Bogle, based on the novel by Tim Winton. Camera, Martin McGrath; editor, Suresh Ayyar; music, Peter Cobbin; production designer, Nicholas McCallum; costume designer, Wendy Cook. Reviewed at Verona 2, Sydney, May 8. Running time: 92 mins.

Brenda Blethyn (Ida Stubbs), Ray Barrett (Maurice Stubbs), Richard Roxburgh (Laurie Jacobs), Miranda Otto (Ronnie).

The inner demons haunting four residents of an isolated valley are reflected by an unseen predator that is attacking livestock in James Bogle's *In The Winter Dark.* A slowly paced but accomplished adaptation of Tim Winton's acclaimed novel, pic should scare up decent business in Australia thanks to a strong cast and eerily fine direction, and make a dent in international arthouses following fest exposure.

Buffs will recognize a debt to William Wellman's classic *Track of the Cat* in this strange story, which was filmed on the fringes of Australia's spectacular Blue Mountains. Opening sequence, revealing the discovery of a woman's body in a forest, establishes a mood of forbidding beauty, as the narrator, in classic film-noir tradition, takes the viewer back "to figure out how it could have been different."

Int'l release: Sept. 10                    Int'l B.O.: $75,000

### Intimates (Chi So) (Hong Kong)

A Golden Harvest release of a United Filmmakers Organization production, in association with China Film Co-production Corp. and Xiaoxiang Film Studio, for Golden Harvest. Produced by Raymond Chow. Directed by Jacob Cheung. Screenplay, Anita Tong. Camera, Yang Lun, Ardy Lam; editor, Kam Ma; music, Steve Ho; art direction, Terrence Fok; costume design, Shirley Chan. Reviewed at Cine Art theater, Hong Kong, Dec. 6, 1997. Running time: 158 mins.

Carina Liu (Wan), Charlie Young (Foon), Gua Ah-leh (Auntie Foon), Theresa Lee (Wai), Winston Chao (Wah).

Anchored by a terrif performance from Carina Liu, *Intimates* is an effective, complexly structured meller. This tale of an undying love affair between two women across 50 years occasionally stumbles but ranks as one of the most ambitious pics, both technically and artistically, from the territory this year. Beyond fests, specialized distribution is not out of the question. Tale centers on a journey of self-discovery as a young woman takes an older women from San Francisco to a retirement home in Guangzhou, China.

Int'l release: Nov. 6, 1997      Int'l B.O.: $500,000

### Island, Alicia

A Bear Hand Films production. Produced by Huy Truong. Directed, written by Ken Yunome. Camera/editor, Truong; art director, Fernando Cuestas. Reviewed at Cannes Festival, May 16. Running time: 180 mins.
Jeff Miller (Daniel), Jane Jepson (Alicia), Cheryl Aden (Lena), Ed Bicarri (Dr. Ruben), Kim Beuche (Audrey).
Everything trite, pretentious, and puerile in current Amerindie filmmaking gets a staggering summation in *Island, Alicia*, a three-hour marathon of arty inanity. A would-be psychodrama about a screwed-up young man who beds the mom and then the daughter in the same dysfunctional family, pic is an inexplicable inclusion in Cannes' main section. With near-nil commercial prospects, its best bet for future exposure may be in any fest that cares to jibe the programmers of *Un Certain Regard*. Story opens with Daniel recounting to his psychiatrist a tale of being sexually preyed upon by an aunt during childhood. In a Manhattan bar Daniel meets an unhappy 40-year-old housewife, Lena, and follows her to her Staten Island home.

### I Still Know What You Did Last Summer

A Sony Pictures release of a Columbia Pictures presentation, in association with Mandalay Entertainment, of a Neal H. Moritz production. Produced by Moritz, Erik Feig, Stokely Chaffin, William S. Beasley. Directed by Danny Cannon. Screenplay, Trey Callaway, based on characters in the film written by Kevin Williamson and the novel by Lois Duncan. Camera, Vernon Layton; editor, Peck Prior; music, John Frizzell; production design, Doug Kraner; costume design, Dan Lester; stunt coordinator, Freddie Hice. Reviewed at UA Westwood, L.A., Nov. 4. MPAA Rating: R. Running time: 101 mins.
Jennifer Love Hewitt (Julie James), Freddie Prinze, Jr. (Ray Bronson), Brandy (Karla Wilson), Mekhi Phifer (Tyrell), Muse Watson (Ben Willis), Matthew Settle (Will Benson), Bill Cobbs (Estes), Jeffrey Combs (Brooks), Jennifer Esposito (Nancy), John Hawkes (Dave).
You can't keep a good man – or a screen ghoul – down, as evidenced in the highly manipulative, predictable scream sequel *I Still Know What You Did Last Summer*. This follow-up to last year's successful teens-in-jeopardy opus piles on the chills, thrills, and body count. Purists will find the pic's obviousness disappointing, but there's no question that the film delivers a sufficient shock quotient to satisfy its youthful target audience and rack up potent B.O. and buoyant action in ancillaries.

The new chapter begins on the first anniversary of the previous encounter. Survivor Julie James is attending college, and Ray Bronson is catching fish on his boat in North Carolina. She's still haunted by nightmares about the hook-handed, slicker-coated killer Ben Willis, who terrorized and murdered her friends before he was apparently killed. A radio promotion

allows Julie and roommate Karla to take a Bahamas vacation for four. Karla invites her squeeze, Tyrell, and Julie calls Ray to join the fun. But he's hesitant; only after hanging up the phone does he decide to go. On his way north with a buddy to surprise her, he stumbles upon a stalled car and a body in the road. A turn of the head later, the familiar hook has impaled his friend. Ray runs for his life and the rest runs to form. The music swells, the hook sweeps, and another victim lies in a pool of blood in the pounding rain.

U.S. release: Oct. 17      U.S. B.O.: $39 million
Int'l release: Nov. 26      Int'l B.O.: $4 million

### It's a Long Road (Ola Ine Dromos) (Greece)

An Alco Film/Greek Film Centre production, in association with Greek Television. Produced by Panos Papadopoulos, Anna Comninou. Directed by Pantelis Voulgaris. Screenplay, Voulgaris, Giorgos Skabardonis. Camera, Giorgos Frentzos; editor, Dinos Katsouridis; music, Stamatis Spanoudakis; production/costume designer, Julia Stavridou. Reviewed at Berlin Festival, Feb. 19. Running time: 118 mins.
Dimitris Katalifos (Archeologist), Thanassis Vengos (Game Warden), Giorgos Armenis (Factory Owner).
Vet Greek helmer Pantelis Voulgaris' latest is a modest, tasty three-parter in which a trio of middle-aged men face emotional and personal crossroads in their lives. Festival programmers should take a look at this elegant item, with Eurotube exposure also indicated.

First story involves an archeologist whose discovery of the remains of an ancient soldier triggers his realization that self-absorption in his work has robbed his personal life. Other segments similarly play like modern parables. Voulgaris is working in a minor key here, but his intimate portraits are filled with compassion and affection.

### It's Your Turn, Laura Cadieux (C't'a ton tour Laura Cadieux) (Canada)

An Alliance presentation of a Cinemaginaire production, with support from Telefilm Canada, OFDC, Viacom Canada. Produced by Denise Robert. Directed, written by Denise Filatrault, based on the novel by Michel Tremblay. Camera, Daniel Jobin; editor, Richard Comeau; music, François Dompierre; production design, Stephane Roy; costume design, Helen Rainbird, Marc Larose. Reviewed at Vancouver Festival, Oct. 6. Running time: 92 mins. (French dialog)
Ginette Reno (Laura Cadieux), Pierette Robitaille (Madame Therrien), Denise Dubois (Madame Brouillette), Adele Reinhardt (Lucille Bolduc), Mireille Thibault (Madame Gladu), Danielle Lorain (Vovonne), Donald Pilon (Oscar Blanchette).
Zesty appetites – for food, sex, fun, and life itself – fill the screen in *It's Your Turn, Laura Cadieux*, a jet-propelled vehicle for some of French Canada's top talents. The hinted-at dreams and disappointments of a bunch of size-large women, most over 50, give heart to this otherwise hilarious farce, tangily adapted from a novel by stage-great Michel Tremblay. The ample star power of Ginette Reno, as the soulful, bellicose, and deeply prejudiced title character, travels easily beyond the Quebec singer-thesp's home base. With careful handling, pic could score even with auds who don't normally venture out for foreign fare. Reno, who was La Belle Provence's top chanteuse until skinny Celine Dion slithered onto the scene, is a veritable force of nature as Laura Cadieux, first seen on her

---

way to a weekly gaggle of similarly well-stuffed Montreal matrons at a doctor's office, where her working-class friends gather for diet injections. But their real intent is to while away their time telling jokes and hashing over old problems. On this particular visit, they especially pick on the only non-fat member of the group who has a skin condition; she also has a transparent crush on the too-dapper Oscar Blanchette, likewise a regular presence.

U.S. release: Oct. 9                     U.S. B.O.: $1.9 million

### I Want You (U.K.)

A Polygram Filmed Entertainment presentation of a Revolution Films production. Produced by Andrew Eaton. Directed by Michael Winterbottom. Screenplay, Eoin McNamee. Camera, Slawomir Idziak; editor, Trevor Waite; music, Adrian Johnston; production design, Mark Tildesley; costume design, Rachael Fleming. Reviewed at Berlin Festival, Feb. 18. Running time: 87 mins.

Rachel Weisz (Helen), Alessandro Nivola (Martin), Luka Petrusic (Honda), Labina Mitevska (Smokey), Carmen Ejogo (Amber), Ben Daniels (Bob).

A dark, fragmented Euro-noir set in a crumbling English beach resort, *I Want You* is an ambitious idea that succeeds more as a stylistic exercise than an involving, fully realized drama. Quite the opposite to director Michael Winterbottom's previous *Welcome to Sarajevo*, the film will appeal more to arthouse patrons than broad public. Opening involves a body dumped off a pier, then rewinds to introduce the key characters and clues to what led to the mysterious incident.

Int'l release: Sept. 16                  Int'l B.O.: $400,000

### I Woke Up Early The Day I Died

A Muse Prods/Cinequanon Pictures Int'l production. Produced by Chris Hanley, Billy Zane. Directed by Aris Iliopulos. Screenplay, Edward D. Wood, Jr. Camera, Michael F. Barrow; editor, Dody Dorn; music, Larry Groupe; production design, Maia Javan. Reviewed at Toronto Festival, Sept. 11. Running time: 89 mins.

Billy Zane (The Thief), Sandra Bernhard (Sandy Sands), Ron Perlman (Caretaker), Tippi Hedren (Maylinda), Andrew McCarthy (Cop), Will Patton (Preacher), Carel Struycken (Undertaker), Max Perlich (Asst. Undertaker), John Ritter (Robert Forrest), Eartha Kitt (Cult Leader), Ann Magnuson (Secretary), Maila Nurmi (Vampira).

If first impressions were enough, *I Woke Up Early the Day I Died* would have a lock on the Midnight Movie Hall of Fame. Said to be based on schlockmeister Ed Wood's final unproduced script, pic boasts a John Waters dream ensemble that includes Tippi Hedren, Eartha Kitt, Christina Ricci, Karen Black, Carel Struycken, and, as a tassel-twirling stripper, Sandra Bernhard. Too bad casting and outré elements aren't enough to goose the episodic script to life. Curiosity and camp factor will take this one only so far on the fest/specialized circuit, then to the discount vid bin. Shot on the run as a virtually silent feature, indie stars Billy Zane as a cross-dressing wacko who escapes from a sanitarium, scores some loot but winds up losing it and going on a berserk rampage of vengeance.

### Jack Frost

A Warner Bros. release of an Azoff Entertainment/Canton Co. production. Produced by Mark Canton, Irving Azoff. Directed by Troy Miller. Screenplay, Mark Steven Johnson, Steve Bloom,

Jonathan Roberts, Jeff Cesario. Camera, Laszlo Kovacs; editor, Lawrence Jordan; music, Trevor Rabin; production design, Mayne Berke; costume design, Sarah Edwards; visual-effects supervisor, Joe Letteri. Reviewed at Cinemark's Tinseltown Westchase, Houston, Texas, Nov. 30. MPAA Rating: PG. Running time: 95 mins.

Michael Keaton (Jack Frost), Kelly Preston (Gabby Frost), Mark Addy (Mac MacArthur), Joseph Cross (Charlie Frost).

Although it faces tough sledding in a crowded market of family-friendly features, *Jack Frost* is a slickly packaged and engagingly sentimental fantasy-comedy that stands out as one of the season's most pleasant surprises. Pic offers a shrewdly balanced mix of humor, high concept, and heart tugging, along with some amusingly impressive special effects from the wizards of Jim Henson's Creature Shop and Industrial Light and Magic. Expect upbeat opening-weekend grosses. After that, however, strong word of mouth will be necessary to avoid a quick B.O. meltdown. Michael Keaton is an inspired choice for title character, even though he hardly appears on camera.

Jack is a Colorado-based rock musician who mostly lives on the road. The gigs are plentiful but breakthrough success remains elusive. Gabby, Jack's wife, is supportive of his struggle, but even she is upset when his workaholic ways cut into time with Charlie, their 12-year-old son. To make amends, Jack gives the boy a harmonica with "magical" qualities. "Whenever you play this," Jack says, "no matter where I am, I can hear you." Driving home in a snowstorm for a family Christmas, Jack swerves off the road and is killed. A year later, Charlie plays a few notes on his harmonica while building a snowman. Jack hears the summons, and comes home. There's a slight catch, however: Jack's spirit now resides within the snowman.

U.S. release: Dec. 11                    U.S. B.O.: $28 million

### Jackie Brown

A Miramax release of an A Band Apart production. Produced by Lawrence Bender. Directed, written by Quentin Tarantino, based on the novel *Rum Punch* by Elmore Leonard. Camera, Guillermo Navarro; editor, Sally Menke; production design, David Wasco; costume design, Mary Claire Hannan. Reviewed at the Avco Cinema, L.A., Dec. 12, 1997. MPAA Rating: R. Running time: 155 mins.

Pam Grier (Jackie Brown), Samuel L. Jackson (Ordell Robbie), Robert Forster (Max Cherry), Bridget Fonda (Melanie), Michael Keaton (Ray Nicolette), Robert De Niro (Louis Gara), Chris Tucker (Beaumont Livingston).

Facing the daunting task of making a third feature that could measure up to *Reservoir Dogs* and *Pulp Fiction*, Quentin Tarantino treads turf that is both familiar and fresh in *Jackie Brown*. Unquestionably too long, and lacking the snap and audaciousness of the pictures that made him the toast of the town, this narratively faithful but conceptually imaginative adaptation of Elmore Leonard's novel *Rum Punch* offers an abundance of pleasures, especially in the realm of characterization and atmosphere. Down-and-dirty pic's B.O. prospects are OK in urban areas, less so elsewhere.

Jackie Brown is a fulsome examination of deceit, treachery, cunning, stupidity, mistrust, risk, and daring among a group of small-timers. Ordell Robbie is a very smooth and lethal arms dealer operating out of a beach pad he shares with blonde, stoned surfer girl Melanie. Trouble lands on Ordell's doorstep when stewardess Jackie Brown (Grier) is busted at LAX smuggling $50,000 into the country for him. Facing a prison term, she decides to cooperate with the authorities.

U.S. release: Dec. 25, 1997     U.S. B.O.: $40 million
Int'l release: March 6     Int'l B.O.: $47 million

## Jane Austen's Mafia!

A Buena Vista release of a Touchstone Pictures presentation of a Tapestry Films production. Produced by Bill Badalato. Directed by Jim Abrahams. Screenplay, Abrahams, Greg Norberg, Michael McManus. Camera, Pierre Letarte; editor, Terry Stokes; music, Gianni Frizzelli; production design, William Elliott; costume design, Mary Malin. Reviewed at Regency II, San Francisco, July 20. MPAA rating: PG-13. Running time: 84 mins.
**Jay Mohr (Anthony Cortino), Billy Burke (Joey Cortino), Christina Applegate (Diane), Pamela Gidley (Pep Gianni), Olympia Dukakis (Sophia), Lloyd Bridges (Vincenzo Cortino), Joe Viterelli (Clamato), Tony Lo Bianco (Marzoni).**

The anarchic, splatterpaint-with-gags approach Jim Abrahams first visited on disaster flicks with *Airplane!* now wreaks havoc on Cosa Nostra epics in *Jane Austen's Mafia!* Its particular target genre being not exactly at peak visibility, this agreeable, if typically hit-and-miss, spoof may not soar to the commercial heights of prior *Naked Gun* romps. But frequent hilarity should translate into palatable mid-range summertime B.O., with excellent ancillary biz to follow. Abrahams takes aim primarily at *The Godfather* trilogy and *Casino.* Ignorance, particularly of the first pics, renders the spoof mirthless while knowledge raises laughter level to a titter.

U.S. release: July 24     U.S. B.O.: $20 million
Int'l release: Aug. 5     Int'l B.O.: $14 million

## Jeanne and the Perfect Guy (Jeanne Et Le Garçon Formidable) (France)

A Les Films du Requin production, in association with Le Studio Canal Plus, France 2 Cinéma, M6 Films, Orsans Prods. Produced by Cyriac Auriol, Pauline Duhault. Directed by Olivier Ducastel. Screenplay, Jacques Martineau. Camera, Mathieu Poirot-Delpech; editor, Sabine Mamou; musical arrangements, Philippe Miller; songs, Martineau; art direction, Louis Soubrier; costume design, Juliette Chanaud; choreography, Sylvie Giron. Reviewed at Berlin Festival, Feb. 16. Running time: 94 mins.
**Virginie Ledoyen (Jeanne), Mathieu Demy (Olivier), Jacques Bonnaffe (François), Valerie Bonneton (Sophie), Frederic Gorny (Jean-Baptiste), Denis Podalydes (Julien).**

As soon as the office cleaners break into song, there's not a shadow of a doubt that *Jeanne and the Perfect Guy* is in Jacques Demy territory as the colorful tuner hangs lightly on the shoulders of a modern fairy-tale musical about love and AIDS. The bigger stretch for many viewers will be swallowing a sunny, upbeat approach to a subject that's hardly a cause for celebration. Offshore sales look tricky for this slice of multihued Gallic whimsy. Jeanne, a receptionist at a travel agency, enjoys the company of men, preferably between the sheets and in constant supply. A quickie on the metro with complete stranger Olivier turns into the love of her life. But he reveals that he's HIV-positive from a contaminated needle.

Int'l release: April 22     Int'l B.O.: $1 million

## Jerry and Tom

A Miramax release of a Lions Gate Films production. Produced by Elinor Reid, Vivienne Leebosh, Michael Paseornek, Saul Rubinek. Directed by Saul Rubinek. Screenplay, Rick Cleveland.

Camera, Paul Sarossy; editor, Sloane Klevin; music, David Buchbinder; production design, costume design, Morganne Newson. Reviewed at Sundance Film Festival, Jan. 19. Running time: 106 mins.
**Joe Mantegna (Tom), Sam Rockwell (Jerry), Maury Chaykin (Billy), Charles Durning (Vic), William H. Macy (Karl), Peter Riegert (Stanley).**

Hit men receive the sort of artistic treatment they scarcely deserve in *Jerry and Tom.* Very well acted and beautifully directed by actor Saul Rubinek in his debut, this reductio ad absurdum of a shopworn mini-genre is too rarefied and conceptual in nature to go far, but a good reception in limited release will give it the rep it needs to enjoy a decent afterlife. As soon as thesps Joe Mantegna and William H. Macy turn up and the rhythms of scripter Rick Cleveland's smartly tailored thug talk establish themselves, it's clear that Mamet country is very nearby. Opening sequence sees Tom, a veteran hit man, and Jerry, his young apprentice – used-car salesmen by day – waiting in a deserted Chicago bar for a phone call giving them the greenlight to execute a bound and hooded man.

U.S. release: Dec. 4     U.S. B.O.: $50,000

## Joey (Australia)

A Roadshow release of a Village Roadshow Pictures presentation of a Pratt Films production, with the participation of the Pacific Film & TV Commission. Produced by Michael Lake. Directed by Ian Barry. Screenplay, Stuart Beattie. Camera, David Burr; editor, Lee Smith; music, Roger Mason; production design, Peta Lawson; costume design, Marion Boyce; animatronics supervisor, John Cox. Reviewed at Village Roadshow screening room, Sydney, Oct. 30, 1997. Running time: 96 mins.
**Jamie Croft (Billy MacGregor), Alex McKenna (Linda Ross), Rebecca Gibney (Penny MacGregor), Ed Begley, Jr. (Ambassador Ted Ross), Ruth Cracknell (Sylvia Vanderberg), Harold Hopkins (Kanga Catcher), Errol O'Neill (Dixon).**

A bland furry-animal pic aimed at small-fry and kids in their early teens, *Joey* is a formulaic adventure in which a farm boy ventures into the big city searching for the kidnapped parents of a baby kangaroo. Given a big boost in Oz, pic is up against formidable holiday fare. With one eye firmly on the Yank market, the producers have contrived to have their young hero team up with a feisty American girl his own age, which may give *Joey* some Stateside exposure, especially in ancillary markets.

The adventure begins on a lushly idealized farm in Queensland where Billy lives with his widowed mother. His favorite pastime is observing a group of kangaroos, and especially baby Joey, but unfortunately the creatures hang out on the farm of brutal, roo-hating neighbor Dixon.

Int'l release: Dec. 26, 1997     Int'l B.O.: $1.3 million

## John Carpenter's Vampires

A Sony Pictures release of a Largo Entertainment/Film Office presentation of a Storm King production. Produced by Sandy King. Directed by John Carpenter. Screenplay, Carpenter, Don Jacoby, Dan Mazur, based on the novel *Vampire$* by John Steakley. Camera, Gary B. Kibbe; editor, Edward A. Warschilka; music, Carpenter; production designer, Thomas A. Walsh; costume designer, Robin Michel Bush; special effects, Darrell D. Pritchett. Reviewed at UGC Odeon, Paris, April 27. Running time: 104 mins.
**James Woods (Jack Crow), Daniel Baldwin (Tony Montoya), Sheryl Lee (Katrina), Thomas Ian Griffith (Valek), Tim Guinee**

---

(Father Adam Guiteau), Maximilian Schell (Cardinal Alba). The pleasures are modest but consistent in *John Carpenter's Vampires*, a part-Western, part-horror flick that doesn't aim too high but nails the range it occupies. A tale of parallel quests, pic centers on a vampire slayer on the Vatican payroll who's intent on destroying a 600-year-old ghoul before the creature gets his hands on a secret weapon that will afford him 24-hour mobility. There's a mild brainy streak running through Carpenter's movie that could tickle slightly older, better-versed horror fans. As the story evolves, these particular vampires seem impervious to the so-called "magic hour" before sunset.

| | |
|---|---|
| U.S. release: Oct. 30 | U.S. B.O.: $20 million |
| Int'l release: April 21 | Int'l B.O.: $6.5 million |

### John Grisham's The Rainmaker

A Paramount release of a Constellation Films presentation of a Douglas/Reuther production, in association with American Zoetrope. Produced by Michael Douglas, Steven Reuther, Fred Fuchs. Directed, written by Francis Ford Coppola, based on the novel by John Grisham. Narration written by Michael Herr. Camera, John Toll; editor, Barry Malkin; music, Elmer Bernstein; production design, Howard Cummings; costume design, Aggie Guerard Rodgers. Reviewed at Paramount, L.A., Nov. 11, 1997. MPAA Rating: PG-13. Running time: 135 mins.
Matt Damon (Rudy Baylor), Claire Danes (Kelly Riker), Jon Voight (Leo Drummond), Mary Kay Place (Dot Black), Mickey Rourke (Bruiser Stone), Danny DeVito (Deck Schifflet), Dean Stockwell (Judge Harvey Hale), Teresa Wright (Miss Birdie), Virginia Madsen (Jackie Lemancyzk), Andrew Shue (Cliff Riker), Roy Scheider (Wilfred Keeley), Danny Glover (Judge Tyrone Kipler).

A carefully constructed, handsomely crafted classic Hollywood production, Francis Ford Coppola's screen version of John Grisham's *The Rainmaker* represents just about all a filmmaker could do with the bestselling author's patented dramatic formulas without subverting them altogether. Although highly predictable, this story of a young Southern lawyer taking on an evil insurance giant exerts an almost irresistible David and Goliath appeal, and proves absorbing. Pic looms as a highly durable B.O. entry.

Rudy Baylor, a Memphis law grad, finds less than ideal work at the questionably legit firm of the aptly named Bruiser Stone. Company leg man Deck Schifflet teaches him the basics of ambulance-chasing. Rudy has also generated a couple of promising clients, Miss Birdie and, notably, Dot Black, whose son is dying of leukemia. The Black's insurance company has repeatedly dodged payment on coverage for the boy's care. With the threat of being taken to court, the insurers' slick lawyer Leo Drummond offers to settle. But the team push ahead with what becomes a wrongful-death suit when the boy dies. Playing on the audience's pleasure in seeing an arrogant and unfeeling corporation being brought down to size, pic methodically presents the clever and lucky ways in which Rudy and Deck peel away layers of deceit until the venal business practices are revealed.

| | |
|---|---|
| U.S. release: Nov. 21, 1997 | U.S. B.O.: $46 million |
| Int'l release: Feb. 13 | Int'l B.O.: $22 million |

### Judas Kiss

A Key Entertainment presentation, in association with Bandeira Entertainment, of a Flynn/Simchowitz production. Produced by Beau Flynn, Stefan Simchowitz, Jonathan King. Directed, written by Sebastian Gutierrez, based on a screen story by Gutierrez, Deanna Fuller. Camera, James Chressanthis; editor, Howard Smith; music, Christopher Young; production design, Jerry Fleming; costume design, Denise Wingate. Reviewed at Toronto Festival, Sept. 16, 1998. Running time: 97 mins.
Simon Baker-Denny (Junior Armstrong), Gil Bellows (Lizard Browning), Carla Gugino (Coco Chavez), Alan Rickman (Det. David Friedman), Til Schweiger (Ruban Rubenbauser), Emma Thompson (Agent Sadie Hawkins), Hal Holbrook (Sen. Rupert Hornbeck), Greg Wise (Ben Dyson), Lisa Eichhorn (Mary-Ellen Floyd), Beverly Penberthy (Patty Hornbeck).

*Judas Kiss* is a wannabe film noir-cum-policier that's badly in need of a rewrite. First-time writer-director Sebastian Gutierrez gets the action and characters onscreen in OK fashion, but most of the words coming out of the actors' mouths wouldn't hard-boil an egg. Despite an interesting cast, pic looks set to get the kiss-off theatrically in mature territories, with direct-to-homevid more likely in some.

A team breaks into an upscale New Orleans apartment and kidnaps Dyson, head of the computer conglom Dyscape. At the last moment, however, another tenant enters the corridor and is fatally shot by Coco. When the group hears on TV that the woman they killed was the wife of powerful Sen. Hornbeck, the kidnapping takes on serious extra dimensions. Hornbeck, who has plenty to hide, puts his own team on the case; also trawling for clues are FBI agent Hawkins and alcoholic police detective Friedman. As the kidnappers lead the cops and the man with the payoff money on a merry trail across town, details emerge that the killing of Hornbeck's wife may not have been such a coincidence.

### Junk Food (Japan)

A Gaga Prods production. Produced by Yoshinori Chiba, Toshiki Kimura. Directed by Takashi Miike. Screenplay by Toshiuki Morioka, from a story by Hitoshi Tanimura. Camera, Hideo Yamamoto; editor, Yasushi Shimamura; music, Chu Ishikawa; production design, Akira Ishige. Reviewed at Toronto Festival, Sept. 15, 1997. Running time: 82 mins.
With: Shizuko Yamamoto, Miyuki Ijima, Akifumi Yamaguchi, Keigo Naruse, Yoichi Okamura, Rumi Otori, Ali Ahmed.

This enigmatic, self-assured study of people on the fringes of postmodern Japanese society is fascinating until it descends into meller antics, swamping its characters in blood and empty attitudinizing. *Junk Food* had the potential for a cult following but it's just too indigestible for offshore auds. Pic interweaves 24 unhappy hours in the lives of various troubled Tokyoites. Things start at dawn with an elderly blind woman going through daily rituals then abruptly shifts to Miyuki, a young woman waking up from a kinky sex-and-drugs fest; mounting her latest casual encounter, she strangles the guy and heads to work.

| | |
|---|---|
| Int'l release: April 18 | Int'l B.O.: $500,000 |

### Just Write

A Curb Entertainment Int'l presentation, in association with Wind Chill Prods, of a Heath McLaughlin production. Produced by McLaughlin. Directed by Andrew Gallerani. Screenplay, Stan Williamson. Camera, Michael Brown; editor, Laura M. Grody; music, Leland Bond; production design, Roger Collins; costume design, Arlene Toback. Reviewed at Aidikoff Screening Room, Beverly Hills, Sept. 2. Running time: 104 mins.
Sherilyn Fenn (Amanda Clark), Jeremy Piven (Harold

McMurphy), JoBeth Williams (Sydney Stone), Jeffrey Sams (Danny), Alex Rocco (Father), Wallace Shawn (Arthur Blake). A slight, occasionally embarrassing indie with a decidedly Hollywood spin, *Just Write* (winner of best film at the 1997 Santa Barbara Festival) nonetheless provides some guilty pleasures and features engaging lead performances from Sherilyn Fenn and Jeremy Piven. Cable and video seem more appropriate venues for the picture, which should have no problem finding an audience there after a short theatrical run.

Piven plays Hollywood tour bus guide Harold McMurphy, who lives in an apartment with his burnt out old man. A film buff and a dreamer, Harold enjoys his tour guide gig, which allows him to show off his knowledge of film history. Harold is sure that something wonderful will happen to him one day. That long-awaited event takes place when he catches the eye of hot new movie star Amanda Clark at a ritzy Hollywood bar. Eager to impress the actress, Harold blurts out that he's a writer with a big-shot agent. Amanda is also a film buff, and she and Harold hit it off. When she asks Harold to do a rewrite on a cheesy pic she's set to star in with Brad Pitt, Harold reluctantly accepts. Does he really have the chops to script a movie?

### Kayla (Canada)

A Film Tonic release of a Cine-Action production. Produced by Claudio Luca, Colin Neale. Directed by Nicholas Kendall. Screenplay, Peter Behrens, based on the novel by Elizabeth Van Steenwik. Camera, John Berrie; editor, Jean-Marie Drot; music, Milan Kymlicka; art director, Stephane Roy; costume designer, Nicoletta Massone. Reviewed at the Centreville Cinema, Montreal, March 19. Running time: 96 mins.
Tod Fennell (Sam MacKenzie), Henry Czerny (Asa Robinson), Meredith Henderson (Jaynie Nightingale), Bronwen Booth (Althea Robinson), Brian Dooley (August Nightingale), Ricky Mabe (Ernie Wallace).
A tried-and-true tale of a boy and his dog, *Kayla* is a reasonably engaging kidpic, but it doesn't have the plot twists or emotional impact to set itself apart from the family-film pack. This Canadian-made period piece doesn't have the bigscreen bark to make much of an impression theatrically, but it should click worldwide with TV webs.

Set in the countryside just southeast of Montreal in the early 1920s, the story revolves around Sam MacKenzie, a 12-year-old whose father, the renowned Arctic explorer Samuel Clearwater MacKenzie, disappeared in the tundra several years back. Sam refuses to believe his dad is dead.
U.S. release: March 13          U.S. B.O.: $20,000

### The Key (Kagi) (Japan)

A Tohokushinsha Film Co. presentation of a Toei Co. production. Produced by Mitsuru Kurosawa, Tetsu Uemura. Directed by Toshiharu Ikeda. Screenplay, Ikeda, Akane Shiratori, Masahiko Kagawa; story by Junichiro Tanizaki. Camera, Yonezo Maeda; editor, Akimasa Kawashima; music, Toshiyuki Honda; production designer, Tadayuki Kuwana. Reviewed at Santa Barbara Festival, March 13. Running time: 95 mins.
Naomi Kawashima (Ikuko Anzai), Akira Emoto (Soichiro Anzai), Mikio Osawa (Kimura), Kaori Tsuji (Toshiko), Kenji Imai (Dr. Soma).
A lyrical meditation on love, sex, the challenges of communication, and the ambiguity of truth, *The Key* is an absorbing, at times surprisingly funny, film. The fifth cinematic

adaptation of Junichiro Tanizaki's novel of the same name, pic's sensual scenes and witty premise notwithstanding, its intellectual tone will likely make it a tough sell to all but the arthouse crowd.

Set in Tokyo circa 1956, the story finds Soichiro Anzai, a middle-aged professor, keeping a detailed diary of his frustrating sexual relationship with his young wife, Ikuko. In a calculated effort to communicate, he locks the diary away but leaves the key for her to find. As expected, she reads the diary, fascinated by her husband's private thoughts.
Int'l release: Oct. 24, 1997          Int'l B.O.: $1.4 million

### Khrustaliov, My Car! (Khroustaliov, Ma Voîture!)

(France-Russia)
A Polygram Film Distribution release of a Sodaperaga (Paris)/Goskino (Moscow) co-production. Produced by Guy Seligmann, Armen Medvedev, Alexandre Golutva. Directed by Alexei Guerman. Screenplay, Svetlana Karmalita, Guerman. Camera, Vladimir Ilyne; editor, Irina Gorokhovskaya; music, Andrei Petrov; production designer, V. Svetozarov, G. Kropatchiov, M. Guerassimov; costume designer, E. Chapkaits. Reviewed at Cannes Festival, May 20. Running time: 150 mins.
Y. Tsurilo (Gen. Klenski), N. Ruslanova (Wife), M. Dementiev (Son), A. Bachirov (Idiot), Y. Yarvet (Swedish Reporter).
On a snowy Moscow night in the early 1950s, a boiler repairman leaves work and comically falls into the hands of Stalin's police. Scenes shift with the disturbing facility of a dream. In a big hospital full of hallways and doors, the General makes his rounds while staff fawn on him. The hospital seems to be a madhouse without rules.

Director Alexei Guerman, one of the most singular talents to emerge from the Soviet Union in the 1970s, returns to the scene after 16 years with the mightily disappointing *Khrustaliov, My Car!* After attempting to finance the project for more than a decade, Guerman seems to explode with long-repressed ideas like a swollen balloon spewing forth a cacophony of images, characters, and camera pyrotechnics while trying to tell a story that is almost impossible to follow. As admirable as many of the bits and pieces are, the details fail to come together or even make any sense to a Western viewer. The French-Russian co-production may arouse initial interest on a curiosity basis but looks set to sink quickly in specialized markets.

### Killer Couple (Coppia Omicida) (Italy)

A Filmauro release of a Filmauro production. Produced by Aurelio De Laurentiis. Directed by Claudio Fragasso. Screenplay, Rossella Drudi, Fragasso. Camera, Blasco Giurato; editor, Ugo De Rossi; music, Pino Donaggio; art director, Francesco Vanorio; costumes, Nicoletta Ercoli. Reviewed at Europa Cinema, Rome, March 31. Running time: 108 mins.
Raoul Bova (Dario), Francesca Schiavo (Luciana), Laura Morante (Carla), Thomas Kretschmann (Domenico), Raz Degan (Vito).
A former French secret service agent has gone bad – his specialty is recruiting nice young couples and turning them into heartless killers. A bloody, if puzzling, opening in Berlin shows what newlyweds armed to the teeth with guns, knives, and bombs can do.

A commercial thriller high on production values but low on psychology, style, and logic, *Killer Couple* revolves around the amusing, if implausible, idea of young marrieds being recruited as international assassins. Helmer Claudio Fragasso (*Palermo-Milan One Way*) is fast establishing himself as Italy's premier director of briskly paced actioners with a glossy, international patina. Pic opened locally with good per-screen biz and should be a hot seller for producer Filmauro, especially at TV markets.

Int'l release: March 20                    Int'l B.O.: $500,000

## Kissing a Fool

A Universal release, presented in association with R.L. Entertainment and Largo Entertainment of a Tag Mendillo/Andrew Form production. Produced by Mendillo, Form, Rick Lashbrook. Directed by Doug Ellin. Screenplay, James Frey, Ellin, story by Frey. Camera, Thomas Del Ruth; editor, David Finfer; music, Joseph Vitarelli; production design, Charles Breen; costume design, Sue Kaufmann. Reviewed at Universal, Universal City, Feb. 19. MPAA Rating: R. Running time: 93 mins.

**David Schwimmer (Max Abbitt), Jason Lee (Jay Murphy), Mili Avital (Samantha Andrews), Bonnie Hunt (Linda), Vanessa Angel (Natasha), Kari Wuhrer (Dara).**

Max is a popular local sports broadcaster with a revolving door of ladies, while Jay is a writer with his first novel on the way. Jay sets his friend up with book editor Samantha, and while they seem ill-matched, the fireworks are so great that they are engaged within two weeks.

A slick, low-laugh-quotient romantic comedy, *Kissing a Fool* offers too few new wrinkles on the tired subject of yuppie commitment-anxiety. Sporting a small, contrived plot, pic looks to strike few sparks theatrically but might settle in as a reasonable vid title. Designed to contrast the dilemma of a compulsive womanizer who doesn't know if he can settle down with just one partner with the angst of an incurable romantic who can't get over a love-of-his-life heartbreak, script winds up hinging upon hokey devices of confrontation and consequent confessions.

U.S. release: Feb. 27                    U.S. B.O.: $4.1 million

## Knockin' on Heaven's Door (Germany)

A Buena Vista Int'l release of a Mr. Brown Entertainment/Buena Vista Int'l Filmproduction production. Produced by Til Schweiger, Tom Zickler, Andre Heinicke. Directed by Thomas Jahn. Screenplay, Jahn, Schweiger; original story by Jahn. Camera, Gero Steffen; editor, Alexander Berner; music, Franz Plasa, Selig; production design, Monika Bauert; costume design, Heike Weber. Reviewed at London Festival, Nov. 17, 1997. Running time: 90 mins.

**Til Schweiger (Martin Brest), Jan Josef Liefers (Rudi Wurlitzer), Thierry van Werveke (Henk), Moritz Bleibtreu (Abdul), Huub Stapel (Frankie "Boy" Beluga), Leonard Lansink (Schneider), Ralph Herforth (Keller), Rutger Hauer (Curtiz).**

Two social mavericks with terminal diseases break out of hospital for a final, glorious journey to the sea in *Knockin' on Heaven's Door*, a slick, energized road movie that's another feather in the cap of New German Cinema. Toplined, co-produced and co-written by local star Til Schweiger, it was Germany's top local pic. Offshore potential could be OK, given a reasonable chance and proper marketing.

Martin (Schweiger) and Rudi (Jan Josef Liefers) meet in a clinic where the former is diagnosed as having a brain tumor and the latter cancer. Determined to go out in a blaze of glory,

the pair bond and, after a tequila bender one night, head north to see the sea, fulfilling a longtime dream of Rudi's.

Int'l release: Feb. 20, 1997                    Int'l B.O.: $26 million

## Knock Off

A TriStar Pictures release of a Knock Films, A.V.V. and MDP Worldwide presentation of a Film Workshop Co. Ltd/Val D'Oro Entertainment production. Produced by Nansun Shi. Directed by Tsui Hark. Screenplay, Steven E. De Souza. Camera, Arthur Wong; editor, Mak Chi Sin; music, Ron Mael, Russell Mael; production design, James Leung, Bill Lui; costumes, Ben Luk, William Fung, Mable Kwan; stunt coordinator, Yuen Bing. Reviewed at Cinemark Tinseltown 290, Houston, Aug. 28. MPAA Rating: R. Running time: 91 mins.

**Jean-Claude Van Damme (Marcus Ray), Rob Schneider (Tommy Hendricks), Lela Rochon (Karen), Paul Sorvino (Johansson), Carmen Lee (Ling Ho), Wyman Wong (Eddie), Glen Chin (Skinny), Michael Fitzgerald Wong (Insp. Han).**

The last blast of the summer is an exuberantly cheesy action opus featuring Jean-Claude Van Damme and Rob Schneider as an improbable pair of gung-ho heroes. At once artfully stylized and brazenly junky, the aptly titled *Knock Off* is a perfunctorily Westernized version of a rock-the-house Hong Kong B-movie. The pic actually gets better as it goes along, thanks in large measure to the pell-mell pacing and quick-cut pizzazz of Tsui Hark, the cult-fave HK filmmaker. Expect so-so domestic B.O., slightly better overseas biz, and an extended afterlife in ancillary venues.

Van Damme and Schneider play business partners who run the Hong Kong branch of V-Six, a designer-label blue jeans company. In a modestly clever twist, it's Schneider who's a deep-cover CIA operative and Marcus has the checkered past: he was manufacturing and exporting "knock-off" brand name merchandise. He still has close friends in the underground, including adoptive brother Eddie. Marcus finds himself torn between his friendship for Tommy and loyalty to Eddie when all hell breaks loose in Hong Kong just before the 1997 transfer of the former British colony. Chinese gangsters, Russian Mafiosi, British Colonial police inspectors, and American intelligence agents add to the confusion and mayhem.

U.S. release: Sept. 4                    U.S. B.O.: $10.3 million
Int'l release: June 24                    Int'l B.O.: $10 million

## Krippendorf's Tribe

A Buena Vista release of a Touchstone Pictures presentation of a Mora-Brezner-Steinberg-Tenenbaum/Dreyfuss-James production. Produced by Larry Brezner. Directed by Todd Holland. Screenplay, Charlie Peters, based on the book by Frank Parkin. Camera, Dean Cundey; editor, Jon Poll; music, Bruce Broughton; production design, Scott Chambliss; costume design, Isis Mussenden. Reviewed at Loews Fountains Theater, Houston, Feb. 21. MPAA Rating: PG-13. Running time: 94 mins.

**Richard Dreyfuss (James Krippendorf), Jenna Elfman (Veronica Micelli), Natasha Lyonne (Shelly Krippendorf), Gregory Smith (Mickey Krippendorf), Carl Michael Linder (Edmund Krippendorf), David Ogden Stiers (Henry Spivey), Lily Tomlin (Ruth Allen), Zakes Mokae (Sulukim).**

Frenetic, formulaic, and instantly forgettable, *Krippendorf's Tribe* is a tepid one-joke comedy about a widowed anthropologist who employs his three children in a plot to fake the existence of an "undiscovered" New Guinea tribe. Despite its marquee allure, pic isn't likely to be discovered by many

---

**...June 11...**

Tom Hanks and Robert Zemeckis announce they'll reteam for dramatic comedy **The Castaway**.

ticket buyers. Expect a fast theatrical play-off, followed by modest action on cassette and cable.

Dreyfuss plays James Krippendorf, a respected academic who's driven to desperate measures by financial imperatives. Krippendorf and his wife, another anthropologist, journey to the wilds of New Guinea, where they try, and fail, to find a lost tribe. Two years after the wife's death, Krippendorf has spent all of his foundation grant to provide for his dysfunctional kids and now has to face the music.

U.S. release: Feb. 27          U.S. B.O.: $7.6 million
Int'l release: March 26        Int'l B.O.: $1.3 million

## Kundun

A Buena Vista release of a Touchstone Pictures presentation of a Cappa/De Fina production. Produced by Barbara De Fina. Directed by Martin Scorsese. Screenplay, Melissa Mathison, based on the life story of the Dalai Lama. Camera, Roger Deakins; editor, Thelma Schoonmaker; music, Philip Glass; production/costume design, Dante Ferretti. Reviewed at Harmony Gold, L.A., Dec. 6, 1997. MPAA Rating: PG-13. Running time: 134 mins.
**Tenzin Thuthob Tsarong (Adult Dalai Lama), Gyurme Tethong (Dalai Lama, age 12), Tulku Jamyang Kunga Tenzin (Dalai Lama, age 5), Tencho Gyalpo (Mother), Tsewang Migyur Khangsar (Father), Sonam Phunstok (Reting Rinpoche), Robert Lin (Chairman Mao).**
Martin Scorsese's haunting meditation on the early life of Tibet's Dalai Lama, *Kundun*, is one from the heart, a majestic spectacle of images and sounds. Bogged down by a routine screenplay, the film fails to provide fresh perspective on the nonviolent culture. The combination of a serious, demanding subject, a cast composed of Tibetan nonprofessionals, and the lack of an involving dramatic structure should spell box-office disappointment for the singular film.

Story begins in 1933 with the death of the 13th Dalai Lama and the search for a successor. Told from the point of view of a child born in a remote rural area, early chapters show the process of finding the religious leader's reincarnation. It sets a mysterious, almost surreal tone. The story gets more somber when it jumps ahead to 1944 and the Dalai Lama learns of Nazism and Hiroshima from magazines and newsreels. At the end of WWII, the Chinese communists move to seize control of Tibet, with Gen. Mao Zedong enforcing a reign of terror embodied by the massacre of innocents and the annihilation of a "society of spirit." Finally, the Dalai Lama has no choice but a journey into exile.

U.S. release: Dec. 25, 1997    U.S. B.O.: $5.5 million
Int'l release: March 13        Int'l B.O.: $10 million

## Kurt and Courtney (U.K., Docu)

A Strength Ltd production. Produced, directed by Nick Broomfield. Camera, Joan Churchill; editor, Mark Atkins; sound, Broomfield; second-unit camera, Alex Vendler. Reviewed at Slamdunk Festival, Jan. 18. Running time: 100 mins.
Docmeister Nick Broomfield's amusing penchant for dwelling on the frequent wild-goose-chase nature of investigative filmmaking becomes a raison d'être with *Kurt and Courtney*, his pic about late rock star Kurt Cobain and Courtney Love. Subject matter – and current publicity about pic's legal dilemmas – will no doubt spur interest for limited theatrical, broadcast, and vid exposure. Yet this undeniably lively, sometimes lurid package must rate in the end as one of

Broomfield's less satisfying efforts.

Film begins with suicide of Cobain then backtracks to sketch his unhappy youth in rural Washington state. By the time he married Love in 1992 his band, Nirvana, had defined the Seattle-based grunge sound worldwide, while she was a well-known punk scene gadfly with her own rising band, Hole. There's no question that the docu is highly unflattering to the musician-cum-actress professionally and in regard to numerous "conspiracy theories" floated in regard to Cobain's demise.

U.S. release: Feb. 27          U.S. B.O.: $700,000
Int'l release: July 3          Int'l B.O.: $300,000

## La Cucaracha

A Flashpoint Ltd presentation of a 723 Production. Produced by Richard C. Mann, Michael A. Candela. Directed by Jack Perez. Screenplay, Jack McManus. Camera, Shawn Mauer; editor, John Pace; music, Martin Davich; production designer, Reiko Kobayashi; costume designer, Elaine Montalvo; casting, Bonni Allen. Reviewed at Cannes Festival, May 14, 1998. Running time: 104 mins.
**Eric Roberts (Walter), Joaquim De Almeida (José Guerra), Victor Rivers (Humberto), Jack McManus (Louis), Tara Crespo (Lourdes).**
A young American hooked on Hemingway plunges into dramatic Mexican adventures in *La Cucaracha*. Despite a bantering, don't-take-me-seriously tone, pic has a curiously dark side that is never fully explored. Vid sales are likely to be the main outlet for this watchable but in no way outstanding vehicle.

Walter is a frustrated New Jersey office worker who one day leaves everything to travel to Santiago, Mexico and "be a writer." The town turns out to be a dusty, dangerous place where he never gets started writing because physical survival becomes top priority. Offered a job as a hit man by the town's leading citizen, José Guerra, Walter lets the illusion of riches tempt him.

## The Land Girls

A Gramercy Pictures release of a Polygram Filmed Entertainment presentation from Intermedia Films, with the participation of the Greenlight Fund and Channel Four Films, of a Greenpoint Film in association with West Eleven Films. Produced by Simon Relph. Directed by David Leland. Screenplay, Keith Dewhurst, Leland, based on the novel by Angela Huth. Camera, Henry Braham; editor, Nick Moore; music, Brian Lock; production design, Caroline Amies; costume design, Shuna Harwood. Reviewed at Sundance Festival, Jan. 20. Running time: 110 mins.
**Catherine McCormack (Stella), Rachel Weisz (Ag), Anna Friel (Prue), Steven Mackintosh (Joe Lawrence), Tom Georgeson (Mr. Lawrence), Maureen O'Brien (Mrs. Lawrence), Paul Bettany (Philip).**
Adding another interesting chapter to the revisionist history of women's contribution to WWII, David Leland's *The Land Girls* pays tribute to Britain's Women's Land Army, a unit composed of femmes who volunteered in the fields for the men gone to war. This traditional period drama is so exquisitely mounted and so splendidly acted that it might overcome the ultra-romantic center that gives the film an aura of soft melodrama. The pic holds special allure for older female audiences, but is so enjoyable on its own terms that, with the right marketing, Gramercy could reach a broader demographic.

---

**... June 12 ...**
John Travolta files $5 million lawsuit against capital-funding companies for misrepresentation – claiming he was a client.

In 1941 the Women's Land Army was formed in England. Answering the call, three women arrive at a remote spot in rural Dorset. Stella is a quiet, romantic woman, about to be married to a naval officer; Ag is a quirky and cerebral Cambridge grad looking to experience a different kind of life; and Prue is a working-class hairdresser whose brazen wit and flirtatious manner camouflage her innocence.

U.S. release: June 12         U.S. B.O.: $250,000
Int'l release: June 12         Int'l B.O.: $2.9 million

## The Land of the Deaf (Strana Gluchich) (Russia)

A Gorky Filmstudio presentation of a Studio Grashdane-Racoon Film production, supported by the Russian State Film Committee. Produced by Sergei Livnev. Directed by Valery Todorovsky. Screenplay, Todorovsky, Yuri Korotkov, from the novella *To Possess and To Belong*, by Renata Litvinova. Camera, Yuri Shaigardanov; editor, Natalia Kutsherenko; music, Alexei Aigi; production design, Sergei Ivanov; costume design, Alexander Osipov. Reviewed at Berlin Festival, Feb. 12. Running time: 119 mins.

**Chulpan Khamatova (Rita), Dina Korzun (Jaja), Maxim Sukhanov (Svinja), Nikita Tiunin (Alyosha), Alexander Yatsko (Albino), Alexei Gorbunov (Boss).**

Two vibrant young women, one of them hearing-impaired, are forced to test their survival skills in contemporary Moscow in Valery Todorovsky's handsome, uneven feature. The personal stories which unfold in the film are much more interesting than the rather perfunctory and familiar scenes featuring Russian gangsters, and the strong performances of the attractive leads are major assets. Further fest exposure and quality tube bookings are indicated for this generally accomplished effort.

Alyosha, the boyfriend of Rita, is a compulsive gambler who owes lots of money. During a meeting with a threatening creditor, the boss of a gang involved in casinos, Rita suddenly fears that Alyosha may be offering her to the gangster in payment of his debts, and high-tails it.

## Lani Loa: The Passage

A Francis Ford Coppola/Wayne Wang presentation of a Chrome Dragon Films production. Produced by John P. Marsh, Sherwood Hu. Directed by Hu. Screenplay, John P. Marsh. Camera, Hou Yong; editor, Nicholas C. Smith; music, Frank Fitzpatrick; production design, James Newport. Reviewed at San Sebastian Festival, Sept. 25. Running time: 89 mins.

**Angus MacFadyen (Turner), Carlotta Chang (Jenny), Ray Bumatai (Kenny), Chris Tashima (Bong).**

The first English-language feature from L.A.-based Chinese director Sherwood Hu, *Lani Loa: The Passage* tosses together Hawaiian exotica, Hong Kong-style gangster action, and otherworldly elements involving the vengeful specter of a murdered bride. Production values and physical direction are sharp enough on this energetic fantasy thriller, but its risible plot and lifeless performances from an uncharismatic cast look more likely to steer it to video than into theaters.

Opening intercuts parallel preparations, on one hand for the wedding of local cop Turner and his native Hawaiian bride, Jenny, and on the other for a bank robbery by a carload of mobsters led by ultraslick Bong. En route to his nuptials, Turner stops in at the bank and unwisely intervenes in the robbery. A car chase ensues, during which Turner pursues the criminals to the farmland where the wedding is to take place. The ceremonial altar becomes a bloodbath, with Jenny brutalized, almost raped, and finally mown down along with most of the guests. Jenny begins appearing in his dreams, eliminating the gangsters one by one as part of a cleanup operation before moving on to the next world. But when the bodies turn up in the light of day, suspicion falls on Turner.

## The Last Contract (Sista Kontraktet) (Sweden)

A Sonet Film release of a FilmLance Int'l (Sweden)/Yellow Cottage (Norway)/Kinoproduction (Finland). Produced by Borje Hansson. Directed by Kjell Sundvall. Screenplay, Mats Arihn, Johan Bogaeus, Hansson, based on a novel by John W. Grow. Camera, Kjell Lagerroos; editor, Darek Hodor; music, Geir Bohren, Bent Aserud; production design, Birgitta Brensin; costume design, Karin Sundvall. Reviewed at Swedish Film Institute, Stockholm, Feb. 23. Running time: 114 mins.

**Mikael Persbrandt (Roger), Michael Kitchen (Killer), Pernilla August (Roger's Wife), Reine Brynolfsson (Bo).**
(Swedish and English dialog)

The first feature to deal with the still-unsolved murder of Swedish Prime Minister Olof Palme, *The Last Contract* is a tight and mostly plausible thriller helmed by Kjell Sundvall. Home-soil box office for his new pic looks very good. The controversial Palme was gunned down while walking through central Stockholm in 1986. Over the years, the slaying has been attributed to everything from a lone gunman, South African agents, Turkish guerrillas, and Swedish police officers to members of the local financial community.

Pic opens with a young police officer, Roger, on the verge of a breakdown. His colleague Bo is ordered to find out what's troubling him and Roger tells how he came to believe someone was plotting to murder the prime minister and how he came close to preventing the crime. Film then flashes back to how the conspiracy was set in motion.

Int'l release: March 3         Int'l B.O.: $1.2 million

## The Last Days (Docu)

An October Films release of a Steven Spielberg presentation, in association with the Survivors of the Shoah Visual History Foundation. Produced by June Beallor, Ken Lipper. Directed by James Moll. Camera, Harris Done; editor, Moll; music, Hans Zimmer; historians, Dr. Michael Berenbaum, Dr. Randolph Braham. Reviewed at Mill Valley Festival, Oct. 10. Running time: 86 mins.

**With: Bill Basch, Alice Lok Cahana, Renee Firestone, Congressman Tom Lantos, Irene Zisblatt.**

Executive-produced by Steven Spielberg as the first theatrical release affiliated with his survivor-testimony-archiving Shoah Foundation, *The Last Days* is a hard-hitting, well-organized documentary grounded in the stories of five Hungarian Jews who lived through the Holocaust. While pic breaks no new ground, it provides a powerful, compact overview of both representative human experiences and larger historical events. Clearly blessed with production resources well above docu average, pic looks likely to reap awards and decent specialized biz when October rolls it out in early 1999; long broadcast and educational shelf lives will follow.

The now-elderly but quite hale survivors here are all current U.S. citizens originally born in prewar Hungary, which had one of the most assimilated and patriotic Jewish populations in Europe. So the subjects, who were then in their

---

...**June 13**...
**Six Days Seven Nights**, with Harrison Ford and Anne Heche, has a heady $23.6 million premiere in the U.S.

teens, were amazed when their homeland began aping Germany's anti-Semitic restriction laws and creating its own Nazi-allied movement.

## The Last Days of Disco

A Gramercy release of a Castle Rock Entertainment/Westerly Films presentation. Produced by Whit Stillman. Directed, written by Stillman. Camera, John Thomas; editors, Andrew Hafitz, Jay Pires; music, Mark Suozzo; music supervisor, Peter Afterman; production designer, Ginger Tougas; costumes, Sarah Edwards; choreographer, John Carrafa. Reviewed at Todd-AO, Santa Monica, April 28. MPAA Rating: R. Running time: 113 mins.
**Chloe Sevigny (Alice), Kate Beckinsale (Charlotte), Chris Eigeman (Des), Matt Keeslar (Josh), Mackenzie Astin (Jimmy), Robert Sean Leonard (Tom), Jennifer Beals (Nina).**
One September in "the very early 1980s" a bunch of friends converge on the hottest disco in New York.

The good times don't exactly roll in *The Last Days of Disco*, which is as interesting to watch for its serious disjuncture between style and content as for its cute cast and fabulous soundtrack. Whit Stillman's stiff directorial approach ill suits the sensual ambience of the club scene. External trappings and nostalgia value of the music give Gramercy something flashy to promote, but critical and audience reactions look to be mixed, resulting in just moderate overall B.O.

| | |
|---|---|
| U.S. release: May 29 | U.S. B.O.: $3 million |
| Int'l release: Sept. 10 | Int'l B.O.: $1.3 million |

## Last Night (Canada)

A Cineplex release of a Rhombus Media presentation for Arte and the Canadian Broadcasting Corp. Produced by Niv Fichman, Daniel Iron. Directed, written by Don McKellar. Camera, Douglas Koch; editor, Reginald Harkema; music, Alexina Louie, Alex Pauk; production designer, John Dondertman; costume designer, Lea Carlson. Reviewed at Cannes Festival, May 18. Running time: 94 mins.
**Don McKellar (Patrick Wheeler), Sandra Oh (Sandra), Callum Keith Rennie (Craig Zwiller), Sarah Polley (Jennifer Wheeler), David Cronenberg (Duncan), Tracy Wright (Donna), Genevieve Bujold (Mrs. Carlton).**
It's 6 p.m., and in six hours – give or take a couple of seconds – the world will come to an end. That's the gist of *Last Night*. And while it might appear to be a grim subject for a movie, writer-helmer Don McKellar's bittersweet pic is funny, heart-wrenching and life-affirming. The modestly produced first feature has offbeat appeal that will translate well for specialized play globally and strong sales in ancillary revenue streams.

Produced as part of a 12-segment Arte series on the year 2000, McKellar's take is the most cataclysmic. McKellar casts himself as Patrick, an architect who plans to meet the end alone, quietly, after a family dinner. The other character strands in the interwoven scenario involve a woman attempting to get across town for a suicide pact with her husband; Craig, who's pursuing a laundry list of sexual conquests; and Donna, who's trying to screw up her courage and show her true colors before the final fade. Without forcing the point, the script examines how someone who has withdrawn is forced to feel again. With the stakes higher than ever, the goal for most of the characters is that they exit with their humanity.

U.S. release: Oct. 23                            U.S. B.O.: $300,000

## Last Stop Paradise (Terminus Paradis) (France-Romania)

An MK2 Diffusion release of an MK2 Prods (France)/Le Studio de Création Cinématographique du Ministère de la Culture (Romania) production. Produced by Marin Karmitz. Directed by Lucian Pintilie. Screenplay, Pintilie, Ravsan Popescu, Radu Aldulescu. Camera, Calin Ghibu, Silviu Stavila; editors, Victoria Nae, Claudine Bouche; art director, Calin Papura; costume design, Catalina Ghibu. Reviewed at Club de l'Etoile, Paris, Aug. 31. Running time: 99 mins.
**Costel Cascaval (Mitou), Dorina Chiriac (Norica), Gheorghe Visu (Vatesescu), Victor Rebenguic (Grigore Cafanu), Razvan Vasilescu (Capt. Burci).**
When a rebellious hothead meets a young woman in hotpants, the results are classic yet unpredictable in *Last Stop Paradise*. With this scathing, ultimately touching portrait of l'amour fou at odds with evil and idiocy, ever-provocative Romanian director Lucian Pintilie provides an engaging contempo tale that denounces privilege and champions stubborn individuality. Keenly played pic will be a plus in any fest lineup but will still need lots of critical support to make it into hardtops beyond France and Romania.

Dimitri, known as Mitou, lures Elena, known as Noricato, to join him slug for slug in downing vodka. He tends pigs for a living and she waits table at Papa Gili's sausage stand, a ramshackle roadside dive. She and Gili – a corpulent lecher twice her age – are to be wed in the fall, but that doesn't stop Norica from accompanying Mitou to his minimally equipped apartment. Mitou is due to start two years of military service the next day. He's decided that Norica is his woman and nothing is going to stand in his way. Because Mitou refuses to compromise, he's on a collision course with authority.
Int'l release: Oct. 7                            Int'l B.O.: $75,000

## Late August, Early September (Fin Aout, Debut Septembre) (France)

A Polygram Film Distribution release of a Dacia Films/Cinea production, with the participation of Canal Plus, CNC. Produced by Georges Benayoun, Philippe Carcassonne. Directed, written by Olivier Assayas. Camera, Denis Lenoir; editor, Luc Barnier; music, Ali Sarka Toure; production design, François Renaud Labarthe; costume design, Françoise Clavel. Reviewed at Toronto Festival, Sept. 15. Running time: 111 mins.
**Mathieu Amalric (Gabriel Deshays), Virginie Ledoyen (Anne Rosenwald), François Cluzet (Adrien Willer), Jeanne Balibar (Jenny), Alex Descas (Jeremie), Arsinee Khanjian (Lucie), Mia Hansen-Love (Vera), Nathalie Richard (Maryelle).**
A kaleidoscopic but engrossing study of the shifting sands of friendship among a group of Parisians, *Late August, Early September* reps a major advance by writer-director Olivier Assayas in warmth and maturity. Shot in a slightly grainy, elliptical style but buoyed by terrific ensemble playing from its varied cast, this très-Gallic relationships pic will appeal to upscale auds on the arthouse circuit but will need strong critical support to make much of a theatrical dent outside France.

Central quartet comprises Gabriel, his ex-partner Jenny, his best friend Adrien, and his new g.f. Anne. Adrien, a former bestselling author, is suddenly faced with the reappearance of an illness that is now terminal, which opens up self-doubts about his worth as a writer and his longtime friendship with Gabriel. Unlike Adrien, Gabriel is not a risk-taker: His career path as an editor at a publishing house is steady and secure, and he's still in emotional indecision over his split with the somewhat loopy Jenny and his new relationship with the younger, all-or-nothing Anne.

## Lautrec (France-Spain)

A Les Films du Losange release of a Les Films du Losange, Le Studio Canal Plus, France 3 Cinema (France)/Sociedad General de Cine (Spain) production, with the participation of CNC and Canal Plus. Produced by Margaret Menegoz. Directed, written by Roger Planchon. Camera, Gerard Simon; editor, Isabelle Devinck; music, Jean-Pierre Fouquey; art director, Jacques Rouxel; costume design, Pierre-Jean Larroque. Reviewed at Club Gaumont, Paris, Aug. 19. Running time: 127 mins.

**Regis Royer (Henri de Toulouse-Lautrec), Elsa Zylberstein (Suzanne Valadon), Anemone (Adèle de Toulouse-Lautrec), Claude Rich (Alphonse de Toulouse-Lautrec), Jean-Marie Bigard (Aristide Bruant).**

Vet stage director Roger Planchon paints the short eventful life of Henri de Toulouse-Lautrec with strangely anemic strokes in this lavish, well-cast but emotionally inert costumer. Overlong pic strives to be as buoyant and racy as a cancan dancer but feels more like an anvil landing on a soufflé. Subject matter should facilitate offshore sales before pic settles into quality tube dates and video shelves.

Henri is seen within the first 10 minutes as a newborn with an unexplained bone deficiency and an adult with pince-nez, full beard, and painter's easel. His dad is a well-heeled womanizer, his beloved mom devoutly religious. And Henri? Well, Henri is sweet as can be but awfully short. In Paris, Lautrec undergoes ritual hazing before being accepted into the Beaux-Arts painting classes; makes friends with other young men who prefer the renegade Impressionists; is deflowered by an accommodating artist's model, and launches into a tempestuous affair with fellow painter Suzanne Valadon. Although sincerely smitten by Lautrec, the headstrong Suzanne fears that his style will exert too strong a pull. When he leaves her for good, Henri hits the absinthe, contracts venereal disease, and embarks on an ill-defined decline toward death.

Int'l release: Sept. 9      Int'l B.O.: $3 million

## L.A. Without a Map (U.K.-France-Finland)

A Dan Films/Euro American Films/Marianna Films production. Produced by Julie Baines, Sarah Daniel, Pierre Assouline. Directed by Mika Kaurismaki. Screenplay, Richard Rayner, Kaurismaki, based on the novel *Los Angeles Without a Map* by Rayner. Camera, Michael Amathieu; editor, Ewa J. Lind; music, Sebastien Cortella, Leningrad Cowboys; production design, Caroline Hanania; costume design, Yasmine Abraham. Reviewed at Toronto Festival, Sept. 11. Running time: 106 mins.

**David Tennant (Richard), Vinessa Shaw (Barbara), Julie Delpy (Julie), Vincent Gallo (Moss), Cameron Bancroft (Patterson), James Le Gros (Takowsky), Saskia Reeves (Joy), Joe Dallesandro (Michael). With: Anouk Aimée, Robert Davi, Johnny Depp, Monte Hellman as themselves.**

The lure of fame and fortune has drawn millions to Hollywood and spawned a veritable industry of books and movies about making it or not in the film industry. *L.A. Without a Map*, based on Richard Rayner's autobiographical novel, reps one of the tamer riffs on this theme. Essentially a boy-meets-girl yarn, the picture has some warm moments and funny vignettes but overall lacks the bite or wit to deliver more than modest commercial returns. Ancillary biz might be marginally better for this missed artistic opportunity.

It begins in the North of England, where Richard is the town's undertaker and writes obituaries for the local paper. Barbara – an aspiring actress from Los Angeles – stumbles into the village while vacationing. It's not particularly "meet cute," but they're photogenic together and Richard can't get her one-day visit out of his head. So he packs a bag and hops a plane to Hollywood. Armed only with a matchbook, he shows up at the Japanese restaurant where she waits tables and has told co-workers of the writer she met while touring. Richard's Hollywood education is a series of misadventures involving seedy hustlers, fast-talking agents, and hot-shot directors.

## Leaf on a Pillow (Daun Di Atas Bantal) (Indonesia)

A Christine Hakim Film production. Produced by Hakim. Directed by Garin Nugroho. Screenplay, Nugroho, Armantono. Camera, Nur Hidayat; editor, Sentot Sahid; music, Djaduk Ferianto; costumes, Jujuk Prabowo. Reviewed at Cannes Festival, May 23. Running time: 80 mins.

**With: Kancil, Heru, Sugeng, Christine Hakim, Kabri Wali, Denny Christantra, Sarah Azhari.**

Berlin Forum discovery Garin Nugroho takes the big step up to Cannes with *Leaf on a Pillow*, the fourth feature for the Indonesian helmer. Kaleidoscopic portrait of a bunch of street urchins is a well-worked subject, but Nugroho and his non-pro tykes bring a poetic humanity to the pic, free of preaching and heavy emoting. Limited distribution in some territories could be in the cards, with fests and upscale webs providing further platforms. The movie is a loose collection of incidents focused on a handful of kids who group around Asih, a middle-aged woman who has a small food-supply business and whose aberrant husband visits her only when he wants money.

Int'l release: Aug. 14      Int'l B.O.: $400,000

## Leaving (Bounce Ko Gals) (Japan)

A Shochiku Co. presentation. Produced by Masakatsu Suzuki. Directed, written by Masato Harada. Camera, Yoshitaka Sakamoto; editor, Hirohide Abe; music, Masahiro Kawasaki; art direction, Hiroshi Maruyama. Reviewed at Rotterdam Festival, Feb. 6. Running time: 110 mins.

**Hitomi Sato (Jonko), Yasue Sato (Raku), Yukiko Okamoto (Lisa), Jun Murakami (Sap), Shin Yazawa (Maru), Kaori Momoi (Saki), Koji Yakusho (Oshima).**

Director Masato Harada brings a disarmingly light touch to the dark subject of teen prostitution in *Leaving*. Exposing a generation of material girls without morals or values but with a curiously touching loyalty within their own ranks, the film centers on three Japanese high-school hookers, who use the demand for nubile flesh to finance their affluent lifestyles and expensive shopping careers. This upbeat, hip-looking youth film is structurally messy at times, but could see some specialized theatrical play.

The growing phenomenon of high-school "ko gals" (call girls, in the Nipponized English slang that resembles a Japanese version of Valley Girl-speak) is part of a booming teen-sex industry built around Tokyo's trendy Shibuya district. Against this background, a trio of characters are introduced and followed over the course of one long, eventful night.

Int'l release: Nov. 8, 1997      Int'l B.O.: $900,000

---

**...June 15...**

Col ponies up high-six-figure sum for original spec romantic comedy **Serial Dater**.

## Left Luggage

(Netherlands-Belgium-U.S.)

A Trident release of a Left Luggage BV-Shooting Star-Flying Dutchman Prods (Amsterdam)-Favourite Films (Brussels)-Greystone Films (Los Angeles) co-production. Produced by Ate de Jong, Hans Pos, Dave Schram. Directed by Jeroen Krabbe. Screenplay, Edwin de Vries, based on the novel *The Shovel and the Loom* by Carl Friedman. Camera, Walter Vanden Ende; editor, Edgar Burcksen; music, Henny Vrienten; production design, Hemmo Sportel; costume design, Yan Tax, Bernadette Corstens. Reviewed at Berlin Festival, Feb. 12. Running time: 100 mins.

**Laura Fraser (Chaja), Isabella Rossellini (Mrs. Kalman), Maximilian Schell (Chaja's Father), Jeroen Krabbe (Mr. Kalman), Marianne Sagebrecht (Chaja's Mother), David Bradley (Concierge), Adam Monty (Simcha), Chaim Topol (Mr. Apfelschnitt), Miriam Margolyes (Mrs. Goldman).**

Chaja, a free-spirited 20-year-old student, is the daughter of concentration-camp survivors. Needing cash to avoid eviction she seeks employment as a nanny in the home of a strict Hassidic family where she bridles against the rigid lifestyle.

Actor Jeroen Krabbe's directing debut is a well-intentioned but uneven and overly sentimental film about a young, liberated Jewish woman who finds herself drawn to members of an orthodox Hassidic family in Antwerp in 1972. Pic is undeniably thoughtful and serious, yet surprisingly contrived and unconvincing in crucial details. Despite a strong cast of players, film is likely to perform only modestly.

Int'l release: April 2 Int'l B.O.:$1.7 million

## The Legend of the Pianist on the Ocean (La Leggenda Del Pianista Sull'oceano) (Italy)

A Fine Line Features/Medusa Film release of a Medusa Film production made by Sciarlo. Executive producer, Laura Fattori. Directed, written by Giuseppe Tornatore, adapted from the stage monolog *Novecento*, by Alessandro Baricco. Camera, Lajos Koltai; editor, Massimo Quaglia; music, Ennio Morricone; production design, Francesco Frigeri; costume design, Maurizio Millenotti; digital visual-effects supervisor, David Bush. Reviewed at Cinecitta, Rome, Oct. 26. Running time: 170 mins.

**Tim Roth (Nineteenhundred), Pruitt Taylor Vince (Max), Melanie Thierry (The Girl), Bill Nunn (Danny Boodmann), Peter Vaughan (Music-Shop Owner), Alberto Vasquez (Mexican Machinist), Clarence Williams III (Jelly Roll Morton).**

Giuseppe Tornatore's first English-language feature, *The Legend of the Pianist on the Ocean*, is a physically imposing project of uncommon scope and ambition. Chronicling the extraordinary life of a virtuoso musician born at the dawn of the century on a trans-Atlantic steamer from which he never goes ashore, this watery epic displays many of the same strengths and weaknesses that have characterized the director's previous work, notably great technical skill and a strong visual sense, but a tendency for long-windedness and sentimental overkill.

The title character is an orphan left in a lemon crate of the first-class ballroom of the steamer *Virginian*, presumably by penniless parents from the lower decks. He's raised by a jovial machinist, who names him Danny Boodmann T.D. Lemon Nineteenhundred. Revealing an instinctive talent for tickling the ivories, he starts playing jazz and dance music upstairs for well-heeled passengers, and florid, unconventional tunes of his

own invention downstairs for the huddled masses of immigrants. But despite the offer of recording contracts and concert tours, Danny refuses to leave his floating world. He comes closest to going ashore after falling for a Gotham-bound Italian girl, but his apprehension stops him short.

Int'l release: Oct. 23 Int'l B.O.: $6 million

## Leila (Iran)

A Farazmand Film production, with support from the Hubert Bals Fund, Rotterdam. Produced by Dariush Mehrjui, Faramarz Farazmand. Directed, written by Mehrjui, based on a story by Mahnaz Ansarian. Camera, Mahmoud Kalari; editor, Mostafa Kherqepush; music, Keivan Jahanshahi; art direction, Zhila Mehrjui, Fariar Javaherian, Bita Qazal-Ayaq. Reviewed at Rotterdam Festival, Feb. 2. Running time: 124 mins.

**With: Leila Hatami, Ali Mosaffa, Jamileh Sheikhi, Mohammad Reza Sharifinia, Turan Mehrzad.**

One of the few Iranian features to make the global fest rounds recently that doesn't focus on children, veteran director Dariush Mehrjui's *Leila* is a highly emotional melodrama that deals effectively with adult issues. Examining the family pressure and guilt brought to bear on an affluent young couple when the wife discovers she is infertile, the film divided audiences in Iran.

Not long into her very happy marriage, Leila learns she is unable to have children. She tries homeopathic cures and traditional medicine without success, and flirts halfheartedly with the idea of adoption. But despite assurances from her supportive husband, Reza, that their life will be just as complete as a family of two, Leila's sense of her own inadequacy begins to weigh heavily on her mood.

## Lenny Bruce: Swear to Tell the Truth (Docu)

A Whyaduck production, in association with HBO Documentary films. Produced, directed, written by Robert B. Weide. Editors, Geof Bartz, Weide. Reviewed at Film Forum, N.Y., Oct. 30. Running time: 93 mins.

**Narrator: Robert De Niro.**

A long and loving tribute 10 years in the making, *Lenny Bruce: Swear to Tell the Truth* emotionally argues the performer's place as the most innovative thinker to emerge from the standup comedy circuit. After detailing his transformation from shticky gag man of the 1940s to cultural gadfly of the early 1960s, pic focuses perhaps a bit too much on the ceaseless attempts to prosecute him for speaking his mind by using dirty little words. While it is a resoundingly tragic story, the film is far from somber thanks to generous inclusions of Bruce's still-fresh material. After concluding its successful two-week run at Gotham's Film Forum, pic should enjoy strong success on HBO before becoming a provocative, sought-after vid rental.

The Lenny Bruce shown here is effectively evoked through a well-stitched quilt of photos, interviews with friends and associates (Steve Allen, ex-wife Honey Bruce, and jazz critic Nat Hentoff), unaired TV appearances, and footage of his standup act, emerging as a depressed yet hyperactive mama's boy. Film essentially makes two arguments about Bruce's life: that as a comedian he was without parallel, and that constant police persecution is what ultimately killed him. The first position is much more interesting and persuasive than the second; he was, after all, an extremely self-destructive guy.

U.S. release: Oct. 21 U.S. B.O.: $50,000

## Les Misérables

A Sony Pictures Entertainment release of a Columbia Pictures presentation of a Mandalay Entertainment presentation of a Sarah Radclyffe and James Gorman production. Produced by Radclyffe, Gorman. Directed by Bille August. Screenplay, Rafael Yglesias, based on the novel by Victor Hugo. Camera, Jorgen Persson; editor, Janus Billeskov-Jansen; music, Basil Poledouris; production designer, Anna Asp; costume designer, Gabriella Pescucci. Reviewed at Century Plaza Cinema, L.A., April 22. MPAA Rating: PG-13. Running time: 131 mins.

**Liam Neeson (Valjean), Geoffrey Rush (Javert), Uma Thurman (Fantine), Claire Danes (Cosette), Peter Vaughan (Bishop).**

The third American screen rendition of Victor Hugo's classic novel *Les Misérables* is without a doubt the most emotionally powerful and handsomely mounted production yet. Though the romantic, *Romeo and Juliet*-like plot appears mostly in the last reel, Columbia could profitably use it to lure younger audiences to a period piece that naturally holds stronger appeal for older and more educated viewers. A classy entertainment that does full honor to its source, it should play well as counterprogramming to the season's action-adventure fare.

This version starts with Valjean being released on parole after enduring 20 years of hard labor and cruelty. The harsh treatment has made Valjean a brute with strong survival instincts but no sense of morality. The only things he can rely on are his instinctive wit and sheer physical strength.

| U.S. release: May 1 | U.S. B.O.: $14 million |
| Int'l release: May 14 | Int'l B.O.: $7 million |

## Lethal Weapon 4

A Warner Bros. release of a Silver Pictures production, in association with Doshudo Prods. Produced by Joel Silver, Richard Donner. Directed by Donner. Screenplay, Channing Gibson; story by Jonathan Lemkin, Alfred Gough, Miles Millar, based on characters created by Shane Black. Camera, Andrzej Bartkowiak; editors, Frank J. Urioste, Dallas Puett; music, Michael Kamen, Eric Clapton, David Sanborn; production designer, J. Michael Riva; costume designer, Ha Nguyen; martial-arts choreography, Cory Yuen, Huen Chiu Ku, Chi Wah Ling. Reviewed at Mann Village, L.A., July 6. MPAA Rating: R. Running time: 127 mins.

**Mel Gibson (Martin Riggs), Danny Glover (Roger Murtaugh), Joe Pesci (Leo Getz), Rene Russo (Lorna Cole), Chris Rock (Lee Butters), Jet Li (Wah Sing Ku), Steve Kahan (Capt. Murphy), Darlene Love (Trish Murtaugh), Traci Wolfe (Rianne).**

Detectives Riggs and Murtaugh are up to the sort of mischief in *Lethal Weapon 4* that's made the series a successful popcorn entertainment over the past decade. The quintessence of the buddy cop pic, *LW4* is big on action, playful banter and just enough plot to keep our attention from wandering. It matters little that the film is rife with non sequiturs, nonsense, and nihilistic violence, because its heroes are so darn buoyant and charming. In the current climate of big movies with low entertainment quotients, pic stands out because it delivers the goods, making it a leading prospect for the summer's B.O. crown, with domestic revenue likely to rival earlier installments.

Bare-bones plot centers on a group of transplanted Chinese triad members who are smuggling in families from the mainland. Of course, such penny-ante criminal activity is just the tip of the iceberg in a much more nefarious operation. But the film is as concerned with what's going on in the margins as it is with the evil doings of martial-arts master and triad leader Wah Sing Ku.

| U.S. release: June 10 | U.S. B.O.: $130 million |
| Int'l release: July 16 | Int'l B.O.: $145 million |

## Let's Get Lost (Denmark)

A Per Holst Film presentation of a Dansk Novellefilm production, with support from the Danish Film Institute. Produced by Per Holst. Directed, written by Jonas Elmer. Camera (B&W), Bo Tengberg; editor, Mette Zeruneith; music, Nikolaj Egelund, Povi Kristian; sound (Dolby digital), Niels Arnt Torp; assistant director, Ake Griffenberg. Reviewed at Berlin Film Festival, Feb. 13, 1998. Running time: 92 mins.

**Sidse Babett Knudsen (Julie Mynborg), Bjarne Henriksen (Mogens Krovgaard), Troels Lyby (Thomas Bachausen), Nicolaj Kopernikus Christiansen (Steffan Ficher), Jesper Asholt (Little John), Martin Kongstad (Rene Dalgaard).**

*Let's Get Lost* is an abrasively honest and entertaining first feature that, surprisingly, hasn't found an official festival slot since it was completed in the second half of last year. A surprise commercial success in Denmark, the black-and-white film certainly deserves international exposure. Newcomer Jonas Elmer received funding only for a short film, but was resourceful enough to use the cash to make a full-length feature. Result is an understated but heartfelt examination of a clutch of ordinary folk trying to survive in difficult financial and emotional circumstances.

Julie is in a state because her boyfriend, Rene, is neglecting her; she suspects there's another woman. Elmer's film is about surviving, and its group of idle but amiable dreamers are nothing if not survivors.

## Let's Talk About Sex

A Fine Line Features release of a Deborah Ridpath production. Produced by Ridpath. Directed, written by Troy Beyer. Camera, Kelly Evans; editor, Bill Henry; music, Michael Carpenter; production design, Joe Warson; costume design, Timothy Biel. Reviewed at Aidikoff Screening Room, Beverly Hills, Sept. 9. MPAA Rating: R. Running time: 82 mins.

**Troy Beyer (Jazz), Paget Brewster (Michelle), Randi Ingerman (Lena), Joseph C. Phillips (Michael), Michaline Babich (Morgan), Tina Nguyen (Drew).**

Following the recent indie trend of scripted features presented in documentary style, *Let's Talk About Sex* is a crude piece of filmmaking that's bogged down by laughable melodrama and weak perfs. The salacious material and overall low quality make it nearly impossible to distinguish filmmaker Troy Beyer's debut feature from any latenight, cable soft-core pic. Expect minimal theatrical returns.

Jazz is a Miami advice columnist who's sick of her newspaper gig and wants to get off the ground a TV show featuring women talking about what they desire in relationships. She has a week to film a pilot, so she employs her best friends – the ruthless man-user Michelle and the vulnerable Lena. The trio set out to "find out what makes girls tick," which means listening to women talking about sexual wants and frustrations.

| U.S. release: Sept. 11 | U.S. B.O.: $400,000 |

## Life is Beautiful (La Vita E Bella) (Italy)

A Cecchi Gori Distribuzione release of a Mario and Vittorio Cecchi Gori/Roberto Benigni presentation of a Melampo Cinematografica production. Produced by Elda Ferri, Gianluigi

---

**... June 17 ...**

**Citizen Kane** tops AFI's top-100 pix list.

Braschi. Directed by Roberto Benigni. Screenplay, Vincenzo Cerami, Benigni. Camera, Tonino Delli Colli; editor, Simona Paggi; music, Nicola Piovani; art direction/costume design, Danilo Donati. Reviewed at Anica, Rome, Dec. 11, 1997. Running time: 122 mins.

**Roberto Benigni (Guido), Nicoletta Braschi (Dora), Giustino Durano (Uncle), Sergio Bustric (Ferruccio), Horst Buchholz (Dr. Lessing), Giorgio Cantarini (Giosue).**

Roberto Benigni achieves mixed results with his latest actor-director outing, *Life is Beautiful*, a bittersweet tragicomedy set during World War II about an erudite buffoon, his sweetheart and the infant son he lovingly shelters from the horrors of Nazism. Benigni's films have never quite lived up to the popular star's formidable performing skills, and this most ambitious project yet is no exception. Sluggish, uneven, and lacking in rhythm, it nonetheless has enough pathos and winning humor to ensure national success and a share of foreign sales.

Budgeted at $6.5 million, feature strives to improve on the genre's normally modest production standards. Set in a large Tuscan town in the 1930s, Guido falls for sweet, upper-class schoolteacher Dora and slowly wins her over. Five years later, they are married with a son who's starting to ask questions about anti-Jewish sentiment.

| | |
|---|---|
| Int'l release: Dec. 11, 1997 | Int'l B.O.: $68 million |
| U.S. release: Oct. 23 | $10.5 million |

### Life on Earth (La Vie Sur Terre) (Docudrama, France)

An Haut et Court Distribution release of a La Sept Arte/Haut et Court production, in association with Centre National de la Cinématographie, Procirep. Produced by Caroline Benjo, Carole Scotta. Directed, written by Abderrahmane Sissako. Camera, Jacques Besse; editor, Nadia Ben Rachid; music, Salif Keita, Anovar, Brahem, Balafons et Tamours d'Afrique. Reviewed at Cannes Film Festival, May 21. Running time: 61 mins.

**Abderrahmane Sissako (Dramane), Nana Baby (Nana), Mohamed Sissako (Father), Keita Bina Gaoussou (Postman), Mahamadou Drame (Telephone Employee).**

French-based Mauritanian helmer Abderrahmane Sissako goes back to a small village in Mali to see his father. Life in the sleepy village revolves around the post office, site of the only telephone in town.

*Life on Earth* is probably the most visually stunning film in the "Collection 2000" series. It isn't hard to see why this serious and poetic work was selected for the Cannes Directors Fortnight, despite some tiring repetitions. Its brief running time is more than sufficient for a depiction of an African village as it prepares to enter the new millennium. Specialized TV should be interested in this very original entry.

### Like It Is (U.K.)

A Dangerous To Know release of a Fulcrum production, in association with Channel 4. Produced by Tracey Gardiner. Directed by Paul Oremland. Screenplay, Robert Gray; story by Gray, Oremland, Kevin Sampson. Camera, Alistair Cameron; editor, Jan Langford; music, Don McGlashan; production designer, Tim Sykes; Carl Gardiner. Reviewed at ABC Piccadilly, London, May 5. Running time: 100 mins.

**Roger Daltrey (Kelvin), Dani Behr (Paula), Ian Rose (Matt), Steve Bell (Craig), Christopher Hargreaves (Tony), P.J. Nicholas (Jamie).**

A gay boxer from the North finds love and disillusionment in trendy London in *Like It Is*, a respectable low-budgeter from first-time director Paul Oremland that mostly steers a refreshing middle path between gaucheness and grandstanding. Though the story is hardly original, natural perfs and smooth production values help to bolster the slim pic.

| | |
|---|---|
| U.S. release: Sept. 4 | U.S. B.O.: $70,000 |
| Int'l release: April 17 | Int'l B.O.: $25,000 |

### The Lion King II: Simba's Pride (Direct-To-Video, Animated)

A Buena Vista Home Entertainment release of a Walt Disney Home Video production. Produced by Jeannine Roussel. Directed by Darrell Rooney. Screenplay, Flip Kobler, Cindy Marcus. Director of animation, Steven Trenbirth; editor, Peter N. Lonsdale; music score, Nick Glennie-Smith; art director, Fred Warter. Reviewed on videocassette, Houston, Oct. 14. Running time: 75 mins.

**Voices: Matthew Broderick (Simba), Neve Campbell (Kiara), Andy Dick (Nuka), Robert Guillaume (Rafiki), James Earl Jones (Mufasa), Moira Kelly (Nala), Nathan Lane (Timon), Jason Marsden (Kovu), Suzanne Pleshette (Zira), Ernie Sabella (Pumbaa).**

Disney likely will set a new record for sales of a direct-to-video title when *The Lion King II: Simba's Pride* roars into retail outlets. And don't be surprised if some buyers aren't parents of small children. In marked contrast to most of the studio's small-screen sequels to big-screen animated hits, new pic isn't merely kids' stuff. Not unlike its Oscar-winning predecessor, *Lion King II* has enough across-the-board appeal to entertain viewers of all ages.

Sequel begins where the 1994 original ended, with Simba established as king of beasts in the African Pridelands. With Nala, his loving mate, Simba officiates at the ceremonial introduction of his newborn, Kiara. Much to the dismay of the overly-protective Simba, Kiara is an inquisitive and energetic free spirit who tends to wander off on misadventures. While prowling through the forbidden Outlands, where Scar's minions have been banished, the Lion Princess befriends another rambunctious cub, Kovu. At first, Kovu is a willing pawn in his mother Zira's plans for revenge. But as he grows older and falls in love with Kiara, things get appreciably more complicated.

### A Little Bit of Soul (Australia)

A Columbia TriStar release of a Beyond Films presentation of a Faust Film production. Produced by Peter Duncan, Simon Martin, Martin McGrath, P.J. Voeten. Directed, written by Duncan. Camera, Martin McGrath; editor, Simon Martin; music, Nigel Westlake; production designer, Tony Campbell; costumes, Terry Ryan. Reviewed at Greater Union Theater, Sydney, Aug. 24, 1997. Running time: 83 mins.

**Geoffrey Rush (Godfrey Usher), David Wenham (Richard Shorkinghom), Frances O'Connor (Kate Haslett), Heather Mitchell (Grace Michael), John Gaden (Dr. Somerville), Kerry Walker (Eugene Mason).**

Peter Duncan's sophomore outing is a mini-budgeted, rather talkative comedy that takes a fresh approach to the venerable Faust theme. Some name talent, including Geoffrey Rush, should ensure pic gets a decent start in Oz. Internationally, pic is probably too modestly scaled to find theatrical bookings, so ancillary markets will likely yield best results. *Soul* is very much up-to-the-minute, with Rush playing an ambitious and

---

avuncular politician. Pic centers on research scientists with competing formulas to reverse the ageing process who court the pol's favor only to discover his hellish secret.

### Little Book of Love (Pequeno Dicionario Amoroso) (Brazil)

A Cinéluz and Lumière presentation of a Werneck/Beauchamps/Wainer production. Produced by Sandra Werneck, Marc Beauchamps, Bruno Wainer. Directed by Takashi Miike. Screenplay, Paulo Halm, José Roberto Torero. Camera, Walter Carvalho; editor, Virginia Flores; music, Ed Motta, Joao Nabuco; production design, Claudio Amaral Peixoto; costumes, Pedro Sayad. Reviewed at Vancouver Festival, Sept. 9, 1997. Running time: 91 mins.
**With:** Andrea Beltrao, Daniel Dantas, Monica Torres, Tony Ramos, Gloria Pires, José Wilker.

A terrific concept and solid performances don't compensate for a hackneyed script in this Rio-set romance-by-numbers – make that letters. Idea for this "Little Book of Love" (or "dictionary" in Portuguese) is to break down particulars of a single affair into alphabetically arranged stages. Actual execution, although well received at home, rates no more than a C, nixing chances for offshore importation. Andrea Beltrao plays Luiza, a thirtysomething looking for the Real Thing when she bumps into Gabriel (Daniel Dantas), an amiably rumpled researcher in the midst of a messy divorce. Despite this problem they almost immediately click.

### Little Miracles (Pequenos Milagros) (Argentina , Color/B&W)

A Spanish Television Services presentation of a Promisa S.A. production, with the participation of INCAA. Produced by Omar Romaya, Eliseo Subiela. Directed, written by Eliseo Subiela. Camera, Daniel Rodriguez Maseda; editor, Marcela Saenz; music, Osvaldo Montes; production designer, Margarita Jusid, Ruben Greco. Reviewed at San Francisco Festival, April 28. Running time: 102 mins.
Julieta Ortega (Rosalia), Antonio Birabent (Santiago), Susana Monica Galan (Susana), Paco M (Don Francisco).

Not since Tinkerbell first got clapped back to consciousness has there been such a run on fairy lore, which seems to be the mythic totem du jour. In contrast to recent family-oriented pics, Eliseo Subiela's latest mines that same whimsical theme for grownups. The sweet-tempered *Little Miracles*, however, may be a bit soft to travel as far on international circuits.

His protagonist this time may think she's a "fairy godmother," but she's more like Cinderella. Rosalia lives simply in Buenos Aires, working as a cashier at a supermarket where customers are routinely stumped by her impromptu theological queries.
Int'l release: Sept. 25, 1997          Int'l B.O.: $650,000

### Little Teachers (I Piccoli Maestri) (Italy)

A Cecchi Gori Distribuzione release of a Mario and Vittorio Cecchi Gori presentation of a Cecchi Gori Group Tiger Cinematografica production. Produced by Vittorio and Rita Cecchi Gori. Directed by Daniele Luchetti. Screenplay, Sandro Petraglia, Stefano Rulli, Domenico Starnone, Luchetti, based on the novel by Luigi Meneghello. Camera, Giuseppe Lanci; editor, Patrizio Marone; music, Dario Lucantoni; production design, Giancarlo Basili; costume design, Maria Rita Barbera. Reviewed at Cecchi Gori Group, Rome, Aug. 5. Running time: 114 mins.

Stefano Accorsi (Gigi), Stefania Montorsi (Simonetta), Giorgio Pasotti (Enrico), Diego Gianesini (Lelio), Filippo Sandon (Bene), Manuel Donato (Nello), Stefano Scandaletti (Rodino), Marco Piras (Dante).

Having proved himself a skilled director of sharply scripted social comedies, Daniele Luchetti seems destined to keep following his hits with ambitious misfires. The Italo helmer now follows 1995's *School* with the disappointing *Little Teachers*. Based on Luigi Meneghello's poetic novel about a band of idealistic young college students drawn into the Resistance, this antiheroic take on the World War II partisan movement musters too little passion and emotion to stir much theatrical support.

Chronicle of the final 20 months before Italy's liberation from fascism centers on a group of philosophy-spouting student chums. Identifying empty rhetoric as their prime enemy, they head into the mountains in Nazi-occupied northern Italy. Their early exploits are marked more by enthusiasm than strategy. But as they become part of the real conflict, and some are killed, the eye-opening reality of war changes them. Maintaining an almost jaunty tone in the early going, the film gradually acquires dramatic weight as its protagonists develop a consciousness of the events in which they blithely became involved, and as the barely formed principles of democracy and freedom they set off pursuing become fused by pain and experience into more concrete ideals.
Int'l release: Sept. 4          Int'l B.O.: $1.3 million

### Little Tony (Kleine Teun) (The Netherlands)

A Warner Bros. release of a Graniet Film production. Produced by Marc van Warmerdam, Ton Schippers, Alex van Warmerdam. Directed, written by van Warmerdam, based on his play. Camera, Marc Felperlaan; editor, Stefan Kamp; music, Alex van Warmerdam; art directors, Jelier & Schaaf; costume designer, Leonie Polak. Reviewed at Cannes Festival, May 14. Running time: 95 mins.
Annet Malherbe (Keet), Ariane Schluter (Lena), Alex van Warmerdam (Brand), Sebastian and Tomas te Wierk (Tony).

Dutch director Alex van Warmerdam has proved himself an original observer of bizarre human behavior, unafraid to touch nerves with his scabrous sense of humor. His accomplished fourth feature, *Little Tony*, is both blacker and more tightly focused. A droll comedy about power and possessiveness within a less-than-harmonious ménage a trois, the film steadily darkens its mood as it proceeds unpredictably toward the three-way tangle's drastic solution. The director's last feature traveled widely through specialized distribs, and this one should do the same. The quintessentially Dutch setting is a picture-book farmhouse. Here the illiterate Brand and his wife, Keet, seem basically happy despite her yearning for a child.
Int'l release: April 29          Int'l B.O.: $350,000

### Little Voice (U.K.)

A Miramax Films release of a Miramax/Scala presentation of a Scala Prods production. Produced by Elizabeth Karlsen. Directed, written by Mark Herman, based on the play *The Rise and Fall of Little Voice* by Jim Cartwright. Camera Andy Collins; editor, Michael Ellis; music and arrangements, John Altman; production design, Don Taylor; costume design, Lindy Hemming. Reviewed at Toronto Film Festival, Sept. 18. Running time: 96 mins.

Brenda Blethyn (Mari Hoff), Jane Horrocks (Laura Hoff aka L.V.), Michael Caine (Ray Say), Jim Broadbent (Mr. Boo), Ewan McGregor (Billy), Annette Badland (Sadie).

*Little Voice* is a small picture with a big heart. Intelligently opened up from Jim Cartwright's London legit hit, without losing the intimacy, this broad, northern English working-class comedy centers on a repressed young woman with a gift for mimicking musical show-stoppers. The film has everything going for it, with the exception of a somewhat lopsided structure in which the climax comes two-thirds of the way through, and a romantic subplot that plays like an afterthought. Nevertheless, smooth direction by Mark Herman and juicy performances by a host of Brit character actors ensure an entertaining ride, signaling warm curtain calls on a limited basis, especially among older, more discerning auds.

Jane Horrocks encores her title role from the 1992 National Theatre production of *The Rise and Fall of Little Voice*, with spot-on vocal impersonations that extend from Judy Garland and Marilyn Monroe to Shirley Bassey and Marlene Dietrich. Horrocks is Laura Hoff (nicknamed "L.V." – "Little Voice"), the withdrawn daughter of Mari, an ageing white-trash widow in a northern seaside town. Traumatized by the death of her father, with whom she shared a love of song, Laura spends most of the time alone, listening to her dad's vintage disc collection. Downstairs, liberated from domesticity, mom is in sexual overdrive, with sleazy talent agent Ray Say. When he hears Laura singing, he smells a chance of the big time and persuades both local niterie owner Mr. Boo and Mari to give Laura a chance on stage. The big questions are whether Laura will play along, and whether her private gift will translate as a public performance.

U.S. release: Dec. 4                    U.S. B.O.: $700,000

## Living in Paradise (Vivre Au Paradis) (France-Belgium-Norway-Algeria)

A 3B Prods (Paris)/Alinea Film (Brussels)/Exposed Films (Oslo)/WFE (Algiers) co-production. Produced by Jean Brehat, Rachid Bouchareb. Directed by Bourlem Guerdjou. Screenplay, Olivier Lorelle, Olivier Douyere, Guerdjou, based on a book by Brahim Benaicha. Camera, Georges Lechaptois; editor, Sandrine Deegen; production design, Laurent Perod; costume design, Khadija Zeggai. Reviewed at Venice Festival, Sept. 9. Running time: 104 mins. (Arabic and French dialog)

Roschdy Zem (Lakhdar), Fadila Belkebla (Nora), Omar Bekhaled (Rachid), Farida Rahouadj (Ouarda), Hiam Abbass (Aicha).

Bourlem Guerdjou's beautiful and moving film is set in the 'burbs of Paris in the early 1960s, when the Algerian War was creating tensions among the Arab community in France. Centering on a husband who works himself to the bone to buy an apartment for his family while his wife turns to political activism, *Living in Paradise* is a reminder of the harm unbridled racism can inflict on a community. Further fest exposure is a given, and quality tube programmers will want to schedule this one.

Pic begins with Algerian immigrant Lakhdar living in squalid circumstances while he labors on a building site. He is better educated than many of the other Algerians: he can read and write. But he misses his wife and two children so much that he persuades them to come and live with him. Nora, his wife, is appalled by the squalor. Though traditionally accustomed to a subservient role, she begins to become politically active in the fight for better living and working conditions.

## Living Out Loud

A New Line Cinema release of a Jersey Films production. Produced by Danny DeVito, Michael Shamberg, Stacey Sher. Directed, written by Richard LaGravenese. Camera, John Bailey; editors, Jon Gregory, Lynzee Klingman; music, George Fenton; production design, Nelson Coates; costume design, Jeffrey Kurland; sound, Petur Hliddal. Reviewed at Loews Cineplex Copley Place, Boston, Sept. 8. MPAA Rating: R. Running time: 93 mins.

Holly Hunter (Judith), Danny DeVito (Pat), Queen Latifah (Liz Bailey), Martin Donovan (Bob Nelson), Richard Schiff (Philly), Elias Koteas (Kisser).

This feminist comedy shot through with fantasies about the travails of newly single womanhood strikes some rich chords, but doesn't quite put together a complete tune. Uneven New Line release will face an uphill commercial battle against other upscale fall fare, although it could develop a following amongst thirtysomething women.

Premise has Judith finding herself alone in the world when her doctor husband dumps her for a younger woman. Pat is the elevator operator in Judith's exclusive Gotham apartment building, a man with big dreams and equally big gambling debts. The two lonely souls reach out to each other, although Judith finds it hard to take Pat seriously as a prospective partner. Despite fine work by Hunter and DeVito in their roles, LaGravenese paints himself into a corner with this central relationship. With no realistic expectation of a conventional romantic happy ending, pic is hemmed in without a clear direction out.

U.S. release: Oct. 30                    U.S. B.O.: $12 million

## Lock, Stock and Two Smoking Barrels (U.K.)

A Polygram Filmed Entertainment release of a Steve Tisch Co./SKA Films presentation. Produced by Matthew Vaughan. Directed, written by Guy Ritchie. Camera, Tim Maurice-Jones; editor, Niven Howie; original music, David A. Hughes, John Murphy; production design, Iain Andrews, Eve Mavrakis; costume design, Stephanie Collie; stunt coordinator, Glenn Marks. Reviewed at BAFTA, London, July 2. Running time: 105 mins.

Jason Flemyng (Tom), Dexter Fletcher (Soap), Nick Moran (Eddy), Jason Statham (Bacon), Steven Mackintosh (Winston), Vinnie Jones (Big Chris), Sting (J.D.), P.H. Moriarty (Hatchet Harry), Steve Sweeney (Plank), Frank Harper (Dog), Peter McNicholl (Little Chris).

With visual style to spare, and a cast and plot you need a computer to keep track of, British writer-director Guy Ritchie's debut *Lock, Stock and Two Smoking Barrels* lacks nothing in energy. This London crime caper is peopled by brutes and half-wits speaking in a cockney version of Damon Runyonese. It falls, however, some way short, relying increasingly on plot twists and outré violence to sustain pacing and interest.

It's a pranky, often entertaining but not very pleasant night out at the movies. Set in a grubby, working-class armpit of London's East End, the complex story centers on four layabouts who cook up a scheme to make some big money by having one of them, cardsharp Eddy, enter a game with gangster/porn king Hatchet Harry. But things go drastically wrong and Eddy loses his bundle of half a million pounds. Desperate to raise some quick cash, he overhears a plan by mob neighbors to rob a marijuana outlet and arranges with his cronies to get there first and make off with the cash and plants.

Int'l release: Aug. 28                    Int'l B.O.: $23 million

---

**. . . June 20 . . .**

Fox's **The X-Files** and Disney's **Mulan** dominate the box office in the U.S.

## Lost in Space

A New Line Cinema release of a Prelude Pictures production, in association with Irwin Allen Prods. Produced by Mark W. Koch, Stephen Hopkins, Akiva Goldsman, Carla Fry. Directed by Hopkins. Screenplay, Goldsman. Camera, Peter Levy; editor, Ray Lovejoy; music, Bruce Broughton; production designer, Norman Garwood; costume designer, Vin Burnham, Robert Bell, Gilly Hebden; visual-effects supervisor, Angus Bickerton. Reviewed at Variety Club, April 1. MPAA Rating: PG-13. Running time: 131 mins.

William Hurt (John Robinson), Mimi Rogers (Maureen Robinson), Heather Graham (Judy Robinson), Lacey Chabert (Penny Robinson), Jack Johnson (Will Robinson), Gary Oldman (Dr. Smith), Matt LeBlanc (Don West), Jared Harris (Old Will).

One of the most endearingly dumb baby-boomer tube faves finally makes it to the big screen with *Lost in Space*. New Line's most commercially ambitious, and costly, production reps a considerable risk, although a strong opening seems assured. Still, word of mouth is likely to taper fast for a pic that provides one hour's decent, eye-filling ride, then crashes and burns amid some terrible writing. The updated *Swiss Family Robinson* places a traditional, all-American nuclear family – plus one romantic-interest hunk for the eldest daughter, a duplicitous stowaway, and one loyal robot – on a spaceship that is off course.

U.S. release: April 3      U.S. B.O.: $69 million
Int'l release: April 9      Int'l B.O.: $60 million

## Louisa May Alcott's Little Men (Canada)

A Legacy release of a Brainstorm Media, in association with Image Organization presentation of an Allegro Films production. Produced by Pierre David, Franco Battista. Directed by Rodney Gibbons. Screenplay, Mark Evan Schwartz, based on the novel by Louisa May Alcott. Camera, Georges Archambault; editor, Andre Corriveau; music, Milan Kymlicka; production designer, Donna Noonan; costume designer, Janet Campbell. Reviewed at Samuel Goldwyn Cinemas, L.A., May 2. MPAA Rating: PG. Running time: 98 mins.

Michael Caloz (Nat Blake), Mariel Hemingway (Jo Bhaer), Ben Cook (Dan), Ricky Mabe (Tommy Bangs), Chris Sarandon (Fritz Bhaer), Gabrielle Boni (Nan Harding), Michael Yarmoush (Emil).

A straightforward, not particularly engrossing story of camaraderie among boys, *Louisa May Alcott's Little Men* seems a calculated attempt to benefit from Gillian Armstrong's well-received *Little Women*. But whereas that film's success was enhanced by a combination of strong casting and the novel's long-standing reputation, new pic will have an uphill B.O. battle, in part because the book is not as well known.

Though it's wholesome family fare, *Little Men* is probably too sentimental and has neither the directorial nuances nor the acting strengths of the earlier production. New tale follows the adventures of Nat and Dan, two street urchins with a penchant for trouble. About to be apprehended for petty theft, Nat becomes the recipient of a kindly benefactor's goodwill and goes to live at Plumfield, the happy, peaceful school run by Jo and Fritz Bhaer. Meanwhile, Dan eludes the authorities.

U.S. release: May 8      U.S. B.O.: $100,000

## Louis & Frank

(France-U.S.)

An MK2 Diffusion/Why Not Prods presentation of an MK2 Prods/Why Not Prods production, in association with Eureka Pictures. Produced by Tim Perell, Howard Bernstein, Alexandre Rockwell. Directed, written by Rockwell; editor, Elena Maganini; music, Paolo Conte; production design, Susan Block; costume design, Catherine Thomas. Reviewed at Rotterdam Festival, Feb. 2. Running time: 87 mins.

Steven Randazzo (Louis), Francesco Messina (Frank), Tony Curtis (Lenny Star Springer), Meta Golding (Betsy), Sam Rockwell (Sam), Rockets Redglare (Ralph), Steve Buscemi (Drexel).

With *Louis & Frank*, Alexandre Rockwell attempts a return to the levity and spirit of his 1992 Sundance prizewinner *In the Soup*. But this no-budget, no-ideas French-financed feature about two former doo-wop crooners trying to make a comeback falls resoundingly flat. Saddled with a script by the director that has no more going for it than the washed-up lounge act at its center, the unfunny comedy likely will be forgotten fast.

A onetime regular on the club circuit in New York's Little Italy, Louis Di Buffoni has traded his microphone for a family and a business. His cousin and former singing partner, Frank, has been in Sicily training as a beautician. Returning to Queens full of inspirational talk about pursuing one's dreams, Frank disrupts his cousin's family and business and eventually convinces Louis to start singing professionally again.

Int'l release: July 8      Int'l B.O. $100,000

## Louise (Take 2) (France)

An Initial Prods/Studio Canal Plus/Cine Valse production. Produced by Jean Cazes. Directed, written by Siegfried. Camera, Siegfried, Vincent Buron, Hervé Lode; editor, Herve Schneid; music, Siegfried; set decorator, Giacomo Macchi; costume designer, Emmanuelle Pertus. Reviewed at Cercle Foch, Paris, June 20. Running time: 103 mins.

Elodie Bouchez (Louise), Roschdy Zem (Remi), Gerald Thomassin (Yaya), Antoine de Merle (Gaby).

Siegfried's first feature, *Louise (Take 2)*, speaks for itself. An exhaustingly vibrant, ever-so-now tale of a middle-class waif who taps into adventure by slumming with young thugs in the Paris metro, it careens around with a verve and immediacy that will appeal to youths, but tackles the big existential questions with a flimsy whimsy that may irk adults. Still, occasional bursts of visual bravado amidst the breathless narrative – written, helmed, co-lensed, and engagingly scored by its twentysomething auteur – make it worth a hard look.

Pic, which starts out as a fun-loving romp about shakedown artists before turning into an artsy take on alienation, advocates an outlaw sensibility for its own sake. By chance, Louise meets Remi, a homeless ladies' man with an excellent supply of pickup lines and self-assured charm. There's a spark between the two free spirits, but Louise is already spoken for.

## Love Tangles (Petits Désordres Amoureux)

(France-Switzerland-Spain)

An AB Films Distribution release of a K'ien Prods, Expand Images, Alinea Films, Zen Prods, Les Films de l'Arlequin, Ventura Films (France)/Cisa Services (Switzerland)/Igeldo Komunikazioa (Spain). Executive producer, David Kodsi. Directed by Olivier Peray. Screenplay, Eric Assous, Peray. Camera, Carlo Varini; editor, Anna Ruiz; music, David Moreau; art direction, Giuseppe Ponturo; costume design, Nathalie Raoul. Reviewed at Berlin Festival, Feb. 18. Running time: 97 mins. (French dialog)

---

**...June 21...**

Canada's two largest production companies – Alliance Communications and Atlantis Communications – ink a $127 million merger agreement that promises to create one of North America's largest indie movie and TV production-distribution outfits.

Bruno Putzulu (Lionel), Smadi Wolfman (Claire), Vincent Elbaz (Alain), Sarah Grappin (Sophie), Beatrice Palme (Sylvia), Cecile Tanner (Myriam).

Pitched somewhere between the poise of Patrice Leconte and playful observation of Eric Rohmer, *Love Tangles* is a delight. Schematic, sexy, beautifully played, and scripted with economy, this brightly lensed conte moral about an office Lothario and his female quarry has enough going for it to carve a theatrical career among upscale auds. The Rohmer parallels are immediately obvious as bright young thing Sophie (Sarah Grappin) strikes up a conversation with studious-looking Alain (Vincent Elbaz) at a roadside café about a guy (Bruno Putzulu) at another table who's surrounded by two adoring women.

Int'l release: March 11                Int'l B.O.: $250,000

### Love is the Devil (U.K.)

A Strand Releasing/Artificial Eye release of a BBC Films and British Film Institute presentation, in association with Première Heure (Paris), Uplink (Tokyo), Arts Council of England, of a BFI production. Produced by Chiara Menage. Directed, written by John Maybury. Camera, John Mathieson; editor, Daniel Goddard; music, Ryuichi Sakamoto; production designer, Alan Macdonald; costume designer, Annie Symons; special consultant, Daniel Farson. Reviewed at Cannes Festival, May 18. Running time: 91 mins.

Derek Jacobi (Francis Bacon), Daniel Craig (George Dyer), Tilda Swinton (Muriel Belcher), Anne Lambton (Isabel Rawsthorne), Adrian Scarborough (Daniel Farson), Karl Johnson (John Deakin).

Unconventional, audacious, and uncompromising in every sense, John Maybury's *Love is the Devil* is a very personal interpretation of the destructive relationship between British painter Francis Bacon and his lover and muse, George Dyer. This provocative film's unflinchingly unsympathetic portrayal of the artist – ferociously played by Derek Jacobi – and its often distancing, experimental style, make it clearly an item for niche audiences. But it nonetheless looks certain to become a talked-about release backed by plenty of critical heft and a benchmark for future films about artists.

Opening with Bacon's crowning success, a 1971 retrospective at the Grand Palais in Paris, the film backtracks seven years to recount his meeting in London with Dyer, a small-time criminal from the lower-working-class East End. Unable to obtain permission to use his work from Bacon's estate, Maybury instead has developed a visual style that approximates his morbid, horrific images in boldly inventive ways.

U.S. release: Oct. 9                U.S. B.O.: $350,000
Int'l release: Sept. 18            Int'l B.O.: $750,000

### The Lovers of the Arctic Circle (Los Amantes Del Circulo Polar) (Spain)

A Sogetel presentation of an Alicia Produce/Bailando en la Luna production, in association with Le Studio Canal Plus, Sogepaq, Canal Plus Espana. Produced by Fernando Bovaira, Enrique Lopez Lavigne. Directed, written by Julio Medem. Camera, Gonzalo Berridi; editor, Ivan Aledo; music, Alberto Iglesias; art director, Satur Idarreta. Reviewed at Cines Renoir, Madrid, July 10. Running time: 107 mins.

Najwa Nimri (Ana), Fele Martinez (Otto), Nancho Novo (Alvaro), Maru Valdivieisio (Olga), Peru Medem (Young Otto), Sara Valiente (Young Ana), Beate Jensen (Ula).

Spanish auteur Julio Medem consolidates his reputation for

unsettling cinematic beauty with a philosophical twist in *The Lovers of the Arctic Circle*, an offbeat and intelligent love story that is his most accessible work. Ping-pong structure and complexity of its concerns position the movie outside the mainstream, but pic should do OK at home. The deft combination of head and heart in *Lovers* could bring helmer back from the offshore cold, with fest runs and arthouse showings looking likely.

Typically blending theory with practice, most of the real action takes place at the level of ideas. Credits roll over mysterious images of a crashed airplane in snow, and rest of the movie is an intriguing, leisurely explanation of what these images mean. Two school kids, feisty Ana and dreamy Otto, are united by fate when Ana's mother and Otto's father fall in love. Ana is under the impression that the soul of her dead father has inhabited the boy's body and they are destined to be together. The brother-sister relationship alters as they hit adolescence and sleep together one stormy night. The first kiss occurs over a geography book open at a description of the Arctic Circle, and they end up regularly sleeping together, secretly, in the parental home.

Int'l release: Aug. 28                Int'l B.O.: $3 million

### Lucinda's Spell

A Zero Pictures presentation of a Golden Shadow Pictures production, in association with Motion Picture Capital. Produced by Michael Kastenbaum. Directed, written by Jon Jacobs. Camera, Jaime Reynoso; editor, Clayton Halsey; music, Niki Jack; production designers, Andy Peach, Jana Pasek; costume designer, Keith Sayer. Reviewed at Cannes Festival, May 17. Running time: 105 mins.

Jon Jacobs (Jason, aka First Horn), Christina Fulton (Lucinda Bale), Shannah Battz (Beatruce), Leon Herbert (Maddison), Angie Green (Chickory), Alex Koromzay (Natalie), J.C. Brandy (Betsy).

The winner of the alternative Golden Warrior prize at Cannes' renegade (and virtually unnoticed) Cannes You Dig It sidebar, *Lucinda's Spell* is a lively U.S. indie cross-genre piece that will leave marketing mavens scratching their heads. A ribald saga with supernatural underpinnings, the film is equal parts comedy and social drama that add up to a puzzling, if entertaining, whole. Offbeat pic could develop cult status based on sheer energy alone, but it will require careful handling to maximize its specialized potential from all revenue streams. The mumbo-jumbo plot has something to do with a Druid celebration called Beltane. Jason, a descendant of a great wizard, returns to Earth to find a mate. He lands in New Orleans, where the local witches are preparing their best and most alluring spells to win his favor.

### Luck or Coincidence (Hasards Ou Coincidences)

(France-Canada)

A Film 13/TF1 Films/UGC Images/Neuilly/SDA production. Produced by Claude Lelouch. Directed, written by Lelouch. Camera, Pierre-William Glenn; editor, Hélène de Luze, Stephane Mazalaigue; music, Francis Lai, Claude Bolling; production design, Jacques Bufnoir, costume design, Dominique Borg; choreography, Richard Wherlock. Reviewed at World Film Festival, Montreal, Sept. 3. Running time: 121 mins.

Alessandra Martines (Myriam Lini), Pierre Arditi (Pierre Turi), Marc Hollogne (Marc Deschamps), Geoffrey Holder

---

**. . . June 22 . . .**

Jane is Jane for ever: Maureen O'Sullivan swings her last vine from **Tarzan** to **Hannah and Her Sisters** (as the mother of real-life daughter Mia Farrow).

(Gerry), Laurent Hilare (Laurent), Arthur Cheysson (Serge Lini), Veronique Moreau (Catherine Desvilles), Patrick Labbe (Michel Bonhomme).

Three decades after *A Man and a Woman*, Claude Lelouch continues to mine the territories of romance and fate in *Luck or Coincidence*. Once again his visual sweep and locales are breathtaking, and much of the drama is on target about the ethereal nature of love. One of his better recent efforts, pic should play well in markets where the helmer's work continues to be a presence. But securing distribution in English-speaking territories – where his penchant for grand emotion and theatrical flourish have fallen out of favor – will be difficult.

The new entry is again a cat's cradle of interwoven narrative strands that eventually gel into a precise design. Myriam is a former classical dancer raising a young son, Serge. She meets Pierre, an art broker and forger, by chance in Venice where he's creating a faux Soutine painting for an unsuspecting American client. There is an immediate rapport. Meanwhile, in Montreal, transplanted Frenchman Marc is creating interactive theater and pursuing work as a futurologist. He maintains that one can reliably predict tomorrow via a complex mathematical equation; luck and coincidence are not real factors in his life. Following the filmmaker's bent, the story will evolve to refute Marc's assertion, and he will become a believer in the unpredictable and the heart.

U.S. release: Sept. 9          U.S. B.O.: $100,000
Int'l release: Nov. 18          Int'l B.O.: $1.5 million

## Lulu on the Bridge

A Capitol Films presentation of a Redeemable Features production. Produced by Peter Newman, Greg Johnson, Amy Kaufman. Directed, written by Paul Auster. Camera, Alik Sakharov; editor, Tim Squyres; music, Graeme Revell; Katamandu CD music, John Lurie and the Lounge Lizards; production designer, Kalina Ivanov; costume designer, Adelle Lutz. Reviewed at Cannes Festival, May 11. Running time: 103 mins.

Harvey Keitel (Izzy Mauer), Mira Sorvino (Celia Burns), Willem Dafoe (Dr. Van Horn), Gina Gershon (Hannah), Mandy Patinkin (Philip Kleinman), Vanessa Redgrave (Catherine Moore).

Writer Paul Auster's first solo directorial effort, the quiet, moody, and ponderous *Lulu on the Bridge* centers on a mysterious romantic affair – a kind of American amour fou – between middle-aged musician Izzy and aspiring actress Celia. Izzy sinks into depression after a stray bullet sidelines him from playing his saxophone.

The film is original and intermittently touching, but ultimately frustrating because of the meandering nature of the riddle-like script and Auster's lethargic direction.

Int'l release: Nov. 14          Int'l B.O.: $650,000

## Madeline

A Sony Pictures Entertainment release of a TriStar Pictures presentation of a Jaffilms/Pancho Kohner/Saul Cooper production. Produced by Cooper, Kohner, Allyn Stewart. Directed by Daisy von Scherler Mayer. Screenplay, Mark Levin, Jennifer Flackett, screen story by Malia Scotch Marmo, Levin, Flackett, based on the book by Ludwig Bemelmans. Camera, Pierre Aim; editor, Jeffrey Wolf; music, Michel Legrand; production designer, Hugo Luczyc-Wyhowski; costume designer, Michael Clancy. Reviewed at Sony, Culver City, June

28. MPAA Rating: PG. Running time: 90 mins.

Frances McDormand (Miss Clavel), Nigel Hawthorne (Lord Covington), Hatty Jones (Madeline), Ben Daniels (Leopold), Arturo Venegas (Spanish Ambassador), Stephane Audran (Lady Covington), Kristian de la Osa (Pepito).

Much of the charm of one of the modern classics of children's literature survives in *Madeline*. Stitched together using elements from four of Ludwig Bemelmans' illustrated books about a plucky girl at a small French boarding school, this live-action feature has the requisite adventure, comedy, conflict, and appeal to make the grade. Vast popularity of the books amongst baby boomers and their kids, especially girls, gives the film a fairly sizable audience. Theatrical returns should be decent, with a long life in store on video. Tales recount the escapades of the redheaded heroine, and scripters Mark Levin and Jennifer Flackett have done a reasonable job by making Lord Covington's intention to sell the school the pivot of the drama, then mixing in a host of smaller capers to supply the picture with sufficient incident.

U.S. release: July 10          U.S. B.O.: $30 million
Int'l release: Nov. 14          Int'l B.O.: $1.6 million

## Major League: Back to the Minors

A Warner Bros. release of a James G. Robinson presentation of a Morgan Creek production. Produced by Robinson. Directed, written by John Warren. Camera, Tim Suhrstedt; editors, O. Nicholas Brown, Bryan H. Carroll; music, Robert Folk; production designer, David Crank; costume designer, Mary MacLeod. Reviewed at the Sony Copley Place, Boston, April 17. MPAA Rating: PG-13. Running time: 100 mins.

Scott Bakula (Gus Cantrell), Corbin Bernsen (Roger Dorn), Dennis Haysbert (Pedro Cerrano), Takaaki Ishibashi (Taka Tanakia), Jensen Daggett (Maggie Reynolds), Ted McGinley (Leonard Huff), Bob Uecker (Harry Doyle).

As studios hasten to clear their shelves of product to make way for summer releases, occasionally something decent gets caught in the sweep. This third outing in the *Major League* series, which lacks topliners Tom Berenger and Charlie Sheen, is an amusing film in its own right and should enjoy a happy ancillary life on cable and homevid. Premise is as old as sports movies: An underdog team made up of lovable misfits takes on powerful but arrogant champions, and no fair guessing who wins. Corbin Bernsen returns as Roger Dorn, now owner of the Minnesota Twins and the minor-league South Carolina Buzz. He persuades retiring minor-league player Gus Cantrell to manage the hapless Buzz.

U.S. release: April 17          U.S. B.O.: $3.6 million
Int'l release: May 30          Int'l B.O.: $5 million

## The Man in the Iron Mask

An Invisible Studio/The Fastest Cheapest Best Film Corp./Jerry Seltzer presentation. Produced by William Richert. Directed, written by Richert, based on the story and characters of Alexandre Dumas. Camera, William Barber; editor, Andre Vaillancourt; music, Jim Ervin; production design, Jacques Hebert; costume design, Salvador Perez. Reviewed at Raleigh Studios, L.A., Feb. 4. Running time: 85 mins.

Edward Albert (Athos), Dana Barron (Valliere), Timothy Bottoms (Fouquet), Fannie Brett (Henriette), Meg Foster (Queen Anne), Dennis Hayden (D'Artagnan), William Richert (Count Aramis), Nick Richert (Louis XIV/Philippe), Rex Ryon (Porthos).

---

### ... June 23 ...
Paramount buys rights to TV skein **Hogan's Heroes**.

Alexandre Dumas' Three Musketeers tales have proven to be all-but-surefire source material for many movies but William Richert's low-budget *The Man in the Iron Mask* demonstrates that some stories simply cry out for lavish, big-star treatment. Threadbare production values and sub-par cast here don't do Dumas, or the viewer, any favors, and this is one instance when a pic's indie status doesn't translate into any artistic advantages onscreen. Leonardo DiCaprio and Jeremy Irons, who co-star in the new MGM version, have nothing to worry about.

In pared-down terms, pic sets up the premise of the future King of France being kidnapped as a boy and encased in a dreadful iron mask in the Bastille, while his twin is installed by manipulative court villains as Louis XIV. Ten years later, after the queen makes a deathbed confession of what happened to Count Aramis, the loyal Jesuit engages the help of the recently returned Musketeers to set things right.

### The Man in the Iron Mask

An MGM release of a United Artists presentation. Produced by Randall Wallace, Russell Smith. Directed, written by Wallace, based on the novel by Alexandre Dumas. Camera, Peter Suschitzky; editor, William Hoy; music, Nick Glennie-Smith; production design, Anthony Pratt; costume design, James Acheson. Reviewed at the National, L.A., March 9. MPAA Rating: PG-13. Running time: 132 mins.
**Leonardo DiCaprio (King Louis/Philippe), Jeremy Irons (Aramis), John Malkovich (Athos), Gérard Depardieu (Porthos), Gabriel Byrne (D'Artagnan), Anne Parillaud (Queen Anne), Judith Godreche (Christine).**
The man of the moment, Leonardo DiCaprio, delivers a wonderful double star turn in *The Man in the Iron Mask*. An unusually sober and serious-minded telling of Alexandre Dumas's classic tale, this handsome costumer is routinely made and comes up rather short in boisterous excitement. But the compensations of an involving, old-fashioned narrative and a magnetic and enjoyable cast go a long way toward making this an agreeable middle-of-the-road entertainment. DiCaprio's presence assures a strong opening, and it will be interesting to see how far the film can travel in the wake of *Titanic*.

In Wallace's liberal reworking, the gears of treachery and revenge are set in motion when young King Louis XIV becomes enamored of the beautiful Christine and sends her ardent suitor Raoul to the front and certain death. When he's killed, Louis earns the undying enmity of the boy's father, the former musketeer Athos. He and Porthos join in an ingenious plot in which they spirit out of prison a man who, for six years, has lived in a cell with his head encased in a locked iron mask.

| | |
|---|---|
| U.S. release: March 13 | U.S. B.O.: $57 million |
| Int'l release: March 20 | Int'l B.O.: $123 million |

### Man is a Woman (L'homme Est Une Femme Comme Les Autres) (France)

A Polygram Film Distribution release of a Les Films Balenciaga/M6 Films production, with the participation of Canal Plus, CNC. Produced by Regine Konckier, Jean-Luc Ormières. Directed by Jean-Jacques Zilbermann. Screenplay, Gilles Taurand, Zilbermann, based on a story idea by Zilbermann and Joele Van Effenterre. Camera, Pierre Aim; editor, Monica Coleman; music, Giora Feidman (clarinet solos), Rosalie Becker (soprano); art director, Valerie Grall; costume designer, Edith Vesperini. Reviewed at Max Linder Cinema,

Paris, March 10. Running time: 100 mins. (French, English, and Yiddish dialog)
**Antoine de Caunes (Simon), Elsa Zylberstein (Rosalie), Gad Elmaleh (David), Michel Aumont (Uncle Salomon), Judith Magre (Simon's Mother).**
A gay, secular Jewish man is semi-willingly blackmailed into marrying an Orthodox Jewish woman in the mostly comic *Man is a Woman*. Well-cast and well-acted pic is solidly entertaining but gets bogged down and peters out with a limp conclusion. Helped by popular-name talent, pic should pull in local auds, is a natural for Jewish and gay fests, and could wrangle some urban screens internationally.

Simon is comfortable in his homosexuality. But at his cousin David's wedding, all Simon's relatives want to know is when he's going to find a nice girl. Simon's artistry on his late father's clarinet creates an instant admirer in one wedding guest – Rosalie, a New York-raised French Jew with a soaring soprano voice and a relentlessly chirpy personality.

| | |
|---|---|
| Int'l release: March 17 | Int'l B.O.: $3 million |

### The Man With Rain in His Shoes (Spain-U.K.)

A Handmade Films/Paragon Entertainment Corp. presentation of an Esicma production, in association with CLT-UFA Int'l, Mandarin Films, Wild Rose Prods. Produced by Juan Gordon. Directed by Maria Ripoll. Screenplay, Rafa Russo. Camera, Javier Salmones; editor, Nacho Ruiz-Capillas; music, Luis Mendo, Bernardo Fuster; production designer, Grant Hicks. Reviewed at Madrid Film, Feb. 11. Running time: 89 mins.
**Douglas Henshall (Victor Bukowski), Lena Headey (Sylvia Weld), Penelope Cruz (Louise), Mark Strong (Dave), Eusebio Lazaro (Don Miguel), Gustavo Salmeron (Rafael).**
Deft, witty, and surprisingly assured for a feature debut, Spaniard Maria Ripoll's English-language feel-good romantic comedy *The Man With Rain in His Shoes*, released in the U.K. as *If Only*, makes pleasing, if slightly anodyne, viewing. London-set pic's attempt at a new twist on the theme of twentyish angst is only partially successful, but the movie's familiarity, international flavor, and overall warmth could make it click offshore with the right marketing.

Tight script tells of Victor (Douglas Henshall), a struggling thesp in his twenties who has a private life that's as messy as his red hair. Regretting his breakup with Sylvia (Lena Headey) – who is due to marry Dave (Mark Strong) in two days – Victor gets drunk in the rain and runs into two otherworldly Spanish garbage men, Don Miguel (Eusebio Lazaro) and Rafael (Gustavo Salmeron).

| | |
|---|---|
| Int'l release: Nov. 27 | Int'l B.O.: $150,000 |

### Mararia (Spain)

An Alta Films release of an Aiete Films/Ariane Films/Mararia PC production, with the participation of RTVE. Produced by Andres Santana. Directed by Antonio José Betancor. Screenplay, Carlos Alvarez, Betancor, based on the novel by Rafael Arozarena. Camera, Juan Antonio Ruiz Anchia; editor, Guillermo Represa; music, Pedro Guerra; art director, Felix Murcia. Reviewed at Cine Capitol, Madrid, Oct. 29. Running time: 109 mins.
**Carmelo Gomez (Fermin), Ian Glen (Bertrand), Goya Toledo (Mararia), Mirta Ibarra (Herminia), José Manuel Cervino (Marcial).**
Superficially a good old-fashioned melodrama, vet Antonio José Betancor's *Mararia* has enough intelligent idiosyncrasy to free it from the rule book and give it power and charm. Pic is

a terrifically lensed tale about the destructive power of love set amongst the volcanic scenery of the Spanish island of Lanzarote. Its tightly structured script, powerful atmospherics, and good perfs make for gripping viewing that occasionally soars into tragedy. But a lack of marquee glamour could restrict its chances outside standard Spanish territories.

Highly principled Fermin is a young doctor who arrives in a small pueblo around the time of the Spanish Civil War. No sooner has he arrived than he becomes a victim of the smoldering eyes of Mararia. Enter the unprincipled Bertrand, an English surveyor working for the Royal Geographic Society, who proceeds to win over Mararia. When Mararia becomes pregnant by Bertrand, tradition dictates she marry him, but tragedy beckons.
Int'l release: Oct. 23                    Int'l B.O.: $550,000

### Mark Twain's America in 3D (Docu, Imax )
A Sony Pictures Classics release of an Ogden Entertainment presentation. Produced by James Lahti, Stephen Low. Directed by Low. Screenplay, Alex Low; story by Stephen Low. Camera (Imax 3-D), Andrew Kitzanuk; editor, James Lahti; music, Alan Williams; historic stereo photographs, UCR/California Museum of Photography. Reviewed at Edwards' Imax, Irvine, June 27. Running time: 52 mins.
**Narrator: Anne Bancroft.**
Arriving just in time for the July 4 holiday weekend, *Mark Twain's America in 3D* feels like a shameless attempt to lure families looking for historical relevance with the promise of kid-friendly 3-D effects. Sony Pictures Classics' docu is a curiosity even by Imax standards, its content in no way consistent with either the large-screen format or 3-D technology. Purportedly a historical account of Twain's life and times, pic juxtaposes black-and-white stills of the celebrated literary humorist with modern footage of his hometown of Hannibal, Mo. and other locales where contemporary crowds revisit 19th-century traditions. Some of these scenes seem like an excuse to throw in 3-D effects, which are hopelessly out of place.
U.S. release: July 2                    U.S. B.O.: $1 million
Int'l release: July 3                    Int'l B.O.: $500,000

### Martha – Meet Frank, Daniel and Laurence
(U.K.)
A Film Four Distributors/Miramax release of a Channel Four Films presentation of a Banshee production. Produced by Grainne Marmion. Directed by Nick Hamm. Screenplay, Peter Morgan. Camera, David Johnson; editor, Michael Bradsell; music, Ed Shearmur; production designer, costume designer, Anna Sheppard. Reviewed at Century Theatre, London, March 2. Running time: 83 mins.
**Monica Potter (Martha), Rufus Sewell (Frank), Tom Hollander (Daniel), Joseph Fiennes (Laurence), Ray Winstone (Dr. Pedersen).**
A clever idea doesn't fire on all cylinders in *Martha – Meet Frank, Daniel and Laurence*, an upbeat romantic comedy about an American gal's entanglements with three Brits in London. Lack of real chemistry between the leads and unsteady direction by Nick Hamm dampen an otherwise promising screenplay by Peter Morgan. Tagged to a bright and breezy campaign, pic could sidestep mixed critical reactions and clock up reasonable numbers without hitting the jackpot.

In some respects, Martha is a 1990s version of Richard Lester's 60s comedy *The Knack*, with three males, repping aspects of the era's zeitgeist, thrown into confusion by an out-of-town femme. This being the late 1990s, *Martha* has none of the innocent swagger of Lester's classic, nor its cinematic pranks; instead, Morgan's script aims for a sophisticated, hall-of-mirrors approach in a cappuccino-drinking, laddish, neo-deco London that's recognizably of the times.
Int'l release: May 8                    Int'l B.O.: $3 million

### The Mask of Zorro
A Sony Pictures Entertainment release of a TriStar Pictures presentation of an Amblin Entertainment production, in association with Zorro Prods. Produced by Doug Claybourne, David Foster. Directed by Martin Campbell. Screenplay, John Eskow, Ted Elliott, Terry Rossio, story by Elliott, Rossio, Randall Jahnson. Camera, Phil Meheux; editor, Thom Noble; music, James Horner; production design, Cecilia Montiel; costume design, Graciela Mazon; sword master, Robert Anderson; stunt coordinator, Glenn Randall, Jr. Reviewed at Sony, Culver City, June 23. MPAA Rating: PG-13. Running time: 136 mins.
**Antonio Banderas (Alejandro Murrieta), Anthony Hopkins (Don Diego), Catherine Zeta Jones (Elena), Stuart Wilson (Don Rafael Montero), Matt Letscher (Capt. Harrison Love), Maury Chaykin (Warden), Pedro Armendariz (Don Pedro), L.Q. Jones (Three-Finger Jack).**
*The Mask of Zorro* stands as a pointed riposte to those who say they don't make 'em like that anymore. The return of the legendary swordsman is well served by a grandly mounted classic-style production. Somewhat overlong pic lacks the snap and concision that would have put it over the top as a bang-up entertainment, but it's closer in spirit to a vintage swashbuckler than anything out of Hollywood in quite some time. Domestic B.O. will likely fall in the very strong rather than blockbuster league, with even better results looming offshore.

It's 1821, and the rebellion against colonial Spanish rule in Mexico is coming to a close. Masked man Zorro (aristocrat Don Diego) spectacularly rescues three peasants about to be executed by Spanish governor, Don Rafael Montero. With the battle won, Don Diego resolves to let his secret identity lapse and devote himself to his wife and baby daughter. But Montero is not about to leave without exacting revenge: causing his wife's death, kidnapping his child Elena, and tossing the ex-avenger into a dungeon. Twenty years later, Montero returns with a devious scheme to buy the California territory and Elena, raised believing he is her father. Don Diego recruits an outlaw, Alejandro Murrieta, to take on his mantle, schooling him in fighting skills and the social graces. Alejandro makes his debut as the reincarnation of Zorro and worms his way into Montero's inner circle posing as a wealthy don sympathetic to his land grab.
U.S. release: July 17                    U.S. B.O.: $93 million
Int'l release: July 24                    Int'l B.O.: $112 million

### Meet Joe Black
A Universal release of a City Light Films production. Produced by Martin Brest. Directed by Brest. Screenplay, Ron Osborn, Jeff Reno, Kevin Wade, Bo Goldman, suggested by the play *Death Takes a Holiday*, written by Alberto Casella and adapted by Walter Ferris, and the motion picture screenplay by Maxwell Anderson and Gladys Lehman. Camera, Emmanuel Lubezki; editors, Joe Hutshing, Michael Tronick; music, Thomas Newman; production design, Dante Ferretti; costume design,

Aude Bronson-Howard, David C. Robinson. Reviewed at Universal, Universal City, Oct. 30. MPAA Rating: PG-13. Running time: 180 mins.

**Brad Pitt (Joe Black), Anthony Hopkins (William Parrish), Claire Forlani (Susan Parrish), Jake Weber (Drew), Marcia Gay Harden (Allison), Jeffrey Tambor (Quince), David S. Howard (Eddie Sloane).**

In half the time it takes to "Meet Joe Black," many good films chart an entire life story. By contrast, this thoroughly over-elaborated whimsy dawdles distractedly in delineating one man's confrontation with mortality, which presents itself in the person of a handsome young stranger. What might have been an effective fantasy with a certain sophistication and insouciance is instead weighed down by ponderous pacing and overstuffed production values. The release could do some solid midrange business on the basis of Brad Pitt's name and the public's seemingly endless appetite for stories relating to angels and the afterlife, no matter how mediocre. But whatever B.O. it does cannot possibly match its pretensions.

Brest and his writers have taken the central premise of *Death Takes a Holiday* – Death assuming human form for a few days to get a taste of what life is like, and falling in love along the way – and spun it in different, much more detailed ways. No matter the new film's failings, its inventions can represent only improvements, as the earlier film now comes off as deadly dull.

New York media tycoon William Parrish begins hearing a strange, disembodied voice, and shortly suffers a heart seizure. In short order, the voice materializes to the mystified William in the guise of the fellow from the coffee shop. In the communications baron's plush library, the visitor, who goes by the name of Joe Black, informs the older man, a widower whom he has chosen for his exceptional character, that he can buy some time if he will act as his guide to all things earthly.

| | |
|---|---|
| U.S. release: Nov. 13 | U.S. B.O.: $43 million |
| Int'l release: Dec. 11 | Int'l B.O.: $9.5 million |

## Meet the Deedles

A Buena Vista release of a Walt Disney Pictures presentation of a DIC Entertainment/Peak production. Produced by Dale Pollock, Aaron Meyerson. Directed by Steve Boyum. Screenplay, Jim Herzfeld, Pollock. Camera, David Hennings; editor, Alan Cody; music, Steve Bartek; production designer, Stephen Storer; costume designers, Alexandra Welker, Karyn Wagner; visual-effects supervisor, Tim Landry. Reviewed at Crest Theater, L.A., March 21. MPAA Rating: PG. Running time: 92 mins.

**Steve Van Wormer (Stew Deedle), Paul Walker (Phil Deedle), A.J. Langer (Lt. Jesse Ryan), John Ashton (Capt. Douglas Pine), Dennis Hopper (Frank Slater), Eric Braeden (Elton Deedle), Richard Lineback (Crabbe), Robert Englund (Nemo).**

A sophomoric comedy about a pair of surfer dudes who find themselves adrift in Wyoming, *Meet the Deedles* follows in the wake of the *Bill & Ted* films and *Wayne's World*. But unlike those hits, there's nothing excellent about this adventure. *Deedles* lacks the truly hilarious scenes and memorable catch-phrase lexicon that make an impact. Commercial prospects look just fair, with the film likely to appeal only to teenagers, and probably not in a big way. At the center of the story are Stew and Phil Deedle, fraternal twins, superior surfers, and frequent troublemakers. Facing expulsion from school, they meet with their wealthy, disappointed father, who decides that a stint at a Wyoming summer camp will turn his boys into men.

| | |
|---|---|
| U.S. release: March 27 | U.S. B.O.: $4.4 million |

## Mektoub (Morocco-France)

A Shem's (Morocco)/Playtime (France) production, with support from CCM, Agence de Coopération Culturelle et Technique, Hubert Bals Fund. Directed, written by Nabil Ayouch. Camera, Vincent Mathias; editor, Jean Robert Thomann; music, Henri Agoel, Pierre Boscheron. Reviewed at Rotterdam Festival, Jan. 31. Running time: 91 mins.

**With: Rachid El Ouali, Amal Chabli, Mohamed Miftah, Faouzi Bensaidi, Mohamed Zouhair.**

Two Americanized Moroccans return to a country plagued by injustice, corruption, and the abuse of power in *Mektoub*, which is based on a widely publicized tabloid crime. Winner of the best first feature prize at the Cairo Film Festival, newcomer Nabil Ayouch's pacey thriller is rather conventional and a little naïve at times, but the solidly constructed, compelling pic should make the rounds of North African film events in the coming months.

Back in Casablanca after 10 years of training in the U.S., Taoufik plans to set up an ophthalmology practice with his wife, Sophia. But during dinner at a swanky hotel in Tangier, his drink is drugged, and Sophia is abducted, raped, and dumped on the street. Attempting to avenge the crime, Taoufik pockets a gun belonging to his jaded cop brother, Kemal.

| | |
|---|---|
| Int'l release: Nov, 19, 1997 | Int'l B.O.: $750,000 |

## Melody for a Hustler (Cantique De La Racaille) (France)

A Pyramide release of an April Films/M6 Films/Le Studio Canal Plus/Les Films du Garage production, with the participation of M6, Studio Images 4, Arcapix, Procirep, CNC. Produced by Jean-Pierre Alessandri. Directed by Vincent Ravalec. Screenplay, Ravalec, based on his novel. Camera, Philippe Lesourd; editor, Yvon Lemière; music, Robert Miny; costumes, Laurence Lapoyade, Valentine Breton de Lois. Reviewed at Cannes Festival, May 16. Running time: 104 mins.

**Yvan Attal (Gaston), Virginie Lanoue (Marie-Pierre), Yann Collette (Gilles), Benaissa Ahaouari (Said), Samy Naceri (Joel), Marc Lavoine (Bruno).**

Gaston is a local hood with big ambitions. He has hooked up with 16-year-old Marie-Pierre, whom he picked up hitch-hiking, and he pulls her into his web by pretending to be a millionaire businessman.

Gallic novelist Vincent Ravalec makes a striking debut with his first directing effort, *Melody for a Hustler*, an offbeat but captivating meditation on the evils of the market-driven modern world. The portrait of a small-time crook who transforms himself into a yuppie chef d'entreprise is wryly humorous, moves along at a good clip, and is filled with all kinds of eye-catching visual flourishes. Pic will likely make some music in theaters on its home turf and draw festival interest, but will have more trouble coming up with a memorable box-office tune internationally.

| | |
|---|---|
| Int'l release: Oct. 14 | Int'l B.O.: $60,000 |

## Melvin Van Peebles' Classified X (France-U.S., Docu)

A Les Films D'Ici/Yeah Inc./Ecoutez Voie/La Sept Arte production in association with Channel 4 and TP, with the participation of Centre National de la Cinématographie and Procirep. Produced by Yves Jeanneau, Christine Le Goff, Judy Eley. Directed by Mark Daniels. Screenplay, Melvin Van Peebles. Camera, Daniels; editors, Catherine Mabilat, Janice Jones; art direction, Patrick Durand. Reviewed at Sundance Festival, Jan. 25. Running time: 53 mins.

---

**... June 26 ...**

Richard Gere and Julia Roberts will reteam with **Pretty Woman** director Gary Marshall in romantic comedy **Runaway Bride** for Paramount.

**Narrator: Melvin Van Peebles.**
Pioneering U.S. black filmmaker Melvin Van Peebles casts an acerbic, unapologetically personal eye over the history of African-American screen imagery in *Classified X*. While short docu feature breaks no new ground, Van Peebles' distinctive analyses and his ever-growing importance to new black helmers via 1971's breakthrough *Sweet Sweetback's Baadasssss Song* make this a package with shelf life for cinematheques, schools, and select broadcaster webs. A bit halting in his on-camera delivery, Van Peebles nonetheless fires off a series of incisive commentaries that occasionally border on the excessively academic in tone. Excerpts from more than 70 features – none identified, unfortunately – chart Hollywood's history of racist stereotyping from even before D.W. Griffith's notorious KKK-championing *Birth of a Nation*. Scaredy-cat comedy-relief types, jungle "savages," mammies, and minstrels gave way after WWII to "The New Negro" – a put-upon "keeper of conscience" for the white protagonists.

## Ménage à Trois (Retro Vtroyom) (Russia)
A Mirabelle Film production. Produced by Mira Todorovskaya. Directed by Pyotr Todorovsky. Screenplay, Todorovsky, Timur Suleimenov, Mira Todorovskaya. Camera, Nikolai Nemolyaev; editor, Alla Strelnikova; music, Aleksei Aygi; songs, Todorovsky; art direction, Leonard Svinitsky. Reviewed at Berlin Festival, Feb. 15. Running time: 96 mins.
**Elena Yakovleva (Rita), Sergei Makovetsky (Sergei), Yevgeni Sidikhin (Kostya), Yekaterina Dvidubskaya (Zina), Tatyana Ivchenko (Raya).**
Sergei turns up unannounced from the provinces at the Moscow apartment of Kostya, who's married to photographer Rita. Sergei has left his wife back in the war-torn Caucasus.
This remake of Abram Room's controversial 1927 silent *Bed and Sofa* has an amazing freshness and vitality that redeems its paper-thin plot and sometimes fanciful tone, signaling limited arthouse play in auteur-friendly territories and fest slots elsewhere. Director Todorovsky dresses up this mightily flimsy plot in a charming, emotionally seductive wrapping. Strip the credits off *Ménage à Trois* and you'd think it was the work of Todorovsky fils (Valeri) rather than his 72-year-old pere, Pyotr.

## Men Cry Bullets
An Idiot Films production. Produced by Harry Ralston, Tamara Hernandez, Jessica Rains. Directed, written by Hernandez. Camera, Michael Grady; editors, Garth Grinde, Scott Balcerek; production designer, Ivana Letica. Reviewed at South by Southwest Festival, Austin, Texas, March 20. Running time: 105 mins.
**Steven Nelson (Billy), Honey Lauren (Gloria), Jeri Lynn Ryan (Lydia), Harry Ralston (Freddy Fishnets), Michael Mangiamele (The Paper Boy).**
By turns campy and creepy, *Men Cry Bullets* is a muddled mix of absurdist farce and overheated melodrama. Writer-director Tamara Hernandez's first full-length effort was named best narrative feature at the recent South by Southwest Film Festival. Even so, pic will be hard-pressed to find an audience beyond what's left of the midnight-movie circuit. Hernandez tries to reverse traditional gender roles in her story about an abusive relationship between Billy, an anxious waif who wants to be a female impersonator, and Gloria, a cruel and capricious novelist who enjoys rough sex even more than a good bar-room brawl.

## Men With Guns (Canada)
A Norstar Entertainment presentation of a Peter R. Simpson production, with the participation of the Movie Network. Produced by Ilana Frank. Executive producers, Peter R. Simpson, Antony I. Ginnane. Co-executive producer, Donal Logue. Directed by Kari Skogland. Screenplay, Lachy Hulme. Camera, Danny Nowak; editors, Susan Maggi, Nick Rotundo; music, Eric Cadesky; art direction, Jasna Stefanovic; costume design, Tamara Winston; sound, Ross Redfern; line producer, Sandra Cunningham; assistant director, Fergus Barnes; casting, Heidi Levitt. Reviewed at Rotterdam Festival, Feb. 1, 1998. Running time: 89 mins.
**Donal Logue (Goldman), Gregory Sporleder (Lucas), Callum Keith Rennie (Mamet), Max Perlich (Easy Gary), Paul Sorvino (Horace Burke), Joseph Griffin (Mickey Burke).**
Perennial losers eager to move up from small-time crime, Eddie (Donal Logue) and Lucas (Gregory Sporleder) are sent to a remote farm to collect a debt. But the hardened thugs they meet there are unwilling to oblige.
Just when you thought the last of the Tarantino wannabes had reared their ugly heads, along comes Canada's Kari Skogland. Her *Men With Guns* marshals enough attitude, over-constructed dialog, posturing performances, and bludgeoning ultraviolence to make Q.T. seem like Marguerite Duras. Interesting purely as a trip by a distaff director into predominantly male territory, this stylishly made but humorless tale of inept crims in over their heads is too bereft of original ammunition to hit theatrical targets.

## Mercury Rising
A Universal release of a Universal and Imagine Entertainment presentation of a Brian Grazer production. Produced by Grazer, Karen Kehela. Directed by Harold Becker. Screenplay, Lawrence Konner, Mark Rosenthal, based on the novel *Simple Simon* by Ryne Douglas Peardon. Camera, Michael Seresin; editor, Peter Honess; music, John Barry; production designer, Patrizia von Brandenstein; costume designer, Betsy Heimann; visual-effects supervisor, Michael Owens. Reviewed at Universal, Universal City, March 31. MPAA Rating: R. Running time: 112 mins.
**Bruce Willis (Art Jeffries), Alec Baldwin (Nicholas Kudrow), Miko Hughes (Simon), Chi McBride (Tommy Jordan), Kim Dickens (Stacey), Peter Stormare (Shayes), Kevin Conway (Lomax).**
*Mercury Rising* won't raise many viewers' temperatures. A somber suspenser with an oddly disconnected assortment of characters and a lack of freshly conceived action, this tale of a maverick FBI agent who takes on malevolent government forces to protect an orphaned autistic child serves up some dramatic moments but never legitimately convinces. Pic will be one of Bruce Willis' modest performers in between more muscular outings.
Art Jeffries seems tailor-made for Willis: A tough, no-strings-attached specialist in undercover work not afraid to stand his ground even in the face of official censure. As Art treads water, eavesdropping on wiretaps, focus shifts to Simon, an autistic 9-year-old who is able to decipher a code hidden within an innocuous children's magazine puzzle. Reaching government functionaries to collect a prize, Simon sets off alarm bells at the highest security levels.

| | |
|---|---|
| U.S. release: April 3 | $33 million |
| Int'l release: April 9 | $56 million |

---

### ... June 27 ...
The U.S. scores a smashing victory at the 45th Cannes International Advertising Festival, which ended today with Americans scooping 13 of the 24 top awards.

## Midnight (Meia Noite) (France-Brazil)

A Haut & Court, La Sept-Arte (France)/VideoFilmes, RioFilme (Brazil) production. Produced by Carole Scotta, Caroline Benjo, Simon Arnal. Executive producer, Beth Pesco. Directed by Walter Salles, Daniela Thomas. Screenplay, Salles, Thomas, Joao Emanuel Carneiro. Camera, Walter Carvalho; editor, Felipe Lacerda; music, Antonio Pinto, Eduardo Bid, Nana Vasconcellos; art director, Carla Caffe. Reviewed at Locarno Festival, Aug. 12. Running time: 66 mins.

**Fernanda Torres (Maria), Luis Carlos Vasconcellos (Joao), Carlos Vereza (Pedro).**

Two sides of Rio's divided society bring hope to each other on the eve of the millennium in *Midnight*, the Brazilian entry in the "2000 Seen By…" series. Co-directed by Walter Salles and Daniela Thomas, this impressive short feature – sexy, cruel, dramatic, and romantic by turns – has the feel of a full-length work and helmers are set to expand the running time by around 20 minutes for theatrical release. As the city already parties to celebrate the magical date, Joao, a young man, rots in a dank Rio jail. Determined to escape a life behind bars, he murders his best friend and cell mate, Pedro, and escapes in the confusion. Meanwhile, across town in a comfortable apartment, Maria, a speech therapist, awakes to find a note left by her lover, Pedro, who's suddenly upped and left her during the night. Later that night, as the millennium arrives, Joao's and Maria's paths finally cross, with both ecstatic and tragic results.

## The Mighty

A Miramax Films release of a Scholastic/Simon Fields production. Produced by Jane Startz, Fields. Executive producers, Bob Weinstein, Harvey Weinstein, Julie Goldstein. Directed by Peter Chelsom. Screenplay, Charles Leavitt, based on the book *Freak the Mighty* by Rodman Philbrick. Camera, John de Borman; editor, Martin Walsh; music, Trevor Jones; production designer, Caroline Hanania; costume designer, Marie Sylvie Deveau. Reviewed at ShoWest, Las Vegas, March 12. MPAA Rating: PG-13. Running time: 100 mins.

**Sharon Stone (Gwen Dillon), Elden Henson (Max Kane), Kieran Culkin (Kevin Dillon), Gena Rowlands (Gram), Harry Dean Stanton (Grim), Gillian Anderson (Loretta Lee), James Gandolfini (Kenny Kane).**

Most movies about young teens get it wrong. Adolescence is a war zone where levels of cruelty are boundless and where most people are physically and psychologically ill-prepared to cope with the brutality. *The Mighty*, based on the kid-lit fave *Freak the Mighty*, is an exception. It "gets" the milieu, and the saga soars as the filmmakers inventively visualize the aspirations of its two young outcasts. A deft work of sleight-of-hand that translates across generations, the pic has the potential to be a breakout success when it's released in the fall. Ancillary action also looks upbeat, particularly in videocassette, where such fare has been consistently strong.

Kevin is assigned as reading tutor to Max, who is virtually illiterate. With a copy of the Arthurian legend, Kevin explains the process of reading and comprehension to his pupil in a way that finally makes sense. It's an act of giving that's important for both, because it works toward their unconscious striving for normalcy. Chelsom's offbeat sensibility finds voice in a story that demands extremes of triumph and tragedy. Yet he makes few obvious stops.

U.S. release: Oct. 9 — U.S. B.O.: $2.6 million
Int'l release: Nov. 19 — Int'l B.O.: $3 million

## Mighty Joe Young

A Buena Vista release of a Walt Disney presentation, in association with RKO pictures. Produced by Ted Hartley and Tom Jacobson. Directed by Ron Underwood. Screenplay, Mark Rosenthal, Lawrence Konner, based on a screenplay by Ruth Rose and a story by Merian C. Cooper. Camera, Don Peterman, Oliver Wood; editor, Paul Hirsch; music, James Horner; production design, Michael Cornblith; costume design, Molly Maginnis; creature design, Rick Baker; visual-effects supervisor, Hoyt Yeatman. Reviewed at Beverly Connection, L.A., Dec. 5, 1998. MPAA Rating: PG. Running Time: 114 mins.

**Charlize Theron (Jill Young), Bill Paxton (Gregg O'Hara), Rade Sherbedgia (Strasser), Peter Firth (Garth), David Paymer (Harry Ruben), Regina King (Cicily Banks), Robert Wisdom (Kweli), Naveen Andrews (Pindi), Dr. Ruth Young (Linda Purl), Dr. Baker (Lawrence Pressman).**

*Mighty Joe Young* is wholesome, well-crafted, old-fashioned family fare. Redo of 1949 yarn of an oversized African gorilla out of his element in urban America, pic makes the most of modern technology, adding color, computer graphics, and animatronics to a rather predictable story. Positioned as the major live-action family adventure of the season, *Mighty Joe* ought to have no trouble finding its footing.

Scientist Ruth Young is studying apes in Tanzania that include young Joe, whose rare genetic mutation makes him grow faster than his peers. But this seeming Eden is invaded by vicious poachers who plan to snatch the baby gorilla for sale on the black market. The attempt fails but during the raid both Dr. Ruth and Joe's mother are killed, leaving the ape and young Jill, Ruth's daughter, orphaned.

Years pass and the girl becomes a woman, living in seclusion with Joe until scientist Gregg O'Hara finds proof of their existence and tracks them down, inadvertently prompting the poachers' return. Jill is reluctantly convinced to pack up will Joe for the presumably safer environs of a California wildlife preserve. But a black marketeer posing as a benefactor is cooking up an evil scheme that results in an ape escape and an amusing chase through Hollywood.

U.S. release: Dec. 25 — U.S. B.O.: $20 million

## Minotaur (U.S.-Israel)

A Cinema Pardes/Top Line Communications presentation of a Minotaur production. International sales: Redwood Communications, Venice, Calif. Produced by Micky Rabinowitz, David Silber, Shai Bar Levi, Dan Turgerman, Irving S. White. Directed by Jonathan Tammuz. Screenplay, White, Dan Turgerman, based on the novel by Benjamin Tamuz. Camera, David Gurfinkel; editor, Zohar M. Sela; music, Amotz Plessner; production design, Roshelle Berliner; costumes, Rosemary Ponzo. Reviewed at Cannes Festival, May 13. Running time: 81 mins.

**Mili Avital (Thea), Dan Turgerman (Alex), George Corraface (Nicos), Josh Lucas (G.R.), Anat Atzmon (Mother), Mike Burstein (Mossad Agent), Catherine Kelner (Kim).**

*Minotaur* is a brooding romantic thriller about an undercover Israeli agent on assignment in the U.S. who falls in love and, as a result, compromises his security. Despite some intriguing elements, pic has an attenuated feel to it that prevents it from being completely satisfying. A more expansive and more interesting film could have been made from this material, which, as it stands, has limited box-office potential. Based on a novel by Benjamin Tamuz, film establishes Dan Turgerman as

**… June 28 …**

South African filmmaker Anant Singh is looking for a powerful actor to play Nelson Mandela in **Long Walk to Freedom**.

Alex Abramov, a dedicated Mossad agent currently working undercover in New York. Still haunted by tragic childhood memories, Alex is, of necessity, a loner. Details of his current assignment are sketchy, but he's after some bad guys who are on to him.

### The Misadventures of Margaret (U.K.-France)

A TF1 Int'l and Granada presentation with the participation of the European Co-Production Fund (U.K.) of a Lunatics & Lovers/Granada production in co-production with Mandarin and TF1 Films with the participation of Canal Plus in association with Film 50. Produced by Ian Benson. Directed, written by Brian Skeet, based on the novel *Rameau's Niece* by Cathleen Schine. Camera, Romain Winding; editor, Clare Douglas; music, St Etienne; production design, Martin Childs; costume design, Edi Giguere; makeup and hair design, Jan Sewell. Reviewed at Sundance Festival, Jan. 19. Running time: 105 mins.

**Parker Posey (Margaret Nathan), Jeremy Northam (Edward Nathan), Craig Chester (Richard Lane), Elizabeth McGovern (Till Turner), Brooke Shields (Lily), Corbin Bernsen (Art Turner).**

A lamentable attempt to recapture the appeal of classic Hollywood romantic comedies, *The Misadventures of Margaret* falls flat on its face right out of the gate and never gets back on its feet. Arch, unfunny, and annoying, this mostly Gotham-set British-French co-production makes even its most talented cast members look bad and has dire commercial prospects. Based on a novel by Cathleen Schine, this first feature by Brian Skeet tries to be oh-so-naughty by taking a sexually frank approach to the sort of material that used to be handled with discretion and innuendo. But making all the women unpleasantly catty sex-on-the-brain neurotics and throwing in a liberal dose of male nudity rep just a couple of the many misguided gambits in a film that emerges as a curdled version of Hollywood's sophisticated "divorce comedies."

### Miss Monday (U.S.-Japan-U.K.)

A Lakeshore Int'l presentation of a Mondo Paradiso Films (U.S.)/Sunny Side Up (Japan)/Metropolitan Films (U.K.) production. Produced by Steve Smith. Directed by Benson Lee. Screenplay, Lee, Richard Morel, Paul Leyden. Camera, Mike Coles; editor, Tula Goenka; music, Woody Pak; production designer, Julian Weaver; costume designer, Julian Day. Reviewed at Cannes Festival, May 19. Running time: 90 mins.

**Andrea Hart (Gloria), James Hicks (Roman), Alex Giannini (Steven), Louise Barrett (Debbie), Julie Alanagh-Brighten (Marianne), Nick Moran (Jeremy).**

Frustrated writer Roman hammers away at his typewriter, attempting to breathe life into his female lead, Marianne, a gorgeous, successful businesswoman, who has fought her way to the top. However, his attempts at serious social drama keep taking a farcical – but relentlessly unfunny – turn.

Glaswegian thesp Andrea Hart deservedly won an acting award at Sundance earlier this year for her harrowing role as a tough career woman given to bulimic binging in Benson Lee's London-set feature debut, *Miss Monday.* But while her performance gives the film some tangible dramatic rewards, the clumsily incompatible, smugly comic tone of a cumbersome framing device in which a screenwriter searches for real-life inspiration all but limits it to some fest play and cable dates.

### Mr. Fifteen Balls (Il Signor Quindicipalle) (Italy)

A Medusa release of a Videomaura, Filmone, Medusa Film production. Produced by Bruno Altissimo, Claudio Saraceni. Directed by Francesco Nuti. Screenplay, Nuti, Mario Rellini, Malu Di Lonardo. Camera, Danilo Desideri; editor, Ugo De Rossi; music, Giovanni Nuti; production/costume design, Enrico Serafini. Reviewed at Barberini Cinema, Rome, Sept. 30. Running time: 105 mins.

**Francesco Nuti (Cecco), Sabrina Ferilli (Sissi), Novello Novelli (Maestro), Antonio Petrocelli (Giampiero), Giulia Weber (Guilia)**

Growing up in the 1950s in a small factory town, Cecco, under his father's watchful eye, learns to send 15 billiard balls into the pockets with a single stroke of a broomstick. Hired to play Cecco's nonexistent, very religious fiancée in front of his houseful of conservative female relations, happy hooker Sissi soon gets into the homey feeling and fantasizes about marriage and lots of kids, but Cecco frets she won't be able to give up the streetlife.

A slight romantic comedy enlivened by scenes of crack exhibition pool-playing and a sassy perf by Sabrina Ferilli as a $1,000 call girl, *Mr. Fifteen Balls* has put Francesco Nuti back on local charts after a long absence, opening better than any of the director-star's pix in years. A former box-office champ long eclipsed by fellow Tuscan comic Roberto Benigni, Nuti once again bets on billiards, the game that launched him as an actor in *Me, Chiara and Darkness.* However, beyond the land where Tuscan comics rule, audience interest will be dampened by pic's many repetitions and plain-Jane shooting style.

Int'l release: Oct. 2 — Int'l B.O.: $6 million

### Mr. Magoo

A Buena Vista release of a Walt Disney Pictures presentation of a Ben Myron production. Produced by Ben Myron. Directed by Stanley Tong. Screenplay, Pat Proft, Tom Sherohman, based on the character owned by UPA Prods of America. Camera, Jingle Ma; editors, Stuart Pappe, David Rawlins, Michael R. Miller; music, Michael Tavera; production design, John Willett; costume design, Tom Bronson. Reviewed at Loews Memorial City, Houston, Dec. 17, 1997. MPAA Rating: PG. Running time: 87 mins.

**Leslie Nielsen (Quincy Magoo), Kelly Lynch (Luanne Leseur), Matt Keeslar (Waldo), Nick Chinlund (Bob Morgan), Stephen Tobolowsky (Stupak), Ernie Hudson (Gus Anders), Malcolm McDowell (Austin Cloquet), Miguel Ferrer (Ortega Peru).**

By turns frenetic and flat-footed, *Mr. Magoo* is an uninspired live-action comedy based on the 1950s UPA cartoons about the misadventures of a near-sighted eccentric. Despite the abundance of slapstick and an overall skew toward younger viewers, pic may hold little appeal for pre-teens. Older ticket buyers aren't likely to care much, either. Expect a fast fade from theaters, and only slightly longer visibility on video store shelves.

Quincy Magoo is a sight-impaired millionaire who's too stubborn to admit he needs eyeglasses. Despite the best intentions, he has a habit of strolling into trouble, in this case as prime suspect in the theft of a precious stone from a museum.

U.S. release: Dec. 25 — U.S. B.O.: $21 million
Int'l release: April 3 — Int'l B.O.: $19 million

**Mr. Zhao (Zhao Xiansheng)** (China-Hong Kong)
A Beijing Zhang Tian Culture & Media Center (China)/Nam
Kwong Development (Hong Kong) production. Produced by
Yang Hongguang. Directed by Lu Yue. Screenplay, Shu Ping.
Camera, Wang Tianlin; editor, Zhai Ru; art director, An Bin;
associate producers, Liu Xiaodong, Liu Xiaodian. Reviewed at
Locarno Festival, Aug. 14. Running time: 88 mins.
Shi Jingming (Zhao Qiankum), Zhang Zhihua (Zhou
Ruomin), Chen Yinan (Tian Jing), Jiang Wenli (The Woman).
(Mandarin and Shanghainese dialog)
Mainland Chinese cinema takes a major step forward with *Mr.
Zhao*, a trenchantly observed study of a habitual womanizer
that's shot through with a delicious sense of irony and genuine
warmth. In line with several other recent pics showing modern
urban life in China, this directorial debut by noted
cinematographer Lu Yue makes no concessions to Western
tastes for "exotic" rural or historical settings, instead portraying
contempo relationships in a real but always cinematic way.
Structurally bold pic may alienate some auds, signaling fest
dates and quality tube sales. Film deservedly copped the top
Golden Leopard award at its Locarno world preem.

Zhao, a Shanghai doctor, is caught in bed with his mistress,
Tian Jing, by his wife, an uneducated factory worker, who is
shattered by Zhao's betrayal and his seeming inability to
explain his actions.

**Modulations** (Docu)
A George Gund presentation of a Calpirinha Prods film.
Produced by Gund. Directed by Iara Lee. Consulting writer,
Peter Shapiro. Camera, Marcus Burnett, Paul Yates; editor, Paula
Heredia; sound montage, Mark Jan Wlodarkiewicz. Reviewed at
Sundance Festival, Jan. 21. Running time: 73 mins.
Brazilian-born U.S. documaker Iara Lee's *Modulations*
concentrates on current musical craze electronica's major
players and history. Though still a bit of an overload, its often
exciting match of style and subject should perform well with
youthful urban and college auds worldwide.

To what can this boom in electronic dance music be traced
to? The huge number of interviewees here have many opinions.
Among precursors discussed are avant-garde composers John
Cage and Karlheinz Stockhausen; Robert Moog, inventor of the
Moog Synthesizer; 1970s German art-rock bands like
Kraftwerk; Eurodisco innovator Giorgio Moroder; industrial-
noise units such as Britain's Throbbing Gristle, and the early
hip-hop disc jockeys who manipulated vinyl on their
turntables to create "scratch" music.
U.S. release: Sept. 4                    U.S. B.O.: $150,000

**Money No Enough (Riu Bo Gao Eng)** (Singapore)
A Shaw Organisation release of a JSP Entertainment production.
Produced by J.P. Tan. Directed by Tay Teck-lock. Screenplay, Jack
Neo. Camera, Kamis; editor, A. Supranamian; art
director/costumes, Anthony Ng. Reviewed at Golden Village
Yishun 8, Singapore, July 20. Running time: 98 mins. (Hokkien,
Singlish, and Mandarin dialog)
Jack Neo (Chew Wah-keong), Mark Lee (Ong), Henry Thia
(Hui), Patricia Mok, Vivian Tok.
A boisterous, on-the-nose comedy about three cash-strapped
Singaporeans living in government projects, *Money No Enough*
is initially fresh and amusing but ultimately too one-note and
local in its humor to travel far beyond East Asia. Low-budget
pic has made history in the tiny island republic by taking

S$5 million ($3 million) in its first two months, becoming the
all-time top Chinese-lingo grosser and even beating out such
Hollywood blockbusters as *Independence Day* and *Twister* on
the B.O. charts.

Central trio are Chew Wah-keong, a married-with-kids 40-
year-old who's permanently up to his ears in bills; Ong, a
longhaired doofus who renovates apartments; and pudgy Hui,
a waiter at a sidewalk café. When Chew is suddenly passed over
for promotion at the trading company where he works, he
blows his top and quits. Ong, meanwhile, has borrowed 40
grand from a loan shark and is likely to have his legs broken if
he doesn't repay in two weeks. Hui's problems are more
personal than pecuniary: how to pull women when you have
zero career prospects and a face like a teapot.

**Montana**
An Initial Entertainment Group presentation of a Zeta
Entertainment and No Bones production. Produced by Sean
Cooley, Zane W. Levitt, Mark Yellen. Directed by Jennifer
Leitzes. Screenplay, Erich Hoeber, Jon Hoeber. Camera, Ken
Kelsch; editor, Norman Buckley; music, Cliff Eidelman;
production designer, Daniel Roth. Reviewed at Sundance
Festival, Jan. 16. Running time: 99 mins.
Kyra Sedgwick (Claire), Stanley Tucci (Nick), Robbie Coltrane
(The Boss), Robin Tunney (Kitty), Philip Seymour Hoffman
(Duncan), John Ritter (Dr. Wexler), Ethan Embry (Jimmy).
Claire calmly strolls out of a swank Manhattan restaurant,
brutally elbows an Asian man and, with the help of colleague
Nick, stuffs him in their car trunk and drives off. When they
spot another Asian fellow and realize they've made a mistake,
they put him in the trunk and dump out their bewildered first
victim. The Iago-like Duncan convinces the Boss that Claire
and Nick have actually tricked him and taken money. Thus is
set up a cat-and-mouse game which sees the Boss' goons
pursuing Claire, Nick, and Kitty hither and yon, with the
hunted trio using every shred of their ingenuity to slither out
of numerous jams.

Yet another comically hip riff on modern gangsters and hit
men, *Montana* offers too few new ideas on the genre to be
worth the trip. Feminist slant on traditionally male territory,
some occasionally effective oddball humor, a fine cast and a
degree of stylistic ambition lend this sleek-looking indie a
certain minor interest, but not enough to position it
meaningfully from a commercial p.o.v.

**Monument Avenue**
A Filmline Int'l/Phoenician Films/Clinica Estetico/Tribeca
Independent Films presentation of a Spanky Pictures/Apostle
production. Produced by Nicolas Clermont, Elie Samaha, Joel
Stillerman, Ted Demme, Jim Serpico. Directed by Demme.
Screenplay, Mike Armstrong. Camera, Adam Kimmel; editor,
Jeffrey Wolf; music supervisor, Amanda Scheer-Demme;
production design, Ruth Ammon; costume design, Deborah
Newhall. Reviewed at Sundance Festival, Jan. 20. Running time:
93 mins.
Denis Leary (Bobby O'Grady), Jason Barry (Seamus), Billy
Crudup (Teddy), John Diehl (Digger Bruce), Greg Dulli
(Shang), Noah Emmerich (Red Doherty), Ian Hart (Mouse
Murphy), Famke Janssen (Katy O'Connor), Colm Meaney
(Jackie O'Hara), Martin Sheen (Hanolon), Jeanne Tripplehorn
(Annie).
While credible in its portrayal of small-time crime among Irish

lowlifes in Boston, *Monument Avenue*, formerly known as *Snitch*, is irredeemably stuck in the boys-will-be-boys genre that has become more than a bit shopworn since *Mean Streets*. Well acted and ultimately involving despite the obnoxiously immature, all-too-familiar shenanigans of the reckless, boozing, violence-prone characters, this study of the difficulty of breaking traditional cycles of criminal activity reps a fair bet for interested indie distribs and specialized audiences.

Bobby O'Grady, a thirtysomething on the outside but emotionally an adolescent who spends most evenings coked-up with his buddies, is a senior member of a gang run by Jackie O'Hara, a big bully of the old school who demands absolute, unquestioning loyalty. Bobby's specialty is car theft, but the jobs are infrequent. Story's final act delineates Bobby's slow, dim moral awakening, triggered by the tragic, senseless murder of one of the gang.

U.S. release: Sept. 25　　　　　　U.S. B.O.: $300,000

## Mooncalf (Dis-Moi Que Je Rêve) (France)

A Rezo Films release of a Cinea/Rhone-Alpes Cinema/Euskal Media production, with the participation of the Région Rhone-Alpes, Centre National de la Cinématographie, Canal Plus. Produced by Philippe Carcassonne. Directed, written by Claude Mourieras. Camera, William Lubtchansky; editor, Monique Dartonne; music, Bertrand Lenclos; production designer, Wouter Zoon; costume designer, Brigitte Lauber. Reviewed at Cannes Festival, May 18. Running time: 96 mins.

**Muriel Mayette (Jeanne), Frederic Pierrot (Luc), Vincent Deneriaz (Julien), Cedric Vieira (Jules), Julien Charpy (Yannick), Stephanie Frey (Marion).**

Claude Mourieras' feature – the tale of an inbred farming family in a spectacular Alpine backwater – puts a new spin on dysfunctional family relationships. The new pic, which has won France's prestigious Jean Vigo prize, is likely to move audiences and should play the fest route as well as find niche distribution in some territories.

Mourieras is working with sensitive themes, exploring the place of the mentally and physically retarded in so-called normal society and the way families have to come to terms with "problem" children. The Ducrets are a close-knit family, fiercely protective of one another. Luc wanted to be a cosmonaut but wound up farming cows. Wife Jeanne has never acknowledged the shame over their decision to abandon their severely deformed firstborn at birth. Luc and Jean have not told their other three children about Jules and almost seem to have wiped out his existence.

Int'l release: June 3　　　　　　Int'l B.O.: $150,000
U.S. release: Sept. 25　　　　　　U.S. B.O.: $50,000

## Motello (Denmark)

A Polygram presentation of a Graested Film & Fjernsyn production, in association with Zentropa Entertainments. Produced by Mikael Wikke, Steen Rasmussen. Directed, written by Wikke, Rasmussen. Camera, Steffen Led Sorensen; editor, Jesper Osmund Christensen; music, Tango Orkestret, with Carl Quist Moller; production designer, Soren Skjaer; costume designer, Margrethe Rasmussen. Reviewed at Gothenburg Festival, Sweden, Feb. 8. Running time: 85 mins.

**Allan Olsen (Willy), Sidse Babett Knudsen (Julie), Bent Warburg (Ford Fordson), Solbjorg Hojfeldt (Gertrud Fordson), Bjarne Henriksen (Mac Fordson), Victor Hugo Diaz (Victor Othello), Steen Rasmussen (Rosenkrantz), Mikael**

**Wikke (Bendt Gyldenstjerne).**

A funny and often clever black comedy about two cops investigating a death at a motel, *Motello* is the new pic from the duo behind *Russian Pizza Blues*. This feature should generate healthy business on home turf and, with its witty use of Shakespearean motifs, could work overseas as well. Pic starts with Ford Fordson (Bent Warburg), owner of motorway motel Motello, being chilled to death in the establishment's deep freeze. Two cops, Rosenkrantz (Rasmussen) and Gyldenstjerne (Wikke), are assigned the case, somewhat hindered by the fact that Gyldenstjerne has to bring his 1-year-old son with him because his wife walked out the same day.

Int'l release: Feb. 20　　　　　　Int'l B.O.: $50,000

## Mouse Hunt

A DreamWorks Pictures release. Produced by Alan Riche, Tony Ludwig, Bruce Cohen. Directed by Gore Verbinski. Screenplay, Adam Rifkin. Camera, Phedon Papamichael; editor, Craig Wood; music, Alan Silvestri; production design, Linda DeScenna; costume design, Jill Ohanneson; visual-effects supervisor, Charles Gibson; mouse and cat creature design, Stan Winston Studios. Reviewed at GCC Meyerland Cinema, Houston, Dec. 16, 1997. MPAA Rating: PG. Running time: 97 mins.

**Nathan Lane (Ernie Smuntz), Lee Evans (Lars Smuntz), Vicki Lewis (April Smuntz), Maury Chaykin (Alexander Falko), Michael Jeter (Quincy Thorpe), William Hickey (Rudolph Smuntz), Christopher Walken (Caesar).**

*Mouse Hunt* is the cat's meow. Blending the graceful slapstick of Laurel and Hardy with the mock-Gothic visuals of *The Addams Family*, this often screamingly funny comedy about a resilient rodent has enough across-the-board appeal to click with audiences of all ages.

Estranged brothers Ernie and Lars are reunited by the death of their father, a string manufacturer. Ernie wants to sell the old man's factory, but Lars wants to preserve the family business. It takes a while for Adam Rifkin's clever screenplay to place Ernie and Lars in the mansion, and in conflict with the mouse. But once the brothers start to match wits with the rodent, pic becomes an amusingly twisted live-action cartoon.

U.S. release: Dec. 19, 1997　　　　U.S. B.O.: $62 million
Int'l release: Jan. 1　　　　　　Int'l B.O.: $60 million

## Mulan (Animated)

A Buena Vista release of a Walt Disney Pictures presentation. Produced by Pam Coats. Directed by Barry Cook, Tony Bancroft. Screenplay, Rita Hsiao, Christopher Sanders, Philip Lazebnik, Raymond Singer, Eugenia Bostwick-Singer, based on a story by Robert D. San Souci. Editor, Michael Kelly; songs: music, Matthew Wilder; lyrics, David Zippel; score, Jerry Goldsmith; production designer, Hans Bacher. Reviewed at Walt Disney, Burbank, May 3. MPAA Rating: G. Running time: 88 mins.

**Voices: Ming-Na Wen (Mulan), Lea Salonga (Singing Mulan), Eddie Murphy (Mushu), B.D. Wong (Shang), Donny Osmond (Singing Shang), Harvey Fierstein (Yao), Jerry S. Tondo (Chien-Po), Gedde Watanabe (Ling), Matthew Wilder (Singing Ling), James Hong (Chi Fu), Miguel Ferrer (Shan-Yu), Pat Morita (The Emperor), June Foray (Grandmother Fa), Marni Nixon (Singing Grandmother Fa).**

Quite likely the first animated cross-dressing action musical, *Mulan* plays out as a rich dramatic tapestry lightly stained by some strained comedy, rigorous political correctness, and perhaps more adherence to Disney formula than should have been the case in what is otherwise one of its most adventurous and serious animated features. About a tradition-bucking young woman in Ancient China who disguises herself as a man to serve in the army, this is a female empowerment story par excellence, as well as a G-rated picture that may have strong appeal for many adults.

A Disney rarity as it's not based on well-known material or characters – but purportedly a Chinese legend – it should generate strong response and business. Historically, *Mulan* reps a full turn of the circle from such age-old Disney classics as *Snow White and the Seven Dwarfs*, *Cinderella*, and *Sleeping Beauty*, in which passive heroines were rescued by blandly noble princes. Here, it's the girl who does the rescuing, saving not only the prince but the emperor from oblivion, and this in a culture where women were expected to obey strictly prescribed rules.

U.S. release: June 19     U.S. B.O.: $120 million
Int'l release: June 19     Int'l B.O.: $150 million

## My Dearest Friends (I Miei Piu Cari Amici) (Italy)

A Cecchi Gori Distribuzione release of a Cecchi Gori production. Produced by Vittorio and Rita Cecchi Gori. Directed by Alessandro Benvenuti. Screenplay, Benvenuti, Alberto Ongaro. Camera, Maurizio Calvesi; editor, Carla Simoncelli; music, Patrizio Fariselli; art director/costume designer, Eugenio Liverani. Reviewed at Ariston Cinema, Rome, April 13. Running time: 112 mins.

**Alessandro Benvenuti (Alessio), Eva Robins (Loretta), Athina Cenci (Martha), Alessandro Gassman (Rossano), Vito (Oscar), Zuzzurro (Bric), Gaspare (Brac).**

Six down-and-out actors accept a mysterious invitation to a medieval castle from their long-lost ex-friend Alessio (Benvenuti). They still hate their host for having cannibalized their lives 15 years ago for his hit play *My Dearest Friends*. Now he seems anxious to make amends with a new performance in which they will play themselves.

Belonging to the upper crust of the Cecchi Gori comedy stable, actor-director Alessandro Benvenuti and his stock company of thesps deliver a pleasant, fast-talking comedy with haunted-house undertones in *My Dearest Friends*. The elaborate dialog laced with irony may fly over the heads of some viewers, who can instead enjoy pic's spate of earthy low humor. The well-made, fast-paced, and funny movie is worth a look for foreign markets.

Int'l release: April 3     Int'l B.O.: $1 million

## My Giant

A Sony Pictures Entertainment release of a Columbia Pictures/Castle Rock Entertainment presentation of a Face production. Produced by Billy Crystal. Directed by Michael Lehmann. Screenplay, David Seltzer; story by Crystal, Seltzer. Camera, Michael Coulter; editor, Stephen Semel; music, Marc Shaiman; production designer, Jackson DeGovia; costume designer, Rita Ryack. Reviewed at UA Westwood, L.A., March 17. MPAA Rating: PG. Running time: 103 mins.

**Billy Crystal (Sam Kanin), Kathleen Quinlan (Serena Kanin), Gheorghe Muresan (Max), Joanna Pacula (Lillianna), Zane Carney (Nick Kanin), Rider Strong (Justin Allen), and Steven Seagal as himself.**

What makes agent Sammy Kanin run is the prospect of

anything or anyone who will raise his professional profile. A natural salesman with a winning personality, he's been stuck in the minor leagues because he's incapable of distinguishing gold from pyrites. However, he stumbles onto the real thing in Romania in the form of the 7-foot, 7-inch Max, a ward of the local monks.

As a filmmaker and performer, Billy Crystal has a near-obsessive need to do the right thing. In *My Giant*, which he produced from his and David Seltzer's original idea, good intentions largely work against the material's strengths. A reliance on a laugh or a clever remark too often interferes with emotion in the story of a gentle man whose innate decency turns a desperate cynic into a mensch. Those conflicting forces chafe badly, resulting in an uneven film with limited commercial appeal. Expect soft theatrical results and modest play in ancillaries.

U.S. release: April 10     U.S. B.O.: $8.1 million

## My Name is Joe (U.K.-Germany)

A Parallax Pictures/Road Movies Vierte Prod. production, with the support of the Scottish Arts Council National Lottery Fund, the Glasgow Film Fund, Filmstiftung NRW. Produced by Rebecca O'Brien. Directed by Ken Loach. Screenplay, Paul Laverty. Camera, Barry Ackroyd; editor, Jonathan Morris; music, George Fenton; production designer, Martin Johnson; costume designer, Rhona Russell. Reviewed at Cannes Festival, May 15. Running time: 105 mins.

**Peter Mullan (Joe Kavanagh). Louise Goodall (Sarah Downie), David McKay (Liam), Annemarie Kennedy (Sabine), David Hayman (McGowan), Gary Lewis (Shanks).**

Joe Kavanagh is a reformed alcoholic who's first seen addressing an AA meeting. Unemployed, he does odd jobs for cash and tries to run a chaotic, no-hope soccer team, among whose players is Liam, who owes a tidy sum to a local hood. He's also taking the first awkward steps in a relationship with career woman Sarah.

Emotionally dense, often moving, but finally flawed by a lack of focus, *My Name is Joe* is more boilerplate-British Ken Loach than the fully realized excursion to new territory promised by its opening. This Glasgow-set tale of working-class characters caught in a downward spiral looks like it will please the helmer's aficionados but still will be a tough sell beyond specialized venues.

Int'l release: Oct. 14     Int'l B.O.: $4.5 million

## Naturally Native

A Red-Horse Native production. Produced by Valerie Red-Horse, Dawn Jackson, Yvonne Russo. Directed by Jennifer Wynne Farmer, Red-Horse. Screenplay, Red-Horse. Camera, Bruce Finn; editor, Lorraine Salk; music, Murielle Hamilton; production design, Kee Miller; costume design, Irene Fredericks. Reviewed at Sundance Festival, Jan. 16. Running time: 107 mins.

**Valerie Red-Horse (Vickie Lewis Bighawk), Irene Bedard (Tanya Lewis), Kimberly Norris Guerrero (Karen Lewis), Pato Hoffmann (Steve Bighawk), Mary Kay Place (Madame Celste), Max Gail (Mr. Carlson).**

Billed as the first feature entirely financed by an Indian tribe, Connecticut's Mashantucket Piquots, *Naturally Native* can't be faulted for its dogged earnestness in treating the day-to-day travails of three sisters learning new self-awareness and the realities of the business world. Pic is at once deeply felt and clumsily plotted, a better bet for civics class than the multiplex.

---

**... July 2 ...**
October drops Todd Solondz's controversial **Happiness** from its release slate.

Future, despite bushels of good intentions and disarming honesty, isn't bright.

Vickie seeks backers for home-grown cosmetics based on old tribal remedies. She's joined in this quest by younger sisters Tanya and Karen. Siblings were adopted at birth outside of their tribe and are haunted by feelings of not belonging.

## The Negotiator

A Warner Bros. release of a Regency Enterprises presentation of a Mandeville Films/New Regency production, in association with Taurus Films. Produced by David Hoberman, Arnon Milchan. Directed by F. Gary Gray. Screenplay, James DeMonaco, Kevin Fox. Camera, Russell Carpenter; editor, Christian Wagner; music, Graeme Revell; production design, Holger Gross; costume design, Francine Jamison-Tanchuck; stunt coordinator, Joel Kramer. Reviewed at Plaza Theater, L.A., July 18. MPAA Rating: R. Running time: 138 mins.
**Samuel L. Jackson (Danny Roman), Kevin Spacey (Chris Sabian), David Morse (Cmdr. Adam Beck), Ron Rifkin (Cmdr. Frost), John Spencer (Chief Al Travis), J.T. Walsh (Terence Niebaum), Regina Taylor (Karen Roman), Paul Giamatti (Rudy).**

The teaming of Samuel L. Jackson and Kevin Spacey, in roles that call for a battle of wits and wills, proves shrewd and the best element of *The Negotiator*. Inspired by a real case, this action thriller gives the familiar construct of a falsely accused man who's forced to violate the law in order to prove his innocence. Though pic is slightly impaired by an overlong, overbaked production, expect midrange numbers for the entertaining suspenser whose serious issues are likely to appeal to audiences tired of mindless fare.

Praised by supervisors and celebrated by the news media for his courage under fire, hostage negotiator Danny Roman goes back to "routine" cop duties. It doesn't last long as his partner is gunned down, minutes before he was to meet Roman with info and names involved in departmental embezzlement. Found at the scene of the crime, Roman is under suspicion and asked to relinquish his badge and gun. Facing charges of murder and embezzlement, he resorts to a desperate gambit: He goes to the Chicago Internal Affairs headquarters and, after a direct confrontation with his chief interrogator Niebaum, he takes him and three others hostage. Roman decides he needs an unbiased listener and demands Chris Sabian, a respected negotiator from another precinct, to mediate. But defined rules are hard to break.

U.S. release: July 29     U.S. B.O.: $45 million
Int'l release: Sept. 25     Int'l B.O.: $22 million

## Neil Simon's The Odd Couple II

A Paramount Pictures release of a Cort/Madden production. Produced by Neil Simon, Robert W. Cort, David Madden. Directed by Howard Deutch. Screenplay, Neil Simon. Camera, Jamie Anderson; editor, Seth Flaum; music, Alan Silvestri; production designer, Dan Bishop; costume designer, Lisa Jensen. Reviewed at AMC Meyer Park, Houston, March 12. MPAA rating: PG-13. Running time: 96 mins.
**Jack Lemmon (Felix Ungar), Walter Matthau (Oscar Madison), Christine Baranski (Thelma), Barnard Hughes (Beaumont), Jonathan Silverman (Brucey Madison), Jean Smart (Holly), Doris Belack (Blanche Madison Povitch), Ellen Geer (Frances Ungar Melnick), Jay O. Sanders (Leroy), Lisa Waltz (Hannah Ungar).**

Thirty years later, retired sportswriter and incurable slob Oscar Madison is living in Florida. It's been 17 years since he's seen former roommate, the obsessively neat Felix Ungar. So when Brucey, Oscar's son, calls from Los Angeles to announce his impending marriage to Hannah, Felix's daughter, Oscar views the union as a mixed blessing.

Given the enduring popularity of the original 1965 play, *Neil Simon's The Odd Couple II* may attract enough ticketbuyers to post decent opening-weekend numbers. But this long-overdue sequel to the smash-hit 1968 feature offers too little, too late. A curiously tepid trifle that relies heavily on the trademark shtick of stars Jack Lemmon and Walter Matthau, pic won't find a big audience until it surfaces in video and cable.

U.S. release: April 10     U.S. B.O.: $19 million
Int'l release: Aug. 19     Int'l B.O.: $700,000

## The Nephew (Ireland)

An Irish DreamTime/World 2000 Entertainment production. Produced by Pierce Brosnan, Beau St. Clair. Directed by Eugene Brady. Screenplay, Jacqueline O'Neill, Sean P. Steele. Camera, Jack Conroy; editor, J. Patrick Duffner; music, Stephen McKeon; production designer, John Decuir. Reviewed at Cannes Festival, May 16. Running time: 106 mins.
**Hill Harper (Chad), Aislin McGuckin (Aislin), Pierce Brosnan (Joe Brady), Donal McCann (Tony Egan), Sinead Cusack (Brenda O'Boyce), Niall Tobin (Sean).**

Actor Pierce Brosnan makes his producing bow in *The Nephew*. Director Eugene Brady's dramatic treatment of good sitcom material makes for a strange beast – half culture clash, half family melodrama. Pic's emphasis on human relations and a warm ending, as well as its widescreen, tourist-board visuals, should help the film find its way to theatrical release for family audiences.

Set against the lush backdrop of an emerald islet, this is the unlikely tale of the tumult caused when the inbred denizens discover they have a young American cousin who is talented, handsome, and black. When Chad Egan-Washington shows up on the Irish island to scatter his mother's ashes, his misanthropic uncle Tony Egan is shocked. Having broken off contact with his sister 20 years back, he had no idea she had married a black New Yorker or ran a grocery store in Hell's Kitchen.

Int'l release: Aug. 28     Int'l B.O.: $700,000

## New Rose Hotel

An Edward R. Pressman Film Corp. production, in association with Quadra Entertainment. Produced by Edward R. Pressman. Directed by Abel Ferrara. Screenplay, Ferrara, Christi Zois, from a story by William Gibson. Camera, Ken Kelsch; editors, Anthony Redman, Jim Moll; music, Schooly D.; production design, Frank De Curtis; costume design, David C. Robinson. Reviewed at Venice Festival, Sept. 8. Running time: 92 mins.
**Christopher Walken (Fox), Willem Dafoe (X), Asia Argento (Sandii), Yoshitaka Amano (Hiroshi), Annabella Sciorra (Madame Rosa), Gretchen Mol (Hiroshi's Wife). With: John Lurie, Ryuichi Sakamoto.**

Abel Ferrara's latest effort is a well-made and fiercely well-performed erotic drama that perversely fails to deliver on the thriller aspects promised. Centered on a socko performance from Italo actress Asia Argento, the film, which focuses on industrial espionage and corporate skullduggery, is unlikely

---

**... July 3 ...**
Teen thesp Anna Paquin signs on for Miramax Films' romantic comedy **She's All That**.

to find new fans for the wayward Ferrara, though his core of supporters – particularly in France and Italy – will be keen to see what he's wrought from William Gibson's short story included in the anthology *Burning Chrome.*

Similar to Ernest Hemingway's *The Killers*, it consists of a monologue, as a man, expecting to be murdered, waits at the titular hotel and recalls the events that led up to this moment. Ferrara retains the essence of the original, while rejecting the flashback structure. Pic starts off with mysterious corporate raider Fox, together with his deputy, X, plotting to lure Hiroshi, a scientific genius, away from his employer. Fox's plan is simple. He offers slinky chanteuse Sandii $1 million if she'll seduce Hiroshi away from the company. Ferrara abruptly abandons the thriller aspects of the plot. There are no scenes involving Sandii and Hiroshi; we only hear, through dialog, that she succeeded – and then betrayed her employers.

### The Newton Boys

A 20th Century Fox presentation of a Detour Films production. Produced by Anne Walker-McBay. Directed by Richard Linklater. Screenplay, Linklater, Claude Stanush, Clark Lee Walker, based on Stanush's book. Camera, Peter James; editor, Sandra Adair; music, Edward D. Barnes; production design, Catherine Hardwicke; costume design, Shelley Komarov. Reviewed at 20th Century Fox, L.A., March 11. MPAA Rating: PG-13. Running time: 122 mins.
**Matthew McConaughey (Willis Newton), Skeet Ulrich (Joe Newton), Ethan Hawke (Jess Newton), Vincent D'Onofrio (Doc Newton), Julianna Margulies (Louise Brown), Dwight Yoakam (Brentwood Glasscock), Chloe Webb (Avis Glasscock).**
A radical departure from the director's previous youth-angst movies, Richard Linklater's *The Newton Boys* is a chronicle of four real-life siblings who entered collective mythology as Depression-era bank robbers. An extremely handsome production that meticulously evokes the 1920s, and a likeable male-dominated cast, only partially compensate for a story that's too diffuse and lacks a discernible point of view that would make it dramatically engaging. Fox should expect modest returns domestically (and weaker ones overseas) for period film that doesn't have erotic appeal.

Spanning five years, 1919-24, script establishes the context of a post-WWI rural society on the verge of dramatic change, catapulted by forces of technology, urbanization and industrialization. At the outset, the Newtons are poor, struggling farmers with a chip on their shoulders.

U.S. release: March 27          U.S. B.O.: $10.5 million
Int'l release: June 19          Int'l B.O.: $1 million

### Next Stop Wonderland

A Miramax release of a Robbins Entertainment production. Produced by Mitchell B. Robbins. Directed by Brad Anderson. Screenplay, Anderson, Lyn Vaus. Camera, Uta Briesewitz; editor, Anderson; music, Claudio Ragazzi; production design, Chad Detweiller. Reviewed at Sundance Festival, Jan. 17. Running time: 111 mins.
**Hope Davis (Erin Castleton), Alan Gelfant (Alan Monteiro), Victor Argo (Frank), Jon Benjamin (Eric), Cara Buono (Julie), Larry Gilliard, Jr. (Brett), Phil Hoffman (Sean), Roger Rees (Ray Thornback), Holland Taylor (Piper Castleton).**
Low on plot but high on charm and personality, *Next Stop Wonderland* is a sly, hand-crafted indie that is very alive and attentive to its characters' feelings and foibles. Brad Anderson's

second feature is individualistic and appealing. Although pic is probably too light to carve out significant commercial territory, it should connect with a certain niche audience, particularly among young female viewers. Focus here is on Erin, an attractive, thirtyish registered nurse who sinks into a prolonged funk when her political-activist boyfriend dumps her. Her mother, who runs a successful modeling agency, places a personal ad in the paper for her.
U.S. release: Aug. 21          U.S. B.O.: $3.5 million

### A Night at the Roxbury

A Paramount release, presented in association with SNL Studios, of a Lorne Michaels and Amy Heckerling production. Produced by Michaels, Heckerling. Directed by John Fortenberry. Screenplay, Steve Koren, Will Ferrell, Chris Kattan. Camera, Francis Kenny; editor, Jay Kamen; music, David Kitay; production design, Steven Jordan; costume design, Mona May. Reviewed at AMC 1000, San Francisco, Sept. 29. MPAA rating: PG-13. Running time: 81 mins.
**Will Ferrell (Steve Bubati), Chris Kattan (Doug Bubati), Molly Shannon (Emily), Dan Hedaya (Mr. Bubati), Loni Anderson (Mrs. Bubati), Elisa Donovan (Cambi), Gigi Rice (Viveca), Lochlyn Munro (Craig), Dwayne Hickman (Mr. Sanderson), and Richard Grieco as himself.**
One of the few reliably funny skits on *Saturday Night Live* in recent years has had Will Ferrell and Chris Kattan as two seemingly coke-addicted, desperately "hip" losers who trawl through Manhattan clubland, rebuffed over and over by all womankind. Of course, a three-minute sketch is one thing, a feature another. This one stands just a peg higher, as an amiable, if flyweight, diversion. With fall screens dominated by grown-up fare, *Roxbury* should score good short-term change from younger auds, then hale ancillary returns.

Basic shtick is that hair-gelled, silver-chained, satin-blazer-wearing brothers Steve and Doug Bubati cruise niteries to the endless thump of disco tunes, alienating every "babe" they try to pick up. Pic relocates duo from NYC to sunny Beverly Hills. What the boys dream about is opening their own club, one modeled on top local discotheque the Roxbury. A car accident with former *21 Jump Street* co-star Richard Grieco at last provides them with the desired entrance clout. Pair then find themselves embraced by the venue's owner (unbilled Armand Assante), as well as pursued by two slinky gold-diggers who mistake them for rich businessmen. This idyll can't last, and subsequent fallout finds Steve elbowed by Dad toward wedlock with pushy neighbor Emily, while Doug pouts on the sidelines.
U.S. release: Oct. 2          U.S. B.O.: $30 million

### Nightwatch

A Miramax Films release of a Dimension Films presentation of a Michael Obel production. Produced by Obel. Directed by Ole Bornedal. Screenplay, Steven Soderbergh, Bornedal, based on the film *Nattevagten* by Bornedal. Camera, Dan Lausten; editor, Sally Menke; music, Joachim Holbeck; production designer, Richard Hoover; costume designer, Louise Mingenbach; special-effects makeup, Steve Johnson, Kenny Meyers. Reviewed at the Aidikoff Screening Room, Beverly Hills, April 6, 1998. MPAA Rating: R. Running time: 101 mins.
**Ewan McGregor (Martin Bells), Nick Nolte (Insp. Thomas Cray), Josh Brolin (James Gallman), Patricia Arquette (Katherine), Alix Koromzay (Joyce), John C. Reilly (Insp. Bill Davis), Brad Dourif (Duty Doctor).**

---

**...July 4...**

MTV pulls its channel off the air in Amsterdam, leaving the city the only European capital that cannot receive the international music channel.

John Huston once noted that it was all right to steal from others when making movies – the fatal mistake was stealing from oneself. It's a piece of advice Ole Bornedal decided not to heed in remaking his Danish chiller *Nattevagten*. The new outing – which retains the essential twists of the original – has been physically enhanced with American production values and a marquee cast, but much of the earlier film's humanity and mordant humor have been lost in translation. Result, *Nightwatch*, is a story that's gone from arthouse to grind-house; rather rapid theatrical play will attract devotees of shock horror, with OK, if limited, ancillary action in that genre niche.

University student Martin (Ewan McGregor) takes a job as the night watchman in the city morgue to earn some extra money. He ignores vaguely sinister warnings from the former guard that it's a place where strange things happen. Then, strange things happen.

U.S. release: April 17  U.S. B.O.: $1.2 million
Int'l release: May 15  Int'l B.O.: $5 million

## No Looking Back

A Gramercy/20th Century Fox release of a Polygram Filmed Entertainment Group presentation of a Marlboro Road Gang/Good Machine/South Fork Pictures production. Produced by Ted Hope, Michael Nozik, Edward Burns. Directed, written by Burns. Camera, Frank Prinzi; editor, Susan Graef; music, Joe Delia; production designer, Therese DePrez; costume designer, Sara Jane Slotnick. Reviewed at Polygram, Beverly Hills, March 3. MPAA Rating: R. Running time: 96 mins.
Lauren Holly (Claudia), Edward Burns (Charlie), Jon Bon Jovi (Michael), Blythe Danner (Claudia's Mother), Connie Britton (Kelly), Jennifer Esposito (Teresa).

Good-looking Charlie returns to his sleepy Eastern seaboard hometown with the sole aim of winning back the girlfriend he unceremoniously abandoned three years before, only to find that Claudia is "basically" engaged to Michael, his best friend since first grade.

A minor character and mood piece, *No Looking Back* reps a watchable but unexciting sidestep for writer-director-star Edward Burns. Effectively evocative of dead-end small-town life, handsomely crafted working-class pic is nonetheless too bereft of incident, complexity, and surprise to generate much interest, spelling blah B.O. in limited release.

U.S. release: March 27  U.S. B.O.: $250,000

## The Object of my Affection

A 20th Century Fox release of a Laurence Mark production. Produced by Mark. Directed by Nicholas Hytner. Screenplay, Wendy Wasserstein, based on the novel by Stephen McCauley. Camera, Oliver Stapleton; editor, Tariq Anwar; music, George Fenton; production designer, Jane Musky; costume designer, John Dunn. Reviewed at the Chinese, L.A., April 7. MPAA Rating: R. Running time: 112 mins.
Jennifer Aniston (Nina Borowski), Paul Rudd (George Hanson), Alan Alda (Sidney Miller), Nigel Hawthorne (Rodney Fraser), John Pankow (Vince McBride), Tim Daly (Dr. Robert Joley), Steve Zahn (Frank Hanson).

A very vanilla romantic tale about an attempt at a design for living between a gay man and a pregnant woman, *The Object of My Affection* tries to mix the messy realities of mismatched relationships with the structural neatness of a musical-comedy, with mild, occasionally diverting results. The plot's hokey

contrivances and the theatrical shtick tend to prevail over the sporadic moments of insight and emotional truth. An attractive cast, a few pleasant chuckles, and low-voltage sexual frissons don't look to be enough to turn this into anything more than a modest B.O. performer.

Wendy Wasserstein's script throws the principal characters together at an upscale dinner party hosted by a literary agent and his quip-witted wife. Stepsister Nina inadvertently informs the nice, attractive George that his lover Robert, also in attendance, is dumping him. This leads to a growing friendship. But what Nina and George don't count on is falling, sort of, in love.

U.S. release: April 17  U.S. B.O.: $29 million
Int'l release: May 8  Int'l B.O.: $16 million

## Occasional Coarse Language (Australia)

A Roadshow release of a Village Roadshow-Flickering Films presentation of a Very Chancy Material production. Produced by Trish Piper. Directed, written by Brad Hayward. Camera, John Biggins; editor, Simon Martin; music supervisor, Brett Oaten; production design, Rebecca Barry. Reviewed at Village Roadshow, Sydney, Nov. 3. Running time: 81 mins.
Sara Browne (Min), Astrid Grant (Jaz), Nicholas Bishop (David), Michael Walker (Stanley), Lisa Denmeade (Claire), Michelle Fillery (Alex), Belinda Hoare (Soph), Shannon Faith (Monica).

This low-budgeter about 21-year-old women who inhabit the inner suburbs of Sydney succeeds as a seemingly accurate and all-too-realistic depiction of rather depressing lifestyles. Tyro writer-director Brad Hayward's rough cut impressed execs of Village Roadshow, who provided the cash for post-production, including the addition of a potent musical soundtrack.

Story's central focus is Min, a plain Jane who worries about her weight, her dad's surgery, she's broken up with her boyfriend, moved out of the house, and lost her job. Her best friend, Jaz, suggests Min take a vacant room in the house rented by David, who's also getting over a broken relationship. Min soon discovers he's not only a snooty intellectual, he's also "getting over" his broken romance by inviting a different woman to bed each night. Jaz complains to Min about b.f. Stanley's lack of sexual prowess, so she's surprised when Stanley confides in her with similar complaints about Jaz. When Jaz discovers Min has been talking to Stanley, she angrily dumps her friend – and Min and Stanley start seeing each other.

Int'l release: Nov. 26  Int'l B.O.: $600,000

## Of Freaks and Men (Pro Ourodov I Lioudiei)
(Russia)

A CTB production. Executive producer, Maksim Volodin. Produced by Serguei Selyanov, Oleg Botogov. Directed, written by Alexei Balabanov. Camera, Sergei Astakhov; editor, Marina Lipartia; production designer, Vera Zelinskaya; costume designer, Nadya Vasilyeva. Reviewed at Cannes Festival, May 20. Running time: 93 mins.
Igor Shibanov (Radlov), Sergei Makovetsky (Johann), Dinara Drukarova (Lisa), Lika Nevolina (Ekaterina Kirillovna), Victor Sukhorukov (Victor Ivanovich), Alyesha De and Chingiz Tsydendabayev (Kolya and Tolya), Vadim Prokhorov (Pytilov), Alexandr Mezentsev (Dr. Stasov).

Insinuating itself into the viewer's mind in the way its nefarious lead characters corrupt and undermine two families in turn-of-the-century Russia, *Of Freaks and Men* is both a dark gem

---

**...July 5 ...**
Johnny Speight, British comedy writer and creator of Alf Garnett and his subsequent U.S. reincarnation Archie Bunker, dies.

and a perplexing marketing conundrum. Pic will get kudos, but it's too much ribald fun for "serious" artfilm lovers and too offbeat in its subject matter and stylized cinematography to catch any significant arthouse B.O.

Two St. Petersburg families, one high-society and the other middle-class, come into contact with the strange, dour Johann, a professional producer of pornography. What binds them to the smut merchant is his hold on Radlov's seemingly innocent daughter and Radlov's secret relationship with Grunya, Johann's sister. Johann's henchman Victor creeps between the households, peddling photos and developing his own lust for the illicit. The objects of his affection are Dr. Stasov's adopted conjoined twins, Kolya and Tolya. Everyone appears to have some aberrant sexual quirk.

## Of Lost Love (Del Perduto Amore) (Italy)

A CDI/Buena Vista Int'l Italia release of a Clemi Cinematografica production, in association with RAI Cinemafiction. Produced by Giovanni Di Clemente. Directed by Michele Placido. Screenplay, Domenico Starnone, Placido. Camera, Blasco Giurato; editor, Francesca Calvelli; music, Carlo Crivelli; production design, Paola Comencini; costume design, Claudio Cordaro. Reviewed at Apollo Cinema, Rome, Aug. 27. Running time: 98 mins.
Giovanna Mezzogiorno (Liliana), Fabrizio Bentivoglio (Antonio), Rocco Papaleo (Cucchiaro), Enrico Lo Verso (Dr. Satriano), Rino Cassano (Don Gaetano), Michele Placido (Don Gerardo), Piero Pischedda (Gerardo), Sergio Rubini (Italo), Lorenzo Gentile (Don Vincenzo).

Actor-turned-director Michele Placido weaves a romantic tale about a feisty young woman whose Communist principles and crusades make her an unpopular presence in conservative southern Italy in the late 1950s. Inspired by Liliana Rossi who dedicated her short, intense life to voluntary teaching, community assistance, and politics, *Of Lost Love* sufficiently recovers from its awkward opening stretch and schematic flashback structure to become an engrossing, if old-fashioned, period piece that should figure on fest slates.

Present-day opener has priest Don Gerardo preaching about sins while reflecting on his own failings. Backtracking to his childhood in 1958, the drama wades through some stodgy exposition, sketching his expulsion from school over a presumed homosexual encounter, and the efforts to set him on a righteous path.

Gerardo is drawn to twentysomething Liliana, an outspoken member of the Communist party. Despite the hostility of the community, Liliana establishes a school. But her teaching of such advanced ideas as birth control and equality between the sexes creates resentment. The confusion caused by Gerardo's incipient love, his religious vocation, and his conditioned disapproval of her red-flag-waving is aggravated when he learns of her clandestine affair with a married doctor.

Int'l release: Sept. 18    Int'l B.O.: $400,00

## O.K. Garage

A Talana Prods/Rialto Film production. Produced by Keith Rotman. Directed, written by Brandon Cole. Camera, Rob Sweeney; editor, Suzanne Pillsbury; music, Evan Lurie; production designer, Frankie D.; costume designer, Kevin Scott. Reviewed at L.A. Independent Festival, April 19. Running time: 90 mins.
John Turturro (Johnny), Lili Taylor (Rachel), Will Patton (Sean), Gemma Jones (Mrs Wiggins), Joe Maher (Lilly), Paul Calderon (Carl), Richard Bright (Louis), Olek Krupa (Yannick).

Brandon Cole's *O.K. Garage* is a comic tale about the daily frustrations and romantic aspirations of ordinary urban dwellers. Pic's mixture of revenge and quirky romance doesn't always work, but the three gifted leads endow the modern-day fantasy with offbeat charm. Better written than directed, this modestly executed yarn is a likely bet for the specialized theatrical market.

Rachel, an inner-city school teacher, has car trouble and pulls in at the O.K. Garage. Yannick, the owner, promises to fix the car, but soon after Rachel leaves, it's established that he's a small-time crook who prides himself on ripping off his customers.

## Olympia

A Big Tomato production. Produced by Adrienne Gruben, Nancy Schafer, Jason Silverman. Director, Robert Byington. Screenplay, Byington, Bill Stout, Johnny McAllister, based on the story *Javelkemeiche* by Byington. Camera, Paul Kloss; editor, Garrett Savage; music, Lisa Hunsacker; production design, Gigi Causey; costume design, Hunsacker. Reviewed at Laemmle Monicas, Santa Monica, Jan. 13. Running time: 76 mins.
Carmen Nogales (Olympia Miraflores), Jason Andrews (Bill Daniel), Damian Young (Ed Pedernales), Patricia Fiske (Mom).

A yarn about pursuing one's dreams, however improbable, the modestly budgeted *Olympia* combines goofball situations and serious themes, to disarming effect. While pic has limited commercial prospects, filmmaker Robert Byington displays talent and the potential for wider commercial reach.

The story turns on title character Olympia Miraflores, a Mexican television soap star obsessed with competing in the Olympics in the javelin throw. Neither her fans nor her trainer-manager particularly like the idea.

## One Against All (Seul Contre Tous) (France)

A Les Cinémas de la Zone presentation of a Cinémas de la Zone/Lovestreams Prods co-production, with the participation of CNC. Produced, written, directed by Gaspar Noe. Camera, Dominique Colin; editors, Lucille Hadzihalilovic, Noe. Reviewed at Cannes Festival, May 16. Running time: 81 mins.
Philippe Nahon (The Butcher), Frankyie Pain (His Mistress), Blandine Lenoir (Cynthia), Martine Audrain (Mother-in-Law).

A guy who's never gotten a break decides to get even in the delectably sordid *One Against All*, an ultra-widescreen slice of jaundice that creates its own unrelentingly tawdry, hermetic universe. Pic does an outstanding job of burrowing into the mind of an essentially decent, average man as he rationalizes his escalating anger. Gaspar Noe's abrasive, ironic, and uncomfortably funny pic unquestionably constitutes a marketing headache.

Pic is narrated by the unnamed man (Philippe Nahon), who was orphaned during the war, went to work at 14, and eventually opened a butcher's shop. The butcher is "starting over," following prison time, with an obese, shrewish bar owner, who is very pregnant with his child. It's January 1980 in a housing project in a suburb of Lille, where the butcher and his emasculating mistress have moved in with her mother. Unable to find work and fed up with the two women, the butcher has a knock-down fight with his mistress and hitchhikes back to the outskirts of Paris.

---

### ... July 6 ...

Francis Ford Coppola awarded $20 million in **Pinocchio** lawsuit... Happy trails for singing cowboy Roy Rogers in his last round-up.

## One Evening After the War (Un Soir Après La Guerre) (France-Cambodia)

A JBA (France) production, in association with Thelma Film AG (Switzerland), Compagnie Mediterranéenne de Cinéma (Belgium), La Direction du Cinéma au Cambodge (Cambodia). Produced by Jacques Bidou. Directed by Rithy Panh. Screenplay, Panh, Eve Duboise. Camera, Christophe Pollock; editor, Marie-Christine Rougerie; music, Marc Marder. Reviewed at Cannes Festival, May 19. Running time: 108 mins.
Chea Lyda Chan (Srey Poeuv), Narith Roeun (Savannah), Ratha Keo (Maly), Sra N'Gath Kheav (Le Meut), Mol Sovanna (Phal).

A classically proportioned tragedy about the aftermath of Cambodia's two decades of war, *One Evening After the War* follows helmer Rithy Panh's *The Rice People* in bringing handsome French production values to a Southeast Asian milieu of stark poverty and social turmoil. Well acted and very assured in its narrative handling and visual mounting, pic offers both insight and emotional payoff. Its neo-realist-tinged drama and poised style suggest pic is best suited to upscale Euro arthouses and fests.

Panh's sophomore outing concerns the difficulties faced by soldiers returning from far-flung war zones to newly pacified Phnom Penh in the early 1990s. Rid of the Khmer Rouge, the country now abounds in gangsters and prostitutes. Savannah has at least survived the conflict with his limbs intact, but, suddenly thrown back into the bustling city, he's at a loose end. Rejecting the lure of petty crime, he tries to make his way as a kickboxer, while living with an uncle who's the only one of his large family left after Pol Pot's genocidal reign.
Int'l release: Dec. 16                Int'l B.O.: $25,000

## One Tough Cop

A Stratosphere Entertainment release of a Patriot Pictures production. Produced by Michael Bregman, Martin Bregman. Directed by Bruno Barreto. Screenplay, Jeremy Iacone, inspired by the novel by Bo Dietl. Camera, Ron Fortunato; editor, Ray Hubley; music, Bruce Broughton; production design, Perri Gorrara; costume design, Martha Mann, Sue Gandy. Reviewed at Variety Club, San Francisco, Sept. 24. Running time: 90 mins.
Stephen Baldwin (Bo Dietl), Chris Penn (Duke Finnerty), Mike McGlone (Richie La Cassa), Gina Gershon (Joey O'Hara), Paul Guilfoyle (Frank "Hot" Salvano), Amy Irving (FBI Agent Jean Devlin), Victor Slezak (FBI Agent Bruce Payne), Luis Guzman (Popi).

Attempting a more commercial project, vet Brazilian helmer Bruno Barreto stumbles with a crime actioner every bit as generic as its title. "Inspired" by real-life Big Apple detective Bo Dietl's career, *One Tough Cop* recycles hoary cliches bluntly and cluelessly. Fastest-paced aspect is likely to be pic's theatrical in-and-out; genre item should do OK in ancillary markets.

Dietl was evidently a slug-first, due-process-later kinda cop. He and hard-drinking, hot-tempered partner Duke routinely exasperate their NYPD superiors, but are nonetheless considered amongst the city's best. Focal case in the film involves a nun found raped, beaten, and grotesquely mutilated at her Harlem convent school – though the nun is never seen again post-ambulance, her fate barely discussed, and the perpetrator's identity never particularly germane to the plot arc. But it does provide some chase segs, and a vehicle for cop duo to get in hot water re their inappropriate social contacts with mob figures. Two cold-blooded FBI agents play this card

to pressure Bo and Duke for federal investigative purposes.
U.S. release: Oct. 9                U.S. B.O.: $1.3 million

## One True Thing

A Universal release of a Monarch Pictures/Ufland production. Produced by Harry Ufland, Jesse Beaton. Directed by Carl Franklin. Screenplay, Karen Croner, based on the novel by Anna Quindlen. Camera, Declan Quinn; editor, Carole Kravetz; music, Cliff Eidelman; production designer, Paul Peters; costume design, Donna Zakowska. Reviewed at Universal, Universal City, Aug. 24. MPAA Rating: R. Running time: 127 mins.
Meryl Streep (Kate Gulden), Renee Zellweger (Ellen Gulden), William Hurt (George Gulden), Tom Everett Scott (Brian Gulden), Lauren Graham (Jules), Nicky Katt (Jordan Belzer), Gerrit Graham (Oliver Most).

As sensitively written, fluidly directed, and expertly acted as it is, *One True Thing* has trouble breaking free of its limitations as a small-scale, modestly aimed family drama. Nicely judged artistically and pitched to reveal many small truths about parent-child relationships, pic is held in sharp focus by Renee Zellweger's central performance and reps an unexpected and admirable change of pace for director Carl Franklin. This sort of domestic material's been done most often for television in recent years, and its muted nature presents an imposing challenge to move pic beyond a modest, femme-dominated theatrical audience.

Not long out of Harvard, Ellen Gulden is trying to make a name for herself with investigative magazine pieces. Her father, George, calls to say that mother Kate is about to undergo cancer surgery and Ellen has to supervise her care. Ellen doesn't initially see the point and agrees only to have some distance from her difficult relationship with boyfriend Jordan. She'll just continue her magazine writing from home. The main problem is that Ellen has come to view her mom's world as unbearably boring, defined by dreary housekeeping duties and silly relationships with chattering cronies. By contrast, Ellen idealizes her intellectual father. But as Kate's condition worsens, Ellen begins to recognize both the need for her presence and some dark family truths.
U.S. release: Sept. 18                U.S. B.O.: $23 million

## On Guard! (Le Bossu) (France-Italy-Germany)

An AMLF release of an Aliceleo, TF1 Films Prod, DA Films, Prima (France)/CGG Tiger Cinematografica (Italy)/Gemini Film Produktion (Germany) production. Produced by Patrick Godeau. Directed by Philippe de Broca. Screenplay, Jean Cosmos, Jerome Tonnerre, de Broca, based on the novel by Paul Feval. Camera, Jean-François Robin; editor, Henri Lanoe; music, Philippe Sarde; art direction, Bernard Vezat; costume design, Christian Gasc; stunts/fencing adviser, Michel Carliez. Reviewed at UGC Normandie, Paris, Nov. 6, 1997. Running time: 128 mins.
Daniel Auteuil (Lagardere), Fabrice Luchini (Gonzague), Vincent Perez (Nevers), Marie Gillain (Aurore), Yann Collette (Peyrolles), Jean-François Stevenin (Cocardasse), Philippe Noiret (Philippe d'Orleans).

A humor-bedecked historical romp, *On Guard!* is consistently enjoyable, if rarely exceptional, mass entertainment. Philippe de Broca's swashbuckling 17th-century saga of delayed revenge provides plum roles for Daniel Auteuil and Fabrice Luchini as, respectively, the versatile hero and delectably hissable villain. This seventh screen adaptation of Paul Feval's 1857 serialized

---

**... July 7 ...**
John Travolta inks to star in Columbia's drama **The Shipping News**, based on the bestselling novel.

novel is a refreshing bigscreen experience.

Lagardere, a former street urchin schooled in fencing and circus arts, goes from accepting money to kill the Duke of Nevers to becoming his trusted friend and bodyguard. The greedy Gonzague enlists brigands to slaughter Nevers, his wife, and his child. Dying from a fatal stab in the back, Nevers entrusts Lagardere with the infant and asks his friend to avenge him... no matter how long it takes. Years will pass before Lagardere has his opportunity, getting to the inner circle disguised as a "bossu" – a hunchback.

Int'l release: Dec. 3, 1997     Int'l B.O.: $14 million
U.S. release: March 20     U.S. B.O.: $300,000

### Open Bodies (Les Corps Ouverts) (France)

A Magouric release of a Lancelot Films/Michka Prods production. Produced by Christian Tison. Directed by Sebastien Lifshitz. Screenplay, Stephane Bouquet, Lifshitz. Camera, Pascal Poucet; editors, Stephanie Mahet, Jeanne Moutard; music, Akhenaton, L'Orient, Imaginaire, Rob Dougan, Ala; art director, Valerie Mrejen; costume designer, Elisabeth Mehu. Reviewed at Videothéque de Paris, Paris, May 4. Running time: 45 mins.
**Yasmine Belmadi (Remi), Pierre-Loup Rajot (Marc), Margot Abascal (Young Woman).**
A kind and decent 18-year-old boy explores his still-fluid sexuality in *Open Bodies*, a slight but well-limned slice of life. Sebastien Lifshitz's deftly edited effort has enjoyed busy rotation on the French festival circuit in recent months and won the prestigious Prix Jean Vigo for 1998.

The offspring of a French mother and a North African father, teenager Remi is majoring in commerce and management, trying to be a good son to his seriously ill father and working part-time in an Arab grocery. One day he answers an ad to appear in a film. With the camera tucked up close to his face, the director, Marc, auditions him and casts him to "appear" in his bed.

Int'l release: June 24     Int'l B.O.: $50,000

### Open Your Eyes (Abre Los Ojos) (Spain-France-Italy)

A Sogepaq release of a Sogetel, El Escorpion (Spain)/Les Films Alain Sarde (France)/Lucky Red (Italy) production, in association with Canal Plus Spain. Cuerda. Produced by José Luis Cuerda. Directed by Alejandro Amenabar. Screenplay, Amenabar, Mateo Gil. Camera, Hans Burmann; editor, Maria Elena Sainz de Rojas; music, Amenabar, Mariano Marin; art direction, Wolfgang Burmann. Reviewed at Cine Cite, Madrid, Dec. 12, 1997. Running time: 117 mins.
**Eduardo Noriega (Cesar), Penelope Cruz (Sofia), Chete Lera (Antonio), Fele Martinez (Pelayo), Najwa Nimri (Nuria).**
Floppy-haired, doe-eyed Cesar is a rich yuppie who makes it a point of honor to sleep with women only once before abandoning them.

An ambitiously complex, disturbing, and terrific-looking thriller, *Open Your Eyes* is helmer Alejandro Amenabar's much-awaited follow-up to his award-winning 1995 debut, *Thesis*. Pic shows him breaking traditional formats, mixing in a bit of sci-fi, throwing it all up in the air, and seeing what happens. Result just barely sidesteps art-school pretentiousness and could be too perplexing for mainstream tastes. But its strong script and hot cast should make pic a subject of interest at home, as well as opening the eyes of offshore arthouse auds to one of Spain's brightest young talents.

Int'l release: Dec. 19, 1997     Int'l B.O.: $8.5 million

### The Opposite of Sex

A Sony Pictures Classics release of a Rysher Entertainment presentation of a David Kirkpatrick/Michael Besman production. Produced by Kirkpatrick, Besman. Directed, written by Don Roos. Camera, Hubert Taczanowski; editor, David Codron; music, Mason Daring; production design, Michael Clausen; costume design, Peter Mitchell. Reviewed at Sundance Festival, Jan. 22. Running time: 105 mins.
**Christina Ricci (Dedee Truitt), Martin Donovan (Bill Truitt), Lisa Kudrow (Lucia), Lyle Lovett (Sheriff Carl Tippett), Johnny Galecki (Jason), Ivan Sergei (Matt Mateo).**
An odd-tasting stew of provocative sexual hijinx, trash talk, lower-class vengeance, p.c. sendups, and the search for true love. Determined to cut through the thicket of political correctness with rapier wit and rude humor, *The Opposite of Sex* ends up being more of a bumpy romp than a good roll in the hay. An acerbic, bitchy comedy about the momentary ups and prolonged downs of sexual entanglements, initial directorial outing by writer Don Roos provokes quite a few laughs that could make this an audience pleaser in niche specialized play.

Ricci stars and narrates as Dedee, a 16-year-old Louisiana swamp tramp who, after burying her stepfather, hightails it to Indiana, where she barges in on her half-brother Bill, a strait-laced "homo" schoolteacher seeing the very good-looking Matt. On the make, Dedee bluntly accuses Matt of being prejudiced and discriminatory in not sleeping with women and thereby succeeds in prodding him into an affair.

U.S. release: May 22     U.S. B.O.: $6.4 million
Int'l release: Aug. 14     Int'l B.O.: $1.7 million

### Orphans (U.K.)

A Channel Four Films presentation, in association with the Scottish Arts Council and the Glasgow Film Fund, of an Antonine Green Bridge production. Produced by Frances Higson. Directed, written by Peter Mullan. Camera, Grant Scott Cameron; editor, Colin Monie; music, Craig Armstrong; production design, Campbell Gordon; costume design, Lynn Aitken. Reviewed at Cannes Festival, May 21, 1998. Running time: 101 mins.
**Douglas Henshall (Michael), Gary Lewis (Thomas), Stephen Cole (John), Rosemarie Stevenson (Sheila), Frank Gallagher (Tanga), Alex Norton (Hanson).**
Grief prompts some bizarre behavior in *Orphans*, the feature-writing-directing debut of Scottish actor Peter Mullan, who turned heads in Cannes with his prize-winning performance in Ken Loach's *My Name is Joe*. While the narrative grasp is a little too unrefined to land much commercial exposure, strong directorial instincts are by no means absent from this original view of a family coming to terms with death. Full of authentic surprises and clearly the fruit of a very dark sense of humor, the eccentric black comedy-drama is an impressive debut. The opening intros four adult siblings come to bury their mother. The film then veers progressively further off-kilter as they go through a long night of pain and purification before her funeral the following day.

### Oscar and Lucinda

A Fox Searchlight release, in association with the Australian Film Finance Corp. and the New South Wales Film & Television Office, of a Dalton Films production, produced in association with Meridian Films. Produced by Robin Dalton, Timothy

White. Directed by Gillian Armstrong. Screenplay, Laura Jones, based on the novel by Peter Carey. Camera, Geoffrey Simpson; editor, Nicholas Beauman; music, Thomas Newman; production design, Luciana Arrighi; costume design, Janet Patterson. Reviewed at 20th Century Fox, L.A., Nov. 17, 1997. MPAA Rating: R. Running time: 132 mins.

Ralph Fiennes (Oscar Hopkins), Cate Blanchett (Lucinda Leplastrier), Ciaran Hinds (Rev. Dennis Hasset), Tom Wilkinson (Hugh Stratton), Richard Roxburgh (Mr. Jeffris), Clive Russell (Theophilus), Bille Brown (Percy Smith), Josephine Byrnes (Miriam Chadwick), Barnaby Kay (Wardley-Fish), Barry Otto (Jimmy D'Abbs). Narrator: Geoffrey Rush

*Oscar and Lucinda* is a poetic saga whose physical production is just as impressive as its spiritual aspirations. Director Gillian Armstrong's meticulous attention to visual detail and her sharp observational powers about human conduct inform this Victorian-era romance of two eccentric soulmates, reckless dreamers and gamblers. Pic is highly dependent on strong critical support, and poses an imposing marketing challenge to transcend arthouse and enter the mainstream.

Faithful adaption of Peter Carey's 1988 Booker Prize novel is told in flashback by Oscar's great-grandson (narrated by Geoffrey Rush). Pic opens with title characters' respective childhoods, crosscutting between Oscar's lonely boyhood in rural England under stern supervision of preacher father, and Lucinda's on an Australian farm, tutored by a strong-willed mother. When Oscar trains for the ministry, he realizes that he "simply does not fit." Lonely and repressed, he meets a mate who intros him to the horses. The act of gambling finally makes him come alive – giving his winnings to the poor.

Oscar's fateful meeting with the woman occurs shipboard en route to a ministry in the Australian outback; Lucinda is returning from London with machinery for her glass factory. The two outcasts connect upon recognizing each other's "pathological" behavior. A most peculiar bond evolves, one that's based on trust and is intimately romantic without being carnal.

| U.S. release: Dec. 31, 1997 | U.S. B.O.: $1.9 million |
| Int. release: Jan. 22 | Int'l B.O.: $2.5 million |

## The Other Side of the Tracks (De L'autre Côté Du Periph) (Docu, France)

A France 2/Little Bear production. Produced by Frederic Bourboulon, Denis Poncet. Directed by Bertrand Tavernier, Nils Tavernier. Screenplay, Bertrand Tavernier. Camera, Nils Tavernier, Eric Philbert; editor, Luce Grunenwaldt; music, Positif, Toure Kunda, Super Diamono de Dakar. Reviewed at the Montreal Int'l Festival of New Cinema & New Media, Oct. 15. Running time: 150 mins.

A 2½ -hour documentary on the tough living conditions in poor suburbs of Paris does not sound like a particularly appetizing cinematic treat, but seasoned Gallic helmer Bertrand Tavernier and his son Nils manage to turn a stale lesson in sociology into an intriguing piece of cinema verité-style filmmaking. By moving into the neighborhood and building close ties with the folks they're filming, they provide a rare glimpse of the real people behind headlines of violence, poverty, and discontent in the housing projects. *The Other Side of the Tracks* is fascinating viewing for the most part, but its length and its discussion of specific domestic French political squabbles will severely limit its reach.

Tavernier et fils spent months in the 'hood, gaining the trust

of the largely immigrant (mainly North African) population. They query school teachers, public officials, local cops, and politicians, and the interviews provide a host of quite different views on the dire social problems in the area: a chronic shortage of low-cost housing, rampant unemployment, inadequate schools, and social centers, and the usual strained relations between the residents and the police.

## Our God's Brother (Italy-Poland-Germany)

A Trans World Films, RAI (Rome)/Film Studio Tor, TVP (Warsaw)/Tellex Film (Dresden) co-production. Produced by Giacomo Pezzali, Georg Stingl, Krzysztof Zanussi. Directed by Zanussi. Screenplay, Mario di Nardo, Zanussi, based on the play *Brat Naszego Boga* by Karol Wojtyla, translated by Boleslaw Taborski. Camera, Ryszard Lenczewski; editor, Marek Denys; music, Wojciech Kilar; production design, Ewa Braun, Grzegorz Piatkowski; costumes, Malgorzata Stefaniak. Reviewed at Venice Festival, Sept. 5, 1997. Running time: 123 mins.

Scott Wilson (Adam Chmielowski), Christoph Waltz (Max), Wojciech Pszoniak (The Stranger), Grazyna Szapolowska (Helena), Riccardo Cucciolla (The Monk), Jerry Flynn (Lucjan).

Krzysztof Zanussi has made a reverential screen adaptation of a play written in 1949 by Karol Wojtyla, better known today as Pope John Paul II. The inspired new film is likely to have a long life as a teaching tool for Catholic audiences worldwide and be in demand as a video title but regular theatrical bookings appear limited.

Wojtyla wrote *Our God's Brother* as a tribute to Adam Chmielowski, a painter-turned-priest who gave up a comfortable bourgeois life to work amongst the poor and whom he, as Pope, recently canonized as Saint Brother Albert. In 1863 the young Chmielowski takes part in an uprising against the occupying Russians, in which he loses a leg. After the conflict he turns successfully to painting but finds the social world stuffy. When Chmielowski stumbles across a band of homeless people living in abject poverty, helping them becomes his obsession and will lead him to the priesthood.

## Out of Order (A Miniszter Felrelep) (Hungary)

An InterCom release of an Andrew G. Vajna presentation of an InterCom production. Produced by Vajna. Directed by Andras Kern, Robert Koltai. Screenplay, Jim Adler, Kern, Koltai, from the stage play *Out of Order* by Ray Cooney. Camera, Elemer Ragalyi; editor, Eva Gardos; music, Laszlo Des; art direction, Jozsef Romvari; costume design, Lucia S. Hegyi, Bela Sumeghy. Reviewed at Hungarian Film Week, Budapest, Feb. 7. Running time: 100 mins.

With: Andras Kern (Peter Vitt), Robert Koltai (Sandor), Sandor Gaspar, Judit Hernadi, Ivan Kamaras, Ferenc Kallai, Gabor Reviczky, Dorottya Udvaros (Wife), Kata Dobo (Tunde).

Peter Vitt, a smooth, right-wing minister in a perilous coalition government is having an affair with his assistant's secretary. Telling his wife he'll be working late, Vitt arranges to meet the woman at an hotel and gets an unwanted corpse in the bargain. Hollywood producer Andy Vajna has hit a home run on his native Magyar soil with *Out of Order*, an old-fashioned farce. After seven weeks of release, the pic, produced and distribbed by Vajna's own Budapest-based company InterCom, had racked up a giant 530,000 admissions locally.

Though it's pleasantly amusing, and has one of those

clockwork plots with people hiding in every room and closet, this reworking of a legit item by Ray Cooney depends for much of its fun on recognizing the stellar Hungarian players going through their shtick rather than anything very original or belly-clutching. Offshore, however, viewers should wait for Vajna's planned U.S. remake.

Int'l release: Dec. 17     Int'l B.O.: $1.1 million

## Out of Sight

A Universal Pictures release of a Jersey Films production. Produced by Danny DeVito, Michael Shamberg, Stacy Sher. Directed by Steven Soderbergh. Screenplay, Scott Frank, based on the novel by Elmore Leonard. Camera, Elliot Davis; editor, Anne V. Coates; music, David Holmes; production designer, Gary Frutkoff; costume designer, Betsy Heimann. Reviewed at Beverly Connection, L.A., June 18. MPAA Rating: R. Running time: 122 mins.

**George Clooney (Jack Foley), Jennifer Lopez (Karen Sisco), Ving Rhames (Buddy Bragg), Don Cheadle (Maurice "Snoopy" Miller), Dennis Farina (Marshall Sisco), Albert Brooks (Richard Ripley), Steve Zahn (Glenn Michaels), Luis Guzman (Chino), Catherine Keener (Adele), Nancy Allen (Midge). With: Michael Keaton, Samuel L. Jackson.**

Jack Foley's latest bank robbery goes smoothly until he reaches his car a dead battery. Back in prison, he begins to plot out his next heist with an ill-assortment of characters.

   Out of Sight, a sly, sexy, vastly entertaining film version of Elmore Leonard's playful crime novel, is director Steven Soderbergh's most ambitious and accomplished work. Brimming with offbeat characters, this reflexively witty crime caper boasts the sort of bright, snappy dialog that's rarely heard in a mainstream picture. Pic should do reasonably well at the B.O., though its complex structure, subtle humor and deliberate pacing – all contributing factors to the overall artistic impact – will prevent it from matching the success of Get Shorty.

U.S. release: June 26     U.S. B.O.: $37.5 million
Int'l release: Sept. 17     Int'l B.O.: $35.5 million

## The Outskirts (Okraina) (Russia)

A Morning of the XXI Century Studio/Goskino of Russia presentation. Produced, directed by Petr Lutsik. Screenplay, Lutsik, Alexei Samorjadov. Camera, Nikolai Ivasiv; editor, Svetlana Guralskaya; music, Georgy Sviridov, Gavriil Popov; production design, Andrei Bessolitsyn; creative consultant, Aleksei Rybakov. Reviewed at Mill Valley Festival, Oct. 4. Running time: 95 mins.

**Yuri Dubrovin (Philip Safronov), Nikolai Olyalin (Kolka Poluyanov), Alexei Pushkin (Panka Morozov), Alexei Vanin (Vasily Perfiliev), Rimma Markova (Panka's Mother), Victor Stepanov (The Master).**

Award-winning scenarist Petr Lutsik takes aim at reckless capitalism – as well as the increasing Westernization of Russia – with a disquieting allegory that in both themes and aesthetic is an audacious throwback to pre-WWII Soviet cinema formalism. Unquestionably one of the most striking Russian features in recent years, The Outskirts should get ample fest-circuit mileage, though making offshore arthouse inroads would require considerable distributor chutzpah.

   The residents of a remote village discover that oil rights to their land have been sold when the landscape is overrun with thugs, machinery, and pollutants that kill fish and game. Most

accept it grimly, but a few elderly men form a vigilante party to hunt down the four "smart Alec" authority figures who put their seals on the certificate of sale. The creaky posse sets out across the bleak, wintry terrain, first traveling by foot, then motorbike, train and so on. But their comic exterior soon gives way to violence and death. For all its ambiguities, The Outskirts is a pointed statement about how Russian exploitation hasn't really changed through Czarist, communist, and glasnost eras.

## Paljas

A Videovision Entertainment/Sonneblom Films presentation, in association with M-Net, of a Distant Horizon production. Produced by Anant Singh. Directed by Katinka Heyns. Screenplay, Chris Barnard. Camera, Koos Roets; editor, Avril Beukus; music, Sue Grealy; production design, Birrie Le Roux; costume design, Diana Cilliers. Reviewed at AFM, Santa Monica, Feb. 27. Running time: 119 mins. (In Afrikaans with English subtitles)

**Marius Weyers (Hendrik MacDonald), Aletta Bezuidenhout (Katrina MacDonald), Liezel van der Merwe (Emma MacDonald), Larry Leyden (Willem MacDonald), Jan Ellis (Nollie), Ian Roberts (Frans), Ellis Pearson (Manuel), Gerard Rudolff (Jan Mol).**

A stunning look at small-town intolerance and an unusual solution for a South African Boer family form the bedrock of Paljas. The country's submission for the foreign-language Oscar is a handsomely made, compelling drama with upbeat potential as an arthouse hit in top international territories. Pic is a tad too long, but deft cutting would significantly improve its commercial chances and bring home its points more forcefully.

   Set in rural Toorwater, the tale revolves around Hendrik MacDonald, the railroad depot manager, and his troubled family, including young son Willem who stopped talking because of some undisclosed shock two years earlier. One morning they awake to the sounds of wild animals and discover on their doorstep an abandoned circus train, off-loaded at the wrong station. The rough-and-tumble ways of the gypsy lot chafe with the locals, but during their brief stay the troupe has an incalculable effect on the railroad family. Only later will Hendrik realize that they brought the "paljas" to the household. That difficult-to-translate term means magic, or the ability to make things right.

Int'l release: Jan. 30     Int'l B.O.: $750,000

## Palmetto

A Sony Pictures release from Columbia Pictures of a Castle Rock Entertainment presentation of a Rialto Film production. Produced by Matthias Wendlandt. Directed by Volker Schlondorff. Screenplay by E. Max Frye, based on the novel Just Another Sucker by James Hadley Chase. Camera, Thomas Kloss; editor, Peter Przygodda; music, Klaus Dolinger; production design, Claire Jenora Bowin; costume design, Terry Dresbach. Reviewed at Variety Club, San Francisco, Feb. 10. MPAA Rating: R. Running time: 114 mins.

**Woody Harrelson (Harry Barber), Elisabeth Shue (Rhea Malroux), Gina Gershon (Nina), Rolf Hoppe (Felix Malroux), Michael Rapaport (Donnelly), Chloe Sevigny (Odette).**

Some first-class talent travels coach in the low-flying suspenser Palmetto. Adding no particular novelty or inspiration to the by-now-overtilled steamy neo-noir sweepstakes, Volker Schlondorff's film looks to do middling-fair domestic biz, with best returns likely from the usual ancillary.

Harry Barber gets sprung from prison when it's revealed he was framed. Understandably bitter about his two years of incarceration, he plans to remake his life in Miami, when former g.f. Nina surfaces, dragging him back to the title burg. He chances upon undulating blonde Rhea Malroux, young wife to the area's richest old man. She has a "job" for Harry, with a $50,000 payoff: He'll pretend to be the kidnapper in the fake abduction of Rhea's teenage stepdaughter Odette.

| | |
|---|---|
| U.S. release: Feb. 20 | U.S. B.O.: $6 million |
| Int'l release: April 2 | Int'l B.O.: $500,000 |

### Pants On Fire

An Elevator Pictures presentation. Produced by Stephen Apicella. Directed, written by Rocky Collins. Camera, Rufus Standefer; editor, Sherry Daniel; music, Robert Miller; production designer, Maria Wagner; art director, Glenn Reed; costume designer, Azan Kung. Reviewed at Raleigh Studios, L.A., April 2. (L.A. Independent Festival.) Running time: 107 mins.
**Christy Baron (Julie Hammer), Harry O'Reilly (Max Hammer), Neil Maffin (Barry Grogan), Arija Bareikis (Nicki), Leland Gantt (Allen), Eileen Brennan (Mom), Mark Margolis (Malcolm Preston), Darrell Larson (Ralph Blaylock).**

A tale of suburban infidelity delectably set at the nexus between dark comedy and high melodrama, *Pants on Fire* hits notes rarely heard in American indie fare. Ambitious in its comic depiction of human foibles and the difficulty of thinking straight when libidos get the upper hand, feature debut by former documaker Rocky Collins reveals considerable talent and should play well with savvy fest audiences. Pic could snag some limited theatrical play, but lack of names and difficulty in describing the film would make marketing an uphill struggle.

Storyline is the stuff of innumerable pulp romantic dramas but Collins' boldfaced presentation sets the film apart. Teachers Julie Hammer and Barry Grogan indulge in a classroom quickie, barely eluding the attention of nearby staff and students. At home, however, Julie is the adoring wife of the sharp and aggressive Max, a deputy district attorney running for election as D.A.; the last thing he needs right now is distraction in his personal life.

### Paparazzi (France)

An AMLF release of a Rigolo Films 2000/Le Studio Canal Plus/TF1 Films production. Produced by Olivier Granier, Dominique Farrugia. Directed by Alain Berberian. Screenplay, Daniele Thompson, Berberian, Jean-François Halin, Simon Michel, Vincent Lindon, Patrick Timsit. Camera, Vincenzo Marano; editor, Catherine Renault; music, Franck Roussel; art director, Olivier Radot; costume designer, Cristine Guegan. Reviewed at Cannes Festival, May 23. Running time: 104 mins.
**Patrick Timsit (Franck), Vincent Lindon (Michel), Catherine Frot (Evelyne), Isabelle Gelinas (Sandra), Elise Tielrooy (Benedicte), Nathalie Baye (Nicole).**

With its title having become a dirty word in the wake of the Princess Diana tragedy, Gallic comedy *Paparazzi* lives dangerously by milking humor from the exploits of kamikaze celebrity photographers. But the film's moral distance from its protagonists' profession goes some way toward allaying the problem, and the chemistry and charm of leading duo Patrick Timsit and Vincent Lindon goes further still. However, this looks more likely to spark remake interest than to travel far under its own steam.

Photographed next to a philandering TV star while he should have been working, humble nightwatchman Franck is fired when pic makes the cover of a national gossip magazine. Too ashamed to tell his wife, he goes to the mag's editors to demand compensation. Instead, Franck falls in with ace paparazzo Michel, who makes the unwitting stooge his accomplice in ambushing celebs.

| | |
|---|---|
| Int'l release: April 29 | Int'l B.O.: $5 million |
| U.S. release: Nov. 13 | U.S. B.O.: $40,000 |

### Paradise Falls

A Maceo Prods presentation. Produced by Sean Bridgers, Nick Searcy, Peter Wentworth. Directed by Nick Searcy. Screenplay, Sean Bridgers, Sue Ellen Bridgers. Camera, Mark Petersen; editor, Robert F. Landau; music, the Red Clay Ramblers; production designer, Jamie Arbuckle; costume designer, Susan Brown Strauss. Reviewed at Hollywood Festival, Aug. 8. Running time: 101 mins.
**Sean Bridgers (Henry Bancroft), Christopher Berry (Oshel Hooper), Nick Searcy (Jake Kyler), Sonny Shroyer (Bert Kyler), Claire Eye (Clarice Kyler), Judy Simpson Cook (Mrs. Bancroft), Chloe Searcy (Sissy Bancroft).**

*Bonnie and Clyde* on a budget, *Paradise Falls* reps an impressive, if rough-hewn, feature debut. Set in the rural American South during the Depression, this co-winner of the best picture award at the Hollywood Film Festival is a textured tale of lives riven by economic hardship and desperation that leads to lawlessness. While the filmmakers make much of their locations and story, the film cannot overcome its modest resources and absence of marquee names, which will put a definite crimp on its commercial potential. Its qualities indicate niche theatrical bookings, but pic's primary revenue will come from small-screen sales.

The basic scenario charts familiar terrain. Henry Bancroft and Oshel Hooper are farmers' sons with more dreams than prospects. Oshel's disillusionment stems from more than just failed crops: His father died during World War I, and he views society as chaotic, spinning wild yarns of robbing the rich (or their minions) and giving back to "the people" to right the balance. It's only when Henry realizes that his father's farm is about to be taken over by the bank that he starts to take his buddy's cant seriously.

### The Parent Trap

A Buena Vista release of a Walt Disney Pictures production. Produced by Charles Shyer. Directed by Nancy Meyers. Screenplay, David Swift, Meyers, Charles Shyer, based on the book *Das Doppelte Lottchen* by Erich Kastner. Camera, Dean A. Cundey; editor, Stephen A. Rotter; music, Alan Silvestri; production design, Dean Tavoularis; costume design, Penny Rose; special-effects coordinator, Cliff Wenger; casting, Ilene Starger. Reviewed at Cinemark Tinseltown USA, Houston, July 22. MPAA Rating: PG. Running time: 127 mins.
**Lindsay Lohan (Hallie Parker/Annie James), Dennis Quaid (Nick Parker), Natasha Richardson (Elizabeth James), Elaine Hendrix (Meredith Blake), Lisa Ann Walter (Chessy), Simon Kunz (Martin), Ronnie Stevens (Grandfather).**

The recycled hits just keep on coming with Disney launching a remake of its golden oldie *The Parent Trap* – updating the 1961 comedy about reunited twin sisters who want to reconnect their divorced parents. New pic is slick, sentimental, and exceptionally well cast, with enough cross-generational appeal

---

**... July 11 ...**
Bill Cosby to team with kids cable web Nickelodeon to produce an animated pre-school series called **Little Bill**, based on a book series written by Cosby.

to suggest strong commercial potential. On the downside, however, audiences may have trouble accepting a few of the plot elements carried over from the original.

Story begins at a Maine summer camp, where 11-year-old Hallie Parker and Annie James develop an immediate and intense dislike for each other. That they look exactly alike only serves to intensify their animosity. It takes a very long time for the girls to realize they are twin sisters. Years earlier, their parents, Nick and Elizabeth, met and impulsively wed. When the marriage soured, Nick claimed Hallie and brought her to live with him on his Napa Valley vineyard. Elizabeth claimed Annie and raised her in London while earning fame and fortune as a wedding-gown designer. As a result of this divorce settlement, neither twin has ever seen – or even known – her other birth parent. So, Hallie and Annie decide to switch identities. Despite a few awkward moments, the ruse works for a while. But when Nick announces his plans to remarry, Hallie and Annie spill the beans.

| | |
|---|---|
| U.S. release: July 29 | U.S. B.O.: $66 million |
| Int'l release: Sept. 25 | Int'l B.O.: $15 million |

## Pariah

A Poor Boy Prods presentation. Produced by Shaun Hill, Vince Rotonda. Directed, written by Randolph Kret. Camera, Nils Erickson, editor, Bill DeRonde; music, Scott Grusin; production design, Joint Effort; costumes, Carrie Niccol, Julie Colella. Reviewed on videotape, L.A., Jan. 14. Running time: 105 mins.
**Damon Jones (Steve), Dave Oren Ward (Crew), David Lee Wilson (David Lee), Aimee Chaffin (Sissy), Angela Jones (Angela), Anna Padgett (Lex), Dan Weene (Joey), Ann Zupa (Babe).**

Hate crimes and the activities of a skinhead gang center the searing drama *Pariah*. More than simply a chronicle of violence, the film attempts to come to grips with the subculture through the device of planting a mole in its midst. The pic's strength and its weakness come from its rawness, and while the subject matter limits it to specialized play, within that niche *Pariah* has upbeat commercial prospects and should see solid follow-up in ancillaries.

What sets the piece in motion is a random (graphically presented) assault on an interracial couple that ends in the gang rape of Sam. The woman subsequently commits suicide, unable to come to terms with the senseless act. Her boyfriend, Steve, vows revenge. But frustrated by legal channels, he decides to destroy the group by posing as a kindred spirit.

## Parting Shots (U.K.)

A Scimitar Films production. Produced, directed by Michael Winner. Screenplay, Winner, Nick Mead. Camera, Ousama Rawi; editor, Arnold Crust; music, Les Reed, Chris Rea; production design, Crispian Sallis. Reviewed at Cannes Festival, May 18. Running time: 98 mins.
**Chris Rea (Harry Sterndale), Felicity Kendal (Jill Saunders), John Cleese (Maurice Walpole), Bob Hoskins (Gerd Layton), Ben Kingsley (Renzo Locatelli), Diana Rigg (Lisa), Oliver Reed (Jamie), Joanna Lumley (Fred).**

A stellar cast distinguishes, but fails to rescue, this comic variation on *Death Wish* from vet Brit producer-director Michael Winner. The oft-told tale of a man who believes he only has a short time to live and sets about fulfilling his wildest dreams is given a modest twist by having the protagonist turn

into a revenge killer. Pic chugs along with few surprises. It should post reasonable opening figures in England because of the cast, but word of mouth, and international reception, will be unenthusiastic.

Rea plays Harry, a wedding photographer with a long list of life grievances: He was bullied at school, his best friend stole his ideas, his wife betrayed him, and he lost all his money in a shady investment. When his doctor tells him he has only six weeks left to live, he decides to get back at everyone.

## Passion (Szenvedely) (Hungary)

A Budapest Filmstudio-Magyar TV production. Produced by Eva Schulze, Jolan Arvai, Ferenc Kardos, Gyorgy Feher. Directed by Feher. Screenplay, Feher, Bela Tarr, Istvan Kardos, based on *The Postman Always Rings Twice*, by James M. Cain. Camera, Miklos Gurban; editor, Maria Czeilik; production design, Tamas Vayer; costume design, Gyula Pauer. Reviewed at Hungarian Film Week, Budapest, Feb. 7. Running time: 149 mins.
**Ildiko Bansagi (Wife), Janos Derzsi (Lover), Dzsoko Rozsics (Husband).**

The fourth screen version of James M. Cain's grim novel of crime and passion, *Passion* is a visually powerful and dramatically potent depiction of the timeless story of lovers who plot to kill the woman's older husband. Magyar helmer Gyorgy Feher homes in on only parts of Cain's story, and dialog is used sparingly in favor of dank, dark, grainy black-and-white images. *Passion*, which is not without serious flaws, will be an almost impossibly hard commercial sell anywhere in the world, though it might make its mark at fests in the coming months. In this version, story begins with the stranger already employed by the old man, who suspects his wife is having an affair with his employee. Only later is their sexual hunger sated with a steamy coupling – a rape that turns into mutual satisfaction.

## Patch Adams

A Universal Pictures release of a Blue Wolf, Farrell/Minoff, Bungalow 78 production. Produced by Barry Kemp, Mike Farrell, Marvin Minoff, Charles Newirth. Directed by Tom Shadyac. Screenplay, Steve Oedekerk, based on the book *Gesundheit: Good Health is a Laughing Matter* by Hunter Doherty Adams. Camera, Phedon Papamichael; editor, Don Zimmerman; music, Marc Shaiman; production design, Linda Descenna; costume design, Judy Ruskin-Howell. Reviewed at Meyerland Plaza, Houston, Dec. 12. MPAA Rating: PG-13. Running Time: 115 mins.
**Robin Williams (Hunter "Patch" Adams), Daniel London (Truman), Monica Potter (Carin), Philip Seymour Hoffman (Mitch), Bob Gunton (Dean Walcott), Josef Sommer (Dr. Eaton), Irma P. Hall (Joletta), Harve Presnell (Dean Anderson), Jake Bowen (Bryan), Peter Coyote (Bill Davis), Michael Jeter (Rudy), Harold Gould (Arthur Mendelson), Richard Kiley (Dr. Titan).**

Shamelessly sappy and emotionally manipulative, *Patch Adams* is an aggressively heartwarming comedy-drama that will be roasted by critics but embraced by ticketbuyers. Robin Williams pulls out all the stops in a role that allows him to careen between extremes of silliness and sentimentality. He overworks the schtick in this slickly packaged Hollywood hokum. Still, prospects are good for a healthy, if not record-breaking, theatrical run and extended shelf life on video and cable.

Pic begins in 1969 with title character checking himself into a mental hospital after a failed suicide attempt. He discovers his gift for healing himself while lifting other patient's spirits. Two years later, he's a first-year med student, burning to "treat the patient as well as the disease." That attitude puts him in conflict with the dean, but top grades, boundless energy and optimism, and a peerless rating with staff and terminal-ward patients save him repeatedly from expulsion. His drive leads him to start an off-campus free clinic which will ultimately challenge all that he innately believes.

U.S. release: Dec. 25          U.S. B.O.: $46 million

## Paulie

A DreamWorks Pictures release of a Mutual Film Co. production. Produced by Mark Gordon, Gary Levinsohn, Allison Lyon Segan. Directed by John Roberts. Screenplay, Laurie Craig. Camera, Tony Pierce-Roberts; editor, Bruce Cannon; music, John Debney; production designer, Dennis Washington; costume designer, Mary Zophres; animal-stunt coordinator, Boone Narr; animatronic characters, Stan Winston. Reviewed at Century Plaza, L.A., April 11. MPAA Rating: PG. Running time: 91 mins.

Gena Rowlands (Ivy), Tony Shalhoub (Misha), Cheech Marin (Ignacio), Bruce Davison (Dr. Reingold), Jay Mohr (Paulie [voice]/Benny), Trini Alvarado (Marie), Buddy Hackett (Artie), Matt Craven (Warren Alweather).

A talking parrot's *Pilgrim's Progress*, Paulie has moments of minor charm but lacks the magic fully to capture the imaginations of either children or adults. Too sophisticated and dialog-heavy for very young kids, this DreamWorks release should post healthy returns for the first weekend or two, but looks unlikely to become a must-see family event. Misha, a janitor at an animal-research lab, takes pity on a Blue-crown Conure parrot caged in a dingy basement and is amazed to discover that the bird can not only "talk" in the manner expected of parrots, but can converse. Paulie spins the tale of his varied odyssey, one that begins in flashback and progresses forward.

U.S. release: April 17          U.S. release: $27 million
Int'l release: July 4          Int'l B.O.: $5.5 million

## The Pear Tree (Derakht-E Golabi) (Iran)

Produced by Dariush Mehrjui, Faramarz Farazmand, Farabi Cinema Foundation. Directed by Dariush Mehrjui. Screenplay, Mehrjui, Goli Taraqi, based on a story by Taraqi. Camera, Mahmoud Kalari; editor, Mostafa Kherqepoosh; art direction, Faryar Javaherian, Bita Qezal Eyaq. Reviewed at Fajr Festival, Tehran, Feb. 11. Running time: 96 mins.

Homayoun Ershadi (Mahmoud), Golshifte Farahani (M), Mohammad Reza (Young Mahmoud). With: Nematollah Gorji, Jafar Bozorgi, Maryam Majd, Maryam Moqbeli.

If Abbas Kiarostami's 1997 Palme d'Or-winning *Taste of Cherry* sometimes suggested the dark, despairing side of Ingmar Bergman, Dariush Mehrjui's *The Pear Tree* recalls the Swedish master's brighter, bittersweet side. A lush, golden evocation of first love and temps perdu, pic, a memory drama par excellence, is one of the most captivating of recent Iranian accomplishments, and should find numerous admirers at fests and arthouse sites globally.

*The Pear Tree* has a personal, reflective air that enhances its narrative assets. After a contemporary intro in which Mahmoud, a celebrated middle-aged writer, paces around his country villa snared by writer's block, pic flashes back to a

memory that eventually sets his creative juices flowing. At age 11, Mahmoud is awkward, lacking in confidence, and completely in thrall to a self-possessed female cousin three years his senior.

## Pecker

A Fine Line release of a Polar Entertainment presentation. Produced by John Fiedler, Mark Tarlov. Directed, written by John Waters. Camera, Robert Stevens; editor, Janice Hampton; music, Stewart Copeland; production design, Vincent Peranio; costume design, Van Smith. Reviewed at New Line, L.A. July 10. MPAA Rating: R. Running time: 87 mins.

Edward Furlong (Pecker), Christina Ricci (Shelley), Mary Kay Place (Joyce), Martha Plimpton (Tina), Brendan Sexton III (Matt), Bess Armstrong (Dr. Klompus), Patricia Hearst (Lynn Wentworth), Mark Joy (Jimmy), Lili Taylor (Rorey Wheeler).

Shockmeister John Waters has, surprisingly, made a sentimental movie with *Pecker*. Sweet story centers on a working-class teenager who becomes a superstar photographer despite himself. This amiably light satire doesn't have much new to say about the culture of celebrity, nor is it biting enough in the manner of the helmer's previous efforts. Expect modest returns for a pleasant but ephemeral spoof that may disappoint Waters' hard-core fans.

Furlong plays the title role, so named for his childhood habit of "pecking" at his food. A congenial, slightly goofy adolescent, Pecker works in a Baltimore sandwich shop, where he cultivates his hobby, snapping photographs of his customers. Pecker's family is "culturally challenged": His mom dispenses fashion tips to the homeless at her thrift shop; his older, gay-friendly sister, Tina, hires go-go boys to dance at the local club; and his younger sister, Little Chrissy, is addicted to sugar. Pecker stumbles into fame when his work is "discovered" by Rorey Wheeler, a savvy New York art dealer. Never mind that his photographs are amateurish, grainy, and slightly out of focus; they somehow strike a chord with the New York's artsy crowd, and soon there is a big public show and instant fame.

U.S. release: Sept. 25          U.S. B.O.: $2.2 million
Int'l release: Dec. 12          Int'l B.O.: $150,000

## Pep Squad

A Troma Entertainment release of a Steve Balderson production. Produced, directed, written, edited by Steve Balderson. Camera, Rhet W. Bear; music, Johnette Napolitano; production designers, Angela Meyer, Beth Duvall; costume designer, Steve Balderson. Reviewed at Cannes Festival, May 14. Running time: 92 mins.

Jennifer Dreiling (Beth), Brooke Balderson (Cherry), Amy Kelly (Terra), Adrian Pejol (Scott), Summer Makovkin (Julie), Eric Sherman (Lester the Molester), Betty O (Miss Nelson).

Dorothy and Toto might not be so enthusiastic about returning to today's Kansas, as depicted with malice aforethought by native son Steve Balderson in the dark comedy *Pep Squad*. First-time filmmaker has obviously boned up on Warhol and Waters and takes a few hints from De Palma's *Carrie*. Result is choppy and derivative in places, accomplished and funny in others. More gung-ho than ho-ho, pic – whose natural habitat is drive-ins, midnight shows, cable, and video – suggests that the 23-year-old helmer will "graduate" and bring home better grades next time. There are eight candidates for senior-class prom queen at Oak Hill High… but not for long.

---

**. . . July 13 . . .**
Godzilla sets opening-day records in Japan.

## A Perfect Murder

A Warner Bros. release of a Kopelson Entertainment production. Produced by Arnold Kopelson, Anne Kopelson, Christopher Mankiewicz, Peter Macgregor-Scott. Directed by Andrew Davis. Screenplay, Patrick Smith Kelly, based on the play *Dial M for Murder* by Frederick Knott. Camera, Dariusz Wolski; editors, Dennis Virkler, Dov Hoenig; music, James Newton Howard; production designer, Philip Rosenberg; costume designer, Ellen Mirojnick. Reviewed at Directors Guild, L.A., May 27. MPAA Rating: R. Running Time: 105 mins.

**Michael Douglas (Steven Taylor), Gwyneth Paltrow (Emily Bradford), Viggo Mortensen (David Shaw), David Suchet (Det. Mohamed Karaman), Sarita Choudhury (Raquel Martinez), Constance Towers (Sandra Bradford).**

*A Perfect Murder*, based on the play and subsequent Hitchcock film *Dial M for Murder*, freely adapts a lesser work by the master and only serves to prove that even that minor bygone film is superior to high gloss, misconceived modernization. The notion of a crime of passion executed with icy precision has been superseded by issues of commerce and rendered a cold and cynical piece. The upshot is a few thrills, too many twists, and box office that may see some initial fire, followed by rapid erosion.

Emily is married to commodities trader Stephen Taylor but romantically entangled with bohemian painter David Shaw. Stephen knows about the affair. On the pretense of buying some artwork, he visits David at his loft and confronts him with a dossier that includes a string of aliases, jail time and a series of past scams involving wealthy, lonely women. Stephen's willing to forgive and forget if David will do him one favor – he'd like him to murder Emily. He'll also throw in $500,000 for David's trouble.

U.S. release: June 5  
Int'l release: July 9  
U.S. B.O.: $68 million  
Int'l B.O.: $61 million

## Permanent Midnight

An Artisan Entertainment Release of a JD Prods production. Produced by Jane Hamsher, Don Murphy. Directed, written by David Veloz, based on the book by Jerry Stahl. Camera, Robert Yeoman; editors, Steven Weisberg, Cara Silverman; music, Daniel Licht; production design, Jerry Fleming; costume design, Louise Mingenbach, Lori Eskowitz. Reviewed at Toronto Festival, Sept. 11. Running time: 85 mins.

**Ben Stiller (Jerry Stahl), Elizabeth Hurley (Sandra), Maria Bello (Kitty), Owen Wilson (Nicky), Lourdes Benedicto (Vola), Peter Greene (Gus), Janeane Garofalo (Jana), Jerry Stahl (Dr. Murphy).**

Stahl, just out of detox, is raring to share his story and unloads on fellow urban casualty Kitty.

Ben Stiller is an angst-ridden junkie in *Permanent Midnight*, based on TV scribe Jerry Stahl's tell-all about taking Hollywood meetings on a $6,000-a-week heroin habit. But Stiller's attempted image makeover, though admirable, doesn't make it. His performance is strictly from the clenched-teeth school. B.O. prospects look as gloomy as subject matter.

U.S. release: Sept. 16  
U.S. B.O.: $1.2 million

## Phantoms

A Miramax release of a Dimension Films presentation of a Neo Motion Pictures production, in association with Raven House. Produced by Joel Soisson, Michael Leahy, Robert Pringle, Steve Lane. Directed by Joe Chappelle. Screenplay, Dean Koontz, based on his novel. Camera, Richard Clabaugh; editor, Randolph K. Bricker; music, David Williams; production design, Deborah Raymond, Dorian Vernacchio; costume design, Dana K. Litwak. Reviewed at Worldwide Cinema, New York, Jan. 21. MPAA Rating: R. Running time: 95 mins.

**Peter O'Toole (Timothy Flyte), Rose McGowan (Lisa Pailey), Joanna Going (Jenny Pailey), Liev Schreiber (Deputy Stu Wargle), Ben Affleck (Sheriff Bryce Hammond), Nicky Katt (Deputy Steve Shanning), Clifton Powell (Gen. Copperfield).**

*Phantoms* is a crackling good frightfest that is a departure from current trend toward knowing, jokey, teen-oriented slasher fare. Rather, it serves up a full helping of spooky dread and supernatural terror, spiced with impressive special effects. Scripted by Dean Koontz from his novel, and helmed with considerable savvy and polish by Joe Chappelle, pic has the goods to scare up plenty of business at the B.O. and in all ancillaries.

Sisters Lisa and Jenny Pailey arrive in picturesque Snowfield, Colo. for a ski vacation, to find their landlady dead on the kitchen floor and burg's streets empty. A few boos later, the sisters run into Sheriff Bryce Hammond and deputies Stu Wargle and Steve Shanning. The five are drawn into an old hotel where they find the scrawled words "Timothy Flyte" and "the Ancient Enemy." Calling the Army for reinforcements, Timothy Flyte is discovered to be an erstwhile British prof reduced to writing for tabloids because his theory of an evil underground empire was laughed off by colleagues.

U.S. release: Jan. 23  
Int'l release: June 4  
U.S. B.O.: $5.5 million  
Int'l B.O.: $2.5 million

## The Pharmacist (Die Apothekerin) (Germany)

A Senator Film release of a Senator Film Produktion production. Produced by Guenter Rohrbach, Hanno Huth. Directed by Rainer Kaufmann. Screenplay, Ralf Hertwig, Kathrin Richter, based on the novel by Ingrid Noll. Camera, Klaus Eichhammer; editor, Ueli Christen; music, Ludwig Eckmann, Maximilian Geller; art direction, Knut Loewe; costume design, Katharina von Martius. Reviewed at Berlin Festival, Feb. 13. Running time: 103 mins.

**Katja Riemann (Hella Moormann), Juergen Vogel (Levin Graber), Richy Mueller (Dieter Krosmansky), Isabella Parkinson (Margot Krosmansky), Dagmar Manzel (Dorit Meissen), Joachim Tomaschewsky (Hermann Graber).**

Slickly mounted and highly cinematic, *The Pharmacist* is a black comedy-thriller played with gusto by its star cast and helmed with De Palma-like glee by Rainer Kaufmann. As the titular test-tuber whose skills prove useful on a variety of victims, German star Katja Riemann has her best leading role in a solidly commercial movie that deserves a dose of offshore theatrical play.

Hella, an attractive but tightly wound small-town pharmacist, meets the spoiled, childlike Levin, who shares her taste for fast cars, and sooner than you can say "apothecary" the pair are having a wild time – with a little help from Hella's medicine box. Levin has an unresolved problem: He owes a heap of money to drug-dealer Dieter. He suggests to Hella that they poison his monied grandfather, inherit his manse, and pay off Dieter. Hella is horrified, and when the grandfather suddenly drops dead, she suspects Levin murdered him anyway.

Int'l release: Oct. 2, 1997  
Int'l B.O.: $9.5 million

---

**...July 14...**  
NBC and Turner Broadcasting buy package of WB films, including **Lethal Weapon 4.**

## Phoenix

A Lakeshore Entertainment presentation of a Paradox Films production. Produced by Victoria Nevinny, Tracie Graham. Directed by Danny Cannon. Screenplay, Eddie Richey. Camera, James L. Carter; editor, Zach Staenberg; music, Graeme Revell; production designer, Charles Breen; costume designer, Alexandra Walker. Reviewed at Cannes Festival, May, 14. Running time: 104 mins.

Ray Liotta (Harry Collins), Anthony LaPaglia (Mike Henshaw), Anjelica Huston (Leila), Daniel Baldwin (James Nutter), Jeremy Piven (Fred Shuster), Tom Noonan (Chicago), Xander Berkely (Clyde Webber), Giancarlo Esposito (Louie), Kari Wuhrer (Katie Shuster).

It's just a matter of degree that separates the good cops from the bad ones in *Phoenix*. And though the film attempts to give its genre material a hip, complex spin, the efforts are largely tiresome and uninspired. Technically, pic has a bigscreen sheen, but, because it covers all-too-familiar territory, it would be better served as a pay-cable premiere with some modest video afterlife.

Plot centers on four Phoenix detectives, particularly gambling addict Harry Collins and the pliantly corruptible Mike Henshaw. Harry's in way over his head to loan sharks and eventually is driven to hit a crime czar's club with his fellow officers to get the cash to pay his debt. But lurking in the background is a sanctimonious internal affairs officer ready to pounce on his prey.

U.S. release: Sept. 4      U.S. B.O.: $60,000

## Pi

A Live Entertainment release of a Truth & Soul/Harvest Filmworks/Plantain Films presentation of a Protozoa Films production. Produced by Eric Watson. Executive producer, Randy Simon. Directed, written by Darren Aronofsky. Camera (B&W, 16mm), Matthew Libatique; editor, Oren Sach; original score, Clint Mansell; production design, Matthew Marraffi. Reviewed at Sundance Festival, Jan. 19. Running time: 85 mins.

Sean Gullette (Max Cohen), Mark Margolis (Sol Robeson), Ben Shenkman (Lenny Meyer), Pamela Hart (Marcy Dawson), Stephen Pearlman (Rabbi Cohen), Samia Shoaib (Devi).

*Pi* reps a striking debut feature for writer-director Darren Aronofsky. Though pic is somewhat limited in terms of narrative and emotional drive – not to mention commercial prospects – by dint of its very originality as a vaguely sci-fi, Kafkaesque B&W religio-mathematical thriller, there's no question it will turn heads in anticipation of this helmer's next move. Wide fest pickup and possible cult status are likelier than theatrical play.

Sean Gullette plays Max, a genius mathematician who spends nearly all his time cloistered amid the gizmo-clutter of his squalid NYC flat. Obsessed with the idea that "everything can be understood in terms of numbers," he's bent on finding the pattern hidden beneath man's ultimate disorderly system: the stock market. This quest – and periodic, piercing headache "attacks" – keeps him in hermit-like withdrawal from various well-meaning neighbors, and anyone else.

U.S. release: July 10      U.S. B.O.: $3.2 million

## Pick A Card (Afula Express) (Israel)

A Norma Prods presentation. Produced by Assaf Amir. Directed by Julie Shles. Screenplay, Amit Leor. Camera, Itzik Portal; editor, Maor Keshet; music, Yuval Shafrir; art direction, Eva Gronowitz. Reviewed at the American Film Institute, L.A., Jan. 29. Running time: 96 mins.

Zvika Hadar (David), Esti Zackheim (Batya), Aryeh Moskuna (Shimon), Orly Perl (Vickie).

Devoid of overt politics or explicit ideology, *Pick a Card* is a new kind of Israeli film: A fresh dramatic comedy about ordinary people who simply refuse to be defeated by their harsh reality. Helmer Julie Shles also endows her tale with the kind of enchanting magic one associates with the work of Fellini. Winner of six Israeli Academy Awards including best picture, *Pick a Card* is a likely candidate for a limited theatrical distribution in U.S. cities. Style and content beautifully cohere in this vastly enjoyable film. Shles weaves a tale, both absurd and exhilarating, of four ordinary people who reside in a poor Tel Aviv quarter.

## A Place Called Chiapas (Canada , Docu)

A Canada Wild Prods, in association with the Canadian Broadcasting Corp. Produced by Nettie Wild, Betsy Carson, Kirk Tougas. Directed by Wild. Screenplay, Wild, Manfred Becker. Camera, Kirk Tougas, Wild; editor, Becker; music, Joseph Pepe Danza, Salvador Ferreras, Celso Machado, Laurence Mollerup. Reviewed at Berlin Festival, Feb. 20, 1998. Running time: 89 mins.

*A Place Called Chiapas* is an exemplary documentary that vividly and lucidly explores a modern Mexican standoff. It deserves niche theatrical release, and is a must for tube programming and further fest exposure.

Filmmaker Nettie Wild notes that in Canada, the North American Free Trade Agreement was a matter for debate; in the state of Chiapas, one of the poorest in Mexico, it provoked a revolution. On the day NAFTA began, the Zapatista National Liberation Army (EZLN), under the leadership of the mystery man Marcos, took over five towns and more than 500 ranches in Chiapas, ousting landlords, stranding tourists, and causing the Mexican government to send in 30,000 troops. A cease-fire ensued and an uneasy standoff resulted.

U.S. release: Nov. 4      U.S. B.O.: $50,000

## A Place in the Heart (A La Place Du Coeur) (France)

An Agat Films production, in association with La Sept Cinema, France 2 Cinema, Le Studio Canal Plus, Diaphana. Producer, Gilles Sandoz. Directed by Robert Guediguian. Screenplay, Jean-Louis Milesi, Guediguian. Camera, Bernard Cavalie; editor, Bernard Sasia; art director, Michel Vandestien. Reviewed at Toronto Festival, Sept. 16. Running time: 112 mins.

Ariane Ascaride (Marianne), Christine Bruecher (Francine), Jean-Pierre Darroussin (Joel), Gerard Meylan (Franck), Alexandre O. Gou (Bebe), Laure Raoust (Clim), Veronique Balme (Sophie).

Though it's a rung down from the marvelously observed *Marius and Jeannette*, Robert Guediguian's latest foray into the lives and emotions of Marseilles' working class is still a warmly textured slice of humanist cinema that manages to spring some surprises within its resolutely non-dramatic structure. A look at an average blue-collar family through the prism of a daughter's love affair with a black man, it's probably too slight to make much impact on the arthouse circuit, but it shows the 45-year-old helmer still reaching into new territory stylistically. Quality tube sales look assured.

Clim patiently explains that her nickname is derived from

---

Clementine before introducing her lover, Bebe – at 18 two years older than her. He's in prison on a phony charge of rape and Clim visits him to reveal that she's pregnant. Bebe is the adopted son of a white couple – hard-drinking docker Franck and Bible-bashing Francine – who also adopted Bebe's sister. Clim's family is more caring and better adjusted.

Int'l release: Dec. 9                         Int'l B.O.: $900,000

## Place Vendôme (France)

An AMLF release of a Les Film Alain Sarde/TF1 Films Production/Les Films de l'Etang/Alhena Films/Angel's Company production, with the participation of Canal Plus, CNC, Studio Images 3: Produced by Alain Sarde. Directed by Nicole Garcia. Screenplay, Garcia, Jacques Fieschi. Camera, Laurent Dailland; editors, Luc Barnier, Françoise Bonnot; music, Richard Robbins; art director, Thierry Flamand; costume design, Nathalie du Roscoat, Elisabeth Tavernier. Reviewed at Planet Hollywood, Paris, Sept. 1. Running time: 117 mins.
**Catherine Deneuve (Marianne), Jean-Pierre Bacri (Jean-Pierre), Emmanuelle Seigner (Nathalie), Jacques Dutronc (Battistelli), Bernard Fresson (Vincent Malivert), François Berleand (Eric Malivert), Philippe Clevenot (Kleiser).**

An elaborate and elegant suspenser that gives Catherine Deneuve plenty of leeway, *Place Vendôme* features coveted gemstones and the no-nonsense factions that want them. Taut and nuanced with memorable, central characters and an appealingly melancholy tone, helmer/co-scripter Nicole Garcia's feature has what it takes to satisfy arthouse patrons worldwide.

A posh square in the heart of Paris, Place Vendôme houses a select group of venerable jewelers, among them Vincent Malivert. His operation has seen better times. Eric, the firm's artistic director, complains they're short on raw materials to craft luxury accessories. A trip to London to meet with reps of the De Beers empire makes it clear that Vincent is suspected of dubious practices. It's implied he may have fenced stolen diamonds. When Vincent meets with an untimely death, his wife, Marianne, a dissolute alcoholic who spends most of her time drying out in an upscale clinic, sobers up. A former gem dealer who hasn't lost her appraiser's eye, she can't bring herself to sign the papers that will save the firm from bankruptcy. Instead, Marianne sets out on a multilayered adventure that is part detective work, part instinct, and part a date with destiny.

Int'l release: Oct. 7                         Int'l B.O.: $6 million
U.S. release: Dec. 18                        U.S. B.O.: $60,000

## The Players Club

A New Line Cinema release of an Ice Cube/Pat Charbonnet production. Produced by Patricia Charbonnet. Written, directed by Ice Cube. Camera, Malik Sayeed; music, Hidden Faces; music supervisor, Frank Fitzpatrick; production designer, Dina Lipton; costume designer, Dahlia Foroutan. Reviewed at GCC Meyerland Cinema, Houston, April 2. MPAA rating: R. Running time: 104 mins.
**LisaRaye (Diana Armstrong/Diamond), Bernie Mac (Dollar Bill), Monica Calhoun (Ebony), A.J. Johnson (Li'l Man), Ice Cube (Reggie), Alex Thomas (Clyde), Jamie Foxx (Blue), Dick Anthony Williams (Mr. Armstrong), Tiny Lister (XL), John Amos (Freeman).**

Ice Cube continues his evolution from hard-core rapper to multihyphenate filmmaker with *The Players Club*, a messy but lively B movie that recalls the more spirited comedy-dramas of the 1970s blaxploitation era. While pic has limited crossover appeal, it looms as a midrange performer in urban markets, with respectable ancillary action down the line.

Focus is Diana, an African-American single mother who dreams of becoming a broadcast journalist. To pay for her college tuition, she lands a job as a stripper at the Players Club, a rowdy joint operated by a grandiloquent hustler named Dollar Bill. The movie emphasizes that, even though she doffs her clothes and performs the occasional table dance, Diana is most assuredly not a prostitute.

U.S. release: April 8                        U.S. B.O.: $23 million
Int'l release: June 18                       Int'l B.O.: $130,000

## Pleasantville

A New Line Cinema release of a Larger Than Life production. Produced by Jon Kilik, Robert J. Degus, Steven Soderbergh, Gary Ross. Directed, written by Ross. Camera, John Lindley; editor, William Goldenberg; music, Randy Newman; production design, Jeannine Oppewall; costume design, Judianna Makovsky; visual-effects supervisor, Chris Watts; color-effects designer, Michael Southard. Reviewed at Toronto Festival, Sept. 16. MPAA Rating: PG-13. Running time: 123 mins.
**Tobey Maguire (David/Bud), Jeff Daniels (Mr. Johnson), Joan Allen (Betty), William H. Macy (George), J.T. Walsh (Big Bob), Reese Witherspoon (Jennifer/Mary Sue), Don Knotts (TV Repairman), Paul Walker (Skip), Marley Shelton (Margaret), Jane Kaczmarek (Mother).**

Ingeniously conceived and impressively executed, *Pleasantville* is a provocative, complex, and surprisingly anti-nostalgic parable wrapped in the beguiling guise of a commercial high-concept comedy. Screenwriter Gary Ross is nothing if not ambitious in his feature-directing debut. And while he occasionally blunts the satirical edge of his material by obfuscating his intentions, pic shapes up as a significant autumn B.O. contender with even rosier ancillary prospects.

For the awkward, introverted David, *Pleasantville*, a 1950s-era sitcom, represents an addictively comforting black-and-white view of smal-town nuclear family life. He, and sister Jennifer, are magically transported into *Pleasantville* thanks to the high-tech remote-control unit provided by a vaguely sinister TV repairman. They assume the identities of Bud and Mary Sue, the model teen children of paradigmatic parents: George, a chipper businessman, and Betty, an impeccably coifed housewife. They struggle to fit into a world where the people, the weather, and the overall mood are, well, pleasant.

Since David is well-versed in *Pleasantville* trivia, he finds it relatively easy. But Jennifer is far more discontented – at least until she meets Skip, a hunky high-school senior who's eager to go steady with Mary Sue. When they drive to the local lovers' lane for some innocent hand-holding, Jennifer takes control. And with that, a bold new life force is introduced to Pleasantville. At first, only flowers reveal their natural colors. But then the virus starts to spread, and soon some of the other sexually awakened teens blossom with vibrant flesh tones. While introducing the joys of real-world passions, David and Jennifer inadvertently unleash much darker forces: intolerance, paranoia, even mob violence.

U.S. release: Oct. 23                        U.S. B.O.: $39 million
Int'l release: Nov. 29                       Int'l B.O.: $100,000

## Pleasure (and its Little Inconveniences) (Le Plaisir) (France-Italy-Luxembourg-Belgium)

A Polygram Film Distribution release of a Noe Prods, M6 Films (France)/3emme (Italy)/Samsa Film (Luxembourg)/Artemis Prods (Belgium) production. Produced by Frederique Dumas, Marc Baschet. Directed by Nicolas Boukhrief. Screenplay, Boukhrief, Dan Sasson. Camera, Jean-Max Bernard; editor, Jacqueline Mariani; music, Nicolas Baby; art director, Jean-Vincent Puzos. Reviewed at UGC Odeon, Paris, Aug. 8. Running time: 99 mins.

**Vincent Cassel (Michael), Francis Renaud (Raphael), Julie Gayet (Vera), Mathieu Kassovitz (Roland), Caroline Cellier (Hélène), Michele Placido (Carlo), Foued Nassah (Marcel), Florence Thomassin (Lise).**

What goes around comes around in *Pleasure (and its Little Inconveniences)*, a narrative roundelay in seven segments during which eight characters seek to appease their loneliness and live – or die – with the consequences. Intellectually ambitious but uneven in execution, helmer and co-scripter Nicolas Boukhrief's sophomore outing aims to evoke strong emotions. Strong lineup of thesps, however, may translate into some offshore sales.

Lady-killer Michael strangles a woman before the opening credits. Pic then takes a fresh starting point, after which one character from each episode pulls the narrative forward, linked via sex to a new character à la Schnitzler's *La Ronde*.

Int'l release: Aug. 5                    Int'l B.O.: $300,000

## Plump Fiction

A Legacy release of a Rhino Films presentation. Produced by Gary Binkow. Directed, written by Bob Koherr. Camera, Rex Nicholson; editor, Neil Kirk; production designer, Jacques Herbert; costume designer, Vincent Lapper. Reviewed at Sunset screening room, L.A., May 8. MPAA Rating: R. Running time: 82 mins.

**Tommy Davidson (Julius), Julie Brown (Mimi), Paul Dinello (Jimmy), Sandra Bernhard (Bunny Roberts), Colleen Camp (Viv), Pamela Segall (Vallory), Matthew Glave (Nicky), Jennifer Rubin (Kandi Kane), Robert Costanzo (Montello).**

Quentin Tarantino's *Pulp Fiction* may appear ripe for spoofing: In reality, however, the patented looniness of *Pulp Fiction* makes it virtually spoof-proof. *Plump Fiction* is a shallow and surprisingly unimaginative attempt to parody Tarantino's work. It should have anemic and brief B.O.

*Plump Fiction* is lamentably predictable. Revisiting most of the celebrated scenes of *Pulp Fiction*, the new pic also throws in a potpourri of references to other indie pics like *Reservoir Dogs*, as well as to commercial hits like *Natural Born Killers*, *Forrest Gump*, and *Nell*.

U.S. release: May 15                    U.S. B.O.: $75,000

## The Polish Bride (De Poolse Bruid) (The Netherlands)

An RCV Film Distribution release of a Motel Films/Ijswater Films production. Produced by Jeroen Beker, Frans van Gestel. Directed by Karim Traidia. Screenplay, Kees van der Hulst. Camera, Jacques Laureys; editor, Chris Teerink; music, Fons Merkies; art direction, Anne Winterink. Reviewed at Rotterdam Festival, Feb. 3. Running time: 86 mins.

**Jaap Spijkers (Henk), Monic Hendrickx (Anna). With: Rudi Falkenhagen, Roef Ragas, Hakim Traidia.**

The standout entry in a quartet of low-budget Dutch features

known collectively as "Route 2000," first-time director Karim Traidia's *The Polish Bride* is a delicate two-handed chamber piece about the slow-kindling love between a hermitlike farmer and a battered refugee. Impressively modulated and affecting, this winner of the audience award at the Rotterdam Festival should segue to further fest dates and wide TV sales.

Edgy opening swiftly establishes the plight of title character Anna as she staggers, beaten and bleeding, through the streets of a small town and collapses at the feet of stoic farmer Henk. He takes the frightened girl in and cleans her up, with the unlikely couple keeping a circumspect distance from each other as she recovers.

Int'l release: March 25                    Int'l B.O.: $600,000

## Polish Wedding

A Fox Searchlight release, in association with Lakeshore Entertainment, of a Fox Searchlight presentation of an Addis/Wechsler production. Produced by Tom Rosenberg, Julia Chasman, Geoff Stier. Directed, written by Theresa Connelly. Camera, Guy Dufaux; editors, Curtiss Clayton, Suzanne Fenn; music, Luis Bacalov; production design, Kara Lindstrom; costume design, Donna Zakowska. Reviewed at Sundance Festival, Jan. 17. Running time: 107 mins.

**Lena Olin (Jadzia Pzoniak), Gabriel Byrne (Bolek Pzoniak), Claire Danes (Hala Pzoniak), Adam Trese (Russell Schuster), Mili Avital (Sofie Pzoniak), Rade Serbedzija (Roman), Daniel Lapaine (Ziggi).**

A throwback to family comedies of yesteryear, *Polish Wedding* provides a schmaltzy, old-fashioned chronicle of one large Polish-American family living in a Detroit neighborhood. An extremely attractive and hard-working cast struggles valiantly to overcome a broadly told, cliche-ridden script.

Filmmaker Theresa Connelly constructs a portrait of a family that, while boisterously turbulent, still manages to keep a unified facade and maintain its motto that there's nothing more important than "making life and making love." Olin stars as Jadzia Pzoniak, a middle-aged matriarch who runs her family with an iron fist. An extremely proud woman who cleans toilets for a living, Jadzia boasts of giving birth to five children, "four of them real men," as she says. While the boys always obey her, her beautiful adolescent daughter, Hala, proves strong-willed and independent.

U.S. release: July 27                    U.S. B.O.: $700,000
Int'l release: Nov 5                    Int'l B.O.: $50,000

## Possums

An HSX Films/Kushner-Locke presentation of an HSX Films production. Produced by Leanna Creel. Directed, written by J. Max Burnett. Camera, Christopher Duskin; editor, Karen Lee Smith; music, Justin Caine Burnett; production design, Chuck Price; costume design, Jane Montgomery. Reviewed at Seattle Festival, June 13. Running time: 97 mins.

**Mac Davis (Will Clark), Cynthia Sikes (Elizabeth Clark), Gregory Coolidge (Jake Malloy), Andrew Prine (Charlie Lawton), Dennis Burkley (Orville Moss), Monica Lacy (Sarah Jacobs).**

A sweet-tempered sports flick with "sleeper" written all over it, *Possums* reps a stellar turn for Mac Davis, playing a small-town sports announcer who single-handedly keeps the local high-school football team alive. It's also a startling debut for helmer-scripter J. Max Burnett, who doesn't hit a wrong note in the gently detailed family drama. Stereotype-free pic will resonate best in ex-urban areas and, down the line, it should be a hot direct-order video title.

Will Clark is a hardware-store owner and lifelong booster of the Possums, the increasingly pathetic pigskin kickers of Nowata, Okla. – a town that, itself, is on the verge of drying up and blowing away. The town's smarmy mayor is ready to pull the plug on the school's pricey sports program.

## The Postman

A Warner Bros. release of a Tig production. Produced by Jim Wilson, Steve Tisch, Kevin Costner. Directed by Costner. Screenplay, Eric Roth, Brian Helgeland, based on the novel by David Brin. Camera, Stephen Windon; editor, Peter Boyle; music, James Newton Howard; production design, Ida Random; costume design, John Bloomfield; stunt coordinator, Norman Howell. Reviewed at Warner Bros., Burbank, Dec. 6, 1997. MPAA Rating: R. Running time: 177 mins.
**Kevin Costner (The Postman), Will Patton (Bethlehem), Larenz Tate (Ford), Olivia Williams (Abby), James Russo (Idaho), Tom Petty (Mayor), Scott Bairstow (Luke).**
A big-canvas rendering of a passionately expressed vision of what the United States was, and is meant to be, *The Postman* is a rare epic film that is actually substantive. The clarity with which its ideas are articulated proves variable, and the hokiness and straight-faced sincerity of some of them will make the film an easy target for highbrow and cynical critics. At the same time, this involving, impressively filmed futuristic drama could catch on in Middle America if adverse advance impressions can be overcome quickly. In other words, B.O. outlook for this ruggedly entertaining effort is quite questionable.

Set 16 years in the future in the wake of devastating war, this adaptation of David Brin's 1985 sci-fi novel bears superficial resemblance to such post-apocalyptic landmarks as *The Road Warrior*. Although *The Postman* conveys a thoroughly imagined vision of a future society, its basic concerns are actually far from those of traditional sci-fi, as it quickly comes to feel more like a Western than anything else. A nameless vagabond delivers an amateurish one-man show of Shakespeare for the inhabitants of a town before being press-ganged into the marauding Holnists. The group's fascist agenda includes weeding out of the weak and the ethnically "deficient and impure" and, above all, the eradication of any and all vestiges of the old USA.

| | |
|---|---|
| U.S. release: Dec. 25, 1997 | U.S. B.O.: $17.5 million |
| Int'l release: Feb. 12 | Int'l B.O.: $9.5 million |

## The Powder Keg (Bure Baruta) (France-Yugoslavia-Greece-Macedonia-Turkey)

A MACT Prods/Ticket Prods (Paris)/Stefi S.A. (Athens)/Mine Films (Turkey)/Gradski Kina (Macedonia)/Vans Films (Belgrade) co-production. Produced by Goran Paskaljevic. Directed by Paskaljevic. Screenplay, Dejan Dukovski, Paskaljevic, Filip David, Zoran Andric, based on the play by Dukovski. Camera, Milan Spasic; editor, Petar Putnikovic; music, Zoran Simjanovic; production design, Milenko Jeremic; costume design, Zora Mojsilovic Popovic, Suna Ciftci. Reviewed at Venice Festival, Sept. 7. Running time: 102 mins.
**Miki Manojlovic (Mane), Nebojsa Glogovac (Taxi Driver), Ana Sofrenovic (Woman on Train), Dragan Nikolic (First Boxer), Lazar Ristovski (Second Boxer), Velimir Bata Stojkovic (Bus Driver).**

*The Powder Keg*, a devastating microcosm of life in contemporary Belgrade, is arguably the best film to date of director Goran Paskaljevic. Pic intros a gallery of characters who live in Belgrade during one hectic, at times frightening, night. Savagely funny, uncompromisingly critical, and impeccably staged and acted, the film is filled with insight into the makeup of the Serbian character. It should perform well in Euro arthouses, with chances good for other specialized distribution. Eurotube programmers will be eager for this one.

Opener is a direct nod to *Cabaret*, with an emcee in heavy makeup, cheerfully warning the viewer that "tonight I'm going to fuck with you." Segue to Mane, who's returned to the country in hopes of reconciling with his estranged wife. The taxi driver bringing him from the airport seriously questions his sanity. Amongst the characters intro'd are a family of Bosnian Serb refugees forced to live in a garage without utilities; a middle-aged boxer so damaged by life that he kills his best friend; an angry young man who hijacks a bus when the driver dallies; a VW driver moved to extreme road rage; a former student firebrand who traffics in alcohol, cigarettes, and drugs; and a youth attacked by a mob who mistake him for a car thief. What's most disturbing, perhaps, is that the incidents portrayed in the film could occur in almost any big city in the world. We are, Paskaljevic suggests, all sitting on a powder keg.

| | |
|---|---|
| Int'l release: Oct. 22 | Int'l B.O.: $350,000 |

## Practical Magic

A Warner Bros. release presented in association with Village Roadshow Pictures of a Di Novi Pictures production, in association with Fortis Films. Produced by Denise Di Novi. Directed by Griffin Dunne. Screenplay, Robin Swicord, Akiva Goldsman, Adam Brooks, based on the novel by Alice Hoffman. Camera, Andrew Dunn; editor, Elizabeth Kling; music, Alan Silvestri; production design, Robin Standefer; costume design, Judianna Makovsky; special-effects supervisor, Burt Dalton. Reviewed at Village Theater, L.A., Oct. 12. MPAA Rating: PG-13. Running time: 105 mins.
**Sandra Bullock (Sally Owens), Nicole Kidman (Gillian Owens), Dianne Wiest (Aunt Jet), Stockard Channing (Aunt Frances), Aidan Quinn (Gary Hallet), Goran Visnic (Jimmy), Evan Rachel Wood (Kylie), Alexandra Astrip (Antonia), Mark Feuerstein (Michael).**
Though not as embarrassingly silly as the 1993 *Hocus Pocus*, Griffin Dunne's slight, undernourished *Practical Magic* doesn't improve Hollywood's record on witchcraft. Part comedy, part family drama, part romance, part special-effects mystery-adventure, and not entirely satisfying on any of these levels, this hodgepodge suffers from conflicting sensibilities. Sandra Bullock – whose company co-produced – has a track record of making commercially accessible movies out of bland, schmaltzy material, and her new vehicle should prove no different; it's likely to reach midrange success.

Sally and Gillian, who are raised by their aunts after their parents' deaths, grow up in an eccentric mansion in which there are basically no rules. However, they soon learn the meaning of ostracism, as they are treated by the town's folks as outcasts, if not freaks. They also realize that the invocation of witchcraft carries with it a curse – their family's loved men are all doomed to untimely deaths.

| | |
|---|---|
| U.S. release: Oct. 16 | U.S. B.O.: $46.5 million |
| Int'l release: Nov. 19 | Int'l B.O.: $8 million |

## Praise (Australia)

An Emcee Film production. Produced by Martha Coleman. Directed by John Curran. Screenplay, Andrew McGahan, based on his novel. Camera, Dion Beebe; editor, Alexandre de Franceschi; music, Dirty Three; production design, Michael Philips; costume design, Emily Seresint. Reviewed at Toronto Festival, Sept. 12. Running time: 97 mins.
Peter Fenton (Gordan Buchanan), Sacha Holder (Cynthia Lamond), Marta Dusseldorp (Rachel), Joel Edgerton (Leo), Yvette Duncan (Molly), Ray Bull (Vass).

A feature debut that packs a knockout punch, the Australian *Praise* is a surprise for both its potent content and technical skill. The story of young down-and-outers is unsparing in detail, yet possesses a sly sense of humor that allows us to get under the skin of its characters rather than dismiss them. This stunning first film should score top marks with critics, which will pave the way for upbeat niche returns internationally of the order of such recent tough-minded entertainment as *Once Were Warriors* and *Leaving Las Vegas*.

Twentysomething Gordon has chucked his convenience-store gig to drink and hang out in his flea-pit Brisbane apartment-hotel with the other marginals. Cynthia, a former co-worker, invites him over to her parents' house for a party, and when he arrives he discovers he's the only guest. They proceed to spend days drinking, doing drugs, and just gabbing. Finally, she proposes sex and the two go at it with the same sort of excess that characterized their use of chemical stimulants. This unusual co-dependent relationship is cemented when Cynthia decides to stay with Gordon rather than follow her family to another city.

## A Price Above Rubies

A Miramax release of a Lawrence Bender production. Produced by Bender, John Penotti. Directed, written by Boaz Yakin. Camera, Adam Holender; editor, Arthur Coburn; music, Lesley Barber; production design, Dan Leigh; costume design, Ellen Lutter. Reviewed at Sundance Festival, Jan. 22. Running time: 117 mins.
Renee Zellweger (Sonia), Christopher Eccleston (Sender), Glenn Fitzgerald (Mendel), Allen Payne (Ramon), Julianna Margulies (Rachel), Edie Falco (Feiga), John Randolph (Rebbe), Kim Hunter (Rebbitzn).

As a young woman who questions her religious background and embarks on a personal odyssey, Renee Zellweger gives, in *A Price Above Rubies*, an utterly convincing and captivating performance. Sophomore effort by Boaz Yakin represents a more mature and substantial work, but suffers from predominantly one-dimensional portraiture and a context that's not grounded enough in realistic detail. Pic will need strong critical support and extra muscle to play well beyond the big urban centers. Set in Brooklyn's Orthodox Jewish community, the story depicts the pressures of a restrictive life on an individualistic woman who refuses to conform.
U.S. release: March 25          U.S. B.O.: $1.1 million

## Pride (Unmei No Toki) (Japan)

A Tokyo Film Production Inc./Toei Film Co. production. Produced by Masao Sato, Kanji Nakagawa. Directed by Shunya Ito. Screenplay, Hiroo Matsuda, Ito. Camera, Yudai Kato; editor, Takeo Araki; music, Michiru Oshima; production design, Akira Naito. Reviewed at Brisbane Festival, Aug. 8. Running time: 161 mins. (Japanese, English and Hindi dialog)

Masahiko Tsugawa (Gen. Hideki Tojo), Ayumi Ishida (Katsuko Tojo), Scott Wilson (Joseph Keenan), Ronny Cox (Sir William Webb), Suresh Oberoi (Indian Judge), Eiji Okuda (Ichiro Kiyose), Naho Toda (Akiko Shintani).

The Tokyo Trial (1946-48), in which Prime Minister Hideki Tojo and 27 other officials of his government were arraigned before the International Military Tribunal for crimes against humanity, conspiracy, and aggression, is re-examined in this powerful, controversial, revisionist courtroom drama. Pic has been a major success in Japan since it opened in late May. For Western viewers, the provocatively titled *Pride* is filled with material diametrically opposed to the "official" view of history. There's a distinct anti-U.S. bias to the movie, yet the material is so fascinating that it deserves to be seen and discussed at fests and other film events.

According to the film, the trial was unfair and the results preordained. Tojo is presented as a pacifist reluctantly drawn into the war when he felt he had no option, fiercely loyal to the emperor he literally worshipped as a god. Throughout the pic, Tojo's apparently sincere and reasoned arguments are contrasted with the bitter antagonism of U.S. prosecutor Keenan, who sees himself on a mission to restructure the crushed nation to prevent Japan from being a military threat again. Pic's different spin on famous events of the Pacific war is at times quite disturbing but is nonetheless fascinating and makes for most effective drama.
Int'l release: May 23          Int'l B.O.: $10 million

## Primary Colors

A Universal release of a Universal/Mutual Film Co. presentation. Produced, directed by Mike Nichols. Screenplay, Elaine May, based on the novel by Anonymous (Joe Klein). Camera, Michael Ballhaus; editor, Arthur Schmidt; music, Ry Cooder; production design, Bo Welch; costume design, Ann Roth. Reviewed at Universal, Universal City, March 10. MPAA Rating: R. Running time: 143 mins.
John Travolta (Gov. Jack Stanton), Emma Thompson (Susan Stanton), Billy Bob Thornton (Richard Jemmons), Kathy Bates (Libby Holden), Adrian Lester (Henry Burton), Maura Tierney (Daisy), Larry Hagman (Gov. Fred Picker), Diane Ladd (Mamma Stanton), Rob Reiner (Izzy Rosenblatt), Tony Shalhoub (Eddie Reyes).

A modern immorality tale with a keen edge, *Primary Colors* can hardly help but fascinate as a rare example of a film à clef. Frequently funny, wonderfully performed, eerily evocative of recent history, and gratifyingly blunt in its assessment of American politics, pic still comes short of being an entirely credible portrait of its subject. Speculation about the film's commercial prospects has centered on the public's customary aversion to political movies and a suspicion that recent history may have outstripped what's on view. But curiosity, John Travolta's star power, heavy press coverage on and off the entertainment pages, and film's undeniable entertaining qualities should propel it to hefty domestic grosses; foreign outlook is less encouraging.
U.S. release: March 20          U.S. B.O.: $39 million
Int'l release: March 27          Int'l B.O.: $12 million

## The Prince Of Egypt (Animated)

A DreamWorks Pictures release and production. Produced by Penney Finkelman Cox, Sandra Rabins. Directed by Brenda Chapman, Steve Hickner, Simon Wells. Screenplay, Philip

LaZebnik; supervising editor, Nick Fletcher; music, Hans Zimmer; songs, Stephen Schwartz; production design, Darek Gogol; costume design, Kelly Kimball; additional screenplay material, Nicholas Meyer. Reviewed at Camera 3, San José, Dec. 9. MPAA rating: PG. Running time: 97 mins.

**Voices: Val Kilmer (Moses), Ralph Fiennes (Rameses), Michelle Pfeiffer (Tzipporah), Sandra Bullock (Miriam), Jeff Goldblum (Aaron), Danny Glover (Jethro), Patrick Stewart (Seti), Helen Mirren (The Queen), Steve Martin (Hotep), Martin Short (Huy).**

Far more than a cartoon rendering of the beloved Bible story, DreamWorks' *The Prince of Egypt* proves an outstanding artistic achievement that further ups the ante in high-stakes feature animation. At once rich in historic and character detail and full of eye-popping tableaux, this new spin on the Moses saga sometimes out-DeMilles his 1956 epic, *The Ten Commandments*. The PG-rated pic's dour tone and admirable refusal to play down to little ones with farcical time-outs will hobble it at the box office. Discerning adults would appear to be target audience for a film that will be more admired than enjoyed. B.O. Promised Land will be deferred until cable and TV playdates, when the story's timeless appeal will translate into perennial holiday bookings as well as video.

A seamless combination of traditional animation and state-of-the-art CGI, pic opens masterfully with a musical prologue establishing both the majesty and ruthlessness of Ancient Egypt. Moses is saved from Pharaoh's forces when his mother launches him down the Nile. Central conflicts emerge as Pharaoh reminds Rameses of his duties as divine successor, and Moses, after a chance meeting with his slave sister Miriam, begins to question his own lineage. With Rameses and Moses rewritten as hellion stepbrothers, pic shrewdly milks filial love-gone-sour aspects .

To head off criticism from scholars for license taken, *Prince* opens with disclaimer that all to follow is true to the "essence and values" of the story.

U.S. release: Dec. 18 — Domestic B.O. $55 million
Int'l release: Dec. 17 — Int'l B.O.: $45 million

## Princess Mononoke (Mononoke Hime) (Japan, animated)

A Miramax Films release of a Tokuma Shoten Co./Nippon Television Network/Dentsu/Studio Ghibli production. Produced by Toshio Suzuki. Directed, written by Hayao Miyazaki. Animation direction, Masashi Ando, Kitaro Kosaka, Yoshifumi Kondo. Camera, Atsushi Okui; editor, Takeshi Seyama, Miyazaki; music, Joe Hisaishi. Reviewed at Ticketmaster, L.A., Jan. 27. Running time: 133 mins.

**Voices: Yoji Matsuda (Ashitaka), Yuriko Ishida (San), Yuko Tanaka (Lady Eboshi), Kaori Kobayashi (Jiko), Masahiko Nishimura (Koroku), Tsunehiko Kamijyo (Gonza).**

Japan's all-time box-office champ, *Princess Mononoke*, (grossing $150 million) is a rich cartoon fable of bygone gods locking horns with man and industry, which threatens to unbalance the forces of nature. Though set in the 14th century, its ecological bias and feminist slant provide a modern resonance. But the picture – steeped in Asian folklore – will require shrewd translation to connect with Western audiences. A few deft brush strokes could result in strong theatrical returns and extremely buoyant cassette sales. A bold experiment for Hayao Miyazaki – whose earlier work had more gentle, youthful themes – it's not only more sharply drawn, it

has an extremely complex and adult script.

In the opening, Prince Ashitaka is valiantly fighting off a demon god – a giant boar seemingly possessed by wormlike creatures. After he slays the beast, the village oracle begs its forgiveness, but it has already infected the prince with a fatal disease. Ashitaka must venture to the west to have the malediction lifted. The journey evolves into a mystical and violent pilgrim's progress. Eventually he arrives at the great forest and is befriended by Lady Eboshi, who operates a giant ironworks. Ashitaka finds himself thrust into the middle of a great struggle between the factory and the forest families of boars, wolves, and the like who are being killed off to make way for industrial expansion. Allegiances are further clouded by the arrival of the title character (aka San) who not only runs with the wolves, but also considers herself one of them.

Int'l release: July 12, 1997 — Int'l B.O.: $145 million

## Progeny

A Fries Film Group presentation of a Jack F. Murphy/Henry Seggerman production. Produced by Murphy, Seggerman. Directed by Brian Yuzna. Screenplay, Aubrey Solomon. Camera, James Hawkinson; editors, Harry B. Miller III, Christopher Roth; music, Steven Morrell; production designer, Anthony Tremblay; costume designer, Warden Neil; alien-creature design, Screaming Mad George. Reviewed at Cannes Festival, May 14, 1998. Running time: 100 mins.

**Arnold Vosloo (Craig Burton), Jillian McWhirter (Sherry Burton), Brad Dourif (Dr. Clavell), Lindsay Crouse (Psychiatrist), Wilford Brimley (Gynecologist).**

A cross between *Rosemary's Baby* and *Alien* with a pinch of *ER* thrown in, *Progeny* has all the outward trappings of Brian Yuzna's best horror work, including scary creatures waving long tentacles and an unnerving way of getting under the skin. Yet pic covers such familiar narrative ground that it fails fully to ignite. Genre fans should be happy to ride the wave of skillfully timed thrills and familiar-looking monsters.

Craig and Sherry Burton are in bed making love when a burst of light causes their bodies to separate and float through the air. They don't remember what happened until they are hypnotized by a psychiatrist and a UFO investigator. In dream they recall how Sherry was abducted to an outer-space operating room and penetrated by slimy, tentacled aliens wielding long steel instruments.

## The Proposition

A Polygram Films release of a Polygram Filmed Entertainment presentation of an Interscope Communications production. Produced by Ted Field, Diane Nabatoff, Scott Kroopf. Directed by Lesli Linka Glatter. Screenplay, Rick Ramage. Camera, Peter Sova; editor, Jacqueline Cambas; music, Stephen Endelman; production design, David Brisbin; costume design, Anna Sheppard. Reviewed at Polygram, Beverly Hills, March 10. MPAA Rating: R. Running time: 110 mins.

**Kenneth Branagh (Father Michael McKinnon), Madeleine Stowe (Eleanor Barret), William Hurt (Arthur Barret), Neil Patrick Harris (Roger Martin), Robert Loggia (Hannibal Thurman), Blythe Danner (Syril Danning).**

Father Michael McKinnon, fresh from Britain, joins the clergy at wealthy St. Jude's. Arthur and Eleanor Barret, two prominent parishoners, have reached the point in their marriage where they are determined to have a child at all costs, even though Arthur's sterility will force them to go outside conventional means to do so.

An original, peculiar story that plays like a labored adaptation of some obscure novel, *The Proposition* is an offer most people will be able to refuse. Powerful in a handful of scenes and with an appealing cast, this tale of an upper-class 1930s couple's efforts to adopt a child by any means gets stuck in a bog of feminist impulses, unrequited love, religious confusion, and unlikely crime. Result is a far-fetched and overly contrived melodrama that doesn't work on any level, making for a dim B.O. forecast.

| | |
|---|---|
| U.S. release: March 27 | U.S. B.O.: $150,000 |
| Int'l release: May 21 | Int'l B.O.: $1.3 million |

## Psycho

A Universal release of an Imagine Entertainment production. Produced by Brian Grazer, Gus Van Sant. Directed by Gus Van Sant. Screenplay, Joseph Stefano, based on the novel by Robert Bloch. Camera, Christopher Doyle; editor, Amy Duddleston; music, Bernard Herrmann; music-adaptor/producer, Danny Elfman; production design, Tom Foden; costume design, Beatrix Aruna Pasztor. Reviewed at Sony 19th Street East, New York, Dec. 4. MPAA rating: R. Running time: 109 mins.

**Vince Vaughn (Norman Bates), Anne Heche (Marion Crane), Julianne Moore (Lila Crane), Viggo Mortensen (Sam Loomis), William H. Macy (Milton Arbogast), Robert Forster (Dr. Simon), Chad Everett (Tom Cassidy), Rita Wilson (Caroline), James Remar (Patrolman), James LeGros (Car Dealer).**

Imitation, in the case of Gus Van Sant's *Psycho*, may be the sincerest form of flattery, but it's hardly the most scintillating. A faithful-unto-slavish remake of the 1960 Hitchcock classic, pic contains nothing to outrage or offend partisans of the original, yet neither does it stand to add much to their appreciation. And as for introducing a new generation to the granddaddy of all slasher films, forget about it: To the *Scream* kids, sincerity is out anyway, and the thrills here are strictly old hat. With an audience limited mainly to Hitch fans and first-weekend curiosity seekers, pic hardly stands to reduce the body count at beleaguered Universal.

The reason the conceit backfires is that the original depended on narrative surprises that can't possibly be replicated today and that were superseded decades ago. This *Psycho* is in color, which reduces the dream-like mood as well as the schematic visual rigor of Hitchcock's design.

The story is still the same. Marion Crane, who's having an affair with commitment-shy Sam Loomis, steals a load of cash and hits the road. Taking refuge in the motel owned by conflicted mama's boy Norman Bates, she's murdered during a nocturnal shower. Her disappearance prompts inquiries by a private eye as well as Sam and Marion's sister Lila, who discover the morbid bond linking Norman to his mysterious mom. The film's most famous scene, the shower knife-murder, Van Sant restages with slightly more nudity and realism.

| | |
|---|---|
| U.S. release: Dec. 4 | U.S. B.O.: $20 million |

## The Quarry (Belgium-France-Netherlands-Spain)

A Man's Film/Tchin Tchin/Studio Nieuwe Gronden/Wanda Films production. Produced, directed, written by Marion Hansel, based on the novel by Damon Galgut. Camera, Bernard Lutic; editor, Michele Hubinon; music, Takashi Kako; art director, Thierry Leproust; costume design, Yann Tax. Reviewed at World Film Festival, Montreal, Sept. 1. Running time: 114 mins.

**John Lynch (The Man), Jonne Phillips (Capt. Mong), Oscar Petersen (Valentine April), Sylvia Esau (The Woman), Jodi Abrahams (Small), Serge-Henri Valcke (Rev. Frans Niemand).**

The attempt to create a modern parable about identity and responsibility falls short of its target in the Euro co-production *The Quarry*. While the film is intriguing in parts, it is too oblique to reach a wide audience, and will find only limited exposure on the fest circuit and scattered sales aimed at the arthouse crowd. Pic shared top prize in Montreal and an award for Takashi Kako's music score.

Set in the South African outback, story centers on an escaped criminal. He receives a ride from a minister who makes sexual advances; he accidentally kills him in the ensuing scuffle and buries him in an inactive quarry. Taking on the reverend's identity, he arrives at the remote northern outpost where the dead man was to assume a post. With his simple manner, he's able to satisfy the townspeople's hunger for spiritual guidance and serve the community. But petty thieves discover that he's an impostor, and the threat of exposure unbalances the situation.

## Quest For Camelot (Animated)

A Warner Bros. production. Produced by Dalisa Cooper Cohen. Directed by Frederick Du Chan. Screenplay, Kirk De Micco, William Schifrin, Jacqueline Feather, David Seidler, based on the novel *The King's Damsel* by Vera Chapman. Editor, Stanford C. Allen; music, Patrick Doyle; original songs, David Foster, Carole Bayer Sager; production design, Steve Pilcher; supervising animator, Russell Hall. Reviewed at Sony State Theater, N.Y., April 25. MPAA Rating: G. Running time: 85 mins.

**Voices: Jessalyn Gilsig (Kayley), Cary Elwes (Garrett), Gary Oldman (Ruber), Eric Idle (Devon), Don Rickles (Cornwall), Jane Seymour (Juliana), Pierce Brosnan (King Arthur), Bronson Pinchot (Griffin), Jaleel White (Bladebeak), Gabriel Byrne (Lionel), John Gielgud (Merlin).**

Warner Bros.' fully animated feature *Quest for Camelot* is a lightweight, likeable fantasy that offers a playfully feminist twist to Arthurian legends. With no other high-profile kid-oriented fare on the playing field, the handsomely mounted pic should score respectably midrange B.O. before hitting the jackpot as a sell-through video title.

This *Camelot* reduces King Arthur and Merlin to supporting players, focusing on Kayley, a plucky girl who dreams of following her late father as a Knight of the Round Table. Kayley's brave father was killed defending his king against an attack by the wicked Ruber, would-be usurper. Several years on, Ruber once again is making a bid for King Arthur's throne, having managed through chicanery to snatch Excalibur, Arthur's legendary magical sword. Kayley vows to find the sword before Camelot is overrun. As she journeys through the haunted forest, she finds a reluctant ally in Garrett, a young man who, despite being blind, knows the lay of the land. At first, Garrett grumpily demands to be left alone. But when he discovers that Kayley is the daughter of Sir Lionel, the knight who trained him to fight, he agrees to help.

| | |
|---|---|
| U.S. release: May 15 | U.S. B.O.: $22.5 million |
| Int'l release: May 28 | Int'l B.O.: $20 million |

## The Race to Save 100 Years (Docu, B&W/Color)

A Warner Bros./ Turner Entertainment production. Produced by Mary Adair Kaiser. Directed by Scott Benson. Screenplay, Adair Kaiser, John de Groot. Camera, Joseph Montgomery, John

Simmons; editor, de Groot; restoration film editor, Ron Ratberg. Reviewed at Santa Barbara Festival, March 14. Running time: 57 mins.

**With: Martin Scorsese, Kevin Brownlow, Robert Rosen, Mary Lea Bandy, James H. Billington.**

A worthy introduction to cinema history, *The Race to Save 100 Years* highlights the urgent need to make strides in film preservation. Featuring the participation of a panel of experts, docu is likely to turn up on the museum and college circuit, as well as TV. Film opens with disheartening images of decayed nitrate film rusting away in abandoned vaults, to illustrate the graphic results of years of neglect.

### Radiance (Australia)

A Polygram Filmed Entertainment release of an Eclipse Films production. Produced by Ned Lander, Andrew Myer. Directed by Rachel Perkins. Screenplay, Louis Nowra, based on his play. Camera, Warwick Thornton; editor, James Bradley; music, Alistair Jones; production designer, Sarah Stollman; costume designer, Tess Schofield. Reviewed at Cannes Festival, May 17. Running time: 83 mins.

**Rachael Maza (Cressy), Deborah Mailman (Nona), Trisha Morton-Thomas (Mae).**

Three sisters reunite to bury their mother and unearth their past in documaker Rachel Perkins' polished feature debut, *Radiance*. A fiery, Southern-style melodrama that builds slowly but surely to an emotionally charged conclusion, the film skillfully touches on indigenous questions regarding displacement, heritage, land, and belonging. International prospects stand to benefit greatly from a strategic festival platform.

Adapted by Louis Nowra from his play, the material never entirely disguises its theatrical origins. But this does not seem inappropriate given Perkins' richly operatic handling of the drama. Mae, who's stayed in the house to care for their prematurely senile mother, resents convent-raised sister Cressy, who has pursued a successful career as an opera diva. Youngest sister Nona is an exuberant party girl.

Int'l release: Oct. 8                    Int'l B.O.: $300,000

### Radio Freccia (Italy)

A Medusa Film release of a Fandango production in association with Medusa Film. Produced by Domenico Procacci. Directed by Luciano Ligabue, with collaboration of Antonello Grimaldi. Screenplay, Antonio Leotti, Ligabue, based on the short stories *Fuori e dentro il borgo* by Ligabue. Camera, Arnaldo Catinari; editor, Angelo Nicolini; music, Ligabue; production/costume design, Stefano Giambanco. Reviewed at Venice Festival, Sept. 12. Running time: 112 mins.

**Stefano Accorsi (Freccia), Luciano Federico (Bruno), Alessio Modica (Iena), Enrico Salimbeni (Tito), Roberto Zibetti (Boris), Francesco Guccini (Adolfo), Patrizia Piccinini (Marzia).**

Popular Italian rock star Luciano Ligabue moves into directing with *Radio Freccia*, adapted from his autobiographical short stories about his youth in 1970s small-town Italy. Avoiding the usual pitfalls of inexperience, Ligabue appears to have taken full advantage of an attentive producer, a talented d.p., and backup from a more seasoned director, making for a polished, visually stylish production. Loaded with engaging individual scenes and keenly observed moments, it lacks the overall control to bring the elements together, but has enough energy

and spirit to speak to young audiences.

Opening in 1993 with the closure of a provincial free-radio station, the story backtracks as DJ Bruno recounts its birth 18 years earlier. Nucleus of the band of sex-and-drug-era vitelloni involved in establishing the station is Freccia, whose death from a heroin overdose will prompt the rechristening of the network in his name. Freccia drifts into heroin almost out of boredom and dissatisfaction, then kicks the habit with the help of a selfless woman, but succumbs again fatally after a bad case of unrequited love.

The film fails to display much of a point of view about the era of social change it depicts, but Ligabue's script has the genuine feeling of a first-hand account.

Int'l release: Oct. 16                    Int'l B.O.: $5 million

### The Rain Soldier (Deszczowy Zolnierz) (Poland-Germany)

A Saco Films, Agencja Produkcji Filmowej, TV Polska (Warsaw)/Projekt 4 (Berlin)/WFF (Wroclaw) co-production. Produced by Wieslaw Saniewski, Christine Hamer-Swiecznik, Andrzej Stachecki. Directed, written by Saniewski. Camera, Przemyslaw Skwirczynski; editor, Urszula Jablonska; music, Jerzy Satanowski; production design, Christine Hamer-Swiecznik; costume design, Alicja Wasilewska. Reviewed at Berlin Festival, Feb. 19. Running time: 96 mins. (Polish dialog)

**Antonina Choroszy (Anna Bracka), Mariusz Bonaszewski (Witek), Jan Nowicki (Jan Szymanski), Lukasz Nowicki (Young Jan Szymanski), Artur Zmijewski (Jerzy).**

The past returns to haunt the present in this eerie, well-made meller from Poland, which starts off as a legal thriller and abruptly segues into a supernatural yarn. Pic copped a couple of prizes, including the Indie Filmmakers Award, last year at the Houston fest, and is a natural for Eurotube programmers.

Lawyer Anna Bracka is launching an investigation into high-level corporate corruption. When her lover, Jerzy, proposes she accept a bribe to lose the case, she angrily refuses and he brutally abuses her. Distraught, she drives off into a rainy, windswept night and nearly hits a man in the road. The stranger, who's carrying a gun, appears to have lost his memory. When it returns, he reveals that the gun was owned by Jan Szymanski – Anna's father, a retired military prosecutor. Witek, it's revealed, was a true idealist. He wouldn't betray his beliefs, just as, in the present, Anna refuses to betray her ideals and take the easy option offered her by Jerzy.

### A Rat's Tale (Die Story Von Monty Spinnerratz) (Germany)

A Legacy Films release of a Monty Film production. Produced by Hans Peter Clahsen. Directed by Michael F. Huse. Screenplay, Werner Morgenrath, Peter Scheerbaum, based on the book by Tor Seidler. Camera, Piotr Lenar; editor, Timothy McLeish; music, Frederic Talgorn; production designer, Austen Spriggs; costumes, Eun-Young Kim; marionette designers, Hannelore Marschall-Oehmichen, Jurgen Marschall. Reviewed at Goldwyn Pavilion, L.A., March 14. MPAA Rating: G. Running time: 89 mins.

**Lauren Hutton (Evelyn Jellybelly), Beverly D'Angelo (Mrs. Dollart), Jerry Stiller (Prof. Plumpingham), Josef Ostendorf (Lou Dollart). Voices: Dee Bradley Baker (Monty Mad-Rat), Lynsey Bartilson (Isabella Noble-Rat).**

Beneath the bustling streets of Manhattan is a thriving community of rodents and assorted creatures whose society strikingly mirrors that of the humans above ground. These cuddly varmints, the creations of Germany's Augsburger Puppet Theatre, inhabit a world of eco-conscious star-crossed lovers in *A Rat's Tale*, based on the kids' yarn by Tor Seidler. Though well intentioned and visually unusual, the film will appeal almost exclusively to the youngest moviegoers, and will translate into much stronger biz on video than in theaters. In Germany, where the Augsburger troupe is acclaimed, the pic opened in early 1997 and did solid biz, grossing more than $3 million.

Essentially a tale of young love, pic centers on the cute couple of Monty, an artist, and upper-crust politician's daughter Isabella. They meet when Monty rescues her from the rain and inducts her into the rapid transit of Gotham's sewer system. They're mutually smitten, but Isabella's family will not approve of her dating beneath her station.

Int'l release: March 27, 1997 — Int'l B.O.: $3.1 million
U.S. release: March 20 — U.S. B.O.: $60,000

### Razor Blade Smile (U.K.)

A Palm Pictures/Manga Live presentation of an Eye Deal Image Prods (London) production, in association with Beatnik Pictures. Produced by Jake West, Robert Mercer. Directed, written, edited by West. Camera, James Solan; music, Richard Wells; production design, Neil Jenkins; costume stylist, Dena Costello. Reviewed at Vancouver Festival, Oct. 4. Running time: 101 mins.
**Eileen Daley (Lilith Silver), Christopher Adamson (Sethane Blake), Kevin Howarth (Platinum), Jonathan Coote (Ray Price), David Warbeck (Horror Movie Man), Heidi James (Ariauna).**
Cheesiness is its own reward in *Razor Blade Smile*, an over-the-top vampire romp sure to have Bela Lugosi turning in his grave. Pic's canny combo of omnisexual romping and campy violence makes up for any debits in the acting and plotting departments, with stylish design and a sizzling lead, in the form of scream queen Eileen Daley, sure to draw blood from the latenight crowd before opening up a healthy video vein.

After Lilith loses a loved one in a duel with the cruel Sir Sethane Blake a century ago, Blake shoots her and then revives the lass using his canine-incisors method. In decadent modern London, leather-clad Lilith barely stands out. Her durability, cunning, and carnal needs make her chosen career of hit woman an apt fit. Story involves a conspiratorial group that has infiltrated the highest levels of business and government. But now somebody's bumping off the so-called Illuminati, and black-haired Lilith seems to be doing a lot of the bumping.

### Reach The Rock

A Gramercy Pictures release of a John Hughes and Ricardo Mestres production. Produced by Hughes, Mestres. Directed by William Ryan. Screenplay, John Hughes. Camera, John Campbell; editor, Jerry Greenberg; music, John McEntire; music supervisor, John Hughes III; production design, Jeffrey Townsend; costume design, Ellen Ryba. Reviewed at Music Hall, Beverly Hills, Oct. 5. Running time: 100 mins.
**William Sadler (Quinn), Alessandro Nivola (Robin), Bruce Norris (Ernie), Karen Sillas (Donna), Brooke Langton (Lise), Richard Hamilton (Ed), Norman Reedus (Danny).**
A quirky little indie about a young man's quest for personal redemption, *Reach the Rock* offers an intriguing premise and a few laughs but ultimately falls short of its goals.

Modest pic aspires to, but never attains, an emotional connection with its audience. Theatrical life will consequently be exceptionally short.

Robin Fleming is a young man whose penchant for troublemaking lands him in the Shermer, Ill. slammer one hot summer night after a random act of vandalism. A small, virtually deserted town, Shermer has a police force of two: gruff sergeant Phil Quinn and his dimwitted deputy, Ernie. The older blames his subordinate for the death of his nephew in a drunken swimming accident four years earlier. Robin steals a key and slips away, wreaking more havoc on the town. Robin's goals are twofold: to persuade his ex-girlfriend Lise to come down and bail him out, and to force a verbal confrontation with Quinn, finally wearing down the cop's resistance with humor and trickery.

U.S. release: Oct. 16 — U.S. B.O.: $30,000

### The Real Howard Spitz (U.K.-Canada)

A Mob Film Co. release of a Metrodome/Imagex production, in association with Telefilm Canada, and with the participation of the Nova Scotia Film Development Corp. Produced by Paul Brooks, Christopher Zimmer. Directed by Vadim Jean. Screenplay, Jurgen Wolff. Camera, Glen MacPherson; editor, Pia di Ciaula; music, David A. Hughes, John Young; production design, Chris Townsend; costumes, Martha Curry. Reviewed at Virgin Trocadero, London, Aug. 3. Running time: 102 mins.
**Kelsey Grammer (Howard Spitz), Amanda Donohoe (Laura Kershaw), Genevieve Tessier (Samantha Kershaw), Joseph Rutten (Lou), Patrick McKenna ("Howard Spitz"), Kay Tremblay (Theodora Winkle), David Christofel (Bill).**
Kelsey Grammer is the best thing in *The Real Howard Spitz*, but he's pushing water uphill all the way in this flimsy family comedy that's never more than amiable. Grammer retranslates his *Frasier* persona into a testy scribe who secretly loathes tykes, providing a modest amount of amusement in a pic that has "ancillary" written all over it.

Howard Spitz is a seedy, indebted writer of equally seedy hard-boiled detective novels whose latest manuscript is so bad that his long-suffering agent, Lou, suggests he switch to penning self-help manuals. After a chance encounter with kidtome grande dame Theodora Winkle, Howard instead is inspired to turn his hand to children's books, creating the bovine shamus Crafty Cow. Schooled in what kids want to read by the precocious Samantha – whom he got to know in the local library – Howard hits pay dirt. As payback, Samantha requires Howard (a former private dick) to track down her father.

Int'l release: Aug. 28 — Int'l B.O.: $25,000

### The Redemption (Lunastus) (Finland)

A Kinoproduction production, in association with YLE, Swedish Television 1 Drama. Produced by Claes Olsson. Directed by Olli Saarela. Screenplay, Saarela, Heikki Vuento. Camera, Antti Hellstedt; editor, Tuuli Kuittinen; music, Tuomas Kantelinen; art director, Risto Karhula. Reviewed at Rouen Festival of Nordic Cinema, France, March 28, 1998. Running time: 72 mins.
**With: Kari Heiskanen, Jussi Puhakka, Jussi Lehtonen.**
A moody, well-acted first feature, set during the 1918 civil war that followed Finland's declaration of independence from Russia, *The Redemption* is a tense and dour drama with a few unexpected twists that pack a punch.

A bone-weary Lutheran priest in a small village has been tending his motley parish as best he can, faced with scarce supplies and scarcer enthusiasm for the Lord's teachings. Convinced he's a sinner whose professorial efforts are wasted on the local school children, the priest is put in charge of a prisoner – a young soldier fighting for the Reds.

### The Red Violin (Le Violon Rouge) (Canada-Italy)

A Fine Line release of a New Line Int'l/Channel Four Films/Telefilm Canada presentation of a Rhombus Media/Mikado/Sidecar Films production. Produced by Niv Fichman. Directed by François Girard. Screenplay, Don McKellar, Girard. Camera, Alain Dostie; editor, Gaetan Huot; music, John Corigliano; solo violin, Joshua Bell; production design, François Seguin; costume design, Renee April. Reviewed at Venice Festival, Sept. 2. Running time: 131 mins. (English, Italian, German, French, and Mandarin dialog.) **Samuel L. Jackson (Charles Morritz), Don McKellar (Evan Williams), Carlo Cecchi (Nicolo Bussotti), Irene Grazioli (Anna Bussotti), Jean-Luc Bideau (Georges Poussin), Christoph Koncz (Kaspar Weiss), Jason Flemyng (Frederick Pope), Greta Scacchi (Victoria Byrd), Sylvia Chang (Xiang Pei), Liu Zi Feng (Chou Yuan), Colm Feore (Auctioneer).**
A saga of love and music spanning three centuries, Canadian director François Girard's follow-up to *Thirty Two Short Films About Glenn Gould* is nothing if not ambitious. Unfortunately, the episodic pic, which follows the fortunes of a perfectly crafted violin that is linked to a bloody secret, fails on a number of counts, mostly because individual stories aren't very gripping. Distrib will have to market this one carefully to find an appreciative audience, and may not be helped by mixed critical response.

Pic is structured around an auction in Montreal in which a number of valuable instruments, including a Stradivarius, are on the block; but the pièce de resistance is the famous Red Violin, crafted in 1681 by Italian master Nicolo Bussotti. The instrument is, according to an expert, "the perfect marriage of science and beauty" and "the single most perfect acoustic machine" – quite a wrap.

Complex flashback structure intercuts between investigations of the instrument's authenticity, while stories centering on the violin's colorful past unreel chronologically, beginning with its production and the trauma endured by Bussotti when his wife dies in childbirth then moving through time to Austria, England, and China.

| | |
|---|---|
| U.S. release: Nov. 6 | U.S. B.O.: $1.2 million |
| Int'l release: Oct. 23 | Int'l B.O.: $200,000 |

### Relax It's Just Sex

An Atlas Entertainment production. Produced by Steven J. Wolfe, Megan O'Neill, Harold Warren. Directed, written by P.J. Castellaneta. Camera, Lon Magdich; editor, Tom Seid; music, Lori Eschler Frystak; music supervision, Ricky Frystak; production design, Timm Bergen; costume design, Sharon Lynch. Reviewed at Sundance Festival, Jan. 19. Running time: 110 mins.
**Jennifer Tilly (Tara Ricotto), Mitchell Anderson (Vincey Sauris), Cynda Williams (Sarina Classer), Lori Petty (Robin Moon), Serena Scott Thomas (Megan Pillsbury), Eddie Garcia (Javi Rogero), T.C. Carson (Buzz Wagner), Billy Wirth (Jared Baroziak), Susan Tyrell (Alicia Pillsbury), Seymour Cassell (Emile Pillsbury), Paul Winfield (Auntie Miriam).**
P.J. Castellaneta's *Relax It's Just Sex* is a 1990s romantic comedy that deals with the affairs and intrigues of the heart amongst a social clique composed of gays and straights. Despite vibrantly funny dialog, and terrific ensemble acting, more than simple cuts would be necessary for the film to be a serious theatrical contender. Structured à la *La Ronde*, pic has characters address the camera directly, beginning a vignette that involves another character. Predictably, in the first collective scene, a dozen friends voice their opinions about AIDS.

### The Replacement Killers

A Sony Pictures release of a Columbia Pictures presentation of a Bernie Brillstein/Brad Grey and WCG Entertainment production. Produced by Grey, Brillstein. Directed by Antoine Fuqua. Screenplay, Ken Sanzel. Camera, Peter Lyons Collister; editor, Jay Cassidy; music, Harry Gregson-Williams; production design, Naomi Shohan; costume design, Arianne Phillips; sound, Douglas B. Arnold; stunt coordinator, Allan Graf; casting, Wendy Kurtzman. Reviewed at Sony Studios, Culver City, Jan. 30. MPAA Rating; R. Running time: 86 mins.
**Chow Yun-Fat (John Lee), Mira Sorvino (Meg Coburn), Michael Rooker (Stan "Zeedo" Zedkov), Jurgen Prochnow (Michael Kogan), Kenneth Tsang (Terence Wei), Randall Duk Kim (Alan Chan).**
The realization that there is something innately cockeyed about *The Replacement Killers* sets in with the awareness that the movie isn't about what its title indicates: The lead characters portrayed by Asian action-hero Chow Yun-Fat and Mira Sorvino are actually the targets of the titular assassins. A Westernization of the Hong Kong movies of Chow, here making his American film debut, and exec-producers John Woo and Terence Chang, this mechanical effort is studied rather than heartfelt, and will disappoint aficionados and thwart potential fans. Result will be tepid box-office returns. Follow up in ancillaries should be OK, but it remains a niche genre item.

Chow is on familiar ground as John Lee, a hired gun with a debt to pay. His final mission is to murder the 7-year-old son of the cop. However, when he has the boy in his sights, a crisis of conscience prevents him from pulling the trigger. Lee knows his decision will make him a target of whomever is brought in to finish the job.

| | |
|---|---|
| U.S. release: Feb. 6 | U.S. B.O.: $19 million |
| Int'l release: Jan. 22 | Int'l B.O.: $20 million |

### Requiem (Switzerland-France-Portugal)

A CAB Production/Filmograph/ Gemini Films/Madragoa Filmes co-production, in association with Swiss Romand TV TSR, WDR. Produced by Gerard Ruey, Jean-Louis Porchet, Alain Tanner, Paulo Branco. Directed by Tanner. Screenplay, Tanner, Bernard Comment, based on the novel by Antonio Tabucchi. Camera, Hugues Ryffel; editor, Monica Goux; music, Michel Wintsch; production designer, Joao Torres; costume designer, Isabel Quadros. Reviewed at Cannes Festival, May 17. Running time: 99 mins.
**Francis Frappat (Paul), Andre Marcon (Pierre), Alexandre Zloto (Father), Myriam Szabo (Isabel).**
Vet Swiss director Alain Tanner returns to Portugal with an adaptation of Italo writer Antonio Tabucchi's *Requiem*. The film, like the novel, is a salute to Portuguese scribe Fernando Pessoa, who appears as a mysterious character in this quiet, unhurried work. Meticulously shot, heavy on atmosphere, and 100% cerebral, pic offers little to rouse the enthusiasm of even

arthouse regulars.

Set on the hottest day of August, with no one on the deserted streets besides a few extras, the story stretches from noon to midnight as French writer Paul waits for an appointment with "a ghost." He whiles away the day meeting long-dead friends from his memories, who materialize out of nowhere with complete naturalness.

Int'l release: June 3                    Int'l B.O.: $150,000

## Restaurant

A Palisades Pictures presentation, in association with Giv'en Films, of a Chaiken Films production. Produced by H.M. Coakley, Shana Stein, Eric Bross. Directed by Bross. Screenplay, Tom C. Cudworth. Camera, Horacio Marquinez; editor, Keith Reamer; music, Theodore Shapiro; production designer, Steven McCabe; costume designer, Elizabeth Shelton. Reviewed at L.A. Independent Festival, April 17. Running time: 107 mins.

**Adrien Brody (Chris Calloway), Elise Neal (Jeanine), David Moscow (Reggae), Simon Baker-Denny (Kenny), Catherine Kellner (Nancy), Malcolm Jamal Warner (Steven).**

A flawed but dynamic ensemble piece about a bunch of young creative types waiting tables and tending bar while waiting for their big breaks, *Restaurant* is a tasty meal spoiled only by a heavy sauce of pretension and forced social commentary. Energetically directed and vividly performed, pic is potent and topical enough to spark reasonable critical support, making it a fair bet for specialized theatrical distribution.

At J.T. McClure's, a popular Hoboken, N.J. restaurant and watering hole, most of the attractive young staff harbor artistic aspirations. Amid the swirl of activity on a busy evening, director Eric Bross and writer Tom C. Cudworth deftly introduce the key players: Chris, an alcoholic bartender now on the wagon, whose autobiographical play is in rehearsals at a local theater; Kenny, a callow playboy who infuriated Chris by sleeping with his ex-girlfriend Leslie; Jeanine, a waitress and accomplished singer who awakens Chris to the possibility of a new romance; and Reggae (David Moscow), Chris' best friend and fellow "Newark Boy" who works as a chef.

## Return To Paradise

A Polygram Films release of a Polygram Filmed Entertainment presentation of a Propaganda Films production, in association with Tetragram. Produced by Alain Bernheim, Steve Golin. Directed by Joseph Ruben. Screenplay, Wesley Strick, Bruce Robinson. Camera, Reynaldo Villalobos; editors, Andrew Mondshein, Craig McKay; music, Mark Mancina; production design, Bill Groom. Reviewed at Polygram, Beverly Hills, July 29. MPAA Rating: R. Running time: 109 mins.

**Vince Vaughn (Sheriff), Anne Heche (Beth), Joaquin Phoenix (Lewis), David Conrad (Tony), Vera Farmiga (Kerrie), Nick Sandow (Ravitch), Jada Pinkett Smith (M.J. Major).**

An undernourished melodrama about the moral dilemma confronted by two young men whose buddy faces a death sentence in Southeast Asia, *Return to Paradise* offers a disappointingly conventional treatment of an intriguing story that needed more narrative zing or greater thematic complexity. Pic's dramatic fulcrum provides a measure of undeniable gravity and ticking-clock suspense, but middle-of-the-road approach positions this closer to erstwhile issue-oriented TV movies than to the kind of edgy, suspenseful fare that lures young viewers into theaters.

Two years after saying good-bye to earnest do-gooder Lewis, who stayed in Asia to help save endangered orangutans in Borneo, Sheriff is informed of his arrest for carrying hash and subsequent trial in Malaysia. The conviction comes with a death sentence due to be carried out in eight days. He will be spared only if one or both of his drug-using cohorts comes back to do time.

U.S. release: Aug. 14                    U.S. B.O.: $8 million
Int'l release: Nov. 6                    Int'l B.O.: $800,000

## Return With Honor (Docu, Color/B&W)

A Sanders & Mock production. Produced by Freida Lee Mock, Terry Sanders. Directed by Lee Mock, Sanders. Screenplay, Mock, Sanders, Christine Z. Wiser. Camera, Eddie Marritz, Sanders; editor, Greg Byers; music, Charles Bernstein. Reviewed at Mill Valley Festival, Oct. 4. Running time: 101 mins.

Vet nonfiction helmers Freida Lee Mock's and Terry Sanders' *Return With Honor* is a potent look back at the experiences of American POWs in North Vietnam, one made strikingly immediate by the unprecedented amount of hitherto-unavailable enemy propaganda footage. A Vietnam War docu that scarcely references the big question of U.S. involvement, pic features highly dramatic content that may attract a larger-than-usual aud in theatrical release, with broadcast showcasing sure to follow.

Pic dives into the recollections of its eight principal interviewees. These onetime POWs include high-ranking "top guns," as well as lesser-sung servicemen. This vocal testimony would be powerful enough abetted only by the still photos and Western military footage. But the most stunning element is the additional deployment of reels only recently released by the now-friendly Vietnamese government.

## The Revengers' Comedies (U.K.-France)

A J&M Entertainment/BBC Films presentation, in association with the Arts Council of England and France 2 Cinema in association with Canal Plus, Sofica, Sofinergie 4, of an Artisan Films (U.K.)/IMA Films (France) production. Produced by Simon Bosanquet. Directed, written by Malcolm Mowbray, based on the plays by Alan Ayckbourn. Camera, Romain Winding; editor, Barrie Vince; music, Alexandre Desplat; production design, Stuart Walker; costume design, Anushia Nieradzik. Reviewed at Pasquino Cinema, Rome, Jan. 3. Running time: 82 mins.

**Sam Neill (Henry Bell), Helena Bonham Carter (Karen Knightly), Kristin Scott Thomas (Imogen Staxton-Billing), Rupert Graves (Oliver Knightly), Martin Clunes (Anthony Staxton-Billing), Steve Coogan (Bruce Tick), John Wood (Col. Marcus), Liz Smith (Winnie).**

A tony cast adds polish to the old-fashioned but not unamusing *The Revengers' Comedies*. Condensed from a pair of plays by Alan Ayckbourn, this mix of dry British wit, sophisticated farce and arch eccentricity is the kind of material that can sparkle onstage but often sits uneasily onscreen, and tends to have limited pull with today's audiences. The stylishly played black comedy lacks acid barbs and bite and appears unlikely to become a strong theatrical entry.

Depressed businessman Henry Bell and orphaned aristocrat Karen Knightly meet and save each other's lives one night when both are planning suicidal leaps. As they compare their unhappy plights over drinks, Karen hatches a reciprocal revenge plot. She will punish Bruce Tick, the condescending upstart who maneuvered Henry's job away from him, while he

---

**. . . July 25 . . .**

Rupert Murdoch, who had failed twice to buy into Silvio Berlusconi's TV empire, now holding talks with Italy's telco Telecom Italia.

sets out to destroy Imogen Staxton-Billing, the woman who caused husband Anthony to stray.

Int'l release: Dec. 12, 1997      Int'l B.O.: $2.1 million

## Ride

A Dimension Films release of a Hudlin Bros. production. Produced by Reginald Hudlin, Warren Hudlin. Directed, written by Millicent Shelton. Camera, Frank Byers; editor, Earl Watson; music, Dunn Pearson, Jr.; music supervisors, Bill Stephney, Byron Phillips; production design, Bryan Jones; costume design, Richard Owings. Reviewed at Beverly Connection, L.A., March 26. MPAA Rating: R. Running time: 83 mins.

**Malik Yoba (Poppa), Melissa De Sousa (Leta), John Witherspoon (Roscoe), Fredro Starr (Geronimo), Cedric the Entertainer (Bo), Sticky Fingaz (Brotha X), Kellie Williams (Tuesday), Idalis de Leon (Charity), Julia Garrison (Blacke), Guy Torrey (Indigo), Reuben Asher (Casper), Downtown Julie Brown (Bleau Kelly).**

A road comedy, *Ride* offsets its predictable storyline with a few genuinely funny bits of dialog and some earnest performances. Propelled by a popular rap and hip-hop soundtrack, it should score with young urban audiences, even if crossover and international prospects are slight. Ancillary cable and video outlook is solid.

New Yorker Leta, an aspiring director just out of film school, accepts her first job as an assistant to musicvideo helmer Bleau Kelly. Assembling a group of young street talents for an upcoming video to be shot in Florida, Leta makes her first trip to Harlem and finds more than she bargained for. An inner-city activist named Poppa introduces Leta to the undisciplined bunch of would-be artists.

U.S. release: March 27      U.S. B.O.: $5.5 million

## The Ride

A World Wide Pictures release. Produced by Laurie Leinonen. Directed, written by Michael O. Sajbel, based on a screenplay by David Bowen. Camera, Michael T. Balog; editor, Michael Fallavollita; music, James Covell; production designer, Jo-Ann Chorney; costume designer, Gina Aller; stunt coordinator, Eddie Matthews. Reviewed on videotape, L.A., March 6. MPAA Rating: PG. Running time: 101 mins.

**Michael Biehn (Smokey Banks), Brock Pierce (Danny O'Neil), Jennifer Blanc (Linnette Stillwell), Chris Owen (Steve), Clarence Felder (Mike Stillwell), Jennifer O'Neill (Ellen Stillwell).**

The cowboy remains the most enduring American movie hero. But he's been battered and bruised over the years, and in the contemporary *The Ride*, it takes a passel of trouble to get him to show his true grit. A tad on the syrupy side, pic is an uplifting yarn about rodeo and kids aimed at families; it should do well in the country's heartland and be a potent mover on video.

Smokey Banks is a one-time bull-riding champ who's seen considerably better days. A gambler and a boozer, he's low on cash and running a high tab with a couple of mean hombres. Getting a bit too feisty in a bar, he winds up before a judge who sentences him to hard time in community service at a ranch camp for underprivileged and orphaned kids. One of the brood, terminally-ill Danny, knows the man's history of triumphs and presses him to teach him how to stay in the saddle.

U.S. release: Dec. 5, 1997      U.S. B.O.: $250,000

## River Red

A Drilling Films presentation, in association with Miller Entertainment Group and Frontier Films. Produced by Eric Drilling, Steven Schlueter, Avram Ludwig. Directed, written by Drilling, based on his play. Camera, Steven Schlueter; editor, Paul Streicher; music, Johnny Hickman; production design, Roshelle Berliner; costume design, Cindy Evans. Reviewed at Sundance Film Festival, Jan. 20. Running tme: 104 mins.

**Tom Everett Scott (Dave Holden), David Moscow (Tom Holden), Cara Buono (Rachel), David Lowery (Billy), Denis O'Hare (Daniel Holden), Leo Burmester (Judge Harold Perkins).**

Social drama and American gothic meet at the junction of *River Red*. And while there's no reason these two dramatic elements shouldn't flow, filmmaker Eric Drilling lacks the experience and focus to make the strands of his knotted yarn mesh. The absence of a compelling narrative in this dour piece limits its commercial prospects, making more than token theatrical distribution unlikely. Set in rural New England, pic wastes no time in establishing a history of abuse and alcoholism in a single-parent family. In a misguided act, David Holden fatally stabs his father in order to protect his brother Tom from ongoing physical harm.

## Ronin

An MGM release of a United Artists presentation of an FGM Entertainment production. Produced by Frank Mancuso, Jr. Directed by John Frankenheimer. Screenplay, J.D. Zeik, Richard Weisz, story by Zeik. Camera, Robert Fraisse; editor, Tony Gibbs; music, Elia Cmiral; production design, Michael Z. Hanan; costume designer, May Routh; car-stunt coordinator, Jean-Claude Lagniez; car-stunt technical coordinator, Patrick Ronchin. Reviewed at MGM, Santa Monica, Aug. 27. MPAA Rating: R. Running time: 118 mins.

**Robert De Niro (Sam), Jean Reno (Vincent), Natascha McElhone (Deirdre), Stellan Skarsgard (Gregor), Sean Bean (Spence), Skipp Sudduth (Larry), Michael Lonsdale (Jean-Pierre), Jonathan Pryce (Seamus), Feodor Atkine (Mikhi), Katarina Witt (Natacha Kirilova), Bernard Bloch (Sergi).**

*Ronin* reps a pleasurable throwback to the sort of gritty, low-tech international thriller that was a staple of the 1960s. Even though the characters are virtual cut-outs and the story is ultimately without meaning or resonance, film offers enough potent action, intriguing shifting loyalties, and scenic French locations to hold the interest; all the picture lacks is a world-weary, existential ennui. MGM should reap decent returns in a relatively open field for actioners in late September, while significantly better coin lies in wait overseas.

Beginning on a shadowy Montmartre street as the scruffy Sam arrives for an appointment at a seedy bar, plot snaps to attention as Irish ringleader Deirdre presides over a planning meeting for an ambush at which the ad hoc group will attempt to retrieve a mysterious briefcase from some criminals. Working strictly for the money without knowing who is hiring them or the targets, the gang consists of the usual cross-section of specialists: American strategist Sam, French coordinator Vincent, German electronics/surveillance whiz Gregor, and British military vet and weapons adviser Spence.

U.S. release: Sept. 25      U.S. B.O.: $41 million
Int'l release: Nov. 13      Int'l B.O.: $27 million

---

### ... July 26 ...

The demise of U.K. theatrical distributor First Independent Films looks set to spark a bidding war for British rights to the company's one leftover pic, hot Irish comedy **Waking Ned**.

## The Rooster (Gallo Cedrone) (Italy)

A Cecchi Gori Distribuzione release of a Mario and Vittorio Cecchi Gori presentation of a Cecchi Gori Group Tiger Cinematografica production. Produced by Vittorio and Rita Cecchi Gori. Directed by Carlo Verdone. Screenplay, Verdone, Leo Benvenuti, Piero De Bernardi, Pasquale Plastino. Camera, Danilo Desideri; editor, Antonio Siciliano; music, Fabio Liberatori; art director, Maurizio Marchitelli; costume design, Tatiana Romanoff. Reviewed at Roma Cinema, Rome, Oct. 9. Running time: 94 mins.

**Carlo Verdone (Armando Feroci), Regina Orioli (Martina), Paolo Triestino (Franco Feroci), Ines Nobili (Marcella Feroci), Enrica Rosso (Egle), Giorgia Brugnoli (Morena Feroci).**

With a nod to veterans like Vittorio Gassman and Alberto Sordi, actor-director Carlo Verdone struts his stuff as a vain, skirt-chasing vulgarian in *The Rooster*. While the Roman comedy king is no more attentive than usual to the construction of anything too complex outside his own character, this remains a sturdy showcase for his well-oiled shtick and promises to be one of the major homegrown commercial performers of Italy's fall season.

Verdone's knack for affectionately pinpointing often-unattractive Italian foibles has endeared him to domestic audiences but limits his films to primarily local consumption. Opening in an Arab country where Armando Feroci has been condemned to death by Islamic fundamentalists, the story backtracks to recap 17 years of his life, as news of the sentence ricochets among his friends, relatives, and acquaintances in Italy. An inveterate curb-crawler, he routinely accosts women with lewd suggestions from his red convertible and eventually oversteps the line by cruising a veiled Arab woman in the desert while driving a Red Cross missionary jeep. These scenes of gross political incorrectness provide some of the biggest laughs.

Int'l release: Oct. 9          Int'l B.O.: $13.5 million

## The Rose Seller (La Vendedora De Rosas)
(Colombia)

A Producciones Filmamento production. Produced by Erwin Goggel. Directed by Victor Gaviria. Screenplay, Gaviria, Carlos Henao, Diana Ospina. Camera, Rodrigo Lalinde; editor, Agustin Pinto; music, Luis F. Franco; art director, Ricardo Duque; costume designer, Karina Blumencwejg. Reviewed at Cannes Festival, May 13. Running time: 116 mins.

**With: Leidy Tabares (Monica), Marta Correa, Mileider Gil, Diana Murillo, Liliana Giraldo, Yuli Garcia, Alex Bedoya.**

Director Victor Gaviria transports the Hans Christian Andersen tale *The Little Match Girl* to the bruising streets of Colombia in *The Rose Seller*. A shapeless slice of neo-realist drama dealing with a band of runaway urchins in a tough world of drugs, theft, violence, and precocious sexuality, the film musters some potency, but is far too rambling and unfocused in getting there. Lacking the narrative muscle of other Latin American street-kid sagas like *Pixote*, it looks unlikely to bloom commercially beyond fest trail. Gaviria substitutes flowers for matches in his dreamy reworking of the melancholy fable, centering the drama on 13-year-old Monica (Leidy Tabares) – one of a group of kids from poor families, she sells roses in local nightspots. She hangs out with other waifs and, with her faithless dealer boyfriend, smokes grass, sniffs glue, and hallucinates about her dead grandmother.

Int'l release: Aug. 13          Int'l B.O.: $1.1 million

## Rosie (Belgium)

A Prime Time production. Produced by Antonino Lombardo. Directed, written by Patrice Toye. Camera, Richard von Oosterhout; editor, Ludo Trouch; music, John Parish; art director, Johan van Essche. Reviewed at Toronto Festival, Sept. 12. Running time: 97 mins.

**Aranka Coppens (Rose), Sara de Roo (Irene), Frank Vercruyssen (Michel), Dirk Roofthooft (Bernard), Joost Wijnant (Jimi).**

Belgian-produced *Rosie* is a scrupulously unsentimental case study of a 13-year-old who, tired of home-front lies and confrontations, takes refuge in her own fantasy world. Her story, the most incisive look at adolescent angst since Peter Jackson's *Heavenly Creatures*, looks to be a shoo-in on fest and arthouse circuits.

Pic opens with Rosie being packed off to reform school for having committed unspeakable acts. She's unrepentant. As Rosie adjusts to her new surroundings, we flash back to the events that culminated in her present predicament. Her problems stem from basic rejection. She never knew her father, and her mother, not wanting to scare off possible suitors, passes Rosie off as her kid sister. The adults in Rosie's life are self-involved; they don't look up when she comes home scraped and bloody after being knocked down by a car. What's a girl to do but panhandle, shoplift, and go joy-riding? Two things set this film apart from the usual run of alienated-teen pics: Coppens' tempered turn as love-starved outsider and Toye's refusal to play favorites in the brewing generational conflict.

Int'l release: Oct. 21          Int'l B.O.: $200,000

## Rounders

A Miramax release of a Spanky Pictures production. Produced by Joel Stillerman, Ted Demme. Directed by John Dahl. Screenplay, David Levien, Brian Koppelman. Camera, Jean Yves Escoffier; editor, Scott Chestnut; music, Christopher Young; production design, Rob Pearson; costume design, Terry Dresbach. Reviewed at Cineplex Showcase, L.A., Aug. 25. MPAA Rating: R. Running time: 120 mins.

**Matt Damon (Mike McDermott), Edward Norton (Worm), John Turturro (Joey Knish), Gretchen Mol (Jo), Famke Janssen (Petra), John Malkovich (Teddy KGB), Martin Landau (Abe Petrovsky), Michael Rispoli (Grama).**

*Rounders* wins a few hands but doesn't walk off with the pot. Intermittently engaging but dramatically slack, this tale of a law student's discovery of his true calling as a world-class poker player is more interesting around the edges than it is at its core, thanks to the dull nature of the lead character played by Matt Damon. After festival launches in Montreal and Venice, Miramax should expect some reasonable short-term winnings here rather than a big haul.

Confident college boy Mike McDermott loses his life savings by pushing his luck in a game against a crafty Russian hood, Teddy KGB. Nine months later, Mike is hitting his law books, having renounced his cardsharping. But g.f. Jo's antennae are raised when Worm, Mike's wise-ass old friend, is released from jail. Worm immediately steers Mike in the direction of the nearest easy-mark card game. Being reminded of the thrill of winning at the tables makes him feel revived and his admission of this is sufficiently insulting to Jo that she walks out.

U.S. release: Sept. 11          U.S. B.O.: $23 million
Int'l release: Nov. 19          Int'l B.O.: $2 million

---

### ...July 27...
**Touched by an Angel** star Della Reese settles her feud with CBS over salary.

## Rudolph The Red-Nosed Reindeer: The Movie
(Animated)
A Legacy release of a Goodtimes Entertainment presentation of a Cayre Brothers/Tundra production. Produced, directed by Bill Kowalchuk. Screenplay, Michael Aschner; Rudolph the Red-Nosed Reindeer story by Robert L. May, song by Johnny Marks. Editor, Tom Hok; music and lyrics, score by Michael Lloyd, Al Kasha; character design, Phil Mendez. Reviewed on videocassette, L.A., Oct. 15. MPAA Rating: G. Running time: 83 mins.
**Voices: John Goodman (Santa Claus), Eric Idle (Slyly the Fox), Bob Newhart (Leonard the Polar Bear), Debbie Reynolds (Mrs. Claus), Richard Simmons (Boone), Whoopi Goldberg (Stormella), Eric Pospisil (Young Rudolph), Kathleen Barr (Adult Rudolph).**
As bland as the lowest-end Saturday morning TV cartoons, this first animated version of the popular 60-year-old Christmas story about a reindeer who's "different" will be palatable only to the very youngest of viewers. Boringly executed in all departments, this holiday-themed musical opened two holiday seasons early, presumably to take advantage of booking opportunities, and the number of parents who choose to give their kids an advance taste of Christmas cheer in October will assuredly be very limited. Prospects are brighter for video release, which will take place in mid-November.

Taking its cues directly from the perennial song, Michael Aschner's script marginally fleshes out and dramatizes Rudolph's sense of social ostracism and adds some young love, but lacks any sense of surprise or inventiveness; this, combined with the lack of any captivating qualities in the animation or music, makes for a very humdrum experience even by kidpic standards.
U.S. release: Oct. 16          U.S. B.O.: $100,000

## The Rugrats Movie (Animated)
A Paramount release of a Nickelodeon Movies presentation of a Klasky/Csupo production. Produced by Arlene Klasky, Gabor Csupo. Directed by Norton Virgien, Igor Kovalyov. Screenplay, David N. Weiss, J. David Stem. Supervising editor, John Bryant; music, Mark Mothersbaugh, Jamshied Sharifi; art director, Dima Malanitchev. Reviewed at Paramount Studios, L.A., Nov. 7. MPAA rating: G. Running time: 79 mins.
**Voices: E.G. Daily (Tommy Pickles), Christine Cavanaugh (Chuckie Finster), Kath Soucie (Phil/Lil De Ville), Cheryl Case (Angelica Pickles), Tara Charendoff (Dil Pickles), Melanie Chartoff (Didi Pickles), Jack Riley (Stu Pickles), Joe Alaskey (Grandpa Pickles), Phil Proctor (Howard De Ville), Whoopi Goldberg (Ranger Margaret), David Spade (Ranger Frank).**
Aimed squarely at moppets with minuscule attention spans, *The Rugrats Movie* is a fast and frenetic animated feature that should delight young aficionados of the long-running Nickelodeon TV series. Trouble is, pic lacks the cross-generational appeal of recent Disney-produced B.O. blockbusters and may be ill-equipped to compete for long against other family-oriented holiday releases. However, after a respectable but likely unspectacular theatrical run, *Rugrats* will rake in the jack as a priced-for-purchase video release.

*The Rugrats* focuses on the misadventures of precocious toddlers, ranging in age from 1 to 3, in a suburban neighborhood. Tommy, the unofficial leader of the group, is a plucky little fellow who appears perfectly cast in the opening fantasy sequence as "Okie-Dokie Jones," the whip-cracking raider of a lost ark. When playtime is over, however, Tommy must face the real-life challenge of coping with a new baby brother, Dil.

As he finds himself vying with the ever-wailing Dil for his parents' attention, Tommy is consoled by the timorous Chuckie (his best friend), twins Phil and Lil, and Angelica. Complications ensue when Tommy, his friends, and his baby brother take a spin in his inventor-father's latest contraption, the Reptar Wagon, "the ultimate in toddler transportation." Unfortunately, the wagon transports the toddlers all the way to a forest far from the neighborhood.
U.S. release: Nov. 20          U.S. B.O.: $86 million

## Run Lola Run (Lola Rennt) (Germany)
A Prokino release of a Bavaria Film Int'l/German Independents presentation of an X Film Creative Pool production, with the support of Filmstiftung NRW, FFA Filmboard Berlin-Brandenburg, FFF Bayern, BMI, and with the participation of WDR, Arte. Produced by Stefan Arndt. Directed, written by Tom Tykwer; editor, Mathilde Bonnefoy; music, Tykwer, Johnny Klimek, Reinhold Heil; production design, Alexander Manasse; costume design, Monika Jacobs; animation sequences, Gil Alkabetz. Reviewed at Venice Festival, Sept. 3. Running time: 81 mins.
**Franka Potente (Lola), Moritz Bleibtreu (Manni), Herbert Knaup (Lola's Father), Armin Rohde (Mr. Schuster), Joachim Krol (Norbert von Au), Nina Petri (Jutta Hansen), Heino Ferch (Ronnie).**
Cleverly juggling the elements and encounters of a simple thriller scenario by using multiple viewpoints and a domino effect to create different destinies, *Run Lola Run* is a breathless race against the clock. After earning festival plaudits with early features, German filmmaker Tom Tykwer looks to make a wider impact with this highly accomplished, compact feature, which, while it may be light on depth, is rich in humor, rhythm, energy, and inventiveness.

With unfaltering confidence, Tykwer makes the mix of aggressively hip, music video language, character development, and dramatic complexity work in his ambitious picture. He trowels on with split screen, fast and slow motion, rapid montage, jump cuts, whip pans, still photographs, animation, and shifts among color, B&W, and video. Even with all this almost show-offy virtuosity, the characters are nuanced and involving, and the drama cranks up plenty of urgency.

Tykwer concocts three "what if?" variations on the same story. Lola receives a call from her panicked lover, Manni, an errand boy for a local criminal. He's bungled a money drop, leaving the bag on the subway in his haste to avoid ticket inspectors. He now has 20 minutes to come up with 100,000 deutsche marks or face the dire consequences. The call sends Lola flying downstairs and into the Berlin streets. She heads for the bank run by her unsympathetic father to lean on him for the cash, but interrupts a confrontation with his pregnant mistress, coming away rejected and empty-handed. Rendezvousing with Manni, she finds him midway through a supermarket holdup and steps in to save his skin . What should be the tragic final act becomes merely a junction from which the story starts again, each time taking a new tangent and leading to another outcome.
Int'l release: Sept. 24          Int'l B.O.: $15 million

---

**... July 28 ...**
CBS buys **The Mask of Zorro** rights for $30 million.

## Rush Hour

A New Line Cinema release of an Arthur Sarkissian and Roger Birnbaum production. Produced by Birnbaum, Sarkissian, Jonathan Glickman. Directed by Brett Ratner. Screenplay, Jim Kouf, Ross Lamanna, story by Lamanna. Camera, Adam Greenberg; editor, Mark Helfrich; music, Lalo Schifrin; production design, Robb Wilson King; costume design, Sharen Davis; stunt coordinators, Terry Leonard, Jackie Chan; casting, Matt Barry. Reviewed at Magno Review, New York, Aug. 28. MPAA Rating: PG-13. Running time: 98 mins.
Jackie Chan (Det. Insp. Lee), Chris Tucker (Det. James Carter), Tom Wilkinson (Thomas Griffin), Elizabeth Pena (Tania Johnson), Philip Baker Hall (Capt. Diel), Mark Rolston (Agent Russ), Tzi Ma (Consul Han); Ken Leung (Sang).

Jackie Chan is poised to score his biggest American hit with *Rush Hour*, a frankly formulaic but raucously entertaining action comedy that comes equipped with the additional hook of up-and-comer Chris Tucker. Cast as an odd couple of cops who join forces to find a Chinese consul's kidnapped daughter, the two leads should be laughing all the way to the bank when the grosses start rolling in. Foreign release likely will generate even more impressive coin, and homevid income will sweeten the pot.

Pic represents a savvy career move for Chan. This time out, he gets a chance to broaden his appeal beyond his loyal cult simply by doing what he does best. Tucker's manic, motor-mouth style of comedy is an effective counterbalance to Chan's rapid-fire acrobatics.

Carter yearns to join the FBI, and thinks he's gotten a big break when his disapproving chief assigns him to the bureau for a major case. But the feds simply want Carter to "baby-sit" Lee, who has flown to L.A. to help his old friend the Chinese consul recover his abducted 11-year-old daughter. The FBI agents in charge view Lee as little more than a nuisance, and expect Carter to keep the Hong Kong detective far out of harm's way. Not surprisingly, Lee and Carter are the ones who identify, and ultimately neutralize, the villains.

| | |
|---|---|
| U.S. release: Sept. 18 | U.S. B.O.: $136 million |
| Int'l release: Sept. 24 | Int'l B.O.: $25.5 million |

## Rushmore

A Buena Vista release of a Touchstone Pictures presentation of an American Empirical production. Produced by Barry Mendel, Paul Schiff. Directed by Wes Anderson. Screenplay, Anderson, Owen Wilson. Camera, Robert Yeoman; editor, David Moritz; music, Mark Mothersbaugh; production design, David Wasco. Reviewed at Telluride Festival, Sept. 6. MPAA Rating: R. Running time: 89 mins.
Jason Schwartzman (Max Fischer), Bill Murray (Herman Blume), Olivia Williams (Rose Cross), Seymour Cassel (Bert Fischer), Brian Cox (Dr. Guggenheim), Mason Gamble (Dirk Calloway), Sara Tanaka (Margaret Yang), Stephen McCole (Magnus Buchan).

A wickedly funny high-school comedy, *Rushmore* is a bracingly fresh and original sophomore outing from the director and writers of the critical fave *Bottle Rocket*. This tart tale of an audaciously clever prep-school kid going over the edge because of an infatuation with a beautiful teacher has all the makings of a cult hit. All the same, its somewhat brainy humor and serious take on the implications of its characters' malicious activities set it apart from standard-issue teen comedies, and special effort will be needed to position the picture properly in order for it to find a potentially substantial audience when it opens in February 1999.

Max Fisher is one of the worst students at Rushmore Academy, a leafy private school. Unable to apply himself scholastically, Max throws himself into extracurricular activities, inventing new clubs, teams, and groups to head. The precocious 15-year-old considers himself the equal of any adult, and distinguishes himself as a dramatist by putting on a brutal David Mamet-like play. Max becomes infatuated with English widow Rose Cross, who teaches at the school. His inability to bed her via charm, brains or cunning leads to his descent into despair and vengeful behavior. Max's rival, it turns out, is a local industrial tycoon, Herman Blume, one of the few adults to recognize Max's special gifts. Blume invests in one of Max's more harebrained schemes, the construction of an aquarium on the school's baseball field.

| | |
|---|---|
| U.S. release: Dec. 11 | U.S. B.O.: $80,000 |

## Sada (Japan)

A Shochiku Co. release and production, in cooperation with PSC. Produced by Kyoko Obayashi. Directed, edited by Nobuhiko Obayashi. Screenplay, Yuko Nishizawa. Camera, Noritaka Sakamoto; editor, Obayashi; music, Sotaro Manabi; production design, Koichi Takeguchi; costume design, Chieko Okano. Reviewed at Berlin Festival, Feb. 21. Running time: 132 mins.
Hitomi Kuroki (Sada Abe), Tsurutaro Kataoka (Tatsuzo Kikumto), Norihei Miki (Takuzo), Kippei Shena (Masaru Okada), Negishi Toshie (Yoshi Kikumoto), Bengal (Sanosuke Tachibana), Kyusaka Shimada (Takiguchi).

The celebrated case of Sada Abe, who in 1936 became an overnight celebrity in Japan after strangling her lover and slicing off his penis, was memorably filmed in 1976 by Nagisa Oshima as *In the Realm of the Senses*. That film is still unique in movie history for its graphic and frank sexual depictions. In contrast, Nobuhiko Obayashi's stylish new film is discretion itself as it explores the background of the notorious case. Likely to split reviewers, pic made a good start when it copped the international film critics (Fipresci) prize at the Berlin film fest. Obayashi's intention here seems to be not only to present a rounded portrait of the film's tragic protagonist, but also to pay tribute to various film genres of the past. Bursting with invention and trickery, the film constantly calls attention to itself and, at the same time, distances the audience. Sada's life is sketched in broad brush strokes. She was born in 1905 into a poor household, and at 14 was violently raped. Not long afterward, Sada is forced into prostitution. Over the years, she has hundreds of customers until, at the age of 29, she's taken up by the kindly Tachibana, a member of the Nagoya City Council, and becomes his mistress.

| | |
|---|---|
| Int'l release: April 11 | Int'l B.O.: $700,000 |

## Safe Men

An Andell Entertainment production, in association with Blue Guitar Films. Produced by Andrew Hauptman, Ellen Bonfman, Jeffrey Clifford, Jonathan Cohen. Directed, written by John Hamburg. Camera, Michael Barrett; editor, Suzanne Pillsbury; music, Theodore Shapiro; production design, Anthony Gasparro; costume design, Cat Thomas. Reviewed at Sundance Festival, Jan. 18. Running time: 94 mins.
Sam Rockwell (Sam), Steve Zahn (Eddie), Paul Giamatti (Veal Chop), Michael Schmidt (Bernie, Jr.), Michael Lerner (Big Fat Bernie Gayle), Harvey Fierstein (Leo).

---

**... July 29 ...**
Director-choreographer Jerome Robbins, 79, taps out after **Gypsy, Fiddler on the Roof,** and **West Side Story** to name a few... Walter Cronkite will cover John Glenn's return into space.

Technically raw and narratively bumpy, *Safe Men* is a high-concept comedy that has all the merits and weaknesses of low-budget indie filmmaking. Intermittently funny pic is distinguished by its colorful cast, but it's doubtful that a major distributor will pick up on a spotty, not-quite-ready movie.

Premise of John Hamburg's debut feature is not bad: set in Providence, R.I., Sam and Eddie are two untalented singers who, when mistaken for safecrackers, are pulled into a netherworld of crime – in this case, the Jewish Mafia. The city's underworld appears to be dominated by two men, Big Fat Bernie Gayle and rival Good Stuff Leo.

U.S. release: Aug. 7                    U.S. B.O.: $40,000

### The Saltmen of Tibet (Die Salzmanner Von Tibet) (Switzerland-Germany, Docu)

A Catpics Coprods (Switzerland)/Duran Film (Germany) production. Produced by Alfi Sinniger. Directed, written by Ulrike Koch. Camera, Pio Corradi; editor, Magdolna Rokob; music, Stefan and Frank Wulff. Reviewed at Vienna Festival, Oct. 24, 1997. Running time: 108 mins.

Filmer Ulrike Koch and a skeleton crew smuggled camera gear into Tibet to document four men and 160 yak on their annual spring pilgrimage to remote lakes where they gather raw salt, continuing an imperiled ritual that goes back more than 2,000 years. This leisurely yet riveting look at the majestic vistas and tradition-bound people of a still-isolated and increasingly threatened enclave is a haunting, ethno-graphic study. Via song, prayer, conversation, and concerted trekking, viewers share in the humor and faith of a hard-working yet easygoing population following nomadic tradition on the "roof of the world." Once they reach their destination, the men mold moist salt into little pointed mounds with special shovels, patiently shaping the salt mounds until they look like a sea of miniature glaciers.

U.S. release: July 22                   U.S. B.O.: $170,000
Int'l release: Oct. 2, 1997            Int'l B.O.: $150,000

### Same Old Song (On Connaît La Chanson)

(France-Switzerland-U.K.)

An AMLF release of an Arena Films, Camera One, France 2 Cinema (France)/Vega Film (Switzerland)/Greenpoint Films (U.K.) production. Produced by Bruno Pesery. Directed by Alain Resnais. Screenplay, Agnes Jaoui, Jean-Pierre Bacri. Camera, Renato Berta; editor, Herve de Luze; music, Bruno Fontaine; art direction, Jacques Saulnier; costume design, Jackie Budin; post-synch engineer, Jacques Levy. Reviewed at Club Gaumont, Paris, Oct. 10, 1997. Running time: 122 mins.

Pierre Arditi (Claude), Sabine Azema (Odile Lalande), Jean-Pierre Bacri (Nicolas), Andre Dussollier (Simon), Agnes Jaoui (Camille Lalande), Lambert Wilson (Marc Duveyrier).

Audacious, delightful, and just about perfect from first note to last, Alain Resnais' *Same Old Song* presents a familiar tune in a clever new arrangement. A sly, urban melodrama full of amusing twists and turns, pic plugs snippets of lip-synched popular songs into the mouths of its dissimulating and prevaricating characters. The device is a great conveyor of both pathos and yocks. There's little doubt that *Same Old Song* will do dynamite business at Gallic wickets where locals will fall for its hooks, lines, and synchers. However, devoted and ingenious handling is essential if pic is to score offshore.

While finishing her history dissertation, Camille gives lecture tours of Paris. Nicolas, a businessman, is back in Paris

after eight years. He and Camille's sister, Odile, were an item but now he's married with kids, and Odile is hitched to the callow Claude. Simon, a regular at Camille's tours, says he's doing research for historical radio dramas. Odile is thinking of buying a lavish penthouse apartment brokered by suave real estate agent Marc. Marc and Camille embark on an affair, while Simon pines for her from afar. Into this basic network of six characters float obstacles, misunderstandings, petty and not-so-petty betrayals, and a consistently entertaining range of star-crossed, often ironic, developments.

Pic was written by Agnes Jaoui and Jean-Pierre Bacri, the prolific writer-performers who adapted Alan Ayckbourn's 16-part legit play *Intimate Exchanges* into Resnais' 1993 *Smoking/No Smoking*, which swept the French Cesars.

Int'l release: Nov. 12, 1997           Int'l B.O.: $19.8 million
U.S. release: March 27                 U.S. B.O.: $135,000

### Saving Private Ryan

A DreamWorks Pictures/Paramount release of an Amblin Entertainment production, in association with Mutual Film Co. Produced by Steven Spielberg, Ian Bryce, Mark Gordon, Gary Levinsohn. Directed by Spielberg. Screenplay, Robert Rodat. Camera, Janusz Kaminski; editor, Michael Kahn; music, John Williams; production designer, Tom Sanders; costume designer, Joanna Johnston; special-effects supervisor, Neil Corbould; stunt coordinator, Simon Crane; military adviser, Capt. Dale Dye. Reviewed at Harmony Gold, L.A., July 1. MPAA Rating: R. Running time: 169 mins.

Tom Hanks (Capt. John Miller), Edward Burns (Pvt. Reiben), Tom Sizemore (Sgt. Horvath), Jeremy Davies (Cpl. Upham), Vin Diesel (Pvt. Caparzo), Adam Goldberg (Pvt. Mellish), Barry Pepper (Pvt. Jackson), Giovanni Ribisi (T/4 Medic Wade), Matt Damon (Pvt. James Ryan), Dennis Farina (Lt. Col. Anderson), Ted Danson (Capt. Hamill), Harve Presnell (Gen. George Marshall), Paul Giamatti (Sgt. Hill).

*Saving Private Ryan* relates the kind of wartime stories that fathers never tell their families. A searingly visceral combat picture, Steven Spielberg's World War II drama is arguably second to none as a vivid, realistic, and bloody portrait of armed conflict. Grim, sometimes moving, and just occasionally windy film is unusually demanding and serious for a mainstream midsummer attraction, as well as a questionable bet for some women and more conventional thrill-seeking teens. Backed by strong reviews, DreamWorks' gamble could just as easily pay off handsomely as a shrewd piece of counter-programming as it could land in a commercial middle ground.

Plunging the viewer headlong into battle, Spielberg wrenchingly presents combat from the grunts' p.o.v. as it is fought inch by inch in all its arbitrariness and surreality. No sooner have Capt. Miller and his men paused for a smoke than they are ordered to try to locate a James Ryan, who parachuted into France the night before. The reason: His three brothers have all recently been killed in combat, and the war dept. has taken a benevolent interest in the family's situation. The story itself is somewhat irksome in its far-fetched, even contrived nature, but the film packs a heavy emotional punch at many moments, as the tenuousness of life and the abruptness of loss assert themselves. Spielberg has made an amazing piece of pure, visceral cinema, akin to a great silent film, in which the words are basically superfluous.

U.S. release: July 24                   U.S. B.O.: 191 million
Int'l release: Sept. 11                 Int'l B.O.: $235 million

---

## Savior

A First Independent release of an Initial Entertainment Group presentation of an Oliver Stone production. Produced by Oliver Stone, Janet Yang. Directed by Peter Antonijevic. Screenplay, Robert Orr. Camera, Ian Wilson; editors, Ian Crafford, Gabriella Cristiani; music, David Robbins; production design, Vladislav Lasic; costume design, Boris Caksiran. Reviewed at Virgin Haymarket, London, June 20. MPAA Rating: R. Running time: 103 mins.
**Dennis Quaid (Josh Rose/Guy), Nastassja Kinski (Maria), Stellan Skarsgard (Peter), Natasa Ninkovic (Vera), Sergej Trifunovic (Goran), Nebojsa Glogovac (Vera's Brother).**
(English and Serbian dialog)
*Savior* is a chamber-size but often extremely powerful war drama about a mercenary who exorcises his personal demons by rescuing a baby from the war in Bosnia. Grim but engrossing pic – the first 100% U.S.-funded movie to touch on the Yugoslav conflict – has little going for it commercially but is an impressive addition to the war-as-existential-battlefield genre.

The power of *Savior* comes from the almost offhand way in which sectarian violence and hatred are portrayed. In 1993, Joshua, a former U.S. military official turned mercenary, is in Bosnia, fighting on the Serbian side alongside his buddy Peter. When his friend is killed by a young girl with a hand grenade, he hardly thinks twice about shooting. Joshua accompanies Goran, a Muslim-hating Serb, to an exchange of prisoners where they receive Vera, a pregnant Serbian woman who's been raped by Muslim captors. Goran accuses her of sleeping with the enemy.

When Vera goes into labor, he threatens to shoot the baby when it pops out. Vera rejects the kid, and her family reject her, forcing Joshua to drive mother and squealing child to a refugee center. First they are hunted by her father and brother; later, when Joshua decides to smuggle Vera and the baby out of the country, they run into a marauding Croatian killing squad.

| | |
|---|---|
| U.S. release: Nov. 20 | U.S. B.O.: $30,000 |
| Int'l release: May 15 | Int'l B.O.: $150,000 |

## The School of Flesh (L'École De La Chair)

(France)
A Pyramide Films release of a Fabienne Vonier presentation of a co-production by Orsans Productions/V.M.P./La SEPT Cinema/Bel Age Distribution/Samsa Film. Produced by Vonier. Directed by Benoît Jacquot. Screenplay, Jacques Fieschi, based on the novel by Yukio Mishima. Camera, Caroline Champetier; editor, Luc Barnier; production design, Katia Wyszkop; costume design, Corinne Jorry-Horlait. Reviewed at the Cannes Festival, May 21. Running Time: 102 mins.
**Isabelle Huppert (Dominique), Vincent Martinez (Quentin), Vincent Lindon (Chris), Marthe Keller (Laurence Thorpe), François Berleand (Soukaz), Daniele Dubroux (Daniele), Bernard Le Coq (David Cordier).**
Dominique is a career woman out on the town when she spots Quentin working behind the bar at a quiet night spot. Though she feigns disinterest, it's obvious that a lot of eye contact is being exchanged.

French filmmaker Benoît Jacquot turns his attention to un amour fou in his latest film, *The School of Flesh*. An elegant rumination on the attraction and chemistry between an older woman and younger man, the film is a skillful blend of fire and ice that subtly conveys the emotional extremes fraught in the

relationship. Decidedly for adult auds, the pic has definite specialized appeal outside France and should broaden the director's commercial rep and prestige.

| | |
|---|---|
| Int'l release: Nov. 18 | Int'l B.O.: $800,000 |
| U.S. release: Nov. 6 | U.S. B.O.: $50,000 |

## Scotch and Milk

Produced by Robert Bauer, Francesca Silvestri. Co-producer, Adrienne Gruben. Directed, written by Adam Goldberg. Additional dialog by the cast. Camera, Mark Putnam; editors, Annette Davey, Goldberg, Max Heller; music supervisor, Andrew Leary; production designer, Jeffrey Texas Schell; costume designer, Carol Katt. Reviewed at L.A. Independent Festival, April 19. Running time: 117 mins.
**Adam Goldberg (Jim), Nicky Katt (Ray), Clea Lewis (Ilsa), Giovanni Ribisi (Marty), Cole Hauser (Johnny), Rio Hackford (Stanley), Hubert Selby Jr. (Cubby), Robert Pastorelli (The Skipper).**
A film drenched in booze, cigarettes, jazz, and noir, *Scotch and Milk* reps an exceedingly elegant wallow in a lifestyle almost entirely defined by romantic notions of 1950s hipsterdom. Slight of story and bearing signs of having been motivated by therapeutic reasons as much as artistic ones, debut feature by writer-director-star Adam Goldberg nonetheless boasts a strong professional patina crowned by Mark Putnam's outstanding B&W lensing. Commercial prospects for this obviously personal project are extremely limited, but pic should serve as a good calling card for the talents of a number of its participants.

Jim is a would-be swinger type in his late twenties who, while suffering from lost-love distress and vainly trying to write, lives a brooding bachelor life in a seedy downtown L.A. apartment. Although the streets are atmospherically empty, Jim does have a number of like-minded buddies; qualifications for membership are chain smoking, the ability to drink round the clock, and lack of regular employment or relationships.

## Scream 2

A Miramax release of a Dimension Films presentation, in association with Craven/Maddalena Films, of a Konrad Pictures production. Produced by Cathy Konrad, Marianne Maddalena. Directed by Wes Craven. Screenplay, Kevin Williamson, based on characters created by Williamson. Camera, Peter Deming; editor, Patrick Lussier; music, Marco Beltrami; production design, Bob Ziembicki; costume design, Kathleen Detoro; special makeup effects, Kamar Bitar. Reviewed at Culver Studios, Culver City, Dec. 2, 1997. MPAA Rating: R. Running time: 120 mins.
**David Arquette (Dewey Riley), Neve Campbell (Sidney Prescott), Courteney Cox (Gale Weathers), Sarah Michelle Gellar (Cici Cooper), Jamie Kennedy (Randy Meeks), Laurie Metcalf (Debbie Salt), Elise Neal (Hallie), Jerry O'Connel (Derek), Liev Schreiber (Cotton Weary), David Warner (Gus Gold).**
There are certain tacit rules to be followed in making a sequel, notes a character in *Scream 2*. He cites a couple of the more banal truisms, but there's no question that the filmmakers – all veterans of the phenomenally successful original – have not only thought long and hard about stepping back into familiar territory but have been ultra-diligent about keeping the second outing on course. Visceral, witty, and appropriately redundant, the sequel has a winning commercial recipe that's certain to cook up excellent returns in all areas.

The continuation relocates to Windsor College in small-town Ohio. Sidney and Randy are attempting to escape the notoriety created by last year's tabloid-sensation murder and mayhem. A book on the incident by reporter Gale Weathers was a bestseller and has been adapted for the screen. The film-within-a-film provides a neat intro, deftly seguing into the continuing story. A young couple attending the premiere of the movie become the first victims of a copycat killer. Sidney is thrown back into the limelight, Gale is assigned the news story, and former deputy Dewey flies crosscountry to protect the imperiled young woman. The rest is an intrigue of finger-pointing and terror as the elusive masked killer is tracked.

U.S. release: Dec. 12, 1997    U.S. B.O.: $101.3 million
Int. release: Jan. 16    Int'l B.O.: $69 million

### Secret Defense (France-Switzerland-Italy)

A Pierre Grise Distribution release of a Pierre Grise Prods, La Sept Cinema (France)/T&C Film (Switzerland)/Alai Films (Italy) production, with the participation of Canal Plus. Produced by Martine Marignac, Maurice Tinchant. Directed by Jacques Rivette. Screenplay, Pascal Bonitzer, Emmanuelle Cuau, Rivette. Camera, William Lubitchansky; editor, Nicole Lubitchansky; music, Jordi Savall; art director, Manu de Chauvigny; costume designer, Anne Autran. Reviewed at Le Balzac, Paris, March 6. Running time: 173 mins.
**Sandrine Bonnaire (Sylvie), Jerzy Radziwilowicz (Walser), Laure Marsac (Veronique/Ludivine), Gregoire Colin (Paul), Françoise Fabian (Genevieve).**

In *Secret Defense* veteran helmer Jacques Rivette maintains a tricky, elongated rhythm that lovers of highbrow cinema will find perfectly enthralling. This two-tiered murder mystery, cloaked in family and business relationships more equivocal than loving, takes almost three hours to spill its guts. Precise direction keeps suspense taut as a complex skein of emotions, appearances, and delayed consequences plays out with methodical, frequently graceful strokes.

While working late at the lab, cancer researcher Sylvie catches her younger brother, Paul, stealing a gun she keeps in a drawer. A just-surfaced photo, taken on a railroad platform, has convinced Paul that their father didn't die accidentally. He plans to avenge the murder the old-fashioned way.

Int'l release: March 18    Int'l B.O.: $150,000

### Sekal Has To Die (Je Treba Zabit Sekala) (Czech Republic-Poland-Slovakia-France)

A Falcon release of a Buc-film production, in association with Czech Television, Apple Film Production, Pro Art Production Slovakia, CDP, Barrandov Biografia, Polish Television, Canal Plus Poland, Markiza TV. Produced by Jaroslav Boucek. Directed by Vladimir Michalek. Screenplay, Jiri Krizan. Camera, Martin Strba; editor, Jiri Brozek; music, Michal Lorenc; set design, Jiri Sternwald; costume design, Mona Hafsahl. Reviewed at Karlovy Vary Festival, July 3. Running time: 110 mins.
**Boguslaw Linda (Sekal), Olaf Lubaszenko (Jura Baran), Jiri Bartoska (Father Flora), Agnieszka Sitek (Anezka), Vlasta Chramostova (Marie), Milan Riehs (Mayor), Ludovit Cittel (Zaprdek), Anton Sulik (Vcelny), Jiri Holy (Old Oberva), Martin Sitta (Young Oberva).**

With a thoughtful script, elegiac lensing, a masterful music score, and a triumvirate of exquisite performances, this central European *High Noon* is a first-class wartime morality drama. But a slackening of tension in the drawn-out second half ultimately lets the viewer down, denying the tragic catharsis promised. Still, commercial prospects in home territories look solid, along with further theatrical pickup and classy tube sales.

Jura Baran is a Nazi resister already semi-numbed by defeat. He arrives in a small Czech village to hide out, armed with a letter of introduction to the mayor. The petty bureaucrat sets him up as a blacksmith. As a Lutheran in dogmatically Catholic territory, he soon crosses paths with Sekal, an amoral opportunist who gobbles up local farms by turning in the owners to the Nazis. Sekal is the most outwardly unsavory of the villagers, a sneer barely covering the explosive cocktail of emotions eating at him.

Scorned by his father, Sekal covets the respectability and family life of his younger half-brother. With the complicity of his only companion, the dwarf Zaprdek, Sekal makes good on his threats to the farmers. But when two farms don't ease his soul, Sekal demands the mayor's daughter as his bride. Enough is enough, and the farmers elect Baran to kill Sekal.

At Karlovy Vary, *Sekal Has To Die* took home two awards, including best actor for Polish actor Olaf Lubaszenko.

Int'l release: Sept. 3    Int'l B.O.: $100,000

### Senseless

A Dimension Films release of a Mandeville Films, Gold/Miller production. Produced by David Hoberman. Albert Beveridge. Directed by Penelope Spheeris. Screenplay, Greg Erb, Craig Mazin. Camera, Daryn Okada; editor, Ross Albert; music, Yello; production design, Peter Jamison; set decoration, Linda Spheeris; costume design, Betsy Cox; casting, Junie Lowry Johnson. Reviewed at Hollywood Galaxy, L.A., Feb. 3. MPAA Rating: R. Running time: 93 mins.
**Marlon Wayans (Darryl Witherspoon), David Spade (Scott Thorpe), Matthew Lillard (Tim LaFlour), Brad Dourif (Dr. Wheedon), Tamara Taylor (Janice), Rip Torn (Randall Tyson).**

*Senseless* takes dozens and dozens of shots on goal from every conceivable angle, but only racks up a handful of comic points. Apparently laboring under the impression that the harder he works, the funnier he'll be, Marlon Wayans seems to be trying to steal the crown of spaz comedy from Jim Carrey, but only manages to overstay his welcome. This over-strenuous tale about a young black man's quest for success in the whitebread world of university and corporate economics could score some quick change, but doesn't look at all leggy.

Bed-Stuy-bred college student Darryl Witherspoon is frantically but cheerfully balancing a number of menial and demeaning jobs on and off campus to pay the bills. He hopes to vault into the financial stratosphere by winning the annual junior analyst competition, which guarantees a big-money job with the snooty Smythe-Bates brokerage firm. But the odds seem stacked against him. For cash, he becomes the only guinea pig for an experimental drug being developed on campus that promises to heighten the senses by five times, and the effect of the potion is predictable.

U.S. release: Feb. 20    U.S. B.O.: $13 million

### Serial Lover (France)

A Rezo Films release of a Les Films de la Suane/Le Studio Canal Plus/France 2 Cinema/Captain Movies production. Produced by Philippe Rousselet. Directed by James Huth. Screenplay, Huth, Romain Berthomieu, Hugo Jacomet. Camera, Jean-Claude Thibaut; editor, Scott Stevenson; music, Bruno Coulais;

production designer, Pierre-Emmanuel Chatiliez. Reviewed at Planet Hollywood, Paris, April 8. Running time: 83 mins.
**Michele Laroque (Claire Doste), Albert Dupontel (Eric Cellier), Elise Tielrooy (Alice Doste), Michel Vuillermoz (Charles Thiriot), Zinedine Soualem (Prince Hakim), Antoine Basler (Sacha Peters), Gilles Privat (Ruitchi Di Chichi).**

With a deliberate nod to pulp novels and a level of invention that's cause for celebration, first-time helmer and co-scripter James Huth plays for laughs – and gets them – in *Serial Lover*. This twisted comedy, about a woman whose dinner party with her three favorite suitors backfires with sardonically jubilant results, is deeply stylish light entertainment that could have sleeper potential with the same international crowd that appreciated *Delicatessen*.

Claire, an editor at a publishing house, lives in a fab duplex done up in 1950s pastels. Anglophone dandy Sacha, upright physician Charles and easygoing Hakim all think they're arriving for a romantic tête-à-tête, only to learn that Claire, on the eve of her 35th birthday, wants to pick the man she'll marry.

| | |
|---|---|
| Int'l release: April 22 | Int'l B.O.: $900,000 |
| U.S. release: Nov. 20 | U.S. B.O.: $40,000 |

## Shadrach

A Millennium Films presentation, in association with Nu Image, of a Bridget Terry production. Produced by Terry, John Thompson, Boaz Davidson. Directed by Susanna Styron. Screenplay, Styron, Terry, based on the short story by William Styron. Camera, Hiro Narita; editor, Colleen Sharp; music, Van Dyke Parks; production designer, Burton Rencher; costume designer, Dona Granata. Reviewed at L.A. Independent Festival, April 17. Running time: 86 mins.
**Harvey Keitel (Vernon), Andie MacDowell (Trixie), John Franklin Sawyer (Shadrach), Scott Terra (Paul), Daniel Treat (Little Mole), Monica Bugajski (Edmonia).**

Susanna Styron, daughter of writer William Styron, makes an unexciting feature debut with *Shadrach*, an adaptation of her father's 1978 short story. Set in the South at the height of the Depression, tale centers on a large, poor family as they face a moral dilemma. Theatrical prospects are dim for a picture whose old-fashioned, earnest sensibility and level of execution are more suitable for the small screen.

Paul Whitehurst (voiced by Martin Sheen) reflects upon three momentous days in the summer of 1935 when, at the age of 10, he experienced some bizarre, unanticipated events that precipitated his coming of age. Shadrach, a 99-year-old former slave, appears out of the blue at the Dabney household with the request he be buried on the plantation where he was born into slavery. Shadrach presents it as a personal wish, but also as a moral right. However, it's a strict violation of Virginia law. Remainder of the saga details how Vernon overcomes his innate racism, harsh poverty, and discriminatory law to grant the final wish.

| | |
|---|---|
| U.S. release: Sept. 23 | U.S. B.O.: $110,000 |
| Int'l release: Sept. 11 | Int'l B.O.: $60,000 |

## Shakespeare in Love

A Miramax/Universal release of a Bedford Falls production. Produced by David Parfitt, Donna Gigliotti, Harvey Weinstein, Edward Zwick, Marc Norman. Directed by John Madden. Screenplay, Marc Norman, Tom Stoppard. Camera, Richard Greatrex; editor, David Gamble; music, Stephen Warbeck; production design, Martin Childs; costume design, Deborah

Scott; makeup/hair designer, Lisa Westcott. Reviewed at Music Hall, Beverly Hills, Dec. 3. MPAA rating: R. Running time: 122 mins.
**Joseph Fiennes (Will Shakespeare), Gwyneth Paltrow (Viola De Lesseps), Geoffrey Rush (Philip Henslowe), Judi Dench (Queen Elizabeth), Simon Callow (Tilney), Colin Firth (Lord Wessex), Imelda Staunton (Nurse), Ben Affleck (Ned Alleyn), Tom Wilkinson (Hugh Fennyman), Martin Clunes (Richard Burbage), Rupert Everett (Marlowe).**

With *Shakespeare in Love*, director John Madden does for adults what Baz Luhrmann did for teens in *Romeo and Juliet* – he makes Shakespeare accessible, entertaining, and fun. Exquisitely acted, tightly directed, and impressively assembled, this lively period piece is the kind of arty gem with potentially broad appeal. Nevertheless, it helps to know Shakespeare's work, a prerequisite that may limit its success.

While the film's storyline is labyrinthine, its premise is fairly simple: William Shakespeare has writer's block and needs a muse to unlock his creative abilities. When he falls for the lovely Viola De Lesseps, his passion is released, and his ineptly titled *Romeo and Ethel, the Pirate's Daughter* becomes *Romeo and Juliet*. In true Shakespearean fashion, their romance is hampered by various complications: Viola is betrothed to the insufferable Lord Wessex. A keen fan of drama and of Shakespeare in particular, Viola is determined to audition. Disguised as one Thomas Kent, she wins the part of Romeo. Later she appears as Viola, and the playwright is smitten. The confusion over sexual identity is expertly played out.

| | |
|---|---|
| U.S. release: Dec. 11 | U.S. B.O.: $6.5 million |

## Shattered Image

A Seven Arts Pictures/Schroeder Hoffman production, in association with Fireworks Entertainment. Produced by Barbet Schroeder, Susan Hoffman. Directed by Raul Ruiz. Screenplay, Duane Poole. Camera, Robbie Muller; editor, Michael Duthie; music, Jorge Arriagada; production design, Robert DeVico; costume design, Francine LeCoultre. Reviewed at World Film Festival Montreal, Aug. 28. Running time: 102 mins.
**Anne Parillaud (Jessie), William Baldwin (Brian), Lisanne Falk (Paula/Laura), Graham Greene (Conrad/Mike), Billy Wilmott (Lamond), O'Neil Peart (Simon), Leonie Forbes (Isabel), Bulle Ogier (Mrs. Ford).**

While *Shattered Image* marks the U.S. debut of prolific Euro-based helmer Raul Ruiz, the psychological suspenser is thoroughly consistent with his previous work. An intricately plotted tale of a hit woman trying to get a grip on reality, stylishly mounted pic belongs to the realm of art movies. Given the lack of any startling virtues to set it apart from the generic pack, it's more likely to score in situations, primarily European, where Ruiz is already a fave than to break new ground.

As the story opens, Jessie follows a businessman into the men's room at a chic restaurant and blows him to kingdom come. But her precision clearly masks some heavy problems. When she goes home and falls asleep, a different version of herself emerges. The second Jessie, softer and not as harshly made up, wakes up remembering the previous scene as a nightmare. She's bound for a Jamaican honeymoon with her new husband, Brian. When they arrive, the reasons for his extreme solicitude and her paranoid skittishness become apparent. She was the victim of a brutal rape and bears the wrist scars of a would-be suicide. When Jessie drifts off again, she's in Seattle, with no scars on her wrist as she plans another murder.

Casing an antiques store, she meets a man she recognizes from her dream and immediately has the hots for him. It's Brian.
U.S. release: Dec. 4                    U.S. B.O.: $80,000

### Shooting The Moon (L'Albero Delle Pere) (Italy)

An Istituto Luce release of a 3emme Cinematografica/Istituto Luce/RAI Cinemafiction production, in collaboration with Tele. Produced by Leo Pescarolo, Guido de Laurentiis. Directed, written by Francesca Archibugi. Camera, Luca Bigazzi; editor, Esmeralda Calabria; music, Battista Lena; production design, Mario Rossetti; costume design, Paola Marchesin. Reviewed at Venice Film Festival, Sept. 3. Running time: 90 mins.
**Valeria Golino (Silvia), Sergio Rubini (Massimo), Stefano Dionisi (Roberto), Niccolo Senni (Siddhartha), Francesca di Giovanni (Domitilla).**
*Shooting the Moon,* an unblinking examination of a young teenager forced to make adult decisions, is an accessible Italo film that should perform decently in Euro arthouses and has a shot at specialized distribution elsewhere. Set in Rome, pic homes in on a 14-year-old boy, Siddhartha. Apart from the burden of his name, he is saddled with a hopelessly unreliable mother and is forced to grow up fast. Mother Silvia is a heroin addict; Siddhartha's video-filmmaker father, Massimo, left years earlier. Since the marriage broke up, Silvia has had a relationship with a yuppie lawyer, Roberto, resulting in little Domitilla, now 4 years old.

The boy adores his little half-sister. He's faced with an agonizing decision when the little girl, rummaging through her mother's things, pricks herself on a used needle. Unwilling to seek help and advice from his father or from Roberto, he turns to the Internet for information. Siddhartha is advised to have the little girl tested for AIDS and various forms of hepatitis – not so easy to do if you're not an adult, as he soon discovers when faced with sympathetic but unhelpful medical bureaucrats.
Int'l release: Sept. 4              Int'l B.O.: $1.5 million

### Short Sharp Shock (Kurz Und Schmerzlos)

(Germany)
A Polygram Filmed Entertainment GmbH release of a Wueste Filmproduktion production, in association with ZDF. Produced by Ralph Schwingel, Stefan Schubert. Directed, written by Fatih Akin. Camera, Frank Barbian; editor, Andrew D. Bird; music, Ulrich Kodjo Wendt; art director, Guido Amin Fahim; costumes, Ingeborg Moritoris. Reviewed at Locarno Festival, Aug. 8. Running time: 96 mins. (German and Turkish dialog)
**Mehmet Kurtulus (Gabriel), Aleksandar Jovanovic (Bobby), Adam Bousdoukos (Costa), Regula Grauwiller (Alice), Idil Uner (Ceyda), Ralph Herforth (Muhamer).**
Following on the heels of other Euro counterparts, German cinema gets its first real *Boyz N the Hood* with *Short Sharp Shock,* a punchy, gritty tale of three pals in multi-ethnic Hamburg whose friendship is tested in the city's criminal milieu. Though the film becomes more of a conventional, tragic melodrama in its second half, the strong central performances and tight direction by freshman Fatih Akin make this an agreeable ride. Foreign sales, however, could be tricky.

Central trio is Gabriel, a tough, lantern-jawed Turk; Costa, a shaggy-haired, somewhat goofy Greek who goes out with Gabriel's sister, Ceyda; and Bobby, a handsome but dangerous Serb. They used to be in a gang together, but Gabriel, who's just come out of prison, announces he wants to start over in life. Still, old habits die hard. Major trouble rears its head when Bobby starts doing jobs for an Albanian mobster, Muhamer. When Costa also joins the gang, Gabriel tries to save his two friends from themselves, even at the cost of imperiling his dream of retiring to Turkey and setting up a restaurant by the sea.
Int'l release: Oct. 15              Int'l B.O.: $400,000

### Siberia (The Netherlands)

A Warner Bros. release of a Siberia Experience production, in association with Partners of the Siberia Experience, Dutch Filmfund, CoBofund, NPS Television. Produced by Clea de Koning. Directed by Robert Jan Westdijk. Screenplay, Westdijk, Jos Driessen. Camera, Bert Pot; editor, Herman P. Koerts; music, Junkie XL; art director, Anouk Damoiseaux; costume designer, Ciska Nagel; assistant director, Tom Raeymaekers. Reviewed at Cannes Festival, May 21, 1998. Running time: 91 mins. (Dutch and English dialog)
**Hugo Metsers (Hugo), Roeland Fernhout (Goof), Vlatka Simac (Lara), Johnny Lion (Freddy), Nicole Eggert (Kristy).**
Dutch director Robert Jan Westdijk makes a sure-footed transition to a more substantial budget with his sophomore feature, *Siberia.* Centering on two charming rogues who seduce and rob female tourists in Amsterdam, and the cool Russian beauty who sabotages their operation, this punchy drama relies a little heavily on visual and editing tricks to create atmosphere. But the volatile dynamic among the main trio and the plot's unexpected turns will secure sales in Euro territories.

Taking full advantage of a town known for its libertarian attitude toward sex and drug-taking, young roommates Hugo and Goof have made a thriving cottage industry out of befriending backpackers, taking them to bed, and lifting their cash and valuables. The scam runs like clockwork until they encounter smooth operator Lara.
Int'l release: Aug. 27              Int'l B.O.: $250,000

### Side Streets

A Merchant Ivory Prods/CEO Films presentation of a Cornerstone Films production. Produced by Bruce Weiss. Directed by Tony Gerber. Screenplay, Lynn Nottage, Gerber. Camera, Russell Lee Fine; editor, Kate Williams; music, Evan Lurie; production design, Stephen McCabe; Paul Cheponis; costume design, Kasia Walicka Maimone. Reviewed at Venice Festival, Sept. 6. Running time: 131 mins.
**Valeria Golino (Sylvie Otti), Shashi Kapoor (Vikram Raj), Leon (Errol Boyce), Art Malik (Bipin Raj), Shabana Azmi (Chandra Raj), Mirjana Penezic Jokovic (Elena Iscovescu), John Ortiz (Ramon), David Vadim (Josif Iscovescu), Rosario Dawson (Marisol Hidalgo), Aunjanue Ellis (Brenda Boyce), Gary Perez (Victor), Miho Nikaido (Yuki Shimamura), Victor Argo (Albani Krug).**
Interconnecting stories set during a sweltering summer day in the five boroughs of New York City, *Side Streets* is an entertaining mosaic of life in the multicultural melting pot that refreshingly paints its wide race-and-class canvas without getting mired in p.c. concerns. Ambitious, mostly successful first feature from New Yorker Tony Gerber is overlong, and too unhurried about resolving its various strands.

In Manhattan, fashion designer Sylvie struggles to emerge from the shadow of her celebrated mother, facing eviction from her Soho apartment and the dead end in her relationship.

---

On Staten Island, Indian limo driver Bipin attempts to placate his frazzled wife who is fed up with being treated like a servant by Bipin's visiting brother, a pompous former Bollywood star. In the Bronx, humble Puerto Rican baker's daughter Marisol mistakenly sees her lover, Ramon, as her escape route to a life of glamour and success. But when these and the other stories are tied up, the conclusions have a warmth and spirit that is genuinely winning. Destined for perhaps only marginal theatrical exposure, this likeable pic will make an impressive calling card for future directing work.

### The Siege

A 20th Century Fox release of a Lynda Obst production. Produced by Obst, Edward Zwick. Directed by Zwick. Screenplay, Lawrence Wright, Menno Meyjes, Zwick; story by Wright. Camera, Roger Deakins; editor, Steven Rosenblum; music, Graeme Revell; production design, Lilly Kilvert; costume design, Ann Roth; stunt coordinator, Joel J. Kramer. Reviewed at Plaza Theater, L.A., Oct. 27. MPAA Rating: R. Running time: 116 mins.

Denzel Washington (Anthony Hubbard), Annette Bening (Elise Kraft/Sharon Bridger), Bruce Willis (Gen. William Devereaux), Tony Shalhoub (Frank Haddad), Sami Bouajila (Samir Nazhde), David Proval (Danny Sussman).

A potentially provocative idea is played out to diminishing returns in *The Siege*. Opening reels concerning the FBI's efforts to thwart terrorists in New York City possess some grit, power, and verve. But as the stakes mount when a power-hungry general gets carried away with martial law, Edward Zwick's attempt to extend recent history into a hypothetical nightmare scenario descends into stock, generalized action and cartoon-like confrontations. Grim tone and pat resolutions leave an acrid taste by fade-out, so expect weak word of mouth to lead to a quick B.O. slide after likely solid, star-driven opening frame.

FBI Terrorism Task Force chief Anthony Hubbard mobilizes his Gotham-based team to get to the bottom of a false-alarm bomb threat and hostage situation, and then a real one that results in a bus in Brooklyn blowing up. Hub crosses paths, and trades barbs, with National Security Agency operative Elise Kraft, a Middle East specialist. Hub has her "arrested" to get her out of his hair, but in the long run the two agents need each other to try to crack a difficult case in which the enemy is all but invisible. Gen. Devereaux warns against the Army being sent in as domestic police, but he winds up heading the massive force deployed on the streets of Manhattan and Brooklyn when the President declares martial law. Tanks are sent rumbling into neighborhoods, and adult Arab males are thrown into barbed-wire-enclosed detention camps.

U.S. release: Nov. 6          U.S. B.O.: $40 million
Int'l release: Nov. 20          Int'l B.O.: $12 million

### The Silence (Le Silence) (Iran-France)

An MK2 Prods (France)/Makhmalbaf Prods (Iran) co-production. Produced by Marin Karmitz. Directed, written, edited by Mohsen Makhmalbaf. Camera, Ebrahim Ghafori. Reviewed at Venice Festival, Sept. 6. Running time: 76 mins.

Tahmineh Normatova (Khorshid), Nadereh Abdelahyeva (Nadereh), Golbibi Ziadolahyeva (Mother), Araz M. Mohamadli (Wandering Musician).

Filmed in and around a small town in Tadjikistan, this lyrical mood piece from Iranian helmer Mohsen Makhmalbaf explores the almost surreal world of a 10-year-old blind boy who tunes musical instruments to earn money. Lacking formal narrative, the film consists of a repetitive series of images as Makhmalbaf's camera follows the young protagonist through his daily routine, a world that, despite the film's title, is not a silent one. Khorshid has to use his ears to find his way through life.

Even fans of Iranian cinema may find this a slight entry, not destined to travel any further than the helmer's name can take it. The story is elliptical almost to the point of frustration. Khorshid lives with his mother; his father left some years earlier for Russia. They rent a house by a river, but the rent's overdue and the landlord is threatening eviction. Every day Khorshid travels by bus to the town where he works for a maker of stringed instruments. As a tuner, he's not performing well and is threatened with the sack.

Int'l release: Sept. 9          Int'l B.O.: $80,000

### Simon Birch

A Buena Vista release of a Hollywood Pictures presentation, in association with Caravan Pictures, of a Roger Birnbaum/Laurence Mark production. Produced by Mark, Birnbaum. Directed, written by Mark Steven Johnson, suggested by the novel *A Prayer for Owen Meany* by John Irving. Camera, Aaron E. Schneider; editor, Betsy Heimann; music, Marc Shaiman; production design, David Chapman; costume design, Betsy Heiman, Abram Waterhouse. Reviewed at AMC Kabuki, San Francisco, Aug. 27. MPAA Rating: PG. Running time: 113 mins.

Ian Michael Smith (Simon Birch), Joseph Mazzello (Joe Wenteworth), Ashley Judd (Rebecca Wenteworth), Oliver Platt (Ben Goodrich), David Strathairn (Rev. Russell), Dana Ivey (Grandmother Wenteworth), Beatrice Winde (Hilde Grove), Jan Hooks (Miss Leavey), Jim Carrey (Adult Joe).

John Irving's novels – which juicily mix comedy, melodrama, real-world issues, and fable – seem like "natural" screen material. But as prior adaptations have proved, capturing his mercurial tonal shifts isn't easy. Drastically reducing 1989's *A Prayer for Owen Meany* in narrative scale and complexity – Irving himself demanded renaming the character, as well as "suggested by" rather than "based on" credit – *Simon Birch* might as well say its B.O. prayers right. Without the original moniker to draw bestseller fans, the syrupy hash by first-time director Mark Steven Johnson looks weak as both mainstream and arthouse fare.

Book has been reduced to familiar summer-that-changed-my-life childhood memory piece. Setting is Gravestown, N.H., where Joe is raised by his loving mom, Rebecca, who has refused to divulge – even to him – his father's identity. His best friend is title character: born so tiny his mother barely noticed the delivery, he grows into a pint-size pre-adolescent whom adults ridicule and fellow kids cluck over or treat like a "doll." Simon is convinced of his role as "God's instrument," fated to be a hero some day.

U.S. release: Sept. 11          U.S. B.O.: $18.2 million
Int'l release: Dec. 11          Int'l B.O.: $200,000

### A Simple Plan

A Paramount release of a Paramount/Mutual Film Co. production, in association with Savoy Pictures. Produced by James Jacks, Adam Schroeder. Directed by Sam Raimi. Screenplay, Scott B. Smith, based on his novel. Camera, Alar

Kivilo; editors, Arthur Coburn, Eric L. Beason; music, Danny Elfman; production design, Patrizia von Brandenstein; costume design, Julie Weiss. Reviewed at Toronto Festival, Sept. 12. MPAA Rating: R. Running time: 121 mins.

**Bill Paxton (Hank), Billy Bob Thornton (Jacob), Brent Briscoe (Lou), Bridget Fonda (Sarah), Jack Walsh (Tom Butler), Chelcie Ross (Carl), Becky Ann Baker (Nancy), Gary Cole (Baxter).**

There's a temptation to lump *A Simple Plan* with the Coen brothers' *Fargo*. Both are slices of life about outlandish crimes and Average Joe felons in over their heads; and both blend Grand Guignol and beautiful but foreboding snowscapes. The key differences are in emphasis and tone: *Fargo* is deadpan noir; *A Simple Plan* is a more robust Midwestern Gothic that owes as much to Poe as to Chandler. Director Sam Raimi's core audience will be disappointed in pic's brooding tone and relative reserve, while others will be shocked by helmer's signature mix of mirth and mayhem. Paramount would do well to platform out and take advantage of supportive reviews and word of mouth.

Pic opens in a small Minnesota town on New Year's Eve. An impromptu fox hunt leads to a freakish find in a remote field: the wreckage of a small plane and, behind a decaying corpse, more than $4 million in crisp hundreds. The debate over "the right thing to do" doesn't last long. Unemployed Jacob and buddy Lou see the money as manna from heaven; Hank, Jacob's comparatively well-heeled brother, initially resists, but is won over by the argument that the green, probably from a drug deal gone bad, has no traceable owner. In the tradition of *The Treasure of the Sierra Madre*, greed, paranoia, and plain bad luck play roles, and the body count begins to mount at an alarming rate.

U.S. release: Dec. 11          U.S. B.O.: $2 million

## Sitcom (France)

A Mars Films release of a Fidelité Prods presentation and production. Produced by Olivier Delbosc, Marc Missonnier. Directed, written by François Ozon. Camera, Yorik Le Saux; editor, Dominique Petrot; music, Eric Neveux; art director, Angelique Puron; costume designer, Herve Poeydemenge; rat wrangler, Bruno Salvatore. Reviewed at Club de l'Etoile, Paris, April 6, 1998. Running time: 79 mins.

**Evelyne Dandry (Hélène), François Marthouret (Jean), Marina de Van (Sophie), Adrien de Van (Nicolas), Stephane Rideau (David), Lucia Sanchez (Maria), Julien-Emmanuel Eyoum Deido (Abdu).**

A pet rat sets off a chain reaction of debauchery in a prim and proper nuclear family in *Sitcom*, a sort of "*Mouse Hunt* Meets the Marquis de Sade." Pic is marginal, but its commercial prospects are promising in outlets that relish notoriety and jaunty depictions of homosexuality, bisexuality, S&M, incest, and the sight of at least one memorably proportioned erect member.

Unfortunately Ozon, an original, iconoclastic storyteller, hasn't completely thought out his premise: The 79-minute endeavor runs out of steam about an hour in. Movie kicks off in the setting of a bucolic suburban home where mom, dad, brother, and sister live in bourgeois harmony. Model father Jean is greeted with a birthday surprise party thrown by his extended family. Dad responds by opening fire on his loved ones.

Int'l release: May 27       Int'l B.O.: $1.1 million
U.S. release: Sept. 18       U.S. B.O.: $40,000

## Six Days, Seven Nights

A Buena Vista release of a Touchstone Pictures presentation, in association with Caravan Pictures, of a Roger Birnbaum/Northern Lights Entertainment production. Produced by Ivan Reitman, Wallis Nicita, Birnbaum. Directed by Reitman. Screenplay, Michael Browning. Camera, Michael Chapman; editors, Sheldon Kahn, Wendy Greene Bricmont; music, Randy Edelman; production designer, J. Michael Riva; costume design, Gloria Gresham; stunt coordinator, Doug Coleman. Reviewed at Harmony Gold, L.A.. MPAA Rating: PG-13. Running time: 101 mins.

**Harrison Ford (Quinn Harris), Anne Heche (Robin Monroe), David Schwimmer (Frank Martin), Jacqueline Obradors (Angelica), Temuera Morrison (Jager), Allison Janney (Marjorie), Douglas Weston (Philippe).**

*Six Days, Seven Nights* is a passable romantic comedy in which enforced proximity makes the heart grow fonder. Sprinkled with just enough laughs, close shaves, and compromising positions to keep audiences mildly interested, this old-fashioned popcorn picture is agreeably breezy and colorful. B.O. looks to be sturdy, if not stellar, for this well-tooled, utterly mainstream entertainment, and much-bruited concern about public acceptance of Anne Heche as a romantic heroine should become a moot point.

Harrison Ford plays a South Pacific cargo pilot who becomes stranded on a deserted island with a neurotic, high-powered New York magazine editor. Robin Monroe is a workaholic associate editor of a mag whisked off by her b.f., Frank, for a week's vacation on a remote, paradisiacal isle. But, career girl that she is, Robin cannot refuse an emergency assignment on an all-important one-day photo shoot in nearby Tahiti, and enlists the help of island rat Quinn Harris to fly her there in his old DeHavilland Beaver.

U.S. release: June 12       U.S. B.O.: $74 million
Int'l release: June 22       Int'l B.O.: $84 million

## Six-String Samurai

A Palm Pictures release of an Overseas Filmgroup presentation of an HSX Film production. Produced by Leanna Creel. Directed by Lance Mungia. Screenplay, Mungia, Jeffrey Falcon. Camera, Kristian Bernier; editor, James Frisa; music, Brian Tyler; production/costume design, Falcon. Reviewed at AFM, Santa Monica, Feb. 28. Running time: 91 mins.

**Jeffrey Falcon (Buddy), Justin McQuire (The Kid), Stephane Gauger (Death), John Sakisian (Russian General), Gabrille Pimenter (Little Man).**

In the singular world of *Six-String Samurai*, the Ruskies dropped the bomb in 1957 and amid the devastation Elvis was made king. Four decades later, Elvis has left the building... permanently. A rock 'n' roll *Mad Max* served up Cantonese style, this is one wildly original and highly entertaining American indie with genuine commercial appeal. This samurai cuts a mean figure, with fierce theatrical crossover potential and boffo prospects in ancillaries.

The protagonist, Buddy, is one of many aspirants for the vacated throne. From somewhere in the barren, dusty Southwest, he's making the trek to Las Vegas, where there will be a showdown between warrior-musicians to see who will be worthy of wearing the crown and cape. His most lethal challenge comes from Death, a dark presence in a black top hat with a trio of archers as side men.

U.S. release: Sept. 18       U.S. B.O.: $130,000

---

**... August 5 ...**

Director Paul Verhoeven inks to helm Phoenix Pictures' **Official Assassins.**

## Slam

A Trimark release of an Off Line Entertainment Group production. Produced by Henri Kessler, Marc Levin, Richard Stratton. Directed by Marc Levin. Screenplay, Stratton, Levin, Sonja Sohn, Saul Williams. Camera, Marc Benjamin; editor, Emir Luis. Reviewed at Sundance Festival, Jan. 20. Running time: 100 mins.

Saul Williams (Ray Joshua), Sonja Sohn (Lauren Bell), Bonz Malone (Hopha).

Marc Levin's *Slam* is a landmark film that defies categorization. Part gritty prison drama, part inner-city ghetto chronicle, pic is a compassionate plea for black males to take a new direction to change their status in American society. This emotionally powerful and technically innovative film deserves to be seen on the bigscreen, though its raw intensity and realistically downbeat tone might limit its appeal.

Levin, an accomplished documentarian, makes a stunning feature debut with a film that inventively blends conventions of fiction and documentary. Ray Joshua, a product of a housing project in Washington, D.C., lives in the war zone known as "Dodge City." The street-smart Ray lives by his wits, and minor marijuana dealings. Endowed with a natural talent for words, he expresses himself through the poems he passionately composes. One summer night, while he is talking to Big Mike, his drug connection, the latter is gunned down. When the police arrive, Ray is busted for suspicion of murder as well as possession of pot.

| U.S. release: Oct. 9 | U.S. B.O.: $700,000 |
| Int'l release: Nov. 11 | Int'l B.O.: $100,000 |

## Slappy And the Stinkers

A TriStar release of a Bubble Factory presentation of a Sheinberg production. Produced by Sid, Bill, and Jon Sheinberg. Directed by Barnet Kellman. Screenplay, Bob Wolterstorff, Mike Scott. Camera, Paul Maibaum; editor, Jeff Wishengrad; music, Craig Safan; production design, Ivo Cristante; costume design, Jami Burrows. Reviewed at Raleigh Studios, Jan. 10. MPAA rating: PG. Running time: 78 mins.

B.D. Wong (Morgan Brinway), Bronson Pinchot (Roy), Jennifer Coolidge (Harriet), Joseph Ashton (Sonny), Gary LeRoi Gray (Domino), Carl Michael Lindner (Witz), Scarlett Pomers (Lucy), David Dukes (Spencer Dane, Sr.), Spencer Klein (Spencer Dane, Jr.), Sam McMurray (Boccoli).

Filled to the gills with slapstick humor, *Slappy and the Stinkers* could well have been sold as *The Little Rascals* meets *Free Willy*. Innumerable pratfalls and gross-out humor successfully distract and entertain the under-12 set, to whom pic is sure to appeal. Adults, however, may have a hard time sitting through *Slappy*, which suggests that pic's real market is on video.

Action unfolds at Dartmoor Academy where stuffy, overbearing principal Morgan Brinway forces second graders to study opera. In the spirit of rebellion, five unruly kids – whom Brinway dubs "Stinkers" – abandon class and wreak playful havoc on the school grounds. A notorious animal thief named Boccoli wants to steal Slappy the sea lion and sell him to a circus, while wacky school groundskeeper Roy mistakes Slappy for a giant gopher and plans to destroy him.

| U.S. release: Jan. 23 | U.S. B.O.: $80,000 |

## Sliding Doors (U.K.-U.S.)

A Miramax release of a Miramax and Paramount presentation, in association with Intermedia Films, of a Mirage production.

Produced by Sydney Pollack, Philippa Braithwaite, William Horberg. Directed, written by Peter Howitt. Camera, Remi Adefarasin; editor, John Smith; music, David Hirschfelder; production design, Maria Djurkovic; costume design, Jill Taylor. Reviewed at Sunset screening room, L.A., Jan. 13. MPAA Rating: R. Running time: 108 mins.

Gwyneth Paltrow (Helen), John Hannah (James), John Lynch (Gerry), Jeanne Tripplehorn (Lydia), Zara Turner (Anna).

*Sliding Doors* is a frothy, lightweight romantic comedy that strives to seem richer and more complex than it really is. Peter Howitt, making his bigscreen writing-directing debut, has whipped up a concoction with enough quick wit and charm to make this a surefire audience pleaser with a good commercial spin.

Picture plays out on parallel tracks. On one, Helen arrives home early to find Gerry in the sack with his former g.f., Lydia; in real life she only vaguely suspects something based on odd hints. The other view, Helen's pain at being betrayed by Gerry, is gradually offset by the amusing and increasingly amorous attentions of James.

| U.S. release: April 24 | U.S. B.O.: $12 million |
| Int'l release: May 1 | Int'l B.O.: $55 million |

## Slums of Beverly Hills

A Fox Searchlight release of a South Fork Pictures production. Produced by Michael Nozik, Stan Wlodkowski. Directed, written by Tamara Jenkins. Camera, Tom Richmond; editor, Pamela Martin; music, Rolfe Kent; production designer, Dena Roth; costume designer, Kirsten Everberg. Reviewed at Cannes Festival, May 21. Running time: 90 mins.

Natasha Lyonne (Vivian), Alan Arkin (Murray), Marisa Tomei (Rita), Kevin Corrigan (Eliot), Eli Marienthal (Rickey), David Krumholtz (Ben), Jessica Walter (Doris), Carl Reiner (Mickey).

A notch or two above a TV sitcom, *Slums of Beverly Hills*, Tamara Jenkins' semi-autobiographical feature debut, is a bawdy, broad comedy about an eccentric, downwardly mobile Jewish family, centering on the coming of age of a bright adolescent girl. Rude, vulgar, and sporadically funny, the film should play well with young urban dwellers, but is less likely to excite mature viewers because of its rough surface and mediocre execution.

Set in 1976, movie is conceived in the vein of neurotic Jewish comedies with two notable exceptions: The story is refreshingly told from a female p.o.v., and it's not nearly as accomplished, poignant or funny as earlier works. Head of this yarn's dysfunctional clan is benevolent patriarch Murray, a single, divorced father in constant search of a better lifestyle for his three children.

| U.S. release: Aug. 14 | U.S. B.O.: $5.5 million |
| Int'l release: Sept. 11 | Int'l B.O.: $150,000 |

## Small Soldiers

A DreamWorks release of a DreamWorks/Universal presentation. Produced by Mike Finnell, Colin Wilson. Directed by Joe Dante. Screenplay, Gavin Scott, Adam Rifkin, Ted Elliott, Terry Rossio. Camera, Jamie Anderson; editor, Marshall Harvey; music, Jerry Goldsmith; production design, William Sandell; costume design, Carole Brown-James; animatronic design, Stan Winston; visual-effects supervisor, Stefen Fangmeier; military adviser, Dale Dye. Reviewed at Loews Cineplex Century City, L.A., July 7. MPAA Rating: PG-13. Running time: 99 mins.

Kirsten Dunst (Christy Fimple), Gregory Smith (Alan Abernathy), Jay Mohr (Larry Benson), Phil Hartman (Phil Fimple), Kevin Dunn (Stuart Abernathy), Denis Leary (Gil Mars), David Cross (Irwin Wayfair), Ann Magnuson (Irene Abernathy). Voices: Tommy Lee Jones (Maj. Chip Hazard), Frank Langella (Archer), Ernest Borgnine (Kip Killagin), Jim Brown (Butch Meathook), Bruce Dern (Link Static), George Kennedy (Brick Bazooka), Clint Walker (Nick Nitro).

The notion of technology running amok fuels *Small Soldiers*. When children's action toys, implanted with faulty military microchips, begin to move, speak, and learn, they turn on their human owners with a lethal vengeance. It's an adult's paranoid dream come to life, so setting it in a juvenile context may have inadvertently undone the foundation of the story. And while pic's sense of a toy store turned upside down, courtesy of dazzling f/x, will draw young viewers, ultimately the film's mean-spiritedness and serious underpinnings will turn off its core audience. Result will be rapid commercial erosion and disappointing theatrical B.O.; ancillary movement, particularly on video, could provide the pic with a more vital afterlife.

In the workshop of a toy company, its two top developers are trying to second-guess the whims of Globotech – the former defense-industry conglomerate that's acquired the company as part of its transition to peacetime industrialization. Stipulating that new action figures function in the lifelike manner of their promo reel, Globotech chief offers up his arsenal of techno wizardry to ensure this is accomplished.

U.S. release: July 10          U.S. B.O.: $55 million
Int'l release: Aug. 13        Int'l B.O.: $32.5 million

## Smoke Signals

A Miramax release of a Shadow Catcher Entertainment production. Produced by Scott Rosenfelt, Larry Estes. Directed by Chris Eyre. Screenplay, Sherman Alexie, based on stories from his book *The Lone Ranger and Tonto Fistfight in Heaven*. Camera, Brian Capener; editor, Brian Berdan; music, BC Smith; production design, Charles Armstrong; costume design, Ron Leamon. Reviewed at Sundance Festival, Jan. 16,. Running time: 88 mins. Adam Beach (Victor Joseph), Evan Adams (Thomas Builds-the-Fire), Irene Bedard (Suzy Song), Gary Farmer (Arnold Joseph), Tantoo Cardinal (Arlene Joseph).

"It's a good day to be indigenous," a radio announcer on the desolate Coeur d'Alene Indian reservation dryly intones at the beginning of *Smoke Signals*, and the remark serves not only as an accurate indication of the quirky, self-deprecating humor to be found throughout the film, but as a sort of prophetic blessing on this evidently first fictional feature written, directed, and co-produced by Native Americans. A light, entertaining treatment of serious themes that speaks with a distinctive voice and avoids being solemn and pretentious, pic won both the Audience Award and Filmmakers' Trophy at the Sundance Festival.

Subjects at hand include the poverty of life on the reservations, Indian stereotyping, and the problem of coming to terms with an irresponsible, absent father. Victor (Adam Beach), an athletic, seemingly tough young man, learns his father has died in Arizona. Thomas, the reservation nerd and storyteller, offers to pay for Victor's trip provided that he can go along. Thus begins a picaresque road trip, studded with off-kilter humor and revelation.

U.S. release: June 26          U.S. B.O.: $6.9 million
Int'l release: Dec. 3         Int'l B.O.: $250,000

## Snake Eyes

A Paramount/Buena Vista Int'l release of a DeBart production. Produced by Brian De Palma. Directed by De Palma. Screenplay, David Koepp, story by De Palma, Koepp. Camera, Stephen H. Burum; editor, Bill Pankow; music, Ryuichi Sakamoto; production design, Anne Pritchard; costume design, Odette Gadoury; visual-effects supervisor, Eric Brevig. Reviewed at Paramount, L.A., Aug. 3. MPAA Rating: R. Running time: 99 mins. Nicolas Cage (Rick Santoro), Gary Sinise (Kevin Dunne), John Heard (Gilbert Powell), Carla Gugino (Julia Costello), Stan Shaw (Lincoln Tyler), Kevin Dunn (Lou Logan), Luis Guzman (Cyrus).

*Snake Eyes* is snakebit. After a razzle-dazzle opening, this hyperactive thriller about a corrupt cop's investigation of a political assassination devolves into a stylistic exercise by director Brian De Palma, one whose wispy threads of dramatic plausibility and character involvement unravel completely by the time of the incredibly silly finale. This late-summer release offers a true test of Nicolas Cage's star status and ability to open a picture; initial roll of the dice will likely be a winner, followed by a quick loss of luck.

Homicide detective Rick Santoro bounds through stadium hallways, hits on a between-rounds placard babe, stops at the dressing room of the champ, jumps an escalator to shake down a small-time hood for gambling money, heads into the arena filled with thousands of expectant fans, chats on his cellphone with his wife and girlfriend, takes a ringside seat next to boyhood friend Navy Cmdr. Kevin Dunne, and watches the first round of the fight, which concludes with a knockout of the champ and the sniper shooting of the U.S. Secretary of Defense. This one, long, uninterrupted tracking shot is an indisputably impressive tour de force on numerous levels, particularly in that Cage is on the move and running his mouth to a wide assortment of characters virtually throughout the sequence. Although Dunne manages to nail the apparent assassin, a Palestinian extremist, Santoro has the stadium doors locked in hopes of finding other suspects among the 14,000 fight fans. His suspicions are aroused when a videotape replay reveals that the champ went down from a phantom punch.

U.S. release: Aug. 7          U.S. B.O.: $56 million
Int'l release: Aug. 21        Int'l B.O: $44 million

## Snow

A Winter Light Films production. Produced, directed, written by Eric Tretbar. Camera, Philip Harder; editor, Daniel J. Geiger; music, Chan Poling, Tretbar; art director, Heather Keena; costume designer, Jeannine Bourdaghs; assistant director, Peter Rudrud. Reviewed at Raleigh Studios, L.A., April 8. Running Time: 81 mins. Shane Barach (Thomas), Rose Mailutha (Sabina), Lara Miklasevics (Jessica), Erika Remillard (Robbie), John Crozier (Spike).

It doesn't get much more bleak than Minneapolis during mid-winter, and *Snow* aptly captures that quality of gloom in an engaging tale of aimless youth. A subtly observed piece, the film has a quiet authority that's compelling, but its modest physical trappings will limit its commercial potential. Filming in black-and-white on 16mm provides the material with an old-fashioned realism that will limit its prospects to niche, non-mainstream venues. Focus is on Thomas, a one-time rock musician who's been delaying making a decison about the future. He's having second thoughts about his relationship with Jessica but hasn't found the energy to commit or move on. He's stuck, he's stalling, he's unmotivated.

## Soldier

A Warner Bros. release, presented in association with Morgan Creek, of a Jerry Weintraub production in association with Impact Pictures. Produced by Weintraub. Directed by Paul Anderson. Screenplay, David Webb Peoples. Camera, David Tattersall; editor, Martin Hunter; music, Joel McNeely; production design, David L. Snyder; costume design, Erica Edell Phillips; visual-effects supervisor, Ed Jones; makeup supervisor, Steve Laporte; stunt coordinator, Dick Ziker. Reviewed at AMC Mercado 20, San Jose, Sept. 21. MPAA Rating: R. Running time: 98 mins.

**Kurt Russell (Todd), Jason Scott Lee (Caine 607), Connie Nielsen (Sandra), Sean Pertwee (Mace), Michael Chiklis (Jimmy Pig), Gary Busey (Church), Jason Isaacs (Col. Mekum).**

James Cameron can rest easy – his *Terminator* epics are tough to replicate. Genre specialists Paul Anderson and David Webb Peoples attempt to usurp the franchise with *Soldier*, a big, brutal sci-fi entry that's every bit as single-minded and vacuous as its programmed-to-grunt futureworld noncoms. A pumped-up Kurt Russell, who utters no more than a dozen syllables throughout, obviously aims to put Arnie out of work. His star appeal and pic's nonstop mayhem should draw enough indiscriminate action fans to launch this one; thereafter, derivative heroics and done-to-death post-apocalyptic setting will spell a fast slide to ancillary afterlife.

Opener is promisingly slam-bam, bleakly funny, showing infants classified 1A from birth, then placed in a day-care center and military academy designed to promote savagery. Young Todd is tops in his class, growing up to be the ultimate weapon in earthly and interplanetary skirmishes. But at age 40 he's deemed obsolete by military leaders who have furthered the process through genetic engineering. Todd and two others are pitted against next-generation Caine 607 and literally left on the scrap heap. Dumped on a garbage planet at the far corner of the galaxy, he's nursed back to health by ragtag homesteaders. When Caine and his squad stop by for a little hands-on training, the villagers decide to overlook Todd's personality flaws. Even if he's not much of a talker, he's a good man to have around in a firefight.

U.S. release: Oct. 23 — U.S. B.O.: $14.5 million
Int'l release: Nov. 27 — Int'l B.O.: $4.9 million

## A Soldier's Daughter Never Cries

An October Films release of a Merchant Ivory production. Produced by Ismail Merchant. Directed by James Ivory. Screenplay, Ivory, Ruth Prawer Jhabvala, based on the book by Kaylie Jones. Camera, Jean-Marc Fabre; editor, Noelle Boisson; music, Richard Robbins; production design, Jacques Bunoir, Pat Garner; costume designer, Carol Ramsey. Reviewed at Ticketmaster, L.A. July 30. MPAA Rating: R. Running time: 127 mins.

**Kris Kristofferson (Bill Willis), Barbara Hershey (Marcella Willis), Leelee Sobieski (Channe Willis), Jesse Bradford (Billy "Benoit" Willis), Anthony Roth Costanzo (Francis Fortescue), Dominique Blanc (Candida), Jane Birkin (Mrs. Fortescue), Virginie Ledoyen (Benoit's Mother), Samuel Gruen (Benoit), Luisa Conlon (Young Channe).**

There's something fresh in the new Ismail Merchant–James Ivory production, *A Soldier's Daughter Never Cries*. Based on Kaylie Jones' 1990 autobiographical novel, the touching drama offers a multilayered, intergenerational view of an expatriate American family living in Paris in the 1960s and 1970s. Given the right handling, October could score with this nicely mounted, superbly acted picture, which will appeal to the art crowd that has supported Merchant Ivory productions over the last two decades.

Told from daughter Channe's point of view, film focuses on her relationships with father, Bill Willis, a successful expatriate writer haunted by his war experiences. But the yarn doesn't neglect the other members of the family: Marcella, Bill's fun-loving, poker-playing wife, and Benoît, a French orphan who, as the yarn begins, is brought to the family for adoption. The second act records the intense friendship that evolves between Channe and a sensitive, artistic boy, Francis Fortescue, who's fatherless and lives with his expatriate British mother. Channe admires Francis' dramatic skills and sophistication, but their bond becomes strained when she begins to show romantic interest in other boys. The children's world is suddenly transformed when her father announces their return to the U.S. Last and most emotional segment is set in the 1970s on the East Coast and chronicles Bill's deteriorating health and the painful coming of age of Billy and Channe.

U.S. release: Sept. 18 — U.S. B.O.: $1.8 million

## Sombre (France)

A Zelie Prods production, in association with La Sept Cinema and Monteurs' Studio, with the participation of Canal Plus, CNC. Produced by Catherine Jacques. Directed by Philippe Grandrieux. Screenplay, Grandrieux, Pierre Hodgson, Sophie Fillières. Camera, Sabine Lancelin, Grandrieux; editor, Françoise Tourmen; music, Alan Vega; art director, Gerbaux; costumes, Ann Dunsford-Varenne. Reviewed at Locarno Festival, Aug. 9. Running time: 112 mins.

**Marc Barbe (Jean), Elina Lowensohn (Claire), Geraldine Voillat (Christine).**

Guaranteed to send auds either straight to the exit or into paroxysms of rapture, *Sombre* is an impossibly arty, totally noncommercial construct that ends up, for those prepared to stay the course, as a surprisingly creepy look into the tortured mind of a serial killer. A small career in more outré festival slots beckons this first feature by former video-installation artist Philippe Grandrieux.

Though unprized at Locarno, the film provoked the most heated discussion among competing titles, plus an official statement: "Half of the jury would like to call attention to *Sombre*. Our jury split between those who were morally offended by the film and those who saw a purpose in its darkness, and in the strength of its mise-en-scène and images."

Central character, Jean, drives around France, casually strangling women. Story proper begins when he picks up Claire, whose car has broken down, and the two set off with Claire's racier sister, Christine, to escape the women's cloistered family life. Though it's clear Jean is a major weirdo, the sisters stick with him.

## Some Girls

A Millennium Films presentation, in association with Nu Image, of a Virile production. Produced by Boaz Davidson, Abra Edelman, Gay Ribisi. Directed by Rory Kelly. Screenplay, Marissa Ribisi, Brie Shaffer. Camera, Amy Vincent; editor, Melissa Kent;

music supervisor, Bill Ewart; production designer, Martina Buckley; costume designers, Isis Mussenden, Denise Martinez. Reviewed at L.A. Independent Festival, April 19. Running time: 95 mins.
**Marissa Ribisi (Claire), Juliette Lewis (April), Giovanni Ribisi (Jason), Jeremy Sisto (Chad), Pamela Segall (Jenn), Michael Rapaport (Neil).**
A labored portrait of young Angelenos searching for relationships, *Some Girls* falls short of director Rory Kelly's debut effort, *Sleep With Me*. New pic is felled by a thoroughly unlikable bunch of central characters whom even decent dialog and a few funny scenes cannot render appealing. Nevertheless, recognizable cast, buoyed by an appealing soundtrack, could spell limited theatrical play. At the center of the story is hopelessly romantic, desperately insecure Claire. Still healing from her last breakup, Claire meets the smooth-talking Chad.

## Some Nudity Required (Docu)
An Only Child production. Produced by Odette Springer. Directed, written by Springer, Johanna Demetrakas. Camera, Alain Bertrancourt, Sandra Chandler; editor, Kate Amend; music, Springer; music supervisor, Paul di Franco; sound, Ted Gordon. Reviewed at Sundance Festival, Jan. 16. Running time: 82 mins.
Odette Springer, former music supervisor for Concorde/New Horizons, holds the mirror up in the intriguing *Some Nudity Required*, an insightful, entertaining docu memoir on life in the exploitation film biz that's made-to-order for arthouse habitués. Classical-music-trained Springer, who shared writer-director chores with Johanna Demetrakas, adopts a self-analytical approach, shored up by interviews with exploitation vets and scream queens. Still, Springer asks the hard questions and doesn't shy away from more perverse aspects of the trade.

## Sour Grapes
A Sony Pictures Entertainment release of a Columbia Pictures presentation of a Castle Rock production. Produced by Laurie Lennard. Directed, written by Larry David. Camera, Victor Hammer; editor, Priscilla Nedd-Friendly; production designer, Charles Rosen; costume designer, Debra McGuire. Reviewed at Sony, Culver City, April 8. MPAA Rating: R. Running time: 91 mins.
**Steven Weber (Evan Maxwell), Craig Bierko (Richie Maxwell), Matt Keeslar (Danny Pepper), Karen Sillas (Joan), Robyn Peterman (Roberta), Viola Harris (Selma Maxwell), Jennifer Leigh Warren (Millie).**
The comic premise of *Sour Grapes* is ingenious. Imagine your best friend hit the jackpot after you had lent him the money to play. The resulting strife is palpable, and sitcom vet Larry David takes the situation to comic extremes. While he doesn't always hit a bullseye, he's generally on target. The film does suffer slightly from a first-timer's awkwardness, but nonetheless delivers enough laughter and truth to generate solid returns from all revenue streams and turn the pic into a surprise spring hit.
    The pic gets on track as the two young men plot a trip to Atlantic City. Richie is an unrepentant adolescent and the perfect boy to his adoring mother (Viola Harris). Cousin Evan takes on the mantle of maturity. Richie delights in finding ways to get his relative to unwind. A few days of gambling and shows with their girlfriends would seem to be a perfect plan. After

losing most of their wad at the tables, they sit down at the slot machines. Down to his last quarter, Richie turns to Evan for two more coins for one last pull. The cylinders spin, coming to rest on three clusters of grapes.
U.S. release: April 17                    U.S. B.O.: $250,000

## The Southern Lighthouse (El Faro Del Sur)
(Argentina-Spain)
An Alta Films release of an Artear (Argentina)/Prime Films (Spain) production, in association with Via Digital. Directed, written by Eduardo Mignogna. Camera, Marcelo Camorino; editors, Juan Carlos Macias, Nacho Ruiz Capillas; music, Baby Lopez Furst; art director, Abel Facello. Reviewed at Cines Princesa, Madrid, May 24. Running time: 109 mins.
**Ingrid Rubio (Meme), Ricardo Darin (Andy), Jimena Baron (Young Aneta), Florencia Bertotti (Aneta), Mariano Martinez (Javier), Norberto Diaz (Fernando), Norma Aleandro (Dolores).**
After *Autumn Sun*, his prize-winning 1996 study of love in middle age, Argentine helmer Eduardo Mignogna returns with *The Southern Lighthouse*, a sporadically charming but over-long study of sisterly love. Though intermittently powerful, plot is too drawn out to sustain interest, and schmaltzy music and picture-postcard photography end up detracting from the powerful emotions helmer clearly wants to generate. Pic is unlikely to break beyond Spanish-speaking territories.
    Meme and 10-year-old sister Aneta are orphaned after a car crash. As a result of the accident, Meme has a limp, which seriously affects her self-esteem. The sisters are thrown on the mercy of their two spinster aunts in Uruguay, from whom they run away. After they arrive in Buenos Aires, Meme becomes a surrogate mother to Aneta, as well as experiencing late-teen growing pains and boy trouble because of her bad leg.
Int'l release: May 22                    Int'l B.O.: $3 million

## Southie
An American World Pictures presentation of a Prophecy Pictures production. Produced by Bill McCutchen, Hugh Wilson. Directed by John Shea. Screenplay, Shea, James Cummings, Dave McLaughlin. Camera, Allen Baker; editor, Tracy Granger; music, Wayne Sharp; production designer, G.W. Mercier; costume designer, Liz McGarrity. Reviewed at Seattle Festival, June 10. Running time: 95 mins.
**Donnie Wahlberg (Danny Quinn), Rose McGowan (Kathy Quinn), Anne Meara (Mrs. Quinn), James Cummings (Joey Ward), Amanda Peet (Marianne), Will Arnett (Whitley), Lawrence Tierney (Colie Powers).**
*Southie*, a carbon-copy crime drama, won the juried American Independent award at this year's Seattle Festival, an odd choice since it was arguably the least original contender. Bottom-drawer plot of a South Boston bad boy returning to tie up loose ends reads like every other *Mean Streets* knockoff in the past decade, with no scene, development or performance standing out from undifferentiated din. With the low-budget gangster genre seemingly played out for the moment, this will be a hard sell in any market.
    Danny Quinn is the prodigal son who made it all the way to New Yawk before money or luck ran out. Conflict-ridden story sticks Danny between his pals, who open a "private" casino with the help of one Irish Mafia crowd, while his family is beholden to another one, headed by a crusty old-timer played by Lawrence Tierney, doing his best Godfather shtick.

---

**...August 9...**
**Snake Eyes** takes $16 million plus in its first weekend in the U.S.

## Spanish Fly

A Miramax release of a Juan Alexander production for Portman Films. Produced by Alexander. Co-producers, Nella Banfi, Cat Villiers. Directed, written by Daphna Kastner. Camera, Arnaldo Catinari; editor, Caroline Biggerstaff; music, Mario de Benito; production design, Alain Bainee; costume design, José Maria de Cossio. Reviewed at Cannes Film Festival, May 15. Running time: 91 mins.

**Daphna Kastner (Zoe), Toni Canto (Antonio Molina), Martin Donovan (Carl Livingston), Danny Huston (John), Marianne Sagebrecht (Rosa), Antonio Castro (Julio).**

Actress-filmmaker Daphna Kastner's *Spanish Fly* marks a step backward from her debut romantic comedy, *French Exit*. The tale of a woman researching a book on male machismo in Spain is a tad too sincere and tinged with forced drama to play in the big leagues. Pic has limited theatrical prospects prior to finding its small-screen niche. Zoe is in the midst of interviewing men in Madrid. A piece she did for *Vanity Fair* has evolved into a book, and her anxious behavior suggests the original work had more style than substance. Only Antonio seems at all interested in giving her the straight goods. But it don't jibe with her thesis.

## Species II

A Metro-Goldwyn-Mayer release of an FGM production. Produced by Frank Mancuso, Jr. Directed by Peter Medak. Screenplay, Chris Brancato, based on characters created by Dennis Feldman. Camera, Matthew F. Leonetti; editor, Richard Nord; music, Edward Shearmur; production designer, Miljen Kreka Kljakovic; costume designer, Richard Bruno; creatures/makeup effects, Steve Johnson; original Species design, H.R. Giger. Reviewed at AMC Studio 30, Houston, April 11. MPAA Rating: R. Running time: 93 mins.

**Michael Madsen (Press Lennox), Natasha Henstridge (Eve), Marg Helgenberger (Dr. Laura Baker), Mykelti Williamson (Dennis Gamble), George Dzundza (Col. Carter Burgess, Jr.), James Cromwell (Sen. Ross), Justin Lazzard (Patrick Ross), Richard Belzer (The President).**

Lightning isn't likely to strike twice with *Species II*, a half-baked rehash of the hit 1995 sci-fi shocker about a half-human, half-alien beauty with a murderous urge to mate. An unsavory and unsatisfying blend of dumb plotting, leering lasciviousness, and full-bore gore, pic should warp-speed to video shelves after making a minor blip on the B.O. radar screen.

Henstridge returns as another half-breed, Eve, who's been cooked up in a top-secret government lab to help scientists develop a way to battle other evil extraterrestrials.

U.S. release: April 10 — U.S. B.O.: $19 million
Int'l release: May 29 — Int'l B.O.: $16 million

## Sphere

A Warner Bros. release of a Baltimore Pictures/Constant c production in association with Punch Prods Produced by Barry Levinson, Michael Crichton, Andrew Wald. Directed by Levinson. Screenplay, Stephen Hauser, Paul Attanasio, adaptation by Kurt Wimmer, based on the novel by Michael Crichton. Camera, Adam Greenberg; editor, Stu Linder; music, Elliot Goldenthal; production design, Norman Reynolds; costume design, Gloria Gresham; visual-effects supervisor, Jeffrey A. Okun. Reviewed at Century Plaza, L.A., Feb. 9. MPAA Rating: PG-13. Running time: 133 mins.

**Dustin Hoffman (Dr. Norman Goodman), Sharon Stone (Beth Halperin), Samuel L. Jackson (Harry Adams), Peter Coyote (Barnes), Liev Schreiber (Ted Fielding), Queen Latifah (Fletcher).**

*Sphere* is an empty shell. Derivative of any number of famous sci-fi movies and as full of false promises as the Wizard of Oz, this portentous underwater *Thing* swims along with reasonable good humor for its first hour, then descends into mechanical and routine "suspense" sequences that fail to deliver what genre fans demand. Major star names will have to deliver the B.O. goods opening weekend, because attendance will plummet fast when the word gets out.

Psychologist Dr. Norman Goodman is summoned to a remote Pacific site where group leader Barnes throws him together with biochemist Beth Halperin, mathematician Harry Adams, and astrophysicist Ted Fielding. The hastily assembled crew is taken a thousand feet down, where they view an amazing sight: a submerged spacecraft nearly a half-mile long that crashed 288 years earlier.

U.S. release: Feb. 13 — U.S. B.O.: $37 million
Int'l release: March 12 — Int'l B.O.: $36 million

## Spice World (U.K.)

A Polygram/Sony release of a Spice Girls presentation, in association with Polygram Filmed Entertainment and Icon Entertainment Int'l, of a Fragile Films production. Produced by Uri Fruchtman, Barnaby Thompson. Directed by Bob Spiers. Screenplay, Kim Fuller, based on an idea by the Spice Girls and Kim Fuller; additional writing, Jamie Curtis. Camera, Clive Tickner; editor, Andrea MacArthur; music, Paul Newcastle; production design, Grenville Horner; costume design, Kate Carin; choreographer, Priscilla Samuels. Reviewed at Empire Theatre, London, Dec. 16, 1997. Running time: 92 mins.

**Mel B, Emma, Mel C, Geri, Victoria (The Spice Girls), Richard E. Grant (Clifford), Alan Cumming (Piers), George Wendt (Producer), Claire Rushbrook (Deborah), Mark McKinney (Graydon), Richard O'Brien (Damien), Roger Moore (Chief), Barry Humphries (Kevin McMaxford), Jason Flemyng (Brad), Meatloaf (Dennis), Stephen Fry (Judge), Richard Briers (Bishop). As themselves: Elvis Costello, the Dream Boys, Bob Geldof, Bob Hoskins, Elton John, Jonathan Ross.**

A bright and breezy movie that's as timely but evanescent as the Cool Britannia culture it celebrates, *Spice World* will delight the Fab Five's pre-pubescent fans, recall fond memories of the 1960s to those who actually lived through them, and be quickly forgotten. More retro than the genuinely groundbreaking *A Hard Day's Night* it apes, pic manages to paper over its weak script with enough decibels and optimistic energy to light up a city. Result should mop up juicy, though not stratospheric, business in fast playoff.

Picture is not so much a story as a series of musical opportunities dotted with celeb cameos, following the Spices through five days leading up to their first live gig in London's Royal Albert Hall. En route, the movie takes potshots at the tabloid press, the capital's glitterati, and the media in general, as well as stirring in beaucoup filmic refs to amuse oldsters while the young'uns are transfixed by the girls and their music.

U.S. release: Jan. 23 — U.S. B.O.: $29 million
Int'l release: Dec. 24, 1997 — Int'l B.O.: $49 million

## Spring in my Hometown (South Korea)

A Korean Film Art Center/Baek Du-Daegan Co. Ltd production. Directed, written by Kwangmo Lee. Camera, Hyungkoo Kim; editor, Sungwon Ham; music, Il Won; production design, Jae

Hee Song; sound, Seungshul Lee. Reviewed at Cannes Festival, May 15, 1998. Running time: 110 mins.

**With: Sungki Ahn, Yoojung Bae, Oksook Song, Seonhoi Yoo, In Lee.**

Kwangmo Lee's exquisite first feature is one of those slowly paced, minimalist Asian pics which play well at festivals but rarely make it into Western arthouse cinemas. Buffs will revel in the film's placid beauty, but patience is needed for full appreciation of the film and the director's penchant for staging key scenes in extreme long shot will make even TV exposure problematic.

The film spans 1952-53 in a tiny backwater far from the battleground of the Korean War. However, the conflict impinges on the traditional lives of these villagers via the unwanted presence of American troops and their fraternization with local women. Pic is seen from the inquisitive perspective of a little boy and his best friend who delight on spying on the Yank soldiers.

## Star Kid

A Trimark release of a Jennie Lew Tugend presentation of a Manny Coto production. Produced by Tugend. Directed, written by Manny Coto. Camera, Ronn Schmidt; editor, Bob Ducsay; music, Nicholas Pike; production design, C.J. Strawn; costume design, Ileane Meltzer; special makeup effects, Thomas R. Burman, Bari Dreiband-Burman; visual effects, Thomas C. Rainone. Reviewed at Todd-AO, Santa Monica, Jan. 8. Running time: 101 mins.

**Joseph Mazzello (Spencer Griffith), Joey Simmrin (Turbo Bruntley), Alex Daniels (Cybersuit), Brian Simpson (Bloodwarrior), Richard Gilliland (Rolan Griffith), Corinne Bohrer (Teacher).**

A family film that at best feels a lot like a videogame, *Star Kid* has entertaining special effects and cartoonishly gory battle scenes that should strike a responsive chord with pre-adolescent boys. But apart from that demographic, pic is unlikely to find much of an audience; its plot is thin, characters stock, and action sequences frequently formulaic.

The story centers on skinny, introverted seventh-grader Spencer Griffith, who spends recess trying to escape Turbo, the class bully. Though his teacher encourages him to face his fears, Spencer can no more summon the courage to talk to a pretty girl he admires than he can steel himself to fight the bully. That changes one night when Spencer spots a meteor crashing into the local junkyard. He ventures into the area to find Cybsorsuit, an amiable robot searching for a biotic host or organic life form to inhabit its android shell. Somewhat unwittingly, Spencer volunteers and once inside Cy finds he's endowed with superpowers.

U.S. release: Jan. 16          U.S. B.O.: $7 million
Int'l release: May 15          Int'l B.O.: $2 million

## Star Trek: Insurrection

A Paramount release of a Rick Berman production. Produced by Berman. Directed by Jonathan Frakes. Screenplay, Michael Piller, from story by Piller, Berman, based on *Star Trek* created by Gene Roddenberry. Camera, Matthew F. Leonetti; editor, Peter E. Berger; music, Jerry Goldsmith; production design, Herman Zimmerman; costume design, Sanja Milkovic Hays; makeup design, Michael Westmore; stunt coordinator, Rick Avery; visual-effects supervisors, Adam Howard, Jim Rygiel. Reviewed at the Cinemark Tinseltown Westchase, Houston, Dec. 9. MPAA Rating: PG. Running time: 100 mins.

**Patrick Stewart (Capt. Jean-Luc Picard), Jonathan Frakes (Cmdr. William Riker), Brent Spiner (Lt. Cmdr. Data), LeVar Burton (Lt. Geordi La Forge), Michael Dorn (Lt. Cmdr. Worf), Gates McFadden (Dr. Beverly Crusher), Martina Sirtis (Lt. Cmdr. Deanna Troi), F. Murray Abraham (Ru'afro), Donna Murphy (Anji), Anthony Zerbe (Adm. Dougherty).**

The *Star Trek* feature franchise continues apace with a ninth chapter aimed primarily at an audience of fans. A distinct comedown from its immediate prior installment, *Star Trek: Insurrection* plays less like a stand-alone sci-fi adventure than an expanded episode of *Star Trek: The Next Generation*. Still, it strikes a deft balance of predictable heroics and quirky humor to ensure respectable if not spectacular theatrical biz. Down the road, pic should live long and prosper in ancillary venues.

The Ba'ku, peaceful inhabitants of an idyllic planet, have been ordered to relocate, thanks to an ends-justify-means alliance between Federation leaders and new allies, the Son'a. Capt. Jean-Luc Picard leads the Enterprise crew to the Ba'ku planet, discovering its 600 inhabitants long ago rejected advanced technology and, thanks to the metaphasic radiation permeating their planet, remain eternally youthful. Picard and his fellow officers begin to enjoy the same benefits of this natural phenomenon. Ru'afro, the visually hideous leader of the Son'a, wants to replace the Ba'ku, so his people can gain control of the radiation. Picard isn't so easily swayed.

U.S. release: Dec. 11          U.S. B.O.: $54 million
Int'l release: Dec. 24          Int'l B.O.: $1.1 million

## Stephen King's The Night Flier

A New Line Cinema release of a New Amsterdam Entertainment/Stardust Int'l/Medusa Film presentation of a Richard P. Rubinstein production. Produced by Rubinstein, Mitchell Galin. Directed by Mark Pavia. Screenplay, Pavia, Jack O'Donnell, based on a story by Stephen King. Camera, David Connell; editor, Elizabeth Schwartz; music, Brian Keane; production design, Burton Rencher; costume design, Pauline White. Reviewed at New Line, L.A., Feb. 4. MPAA Rating: R. Running time: 97 mins.

**Miguel Ferrer (Richard Dees), Julie Entwisle (Katherine Blair), Dan Monahan (Merton Morrison), Merton H. Moss (Dwight Renfield), John Bennes (Ezra Hannon), Beverly Skinner (Selida McCamon).**

*Stephen King's The Night Flier* is a creepy vampire tale that offers some clever commentary on bloodthirsty tabloid journalists. While not the most memorable King adaptation, it's far from the worst, and with King's name emblazoned in the title, pic may profit from scribe's following in limited theatrical release before it segues to a long and comfortable video life.

In the hectic offices of the tabloid *Inside View*, a rivalry develops between veteran reporter and paparazzo Richard Dees and eager young rookie Katherine Blair. In a pair of recent murders, an unidentified Cessna pilot has landed on small, isolated airfields to feed on the blood of local residents. When Dees passes on the story, it's given to Blair. But when another murder takes place, Dees changes his mind.

U.S. release: Feb. 6          U.S. B.O.: $125,000
Int'l release: Sept. 26, 1997          Int'l B.O.: $1.3 million

## Stepmom

A Sony Pictures Entertainment release of a Columbia Pictures presentation of a Wendy Finerman and 1492 production.

---

Produced by Finerman, Chris Columbus, Mark Radcliffe, Michael Barnathan. Directed by Columbus. Screenplay, Gigi Levangie, Jessie Nelson, Steven Rogers, Karen Leigh Hopkins, Ron Bass; story by Levangie. Camera, Donald M. McAlpine; editor, Neil Travis; music, John Williams; production design, Stuart Wurtzel; costume design, Joseph G. Aulisi. Reviewed at Sony, Culver City, Nov. 17. MPAA Rating: PG-13. Running time: 124 mins.

**Julia Roberts (Isabel), Susan Sarandon (Jackie), Ed Harris (Luke), Jena Malone (Anna), Liam Aiken (Ben), Lynn Whitfield (Dr. Sweikert), Darrell Larson (Duncan Samuels).**

Tears are jerked with strenuously sincere calculation in *Stepmom*, which sees some very talented thesps working over the most mawkish conventions as if they were freshly minted. The combined efforts of five screenwriters ensured that not a single cliche of the modern feel-good tragic melodrama genre has gone unturned, resulting in a soggy heart-tugger that will be last on any guy's Christmas want-see list but will attract, and connect with, more than enough women to make it a solid hit.

Isabel is a New York fashion photographer, so fabulously talented that she can dash off her shoots in three minutes flat. Having just moved into the apartment of b.f. Luke Harrison, she is instantly saddled with his kids. Less thrilled is Luke's ex-wife Jackie, a suburban supermom who finds Luke's new woman young, self-involved, and clueless about kids; Isabel, not unjustifiably, finds her "imperious." However, when Jackie is called into her doctor's office and hears, "It's spread," it quickly dawns that the movie has a *Terms of Endearment* destination in mind, one of cloying sentimentality to be arrived at with clear, if teary, eyes.

U.S. release: Dec. 25                    U.S. B.O.: $35 million

## Still Crazy (U.K.)

A Columbia TriStar Films/Sony Pictures release of a Columbia Pictures presentation, in association with the Greenlight Fund, of a Marmot Tandy Prods production. Produced by Amanda Marmot. Directed by Brian Gibson. Screenplay, Dick Clement, Ian La Frenais. Camera, Ashley Rowe; editor, Peter Boyle; music, Clive Langer; production design, Max Gottlieb; costume design, Caroline Harris. Reviewed at Virgin Haymarket, London, Oct. 30. Running time: 95 mins.

**Stephen Rea (Tony Costello), Billy Connolly (Hughie), Jimmy Nail (Les Wickes), Timothy Spall (David "Beano" Baggot), Bill Nighy (Ray Simms), Juliet Aubrey (Karen Knowles), Helena Bergstrom (Astrid Simms), Bruce Robinson (Brian Lovell), Hans Matheson (Luke Shand), Phil Daniels (Neil Gaydon).**

The *Full Monty* formula gets a fresh and inventive spin in *Still Crazy*, a chucklesome, warmly observed comedy about five middle-aged losers who reassemble their 1970s rock band. Shot and played in a low-key, almost offhand style, but with plenty of typically British humor from the pens of veteran scripters Dick Clement and Ian La Frenais, this small, character-driven item has the makings of a local click that could work internationally, though careful marketing and word of mouth will be crucial.

Pic is a slowly engrossing portrait of ex-rockers whose comeback is dogged by the same tensions that led to their acrimonious breakup 21 years earlier. Strange Fruit was a classic rock band, riven by drugs, booze, egos, and sex, that was finished in 1977 by "divine intervention" at an open-air festival – when a bolt of lightning canceled the gig. One day the son

of the fateful fest promoter bumps into keyboard player Tony and suggests the Fruits hold a reunion concert at the same outdoor venue. In London, Tony contacts their former PA, Karen, and the pair set about rounding up the group. Guitarist-composer Les is running a one-man roofing business; addled lead singer Ray is living in an English country manse with his second wife; corpulent drummer Beano works in a flower nursery in permanent fear of the tax authorities. All are flat broke. Guts of the picture is the band's odyssey marked by embarrassing disasters, the resurgence of old frictions, a growing re-attraction between Tony and Karen, and the pursuit of Beano by a mystery lady.

U.S. release: Dec. 11               U.S. B.O.: $25,000
Int'l release: Oct. 31             Int'l B.O.: $1.5 million

## Storefront Hitchcock (Concert Docu)

An Orion Pictures presentation of a Clinica Estetico production. Produced by Peter Saraf. Directed by Jonathan Demme. Camera, Anthony Jannelli; editor, Andy Keir; creative adviser, Kirsten Coyne. Reviewed at San Francisco Festival, April 28. Running time: 77 mins.

**With: Robyn Hitchcock, Deni Bonet, Tim Keegan.**

The eccentric appeal of Brit singer-songwriter Robyn Hitchcock gets a nice showcase in Jonathan Demme's performance-record feature. While unlikely to have the same impact as helmer's earlier breaks from major studio projects, pic should scare up some change in limited release, then enjoy decent shelf life via rep-house, vid, and cable circuits.

Never much noticed at home, Hitchcock first won U.S. cult attention as part of the Cambridge-bred Soft Boys in the late 1970s. Going solo, he was a U.S. modern-rock radio staple through the late 1980s. As a lyricist, Hitchcock spins out surreal, often humorous juxtapositions. As a melodist, he's indebted to the breadth of a U.K. Oddjob Rock Troubadour tradition stretching from novelty-pop Herman's Hermits to ex-Pink Floyd nutty experimenter Syd Barrett and wispy romantics like Nick Drake.

U.S. release: Nov. 18                U.S. B.O.: $30,000

## The Storm Riders (Fung Wan: Hungba Tinha)
(Hong Kong)

A Golden Harvest release of a Golden Harvest Pictures Ltd presentation, in association with Centro Digital (Hong Kong) and Tian Shan Film Studio (China), of a Bob & Partners Co. production. Produced by Raymond Chow, John Chu. Directed by Andrew Lau. Screenplay, Manfred Wong, based on a screenplay by Chau Ting, based on the manga by Ma Wing-shing. Camera, Lau; editors, Mak Chi-sin, Pang Fat; music supervisor, Chan Kwong-wing; production design, Wong Ka-nang; costume design, Lee Pik-kwan; martial-arts director, Dion Lam; visual-effects director, Wong Kin-ming. Reviewed at Golden Village Pavilion, Singapore, July 25. Running time: 126 mins.

**Aaron Kwok (Cloud), Ekin Cheng (Wind), Sonny Chiba (Lord Conqueror), Kristy Yang (Charity), Shu Qi (Muse), Michael Tse (Frost), Anthony Wong (Sword Saint), Lawrence Cheng (Jester).**

An ambitious attempt to replicate a popular martial arts manga on the bigscreen with elaborate CGI work and location shooting in China, *The Storm Riders* largely succeeds on the tech front but, like many genre pics, hits problems compressing its complex story. Heavily promoted, star-laden pic got off to a good start in Hong Kong. On the strength of helmer Andrew Lau's name, this entertaining extravaganza should roll into fantasy-fest slots and play the midnight circuit.

Martial arts king Lord Conqueror is informed by acolytes that he can remain invincible by adopting two young disciples, children Wind and Cloud. They will help him, 10 years hence, in a duel with his only remaining threat, the Sword Saint. He promptly kidnaps the kids. A decade later, Lord Conqueror pairs the grown Wind with his daughter, Charity, much to the chagrin of Cloud.

In a subsequent duel between the young men, Charity is accidentally killed, and Cloud later loses his arm in a fight with his master. In grace, Cloud is tended to by Muse, and her father, a herbalist doctor who gives his left arm so Cloud can fight another day. L.C. Wind is sent on a mission for Lord Conqueror's imminent duel with the Sword Saint. En route, however, he learns it's actually heading into a trap.

Int'l release: July 18                    Int'l B.O.: $13 million

## Street Heart (Le Coeur Au Poing) (Canada)

A France Film release of a Cité-Amerique production. Produced by Lorraine Richard. Directed by Charles Biname. Screenplay, Biname, Monique Proulx. Camera, Pierre Gill; editor, Claude Palardy; music, Richard Gregoire, Yves Desrosiers; art direction, Danielle Labrie; costume design, Daniel Lalande. Reviewed at the Quartier Latin Cinema, Montreal, March 11. Running time: 101 mins.

Pascale Montpetit (Louise), Guy Nadon (Julien), Anne-Marie Cadieux (Paulette), Guylaine Tremblay (Marlene), Rita Lafontaine (Rita).

With *Street Heart*, Montreal helmer Charles Biname returns to the same seamy downtown streets he first visited in 1995's *Eldorado*. This is a mighty stylish exercise, but the story is simply not compelling. Pic's real revelation is Quebec thesp Pascale Montpetit, who energizes the slight script with a powerhouse performance. *Street Heart* will click with hip young auds on its home turf. Beyond the fest circuit it won't make much of a dent.

Louise is not a happy camper. She's suffering from a serious lack of quality relationships and has a desperate craving to connect emotionally. Her sister, Paulette, is a cold, career-oriented type who has scant patience for Louise's bohemian lifestyle. Louise's lover, Julien, is a passionate, poetic fellow but, unfortunately, married with a child.

U.S. release: March 13                    U.S. B.O.: $150,000

## A Stranger in the Kingdom

A Whiskeyjack Pictures/Kingdom Come Pictures presentation, in association with Northflow Partners II. Produced, directed by Jay Craven. Screenplay, Don Bredes, Craven, based on the novel by Howard Frank Mosher. Camera, Philip Holahan; editor, Elizabeth Schwartz; music, the Horse Flies; production/costume design, Stephanie Kerley Schwartz. Reviewed at Hollywood Festival, Aug. 9. Running time: 112 mins.

David Lansbury (Charlie Kinneson), Ernie Hudson (Rev. Walter Andrews), Martin Sheen (Sigurd Moulton), Bill Raymond (Resolved Kinneson), Sean Nelson (Nat Andrews), Jean Louisa Kelly (Athena Allen), Jordan Bayne (Claire LaRivierre), Henry Gibson (Zack Burrows).

A handsome, sober social drama, *A Stranger in the Kingdom* is long on good intentions and a tad flat when it comes to dramatic tension. Though it looks great on the big screen, its subject matter, leisurely pacing, and even the cast seem better suited to television. Securing theatrical bookings will be an uphill struggle for the filmmakers, who might see more returns from cable sales and video biz.

Set in the 1950s in a rural Vermont town, the story hinges on the arrival of a new minister. A former army chaplain, Walter Andrews also happens to be black. That fact somehow eluded the people who hired him over the phone. A couple of the townsfolk are openly hostile to the churchman and his son, but most feign tolerance, harboring the belief that he will pass through and the unfortunate interlude will be quickly forgotten. However, when Claire LaRivierre – a young woman with a notorious reputation – is discovered murdered in the nearby woods, the specter of guilt falls on Andrews. He had befriended and sheltered her from a former, abusive employer.

## Strike! (U.S.-Canada)

A Miramax presentation of a Redeemable Features production, in association with Alliance Communications. Produced by Ira Deutchman, Peter Newman. Directed, written by Sarah Kernochan. Camera, Anthony Janelli; editor, Peter C. Frank; music, Graeme Revell; production design, John Kasarda; costumes, Julie Ganton Whitfield, Ann Hould-ward. Reviewed at Granville Cinemas, Vancouver, Aug. 14, 1998. Running time: 110 mins.

Lynn Redgrave (Miss McVane), Gaby Hoffman (Odie), Kirsten Dunst (Verena), Monica Keena (Tinka), Merritt Wever (Momo), Heather Matarazzo (Tweety), Rachael Leigh Cook (Abby), Vincent Kartheiser (Snake), Tom Guiry (Frosty), Matthew Lawrence (Dennis).

Below the surface of this marketing headache lies a mildly effective coming-of-age saga that could speak to today's girls, and to Boomer survivors of the period depicted. Pic tells the tale of an all-female boarding school that revolts when forced to go co-ed in the early 1960s, but the impenetrable title and uneven tone seem to make it hard for *Strike!* to find an appreciative audience. A happier graduation to vid is assured.

Gaby Hoffman is Ondine, aka Odie, who gets shipped to Miss Godard's School for Girls when caught trysting with her randy boyfriend. Once there, she reluctantly falls in with trouble-making Verena, brainy Momo, boy-mad Tinka, and food-obsessed Tweety. Despite herself, Odie starts enjoying this largely monosexual environment, with its emphasis on academic achievement. But the financially strapped school is threatened with annexation by a more powerful boys' academy. The mixed reaction this gets from the girls is the crux of the movie.

U.S. release: Aug. 14                    U.S. B.O.: $1.1 million

## Such a Long Journey (Canada-U.K.)

A Red Sky release of a Film Works/Amy Int'l Artists presentation. Produced by Paul Stephens, Simon MacCorkindale. Directed by Sturla Gunnarsson. Screenplay, Sooni Taraporevala, based on the novel by Rohinton Mistry. Camera, Jan Kiesser; editor, Jeff Warren; music, Jonathan Goldsmith; production design, Nitin Desai; costume design, Lovleen Bains. Reviewed at Toronto Festival, Sept. 13. Running time: 112 mins.

Roshan Seth (Gustad Noble), Soni Razdan (Dilnavaz Noble), Om Puri (Ghulam), Naseeruddin Shah (Jimmy Bilimoria), Ranjit Chowdhry (Pavement Artist), Sam Dastor (Dinshawji).

Friendship and good intentions – and how they can lead to bad ends – inform this adaptation of Rohinton Mistry's sprawling novel *Such a Long Journey.* Set in Bombay in 1971, the film falls short of its source material's power by emphasizing the unflagging decency of its central character and losing sight of the book's biting irony. Pic can expect no more than tame returns in upscale niche theatrical distribution and in ancillary exploitation.

Gustad Noble is a middle-aged Parsee bank worker. He's toiled hard all his life for his family, which includes a sickly young daughter and a son who's split from the clan over his schooling. His life appears dull, consumed by the minutiae of home, work, and the bustle of the big city. A letter from Jimmy Bilimoria, a friend with political connections who mysteriously vanished several years earlier, rocks the household balance. Jimmy implores his friend to launder money through the bank for a patriotic cause. The country's in the throes of war with Pakistan over Bangladesh, and the implication is that the lucre will be diverted toward that effort. The act – likely Gustad's first illegal action – subtly changes him. He begins to perceive and respond to the events surrounding him as challenges to be remedied, and this outlook renews his zest for life.

## Sue

An AMKO Prods production. Produced, directed, written by Amos Kollek. Camera, Ed Talavera; editor, Liz Gazzara; music, Chico Freeman; production design, Charlotte Bourke; costume design, Seth Hanson. Reviewed at Toronto Festival, Sept. 12, 1997. Running time: 90 mins.
**Anna Thomson (Sue), Matthew Powers (Ben), Tahnee Welch (Lola), Tracee Ross (Linda), Austin Pendleton (Bob).**

As the title character in writer-director Amos Kollek's *Sue,* Anna Thomson offers a haunting portrayal of a lonely Manhattanite who slowly descends into madness. But the indie production itself is an unsatisfying mix of gritty realism, poignant sentiment, and scenes that, perhaps inadvertently, play like deadpan comedy. Pic lacks commercial potential, even as a homevideo release, but may generate interest on fest circuit. Sue is a fairly attractive woman in her mid-to-late thirties, but her air of detached bewilderment indicates she is perilously close to the edge. As the drama slowly unfolds, it's revealed that Sue is an unemployed office worker who spends many of her days going to job interviews that never pan out. She's behind in rent and impulsively accepts a hard-bitten prostitute as a short-term roommate.

Int'l release: Sept. 10      Int'l B.O.: $800,000
U.S. release: Nov. 22      U.S. B.O.: $35,000

## The Sugar Factory (Australia)
An Australian Film Finance Corp. presentation of an Imagine Films production, assisted by the Australian Film Commission, NSW Film & TV Office. Produced by Jenny Woods. Directed, written by Robert Carter, based on his novel. Camera, Andrew Lesniw; editor, Wayne Le Clos; music, Peter Best; production design, Nicholas McCallum; costume design, Theresa Jackson. Reviewed at Leura screening room, Leura, Australia, April 18. Running time: 91 mins.
**Matt Day (Harris Berne), Rhondda Findleton (Helen MacMillan), John Waters (Sam Lejeune), Tony Hayes (Marlo), Michela Noonan (Angela), Glen Shea (Joe), Sam Healy (Stephanie).**

Aussie author Robert Carter brings his widely praised novel *The Sugar Factory* to the big screen in his film directing debut. This modestly conceived low-budgeter centers on a confused,

traumatized teenager who undergoes therapy. But despite the intelligence and dedication on display here, pic will struggle to find an audience – to date it's been bypassed by Aussie distribs.

Harris Berne, 17, has been "different" since childhood, when his favorite activity was sitting under his parents' house pounding sandstone into fine grain ("sugar," he called it) with a galvanized bolt. A loner, Harris becomes smitten with Helen, a divorced woman with two children. While baby-sitting them, the little girl hides in a refrigerator during a game of hide-and-seek, and expires. The devastated Harris is sent to the Cottage, a halfway house for disturbed teens. Helped by a psychiatrist, he begins to address his demons and the root of his emotional trauma.

## A Summer by the River (Kuningasjatka) (Finland)
A Buena Vista Int'l release of a Fennada Filmi production. Produced by Kari Sara. Directed, written by Markku Polonen. Camera, Kari Sohlberg; editor, Jukka Nykanen; music, Vesa Makinen; production designer, Minna Santakari; costume designer, Tiina Kaukanen. Reviewed at Skandia Cinema, Stockholm, Sweden, March 12. Running time: 86 mins.
**Pertti Koivula (Tenho), Simo Kontio (Topi), Esko Nikkari (Hannes), Anu Palevaara (Hikka), Peter Franzin (Kottarainen).**

Intentionally recalling Scandi pictures of the 1950s in look and feel, *A Summer by the River* is a charming coming-of-ager that's been a B.O. hit on home turf in Finland and could generate some foreign interest. Set in the mid-1950s, new pic centers on Tenho who, after his wife dies, takes his 10-year-old son, Topi, to eastern Finland and gets a summer job as a logger. The work is hard, and the cynical, sometimes brutal loggers initially harass Tenho. During the course of the summer, however, he earns their respect.

Int'l release: Feb. 15      Int'l B.O.: $1.8 million

## Summer of the Monkeys (Canada)
A BWE Distribution presentation of an Edge Prods production. Produced by David Doerksen. Directed by Michael Anderson. Screenplay, Greg Taylor, Jim Strain, based on the book by Wilson Rawls. Camera, Michael Storey; editor, Lenka Svab; music, George Blondheim; production design, Seamus Flannery; costume design, Lynda Kemp. Reviewed at Toronto Festival, Sept. 12. Running time: 101 mins.
**Michael Ontkean (John Lee), Leslie Hope (Sara Lee), Wilford Brimley (Grandpa Sam Ferens), Corey Sevier (Jay Berry Lee), Katie Stuart (Daisy Lee), Don Francks (Bayliss Hatcher), Andre Therein (Jobert).**

There's not much to *Summer of the Monkeys.* The family film set at the turn-of-the-century is dripping with old-fashioned values and warmth in the tradition of *The Waltons* and effectively ambles through its relatively cut-and-dried story. The absence of contemporary resonance severely limits theatrical prospects, but it would seem a natural for TV sales both domestically and abroad that could motivate some modest video movement.

Film's focus is the near-picture-perfect Lee family. Father John is a hard-working farmer who prays for good weather, his wife is attentive, and their children include the precocious Jay Berry and the crippled Daisy. In the nearby town, Gramps runs the general store. Jay Berry's dream is to save up enough money working at the store during summer recess to buy a pony, and he sees his chance to earn some extra money when a quartet of circus monkeys escape into the wilds after a train wreck. The young boy stumbles onto their newfound enclave near the farm but capturing them and collecting the posted reward prove to be a bit of a challenge. Along the way, Jay learns some valuable life lessons that will presumably form the bedrock for his adult character.

U.S. release: Sept. 18                    U.S. B.O.: $50,000

## Sun Bird (China)

A Yunnan Nationality Film Studio production. Directed by Wang Xueqi, Yang Liping. Screenplay, Yang. Camera, Zhang Li; editor, Yuxi Zhang Haihong; music, Zhao Jiping; art director, Cao Bin. Reviewed at World Film Festival, Montreal, Sept. 3. Running time: 100 mins.
**Yang Liping (Tana), Wang Xueqi (Yuan Wen).**
Filled with entrancing, spectacular dance sequences, *Sun Bird* looks great. The trouble is that the drama surrounding the choreographed sequences is not nearly as captivating as the onstage performances of co-director Yang Liping. Based in part on her life story, this tale of a young girl from a remote village who becomes a dance star and suffers an emotional breakdown is full of dramatic possibility. But the film's main characters are curiously cold and lifeless. Chances of *Sun Bird* taking flight beyond the fest horizon are slim. Pic won the Special Grand Prix of the Jury at Montreal.

Tana is having trouble with her eyesight, and doctors suggest her problem may well be psychological. She is haunted by memories of her difficult childhood in a remote mountain village; in fact, most of her dances seem to be drawn from her rural background. She lost both parents at a young age and is particularly scarred by the death of her mother during childbirth. Life in the village rotated around various dance rituals, notably fertility dances. Tana's obsession with the tribal chief who led the dance ceremonies makes it hard for her to build relationships as an adult. Her manager and lover, Yuan Wen, is unable to break through her psychic defenses.

## Surrender Dorothy

A Rich Entertainment presentation. Produced by Richard Goldberg. Directed, written, edited by Kevin DiNovis. Camera, Jonathan Kovel; music, Christopher Matarazzo; production design, Michael Doyle. Reviewed at Slamdance Festival, Park City, Utah, Jan. 21. Running time: 87 mins.
**Peter Pryor (Trevor), Kevin DiNovis (Lanh/Dorothy), Jason Centeno (Denis), Elizabeth Casey (Vicky), Marcos Muniz (Angel).**
Slamdance Grand Prize winner *Surrender Dorothy* is a disturbing, hard-edged tale of physical abuse and sexual aberration that pulls no punches. The graphic, psychologically wrenching film – shot in black-and-white – is decidedly for niche tastes. Nonetheless, the assurance of the storytelling and indelible performances make this a distinctive, compelling story with specialized potential that heralds an exciting young talent in Kevin DiNovis.

Film focuses on two men who are drawn together by need and circumstance. Trevor works at a dead-end job at an upscale restaurant. Lanh is a heroin addict living on his wiles and whatever he can scam or steal. Having robbed a dealer, Lanh almost literally bumps into Trevor, who takes pity on the desperate man and offers him shelter. But even if the initial act was generously motivated, the relationship evolves into a twisted master-servant dynamic.

## Susan's Plan

A Kushner-Locke presentation of a Landis/Belzberg/Wyman production. Produced by Leslie Belzberg, Brad Wyman, John Landis. Directed, written by Landis. Camera, Ken Kelsch; editor, Nancy Morrison; music, Peter Bernstein; production design, Stuart Blatt; costume design, Deborah Nadoolman. Reviewed at AFI Festival, Oct. 29. Running time: 89 mins.
**Nastassja Kinski (Susan Holland), Billy Zane (Sam), Michael Biehn (Bill), Rob Schneider (Steve), Lara Flynn Boyle (Betty Johnson), Dan Aykroyd (Bob), Paul (Adrian Paul), Thomas Haden Church (Dr. Chris Stillman), Bill Duke (Det. Scott), Lisa Edelstein (Penny Byers).**
Greed is good and fitfully funny in John Landis' filigree, *Susan's Plan*. This yarn of a woman out to murder her ex-husband and collect on his insurance policy is largely nonsensical, but Landis keeps the action antic, which is almost enough to sweep pic's myriad shortcomings under the carpet. Independently made lightweight suspenser is a niche theatrical outing with modest B.O. potential but should enjoy a longer sales life in cable rotation and as a subsequent video rental.

The story hits the ground running with Susan and current squeeze Sam, an insurance salesman, plotting the demise of her reprehensible former husband, Paul. Sam recruits Bill and Steve, marginals who owe him a favor, to do the job, while Susan enlists her hairdresser, Betty, to lure the victim to a fateful appointment. When Paul arrives for an early-morning assignation, the low-rent gunmen jump out in stocking caps and plug him three times at pointblank range. But this is supposed to be a comedy, so, naturally, the bullets miss every vital organ. Plan B is to have lunkheaded biker Bob sneak into intensive care and smother the recuperating Paul with a pillow. Meanwhile, Betty is to keep the attending physician occupied by every means possible.

## Suzie Washington (Austria)

A Filmladen release of an Allegro Film production. Produced by Helmut Grasser. Directed, written by Florian Flicker, story by Michael Sturminger, Flicker. Camera, Robert Neumuller; editor, Monika Willi; music, Andi Haller; art director, Christoph Kanter; costume design, Heidi Melinc. Reviewed at San Sebastian Festival, Sept. 19. Running time: 87 mins.
**Birgit Doll (Nana), August Zirner (Herbert Korn), Karl Ferdinand Kratzl (Fugitive), Wolfram Berger (Lodge Manager).** (English and German dialog)
Austrian director Florian Flicker, who clocked some festival miles with his imaginative low-budget sci-fi debut, *Half World*, in 1993, follows with *Suzie Washington*, an intense, compelling road movie about the flight of an illegal immigrant. Tightly scripted, confidently directed, and persuasively performed, the drama cleverly uses the postcard scenery of the Austrian countryside to create a seemingly hospitable but rather chilly wonderland for its latter-day Alice without a visa. Limited European theatrical dates and wider foreign-language TV slots should follow.

The film follows a carefully mapped path from crowded civilization in the chaotic airport-set opening to unpopulated mountain wilderness in its closing scenes near the Austrian-German border. Having struggled for years to get out of her former Soviet homeland, teacher Nana is detained by officials at Vienna airport with a fake visa as she tries to board a connecting flight to the U.S. But while awaiting deportation, she seizes the opportunity to escape during the confusion of a

---

police incident involving a fellow illegal alien. Jumping on a tour bus, Nana encounters Suzie Washington, an American traveler whose name she later appropriates as she flees across the countryside.

## Sweety Barrett (Ireland)

A Handmade Films presentation of a Temple Films/Peter Rommel Prods/Icelandic Film Corp. production. Produced by Ed Guiney. Directed, written by Stephen Bradley. Camera, Thomas Mauch; editor, Dermot Diskin; music, Stephen McKeon; production design, Nathan Crowly, Paki Smith; costumes, Lorna Marie Mugan. Reviewed at Toronto Film Festival, Sept. 13. Running time: 92 mins.

**Brendan Gleeson (Sweety Barrett), Liam Cunningham (Det. Mannix Bone), Lynda Steadman (Anne King), Andy Serkis (Leo King), Dylan Murphy (Conor King), Tony Rohr (Flick Hennessy).**

Anchored by a riveting performance from Brendan Gleeson, *Sweety Barrett* is a strange, intriguing morality tale that is as original as it is emotionally satisfying. First-time helmer Stephen Bradley skillfully builds the drama in this adult fable about a simple man stuck in a corrupt Irish town. The languid pace will not help the film's commercial prospects, but the standout turn by Gleeson and the accessible appeal of this evocative story should stir up some theatrical interest.

Sweety Barrett has just lost his circus job of swallowing various objects. He meets a bootlegger, Flick Hennessy, who sets him up in a hostel in the port town of Dockery and hires him to do odd jobs. When Sweety meets Anne King and her 6-year-old son Conor, the huge, simple man, immediately hits it off with the boy. In short order, life becomes a lot more complicated for Sweety. He bumps heads with the town's demented police chief, Mannix Bone, who routinely beats up locals, exacts graft from businessmen, and tosses enemies into jail on trumped-up charges.

## A Tale of Autumn (Conte D'Automne) (France)

A Les Films du Losange release of a Les Films du Losange/La Sept Cinema production, with the participation of Canal Plus, Sofilmka, Rhone-Alpes Cinema. Produced by Margaret Menegoz. Directed, written by Eric Rohmer. Camera, Diane Baratier; editor, Mary Stephen; music, Claude Marti, Gerard Pansanel, Pierre Peyras, Antonello Salis. Reviewed at Club Gaumont, Paris, Aug. 4. Running time: 112 mins.

**Marie Riviere (Isabelle), Beatrice Romand (Magali), Alain Libolt (Gerald), Didier Sandre (Etienne), Alexia Portal (Rosine).**

The fourth installment in Eric Rohmer's seasonal-themed series, *A Tale of Autumn* flirts with various semi-devious approaches to matchmaking among the over-40 set. A deftly layered meditation on men, women, friendship, and the prospect of romance in the Rhône Valley, pic will definitely tickle helmer's fans but do nothing to dispel the received wisdom that French movies are slow-moving and talky. Offshore sales are a foregone conclusion.

Pic unspools in a leisurely and deliberate manner, introducing characters and laying essential groundwork, before coming to life – after which its quirky pleasures build to a satisfying denouement. Best friends Magali and Isabelle have known each other since childhood. Magali, a widow, proudly tends the vineyard she inherited from her parents, but feels lonely out in the country since her two grown children left

home. She admits she'd relish companionship, but her prospects for meeting an available man seem slim. Bookshop owner Isabelle lives in town with her husband of 24 years, and they will soon be marrying their daughter. Determined to find a suitable guy for Magali, Isabelle secretly places a lonely hearts ad and filters the responses. Using her own name but appropriating Magali's bio, Isabelle starts to "date" respondent Gerald. Once she begins the "test drive," the crafty humor of her machination – and the film itself – kick in.

Int'l release: Sept. 23                    Int'l B.O.: $3.5 million

## Talk of Angels

A Miramax Films release of a Polaris Pictures Ltd production. Produced by Patrick Cassavetti. Directed by Nick Hamm. Screenplay, Ann Guedes, Frank McGuinness, based on the novel *Mary Lavelle* by Kate O'Brien. Camera, Alexei Rodionov; editor, Gerry Hambling; music, Trevor Jones; production design, Michael Howells; costume design, Liz Waller, Lala Huete. Reviewed at Sony, Culver City, Oct. 21. MPAA rating: PG-13. Running time: 96 mins.

**Polly Walker (Mary Lavelle), Vincent Perez (Francisco Areavaga), Franco Nero (Dr. Vicente Areavaga), Marisa Paredes (Don Consuelo), Leire Berrocal (Milagros), Penelope Cruz (Pilar), Frances McDormand (Conlon), Ruth McCabe (O'Toole), Francisco Rabal (Don Jorge).**

A love story set against the backdrop of the Spanish Civil War, *Talk of Angels* has several elements of a romantic epic but none of the passion or power. Despite a prominent international cast, pic's central romance suffers from a lack of chemistry. Pic, which lacks recognizable American stars and has been in a holding pattern on Miramax's release sked for eons, will be overshadowed in the domestic marketplace. Overseas prospects are marginally better.

Based on Kate O'Brien's novel *Mary Lavelle*, *Talk of Angels* is the story of a young Irish governess who has left her homeland to spend a year working for the Areavagas, a wealthy family in Spain. Already entranced by the country's beauty and history, Mary soon becomes intrigued with the family's handsome son, Francisco, who, though married, reciprocates. With Spain on the brink of war and riots erupting in the streets, Francisco and Mary must decide whether they can pursue their forbidden love, doomed though it may be.

U.S. release: Oct. 30                    U.S. B.O.: $20,000

## Tango (Spain-Argentina)

An Alma Ata Int'l Pictures (Spain)/Argentina Sono Film (Argentina) production, in association with Astrolabio Producciones, Terraplen Producciones, Adela Pictures, Beco Films, Hollywood Partners. Produced by José Maria Calleja de la Fuente, Alejandro Bellaba. Directed, written by Carlos Saura. Camera, Vittorio Storaro; editor, Julia Juaniz; music, Lalo Schifrin; production design, Emilio Basaldua; choreographers, Juan Carlos Copes, Carlos Rivarola, Ana Maria Stekelman. Reviewed at Impala screening room, Madrid, April 30. Running time: 112 mins.

**Miguel Angel Sola (Mario Suarez), Cecilia Narova (Laura Fuentes), Mia Maestro (Elena Flores), Juan Carlos Copes (Carlos Nebbia), Juan Luis Galiardo (Angelo Larroca), and Julio Bocca as himself.**

Carlos Saura returns to terrain he has made his own with the musical *Tango*, a part-fictional, part-documentary study of Argentina's national dance. Powerful, intelligent, and stunningly lensed by Vittorio Storaro, pic is more than the mere homage of *Sevillanas* and *Flamenco*, and, though purists may complain that there are a few philosophical conversations too many, sales prospects worldwide look solid.

Mario Suarez is a forty-something tango artist whose best years are behind him. His wife, Laura, has left him and he throws himself into his work, leaving his apartment and moving to the outskirts of Buenos Aires, to prepare a film about tango. It is, of course, in the dance pieces that the film's true power resides. Original music by Lalo Schifrin blends seamlessly into a healthy smattering of tango classics that show the uninitiated that tango is not only about passion, but about danger and sorrow, too.

Int'l release: Feb. 12       Int'l B.O.: $2.2 million

## Tangos are for Two (Sus Ojos Se Cerraron)
(Spain-Argentina)

A Buena Vista Int'l release of a Rocabruno, Aurum Prods (Spain)/Patagonik (Argentina) production, in association with BVI Films Prods and Aleph Prods, with the participation of Antena 3 TV (Spain), Telefe (Argentina). Directed by Jaime Chavarri. Screenplay, Oscar Plasencia, Raul Brambilla. Camera (color), Carles Cusi; editor, Pedro del Rey; music, Luis Maria Serra, Daniel Barrardi, Rodolfo Medero; production design, Daniel Feijoo. Reviewed at Palacio de la Musica, Madrid, Jan. 22, 1997. Running time: 91 mins.

**Aitana Sanchez-Gijon (Juanita), Dario Grandinetti (Renzo Franchi), Juan Echanove (Gustavo), Ulises Dumont (Anibal).**
Part musical and part melodrama, vet director Jaime Chavarri's *Tangos are for Two* makes for pleasant, if unchallenging, viewing. The real stars are pic's passion-drenched tangos, but the successfully captured mood of nostalgia should mean reasonable home B.O. amongst the over-forties and other lovers of dark-eyed, frilly-shirted excess. Offshore feet could tap, too, given the right marketing, though the magnificent tango lyrics are unlikely to work in subtitles. Chavarri sets out to celebrate the Argentine musical form as performed by superstar Carlos Gardel. In 1930s Buenos Aires, Juanita is a factory worker, going out with Gustavo but obsessed with Gardel.

Int'l release: April 23       Int'l B.O.: $140,000

## Tarzan and the Lost City

A Warner Bros. presentation of a Dieter Geissler/Alta Vista production, in association with Village Roadshow Pictures–Clipsal Film Partnership. Produced by Stanley Canter, Dieter Geissler, Michael Lake. Directed by Carl Schenkel. Screenplay, Bayard Johnson, J. Anderson Black, based on the stories by Edgar Rice Burroughs. Camera, Paul Gilpin; editor, Harry Hitner; music, Christopher Franke; production designer, Herbert Pinter; costume designer, Jo Katsaras-Barklem. Reviewed at Sony Copley Place, Boston, April 24. MPAA Rating: PG. Running time: 84 mins.

**Casper Van Dien (Tarzan), Jane March (Jane), Steven Waddington (Nigel Ravens), Winston Ntshona (Mugambi), Rapulana Seiphemo (Kaya), Ian Roberts (Capt. Dooley).**
There's a reason *Tarzan and the Lost City* was released with little or no fanfare. This silly adventure comes across more like a sequel to *George of the Jungle*, but without the laughs. Box-office action will soon be as scarce as a map to the Lost City. The story picks up in England in 1913, on the eve of Tarzan's marriage to Jane. Instead of exchanging vows, he rushes back to the jungle where the evil explorer Nigel Ravens is killing and burning his way to the lost city of Opar, supposedly the cradle of civilization. Jane is soon in pursuit, and the rest of this brief film has them chasing each other through the jungle.

U.S. release: April 24     U.S. B.O.: $2.2 million
Int'l release: April 29     Int'l B.O.: $1.7 million

## Taxi (France)

An ARP Selection release of a Luc Besson presentation of an ARP, TF1 Films Prod, Le Studio Canal Plus production. Produced by Luc Besson, Laurent Petin. Directed by Gerard Pires. Additional direction, Gerard Krawczyk. Screenplay, Luc Besson. Camera, Jean-Pierre Sauvaire; editor, Veronique Lange; music, IAM; art director, Jean-Jacques Gernolle; stunt coordinator, Michel Julienne; assistant director, Stephane Gluck. Reviewed at UGC Odéon, Paris, Apr. 14. Running time: 86 mins.

**Samy Naceri (Daniel), Frederic Diefenthal (Emilien), Marion Cotillard (Lilly), Emma Sjoberg (Petra), Manuela Gourary (Camille).**
Written and co-produced by Luc Besson, and shot in the streets of Marseilles with famous racing drivers handling the real-time stunts, *Taxi* is a basically harmless but overwhelmingly stupid ride. Pic is certain to rack up fares with the undiscriminating arcade-game crowd. Insofar as high-speed chases and car crashes are a universal language, international B.O. could rep a modest pile-up of money.

Story focuses on Daniel, a former pizza-delivery man who drives a souped-up taxi. Rather than lose his license for a speeding offense, Daniel makes a deal with the arresting officer, Emilien, to serve as his personal chauffeur. The two unlikely allies literally chase down a bunch of German bank robbers.

Int'l release: April 14     Int'l B.O.: $43.5 million
U.S. release: Nov. 13     U.S. B.O.: $250,000

## Telling You

A Miramax release of a CineTel presentation of a Division 1 Entertainment production. Produced by David DuPuy. Directed by Robert DeFranco. Screenplay, DeFranco, Marc Palmieri; story by Palmieri, Denis Flood. Camera, Mark Doering-Powell; editor, Louis Cioffi; music, Russ Landau; production design, Sandy Espinet; costume design, Andrea Tiano. Reviewed at Hollywood Festival, Aug. 7. Running time: 94 mins.

**Peter Facinelli (Phil Fazzulo), Dash Mihok (Dennis Nolan), Jennifer Love Hewitt (Deb Friedman), Frank Medrano (Sal Lombardo), Richard Libertini (Mr. P), Robert DeFranco (Steve Fagan), Matthew Lillard (Adam Ginesberg), Rick Rossovich (McQueeney).**
Falling into the oddball American genre of hanging-out pics (*Marty, Diner, Clerks*) is the indie production *Telling You*. Recently acquired by Miramax, pic focuses on a couple of New Jersey high-school hot shots, Phil and Dennis, who took a wrong turn after college and wound up working at their neighborhood pizza joint. They realize that they've been passed by the nerds and geeks they used to mock.

Though the film lacks the punch, craft or insight to reach a wide audience, its predominantly fresh cast and creative team demonstrate the sort of nascent skills that bode well for follow-up work. Essentially a calling-card production, the film could find limited niche theatrical life and ancillary biz domestically, and score some fest and specialized dates internationally.

## The Terrorist (India)

A Moderne Gallerie Motion Pictures (U.S.)/Indian Image Prods (India) presentation of an Indian Image Prods production. Produced by A. Sriram, Abhijeeth. Directed by Santosh Sivan. Screenplay, Sivan, Ravi Deshpande, Vijay Deveshwar. Camera, Sivan; editor, A. Skreekar Prasad; music, Sonu Sisupal, Rajamani; production design, Shyam Sunder; costume design, Anuradha. Reviewed at Toronto Festival, Sept. 17. Running time: 100 mins.

**With: Ayesha Dharkar (Malli), Vishnu Vardhan, Bhanu Prakash, K. Krishna, Sonu Sisupal.** (Tamil dialog)

While the title seems to promise a politically charged thriller, *The Terrorist* is something else entirely. This richly lensed meditation on the value of life vs. the satisfaction of commitment centers on a distaff freedom fighter who's tapped to kill a dignitary, embarking on a physical and spiritual journey in the week leading up to the act. Winner of best film and editing prizes in India, pic may be too moody and claustrophobic for some, but reps an audacious helming bow by cinematographer Santosh Sivan.

A veteran of 30 covert operations for a well-organized resistance outfit, beautiful 19-year-old Malli has killed before but is compassionate enough to be haunted by the death of her brother, the latest in her family to die for the cause. Chosen from an elite group of teenage terrorists to be a "thinking bomb" that dispatches a never-seen VIP, she begins the mundane but dangerous tasks involved in traveling to the city where the deed will be done.

## The Theory of Flight (U.K.)

A Fine Line Features release of a Distant Horizon/BBC Films production. Produced by Helena Spring, Ruth Caleb, David M. Thompson, Anant Singh. Directed by Paul Greengrass. Screenplay, Richard Hawkins. Camera, Ivan Strasburg; editor, Mark Day; music, Rolfe Kent; production design, Melanie Allen; costume design, Dinah Collin. Reviewed at Toronto Festival, Sept. 10. Running time: 99 mins.

**Helena Bonham Carter (Jane Hatchard), Kenneth Branagh (Richard), Gemma Jones (Anne), Holly Aird (Julie), Ray Stevenson (Gigolo).**

A risky idea only occasionally gets both wheels off the ground in *The Theory of Flight*, a sometimes wryly amusing, oftimes dramatically awkward story about a woman in a wheelchair who's determined to lose her virginity before she expires. Pic's hairline flirtation with good taste is mostly kept on course by a terrif lead performance from Helena Bonham Carter, despite the miscasting of Kenneth Branagh and a script that changes gears too many times really to soar. Theatrical prospects look shakier than small-screen ones.

Richard is an artist-cum-dreamer who aspires to human flight but ends up falling off buildings. One stunt in central London lands him with 120 hours of community service, during which he is assigned to Jane, a young woman dying of motor neurone disease. Jane's salty language and fiercely independent attitude have put off a string of social workers. Jane makes it clear that she doesn't want any namby-pamby treatment. When he shows her his latest obsession, a rickety WWI-style biplane he's been building at a remote country hideaway, she reveals her inner secret – she wants to be deflowered.

U.S. release: Dec. 23 U.S. B.O.: $30,000

## There's Something About Mary

A 20th Century Fox release. Produced by Frank Beddor, Michael Steinberg, Charles B. Wessler, Bradley Thomas. Directed by Peter Farrelly, Bobby Farrelly. Screenplay, Ed Decter, John J. Strauss, Peter Farrelly, Bobby Farrelly, story by Decter, Strauss. Camera, Mark Irwin; editor, Christopher Greenbury; music, Jonathan Richman; art director, Arlan Jay Vetter; visual consultant, Sidney J. Bartholomew, Jr.; costume designer, Mary Zophres. Reviewed at the Exchange, Glendale, June 27. MPAA Rating: R. Running time: 118 mins.

**Cameron Diaz (Mary Jenson), Matt Dillon (Pat Healy), Ben Stiller (Ted Stroehmann), Lee Evans (Tucker), Chris Elliott (Dom), Lin Shaye (Magda), Jeffrey Tambor (Sully), W. Earl Brown (Warren).**

Crudely made, somewhat overlong, and larded with plenty of things that don't work, *There's Something About Mary* stands as proof positive that a comedy can be far from perfect and still hit the bullseye if it delivers when it counts in its big scenes. And deliver it does, in episodes and a general outlook of spectacular irreverence, rudeness, and cheek. Add the disarmingly game and gorgeous Cameron Diaz, and the result is a wildly commercial comic cocktail from Peter and Bobby Farrelly that could easily surpass the cosmic B.O. of their first film, *Dumb and Dumber.*

Ted is still mooning about what might have been 13 years earlier at his senior prom when his date with class cutie Mary was interrupted by a stuck zipper. He hires a sleazy private dick, Pat Healy, to find her. But when Pat lays eyes on Mary in Miami and sees she's not only sexy and loves sports but is unattached, he reports back to Ted that his inamorata now weighs 200 pounds and is confined to a wheelchair in a housing project.

U.S. release: July 15 U.S. B.O.: $174.5 million
Int'l release: Aug. 27 Int'l B.O.: $153.5 million

## Things I Left in Havana (Las Cosas Que Deje En La Habana) (Spain)

An Altafilms release of a Sogetel/Tornasol Films production, in association with Canal Plus Espana, Sogepaq. Produced by Gerardo Herrero. Directed by Manuel Gutierrez Aragon. Screenplay, Gutierrez Aragon, Senel Paz. Camera, Teo Escamilla; editor, Jose Salcedo; music, Jose Maria Vitier; art direction, Miguel Lopez Pelegrin. Reviewed at Cines Renoir, Madrid, Jan. 9. Running time: 110 mins.

**Jorge Perugorria (Igor), Violeta Rodriguez (Nena), Kiti Manver (Azucena), Broselianda Hernandez, (Ludmila), Isabel Santos (Rosa).**

Vet Manuel Gutierrez Aragon delivers his best pic with *Things I Left in Havana*, a lively and intelligent study of the effects of immigration that's saccharin-free. Co-winner of the Silver Spike at the Valladolid fest, pic combines an energetic young cast with accomplished direction, quality production values, and a strong storyline. It should prove a solid B.O. winner at home with good specialized sales prospects offshore. Tales centers on three sisters who've come to Madrid from Havana without papers and are put to work in a fur store. One is set up with an arranged marriage but the groom has his eye on a different sibling.

Int'l release: Jan. 16 Int'l B.O.: $1.5 million

## This is my Father

A Filmline Int'l/Hummingbird Communication production. Produced by Nicolas Clermont, Philip King. Directed, written by

Paul Quinn. Camera, Declan Quinn; editor, Glenn Berman; music, Donal Lunny; production design, Frank Conway; costume design, Consolata Boyle. Reviewed at World Film Festival, Montreal, Aug. 31. Running time: 120 mins.
**Aidan Quinn (Kieran O' Day), James Caan (Kieran Johnson), Stephen Rea (Father Quinn), John Cusack (Eddie Sharp), Moya Farrelly (Fiona Flynn), Jacob Tierney (Jack), Colm Meaney (Seamus Kearney), Donal Donnelly (John Maney).**
The first feature by Paul Quinn – collaborating with brothers Aidan and Declan – is an ambitious multigenerational tale of love, family and tragedy that's effective despite a rough-hewn narrative quality. Even with the unprecedented success of *Titanic*, the large-scale romance of *This is my Father* remains slightly out of step with current moviegoing tastes. Nonetheless, the pic has the potential for good theatrical returns in domestic and international markets, and similar prospects in ancillary venues.

Middle-aged schoolteacher Kieran Johnson stumbles across a cache of photos from his mother's past that suggest his biofather may have been an Irish farmer, not a French seaman as he was told. He goes to Ireland to trace his past, encountering cautious and ambivalent townspeople. Clearly, his parents' story represents unpleasant memories for the villagers. The setup to the historic saga is unquestionably clunky. But flashback section provides a natural stride – and real drama. Kieran's mother, Fiona Flynn, was the proverbial wild rose. Poor-as-dirt tenant farmer Kieran O'Day spots the lass and uncharacteristically steps forward boldly with an invitation to the village dance. The event is pretty much a fiasco. Luckily, the young woman sees the farmer's inherent goodness and not his temper. She gives Kieran his first dance lesson. It's the stuff of true love.

## Those Who Love Me Can Take The Train (Ceux Qui M'aiment Predront Le Train) (France)
A Bac Films release of a Charles Gassot presentation of a Telema/ Studio Canal Plus/France 2 Cinema/France 3 Cinema/Azor Films production, with the participation of CNC and Procirep. Produced by Charles Gassot. Directed by Patrice Chereau. Screenplay, Daniele Thompson, Chereau, Pierre Trividic, from a story idea by Thompson. Camera, Eric Gautier; editor, François Gedigier; art director, Richard Peduzzi, Sylvain Chauvelot; costume designer, Caroline de Vivaise. Reviewed at Club 13, Paris, May 6. Running time: 122 mins.
**Pascal Greggory (François), Jean-Louis Trintignant (Lucien/Jean-Baptiste), Valeria Bruni-Tedeschi (Claire), Charles Berling (Jean-Marie), Bruno Todeschini (Louis), Sylvain Jacques (Bruno), Vincent Perez (Viviane), Roschdy Zem (Thierry), Dominique Blanc (Catherine).**
*Those Who Love Me Can Take The Train* is a vivid and emotionally draining enssembler that makes the average Woody Allen film seem like a picnic for the well-adjusted. Helmer Patrice Chereau has his distinguished thesps do everything except tie themselves to the tracks as their characters travel via train to the funeral of a painter. An enthusiastic local reception seems assured, but crix and auds beyond France will be sharply divided on the merits of so much overwrought soul-searching by not-terribly-pleasant people.

The friends and associates of minor painter Jean-Baptiste Emmerich frenetically convene at a Paris railroad station, for the trip to Limoges, where the deceased wished to be buried. Amongst them are nearly a dozen characters who have, or have

had, problems with drugs, HIV infection, fidelity, unwanted pregnancy, suicide – you name it. Jean-Baptiste was a manipulative man possessed of a multilayered sexuality that captivated men and women alike.
Int'l release: May 13     Int'l B.O.: $2.7 million
U.S. release: Oct. 23     U.S. B.O.: $30,000

## Three Men and a Leg (Tre Uomini E Una Gamba) (Italy)
A Medusa Film release of a Rodeo Drive/A.GI.DI. production in association with Medusa Film. Produced by Marco Poccioni, Marco Valsania, Paolo Guerra. Directed by Aldo, Giovanni, and Giacomo, Massimo Venier. Screenplay, Aldo, Giovanni, and Giacomo, Venier, Giorgio Gherarducci, Lucio Martignoni. Camera, Giovanni Fiore Coltellacci; editor, Marco Spoletini; music, Phil Palmer, Marco Forni; costume design, Stefano Giovani. Reviewed at Cola di Rienzo Cinema, Rome, Dec. 30, 1997. Running time: 99 mins.
**Aldo Baglio (Aldo), Giovanni Storti (Giovanni), Giacomo Poretti (Giacomo), Marina Massironi (Chiara), Carlo Croccolo (Eros).**
Talented legit and small-screen comic trio Aldo, Giovanni, and Giacomo have fashioned a road-worthy vehicle for their well-honed shtick in *Three Men and a Leg*. This small but satisfying road movie is doing brisk national business thanks to the stars' stalwart following but looks to kindle limited interest offshore. Story chronicles a car trip from Milan to southern Puglia, where the three stooges, all sales clerks in a hardware store, are set to rendezvous with their overbearing, nouveau-riche boss, Eros. Aldo and Giovanni are married to two of his shrewish daughters, while Giacomo is about to get hitched to a third. Their cargo is Eros' beloved pet pooch and a valuable wooden sculpture of a leg.
Int'l release: Dec. 15, 1997     Int'l B.O.: $25.5 million

## 3 Ninjas: High Noon on Mega Mountain
A Sony Pictures Entertainment release of a TriStar presentation of a Sheen Prods production, in association with Leeds/Ben-Ami Prods. Produced by James Kang, Yoram Ben-Ami. Directed by Sean McNamara. Screenplay, McNamara, Jeff Phillips. Camera, Blake T. Evans; editor, Annamaria Szanto; music, John Coda; production designer, Chuck Connor; costume designer, Miye Matsumoto. Reviewed at AMC Studio 30, Houston, April 7. MPAA Rating: PG. Running time: 93 mins.
**Hulk Hogan (Dave Dragon), Loni Anderson (Medusa), Jim Varney (Lothar Zogg), Mathew Botuchis (Rocky), Michael J. O'Laskey II (Colt), J.P. Roeske II (Tum Tum), Victor Wong (Grandpa Mori).**
Only small children with limited attention spans will be impressed by the lackluster kung-foolishness in *3 Ninjas: High Noon at Mega Mountain*. This fourth episode in the kid-friendly franchise is a considerable improvement over its immediate predecessor, but even with a bigger budget, a few grownup "guest stars", and three new youngsters, *Mega Mountain* won't amount to a hill of beans at the box office. Given the series' past track record, homevideo prospects are mildly bright.

Grandpa Mori, a retired ninja, teaches fighting skills to his three grandchildren: 15-year-old Rocky, 14-year-old Colt, and 8-year-old Tum Tum. The boys get a chance to test their abilities during a trip to Mega Mountain amusement park when it's invaded by an army of ninjas led by Medusa, a haughty villainess, and Lothar, her surly chief henchman. The bad guys don't count on the presence of Dave Dragon, a faded TV star who's making a farewell appearance at the park, and the three black-belted boys.

### Tiger-Stripe Woman Waits for Tarzan (Tigerstreifenbaby Wartet Auf Tarzan) (Germany)

A Moana Film production, in association with Westdeutsches Rundfunk production. Produced by Rudolf Thome. Directed by Thome. Screenplay, Thome, Peter Lund. Camera, Carsten Thiele; editor, Doerte Voelz-Mammarella; music, Wolfgang Boehmer; art director, Armgard Meyer, Nia Dryhurst, Barbara Rolfs; costume designer, Gioia Raspe. Reviewed at Berlin Festival, Feb. 16. Running time: 117 mins.
Herbert Fritsch (Frank Mackay), Cora Frost (Luise), Valeska Hanel (Laura Luna), Irm Hermann (Birgit Kirchstein), Ruediger Vogler (Franz), Tilo Werner (Theo).

Those who find German iconoclast Rudolf Thome's pics an acquired taste won't have to struggle so hard with *Tiger-Stripe Woman Waits for Tarzan*, his most approachable movie in a decade. It's a semi-fairytale centered on various women falling for an unprepossessing guy with a spiritual mission. Luise and Theo pick up a mysterious blond guy, Frank, and give him a lift to Berlin, where Luise comes on to him. Frank, however, is more interested in tracking down Laura Luna, author of the book *Tiger-Stripe Woman Waits for Tarzan*, as he's fallen in love with her picture and wants to take her back to the future, a time when women have died out.

### Titanic

A Paramount/20th Century Fox release of a Lightstorm Entertainment production. Produced by James Cameron, Jon Landau. Directed, written by Cameron. Camera, Russell Carpenter; editors, Conrad Buff, Cameron, Richard A. Harris; music, James Horner; Randy Gerston; production design, Peter Lamont; art direction, Martin Laing; costume design, Deborah L. Scott; visual-effects supervisor, Robert Legato; *Titanic* deep-dive camera, Cameron; stunt coordinator, Simon Crane. Reviewed at Paramount, L.A., Oct. 31, 1997. MPAA Rating: PG-13. Running time: 194 mins.
Leonardo DiCaprio (Jack Dawson), Kate Winslet (Rose DeWitt Bukater), Billy Zane (Cal Hockley), Kathy Bates (Molly Brown), Frances Fisher (Ruth DeWitt Bukater), Gloria Stuart (Old Rose), Bill Paxton (Brock Lovett), Bernard Hill (Capt. Smith), Jonathan Hyde (Bruce Ismay), Victor Garber (Thomas Andrews), David Warner (Spicer Lovejoy), Suzy Amis (Lizzy Calvert).

This *Titanic* arrives at its destination, as a spectacular demonstration of what modern technology can contribute to dramatic storytelling. The dynamic of the central love story, between a brash lad from steerage and an upper-class young lady, is as effective as it is corny, and will definitely help put the pic over with the public. This fast-paced three-hour extravaganza is certain to do exceptionally well at the box office, and Paramount's $60 million investment has to be one of the bargain deals of the century. Whether Fox can come near to break-even in the rest of the world is another matter.

Capitalizing on the 1985 discovery of *Titanic*'s remains, Cameron frames the period drama with a contemporary yarn in which explorer Brock Lovett uses deep-sea submersibles to retrieve artifacts from the vessel. Instead of finding gems, Lovett turns up an intriguing drawing of a nude woman

wearing a fabulous necklace. It comes to the attention of a 102-year-old woman named Rose – the woman in the portrait – and she's taken to Lovett's ship to confirm details and, at length, tell her story.

First shots of *Titanic* taking on passengers at Southampton are stunning. Cameron's camera takes an immediate interest in Rose DeWitt Bukater, a society girl returning to Philadelphia to marry snob fiancé Cal Hockley; and penniless, devil-may-care Jack Dawson, who wins his ticket in a dockside card game. Rose, feeling hopelessly trapped, is rescued from jumping by none other than Jack. To repay him, Cal invites the scruffy dog to dinner in first class, where Jack parries his hosts' insults. Later, he spirits Rose to third class, where they join in spirited dancing with the immigrants. Rose asks Jack, who sketched on the streets of Paris, to draw her in the nude wearing the priceless blue diamond. Later, they find the place to consummate their passion – American style – in the back seat of a luxury car in the ship's hold. After the ship hits the iceberg, the sinking represents uninterrupted excitement and spectacle. Cameron still steers his attention away from the general calamity to pile on more complications for Jack and Rose.

| | |
|---|---|
| U.S. release: Dec. 18, 1997 | U.S. B.O.: $600.8 million |
| Int'l release: Dec. 18, 1997 | Int'l B.O.: $1.23 billion |

### Titanic Town (U.K.)

A Pandora Cinema/BBC Films presentation, in association with British Screen and the Arts Council of Northern Ireland's Lottery Fund, of a Company Pictures production. Produced by George Faber, Charles Patterson. Directed by Roger Michell. Screenplay, Anne Devlin, based on the novel by Mary Costello. Camera, John Daly; editor, Kate Evans; music, Trevor Jones; production designer, Pat Campbell; costume designer, Hazel Pethig. Reviewed at Cannes Festival, May 19. Running time: 100 mins.
Julie Walters (Bernie McPhelimy), Ciaran Hinds (Aidan McPhelimy), Nuala O'Neill (Annie McPhelimy), James Loughran (Thomas McPhelimy), Barry Loughran (Brendan McPhelimy), Elizabeth Donaghy (Sinead McPhelimy), Ciaran McMenamin (Dino/Owen), Jaz Pollock (Patsy French).

Julie Walters gives a corker of a performance as a feisty Belfast housewife-turned-peace activist in *Titanic Town*, based on Mary Costello's autobiographical novel. While recent films about the Northern Irish conflict have floundered, the ability of this touching drama to elicit pathos, irony, and warm humor out of a tragic situation should ensure a small sprinkling of theatrical sales and wide TV berths.

Bernie McPhelimy and her family move during the height of the trouble in Northern Ireland into a housing-estate home in a Catholic neighborhood of Belfast famous as the place where the *Titanic* was built. Helicopters, tanks, and flying bullets exist side-by-side with normal neighborhood life. But when an old friend is caught in the crossfire and killed, Bernie's outspokenness leads her to a meeting of an ineffectual women's peace group.

### Today or Never (Aujourd'hui Ou Jamais) (Canada)

A Remstar Distribution release of a Vent d'Est production, with the participation of the Canadian Cable Distribution Fund, Telefilm Canada, Sodec. Produced by Bernard Lalonde. Directed by Jean Pierre Lefebvre. Screenplay, Lefebvre, Marcel Sabourin. Camera, Robert Vanherweghem; editors, Barbara Easto, Lefebvre; music, Daniel Lavoie; costumes, Nicole Pelletier.

---

**... August 20 ...**
Denzel Washington will make his directing debut with Fox Searchlight's **Finding Fish**.

Reviewed at the Complexe Desjardins, Montreal, Oct. 16.
Running time: 106 mins.
**Marcel Sabourin (Abel Gagne), Jean-Pierre Ronfard (Antoine), Claude Blanchard (Napoleon), Julie Menard (Mylene/Monique), Micheline Lanctot (Arlette). With: Sean Gallagher, Sarah Mennel.**
Jean Pierre Lefebvre, a key figure in Quebec cinema during the 1960s and 1970s, returns with his first feature in seven years, an unabashed throwback to the auteur style of that earlier period of French-Canadian filmmaking. *Today or Never* is a warm, poetic meditation on death, family ties, and friendship. The touching film is anchored by two fine performances from veteran thesps Marcel Sabourin and Claude Blanchard. But the same qualities that make the picture such a pleasure to watch will likely not endear it to today's auds, and effort's commercial prospects are further dampened by languid pacing.

Abel is one unhappy guy. A 55-year-old pilot, he has not taken to the air in the 15 years since his best friend and co-pilot died in a plane crash. Abel runs a small airfield in Quebec's rural Eastern Townships with Antoine and, at the start, he's ready to return to the skies in his vintage Tiger Moth biplane. But his flight is grounded by a couple of unforeseen events. Bank reps drop by to tell him that they'll be seizing his assets the next day if he doesn't pay off a longstanding debt. Then his father, Napoleon, suddenly shows up at the airfield 50 years after deserting his family to move to Brazil. Abel doesn't take too kindly to the surprise reappearance. Much of the rest of the film chronicles Abel's painful path toward coming to terms with his father.

## Tomorrow Never Dies

An MGM release from United Artists of an Albert R. Broccoli's Eon Prods Ltd presentation. Produced by Michael G. Wilson, Barbara Broccoli. Directed by Roger Spottiswoode. Screenplay, Bruce Feirstein. Camera, Robert Elswit; editors, Dominique Fortin, Michel Arcand; music, David Arnold; production design, Allan Cameron; costume design, Lindy Hemming; special-effects supervisor, Chris Corbould; stunt supervisor, Dickey Beer. Reviewed at the National, L.A., Dec. 10, 1997. MPAA Rating: PG-13. Running time: 119 mins.
**Pierce Brosnan (James Bond), Jonathan Pryce (Elliot Carver), Michelle Yeoh (Wai Lin), Teri Hatcher (Paris Carver), Joe Don Baker (Wade), Ricky Jay (Henry Gupta), Gotz Otto (Stamper), Judi Dench (M), Desmond Llewelyn (Q), Vincent Schiavelli (Dr. Kaufman).**
There's plenty of bang-bang but modest kiss-kiss in *Tomorrow Never Dies*, a solid but somewhat by-the-numbers entry in the James Bond cycle. An imaginatively conceived media-magnate villain and an unusually active female partner for the hero help distinguish this installment in the series. Latest effort may not quite match *Goldeneye*, but it will perform handsomely, with Asian territories benefiting from the winning co-starring turn by Malaysian-Hong Kong favorite Michelle Yeoh.

Scenarist Bruce Feirstein has cooked up a delicious villain for the post-Cold War 1990s, a megalomaniacal communications tycoon, Elliot Carver, whose network of satellites enables him to reach into every corner of the globe and whose strategy for domination involves manipulating world crises that will be reported exclusively on his network. Carver manufactures an international conflict when his high-tech stealth battleship sinks a British naval vessel and pins the blame on the Chinese.

With tensions rising between East and West, Bond is sent to Hamburg to infiltrate a Carver bash, and it just happens that Carver's wife Paris is an old flame. 007 also makes the acquaintance of a striking Chinese woman, Wai Lin, whose journalistic credentials are as transparent as Bond's as a banker. The two secret agents unite in an effort to prevent World War III by disarming Carver's stealth ship, from which a cruise missile is about to be launched on Beijing.

| | |
|---|---|
| U.S. release: Dec. 19, 1997 | U.S. B.O.: 125 million |
| Int'l release: Dec. 12, 1997 | Int'l B.O.: $212 million |

## Too Much (Little) Love [Trop (Peu) D'amour]

(France)
An Alain Sarde production, in association with Canal Plus. Produced by Alain Sarde. Directed, written by Jacques Doillon. Camera, Christophe Pollock; editor, Catherine Quesemand. Reviewed at Berlin Festival, Feb. 13. Running time: 119 mins.
**Lambert Wilson (Paul), Elise Perrier (Emma), Alexia Stresi (Margot), Lou Doillon (Camille), Jeremy Lippmann (David).**
Jacques Doillon's latest film is a frustrating mixture of the excellent and the awful. On one hand are outstanding performances and an intriguing theme, but the director indulges himself – in a very Gallic way – in seriously overextended dialog scenes that entertain for a while but eventually become tedious. As a result, *Too Much (Little) Love* is only fitfully engaging, and far less accessible than the director's previous *Ponette*. Pic has a bleak commercial future outside selected Euro territories.

Premise seems promising. Emma, a fiercely intelligent and emotional 17-year-old, is a passionate admirer of the work of filmmaker Paul, whose movies, she claims, have "saved her." This intellectual groupie catches Paul's attention when she sends him an outline for a proposed film.

Int'l release: March 25            Int'l B.O.: $70,000

## Too Tired to Die

A Dream Search Entertainment presentation of a Black Swan production. Produced by Victor Hwang, Donna Bascom, Connie Kaiserman. Directed, written by Wonsuk Chin. Camera, Jim Denault; editor, Merril Stern; music, Mader; production design, Lisa Albin; costume design, Melissa Toth;. Reviewed at Sundance Festival, Jan. 20. Running time: 97 mins.
**Takeshi Kaneshiro (Kenji), Mira Sorvino (Death/Jean), Jeffrey Wright (Balzac Man), Michael Imperioli (Fabrizio), Geno Lechner (Pola), Ben Gazzara (John Sage).**
A quirky little cross-cultural item, *Too Tired to Die* is a cinephile's wet dream, a pop artifact that trades in equal measures of contempo Asian rootlessness, European artfilm doodlings, and downtown New York hipsterism. A colorful cast and a stream of eclectic references will keep buffs amused, making this a tasty offering for fests and highly specialized urban bookings, but far too inside and ephemeral for wider play.

Opening is a wonderfully realized B&W silent sequence depicting a young man being pursued by Death through Old Baghdad. Back in modern Manhattan, Japanese twenty-something Kenji is in bed in a barely furnished apartment. Rousing himself sufficiently to visit a local café, he engagingly converses at length with an Italian friend and a mysterious young German woman, Pola. But Death is always hovering around in various guises; before it's over, she appears as a Chinese woman, a disco dolly, a Japanese geisha, and a devil in a red dress, among other impersonations.

## Torrente, The Dumb Arm of the Law (Torrente, El Brazo Tonto De La Ley) (Spain)

A Columbia TriStar release of a Rocabruno Producciones production, in association with Cartel, with the participation of Via Digital. Producer, Andres Vicente Gomez. Directed, written by Santiago Segura. Camera, Carles Gusi; editor, Fidel Collados; music, Roque Banos; art directors, Arri, Biaffra, Los Zombis de Sahuayo. Reviewed at Cine Capitol, Madrid, March 12. Running time: 98 mins.
**Santiago Segura (Torrente), Javier Camara (Rafi), Neus Asensi (Amparito), Chus Lampreave (Reme), Tony Leblanc (Father).**

Spanish wit and canny self-publicist Santiago Segura makes his feature debut with the deliriously non-p.c. *Torrente, The Dumb Arm of the Law*, a tremendously enjoyable comedy-thriller that comes with top production-backing values. Home auds will love it; in non-Spanish-speaking territories, only clever marketing will prevent this one-man vehicle from collapsing under the weight of local jokes and subtitling difficulties.

Plot is typical low-budget action thriller. Down-and-out ex-cop Torrente, who continues to work as though he hadn't been fired, lives with his aged father, whom he sends out in a wheelchair every day to beg, even though the old man can walk. Meanwhile, Torrente makes friends with gun-worshipping nerd Rafi in order to score with Rafi's nymphomaniac cousin, Amparito.
Int'l release: March 13                    Int'l B.O.: $14 million

## To the Limit (Al Limite) (Spain-France)

A Columbia TriStar release of a Cartel, Enrique Cerezo (Spain)/ACT-Auditel (France) production, in association with TVE. Produced by Enrique Cerezo, Eduardo Campoy. Directed by Campoy. Screenplay, Agustin Diaz Yanes, Luis Marias, Carlos Perez-Merinero. Camera, Armand Marco; editor, Luis Manuel del Valle; music, Mario de Benito; art direction, Javier Fernandez. Reviewed at Cines El Mirador, Seville, Dec. 20, 1997. Running time: 95 mins.
**Juanjo Puigcorbe (Javier Barea), Lydia Bosch (Maria Ramos), Beatrice Dalle (Elena), Bud Spencer (Elorza).**

Spanish producer Eduardo Campoy returns to helming after a five-year layoff with the ambitious serial-killer movie *To the Limit*. Though slickly made and visually strong, pic all too clearly shows its roots in the predominantly U.S. genre and ends up as no more than an exercise in style. A pre-Christmas release slot and good marketing translated into respectable home B.O., but the movie's lack of an authentic sense of place is more likely to hinder than help foreign sales.
Int'l release: Dec. 11, 1997                  Int'l B.O.: $800,000

## The Town (Kasaba) (Turkey)

An NBC Film production. Produced by Nuri Bilge Ceylan. Directed, written by Nuri Bilge Ceylan, based on a story by Emine Ceylan. Camera, Nuri Bilge Ceylan; editor, Ayhan Ergursel; music, Ali Kayaci; art director, Ebru Yapici. Reviewed at Istanbul Festival, April 29. Running time: 79 mins.
**With: Mehmet Emin Toprak, Kavva Saglam, Cihat Butun, Fatma Ceylan and Emin Ceylan.**

A remarkable first feature from director Nuri Bilge Ceylan, *The Town* is a strikingly original, vibrantly sensitive look at an extended family living in a remote Turkish village. After its premier in Berlin's Forum, pic won multiple kudos in the National Competition of the recent Istanbul fest, including the Fipresci (international critics jury) prize. Further fest prospects are bright for this very personal, refined work, which in many ways recalls the craftsmanship and sensitivity of the best Iranian films.

Structured around the four seasons, pic opens in wintertime. A young teacher, distractedly gazing out of the window, has his young pupils read from a patriotic textbook extolling the rules of social life and the family as the nucleus of Turkish society. Ceylan begins to introduce conflicts in this happy picture with subdued irony.

## Train of Life (Train De Vie) (France-Belgium-Romania-Netherlands)

An AB Int'l Distribution release of a Noe Prods, Le Studio Canal Plus (France)/Raphael Films (Belgium)/7I A (Romania)/Hungry Eye Lowland Pictures (Netherlands) production. Produced by Frederique Dumas, Marc Baschet, Cedomir Kolar, Ludi Boeken, Eric Dussart. Directed, written by Radu Mihaileanu. Camera, Yorgos Arvanitis, Laurent Dailland; editor, Monique Rysselinck; music, Goran Bregovic; art director, Cristi Niculescu; costume design, Viorica Petrovici. Reviewed at Club Gaumont, Paris, July 7, 1998. Running time: 102 mins.
**Lionel Abelanski (Schlomo), Rufus (Mordechai), Clement Harari (Rabbi), Michel Muller (Yossi), Bruno Abraham-Kremer (Yankele), Agathe de La Fontaine (Esther), Johan Leysen (Schmecht), Marie-Jose Nat (Sura).** (French and German dialog)

Somewhere in Central Europe in summer 1941, the inhabitants of an isolated shtetl take the initiative to deport themselves in *Train of Life*. Tragicomic account of how Yiddish-speaking Jews secure a train, sew phony Nazi uniforms, and divvy up into fake captors and captives in an attempt to reach Palestine blends broad humor, wishful thinking, and astute psychological observation in a bittersweet but flawed package. A fable that's charming and clever in places but schmaltzy and stereotypical in others, this train will make plenty of scheduled stops at fests before chugging to TV. Pic won an international critics prize at Venice.

Village eccentric Schlomo runs to the local council with rumors that villagers are being rounded up by the Nazis and herded aboard trains, never to be heard from again. Schlomo suggests they "deport" themselves and make a break for the Promised Land. According to language skills and appearance, some residents are assigned to play Germans while the bulk will play Jews. The village accountant raids communal coffers to purchase a rickety train, and identity papers are forged. After preparations, the whole town pulls up stakes in the middle of the night. The fake Nazis end up enjoying the measure of power their role affords. The Jews in their care find themselves resenting and plotting against their overlords. First run-in with real Germans is both frightening and funny, and there's the small matter of resistance fighters determined to dynamite the train.
Int'l release: Sept. 16                     Int'l B.O.: $1.4 million

## Traps (Pasti, Pasti, Pasticky) (Czech Republic)

A Cineart production, in association with CNTS/TV Nova/KF. Produced by Viktor Schwarcz. Directed by Vera Chytilova. Screenplay, Chytilova, Michel Laznovsky, Tomas Hanak, David Vavra, based on a story by Chytilova, Eva Kacirkova. Camera, Stepan Kucera; editor, Ivana Kacirkova; production design, Frantisek Vokral; costume design, Tereza Kucerova. Reviewed at Venice Festival, Sept. 10, 1998. Running time: 122 mins.

Miroslav Donutil (Dohnal), Zuzana Stivinova (Lenka), Tomas Hanak (Petr), Dasa Blahova (Chief), Katerina Hajna (Ingrid), Eva Holubova (Anna), Daniela Trebicka (Mrs. Dohnal).

A feminist comedy about rape and retribution from veteran Czech helmer Vera Chytilova, *Traps* is great fun in spots but overstays its welcome. Faster pacing and tighter cutting might have turned this decidedly promising material into a comedy classic, but Chytilova's languid storytelling is, in the end, a liability. It takes a particularly long time to establish the characters and get to the incident that triggers the action – the violation of Lenka, a young veterinarian, by Dohnal, a government minister responsible for the environment. Lenka pretends to have amnesia and no knowledge of what happened. It's a big stretch that these supposedly bright guys would fall for her story and take her back to her isolated house, but that's just what they do. There, she offers them drugged beer and, when they're out cold, castrates them. The sequence in which they awake and gradually realize what's happened to them is the film's funniest segment, and is expertly played for top comic effect by Donutil and Hanak.

Int'l release: Oct. 15                 Int'l B.O.: $300,00

### T-Rex: Back to the Cretaceous (Imax 3-D)

An Imax presentation. Produced by Antoine Compin, Charis Horton. Directed by Brett Leonard. Screenplay, Andrew Gellis, Jeanne Rosenberg; story by Gellis, David Young. Camera, Andrew Kitzanuk; editor, Jonathan Shaw; music, William Ross; stereographer/camera operator, Noel Archambault; technical adviser, Dr. Philip Currie. Reviewed at the California Science Center, L.A., Oct. 4. Running time: 45 mins.
Peter Horton (Dr. Donald Hayden), Liz Stauber (Ally Hayden), Kari Coleman (Elizabeth Sample), Laurie Murdoch (Barnum Brown), Tuck Milligan (Charles Knight).

The Imax process finds creatures worthy of its size in *T-Rex: Back to the Cretaceous*, a sensory treat that makes sometimes eye-popping use of the 3-D format. It's a simple story of how the neglected teenage daughter of a famous palaeontologist finds her own path to the world of dinosaurs. A technically impressive picture, it's bound to follow the surprising *Everest* as the next big thing in the family-friendly Imax field.

Dr. Donald Hayden and assistant, Elizabeth, return from a Canadian expedition with an oblong fossil that may just be a Tyrannosaurus egg. However, the two are more than a bit careless with the egg, which emits some mysterious dust when knocked to the floor by daughter Ally. After-hours in the museum, a T-Rex skeleton magically comes to life and roars right into the camera, whereupon Ally finds herself able to "enter" the museum exhibits and travel back in time. The effects are all terrific, and the experience of having a T-Rex baring her teeth at you in 3-D from a screen several stories tall is potent and lifelike. The enterprise indicates the vast potential for Imax 3-D to move further into narrative, special effects, and computer-generated imaging on future projects.

U.S. release: Oct. 23                 U.S. B.O.: $2.6 million
Int'l release: Oct. 29                 Int'l B.O.: $1 million

### The Trio (Das Trio) (Germany)

A Warner Bros. release of a Next Film production, in association with NDR, ORF, Arte. Produced by Laurens Straub. Directed by Hermine Huntgeburth. Screenplay, Horst Sczerba, Volker Einrauch, Huntgeburth. Camera, Martin Kukula; editor, Ingrid Martell; music, Niki Reiser; art director, Katharina

Woeppermann; costumes, Peri de Braganca. Reviewed at Cannes Festival, May 21, 1998. Running time: 98 mins.
Goetz George (Zobel), Christian Redl (Karl), Jeanette Hain (Lizzi), Felix Eitner (Rudolf), Angelika Bartsch (Dorothee).

Though it takes a while to get into gear, *The Trio* is, finally, a likeable relationship movie spinning on the theme of cohabiting sexualities. Relaxedly played by its four leads, and dominated by a funny-sad performance by vet Goetz George as a rapacious, ageing queen, pic could have limited arthouse legs offshore with the right marketing, easily crossing over between straight and gay auds. Titular trio is a group of travelers who live in a caravan and exist by pickpocketing: Zobel, a hairy hunk of beef; his tired lover, Karl; and Zobel's foxy daughter, Lizzi. When Karl dies as a result of a car accident during a bungled sting, his place in the curious ménage is taken by the ambitious young Rudolf, for whom both father and daughter get the hots.

Int'l release: Jan. 29                 Int'l B.O.: $600,000

### Tropic Of Emerald (The Netherlands)

An Emerald Films production. Directed by Orlow Seunke. Screenplay, Seunke, Mieke de Jong. Camera, Tom Erisman; editor, Seunke; music, Menno Daams. Reviewed at Cannes Festival, May 16. Running time: 127 mins.
Pierre Bokma (Theo), Esmée de la Bretonière (Ems), Christine Hakim (Suti), Bram van der Vlugt (Herman), Frans Tumbuan (Boon). (Dutch, English and Indonesian dialog)

In *Tropic of Emerald*, Dutch helmer Orlow Seunke crafts a fascinating historical epic set in 1940s Indonesia. Weaving historical events into a tropical love story, pic sprawls from the pre-war colonial heyday when Dutch plantation owners ruled, to the Japanese invasion and prison camps, ending with the natives' violent struggle for independence. Sympathetic to both sides, this well-lensed epic goes surprisingly deep into the social and political climate. Echoing as it does the current violence in Indonesia, it might find a foothold in some theatrical markets, as well as TV and video in its longer three-hour version.

Screenplay centers on the beautiful nightclub singer Ems, a native Indo-European married to elderly club owner Herman. A strong-willed spitfire, Ems is fiercely loyal to her land but is torn between her European and poor island roots. She falls deeply in love with Theo, a good-looking young Dutchman who has come to work on his uncle's rubber plantation.

Int'l release: Oct. 2, 1997                 Int'l B.O.: $150,000

### The Truman Show

A Paramount release of a Scott Rudin production. Produced by Rudin, Andrew Niccol, Edward S. Feldman, Adam Schroeder. Directed by Peter Weir. Screenplay, Niccol. Camera, Peter Biziou; editors, William Anderson, Lee Smith; music, Burkhard Dallwitz, Philip Glass; production designer, Dennis Gassner; special design consultant, Wendy Stites; costume designer, Marilyn Matthews; digital-visual-effects supervisor, Brad Kuehn. Reviewed at Paramount, L.A., April 23. MPAA Rating: PG. Running time: 102 mins.
Jim Carrey (Truman Burbank), Laura Linney (Meryl), Noah Emmerich (Marlon), Natascha McElhone (Lauren/Sylvia), Holland Taylor (Truman's Mother), Ed Harris (Christof), Una Damon (Chloe), Paul Giamatti (TV Director).

A gemlike picture crafted with rare and immaculate precision, *The Truman Show* amusingly and convincingly presents a nuclear community as a vast television studio. An out-standingly successful change of pace for comic Jim Carrey and a tour de force for director Peter Weir, this clever commentary on media omnipotence is daringly offbeat for a Hollywood studio, although all of its ideas will be perfectly accessible to the most general audiences. At the very least, Carrey's drawing power and widespread critical support spell strong early-summer B.O.

Truman Burbank is a virtual caricature of a clean-cut, "normal" guy. Married to the perky Meryl, they live in the spotless, planned community of Seahaven, an antiseptic island "paradise" where people are forever cheery and nothing untoward ever happens. But he harbors a secret wanderlust, stimulated by his fleeting romance with Lauren, a beautiful student literally snatched from his embrace. A fable about a man whose entire life, unbeknownst to him, has been the subject of a staggeringly popular, 24-hour-per-day TV show, pic trades in issues of personal liberty vs. authoritarian control, safe happiness vs. the excitement of chaos, manufactured emotions, the penetration of media to the point where privacy vanishes, and the fascination of fabricated images over plain sight.

U.S. release: June 5  U.S. B.O.: $125.5 million
Int'l release: Sept. 24  Int'l B.O.: $119 million

## 20 Dates

A Phoenician Films presentation. Produced by Mark McGarry, Jason Villard. Directed, written by Myles Berkowitz. Camera, Adam Biggs; editors, Michael Elliot, Lisa Cheek. Reviewed at Slamdance Festival, Park City, Utah, Jan. 19. Running time: 92 mins.

**Myles Berkowitz (Myles), Elisabeth Wagner (Elisabeth), Richard Arlook (The Agent), Elie Samaha (Voice of Film Producer), and Tia Carrere and Robert McKee as themselves**

The conceit of *20 Dates* is that a tyro filmmaker in search of a girlfriend convinces a producer to finance the quest. He offers a picture in which, hopefully, after a score of romantic rendezvous, he'll find true love and a darn good movie. By blurring the lines between cinéma vérité and fiction, writer-director Myles Berkowitz has created a winning entertainment with the potential for some mainstream crossover and brisk action in ancillaries. The film was awarded the audience prize at Slamdance.

This is a mockumentary of inordinate skill, in which one is hard-pressed to sort the fiction from the fact as Berkowitz records his brief encounters, locks horns with his agent and producer, and suffers rude comments from his friends. For something so assiduously hewn from life, *20 Dates* has a surprisingly effective and strong dramatic arc.

## 23 (Germany)

A Buena Vista Int'l release of a Claussen & Woebke Filmproduktion production. Produced by Jakob Claussen, Thomas Woebke. Directed by Hans-Christian Schmid. Screenplay, Schmid, Michael Gutmann. Camera, Klaus Eichhammer; editor, Hansjoerg Weissbrich; music, Norbert Juergen Schneider; art director, Ingrid Henn; costumes, Peri de Braganca. Reviewed at Locarno Festival, Aug. 6. Running time: 96 mins.

**August Diehl (Karl Koch), Fabian Busch (David), Dieter Landuris (Pepe), Jan-Gregor Kremp (Lupo).**

Though based on a true story, there is an agreeable sense of stylistic freedom to *23* that gives it an edge as a movie rather than simply a fact-based drama. This slickly mounted,

enjoyable thriller about young computer hackers who sold secrets to the Russians will entertain auds in search of quality commercial fare.

After the death of his right-wing father, Karl Koch gets the chance and resources to let his rebelliousness bloom. In thrall to Robert Anton Wilson's cult book *Illuminatus!* – which proposes a hidden, parallel world of government conspiracies and political murders – Karl and pal David start seeing proof of Wilson's theories, both in the appearance of the mystical number 23, and in current events. Working on antiquated computers, the pair hack into minor-league data and, with the help of Pepe, sell some of it to Soviets in East Berlin.

What started out as a prank turns serious when the Russians demand military data. Karl and David start working from hotel rooms to escape detection by the police, and accidentally access a U.S. government database. By now, Karl is close to the brink and thinks his hacking is responsible for disasters like Chernobyl. His eventual breakdown leads to a tragic coda.

## Twilight

A Paramount release of a Cinehaus production. Produced by Arlene Donovan, Scott Rudin. Directed by Robert Benton. Screenplay, Benton, Richard Russo. Camera, Piotr Sobocinski; editor, Carol Littleton; music, Elmer Bernstein; production design, David Gropman; costume design, Joseph G. Aulisi. Reviewed at Paramount, L.A., Feb. 25. MPAA Rating: R. Running time: 94 mins.

**Paul Newman (Harry Ross), Susan Sarandon (Catherine Ames), Gene Hackman (Jack Ames), Reese Witherspoon (Mel Ames), Stockard Channing (Verna), James Garner (Raymond Hope), Giancarlo Esposito (Reuben), Liev Schreiber (Jeff Willis).**

Very much befitting its title, *Twilight* is an autumnal murder mystery awash with rueful intimations of mortality. As a suspenser it's a sometimes clunky and unconvincing recycling of standard private-detective conventions. But the truly stellar cast ensures that whatever is happening onscreen, however incredible, will still be worth watching. Younger audiences are unlikely to connect with the old-fashioned format and ageing thesps, but enough traditionally minded fans should turn out for this beautifully crafted effort to deliver OK short-term B.O.

Newman plays longtime cop and, more recently, private dick Harry Ross. Divorced, broke, and formerly alcoholic, Harry is reduced to living above the garage on the estate of his movie-star friends Jack and Catherine Ames. Harry does odd jobs for the family in exchange for lodging.

U.S. release: March 6  U.S. B.O.: $15 million
Int'l release: May 20  Int'l B.O.: $5.5 million

## 2 Seconds (Canada)

A France Film release of a Max Films production, with the participation of the Cable Distribution Fund, Telefilm Canada, Sodec, Quebec Government, Canadian Government, and in association with Radio-Canada. Produced by Roger Frappier. Directed, written by Manon Briand. Camera, James Gray; editor, Richard Comeau; music, Sylvain-Charles Grand, Dominique Grand; art director, Pierre Allard; costumes, Suzanne Harel. Reviewed at World Film Festival, Montreal, Sept. 1. Running time: 100 mins.

**Charlotte Laurier (Laurie), Dino Tavarone (Lorenzo), Jonathan Bolduc (Young Lorenzo), Suzanne Clement (La Bella), Yves Pelletier (Steff).**

---

**. . . August 24 . . .**
Character actor E.G. Marshall, of TV's **The Defenders** fame, adjourns.

A refreshingly light pic, *2 Seconds* is a reasonably engaging portrait of a mountain-bike racer in the throes of crisis. The main attraction of this rather slim piece of filmmaking is a warm, appealing performance by Quebec thesp Charlotte Laurier. But this first feature from Montreal helmer Manon Briand is simply too slight to set itself apart from the indie pack and make much of a mark theatrically.

The title refers to the crucial moment of hesitation Laurie experiences at the start of a race. Unceremoniously fired from the mountain-bike racing team after a poor finish, she's confused and upset, heading home to Montreal, where she moves in with her nerdy, ultra-goofy brother, Steff. She takes her bike to an out-of-the-way repair shop run by a crusty old Italian named Lorenzo, and, despite a testy first meeting, Laurie and Lorenzo become good pals thanks to their shared love of bike racing. She also takes a day job as a bicycle courier.

U.S. release: Sept. 11                    U.S. B.O.: $200,000

## The Underground Orchestra (Het Ondergronds Orkest) (The Netherlands, Docu)

A Cinemien release of a Pieter van Huystee Film & TV production, in co-production with VPRO Television. Produced by Pieter van Huystee. Directed by Heddy Honigmann. Screenplay and research, Honigmann, Nosh van der Lely. Camera, Eric Guichard; editor, Mario Steenbergen; assistant director, van der Lely. Reviewed at Rotterdam Film Festival, Feb. 4. Running time: 108 mins. (French and Spanish dialog.)

Ostensibly looking at the musicians who entertain in the Paris metro, The Underground Orchestra broadens its gaze to become a stirring account of survival in exile, providing a glimpse into the lives of talented people displaced by war, poverty, and hostile political regimes. Dutch director Heddy Honigmann's warmly observed film should generate strong demand. Focus is four acts that play on the platforms and in the moving trains of the Paris metro: a Venezuelan harpist; a vocal trio of African origin; a violinist who fled former Yugoslavia and a job with the National Opera; and a Romanian family orchestra.

## Under Heaven

A Banner Entertainment release. Produced by Robin Schorr, Brian Swardstrom, Mickey Liddell. Directed, written by Meg Richman. Camera, Claudio Rocha; editor, Deborah Zeitman; music, Marc Olsen; production design, Sharon Lomofsky; costume design, Ron Leamon. Reviewed at Sundance Festival, Jan. 19. Running time: 112 mins.
Joely Richardson (Eleanor), Aden Young (Buck), Molly Parker (Cynthia), Kevin Phillip (John), Krisha Fairchild (Cynthia's Mother).
A modern reworking of Henry James' The Wings of the Dove, Meg Richman's feature directorial debut is an unexciting romantic melodrama centering on a working-class couple who manipulate a rich woman dying of cancer. Pic is marred by an obvious narrative, shallow psychological motivations, and pat ending. Since Iain Softley's highly acclaimed version of *Wings* is in current release, distrib has problem that inevitable comparisons are not likely to favor Richman's adaptation.

Set in contemporary Seattle, story begins with Cynthia and Buck, a couple of young musicians struggling to make a living. Strong-willed and ambitious, Cynthia is determined not to repeat the mistake of her mother (Krisha Fairchild), who got married young to the wrong guy. When Cynthia realizes that Buck is a loser who can't shake his drug addiction, she breaks up with him.

U.S. release: June 19                    U.S. B.O.: $40,000

## The Unknown Cyclist

A Trident Releasing release of a Dream Vision Entertainment III presentation of a Watermark Film. Produced by Matthew Carlistle, Betsy Pool. Directed by Bernard Salzman. Screenplay, Howard Skora, Pool, Matthew Carlisle. Camera, Salzman, Mike Fash; editor, Irit Raz; music supervisor, Donald Markowitz; production designer, Stewart Campbell; costumes, Marcy Froelich. Reviewed at Roxie Cinema, San Francisco, June 2 (Lesbian & Gay Festival). Running time: 96 mins.
Lea Thompson (Melissa Cavatelli), Vincent Spano (Frank Cavatelli), Danny Nucci (Gaetan Amador), Stephen Spinella (Doug Stein), Michael J. Pollard (Gabe Sinclair), Lainie Kazan (Rachel).
Four squabbling survivors join an AIDS bike-a-thon to scatter their late friend's ashes in the amiable, if pat, *The Unknown Cyclist*. By-the-numbers laughter and tears, plus cast's modest marquee value, make this slick, earnest contrivance best suited for broadcast berths.

At a West Hollywood wake, partygoers celebrate the departed founder of a local community center. He left behind two "widows" – ex-wife Melissa, a blocked writer, and Doug. The group is unhappily surprised by Chris' last wish – that they all sign up for a 450-mile, five-day charity ride up the California coast, releasing his ashes en route.

## Up 'n' Under (U.K.)

An Entertainment Film Distributors release of an Entertainment Film Distributors presentation of a Touchdown production, in association with Lluniau Llivv. Produced by Mark Thomas. Directed, written by John Godber, based on his play. Camera, Alan M. Trow; editor, Chris Lawrence; music, Mark Thomas; production design, Hayden Pearce; costume design, Pamela Moore. Reviewed at Planet Hollywood, London, Jan. 20, 1998. Running time: 100 mins.
Gary Olsen (Arthur), Richard Ridings (Frank), Samantha Janus (Hazel), Ralph Brown (Phil), Neil Morrissey (Steve), Adrian Hood (Tommy), David MacCreedy (Tony), Tony Slattery (Reg Welch), Brian Glover (Jack), Griff Rhys Jones (Ray Mason).
A laddish comedy about a bunch of no-hopers being whipped into shape to beat a hotshot amateur rugby team, Up 'n' Under is a game try that still ends up in the second division. Unfortunately coming hard on the heels of the similarly male-menopausal The Full Monty, this screen version of John Godber's 1984 play is likeable enough and scores some points on the laugh scale, but it lacks the overall wit, characterization and tony performances that made *Monty* a success. Distrib should see reasonable returns locally on the strength of its TV-name cast, but foreign results look more questionable.

Arthur, a beer-bellied ex-Rugby League player with a penny-ante decorating business, rises to a challenge from greaseball enemy Reg Welch. Reg, who manages the gung-ho rugby team, bets Arthur he can't train any other team in the North to beat the Cobblers. Arthur stakes his life's savings and selects the most hopeless team in the region, the Wheatsheaf Arms.

Int'l release: Jan. 25                    Int'l B.O.: $6.0 million

---

## Urban Legend

A TriStar release of a Phoenix Pictures presentation of a Neal H. Moritz/Gina Matthews production. Produced by Neal H. Moritz, Gina Matthews, Michael McDonnell. Directed by Jamie Blanks. Screenplay, Silvio Horta. Camera, James Chressanthis; editor, Jay Cassidy; music, Christopher Young; production design, Charles Breen; costume design, Mary Claire Hannan. Reviewed at UA Westwood, L.A., Sept. 17. MPAA Rating: R. Running time: 100 mins.

Jared Leto (Paul), Alicia Witt (Natalie), Rebecca Gayheart (Brenda), Michael Rosenbaum (Parker), Loretta Devine (Reese), Joshua Jackson (Damon), Tara Reid (Sasha), John Neville (Dean Adams), Robert Englund (Prof. Wexler), Natasha Gregson Wagner (Michelle Mancini).

Legend has it that killers return to the scene of the crime. And so it is with studio execs who revisit familiar material in order to replicate their earlier successes. In this case, *Urban Legend*, a formulaic teen horror film, retreads some of the same thematic ground as last year's hit *I Know What You Did Last Summer*, whose sequel is due out later this fall. But because it adds little new to the formula and lacks the star power of the earlier film, this new pic should expect middling B.O., followed by a healthy video shelf life.

Set in the fictitious Pendleton U., the film finds a close-knit group of friends debating the veracity of a campus legend. Some 25 years ago, Pendleton was supposedly the scene of a grotesque student massacre by a deranged professor, yet no evidence of the crime remains. Coincidentally, these same students have enrolled in a class on American folklore taught by the enigmatic Professor Wexler. Exposing urban myths as "cultural admonitions," Wexler urges his students to interrogate the tales they have come to believe. Before long, a lunatic begins a killing spree in the tradition of various urban legends.

U.S. release: Sept. 25 — U.S. B.O.: $37.5 million
Int'l release: Nov. 27 — Int'l B.O.: $3.5 million

## U.S. Marshals

A Warner Bros. release of a Kopelson Entertainment/Keith Barish production. Produced by Arnold and Anne Kopelson. Directed by Stuart Baird. Screenplay, John Pogue, based on the characters created by Roy Huggins. Camera, Andrzej Bartkowiak; editor, Terry Rawlings; music, Jerry Goldsmith; production design, Maher Ahmad; costume design, Louise Frogley. Reviewed at Warner Bros., Burbank, Feb. 26. MPAA Rating: PG-13. Running time: 133 mins.

Tommy Lee Jones (Marshal Sam Gerard), Wesley Snipes (Mark Sheridan), Robert Downey, Jr. (John Royce), Kate Nelligan (U.S. Marshal Walsh), Joe Pantoliano (Dep. Marshal Cosmo Renfro), Irene Jacob (Marie), Daniel Roebuck (Biggs), Latanya Richardson (Cooper).

*U.S. Marshals* is a disappointing sequel to the 1993 Oscar-nominated *The Fugitive*. Granted, it would have been hard to match that level of accomplishment under any circumstances. Tommy Lee Jones reprises his Oscar-winning role as chief deputy marshal Sam Gerard, a dogged pursuer who this time around is chasing the ruthless and mysterious Sheridan, accused of murdering two agents. Joined by his tightly knit team, he is obsessively committed to capturing the deceptive and cunning fugitive. Gerard's elite law enforcement crew is newly joined by Cooper, a black woman, and John Royce, a cocky, hip-shooting special agent.

U.S. release: March 6 — U.S. B.O.: $57.5 million
Int'l release: April 2 — Int'l B.O.: $45 million

## The Velocity of Gary

A Cineville production, in association with Ventana Rosa Prods. Produced by Dan Lupovitz. Directed by Dan Ireland. Screenplay, James Still, based on his play. Camera, Claudio Rocha; editor, Louis Colina; production design, Amy Ancona; costume design, Tim Chappel; casting, Laurel Smith. Reviewed at San Sebastian Festival, Sept. 22. Running time: 100 mins.

Salma Hayek (Mary Carmen), Vincent D'Onofrio (Valentino), Thomas Jane (Gary), Olivia d'Abo (Veronica), Chad Lindberg (Kid Joey), Lucky Luciano (The King).

A bittersweet melodrama about love, death and unorthodox family ties in the age of AIDS, *The Velocity of Gary* has neither the style nor the substance to go anywhere fast. The cast struggles to get a handle on their poorly defined characters, while director Dan Ireland strains to crank up the outrageousness and campy humor in the opening stretch, then works just as hard to get the pathos churning later on. But almost nothing clicks in this trite, New York-set tale of a troubled love triangle that looks destined for a quick trip to video.

Essentially miscast, D'Onofrio plays Valentino, a bisexual porn star replete with lank, greasy hair. No more in tune with her character is Hayek as his inamorata, Mary Carmen, a spitfire waitress with a penchant for lip-synching Diana Ross songs. Their relationship hits a bump when Valentino falls for hunky midwestern stud Gary.

## Velvet Goldmine (U.K.-U.S.)

A Miramax release of a Zenith Prods/Killer Films production, in association with Single Cell Pictures for Newmarket Capital Group, Goldwyn Films, Miramax Films, Zenith Prods, Channel Four Films. Produced by Christine Vachon. Directed, written by Todd Haynes. Story by Haynes, James Lyons. Camera, Maryse Alberti; editor, Lyons; music, Carter Burwell; production designer, Christopher Hobbs; costume designer, Sandy Powell. Reviewed at Cannes Festival, May 21. Running time: 123 mins.

Ewan McGregor (Curt Wild), Jonathan Rhys Meyers (Brian Slade), Toni Collette (Mandy Slade), Christian Bale (Arthur Stuart), Eddie Izzard (Jerry Divine), Emily Woof (Shannon).

Iconoclastic American indie filmmaker Todd Haynes takes a personalized look at British glam rock of the early 1970s in *Velvet Goldmine*, a constantly imaginative, stylistically lively but dramatically inert chronicle of cultural and sexual rebellion. Structured as a *Citizen Kane*-like investigation into the life and career of a vanished superstar rocker, boldly conceived film boasts an arresting first half but bogs down as the multilayering of the storytelling technique becomes more burden than assist. The film's studied approach and particularized take suggest a limited B.O. future rather than widespread acceptance.

In a very grim 1984, Brit newspaper reporter Arthur Stuart is assigned to write a "Whatever Happened to…?" feature. With the Kane interview structure kicking in, Arthur first visits the man who discovered subject Brian Slade.

U.S. release: Nov. 6 — U.S. B.O.: $1.1 million
Int'l release: Oct. 30 — Int'l B.O.: $1.5 million

## Very Bad Things

A Polygram Films release of a Polygram Filmed Entertainment presentation, in association with Initial Entertainment Group, of an Interscope Communications production, in association with

---

**...August 26...**

**ER**'s Noah Wyle will play Apple Computer's Steve Jobs and Anthony Michael Hall will play Microsoft's Bill Gates for **Pirates of Silicon Valley**.

BallPark Prods. Produced by Michael Schiffer, Diane Nabatoff, Cindy Cowan. Directed, written by Peter Berg. Camera, David Hennings; editor, Dan Lebental; music, Stewart Copeland; production design, Dina Lipton; costume design, Terry Dresbach. Reviewed at Toronto Festival, Sept. 12. MPAA Rating: R. Running time: 100 mins.
**Christian Slater (Robert Boyd), Cameron Diaz (Laura Garrety), Daniel Stern (Adam Berkow), Jeanne Tripplehorn (Lois Berkow), Jon Favreau (Kyle Fisher), Jeremy Piven (Michael Berkow), Leland Orser (Charles Moore).**
A darkly comic twist on the stag-party-gone-wrong, *Very Bad Things* spreads its genuinely outrageous, belly-laugh moments pretty thinly across an average, suburban-white-rage buddies comedy. Benefiting considerably from top casting, this first directorial outing by Peter Berg is an uneven stab at graveyard humor that badly needed a more stylish hand at the helm. Curiosity should see this one start off with reasonable numbers, but looks unlikely to be a bad-taste breakout hit.

Kyle, days before his marriage to Laura, sets off with his friends set for a night of drink and drugs in Las Vegas; however, the fun stops when a hired stripper accidentally skewers her brains on a coat hook. Robert, the only cool head among the panicking pardners, takes charge, calmly gutting a hotel security man who comes to tell them to keep the noise down. He assures his hysterical pals that the smart play is to chop up the bodies and bury them in the desert. Oddly, it's basically a very conventional movie gussied up with a few jaw-dropping moments. Each morally transgressive moment has to be analyzed and justified with (often overheated) dialog before moving on to the story's next stage.
U.S. release: Nov. 25                     U.S. B.O.: $9.5 million

## Viola Kisses Everybody (Viola Bacia Tutti) (Italy)

A Cecchi Gori Distribuzione release of a Cecchi Gori Group Tiger Cinematografica production. Produced by Vittorio and Rita Cecchi Gori. Directed by Giovanni Veronesi. Screenplay, Veronesi, Rocco Papaleo. Camera, Fabio Cianchetti; editor, Cecilia Zanuso; music, Pivio and Aldo De Scalzi; art director, Sonia Peng; costume designer, Carolina Olcese. Reviewed at Quirinale Cinema, Rome, Jan. 16. Running time: 91 mins.
**Asia Argento (Viola), Massimo Ceccherini (Max), Valerio Mastandrea (Samuele), Rocco Papaleo (Swing), Franco Califano (Samuele's Father), Daria Nicolodi (Sibilla).**
*Viola Kisses Everybody* is an embarrassingly unfunny road comedy whose only attractions are Dario Argento's daughter, Asia, as the sexy leader of a band of accidental outlaws, and current B.O. champ actor-director Leonardo Pieraccioni in a one-minute walk-on. This Cecchi Gori production would have looked bad as a series of TV sketches, though locally Argento's fans have helped to make the film a reasonable success.

Pic dispenses with plot to focus on its cast. The "narco-epileptic" Swing and goofy Max join their pal Samuele, a nice Jewish boy who works in his dad's restaurant, on a sun-and-sex vacation aboard a big modern camper borrowed from Papa.
Int'l release: Jan. 23                     Int'l B.O.: $3 million

## Voices of the Children (Docu)

A Terezin Foundation Inc. presentation. Produced by Jiri Jezek, Robert Kanter. Directed, written by Zuzana Justman. Camera, Ervin Sanders, Austin de Besche; editor, David Charap; music, Peter Fish. Reviewed on videocassette, Sept. 14, 1997. Running time: 80 mins.

It seems unlikely that a Holocaust docu could break new ground but *Voices of the Children* turns out to be an important contribution to the cinematic and historical record. While commercial theatrical prospects are negligible, it should enjoy a rich ancillary life at festivals on homevid and TV.

Focus is on the memories of three survivors of the Terezin concentration camp in the present Czech Republic. Terezin was a notorious "showplace" camp used for propaganda purposes by the Nazis. The three survivors were all children during the war, and lax standards at Terezin allowed many of their diaries, drawings, and other creations to survive.

## Wag the Dog

A New Line Cinema release of a Tribeca/Baltimore Pictures/ Punch production. Produced by Jane Rosenthal, Robert De Niro, Barry Levinson. Directed by Levinson. Screenplay, Hilary Henkin, David Mamet, based on the novel *American Hero* by Larry Beinhart. Camera, Robert Richardson; editor, Stu Linder; music, Mark Knopfler; production design, Wynn Thomas; costume design, Rita Ryack. Reviewed at Sony, New York, Dec. 8, 1997. MPAA Rating: R. Running time: 97 mins.
**Dustin Hoffman (Stanley Motss), Robert De Niro (Conrad Brean), Anne Heche (Winifred Ames), Woody Harrelson (Sgt. William Schumann), Denis Leary (Fad King), Willie Nelson (Johnny Green), Andrea Martin (Liz Butsky), Kirsten Dunst (Tracy Lime), William H. Macy (Mr. Young).**
Glib cynicism isn't a tremendously appealing quality, but in *Wag the Dog* it at least has the benefit of comic precision and polished execution. Pic satirizes media culture in a way that hardly delivers real insight or pungency, but shrewdly flatters the educated viewer's knowingness. That, plus welcome concision and a deftly hilarious turn by Dustin Hoffman, should help build a solid constituency for pic, especially given a careful rollout and maximum use of critical kudos.

The first question to be answered at the B.O. is exactly how far outside the nation's media centers pic's insiderish, referential comedy will play; premise, eerily timely, concerns D.C. pollsters joining with Hollywoodians to create a quick TV war to distract from presidential peccadilloes. Two weeks before re-election, the President is accused of accosting a Girl Scout. Before the news reaches the media his advisers call in spinmeister Conrad Brean, who specializes in near-impossible image rescues. Brean has the President extend his China tour while creating a press diversion involving rumors of a mythical cancelled contract for bombers complete with a quick, official denial. But for the crisis itself, Brean enlists Hollywood producer Stanley Motss who jumps at the chance of simulating a hot war with unlikely Albania as the enemy.
U.S. release: Dec. 25, 1997              U.S. B.O.: $43 million
Int'l release: Jan. 29                    Int'l B.O.: $20 million

## Waiting for a Tenor (Veranda For En Tenor) (Sweden)

A Svensk Filmindustri release of a Migma Film production, in association with Svensk Filmindustri, the Swedish Film Institute. Produced by Anna Eriksson. Directed by Lisa Ohlin. Screenplay, Klas Ostergren, Ohlin, from a short story by Ostergren. Camera, Anders Bohman; editor, Asa Mossberg; music, Bendik Hofseth; production design, Jan Olof Agren; costume design, Sven Lundin. Reviewed at Svensk Filmindustri, Stockholm, Aug. 14. Running time: 95 mins.
**Johan Hison Kjellgren (Thomas), Krister Henriksson**

---

(Hoffman/Henning), Lena B. Erikson (Revisom), Jessica Liedberg (Penny), Chatarina Larsson (Ingalill), Hans Lindgren (Verner), Jonas Falk (Ake).

The most impressive Swedish film so far this year, *Waiting for a Tenor* is an intricate and cinematically challenging story of two friends who finally try to come to terms with the events that shaped their lives. This demanding feature debut by Lisa Ohlin won't be a runaway success at the box office but is a natural for the festival circuit.

Pic starts with author Thomas quarreling with his wife and exiting for the neighborhood bar where he encounters childhood friend Hoffman, whom he hasn't seen for more than 35 years. Hoffman, an actor, is now an alcoholic and clearly dying of cancer. Hoffman mentions *Waiting for a Tenor*, a successful play that Thomas wrote way back. Hoffman suggests the two of them collaborate to turn it into a movie, with Hoffman playing the lead role of opera lover Henning. Thomas manages to get financing, and the pair write the script. Both the writing and subsequent making of the film awaken a pile of memories for the two men.

Int'l release: Sept. 11                    Int'l B.O.: $60,000

## Waiting for Sunset (Norway)

A Norsk Film/Yellow Cottage production, in association with Tag/Traum Filmproduction, Schibsted Film, Crone Film Produktion. Produced by Aage Aaberge. Executive producer, Espen Hoilund Carlsen. Directed by Leidulv Risan. Screenplay, Arthur Johansen, Risan, Allan Oberholzer. Camera, Axel Block; editor, Janus Billeskov Jansen; music, Geir Behren, Bent Aserud; production designer, Per Hjorth; casting, Ulla Wagner. Reviewed on videotape, L.A., March 5. Running time: 92 mins.
**Robert Mitchum (Ernest Bogan), Cliff Robertson (Ted Roth), Erland Josephson (August Lind), Espen Skjonberg (Carl Berner), Hanna Schygulla (Eva Lehwe), Nadja Tiller (Gertrude Boman).**

An appropriately elegiac work, *Waiting for Sunset* tells of four former classmates reunited by the imminent death of one of their group. The seniors are otherwise in top form, though diminished by material that's unduly maudlin and predictable. Buffs will appreciate the opportunity to catch one of the last performances of Robert Mitchum, but the film is unlikely to draw from outside that niche, resulting in limited theatrical performance. Ancillary activity – particularly cable and TV sales – will remain the pic's most vital venue.

The ailing member of the quartet is Carl, diagnosed with a fatal disease after passing out on an Oslo street. He awakes to see his former cronies who long ago made a pact that entitles Carl to one last fantasy wish.

## Waking Ned Devine (U.K.)

A Fox Searchlight Pictures release of a Tomboy Films production, in association with the Gruber Brothers, Mainstream SA, Bonaparte Films, the Isle of Man Film Commission, Overseas Film Group. Produced by Glynis Murray, Richard Holmes. Directed, written by Kirk Jones. Camera, Henry Braham; editor, Alan Strachan; music, Shaun Davey; production design, John Ebden; costume design, Rosie Hackett. Reviewed at Toronto Festival, Sept. 15. Running time: 91 mins.
**Ian Bannen (Jackie O'Shea), David Kelly (Michael O'Sullivan), Fionnula Flanagan (Annie O'Shea), Susan Lynch (Maggie), James Nesbitt (Pig Finn), Maura O'Malley (Mrs. Kennedy), Robert Hickey (Maurice), Paddy Ward (Brendy), James Ryland**

(Dennis Fitzgerald), Fintan McKeown (Pat Mulligan), Eileen Dromey (Lizzy Quinn).

The shamrock and blarney are thick in *Waking Ned Devine*, a warmly observed comedy of manners centered on a tiny Irish village that wins the national lottery. Strongly steeped in the tradition of Ealing comedies, though thinly plotted, it's a genial, feel-good item that should prove a moderate success in territories that respond to folksy Irish humor.

In the sleepy burg of Tully More, two crafty old-timers, Jackie and Michael, read in the paper that one of their fellow villagers has hit the lotto jackpot. Sniffing around for signs of sudden wealth, Jackie finally stumbles on the truth: The winner was Ned Devine. The only problem, as Jackie discovers when he visits the oldster's cottage, is that Ned is dead – from shock at the news, the winning ticket still in his hand. Jackie hits on a devious scheme: Michael will pose as Ned and they'll split the proceeds, which Jackie reckons at about £500,000. Only when the lotto man arrives from Dublin to check out the winner's credentials do the friends hear the big news: The winnings amount to £6,894,620.

U.S. release: Nov. 20              U.S. B.O.: $5.3 million
Int'l release: Nov. 6             Int'l B.O.: $350,000

## The Wall (France)

A Collection 2000 Seen By presentation of a La Sept ARTE/Haut & Court/WFE co-production, in association with Centre National de la Cinématographie, PROCIREP. Produced by Pierre Chevalier, Carole Scotta, Caroline Benjo, Simon Arnal. Directed, written by Alain Berliner. Camera, Yves Cape; editor, Sandrine Deegen; music, Alain Debaisieux; production designer, Pierre-François Limbosch. Reviewed at Cannes Festival, May 18. Running time: 67 mins.
**Daniel Hanssens (Albert), Mil Seghers (Father), Pascale Bal (Wendy)**

In the land of Magritte and surrealism – Belgian helmer Alain Berliner reminds us in *The Wall* – anything can happen on the eve of the year 2000, even the overnight erection of a wall between the country's bickering Flemish and French-speaking sides. This hourlong entry in the "Collection 2000" series is basically a one-joke production overwhelmed by a political tract as heavy as cement. Though pic is good as a quickie lesson on Belgian social tensions, one might have expected a better-developed and more comic result from the director of *Ma vie en rose*. Euro TV will be its main market.

Albert is the popular owner of a take-out French-fry joint positioned exactly on Belgium's "linguistic border." He's from the French side, but speaks both lingoes. On the eve of the millennium, the authorities decide to solve the problem for once and all by putting up their own Berlin Wall – which cuts Albert's stand in half.

## The Waterboy

A Buena Vista release of a Touchstone Pictures presentation of a Robert Simonds/Jack Giarraputo production. Produced by Simonds, Giarraputo. Executive producer, Adam Sandler. Directed by Frank Coraci. Screenplay, Tim Herlihy, Adam Sandler. Camera, Steven Bernstein; editor, Tom Lewis; music, Alan Pasqua; production design, Perry Andelin Blake; costume design, Tom Bronson. Reviewed at Regency II, San Francisco, Nov. 2. MPAA Rating: PG-13. Running time: 88 mins.
**Adam Sandler (Bob Boucher), Kathy Bates (Mama Boucher), Henry Winkler (Coach Klein), Fairuza Balk (Vicki Vallencourt),**

---

Jerry Reed (Red Beaulieu), Larry Gilliard, Jr. (Derek Wallace), Blake Clark (Farmer Fran), Rob Schneider (Townie).
After decent gains made with *The Wedding Singer*, an amiable crossover vehicle, Adam Sandler scrambles back to his Cajun Boy persona for *The Waterboy*. The formulaic mix of mirth and mayhem is aimed way down the MTV food chain, members of which will lap it up for solid opening returns and ancillary action. But don't expect the word-of-mouth build of *There's Something About Mary*: This yahoos-on-the-bayou farce is neither inventive nor outrageous enough.

The big laughs come from a ragtag football team. As for Sandler, he remains an acquired (lack of) taste. His stammering simp and recycled Jerry Lewis shtick would test the patience of even the French. In spots, the comic steps out of character, his eyes darting sideways to see if anyone is laughing. Needless to say, lack of confidence in material this broad doesn't add anything to his delivery.

Sandler plays Bobby Boucher, your proverbial water/whipping boy for Louisiana U.'s football team. Bobby is used as tackling dummy by the coach and players. Fired for hitting back, he returns to Mama Boucher's arms and then signs on with the underdog Mud Dogs. Bobby's temper tantrums make him a natural as defensive tackle. He transfers his pent-up anger to the opposing team and, following the formula, overcomes 11th-hour adversity to lead his team to victory in the Big Game.

U.S. release: Nov. 6                    U.S. B.O.: $148 million

## Water Easy Reach (En Dag Til I Solen) (Norway)
A BulBul Film production, in association with Liberator Prods, Babel Films, La Sept-Arte, Norsk Film, Audiovisuelt Produksjonsfond, Nordisk Film & TV Fond, TV2 (Norway). Produced by Finn Gjerdrum. Directed, written by Bent Hamer. Camera, Phillip Ogaard; editor, Skafti Gudmundsson; music, the Flesh Quartet; art director, Juan Botella; costumes, Sonia Grande. Reviewed at Toronto Film Festival, Sept. 11. Running time: 95 mins.
Eric Magnusson (Almar), Nicholas Hope (Windy), Ingrid Rubio (Marta), Francisco Rabal (Molina).
Norwegian helmer Bent Hamer follows his lauded 1995 debut, *Eggs*, with this tasty but small-proportioned meditation on culture clash and discovery, as a young sailor awaiting the repair of a watch hangs with the locals in a rugged, picturesque Spanish port. Episodic and elliptical pic finally proves too fragile a vessel to sail to significant commercial destinations, though fest berths will be in easy reach.

Apparently distracted by an eclipse, 20-year-old rookie sailor Almar drops an ornate gold pocket watch and dives into the sea to retrieve it. Told by a fussy watchmaker at his next port of call that the timepiece must be soaked in "sweet" water for 24 hours as a first step to repair, Almar reluctantly jumps ship in Galacia and begins his quiet vigil. In short order, he meets frazzled Australian sailor Windy, who regales the lad with stories of his travels and introduces him to lighthouse keeper Molina, a robust sort who likes mother's milk from the source and a cherished Norwegian calypso record.

Int'l release: March 6                    Int'l B.O.: $60,000

## The Way We Laughed (Cosi Ridevano) (Italy)
A Cecchi Gori Distribuzione release of a Mario and Vittorio Cecchi Gori presentation of a Cecchi Gori Group Tiger Cinematografica production. Produced by Vittorio and Rita Cecchi Gori. Directed, written by Gianni Amelio. Camera, Luca Bigazzi; editor, Simona Paggi; music, Franco Piersanti; production design, Giancarlo Basili; costume design, Gianna Gissi. Reviewed at Venice Festival, Sept. 9. Running time: 126 mins.
Enrico Lo Verso (Giovanni), Francesco Giuffrida (Pietro), Fabrizio Gifuni (Pelaia), Rosaria Danze (Lucia), Claudio Contartese (Rosario), Domenico Ragusa (Simone), Simonetta Benozzo (Ada).
A bittersweet story of fraternal love, sacrifice, and devotion that attempts to chart Italy's transformation and resulting loss of innocence, *The Way We Laughed* unfolds from the late 1950s through 1964, as the country shook off the vestiges of postwar poverty and became an industrial power. Like director Amelio's *Lamerica*, this meticulously crafted feature deals with immigrants' dreams of a new world of opportunity, but it fails to build dramatic backbone. Overly protracted and lacking in narrative fluidity, pic appears unlikely to achieve an international profile.

The film opens with the illiterate Sicilian Giovanni arriving in Turin where his brother Pietro has settled. The selflessly devoted Giovanni has an all-consuming emotional investment in steering his brother through school to a teaching career and a life of enlightenment. But Pietro lacks commitment. Giovanni, meantime, comes alive in the new environment. He devises a scheme to sublet slum quarters and collect rent from other Southern immigrants and later becomes president of a worker's cooperative. Given that the character is set up as sweet-natured and simple, his transition into an exploitative boss figure is difficult to swallow.

Int'l release: Oct. 2                    Int'l B.O.: $1.4 million

## The Wedding Singer
A New Line Cinema release of a Robert Simonds/Brad Grey production. Produced by Simonds, Jack Giarraputo. Directed by Frank Coraci. Screenplay, Tim Herlihy. Camera, Tim Suhrstedt; editor, Tom Lewis; music, Teddy Castellucci; production design, Perry Andelin Blake; art direction, Alan Au; costume design, Mona May. Reviewed at New Line, L.A., Jan. 3. MPAA Rating: PG-13. Running Time: 96 mins.
Adam Sandler (Robbie Hart), Drew Barrymore (Julia Sullivan), Christine Taylor (Holly), Allen Covert (Sammy), Matthew Glave (Glen Gulia), Ellen Albertini Dow (Rosie), Angela Featherstone (Linda), Alexis Arquette (George). With: Jon Lovitz, Steve Buscemi, Billy Idol.
The aptly named Robbie Hart is good at what he does – singing the hits of the 1980s and elevating the fun level at weddings, bar mitzvahs, and other celebrations. *The Wedding Singer* captures that joie de vivre in an unabashedly romantic comedy that has hit written all over it. A spirited, funny, and warm saga, the picture serves up Adam Sandler and Drew Barrymore in a way that enhances their most winning qualities. Commercial prospects are buoyant, with strong odds for the film to be the first genuine success story of 1998 and to show very good legs in international play.

What separates the title character from the pack is that in addition to his whole-hearted renditions, he has the "touch." Robbie knows how to keep the party going, instinctively understands what to say and when, and knows how to disarm a ticking bomb in the form of a surly or soused relative or guest. His spirit is naturally infectious. Julia Sullivan shares that

---

... **August 29** ...
**Lock, Stock and Two Smoking Barrels**, from first-time writer-director Guy Ritchie, went into its first U.K. weekend as a front-runner, hauling in $1.79 million.

open, ingenuous quality. A waitress at events where Robbie performs, she's hardly a world beater. After Robbie is stood up at his own wedding, all doubt is erased that these two are the right people with the wrong mates.

| U.S. release: Feb. 13 | U.S. B.O.: $81 million |
|---|---|
| Int'l release: April 15 | Int'l B.O.: $41 million |

### Weekend (Norway)

A Film 21 presentation of an Olav Oen production. Produced by Oen. Directed by Erik Gustavson. Screenplay, Arne Berggren, Gustavson. Camera, Philip Ogaard; editor, Wadt Thomsen; music, Randall Meyers; production designer, Billy Johansson; costume designer, Silje Fjelberg. Reviewed at Berlin Festival, Feb. 13. Running time: 87 mins.

**Camilla Strom Henriksen (TK), Kim Kolstad (Allan), Kai Remlov (Dr. Kai Strand), Lene Bragli (Berit Strand), Thea Westby (Cecilie Strand).**

*Weekend* is a tense, edgy, kidnap drama in which initial perceptions are completely confounded by later-stage plot developments. Pic has a reasonable chance at distribution in selected territories, with quality tube exposure definitely in the mix.

TK is a hard-faced, disturbed young woman who brandishes a large gun. Her lover, Allan, pretty much does what she says. The drugged-out teen couple, having apparently broken into an upscale suburban Oslo home, face the unexpected return of a doctor and his wife. In flight, they steal the family vehicle unaware that the couple's 9-year-old daughter, Cecilie, is in the back seat.

| Int'l release: Jan. 23 | Int'l B.O.: $80,000 |
|---|---|

### Welcome Back, Mr. McDonald (Radio No Jikan) (Japan)

A Fuji Television Network/Toho Co. production, in association with Premier Int'l. Produced by Chiaki Matsushita, Hisao Masuda, Takashi Ishihara, Kanjiro Sakura. Directed, written by Koki Mitani, based on the play *Radio no jikan* (*Radio Time*) by Mitani and Tokyo Sunshine Boys. Camera, Kenji Takama, Junichi Tozawa; editor, Hirohide Abe; music, Takayuki Hattori; art direction, Tomio Ogawa. Reviewed at Berlin Festival, Feb. 15. Running time: 103 mins.

**Toshiaki Karasawa (Kudo), Kyoka Suzuki (Miyako Suzuki), Masahiko Nishimura (Ushijima), Keiko Toda (Nokko Senbon), Takehiko Ono (Ben Noda), Shiro Namiki (Suguru Hosaka).**

Japanese cinema's first screwball comedy, *Welcome Back, Mr. McDonald* is a total, joyous delight. A fast-paced, inventively scripted ensembler set during the chaotic live broadcast of a radio play, film builds into an engrossing portrait of human foibles that's bighearted toward its characters while also pulling the rug from under the stolid feet of Japanese society. Mix of yocks and genuinely heart-tugging moments could build an offshore career among upscale auds.

A major hit with auds at its Berlin Forum screenings, pic also has rosy remake potential. Almost totally set in the corridors and studio of a Tokyo radio station, pic begins close to midnight with the end of the rehearsal of a play, *A Woman of Fate*, due to air within a matter of minutes. A trashy weepy written by housewife Miyako, it's the winning entry in a competition run by the station – or more accurately, the only entry.

| Int'l release: Nov. 8, 1997 | Int'l B.O.: $4.5 million |
|---|---|

### West Beirut (West Beyrouth) (France-Lebanon-Belgium-Norway)

A Tadrart Films release of a 3B Prods, La Sept/Arte (France)/ Douri Films (Lebanon)/Cine Libre (Belgium)/Exposed Film Prods, Bjorn Eivind Aarskog (Norway) co-production. Produced by Rachid Bouchareb, Jean Brehat. Directed, written by Ziad Doueiri. Camera, Ricardo Jacques Gale; editor, Dominique Marcombe; music, Stewart Copeland; art director, Hamze Nasrallah; costume design, Pierre Matard. Reviewed at Cannes Festival, May 20. Running time: 109 mins.

**Rami Doueiri (Tarek), Mohamad Chamas (Omar), Rola Al Amin (May), Carmen Lebbos (Hala), Joseph Bou Nassar (Riad).** (Arabic and French dialog)

Lebanese scripter-helmer Ziad Doueiri makes a richly assured debut with *West Beirut*, Lebanon's answer to *Hope and Glory*. Lively, historically freighted coming-of-age tale is a technically polished, frequently funny, and emotionally affecting work. Pic's geographical setting, no-name cast, and Arabic dialog may sound daunting to potential distribs, but pic actually fits nicely into the current wave of 1970s-set tales. While hardtops are deciding whether to take the plunge, fests won't have to think twice.

Self-assured class clown Tarek is bounced from class by his French teacher on April 13, 1975, just in time to observe the bloody massacre of 30 bus passengers by masked gunmen that marked the start of civil war. The next day's papers do little to clarify what's going on, but it's already impossible for Muslims to cross into East Beirut, and school is closed, apparently for good. His mother is ready to pull up stakes but his father refuses to believe the current troubles will last long.

### What Dreams May Come

A Polygram Films release of a Polygram Filmed Entertainment presentation of an Interscope Communications production, in association with Metafilmics. Produced by Stephen Simon, Barnet Bain. Directed by Vincent Ward. Screenplay, Ron Bass, based on the novel by Richard Matheson. Camera, Eduardo Serra; editors, David Brenner, Maysie Hoy; music, Michael Kamen; production design, Eugenio Zanetti; costume design, Yvonne Blake; visual-effects supervisor, Stuart Robertson. Reviewed at Polygram, Beverly Hills, Sept. 24, 1998. MPAA Rating: PG-13. Running time: 113 mins.

**Robin Williams (Chris Nielsen), Cuba Gooding, Jr. (Albert), Annabella Sciorra (Annie Nielsen), Max von Sydow (The Tracker), Jessica Brooks Grant (Marie Nielsen), Josh Paddock (Ian Nielsen), Rosalind Chao (Leona).**

A feel-good *Orpheus*, *What Dreams May Come* represents a heaped serving of metaphysical gobbledygook wrapped in a physically striking package. With Robin Williams leading an extensive tour of the afterlife as imagined through a gallery-full of vivified 19th-century romantic paintings, Vincent Ward's ambitious film tilts toward sentimentality, becoming hopelessly mired in an eagerness to remain likeable and upbeat in the face of subject matter that calls for considerably more gravity. This attempt to rally a mass audience around the weighty themes of mortality and eternal love – reportedly costing $85 million – looks to fall short of the commercial mark despite its audience-pleasing aspirations.

In tackling Richard Matheson's 20-year-old tome about a man's effort to reunite with his wife after death, the picture spreads out every conceivable safety net for its walk on the spiritual highwire, going directly for the tear ducts at the outset

---

**. . . August 30 . . .**

The Sarajevo International Film Festival, which was first staged in 1995 while the war in Bosnia was still raging, closed today.

via the deaths of children and a pet dog, for God's sake, and reducing the perennial theme of transcendent love to the easily digestible pop slogan "You must never give up."

Chris, recently deceased, finds himself in a strange world of brilliant colors, dramatic landscapes, and remarkably familiar visions that he soon understands are elaborations upon the paintings his wife restored or created. The "never give up" ethic kicks in when Chris engages the gruff man called "The Tracker" to guide him, as it were, across the River Styx and into hell to rescue his Eurydice.

U.S. release: Oct. 2                                 U.S. B.O.: $55.5 million
Int'l release: Oct. 15                               Int'l B.O.: $20 million

## Whatever

A Sony Pictures Classics release of a Circle/DuArt Films and Anyway Prods presentation. Produced by Ellin Baumel, Michelle Yahn, Kevin Seglla, Susan Skoog. Directed, written by Skoog. Camera, Michael Barrow, Michael Mayers; editor, Sandi Guthrie; production design, Dina Goldman. Reviewed at Sundance Festival, Jan. 19. Running time: 112 mins.
**Liza Weil (Anna Stockard), Chad Morgan (Brenda Talbot), Kathryn Rossetter (Carol Stockard), Frederic Forrest (Mr. Chaminsky), Gary Wolf (Eddie), Dan Montano (Zak).**
Revisiting the territory of numerous Stateside coming-of-age movies, Susan Skoog's well-executed *Whatever* has the novelty of telling the story from a distinctly female point of view, centering on one girl as she's about to cross the inevitably painful threshold. Pic lacks both gritty realism and subtlety, but its overtly melodramatic format, universal concerns, strong production values, and bouncy period music should broaden its appeal among female viewers. Skoog shrewdly sets the story in a New Jersey suburb of the early 1980s, so that she can explore the subculture of sex-drugs-music without dealing with the lethal effects of AIDS.

U.S. release: July 10                                U.S. B.O.: $350,000

## Who Am I? (Ngo Hai Sui) (Hong Kong)

A Columbia TriStar release of a Golden Harvest production. Produced by Barbie Tung. Directed, written by Jackie Chan. Directed by Benny Chan. Screenplay, Susan Chan, Lee Reynolds. Camera, Poon Hang Sang; editors, Peter Cheung, Yau Chi Wai; music, Nathan Wang; costume design, Thomas Chong; stunt coordinator, Jackie Chan. Reviewed at American Film Market, Santa Monica, Feb. 28. Running time: 120 mins.
**Jackie Chan (Jackie, aka Whoami), Michelle Ferre (Christine), Mirai Yamamoto (Yuki), Ron Smerczak (Morgan), Ed Nelson (Gen. Sherman), Washington Sixolo (Village Chief).**
Jackie Chan's latest is an attempt by the actor-filmmaker to try something new while giving his fans the type of picture they've grown to expect. The effort doesn't quite work: It's as if Chan got onto one track but developed cold feet, then fell back on the tried and true. Unless trimmed and reshaped for international auds, *Who Am I?* is destined for fast theatrical playoff and diminished response in ancillaries. Pic reaped a disappointing $5 million since debuting in Hong Kong in January.

Chan portrays a member of a commando group dropped into South Africa to kidnap a scientific research team. U.S. government officials are determined to keep a lid on the assignment; just to be sure, it's been arranged that the team will die in a plane crash once the mission's completed. But Chan survives, albeit with all memory erased. Rescued by

aboriginals, his plaintive question is mistaken for a name, and he becomes "Whoami." When his past starts to return, the plot quickens, the stunts escalate, and the venue changes radically as he heads for Rotterdam to thwart the evildoers and regain his memory.

Int'l release: Jan. 21                                Int'l B.O.: $11.5 million

## Why Do Fools Fall in Love

A Warner Bros. release of a Rhino Films production. Produced by Paul Hall, Stephen Nemeth. Directed by Gregory Nava. Screenplay, Tina Andrews. Camera, Ed Lachman; editor, Nancy Richardson; music, Stephen James Taylor; music supervisor, Christopher Brooks; production design, Cary White; costume design, Elisabetta Beraldo; choreographer, Russell Clark. Reviewed at Warner Bros., Burbank, Aug. 5. MPAA Rating: R. Running time: 115 mins.
**Halle Berry (Zola Taylor), Vivica A. Fox (Elizabeth Waters), Lela Rochon (Emira Eagle), Larenz Tate (Frankie Lymon), Paul Mazursky (Morris Levy), Pamela Reed (Judge Lambrey), Alexis Cruz (Herman Santiago), Miguel A. Nunez, Jr. (Young Little Richard), and Little Richard as himself.**
It takes until the final scenes of this *Rashomon*-like account of the life of 1950s doo-wop singer Frankie Lymon for Gregory Nava's film to find its proper tone of darkly farcical comedy. Up to then, *Why Do Fools Fall in Love* lurches around between standard rock 'n' roll biopic, cautionary tale, and overheated courtroom drama, as the dead crooner's three would-be widows do everything but tear one another's hair out in pursuit of royalties. Pic is too ill defined to emerge from the pack of B.O. also-rans.

Leapfrogging between the 1950s, when Frankie Lymon & the Teenagers scored a phenomenal hit with the titular tune, and the 1980s, when three women stepped forward with questionable but undismissible legal claims to their alleged ex-husband's estate, film hits the notes familiar from so many previous music sagas: the humble beginnings, sudden success, expansion of ego and sexual horizons on tour, dissension among longtime friends within the group, eventual disintegration via drugs and financial irresponsibility, attempts at a comeback, and wasteful early death.

U.S. release: Aug. 28                                U.S. B.O.: $12.5 million

## Wicked

A Frankenstein Entertainment production. Produced by Frank Beddor. Directed by Michael Steinberg. Screenplay, Eric Weiss. Camera, Bernd Heinl; editor, Daniel Gross; music, Eric Martinez; music supervisor, Diane DeLouise Wessel; production design, Dominic Watkins; costume design, Sara Jane Slotnick. Reviewed at Sundance Festival, Jan. 17. Running time: 96 mins.
**Julia Stiles (Ellie Christianson), William R. Moses (Ben Christianson), Patrick Muldoon (Lawson Smith), Vanessa Zima (Inger Christianson), Michael Parks (Det. Boland), Chelsea Field (Karen Christianson).**
Chockablock with nods to Lynch and De Palma, bleakly amusing thriller will appeal to specialty crowds, but is too arty and deliberately plotted to cross over as the next *Scream* machine. Strong reviews should assure latenight cult interest and bright ancillary afterlife for *Wicked*.

Ellie, your not-so-typical 14-year-old, wants to play house with malleable, eager-to-appease Dad. She gets the chance when cheating mom turns up dead, bludgeoned to death by one of several tract-community suspects. Killer's identity

---

emerges, *Vertigo*-style, midway through pic. Pic works best as suburban-Gothic spin on *Lolita*, with father-fixated Stiles drawing immediate suspicion for her willful behavior and inappropriate advances.

## Wide Awake

A Miramax release of a Woods Entertainment production. Produced by Cary Woods, Cathy Konrad. Directed, written by M. Night Shyamalan. Camera, Adam Holender; editor, Andrew Mondshein; music, Edmund Choi; production design, Michael Johnston; costume design, Bridget Kelly. Reviewed at Sony, Culver City, Feb. 24. MPAA Rating: PG. Running time: 88 mins.
Joseph Cross (Josh Beal), Timothy Reifsnyder (Dave O'Hara), Dana Delaney (Mrs. Beal), Dennis Leary (Mr. Beal), Robert Loggia (Grandpa Beal), Rosie O'Donnell (Sister Terry), Camryn Manheim (Sister Sophia).
Centering on a young boy's painful adjustment to the death of his beloved grandfather, *Wide Awake* is an earnest coming-of-age tale with explicitly moral and spiritual overtones. Representing a serious, rather old-fashioned family entertainment, pic should enjoy moderate appeal among young children and their parents, with possibly stronger performance in ancillary markets. Fifth-grader Joshua Beal is closer to his charismatic grandfather than to his kind but restrained yuppie parents. When he dies, Josh is not only devastated, but refuses to adjust to a new reality.

U.S. release: March 20          U.S. B.O.: $300,000

## Wildside (Vildspor) (Denmark-Iceland)

A Balboa 2 (Copenhagen)/Icelandic Film Corp. (Reykjavik) co-production, with support from the Danish Film Institute. Produced by Henrik Danstrup. Directed by Simon Staho. Screenplay, Nikolaj Coster Waldau, Staho. Camera, Jon Karl Helgason; editor, Anne Osterud; music, Hilmar Orn Hilmarson; production design, Arni Pall Johansson; costume design, Dora Einars Bergmann, Ragna Frodadottir. Reviewed at Cannes Festival, May 18. Running time: 95 mins.
Nikolaj Coster Waldau (Oskar "Ossy" Mikkelsen), Mads Mikkelsen (Jimmy), Nukaka (Jona), Palina Jonsdottir (Anna), Saevar Orn (Thorbjorn). (Danish, Icelandic, and English dialog)
*Wildside* is a solidly crafted thriller with links to classic film noir, though the bleakly beautiful Icelandic settings invest this tale of friendship and betrayal with a distinct ambience. There's strong material here for Eurotube programmers, and a vid shelf life is also indicated.
Ossy, an unwelcome visitor from the past, arrives wearing trendy clothes and a wicked smile to destroy the comfortable suburban family life of his former buddy, Jimmy. Copenhagen-born Ossy and Jimmy, friends since they were 18 and Jimmy accidentally killed a man who was beating up his pal, fled Denmark and lived the high life in the Far East. In Thailand they were involved in drug smuggling until Jimmy called it quits. But Jimmy's new, peaceful suburban life with Anna and their young son changes when Ossy turns up, eager to resume the partnership and seeking the reformed Jimmy's help to pull off a drug deal.

Int'l release: May 1          Int'l B.O.: $200,000

## Wild Things

A Sony Pictures Entertainment release of a Columbia Pictures/Mandalay Entertainment presentation. Produced by Rodney Liber, Steven A. Jones. Directed by John McNaughton. Screenplay, Stephen Peters. Camera, Jeffrey L. Kimball; editor, Elena Maganini; music, George S. Clinton; production designer, Edward T. McAvoy; costume designer, Kimberly A. Tillman. Reviewed at UA Westwood, L.A., March 16. MPAA Rating: R. Running time: 108 mins.
Kevin Bacon (Ray Duquette), Matt Dillon (Sam Lombardo), Neve Campbell (Suzie Toller), Theresa Russell (Sandra Van Ryan), Denise Richards (Kelly Van Ryan), Daphne Rubin-Vega (Gloria Perez), Robert Wagner (Tom Baxter), Bill Murray (Ken Bowden), Carrie Snodgress (Ruby).
In the blue-chip Florida enclave of Blue Bay, the sex is as steamy as the climate. *Wild Things* captures the passions of the area's haves and have-nots and gives them a wicked comic spin audiences won't quickly forget. Sly, torrid, and original, pic is certain to shake up an otherwise complacent marketplace. That will translate into upbeat theatrical returns for the eccentric item and strong action in ancillaries.
Imagine *Double Indemnity* cast young, *Twin Peaks* basked in sunshine, and a lethal *Grosse Pointe Blank* and you have a fair indication of the viewing experience. On the surface, it's about high-nosed teen socialite Kelly Van Ryan discovering her sexuality and finding out she can't get whatever she wants: Her moves on guidance counselor Sam Lombardo have been met with indifference. But that doesn't stop her from crying rape.

U.S. release: March 20          U.S. B.O.: $30 million
Int'l release: April 10          Int'l B.O.: $37 million

## Williamstowne

A Woodleaf production of a Richard Horian film. Produced, directed, written by Richard Horian. Camera, Richard Brooks; editor, Mark Harris; music, Ralph Vaughan Williams; production design, Marcus Abbott; costume design, Shana Schoepke. Reviewed at Raleigh Studios, L.A., Nov. 3. Running time: 91 mins.
Deni Delory (Sara McCo`naghy), Richard Horian (Jack), Lynn Britt (Sarah's Mother), Brian Heath (Sarah's Father), Cheri Severns (Rebecca), Noah Bean (Tom).
Occasionally beautiful and frequently frustrating, *Williamstowne* is an ambitious experiment that doesn't always work. With scenes and staging precisely choreographed to the music of Ralph Vaughan Williams, this "ballet without dance" unfolds almost entirely without dialog. While its unique approach may fascinate some, pic's peculiarities will make it a tough sell even to the arthouse crowd.
Set in the mid-1800s, Richard Horian's film tells the story of a young woman who returns from the grave to visit her loved ones on the anni of her accidental death. Deceased for 10 years, Sarah McConaghy appears every spring to wander through the village as a presence unseen but keenly felt by her husband, Jack, her parents, and the townsfolk. Because her spirit is not at peace, her presence, though benign, tortures her loved ones, and the close-knit community must find a way to lay her to rest.
Because multihyphenate Horian insists upon so closely following Vaughan Williams' music, he restricts his film and constricts his actors. The two fixed rules to which he adheres rigorously – no music edits and no tempo alterations – ultimately mean that Horian has privileged the music over all else, including plot structure, character development, dramatic pacing, and narrative logic.

## Wind With the Gone (El Viento Se Llevo Lo Que) (Argentina-France-Netherlands-Spain)

An Agresti Film (Argentina)/DMVB Films (France)/Studio Nieuwe Gronden (Netherlands)/Maestranza Film, Sogedasa, H&A (Spain) production, in collaboration with Surf Film (Italy). Produced by Thierry Forte, Alejandro Agresti, Facundo Narducci, Antonio P. Perez, Sarah Halioua. Directed, written by Agresti. Camera, Mauricio Rubinstein; editor, Alejandro Brodershon; music, Paul Michael van Brugge; art director, Floris Vos; costume design, Mariana Brik, Micaela Salegh. Reviewed at San Sebastian Festival, Sept. 25. Running time: 91 mins. (Spanish/French dialog)

Vera Fogwill (Soledad), Angela Molina (Donna Maria), Fabian Vena (Pedro), Jean Rochefort (Edgar Wexley), Ulises Dumont (Antonio), Carlos Roffe (Amalfi), Sergio Povez Campos (Caruso).

Argentine director Alejandro Agresti couples an elliptical examination of the fragmentation and filtering of information in his country with a paean to the power of cinema to bring people together in *Wind With the Gone*, which was the widely disputed winner of San Sebastian's top prize. This playfully surreal comedy-drama is perhaps too eager in entirely exposing its inventive premise so early, leaving only less original developments to follow. But its absurdist humor and curious characters retain an eccentric charm throughout that will ensure further fest bookings.

Tired of being molested by passengers and exploited by her boss, twentysomething Buenos Aires taxi driver Soledad steals a cab and aimlessly drives south across rugged mountain country to the isolated dustbowl town of Rio Pico, whose inhabitants she quickly realizes are all a little off-kilter. The village's only contact with the outside world is the local cinema. Soledad takes a room at the village inn run by Dona Maria. When the locals learn she briefly studied journalism, they convince her to host their own newsreels documenting life in the town. Her debut as news anchor sparks a romance with film critic Pedro, whose grasp of reality seems tenuous even by Rio Pico standards but who appears to understand Soledad better than anyone. The arrival of a washed-up French film star in the tiny hamlet in response to reams of fan mail serves to reawaken Dona Maria's belief in love.

## With Friends Like These...

A Robert Greenhut/Parkway/Quadrant production. Produced by Greenhut, Amy Lemisch. Directed, written by Philip Messina. Camera, Brian J. Reynolds; editor, Claudia Finkle; music, John Powell; production designer, Beth DeSort; costume designers, Mary Kay Stolz, Joanna Bendel. Reviewed at Harmony Gold, L.A., Feb. 18. Running time: 105 mins.

Adam Arkin (Steve Hersh), Robert Costanzo (Johnny DiMartino), Beverly D'Angelo (Theresa Carpenter), Elle Macpherson (Samantha Mastandrea), Amy Madigan (Hannah DiMartino), Laura San Giacomo (Joan Hersh), David Strathairn (Armand Minetti), Jon Tenney (Dorian Mastandrea), Jon Polito (Rudy Ptak), Bill Murray (Maurice Melnick), and Martin Scorsese as himself.

The insecure world of character actors is humorously and knowingly explored in *With Friends Like These...* Blessed with a great premise – four small-timers, all friends, are up for the same part in Martin Scorsese's next gangland picture – Philip Messina's genial film generates some nice laughs as well as an involving sympathy for the characters. Viewers will have no trouble warming up to the likeable lugs (pic won the audience award at the Santa Barbara fest), suggesting some commercial potential in indie arenas.

The four middle-aged guys at the center are all-purpose "ethnic" second bananas – serious actors who idolize De Niro, Pacino, and Hoffman but make a living playing "goombah hit men" on TV skeins. When Johnny De Martino, a fat, bald, over-excitable fellow, is privately approached to audition for Al Capone in the next Scorsese pic, he practically faints before starting to panic. He can't contain his good fortune and soon his buddies know about it and line up, too.

## Without Limits

A Warner Bros. release of a Cruise-Wagner production. Produced by Tom Cruise, Paula Wagner. Directed by Robert Towne. Screenplay, Towne, Kenny Moore. Camera, Conrad L. Hall; editors, Claire Simpson, Robert K. Lambert; original score, Randy Miller; production design, William Creber; costume design, Grania Preston; technical adviser, Patrice Donnelly. Reviewed at Warner Bros., Burbank, March 11. MPAA Rating: PG-13. Running time: 117 mins.

Billy Crudup (Steve Prefontaine), Donald Sutherland (Bill Bowerman), Monica Potter (Mary Marckx), Jeremy Sisto (Frank Shorter), Matthew Lillard (Roscoe Devine), Billy Burke (Kenny Moore), Judith Ivey (Barbara Bowerman).

The second bigscreen biopic of track star Steve Prefontaine to appear in as many years, Robert Towne's *Without Limits* reps a distinct improvement over Steve James' *Prefontaine*. But as it covers basically the same dramatic events and creates essentially the same emotional reaction, even positive reviews and a strong marketing push will have trouble attracting a wide public.

Whereas many successful sports stories are about underdogs, Prefontaine's is different in that he was so damn good that he rarely had serious competition. And as opposed to tales about long shots, in which the subjects rise from obscurity to unlikely triumphs, the most dramatic moments of any telling of Prefontaine's life are all downers – his deflating loss at Munich and his premature, seemingly arbitrary death. The rest is nearly uninterrupted excellence. Pre's push-pull relationship with Bowerman, a future founder of Nike, remains at the core of the story.

U.S. release: Sept. 11                                    U.S. B.O.: $800,000

## Without Words (Docu, B&W/Color)

An Independent Television Service presentation. Produced, directed, written by Lisa Lewenz. Camera (B&W/color), Ella Lewenz (historical footage), Lisa Lewenz (contemporary footage); editors, Penelope Falk, Anand Kamalaker; Ruth Schell, Lisa Lewenz; music, Paul Bartholomew, Lisa Lewenz, Lewis Spratlan, Bob Telson. Reviewed at Sundance Festival, Jan. 20, 1998. Running time: 62 mins.

A remarkable example of finding home movies in the attic that open a window on an entire world, *A Letter Without Words* provides a glimpse of Germany between the wars that is privileged. Consisting mostly of footage taken by the present filmmaker's wealthy grandmother between 1914 and 1938, Lisa Lewenz's concise, highly evocative docu will fascinate anyone with an interest in 20th-century history and, despite its hour-long running time, could find limited theatrical and special-interest bookings before PBS broadcast and video release.

---

### ...September 2...

In a first, two studios, Fox and Disney, pass the $500 million mark at the summer box office.

Ella Lewenz, born in 1883, was the daughter of an eminent Jewish banker. One of the first Germans to acquire a home-movie camera, as the years went by, Ella gained sufficient ambition and expertise to edit, title, and date her work. Granddaughter Lisa discovered the cache in 1981 and began delving into it. Lisa's sense of discovery is intimately intertwined with the unveiling of the footage itself; raised Episcopalian, she didn't learn of her family's Jewish roots until she was 13, and never knew her grandmother.

### The Wonderful Ice Cream Suit

A Buena Vista release of a Walt Disney Pictures presentation. Produced by Roy E. Disney, Stuart Gordon. Directed by Gordon. Screenplay, Ray Bradbury, based on his short story and play. Camera, Max Ahlberg; editor, Andy Horvitch; music, Mader; production design, Stuart Blatt; costume design, Marie France; choreography, Miranda Garrison. Reviewed at Sundance Festival, Jan. 23. MPAA Rating: PG. Running time: 77 mins.
**Joe Mantegna (Gomez), Esai Morales (Dominguez), Edward James Olmos (Vamenos), Clifton Gonzalez Gonzalez (Martinez), Gregory Sierra (Villanazul), Liz Torres (Ruby Escadrillo), Sid Caesar (Sid Zellman), Howard Morris (Leo Zellman).**
Ray Bradbury's 1957 *Saturday Evening Post* story *The Magic White Suit* has been successfully adapted as a television drama, a play, and a stage musical. But the author's adaptation for yet a fourth medium finds the magic missing. Very broad, rather hokey exercise in slapstick whimsy was produced with vidcassette release in mind, and heavy Disney promotion will sell a few tapes. But pic's lukewarm appeal for both kids and adults renders theatrical release unwise. Middle-aged barrio sharpster Gomez has his heart set on buying the gorgeous white suit. But he's a bit short of cash, so he searches out four more men of the same approximate size to each pony up $20 toward its pricetag.

### Woo

A New Line Cinema release of a Gotham Entertainment production, in association with New Deal Prods. Produced by Beth Hubbard, Michael Hubbard. Directed by Daisy V.S. Mayer. Screenplay, David C. Johnson. Camera, Jean Lepine; editors, Nicholas Eliopoulios, Janice Hampton; music, Michael Colombier; production design, Ian Mayhew; costume design, Michael Clancy. Reviewed at MGM, New York, April 25. MPAA Rating: R. Running Time: 84 mins.
**Jada Pinkett Smith (Woo), Tommy Davidson (Tim), Duane Martin (Frankie), Michael Ralph (Romaine), Darrel M. Heath (Hop), Dave Chappelle (Lenny), Paula Jai Parker (Claudette), LL Cool J (Darryl).**
A half-baked hybrid of *After Hours* and *Blind Date*, *Woo* is a graceless, gratingly unfunny comedy that brings out the worst in all involved. Positioned to make a quick score in urban markets before the onslaught of summer blockbusters, pic may find its shelf life even briefer than expected. Formulaic farce centers on a mismatched couple: Woo, a gorgeous extrovert who's absolutely convinced of her own wonderfulness, and Tommy, an insecure, straight-laced law clerk in need of loosening up. The couple are thrown together on a blind date arranged by Woo's cousin and Tim's best buddy.
U.S. release: May 8 — U.S. B.O.: $8 million
Int'l release: Aug. 20 — Int'l B.O. $75,000

### The Wounds (Rane) (Serbia-France)

A Cobra Film Dept (Belgrade)/Pandora Film (Paris) production. Produced by Dragan Bjelogrlic. Directed, written by Srdjan Dragojevic. Camera, Dusan Joksimovic; editor, Petar Markovic; music, Aleksandar Sasa Habic; production designer, Aleksandar Denic. Reviewed at Toronto Festival, Sept. 19. Running time: 103 mins.
**Dusan Pekic (Pinki), Milan Maric (Kraut), Dragan Bjelogrlic (Dickie), Branka Katic (Suki), Predrag Miki Manojlovic (Stojan), Vesna Trivalic (Lidija), Andreja Jovanovic (Dijabola).**
A jolting bumper-car ride across five years of recent Yugoslav history through the story of two on-the-make teenagers, Srdjan Dragojevic's *The Wounds* plays at times like a Serbian *Trainspotting*. Latest feature from the director of *Pretty Village, Pretty Flame* is a more in-your-face, blackly comic look at the country's recent past, lensed in a style halfway between frantic Balkan tragicomedy and MTV. Often scary rawness of the emotions on display makes for a powerful viewing experience.
Film opened in Belgrade in May and in its first three months racked up some 300,000 admissions, despite the Serbian government ordering a total publicity blackout in state-controlled media after a week in release.
Pinki, the film's narrator, and Kraut, are two kids high on drugs who are hot-rodding through Belgrade's streets at a time when the city is celebrating the end of war. In short order, we meet Pinki's family, led by his excitable father, and the two boys' Slovenian friend, Dijabola, butt of their jokes, as we flash back to 1991 and the tide of Serbian nationalism engulfing the country.
Int'l release: May 14 — Int'l B.O.: $800,000

### Wrongfully Accused

A Warner Bros. release of a James G. Robinson presentation of a Morgan Creek production, in co-production with Constantin Film. Produced by Robinson, Bernd Eichinger, Pat Proft. Co-executive producer, Robert Kulzer. Directed, written by Proft, based on characters created by Roy Huggins. Camera, Glen MacPherson; editor, James R. Symons; music, Bill Conti; production design, Michael Bolton; stunt coordinator, Guy Bews. Reviewed at UA Westwood, L.A., Aug. 4. MPAA Rating: PG-13. Running time: 85 mins.
**Leslie Nielsen (Ryan Harrison), Richard Crenna (Lt. Fergus Falls), Kelly Le Brock (Lauren Goodhue), Melinda McGraw (Cass Lake), Michael York (Hibbing Goodhue), Sandra Bernhard (Dr. Fridley), Aaron Pearl (Sean Laughrea).**
If indeed the time is right to send up the thriller genre exemplified by *The Fugitive*, the makers of *Wrongfully Accused* certainly don't get the job done. The broad comedy misses its target – except for some accidental hits – creating more mess than mirth in its pie-flinging approach to comedy. Though the film has already grossed more than $5 million in three weeks of release in Germany and Austria, domestic prospects aren't comparably strong. It's unlikely to open to major B.O., but will most certainly be sentenced to a brief commercial term prior to heading to video shelves.
The story, at least initially, is a clone of the Harrison Ford movie inspired by the 1960s TV series. Ryan Harrison is a superstar classical violinist who wields a near-lethal bow. He becomes romantically involved with the wife of his benefactor, and quicker than you can say catgut, his cash cow is murdered by mercenaries and Ryan is set up to take the fall.

## The Wrong Guy (Canada)

A Handmade Films presentation of a Paragon Entertainment Corp. production. Produced by Jon Slan. Directed by David Steinberg. Screenplay, Dave Foley, David Higgins, Jay Kogen. Camera, David A. Makin; editor, Christopher Cooper; music, Lawrence Shragge; production design, Gregory P. Keen; costumes, Delphine White. Reviewed at the Atwater, Montreal, Feb. 20, 1998. Running time: 87 mins.

Dave Foley (Nelson Hibbert), Jennifer Tilly (Lynn Holden), David Higgins (Det. Arlen), Colm Feore (The Killer). With: Kevin McDonald, Joe Flaherty, Kenneth Welsh, Alan Scarfe.

Based on a sketch Dave Foley wrote as a member of comedy troupe the Kids in the Hall, *The Wrong Guy* is occasionally very funny and inspired, but it feels like a good TV skit stretched to feature length. *Fugitive* spoof looks to have the wrong stuff at box office and is more likely to do the right thing in video and TV markets.

Nelson Hibbert is a nerdy exec at a large corporation who is convinced that he's a shoo-in to become company president. When he is passed over for the top job, he goes ballistic, threatening to do bodily harm to the boss. He storms into the man's office only to find him slumped over his desk with a knife in his neck. Figuring that everyone will assume he's the murderer, he concludes that he has no choice but to become a fugitive from the law.

## The X-Files

A 20th Century Fox release of a Ten Thirteen production. Produced by Chris Carter and Daniel Sackheim. Directed by Rob Bowman. Screenplay, Carter, story by Carter, Frank Spotnitz. Camera, Ward Russell; editor, Stephen Mark; music, Mark Snow; production design, Christopher Nowak; costume design, Marlene Stewart; visual-effects supervisor, Mat Beck. Reviewed at the Village, L.A, June 16. MPAA Rating: PG-13. Running Time: 120 mins.

David Duchovny (Fox Mulder), Gillian Anderson (Dana Scully), Martin Landau (Dr. Alvin Kurtzweil), Armin Mueller-Stahl (Conrad Strughold), Blythe Danner (Jana Cassidy), William B. Davis (Cigarette-Smoking Man), John Neville (Well-Manicured Man), Mitch Pileggi (Walter Skinner), Jeffrey DeMunn (Dr. Ben Bronschweig), Terry O'Quinn (Darius Michaud).

One of the rare television-derived features to hit the bigscreen while still on the air, *The X-Files* falls somewhere between standing on its own feet and merely being a glorified TV episode. On the plus side, action plays out on a big canvas with major set pieces impossible for the tube. Conversely, project gives off the unmistakable odor of a calculated marketing ploy designed as a bridge between TV seasons and an attempt to morph the pop series into a movie franchise. Enough of the show's legion of faithfuls will turn up during the initial weeks to set this on a profitable trajectory, with foreign and homevid repping lucrative gravy. Non "X"-philes are unlikely to climb aboard in significant numbers as the films lacks the excitement, scope, and style expected of event movies.

Pics begins in TV-teaser fashion with three startling and intriguing suspense scenes: a ferocious creature kills a caveman in 15,000 B.C.; a young boy falls into a pit (on the same site) and is attacked by a black goo; and Mulder and Scully are trapped in a government building with a ticking bomb. The strands will eventually mesh in an oddly ordinary way and devotees get the added bonus of the answers to some long-standing mysteries cultivated over series' five seasons.

| | |
|---|---|
| U.S. release: June 19 | U.S. B.O.: $84 million |
| Int'l release: July 10 | Int'l B.O.: $100 million |

## Xiu Xiu: The Sent-Down Girl (Tian Yu) (Hong Kong-U.S.)

A Whispering Steppes L.P. production. Produced by Joan Chen, Alice Chan. Directed by Chen. Screenplay, Yan Geling, Chen, based on Yan's novella *Tian yu* (*Heavenly Bath*). Camera, Lu Yue; editor, Ruby Yang; music and lyrics, Johnny Chen; production/costume design, Pan Lai. Reviewed at Berlin Festival, Feb. 19. Running time: 99 mins.

Lu Lu (Wenxiu, aka Xiu Xiu), Lopsang (Lao Jin), Qian Zheng (Li Chuanbei), Gao Jie (Mother), Li Zhizhen (Chief), Gao Qiang (Peddler). (Mandarin dialog)

A chamber yarn of lost innocence during the Cultural Revolution that packs a surprising punch under its naive, almost abstract telling, *Xiu Xiu: The Sent-Down Girl* is a confident behind-the-camera debut by mainland-China-born Joan Chen. It may prove too fragile to make much impact theatrically, but the pic is well worth a look by fest programmers and ancillary buyers. Though the film never directly criticizes the Communist Party, or grandstands any political message, there's still plenty here (not least in the sexual content) to give the authorities pause.

Pic kicks off with teen Xiu Xiu about to leave her family in Chengdu for a spell in a remote corner of Tibet. It's 1975, when the Cultural Revolution was virtually played out, making the disruption of her education and family life all the more tragic. Xiu Xiu is assigned to live with horseman Lao Jin. Film basically describes their platonic love story, as Xiu Xiu's teenage arrogance is worn down by the realities of their tough existence and her ideals are shattered when she realizes she's been tricked by the authorities. Silently observed by the neutered Lao Jin, she trades sex for promises from passers-by and officials, still hoping her favors will earn her the right to return home.

## XXL (France)

A Gaumont release of a Legende Films/Gaumont/TF1 Films/DD Prods/Compagnie Cinématographique Prima production, with the participation of Canal Plus. Produced by Alain Goldman. Directed by Ariel Zeitoun. Screenplay, Florence Quentin. Camera, Philippe Pavans de Ceccaty; editor, Hugues Darmois; music, Goran Beregovic; production design, Dominique Andre; costume design, Edith Vesperini. Reviewed at Rive Gauche Theater, Perpignan, France, Dec. 18, 1997. Running time: 97 mins.

Michel Boujenah (Alain Berrebi), Gérard Depardieu (Jean Bourdalou), Elsa Zylberstein (Arlette Stern), Catherine Jacob (Lorene Benguigui), Maurice Chevit (David Stern), Gina Lollobrigida (Gaby Berrebi).

Following the local B.O. tidal wave of Thomas Gilou's *Would I Lie to You?*, a farce set amongst the Jews of Paris' garment district, comic helmer Ariel Zeitoun's foray into the same area was expected to make a splash. Unfortunately, despite a strong cast that includes standup shtickman Michel Boujenah, a surprisingly trim and vigorous Gérard Depardieu, and a delightful cameo by Gina Lollobrigida as a Jewish mama from hell, *XXL* looks to sink like a stone. The combined weight of unsubtle gags, hammy perfs, stereotypes, and a story that falls apart in the final reel ensures that Zeitoun's latest will end up on the local tube.

Int'l release: Dec. 10, 1977          Int'l B.O.: $1.5 million

## You Can Thank Me Later (Canada)

Danehip Entertainment, in association with Flashpoint Ltd, presents a Dotan-Anbar/Cinequest Films production. Produced by Shimon Dotan, Netaya Anbar. Directed by Dotan. Screenplay, Oren Safdie, based on his play *Hyper-Allergenic*. Camera, Amnon Salomon; editor, Netaya Anbar; music, Walter Christian Rothe; production design, Michael Devine; costume design, Renee April. Reviewed at World Film Festival, Montreal, Sept. 3. Running time: 110 mins.

**Ellen Burstyn (Shirley Cooperberg), Amanda Plummer (Susan Cooperberg), Ted Levine (Eli Cooperberg), Mark Blum (Edward Cooperberg), Mary McDonnell (Diane), Genevieve Bujold (Joelle), Jacob Tierney (Simon Cooperberg), Roch Lafortune (TV Repairman), Genevieve Brouillette (Nurse).**

Conduct under pressure is the source of caustic humor and poignancy in *You Can Thank Me Later*. Set primarily in a hospital room where a family awaits the results of the father's operation, the emotional battlefield is a series of zingers that touch sensitive nerves and tickle the funnybone. Yet Oren Safdie's script falls short of achieving the proper balance and focus to make its extremes come together. The top-notch cast keeps pic interesting and should ensure some theatrical play, though the film's best commercial prospects are in small-screen ancillaries.

Shirley Cooperberg is the strong-willed matriarch of a well-heeled Montreal Jewish family. While her husband is under the surgeon's scalpel, her children arrive at the hospital. Eli is an oft-divorced, failed writer; Susan has been pouring her myriad neuroses onto canvas but has yet to find an appreciative audience; and Edward is a successful producer of touring Broadway plays. They are the picture-perfect embodiment of a dysfunctional family.

## You're Laughing (Tu Ridi) (Italy)

An Istituto Luce release of a Filmtre production, in association with Dania Film, RAI CinemaFiction, and with the participation of Telepiu. Produced by Grazia Volpi. Directed, written by Paolo and Vittorio Taviani, based on the novellas of Luigi Pirandello. Camera, Giuseppe Lanci; editor, Roberto Perpignani; music, Nicola Piovani; production design, Gianni Sbarra; costume design, Lina Nerli Taviani. Reviewed at Anica, Rome, Aug. 31. Running time: 102 mins.

**FELICE: Antonio Albanese (Felice), Sabrina Ferilli (Nora), Luca Zingaretti (Migliori), Giuseppe Cederna (Rambaldi), Elena Ghiaurov (Mariska).**
**TWO KIDNAPPINGS: Turi Ferro (Ballaro), Lello Arena (Rocco), Steve Spedicato (Vincenzo).**

Returning to the novellas and characters of Luigi Pirandello, Paolo and Vittorio Taviani have crafted a small, simple, and satisfying pic with *You're Laughing*. Typical of Pirandello, the morals remain elusive in this pair of melancholy, often poignant, tales that deal quietly and idiosyncratically with violence. The widely pre-sold film should open its share of arthouse doors.

The heart of the film is the lovely, hour-long *Felice*. Set in 1930s Rome, it tells of former opera baritone Felice, now unhappy in marriage and in an accounting job at the Teatro dell'Opera. Each night, he laughs uproariously in his sleep

but is unable to remember the dreams that prompt his mirth. When Felice dreams of participating in the daily humiliation the crippled co-worker Rambaldi endures at the hands of an arrogant opera director, and then discovers the man has committed suicide, his misery becomes too much. He sets about avenging the death, but during preparations meets Nora, reawakening love and his past triumphs. Second episode, *Two Kidnappings*, opens in contemporary Sicily. The scenario involves the pre-teen son of a Mafia turncoat held hostage by a compassionate mob flunky to deter his father from turning stoolie. The story serves as a frame for a Pirandello tale concerning a kidnapping gone awry.

Pic was planned as a three-parter, but opening episode – starring Omero Antonutti and based on an autobiographical Pirandello story – was dropped from the release version after being shot and edited.

Int'l release: Sept. 4          Int'l B.O.: $800,000

## Your Friends & Neighbors

A Gramercy Pictures release of a Polygram Filmed Entertainment presentation of a Propaganda Film/Fleece production. Produced by Steve Golin, Jason Patric. Directed, written by Neil LaBute. Camera, Nancy Schreiber; editor, Joel Plotch; music, Metallica; production design, Charles Breen; costume design, April Napier. Reviewed at Polygram, Beverly Hills, July 24. MPAA Rating: R. Running time: 99 mins.

**Amy Brenneman (Mary), Aaron Eckhart (Barry), Catherine Keener (Terri), Nastassja Kinski (Cheri), Jason Patric (Cary), Ben Stiller (Jerry).**

*Your Friends & Neighbors*, Neil LaBute's follow-up to *In the Company of Men*, continues his darkly comic exploration of misogyny and other ills as they inform the tangled web of relationships of a group of bright, endlessly loquacious urbanites. What will prevent this contempo (im)morality tale from traveling beyond the indie milieu is not only the relentless unpleasantness of the male characters, but also the static quality of the writing and staging, which approximate a theatrical mode that lacks narrative momentum or dramatic excitement. New pic remains narrowly focused: the battlefield is the bedroom rather than the boardroom. The power games played by the six characters are motivated by below-the-waist sexual politics.

U.S. release: Aug. 19          U.S. B.O.: $4.5 million

## You've Got Mail

A Warner Bros. release of a Lauren Shuler Donner production. Produced by Nora Ephron, Lauren Shuler Donner. Directed by Ephron. Screenplay, Ephron, Delia Ephron, based on the screenplay *The Shop Around the Corner* by Samson Raphaelson and the play *Parfumerie* by Miklos Laszlo. Camera, John Lindley; editor, Richard Marks; music, George Fenton; production design, Dan Davis; costume design, Albert Wolsky. Reviewed at Bruin, L.A., Dec. 8. MPAA rating: PG-13. Running time: 119 mins.

**Tom Hanks (Joe Fox), Meg Ryan (Kathleen Kelly), Parker Posey (Patricia Eden), Greg Kinnear (Frank Navasky), Jean Stapleton (Birdie), Steve Zahn (George Pappas), David Chappelle (Kevin Scanlon), Dabney Coleman (Nelson Fox), John Randolph (Schuyler Fox).**

*You've Got Mail* is an attractively wrapped package addressed to holiday audiences. The reteaming of *Sleepless in Seattle* combo Tom Hanks and Meg Ryan with director Nora Ephron

---

**... September 5 ...**

The restored director's cut of Orson Welles' **Touch of Evil** unveils at Telluride Film Festival.

puts a fine contempo spin on a time-tested premise – the story of anonymous, affectionate pen pals who dislike each other in person. This winning romantic comedy will be propelled to hefty B.O.

Joe Fox is opening a mammoth bookstore across the street from Kathleen Kelly's boutique children's bookshop, thus setting up a David vs. Goliath confrontation. When Joe and Kathleen meet, romantic sparks fly, but when she learns he's the mercenary entrepreneur, her appreciation of his charm gives way to disapproval of his soulless guile. Unwittingly, however, Joe and Kathleen are each other's cyber soulmates, exchanging daily e-mail under pseudonymous names. Their correspondence takes an unexpected turn when "Shopgirl" (Kathleen's moniker) tells "NY152" (Joe's) that she's facing a professional crisis. Joe advises her to "go to the mattress" and attack the enemy, unmindful that the enemy is himself.

| | |
|---|---|
| U.S. release: Dec. 18 | U.S. B.O.: $63.5 million |
| Int'l release: Dec. 24 | Int'l B.O.: $4 million |

### Zacharia Farted (Canada)

A Windowshot Productions production, in association with Jupiter Films, with support from Telefilm Canada. Produced by Damon Vignale, Colin Cunningham. Directed by Michael Rohl. Screenplay by Cunningham. Camera, Brian Whittred; editor, Rick Benwick; music, Jim Guttridge, Daryl Bennett; production designer, Andre Ricard. Reviewed at Vancouver Festival, Sept. 28. Running time: 110 mins.
**Colin Cunningham (Michael), Benjamin Ratner (Brian), Madison Graie (Corey), Betty Linde (Jean), C. Ernst Harth (Wayne Newton), Willie John Hanna (Martin Yellowcrow).**

Despite its irreverent title, *Zacharia Farted* is an all-aces mainstream calling card, mixing flat-out physical comedy with tender emotional material. On a mostly-air budget, first-time helmer Michael Rohl convincingly turns rural B.C. into Nevada and northern California for a road trip that actually goes somewhere, thanks to a tight, funny script. Pic slayed auds at world preem in Vancouver, and it definitely has enough gas to head south.

Story centers on Mutt-and-Jeff relationship of uptight Michael and his new age buddy, Brian – the kind of guy who plays ocean-sound tapes at the seaside. When Brian loses his job greeting car customers at a San Francisco garage, he talks Michael into ditching a bitchy g.f. for some much-needed R&R in the woods. Their ad-hoc fishing trip is soon interrupted, though, when they stumble upon an unmarked headstone, with only a nearby key, and its PUMZACH inscription, as a clue. Brian is immediately convinced that his life's mission is to figure out who's in the grave, so he drags his reluctant, straight-arrow pal over the Nevada border, in search of an Indian shaman to help them decipher the key's hardware code.

### Zero Effect

A Sony Pictures release of a Columbia Pictures/Castle Rock Entertainment production of a Manifest Film production. Produced by Lisa Henson, Janet Yang, Jake Kasdan. Directed, written by Kasdan. Camera, Bill Pope; editor, Tara Timpone; music, the Greyboy Allstars; production design, Gary Frutkoff; Philip J. Messina; costume design, Kym Barrett. Reviewed at Sony, Culver City, Jan. 6, 1998. MPAA Rating: R. Running time: 115 mins.
**Bill Pullman (Daryl Zero), Ben Stiller (Steve Arlo), Ryan O'Neal (Gregory Stark), Kim Dickens (Gloria Sullivan), Angela Featherstone (Jess).**

*Zero Effect* is a melange of hip humor, whodunit, and pop psychoanalysis. A roller-coaster of ideas and tones, filmmaker Jake Kasdan's debut feature is scattershot entertainment that misses as often as it hits its targets. Buoyed by an eccentric lead performance from Bill Pullman, the film is set for a specialized niche akin to the audience for last year's *Grosse Pointe Blank*. But pic won't be as successful, with only OK theatrical prospects, dim overseas potential, and mild cable and cassette movement. Nonetheless, there's an idiosyncratic talent at work here with the potential to blossom. Daryl Zero is the self-proclaimed greatest living private detective. The shamus' latest assignment is a blackmail case involving wealthy businessman Gregory Stark.

| | |
|---|---|
| U.S. release: Jan. 30 | U.S. B.O.: $4.5 million |
| Int'l release: July 18 | Int'l B.O.: $300,000 |

---

*Never do today what you can put off till tomorrow.* (Humphrey Bogart, The African Queen)

---

**...September 6...**

Japan's film emperor Akira Kurosawa, 88, says sayonara after a career of samurais and a profound influence on U.S. westerns and George Lucas' **Star Wars** space opera.

**Above:** James Cameron, Oscars 1998

**Above:** Kim Basinger, Helen Hunt, Jack Nicholson, Oscars 1998

**Below:** The European Academy Awards, London, December 1998

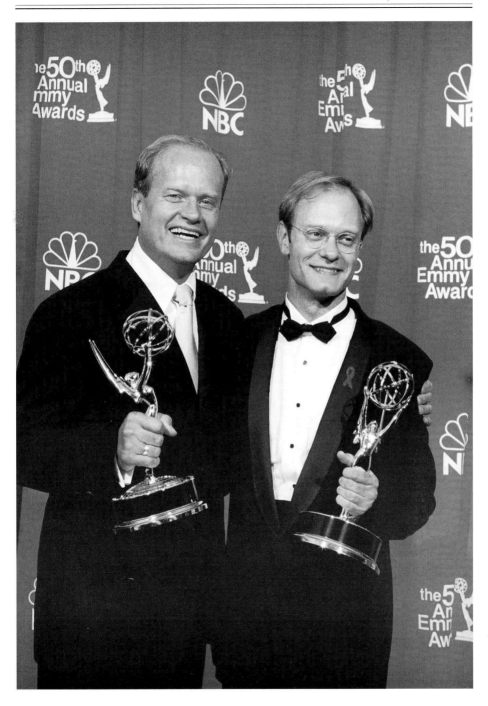

**Above:** Kelsey Grammer and David Hyde Pierce
from *Frasier*, Emmys 1998

**Above:** *The Mousetrap*, original production (left) and from 1996 (right)

**Below:** *Art* (New York, Broadway)

**Above:** *The Lion King* (New York, Broadway)
**Below:** *Les Misérables* (London, West End)

**Below:** *The Phantom of the Opera* (London, West End)

**Above:** Cher, No. 1 best-selling UK single 1998

**Above:** Natalie (left) and Nicole from All Saints at MTV Europe Awards

**Above:** Madonna
**Below:** George Michael at MTV Europe Awards

**Above:** Lew Grade, died December 13 at 91          **Below:** Frank Sinatra, died May 14 at 82

# Future Films

As a paper of record, *Variety* tracks the elaborate mating dance involved in every film production, from the acquisition of a novel or a screenplay, through casting and pre-production, the travails of shooting, and the often torturous post-production phase. For many readers, our regular listings of "films in the future" in *Daily Variety* contain the first clues to the quantity and caliber of the forthcoming year in the cinema. Such lists are fraught with peril: stars climb aboard and stars drop out, directors may ankle only a week or two into the shoot, even the film's title can change. By the time you consult this checklist, many of the films will have been released; others may see the light of day only in a video store a year or more into the millennium. By and large, however, this is the lineup for 1999. *The date after each title indicates commencement of principal photography.*

**All About my Mother (Todo Sobre mi Madre)** (Renn Prods) 6/23, Madrid. **Penelope Cruz, Marisa Paredes, Cecilia Roth, Antonia San Juan.** PROD, Agustin Almodovar; DIR-SCR, Pedro Almodovar.
Black comedy.

**American Beauty** (The Jinks/Cohen Company) 12/14, Los Angeles. **Kevin Spacey, Annette Bening, Thora Birch, Wes Bentley, Mena Suvari.** PROD, Bruce Cohen, Dan Jinks; DIR, Sam Mendes; SCR, Alan Ball; CAM, Conrad Hall; PD, Naomi Shohan; COS, Julie Weiss; CAST, Debra Zane; DISTRIB, DreamWorks.
Harried exec decides you can go home again. Boy does he find out differently in this black comedy.

**Angela's Ashes** (Angelus Films/Dirty Hands Prods/Scott Rudin Prods/Manhattan Project/ Paramount Pics) 9/28. **Emily Watson, Robert Carlyle.** PROD, Scott Rudin, David Brown; DIR, Alan Parker; SCR, Laura Jones; CAM, Michael Seresin; PD, Geoffrey Kirkland; DISTRIB, Par.
Frank McCourt's Pulitzer Prize memoir of growing up in abject poverty in Ireland.

**Any Given Sunday** (Illusion Ent. Group/Shuler Donner-Donner Prods) 1/99, Miami. **Al Pacino, Cameron Diaz, Dennis Quaid, Lauren Holly, Sean "Puffy" Combs, Tom Arnold.** PROD, Lauren Shuler-Donner, Oliver Stone, Dan Halsted, Clayton Townsend; DIR, Oliver Stone; SCR, Josh Logan; DISTRIB, WB.
The grit of the gridiron as ambition and desperation guide the lives of an ageing star, a young owner, a losing coach, and a hopeful in the wings.

**The Astronaut's Wife** (New Line Cinema) 8/14, Los Angeles. **Blair Brown, Nick Cassavetes, Johnny Depp, Clea DuVall, Joe Morton, Donna Murphy, Tom Noonan, Charlize Theron.** PROD, Mark Johnson, Andrew Lazar; DIR-SCR, Rand Ravich; CAM, Allen Daviau; ED, Steve Mirkovich; PD, Jan Roelfs; COS, Isis Mussenden; DISTRIB, New Line.
Houston we have a problem. An accident on a space mission that changes the orbits of a handful of lives.

**The Beach** (Figment Films) 1/15, United Kingdom, Southeast Asia, Thailand, Australia. **Leonardo DiCaprio, Virginie Ledoyen, Guillame Canet, Tilda Swinton.** PROD, Andrew Macdonald; DIR, Danny Boyle; SCR, John Hodge, Alex Garland; DISTRIB, Fox.
Young American's spiritual quest in the Far East goes dramatically askew in adaptation of cult novel.

**Bone Collector** (Collector of Bones Prods) 9/21, Montreal. **Denzel Washington, Angelina Jolie, Queen Latifah, Ed O'Neill, Michael Rooker.** PROD, Martin Bregman, Michael Bregman, Louis Stroller; DIR, Phillip Noyce; SCR, Jeremy Iacone, Chris Crowe; CAM, Dean Semler; ED, Bill Hoy; PD, Nigel Phelps; DISTRIB, U.
The evidence has eerie consequences for a forensics expert.

**Bowfinger's Big Thing** (Imagine Ent) 6/15, Los Angeles. **Steve Martin, Eddie Murphy, Robert Downey, Jr., Heather Graham, Christine Baranski, Jamie Kennedy, Terence Stamp.** PROD, Brian Grazer; DIR, Frank Oz; SCR, Steve Martin; CAM, Ueli Steiger; ED, Rick Pearson; PD, Burton Rencher; COS, Joseph Aulisi; DISTRIB, U.
Film producer juggles hype and buzz to entice a big star to be in his next movie.

---

**Bringing Out the Dead** (Par/Touchstone) 9/15, New York City. **Nicolas Cage, Patricia Arquette, John Goodman, Ving Rhames, Tom Sizemore, Marc Anthony, Mary Beth Hurt, Aida Turturro.** PROD, Scott Rudin, Barbara DeFina; DIR, Martin Scorsese; SCR, Paul Schrader; CAM, Robert Richardson; ED, Thelma Schoonmaker; PD, Dante Ferretti; DISTRIB, Par.
On the edge in Gotham with paramedics whose intense work takes a personal toll.

**Double Jeopardy** (Par) 7/15, Vancouver. **Tommy Lee Jones, Ashley Judd, Bruce Greenwood, Annabeth Gish, Roma Maffia.** PROD, Leonard Goldberg; DIR, Bruce Beresford; SCR, Douglas Cook, David Weisberg; CAM, Peter James; ED, Mark Warner; PD, Howard Cummings; COS, Linda Bass; DISTRIB, Par.
A woman wrongfully convicted of murder has deadly intentions for the real killer when she's paroled.

**Dudley Do-right** (Davis Ent./Joseph Singer Ent./U) 9/8, Vancouver. **Brendan Fraser, Sarah Jessica Parker, Alfred Molina, Eric Idle, Robert Prosky, Alex Rocco.** PROD, John Davis, Joseph Singer; DIR-SCR, Hugh Wilson; CAM, Donald Thorin; ED, Don Brochu; PD, Bob Ziembicki; COS, Lisa Jensen; DISTRIB, U.
He always gets his man but Canada's Royal Mounted have rarely bumbled into it in quite the comic manner of this lantern-jaw hero.

**End of Days** (Lucifilms/Beacon Communications) 11/21, Los Angeles, New York. **Arnold Schwarzenegger, Robin Tunney, Gabriel Byrne, Kevin Pollak.** PROD, Armyan Bernstein, Bill Borden; DIR-CAM, Peter Hyams; SCR, Andrew Marlowe; PD, Richard Holland; COS, Bobbie Mannix; DISTRIB, U.
Apocalyptic yarn pitting "mooscles" against the devil himself in this fantasy thriller.

**Est-Ouest** (UGC) 9/1, France, Bulgaria, Ukraine. **Catherine Deneuve, Sandrine Bonnaire, Oleg Menshikov, Sergei Bodrov.** PROD, Yves Marmion; DIR-SCR, Regis Wargnier; CAM, Laurent Dailland; ED, Herve Schneid, COMP, Patrick Doyler; PD, Roseitsa Baneva; COS, Pierre Yves Gayraud; DISTRIB, UGC.
Tale of sisters whose family ties take them to post-Second World War Russia.

**Eyes Wide Shut** (WB) 11/4/96, London. **Tom Cruise, Nicole Kidman, Sydney Pollack, Todd Field, Marie Richardson, Alan Cumming, Rade Serbedzija, Leslee Sobieski.** PROD, Stanley Kubrick; DIR, Stanley Kubrick; SCR, Stanley Kubrick, Frederic Raphael; CAM, Larry Smith; DISTRIB, WB.

Husband and wife analysts mix business with pleasure and obsession in what promises to be an original blend of drama and comedy.

**Father Damien** (Era Film/Jos Stelling Films) 6/7, Hawaii. **David Wenham, Derek Jacobi, Kris Kristofferson, Sam Neill, Leo McKern, Aden Young, Kate Soberano.** PROD, Tharsi Vanhuysse; DIR, Paul Cox; SCR, John Briley; CAM, Nino Martinetti; ED, John Scott; PD, Jan Petitjean; COMP, Paul Grabowski.
True story of Belgian priest who ministered to the leper colonies of Hawaii.

**Felicia's Journey** (Icon Prods/Marquis Film/Alliance Communications) 9/21, Ireland. **Bob Hoskins, Elaine Cassidy, Peter McDonald, Arsine Khanjian.** PROD, Bruce Davey; DIR-SCR, Atom Egoyan; CAM, Paul Sarossy; ED, Susan Shipton; PD, Jim Clay; COS, Sandy Powell; DISTRIB, Artisan.
Young Irish woman goes to London to find the man who betrayed her and gets caught up in a dangerous game in this thriller.

**50 Violins** (Craven-Maddalena Films/Fifty Fiddles) 10/26, New York. **Meryl Streep, Angela Bassett, Aidan Quinn, Gloria Estefan, Jane Leeves, Cloris Leachman, Kieran Culkin, Isaac Stern, Itzhak Perlman, Arnold Steinhardt, Mark O'Connor, Michael Tree, Diane Monroe, Karen Briggs.** PROD, Marianne Maddalena, Stuart Besser, Susan Kaplan, Alan Miller, Walter Scheuer; DIR, Wes Craven; SCR, Pamela Gray; CAM, Peter Deming; ED, Patrick Lussier; PD, Bruce Miller; COS, Susan Lyall; COMP, Mason Daring; DISTRIB, Miramax.
True story of a woman who set up a Harlem violin class and made a difference; was previously a docu subject that earned an Oscar nom.

**Fight Club** (Fox 2000) 6/8, Los Angeles. **Brad Pitt, Edward Norton, Helena Bonham Carter, Meat Loaf, Jared Leto.** PROD, Art Linson, Cean Chaffin, Ross Bell; DIR, David Fincher; SCR, Jim Uhls; CAM, Jeff Cronenweth; ED, Jim Haygood; PD, Alex McDowell; COS, Michael Kaplan; DISTRIB, Fox.
Young men become entangled in illegal and brutal underworld of boxing.

**Flawless** (Tribeca Prods/MGM), 10/5, Manhattan. **Robert De Niro, Philip Seymour Hoffman, Barry Miller, Rory Cochrane, Daphne Rubin-Vega.** PROD, Joel Schumacher, Jane Rosenthal; DIR-SCR, Joel Schumacher; CAM, Declan Quinn; ED, Mark Stevens; PD, Jan Roelfs; COS, Daniel Orlandi; DISTRIB, MGM.
After a near-fatal stroke, a security guard's rehab leads

him down some unexpected mean streets in this off-beat thriller.

**For Love of the Game** (U) 10/8, Manhattan, Los Angeles. **Kevin Costner, Kelly Preston, Jena Malone.** PROD, Amy Robinson, Armyan Bernstein; DIR, Sam Raimi; SCR, Dana Stevens; CAM, John Bailey; ED, Arthur Coburn, Eric Beason; PD, Neil Spisak; COS, Judianna Makovsky; DISTRIB, U.
Kevin Costner back to basic baseball as a pitcher at the end of his career and a long-time relationship.

**Girl Interrupted** (Red Wagon Prods/3 Arts Ent./Col) 1/99. **Winona Ryder, Angelina Jolie, Brittany Murphy, Clea DuVall, Whoopi Goldberg, Vanessa Redgrave.** PROD, Cathy Konrad, Winona Ryder, Carol Bodie, Douglas Wick; AP, Susanna Kaysen; DIR, James Mangold; SCR, James Mangold, Anna Hamilton Phelan, Susan Shilliday, Lisa Loomer; DISTRIB, Sony.
Upon leaving a psychiatric hospital, a woman finds readjusting to society more difficult than she had imagined.

**The Green Mile** (Castle Rock Ent.) 7/20, Los Angeles, North Carolina, Tennessee. **Tom Hanks, Michael Clarke Duncan, David Morse, Bonnie Hunt, James Cromwell, Michael Jeter, Graham Greene, Sam Rockwell, Patricia Clarkson, Harry Dean Stanton.** PROD, David Valdes; DIR-SCR, Frank Darabont; CAM, David Tattersall; ED, Richard Frances-Bruce, Robert Leighton; PD, Terence Marsh; COS, Karyn Wagner; COMP, Thomas Newman; DISTRIB, WB.
Inside the walls of a prison a death-row inmate and a guard develop an unusually strong bond in this poignant drama.

**Hanging Up** (Laurence Mark Prods/Col.) 2/99, Los Angeles. **Meg Ryan, Lisa Kudrow, Diane Keaton.** EXP, Bill Robinson, Delia Ephron; PROD, Laurence Mark, Nora Ephron; DIR, Diane Keaton; SCR, Delia Ephron, Nora Ephron; DISTRIB, Sony.
Three sisters are reunited at the deathbed of their father.

**The Haunting of Hill House** ("The Haunting of Hill House," Raleigh/Manhattan Studios) 11/30, Los Angeles, England. **Lili Taylor, Liam Neeson, Catherine Zeta-Jones, Owen Wilson, Marian Seldes, Alix Koromzay.** PROD, Susan Arnold, Donna Roth, Colin Wilson; DIR, Jan de Bont; SCR, David Self; CAM, Karl Walter Lindenlaub; ED, Michael Kahn; PD, Eugenio Zanetti; COS, Ellen Mirojnick; DISTRIB, DreamWorks.
Third screen version of Shirley Jackson's suspenser is a serious, intense haunted house opus.

**History is Made at Night** (Scala Prods/IMA Films/Smile Ent.) 11/2, Helsinki. **Bill Pullman, Irene Jacob, Bruno Kirby, Glenn Plummer.** PROD, Jonathan Karlsen, Kerry Rock; DIR, Ilkka Jarvilaturi; SCR, Patrick Amos, Jean-Pierre Gorin; CAM, Michael Amathieu; PD, Zoe MacLeod; COS, Marjatta Nissinen.
Romantic thriller a la *Beat the Devil.*

**Isn't She Great** (Lobell/Bergman Prods) 5/20, Montreal, New York City. **Bette Midler, Nathan Lane, Stockard Channing, David Hyde Pierce, John Cleese.** PROD, Michael Lobell; DIR, Andrew Bergman; SCR, Paul Rudnick; CAM, Karl Walter Lindenlaub; ED, Barry Malkin; PD, Stuart Wurtzel; COS, Julie Weiss; DISTRIB, U.
An unusual and irreverent bio of trash novelist Jacqueline Susann and her acerbic literary circle.

**Joan of Arc** (Gaumont/Seaside Prods) 6/15, France, Czech Republic. **Milla Jovovich, Dustin Hoffman, Faye Dunaway, John Malkovich, Desmond Harrington, Tcheky Karyo.** PROD, Patrice Ledoux; DIR, Luc Besson; SCR, Andrew Birkin, Luc Besson; CAM, Thierry Arbogast; ED, Sylvie Landra; PD, Hughes Tissandier; COS, Catherine Leterier; COMP, Eric Serra; DISTRIB, Sony.
Historic drama about the young woman who heard voices, led her country to victory, and became a sainted martyr.

**Killing Mr. Tingle** (Tingle Prods) 5/10, Los Angeles. **Helen Mirren, Katie Holmes, Marisa Coughlan, Barry Watson, Liz Stauber, Jeffrey Tambor, Lesley Ann Warren, Molly Ringwald, Viveca A. Fox, Michael McKean.** PROD, Cathy Konrad; DIR-SCR, Kevin Williamson; CAM, Jerzy Zielinski; PD, Naomi Shohan; COS, Susie Desanto; DISTRIB, Miramax.
*Scream* scribe concocts a cat's cradle of murder with a black-comic edge.

**The King and I** (Morgan Creek Prods, in association with Rankin/Bass Prods) Animated, 3/19/97. PROD, James G. Robinson, Arthur Rankin, Peter Bakalian; DIR, Richard Rich; SCR, Peter Bakalian, Jacqueline Feather, David Seidler; SCR ADAPTATION, Arthur Rankin; DISTRIB, WB.
The familiar saga with a new toon and tunes.

**Lake Placid** (BEI Lake Placid Prods) 7/24, Vancouver. **Bill Pullman, Bridget Fonda, Oliver Platt, Brendan Gleason.** PROD, David E. Kelly, Michael Pressman; DIR, Steve Miner; SCR, David E. Kelly; CAM, Daryn Okada; PD, John Willett; DISTRIB, Fox.
Murder in the backwoods finds a research scientist and

game warden joining forces to solve the mystery and create some inter-personal sparking.

**Magnolia** (Ghoulardi Films/New Line Cinema) 1/11, Los Angeles. **Julianne Moore, William H. Macy, Tom Cruise, Luis Guzman, Philip Baker Hall, Philip Seymour Hoffman, Ricky Jay, John C. Reilly, Melora Walters, Henry Gibson, April Grace, Felicity Huffman.** PROD, Paul Thomas Anderson, JoAnne Sellar; DIR-SCR, Paul Thomas Anderson; CAM, Robert Elswit; ED, Dylan Tichenor; PD, Bob Ziembicki; COS, Mark Bridges.
*Boogie Nights* filmmaker Anderson returns to the valley for this contempo saga of interwoven lives.

**Man on the Moon** (Jersey Films/U) 7/27, Los Angeles, New York. **Jim Carrey, Danny DeVito, Courtney Love, Paul Giamatti, Vince Schiavelli.** PROD, Danny DeVito, Michael Shamberg, Stacey Sher; DIR, Milos Forman; SCR, Scott Alexander, Larry Karaszewski; CAM, Anastas Michos; ED, Lynzee Klingman; PD, Patricia Von Brandenstein; COS, Jeffrey Kurland; DISTRIB, U.
The life and times of cutting-edge comic Andy Kaufman who burned bright and burned fast.

**Mission: Impossible sequel** (Par) 2/99, Sydney, Australia. **Tom Cruise, Ving Rhames, Dougray Scott, Steve Zhan, Thandie Newton, Luther Stickell.** PROD, Tom Cruise, Paula Wagner; DIR, John Woo; SCR, Michael Tolkin, David Marconi, William Goldman; DISTRIB, Par.
Your mission: Hold onto your hats for a pyrotechnic ride and damn the plot.

**Mr. Accident** (Happy Brand Films) 11/2, Sydney. **Yahoo Serious, Helen Dallimore, David Field, Grant Piro, Gary MacDonald.** PROD, Yahoo Serious, Warwick Ross; DIR, Yahoo Serious; SCR, Yahoo Serious, David Roach; CAM, Steve Arnold; ART, Kerri Ainsworth; COS, Anna Borghesi; DISTRIB, MGM.
Oz comic returns as a man who stumbles onto a nefarious big-biz scheme and winds up taking the blame before he can clear himself.

**Muppets From Space** (S/H Prods) 11/9, Wilmington, North Carolina. **Gonzo, Kermit the Frog, Miss Piggy, Rizzo, Fozzie Bear, Jeffrey Tambor, Andie MacDowell, David Arquette, Ray Liotta, Pat Hingle.** PROD, Brian Henson, Martin G. Baker; DIR, Tim Hill; AD, Michele Ziegler; SCR, Jerry Juhl, Joseph Mazzarina, Ken Kaufman; CAM, Alan Caso; ED, Michael Stevenson; PD, Stephen Marsh; COS, Polly Smith; CHOR, Tony Basil; DISTRIB, Sony.
Federal agents suspect one of the brood is from another planet and go in relentless pursuit of the furry friends.

**Mystery Men** (Universal Pictures/Lawrence Gordon Prods) 10/21, Los Angeles. **Hank Azaria, Claire Forlani, Janeane Garofalo, Greg Kinnear, Jennifer Lewis, William H. Macy, Kel Mitchell, Lena Olin, Paul Reubens, Geoffrey Rush, Ben Stiller, Wes Studi, Tom Waits, Eddie Izzard, Pras.** PROD, Lawrence Gordon, Lloyd Levin, Mike Richardson; DIR, Kinka Usher; SCR, Neil Cuthburt; CAM, Stephen Burum; ED, Conrad Buff; PD, Kirk Petruccelli; COS, Marilyn Vance; DISTRIB, U.
Action comedy in which a mad scientist puts the city in peril and only a band of oddball super heroes can stop him.

**The Ninth Gate** (Artisan Ent.) 6/11, Paris, Spain, New York. **Johnny Depp, Lena Olin, Frank Langella, James Russo.** PROD, Inaki Nunez, Alain Vannier, Roman Polanski; DIR, Roman Polanski; SCR, Roman Polanski, John Brownjohn, Enrique Urbizu; DISTRIB, Artisan.
Title is an occult passageway and navigating successfully tests the steel of the characters.

**Runaway Bride** (Par/Walt Disney Pictures/Interscope/Lakeshore ) 10/19, New York, Maryland. **Julia Roberts, Richard Gere, Joan Cusack, Rita Wilson, Hector Elizondo, Paul Dooley.** PROD, Ted Field, Tom Rosenberg, Scott Kroopf, Robert Cort; DIR, Garry Marshall; SCR, Sara Parriott, Josann McGibbon, Leslie Dixon, Audrey Wells; ED, Bruce Green; PD, Mark Friedberg; COS, Albert Wolsky; DISTRIB, Par; FOREIGN, Buena Vista International.
A reporter on the trail of a woman who chronically gets cloud feet on the way to the altar in a romantic-comedy that resonates of *It Happened One Night.*

**St. Pauli Nacht** (Shark Film) 9/14, Hamburg. **Benno Fuhrmann, Doreen Jacobi, Armin Rohde, Oliver Stokowski, Florian Lukas.** PROD, Kirsten Hager, Eric Moss; DIR, Soenke Wortmann; SCR, Frank Goehre; CAM, Tom Faehrmann; ED, Hans Funk; PD, Thomas Freudenthal; DISTRIB, BVI.
Youth comedy with a hip-flip set, as with director's *The Campus* at, ironically, an institute of higher learning.

**Sixth Sense** (The Kennedy/Marshall Company) 9/21, Philadelphia. **Bruce Willis, Toni Collette, Olivia Williams, Haley Joel Osment, Donnie Wahlberg.** PROD, Frank Marshall, Kathleen Kennedy, Barry Mendel; DIR-SCR, M. Night Shyamalan; CAM, Tak Fujimoto; ED, Andy Mondshein; PD, Larry Fulton; COS, Joanna Johnston; DISTRIB, BV.
Child psychologist gets in over his head when a young boy begins to channel spirits during their sessions.

---

**...September 10 ...**
George Miller to direct a 4th installment of **Mad Max**.

**The Summer of Sam** (40 Acres and a Mule Filmworks/ Caminer-Gallagher Prods) 7/20, New York. **John Leguizamo, Jennifer Esposito, Adrien Brody, Patti LuPone, Mira Sorvino, Bebe Neuwirth, John Savage.** PROD, John Andrew Gallagher, Sylvia Caminer, John Kilik, Spike Lee; DIR, Spike Lee; SCR, Spike Lee, Michael Imperioli, Victor Colicchio; CAM, Ellen Kurus; ED, Barry Alexander Brown; PD, Theresa De Prez; COS, Ruth E. Carter; DISTRIB, BV.
A city in the grip of fear as the victims of true-life serial killer Son of Sam mount in the summer of 1977.

**Supernova** (United Artists/Imperial Ent.) 4/13, Los Angeles. **James Spader, Angela Bassett, Robert Forster, Lou Diamond Phillips, Robin Tunney.** PROD, Dan Chuba, Jamie Dixon, Ash Shah; DIR, Walter Hill; SCR, David Campbell Wilson, Cathy Rabin; CAM, Lloyd Ahern; ED, Freeman Davis; PD, Marek Dobrowolski; COS, Bob Ringwood; DISTRIB, MGM.
Futuristic thriller involving a space rescue and a passenger who becomes an unwanted guest.

**The Talented Mr. Ripley** (Mirage Enterprises/ Timnick Films) 8/10, Rome, Venice, Naples. **Matt Damon, Gwyneth Paltrow, Jude Law, Cate Blanchett, Phillip Seymour Hoffman, Phillip Baker Hall, Sergio Rubini.** PROD, Bill Horberg, Tom Sternberg; DIR-SCR, Anthony Minghella; CAM, John Seale; ED, Walter Murch; PD, Roy Walker; COS, Ann Roth, Gary Jones; COMP, Gabriel Yared; DISTRIB, Par.
Previously filmed in France as *Purple Noon*, psychological thriller centers on a charmer with a deadly bite, socially speaking.

**The Taste of Sunshine** (Alliance/Kinowelt) 7/14, Budapest, Vienna, Berlin, Paris. **Ralph Fiennes, Jennifer Ehle, Rachel Weisz, Molly Parker, William Hurt, Rosemary Harris, Debra Unger.** Robert Lantos, Andras Hamori; DIR, Istvan Szabo; SCR, Istvan Szabo, Israel Horovitz; CAM, Lajos Koltai; DISTRIB, Alliance.
The "*English Patient*" is Hungarian in this period drama of love and war.

**Titus** (Clear Blue Sky Prods) 10/5, Rome, Italy. **Anthony Hopkins, Jessica Lange, Alan Cumming, Jonathan Rhys Meyer, Harry J. Lennix, Colm Feore, Angus MacFayden, Matthew Rhys, Laura Fraser, James Frain, Colin Wells, Kenny Doughty, Blake Ritson, Constantine Gregory, Osheen Jones.** PROD, Conchita Airoldi; DIR-SCR, Julie Taymor; CAM, Luciano Tavoli; ED, Francoise Bonnot; PD, Dante Ferretti; COS, Milena Canonero; COMP, Elliot Goldenthal; DISTRIB, Overseas Film Group.
An epic staging of Shakespeare's *Titus Andronicus*.

**Town and Country** (Avery Pix) 6/23, Los Angeles, New York, Paris, Sun Valley. **Warren Beatty, Diane Keaton, Andie MacDowell, Goldie Hawn, Gary Shandling, Jenna Elfman, Charlton Heston.** PROD, Simon Fields, Andrew Karsch, Fred Roos; DIR, Peter Chelsom; SCR, Michael Laughlin; CAM, William Fraker; ED, David Moritz; PD, Caroline Hanania; COS, Molly Maginnis; DISTRIB, New Line.
The mating game with relationships falling apart, dalliances, and the *Shampoo* set older but not much wiser.

**What Becomes of the Broken Hearted?** (Sequel Prods/South Pacific Pictures/Polygram) 9/6, Auckland, New Zealand. **Temuera Morrison, Rena Owen, Nancy Brunning, Edna Stirling, Pete Smith.** PROD, Bill Gavin; DIR, Ian Mune, SCR, Alan Duff; CAM, Allen Guilford; ED, Mike Horton; PD, Brett Schwieters.
Continuation of *Once Were Warriors*, centering on the strained relationship between father and son.

**The Wild Wild West** (WB), 5/18, Los Angeles. **Will Smith, Kevin Kline, Kenneth Branagh, Salma Hayek.** PROD, Jon Peters, Barry Sonnenfeld; DIR, Barry Sonnenfeld; SCR, Peter S. Seaman, Jeffrey Price; CAM, Michael Ballhaus; ED, Jim Miller; PD, Bo Welch; COS, Deborah Scott; DISTRIB, WB.
Big-screen version of 1960s TV fave appropriately deals with egomaniacal madman and 1880s undercover cops in the way of his venal plans.

**The World is not Enough** (UA/Danjaq Prods) 1/11, London, England, Turkey. **Pierce Brosnan, Denise Richards, Sophie Marceau, Robert Carlyle.** PROD, Barbara Broccoli, Michael G. Wilson; DIR, Michael Apted; SCR, Neal Purvis, Robert Wade; DISTRIB, MGM.
007 is back and though the script's under wraps, expect another high-octane adventure with a Bond for the millennium.

> *It's simple. PG means the hero gets the girl, 15 means that the villain gets the girl and 18 means everybody gets the girl. (Michael Douglas)*

# Television

TV in its widest sense has always been reported in depth by *Variety*. And as the film and broadcasting industries have interlocked ever more tightly in recent years, so coverage of TV has proved more crucial. We've arrived at a point where the stars of the tube are not just Oprah or "Ally McBeal" but also Rupert Murdoch, Silvio Berlusconi, and Ted Turner. Mighty concerns like France's TF1 and Canal Plus are involved in the financing of American pictures, while Italy's RAI is a co-producer with several countries in Europe.

Cable and satellite have played havoc with the traditional, often complacent lineup of terrestrial broadcasters, in the U.S. and around the world. As a result, the major TV industry gatherings of the year (NATPE, MIP-TV, MIPCOM, etc) have grown by leaps and bounds, with ever more channels seeking ever more product to satisfy audiences across all continents.

TV is a field in which *Variety*'s slanguage has prospered, from "feevee" (pay TV, pay cable, subscription TV), and "fin-syn" (defunct financial interest and syndication rules) to "nets" (TV networks) and "sitcom" (*Variety*'s very own word for situation comedy on TV). The Nielsen ratings appear each week, and continue to be devoured avidly by all industry watchers.

## Top all-time U.S. network TV programs

**Title, Telecast, Network, Rating**

| | | | | | | | |
|---|---|---|---|---|---|---|---|
| 1. M*A*S*H (finale) | 2/28/83 | CBS | 60.2 | 26. Bob Hope Christmas Show | 1/14/71 | NBC | 45.0 |
| 2. Dallas | 11/21/80 | CBS | 53.3 | 27. Roots, Part 3 | 1/25/77 | ABC | 44.8 |
| 3. Roots, Part 8 | 1/30/77 | ABC | 51.1 | 28. Super Bowl XI | 1/9/77 | NBC | 44.4 |
| 4. Super Bowl XVI | 1/24/82 | CBS | 49.1 | 28. Super Bowl XV | 1/25/81 | NBC | 44.4 |
| 5. Super Bowl XVII | 1/30/83 | NBC | 48.6 | 30. Super Bowl VI | 1/16/72 | CBS | 44.3 |
| 6. XVII Winter Olympics | 2/23/94 | CBS | 48.5 | 31. XVII Winter Olympics | 2/25/94 | CBS | 44.2 |
| 7. Super Bowl XX | 1/26/86 | NBC | 48.3 | 31. Roots, Part 2 | 1/24/77 | ABC | 44.1 |
| 8. Gone With the Wind, Pt 1 | 11/7/76 | NBC | 47.7 | 33. Beverly Hillbillies | 1/8/64 | CBS | 44.0 |
| 9. Gone With the Wind, Pt 2 | 11/8/76 | NBC | 47.4 | 34. Roots, Part 4 | 1/26/77 | ABC | 43.8 |
| 10. Super Bowl XII | 1/15/78 | CBS | 47.2 | 34. Ed Sullivan | 2/16/64 | CBS | 43.8 |
| 11. Super Bowl XIII | 1/21/79 | NBC | 47.1 | 36. Super Bowl XXIII | 1/22/89 | NBC | 43.5 |
| 12. Bob Hope Christmas Show | 1/15/70 | NBC | 46.6 | 37. Academy Awards | 4/7/70 | ABC | 43.4 |
| 13. Super Bowl XVIII | 1/22/84 | CBS | 46.4 | 38. The Thorn Birds, Part 3 | 3/29/83 | ABC | 43.2 |
| 13. Super Bowl XIX | 1/20/85 | ABC | 46.4 | 39. The Thorn Birds, Part 4 | 3/30/83 | ABC | 43.1 |
| 15. Super Bowl XIV | 1/20/80 | CBS | 46.3 | 40. NFC Championship Game | 1/10/82 | CBS | 42.9 |
| 16. The Day After | 11/20/83 | ABC | 46.0 | 41. Beverly Hillbillies | 1/15/64 | CBS | 42.8 |
| 16. Super Bowl XXX | 1/28/96 | NBC | 46.0 | 42. Super Bowl VII | 1/14/73 | NBC | 42.7 |
| 17. Roots, Part 6 | 1/28/77 | ABC | 45.9 | 43. The Thorn Birds, Part 2 | 3/28/83 | ABC | 42.5 |
| 17. The Fugitive (finale) | 8/29/67 | ABC | 45.9 | 44. Super Bowl IX | 1/12/75 | NBC | 42.4 |
| 20. Super Bowl XXI | 1/25/87 | CBS | 45.8 | 44. Beverly Hillbillies | 2/26/64 | CBS | 42.4 |
| 21. Roots, Part 5 | 1/27/77 | ABC | 45.7 | 45. Super Bowl X | 1/18/76 | CBS | 42.3 |
| 22. Super Bowl XXVIII | 1/29/94 | NBC | 45.5 | 45. Airport | 11/11/73 | ABC | 42.3 |
| 22. Cheers (finale) | 5/20/93 | NBC | 45.5 | 45. Love Story | 10/1/72 | ABC | 42.3 |
| 24. Ed Sullivan | 2/9/64 | CBS | 45.3 | 45. Cinderella | 2/22/65 | CBS | 42.3 |
| 25. Super Bowl XXVII | 1/31/93 | NBC | 45.1 | 50. Roots, Part 7 | 1/29/77 | ABC | 42.2 |

---

**... September 12 ...**
Peter Hoffman's Seven Arts Pictures in advanced negotiations with Rysher
Entertainment to buy all international rights to **Onegin**, starring Ralph Fiennes.

# 1997-98 TV season (series)

**Title, Day, Network, Rating**

| | | | |
|---|---|---|---|
| 1. Seinfeld | Thur | NBC | 22.0 |
| 2. ER | Thur | NBC | 20.7 |
| 3. Veronica's Closet | Thur | NBC | 16.8 |
| 4. Friends | Thur | NBC | 16.4 |
| 5. NFL Monday Night Football | Mon | ABC | 14.9 |
| 6. Touched by an Angel | Sun | CBS | 14.3 |
| 7. 60 Minutes | Sun | CBS | 13.9 |
| 8. Union Square | Thur | NBC | 13.6 |
| 9. CBS Sunday Movie | Sun | CBS | 13.3 |
| 10. Just Shoot Me | Tue/Thu | NBC | 12.0 |
| 10. Home Improvements | Tues | ABC | 12.0 |
| 10. Frasier | Tues | NBC | 12.0 |
| 13. NFL Monday Showcase | Mon | ABC | 11.6 |
| 14. Dateline NBC | Tues | NBC | 11.5 |
| 15. Dateline NBC | Mon | NBC | 11.4 |
| 16. The Drew Carey Show | Wed | ABC | 11.1 |
| 17. 20/20 | Fri | ABC | 10.9 |
| 18. NYPD Blue | Tues | ABC | 10.8 |
| 19. The X-Files | Sun | Fox | 10.6 |
| 20. Primetime Live | Wed | ABC | 10.5 |
| 21. Law and Order | Wed | NBC | 10.2 |
| 22. 20/20 | Mon | ABC | 10.0 |
| 23. King of the Hill | Sun | Fox | 9.8 |
| 23. Diagnosis Murder | Thur | CBS | 9.8 |
| 25. Mad About You | Tues | NBC | 9.7 |
| 26. Dateline NBC | Fri | NBC | 9.5 |
| 26. NBC Sunday Night Movie | Sun | NBC | 9.5 |
| 26. Dharma & Greg | Wed | ABC | 9.5 |
| 26. Cosby | Mon | CBS | 9.5 |
| 30. Walker, Texas Ranger | Sat | CBS | 9.3 |
| 30. The Simpsons | Sun | Fox | 9.3 |
| 30. Hiller and Diller | Tues/Fri | ABC | 9.3 |
| 33. Dateline NBC | Sun | NBC | 9.2 |
| 33. Everybody Loves Raymond | Mon | CBS | 9.2 |
| 35. Soul Man | Tues | ABC | 9.1 |
| 36. Lateline | Tues | NBC | 9.0 |
| 37. Chicago Hope | Wed | CBS | 8.9 |
| 37. Promised Land | Thur | CBS | 8.9 |
| 37. JAG | Tues | CBS | 8.9 |
| 40. Two Guys, a Girl & a Pizza Place | Wed | ABC | 8.8 |
| 40. Ellen | Wed | ABC | 8.8 |
| 42. ABC Sunday Movie | Sun | ABC | 8.5 |
| 42. Third Rock from the Sun | Wed | NBC | 8.5 |
| 44. Spin City | Wed | ABC | 8.4 |
| 44. CBS Tuesday Movie | Tues | CBS | 8.4 |
| 44. Caroline in the City | Mon | NBC | 8.4 |
| 47. Kids Say the Darndest Things | Fri | CBS | 8.3 |
| 47. The Nanny | Wed | CBS | 8.3 |
| 49. The Magnificent Seven | Sat | CBS | 8.2 |
| 49. 20/20 | Thur | ABC | 8.2 |
| 49. Something So Right | Tues | Tues | 8.2 |
| 49. Beverly Hills, 90210 | Fox | Fox | 8.2 |
| 49. Ally McBeal | Mon | Fox | 8.2 |

*One ratings point = approx. 1.5 million viewers*

# 1997-98 TV season (original movies/mini-series)

**Title, Telecast, Network, Rating**

| | | | |
|---|---|---|---|
| 1. I Know What the Deaf Man Heard | 11/23/97 | CBS | 23.0 |
| 2. Merlin, Part 1 | 4/26/98 | NBC | 21.7 |
| 3. Merlin, Part 2 | 4/27/98 | NBC | 20.6 |
| 4. Cinderella | 11/1/97 | ABC | 18.4 |
| 5. Borrowed Hearts | 11/30/97 | CBS | 18.4 |
| 6. Before Women Had Wings | 3/15/98 | ABC | 18.2 |
| 7. The Wedding, Part 1 | 2/22/98 | ABC | 16.8 |
| 8. Ellen Foster | 12/14/97 | CBS | 16.5 |
| 9. The Echo of Thunder | 4/19/98 | CBS | 16.4 |
| 10. The Long Way Home | 3/1/98 | CBS | 15.7 |
| 11. A Thousand Men and a Baby | 12/7/97 | CBS | 15.4 |
| 12. The Wedding, Part 2 | 2/23/98 | ABC | 15.6 |
| 13. Bella Mafia, Part 1 | 11/17/97 | CBS | 14.8 |
| 14. The Love Letter | 2/1/98 | CBS | 14.4 |
| 15. Bella Mafia, Part 2 | 11/19/97 | CBS | 13.8 |
| 16. The Patron Saint of Liars | 4/5/98 | CBS | 13.7 |
| 17. Chance of a Lifetime | 3/29/98 | CBS | 13.6 |
| 18. Get to the Heart: The Barbara Mandrell Story | 9/28/97 | CBS | 13.6 |
| 19. To Live Again | 3/8/98 | CBS | 13.3 |
| 20. Final Descent | 10/12/97 | CBS | 12.9 |

> *We all steal but if we're smart we steal from great directors. Then, we can call it influence. (Krzysztof Kieslowski)*

---

**... September 13 ...**

Brad Anderson's **Next Stop, Wonderland** wins the Grand Prix at the 24th Deauville Festival of American Cinema.

# 1998-99 TV season (through Jan. 10/99)

**Title, Day, Network, Rating**

| | | | | | | | | |
|---|---|---|---|---|---|---|---|---|
| 1. ER | Thur | NBC | 19.3 | 26. CBS Tuesday Movie | Tues | CBS | 9.5 |
| 2. Friends | Thur | NBC | 16.2 | 28. Walker, Texas Ranger | Sat | CBS | 9.4 |
| 3. Frasier | Tues | NBC | 15.9 | 29. Ally McBeal | Mon | Fox | 9.3 |
| 4. Veronica's Closet | Thur | NBC | 14.5 | 30. Dateline NBC | Tues | NBC | 9.1 |
| 5. NFL Monday Night Football | Mon | ABC | 13.9 | 31. Cosby | Mon | CBS | 9.0 |
| 6. Jesse | Thur | NBC | 13.7 | 31. Dateline NBC | Sun | NBC | 9.0 |
| 7. Touched by an Angel | Sun | CBS | 13.4 | 31. The Hughleys | Tues | ABC | 9.0 |
| 8. 60 Minutes | Sun | CBS | 13.2 | 34. Just Shoot Me | Tues | NBC | 8.9 |
| 9. Providence | Fri | NBC | 13.1 | 35. King of Queens | Mon | CBS | 8.8 |
| 10. CBS Sunday Movie | Sun | CBS | 12.8 | 35. NFL Monday Blast | Mon | ABC | 8.8 |
| 11. Dateline NBC | Fri | NBC | 12.7 | 37. NBC Sunday Night Movie | Sun | NBC | 8.6 |
| 12. NYPD Blue | Tues | ABC | 12.1 | 37. Promised Land | Thur | CBS | 8.6 |
| 13. Home Improvements | Tues | ABC | 10.5 | 39. Dateline NBC | Wed | NBC | 8.5 |
| 13. 20/20 | Fri | ABC | 10.5 | 39. Sabrina, the Teenage Witch | Fri | ABC | 8.5 |
| 15. The Drew Carey Show | Wed | ABC | 10.4 | 39. Two Guys, a Girl | | | |
| 15. Everybody Loves Raymond | Mon | CBS | 10.4 |    & a Pizza Place | Wed | ABC | 8.5 |
| 17. The X-Files | Sun | Fox | 10.0 | 42. The Simpsons | Sun | Fox | 8.4 |
| 18. JAG | Tues | CBS | 9.9 | 43. 20/20 | Sun | ABC | 8.3 |
| 19. Dharma & Greg | Wed | ABC | 9.8 | 43. Whose Line Is It Anyway? | Wed | ABC | 8.3 |
| 19. NFL Monday Showcase | Mon | ABC | 9.8 | 45. 48 Hours | Thur | CBS | 8.2 |
| 19. 20/20 | Wed | ABC | 9.8 | 45. Nash Bridges | Fri | CBS | 8.2 |
| 22. Becker | Mon | CBS | 9.7 | 45. The Secret Lives of Men | Wed | ABC | 8.2 |
| 22. Dateline NBC | Mon | NBC | 9.7 | 48. Kids Say the Darndest | | | |
| 22. Law and Order | Wed | NBC | 9.7 |    Things | Fri | CBS | 8.1 |
| 25. Spin City | Wed | ABC | 9.6 | 48. Dateline NBC | Fri | NBC | 8.1 |
| 26. Diagnosis Murder | Thur | CBS | 9.5 | 50. Sports Night | Tues | ABC | 8.0 |

# France: top 10 TV programs: 1998

| Program | Channel | Date | (% audience) |
|---|---|---|---|
| 1. World Cup: Brazil/France | TF1 | July 12 | 39.3 |
| 2. World Cup: presentation ceremony | TF1 | July 12 | 37.9 |
| 3. World Cup: France/Croatia | TF1 | July 8 | 33.8 |
| 4. World Cup: France/South Africa | France 3 | June 12 | 25.8 |
| 5. World Cup news | TF1 | July 12 | 25.6 |
| 6. World Cup: Brazil/Netherlands | France 2 | July 7 | 24.9 |
| 7. *Mrs. Doubtfire* | TF1 | March 17 | 24.9 |
| 8. *The Count of Monte Christo* | TF1 | Sept 28 | 24.5 |
| 9. *Les Trois frères* | TF1 | March 24 | 24.3 |
| 10. *Un Amour de Cousine* | TF1 | Dec 21 | 24.2 |

*Source: Médiamat Médiamétrie*

# Germany: top 10 TV programs: 1998

| Program | Channel | Date | Viewers (millions) |
|---|---|---|---|
| 1. World Cup: Germany/U.S. | ARD | June 15 | 24.37 |
| 2. World Cup: Germany/Iran | ARD | June 25 | 24.32 |
| 3. World Cup: France/Brazil | ARD | July 12 | 24.06 |
| 4. World Cup: Germany/Croatia | ARD | July 4 | 23.26 |

---

**... September 14 ...**
**Frasier** basks in glow after winning an unprecedented fifth consecutive
Outstanding Comedy Emmy.

| | | | |
|---|---|---|---|
| 5. World Cup: Brazil/The Netherlands (penalties) | ZDF | July 7 | 20.11 |
| 6. World Cup: Germany/Mexico | ZDF | June 29 | 19.48 |
| 7. World Cup: Brazil/The Netherlands (extra time) | ZDF | July 7 | 19.33 |
| 8. World Cup: France/Croatia | ARD | July 8 | 18.25 |
| 9. World Cup: Brazil/The Netherlands (the game) | ZDF | July 7 | 17.73 |
| 10. World Cup: Germany/Yugoslavia | ZDF | June 21 | 17.30 |

*Period: Jan. 1-Dec. 11 1998*

# Italy: top 10 TV programs: 1998

| Program | Channel | Date | Viewers (millions) |
|---|---|---|---|
| 1. World Cup: Italy/Cameroon | RAI1 | June 17 | 23.634 |
| 2. World Cup: Italy/France | RAI1 | July 3 | 21.407 |
| 3. World Cup: Italy/France (post-match discussion) | RAI1 | July 3 | 19.821 |
| 4. World Cup: Italy/Norway | RAI1 | June 27 | 19.797 |
| 5. World Cup: Italy/Cameroon (post-match discussion) | RAI1 | June 17 | 18.825 |
| 6. World Cup: Italy/Chile | RAI1 | June 11 | 18.000 |
| 7 .World Cup: Italy/Austria | RAI1 | June 23 | 17.459 |
| 8 .World Cup: Italy/Norway (post-match discussion) | RAI1 | June 27 | 15.973 |
| 9. World Cup: Brazil/France | RAI1 | July 12 | 15.693 |
| 10. San Remo Music Festival | RAI1 | Feb 28 | 15.588 |

*Period: Jan. 1-20 Dec.1 1998*

# U.K.: top 50 TV programs: 1998

| Program | Channel | Date | Viewers (000's) |
|---|---|---|---|
| 1. World Cup: Argentina/England | ITV | June 30 | 23,782 |
| 2. World Cup: Romania/England | ITV, | June 22 | 19,480 |
| 3. World Cup: Columbia/England | BBC1 | June 26 | 19,131 |
| 4. World Cup: post-match analysis | ITV | June 22 | 19,067 |
| 5. Coronation Street | ITV | November 16 | 18,620 |
| 6. Coronation Street | ITV | November 18 | 18,524 |
| 7. Coronation Street | ITV | January 4 | 18,371 |
| 8. Coronation Street | ITV | January 16 | 17,392 |
| 9. Eastenders | BBC1 | December 29 | 16,907 |
| 10. Heartbeat | ITV | February 22 | 16,451 |
| 11. Celebrity Stars in Their Eyes | ITV | December 2 | 16,337 |
| 12. EastEnders | BBC1 | December 28 | 15,941 |
| 13. EastEnders | BBC1 | December 3 | 15,758 |
| 14. Casualty | BBC1 | February 28 | 15,741 |
| 15. World Cup: Brazil/France | BBC1 | July 12 | 15,647 |
| 16. Men Behaving Badly | BBC1 | December 28 | 15,193 |
| 17. *Forrest Gump* | BBC1 | January 1 | 15,080 |
| 18. EastEnders | BBC1 | December 25 | 15,043 |
| 19. World Cup: France/Croatia | BBC | July 8 | 14,621 |
| 20. World Cup: Brazil/Holland | ITV | July 7 | 14,095 |
| 21. EastEnders | BBC1 | January 7 | 14,016 |
| 22. You've Been Framed | ITV | September 13 | 13,859 |
| 23. EastEnders | BBC1 | January 9 | 13,811 |
| 24. Goodnight Mr. Tom | ITV | October 25 | 13,811 |
| 25. Birds of a Feather | BBC1 | January 19 | 13,303 |
| 26. World Cup Winner's special | ITV | July 12 | 13,279 |
| 27. Emmerdale | ITV | July 12 | 13,276 |

**. . . September 15 . . .**
**Saving Private Ryan** bows in U.K. to $4.4 million.

| | | | |
|---|---|---|---|
| 28. National Lottery Live | BBC1 | February 28 | 13,195 |
| 29. The Cruise | BBC1 | January 13 | 12,863 |
| 30. London's Burning | ITV | January 11 | 12,823 |
| 31. Diana: Secrets/Crash | ITV | June 3 | 12,786 |
| 32. World Cup Scotland/Morocco | BBC1 | June 23 | 12,670 |
| 33. Emmerdale | ITV | May 7 | 12,634 |
| 34. Airline | ITV | March 20 | 12,559 |
| 35. Emmerdale | ITV | January 14 | 12,522 |
| 36. Who Wants to Be a Millionaire | ITV | September 13 | 12,472 |
| 37. Inspector Morse | ITV | November 11 | 12,393 |
| 38. The Bill | ITV | January 30/1 | 12,338 |
| 39. They Think It's All Over | BBC1 | December 25 | 12,313 |
| 40. Dinnerladies | BBC1 | November 12 | 12,238 |
| 41. Holidays from Hell | ITV | November 2 | 12,179 |
| 42. World Cup Pre match | ITV | June 30 | 12,135 |
| 43. Police, Camera Action | ITV | January 20 | 12,112 |
| 44. World Cup Brazil/Scotland | BBC1 | June 10 | 12,092 |
| 45. Before They Were Famous | BBC1 | December 25 | 11,933 |
| 46. Coming Home | ITV | April 13 | 11,872 |
| 47. Where the Heart Is | ITV | June 7 | 11,834 |
| 48. Airport | BBC1 | January 21 | 11,757 |
| 49. Harry Enfield and Chums | BBC | December 28 | 11,786 |
| 50. Only Fools and Horses | BBC1 | January 2 | 11,639 |

*Source: Taylor Nelson Sofres*

# Golden Globe TV nominations: 1998

Television series – drama: *ER* (NBC); *Felicity* (WB); *Law & Order* (NBC); *The Practice* (ABC); *The X-Files* (Fox)

Television series – musical or comedy: *Ally McBeal* (Fox); *Dharma & Greg* (ABC); *Frasier* (NBC); *Just Shoot Me* (NBC); *Spin City* (ABC)

Performance by an actress in a television series – drama: Gillian Anderson, *The X-Files*; Kim Delaney, *NYPD Blue*; Roma Downey, *Touched by an Angel*; Julianna Margulies, *ER*; Keri Russell, *Felicity*

Performance by an actor in a television series – drama: David Duchovny, *The X-Files*; Anthony Edwards, *ER*; Lance Henriksen, *Millennium*; Dylan McDermott, *The Practice*; Jimmy Smits, *NYPD Blue*

Performance by an actress in a television series – musical or comedy: Christina Applegate, *Jesse*; Jenna Elfman, *Dharma & Greg*; Calista Flockhart, *Ally McBeal*; Laura San Giacomo, *Just Shoot Me*; Sarah Jessica Parker, *Sex and the City*

Performance by an actor in a television series – musical or comedy: Michael J. Fox, *Spin City*; Thomas Gibson, *Dharma & Greg*; Kelsey Grammer, *Frasier*; John Lithgow, *3rd Rock from the Sun*; George Segal *Just Shoot Me*

Mini-series or motion picture made for television: *The Baby Dance* (Showtime); *From the Earth to the Moon* (HBO); *Gia* (HBO); *Merlin* (NBC); *The Temptations* (NBC)

Performance by an actress in a mini-series or a motion picture made for television: Stockard Channing, *The Baby Dance*; Laura Dern, *The Baby Dance*; Angelina Jolie, *Gia*; Ann-Margret, *Life of the Party: The Pamela Harriman Story*; Miranda Richardson, *Merlin*

Performance by an actor in a mini-series or a motion picture made for television: Peter Fonda, *The Tempest*; Sam Neill; *Merlin*; Bill Paxton, *A Bright Shining Lie*; Patrick Stewart, *Moby Dick*; Stanley Tucci, *Winchell*

Performance by an actress in a supporting role in a series, mini-series or motion picture made for television: Helena Bonham-Carter, *Merlin*; Faye Dunaway, *Gia*; Jane Krakowski, *Ally McBeal*; Wendie Malick, *Just Shoot Me*; Camryn Manheim, *The Practice*; Susan Sullivan, *Dharma & Greg*

Performance by an actor in a supporting role in a series, mini-series or motion picture made for television: Don Cheadle, *The Rat Pack*; Joe Mantegna, *The Rat Pack*; Gregory Peck, *Moby Dick*; David Spade, *Just Shoot Me*; Noah Wyle, *ER*

# Golden Globe TV Awards: 1998

Television series – drama: *The Practice*, 20th Century Fox TV/David E. Kelley Prods; ABC
Television series – musical or comedy: *Ally McBeal*, David E. Kelley/20th Century Fox TV; FOX
Performance by an actress in a television series – drama: Keri Russell, *Felicity*
Performance by an actor in a television series – drama: Dylan McDermott, *The Practice*
Performance by an actress in a television series – musical or comedy: Jenna Elfman, *Dharma and Greg*
Performance by an actor in a television series – musical or comedy: Michael J. Fox, *Spin City*
Mini-series or motion picture made for television: *From the Earth to the Moon*,
HBO/Imagine Ent./Clavius Base; HBO
Performance by an actress in a mini-series or a motion picture made for television: Angelina Jolie, *Gia*
Performance by an actor in a mini-series or a motion picture made for television: Stanley Tucci, *Winchell*
Performance by an actress in a supporting role in a series, mini-series or motion picture made for television: Faye Dunaway, *Gia*
Camryn Manheim, *The Practice*
Performance by an actor in a supporting role in a series, mini-series or motion picture made for television: Don Cheadle, *The Rat Pack*; Gregory Peck, *Moby Dick*

# British Academy of Film and Television Awards: 1998

Best TV Actor: Simon Russell Beale, *A Dance to the Music of Time*
Best TV Actress: Daniella Nardini, *This Life*
Best Light Entertainer: Paul Whitehouse, *The Fast Show*
Best Drama Series: *Jonathan Creek*
Best Drama Serial: *Holding On*
Best Single TV Drama: *No Child of Mine*
Best Comedy Series: *I'm Alan Partridge*
Best Comedy Performance: Steve Coogan, *I'm Alan Partridge*
Best Factual Series: *The Nazis: A Warning from History*
Best Light Entertainment Series: *The Fast Show*
Best TV Documentary: *The Grave*
Best News Coverage: *Valentina's Story*
Best Foreign TV Program: *Friends* (U.S.)
Dennis Potter Award: Kay Mellor
Lew Grade Audience Award: *A Touch of Frost*
Richard Dimbleby Award: David Dimbleby

# Golden Rose Festival, Montreux: 1998

**GOLDEN ROSE:** *Yo-Yo Ma Inspired by Bach: Six Gestures* (Rhombus, Canada)
**COMEDY**
Silver Rose – Special Prize of the City of Montreux: *Harry Enfield & Chums* (Tiger Aspect, U.K.)
Bronze Rose: *The Chamber Quintet* (Matar, Israel)
**MUSIC**
Silver Rose: *The Canadian Brass: A Christmas Experiment* (Rhombus, Canada)
Bronze Rose: *Gael Force* (Tyrone/RTE, Ireland)
Special mention: *Il Segreto di Pulcinella* (RTSI, Ch)
**SITCOMS**
Silver Rose: *Operation Good Guys: Frisk'em* (BBC2, U.K.)
Bronze Rose: *Father Ted: Are You Right There?* (Channel 4, U.K.)
**GAME SHOWS**
Silver Rose: *Happy Family Plan* (TBS, Japan)
Bronze Rose: *Ice Warriors* (LWT, U.K.)
**PRESS PRIZE "EX AEQUO"**
*David Blaine: Street Magic* (David Blaine Productions, U.S.)
*Operation Good Guys: Frisk'em* (BBC2, U.K.)
**VARIETY**
Silver Rose: *Cronicas Marcianas* (Gestmusic Zepp)
Bronze Rose: *David Blaine: Street Magic* (David Blaine Productions, U.S.)
**ARTS & SPECIALS**
Silver Rose: *Queen – "Béjart: Ballet for Life"* (Queen Prod. U.K.)
Bronze Rose: *Fame and Fortune: Ozzy Osbourne* (Channel 5, U.K.)
**UNDA PRIZE**
*Yo-Yo Ma Inspired by Bach: Six Gestures* (Rhombus, Canada)

---

**...September 17...**
DreamWorks buys **The Castle** pitch for George Clooney to produce.

# The Emmys

Nicknamed "Oscar's kid sister" by *Variety*, the Emmy statuette was born on January 25, 1949, with awards going to the "Best Film Made for Television" and to the "Most Popular Programs", along with nods to "Most Outstanding Personality", for the best Station (KTLA in those days). As television has expanded in range and influence beyond anyone's dreams (or nightmares), so the Emmys have grown in scope to comprise some 250 different awards, covering every conceivable kind of programme and technical craftsmanship. Whether it's daytime or primetime, sports or news, films or documentaries, the Emmys acknowledge its achievement. Contenders for nomination are chosen by a broad popular vote of members of NATAS (the National Academy of Television Arts and Sciences). *Variety* Editor-in-Chief Peter Bart likes telling the story of the paper's mounting an industry-wide search for the first Emmy winner – an obscure ventriloquist and puppeteer named Shirley Dinsdale, who was a naive 22-year-old when she won her award. Though her show was promptly picked up by NBC, alas, it flopped. One loyal *Variety* reader found Dinsdale living quietly in Stony Brook, New York, and she told our newspaper, "I didn't know what an Emmy was when I got it and I certainly didn't understand it afterward." Today, an Emmy can help make or break a series, and represents the ultimate accolade for anyone working in American television.

## 1948
Most popular program: *Pantomime Quiz*, KTLA
Best film made for television: *The Necklace* (*Your Show Time* series)
Outstanding personality: Shirley Dinsdale and puppet Judy Splinters, KTLA
Technical award: Charles Mesak
Station award: KTLA
Special award: Louis McManus

## 1949
Live show: *The Ed Wynn Show*, KTTV (CBS)
Outstanding live personality: Ed Wynn, KTTV (CBS)
Kinescope show: *Texaco Star Theater*, KNBH (NBC)
Outstanding kinescope personality: Milton Berle, KNBH (NBC)
Film made for and viewed on television: *The Life of Riley*, KNBH (NBC)
Children's show: *Time for Beany*, KTLA
Sports coverage: *USC-UCLA Football*, KECA-TV (ABC) (winner, according to contemporary press accounts); *Wrestling*, KTLA (Official ATAS winner)
Public service, cultural or educational program: *Crusade in Europe*, KECA-TV (ABC), KTTV (CBS)
Technical award: Harold W. Jury
Commercial: Lucky Strike, N.W. Ayer
Station achievement: KTLA

## 1950
Dramatic show: *Pulitzer Prize Playhouse*, KECA-TV (ABC)
Variety show: *The Alan Young Show*, KTTV (CBS)
Cultural show: *Campus Chorus and Orchestra*, KTSL
Game and audience-participation show: *Truth or Consequence*, KTTV (CBS)
Children's show: *Time for Beany*, KTLA
Sports program: *Rams Football*, KNBH (NBC)
News program: *KTLA Newsreel*, KTLA
Educational show: *KFI-TV University*, KFI-TV
Special event: *Departure of Marines for Korea*, KFMB-TV (San Diego), KTLA
Public service: *City at Night*, KTLA
Outstanding personality: Groucho Marx, KNBH (NBC)
Actor: Alan Young, KTTV (CBS)
Actress: Gertrude Berg, KTTV (CBS)
Technical achievement: KNBH (NBC)
Station achievement: KTLA

## 1951
Dramatic show: *Studio One*, CBS
Variety show: *Your Show of Shows*, NBC
Comedy show: *The Red Skelton Show*, NBC
Actor: Sid Caesar
Actress: Imogene Coca
Comedian or comedienne: Red Skelton, NBC

---

**...September 18...**
NBC buys rights to **Antz** and **The Prince of Egypt**.

Special achievement awards: Senator Estes Kefauver, AT&T; Jack Burrell, KNBH

## 1952

Dramatic program: *Robert Montgomery Presents*, NBC
Situation comedy: *I Love Lucy*, CBS
Mystery, action or adventure program: *Dragnet*, NBC
Variety program: *Your Show of Shows*, NBC
Public-affairs program: *See It Now*, CBS
Children's program: *Time for Beany*, KTLA
Audience-participation, quiz or panel program: *What's My Line?*, CBS
Actor: Thomas Mitchell
Actress: Helen Hayes
Comedian: Jimmy Durante, NBC
Comedienne: Lucille Ball, CBS
Outstanding personality: Bishop Fulton J. Sheen

## 1953

New program: (tie) *Make Room for Daddy*, ABC and *U.S. Steel Hour*, ABC
Dramatic program: *U.S. Steel Hour*, ABC
Situation comedy: *I Love Lucy*, CBS
Mystery, action or adventure program: *Dragnet*, NBC
Variety program: *Omnibus*, CBS
Program of news or sports: *See It Now*, CBS
Public-affairs program: *Victory at Sea*, NBC
Audience-participation, quiz or panel program: (tie) *This Is Your Life*, NBC, and *What's My Line?*, CBS
Children's program: *Kukla, Fran & Ollie*, NBC
Outstanding personality: Edward R. Murrow, CBS
Male star in a regular series: Donald O'Connor, *Colgate Comedy Hour*, NBC
Female star in a regular series: Eve Arden, *Our Miss Brooks*, CBS
Supporting actor in a regular series: Art Carney, *The Jackie Gleason Show*, CBS
Supporting actress in a regular series: Vivian Vance, *I Love Lucy*, CBS

## 1954

Single program of the year: *Operation Undersea*, *Disneyland*, ABC
Dramatic series: *U.S. Steel Hour*, ABC
Situation-comedy series: *Make Room for Daddy*, ABC
Mystery or intrigue series: *Dragnet*, NBC
Western or adventure series: *Stories of the Century*, Syndicated
Cultural, religious or educational program: *Omnibus*, CBS
Variety series: *Disneyland*, ABC
Daytime program: *Art Linkletter's House Party*, CBS
Audience guest participation or panel

program: *This Is Your Life*, NBC
Children's program: *Lassie*, CBS
Sports program: *Gillette Cavalcade of Sports*, NBC
Actor in a regular series: Danny Thomas, *Make Room for Daddy*, ABC
Actress in a regular series: Loretta Young, *The Loretta Young Show*, NBC
Supporting actor in a regular series: Art Carney, *The Jackie Gleason Show*, CBS
Supporting actress in a regular series: Audrey Meadows, *The Jackie Gleason Show*, CBS
Actor in a single performance: Robert Cummings, *Twelve Angry Men*, CBS
Actress in a single performance: Judith Anderson, *Macbeth*, NBC
Male singer: Perry Como, CBS
Female singer: Dinah Shore, NBC
Most outstanding new personality: George Gobel, NBC
News reporter or commentator: John Daly, ABC
Direction: Franklin Schaffner, *Twelve Angry Men*, CBS
Writing in dramatic material: Reginald Rose, *Twelve Angry Men*, CBS
Writing in comedy material: James Allardice, Jack Douglas, Hal Kanter, Harry Winkler, *The George Gobel Show*, NBC

## 1955

Single program of the year: *Peter Pan, Producers' Showcase*, NBC
Dramatic series: *Producers' Showcase*, NBC
Comedy series: *The Phil Silvers Show*, CBS
Action or adventure series: *Disneyland*, ABC
Variety series: *The Ed Sullivan Show*, CBS
Music series: *Your Hit Parade*, NBC
Special event of news program: *A-Bomb Test Coverage*, CBS
Documentary program: *Omnibus*, CBS
Daytime programming: *Matinee Theatre*, NBC
Audience-participation series: *The $64,000 Question*, CBS
Children's series: *Lassie*, CBS
Actor – single performance: Lloyd Nolan, *The Caine Mutiny*
Actress – single performance: Mary Martin, *Peter Pan, Producers' Showcase*, NBC
Actor – continuing performance: Phil Silvers, *The Phil Silvers Show*, CBS
Actress – continuing performance: Lucille Ball, *I Love Lucy*, CBS
Actor in a supporting role: Art Carney, *The Honeymooners*, CBS
Actress in a supporting role: Nanette Fabray, *Caesar's Hour*, NBC
Comedian: Phil Silvers, CBS

---

**. . . September 19 . . .**

**Titanic** continues to steam through the record books: the highest-grossing film in history tops **Independence Day** as the bestselling live-action homevideo release ever.

Comedienne: Nanette Fabray, NBC
Male singer: Perry Como, NBC
Female singer: Dinah Shore, NBC
MC or program host: Perry Como, NBC
News commentator or reporter: Edward R. Murrow, CBS
Specialty act – single or group: Marcel Marceau, NBC
Producer – live series: Fred Coe, *Producers' Showcase,* NBC
Producer – film series: Walt Disney, *Disneyland,* ABC
Director – live series: Franklin Schaffner, *The Caine Mutiny Court-Martial, Ford Star Jubilee,* CBS
Director – film series: Nat Hiken, *The Phil Silvers Show,* CBS
Original teleplay writing: Rod Serling, *Kraft Television Theatre,* NBC
Comedy writing: Nat Hiken, Barry Blitser, Arnold Auerbach, Harvey Orkin, Vincent Bogert, Arnold Rosen, Coleman Jacoby, Tony Webster, Terry Ryan, *The Phil Silvers Show,* CBS
Television adaptation: Paul Gregory, Franklin Schaffner, *The Caine Mutiny Court-Martial, Ford Star Jubilee,* CBS
Commercial campaign: Ford Motor Co.

## 1956

Single program of the year: *Requiem for a Heavyweight, Playhouse 90,* CBS
New program series: *Playhouse 90,* CBS
Series – one hour or more: *Caesar's Hour,* NBC
Series – half hour or less: *The Phil Silvers Show,* CBS
Public-service series: *See It Now,* CBS
Single performance by an actor: Jack Palance, *Requiem for a Heavyweight, Playhouse 90,* CBS
Single performance by an actress: Claire Trevor, *Dodsworth, Producers' Showcase,* NBC
Actor in a drama series: Robert Young, *Father Knows Best,* NBC
Actress in a drama series: Loretta Young, *The Loretta Young Show,* NBC
Comedian in a series: Sid Caesar, *Caesar's Hour,* NBC
Comedienne in a series: Nanette Fabray, *Caesar's Hour,* NBC
Supporting actor: Carl Reiner, *Caesar's Hour,* NBC
Supporting actress: Pat Carroll, *Caesar's Hour,* NBC
Male personality: Perry Como, NBC
Female personality: Dinah Shore, NBC
Coverage/newsworthy event: *Years of Crisis,* CBS
News commentator: Edward R. Murrow, CBS
Direction – one hour or more: Ralph Nelson, *Requiem for a Heavyweight, Playhouse 90,* CBS
Direction – half hour or less: Sheldon Leonard, *The Danny Thomas Show,* ABC
Teleplay writing – half hour or less: James P. Cavanagh, *Alfred Hitchcock Presents,* CBS
Teleplay writing – one hour or more: Rod Serling,

*Requiem for a Heavyweight, Playhouse 90,* CBS
Comedy writing – variety or situation comedy: Nat Hiken, Billy Friedberg, Tony Webster, Leonard Stern, Arnold Rosen, Coleman Jacoby, *The Phil Silvers Show,* CBS

## 1957

Single program of the year: *The Comedian, Playhouse 90,* CBS
New series: *The Seven Lively Arts,* CBS
Drama series: *Gunsmoke,* CBS
Comedy series: *The Phil Silvers Show,* CBS
Dramatic anthology series: *Playhouse 90,* CBS
Music, variety, audience-participation or quiz show: *The Dinah Shore Chevy Show,* NBC
Public-service program or series: *Omnibus,* ABC, NBC
Actor in a single performance – lead or support: Peter Ustinov, *The Life of Samuel Johnson, Omnibus,* NBC
Actress in a single performance – lead or support: Polly Bergen, *The Helen Morgan Story, Playhouse 90,* CBS
Continuing performance in a series by a man who essentially plays himself: Jack Benny, *The Jack Benny Show,* CBS
Continuing performance in a series by a woman who essentially plays herself: Dinah Shore, *The Dinah Shore Chevy Show,* NBC
Continuing performance by a lead actor in a dramatic or comedy series: Robert Young, *Father Knows Best,* NBC
Continuing performance by a lead actress in a dramatic or comedy series: Jane Wyatt, *Father Knows Best,* NBC
Supporting actor in a drama or comedy series: Carl Reiner, *Caesar's Hour,* NBC
Supporting actress in a drama or comedy series: Ann B. Davis, *The Bob Cummings Show,* CBS, NBC
Coverage of an unscheduled newsworthy event: Rikers Island, New York, plane crash, *World News Round-Up,* CBS
News commentary: Edward R. Murrow, *See It Now,* CBS
Direction – one hour or more: Bob Banner, *The Dinah Shore Chevy Show,* NBC
Direction – half hour or less: Robert Stevens *The Glass Eye, Alfred Hitchcock Presents,* CBS
Teleplay writing – one hour or more: Rod Serling, *The Comedian, Playhouse 90,* CBS
Teleplay writing – half hour or less: Paul Monash, *The Lonely Wizard*
Comedy writing: Nat Hiken, Billy Friedberg, Phil Sharp, Terry Ryan, Coleman Jacoby, Arnold Rosen, Sidney Zelinka, A.J. Russell, Tony Webster, *The Phil Silvers Show,* CBS

## 1958-59

Single program of the year: *An Evening with Fred Astaire,* NBC

---

### ... September 20 ...

Despite a full-tilt charge up the Nielsen syndie chart by Jerry Springer, Oprah Winfrey retains the talkshow crown for the September-to-September 1997-98 syndie season.

Dramatic series – one hour or longer: *Playhouse 90*, CBS
Dramatic series – less than one hour: *The Alcoa Hour/Goodyear Playhouse*, NBC
Special dramatic program: *Little Moon of Alban, Hallmark Hall of Fame*, NBC
Comedy series: *The Jack Benny Show*, CBS
Western series: *Maverick*, ABC
Music or variety series: *The Dinah Shore Chevy Show*, NBC
Special music or variety program – one hour or longer: *An Evening with Fred Astaire*, NBC
Public-service program or series: *Omnibus*, NBC
News-reporting series: *The Huntley-Brinkley Report*, NBC
Special news program: *The Face of Red China*, CBS
Panel, quiz or audience-participation series: *What's My Line?*, CBS
Actor in a drama series: Raymond Burr, *Perry Mason*, CBS
Actress in a drama series: Loretta Young, *The Loretta Young Show*, NBC
Actor in a comedy series: Jack Benny, *The Jack Benny Show*, CBS
Actress in a comedy series: Jane Wyatt, *Father Knows Best*, NBC
Single performance by an actor: Fred Astaire, *An Evening with Fred Astaire*, NBC
Single performance by an actress: Julie Harris, *Little Moon of Alban, Hallmark Hall of Fame*, NBC
Supporting actor in a drama series: Dennis Weaver, *Gunsmoke*, CBS
Supporting actress in a drama series: Barbara Hale, *Perry Mason*, CBS
Supporting actor in a comedy series: Tom Poston, *The Steve Allen Show*, NBC
Supporting actress in a comedy series: Ann B. Davis, *The Bob Cummings Show*, NBC
Actor in a variety series: Perry Como, *The Perry Como Show*, NBC
Actress in a variety series: Dinah Shore, *The Dinah Shore Chevy Show*, NBC
News commentator: Edward R. Murrow, CBS
Direction of a single dramatic program – one hour or longer: George Schaefer, *Little Moon of Alban, Hallmark Hall of Fame*, NBC
Direction of a single program of a drama series – under one hour: Jack Smight, *Eddie, Alcoa Hour-Goodyear Theatre*, NBC
Direction of a single program of a comedy series: Peter Tewksbury, *Medal for Margaret, Father Knows Best*, CBS
Direction of a music or variety program: Bud Yorkin, *An Evening with Fred Astaire*, NBC
Writing of a single dramatic program – one hour or longer: James Costigan, *Little Moon of Alban,*

*Hallmark Hall of Fame*, NBC
Writing of a single program of a drama series – less than one hour: Alfred Brenner, Ken Hughes, *Eddie, Alcoa Hour – Goodyear Theatre*, NBC
Writing of a single program of a comedy series: Sam Perrin, George Balzer, Hal Goldman, Al Gordon, *The Jack Benny Show*, CBS
Writing of a single music or variety program: Bud Yorkin, Herbert Baker, *An Evening with Fred Astaire*, NBC

## 1959-60

Drama program: *Playhouse 90*, CBS
Humor program: *Art Carney Special*, NBC
Variety program: *The Fabulous Fifties*, CBS
Public-affairs program: *The Twentieth Century*, CBS
News program: *The Huntley-Brinkley Report*, NBC
Music program: *Leonard Bernstein and the New York Philharmonic*, CBS
Children's program: *Huckleberry Hound*, syndicated
Actor in a series – lead or supporting: Robert Stack, *The Untouchables*, ABC
Actress in a series – lead or supporting: Jane Wyatt, *Father Knows Best*, NBC
Single performance by an actor – lead or supporting: Laurence Olivier, *The Moon and Sixpence*, NBC
Single performance by an actress – lead or supporting: Ingrid Bergman, *The Turn of the Screw, Ford Startime*, NBC
Single performance in a variety or music program or series: Harry Belafonte, *Tonight with Belafonte, The Revlon Revue*, CBS
Directing in drama: Robert Mulligan, *The Moon and Sixpence*, NBC
Directing in comedy: Ralph Levy, Bud Yorkin, *The Jack Benny Hour Special*, CBS
Writing in drama: Rod Serling, *The Twilight Zone*, CBS
Writing in comedy: Sam Perrin, George Balzer, Al Gordon, Hal Goldman, *The Jack Benny Show*, CBS
Writing in documentary field: Howard K. Smith, Av Westin, *The Population Explosion, CBS Report*, CBS

## 1960-61

Program of the year: *Macbeth, Hallmark Hall of Fame*, NBC
Drama program: *Macbeth, Hallmark Hall of Fame*, NBC
Humor program: *The Jack Benny Show*, CBS
Variety program: *Astaire Time*, NBC
Public-affairs program: *The Twentieth Century*, CBS
News program: *The Huntley-Brinkley Report*, NBC
Children's program: *Aaron Copland's Birthday Party, Young People's Concert*, CBS
Lead actor in a series: Raymond Burr, *Perry Mason*, CBS
Lead actress in a series: Barbara Stanwyck, *The Barbara Stanwyck Show*, NBC

---

Single performance by a lead actor: Maurice Evans, *Macbeth, Hallmark Hall of Fame*, NBC

Single performance by a lead actress: Judith Anderson, *Macbeth, Hallmark Hall of Fame*, NBC

Supporting actor or actress in a single program: Roddy McDowall, *Not without Honor, Equitable's American Heritage*, NBC

Supporting actor or actress in a series: Don Knotts, *The Andy Griffith Show*, CBS

Performance in a variety or music program or series: Fred Astaire, *Astaire Time*, NBC

Directing in drama: George Schaefer, *Macbeth, Hallmark Hall of Fame*, NBC

Directing in comedy: Sheldon Leonard, *Danny Thomas Show*, CBS

Writing in drama: Rod Serling, *The Twilight Zone*, CBS

Writing in comedy: Sherwood Schwartz, Dave O'Brien, Al Schwartz, Martin Ragaway, Red Skelton, *The Red Skelton Show*, CBS

Documentary writing: Victor Wolfson, *Winston Churchill – The Valiant Years*, ABC

## 1961-62

Program of the year: *Victoria Regina, Hallmark Hall of Fame*, NBC

Drama program: *The Defenders*, CBS

Humor program: *The Bob Newhart Show*, NBC

Variety or music program: (variety) *The Garry Moore Show*, CBS; (music) *Leonard Bernstein and the New York Philharmonic in Japan*, CBS

News program: *The Huntley-Brinkley Report*, NBC

Educational or public affairs program: *David Brinkley's Journal*, NBC

Daytime program: *Purex Specials for Women*, NBC

Lead actor in a series: E.G. Marshal, *The Defenders*, CBS

Lead actress in a series: Shirley Booth, *Hazel*, NBC

Single performance by a lead actor: Peter Falk, *Dick Powell Theatre*, NBC

Single performance by a lead actress: Julie Harris, *Victoria Regina, Hallmark Hall of Fame*, NBC

Supporting actor: Don Knotts, *The Andy Griffith Show*, CBS

Supporting actress: Pamela Brown, *Victoria Regina, Hallmark Hall of Fame*, NBC

Performance in a variety or music program or series: Carol Burnett, *The Garry Moore Show*, CBS

Directing in drama: Franklin Schaffner, *The Defenders*, CBS

Directing in comedy: Nat Hiken, *Car 54, Where Are You?*, NBC

Writing in drama: Reginald Rose, *The Defenders*, CBS

Writing in comedy: Carl Reiner, *The Dick Van Dyke Show*, CBS

Documentary writing: Lou Hazam, *Vincent Van Gogh: A Self-Portrait*, NBC

## 1962-63

Program of the year: *The Tunnel*, NBC

Drama program: *The Defenders*, CBS

Humor program: *The Dick Van Dyke Show*, CBS

Variety program: *The Andy Williams Show*, NBC

Music program: *Julie and Carol at Carnegie Hall*, CBS

Panel, quiz or audience-participation program: *College Bowl*, CBS

Documentary program: *The Tunnel*, NBC

Children's program: *Walt Disney's Wonderful World of Color*, NBC

Outstanding achievement in news: *The Huntley-Brinkley Report*, NBC

Outstanding program achievement in news commentary or public affairs: *David Brinkley's Journal*, NBC

Outstanding achievement in international reporting or commentary: Piers Anderton, *The Tunnel*, NBC

Lead actor in a series: E.G. Marshal, *The Defenders*, CBS

Lead actress in a series: Shirley Booth, *Hazel*, NBC

Single performance by a leading actor: Trevor Howard, *The Invincible Mr. Disraeli, Hallmark Hall of Fame*, NBC

Single performance by a leading actress: Kim Stanley, *Ben Casey*, ABC

Supporting actor: Don Knotts, *The Andy Griffith Show*, CBS

Supporting actress: Glenda Farrell, *Ben Casey*, ABC

Performance in a variety or music program or series: Carol Burnett, *Julie and Carol at Carnegie Hall* and *Carol & Company*, CBS

Directing in drama: Stuart Rosenberg, *The Defenders*, CBS

Directing in comedy: John Rich, *The Dick Van Dyke Show*, CBS

Writing in drama: Robert Thom, Reginald Rose, *The Defenders*, CBS

Writing in comedy: Carl Reiner, *The Dick Van Dyke Show*, CBS

## 1963-64

Program of the year: *The Making of the President 1960*, ABC

Drama program: *The Defenders*, CBS

Comedy program: *The Dick Van Dyke Show*, CBS

Variety program: *The Danny Kaye Show*, CBS

Music program: *The Bell Telephone Hour*, NBC

News program: *The Huntley-Brinkley Report*, NBC

News or public affairs commentary: *Cuba: P arts I and II – the Bay of Pigs and the Missile Crisis, NBC White Paper*, NBC

Documentary program: *The Making of the*

President 1960, ABC

Children's program: *Discovery '63-'64*, ABC

Lead actor in a series: Dick Van Dyke, *The Dick Van Dyke Show*, CBS

Lead actress in a series: Mary Tyler Moore, *The Dick Van Dyke Show*, CBS

Single performance by a lead actor: Jack Klugman, *The Defenders*, CBS

Single performance by a lead actress: Shelley Winters, *Two Is the Number, Bob Hope Presents the Chrysler Theater*, NBC

Supporting actor: Albert Paulsen, *One Day in the Life of Ivan Denisovich, Bob Hope Presents the Chrysler Theater*, NBC

Supporting actress: Ruth White, *Little Moon of Alban, Hallmark Hall of Fame*, NBC

Performance in a variety or music program or series: Danny Kaye, *The Danny Kaye Show*, CBS

Directing in drama: Tom Gries, *East Side, West Side*

Directing in comedy: Jerry Paris, *The Dick Van Dyke Show*, CBS

Directing in variety or music: Robert Scheerer, *The Danny Kaye Show*, CBS

Drama writing – original: Ernest Kinoy, *The Defenders*, CBS

Drama writing – adaptation: Rod Serling, *It's Mental Work, Bob Hope Presents the Chrysler Theater*, NBC

Writing in comedy or variety: Carl Reiner, Sam Denoff, Bill Persky, *The Dick Van Dyke Show*, CBS

## 1964-65

Entertainment programs: *The Dick Van Dyke Show*, CBS; *The Magnificent Yankee, Hallmark Hall of Fame*, NBC; *My Name Is Barbra*, CBS; *What is Sonata Form?, New York Philharmonic Young People's Concerts with Leonard Bernstein* , CBS

News, documentary, information and sports programs: *I, Leonardo da Vinci, Saga of Western Man*, ABC

Outstanding achievement in entertainment (actors and performers): Leonard Bernstein, *New York Philharmonic Young People's Concerts with Leonard Bernstein* , CBS; Lynn Fontaine, *The Magnificent Yankee, Hallmark Hall of Fame*, NBC; Alfred Lunt, *The Magnificent Yankee, Hallmark Hall of Fame*, NBC; Barbra Streisand, *My Name Is Barbra*, CBS; Dick Van Dyke, *The Dick Van Dyke Show*, CBS

Outstanding achievement in entertainment (writers): David Karp, *The Defenders*, CBS

Outstanding achievement in entertainment (directors): Paul Bogart, *The Defenders*, CBS

Outstanding achievement in news, documentaries, and sports (narrators): Richard Basehart, *Let My People Go*, syndicated

Outstanding achievement in news, documentaries, and sports (directors): John L. Sughrue, *The Louvre*, NBC

Outstanding achievement in news, documentaries, and sports (writers): Sidney Carroll, *The Louvre*, NBC

## 1965-66
### PRIMETIME PROGRAM AWARDS

Drama series: *The Fugitive*, ABC

Single dramatic program: *The Ages of Man*, ABC

Comedy series: *The Dick Van Dyke Show*, CBS

Variety series: *The Andy Williams Show*, NBC

Variety special: *Chrysler Presents the Bob Hope Christmas Special*, NBC

Musical program: Frank Sinatra: *A Man and His Music*, NBC

Children's program: *A Charlie Brown Christmas*, CBS

### PERFORMANCE, DIRECTING, AND WRITING

Actor in a drama series: Bill Cosby, *I Spy*, NBC

Actress in a drama series: Barbara Stanwyck, *The Big Valley*, ABC

Actor in a comedy series: Dick Van Dyke, *The Dick Van Dyke Show*, CBS

Actress in a comedy series: Mary Tyler Moore, *The Dick Van Dyke Show*, CBS

Actor in a drama special: Cliff Robertson, *The Game, Bob Hope Presents the Chrysler Theater*, NBC

Actress in a drama: Simone Signoret, *A Small Rebellion, Bob Hope Presents the Chrysler Theater*, NBC

Supporting actor in a drama: James Daly, *Eagle in a Cage, Hallmark Hall of Fame*, NBC

Supporting actress in a drama: Lee Grant, *Payton Place*, ABC

Supporting actor in a comedy: Don Knotts, *The Andy Griffith Show*, CBS

Supporting actress in a comedy: Alice Pearce, *Bewitched*, ABC

Directing in drama: Sidney Pollack, *The Game, Bob Hope Presents the Chrysler Theater*, NBC

Directing in comedy: William Asher, *Bewitched*, ABC

Directing in variety or music: Alan Handley, *The Julie Andrews Show*, NBC

Writing in drama: Millard Lampell, *Eagle in a Cage, Hallmark Hall of Fame*, NBC

Writing in comedy: Bill Persky, Sam Denoff, *The Dick Van Dyke Show*, CBS

Writing in variety: Al Gordon, Hal Goldman, Sheldon Keller, *An Evening with Carol Channing*, CBS

### THE AREAS

News and documentary program: *American White Paper: United States Foreign Policy*, NBC

Daytime program: *Camera Three*, CBS; *Wild Kingdom*, NBC

Sports program: *ABC's Wide World of Sports*, ABC

**... September 23 ...**
Bruce Springsteen, Billy Joel, and Paul McCartney nominated for
Rock and Roll Hall of Fame.

## 1966-67

PRIMETIME PROGRAM AWARDS
Drama series: *Mission: Impossible*, CBS
Single dramatic program: *Death of a Salesman*, CBS
Comedy series: *The Monkees*, NBC
Variety series: *The Andy Williams Show*, NBC
Variety special: *The Sid Caesar, Imogene Coca, Carl Reiner, Howard Morris Special*, CBS
Music program: *Brigadoon*, ABC
Children's program: *Jack and the Beanstalk*, NBC
PERFORMANCE, DIRECTING, AND WRITING
Actor in a drama series: Bill Cosby, *I Spy*, NBC
Actress in a drama series: Barbara Bain, *Mission Impossible*, CBS
Single performance by a lead actor in a drama: Peter Ustinov, *Barefoot in Athens, Hallmark Hall of Fame*, NBC
Single performance by a lead actress in a drama: Geraldine Page, *A Christmas Memory, ABC Stage 67*, ABC
Actor in a comedy series: Don Adams, *Get Smart*, NBC
Actress in a comedy series: Lucille Ball, *The Lucy Show*, CBS
Supporting actor in a drama: Eli Wallach, *The Poppy Is Also a Flower, Xerox Special*, ABC
Supporting actress in a drama: Agnes Moorehead, *The Wild, Wild West*, CBS
Supporting actor in a comedy: Don Knotts, *The Andy Griffith Show*, CBS
Supporting actress in a comedy: Frances Bavier, *The Andy Griffith Show*, CBS
Directing in drama: Alex Segal, *Death of a Salesman*, CBS
Directing in comedy: James Frawley, *The Monkees*, NBC
Directing in variety or music: Fiedler Cook, *Brigadoon*, ABC
Writing in drama: Bruce Geller, *Mission: Impossible*, CBS
Writing in comedy: Buck Henry, Leonard Stern, *Get Smart*, NBC
Writing in variety: Mel Brooks, Sam Denoff, Bill Persky, Carl Reiner, Mel Tolkin, *The Sid Caesar, Imogene Coca, Carl Reiner, Howard Morris Special*, CBS
THE AREAS
News and documentary program: *China: The Roots of Madness*, syndicated
Daytime program: *Mutual of Omaha's Wild Kingdom*, NBC
Sports program: *ABC's Wide World of Sports*, ABC

## 1967-68

PRIMETIME PROGRAM AWARDS
Single dramatic program: *Elizabeth the Queen, Hallmark Hall of Fame*, NBC
Drama series: *Mission: Impossible*, CBS
Comedy series: *Get Smart*, NBC
Music or variety program: *Rowan and Martin's*

*Laugh-In Special*, NBC
Music or variety series: *Rowan and Martin's Laugh-In*, NBC
PERFORMANCE, DIRECTING, AND WRITING
Actor in a drama series: Bill Cosby, *I Spy*, NBC
Actress in a drama series: Barbara Bain, *Mission: Impossible*, CBS
Actor in a drama special: Melvyn Douglas, *Do Not Go Gentle into That Good Night, CBS Playhouse*, CBS
Actress in a drama special: Maureen Stapleton, *Among the Paths to Eden, Xerox Special*, ABC
Actor in a comedy series: Don Adams, *Get Smart*, NBC
Actress in a comedy series: Lucille Ball, *The Lucy Show*, CBS
Supporting actor in a drama special: Milburn Stone, *Gunsmoke*, CBS
Supporting actress in a drama special: Barbara Anderson, *Ironside*, NBC
Supporting actor in a comedy: Werner Klemperer, *Hogan's Heroes*, CBS
Supporting actress in a comedy: Marion Lorne, *Bewitched*, ABC
Directing in drama special: Paul Bogart, *Dear Friends, CBS Playhouse*, CBS
Directing in comedy: Bruce Bilson, *Get Smart*, NBC
Directing in music or variety: Jack Haley, Jr., *Movin' with Nancy*, NBC
Writing in drama: Loring Mandel, *Do Not Go Gentle into That Good Night, CBS Playhouse*, CBS
Writing in comedy: Allan Burns, Chris Hayward, *He & She*, CBS
Writing in music or variety: Chris Beard, Phil Hahn, Jack Hanrahan, Coslough Johnson, Marc London, Paul Keyes, Allan Manings, David Panich, Hugh Wedlock, Digby Wolfe, *Rowan and Martin's Laugh-In*, NBC
THE AREAS
Daytime program: *Today*, NBC
Sports programming (programs): *ABC's Wide World of Sports*, ABC

## 1968-69

PRIMETIME PROGRAM AWARDS
Single dramatic program: *Teacher, Teacher, Hallmark Hall of Fame*, NBC
Drama series: *N.E.T. Playhouse*, NET
Comedy series: *Get Smart*, NBC
Music or variety series: *Rowan and Martin's Laugh-In*, NBC
Music or variety program: *The Bill Cosby Special*, NBC
PERFORMANCE, DIRECTING, AND WRITING
Actor in a drama special: Paul Scofield, *Male of the Species, Prudential's On Stage*, NBC
Actress in a drama special: Geraldine Page,

*The Thanksgiving Visitor*, ABC

Actor in a drama series: Carl Betz, *Judd for the Defence*, ABC

Actress in a drama series: Barbara Bain, *Mission: Impossible*, CBS

Actor in a comedy series: Don Adams, *Get Smart*, NBC

Actress in a comedy series: Hope Lange, *The Ghost and Mrs. Muir*, NBC

Supporting actor: no winner

Supporting actress: Anna Calder-Marshall, *Male of the Species, Prudential's On Stage*, NBC

Supporting actor in a series: Werner Klemperer, *Hogan's Heroes*, CBS

Supporting actress in a series: Susan Saint James, *The Name of the Game*, NBC

Directing in drama: David Green, *The People Next Door, CBS Playhouse*, CBS

Directing in comedy, variety or music: no winner

Writing in drama: J.P. Miller, *The People Next Door, CBS Playhouse*, CBS

Writing in comedy, variety or music: Alan Blye, Bob Einstein, Murray Roman, Carl Gottlieb, Jerry Music, Steve Martin, Cecil Tuck, Paul Wayne, Cy Howard, Mason Williams, *The Smothers Brothers Comedy Hour*, CBS

**THE AREAS**

Daytime programming: *The Dick Cavett Show*, ABC

Sports programming (programs): *19th Summer Olympic Games*, ABC

## 1969-70

**PRIMETIME PROGRAM AWARDS**

New series: *Room 222*, ABC

Single dramatic program: *A Storm in Summer, Hallmark Hall of Fame*, NBC

Drama series: *Marcus Welby, M.D.*, ABC

Comedy series: *My World and Welcome to It*, NBC

Variety or music program (variety and popular music): *Annie, the Woman in the Life of a Man*, CBS

Variety or music program (classical music): *Cinderella, National Ballet of Canada*, NET

Variety or music series: *The David Frost Show*, syndicated

**PERFORMANCE, DIRECTING, AND WRITING**

Single performance by a lead actor: Peter Ustinov, *A Storm in Summer, Hallmark Hall of Fame*, NBC

Single performance by a lead actress: Patty Duke, *My Sweet Charlie*, NBC

Actor in a drama series: Robert Young, *Marcus Welby, M.D.*, ABC

Actress in a drama series: Susan Hampshire, *The Forsyte Saga*, NET

Actor in a comedy series: William Windom, *My World and Welcome to It*, NBC

Actress in a comedy series: Hope Lange,

*The Ghost and Mrs. Muir*, ABC

Supporting actor in drama: James Brolin, *Marcus Welby, M.D.*, ABC

Supporting actress in drama: Gail Fisher, *Mannix*, CBS

Supporting actor in comedy: Michael Constantin, *Room 222*, ABC

Supporting actress in comedy: Karen Valentine, *Room 222*, ABC

Directing in drama: Paul Bogart, *Shadow Game*, CBS

Directing in comedy, variety or music: Dwight A. Hemion, *The Sound of Burt Bacharach, The Kraft Music Hall*, NBC

Writing in drama: Richard Levinson, William Link, *My Sweet Charlie*, NBC

Writing in comedy, variety or music: Gary Belkin, Peter Bellwood, Herb Sargent, Thomas Meehan, Judith Viorst, *Annie, the Woman in the Life of a Man*, CBS

**THE AREAS**

Daytime programming: *Today*, NBC

Children's programming (programs): *Sesame Street*, NET

Sports programming (programs): *The NLF Games*, CBS; *ABC's Wide World of Sports*, ABC

## 1970-71

**PRIMETIME PROGRAM AWARDS**

Outstanding program: *The Andersonville Trial, Hollywood Television Theatre*, PBS

New series: *All in the Family*, CBS

Drama series: *The Senator, The Bold Ones*, NBC

Comedy series: *All in the Family*, CBS

Variety or music program (popular music): *Singer Presents Burt Bacharach*, CBS

Variety or music program (classical music): *Leopold Stokowski, N.E.T. Festival*, PBS

Variety series – music: *The Flip Wilson Show*, NBC

Variety series – talk: *The David Frost Show*, syndicated

**PERFORMANCE, DIRECTING, AND WRITING**

Single performance by a lead actor: George C. Scott, *The Price, Hallmark Hall of Fame*, NBC

Single performance by a lead actress: Lee Grant, *The Neon Ceiling*, NBC

Actor in a drama series: Hal Holbrook, *The Senator, The Bold Ones*, NBC

Actress in a drama series: Susan Hampshire, *The First Churchills, Masterpiece Theatre*, PBS

Actor in a comedy series: Jack Klugman, *The Odd Couple*, ABC

Actress in a comedy series: Jean Stapleton, *All in the Family*, CBS

Supporting actor in a drama: David Burns, *The Price, Hallmark Hall of Fame*, NBC

Supporting actress in a drama: Margaret Leighton, *Hamlet, Hallmark Hall of Fame*, NBC

---

**... September 25 ...**

Tom Hanks announces he will star in remake of Japanese pic, **Shall We Dance?**

Supporting actor in a comedy: Ed Asner, *The Mary Tyler Moore Show*, CBS

Supporting actress in a comedy: Valerie Harper, *The Mary Tyler Moore Show*, CBS

Directing in drama (special program): Fiedler Cook, *The Price, Hallmark Hall of Fame*, NBC

Directing in drama (single program or series): Daryl Duke, *The Senator, The Bold Ones*, NBC

Directing in comedy: Jay Sandrich, *The Mary Tyler Moore Show*, CBS

Directing in variety or music: Mark Warren, *Rowan and Martin's Laugh-In*, NBC

Writing in drama: Joel Oliansky, *The Senator, The Bold Ones*, NBC

Writing in comedy: James L. Brooks, Allan Burns, *The Mary Tyler Moore Show*, CBS

**THE AREAS**

Daytime programming (programs): *Today*, NBC

Children's programming (programs): *Sesame Street*, PBS

Sports programming (programs): *ABC's Wide World of Sports*, ABC

## 1971-72

**PRIMETIME PROGRAM AWARDS**

Outstanding program: *Brian's Song*, ABC

New series: *Elizabeth R, Masterpiece Theatre*, PBS

Drama series: *Elizabeth R, Masterpiece Theatre*, PBS

Comedy series: *All in the Family*, CBS

Variety or music program (variety and popular music): *Jack Lemmon in 'S Wonderful, 'S Marvelous, 'S Gershwin*, NBC

Variety or music program (classical music): *Beethoven's Birthday: a Celebration in Vienna with Leonard Bernstein*, CBS

Variety series (music): *The Carol Burnett Show*, CBS

Variety series (talk): *The Dick Cavett Show*, CBS

**PERFORMANCE, DIRECTING, AND WRITING**

Single performance by a lead actor: Keith Michell, *Catherine Howard, The Six Wives of Henry VIII*, CBS

Single performance by a lead actress: Glenda Jackson, *Shadow in the Sun, Elizabeth R, Masterpiece Theatre*, PBS

Actor in a drama series: Peter Falk, *Columbo*, NBC

Actress in a drama series: Glenda Jackson, *Elizabeth R, Masterpiece Theatre*, PBS

Actor in a comedy series: Carroll O'Connor, *All in the Family*, CBS

Actress in a comedy series: Jean Stapleton, *All in the Family*, CBS

Supporting actor in a drama: Jack Warden, *Brian's Song*, ABC

Supporting actress in a drama: Jenny Agutter, *The Snow Goose, Hallmark Hall of Fame*, NBC

Supporting actor in a comedy: Ed Asner,

*The Mary Tyler Moore Show*, CBS

Supporting actress in a comedy: (tie) Valerie Harper, *The Mary Tyler Moore Show*, CBS; Sally Struthers, *All in the Family*, CBS

Performer in music or variety: Harvey Korman, *The Carol Burnett Show*, CBS

Directing in drama (series): Alexander Singer, *The Lawyers, The Bold Ones*, NBC

Directing in drama (special): Tom Gries, *The Glass House*, CBS

Directing in comedy: John Rich, *All in the Family*, CBS

Directing in variety or music (series): Art Fisher, *The Sonny and Cher Comedy Hour*, CBS

Directing in comedy, variety or music (special): Walter C. Miller, Martin Charnin, *Jack Lemmon in 'S Wonderful, 'S Marvelous, 'S Gershwin*, NBC

Writing in a drama series: Richard L. Levinson, William Link, *Columbo*, NBC

Writing in a comedy series: Burt Styler, *All in the Family*, CBS

**THE AREAS**

Daytime drama programming (programs): *The Doctors*, NBC

Children's programming (programs): *Sesame Street*, PBS

Sports programming (programs): *ABC's Wide World of Sports*, ABC

## 1972-73

**PRIMETIME AND DAYTIME PROGRAM AWARDS**

New series: *America*, NBC

Drama series: *The Waltons*, CBS

Comedy series: *All in the Family*, CBS

Drama/comedy – limited episodes: *Tom Brown's Schooldays, Masterpiece Theatre*, PBS

Single program: *A War of Children*, CBS

Variety/music series: *The Julie Andrews Hour*, ABC

Variety/music program: *Singer Presents Liza with a "Z,"* NBC

Classical music program: *Sleeping Beauty*, PBS

Daytime drama: *The Edge of Night*, CBS

Daytime program: *Dinah's Place*, NBC

**PERFORMANCE, DIRECTING, AND WRITING**

Lead actor (drama series – continuing): Richard Thomas, *The Waltons*, CBS

Lead actor (drama/comedy – limited episodes): Anthony Murphy, *Tom Brown's Schooldays, Masterpiece Theatre*, PBS

Lead actress (drama series – continuing): Michael Learned, *The Waltons*, CBS

Lead actress (drama/comedy – limited episodes): Susan Hampshire, *Vanity Fair, Masterpiece Theatre*, PBS

Actor in a comedy series: Jack Klugman, *The Odd Couple*, ABC

Actress in a comedy series: Mary Tyler Moore, *The Mary Tyler Moore Show*, CBS

Single performance by a lead actor: Laurence Olivier, *Long Day's Journey into Night*, ABC

Single performance by a lead actress: Cloris Leachman, *A Brand New Life*, ABC

Supporting actor in drama: Scott Jacoby, *That Certain Summer*, ABC

Supporting actress in drama: Ellen Corby, *The Waltons*, CBS

Supporting actor in comedy: Ted Knight, *The Mary Tyler Moore Show*, CBS

Supporting actress in comedy: Valerie Harper, *The Mary Tyler Moore Show*

Supporting performer in music or variety: Tim Conway, *The Carol Burnett Show*, CBS

Directing in drama (series): Jerry Thorpe, *Kung Fu*, ABC

Directing in drama (special): Joseph Sargent, *The Marcus-Nelson Murders*, CBS

Directing in comedy: Jay Sandrich, *The Mary Tyler Moore Show*, CBS

Directing in comedy, variety or music (series): Bill Davis, *The Julie Andrews Hour*, ABC

Directing in comedy, variety or music (special): Bob Fosse, *Singer Presents Liza with a "Z,"* NBC

Writing in drama series: John McGreevey, *The Waltons*, CBS

Writing in a comedy series: Michael Ross, Bernie West, Lee Kalcheim, *All in the Family*, CBS

**THE AREAS**

Outstanding achievement in a daytime drama: Mary Fickett, performer, *All My Children*, ABC

Children's programming (programs): *Sesame Street*, PBS

Sports programming (programs): *ABC's Wide World of Sports*, ABC

**INTERNATIONAL AWARD WINNERS**

Fiction: *La Cabina*, Televisión Española, Spain

Nonfiction: *Horizon: The Making of a Natural History Film*, BBC, U.K.

Directorate award: Charles Curran

## 1973-74

**PRIMETIME PROGRAM AWARDS**

Drama series: *Upstairs, Downstairs, Masterpiece Theatre*, PBS

Comedy series: *M\*A\*S\*H*, CBS

Limited series: *Columbo*, NBC

Special: *The Autobiography of Miss Jane Pittman*, CBS

Music/variety series: *The Carol Burnett Show*, CBS

Comedy/variety or music special: *Lily Tomlin*, CBS

Children's special: *Marlo Thomas and Friends in Free to Be… You and Me*, ABC

**PERFORMANCE, DIRECTING, AND WRITING**

Actor in a drama series: Telly Savalas, *Kojak*, CBS

Actress in a drama series: Michael Learned, *The Waltons*, CBS

Actor in a comedy series: Alan Alda, *M\*A\*S\*H*, CBS

Actress in a comedy series: Mary Tyler Moore, *The Mary Tyler Moore Show*, CBS

Actor in a limited series: William Holden, *The Blue Knight*, NBC

Actress in a limited series: Mildred Natwick, *The Snoop Sisters*, NBC

Actor in a drama: Hal Holbrook, *Pueblo*, ABC

Actress in a drama: Cicely Tyson, *The Autobiography of Miss Jane Pittman*, CBS

Actor of the year – series: Alan Alda, *M\*A\*S\*H*, CBS

Actress of the year – series: Mary Tyler Moore, *The Mary Tyler Moore Show*, CBS

Actor of the year – special: Hal Holbrook, *Pueblo*, ABC

Actress of the year – special: Cicely Tyson, *The Autobiography of Miss Jane Pittman*, CBS

Supporting actor in drama: Michael Moriarty, *The Glass Menagerie*, ABC

Supporting actress in drama: Joanna Miles, *The Glass Menagerie*, ABC

Supporting actor in comedy: Rob Reiner, *All in the Family*, CBS

Supporting actress in comedy: Cloris Leachman, *The Mary Tyler Moore Show*, CBS

Supporting actor of the year: Michael Moriarty, *The Glass Menagerie*, ABC

Supporting actress of the year: Joanna Miles, *The Glass Menagerie*, ABC

Supporting actor in comedy/variety or music: Harvey Korman, *The Carol Burnett Show*, CBS

Supporting actress in comedy/variety or music: Brenda Vaccaro, *The Shape of Things*, NBC

Director of the year – series: Robert Butler, *The Blue Knight*, NBC

Director of the year – special: Dwight Hemion, *Barbra Streisand… and Other Musical Instruments*, CBS

Writer of the year – series: Treva Silverman, *The Mary Tyler Moore Show*, CBS

Writer of the year – special: Fay Kanin, *Tell Me Where It Hurts*, G.E. Theater, CBS

**THE AREAS**

Outstanding achievement in children's programming: Charles M. Schulz, writer, *A Charlie Brown Thanksgiving*, CBS; William Zaharuk, art director, Peter Ramofski, set decorator, *The Borrowers*, Hallmark Hall of Fame, NBC

Sports programs: *ABC's Wide World of Sports*, ABC

Outstanding achievement: *The Dick Cavett Show*, ABC

**DAYTIME AWARDS**

Drama series: *The Doctors*, NBC

---

**... September 27 ...**

Amid much dissension from local crits, Alejandro Agresti's **Wind With The Gone** takes top prize at the San Sebastian Film Festival.

Drama special: *The Other Woman, ABC Matinee Today*, ABC

Daytime actor of the year: Pat O'Brien, *The Other Woman, ABC Matinee Today*, ABC

Daytime actress of the year: Cathleen Nesbit, *The Mask of Love, ABC Matinee Today*, ABC

Daytime director of the year: H. Wesley Kenney, *Miss Kline, We Love You, ABC Afternoon Playbreak*, ABC

**INTERNATIONAL AWARD WINNERS**

Fiction: *Mr. Axelford's Angel*, Yorkshire Television, U.K.

Nonfiction: *Aquarius: Hello Dali!* London Weekend Television, U.K.

## 1974-75

**PRIMETIME PROGRAM AWARDS**

Drama series: *Upstairs, Downstairs, Masterpiece Theatre*, PBS

Comedy series: *The Mary Tyler Moore Show*, CBS

Limited episodes: *Benjamin Franklin*, CBS

Special – drama or comedy: *The Law*, NBC

Comedy/variety or music series: *The Carol Burnett Show*, CBS

Comedy/variety or music special: *An Evening with John Denver*, ABC

Classical music program: *Profile in Music: Beverly Sills, Festival '75*, PBS

Children's special: *Yes, Virginia There is a Santa Claus*, ABC

**PERFORMANCE, DIRECTING, AND WRITING**

Actor in a drama series: Robert Blake, *Baretta*, ABC

Actress in a drama series: Jean Marsh, *Upstairs, Downstairs, Masterpiece Theatre*, PBS

Actor in a comedy series: Tony Randall, *The Odd Couple*, ABC

Actress in a comedy series: Valerie Harper, *Rhoda*, CBS

Actor in a limited series: Peter Falk, *Columbo*, NBC

Actress in a limited series: Jessica Walter, *Amy Prentiss*, NBC

Actor in a special: Laurence Olivier, *Love Among the Ruins, ABC Theatre*, ABC

Actress in a special: Katharine Hepburn, *Love Among the Ruins, ABC Theatre*, ABC

Supporting actor in a drama series: Will Geer, *The Waltons*, CBS

Supporting actress in a drama series: Ellen Corby, *The Waltons*, CBS

Supporting actor in a comedy series: Ed Asner, *The Mary Tyler Moore Show*, CBS

Supporting actress in a comedy series: Betty White, *The Mary Tyler Moore Show*, CBS

Single performance by a supporting actor in a comedy or drama series: Patrick McGoohan, *Columbo*, NBC

Single performance by a supporting actress in a comedy or drama series: Cloris Leachman, *The Mary Tyler Moore Show*, CBS

Supporting actor in a special: Anthony Quayle, *QB VII*, ABC

Supporting actress in a special: Juliet Mills, *QB VII*, ABC

Supporting actor in variety or music: Jack Albertson, *Cher*, CBS

Supporting actress in variety or music: Cloris Leachman, *Cher*, CBS

Directing in drama: Bill Bain, *Upstairs, Downstairs, Masterpiece Theatre*, PBS

Directing in comedy: Gene Reynolds, *M\*A\*S\*H*, CBS

Directing in a special: George Cukor, *Love Among the Ruins, ABC Theatre*, ABC

Writing in drama: Howard Fast, *Benjamin Franklin*, CBS

Writing in comedy: Ed Weinberger, Stan Daniels, *The Mary Tyler Moore Show*, CBS

**DAYTIME AWARDS**

Drama series: *The Young and the Restless*, CBS

Drama special: *The Girl Who Couldn't Lose, ABC Afternoon Playbreak*, ABC

Actor in a drama series: Macdonald Carey, *Days of Our Lives* , NBC

Actress in a drama series: Susan Flannery, *Days of Our Lives* , NBC

Directing in a drama series: Richard Dunlap, *The Young and the Restless*, CBS

**SPORTS AWARD WINNERS**

Sports program: *ABC's Wide World of Sports*, ABC

Sports event: *Jimmy Connors vs. Rod Laver Tennis Challenge*, CBS

**INTERNATIONAL AWARD WINNERS**

Fiction: *The Evacuees*, BBC, U.K.

Nonfiction: *Inside Story: Marek*, BBC, U.K.

Directorate award: Junzo Imamichi

## 1975-76

**PRIMETIME PROGRAM AWARDS**

Drama series: *Police Story*, NBC

Comedy series: *The Mary Tyler Moore Show*, CBS

Limited series: *Upstairs, Downstairs, Masterpiece Theatre*, PBS

Drama special: *Eleanor and Franklin*, ABC

Comedy, variety or music series: *NBC's Saturday Night*, NBC

Comedy, variety or music special: *Gypsy in My Soul*, CBS

Classical music program: *Bernstein and the New York Philharmonic, Great Performances*, PBS

Children's special: *Huckleberry Finn*, ABC

**PERFORMANCE, DIRECTING, AND WRITING**

Actor in a drama series: Peter Falk, *Columbo*, NBC

Actress in a drama series: Michael Learned, *The Waltons*, CBS

---

Actor in a comedy series: Jack Albertson, *Chico and the Man*, NBC

Actress in a comedy series: Mary Tyler Moore, *The Mary Tyler Moore Show*, CBS

Actor in a single performance in a drama or comedy series: Edward Asner, *Rich Man, Poor Man*, ABC

Actress in a single performance in a drama or comedy series: Kathryn Walker, *The Adams Chronicles*, PBS

Actor in a limited series: Hal Holbrook, *Sandburg's Lincoln*, NBC

Actress in a limited series: Rosemary Harris, *Notorious Woman, Masterpiece Theatre*, PBS

Actor in a special: Anthony Hopkins, *The Lindbergh Kidnapping Case*, NBC

Actress in a special: Susan Clark, *Babe* , CBS

Supporting actor in a drama series: Anthony Zerbe, *Harry O*, ABC

Supporting actress in a drama series: Ellen Corby, *The Waltons*, CBS

Supporting actor in a comedy series: Ted Knight, *The Mary Tyler Moore Show*, CBS

Supporting actress in a comedy series: Betty White, *The Mary Tyler Moore Show*, CBS

Directing in a drama series: David Greene, *Rich Man, Poor Man*, ABC

Directing in a comedy series: Gene Reynolds, *M\*A\*S\*H*, CBS

Directing in a special: Daniel Petrie, *Eleanor and Franklin*, ABC

Writing in a drama series: Sherman Yellen, *The Adams Chronicles*, PBS

Writing in a comedy series: David Lloyd, *The Mary Tyler Moore Show*, CBS

**THE AREAS**

Outstanding achievement: *Bicentennial Minutes*, CBS

Outstanding achievement in sports programming: Andy Sidaris, Don Ohlmeyer, Roger Goodman, Larry Kamm, Ronnie Hawkins, Ralph Mellanby, directors, *XII Winter Olympic Games*, ABC

**DAYTIME AWARDS**

Drama series: *Another World*, NBC

Drama special: *First Ladies' Diaries: Edith Wilson*, NBC

Actor in a drama series: *Larry Haines, Search for Tomorrow*, CBS

Actress in a drama series: Helen Gallagher, *Ryan's Hope*, ABC

Directing in a drama series: David Pressman, *One Life to Live*, ABC

**INTERNATIONAL AWARD WINNERS**

Fiction: *The Naked Civil Servant*, Thames Television, U.K.

Nonfiction: *Reach for Tomorrow*, Nippon Television Network, Japan

Directorate award: Talbot Duckmanton

## 1976-77

**PRIMETIME PROGRAM AWARDS**

Drama series: *Upstairs, Downstairs, Masterpiece Theatre*, PBS

Comedy series: *The Mary Tyler Moore Show*, CBS

Limited series: *Roots*, ABC

Special: (tie) *Eleanor and Franklin: The White House Years*, ABC; *Sybil*, NBC

Variety or music series: *Van Dyke and Company*, NBC

Classical program: *American Ballet Theater: Swan Lake, Live from Lincoln Center, Great Performances*, PBS

Children's special: *Ballet Shoes, Piccadilly Circus*, PBS

Outstanding program achievement: *The Tonight Show*, NBC

**PERFORMANCE, DIRECTING, AND WRITING**

Actor in a drama series: James Garner, *The Rockford Files*, NBC

Actress in a drama series: Lindsay Wagner, *The Bionic Woman*

Actor in a comedy series: Carroll O'Connor, *All in the Family*, CBS

Actress in a comedy series: Beatrice Arthur, *Maude*, CBS

Actor for a single performance in a drama or comedy series: Louis Gossett, Jr., *Roots*, ABC

Actress for a single performance in a drama or comedy series: Beulah Bondi, *The Waltons*, CBS

Actor in a limited series: Christopher Plummer, *The Money-changers*, NBC

Actress in a limited series: Patty Duke Astin, *Captains and the Kings*, NBC

Actor in a special: Ed Flanders, *Harry S. Truman: Plain Speaking*, PBS

Actress in a special: Sally Field, *Sybil*, NBC

Supporting actor in a drama series: Gary Frank, *Family*, ABC

Supporting actress in a drama series: Kristy McNichol, *Family*, ABC

Supporting actor in a comedy series: Gary Burghoff, *M\*A\*S\*H*, CBS

Supporting actress in a comedy series: Mary Kay Place, *Mary Hartman, Mary Hartman*, syndicated

Directing in a drama series: David Greene, *Roots*, ABC

Directing in a comedy series: Alan Alda, *M\*A\*S\*H*, CBS

Directing in a special: Daniel Petrie, *Eleanor and Franklin: The White House Years*, ABC

Writing in a drama series: Ernest Kinoy, William Blinn, *Roots*, ABC

Writing in a comedy series: Allan Burns, James L. Brooks, Ed Weinberger, Stan Daniels, David Lloyd, Bob Ellison, *The Mary Tyler Moore Show*, CBS

**DAYTIME AWARDS**

Drama series: *Ryan's Hope*, ABC

Actor in a drama series: Val Dufour, *Search for Tomorrow*, CBS

---

**. . . September 29 . . .**

Hasbro buys Galoob and assumes control over lucrative **Star Wars** toy line.

Actress in a drama series: Helen Gallagher, *Ryan's Hope*, ABC

Directing in a drama series: Lela Swift, *Ryan's Hope*, ABC

**INTERNATIONAL AWARD WINNERS**

Fiction: *The Collection*, Granada Television, U.K.

Nonfiction: *Henry Ford's America*, Canadian Broadcasting

Directorate award: Alphonse Quiment

## 1977-78

**PRIMETIME PROGRAM AWARDS**

Drama series: *The Rockford Files*, NBC

Comedy series: *All in the Family*, CBS

Limited series: *Holocaust*, NBC

Special: *The Gathering*, ABC

Variety or music series: *The Muppet Show*, syndicated

Variety or music special: *Bette Midler – Ol' Red Hair is Back*, NBC

Classical program: *American Ballet Theater: Giselle, Live from Lincoln Center*, PBS

Children's special: *Halloween is Grinch Night*, ABC

Informational series: *The Body Human*, CBS

Informational special: *The Great Whales, National Geographic Specials*, PBS

Outstanding program achievement: *The Tonight Show*, NBC

**PERFORMANCE, DIRECTING, AND WRITING**

Actor in a drama series: Ed Asner, *Lou Grant*, CBS

Actress in a drama series: Sada Thompson, *Family*, ABC

Actor in a comedy series: Carroll O'Connor, *All in the Family*, CBS

Actress in a comedy series: Jean Stapleton, *All in the Family*, CBS

Actor in a limited series: Michael Moriarty, *Holocaust*, NBC

Actress in a limited series: Meryl Streep, *Holocaust*, NBC

Actor for a single performance in a series: Barnard Hughes, *Lou Grant*, CBS

Actress for a single performance in a series: Rita Moreno, *The Rockford Files*, NBC

Actor in a special: Fred Astaire, *A Family Upside Down*, NBC

Actress in a special: Joanne Woodward, *See How She Runs*, CBS

Supporting actor in a drama series: Robert Vaughn, *Washington: Behind Closed Doors*, ABC

Supporting actress in a drama series: Nancy Marchand, *Lou Grant*, CBS

Supporting actor in a comedy series: Rob Reiner, *All in the Family*, CBS

Supporting actress in a comedy series: Julie Kavner, *Rhoda*, CBS

Directing in a drama series: Marvin J. Chomsky, *Holocaust*, NBC

Directing in a comedy series: Paul Bogart, *All in the Family*, CBS

Directing in a special: David Lowell Rich, *The Defection of Simas Kudirka*, CBS

Writing in a drama series: Gerald Green, *Holocaust*, NBC

Writing in a comedy series: Bob Weiskopf, Bob Schiller, Barry Harman, Harve Brosten, *All in the Family*, CBS

**DAYTIME AWARDS**

Drama series: *Days of Our Lives*, NBC

Actor in a drama series: James Pritchett, *The Doctors*, NBC

Actress in a drama series: Laurie Heinemann, *Another World*, NBC

Directing in a drama series: Richard Dunlap, *The Young and the Restless*, CBS

**INTERNATIONAL AWARD WINNERS**

Fiction: *The Fly*, Televisie Radio Omroep Stichting, Netherlands

Nonfiction: *Four Women*, Canadian Broadcasting

Directorate award: Prix Italia

## 1978-79

**PRIMETIME PROGRAM AWARDS**

Drama series: *Lou Grant*, CBS

Comedy series: *Taxi*, ABC

Limited series: *Roots: The Next Generation*, ABC

Special: *Friendly Fire*, ABC

Variety or music series: *Steve & Eydie Celebrate Irving Berlin*, NBC

Informational program: *Scared Straight!*, syndicated

Classical program: *Balanchine IV, Dance in America, Great Performances*, PBS

Children's special: *Christmas Eve on Sesame Street*, PBS

Outstanding program achievement – special events: *The 51st Annual Academy Awards*, ABC

Outstanding program achievement – special class: (tie) *The Tonight Show*, NBC; *Lifeline*, NBC

**PERFORMANCE, DIRECTING, AND WRITING**

Actor in a drama series: Ron Leibman, *Kaz*, CBS

Actress in a drama series: Mariette Hartley, *The Incredible Hulk*, CBS

Actor in a comedy series: Carroll O'Connor, *All in the Family*, CBS

Actress in a comedy series: Ruth Gordon, *Taxi*, ABC

Actor in a limited series or a special: Peter Strauss, *The Jericho Mile*, ABC

Actress in a limited series or a special: Bette Davis, *Strangers: The Story of a Mother and Daughter*, CBS

Supporting actor in a comedy/variety or music series: Robert Guillaume, *Soap*, ABC

Supporting actress in a comedy/variety or music series: Sally Struthers, *All in the Family*, CBS

Supporting actor in a drama series: Stuart Margolin,

*The Rockford Files*, NBC

Supporting actress in a drama series: Kristy McNichol, *Family*, ABC

Supporting actor in a limited series or a special: Marlon Brando, *Roots: The Next Generation*, ABC

Supporting actress in a limited series or a special: Esther Rolle, *Summer of My German Soldier*, ABC

Directing in a drama series: Jackie Cooper, *The White Shadow*, CBS

Directing in a comedy/variety or music series: Noam Pitlik, *Barney Miller*, ABC

Directing in a limited series or a special: David Greene, *Friendly Fire*, ABC

Writing in a drama series: Michelle Gallery, *Lou Grant*, CBS

Writing in a comedy/variety or music series: Alan Alda, *M\*A\*S\*H*, CBS

**DAYTIME AWARDS**

Drama series: *Ryan's Hope*, ABC

Actor in a drama series: Al Freeman, Jr., *One Life to Live*, ABC

Actress in a drama series: Irene Dailey, *Another World*, NBC

Directing in a drama series: Jerry Evans, Lela Swift, *Ryan's Hope*, ABC

**INTERNATIONAL AWARD WINNERS**

Documentary: *The Secret Hospital*, Yorkshire TV, U.K.

Performing arts: *Elegies for the Deaths of Three Spanish Poets*, U.K.

Popular arts: *Rich Little's Christmas Carol*, Canadian Broadcasting

Drama: *On Giants' Shoulders*, BBC, U.K.

Directorate award: Dr. Frank Stanton

## 1979-80

**PRIMETIME PROGRAM AWARDS**

Drama series: *Lou Grant*, CBS

Comedy series: *Taxi*, ABC

Limited series: *Edward & Mrs. Simpson*, syndicated

Variety or music program: *Baryshnikov on Broadway*, ABC

Special: *The Miracle Worker*, NBC

Classical program: *Live from Studio 8H: A Tribute to Toscanini*, NBC

Informational program: *The Body Human: The Magic Sense*, CBS

Outstanding program achievement – special events: *The 34th Annual Tony Awards*, CBS

Outstanding program achievement – special class: *Fred Astaire: Change Partners and Dance*, PBS

Animated program: *Carlton Your Doorman*, CBS

**PERFORMANCE, DIRECTING, AND WRITING**

Actor in a drama series: Edward Asner, *Lou Grant*, CBS

Actress in a drama series: Barbara Bel Geddes, *Dallas*, CBS

Actor in a comedy series: Richard Mulligan, *Soap*, ABC

Actress in a comedy series: Cathryn Damon, *Soap*, ABC

Actor in a limited series or a special: Powers Boothe, *Guyana Tragedy: The Story of Jim Jones*, CBS

Actress in a limited series or a special: Patty Duke Astin, *The Miracle Worker*, NBC

Supporting actor in a drama series: Stuart Margolin, *The Rockford Files*, NBC

Supporting actress in a drama series: Nancy Marchand, *Lou Grant*, CBS

Supporting actor in a limited series or a special: George Grizzard, *The Oldest Living Graduate*, NBC

Supporting actress in a limited series or a special: Mare Winningham, *Amber Waves*, ABC

Supporting actor in a comedy, variety or music series: Harry Morgan, *M\*A\*S\*H*, CBS

Supporting actress in a comedy, variety or music series: Loretta Swit, *M\*A\*S\*H*, CBS

Directing in a drama series: Roger Young, *Lou Grant*, CBS

Directing in a comedy series: James Burrows, *Taxi*, ABC

Directing in a limited series or a special: Marvin J. Chomsky, *Attica*, ABC

Writing in a drama series: Seth Freeman, *Lou Grant*, CBS

Writing in a comedy series: Bob Colleary, *Barney Miller*, ABC

**DAYTIME AWARDS**

Drama series: *Guiding Light*, CBS

Actor in a drama series: Douglass Watson, *Another World*, NBC

Actress in a drama series: Judith Light, *One Life to Live*, ABC

Directing in a drama series: Lela Swift, *Ryan's Hope*, ABC

**INTERNATIONAL AWARD WINNERS**

Documentary: *Fighting Back*, Canadian Broadcasting

Performing arts: *L'Oiseau de feu*, Société Radio, Canada

Popular arts: *Not the Least of the Nine O'Clock News*, BBC, U.K.

Drama: *A Rod of Iron*, Yorkshire TV, U.K.

Directorate award: Lord Grade of Elstree

Founder's award: Jim Henson

## 1980-81

**PRIMETIME PROGRAM AWARDS**

Drama series: *Hill Street Blues*, NBC

Comedy series: *Taxi*, ABC

Limited series: *Shogun*, NBC

Variety, music or comedy program *Lily: Sold Out*, CBS:

Drama special: *Playing for Time*, CBS

Classical program in the performing arts: *Live from Studio 8H: An Evening of Jerome Robbins' Ballets with Members of the New York City Ballet*, NBC

Informational series: *Meeting of Minds*, PBS
Informational special: *The Body Human: The Bionic Breakthrough*, CBS
Children's program: *Donahue and Kids*, NBC
Animated program: *Life is a Circus, Charlie Brown*, CBS
**PERFORMANCE, DIRECTING, AND WRITING**
Actor in a drama series: Daniel J. Travanti, *Hill Street Blues*, NBC
Actress in a drama series: Barbara Babcock, *Hill Street Blues*, NBC
Actor in a comedy series: Judd Hirsch, *Taxi*, ABC
Actress in a comedy series: Isabel Sanford, *The Jeffersons*, CBS
Actor in a limited series or a special: Anthony Hopkins, *The Bunker*, CBS
Actress in a limited series or a special: Vanessa Redgrave, *Playing for Time*, CBS
Supporting actor in a drama series: Michael Conrad, *Hill Street Blues*, NBC
Supporting actress in a drama series: Nancy Marchand, *Lou Grant*, CBS
Supporting actor in a comedy, variety or music series: Danny DeVito, *Taxi*, ABC
Supporting actress in a comedy, variety or music series: Eileen Brennan, *Private Benjamin*, CBS
Supporting actor in a limited series or a special: David Warner, *Masada*, ABC
Supporting actress in a limited series or a special: Jane Alexander, *Playing for Time*, CBS
Directing in a drama series: Robert Butler, *Hill Street Blues*, NBC
Directing in a comedy series: James Burrows, *Taxi*, ABC
Directing in a limited series or a special: James Goldstone, *Kent State*, NBC
Writing in a drama series: Michael Kozoll, Steven Bochco, *Hill Street Blues*, NBC
Writing in a comedy series: Michael Leeson, *Taxi*, ABC
**DAYTIME AWARDS**
Drama series: *General Hospital*, ABC
Actor in a drama series: Douglass Watson, *Another World*, NBC
Actress in a drama series: Judith Light, *One Life to Live*, ABC
Directing in a drama series: Marlena Laird, Alan Pultz, Phillip Sogard, *General Hospital*, ABC
**INTERNATIONAL AWARD WINNERS**
Documentary: *Charters pour l'enfer (Charters to Hell)*, Société National de Télévision Française, France
Performing arts: *Sweeney Todd: Scenes from the Making of a Musical*, London Weekend TV, U.K.
Popular arts: *Vinicius para criancas or carca de Noe (Noah's Ark)* TV Globo, Brazil
Drama: *A Town Like Alice*, Channel 7, Australia

Directorate award: Sir Huw Wheldon
Founder's award: Roone Arledge, Ms. Shaun Sutton

## 1981-82
**PRIMETIME PROGRAM AWARDS**
Drama series: *Hill Street Blues*, NBC
Comedy series: *Barney Miller*, ABC
Limited series: *Marco Polo*, NBC
Drama special: *A Woman Called Golda*, syndicated
Variety, music or comedy program: *Night of 100 Stars*, ABC
Classical program in the performing arts: *La Bohème, Live from the Met*, PBS
Informational series: *Creativity with Bill Moyers*, PBS
Informational special: *Making of Raiders of the Lost Ark*, PBS
Children's program: *The Wave*, ABC
Animated program: *The Grinch Grinches the Cat in the Hat*, ABC
**PERFORMANCE, DIRECTING, AND WRITING**
Actor in a drama series: Daniel J. Travanti, *Hill Street Blues*, NBC
Actress in a drama series: Michael Learned, *Nurse*, CBS
Actor in a comedy series: Alan Alda, *M\*A\*S\*H*, CBS
Actress in a comedy series: Carol Kane, *Taxi*, ABC
Actor in a limited series or a special: Mickey Rooney, *Bill*, CBS
Actress in a limited series or a special: Ingrid Bergman, *A Woman Called Golda*, syndicated
Supporting actor in a drama series: Michael Conrad, *Hill Street Blues*, NBC
Supporting actress in a drama series: Nancy Marchand, *Lou Grant*, CBS
Supporting actor in a comedy, variety or music series: Christopher Lloyd, *Taxi*, ABC
Supporting actress in a comedy, variety or music series: Loretta Swit, *M\*A\*S\*H*, CBS
Supporting actor in a limited series or a special: Laurence Olivier, *Brideshead Revisited, Great Performances*, PBS
Supporting actress in a limited series or a special: Penny Fuller, *The Elephant Man*, ABC
Directing in a drama series: Harry Harris, *Fame*, NBC
Directing in a comedy series: Alan Rafkin, *One Day at a Time*, CBS
Directing in a limited series or a special: Marvin J. Chomsky, *Inside the Third Reich*, ABC
Writing in a drama series: Steven Bochco, Anthony Yerkovich, Jeffrey Lewis, Michael Wagner, Michael Kozoll, *Hill Street Blues*, NBC
Writing in a comedy series: Ken Estin, *Taxi*, ABC
**DAYTIME AWARDS**
Drama series: *Guiding Light*, CBS
Actor in a drama series: Anthony Geary,

---

*General Hospital*, ABC
Actress in a drama series: Robin Strasser, *One Life to Live*, ABC
Directing in a drama series: Marlena Laird, Alan Pulitz, Philip Sogard, *General Hospital*, ABC
**INTERNATIONAL AWARD WINNERS**
Documentary: *Is There One Who Understands Me? The World of James Joyce*, Radio Telefis Eireann, Ireland
Performing arts: *A Lot of Happiness*, Granada TV, U.K.
Popular arts: *Death and Life Severinian*, TV Globo, Brazil
Drama: *A Voyage 'Round My Father*, Thames TV, U.K.
Directorate award: Akio Morita
Founder's award: Michael Landon

## 1982-83
**PRIMETIME PROGRAM AWARDS**
Drama series: *Hill Street Blues*, NBC
Comedy series: *Cheers*, NBC
Limited series: *Nicholas Nickleby*, syndicated
Drama special: *Special Bulletin*, NBC
Variety, music or comedy program: *Motown 25: Yesterday, Today, Forever*, NBC
Classical program in the performing arts: *Pavarotti in Philadelphia: La Bohème*, PBS
Informational series: *The Barbara Walters Specials*, ABC
Informational special: *The Body Human: The Living Code*, CBS
Animated program: *Ziggy's Gift*, ABC
Children's program: *Big Bird in China*, NBC
**PERFORMANCE, DIRECTING, AND WRITING**
Actor in a drama series: Ed Flanders, *St. Elsewhere*, NBC
Actress in a drama series: Tyne Daly, *Cagney & Lacey*, CBS
Actor in a comedy series: Judd Hirsch, *Taxi*, NBC
Actress in a comedy series: Shelley Long, *Cheers*, NBC
Actor in a limited series or a special: Tommy Lee Jones, *The Executioner's Song*, NBC
Actress in a limited series or a special: Barbara Stanwyck, *The Thorn Birds*, ABC
Supporting actor in a drama series: James Coco, *St. Elsewhere*, NBC
Supporting actress in a drama series: Doris Roberts, *St. Elsewhere*, NBC
Supporting actor in a comedy, variety or music series: Christopher Lloyd, *Taxi*, NBC
Supporting actress in a comedy, variety or music series: Carol Kane, *Taxi*, NBC
Supporting actor in a limited series or a special: Richard Kiley, *The Thorn Birds*, ABC
Supporting actress in a limited series or a special: Jean Simmons, *The Thorn Birds*, ABC
Performance in a variety or music program: Leontyne Price, *Leontyne Price, Zubin Mehta and the New York*

*Philharmonic, Live from Lincoln Center*, PBS
Directing in a drama series: Jeff Bleckner, *Hill Street Blues*, NBC
Directing in a comedy series: James Burrows, *Cheers*, NBC
Directing in a limited series or a special: John Erman, *Who Will Love My Children?*, ABC
Writing in a drama series: David Milch, *Hill Street Blues*, NBC
Writing in a comedy series: Glen Charles, Les Charles, *Cheers*, NBC
**DAYTIME AWARDS**
Drama series: *The Young and the Restless*, CBS
Actor in a drama series: Robert Woods, *One Life to Live*, ABC
Actress in a drama series: Dorothy Lyman, *All My Children*, ABC
Directing in a drama series: Allen Fristoe, Norman Hall, Peter Miner, David Pressman, *One Life to Live*, ABC
**INTERNATIONAL AWARD WINNERS**
Documentary: *The Miracle of Life*, Swedish Television, SVT, Sweden
Performing arts: *Dangerous Music*, HTV, Wales, U.K.
Popular arts: *Blackadder: The Archbishop*, BBC, U.K.
Drama: *King Lear*, Granada, TV, U.K.
Children's programming: *Fraggle Rock*, Canadian Broadcasting
Directorate award: Robert Marinho
Founder's award: Herbert Brodkin

## 1983-84
**PRIMETIME PROGRAM AWARDS**
Drama series: *Hill Street Blues*, NBC
Comedy series: *Cheers*, NBC
Limited series: *Concealed Enemies, American Playhouse*, PBS
Variety, music or comedy program: The Kennedy Center Honors, CBS
Drama/comedy special: *Something about Amelia*, ABC
Classical program in the performing arts: *Placido Domingo Celebrates Seville, Great Performances*, PBS
Informational series: *A Walk through the 20th Century with Bill Moyers*, PBS
Informational special: *America Remembers John F. Kennedy*, syndicated
Animated program: *Garfield on the Town*, CBS
Children's program: *He Makes Me Feel Like Dancin'*, NBC
**PERFORMANCE, DIRECTING, AND WRITING**
Actor in a drama series: Tom Selleck, *Magnum, P.I.*, CBS
Actress in a drama series: Tyne Daly, *Cagney & Lacey*, CBS
Actor in a comedy series: John Ritter, *Three's Company*, ABC

Actress in a comedy series: Jane Curtin, *Kate & Allie*, CBS

Actor in a limited series or a special: Laurence Olivier, *King Lear*, syndicated

Actress in a limited series or a special: Jane Fonda, *The Dollmaker*, ABC

Supporting actor in a drama series: Bruce Weitz, *Hill Street Blues*, NBC

Supporting actress in a drama series: Alfre Woodard, *Hill Street Blues*, NBC

Supporting actor in a comedy series: Pat Harrington, *One Day at a Time*, CBS

Supporting actress in a comedy series: Rhea Perlman, *Cheers*, NBC

Supporting actor in a limited series or a special: Art Carney, *Terrible Joe Moran*, CBS

Supporting actress in a limited series or a special: Roxana Zal, *Something about Amelia*, ABC

Performance in a variety or music program: Cloris Leachman, *Screen Actors Guild 50th Anniversary Celebration*, CBS

Directing in a drama series: Corey Allen, *Hill Street Blues*, NBC

Directing in a comedy series: Bill Persky, *Kate & Allie*, CBS

Directing in a limited series or a special: Jeff Bleckner, *Concealed Enemies, American Playhouse*, PBS

Writing in a drama series: John Ford Noonan, John Masius, Ron Fontana, *St. Elsewhere*, NBC

Writing in a comedy series: David Angel, *Cheers*, NBC

**DAYTIME AWARDS**

Drama series: *General Hospital*, ABC

Actor in a drama series: Larry Bryggman, *As the World Turns*, CBS

Actress in a drama series: Erika Slezak, *One Life to Live*, ABC

Directing in a drama series: Larry Auerbach, George Keathley, Peter Miner, David Pressman, *One Life to Live*, ABC

**INTERNATIONAL AWARD WINNERS**

Documentary: *The Heart of the Dragon: Remembering*, Channel 4, U.K.

Performing arts: *The Tragedy of Carmen*, Channel 4, U.K.

Popular arts: *Fresh Fields*, Thames TV, U.K.

Drama: *The Jewel in the Crown*, Granada TV, U.K.

Children's programming: *Wind in the Willows*, Thames TV, U.K.

Directorate award: Lord Sidney Bernstein

Founder's award: David L. Wolper

## 1984-85

**PRIMETIME PROGRAM AWARDS**

Drama series: *Cagney & Lacey*, CBS

Comedy series: *The Cosby Show*, NBC

Limited series: *The Jewel in the Crown, Masterpiece Theatre*, PBS

Drama/comedy special: *Do You Remember Love?*, CBS

Variety, music or comedy program: *Motown Returns to the Apollo*, NBC

Classical program in the performing arts: *Tosca, Live from the Met*, PBS

Informational series: *The Living Planet: A Portrait of the Earth*, PBS

Informational special: *Cousteau: Mississippi*, syndicated

Animated program: *Garfield in the Rough*, CBS

Children's program: *Displaced Person, American Playhouse*, PBS

**PERFORMANCE, DIRECTING, AND WRITING**

Actor in a drama series: William Daniels, *St. Elsewhere*, NBC

Actress in a drama series: Tyne Daly, *Cagney & Lacey*, CBS

Actor in a comedy series: Robert Guillaume, *Benson*, ABC

Actress in a comedy series: Jane Curtin, *Kate & Allie*, CBS

Actor in a limited series or a special: Richard Crenna, *The Rape of Richard Beck*, ABC

Actress in a limited series or a special: Joanne Woodward, *Do You Remember Love?*, CBS

Supporting actor in a drama series: Edward James Olmos, *Miami Vice*, NBC

Supporting actress in a drama series: Betty Thomas, *Hill Street Blues*, NBC

Supporting actor in a comedy series: John Larroquette, *Night Court*, NBC

Supporting actress in a comedy series: Rhea Perlman, *Cheers*, NBC

Supporting actor in a limited series or a special: Karl Malden, *Fatal Vision*, NBC

Supporting actress in a limited series or a special: Kim Stanley, *Cat on a Hot Tin Roof, American Playhouse*, PBS

Performance in a variety or music program: George Hearn, *Sweeney Todd, Great Performances*, PBS

Directing in a drama series: Karen Arthur, *Cagney & Lacey*, CBS

Directing in a comedy series: Jay Sandrich, *The Cosby Show*, NBC

Directing in a limited series or a special: Lamont Johnson, *Wallenberg: A Hero's Story*, NBC

Writing in a drama series: Patricia Green, *Cagney & Lacey*, CBS

Writing in a comedy series: Ed Weinberger, Michael Leeson, *The Cosby Show*, NBC

**DAYTIME AWARDS**

Drama series: *The Young and the Restless*, CBS

Actor in a drama series: Darnell Williams, *All My Children*, ABC

Actress in a drama series: Kim Zimmer, *Guiding Light*, CBS

---

**... October 4 ...**

Jackie Chan's autobiography, **I am Jackie Chan: My Life in Action**, debuts on the **New York Times** hardcover nonfiction bestseller list at No.15.

Directing in a drama series: John Whitesell II, Bruce Barry, Matthew Diamond, Irene M. Pace, Robert D. Kochman, Joanne Rivituso, Joanne Sedwick, *Guiding Light*, CBS

### INTERNATIONAL AWARD WINNERS
Documentary: *28 Up*, Granada TV, U.K.
Performing arts: *Omnibus: The Treble*, BBC, U.K.
Popular arts: *Spitting Image*, Central Independent Television, U.K.
Drama: *Das Boot*, Bavaria Atelier, West Germany
Children's programming: *Supergran*, Tyne Tees TV, U.K.
Directorate award: Leonard H. Goldson
Founder's award: Sir David Attenborough

## 1985-86
### PRIMETIME PROGRAM AWARDS
Drama series: *Cagney & Lacey*, CBS
Comedy series: *The Golden Girls*, NBC
Mini-series: *Peter the Great*, NBC
Drama/comedy special: *Love Is Never Silent, Hallmark Hall of Fame*, NBC
Variety, music or comedy program: *The Kennedy Center Honors*, CBS
Classical program in the performing arts: *Wolf Trap Presents the Kirov: Swan Lake*, PBS
Informational special: *W.C. Fields Straight Up*, PBS
Informational series: (tie) *Laurence Olivier – A Life, Great Performances*, PBS; *Planet Earth*, PBS
Animated program: *Garfield's Halloween Adventure*, CBS
Children's program: *Anne of Green Gables, Wonderworks*, PBS

### PERFORMANCE, DIRECTING, AND WRITING
Actor in a drama series: William Daniels, *St. Elsewhere*, NBC
Actress in a drama series: Sharon Gless, *Cagney & Lacey*, CBS
Actor in a comedy series: Michael J. Fox, *Family Ties*, NBC
Actress in a comedy series: Betty White, *The Golden Girls*, NBC
Actor in a mini-series or a special: Dustin Hoffman, *Death of a Salesman*, CBS
Actress in a mini-series or a special: Marlo Thomas, *Nobody's Child*, CBS
Supporting actor in a drama series: John Karlen, *Cagney & Lacey*, CBS
Supporting actress in a drama series: Bonnie Bartlett, *St. Elsewhere*, NBC
Supporting actor in a comedy series: John Larroquette, *Night Court*, NBC
Supporting actress in a comedy series: Rhea Perlman, *Cheers*, NBC
Supporting actor in a mini-series or a special: John Malkovich, *Death of a Salesman*, CBS

Supporting actress in a mini-series or a special: Colleen Dewhurst, *Between Two Women*, ABC
Performance in a variety or music program: Whitney Houston, *The 28th Annual Grammy Awards*, CBS
Guest performer in a drama series: John Lithgow, *Amazing Stories*, NBC
Guest performer in a comedy series: Roscoe Lee Browne, *The Cosby Show*, NBC
Directing in a drama series: Georg Stanford Brown, *Cagney & Lacey*, CBS
Directing in a comedy series: Jay Sandrich, *The Cosby Show*, NBC
Directing in a mini-series or a special: Joseph Sargent, *Love Is Never Silent, Hallmark Hall of Fame*, NBC
Writing in a drama series: Tom Fontana, John Tinker, John Masius, *St. Elsewhere*, NBC
Writing in a comedy series: Barry Fanaro, Mort Nathan, *The Golden Girls*, NBC

### DAYTIME AWARDS
Drama series: *The Young and the Restless*, CBS
Actor in a drama series: David Canary, *All My Children*, ABC
Actress in a drama series: Erika Slezak, *One Life to Live*, ABC
Directing in a drama series: Dennis Steinmetz, Rudy Vejar, Frank Pacelli, Randy Robbins, Betty Rothenberg, *The Young and the Restless*, CBS

### INTERNATIONAL AWARD WINNERS
Documentary: *Chasing a Rainbow: The Life of Josephine Baker*, Channel Four, U.K.
Performing arts: *Bejart's Kabuki Ballet*, NHK Japan Broadcasting
Popular arts: *Spitting Image*, Central Independent Television, U.K.
Drama: *Shadowlands*, BBC, U.K.
Children's program: *The Kids of Degrassi Street: Griff Gets a Hand*, Canadian Broadcasting
Directorate award: Herbert Schmertz
Founder's award: Donald L. Taffer

## 1986-87
### PRIMETIME PROGRAM AWARDS
Drama series: *L.A. Law*, NBC
Comedy series: *The Golden Girls*, NBC
Mini-series: *A Year in the Life*, NBC
Drama/comedy special: *Promise, Hallmark Hall of Fame*, CBS
Variety, music or comedy program: *The 1987 Tony Awards*, CBS
Classical program in performing arts: *Vladimir Horowitz: The Last Romantic*, PBS
Informational series: (tie) *Smithsonian World*, PBS; *Unknown Chaplin, American Masters*, PBS

Informational special: Dance in America: *Agnes, the Indomitable De Mille, Great Performances*, PBS

Animated program: *Cathy*, CBS

Children's program: *Jim Henson's The Storyteller: Hans My Hedgehog*, NBC

**PERFORMANCE, DIRECTING, AND WRITING**

Actor in a drama series: Bruce Willis, *Moonlighting*, ABC

Actress in a drama series: Sharon Gless, *Cagney & Lacey*, CBS

Actor in a comedy series: Michael J. Fox, *Family Ties*, NBC

Actress in a comedy series: Rue McClanahan, *The Golden Girls*, NBC

Actor in a mini-series or a special: James Woods, *Promise, Hallmark Hall of Fame*, NBC

Actress in a mini-series or a special: Gena Rowlands, *The Betty Ford Story*, ABC

Supporting actor in a drama series: John Hillerman, *Magnum, P.I.*, CBS

Supporting actress in a drama series: Bonnie Bartlett, *St. Elsewhere*, NBC

Supporting actor in a comedy series: John Larroquette, *Night Court*, NBC

Supporting actress in a comedy series: Jackée Harry, *227*, NBC

Supporting actor in a mini-series or a special: Dabney Coleman, *Sworn to Silence*, ABC

Supporting actress in a mini-series or a special: Piper Laurie, *Promise, Hallmark Hall of Fame*, NBC

Individual performance in a variety or music program: Robin Williams, *A Carol Burnett Special: Carol, Carol, Whoopi & Robin*, ABC

Guest performer in a drama series: Alfre Woodard, *L.A. Law*, NBC

Guest performer in a comedy series: John Cleese, *Cheers*, NBC

Directing in a drama series: Gregory Hoblit, *L.A. Law*, NBC

Directing in a comedy series: Terry Hughes, *The Golden Girls*, NBC

Directing in a mini-series or a special: Glenn Jordan, *Promise, Hallmark Hall of Fame*, NBC

Writing in a drama series: Stevn Bochco, Terry Louise Fisher, *L.A. Law*, NBC

Writing in a comedy series: Gary David Goldberg, Alan Uger, *Family Ties*, NBC

**DAYTIME AWARDS**

Drama series: *As the World Turns*, CBS

Actor in a drama series: Larry Bryggman, *As the World Turns*, CBS

Actress in a drama series: Kim Zimmer, *Guiding Light*, CBS

Drama series directing team: Frank Pacelli, Rudy Vejar,

Betty Rothenberg, Randy Robbins, *The Young and the Restless*, CBS

**INTERNATIONAL AWARD WINNERS**

Documentary: *The Sword of Islam*, Granada TV, U.K.

Performing arts: *The Belle of Amherst*, Thames TV, U.K.

Popular arts: *Alas Smith and Jones*, BBC, U.K.

Drama: *Porterhouse Blue*, Channel Four, U.K.

Children's program: *It's Late: Degrassi Junior High*, CBC, Canada

Directorate award: Jeremy Isaacs

Founder's award: Jacques-Yves Cousteau

## 1987-88

**PRIMETIME PROGRAM AWARDS**

Drama series: *thirtysomething*, ABC

Comedy series: *The Wonder Years*, ABC

Mini-series: *The Murder of Mary Phagan*, NBC

Drama/comedy special: *Inherit the Wind*, NBC

Variety, music or comedy program: *Irving Berlin's 100th Birthday Celebration*, CBS

Classical program in the performing arts: *Nixon in China, Great Performances*, PBS

Informational special: *Dear America: Letters Home from Vietnam*, HBO

Informational series: *Buster Keaton: Hard Act to Follow, American Masters*, PBS

Animated program: *A Claymation Christmas Celebration*, CBS

Children's program: *The Secret Garden, Hallmark Hall of Fame*, CBS

Variety/music events programming: *The 60th Annual Academy Awards*, ABC

**PERFORMANCE, DIRECTING, AND WRITING**

Actor in a drama series: Richard Kiley, *A Year in the Life*, NBC

Actress in a drama series: Tyne Daly, *Cagney & Lacey*, CBS

Actor in a comedy series: Michael J. Fox, *Family Ties*, NBC

Actress in a comedy series: Bea Arthur, *The Golden Girls*, NBC

Actor in a mini-series or a special: Jason Robards, *Inherit the Wind*, NBC

Actress in a mini-series or a special: Jessica Tandy, *Foxfire, Hallmark Hall of Fame*, CBS

Supporting actor in a drama series: Larry Drake, *L.A. Law*, NBC

Supporting actress in a drama series: Patricia Wettig, *thirtysomething*, ABC

Supporting actor in a comedy series: John Larroquette, *Night Court*, NBC

Supporting actress in a comedy series: Estelle Getty, *The Golden Girls*, NBC

---

**. . . October 6 . . .**
Mel Gibson set to produce and star in Wim Wenders' **The Million Dollar Hotel**.

Supporting actor in a mini-series or special: John Shea, *Baby M*, ABC

Supporting actress in a mini-series or special: Jane Seymour, *Onassis: The Richest Man in the World*, ABC

Guest performer in a drama series: Shirley Knight, *thirtysomething*, ABC

Guest performer in a comedy series: Beah Richards, *Frank's Place*, CBS

Individual performance in a variety or music program: Robin Williams, *ABC Presents a Royal Gala*, ABC

Director in a drama series: Mark Tinker, *St. Elsewhere*, NBC

Director in a comedy series: Gregory Hoblit, *Hooperman*, ABC

Director in a mini-series or a special: Lamont Johnson, *Lincoln*, NBC

Writing in a drama series: Paul Haggis, Marshall Herskovitz, *thirtysomething*, ABC

Writing in a comedy series: Hugh Wilson, *Frank's Place*, CBS

**DAYTIME AWARDS**

Drama series: *Santa Barbara*, NBC

Actor in a drama series: David Canary, *All My Children*, ABC

Actress in a drama series: Helen Gallagher, *Ryan's Hope*, ABC

Drama series directing team: Rudy Vejar, Frank Pacelli, Heather Hill, Randy Robbins, Betty Rothenberg, *The Young and the Restless*, CBS

**INTERNATIONAL AWARD WINNERS**

Documentary: *The Last Seven Months of Anne Frank*, TROS-TV, The Netherlands

Performing arts: *Ken Russell's ABC of British Music*, London Weekend TV, U.K.

Popular arts: *The New Statesman*, Yorkshire TV, U.K.

Drama: *A Very British Coup*, Channel Four, U.K.

Young people's program: *Touch the Sun: Captain Johnno*, Australian Children's Television Foundation

Directorate award: Vittorio Boni

Founder's award: Goar Mestre

# 1988-89

**PRIMETIME PROGRAM AWARDS**

Drama series: *L.A. Law*, NBC

Comedy series: *Cheers*, NBC

Mini-series: *War and Remembrance*, ABC

Drama/comedy special: (tie) *Day One*, CBS; *Roe vs. Wade*, NBC

Variety, music or comedy program: *The Tracey Ullman Show*, Fox

Classical program: in the performing arts: *Bernstein at 70!*, Great Performances, PBS

Informational series: *Nature*, PBS

Informational special: *Lillian Gish: The Actor's Life for Me*, American Masters, PBS

Special events: *Cirque du Soleil: The Magic Circus*, HBO; *The 11th Annual Kennedy Center Honors*, CBS; *The 42nd Annual Tony Awards*, CBS, *The American Film Institute Salute to Gregory Peck*, NBC

Animated program – less than one hour: *Garfield: Babes and Bullets*, CBS

Children's program: *Free to Be… A Family*, ABC

**PERFORMANCE, DIRECTING, AND WRITING**

Actor in a drama series: Carroll O'Connor, *In the Heat of the Night*, NBC

Actress in a drama series: Dana Delany, *China Beach*, ABC

Actor in a comedy series: Richard Mulligan, *Empty Nest*, NBC

Actress in a comedy series: Candice Bergen, *Murphy Brown*, CBS

Actor in a mini-series or a special: James Woods, *My Name Is Bill W.*, Hallmark Hall of Fame, ABC

Actress in a mini-series or a special: Holly Hunter, *Roe vs. Wade*, NBC

Supporting actor in a drama series: Larry Drake, *L.A. Law*, NBC

Supporting actress in a drama series: Melanie Mayron, *thirtysomething*, ABC

Supporting actor in a comedy series: Woody Harelson, *Cheers*, NBC

Supporting actress in a comedy series: Rhea Perlman, *Cheers*, NBC

Supporting actor in a mini-series or a special: Derek Jacobi, *The Tenth Man*, Hallmark Hall of Fame, CBS

Supporting actress in a mini-series or a special: Colleen Dewhurst, *Those She Left Behind*, NBC

Individual performance (variety or music program): Linda Ronstadt, *Canciones de mi padre*, Great Performances, PBS

Individual performance (informational programming): Hall Holbrook, host, *Portrait of America*, TBS

Individual performance (special events): Billy Crystal, host, *The 31st Annual Grammy Awards*, CBS

Individual performance (classical music/dance programming): Mikhail Baryshnikov, *Baryshnikov Dances Balanchine*, Great Performances, PBS

Directing in a drama series: Robert Altman, *Tanner '88*, HBO

Directing in a comedy series: Peter Baldwin, *The Wonder Years*, ABC

Directing in a mini-series or a special: Simon Wincer, *Lonesome Dove*, CBS

Writing in a drama series: Joseph Dougherty, *thirtysomething*, ABC

Writing in a comedy series: Diane English, *Murphy Brown*, CBS

---

**... October 7 ...**

Linda Ellerbee, Whoopi Goldberg, and Diane Keaton join together to produce women's liberation movement mini for HBO.

DAYTIME AWARDS

Drama series: *Santa Barbara*, NBC

Actor in a drama series: David Canary, *All My Children*, ABC

Actress in a drama series: Marcy Walker, *Santa Barbara*, NBC

Drama series directing team: Frank Pacelli, Heather Hill, Randy Robbins, Rudy Vejar, Betty Rothenberg, Kathryn Foster, *The Young and the Restless*, CBS

INTERNATIONAL AWARD WINNERS

Documentary: *Four Hours in My Lai*, Yorkshire TV, U.K.

Arts documentary: *Gwen – A Juliet Remembered*, BBC, U.K.

Popular arts: *Alexei Sayle's Stuff: Fun with Magnets*, BBC, U.K.

Performing arts: *La Bohème*, Australian Broadcasting

Drama: *Traffic*, Channel Four, U.K.

Young people: *My Secret Identity*, Sunrise Films, Canada

Directorate award: Ted Turner

Citation: Murray Chercover

Founder's award: Paul Fox

# 1989-90

PRIMETIME PROGRAM AWARDS

Drama series: *L.A. Law*, NBC

Comedy series: *Murphy Brown*, CBS

Mini-series: *Drug Wars: The Camarena Story*, NBC

Drama/comedy special: (tie) *Caroline?*, Hallmark Hall of Fame, CBS; *The Incident*, CBS

Variety, music or comedy series: *In Living Color*, Fox

Variety, music or comedy special: *Sammy Davis, Jr.'s 60th Anniversary Celebration*, ABC

Classical program in the performing arts: *Aida, The Metropolitan Opera Presents*, PBS

Informational series (area award): *Smithsonian World*, PBS

Informational special (area award): *Dance in America: Bob Fosse Steam Heat, Great Performances*, PBS; *Broadway Dreamers: The Legacy of the Group Theatre, American Masters*, PBS

Animated program – one hour or less: *The Simpsons*, Fox

Children's program: *A Mother's Courage: The Mary Thomas Story, The Magical World of Disney*, NBC

PERFORMANCE, DIRECTING, AND WRITING

Actor in a drama series: Peter Falk, *Columbo*, ABC

Actress in a drama series: Patricia Wettig, *thirtysomething*, ABC

Actor in a comedy series: Ted Danson, *Cheers*, NBC

Actress in a comedy series: Candice Bergen, *Murphy Brown*, CBS

Actor in a mini-series or a special: Hume Cronyn, *Age-Old Friends*, HBO

Actress in a mini-series or a special: Barbara Hershey,

*A Killing in a Small Town*, CBS

Supporting actor in a drama series: Jimmy Smits, *L.A. Law*, NBC

Supporting actress in a drama series: Marg Helgenberger, *China Beach*, ABC

Supporting actor in a comedy series: Alex Rocco, *The Famous Teddy Z*, CBS

Supporting actress in a comedy series: Bebe Neuwirth, *Cheers*, NBC

Supporting actor in a mini-series or a special: Vincent Gardenia, *Age-Old Friends*, HBO

Supporting actress in a mini-series or a special: Eva Marie Saint, *People Like Us*, NBS

Performance in a variety or music program: Tracey Ullman, *The Best of Tracey Ullman Show*, Fox

Performance in informational programming: *George Burns, A Conversation with…*, Disney

Performance in classical music/dance programming (area award): Brian Boitano, *Carmen on Ice*, HBO; Brian Orser, *Carmen on Ice*, HBO; Katarina Witt, *Carmen on Ice*, HBO

Guest actor in a drama series: Patrick McGoohan, *Columbo*, ABC

Guest actress in a drama series: Viveca Lindfors, *Life Goes On*, ABC

Guest actor in a comedy series: Jay Thomas, *Murphy Brown*, CBS

Guest actress in a comedy series: Swoosie Kurtz, *Carol & Company*, NBC

Directing in a drama series: (tie) Thomas Carter, *Equal Justice*, ABC; Scott Winant, *thirtysomething*, ABC

Directing in a comedy series: Michael Dinner, *The Wonder Years*, ABC

Directing in a mini-series or a special: Joseph Sargent, *Caroline?, Hallmark Hall of Fame*, CBS

Writing in a drama series: David E. Kelley, *L.A. Law*, NBC

Writing in a comedy series: Bob Brush, *The Wonder Years*, ABC

DAYTIME AWARDS

Drama series: *Santa Barbara*, NBC

Actor in a drama series: A. Martinez, *Santa Barbara*, NBC

Actress in a drama series: Kim Zimmer, *Guiding Light*, CBS

Drama series directing team: Michael Gliona, Rick Bennewitz, Robert Schiller, Pamela Fryman, Jeanine Guarneri-Frons, *Santa Barbara*, NBC

INTERNATIONAL AWARD WINNERS

Documentary: *J'ai douze ans et je fais la guerre*, CAPA Production, France

Arts documentary: *Bookmark: From Moscow to Pietushki*, BBC, U.K.

Performing arts: *The Mahabharata*, Channel Four, U.K.

Popular arts: *Norbert Smith: A Life*, Channel Four, U.K.

Drama: *First and Last*, BBC, U.K.

Children and young people: *Living with Dinosaurs*, Channel Four, U.K.

Directorate award: Henrikas Yushkiavitshus

Founder's award: Joan Ganz Cooney

## 1990-91
### PRIMETIME PROGRAM AWARDS
Drama series: *L.A. Law*, NBC

Comedy series: *Cheers*, NBC

Drama/comedy special or mini-series: *Separate but Equal*, NBC

Variety, music or comedy program: *The 63rd Annual Academy Awards*, ABC

Informational series (area award): *The Civil War*, PBS

Informational special (area award): *Edward R. Murrow: This Reporter, American Masters*, PBS

Children's program: *You Can't Grow Home Again: A 3-2-1 Contact Extra*, PBS

Animated program – one hour or less: *The Simpsons*, Fox

Classical program in the performing arts: *Tchaikovsky's 150th Birthday Gala from Leningrad*, PBS

### PERFORMANCE, DIRECTING, AND WRITING
Actor in a drama series: James Earl Jones, *Gabriel's Fire*, ABC

Actress in a drama series: Patricia Wettig, *thirtysomething*, ABC

Actor in a comedy series: Burt Reynolds, *Evening Shade*, CBS

Actress in a comedy series: Kirstie Alley, *Cheers*, NBC

Actor in a mini-series or a special: John Gielgud, *Summer's Lease, Masterpiece Theatre*, PBS

Actress in a mini-series or a special: Lynn Whitfield, *The Josephine Baker Story*, HBO

Supporting actor in a comedy series: Jonathan Winters, *Davis Rules*, ABC

Supporting actress in a comedy series: Bebe Neuwirth, *Cheers*, NBC

Supporting actor in a drama series: Timothy Busfield, *thirtysomething*, ABC

Supporting actress in a drama series: Magde Sinclair, *Gabriel's Fire*, ABC

Supporting actor in a mini-series or a special: James Earl Jones, *Heat Wave*, TNT

Supporting actress in a mini-series or a special: Ruby Dee, *Decoration Day, Hallmark Hall of Fame*, NBC

Guest actor in a drama series: David Opatoshu, *Gabriel's Fire*, ABC

Guest actress in a drama series: Peggy McCay, *The Trials of Rosie O'Neill*, CBS

Guest actor in a comedy series: Jay Thomas, *Murphy Brown*, CBS

Guest actress in a comedy series: Colleen Dewhurst, *Murphy Brown*, CBS

Directing in a drama series: Thomas Carter, *Equal Justice*, ABC

Directing in a comedy series: James Burrows, *Cheers*, NBC

Directing in a mini-series or a special: Brian Gibson, *The Josephine Baker Story*, HBO

Writing in a drama series: David E. Kelley, *L.A. Law*, NBC

Writing in a comedy series: Gary Dontzig, Steven Peterman, *Murphy Brown*, CBS

### DAYTIME AWARDS
Drama series: *As the World Turns*, CBS

Actor in a drama series: Peter Bergman, *The Young and the Restless*, CBS

Actress in a drama series: Finola Hughes, *General Hospital*, ABC

Drama series directing team: Rick Bennewitz, Peter Brinckerhoff, Michael Gliona, Robert Schiller, Jeanine Guarneri-Frons, Pamela Fryman, Robin Raphaelian, *Santa Barbara*, NBC

### INTERNATIONAL AWARD WINNERS
Documentary: *Cambodia: The Betrayal*, Central Independent Television, U.K.

Arts documentary: *Damned in the U.S.A.*, Channel Four, U.K.

Performing arts: *Le Dortoir*, Canadian Broadcasting

Popular arts: *The Curse of Mr. Bean*, Thames Television, U.K.

Drama: *The Black Velvet Gown*, Tyne Tees TV, U.K.

Children and young people: *The Fool of the World and the Flying Ship*, Cosgrove Hall Productions, U.K.

Directorate award: Henry Becton

Founder's award: Adrian Cowell

## 1991-92
### PRIMETIME PROGRAM AWARDS
Drama series: *Northern Exposure*, CBS

Comedy series: *Murphy Brown*, CBS

Mini-series: *A Woman Named Jackie*, NBC

Made-for-TV movie: *Miss Rose White, Hallmark Hall of Fame*, NBC

Variety, music or comedy series: *The Tonight Show*, NBC

Variety, music or comedy special: *Cirque Du Soleil II: A New Experience*, HBO

Informational series (area award): *MGM: When the Lion Roars*, TNT

Informational special (area award): *Abortion: Desperate Choices*, HBO

Animated program – one hour or less: *A Claymation Easter*, CBS

Children's program: *Mark Twain and Me*, Disney

Classical program in the performing arts: *Perlman in Russia*, PBS

---

Radio Days: Clear Channel Communications buys Jacor Communications for $4.4 billion.

PERFORMANCE, DIRECTING, AND WRITING

Actor in a drama series: Chrisopher Lloyd, *Avonlea*, Disney

Actress in a drama series: Dana Delany, *China Beach*, ABC

Actor in a comedy series: Craig T. Nelson, *Coach*, ABC

Actress in a comedy series: Candice Bergen, *Murphy Brown*, CBS

Actor in a mini-series or a special: Beau Bridges, *Without Warning, The James Brady Story*, HBO

Actress in a mini-series or a special: Gena Rowlands, *Face of a Stranger*, CBS

Supporting actor in a comedy series: Michael Jeter, *Evening Shade*, CBS

Supporting actress in a comedy series: Laurie Metcalf, *Roseanne*, ABC

Supporting actor in a drama series: Richard Dysart, *L.A. Law*, NBC

Supporting actress in a drama series: Valerie Mahaffey, *Northern Exposure*, CBS

Supporting actor in a mini-series or a special: Hume Cronyn, *Broadway Bound*, ABC

Supporting actress in a mini-series or a special: Amanda Plummer, *Miss Rose White, Hallmark Hall of Fame*, NBC

Directing in a drama series: Eric Laneuville, *I'll Fly Away*, NBC

Directing in a comedy series: Barnet Kellman, *Murphy Brown*, CBS

Directing in a mini-series or a special: Daniel Petrie, *Mark Twain and Me*, Disney

Writing in a drama series: Andrew Schneider, Diane Frolov, *Northern Exposure*, CBS

Writing in a comedy series: Elaine Pople, Larry Charles, *Seinfeld*, NBC

DAYTIME AWARDS

Drama series: *All My Children*, ABC

Actor in a drama series: Peter Bergman, *The Young and the Restless*, CBS

Actress in a drama series: Erika Slezak, *One Life to Live*, ABC

Drama series directing team: Michael Eilbaum, Bob Schwarz, Casey Childs, Susan Strickler, Carol Sedwick, Mary Madeiras, Janet Andrews, *Another World*, NBC

INTERNATIONAL AWARD WINNERS

Documentary: *To Sell a War*, Canadian Broadcasting

Arts documentary: *José Carreras: A Life Story*, Iambic Productions and Primetime Television, U.K.

Performing arts: *Pictures on the Edge*, Canadian Broadcasting

Popular arts: *Drop the Dead Donkey*, Channel Four, U.K.

Drama: *A Dangerous Man: Lawrence after Arabia*, Enigma Television, U.K.

Children and young people: *Beat That; Hairdressing*, Channel Four, U.K.

Directorate award: Silvio Berlusconi

Founder's award: Bill Cosby

# 1992-93
PRIMETIME PROGRAM AWARDS

Drama series: *Picket Fences*, CBS

Comedy series: *Seinfeld*, NBC

Mini-series: *Prime Suspect 2, Mystery!*, PBS

Made-for-TV movie: *Barbarians at the Gate*, HBO

Variety, music or comedy series: *Saturday Night Live*, NBC

Variety, music or comedy special: *Bob Hope: The First 90 Years*, NBC

Informational series (area award): *Healing and the Mind with Bill Moyers*, PBS

Informational special (area award): *Lucy and Desi: A Home Movie*, NBC

Animated program – one hour or less: *Batman: The Animated Series*, Fox

Children's program (area award): *Avonlea*, Disney; *Beethoven Lives Upstairs*, HBO

Classical program in the performing arts: *Tosca in the settings and at the times of Tosca*, PBS

PERFORMANCE, DIRECTING, AND WRITING

Actor in a drama series: Tom Skerritt, *Picket Fences*, CBS

Actress in a drama series: Kathy Baker, *Picket Fences*, CBS

Actor in a comedy series: Ted Danson, *Cheers*, NBC

Actress in a comedy series: Roseanne Arnold, *Roseanne*, ABC

Actor in a mini-series or a special: Robert Morse, *Tru, American Playhose*, PBS

Actress in a mini-series or a special: Holly Hunter, *The Positively True Adventures of the Alleged Texas Cheerleader-Murdering Mom*, HBO

Supporting actor in a comedy series: Michael Richards, *Seinfeld*, NBC

Supporting actress in a comedy series: Laurie Metcalf, *Roseanne*, ABC

Supporting actor in a drama series: Chad Lowe, *Life Goes on*, ABC

Supporting actress in a drama series: Mary Alice, *I'll Fly Away*, NBC

Supporting actor in a mini-series or a special: Beau Bridges, *The Positively True Adventures of the Alleged Texas Cheerleader-Murdering Mom*, HBO

Supporting actress in a mini-series or a special: Mary Tyler Moore, *Stolen Babies*, Lifetime

Guest actor in a drama series: Laurence Fishburne, *Tribeca*, Fox

Guest actress in a drama series: Elaine Stritch, *Law & Order*, NBC

Guest actor in a comedy series: David Clennon, *Dream On*, HBO

---

**...October 10...**
Antz earned over $40 million dollars after two weeks at the box office.

Guest actress in a comedy series: Tracey Ullman, *Love & War*, CBS

Directing in a drama series: Barry Levinson, *Homicide*, NBC

Directing in a comedy series: Betty Thomas, *Dream On*, HBO

Directing in a mini-series or a special: James Sadwith, *Sinatra*, CBS

Writing in a drama series: Tom Fontana, *Homicide*, NBC

Writing in a comedy series: Larry David, *Seinfeld*, NBC

### DAYTIME AWARDS

Drama series: *The Young and the Restless*, CBS

Actor in a drama series: David Canary, *All My Children*, ABC

Actress in a drama series: Linda Dano, *Another World*, NBC

Drama series directing team: Paul Lammers, Maria Wagner, Dan Hamilton, Charles C. Dyer, Larry Carpenter, Joel Aronowitz, Michael Kerner, *As the World Turns*, CBS

### INTERNATIONAL AWARD WINNERS

Documentary: *Disappearing World: We Are All Neighbours*, Granada TV, U.K.; *Monica and Jonas: The Face of the Informer State*, NHK Japan Broadcasting

Arts documentary: *The Wonderful Horrible Life of Leni Riefenstahl*, Omega Films GMBH and Nomad Films, Germany/Belgium

Performing arts: *Concerto*, Channel Four, U.K.

Popular arts: *Absolutely Fabulous*, BBC, U.K.; *Drop the Dead Donkey*, Channel Four, U.K.

Children and young people: *The Penknife*, NOS/AVRO/Bos Bros., The Netherlands

Drama: *Unnatural Pursuits*, BBC, U.K.

Directorate award: André Rousselet

Founder's award: Richard Dunn

## 1993-94

### PRIMETIME PROGRAM AWARDS

Drama series: *Picket Fences*, CBS

Comedy series: *Frasier*, NBC

Mini-series: *Prime Suspect 3, Mystery!*, PBS

Made-for-TV movie: *And the Band Played on*, HBO

Variety, music or comedy series: *Late Show with David Letterman*, CBS

Variety, music or comedy special: *The Kennedy Center Honors*, CBS

Informational series (area award): *Later with Bob Costas*, NBC

Informational special (area award): *I Am a Promise: The Children of Stanton Street Elementary School*, HBO

Animated program – one hour or less: *The Roman City*, PBS

Children's program: *Kids Killing Kids/Kids Saving Kids*, CBS, Fox

Cultural program: *Vladimir Horowitz: A Reminiscence*, PBS

### PERFORMANCE, DIRECTING, AND WRITING

Actor in a drama series: Dennis Franz, *NYPD Blue*, ABC

Actress in a drama series: Sela Ward, *Sister*, NBC

Actor in a comedy series: Kelsey Grammer, *Frasier*, NBC

Actress in a comedy series: Candice Bergen, *Murphy Brown*, CBS

Actor in a mini-series or a special: Hume Cronyn, *To Dance with the White Dog, Hallmark Hall of Fame*, NBC

Actress in a mini-series or a special: Kirstie Alley, *David's Mother*, CBS

Supporting actor in a drama series: Fyvish Finkel, *Picket Fences*, CBS

Supporting actress in a drama series: Leigh Taylor-Young, *Picket Fences*, CBS

Supporting actor in a comedy series: Michael Richards, *Seinfeld*, NBC

Supporting actress in a comedy series: Laurie Metcalf, *Roseanne*, ABC

Supporting actor in a mini-series or a special: Michael Goorijan, *David's Mother*, CBS

Supporting actress in a mini-series or a special: Cicely Tyson, *Oldest Living Confederate Widow Tells All*, CBS

Guest actor in a drama series: Richard Kiley, *Picket Fences*, CBS

Guest actress in a drama series: Faye Dunaway, *Columbo*, ABC

Guest actor in a comedy series: Martin Sheen, *Murphy Brown*, CBS

Guest actress in a comedy series: Eileen Heckart, *Love & War*, CBS

Directing in a drama series: Daniel Sackheim, *NYPD Blue*, ABC

Directing in a comedy series: James Burrows, *Frasier*, NBC

Directing in a mini-series or a special: John Frankenheimer, *Against the Wall*, HBO

Writing in a drama series: Ann Biderman, *NYPD Blue*, ABC

Writing in a comedy series: David Angel, Peter Casey, David Lee, *Frasier*, NBC

### DAYTIME AWARDS

Drama series: *All My Children*, ABC

Actor in a drama series: Michael Zaslow, *Guiding Light*, CBS

Actress in a drama series: Hillary B. Smith, *One Life to Live*, ABC

Drama series directing team: Bruce Barry, Jo Anne Sedwick, Irene Pace, Brian Mertes, John O'Connell, Matthew Lagle, Scott Riggs, Lisa Connor, *Guiding Light*, CBS

---

## INTERNATIONAL AWARD WINNERS

Documentary: *Life in the Freezer: The Big Freeze*, BBC, U.K.

Arts documentary: *Positive Art*, Australian Broadcasting

Performing arts: *Peter and the Wolf*, BBC, U.K.

Popular arts: *Absolutely Fabulous: Hospital*, BBC, U.K.; *Red Dwarf VI: Gunmen of the Apocalypse*, BBC, U.K.

Drama: *The Bullion Boys*, BBC, U.K.

Children and young people: *Insektors*, France 3, France

Directorate award: Helmut Thoma

Founder's award: Film on Four, Channel Four, U.K.

## 1994-95

### PRIMETIME PROGRAM AWARDS

Drama series: *NYPD Blue*, ABC

Comedy series: *Frasier*, NBC

Mini-series: *Joseph*, TNT

Made-for-TV movie: *Indictment: The McMartin Trial*, HBO

Variety, music or comedy series: *The Tonight Show with Jay Leno*, NBC

Variety, music or comedy special: *Barbra Streisand: The Concert*, HBO

Informational series (area award): *Baseball*, PBS; *TV Nation*, NBC

Informational special (area award): *Taxicab Confessions*, HBO; *U.S. Holocaust Memorial Museum: One Survivor Remembers*, HBO

Animated program – one hour or less: *The Simpsons*, Fox

Children's program (area award): *Going, Going, Almost Gone! Animals in Danger*, HBO

Cultural program: *Verdi's La Traviata with the New York City Opera, Live from Lincoln Center*, PBS

### PERFORMANCE, DIRECTING, AND WRITING

Actor in a drama series: Mandy Patinkin, *Chicago Hope*, CBS

Actress in a drama series: Kathy Baker, *Picket Fences*, CBS

Actor in a comedy series: Kelsey Grammer, *Frasier*, NBC

Actress in a comedy series: Candice Bergen, *Murphy Brown*, CBS

Actor in a mini-series or a special: Raul Julia, *The Burning Season*, HBO

Actress in a mini-series or a special: Glenn Close, *Serving in Silence: The Margarethe Cammermeyer Story*, NBC

Supporting actor in a drama series: Ray Walston, *Picket Fences*, CBS

Supporting actress in a drama series: Julianna Margulies, *ER*, NBC

Supporting actor in a comedy series: David Hyde Pierce, *Frasier*, NBC

Supporting actress in a comedy series: Christine Baranski, *Cybill*, CBS

Supporting actor in a mini-series or a special: Donald Sutherland, *Citizen X*, HBO

Supporting actress in a mini-series or a special: (tie) Judy Davis, *Serving in Silence: The Margarethe Cammermeyer Story*, NBC; Shirley Knight, *Indictment: The McMartin Trial*, HBO

Guest actor in a drama series: Paul Winfield, *Picket Fences*, CBS

Guest actress in a drama series: Shirley Knight, *NYPD Blue*, ABC

Guest actor in a comedy series: Carl Reiner, *Mad About You*, NBC

Guest actress in a comedy series: Cyndi Lauper, *Mad About You*, NBC

Directing in a drama series: Mimi Leder, *ER*, NBC

Directing in a comedy series: David Lee, *Frasier*, NBC

Directing in a mini-series or a special: John Frankenheimer, *The Burning Season*, HBO

Writing in a drama series: Lance A. Gentile, *ER*, NBC

Writing in a comedy series: Chuck Ranberg, Anne Flett-Giordano, *Frasier*, NBC

### DAYTIME AWARDS

Drama series: *General Hospital*, ABC

Actor in a drama series: Justin Deas, *Guiding Light*, CBS

Actress in a drama series: Erika Slezak, *One Life to Live*, ABC

Drama series directing team: Christopher Goutman, Henry Kaplan, Conal O'Brien, James A. Baffico, Barbara Martin Simmons, Shirley Simmons, Robin Maizes, Sybil Costello, *All My Children*, ABC

### INTERNATIONAL AWARD WINNERS

Documentary: *Anne Frank Remembered*, BBC, U.K.; *Contre l'oubli (Lest We Forget)*, France 2, France

Arts documentary: *Kenzaburo Oe's Long Road to Fatherhood*, NHK Japan Broadcasting

Performing arts: *Carmen*, SVT Channel 1, Sweden

Popular arts: *Don't Forget Your Toothbrush*, Channel Four, U.K.

Drama: *The Politician's Wife*, Channel Four, U.K.

Children and young people: *Little Lord Fauntleroy*, BBC, U.K.; *Wise up*, Channel Four, U.K.

Directorate award: John Birt

Founder's award: Don Hewitt

## 1995-96

### PRIMETIME PROGRAM AWARDS

Drama series: *ER*, NBC

Comedy series: *Frasier*, NBC

Mini-series: *Gulliver's Travels*, NBC

Made-for-TV movie: *Truman*, HBO

Variety, music or comedy series: *Dennis Miller Live*, HBO

Variety, music or comedy special: *The Kennedy Center Honors*, CBS

Informational series (area award): *Time Life's Lost*

*Civilizations*, NBC
Informational special (area award): *Survivors of the Holocaust*, TBS
Animated program – one hour or less: *A Pinky & the Brain Christmas Special*, WB
Children's program (area award): *Peter and the Wolf*, ABC
Cultural music/dance program: *Itzhak Perlman: In the Fiddler's House, Great Performances*, PBS

**PERFORMANCE, DIRECTING, AND WRITING**

Actor in a drama series: Dennis Franz, *NYPD Blue*, ABC
Actress in a drama series: Kathy Baker, *Picket Fences*, CBS
Actor in a comedy series: John Lithgow, *3rd Rock from the Sun*, NBC
Actress in a comedy series: Helen Hunt, *Mad About You*, NBC
Actor in a mini-series or a special: Alan Rickman, *Rasputin*, HBO
Actress in a mini-series or a special: Helen Mirren, *Prime Suspect: Scent of Darkness*, PBS
Supporting actor in a drama series: Ray Walston, *Picket Fences*, CBS
Supporting actress in a drama series: Tyne Daly, *Christy*, CBS
Supporting actor in a comedy series: Rip Torn, *The Larry Sanders Show*, HBO
Supporting actress in a comedy series: Julia Louis-Dreyfus, *Seinfeld*, NBC
Supporting actor in a mini-series or a special: Tom Hulce, *The Heidi Chronicles*, TNT
Supporting actress in a mini-series or a special: Greta Scacchi, *Rasputin*, HBO
Guest actor in a drama series: Peter Boyle, *The X-Files*, Fox
Guest actress in a drama series: Amanda Plummer, *The Outer Limits*, Showtime
Guest actor in a comedy series: Tim Conway, *Coach*, ABC
Guest actress in a comedy series: Betty White, *The John Larroquette Show*, NBC
Directing in a drama series: Jeremy Kagan, *Chicago Hope*, CBS
Directing in a comedy series: Michael Lembeck, *Friends*, NBC
Directing in a mini-series or a special: John Frankenheimer, *Andersonville*, TNT
Writing in a drama series: David Morgan, *The X-Files*, Fox
Writing in a comedy series:Joe Keenan, Christopher Lloyd, Rob Greenberg, Jack Burditt, Chuck Ranberg, Anne Flett-Giordano, Linda Morris, Vic Rauseo, *Frasier*, NBC

**DAYTIME AWARDS**

Drama series: *General Hospital*, ABC
Actor in a drama series: Charles Keating,

*Another World*, NBC
Actress in a drama series: Erika Slezak, *One Life to Live*, ABC
Directing in a drama series: Heather Hill, Frank Pacelli, Mike Denney, Kathryn Foster, Betty Rothenberg, Sally McDonald, Dan Brumett, Robin Masick Phillips, Randal Hill, Don Jacob, Bob Welsh, *The Young and the Restless*, CBS

**INTERNATIONAL AWARD WINNERS**

Documentary: *The Pelican of Ramzan the Red*, France; *People's Century-1933: Master Race*, BBC, U.K.; *The Saga of Life: The Unknown World*, Sveriges Television, Sweden
Arts documentary: *The House*, BBC, U.K.
Performing arts: *September Songs: The Music of Kurt Weill*, Canada
Popular arts: *A Close Shave*, BBC, U.K.
Drama: *La colline aux mille enfants*, The Netherlands
Children and young people: *Newsround Extra*, BBC, U.K.; *Wise up* Channel Four, U.K.
Directorate award: Herbert Granath
Founder's award: Reg Grundy

# 1996-97

**PRIMETIME PROGRAM AWARDS**

Drama series: *Law & Order*, NBC
Comedy series: *Frasier*, NBC
Mini-series: *Prime Suspect 5: Errors of Judgement*, PBS
Made-for-TV movie: *Miss Evers' Boys*, HBO
Variety, music or comedy series: *Tracey Takes on...*, HBO
Variety, music or comedy special: *Chris Rock: Bring the Pain*, HBO
Informational series (area award): *A&E Biography*, A&E; *The Great War and the Shaping of the 20th Century*, PBS
Informational special (area award): *Without Pity: A Film about Abilities*, HBO
Animated program – one hour or less: *The Simpsons*, Fox
Children's program (area award): *How Do You spell God?*, HBO
Cultural music/dance program: *Puccini's La Bohème with the New York City Opera*, PBS

**PERFORMANCE, DIRECTING, AND WRITING**

Actor in a drama series: Dennis Franz, *NYPD Blue*, ABC
Actress in a drama series: Gillian Anderson, *The X-Files*, Fox
Actor in a comedy series: John Lithgow, *3rd Rock from the Sun*, NBC
Actress in a comedy series: Helen Hunt, *Mad about You*, NBC
Actor in a mini-series or a special: Armand Assante, *Gotti*, NBC
Actress in a mini-series or a special: Alfre Woodard, *Miss Evers Boys*, HBO

---

**... October 13 ...**
Jodie Foster will get a $15 million paycheck for **Anna and the King**, a retelling of **The King and I**.

Supporting actor in a drama series: Hector Elizondo, *Chicago Hope*, CBS

Supporting actress in a drama series: Kim Delaney, *NYPD Blue*, ABC

Supporting actor in a comedy series: Michael Richards, *Seinfeld*, NBC

Supporting actress in a comedy series: Kristen Johnston, *3rd Rock from the Sun*, NBC

Supporting actor in a mini-series or a special: Beau Bridges, *The Second Civil War*, HBO

Supporting actress in a mini-series or a special: Diana Rigg, *Rebecca*, PBS

Guest actor in a drama series: Pruitt Taylor Vince, *Murder One*, ABC

Guest actress in a drama series: Dianne Wiest, *Avonlea*, Disney

Guest actor in a comedy series: Mel Brooks, *Mad about You*, NBC

Guest actress in a comedy series: Carol Burnett, *Mad about You*, NBC

Directing in a drama series: Mark Tinker, *NYPD Blue*, ABC

Directing in a comedy series: David Lee, *Frasier*, NBC

Directing in a variety or music program: Don Mischer, *Centennial Olympic Games: Opening Ceremonies*, NBS

Directing in a mini-series or a special: Andrei Konchalovsky, *The Odyssey*, NBC

Writing in a drama series: David Milch, Stephen Gaghan, Michael R. Perry, *NYPD Blue*, ABC

Writing in a comedy series: Ellen DeGeneres, Mark Driscoll, Davba Savel, Tracey Newman, Jomathan Stark, *Ellen*, ABC

Writing in a variety or music program: Chris Rock, *Chris Rock: Bring the Pain*, HBO

Writing in a mini-series or a special: Horton Foote, *William Faulkner's Old Man, Hallmark Hall of Fame*, CBS

**DAYTIME AWARDS**

Drama series: *General Hospital*, ABC

Actor in a drama series: Justin Deas, *Guiding the Light*, CBS

Actress in a drama series: Jes Walton, *The Young and the Restless*, CBS

Supporting actor in a drama series: Ian Buchanan, *The Bold and the Beautiful*, CBS

Supporting actress in a drama series: Michelle Stafford, *The Young and the Restless*, CBS

Drama series directing team: Heather Hill, Frank Pacelli, Mike Denney, Kathryn Foster, Betty Rothenberg, Sall McDonald, Dan Brumett, Robin Masick Phillips, Randal Hill, Donald Jacob, *The Young and the Restless*, CBS

Drama series writing team: Agnes Nixon, Lorraine Broderick, Millee Taggart, Hal Corley, Frederick Johnson, Jeff Beldner, Christina Covino, Courtney Simon, Karen L. Lewis, Elizabeth Smith, Michelle Patrick, Bettina F. Bradbury, Judith Donato, Kathleen Klein, Jane Owen Murphy, *All My Children*, ABC

**SPECIAL AWARDS**

NATAS trustees award: Sumner Redstone

ATAS president's award: *Miss Evers' Boys*, HBO

**INTERNATIONAL AWARD WINNERS**

Drama: *Crossing the Floor*, Channel Four (U.K.)

Documentary: *Jerrie & Louise*, CBC (Canada)

Arts documentary: Dancing for Dollars: *The Bolshoi in Las Vegas*, Channel Four (U.K.)

Children's: *Wise up*, Channel Four (U.K.)

Performance arts: *Enter Achilles*, BBC (U.K.)

Popular arts: *Lieberg Zaps Himself*, TROS (Netherlands)

## 1997-98

Comedy series: *Frasier*, NBC

Drama series: *The Practice*, ABC

Mini-series: *From the Earth to the Moon*, HBO

Telefilm: *Don King: Only in America*, HBO

Lead actor in a comedy series: Kelsey Grammer, *Frasier*, NBC

Lead actress in a comedy series: Helen Hunt, *Mad About You*, NBC

Lead actor in a drama series: Andre Braugher, *Homicide: Life on the Street*, NBC

Lead actress in a drama series: Christine Lahti, *Chicago Hope*, CBS

Supporting actor in a comedy series: David Hyde Pierce, *Frasier*, NBC

Supporting actress in a comedy series: Lisa Kudrow, *Friends*, NBC

Supporting actor in a drama series: Gordon Clapp, *NYPD Blue*, ABC

Supporting actress in a drama series: Camryn Manheim, *The Practice*, ABC

Lead actor in a mini-series or a movie: Gary Sinise, *George Wallace*, TNT

Lead actress in a mini-series or a movie: Ellen Barkin, *Before Women Had Wings*, ABC

Guest actor in a comedy series: Mel Brooks, *Mad about You*, NBC

Guest actress in a comedy series: Emma Thompson, *Ellen*, ABC

Guest actor in a drama series: John Larroquette, *The Practice*, ABC

Guest actress in a drama series: Cloris Leachman, *Promised Land*, CBS

Supporting actor in a mini-series or a movie: George C. Scott, *12 Angry Men*, Showtime

Supporting actress in a mini-series or a movie: Mare Winningham, *George Wallace*, TNT

Performance in a variety or music program: Billy Crystal, *The 70th Annual Academy Awards*, ABC

Animated program (one hour or less): *The Simpsons* (*Trash of the Titans*) Fox

Variety, music or comedy series: *Late Show with David Letterman*, CBS

Variety, music or comedy special: *The 1997 Tony Awards*, CBS

Directing for a comedy series: Todd Holland, *The Larry Sanders Show*, HBO

Directing for a drama series: Mark Tinker, *Brooklyn South*, CBS; Paris Barclay, *NYPD Blue*, ABC

Directing for a variety or music program: Louis J. Horvitz, *The 70th Annual Academy Awards*, ABC

Directing for a mini-series or a movie: John Frankenheimer, *George Wallace*, TNT

Writing for a comedy series: Peter Tolan, Garry Shandling, *The Larry Sanders Show*, HBO

Writing for a drama series: Nicholas Wootton, David Milch, Bill Clark, *NYPD Blue*, ABC

Writing for a variety or music program: Eddie Feldmann (head writer), Dennis Miller, David Feldman, Leah Krinsky, Jim Hanna, David Weiss, Jose Arroyo, *Dennis Miller Live*, HBO

Writing for a mini-series or a movie: Kario Salem, *Don King: Only in America*, HBO

Classical music-dance program: *Yo-Yo Ma Inspired by Bach* (PBS)

Children's program (area award: possibility of one or more than one award): *Muppets Tonight*, Disney Channel, *Nick News Special Edition – What Are You Staring at?*, Nickelodeon

Nonfiction special (area award: possibility of one or more than one award): *Discovery Sunday – Vietnam POWs: Stories of Survival*, Discovery Channel

Nonfiction series (area award: possibility of one or more than one award): *The American Experience*, PBS

Cinematography for a series: Constantine Makris, *Law & Order* (*Stalker*), NBC

Cinematography for a mini-series or a movie: Eric Van Haren Noman, *What the Deaf Man Heard*, CBS

Single-camera picture editing for a series: Heather MacDougall, *The X-Files* (*Kill Switch*), Fox

Single-camera picture editing for a mini-series or a movie: Eric Sears, *Gia*, HBO

Multicamera picture editing for a series: Ron Volk, *Frasier* (*Room Service*), NBC

Multicamera picture editing for a mini-series, movie or a special: Richard Daws, Jason Porthouse, *Stomp out Loud*, HBO

Music composition for a series (dramatic underscore): Christophe Beck, *Buffy the Vampire Slayer* (*Becoming, Part1*), WB

Music composition for a mini-series or a movie (dramatic underscore): Bruce Boughton, *Glory & Honor*, TNT

Music direction: Bill Conti, *The 70th Annual Academy Awards*, ABC

Music and lyrics: Alf Clausen, music; Ken Keeler, lyrics, *The Simpsons* (*You're Checkin' in – a Musical Tribute to the Betty Ford Center*), Fox

Main title theme music: Maribeth Derry, Tom Snow, Robbie Buchana, Richard Barton Lewis, *Fame L.A.*, syndicated

Art direction for a series: Graeme Murray, production designer; Greg Lioewen, art director; Shirley Inget, set decorator, *The X-Files* (*The Post-Modern Prometheus*), Fox

Art direction for a mini-series or a movie: Roger Hall, production designer; John King, supervising art director; Mike Boone, art director; Karen Brookes, set decorator, *Merlin (Part 1)*, NBC

Art direction for a variety or music program: Radny Ser, production designer; Edward L. Rubin, art director; Julie Kaye Fanton, set decorator, *Rodgers & Hammerstein's Cinderella*, ABC

Costume design for a series: Dan Moore, *The Magnificent Seven* (*Working Girls*), CBS

Costume design for a mini-series or a movie: Ann Hollowood, *Merlin (Part 1)*, NBC

Costume design for a variety or music program: Jane Ruhm, *Tracey Takes on… Sports*, HBO and LuEllyn Harper, costume supervisor; Monique Long, key costumer, *NewsRadio* (*Sinking Ship*), NBC

Costuming for a mini-series, movie or a special (area award: possibility of one or no award): Amy Stofsky, costume supervisor, *The Pentagon Wars*, HBO

Sound editing for a series: Walter Newman, supervising sound editor; Darren Wright, Rick Camera, sound editors; Darleen Stoker-Kageyama, Cathy Flynn-Morris, dialog editors; Tom Harris, ADR editor; Michael D. Dittrick, music editor; Casey Crabtree, James Bailey, Foley artists, *ER* (*Exodus*), NBC

Sound editing for a mini-series, movie or a special: Michael Graham, supervising sound editor; Greg Schorer, co-supervising sound editor; Kristi Johns, Suzanne Angel, ADR editors; Bill Bell, Mark Friedgen, Bob Costanza, Rob Webber, Gary Macheel, Rick Steele, Lou Thomas, Adriane Marfiak, Anton Holden, Michael Lyle, David Eichorn, Marke Steele, Tim Terusa, Rusty Tinsley, sound editors; Kim Naves, music editor; Tim Chilton, Jill Schachne, Foley artists, *Rough Riders (Part 2)*, TNT

Sound mixing for a comedy series or a special: Paul Lewis, production mixer; Nello Torri, Kurt Kassulke, Peter R. Kelsey, re-recording mixers, *Ally McBeal* (*Boy of the World*), Fox

---

**... October 15 ...**
Tom Wolfe's **A Man in Full** nominated for National Book Award.

Sound mixing for a variety of music series or a special: Edward J. Greene, production mixer; Tom Vicari, music mixer; Robert Douglass, Patrick Baltzell, sound mixers, *The 70th Annual Academy Awards*, ABC

Sound mixing for a drama series: Russell Fager, production mixer; Rusty Russell Smith, William Freesh, re-recording mixers, *Chicago Hope* (*Brain Salad Surgery*), CBS

Sound mixing for a drama, mini-series or a movie: Russell Williams II, production mixer; David E. Fluhr, Adam Jenkins, re-recording mixers, *12 Angry Men*, Showtime

Casting for a series: Lou Digiaimo, Pat Moran, Brett Goldstein, *Homicide: Life on the Street*, NBC

Casting for a mini-series or a movie: Meg Liberman, Marc Hirschfeld, Sharon Klein, Mark Fincannon, Lisa Mae Wells Fincannon, Craig Fincannon, Deborah Brown, *From the Earth to the Moon*, HBO

Choreography: Marguerite Derricks, Peggy Holmes, *Fame L.A.* (Pilot), syndicated

Lighting direction (electronic) for a comedy series: Donald A. Morgan, *Home Improvement* (*A Night to Dismember*), ABC

Lighting direction (electronic) for a drama series, variety series, mini-series, movie or a special: Robert Dickinson, lighting designer; Andy O'Reilly, Matt Ford, Bob Barnhart, lighting directors, *The 70th Annual Academy Awards*, ABC

Special visual effects for a series: Pedro Pires, *Yo-Yo Ma Inspired by Bach* (*The Sound of the Carceri*) (PBS)

Special visual effects for a mini-series or a movie: Tim Webber, visual-effects supervising designer; Stefan Lange, visual-effects cameraman; Matthew Cope, visua-effects shoot coordinator; Richard Conway, physical special-effects supervisor; Tim Greenwood, George Roper, Murray Butler, Angus Wilson, Pedro Sabrosa, William Bartlett, Avtar Bains, visual-effects artists, *Merlin* (*Part 1*), NBC

Technical direction/camera/video for a series: Gene Crowe, technical director; Dave Chameides, Hank Geving, Larry Heider, Bob Hieghton, Don Lenzer, Bill Philbin, camera; Chuck Reilly, John O'Brien, video, *ER* (*Ambush*), NBC

Technical direction/camera/video for a special: Emmett Loughran, technical director; Miguel Armstrong, Juan Barrera, Jim Covello, John Feher, Manny Gutierrez, Jake Ostroff, David Smith, Ron Washburn, camera; William Steinberg, video, *The Metropolitan Opera Presents Carmen*, PBS

Makeup for a series: Todd A. McIntosh, John Vulich, John Maldonado, John Wheaton, Gerald Quist, Margi Latinopoulos, Dayne Johnson, Alan Friedman, Carig Reardon, Michael Blake, Robin Beauchesne, Brigette Myre-Ellis, Mark Shostrom, *Buffy the Vampire Slayer* (*Surprise/Innocence*), WB

Makeup for a mini-series, movie or a special: Aileen Seaton, Mark Coulier, *Merlin*, NBC

Hairstyling for a series: Audree Futterman, *Tracey Takes on... Smoking*, HBO

Hairstyling for a mini-series, movie or special: Vicky Phillips, Lynda Gurasich, *From the Earth to the Moon*, HBO

Main title design: Kasumi Mihori, Billy Pittard, Ed Sullivan, *The Wonderful World of Disney*, ABC

Achievement in nonfiction programming – Cinematography: Richard Chisolm, Paul Goldsmith, Buddy Squires, Jerry Cotts, Nick Caloyianis, Jon Else, *National Geographic Special: America's Endangered Species: Don't Say Good-bye*, NBC and Jim Dutcher, *Wolves at Our Door*, Discovery Channel

Achievement in nonfiction programming – Picture editing: Michael Bloecher, William Haugse, *Assassinated: The Last Days of Kennedy and King*, TBS Superstation; Sam Pollard, *4 Little Girls*, HBO; Arnold Glassman, *Frank Capra's American Dream*, American Movie Classics; Lenny Feinstein, *National Geographic Special: America's Endangered Species: Don't Say Good-bye*, NBC; Amanda Zinoman, *Trauma: Life in the ER* (*Wrong Place, Wrong Time*), TLC; Mike Harvey, Graham Knight, *Vietnam POWs: Stories of Survival*, Discovery Channel

Achievement in nonfiction programming – Sound editing: Patrick M. Griffith, Lisa Hannan, *National Geographic Explorer* (*Rat*), TBS Superstation

Achievement in nonfiction programming – Sound mixing: Jamie Dutcher, *Wolves at Our Door*, Discovery Channel

Commerical: *Apple Computer – Think Different*, TBWA Chiat/Day, ad agency

Individual achievement in animation: Eric Radomski, *Spawn*, HBO

Voiceover performance: Hank Azaria, *The Simpsons*, Fox

**INTERNATIONAL AWARD WINNERS**

Documentary: *Exile in Sarajevo*, Exile Prods, Australia

Arts documentary: *The War Symphonies: Shostakovich Against Stalin*, Rhombus Media/ZDF/Arte/IDTV, Netherlands

Performing arts: *The Judas Tree*, Landseer/Channel Four, U.K.

Popular arts: *The Vicar of Dibley: Love and Marriage*, Tiger Aspects Prods/BBC, U.K.

Drama: *The Tattooed Widow*, SVT, Sweden

Children's and Young People: *Blabbermouth and Sticky*

# Index to TV reviews in *Variety*: 1998

# Theater

Exploring the yellowing pages of *Variety*'s earliest issues, it's evident that theater (and its cheeky cousin, vaudeville) dominated the fledgling world of entertainment during the first two decades of the century. On the one side there was the straight play, opening on Broadway – the "legitimate" theater (quickly dubbed "Legit" in *Variety*'s slanguage). And beyond the fringe, as it were, lay the world of musical theater, descending all the way down to peripheral music halls, old showboats on the Mississippi, and so on – not necessarily "illegitimate" but simply outside the *Variety* bailiwick.

Throughout the century, *Variety* has stayed loyal to the stage, reviewing most of the new productions on Broadway and in London's West End, tracking openings in other major cities, and recording the grosses of shows as they hit "the road" across the United States. As with our film reviews, notices are aimed at a professional readership, but this does not prevent them from aspiring to a serious artistic assessment of the better productions.

This section includes the Tonys and other leading stage awards, some notable Broadway and West End statistics, openings and closings during 1998, and an index to all *Variety*'s theater reviews during the past year.

## Broadway's leggiest performers

| Show | Season | Perfs | Show | Season | Perfs |
|------|--------|-------|------|--------|-------|
| Cats * | 82-83 | 6,773 | Man of La Mancha | 65-66 | 2,328 |
| A Chorus Line | 75-76 | 6,137 | Abie's Irish Rose | 21-22 | 2,327 |
| Oh! Calcutta! | 76-77 | 5,852 | Oklahoma! | 42-43 | 2,212 |
| Les Misérables * | 86-87 | 4,845 | Beauty and the Beast * | 93-94 | 1,962 |
| The Phantom of the Opera * | 87-88 | 4,585 | Pippin | 72-73 | 1,944 |
| 42nd Street | 80-81 | 3,486 | South Pacific | 48-49 | 1,925 |
| Grease | 72-73 | 3,388 | The Magic Show | 73-74 | 1,920 |
| Fiddler on the Roof | 64-65 | 3,242 | Deathtrap | 77-78 | 1,792 |
| Life With Father | 39-40 | 3,224 | Gemini | 76-77 | 1,788 |
| Miss Saigon * | 90-91 | 3,196 | Harvey | 44-45 | 1,775 |
| Tobacco Road | 33-34 | 3,182 | Dancin' | 77-78 | 1,774 |
| Hello, Dolly! | 63-64 | 2,844 | La Cage aux Folles | 83-84 | 1,761 |
| My Fair Lady | 55-56 | 2,717 | | | |
| Annie | 76-77 | 2,377 | | | |

*\* still running*

*Figures as of Dec. 31, 1998*

## Longest-running shows in London

1. *The Mousetrap* (whodunnit): 46 years, 1 month
2. *Cats* (musical): 17 years, 7 months
3. *Starlight Express* (musical): 14 years, 9 months
4. *Les Misérables* (musical): 13 years, 2 months
5. *The Phantom of the Opera* (musical): 12 years, 2 months
6. *Blood Brothers* (musical): 10 years, 5 months
7. *The Woman in Black* (thriller): 9 years, 10 months
8. *Miss Saigon* (musical): 9 years, 3 months
9. *Buddy* (musical): 9 years, 2 months
10. *Grease* (musical): 5 years, 5 months

*As of Dec. 1998*

# Broadway productions opening and closing: 1998

*Patti LaBelle on Broadway* (Concert) Opened Jan. 13 at St. James Theater; closed after 12 performances (limited engagement).

*Ragtime* (Musical with book by Terrence McNally, music by Stephen Flaherty and lyrics by Lynn Ahrens, based on the novel by E.L. Doctorow; directed by Frank Galati) Opened Jan. 18 at Ford Center for the Performing Arts.

*The Capeman* (Musical with music by Paul Simon, book and lyrics by Simon and Derek Walcott; directed and choreographed by Mark Morris) Opened Jan. 29 at Marquis Theater; closed March 28 after 59 previews, 68 performances.

*Freak* (Solo play written and performed by John Leguizamo) Opened Feb. 12 at Cort Theater; closed July 4 after 23 previews, 143 performances.

*Art* (Play by Yasmina Reza, translated by Christopher Hampton; directed by Matthew Warchus) Opened March 1 at Royale Theater.

*The Sound of Music* (Musical revival directed by Susan H. Schulman) Opened March 12 at Martin Beck Theater.

*Cabaret* (Musical revival directed by Sam Mendes) Opened March 19 at the Kit Kat Klub.

*Ah, Wilderness!* (Play revival directed by Daniel Sullivan) Opened March 18 at Vivian Beaumont Theater; closed after 54 performances (subscription engagement).

*The Deep Blue Sea* (Play revival directed by Mark Lamos) Opened March 26 at Roundabout Stage Right; closed May 17 after 29 previews, 61 performances (subscription engagement).

*The Chairs* (Play revival directed by Simon McBurney) Opened April 1 at John Golden Theater; closed June 14 after 9 previews, 75 performances.

*Golden Child* (Play by David Henry Hwang; directed by James Lapine) Opened April 2 at Longacre Theater; closed May 31 after 11 previews, 69 performances.

*Wait Until Dark* (Play revival directed by Leonard Foglia) Opened April 5 at Brooks Atkinson Theater; closed June 28 after 12 previews, 97 performances.

*The Herbal Bed* (Play by Peter Whelan; directed by Michael Attenborough) Opened April 16 at Eugene O'Neill Theater; closed April 26 after 23 previews, 10 performances.

*Honour* (Play by Joanna Murray-Smith; directed by Gerald Gutierrez) Opened April 26 at Belasco Theater; closed June 14 after 28 previews, 57 performances.

*The Beauty Queen of Leenane* (Play by Martin McDonagh; directed by Garry Hynes) Opened April 23 at Walter Kerr Theater.

*High Society* (Musical with music and lyrics by Cole Porter, book by Arthur Kopit, based on the play *The Philadelphia Story* by Philip Barry and the Turner Entertainment Co. motion picture *High Society*; additional lyrics by Susan Birkenhead; directed by Christopher Renshaw) Opened April 27 at St. James Theater; closed Aug. 30 after 28 previews, 144 performances.

*The Judas Kiss* (Play by David Hare; directed by Richard Eyre) Opened April 29 at Broadhurst Theater; closed Aug. 28 after 7 previews, 102 performances.

*Side Man* (Play by Warren Leight; directed by Michael Mayer) Opened June 25 at Roundabout Stage Right Theater.

*Twelfth Night* (Shakespeare revival directed by Nicholas Hytner) Opened July 16 at Vivian Beaumont Theater; closed Aug. 30 after 30 previews, 53 performances (subscription engagement).

*An Evening With Jerry Herman* (Revue with music and lyrics by Herman; directed by Lee Roy Reams) Opened July 28 at Booth Theater; closed Aug. 23 after 13 previews, 28 performances.

*Jerry Seinfeld: I'm Telling You for the Last Time — Live on Broadway* (Solo show) Opened Aug. 8 at Broadhurst Theater; closed Aug. 9 after 10 performances.

*Colin Quinn: An Irish Wake* (Solo show) Opened Aug. 27 at Helen Hayes Theater; closed Sept. 20 after 22 performances.

*Swan Lake* (Ballet directed and choreographed by Matthew Bourne) Opened Oct. 8 at Neil Simon Theater.

*More to Love: A Big Fat Comedy* (Play by Rob Bartlett; directed by Jack O'Brien) Opened Oct. 15 at Eugene O'Neill Theater; closed Oct. 17 after 17 previews and 4 performances.

*Mandy Patinkin in Concert: Mamaloshen* (Solo concert) Opened Oct. 13 at Belasco Theater.

*Aznavour on Broadway* (Solo concert) Opened Oct. 21 at Marquis Theater.

*Footloose* (Musical adapted by Dean Pitchford and Walter Bobbie from the original screenplay by Pitchford, with music by Tom Snow and lyrics by Pitchford, including songs by Eric Carmen, Sammy Hagar, Kenny Loggins and Jim Steinman; directed by Walter Bobbie) Opened Oct. 22 at Richard Rodgers Theater.

**. . . October 19 . . .**
Oliver Stone to direct George Custer drama **Marching to Valhalla** for New Line.

*Getting and Spending* (Play by Michael J. Chepiga; directed by John Tillinger) Opened Oct. 25 at Helen Hayes Theater.

*Sandra Bernhard: I'm Still Here... Damn It!* (Solo show) Opened Nov. 5 at Booth Theater; closed Jan. 3 after 12 previews, 51 performances.

*Little Me* (Musical revival directed by Rob Marshall) Opened Nov. 12 at Roundabout Stage Right Theater (subscription engagement).

*On the Town* (Musical revival directed by George C. Wolfe) Opened Nov. 21 at Gershwin Theater.

*Fool Moon* (Specialty show by Bill Irwin and David Shiner) Opened Nov. 22 at Brooks Atkinson Theater; closed Jan. 3 after

6 previews, 49 performances.

*Peter Pan* (Musical revival directed by Glenn Casale) Opened Nov. 23 at Marquis Theater; closed limited engagement Jan. 3 after 5 previews, 48 performances.

*Electra* (Play revival directed by David Leveaux) Opened Dec. 3 at Ethel Barrymore Theater.

*The Blue Room* (Play by David Hare, adapted from Arthur Schnitzler's *Reigen*; directed by Sam Mendes) Opened Dec. 13 at Cort Theater.

*Parade* (Musical with music and lyrics by Jason Robert Brown, book by Alfred Uhry; directed by Harold Prince) Opened Dec. 17 at Vivian Beaumont Theater.

# London West End productions opening and closing: 1998

## Openings

*2.5 Minute Ride* (Barbican Pit) 21 July
*Alan Davies* (Duchess) 3 March
*Alarms and Excursions* (Gielgud) 14 Sept.
*Amadeus* (Old Vic) 21 Oct.
*Amy's View* (Aldwych) 14 Jan.
*Ann Hompton Callaway and Liz Callaway in Sibli...* (Donmar Warehouse) 10 Aug.
*Annie* (Victoria Palace) 30 Sept.
*Antony and Cleopatra* (National Olivier) 20 Oct.
*As You Like It* (Shakespeare's Globe) 28 May
*Barbara Cook* (Donmar Warehouse) 24 Aug.
*Betrayal* (National Lyttelton) 24 Nov.
*The Best of Times* (Vaudeville) 17 Nov.
*Bib & Bob* (Criterion) 28 April
*Bip* (Old Vic) 17 May
*Black Comedy* (Comedy) 22 April
*The Blue Room* (Donmar Warehouse) 22 Sept.
*Boogie Nights* (Savoy) 20 Oct.
*The Bowler Hat* (Old Vic) 15 May
*Brassed Off* (National Olivier) 8 June
*Brief Lives* (Duchess) 23 March
*Britannicus* (Albery) 4 Nov.
*The Bullet* (Donmar Warehouse) 8 April
*Camino Real* (Young Vic) 3 March
*Cleansed* (Duke of York's) 6 May
*Cleo, Camping, Emmanuelle and Dick* (National Lyttelton) 21 Sept.
*Closer* (Lyric) 31 March
*The Collection* (Donmar Warehouse) 13 May
*Copenhagen* (National Cottesloe) 28 May
*Cymbeline* (Barbican) 20 Jan.
*The Day I Stood Still* (National Cottesloe) 22 Jan.
*The Dead Monkey* (Whitehall) 29 Sept.
*Do You Come Here Often?* (Vaudeville) 8 Jan.

*Doctor Dolittle* (Labatt's Apollo) 14 July
*Elton John's Glasses* (Queens) 10 June
*An Enemy of the People* (National Olivier) 28 April
*Everyman* (Barbican Pit) 16 Feb.
*Fame* (Prince of Wales) 15 Oct.
*Filumena* (Piccadilly) 8 Oct.
*Flight* (National Olivier) 12 Feb.
*Gentlemen Prefer Blondes* (Open Air) 23 July
*The Gift* (Barbican Pit) 23 June
*Girls' Night out* (Victoria Palace) 25 Feb.
*Guiding Star* (National Cottesloe) 11 Nov.
*Hamlet* (Barbican) 28 Aug.
*Harlem Gospel Singers* (Peacock) 4 Nov.
*Haroun and the Sea of Stories* (National Cottesloe) 1 Oct.
*Henry VIII* (Young Vic) 18 Feb.
*The Honest Whore* (Shakespeare's Globe) 13 Aug.
*How I Learned to Drive* (Donmar Warehouse) 24 June
*A Huey P Newton Story* (Barbican Pit) 6 Oct.
*Human Being (P)* (Arts) 7 March
*The Iceman Cometh* (Old Vic) 19 June
*An Ideal Husband* (Albery) 3 March
*An Ideal Husband* (Haymarket) 25 Aug.
*An Ideal Husband* (Lyric) 2 Nov.
*Imelda Stanton and Her Big Band* (Donmar Warehouse) 1 Sept.
*In a Little World of Our Own* (Donmar Warehouse) 4 March
*Into the Woods* (Donmar Warehouse) 16 Nov.
*The Invention of Love* (Haymarket) 3 Nov.
*Issey Ogata* (Lyric) 25 Feb.
*Jackie* (Queens) 22 Oct.
*Jackie Mason's – Much Ado about Everything* (Playhouse) 9 Nov.
*Jasper Carrott in Concert* (Haymarket) 12 Oct.
*Jeff Green* (Apollo) 23 Nov.
*Jesus, My Boy* (Apollo) 10 Dec.

*The Judas Kiss* (Playhouse) 19 March
*The Jungle Book* (Open Air) 4 Aug.
*Kafka's Dick* (Piccadilly) 19 Nov.
*Kat and the Kings* (Vaudeville) 23 March
*A Kind of Alaska* (Donmar Warehouse) 13 May
*Kit and the Widow Rummaging for Fluff* (Vaudeville) 9 Jan.
*Krapp's Last Tape* (Barbican Pit) 10 March
*The Lady Boys of Bangkok* (Queens) 3 Sept.
*Lee Evans* (Apollo) 21 Sept.
*A Letter of Resignation* (Savoy) 20 April
*The London Cuckolds* (National Lyttleton) 24 March
*Loot* (Vaudeville) 12 Aug.
*Love upon the Throne* (Comedy) 10 Nov.
*The Lover* (Donmar Warehouse) 13 May
*Love's Fire* (Barbican Pit) 21 May
*A Mad World, My Masters* (Shakespeare's Globe) 13 Aug.
*Major Barbara* (Piccadilly) 14 May
*The Man Who Came to Dinner* (Barbican) 16 July
*Measure for Measure* (Barbican) 25 May
*The Merchant of Venice* (Shakespeare's Globe) 29 May
*The Merchant of Venice* (Barbican) 8 Dec.
*A Midsummer's Night Dream* (Open Air) 26 May
*The Misanthrope* (Piccadilly) 26 March
*Miss Evers' Boys* (Barbican Pit) 17 Sept.
*Much Ado about Nothing* (Barbican) 18 Feb.
*Much Ado about Nothing* (Playhouse) 5 June
*The Mysteries* (Barbican Pit) 21 Jan.
*Naked* (The Playhouse) 23 April
*New Edna – The Spectacle* (Haymarket) 21 April
*Not about Nightingales* (National Cottesloe) 5 March
*Oh What a Lovely War!* (Roundhouse) 12 Aug.
*Oklahoma!* (National Olivier) 15 July
*The Old Neighborhood* (Duke of York's) 23 June
*Orestela* (Barbican) 12 Oct.
*Othello* (National Lyttleton) 1 May
*Otra Tempestad – Other Tempest* (Shakespeare's Globe) 21 July
*Our Lady of Sligo* (National Cottesloe) 16 April
*Peter Pan* (National Olivier) 17 Dec.
*Phedre* (Palbery) 9 Sept.
*Pidgin Macbeth* (National Cottesloe) 25 July
*Pidgin Macbeth* (Piccadilly) 9 Oct.
*The Pirates of Penzance* (Queens) 21 Dec.
*The Possessed* (Barbican) 27 June
*Postman Pat* (Barbican) 11 Aug.
*The Prime of Miss Jean Brodie* (National Lyttelton) 25 June
*Purgatory* (Barbican Pit) 9 Dec.
*Pygmalion* (Albery) 28 July
*The Real Inspector Hound* (Comedy) 22 April
*Rent* (Shaftesbury) 12 May
*Riders to the Sea* (Barbican Pit) 9 Dec.
*Saturday Night Fever* (London Palladium) 6 May
*Saucy Jack and the Space Vixens* (Queens) 25 March

*The School for Scandal* (Barbican) 29 Oct.
*The Shadow of the Glen* (Barbican Pit) 9 Dec.
*Shopping and Fucking* (Queens) 21 Jan.
*Show Boat* (Prince Edward) 28 April
*Sleeping Around* (Donmar Warehouse) 24 March
*The Snowman* (Peacock) 9 Dec.
*Sooty* (Savoy) 16 Dec.
*Steve Coogan Is the Man Who Thinks He's It* (Lyceum) 29 Oct.
*Steven Berkoff in Shakespeare's Villains* (Haymarket) 7 July
*Sweet Charity* (Victoria Palace) 19 May
*Tarry Flynn* (National Lyttelton) 20 Aug.
*Tell Me* (Donmar Warehouse) 11 March
*Things We Do for Love* (Gielgud) 3 March
*Things We Do for Love* (Duchess) 26 Aug.
*Think No Evil of Us... My Life with Kenneth Williams* (Vaudeville) 23 Feb.
*Timeless* (Donmar Warehouse) 17 March
*Troilus and Cressida* (Open Air) 11 June
*Troilus and Cressida* (Barbican Pit) 5 Nov.
*The Two Gentlemen of Verona* ( Barbican Pit) 21 Dec.
*Uncle Vanya* (Young Vic) 1 April
*The Unexpected Man* (Barbican Pit) 16 April
*The Unexpected Man* (Duchess) 15 June
*Via Dolorosa* (Duke of York's) 8 Sept.
*Waiting for Godot* (Piccadilly) 10 March
*The Weir* (Duke of York's) 23 Feb.
*The Weir* (Duke of York's) 12 Oct.
*West Side Story* (Prince Edward) 6 Oct.
*Whistle Down the Wind* (Aldwych) 1 July

## Closings

*2.5 Minute Ride* (Barbican Pit) 1 Aug.
*Alan Davies* (Duchess) 14 March
*Amy's View* (Aldwych) 18 April
*Ann Hompton Callaway and Liz Callaway in Sibli...* (Donmar Warehouse) 22 Aug.
*Antony and Cleopatra* (National Olivier) 2 Dec.
*As You Like It* (Shakespeare's Globe) 20 Sept.
*Barbara Cook* (Donmar Warehouse) 29 Aug.
*The Best of Times* (Vaudeville) 19 Dec.
*Bib & Bob* (Criterion) 9 May
*Bip* (Old Vic) 31 May
*Black Comedy* (Comedy) 31 Oct.
*The Blue Room* (Donmar Warehouse) 31 Oct.
*The Bowler Hat* (Old Vic) 30 May
*Brassed Off* (National Olivier) 24 June
*Brief Lives* (Duchess) 23 May
*Britannicus* (Albery) 12 Dec.
*Bugsy Malone* (Queens) 17 Jan.
*The Bullet* (Donmar Warehouse) 2 May
*Camino Real* (Young Vic) 25 April
*The Chairs* (Duke of York's) 31 Jan.

*Cleansed* (Duke of York's) 30 May

*Closer* (National Lyttelton) 3 Feb.

*Closer* (Lyric) 31 Oct.

*The Collection* (Donmar Warehouse) 13 June

*Cymbeline* (Barbican) 7 May

*Cyrano de Bergerac* (Lyric) 14 Feb.

*The Day I Stood Still* (National Cottesloe) 27 June

*The Dead Monkey* (Whitehall) 28 Nov.

*A Delicate Balance* (Haymarket) 4 April

*Do You Come Here Often?* (Vaudeville) 21 Feb.

*Elton John's Glasses* (Queens) 11 July

*An Enemy of the People* (National Olivier) 22 Jan.

*An Enemy of the People* (National Olivier) 20 June

*Everyman* (Barbican Pit) 31 March

*Flight* (National Olivier) 30 May

*The Front Page* (Donmar Warehouse) 28 Feb.

*Gentlemen Prefer Blondes* (Open Air) 1 Sept.

*The Gift* (Barbican Pit) 4 July

*Girls' Night out* (Victoria Palace) 2 May

*Hamlet* (Barbican) 29 April

*Hamlet* (Barbican) 3 Sept.

*Harlem Gospel Singers* (Peacock) 27 Nov.

*Henry VIII* (Young Vic) 21 March

*The Honest Whore* (Shakespeare's Globe) 18 Sept.

*How I Learned to Drive* (Donmar Warehouse) 8 Aug.

*A Huey P Newton Story* (Barbican Pit) 17 Oct.

*The Iceman Cometh* (Old Vic) 1 Aug.

*An Ideal Husband* (Gielgud) 21 Feb.

*An Ideal Husband* (Albery) 22 Aug.

*An Ideal Husband* (Haymarket) 10 Oct.

*Imelda Staunton and Her Big Band* (Donmar Warehouse) 5 Sept.

*In a Little World of Our Own* (Donmar Warehouse) 7 March

*The Invention of Love* (National Lyttelton) 25 April

*Issey Ogata* (Lyric) 14 March

*Jackie* (Queens) 14 Nov.

*Jackie Mason's – Much Ado about Everything* (Playhouse) 6 Dec.

*Jasper Carrott in Concert* (Haymarket) 24 Oct.

*Jeff Green* (Apollo) 5 Dec.

*Jesus Christ Superstar* (Lyceum) 28 March

*The Judas Kiss* (Playhouse) 18 April

*Julian Clary Special Delivery* (Vaudeville) 3 Jan.

*The Jungle Book* (Open Air) 22 Aug.

*Kat and the Kings* (Vaudeville) 1 Aug.

*A Kind of Alaska* (Donmar Warehouse) 13 June

*Kit and the Widow Rummaging for Fluff* (Vaudeville) 31 Jan.

*Krapp's Last Tape* (Barbican Pit) 4 April

*The Lady Boys of Bangkok* (Queens) 26 Sept.

*Lee Evans* (Apollo) 21 Nov.

*A Letter of Resignation* (Comedy) 11 April

*A Letter of Resignation* (Savoy) 10 Oct.

*Little Eyolf* (Barbican Pit) 7 Feb.

*The London Cuckolds* (National Lyttleton) 11 Aug.

*Loot* (Vaudeville) 7 Nov.

*The Lover* (Donmar Warehouse) 13 June

*Love's Fire* (Barbican Pit) 6 June

*A Mad World, My Masters* (Shakespeare's Globe) 19 Sept.

*The Magistrate* (Savoy) 28 March

*Major Barbara* (Piccadilly) 27 Sept.

*The Man Who Came to Dinner* (Barbican) 26 July

*Marchtin Guerre* (Prince Edward) 21 Feb.

*Measure for Measure* (Barbican) 30 May

*The Merchant of Venice* (Shakespeare's Globe) 19 Sept.

*Merry Wives of Windsor* (Barbican) 7 Feb.

*A Midsummer Night's Dream* (Open Air) 5 Sept.

*The Misanthrope* (Piccadilly) 7 Aug.

*Miss Evers' Boys* (Barbican Pit) 3 Oct.

*Much Ado about Nothing* (Barbican) 9 May

*Much Ado about Nothing* (Playhouse) 25 July

*Mutabilitie* (National Cottesloe) 17 Feb.

*The Mysteries* (Barbican Pit) 4 April

*Naked* (Playhouse) 30 May

*New Edna – The Spectacle* (Haymarket) 27 June

*Not about Nightingales* (National Cottesloe) 30 April

*Oh What a Lovely War* (Roundhouse) 11 Oct.

*Oklahoma!* (National Olivier) 3 Oct.

*The Old Neighborhood* (Duke of York's) 8 Aug.

*Oliver* (London Palladium) 21 Feb.

*Orestela* (Barbican) 17 Oct.

*Othello* (National Cottesloe) 6 Jan.

*Othello* (National Lyttelton) 13 June

*Otra Tempestad – Other Tempest* (Shakespeare's Globe) 26 July

*Our Lady of Sligo* (National Cottesloe) 4 Aug.

*Peter Pan* (National Olivier) 11 April

*Phedre* (Albery) 12 Dec.

*Pidgin Macbeth* (National Cottesloe) 1 Aug.

*Pidgin Macbeth* (Piccadilly) 30 Oct.

*Popcorn* (Apollo) 2 Sept.

*The Possessed* (Barbican) 5 July

*Postman Pat* (Barbican) 15 Aug.

*The Prime of Miss Jean Brodie* (National Lyttelton) 12 Dec.

*Pygmalion* (Albery) 4 Oct.

*The Real Inspector Hound* (Comedy) 31 Oct.

*Riverdance* (Apollo Labatt's) 10 Jan.

*Saucy Jack and the Space Vixens* (Queens) 6 June

*The School for Scandal* (Barbican) 21 Nov.

*Shopping and Fucking* (Queens) 14 March

*Show Boat* (Prince Edward) 19 Sept.

*Slava's Snowshow* (Old Vic) 3 Jan.

*Sleeping Around* (Donmar Warehouse) 28 March

*The Slow Drag* (Whitehall) 17 Jan.

*Smokey Joe's Café* (Prince of Wales) 3 Oct.

*The Spanish Tragedy* (Barbican Pit) 29 Jan.

*Stepping Out – The Musical* (Albery) 28 Feb.

---

### . . . October 22 . . .

ACNielsen survey shows 24% of all survey applicants are satisfied with every movie they have seen in the past year.

*Steve Coogan Is The Man Who Thinks He's It* (Lyceum)
12 Dec.
*Steven Berkoff in Shakespeare's Villains* (Haymarket) 8 Aug.
*Sweet Charity* (Victoria Palace) 15 Aug.
*Tarry Flynn* (National Lyttelton) 29 Aug.
*Tell Me* (Donmar Warehouse) 14 April
*Things We Do for Love* (Gielgud) 22 Aug.
*Think No Evil of Us... My Life with Kenneth Williams* (Vaudeville) 14 March
*Timeless* (Donmar Warehouse) 21 March
*Troilus and Cressida* (Open Air) 3 Sept.

*Troilus and Cressida* (Barbican Pit) 21 Nov.
*Uncle Vanya* (Young Vic) 2 May
*The Unexpected Man* (Barbican Pit) 9 May
*The Unexpected Man* (Duchess) 22 Aug.
*Via Dolorosa* (Duke of York's) 3 Oct.
*Waiting for Godot* (Piccadilly) 25 April
*Wallace and Gromit – a Grand Night Out* (Sadler's Wells at the Peacock) 10 Jan.
*The Waste Land* (Wilton's Music Hall) 17 Jan.
*The Weir* (Duke of York's) 18 April

# The Tonys 1947–98

Founded by the American Theater Wing in 1947 in memory of Antoinette Perry, the glamorous Tonys are Broadway's equivalent of the Emmys or the Academy Awards. Off-Broadway shows are not eligible for the awards, however, which is a bone of contention at a time when so much of the best American stage work is performed away from the traditional Broadway houses.

## 1947

Actors (dramatic): José Ferrer, *Cyrano de Bergerac;* Fredric March, *Years Ago*
Actresses (dramatic): Ingrid Bergman, *Joan of Lorraine;* Helen Hayes, *Happy Birthday*
Actress, supporting or featured (drama): Patricia Neal, *Another Part of the Forest*
Actor, supporting or featured (musical): David Wayne, *Finian's Rainbow*
Author: Arthur Miller, *All My Sons*
Composer: Kurt Weill, *Street Scene*
Director: Elia Kazan, *All My Sons*
Costumes: Lucinda Ballard, *Happy Birthday/ Another Part of the Forest/ Street Scene/ John Loves Mary/ The Chocolate Soldier*
Scenic designer: David Ffolkes, *Henry VIII*
Choreographers: Agnes de Mille, *Brigadoon;* Michael Kidd, *Finian's Rainbow*
Special awards: Dora Chamberlain, Mr. & Mrs. Ira Katzenberg, Jules Leventhal, Burns Mantle, P.A. MacDonald, Vincent Sardi, Sr.

## 1948

Actors (dramatic): Henry Fonda, *Mister Roberts;* Paul Kelly, *Command Decision;* Basil Rathbone, *The Heiress*
Actresses (dramatic): Judith Anderson, *Medea;* Katharine Cornell, *Antony and Cleopatra;* Jessica Tandy, *A Streetcar Named Desire*
Actor (musical): Paul Hartman, *Angel in the Wings*
Actress (musical): Grace Hartman, *Angel in the Wings*
Play: *Mister Roberts* by Thomas Heggen & Joshua Logan (based on the novel by Thomas Heggen)

Producer: Leland Hayward, *Mister Roberts*
Authors: Thomas Heggen & Joshua Logan, *Mister Roberts*
Costumes: Mary Percy Schenck, *The Heiress*
Scenic designer: Horace Armistead, *The Medium*
Choreographer: Jerome Robbins, *High Button Shoes*
Conductor & musical director: Max Meth, *Finian's Rainbow*
Stage technician: George Gebhardt
Outstanding performance by newcomers: June Lockhart, *For Love or Money;* James Whitmore, *Command Decision*
Outstanding foreign company: The cast of *The Importance of Being Ernest*
Spreading theater to the country while the originals perform in New York: Mary Martin, *Annie Get Your Gun;* Joe E. Brown, *Harvey*
Experiment in theater: Experimental Theater Inc., accepted by John Garfield
Progressive theater operators: Robert W. Dowling, Paul Beisman
Contribution to theater through a publication: Rosalind Gilder, editor, *Theater Arts*
Contribution to development of regional theater: Robert Porterfield, Virginia Barter Theater
Distinguished wing volunteer worker through the war and after: Vera Allen
Special award: George Pierce

## 1949

Actor (dramatic): Rex Harrison, *Anne of the Thousand Days*
Actress (dramatic): Martita Hunt, *The Madwoman of Chaillot*

Actor, supporting or featured (dramatic): Arthur
Kennedy, *Death of a Salesman*
Actress, supporting or featured (dramatic): Shirley
Booth, *Goodbye My Fancy*
Actor (musical): Ray Bolger, *Where's Charley?*
Actress (musical): Nanette Fabray, *Love Life*
Play: *Death of a Salesman* by Arthur Miller
Producers (dramatic): Kermit Bloomgarden & Walter
Fried, *Death of a Salesman*
Author: Arthur Miller, *Death of a Salesman*
Director: Elia Kazan, *Death of a Salesman*
Musical: *Kiss Me Kate*, book by Bella & Samuel
Spewack, music & lyrics by Cole Porter
Producers (musical): Saint-Subber & Lemuel Ayers,
*Kiss Me Kate*
Authors (musical): Bella & Samuel Spewack, *Kiss Me Kate*
Composer & lyricist: Cole Porter, *Kiss Me Kate*
Costumes: Lemuel Ayers, *Kiss Me Kate*
Scenic designer: Jo Mielziner, *Sleepy Hollow/Summer
and Smoke/Anne of the Thousand Days/Death of a
Salesman/South Pacific*
Choreographer: Gower Champion, *Lend an Ear*
Conductor & musical director: Max Meth, *As the
Girls Go*

## 1950

Actor (dramatic): Sidney Blackmer, *Come Back, Little
Sheba*
Actress (dramatic): Shirley Booth, *Come Back, Little
Sheba*
Actor (musical): Ezio Pinza, *South Pacific*
Actress (musical): Mary Martin, *South Pacific*
Actor, supporting or featured (musical): Myron
McCormick, *South Pacific*
Actress, supporting or featured (musical): Juanita Hall,
*South Pacific*
Play: *The Cocktail Party* by T.S. Eliot, produced by
Gilbert Miller
Director: Joshua Logan, *South Pacific*
Musical: *South Pacific*, book by Oscar Hammerstein II
& Joshua Logan, music by Richard Rodgers, lyrics by
Oscar Hammerstein II, produced by Leland Hayward,
Oscar Hammerstein II, Joshua Logan, & Richard
Rodgers
Libretto: Oscar Hammerstein II & Joshua Logan, *South
Pacific*
Score: Richard Rodgers, *South Pacific*
Costumes: Aline Bernstein, *Regina*
Scenic designer: Jo Mielziner, *The Innocents*
Choreographer: Helen Tamiris, *Touch and Go*
Conductor & musical director: Maurice Abravanel,
*Regina*
Stage technician: Joe Lynn, master propertyman,

*Miss Liberty*
Special awards: Maurice Evans, Mrs. Eleanor
Roosevelt, Brock Pemberton

## 1951

Actor (dramatic): Claude Rains, *Darkness at Noon*
Actress (dramatic): Uta Hagen, *The Country Girl*
Actor, supporting or featured (dramatic): Eli Wallach,
*The Rose Tattoo*
Actress, supporting or featured (dramatic): Maureen
Stapleton, *The Rose Tattoo*
Actor (musical): Robert Alda, *Guys and Dolls*
Actress (musical): Ethel Merman, *Call Me Madam*
Actor, supporting or featured (musical): Russell Nype,
*Call Me Madam*
Actress, supporting or featured (musical): Isabel
Bigley, *Guys and Dolls*
Play: *The Rose Tattoo* by Tennesse Williams, produced
by Cheryl Crawford
Director: George S. Kaufman, *Guys and Dolls*
Musical: *Guys and Dolls*, book by Jo Swerling & Abe
Burrows, music & lyrics by Frank Loesser, produced by
Cy Feuer & Ernest H. Martin
Outstanding musical score: Irving Berlin, *Call Me
Madam*
Costumes: Miles White, *Bless You All*
Scenic designer: Boris Aronson, *The Rose Tattoo/The
Country Girl/Season in the Sun*
Choreographer: Michael Kidd, *Guys and Dolls*
Conductor & musical director: Lehman Engel, *The
Consul*
Stage technician: Richard Raven, master electrician,
*The Autumn Garden*
Special award: Ruth Green

## 1952

Actor (dramatic): José Ferrer, *The Shrike*
Actress (dramatic): Julie Harris, *I Am a Camera*
Actor (musical): Phil Silvers, *Top Banana*
Actress (musical): Gertrude Lawrence, *The King & I*
Actor, supporting or featured (dramatic): John
Crombwell, *Point of No Return*
Actress, supporting or featured (dramatic): Marian
Winters, *I Am a Camera*
Actor, supporting or featured (musical): Yul Brynner,
*The King & I*
Actress, supporting or featured (musical): Helen
Gallagher, *Pal Joey*
Play: *The Fourposter* by Jan de Hartog
Musical: *The King & I*, book & lyrics by Oscar
Hammerstein II, music by Richard Rodgers
Director: José Ferrer, *The Shrike/The Fourposter/Stalag 17*
Costumes: Irene Sharaff, *The King & I*

---

Scenic designer: Jo Mielziner, *The King & I*
Choreographer: Robert Alton, *Pal Joey*
Conductor & musical director: Max Meth, *Pal Joey*
Stage technician: Peter Feller, master carpenter, *Call Me Madam*
Special awards: Judy Garland, Edward Kook, Charles Boyer

## 1953

Actor (dramatic): Tom Ewell, *The Seven Year Itch*
Actress (dramatic): Shirley Booth, *Time of the Cuckoo*
Actor, supporting or featured (dramatic): John Williams, *Dial M for Murder*
Actress, supporting or featured (dramatic): Beatrice Straight, *The Crucible*
Actor (musical): Thomas Mitchell, *Hazel Flagg*
Actress (musical): Rosalind Russell, *Wonderful Town*
Actor, supporting or featured (musical): Hiram Sherman, *Two's Company*
Actress, supporting or featured (musical): Sheila Bond, *Wish You Were Here*
Play: *The Crucible* by Arthur Miller, produced by Kermit Bloomgarden
Director: Joshua Logan, *Picnic*
Musical: *Wonderful Town*, book by Joseph Fields & Jerome Chodorov, music by Leonard Bernstein, lyrics by Betty Comden & Adolph Green, produced by Robert Fryer
Costume designer: Miles White, *Hazel Flagg*
Scenic designer: Raoul Pène Du Bois, *Wonderful Town*
Choreographer: Donald Saddler, *Wonderful Town*
Conductor & musical director: Lehman Engel, *Wonderful Town* and Gilbert & Sullivan Season
Stage technician: Abe Kurnit, *Wish You Were Here*
Special awards: Beatrice Lillie, Danny Kaye, Equity Community Theater

## 1954

Actor (dramatic): David Wayne, *The Teahouse of the August Moon*
Actress (dramatic): Audrey Hepburn, *Ondine*
Actor, supporting or featured (dramatic): John Kerr, *Tea and Sympathy*
Actress, supporting or featured (dramatic): Jo Van Fleet, *The Trip to Bountiful*
Actor (musical): Alfred Drake, *Kismet*
Actress (musical): Dolores Gray, *Carnival in Flanders*
Actor, supporting or featured (musical): Harry Belafonte, *John Murray Anderson's Almanac*
Actress, supporting or featured (musical): Gwen Verdon, *Can-Can*
Play: *The Teahouse of the August Moon* by John Patrick, produced by Maurice Evans & George Schaefer

Director: Alfred Lunt, *Ondine*
Musical: *Kismet*, book by Charles Lederer & Luther Davis, music by Alexander Borodin, adapted & with lyrics by Robert Wright & George Forrest, produced by Charles Lederer
Costume designer: Richard Whorf, *Ondine*
Scenic designer: Peter Larkin, *Ondine* and *The Teahouse of the August Moon*
Choreographer: Michael Kid, *Can-Can*
Musical conductor: Louis Adrian, *Kismet*
Stage technician: John Davis, *Picnic*

## 1955

Actor (dramatic): Alfred Lunt, *Quadrille*
Actress (dramatic): Nancy Kelly, *The Bad Seed*
Actor, supporting or featured (dramatic): Francis L. Sullivan, *Witness for the Prosecution*
Actress, supporting or featured (dramatic): Patricia Jessel, *Witness for the Prosecution*
Actor (musical): Walter Slezak, *Fanny*
Actress (musical): Mary Martin, *Peter Pan*
Actor, supporting or featured (musical): Cyril Ritchard, *Peter Pan*
Actress, supporting or featured (musical): Carol Haney, *The Pajama Game*
Play: *The Desperate Hours* by Joseph Hayes, produced by Howard Erskine & Joseph Hayes
Director: Robert Montgomery, *The Desperate Hours*
Musical: *The Pajama Game*, book by George Abbott & Richard Bissell, music & lyrics by Richard Adler & Jerry Ross
Costume designer: Cecil Beaton, *Quadrille*
Scenic designer: Oliver Messel, *House of Flowers*
Choreographer: Bob Fosse, *The Pajama Game*
Conductor & musical director: Thomas Schippers, *The Saint of Bleecker Street*
Stage technician: Richard Rodda, *Peter Pan*
Special award: Proscenium Productions

## 1956

Actor (dramatic): Paul Muni, *Inherit the Wind*
Actress (dramatic): Julie Harris, *The Lark*
Actor, supporting or featured (dramatic): Ed Begley, *Inherit the Wind*
Actress, supporting or featured (dramatic): Una Merkel, *The Ponder Heart*
Actor (musical): Ray Walston, *Damn Yankees*
Actress (musical): Gwen Verdon, *Phoenix '55*
Actor, supporting or featured (musical): Russ Brown, *Damn Yankees*
Actress, supporting or featured (musical): Lotte Lenya, *The Threepenny Opera*
Play: *The Diary of Anne Frank* by Frances Goodrich &

Albert Hackett, produced by Kermit Bloomgarden
Director: Tyrone Guthrie, *The Matchmaker*
Musical: *Damn Yankees* by George Abbott & Douglass
Wallop, music by Richard Adler & Jerry Ross, produced
by Frederick Brisson, Robert Griffith, & Harold S.
Prince in association with Albert B. Taylor
Conductor & musical director: Hal Hastings, *Damn
Yankees*
Scenic designer: Peter Larkin, *Inherit the Wind/No
Time for Sergeants*
Costume designer: Alvin Colt, *Pipe Dream*
Choreographer: Bob Fosse, *Damn Yankees*
Stage technician: Harry Green, electrician & sound
man, *Middle of the Night/Damn Yankees*
Special awards: City Center, Fourth Street Chekhov
Theater, The Shakespearewright, *The Threepenny
Opera*, The Theater Collection of the N.Y. Public
Library

## 1957

Actor (dramatic): Fredric March, *Long Day's Journey
into Night*
Actress (dramatic): Margaret Leighton, *Separate Tables*
Actor, supporting or featured (dramatic): Frank
Conroy, *The Potting Shed*
Actress, supporting or featured (dramatic): Peggy
Cass, *Auntie Mame*
Actor (musical): Rex Harrison, *My Fair Lady*
Actress (musical): Judy Holliday, *Bells Are Ringing*
Actor, supporting or featured (musical): Sydney
Chaplin, *Bells Are Ringing*
Actress, supporting or featured (musical): Edith
Adams, *Li'l Abner*
Play: *Long Day's Journey into Night* by Eugene O'Neill,
produced by Leigh Connell, Theodore Mann, & José
Quintero
Director: Moss Hart, *My Fair Lady*
Musical: *My Fair Lady*, book & lyrics by Alan Jay Lerner,
music by Frederick Loewe, produced by Herman Levin
Conductor & musical director: Franz Allers, *My Fair Lady*
Scenic designer: Oliver Smith, *My Fair Lady*
Costume designer: Cecil Beaton, *My Fair Lady*
Choreographer: Michael Kidd, *Li'l Abner*
Stage technician: Howard McDonald (posthumous),
carpenter, *Major Barbara*
Special awards: American Shakespeare Festival,
Stratford, Connecticut; Jean-Louis Barrault-French
Repertory; Robert Russell Bennett, William
Hammerstein; Paul Shyre

## 1958

Actor (dramatic): Ralph Bellamy, *Sunrise at Campobello*
Actress (dramatic): Helen Hayes, *Time Remembered*

Actor, supporting or featured (dramatic): Henry Jones,
*Sunrise at Campobello*
Actress, supporting or featured (dramatic): Anne
Bancroft, *Two for the Seesaw*
Actor (musical): Robert Preston, *The Music Man*
Actress (musical): Thelma Ritter, *New Girl in Town*,
Gwen Verdon, *New Girl in Town*
Actor, supporting or featured (musical): David Burns,
*The Music Man*
Actress, supporting or featured (musical): Barbara
Cook, *The Music Man*
Play: *Sunrise at Campobello* by Dore Schary, produced
by Lawrence Langner, Theresa Helburn, Armina
Marshall, & Dore Schary
Director: Vincent J. Donehue, *Sunrise at Campobello*
Musical: *The Music Man*, book by Meredith Wilson &
Franklin Lacey, music & lyrics by Meredith Wilson,
produced by Kermit Bloomgarden & Herbert Greene,
in association with Frank Productions
Conductor & musical director: Herbert Greene, *The
Music Man*
Scenic designer: Oliver Smith, *West Side Story*
Costume designer: Motley, *The First Gentleman*
Choreographer: Jerome Robbins, *West Side Story*
Stage technician: Harry Romar, *Time Remembered*
Special awards: New York Shakespeare Festival, Mrs.
Martin Beck

## 1959

Actor (dramatic): Jason Robards, Jr., *The Disenchanted*
Actress (dramatic): Gertrude Berg, *A Majority of One*
Actor, supporting or featured (dramatic): Charlie
Ruggles, *The Pleasure of His Company*
Actress, supporting or featured (dramatic): Julie
Newmar, *The Marriage-Go-Round*
Actor (musical): Richard Kiley, *Redhead*
Actress (musical): Gwen Verdon, *Redhead*
Actor, supporting or featured (musical): Russel Nype,
*Goldilocks*
Actress, supporting or featured (musical): Pat Stanley,
*Goldilocks*
Play: *J.B.* by Archibald MacLeish, produced by Alfred
de Liagre, Jr.
Director: Elia Kazan, *J.B.*
Musical: *Redhead* by Herbert & Dorothy Fields, Sidney
Sheldon, & David Shaw, music by Albert Hague, lyrics
by Dorothy Fields
Conductor & musical director: Salvatore Dell'Isola,
*Flower Drum Song*
Scenic designer: Donald Oenslager, *A Majority of One*
Costume designer: Rouben Ter-Arutunian, *Redhead*
Choreographer: Bob Fosse, *Redhead*
Stage technician: Sam Knapp, *The Music Man*

Special awards: John Gielgud; Howard Lindsay & Russell Crouse; the cast of *La Plume de ma Tante*

## 1960

Actor (dramatic): Melvyn Douglas, *The Best Man*
Actress (dramatic): Anne Bancroft, *The Miracle Worker*
Actor, supporting or featured (dramatic): Roddy McDowall, *The Fighting Cock*
Actress, supporting or featured (dramatic): Anne Revere, *Toys in the Attic*
Actor (musical): Jackie Gleason, *Take Me Along*
Actress (musical): Mary Martin, *The Sound of Music*
Actor, supporting or featured (musical): Tom Bosley, *Fiorello!*
Actress, supporting or featured (musical): Patricia Neway, *The Sound of Music*
Play: *The Miracle Worker* by William Gibson, produced by Fred Coe
Director: Arthur Penn, *The Miracle Worker*
Musical: *Fiorello!* by Jerome Weidman & George Abbott, lyrics by Sheldon Harnick, music by Jerry Bock, produced by Robert E. Griffith & Harold S. Prince; *The Sound of Music* by Howard Lindsay & Russell Crouse, lyrics by Oscar Hammerstein II, music by Richard Rodgers, produced by Leland Hayward, Richard Halliday & Rodgers & Hammerstein
Director (musical): George Abbott, *Fiorello!*
Conductor & musical director: Frederick Dvonch, *The Sound of Music*
Scenic designer (dramatic): Howard Bay, *Toys in the Attic*
Scenic designer (musical): Oliver Smith, *The Sound of Music*
Costume designer: Cecil Beaton, *Saratoga*
Choreographer: Michael Kidd, *Destry Rides Again*
Stage technician: John Walters, chief carpenter, *The Miracle Worker*
Special awards: John D. Rockefeller III, James Thurber & Burgess Meredith, *A Thurber Carnival*

## 1961

Actor (dramatic): Zero Mostel, *Rhinoceros*
Actress (dramatic): Joan Plowright, *A Taste of Honey*
Actor, supporting or featured (dramatic): Martin Gavel, *Big Fish, Little Fish*
Actress, supporting or featured (dramatic): Colleen Dewhurst, *All the Way Home*
Actor (musical): Richard Burton, *Camelot*
Actress (musical): Elizabeth Seal, *Irma la Douce*
Actor, supporting or featured (musical): Dick Van Dyke, *Bye, Bye Birdie*
Actress, supporting or featured (musical): Tammy Grimes, *The Unsinkable Molly Brown*
Play: *Becket* by Jean Anouilh, produced by David Merrick

Director (dramatic): Sir John Gielgud, *Big Fish, Little Fish*
Musical: *Bye, Bye Birdie*, book by Michael Stewart, music by Charles Strouse, lyrics by Lee Adams, produced by Edward Padula in association with L. Slade Brown
Director (musical): Gower Champion, *Bye, Bye Birdie*
Conductor & musical director: Franz Allers, *Camelot*
Scenic designer (dramatic): Oliver Smith, *Becket*
Scenic designer (musical): Oliver Smith, *Camelot*
Costume designer (dramatic): Motley, *Becket*
Costume designer (musical): Adrian & Tony Duquette, *Camelot*
Choreographer: Gower Champion, *Bye, Bye Birdie*
Stage technician: Teddy Van Bemmel, *Becket*
Special awards: David Merrick, The Theater Guild

## 1962

Actor (dramatic): Paul Scofield, *A Man for All Seasons*
Actress (dramatic): Margaret Leighton, *Night of the Iguana*
Actor, supporting or featured (dramatic): Walter Matthau, *A Shot in the Dark*
Actress, supporting or featured (dramatic): Elizabeth Ashley, *Take Her, She's Mine*
Actor (musical): Robert Morse, *How to Succeed in Business without Really Trying*
Actress (musical): Anna Maria Alberghetti, *Carnival*; Diahann Carroll, *No Strings*
Actor, supporting or featured (musical): Charles Nelson Reilly, *How to Succeed in Business without Really Trying*
Actress, supporting or featured (musical): Phyliss Newman, *Subways Are for Sleeping*
Play: *A Man for All Seasons* by Robert Bolt, produced by Robert Whitehead & Roger L. Stevens
Producer (dramatic): Robert Whitehead & Roger L. Stevens, *A Man for All Seasons*
Director (dramatic): Noel Willman, *A Man for All Seasons*
Musical: *How to Succeed in Business without Really Trying*, book by Abe Burrows, Jack Weinstock, & Willie Gilbert, music & lyrics by Frank Loesser, produced by Cy Feuer & Ernest Martin
Author (musical): Abe Burrows, Jack Weinstock, & Willie Gilbert, *How to Succeed in Business without Really Trying*
Producer (musical): Cy Feuer & Ernest Martin, *How to Succeed in Business without Really Trying*
Director (musical): Abe Burrows, *How to Succeed in Business without Really Trying*
Composer: Richard Rodgers, *No Strings*
Conductor & musical director: Elliot Lawrence, *How to Succeed in Business without Really Trying*
Scenic designer: Will Steven Armstrong, *Carnival*

Costume designer: Lucinda Ballard, *The Gay Life*
Choreographer: Agnes de Mille, *Kwamina*
Stage technician: Michael Burns, *A Man for All Seasons*
Special awards: Brooks Atkinson, Franco Zeffirelli, Richard Rodgers

## 1963

Actor (dramatic): Arthur Hill, *Who's Afraid of Virginia Woolf?*
Actress (dramatic): Uta Hagen, *A Man for All Seasons*
Actor, supporting or featured (dramatic): Alan Arkin, *Enter Laughing*
Actress, supporting or featured (dramatic): Sandy Dennis, *A Thousand Clowns*
Actor (musical): Zero Mostel, *A Funny Thing Happened on the Way to the Forum*
Actress (musical): Vivien Leigh, *Tovarich*
Actor, supporting or featured (musical): David Burns, *A Funny Thing Happened on the Way to the Forum*
Actress, supporting or featured (musical): Anna Quayle, *Stop the World – I Want to Get off*
Play: *Who's Afraid of Virginia Woolf?* by Edward Albee, produced by Theater 1963, Richard Barr, & Clinton Wilder
Producer (dramatic): Richard Barr & Clinton Wilder, Theater 1963, *Who's Afraid of Virginia Woolf?*
Director (dramatic): Alan Schneider, *Who's Afraid of Virginia Woolf?*
Musical: *A Funny Thing Happened on the Way to the Forum*, book by Burt Shevelove & Larry Gelbart, music & lyrics by Stephen Sondheim, produced by Harold Prince
Author (musical): Burt Shevelove & Larry Gelbart, *A Funny Thing Happened on the Way to the Forum*
Producer (musical): Harold Prince, *A Funny Thing Happened on the Way to the Forum*
Director (musical): George Abbott, *A Funny Thing Happened on the Way to the Forum*
Composer & lyricist: Lionel Bart, *Oliver!*
Conductor & musical director: Donal Pippin, *Oliver!*
Scenic designer: Sean Kenny, *Oliver!*
Costume designer: Anthony Powell, *The School for Scandal*
Choreographer: Bob Fosse, *Little Me*
Stage technician: Solly Pernick, *Mr. President*
Special awards: W. McNeil Lowry; Irving Berlin; Alan Bennerr, Peter Cook, Jonathan Miller & Dudley Moore for *Beyond the Fringe*

## 1964

Actor (dramatic): Alec Guinness, *Dylan*
Actress (dramatic): Sandy Dennis, *Any Wednesday*
Actor, supporting or featured (dramatic): Hume Cronyn, *Hamlet*
Actress, supporting or featured (dramatic): Barbara

Loden, *After the Fall*
Actor (musical): Bert Lahr, *Foxy*
Actress (musical): Carol Channing, *Hello Dolly!*
Actor, supporting or featured (musical): Jack Cassidy, *She Loves Me*
Actress, supporting or featured (musical): Tessie O'Shea, *The Girl Who Came to Supper*
Play: *Luther* by John Osborne, produced by David Merrick
Producer (dramatic): Herman Shumlin, *The Deputy*
Director (dramatic): Mike Nichols, *Barefoot in the Park*
Musical: *Hello, Dolly!* book by Michael Stewart, music & lyrics by Jerry Herman, produced by David Merrick
Author (musical): Michael Stewart, *Hello, Dolly!*
Producer (musical): David Merrick, *Hello, Dolly!*
Director (musical): Gower Champion, *Hello, Dolly!*
Composer & lyricist: Jerry Herman, *Hello, Dolly!*
Conductor & musical director: Shepard Coleman, *Hello, Dolly!*
Scenic designer: Oliver Smith, *Hello, Dolly!*
Costume designer: Freddy Wittop, *Hello, Dolly!*
Choreographer: Gower Champion, *Hello, Dolly!*
Special award: Eva Le Gallienne

## 1965

Actor (dramatic): Walter Matthau, *The Odd Couple*
Actress (dramatic): Irene Worth, *Tiny Alice*
Actor, supporting or featured (dramatic): Jack Albertson, *The Subject Was Roses*
Actress, supporting or featured (dramatic): Alice Ghostley, *The Sign in Sidney Brustein's Window*
Actor (musical): Zero Mostel, *Fiddler on the Roof*
Actress (musical): Liza Minnelli, *Flora, the Red Menace*
Actor, supporting or featured (musical): Victor Spinetti, *Oh, What a Lovely War*
Actress, supporting or featured (musical): Maria Karnilova, *Fiddler on the Roof*
Play: *The Subject Was Roses* by Frank Gilroy, produced by Edgar Lansbury
Author (dramatic): Neil Simon, *The Odd Couple*
Producer (dramatic): Claire Nichtern, *Luv*
Director (dramatic): Mike Nichols, *Luv* & *The Odd Couple*
Musical: *Fiddler on the Roof*, book by Joseph Stein, music by Jerry Bock, lyrics by Sheldon Harnick, produced by Harold Prince
Author (musical): Joseph Stein, *Fiddler on the Roof*
Producer (musical): Harold Prince, *Fiddler on the Roof*
Director (musical): Jerome Robbins, *Fiddler on the Roof*
Composer & lyricist: Jerry Bock & Sheldon Harnick, *Fiddler on the Roof*
Scenic designer: Oliver Smith, *Baker Street, Luv* & *The Odd Couple*

---

**. . . October 28 . . .**

Tom Cruise joins New Line's ensemble pic **Magnolia**, directed by **Boogie Nights** helmer Paul Thomas Anderson.

Costume designer: Patricia Zipprodt, *Fiddler on the Roof*

Choreographer: Jerome Robbins, *Fiddler on the Roof*

Special awards: Gilbert Miller, Oliver Smith

## 1966

Actor (dramatic): Hal Holbrook, *Mark Twain Tonight!*

Actress (dramatic): Rosemary Harris, *The Lion in Winter*

Actor, supporting or featured (dramatic): Patrick Magee, *Marat/Sade*

Actress, supporting or featured (dramatic): Zoe Caldwell, *Slapstick Tragedy*

Actor (musical): Richard Kiley, *Man of La Mancha*

Actress (musical): Angela Lansbury, *Mame*

Actor, supporting or featured (musical): Frankie Michaels, *Mame*

Actress, supporting or featured (musical): Beatrice Arthur, *Mame*

Play: *Marat/Sade* by Peter Weiss, produced by David Merrick Arts Foundation

Director (dramatic): Peter Brook, *Marat/Sade*

Musical: *Man of La Mancha*, book by Dale Wasserman, music by Mitch Leigh, lyrics by Joe Darion, produced by Albert W. Selden & Hal James

Director (musical): Albert Marre, *Man of La Mancha*

Composer & lyricist: Mitch Leigh & Joe Darion, *Man of La Mancha*

Scenic designer: Howard Bay, *Man of La Mancha*

Costume designer: Gunilla Palmstierna-Weiss, *Marat/Sade*

Choreographer: Bob Fosse, *Sweet Charity*

Special award: Helen Menken (posthumous)

## 1967

Actor (dramatic): Paul Rogers, *The Homecoming*

Actress (dramatic): Beryl Reid, *The Killing of Sister George*

Actor, supporting or featured (dramatic): Ian Holm, *The Homecoming*

Actress, supporting or featured (dramatic): Marian Seldes, *A Delicate Balance*

Actor (musical): Robert Preston, *I Do! I Do!*

Actress (musical): Barbara Harris, *The Apple Tree*

Actor, supporting or featured (musical): Joel Grey, *Cabaret*

Actress, supporting or featured (musical): Peg Murray, *Cabaret*

Play: *The Homecoming* by Harold Pinter, produced by Alexander H. Cohen

Director (dramatic): Peter Hall, *The Homecoming*

Musical: *Cabaret*, book by Joe Masteroff, music by John Kander, lyrics by Fred Ebb, produced by Harold Prince in association with Ruth Mitchell

Director (musical): Harold Prince, *Cabaret*

Composer & lyricist: John Kander & Fred Ebb, *Cabaret*

Scene designer: Boris Aronson, *Cabaret*

Choreographer: Ron Field, *Cabaret*

Costume designer: Patricia Zipprodt, *Cabaret*

## 1968

Actor (dramatic): Martin Balsam, *You Know I Can't Hear You When the Water's Running*

Actress (dramatic): Zoe Caldwell, *The Prime of Miss Jean Brodie*

Actor, supporting or featured (dramatic): James Patterson, *The Birthday Party*

Actress, supporting or featured (dramatic): Zena Walker, *Joe Egg*

Actor (musical): Robert Goulet, *The Happy Time*

Actress (musical): Patricia Routledge, *Darling of the Day*; Leslie Uggams, *Hallelujah, Baby!*

Actor, supporting or featured (musical): Hiram Sherman, *How Now, Dow Jones*

Actress, supporting or featured (musical): Lilliam Hayman, *Hallelujah, Baby!*

Play: *Rosencrantz and Guildenstern Are Dead* by Tom Stoppard, produced by David Merrick Arts Foundation

Director (dramatic): Mike Nichols, *Plaza Suite*

Musical: *Hallelujah, Baby!* book by Arthur Laurentis, music by Jule Styne, lyrics by Betty Comden & Adolph Green, produced by Albert Selden, Hal James, Jane C. Nusbaum, & Harry Rigby

Producer (musical): Albert Selden, Hal James, Jane C. Nusbaum, & Harry Rigby, *Hallelujah, Baby!*

Director (musical): Gower Champion, *The Happy Time*

Composer & lyricist: Jule Styne, Betty Comden & Adolph Green, *Hallelujah, Baby!*

Scenic designer: Desmond Heeley, *Rosencrantz and Guildenstern Are Dead*

Costume designer: Desmond Heeley, *Rosencrantz and Guildenstern Are Dead*

Choreographer: Gower Champion, *The Happy Time*

Special awards: Audrey Hepburn, Carol Channing, Pearl Bailey, David Merrick, Maurice Chevalier, APA-Phoenix Theater, Marlene Dietrich

## 1969

Actor (dramatic): James Earl Jones, *The Great White Hope*

Actress (dramatic): Julie Harris, *Forty Carats*

Actor, supporting or featured (dramatic): Al Pacino, *Does a Tiger Wear a Necktie?*

Actress, supporting or featured (dramatic): Jane Alexander, *The Great White Hope*

Actor (musical): Jerry Orbach, *Promises, Promises*

Actress (musical): Angela Lansbury, *Dear World*

Actor, supporting or featured (musical): Ronald Holgate, *1776*

Actress, supporting or featured (musical): Marian Mercer, *Promises, Promises*
Play: *The Great White Hope* by Howard Sackler, produced by Herman Levin
Director (dramatic): Peter Dews, *Hadrian VII*
Musical: *1776*, book by Peter Stone, music & lyrics by Sherman Edwards, produced by Stuart Ostrow
Director (musical): Peter Hunt, *1776*
Scenic designer: Boris Aronson, *Zorba*
Costume designer: Louden Sainthill, *Canterbury Tales*
Choreographer: Joe Layton, *George M!*
Special awards: The National Theater Company of Great Britain, The Negro Ensemble Company, Rex Harrison, Leonard Bernstein, Carol Burnett

## 1970

Actor (dramatic): Fritz Weaver, *Child's Play*
Actress (dramatic): Tammy Grimes, *Private Lives* (Revival)
Actor, supporting or featured (dramatic): Ken Howard, *Child's Play*
Actress, supporting or featured (dramatic): Blythe Danner, *Butterflies Are Free*
Actor (musical): Cleavon Little, *Purlie*
Actress (musical): Lauren Bacall, *Applause*
Actor, supporting or featured (musical): René Auberjonois, *Coco*
Actress, supporting or featured (musical): Melba Moore, *Purlie*
Play: *Borstal Boy* by Frank McMahon, produced by Michael McAloney & Burton C. Kaiser
Director (dramatic): Joseph Hardy, *Child's Play*
Musical: *Applause*, book by Betty Comden & Adolph Green, music by Charles Strouse, lyrics by Lee Adams, produced by Joseph Kipness & Lawrence Kasha.
Director (musical): Ron Field, *Applause*
Scenic designer: Jo Mielziner, *Child's Play*
Costume designer: Cecil Beaton, *Coco*
Choreographer: Ron Field, *Applause*
Lighting designer: Jo Mielziner, *Child's Play*
Special awards: Sir Noel Coward, Alfred Lunt & Lynn Fontaine, New York Shakespeare Festival, Barbra Streisand

## 1971

Actor (dramatic): Brian Bedford, *The School for Wives*
Actress (dramatic): Maureen Stapleton, *Gingerbread Lady*
Actor, supporting or featured (dramatic): Paul Sand, *Story Theater*
Actress, supporting or featured (dramatic): Rae Allen, *And Miss Reardon Drinks a Little*
Actor (musical): Hal Linden, *The Rothschilds*
Actress (musical): Helen Gallagher, *No, No Nanette*

Actor, supporting or featured (musical): Keene Curtis, *The Rothschilds*
Actress, supporting or featured (musical): Patsy Kelly, *No, No Nanette*
Play: *Sleuth* by Anthony Shaffer, produced by Helen Bonfils, Morton Gottlieb, and Michael White
Producer (dramatic): Helen Bonfils, Morton Gottlieb, and Michael White, *Sleuth*
Director (dramatic): Peter Brook, *A Midsummer Night's Dream*
Musical: *Company*, produced by Harold Prince
Producer (musical): Harold Prince, *Company*
Director (musical): Harold Prince, *Company*
Book (musical): George Furth, *Company*
Lyrics (musical): Stephen Sondheim, *Company*
Score (musical): Stephen Sondheim, *Company*
Scenic designer: Boris Aronson, *Company*
Costume designer: Raoul Pène Du Bois, *No, No Nanette*
Choreographer: Donald Saddler, *No, No Nanette*
Lighting designer: H.R. Poindexter, *Story Theater*
Special awards: Elliot Norton, Ingram Ash, *Playbill*, Roger L. Stevens

## 1972

Actor (dramatic): Cliff Gorman, *Lenny*
Actress (dramatic): Sada Thompson, *Twigs*
Actor, supporting or featured (dramatic): Vincent Gardenia, *The Prisoner of Second Avenue*
Actress, supporting or featured (dramatic): Elizabeth Wilson, *Sticks and Bones*
Actor (musical): Phil Silvers, *A Funny Thing Happened on the Way to the Forum* (Revival)
Actress (musical): Alexis Smith, *Follies*
Actor, supporting or featured (musical): Larry Blyden, *A Funny Thing Happened on the Way to the Forum* (Revival)
Actress, supporting or featured (musical): Linda Hopkins, *Inner City*
Play: *Sticks and Bones* by David Rabe, produced by New York Shakespeare Festival-Joseph Papp
Director (dramatic): Mike Nichols, *The Prisoner of Second Avenue*
Musical: *Two Gentlemen of Verona*, produced by New York Shakespeare Festival-Joseph Papp
Director (musical): Harold Prince & Michael Bennett, *Follies*
Book (musical): *Two Gentlemen of Verona* by John Guare & Mel Shapiro
Score (musical): *Follies*, music & lyrics by Stephen Sondheim
Scenic designer: Boris Aronson, *Follies*
Costume designer: Florence Klotz, *Follies*
Choreographer: Michael Bennett, *Follies*

Lighting designer: Tharon Musser, *Follies*
Special awards: The Theater Guild-American Theater Society, *Fiddler on the Roof*, Ethel Merman, Richard Rodgers

## 1973

Actor (dramatic): Alan Bates, *Butley*
Actress (dramatic): Julie Harris, *The Last of Mrs. Lincoln*
Actor, supporting or featured (dramatic): John Lithgow, *The Changing Room*
Actress, supporting or featured (dramatic): Leora Dana, *The Last of Mrs. Lincoln*
Actor (musical): Ben Vereen, *Pippin*
Actress (musical): Glynis Johns, *A Little Night Music*
Actor, supporting or featured (musical): George S. Irving, *Irene*
Actress, supporting or featured (musical): Patricia Elliot, *A Little Night Music*
Play: *The Championship Season* by Jason Miller, produced by New York Shakespeare Festival-Joseph Papp
Director (dramatic): A.J. Antoon, *The Championship Season*
Musical: *A Little Night Music*, produced by Harold Prince
Director (musical): Bob Fosse, *Pippin*
Book (musical): *A Little Night Music* by Hugh Wheeler
Score (musical): *A Little Night Music*, music & lyrics by Stephen Sondheim
Scenic designer: Tony Walton, *Pippin*
Costume designer: Florence Klotz, *A Little Night Music*
Choreographer: Bob Fosse, *Pippin*
Lighting designer: Jules Fisher, *Pippin*
Special awards: John Lindsay, Mayor of New York City, Actors' Fund of America, Shubert Organization

## 1974

Actor (dramatic): Michael Moriarty, *Find Your Way Home*
Actress (dramatic): Colleen Dewhurst, *A Moon for the Misbegotten*
Actor, supporting or featured (dramatic): Ed Flanders, *A Moon for the Misbegotten*
Actress, supporting or featured (dramatic): Frances Sternhagen, *The Good Doctor*
Actor (musical): Christopher Plummer, *Cyrano*
Actress (musical): Virginia Capers, *Raisin*
Actor, supporting or featured (musical): Tommy Tune, *Seesaw*
Actress, supporting or featured (musical): Janie Sell, *Over Here!*
Play: *The River Niger* by Joseph A. Walker, produced by Negro Ensemble Co., Inc
Director (dramatic): José Quintero, *A Moon for the Misbegotten*

Musical: *Raisin*, produced by Robert Nemiroff
Director (musical): Harold Prince, *Candide*
Book (musical): *Candide* by Hugh Wheeler
Score: *Gigi*, music by Frederick Loewe, lyrics by Alan Jay Lerner
Scenic designer: Franne & Eugene Lee, *Candide*
Costume designer: Franne Lee, *Candide*
Choreographer: Michael Bennett, *Seesaw*
Lighting designer: Jules Fisher, *Ulysses in Nighttown*
Special awards: Liza Minnelli, Bette Midler, Peter Cook & Dudley Moore, *A Moon for the Misbegotten*, *Candide*, Actors' Equity Association, Theater Development Fund, John F. Wharton, Harold Friedlander
Theater award '74: John F. Wharton, veteran theatrical attorney; Harold Friedlander, the industry's foremost printing expert

## 1975

Actor (dramatic): John Kani & Winston Ntshona, *Sizwe Banzi Dead and the Island*
Actress (dramatic): Ellen Burstyn, *Same Time, Next Year*
Actor, supporting or featured (dramatic): Frank Langella, *Seascape*
Actress, supporting or featured (dramatic): Rita Moreno, *The Ritz*
Actor (musical): John Cullum, *Shenandoah*
Actress (musical): Angela Lansbury, *Gypsy*
Actor, supporting or featured (musical): Ted Ross, *The Wiz*
Actress, supporting or featured (musical): Dee Dee Bridgewater, *The Wiz*
Play: *Equus* by Peter Shaffer, produced by Kermit Bloomgarden & Doris Cole Abrahams
Director (dramatic): John Dexter, *Equus*
Musical: *The Wiz*, produced by Ken Harper
Director (musical): Geoffrey Holder, *The Wiz*
Book (musical): *Shenandoah* by James Lee Barrett, Peter Udell, & Philip Rose
Score: *The Wiz*, music & lyrics by Charlie Smalls
Scenic designer: Carl Toms, *Sherlock Holmes*
Costume designer: Geoffrey Holder, *The Wiz*
Choreographer: George Faison, *The Wiz*
Lighting designer: Neil Peter Jampolis, *Sherlock Holmes*
Special award: Neil Simon
Theater award '75: Al Hirschfeld

## 1976

Actor (play): John Wood, *Travesties*
Actress (play): Irene Worth, *Sweet Bird of Youth*
Actor, (featured role – play): Edward Herrmann, *Mrs. Warren's Profession*
Actress (featured role – play): Shirley Knights, *Kennedy's Children*

Actor (musical): George Rose, *My Fair Lady*

Actress (musical): Donna McKechnie, *A Chorus Line*

Actor (featured role – musical): Sammy Williams, *A Chorus Line*

Actress (featured role – musical): Carole Bishop, *A Chorus Line*

Play: *Travesties* by Tom Stoppard, produced by David Merrick, Doris Cole Abrahams, & Burry Fredrik in association with S. Spencer Davids & Eddie Kulukundis

Director (play): Ellis Rabb, *The Royal Family*

Musical: *A Chorus Line*, produced by Joseph Papp, New York Shakespeare Festival

Director (musical): Michael Bennett, *A Chorus Line*

Book (musical): *A Chorus Line* by James Kirkwood & Nicholas Dante

Score: *A Chorus Line*, music by Marvin Hamlisch, lyrics by Edward Kleban

Scenic designer: Boris Aronson, *Pacific Overtures*

Costume designer: Florence Klotz, *Pacific Overtures*

Lighting designer: Tharon Musser, *A Chorus Line*

Choreographer: Michael Bennett & Bob Avian, *A Chorus Line*

Special awards: Mathilde Pincus, Thomas H. Fitzgerald, Circle in the Square, The Arena Stage, Washington, D.C., Richard Burton

Lawrence Langner award: George Abbott

## 1977

Actor (play): Al Pacino, *The Basic Training of Pavlo Hummel*

Actress (play): Julie Harris, *The Belle of Amherst*

Actor (featured role – play): Jonathan Pryce, *Comedians*

Actress (featured role – play): Trazana Beverley, *For Colored Girls Who Have Considered Suicide/When the Rainbow is Enuf*

Actor (musical): Barry Bostwick, *The Robber Bridegroom*

Actress (musical): Dorothy Loudon, *Annie*

Actor (featured role – musical): Lenny Baker, *I Love My Wife*

Actress (featured role – musical): Delores Hall, *Your Arm's Too Short to Box with God*

Play: *The Shadow Box* by Michael Cristofer, produced by Allan Francis, Ken Marsolais, Lester Osterman, & Leonard Soloway

Director (play): Gordon Davidson, *The Shadow Box*

Musical: *Annie*, produced by Lewis Allen, Mike Nichols, Irwin Meyer, & Stephen R. Friedman

Director (musical): Gene Saks, *I Love My Wife*

Book (musical): *Annie* by Thomas Meehan

Score: *Annie*, music by Charles Strouse, lyrics by Martin Charnin

Scenic designer: David Mitchell, *Annie*

Costume designer: Theoni V. Aldredge, *Annie*; Santo Loquasto, *The Cherry Orchard*

Lighting designer: Jennifer Tipton, *The Cherry Orchard*

Choreographer: Peter Genaro, *Annie*

Special awards: Lily Tomlin, Barry Manilow, Diana Ross, National Theatre for the Deaf, Mark Taper Forum, Equity Library Theatre

Lawrence Langner award: Cheryl Crawford

## 1978

Actor (play): Barnard Hughes, *Da*

Actress (play): Jessica Tandy, *The Gin Game*

Actor (featured role – play): Lester Rawlins, *Da*

Actress (featured role – play): Ann Wedgeworth, *Chapter Two*

Actor (musical): John Cullum, *On the Twentieth Century*

Actress (musical): Liza Minnelli, *The Act*

Actor (featured role – musical): Kevin Kline, *On the Twentieth Century*

Actress (featured role – musical): Nell Carter, *Ain't Misbehavin'*

Play: *Da* by Hugh Leonard, produced by Lester Osterman, Marilyn Strauss, & Marc Howard

Director (play): Melvin Bernhardt, *Da*

Musical: *Ain't Misbehavin'*, produced by Emanuel Azenberg, Dasha Epstein, The Shubert Organization, Jane Gaynor, & Ron Dante

Director (musical): Richard Maltby, Jr., *Ain't Misbehavin'*

Book (musical): *On the Twentieth Century* by Betty Comden & Adolph Green

Score: *On the Twentieth Century*, music by Cy Coleman, lyrics by Betty Comden & Adolph Green

Scenic designer: Robin Wagner, *On the Twentieth Century*

Costume designer: Edward Gorey, *Dracula*

Lighting designer: Jules Fisher, *Dancin'*

Choreographer: Bob Fosse, *Dancin'*

Most innovative production of a revival: *Dracula*, produced by Jujamcyn Theater, Elizabeth I. McCann, John Wulp, Victor Lurie, Nelle Nugent, & Maz Weitzenhoffer

Special award: The Long Wharf Theater, New Haven, Connecticut

Theater award '78: To the creators, Charles Moss & Stan Dragoti (of Wells, Rich, Greene, Inc.) of the "I Love New York Broadway Show tours," and its sponsor, the New York State Department of Commerce

Lawrence Langner memorial award for distinguished

---

lifetime achievement in the American theater: Irving Berlin

## 1979

Actor (play): Tom Conti, *Whose Life Is It Anyway?*
Actress (play): Constance Cummings, *Wings*; Carole Shelley, *The Elephant Man*
Actor (featured role – play): Michael Gough, *Bedroom Farce*
Actress (featured role – play): Joan Hickson, *Bedroom Farce*
Actor (musical): Len Cariou, *Sweeney Todd*
Actress (musical): Angela Lansbury, *Sweeney Todd*
Actor(featured role – musical): Henderson Forsythe, *The Best Little Whorehouse in Texas*
Actress (featured role – musical): Carlyn Glynn, *The Best Little Whorehouse in Texas*
Play: *The Elephant Man* by Bernard Pomerance, produced by Richmond Crinkely, Elizabeth I. McCann, & Nelle Nugent
Director (play): Jack Hofsiss, *The Elephant Man*
Musical: *Sweeney Todd*, produced by Richard Barr, Charles Woodward, Robert Fryer, Mary Lea Johnson, & Martin Richards
Director (musical): Harold Prince, *Sweeney Todd*
Book (musical): *Sweeney Todd* by Hugh Wheeler
Score: *Sweeney Todd*, music & lyrics by Stephen Sondheim
Scenic designer: Eugene Lee, *Sweeney Todd*
Costume designer: Franne Lee, *Sweeney Todd*
Lighting designer: Roger Morgan, *The Crucifer of Blood*
Choreographer: Michael Bennett & Bob Avian, *Ballroom*
Special awards: Henry Fonda, Walter F. Diehl, Eugene O'Neill Memorial Theater Center, Waterford, Connecticut, American Conservatory Theater, San Francisco, California
Lawrence Langner memorial award for distinguished lifetime achievement in the American theater: Richard Rodgers

## 1980

Actor (play): John Rubinstein, *Children of a Lesser God*
Actress (play): Phyllis Frelich, *Children of a Lesser God*
Actor (featured role – play): David Rounds, *Morning's at Seven*
Actress (featured role – play): Dinah Manoff, *I Ought to Be in Pictures*
Actor (musical): Jim Dale, *Barnum*
Actress (musical): Patti LuPone, *Evita*
Actor (featured role – musical): Mandy Patinkin, *Evita*
Actress (featured role – musical): Priscilla Lopez, *A Day in Hollywood/A Night in the Ukraine*
Play: *Children of a Lesser God* by Mark Medoff, produced by Emanuel Azenberg, Shubert Organization, Dasha Epstein, & Ron Dante
Director (play): Vivian Matalon, *Morning's at Seven*
Musical: *Evita*, produced by Robert Stigwood
Director (musical): Harold Prince, *Evita*
Book (musical): *Evita* by Tim Rice
Score: *Evita*, music by Andrew Lloyd Webber, lyrics by Tim Rice
Scenic designer: John Lee Beatty, *Talley's Folly*, David Mitchell, *Barnum*
Costume designer: Theoni V. Aldredge, *Barnum*
Lighting designer: David Hersey, *Evita*
Choreographer: Tommy Tune & Thommie Walsh, *A Day in Hollywood/A Night in the Ukraine*
Reproduction (play or musical): *Morning's at Seven*, produced by Elizabeth I. McCann, Nelle Nugent, & Ray Larson
Special awards: Mary Tyler Moore, *Whose Life Is It Anyway?*, Actors Theater of Louisville, Kentucky, Goodspeed Opera House, East Haddam, Connecticut

## 1981

Actor (play): Ian McKellen, *Amadeus*
Actress (play): Jane Lapotaire, *Piaf*
Actor (featured role – play): Brian Backer, *The Floating Light Bulb*
Actress (featured role – play): Swoosie Kurtz, *Fifth of July*
Actor (musical): Kevin Kline, *The Pirates of Penzance*
Actress (musical): Lauren Bacall, *Woman of the Year*
Actor (featured role – musical): Hinton Battle, *Sophisticated Ladies*
Actress (featured role – musical): Marilyn Cooper, *Woman of the Year*
Play: *Amadeus* by Peter Shaffer, produced by Shubert Organization, Elizabeth I. McCann, Nelle Nugent, & Roger S. Berlind
Director (play): Peter Hall, *Amadeus*
Musical: *42nd Street*, produced by David Merrick
Director (musical): Wilford Leach, *The Pirates of Penzance*
Book (musical): *Woman of the Year* by Peter Stone
Score: *Woman of the Year*, music by John Kander, lyrics by Fred Ebb
Scenic designer: John Bury, *Amadeus*
Costume designer: Willa Kim, *Sophisticated Ladies*
Lighting designer: John Bury, *Amadeus*
Choreographer: Gower Champion, *42nd Street*
Reproduction (play or musical): *The Pirates of Penzance*, produced by Joseph Papp & The New York Shakespeare Festival

Special awards: Lean Horn, Trinity Square Repertory Company, Providence, Rhode Island

## 1982

Actor (play): Roger Rees, *The Life and Adventures of Nicholas Nickleby*
Actress (play): Zoe Caldwell, *Medea*
Actor (featured role – play): Zakes Mokae, *'Master Harold'... and the Boys*
Actress (featured role – play): Amanda Plummer, *Agnes of God*
Actor (musical): Ben Harney, *Dreamgirls*
Actress (musical): Jennifer Holliday, *Dreamgirls*
Actor (featured role – musical): Cleavant Derricks, *Dreamgirls*
Actress (featured role – musical): Liliane Montevecchi, *Nine*
Play: *The Life and Adventures of Nicholas Nickleby* by David Edgar, produced by James M. Nederlander, The Shubert Organization, Elizabeth I. McCann, & Nelle Nugent
Director (play): Trevor Nunn/John Caird, *The Life and Adventures of Nicholas Nickleby*
Musical: *Nine*, produced by Michel Stuart, Harvey J. Klaris, Roger S. Berlind, James M. Nederlander, Francine LeFrak, & Kenneth D. Greenblatt
Director (musical): Tommy Tune, *Nine*
Book (musical): *Dreamgirls* by Tom Eyen
Score: *Nine*, music & lyrics by Maury Yeston
Scenic designer: John Napier, Dermot Hayes, *The Life and Adventures of Nicholas Nickleby*
Costume designer: William Ivey Long, *Nine*
Lighting designer: Tharon Musser, *Dreamgirls*
Choreographer: Michael Bennett, Michael Peters, *Dreamgirls*
Special awards: The Guthrie Theater, Minneapolis, Minnesota; The Actors' Fund of America
Theater Award '82: Warner Communications, Radio City Music Hall

## 1983

Actor (play): Harvey Fierstein, *Torch Song Trilogy*
Actress (play): Jessica Tandy, *Foxfire*
Actor (featured role – play): Matthew Broderick, *Brighton Beach Memories*
Actress (featured role – play): Judith Ivey, *Steaming*
Actor (musical): Tommy Tune, *My One and Only*
Actress (musical): Natalia Makarova, *On Your Toes*
Actor (featured role – musical): Charles "Honi" Coles, *My One and Only*
Actress (featured role – musical): Betty Buckley, *Cats*
Play: *Torch Song Trilogy* by Harvey Fierstein, produced by Kenneth Waissman, Martin Markinson, Lawrence

Lane, John Glines, BetMar, & Donald Tick
Director (play): Gene Saks, *Brighton Beach Memories*
Musical: *Cats*, produced by Cameron Mackintosh, The Really Useful Company, Inc., David Geffen, and The Shubert Organization
Director (musical): Trevor Nunn, *Cats*
Book: *Cats* by T.S. Eliot
Score: *Cats*, music by Andrew Lloyd Webber, lyrics by T.S. Eliot
Scenic designer: Ming Cho Lee, *K2*
Costume designer: John Napier, *Cats*
Lighting designer: David Hersey, *Cats*
Choreographer: Tommy Tune, Thommie Walsh, *My One and Only*
Reproduction: *On Your Toes*, produced by Alfred de Liagre, Jr., Roger L. Stevens, John Mauceri, Donald R. Seawell, and Andre Pastoria
Special award: Oregon Shakespeare Festival Association, Ashland, Oregon
Theater award '83: The Theater Collection, Museum of the City of New York

## 1984

Actor (play): Jeremy Irons, *The Real Thing*
Actress (play): Glenn Close, *The Real Thing*
Actor (featured role – play): Joe Mantegna, *Glengarry Glen Ross*
Actress (featured role – play): Christine Baransky, *The Real Thing*
Actor (musical): George Hearn, *La Cage aux folles*
Actress (musical): Chita Rivera, *The Rink*
Actor (featured role – musical): Hinton Battle, *The Tap Dance Kid*
Actress (featured role – musical): Lila Kedrova, *Zorba*
Play: *The Real Thing* by Tom Stoppard, produced by Emanuel Azenberg, The Shubert Organization, Icarus Productions, Byron Goldman, Ivan Bloch, Roger Berlind, & Michael Codron
Director (play): Mike Nichols, *The Real Thing*
Musical: *La Cage aux folles*, produced by Allan Carr, Kenneth D. Greenblatt, Marvin A. Krauss, Steward F. Lane, James M. Nederlander, Martin Richards, Barry Brown, & Fritz Holt
Director (musical): Arthur Laurentis, *La Cage aux folles*
Book (musical): *La Cage aux folles* by Harvey Fierstein
Score: *La Cage aux folles*, music & lyrics by Jerry Herman
Scenic designer: Tony Straiges, *Sunday in the Park with George*
Costume designer: Theoni V. Aldredge, *La Cage aux folles*
Lighting designer: Richard Nelson, *Sunday in the Park with George*

---

Choreographer: Danny Daniels, *The Tap Dance Kid*
Reproduction: *Death of a Salesman*, produced by
Robert Whitehead & Roger L. Stevens
Special awards: Old Globe Theater, San Diego,
California, *La Tragédie de Carmen*, Peter Feller, *A
Chorus Line*

## 1985

Actor (play): Derek Jacobi, *Much Ado About Nothing*
Actress (play): Stockard Channing, *Joe Egg*
Actor (featured role – play): Barry Miller, *Biloxi Blues*
Actress (featured role – play): Judith Ivey, *Hurleyburly*
Actor (musical): Category eliminated for 1985
Actress (musical): Category eliminated for 1985
Actor (featured role – musical): Ron Richardson, *Big
River*
Actress (featured role – musical): Leilani Jones, *Grind*
Play: *Biloxi Blues* by Neil Simon, produced by Emanuel
Azenberg, & the Center Theater Group/Ahmanson
Theater, Los Angeles
Director (play): Gene Saks, *Biloxi Blues*
Musical: *Big River*, produced by Rocco Landesman,
Heidi Landesman, Rick Steiner, M. Anthony Fisher, &
Dodger Productions
Director (musical): Des McAnuff, *Big River*
Book (musical): *Big River* by William Hauptman
Score: *Big River*, music & lyrics by Roger Miller
Scenic designer: Heidi Landesman, *Big River*
Costume designer: Florence Klotz, *Grind*
Lighting designer: Richard Riddel, *Big River*
Choreographer: Category eliminated
Reproduction (play or musical): *Joe Egg*, produced by
The Shubert Organization, Emanuel Azenberg, Roger
Berlind, Ivan Bloch, & MTM Enterprises, Inc.
Special awards: Yul Brynner, New York State Council
on the Arts, Steppenwolf Theater Company, Chicago,
Illinois
Lawrence Langner memorial award for lifetime
achievement in the theater: Edwin Lester, founder &
general manager for 40 years of the Los Angeles Civic
Light Opera

## 1986

Actor (play): Judd Hirsch, *I'm Not Rappaport*
Actress (play): Lily Tomlin, *The Search for Signs of
Intelligent life in the Universe*
Actor (featured role – play): John Mahoney, *The House
of Blue Leaves*
Actress (featured role – play): Swoosie Kurtz, *The
House of Blue Leaves*
Actor (musical): George Rose, *The Mystery of Edwin
Drood*
Actress (musical): Bernadette Peters, *Song & Dance*

Actor (featured role – musical): Michael Rupert, *Sweet
Charity*
Actress (featured role – musical): Bebe Neuwirth,
*Sweet Charity*
Play: *I'm Not Rappaport* by Herb Gardner, produced
by James Walsh, Lewis Allen, & Marin Heinfling
Director (play): Jerry Zaks, *The House of Blue Leaves*
Musical: *The Mystery of Edwin Drood*, produced by
Joseph Papp
Director (musical): Wilford Leach, *The Mystery of
Edwin Drood*
Book (musical): *The Mystery of Edwin Drood* by
Rupert Holmes
Score: *The Mystery of Edwin Drood*, Rupert Holmes
Scenic designer: Tony Walton, *The House of Blue Leaves*
Costume designer: Patricia Zipprodt, *Sweet Charity*
Lighting designer: Pat Collins, *I'm Not Rappaport*
Choreographer: Bob Fosse, *Big Deal*
Special award: American Repertory Theater,
Cambridge, Massachusetts

## 1987

Actor (play): James Earl Jones, *Fences*
Actress (play): Linda Lavin, *Broadway Bound*
Actor (featured role – play): John Randolph, *Broadway
Bound*
Actress (featured role – play): Mary Alice, *Fences*
Actor (musical): Robert Lindsay, *Me and My Girl*
Actress (musical): Maryann Plunkett, *Me and My Girl*
Actor (featured role – musical): Michael Maguire, *Les
Misérables*
Actress (featured role – musical): Frances Ruffelle, *Les
Misérables*
Play: *Fences* by August Wilson, produced by Carole
Shorenstein Hays & The Yale Repertory Theater
Director (play): Lloyd Richards, *Fences*
Musical: *Les Misérables* produced by Cameron
Mackintosh
Director (musical): Trevor Nunn & John Caird, *Les
Misérables*
Book (musical): *Les Misérables* by Alain Boublil &
Claude-Michel Schönberg
Score: *Les Misérables*, music by Claude-Michel
Schönberg, lyrics by Herbert Kretzmer & Alain Boublil
Scenic designer: John Napier, *Les Misérables*
Costume designer: John Napier, *Starlight Express*
Lighting designer: David Hersey, *Les Misérables*
Choreographer: Gillian Gregory, *Me and My Girl*
Best revival: *All My Sons*, produced by Jay H. Fuchs,
Steven Warnick, & Charles Patsos
Special awards: George Abbott, Jackie Mason, San
Francisco Mime Troupe
Lawrence Langner memorial award for lifetime

achievement in the American theater: Robert Preston (posthumous)

## 1988

Actor (play): Ron Silver, *Speed-the-Plow*
Actress (play): Joan Allen, *Burn This*
Actor (featured role – play): B.D. Wong, *M. Butterfly*
Actress (featured role – play): L. Scott Caldwell, *Joe Turner's Come and Gone*
Actor (musical): Michael Crawford, *The Phantom of the Opera*
Actress (musical): Joanna Gleason, *Into the Woods*
Actor (featured role – musical): Bill McCutcheon, *Anything Goes*
Actress (featured role – musical): Judy Kaye, *The Phantom of the Opera*
Play: *M. Butterfly* by David Henry Hwang, produced by Stuart Ostrow & David Geffen
Director (play): John Dexter, *M. Butterfly*
Musical: *The Phantom of the Opera* produced by Cameron Mackintosh & The Really Useful Theater Company, Inc.
Director (musical): Harold Prince, *The Phantom of the Opera*
Book (musical): *Into the Woods* by James Lapine
Score (musical): *Into the Woods*, music & lyrics by Stephen Sondheim
Scenic designer: Maria Björnson, *The Phantom of the Opera*
Costume designer: Maria Björnson, *The Phantom of the Opera*
Lighting designer: Andrew Bridge, *The Phantom of the Opera*
Choreographer: Michael Smuin, *Anything Goes*
Revival: *Anything Goes*, produced by Lincoln Center Theater, Gregory Mosher, & Bernard Gersten
Special awards: Brooklyn Academy of Music, South Coast Repertory of Costa Mesa, CA

## 1989

Actor (play): Philip Bosco, *Lend Me a Tenor*
Actress (play): Pauline Collins, *Shirley Valentine*
Actor (featured role – play): Boyd Gaines, *The Heidi Chronicles*
Actress (featured role – play): Christine Baransky, *Rumors*
Actor (musical): Jason Alexander, *Jerome Robbins' Broadway*
Actress (musical): Ruth Brown, *Black and Blue*
Actor (featured role – musical): Scott Wise, *Jerome Robbins' Broadway*
Actress (featured role – musical): Debbie Shapiro, *Jerome Robbins' Broadway*

Play: *The Heidi Chronicles* by Wendy Wasserstein, produced by The Shubert Organization, Suntory International Corp., James Walsh, & Playwrights Horizons
Director (play): Jerry Zaks, *Lend Me a Tenor*
Musical: *Jerome Robbins' Broadway*, produced by The Shubert Organization, Suntory International Corp., Byron Goldman, & Emanuel Azenberg
Director (musical): Jerome Robbins, *Jerome Robbins' Broadway*
Book (musical): Category eliminated for 1989
Score (musical): Category eliminated for 1989
Scenic designer: Santo Loquasto, *Cafe Crown*
Costume designer: Claudio Segovia & Hector Orezzoli, *Black and Blue*
Lighting designer: Jennifer Tipton, *Jerome Robbins' Broadway*
Choreographer: Cholly Atkins, Henry LeTang, Frankie Manning, & Gayard Nicholas, *Black and Blue*
Revival: *Our Town*, produced by Lincoln Center Theater, Gregory Mosher, & Bernard Gersten
Special awards: Hartford Stage Company, Hartford, Connecticut

## 1990

Actor (play): Robert Morse, *Tru*
Actress (play): Maggie Smith, *Lettice and Lovage*
Actor (featured role – play): Charles Durning, *Cat on a Hot Tin Roof*
Actress (featured role – play): Margaret Tyzack, *Lettice and Lovage*
Actor (musical): James Naughton, *City of Angels*
Actress (musical): Tyne Daly, *Gypsy*
Actor (featured role – musical): Michael Jeter, *Grand Hotel, The Musical*
Actress (featured role – musical): Randy Graff, *City of Angels*
Play: *The Grapes of Wrath* by Frank Galati, produced by The Shubert Organization, Steppenwolf Theater Company, Suntory International Corp., & Jujamcyn Theaters
Director (play): Frank Galati, *The Grapes of Wrath*
Musical: *City of Angels*, produced by Nick Vanoff, Roger Berlind, Jujamcyn Theaters, Suntory International Corp., & The Shubert Organization
Director (musical): Tommy Tune, *Grand Hotel, The Musical*
Book (musical): *City of Angels* by Larry Gelbart
Score (musical): *City of Angels*, music by Cy Coleman, lyrics by David Zippel
Scenic designer: Robin Wagner, *City of Angels*
Costume designer: Santo Loquasto, *Grand Hotel, The Musical*

---

Lighting designer: Jules Fisher, *Grand Hotel, The Musical*
Choreographer: Tommy Tune, *Grand Hotel, The Musical*
Revival: *Gypsy*, produced by Barry & Fran Weissler, Kathy Levin, & Barry Brown
Special award: Seattle Repertory Theater
Tony honor: Alfred Drake

## 1991

Actor (play): Nigel Hawthorne, *Shadowlands*
Actress (play): Mercedes Ruehl, *Lost in Yonkers*
Actor (featured role – play): Kevin Spacey, *Lost in Yonkers*
Actress (featured role – play): Irene Worth, *Lost in Yonkers*
Actor (musical): Jonathan Pryce, *Miss Saigon*
Actress (musical): Lea Salonga, *Miss Saigon*
Actor (featured role – musical): Hinton Battle, *Miss Saigon*
Actress (featured role – musical): Daisy Eagan, *The Secret Garden*
Play: *Lost in Yonkers* by Neil Simon, produced by Emanuel Azenberg
Director (play): Jerry Zaks, *Six Degrees of Separation*
Musical: *The Will Rogers Follies*, produced by Pierre Cossette, Martin Richards, Sam Crothers, James M. Nederlander, Stewart F. Lane, Max Weitzenhoffer, & Japan Satellite Broadcasting, Inc.
Director (musical): Tommy Tune, *The Will Rogers Follies*
Book (musical): *The Secret Garden* by Marsha Norman
Score (musical): *The Will Rogers Follies*, music by Cy Coleman, lyrics by Betty Comden & Adolph Green
Scenic designer: Heidi Landesman, *The Secret Garden*
Costume designer: Willa Kim, *The Will Rogers Follies*
Lighting designer: Jules Fisher, *The Will Rogers Follies*
Choreographer: Tommy Tune, *The Will Rogers Follies*
Revival: *Fiddler on the Roof*, produced by Barry & Fran Weissler, Pace Theatrical Group
Special award: Yale Repertory Theater, New Haven, Connecticut
Tony honor: Father George Moore (posthumous)

## 1992

Actor (play): Judd Hirsch, *Conversations with My Father*
Actress (play): Glenn Close, *Death and the Maiden*
Actor (featured role – play): Larry Fishburne, *Two Trains Running*
Actress (featured role – play): Brid Brennan, *Dancing at Lughnasa*
Actor (musical): Gregory Hines, *Jelly's Last Jam*
Actress (musical): Faith Prince, *Guys and Dolls*

Actor (featured role – musical): Scott Waara, *The Most Happy Fella*
Actress (featured role – musical): Tonya Pinkins, *Jelly's Last Jam*
Play: *Dancing at Lughnasa* by Brian Friel, produced by Noel Pearson, Bill Kenwright, & Joseph Harris
Director (play): Patrick Mason, *Dancing at Lughnasa*
Musical: *Crazy for You*, produced by Roger Horchow & Elizabeth Williams
Director (musical): Jerry Zaks, *Guys and Dolls*
Book (musical): *Falsettos*, by William Finn & James Lapine
Score (musical): *Falsettos*, music & lyrics by William Finn
Scenic designer: Tony Walton, *Guys and Dolls*
Costume designer: William Ivey Long, *Crazy for You*
Lighting designer: Jules Fisher, *Jelly's Last Jam*
Choreographer: Susan Stroman, *Crazy for You*
Revival: *Guys and Dolls* produced by Dodger Productions, Roger Berlind, Jujamcyn Theaters/TV Asahi, Kardana Productions, & The John. F. Kennedy Center for the Performing Arts
Special award: The Goodman Theater of Chicago
Tony honor: *The Fantasticks*

## 1993

Actor (play): Ron Leibman, *Angels in America: Millennium Approaches*
Actress (play): Madeline Kahn, *The Sisters Rosensweig*
Actor (featured role – play): Stephen Spinella, *Angels in America: Millennium Approaches*
Actress (featured role – play): Debra Monk, *Redwood Curtain*
Actor (musical): Brent Carver, *Kiss of the Spider Woman – The Musical*
Actress (musical): Chita Rivera, *Kiss of the Spider Woman – The Musical*
Actor (featured role – musical): Anthony Crivello, *Kiss of the Spider Woman – The Musical*
Actress (featured role – musical): Andrea Martin, *My Favorite Year*
Play: *Angels in America: Millennium Approaches* by Tony Kishner, produced by Jujamcyn Theatres, Mark Taper Forum/Gordon Davidson, Margo Lion, Susan Quint Gallin, Jon B. Platt, The Baruch-Frankel-Viertel Group, Frederick Zollo, & Herb Alpert
Director (play): George C. Wolfe, *Angels in America: Millennium Approaches*
Musical: *Kiss of the Spider Woman – The Musical*, produced by The Live Entertainment Corp. of Canada/Garth Drabinsky
Director (musical): Des McAnuff, *The Who's Tommy*
Book (musical): *Kiss of the Spider Woman – The Musical* by Terrence McNally
Score (musical): *Kiss of the Spider Woman – The*

*Musical,* music by John Kander, lyrics by Fred Ebb & *The Who's Tommy,* music & lyrics by Pete Townshend

Scenic designer: John Arnone, *The Who's Tommy*

Costume designer: Florence Klotz, *Kiss of the Spider Woman – The Musical*

Lighting designer: Chris Parry, *The Who's Tommy*

Choreographer: Wayne Cilento, *The Who's Tommy*

Revival: *Anna Christie,* produced by Roundabout Theater Company & Todd Haimes

Special awards: *Oklahoma! – 50th Anniversary,* La Jolla Playhouse

Tony honors: IATSE, Broadway Cares/Equity Fights AIDS

## 1994

Actor (play): Stephen Spinella, *Angels in America: Perestroika*

Actress (play): Diana Rigg, *Medea*

Actor (featured role – play): Jeffrey Wright, *Angels in America: Perestroika*

Actress (featured role – play): Jane Adams, *An Inspector Calls*

Actor (musical): Boyd Gaines, *She Loves Me*

Actress (musical): Donna Murphy, *Passion*

Actor (featured role – musical): Jarrod Emick, *Damn Yankees*

Actress (featured role – musical): Audra Ann McDonald, *Carousel*

Play: *Angels in America: Perestroika* by Tony Kushner, produced by Jujamcyn Theater & The Mark Taper Forum/Gordon Davidson, Artistic director with Margo Lion, Susan Quint Gallin, Jon B. Platt, The Baruch-Frankel-Viertel Group, Frederick Zollo, in association with the New York Shakespeare Festival, Mordecai/Cole Productions, & Herb Alpert

Director (play): Stephen Daldry, *An Inspector Calls*

Musical: *Passion,* produced by The Shubert Organization, Capital Cities/ABC, Roger Berlind, & Scott Rudin

Director (musical): Nicholas Hytner, *Carousel*

Book (musical): *Passion* by James Lapine

Original musical score: *Passion,* music & lyrics by Stephen Sondheim

Scenic designer: Bob Crowley, *Carousel*

Costume designer: Ann Hould-Ward, *Beauty and the Beast*

Lighting designer: Rick Fisher, *An Inspector Calls*

Choreographer: Sir Kenneth MacMillan, *Carousel*

Revival: *An Inspector Calls,* produced by Noel Pearson, The Shubert Organization, Capital Cities/ABC, & Joseph Harris

Revival (musical): *Carousel,* produced by Lincoln Center Theater, Andre Bishop, Bernard Gersten, The

Royal National Theater, Cameron Mackintosh, & the Rodgers & Hammerstein Organization

Special awards: Jessica Tandy, Hume Cronyn (Lifetime Achievement), McCarter Theater (Regional Theater)

## 1995

Actor (play): Ralph Fiennes, *Hamlet*

Actress (play): Cherry Jones, *The Heiress*

Actor (featured role – play): John Glover, *Love! Valour! Compassion!*

Actress (featured role – play): Frances Sternhagen, *The Heiress*

Actor (musical): Matthew Broderick, *How to Succeed in Business without Really Trying*

Actress (musical): Glenn Close, *Sunset Boulevard*

Actor (featured role – musical): George Hearn, *Sunset Boulevard*

Actress (featured role – musical): Gretha Boston, *Show Boat*

Play: *Love! Valour! Compassion!* by Terrence McNally, produced by Manhattan Theater Club, Lynne Meadow, Barry Grove, & Jujamcyn Theaters

Director (play): Joe Mantello, *Love! Valour! Compassion!*

Musical: *Sunset Boulevard,* produced by The Really Useful Company, Inc.

Director (musical): Harold Prince, *Show Boat*

Book (musical): *Sunset Boulevard* by Don Black & Christopher Hampton

Original musical score: Andrew Lloyd Webber, Don Black, & Christopher Hampton, *Sunset Boulevard*

Scenic designer: John Napier, *Sunset Boulevard*

Costume designer: Florence Klotz, *Show Boat*

Lighting designer: Andrew Bridge, *Sunset Boulevard*

Choreographer: Susan Stroman, *Show Boat*

Revival: *The Heiress,* produced by Lincoln Center Theater, Andre Bishop, & Bernard Gersten

Revival (musical): *Show Boat,* produced by LIVENT (U.S.) Inc./Garth Drabinsky

Special awards: Carol Channing, Harvey Sabinson (Lifetime Achievement), Goodspeed Opera House, East Haddam, Connecticut (Regional Theater), Tony honor: National Endowment for the Arts, Jane Alexander, chairman

## 1996

Actor (play): George Grizzard, *A Delicate Balance*

Actress (play): Zoe Caldwell, *Master Class*

Actor (featured role – play): Ruben Santiago-Hudson, *Seven Guitars*

Actress (featured role – play): Audra McDonald, *Master Class*

Actor (musical): Nathan Lane, *A Funny Thing*

---

Happened on the Way to the Forum
Actress (musical): Donna Murphy, *The King and I*
Actor (featured role – musical): Wilson Jermaine Heredia, *Rent*
Actress (featured role – musical): Ann Duquesnay, *Bring in 'da Noise/Bring in 'da Funk*
Play: *Master Class* by Terrence McNally
Director (play): Gerald Gutierrez, *A Delicate Balance*
Musical: *Rent*
Director (musical): George C. Wolfe, *Bring in 'da Noise/Bring in 'da Funk*
Book (musical): *Rent* by Jonathan Larson
Original musical score: *Rent*, music & lyrics by Jonathan Larson
Scenic designer: Brian Thomson, *The King and I*
Costume designer: Roger Kirk, *The King and I*
Lighting designer: Jules Fisher & Peggy Eisenhauer, *Bring in 'da Noise/Bring in 'da Funk*
Choreographer: Savion Glover, *Bring in 'da Noise/Bring in 'da Funk*
Revival (play): *A Delicate Balance*
Revival (musical): *A Funny Thing Happened on the Way to the Forum*
Special regional theater award: Alley Theater of Houston

## 1997

Actor (play): Christopher Plummer, *Barrymore*
Actress (play): Janet McTeer, *A Doll's House*
Actor (featured role – play): Owen Teale, *A Doll's House*
Actress (featured role – play): Lynne Thigpen, *An American Daughter*
Actor (musical): James Naughton, *Chicago*
Actress (musical): Bebe Neuwirth, *Chicago*
Actor (featured role – musical): Chuck Cooper, *The Life*
Actress (featured role – musical): Lillias White, *The Life*
Play: *The Last Night of Ballyhoo* by Alfred Uhry, produced by Jane Harmon, Nina Keneally, Liz Oliver
Director (play): Anthony Page, *A Doll's House*
Musical: *Titanic*, produced by Dodger Endemol Theatricals, Richard S. Pechter, & The John. F. Kennedy Center
Director (musical): Walter Bobbie, *Chicago*
Book (musical): *Titanic* by Peter Stone
Original musical score: *Titanic*, music & lyrics by Maury Yeston
Orchestrations: Jonathan Tunick, *Titanic*
Scenic designer: Stewart Laing, *Titanic*
Costume designer: Judith Dolan, *Candide*
Lighting designer: Ken Billington, *Chicago*

Choreographer: Ann Reinking, *Chicago*
Revival (play): *A Doll's House*, produced by Bill Kenwright, & Thelma Holt
Revival (musical): *Chicago* , produced by Barry Weissler, Fran Weissler, & Kardana Productions, Inc.
Special regional theater award: Berkeley Repertory Theater

## 1998

Actor (play): Anthony LaPaglia, *A View from the Bridge*
Actress (play): Marie Mullen, *The Beauty Queen of Leenane*
Actor (featured role – play): Tom Murphy, *The Beauty Queen of Leenane*
Actress (featured role – play): Anna Manahan, *The Beauty Queen of Leenane*
Actor (musical): Alan Cumming, *Cabaret*
Actress (musical): Natasha Richardson, *Cabaret*
Actor (featured role – musical): Ron Rifkin, *Cabaret*
Actress (featured role – musical): Audra McDonald, *Ragtime*
Play: *Art* by Yasmina Reza, produced by David Pugh, Sean Connery, & Joan Cullman
Director (play): Garry Hynes, *The Beauty Queen of Leenane*
Musical: *The Lion King*, produced by Disney
Director (musical): Julie Taymor, *The Lion King*
Book (musical): *Ragtime* by Terrence McNally
Original musical score: *Ragtime*, music by Stephen Flaherty, lyrics by Lunn Ahrens
Orchestrations: William David Brohn, *Ragtime*
Scenic designer: Richard Hudson, *The Lion King*
Costume designer: Julie Taymor, *The Lion King*
Lighting designer: Donald Holder, *The Lion King*
Choreographer: Garth Fagan, *The Lion King*
Revival (play): *A View from the Bridge*, produced by Roundabout Theater Company, Todd Haimes, Ellen Richard, Roger Berlind, James M. Nederlander, Nathaniel Kramer, Elizabeth Ireland McCann, Roy Gabay, & Old Ivy Productions
Revival (musical): *Cabaret*, produced by Roundabout Theater Company, Todd Haimes, & Ellen Richard
Special regional theater award: Denver Center Theater Company

---

*Why don't you get out of that wet coat and into a dry martini? (Robert Benchley,* **The Major and the Minor)**

---

**. . . November 8 . . .**

Jean Marais, 84, French icon-actor associated with Cocteau and the beast of his **Belle et la Bête**, leaves his mortal cage.

# Olivier Awards: 1998

Best play: *Closer*, Patrick Marber
Best musical: *Chicago*. Music: John Kander, lyrics:
Fred Ebb, book by Fred Ebb and Bob Fosse
Best new musical: *Beauty and the Beast*. Music: Alan
Menken, lyrics: Howard Ashman and Tim Rice,
book by Linda Woolverton
Best comedy: *Popcorn*, Ben Elton
Best actor (play): Ian Holm, *King Lear*
Best actress (play): Zoë Wanamaker, *Electra*
Best actor (musical): Philip Quast, *The Fix*
Best actress (musical): Ute Lemper, *Chicago*
Best supporting performance (play): Sarah

Woodward, *Tom & Clem*
Best supporting performance (musical): James
Dreyfus, *Lady in the Dark*
Best director: Richard Eyre, *King Lear*
Best choreography: Simon McBurney, *The
Caucasian Chalk Circle*
Best sets: Tim Goodchild, *Three Hours After
Marriage*
Best costumes: Tim Goodchild, *Three Hours After
Marriage*
Best lighting: Rick Fisher, *Chips with Everything* and
*Lady in the Dark*

# Index of theater shows reviewed in *Variety* 1998

Theater Chicago) (Oct. 5-11)
*Death of a Salesman* (Burbank, Ca, Falcon Theater) (Oct. 26-Nov. 1)
*The Deep Blue Sea* (March 30-April 5)
*Deep Space* (May 4-10)
*Dimly Perceived Threats to the System* (Oct. 12-18)
*Dinah Was* (Off Broadway, musical, WPA Theater) (April 13-19)
*Dinah Was* (Off Broadway, musical, Gramercy Theater) (Sept. 7-13)
*Dinner with Friends* (Nov. 9-15)
*Doctor Dolittle* (July 27-Aug. 2)
*Dogeaters* (Sept. 28-Oct. 4)
*Doing Leonard Cohen* (Dec. 7-13)
*Don Carlos* (July 27-Aug. 2)
*Dr. Jekyll and Mr. Hyde* (Dec. 21-Jan. 3)
*Duet! A Romantic Fable* (Nov. 2-8)
*The Dying Gaul* (June 8-14)
*Eddie Izzard: Dress to Kill* (March 30-April 5)
*Elaborate Lives: the Legend of Aida* (Oct. 12-18)
*Eleanor: Her Secret Journey* (Aug. 31-Sept. 6)
*Electra* (Princeton, N.J.) (Sept. 28-Oct. 4)
*Electra* (Broadway) (Dec. 7-13)
*Eliot Ness… In Cleveland* (Feb. 9-15)
*Emphysema (A Love Story)* (Oct. 12-18)
*End of Civilization* (July 20-26)
*An Enemy of the People* (Aug. 3-9)
*An Evening with Jerry Herman* (Aug. 3-9)
*Evita* (Nov. 16-22)
*Eyes for Consuela* (Feb. 16-22)
*Fantastic Mr. Fox* (opera) (Dec. 21-Jan. 3)
*The Fastest Clock in the Universe* (June 1-7)
*Faust: Version 3.0* (Aug. 3-9)
*Filumena* (Oct. 12-18)
*The Fix* (April-6-12)
*A Flea in Her Ear* (March 9-15)
*Flyovers* (June 1-7)
*Follies* (May 11-17)
*Footloose* (Washington, Kennedy Center) (Sept. 7-13)
*Footloose* (Broadway) (Oct. 26-

Nov. 1)
*For the Pleasure of Seeing Her Again* (Nov. 16-22)
*Forbidden Broadway Cleans up Its Act!* (Dec. 7-13)
*Fosse: a Celebration in Song and Dance* (Aug. 17-23)
*Freak* (Feb. 16-22)
*Free Gift/Stations of the Cross* (Sept. 14-20)
*From Above* (April 27-May 3)
*Full Gallop* (March 9-15)
*Galileo* (Nov. 16-22)
*Geometry of Miracles* (April 27-May 3)
*George Gershwin at 100* (Concert, Carnegie Hall) (Sept. 28-Oct. 4)
*Getting and Spending* (Nov. 2-8)
*The Gimmick* (Nov. 23-29)
*A Girl's Life* (March 16-22)
*Give Me Your Answer, Do* (April 27-May 3)
*Golden Child* (April-6-12)
*Gun-shy* (Feb. 9-15)
*Gypsy* (Oct. 5-11)
*Hamlet* (London) (Jan. 19-25)
*Handbag, or the Importance of Being Someone* (Oct. 5-11)
*Harriet's Return* (Feb. 9-15)
*Haroun and the Sea of Stories* (Nov. 16-22)
*Hazelwood Jr. High* (March 9-15)
*Hedwig and the Angry Inch* (Feb. 23-March 1)
*Henry VIII* (March 16-22)
*The Herbal Bed* (April 20-26)
*Hey Mr. Producer* (June 15-21)
*High Society* (May 4-10)
*Homme Fatale: the Joey Stefano Story* (Feb. 16-22)
*Honour* (April 27-May 3)
*Hope Is the Thing with Feathers* (Dec. 14-20)
*House* (Aug. 31-Sept. 6)
*How I Learned to Drive* (London) (July 13-19)
*How I Learned to Drive* (American Repertory Theater Cambridge, Mass.) (Oct. 5-11)
*Hurrah at Last* (June 8-14)
*Hydriotaphia, or the Death of Dr. Browne* (Sept. 28-Oct. 4)
*Icarus* (May 25-31)

*The Iceman Cometh* (April 20-26)
*I Am Yours* (March 9-15)
*I'm Still Here… Damn It!* (April 13-19)
*I Will Come Back* (March 16-22)
*If Memory Serves* (Oct. 19-25)
*Imelda Staunton and Her Big Band* (Sept. 7-13)
*Impossible Marriage* (Oct. 19-25)
*Insomnia* (Oct. 26-Nov. 1)
*Into the Woods* (Dec. 7-13)
*The Invention of Love* (Nov. 9-15)
*Jackie Mason: Much Ado about Everything* (Nov. 16-22)
*Jails, Hospitals and Hip-Hop* (April-6-12)
*Jerry Seinfeld: I'm Telling You for the Last Time – Live on Broadway* (Aug. 17-23)
*Jerusalem: The Musical* (March 9-15)
*Jitney* (Nov. 9-15)
*John Bull's Other Island* (July 27-Aug. 2)
*Jolson: The Musical* (Oct. 19-25)
*The Judas Kiss* (London) (March 23-29)
*The Judas Kiss* (Broadway) (May 4-10)
*June Moon* (Jan. 19-25)
*Just So* (Dec. 7-13)
*Kat and the Kings* (March 30-April 5)
*Kevin's Bed* (May 25-31)
*Killer Joe* (Oct. 26-Nov. 1)
*The King and I* (April 27-May 3)
*King Lear* (Sept. 21-27)
*Kudzu* (May 4-10)
*Labor Day* (San Diego) (Feb. 23-March 1)
*Labor Day* (Off Broadway, New York, City Center Stage I)(June 8-14)
*Lady Windermere's Fan* (Aug. 17-23)
*The Lady's Not for Burning* (June 1-7)
*Last Lists of My Mad Mother* (Feb. 9-15)
*The Lear Project* (July 20-26)
*Let Me Live* (May 4-10)
*Like Stars in My Hands* (March 9-15)
*Lillian* (June 22-28)
*Little Eyolf* (Jan. 12-18)
*Little Malcolm and His Struggle*

*against the Eunuchs* (Nov. 23-29)

*Little Me* (Nov. 16-22)

*Lizzie Borden* (Nov. 16-22)

*The Lonesome West* (Aug. 17-23)

*Long Day's Journey into Night* (Houston, Alley Theater) (March 9-15)

*Long Day's Journey into Night* (New York) (March 30-April 5)

*Long Day's Journey into Night* (Dublin) (April 20-26)

*Love and Understanding* (March 23-29)

*. . . Love, Langston* (Jan. 19-25)

*Love upon the Throne* (Sept. 21-27)

*Love You, Too* (June 8-14)

*Love's Fire* (London Barbican Centre's Pit Theatre) (June 1-7)

*Love's Fire* (Off Broadway-New York) (June 29-July 12)

*Lucia di Lammermoor* (opera) (Dec. 21-Jan. 3)

*Macbeth* (Off Broadway New York)(March 16-22)

*The Magistrate* (Feb. 9-15)

*The Maiden's Prayer* (March 9-15)

*Major Barbara* (Niagara-on-the-Lake, Ontario) (June 1-7)

*Major Barbara* (London) (Aug. 10-16)

*The Man Who Came to Dinner* (May 4-10)

*Mandy Patinkin in Concert: Mamaloshen* (New York, Angel Orensanz Foundation Center for the Arts) (Aug. 3-9)

*Mandy Patinkin in Concert: Mamaloshen* (New York, Belasco Theater) (Oct. 26-Nov. 1)

*Marcel Pursued by the Hounds* (Jan. 19-25)

*Marco Polo Sings a Solo* (Oct. 5-11)

*Mary Stuart* (April 20-26)

*The Mask of Moriarty* (Jan. 26-Feb. 1)

*The Matchmaker* (July 27-Aug. 2)

*The Memory of Water* (Nov. 16-22)

*Mercy* (Dec. 21-Jan. 3)

*Meshugah* (Nov. 2-8)

*Metamorphoses* (Nov. 9-15)

*Mirette* (Aug. 10-16)

*The Misanthrope* (May 11-17)

*The Miser* (Aug. 24-30)

*Mistery School* (March 30-April 5)

*Mizlansky/Zilinsky or "Schmucks"* (Feb. 23-March 1)

*Monster* (May 4-10)

*More to Love: A Big Fat Comedy* (Oct. 19-25)

*Morning Glories* (Jan. 12-18)

*The Most Fabulous Story Ever Told* (Dec. 21-Jan. 3)

*Mr. Peters' Connections* (May 25-31)

*Mr. Puntila and His Man Matti* (Oct. 19-25)

*Much Ado About Nothing* (New York, Brooklyn Academy of Music Majestic Theater) (April-6-12)

*Much Ado about Nothing* (Stratford, Ontario) (June 22-28)

*Much Ado about Nothing* (New York, City Center, Off Broadway)(Nov. 23-29)

*My Favourite Broadway: The Leading Ladies* (Oct. 5-11)

*My One Good Nerve – a visit with Ruby Dee* (Feb. 23-March 1)

*The Mystery of Irma Vep* (Oct. 5-11)

*Mystery School* (Jan. 12-18)

*Naked* (Feb. 23-March 1)

*Nasty Little Secrets* (June 1-7)

*Needfire* (July 13-19)

*Never Land* (Feb. 2-8)

*Never the Sinner* (Feb. 9-15)

*Never Whistle While You're Pissing* (Feb. 16-22)

*A New Brain* (June 22-28)

*The Night of the Iguana* (Aug. 10-16)

*Nijinsky's Last Dance* (Dec. 14-20)

*Nobody Dies on Friday* (May 4-10)

*Not about Nightingales* (London, Royal National Theatre) (March 23-29)

*Not about Nightingales* (Houston) (June 15-21)

*Le Nozze di Figaro* (Nov. 9-15)

*O* (Dec. 21-Jan. 3)

*Oedipus* (Oct. 19-25)

*Oh What a Lovely War* (Sept. 7-13)

*Oklahoma!* (July 20-26)

*The Old Neighbourhood* (Aug. 3-9)

*The Old Settler* (Nov. 16-22)

*On the Town* (Nov. 30-Dec. 6)

*Once in a Lifetime* (June 8-14)

*Only a Kingdom* (Nov. 30-Dec. 6)

*The Orphan Muses* (Jan. 26-Feb. 1)

*Othello* (April 20-26)

*Our Daily Bread* (Feb. 2-8)

*Over the River and through the Woods* (Oct. 12-18)

*The Pajama Game* (May 11-17)

*Panacea* (Nov. 2-8)

*Parade* (Dec. 21-Jan. 3)

*Paramour* (Oct. 5-11)

*Patience* (March 9-15)

*Patti Labelle on Braodway* (Jan. 19-25)

*Pauline and Turgenev* (June 1-7)

*Peer Gynt* (Providence, A Trinity Repertory Company) (Feb. 16-22)

*Peer Gynt* (Washington, Shakespeare Theater) (March 16-22)

*Penn & Teller* (March 30-April 5)

*People's Century 1900-1999* (April 20-26)

*Pericles* (Nov. 16-22)

*Peter Pan* (Dec. 14-20)

*Peter Pan & Wendy* (Jan. 26-Feb. 1)

*Phaedra in Delirium* (Feb. 2-8)

*Phedre* (Oct. 5-11)

*The Play about the Baby* (Sept. 14-20)

*Play on!* (July 13-19)

*The Playboy of the Western World* (July 27-Aug. 2)

*Pot Mom* (July 20-26)

*Power Plays* (Seattle) (March 23-29)

*Power Plays* (Off Broadway) (May 25-31)

*The Prime of Miss Jean Brodie* (Stratford, Ontario) (June 22-28)

*The Prime of Miss Jean Brodie* (London, Royal National Theatre) (Aug. 17-23)

*Private Life* (Feb. 16-22)

*Putting It Together* (Nov. 2-8)

*Queen of the Stardust Ballroom* (Aug. 31-Sept. 6)

*R&J* (Jan. 26-Feb. 1)

*Ragtime* (Broadway) (Jan. 19-25)

*Ragtime* (Chicago Oriental Theater) (Nov. 16-22)

*Real Classy Affair* (Nov. 2-8)

*The Real Inspector Hound/Black Comedy* (May 25-31)

*Red* (Sept. 21-27)

*Rent* (Toronto) (Jan. 5-11)

*Rent* (London, Shaftesbury

Theatre) (May 18-24)

*Retribution* (Nov. 2-8)

*RichardII/RichardIII* (March 2-8)

*The Ride down Mr. Morgan* (Nov. 23-29)

*Risk Everything* (July 20-26)

*Romeo and Juliet* (Sept. 14-20)

*Ronnie Larsen's Peep Show* (April 27-May 3)

*The Royal Tour* (Oct. 19-25)

*A Russian Romance* (Jan. 19-25)

*Safe as Houses* (March 30-April 5)

*Saint Joan* (July 20-26)

*Sakina's Restaurant* (July 27-Aug. 2)

*Sandra Bernhard: I'm Still Here... Damn It!* (Nov. 9-15)

*Sarah Bernhardt Comes to Town* (May 11-17)

*Saturday Night* (Jan. 5-11)

*Saturday Night Fever* (May 11-17)

*Saturn Returns: A Concert* (April 20-26)

*Savion Glover/Downtown* (July 20-26)

*The Scarlet Pimpernel* (Nov. 9-15)

*The School for Scandal* (Jan. 12-18)

*Scotland Road* (Feb. 2-8)

*Secrets Every Smart Traveler Should Know* (April 27-May 3)

*Shadows* (April-6-12)

*Shang-a-lang* (Nov. 23-29)

*Shopping and Fucking* (New York) (Feb. 9-15)

*The Show Goes on* (Jan. 5-11)

*Sibling Revelry* (Aug. 24-30)

*Side Man* (Off Broadway New York)(March 16-22)

*Side Man* (Broadway) (June 29-July 12)

*The Skin of Our Teeth* (July 13-19)

*Slava's Snowshow* (Jan. 12-18)

*Snakebit* (Dec. 14-20)

*Song at Sunset* (Jan. 26-Feb. 1)

*Soon* (Aug. 10-16)

*The Sound of Music* (March 16-22)

*Spirit Dance* (Aug. 17-23)

*Spirit North* (Feb. 2-8)

*St. Nicholas* (March 23-29)

*Star Billing* (Dec. 21-Jan. 3)

*Steel City* (Jan. 19-25)

*Stop Kiss* (Dec. 14-20)

*The Story of Dr. Faust* (March 16-22)

*The Street of Crocodiles* (Aug. 3-9)

*A Streetcar Named Desire* (Dublin, Gate Theatre) (May 18-24)

*A Streetcar Named Desire* (Hartford, Conn.)(Sept. 21-27)

*A Streetcar Named Desire* (San Francisco Opera) (Sept. 28-Oct. 4)

*Stupid Kids* (June 29-July 12)

*Sueno* (March 9-15)

*Sugar Sugar* (July 27-Aug. 2)

*The Summer Moon* (Sept. 14-20)

*Sunset Boulevard* (Dec. 21-Jan. 3)

*Swan Lake* (Oct. 12-18)

*Sweet Bird of Youth* (June 22-28)

*Tallulah's Party* (April 20-26)

*Tennessee Williams' Rootless Beauties* (March 9-15)

*Things We do for Love* (April-6-12)

*This is Our Youth* (Nov. 9-15)

*Three Sisters* (Feb. 16-22)

*'Til the Rapture Comes* (Oct. 12-18)

*Tintypes* (April 20-26)

*Tiny Alice* (June 1-7)

*Trainspotting* (Feb. 2-8)

*La Traviata* (opera) (Dec. 21-Jan. 3)

*Tribe* (July 13-19)

*Twelfth Night* (Montreal) (Feb. 9-15)

*Twelfth Night* (Broadway) (July 20-26)

*The Uneasy Chair* (Oct. 12-18)

*Uncle Tom's Cabin* (Jan. 5-11)

*Uncle Vanya* (April 27-May 3)

*The Unexpected Man* (April 20-26)

*Vernon Early* (June 29-July 12)

*Via Dolorosa* (Sept. 14-20)

*A View from the Bridge* (Aug. 10-16)

*Village* (Aug. 3-9)

*Visiting Mr. Green* (Jan. 5-11)

*Voices in the Dark* (May 4-10)

*Wait until Dark* (Boston, Broadway Tryout)(March 9-15)

*Wait until Dark* (Broadway) (April 6-12)

*Waiting for Godot* (Nov. 23-29)

*The Wake* (Feb. 16-22)

*Waxworks* (May 11-17)

*The Weir* (May 4-10)

*West Side Story* (Oct. 12-18)

*What the World Needs Now... A Musical Fable* (April 13-19)

*Whistle Down the Wind* (July 13-19)

*White Picket Fence* (Feb. 9-15)

*The Whiteheaded Boy* (June 22-28)

*The Widow Judith* (Feb. 16-22)

*The Winter's Tale* (July 27-Aug. 2)

*Wit* (Sept. 28-Oct. 4)

*The Wizard of Oz* (April 6-12)

*Wolf Lullaby* (Nov. 2-8)

*Wunnerful Liberace* (Feb. 23-March 1)

*Yard Gal* (June 1-7)

*You're a Good Man, Charlie Brown* (Dec. 14-20)

*You Never Can Tell* (July 13-19)

*Zorro: The Musical* (Sept. 14-20)

> *– Oh, your mother, I proposed to her once.*
> *– But, that's my father.*
> *– No wonder he turned me down.* (A Day at the Races, Groucho Marx commenting on the portrait of Margaret Dumont's father)

**...November 12...**

Cameron Diaz inks to star in Fine Line's **Invisible Circus.**

# Music

Although never figuring as large in *Variety*'s universe as film and broadcasting, the music scene has been covered for most of this century in fair depth by the paper. Until the 1960s there were several pages each week devoted to music. The section waned because legendary Editor Abel Green paid comparatively little heed to it. During the past few years, current Editor-in-Chief Peter Bart has resurrected *Variety*'s music coverage, in the form of news analysis and longer investigative pieces. Indeed, never before has there been so much synergy between the various sectors of entertainment. Elton John is involved in film production; Madonna and Sting have appeared in starring roles on screen; Andrew Lloyd Webber has a number one single in the U.K. through Boyzone. The rise of MTV and the abiding importance of the Grammys are reflected in this section.

## All-time U.S. bestselling singles

1. "Candle In The Wind 1997," Elton John, MCA (1997)
2. "I Will Always Love You," Whitney Houston, Arista (1992)
3. "Macarena," Los Del Rio, RCA (1995)
4. "We Are The World," Various, Columbia (1985)
5. "Whomp (There It Is)," Tag Team, Life (1993)
6. "I Do It For You," Bryan Adams, A&M (1991)
7. "Gangsta's Paradise," Coolio, (1995)
8. "Hound Dog," Elvis Presley, (1956)
9. "How Do I Live," LeAnn Rines, Curb (1998)
10. "I'll Be Missing You," Puff Daddy, Bad Boy/Arista (1998)

## All-time U.S. bestselling albums

1. *Greatest Hits 1971-1975*, Eagles, Elektra
2. *Thriller*, Michael Jackson, Epic
3. *The Wall*, Pink Floyd, Columbia
4. *Rumours*, Fleetwood Mac, Warner Bros.
5. *Greatest Hits Vols I & II*, Billy Joel, Columbia
6. *Led Zeppelin IV*, Led Zeppelin, Swan Song
7. *Back In Black*, AC/DC, Atco
8. *The Beatles*, The Beatles, Capitol
9. *Boston*, Boston, Epic
10. *No Fences*, Garth Brooks, Capitol Nashville

## Top 10 U.S. singles: 1998

1. "The Boy is Mine," Brandy/Monica
2. "Too Close," Next
3. "You're Still The One," Shania Twain
4. "Nice & Slow," Usher
5. "First Night," Monica
6. "My Way," Usher
7. "My All," Mariah Carey
8. "Body Bumpin'," Public Announcement
9. "No No No Pt. 2," Destiny's Child
10. "Let's Ride," Montell Jordan

## Top 10 U.S. albums: 1998

1. *Titanic*, Soundtrack, Sony Classical
2. *Let's Talk About Love*, Celine Dion, Epic
3. *Backstreet Boys*, Backstreet Boys, Jive
4. *Come on Over*, Shania Twain, Mercury
5. *'N-Sync*, 'N-Sync, RCA
6. *City of Angels*, Soundtrack, Warner/Sunset Reprise
7. *Double Live*, Garth Brooks, Capitol Nashville
8. *Big Willie Style*, Will Smith, Columbia
9. *Savage Garden*, Savage Garden, Columbia
10. *Armageddon*, Soundtrack, Columbia

**. . . November 13 . . .**

Mel Gibson bows distribution arm, Icon Film Distribution, to be housed in London.

## All-time U.K. bestselling singles

1. "Something about.../Candle in the Wind," Elton John, Rocket (1997)
2. "Do They Know it's Christmas?," Band Aid, Mercury (1984)
3. "Bohemian Rhapsody," Queen, EMI (1975)
4. "Mull of Kintyre," Wings, Capitol (1977)
5. "Rivers of Babylon/Brown Girl in the Ring," Boney M, Atlantic (1978)
6. "Relax," Frankie Goes to Hollywood, ZTT (1983)
7. "She Loves You," The Beatles, Parlophone (1963)
8. "You're the One I Want," John Travolta/Olivia Newton John, RSO (1978)
9. "Unchained Melody," Robson & Jerome, RCA (1995)
10. "Mary's Boy Child," Boney M, Atlantic (1978)

## All-time U.K. bestselling albums

1. *Sgt Pepper's Lonely Hearts Club Band*, The Beatles, Parlophone (1967)
2. *Bad*, Michael Jackson, Epic (1987)
3. *Stars*, Simply Red, East West (1991)
4. *Brothers in Arms*, Dire Straits, Vertigo (1985)
5. *Greatest Hits Volume One*, Queen, Parlaphone (1981)
6. *Thriller*, Michael Jackson, Epic (1982)
7. *(What's the Story) Morning Glory?*, Oasis, Creation (1995)
8. *The Immaculate Collection*, Madonna, Sire (1990)
9. *The Very Best of Elton John*, Elton John, Rocket (1990)
10. *...But Seriously*, Phil Collins, Virgin (1989)

## Top 10 U.K. singles: 1998

1. "Believe," Cher, WEA
2. "My Heart Will Go on," Celine Dion, Epic
3. "It's Like That," Run-D.M.C. vs Jason Nevins, SME Communications
4. "No Matter What," Boyzone, Polydor
5. "C'est la vie," B'witched, Epic
6. "How Do I Live?," LeAnn Rimes, Curb/The Hit Label
7. "Chocolate Salty Balls (P.S. I Love You)," Chef, Columbia
8. "Goodbye," Spice Girls, Virgin
9. "Ghetto Supastar (That is What You Are)," Pras Michel featuring ODB & Mya, Interscope
10. "Truly Madly Deeply," Savage Garden, Columbia

## Top 10 U.K. albums: 1998

1. *Talk on Corners*, The Corrs, Atlantic
2. *Ladies & Gentlemen – The Best of George Michael*, George Michael, Epic
3. *Where We Belong*, Boyzone, Polydor
4. *Life thru a Lens*, Robbie Williams, Chrysalis
5. *I've Been Expecting You*, Robbie Williams, Chrysalis
6. *Urban Hymns*, Verve, Hut
7. *Ray of Light*, Madonna, Maverick
8. *Let's Talk about Love*, Celine Dion, Epic
9. *All Saints*, All Saints, London
10. *Titanic – OST*, James Horner, Sony Classical

*Source: CIN (based on guesstimates, BPI certs and record-company data)*

## The 33rd Annual Academy of Country Music Awards

Album of the year: *Carrying Your Love with Me*, George Strait
Single record of the year: "It's Your Love," Tim McGraw & Faith Hill
Song of the year: "It's Your Love," Tim McGraw & Faith Hill
Video of the year: "It's Your Love," Tim McGraw & Faith Hill
Entertainer of the year: Garth Brooks
Top female vocalist: Trisha Yearwood

Top male vocalist: George Strait
Top vocal duo/group: Brooks & Dunn
Top new female vocalist: Lee Ann Womack
Top new male vocalist: Kenny Chesney
Top new vocal duet/group: The Kinleys
Vocal event of the year: Tim McGraw & Faith Hill, "It's Your Love"
Pioneer award: Charlie Daniels
Special achievement award: Garth Brooks (for the HBO Special, "Live in Central Park")

# Billboard Music Awards: 1998

Artist of the year: Usher
Female artist of the year: Shania Twain
Modern rock artist of the year: Everclear
Hot 100 single of the year: Next, "Too Close"
Hot 100 singles artist of the year: Usher
Hot 100 singles female artist of the year: Shania Twain
Hot 100 singles duo or group of the year: Next, "Too Close"
R&B album of the year: Lauryn Hill, *The Miseducation of Lauryn Hill*
R&B single of the year: "Too Close," Next
R&B singles artist of the year: Next, "Too Close"
R&B albums artist of the year: Jay-Z
R&B artist of the year: Usher
New R&B artist of the year: Next, "Too Close"
R&B group of the year: Next, "Too Close"
R&B singles airplay track of the year: "Too Close," Next
Group album of the year: Backstreet Boys, "Backstreet Boys"
Album of the year: *Titanic*
Album artist of the year: Celine Dion
Soundtrack single of the year: "My Heart Will Go On," from *Titanic*, Celine Dion
Female album of the year: *Let's Talk about Love*, Celine Dion
Country artist of the year: Garth Brooks

Country singles sales artist of the year: LeAnn Rimes
Female country artist of the year: LeAnn Rimes
Bestselling country single of the year: "You're Still the One," Shania Twain
Adult contemporary artist of the year: Celine Dion
Adult contemporary group of the year: Backstreet Boys
Contemporary Christian album of the year: LeAnn Rimes, *Sittin' On Top of the World*
Contemporary Christian artist of the year: LeAnn Rimes, *Sittin' On Top of the World*
Billboard Hot 100 award: LeAnn Rimes for "How Do I Live?"
Billboard Hot 100 award for the most No. 1s ever by a female solo artist: Mariah Carey
The Century award: James Taylor
Modern rock track of the year: "Sex and Candy," Marcy Playground
Rock track of the year: "Blue on Black," Kenny Wayne
Blues album of the year: *Trouble Is...*, Kenny Wayne
Rap artist of the year: Mase
Rap single of the year: "Déjà vu (Uptown Baby)," Lord Tariq and Peter Gunz
Adult top 40 track of the year: "Torn," Natalie Imbruglia

# MTV Awards since inception

## 1984
### GENERAL CATEGORY WINNERS
Video of the year: The Cars, "You Might Think"
Male video: David Bowie, "China Girl"
Female video: Cyndi Lauper, "Girls Just Want to Have Fun"
Concept video: Herbie Hancock, "Rockit"
Group video: ZZ Top, "Legs"
Stage performance in a video: Van Halen, "Jump"
Overall performance in a video: Michael Jackson, "Thriller"

### PROFESSIONAL CATEGORY WINNERS
Special effects in a video: Herbie Hancock, "Rockit"
Art direction in a video: Herbie Hancock, "Rockit"
Editing in a video: Herbie Hancock, "Rockit"
Cinematography in a video: The Police, "Every Breath You Take"
Choreography in a video: Michael Jackson,

"Thriller"
Direction in a video: ZZ Top, "Sharp Dressed Man", Tim Newman, director
Most experimental video: Herbie Hancock, "Rockit"

### SPECIAL AWARD WINNERS
Special recognition award: Quincy Jones, in honor of his overall contribution to the entire music universe
Video vanguard awards: The Beatles, David Bowie, Richard Lester
Viewers choice award: Michael Jackson, "Thriller"

## 1985
### GENERAL CATEGORY WINNERS
Video of the year: Don Henley, "The Boys of Summer"
Male video: Bruce Springsteen, "I'm on Fire"

Female video: Tina Turner, "What's Love Got to Do with It?"
Group video: USA for Africa, "We Are the World"
Concept video: Glenn Frey, "Smuggler's Blues"
Overall performance in a video: Philip Bailey and Phil Collins, "Easy Lover"
Stage performance in a video: Bruce Springsteen, "Dancing in the Dark"
New artist in a video: til' tuesday, "Voices Carry"

**PROFESSIONAL CATEGORY WINNERS**
Special effects in a video: Tom Petty and The Heartbreakers, "Don't Come around Here No More," Tony Mitchell, Kathy Dougherty, Peter Cohen
Art direction in a video: Don Henley, "The Boys of Summer," Bryan Jones
Editing in a video: Art of Noise, "Close (to the Edit)," Zbigniew Rybczynski
Cinematography in a video: Don Henley, "The Boys of Summer," Pascal Lebeque
Choreography in a video: Elton John, "Sad Songs," David Atkins
Direction in a video: Don Henley, "The Boys of Summer," John Baptiste Mondino, director
Most experimental video: Art of Noise, "Close (to the Edit)," Zbigniew Rybczynski

**SPECIAL AWARD WINNERS**
Special recognition award: Bob Geldof
Video vanguard awards: David Byrne, Kevin Godley and Lol Creme, Russell Mulcahy
Viewers choice award: USA for Africa, "We Are the World"

## 1986
**GENERAL CATEGORY WINNERS**
Video of the year: Dire Straits, "Money for Nothing"
Male video: Robert Palmer, "Addicted to Love"
Female video: Whitney Houston, "How Will I Know?"
Group video: Dire Straits, "Money for Nothing"
Concept video: a-Ha, "Take on Me"
Overall performance in a video: David Bowie and Mick Jagger, "Dancing in the Streets"
Stage performance in a video: Bryan Adams and Tina Turner, "It's Only Love"
New artist in a video: a-Ha, "Take on Me"

**PROFESSIONAL CATEGORY WINNERS**
Special effects in a video: a-Ha, "Take on Me," Michael Patterson

Art direction in a video: ZZ Top, "Rough Boy," Ron Cobb
Editing in a video: a-Ha, "The Sun Always Shines on TV," David Yardley
Cinematography in a video: a-Ha, "The Sun Always Shines on TV," Oliver Stapleton
Choreography in a video: Prince and the Revolution, "Raspberry Beret," Prince
Direction in a video: a-Ha, "Take on Me," Steven Barron
Most experimental video: a-Ha, "Take on Me," Steven Barron

**SPECIAL AWARD WINNERS**
Special recognition award: Bill Graham and Jack Healey, executive directors Amnesty International
Video vanguard awards: Madonna and Zbigniew Rybcznski
Viewers choice award: a-Ha, "Take on Me"

## 1987
**GENERAL CATEGORY WINNERS**
Video of the year: Peter Gabriel, "Sledgehammer," producer – Adam Whittaker
Male video: Peter Gabriel, "Sledgehammer"
Female video: Madonna, "Papa Don't Preach"
Group video: Talking Heads, "Wild Wild Life"
Concept video: Peter Gabriel/Stephen Johnson, "Sledgehammer"
Stage performance in a video: Bon Jovi, "Livin' on a Prayer"
Overall performance in a video: Peter Gabriel, "Sledgehammer"
New artist in a video: Crowded House, "Don't Dream It's Over"
New video from a film: Talking Heads, "Wild Wild Life"

**PROFESSIONAL CATEGORY WINNERS**
Special effects in a video: Peter Gabriel, "Sledgehammer," Stephen Johnson, Peter Lord
Art direction in a video: Peter Gabriel, "Sledgehammer," Stephen Johnson, Stephen Quay, Tim Quay
Editing in a video: Peter Gabriel, "Sledgehammer," Stephen Johnson, Colin Green
Cinematography in a video: Robbie Nevil, "C'est la vie," Mark Plummer
Choreography in a video: Janet Jackson, "Nasty," Paula Abdul
Direction in a video: Peter Gabriel, "Sledgehammer," Stephen Johnson,
Most experimental video: "Sledgehammer"

## SPECIAL AWARD WINNERS

Special recognition award: Elton John and Bernie Taupin

Video vanguard awards: Julien Temple, Peter Gabriel

Viewers choice award: U2, "With or without You"

## 1988

### GENERAL CATEGORY WINNERS

Video of the year: INXS, "Need You Tonight/Mediate," producers, Julie Stone, Anna Grieves, Michael Hamlyn

Male video: Prince, "U Got the Look"

Female video: Suzanne Vega, "Luka"

Group video: INXS, "Need You Tonight/Mediate"

Concept video: Pink Floyd, "Learning to Fly"

Stage performance in a video: Prince, "U Got the Look"

New artist in a video: Guns 'N Roses, "Welcome to the Jungle"

New video from a film: Los Lobos, "La Bamba"

### PROFESSIONAL CATEGORY WINNERS

Special effects in a video: Squeeze, "Hourglass," Jim Francis, Dave Barton

Art direction in a video: Squeeze, "Hourglass," Clive Crotty, Mick Edwards

Editing in a video: INXS, "Need You Tonight/Mediate," Richard Lowenstein

Cinematography in a video: Sting, "We'll Be Together," Bill Pope

Choreography in a video: Janet Jackson, "The Pleasure Principle," Barry Lather

Direction in a video: George Michael, "Father Figure," Andy Morahan, George Michael

Breakthrough video: INXS, "Need You Tonight/Mediate"

### SPECIAL AWARD WINNERS

Video vanguard awards: Michael Jackson

Viewers choice award: INXS, "Need You Tonight/Mediate"

## 1989

### GENERAL CATEGORY WINNERS

Video of the year: Neil Young, "This Note's for You"

Male video: Elvis Costello, "Veronica"

Female video: Paula Abdul, "Straight Up"

Group video: Living Colour, "Cult of Personality"

Rap video: D.J. Jazzy Jeff & The Fresh Prince, "Parents Just don't Understand"

Dance video: Paula Abdul, "Straight up"

Heavy-metal video: Guns 'N Roses, "Sweet Child 'O Mine"

Postmodern video: R.E.M., "Orange Crush"

Stage video: Living Colour, "Cult of Personality"

New artist video: Living Colour, "Cult of Personality"

Video from a film: U2 with BB King, "When Love Comes to Town"

### PROFESSIONAL CATEGORY WINNERS

Direction in a video: Madonna, "Express Yourself," David Fincher

Choreography in a video: Paula Abdul, "Straight Up"

Special effects in a video: Michael Jackson, "Leave Me Alone," Jim Blashfield

Art direction in a video: Madonna, "Express Yourself," Vance Lorenzini

Breakthrough video: Art of Noise featuring Tom Jones, "Kiss"

### SPECIAL AWARD WINNERS

Video vanguard: George Michael

International video award: Chayanne "Este ritmo se baila asi"

Viewers choice award: Madonna, "Like a Prayer"

## 1990

### GENERAL CATEGORY WINNERS

Video of the year: Sinead O'Connor, "Nothing Compares 2 U"

Male video: Don Henley, "The End of the Innocence"

Female video: Sinead O'Connor, "Nothing Compares 2 U"

Group video: B 52's, "Love Shack"

Rap video: M.C. Hammer, "U Can't Touch This"

Heavy-metal video: Aerosmith, "Janie's Got a Gun"

Postmodern video: Sinead O'Connor, "Nothing Compares 2 U"

Dance video: M.C. Hammer,"U Can't Touch This"

New artist video: Michael Penn, "No Myth"

Video from a film: Billy Idol, "Cradle of Love" ("Ford Fairlane")

### PROFESSIONAL CATEGORY WINNERS

Direction in a video: Madonna, "Vogue," David Fincher

Choreography in a video: Janet Jackson, "Rhythm Nation," Janet Jackson/Anthony Thomas

Special effects in a video: Tears for Fears, "Sowing the Seeds of Love," Jim Blashfield

Cinematography in a video: Madonna, "Vogue," Pascal Lebeque

Art direction in a video: B 52's, "Love Shack," Martin Lasowitz
Breakthrough video: Tears for Fears, "Sowing the Seeds of Love," Jim Blashfield
Editing in a video: Madonna, "Vogue," Jim Haygood

## SPECIAL AWARD WINNERS
Video vanguard: Janet Jackson
Viewers choice award: Aerosmith, "Janie's Got a Gun"

## INTERNATIONAL VIDEO AWARD WINNERS
Midnight Oil "Blue Sky Mine" (Australia), Titas "Flores" (Brazil), Gloria Estefan "Oye mi canto" (Internacional), The Creeps "Ooh I Like It" (Europe), Kome Kome Club "Funk Fujiyama" (Japan)

# 1991
## GENERAL CATEGORY WINNERS
Video of the year: R.E.M., "Losing My Religion"
Male video: Chris Isaak, "Wicked Game"
Female video: Janet Jackson, "Love Will Never Do without You"
Group video: R.E.M., "Losing My Religion"
Rap video: LL Cool J, "Mama said Knock You Out"
Long-form music video: Madonna, "Immaculate Collection"
Metal/hard-rock video: Aerosmith, "The Other Side"
Alternative-music video: Jane's Addiction, "Been Caught Stealing"
Dance video: C+C Music Factory, "Gonna Make You Sweat (Everybody Dance Now)"
New artist video: Jesus Jones, "Right Here, Right Now"
Video from a film: Chris Isaak, "Wicked Game" (Wild at Heart)

## PROFESSIONAL CATEGORY WINNERS
Direction in a video: R.E.M., "Losing My Religion," Tarsem
Choreography in a video: C+C Music Factory, "Gonna Make You Sweat," Jamale Graves
Special effects in a video: Faith No More, "Falling to Pieces," David Faithfull, Ralph Ziman
Cinematography in a video: Chris Isaak, "Wicked Game" (Concept), Rolf Kesterman
Art direction in a video: R.E.M., "Losing My Religion," José Montana
Breakthrough video: R.E.M., "Losing My Religion," Tarsem
Editing in a video: R.E.M., "Losing My Religion," Robert Duffy

## SPECIAL AWARD WINNERS
Video vanguard: Bon Jovi, Wayne Isham
Viewers choice award: Queensryche, "Silent Lucidity"

## INTERNATIONAL VIDEO AWARD WINNERS
Cui Jian "Wild in the Snow" (Asia), Yothu Yindi "Treaty (Filthy Lucre Mix)" (Australia), Sepultera "Orgasmatron" (Brazil), Roxette "Joyride" (Europe), Franco De Vita "No Basta" (Internacional), Flipper's Guitar "Groove Tube" (Japan)

# 1992
## GENERAL CATEGORY WINNERS
Video of the year: Van Halen, "Right Now"
Male video: Eric Clapton, "Tears in Heaven"
Female video: Annie Lennox, "Why"
Group video: U2, "Even Better than the Real Thing"
Rap video: Arrested Development, "Tennessee"
Metal/hard-rock video: Metallica, "Enter Sandman"
Alternative-music video: Nirvana, "Smells Like Teen Spirit"
Dance video: Prince & The New Power Generation, "Cream"
New artist video: Nirvana, "Smells Like Teen Spirit"
Video from a film: Queen, "Bohemian Rhapsody" (Wayne's World)

## PROFESSIONAL CATEGORY WINNERS
Direction in a video: Van Halen, "Right Now," Mark Fenske
Choreography in a video: En Vogue, "My Lovin' (You're Never Gonna Get It)," Travis Payne, Frank Gatson, Lavelle Smith
Special effects in a video: U2, "Even Better than the Real Thing," Simon Taylor
Cinematography in a video: Guns 'N Roses, "November Rain," Mike Southon/Daniel Pearl
Art direction in a video: Red Hot Chili Peppers, "Give It Away," Nick Goodman
Breakthrough video: Red Hot Chili Peppers, "Give It Away," Stephane Sednaoui
Editing in a video: Van Halen, "Right Now," Mitchell Sinoway

## SPECIAL AWARD WINNERS
Video vanguard award: Guns 'N Roses
Viewers choice award: Red Hot Chili Peppers, "Under the Bridge"

## INTERNATIONAL VIDEO AWARD WINNERS
Christina "Jring Mai Glua" (Asia), Diesel "Man Alive" (Australia), Nenhum de Nos "Ao meu Redor"

---

**... November 18 ...**
FX cabler shells out $40 million for theatrical pics, including **The Full Monty** and **Starship Troopers**.

(Brazil), The Cure "Friday I'm in Love" (Europe), El General "Muevelo" (Internacional)

## 1993
### GENERAL CATEGORY WINNERS
Video of the year: Pearl Jam, "Jeremy"
Male video: Lenny Kravitz, "Are You Gonna Go My Way?"
Female video: k.d. lang, "Constant Craving"
Group video: Pearl Jam, "Jeremy"
Rap video: Arrested Development, "People Everyday"
R&B video: En Vogue, "Free Your Mind"
Metal/hard-rock video: Pearl Jam, "Jeremy"
Alternative-music video: Nirvana, "In Bloom (Version 1-Dresses)
Dance video: En Vogue, "Free Your Mind"
New artist in a video: Stone Temple Pilots, "Plush"
Video from a film: Alice in Chains, "Would?"

### PROFESSIONAL CATEGORY WINNERS
Direction in a video: Pearl Jam, "Jeremy," Mark Pellington
Choreography in a video: En Vogue, "Free Your Mind," Frank Gatson/Lavelle Smith/Travis Payne
Special effects in a video: Peter Gabriel, "Steam," Real World Productions/Colossal Pictures
Cinematography in a video: Madonna, "Rain," Harris Savides
Art direction in a video: Madonna, "Rain," Jan Peter Flack
Breakthrough video: Los Lobos, "Kiko & the Lavender Moon," Ondrej Rudavsky
Editing in a video: Peter Gabriel, "Steam," Douglas Jines

### SPECIAL AWARD WINNERS
Viewers choice award: Aerosmith, "Livin on the Edge"

### INTERNATIONAL VIDEO AWARD WINNERS
Indus Creed "Pretty Child (MTV Asia), Titas "Sera que e isso que eu necessito" (MTV Brazil), Luis Miguel "America" (MTV Internacional), George Michael "Killer/Papa Was a Rolling Stone" (MTV Europe)

## 1994
### GENERAL CATEGORY WINNERS
Video of the year: Aerosmith, "Cryin'"
Male video: Tom Petty & The Heartbreakers, "Mary Jane's Last Dance"
Female video: Janet Jackson, "If"

Group video: Aerosmith, "Cryin"
Rap video: Snoop Doggy Dogg, "Doggy Dogg World"
Metal/hard-rock video: Soundgarden, "Black Hole Sun"
Alternative-music video: Nirvana, "Heart-shaped Box"
Dance video: Salt-N-Pepa with En Vogue, "Whatta Man"
New artist in a video: Counting Crows, "Mr. Jones"
R&B video: Salt-N-Pepa with En Vogue, "Whatta Man"
Video from a film: Bruce Springsteen, "Streets of Philadelphia"

### PROFESSIONAL CATEGORY WINNERS
Direction in a video: Jake Scott, R.E.M., "Everybody Hurts"
Special effects in a video: Brett Leonard/Angel Studios, Peter Gabriel, "Kiss That Frog"
Editing in a video: Pat Sheffield, R.E.M., "Everybody Hurts"
Choreography in a video: Frank Garson/Randy Connors, Salt-N-Pepa with En Vouge, "Whatta Man"
Art direction in a video: Bernadette Disanto, Nirvana, "Heart-shaped Box"
Cinematography in a video: Harris Savides, R.E.M., "Everybody Hurts"
Breakthrough video: June Gutterman, R.E.M., "Everybody Hurts"

### SPECIAL AWARD WINNERS
Special recognition award: Rolling Stones
Video vanguard award: Tom Petty
Viewers choice award: Aerosmith, "Cryin'"

### INTERNATIONAL WINNERS
Sepultura "Territory" (MTV Brazil), Take That "Babe" (MTV Europe), Hide "Eyes Love You" (MTV Japan), Los Fabulos Cadillacs "Matador" (MTV Latino)

## 1995
### GENERAL CATEGORY WINNERS
Video of the year: TLC, "Waterfalls"
Male video: Tom Petty & The Heartbreakers, "You Don't Know How It Feels"
Female video: Madonna, "Take a Bow"
Group video: TLC, "Waterfalls"
Rap video: Dr. Dre, "Keep Their Heads Ringin'"
R&B video: TLC, "Waterfalls"

---

**... November 19 ...**
DreamWorks announces it will bow **The Prince of Egypt** in 40 territories within a week of its domestic debut ... **All the President's Men** director Alan J. Pakula dies in freak auto accident.

Hard-rock video: White Zombie, "More Human than Human"
Alternative-music video: Weezer, "Buddy Holly"
Dance video: Michael Jackson & Janet Jackson, "Scream"
New artist in a video: Hootie & The Blowfish, "Hold My Hand"
Video from a film: Seal, "Kiss from a Rose"

**PROFESSIONAL CATEGORY WINNERS**
Direction in a video: Weezer, "Buddy Holly," Spike Jonze
Choreography in a video: Michael Jackson & Janet Jackson, "Scream," Lavelle Smith/Travis Payne/Tina Landon/Sean Cheeseman
Special effects in a video: Rolling Stones, "Love Is Strong," Fred Raimondi
Cinematography in a video: Rolling Stones, "Love Is Strong," Gary Walker/Mike Trim
Art direction in a video: Michael Jackson & Janet Jackson, "Scream," Tom Foden
Breakthrough video: Weezer, "Buddy Holly," Spike Jonze
Editing in a video: Weezer, "Buddy Holly," Spike Jonze

**SPECIAL AWARD WINNERS**
Video vanguard awards: R.E.M.
Viewers choice award: TLC, "Waterfalls"

**INTERNATIONAL AWARD WINNERS**
Denada "Sambutlah" (MTV Asia), Os paralamas do sucesso "Uma Brasileira" (MTV Brazil), U2 "Hold Me, Thrill Me, Kiss Me, Kill Me" (MTV Europe), Chage & Aska "Something There" (MTV Japan), Café Tacuba "La Ingrata" (MTV Latino), Faye Wong "Chess" (MTV Mandarin)

# 1996
**GENERAL CATEGORY WINNERS**
Video of the year: The Smashing Pumpkins, "Tonight, Tonight"
Male video: Beck, "Where It's At"
Female video: Alanis Morissette, "Ironic"
Group video: Foo Fighters, "Big Me"
Rap video: Coolio Featuring LV, "Gangsta's Paradise (Dangerous Minds)"
R&B video: Fugees, "Killing Me Softly"
Hard-rock video: Metallica, "Until It Sleeps"
Alternative-music video: The Smashing Pumpkins, "1979"
Dance video: Coolio, "1, 2, 3, 3 (Sumpin' New)"
New artist in a video: Alanis Morissette, "Ironic"

Video from a film: Coolio Featuring LV, "Gangsta's Paradise (Dangerous Minds)"

**PROFESSIONAL CATEGORY WINNERS**
Direction in a video: The Smashing Pumpkins, "Tonight, Tonight," Jonathan Dayton & Valerie Faris
Choreography in a video: Bjork, "It's Oh So Quiet," Michael Rooney
Special effects in a video: The Smashing Pumpkins, "Tonight, Tonight," Chris Staves
Cinematography in a video: The Smashing Pumpkins, "Tonight, Tonight," Declan Quinn
Art direction in a video: The Smashing Pumpkins, "Tonight, Tonight," K.K. Barrett & Wa
Breakthrough video: The Smashing Pumpkins, "Tonight, Tonight," Jonathan Dayton & Valerie Faris
Editing in a video: Alanis Morissette, "Ironic," Scott Grey

**SPECIAL AWARD WINNERS**
Viewers choice award: Bush, "Glycerine"

**INTERNATIONAL AWARD WINNERS**
Tai Ji Boys "Come Back Home" (MTV Asia), Skank "Garota Nacional" (MTV Brazil), George Michael "Fastlove" (MTV Europe), Colonial Cousins "Sa ni dha pa" (MTV India), Kuroyume "Pistol" (MTV Japan), Soda Stereo "Ella uso mi cabeza como un revolver" (MTV Latino), Nana Tang "Freedom" (MTV Mandarin)

# 1997
**GENERAL CATEGORY WINNERS**
Video of the year: Jamiroquai, "Virtual Insanity"
Male video: Beck, "Devil's Haircut"
Female video: Jewel, "You Were Meant for Me"
Group video: No Doubt, "Don't Speak"
Rap video: The Notorious B.I.G, "Hypnotize"
R&B video: Puff Daddy & the Family, "I'll Be Missing You (Featuring Faith Evans & 112)"
Rock video: Aerosmith, "Falling in Love (Is Hard on the Knees)"
Alternative-music video: Sublime, "What I Got"
Dance video: Spice Girls, "Wannabe"
New artist in a video: Fiona Apple, "Sleep to Dream"
Video from a film: Will Smith, "Men in Black"

**PROFESSIONAL CATEGORY WINNERS**
Direction in a video: Beck, "The New Pollution"
Choreography in a video: Beck, "The New Pollution"
Special effects in a video: Jamiroquai, "Virtual Insanity"

Cinematography in a video: Jamiroquai, "Virtual Insanity"
Art direction in a video: Jamiroquai, "Virtual Insanity"
Breakthrough video: Jamiroquai, "Virtual Insanity"
Editing in a video: Beck, "Devil's Haircut"

**SPECIAL AWARD WINNERS**
Viewer's choice winner: Prodigy, "Breathe"
Video vanguard: Mark Romanek; LL Cool J

**INTERNATIONAL AWARD WINNERS**
Eraserheads "Ang Huling el bimbo" (MTV Asia), Skank "E uma partida de futebol" (MTV Brazil), Prodigy "Breathe" (MTV Europe), Asha Bhonsle "O mere sona re" (MTV India), Chara "Yasashii Kimochi" (MTV Japan), Cafe Tecuba "Chilanga Banda" (MTV Latino), Mavis Fan "Bartender Angel" (MTV Mandarin)

**1998**
**GENERAL CATEGORY WINNERS**
Video of the year: Madonna, "Ray of Light"
Male video: Will Smith, "Just the Two of Us"
Female video: Madonna, "Ray of Light"
Group video: Backstreet boys, "Everybody (Backstreet's Back)"
Rap video: Will Smith, "Gettin' Jiggy with It"
Dance video: Prodigy, "Smack My Bitch Up"
Rock video: Aerosmith, "Pink"
Alternative-music video: Green Day, "Time of Your Life (Good Riddance)"
New artist in a video: Natalie Imbruglia, "Torn"
Video from a film: Aerosmith, "I Don't Want to Miss a Thing"
R&B video: Wyclef Jean Featuring Refugee Allstars, "Gone till November"

**PROFESSIONAL CATEGORY WINNERS**
Direction in a video: Madonna, "Ray of Light"
Choreography in a video: Madonna, "Ray of Light"
Special effects in a video: Madonna, "Frozen"
Art direction in a video: Bjork, "Bachelorette"

Editing in a video: Madonna, "Ray of Light"
Cinematography in a video: Fiona Apple, "Criminal"
Breakthrough video: Prodigy, "Smack My Bitch up"

**VIEWER'S CHOICE**
Puff Daddy & the Family Featuring the Lox, Lil'Kim, the Notorious B.I.G. & Fuzzbubble, "It's All about the Benjamins (Rock Remix)"

# MTV Europe Awards 1998
**London/Milan 13 November 1998**

Male: Robbie Williams
Group: Spice Girls
Dance: Prodigy
Song: Natalie Imbruglia, "Torn"
Rock: Aerosmith
Female: Madonna
Pop "new": Spice Girls
Breakthrough artist: All Saints
Rap: Beastie Boys
Album "new": Madonna, *Ray of Light*
Video: Massive Attack, *Tear Drop*
Select U.K.: Five
Select north: Eagle Eye Cherry
Select central: Thomas D – Franka Potente
Select southern: Bluevertigo
Free your mind: B-92 (Independent Serbian radio station)

> *Sex appeal is fifty per cent what you've got and fifty per cent what people think you've got. (Sophia Loren)*

# The Grammys

The most glamorous and established of all the music awards, the Grammys are even more difficult to call than the Academy Awards. In the words of Thomas O'Neil (author of *Variety*'s *The Grammys: The Ultimate Unofficial Guide to Music's Highest Honor*): "Predicting nominees has been a shattering experience ever since 1995, when it was decreed that the contenders for best record, song, album, and new artist would no longer be chosen by a vote of the 9,000 members of the National Academy of Recording Arts & Sciences. The membership can still cast its ballots and narrow each category down to 20 choices, but the selection of the final five is trusted to a veiled gang of 25 music experts." Just about every category imaginable carries a statuette – rock, rap, country, movie music, jazz, classical, you name it.

## 1958

Album: *The Music from Peter Gunn* (TV series soundtrack) Henry Mancini, RCA

Record: "Nel Blu dipinto di blu (Volare)," Domenico Modugno, Decca

Song (songwriter's award): "Nel Blu dipinto di blu (Volare)," Domenico Modugno, (lyrics collaborator Franco Miggliacci)

Vocal performance, male: Perry Como, "Catch a Falling Star," RCA

Vocal performance, female: Ella Fitzgerald, *Ella Fitzgerald sings the Irving Berlin Song Book*, Verve

Performance by a vocal group or chorus: Louis Prima, Keely Smith, "That Old Black Magic," Capitol

Performance by a dance band: Count Basie, *Basie*, Roulette

Performance by an orchestra: Billy May, *Billy May's Big Fat Brass*, Capitol

Country and western performance: Kingston Trio, "Tom Dooley," Capitol

Composition, more than 5 minutes : "Cross Country Suite," Nelson Riddle

Rhythm and blues performance: Champs, "Tequila," Challenge

Jazz performance, individual: Ella Fitzgerald, *Ella Fitzgerald sings the Irving Berlin Song Book*, Verve

Jazz performance, group: Count Basie, *Basie*, Roulette

Classical performance, orchestra (conductor's award): Felix Slatkin conducting the Hollywood Bowl Symphony, *Gaîté Parisienne*, Capitol

Classical performance, operatic or choral: Roger Wagner Chorale, *Virtuoso*, Capitol

Classical performance, vocal soloist (with or without orchestra): Renata Tebaldi, *Recital of Songs and Arias*, London

## 1959

Album: *Come Dance With Me*, Frank Sinatra, Capitol

Record: "Mack the Knife," Bobby Darin, Atco

Song (songwriter's award): "The Battle of New Orleans," Jimmy Driftwood

New artist: Bobby Darin

Vocal performance, male: Frank Sinatra, *Come Dance With Me*, Capitol

Vocal performance, female: Ella Fitzgerald, "But Not for Me," Verve

Performance by a vocal group or chorus: Mormon Tabernacle Choir, Richard Condi conducting: "Battle Hymn of the Republic," Columbia

Performance by a top 40 artist: Nat King Cole, "Midnight Flyer," Capitol

Rhythm and blues performance: Dinah Washington, "What a Difference a Day Makes," Mercury

Jazz performance, soloist: Ella Fitzgerald, *Ella Swings Lightly*, Verve

Jazz performance, group: Jonah Jones, *I Dig Chicks*, Capitol

Country and western performance: Johnny Horton, "The Battle of New Orleans," Columbia

Folk performance: Kingston Trio, *The Kingston Trio at Large*, Capitol

Performance by a dance band: Duke Ellington, *Anatomy of a Murder*, Columbia

Performance by an orchestra: David Rose and His Orchestra with André Previn, *Like Young*, MGM

Musical composition, more than 5 minutes: *Anatomy of a Murder*, Duke Ellington

Classical performance, orchestra (conductor's award): Charles Munch conducting the Boston Symphony, *Debussy: Images for Orchestra*, RCA

Classical performance, opera cast or choral: Erich Leinsdorf conducting the Vienna Philharmonic (solos: Peters, London, Della, Casa), *Mozart: The Marriage of Figaro*, RCA

Classical performance, vocal soloist (with or without orchestra): Jussi Björling, *Björling in Opera*, London

Special trustees awards for artists and repertoire contribution: Record of the year: "Mack the Knife," Bobby

Darin – Ahmet Ertegun, A&R producer, Atco
Album of the year: *Come Dance with Me*, Frank Sinatra –
Dave Cavanaugh, A&R producer, Capitol

## 1960

Album: *Button Down Mind*, Bob Newhart, Warner Bros.
Record: "Theme from *A Summer Place*," Percy Faith,
Columbia
Song (songwriter's award): "Theme from *Exodus*," Ernest
Gold
New artist: Bob Newhart
Vocal performance, album, male: Ray Charles, *Genius of
Ray Charles*, Atlantic
Vocal performance, single or track, male: Ray Charles,
"Georgia on My Mind," ABC
Vocal performance, album, female: Ella Fitzgerald, *Mack
the Knife, Ella in Berlin*, Verve
Vocal performance, single or track, female: Ella
Fitzgerald, *Mack the Knife*, Verve
Performance by a pop single artist: Ray Charles, "Georgia
on My Mind," ABC
Performance by a vocal group: Eydie Gormé, Steve
Lawrence, "We Got Us," ABC
Performance by a chorus: Norman Luboff Choir, *Songs of
the Cowboy*, Columbia
Performance by a band for dancing: Count Basie, *Dance
with Basie*, Roulette
Performance by an orchestra: Henry Mancini, *Mr. Lucky*, RCA
Country and western performance: Marty Robbins, "El
Paso," Columbia
Folk performance: Harry Belafonte, "Swing Dat
Hammer," RCA
Rhythm and blues performance: Ray Charles, "Let the
Good Times Roll," Atlantic
Jazz composition, more than 5 minutes (composer's
award): *Sketches of Spain*, Miles Davis, Gil Evans, Columbia
Jazz performance, solo or small group: André Previn,
*West Side Story*, Contempo
Jazz performance, large group: Henry Mancini, *The Blues
and the Beat*, RCA
Classical performance, orchestra (conductor's award):
Fritz Reiner conducting the Chicago Symphony, *Bartók:
Music for Strings, Percussion and Celesta*, RCA
Classical opera production: *Puccini: Turandot*, Erich
Leinsdorf conducting the Rome Opera House Chorus and
Orchestra (solos: Tebaldi, Nilsson, Björling, Tozzi) RCA
Classical performance, vocal soloist: Leontyne Price, *A
Program of Song*, RCA
Contemporary classical composition: *Orchestral Suite
from Tender Land*, Aaron Copland, RCA

## 1961

Album: *Judy at Carnegie Hall*, Judy Garland, Capitol

Record: "Moon River," Henry Mancini, RCA
Song (songwriter's award): "Moon River," Henry
Mancini, Johnny Mercer
New artist: Peter Nero
Solo vocal performance, male: Jack Jones, "Lollipops and
Roses," Kapp
Solo vocal performance, female: Judy Garland, *Judy at
Carnegie Hall*, Capitol
Performance by a vocal group: Lambert, Hendricks and
Ross, *High Flying*, Columbia
Performance by a chorus: Johnny Mann Singers (Si
Zentner Orchestra) *Great Band with Great Voices*, Liberty
Rock and roll recording: "Let's Twist Again," Chubby
Checker, Parkway
Rhythm and blues recording: "Hit the Road Jack," Ray
Charles, ABC-Paramount
Original jazz composition (composer's award): "African
Waltz," Galt MacDermot, Riverside
Jazz performance by a soloist or small group,
instrumental: André Previn, *André Previn Plays Harold
Arlen*, Contemporary
Jazz performance by a large group, instrumental: Stan
Kenton, *West Side Story*, Capitol
Country and western recording: "Big Bad John," Jimmy
Dean, Columbia
Folk recording: *Belafonte Folk Singers at Home and
Abroad*, Belafonte Folk Singers, RCA
Instrumental theme or instrumental version of song
(composer's award): "African Waltz," Galt MacDermot,
Roulette
Album, classical: *Stravinsky Conducts, 1960: Le Sacre du
printemps, Pétrouchka*, Igor Stravinsky conducting the
Columbia Symphony, Columbia
Contemporary classical composition (composer's award)
(tie): *Discantos*, Laurindo Almeida, Capitol and
*Movements for Piano and Orchestra*, Igor Stravinsky; and
Columbia
Classical performance, orchestra (conductor's award):
Charles Munch conducting the Boston Symphony, *Ravel:
Daphnis and Chloé*, RCA
Opera recording (conductor's award): *Puccini: Madame
Butterfly*, Gabriele Santini conducting Rome Opera
Chorus and Orchestra (solos: de los Angeles, Björling,
Pirazzini, Sereni) Capitol
Classical performance, vocal soloist: Joan Sutherland
(Molinari-Pradelli conducting the Royal Opera House
Orchestra) *The Art of Prima Donna*, London

## 1962

Album: *The First Family*, Vaughn Meader, Cadence
Record: "I Left My Heart in San Francisco," Tony Bennett,
Columbia
Song (songwriter's award): "What Kind of Fool Am I?,"

Leslie Bricusse, Anthony Newley
New artist: Robert Goulet
Solo vocal performance, male: Tony Bennett, "I Left My Heart in San Francisco," Columbia
Solo vocal performance, female: Ella Fitzgerald, *Ella Swings Brightly with Nelson Riddle,* Verve
Performance by a vocal group: Peter, Paul and Mary, "If I Had a Hammer," Warner Bros.
Performance by a chorus: New Christy Minstrels, *Presenting the New Christy Minstrels,* Columbia
Rock and roll recording: "Alley Cat," Bent Fabric, Atco
Rhythm and blues recording: "I Can't Stop Loving You," Ray Charles, ABC-Paramount
Original jazz composition (composer's award): Vince Guaraldi, "Cast Your Fate to the Winds," Fantasy
Jazz performance by a soloist or small group, instrumental: Stan Getz, "Desafinado," Verve
Jazz performance by a large group, instrumental: Stan Kenton, *Adventures in Jazz,* Capitol
Country and western recording: "Funny Way of Laughin'," Burl Ives, Decca
Folk recording: "If I Had a Hammer," Peter, Paul and Mary, Warner Bros.
Instrumental theme (composer's award): "A Taste of Honey," Bobby Scott, Ric Marlow, Reprise
Album, classical: *Columbia Records Presents Vladimir Horowitz,* Vladimir Horowitz, Columbia
Classical composition by a contemporary composer: Igor Stravinsky, *The Flood*
Classical performance, orchestra (conductor's award): Igor Stravinsky conducting the Columbia Symphony, *Stravinsky: The Firebird Ballet,* Columbia
Opera recording (conductor's award): *Verdi: Aida,* Georg Solti conducting the Rome Opera House Orchestra and Chorus (solos: Price, Vickers, Gorr, Merrill, Tozzi) RCA
Classical performance, vocal soloist (with or without orchestra): Eileen Farrell (Bernstein conducting the New York Philharmonic) *Wagner: Götterdämmerung, Brünnhilde's Immolation Scene; Wesendonck: Songs,* Columbia

## 1963

Album: *The Barbra Streisand Album,* Barbra Streisand, Columbia
Record: "The Days of Wine and Roses," Henry Mancini, RCA
Song (songwriter's award): "The Days of Wine and Roses," Johnny Mercer, Henry Mancini, RCA
New artist: Swingle Singers
Vocal performance, male: Jack Jones, "Wives and Lovers," Kapp
Vocal performance, female: Barbra Streisand, *The Barbra*

*Streisand Album,* Columbia
Performance by a vocal group: Peter, Paul and Mary, "Blowin' in the Wind," Warner Bros.
Performance by a chorus: Swingle Singers, *Bach Greatest Hits,* Philips
Rock and roll recording: "Deep Purple," Nino Tempo, April Stevens, Atco
Rhythm and blues recording: "Busted," Ray Charles, ABC-Paramount
Original jazz composition (composer's award): Ray Brown, Steve Allen, "Gravy Waltz," Dot
Instrumental jazz performance by a soloist or a small group: Bill Evans, *Conversations with Myself,* Verve
Instrumental jazz performance by a large group: Woody Herman Band, *Encore: Woody Herman, 1963,* Philips
Country and western recording: "Detroit City," Bobby Bare, RCA
Folk recording: Peter, Paul and Mary, "Blowin' in the Wind," Warner Bros.
Instrumental theme (composer's award): "More (Theme from *Mondo Cane*)," Riz Ortolani, Nino Oliviero, Norman Newell, United Artists
Album, classical: *Britten: War Requiem,* Benjamin Britten conducting the London Symphony Orchestra and Chorus (solos: Vishnevskaya, Pears, Fischer-Dieskay); David Willocks directing the Bach Choir; Edward Chapman directing the Highgate School Choir, London
Classical composition by a contemporary composer: Benjamin Britten, *War Requiem,* London
Classical performance, orchestra (conductor's award): Erich Leinsdorf conducting the Boston Symphonic Orcestra, *Bartók: Concerto for Orchestra,* RCA
Most promising new classical artist: André Watts, pianist, Columbia
Classical performance, vocal soloist: Leontyne Price, *Great Scenes from Gershwin's Porgy and Bess,* RCA

## 1964

Album: *Getz/Gilberto,* Stan Getz, João Gilberto, Verve
Record: "The Girl from Ipanema," Stan Getz, Astrud Gilberto, Verve
Song (songwriter's award): "Hello Dolly!" Jerry Herman
New artist: Beatles
Vocal performance, male: Louis Armstrong, "Hello Dolly!" Kapp
Vocal performance, female: Barbra Streisand, "People," Columbia
Performance by a vocal group: The Beatles, *A Hard Day's Night,* Capitol
Performance by a chorus: Swingle Singers, *The Swingle Singers Going Baroque,* Philips
Rock and roll recording: "Downtown," Petula Clark, Warner Bros.

Rhythm and blues recording: "How Glad I Am," Nancy Wilson, Capitol

Original jazz composition (composer's award): Lalo Schifrin, "The Cat," Verve

Instrumental jazz performance by a small group or soloist with small group: Stan Getz, *Getz/Gilberto*, Verve

Instrumental jazz performance by a large group or soloist with large group: Laurindo Almeida, *Guitar from Ipanema*, Capitol

Country and western album: *Dang Me/Chu-a-Lug*, Roger Miller, Smash

Country and western single: "Dang Me," Roger Miller, Smash

Country and western song (songwriter's award): "Dang Me," Roger Miller, Smash

New country and western artist: Roger Miller, Smash

Country and western vocal performance, male: Roger Miller, "Dang Me," Smash

Country and western vocal performance, female: Dottie West, "Here Comes My Baby," RCA

Folk recording: *We'll Sing in the Sunshine*, Gale Garnett, RCA

Instrumental composition (other than jazz) (composer's award): Henry Mancini, "*The Pink Panther* Theme," RCA

Album, classical: *Bernstein: Symphony No. 3 ("Kaddish")* , Leonard Bernstein conducting the New York Philharmonic, Columbia

Classical composition by a contemporary composer: Samuel Barber, *Piano Concerto*, Columbia

Classical performance, orchestra (conductor's award): Erich Leinsdorf conducting the Boston Symphony, *Mahler: Symphony No. 5 in C Sharp Minor; Berg: Wozzeck Excerpts* (solo: Phylis Curtin) RCA

Most promising new artist: Marilyn Horne, mezzo-soprano, London

Opera recording (conductor's award): *Bizet: Carmen*, Herbert von Karajan conducting the Vienna Philharmonic Orchestra and Chorus (solos: Price, Corelli, Merrill, Freni) RCA

Classical performance, vocal soloist (with or without orchestra): Leontyne Price (Reiner conducting the Chicago Symphony) *Berlioz: Nuits d'été; Falla: El amor brujo*, RCA

## 1965

Album: *September of My Years*, Frank Sinatra, Reprise

Record: "A Taste of Honey," Herb Alpert and the Tijuana Brass, A&M

Song (songwriter's award): "The Shadow of Your Smile (Theme from *The Sandpiper*)," Paul Francis Webster, Johnny Mandel

New artist: Tom Jones

Vocal performance, male: Frank Sinatra, "It Was a Very Good Year," Reprise

Vocal performance, female: Barbra Streisand, *My Name is Barbra*, Columbia

Performance by a vocal group: Anita Kerr Quartet, *We Dig Mancini*, RCA

Performance by a chorus: Swingle Singers, *Anyone for Mozart?* Philips

Contemporary (R&R) single: "King of the Road," Roger Miller, Smash

Contemporary (R&R) vocal performance, male: Roger Miller, "King of the Road," Smash

Contemporary (R&R) vocal performance, female: Petula Clark, "I Know the Place," Warner Bros.

Contemporary (R&R) performance by a group (vocal or instrumental): Statler Brothers, "Flowers on the Wall," Columbia

Rhythm and blues recording: "Papa's Got a Brand New Bag," James Brown, King

Original jazz composition (composer's award): Lalo Schifrin, "Jazz Suite on the Mass Texts," RCA

Jazz performance by a small group or soloist with small group: Ramsey Lewis Trio, *The "In" Crowd*, Cadet

Jazz performance by a large group or soloist with large group: Duke Ellington Orchestra, *Ellington '66*, Reprise

Country and western album: *The Return of Roger Miller*, Roger Miller, Smash

Country and western single: "King of the Road," Roger Miller, Smash

Country and western song (songwriter's award): "King of the Road," Roger Miller, Smash

New country and western artist: Statler Brothers, Columbia

Country and western vocal performance, male: Roger Miller, "King of the Road," Smash

Country and western vocal performance, female: Jody Miller, "Queen of the House," Capitol

Folk recording: *An Evening with Belafonte/Makeba*, Harry Belafonte, Miriam Makeba, RCA

Instrumental performance (non-jazz): Herb Alpert and the Tijuana Brass, "A Taste of Honey," A&M

Album, classical: *Horowitz at Carnegie Hall, an Historic Return*, Vladimir Horowitz, Columbia

Composition by a contemporary classical composer: Charles Ives, *Symphony No. 4*, Columbia

Classical performance, orchestra (conductor's award): Leopold Stokowski conducting the American Symphony, *Ives: Symphony No. 4*, Columbia

Most promising new recording artist: Peter Serkin, pianist, RCA

Opera recording (conductor's award): *Berg: Wozzeck*, Karl Böhm conducting the Orchestra of German Opera Berlin, (solos: Fischer-Dieskay, Lear, Wunderlich) Deutsche Grammophon

Classical vocal performance (with/without orchestra): Leontyne Price, (Leinsdorf conducting the Boston Symphony) Strauss: *Salome; The Egyptian Helen*, RCA

## 1966

Album: *Sinatra: A Man and His Music*, Frank Sinatra, Reprise
Record: "Strangers in the Night," Frank Sinatra, Reprise
Song (songwriter's award): "Michelle," John Lennon, Paul McCartney, Capitol
Vocal performance, male: Frank Sinatra, "Strangers in the Night," Reprise
Vocal performance, female: Eydie Gormé, "If He Walked into My Life," Columbia
Performance by a vocal group: Anita Kerr Quartet, "A Man and a Woman," Warner Bros.
Performance by a chorus: Ray Conniff and Singers, "Somewhere My Love (Lara's Theme from *Dr. Zhivago*)," Columbia
Contemporary (R&R) recording: "Winchester Cathedral," New Vaudeville Band, Fontana
Contemporary (R&R) solo vocal performance (male or female): Paul McCartney, "Eleanor Rigby," Capitol
Contemporary (R&R) group performance (vocal or instrumental): The Mamas and the Papas, "Monday, Monday," Dunhill
Rhythm and blues recording: "Crying Time," Ray Charles, ABC-Paramount
Rhythm and blues solo vocal performance (male or female): Ray Charles, "Crying Time," ABC-Paramount
Rhythm and blues group performance (vocal or instrumental): Ramsey Lewis, "Hold It Right There," Cadet
Original jazz composition (composer's award): Duke Ellington, "In the Beginning God," RCA
Instrumental jazz performance by a group or soloist with group: Wes Montgomery, "Goin' out of My Head," Verve
Country and western recording: "Almost Persuaded," David Houston, Epic
Country and western vocal performance (male): David Houston, "Almost Persuaded," Epic
Country and western vocal performance (female): Jeannie Seely, "Don't Touch Me," Monument
Country and western song (songwriter's award): "Almost Persuaded," Billy Sherrill, Glenn Sutton, Epic
Folk recording: *Blues in the Street*, Cortelia Clark, RCA
Instrumental theme (composer's award): "*Batman* Theme," Neal Hefti, RCA
Instrumental performance (other than jazz): Herb Alpert and the Tijuana Brass, "What Now My Love?," A&M
Album, classical: *Ives: Symphony No.1 in D Minor*, Morton Gould conducting the Chicago Symphony, RCA
Classical performance, orchestra (conductor's award):

Erich Leinsdorf conducting the Boston Symphony, *Mahler: Symphony No. 6 in A Minor*, RCA
Opera recording (conductor's award): *Wagner: Die Walküre*, Georg Solti conducting the Vienna Philharmonic, London
Classical performance, vocal soloist: Leontyne Price, *Prima Donna*, RCA

## 1967

Album: *Sgt. Pepper's Lonely Hearts Club Band*, Beatles, Capitol
Record: "Up, Up and Away," 5th Dimension, Soul City
Song (songwriter's award): "Up, Up and Away," Jimmy Webb, Soul City
New artist: Bobby Gentry
Vocal performance, male: Glen Campbell, "By the Time I Get to Phoenix," Capitol
Vocal performance, female: Bobbie Gentry, "Ode to Billie Joe," Capitol
Performance by a vocal group: 5th Dimension, "Up, Up and Away," Soul City
Performance by a chorus: Johnny Mann Singers, "Up, Up and Away," Soul City
Contemporary single: "Up, Up and Away," 5th Dimension, Soul City
Contemporary album: *Sgt. Pepper's Lonely Hearts Club Band*, Beatles, Capitol
Contemporary solo vocal performance, male: Glen Campbell, "By the Time I Get to Phoenix," Capitol
Contemporary solo vocal performance, female: Bobbie Gentry, "Ode to Billie Joe," Capitol
Contemporary group performance (vocal or instrumental): 5th Dimension, "Up, Up and Away," Soul City
Rhythm and blues recording: "Respect," Aretha Franklin, Atlantic
Rhythm and blues solo vocal performance, male: Lou Rawls, "Dead End Street," Capitol
Rhythm and blues solo vocal performance, female: Aretha Franklin, "Respect," Atlantic
Rhythm and blues group performance (vocal or instrumental): Sam and Dave, "Soul Man," Stax
Instrumental jazz performance by a small group or soloist with small group (7 or fewer): Cannonball Adderley Quintet, *Mercy, Mercy, Mercy*, Capitol
Instrumental jazz performance by a large group or soloist with large group (8 or more): Duke Ellington, "Far East Suite," RCA
Country and western recording: "Gentle on My Mind," Glen Campbell, Capitol
Country and western solo vocal performance, male: Glen Campbell, "Gentle on My Mind," Capitol
Country and western solo vocal performance, female: Tammy Wynette, "I Don't Wanna Play House," Epic

**. . . November 26 . . .**
Top 10 U.S. music albums sold almost 10 million units during the pre-Thanksgiving Day week.

Country and western performance by a duo, trio or group (vocal or instrumental): Johnny Cash, June Carter, "Jackson," Columbia

Country and western song (songwriter's award): "Gentle on My Mind," John Hartford, RCA

Folk performance: John Hartford, "Gentle on My Mind," RCA

Instrumental theme (composer's award): "Mission: Impossible," Lalo Schifrin, Dot

Instrumental performance: Chet Atkins, *Chet Atkins Picks the Best*, RCA

Album, classical (tie): *Berg: Wozzeck*, Pierre Boulez conducting the orchestra and chorus of the Paris National Opera (solos: Berry Strauss, Uhl, Doench) Columbia; and *Mahler: Symphony No.8 in E Flat Major ("Symphony of a Thousand")*, Leonard Bernstein conducting the London Symphony with soloists and choruses, Columbia

Classical performance, orchestra (conductor's award): Igor Stravinsky conducting the Columbia Symphony, *Stravinsky: Firebird and Pétrouchka Suites*, Columbia

Opera recording: *Berg: Wozzeck*, Pierre Boulez conducting the orchestra and chorus of the Paris National Opera (solos: Berry Strauss, Uhl, Doench) Columbia

Classical performance, vocal soloist: Leontyne Price, *Prima Donna, Vol 2*, RCA

## 1968

Album: *By the Time I Get to Phoenix*, Glen Campbell, Capital

Record: "Mrs. Robinson," Simon and Garfunkel, Columbia

Song (songwriter's award): "Little Green Apples," Bobby Russell

New artist: José Feliciano

Contemporary pop vocal performance, male: José Feliciano, "Light My Fire," RCA

Contemporary pop vocal performance, female: Dionne Warwick, "Do You Know the Way to San José," Scepter

Contemporary pop vocal performance by a duo or group: Simon and Garfunkel, "Mrs. Robinson," Columbia

Contemporary pop performance by a chorus: Alan Copeland Singers, "Mission: Impossible/Norwegian Wood," ABC

Contemporary pop performance, instrumental: Mason Williams, "Classical Gas," Warner Bros.

Rhythm and blues vocal performance, male: Otis Redding, "(Sittin' on) The Dock of the Bay," Volt

Rhythm and blues vocal performance, female: Aretha Franklin, "Chain of Fools," Atlantic

Rhythm and blues performance by a duo or group (vocal or instrumental): The Temptations, "Cloud Nine," Gordy

Rhythm and blues song (songwriter's award): "(Sittin' on) The Dock of the Bay," Otis Redding, Steve Cropper, Volt

Instrumental jazz performance by a small group or soloist with small group: Bill Evans Trio, *Bill Evans at the Montreux Jazz Festival*, Verve

Instrumental jazz performance by a large group or soloist with large group: Duke Ellington, *And His Mother Called Him Bill*, RCA

Country solo vocal performance, male: Johnny Cash, "Folsom Prison Blues," Columbia

Country solo vocal performance, female: Jeannie C. Riley, "Harper Valley P.T.A.," Plantation

Country performance by a duo or group (vocal or instrumental): Flatt and Scruggs, "Foggy Mountain Breakdown," Columbia

Country song (songwriter's award): "Little Green Apples," Bobby Russell

Folk performance: Judy Collins, "Both Sides Now," Elektra

Instrumental theme (composer's award): "Classical Gas," Mason Williams, Warner Bros.

Classical performance, orchestra (conductor's award): Pierre Boulez conducting the New Philharmonia Orchestra, *Boulez Conducts Debussy*, Columbia

Opera recording: *Mozart: Così fan tutte*, Erich Leinsdorf conducting the New Philharmonia Orchestra and Ambrosian Opera Chorus (solos: Price, Troyanos, Raskin, Milnes, Shirley, Flagello) RCA

Classical performance, vocal soloist: Montserrat Caballé, (Cillario conducting the RCA Italian Opera Orchestra and Chorus)*Rossini Rarities*, RCA

## 1969

Album: *Blood Sweat and Tears*, Blood Sweat and Tears, Columbia

Record: "Aquarius/Let the Sunshine in," 5th Dimension, Soul City

Song (songwriter's award): "Games People Play," Joe South

New artist: Crosby, Stills and Nash

Contemporary vocal performance, male: Harry Nilsson, "Everybody's Talkin'," United Artists

Contemporary vocal performance, female: Peggy Lee, "Is That All There Is?" Capitol

Contemporary vocal performance by a group: 5th Dimension, "Aquarius/Let the Sunshine in," Soul City

Contemporary performance by a chorus: Percy Faith Orchestra and Chorus, "Love Theme from *Romeo and Juliet*," Columbia

Contemporary song (songwriter's award): "Games People Play," Joe South

Contemporary instrumental performance: "Variations on a Theme by Erik Satie," Blood Sweat and Tears, Columbia

Rhythm and blues song (songwriter's award): "Color Him Father," Richard Spencer

Rhythm and blues vocal performance, male: Joe Simon,

...**November 27**...

Helena Bonham Carter set to star in **Women Talking Dirty**, the first pic greenlit from Elton John's Rocket Pictures.

"The Chokin' Kind," Sound Stage

Rhythm and blues vocal performance, female: Aretha Franklin, "Share Your Love with Me," Atlantic

Rhythm and blues vocal performance by a duo or group: Isley Brothers, "It's Your Thing," T-Neck

Rhythm and blues instrumental performance: King Curtis, "Games People Play," Atco

Instrumental jazz performance by a small group or soloist with small group (7 or fewer): Wes Montgomery, *Willow Weep for Me*, Verve

Instrumental jazz performance by a large group or soloist with large group (8 or more): Quincy Jones, "Walking in Space," A&M

Country song (songwriter's award): "A Boy Named Sue," Shel Silverstein

Country vocal performance, male: Johnny Cash, "A Boy Named Sue," Columbia

Country vocal performance, female: Tammy Wynette, "Stand by Your Man," Epic

Country performance by a duo or group : Waylon Jennings, Kimberlys, "MacArthur Park," RCA

Country instrumental performance: Danny Davis and the Nashville Brass, *The Nashville Brass Featuring Danny Davis Play More Nashville Sounds*, RCA

Folk performance: Joni Mitchell, *Clouds*, Warner Bros.

Instrumental theme (composer's award): *Midnight Cowboy*, John Barry

Album, classical: *Switched-on Bach* (*Virtuoso Electronic Performance of Branden Concerto No. 3, Air on a G String, Jesu, Joy of Man's Destiny, etc.*, performed on Moog synthesizer) Walter Carlos, Columbia

Classical performance, orchestra (conductor's award): Pierre Boulez conducting the Cleveland Orchestra, *Boulez Conducts Debussy, Vol. 2, Images pour orchestre*, Columbia

Opera recording: *Wagner: Siegfried*, Herbert von Karajan conducting the Berlin Philharmonic (solos: Thomas, Stewart, Stolze, Dernesch, Keleman, Dominguez, Gayer, Ridderbush) Deutsche Gramophon

Classical performance, vocal soloist: Leontyne Price (Schippers conducting the New Philharmonia) *Barber: Two Scenes from "Anthony and Cleopatra"; Knoxville: Summer of 1915*, RCA

## 1970

Album: *Bridge over Troubled Water*, Simon and Garfunkel, Columbia

Record: "Bridge over Troubled Water," Simon and Garfunkel, Columbia

Song (songwriter's award): "Bridge over Troubled Water," Paul Simon

New artist: Carpenters

Contemporary vocal performance, male: Ray Stevens, "Everything Is Beautiful," Barnaby

Contemporary vocal performance, female: Dionne Warwick, "I'll Never Fall in Love Again," Scepter

Contemporary vocal performance by a duo, group or chorus: The Carpenters, "Close to You," A&M

Contemporary song (songwriter's award): "Bridge over Troubled Water," Paul Simon

Contemporary instrumental performance: Henry Mancini, *Theme from "Z" and Other Film Music*, RCA

Rhythm and blues song (songwriter's award): "Patches," Ronald Dunbar, General Johnson

Rhythm and blues vocal performance, male: B.B. King, "The Thrill Is Gone," ABC

Rhythm and blues vocal performance, female: Aretha Franklin, "Don't Play That Song," Atlantic

Rhythm and blues performance by a duo or group (vocal or instrumental): Delfonics, "Didn't I (Blow Your Mind This Time)?," Philly Groove

Jazz performance by a small group or soloist with small group (7 or fewer): Bill Evans, *Alone*, MGM

Jazz performance by a large group or soloist with large group (8 or more): Miles Davis, *Bitches Brew*, Columbia

Country song (songwriter's award): "My Woman, My Woman, My Wife," Marty Robbins

Country instrumental performance: Chet Atkins, Jerry Reed, *Me and Jerry*, RCA

Country vocal performance, male: Ray Price, "For the Good Times," Columbia

Country vocal performance, female: Lynn Anderson, "Rose Garden," Columbia

Country vocal performance by a duo or group: Johnny Cash, June Carter, "If I Were a Carpenter," Columbia

Instrumental composition (composer's award): Alfred Newman, "*Airport* Love Theme"

Album, classical: *Berlioz: Les Troyens*, Colin Davis conducting the Royal Opera House Orchestra and Chorus (solos: Vickers, Veasy, Lindholm) Philips

Classical performance, orchestra (conductor's award): Pierre Boulez conducting the Cleveland Orchestra, *Stravinsky: Le Sacre du printemps*, Columbia

Opera recording: *Berlioz: Les Troyens*, Colin Davis conducting the Royal Opera House Orchestra and Chorus (solos: Vickers, Veasey, Lindholm) Philips

Classical performance, vocal soloist: Dietrich Fischer-Dieskay (Gerlad Moore, accompanist) *Schubert: Lieder*, Deutsche Grammophon

## 1971

Album: *Tapestry*, Carole King, Ode

Record: "It's Too Late," Carole King, Ode

Song (songwriter's award): "You've Got a Friend," Carole King

New artist: Carly Simon

Pop vocal performance, male: James Taylor, "You've Got a

**... November 28 ...**

The prospect of an unprecedented $7 billion box-office year in the U.S. gains momentum as 1998 climbed to $6 billion.

Friend," Warner Bros.

Pop vocal performance, female: Carole King, "Tapestry," Ode

Pop vocal performance by a duo, group or chorus: Carpenters, *Carpenters*, A&M

Pop instrumental performance: Quincy Jones, *Smackwater Jack*, A&M

Rhythm and blues song (songwriter's award): "Ain't No Sunshine," Bill Withers

Rhythm and blues vocal performance, male: Lou Rawls, "A Natural Man," MGM

Rhythm and blues vocal performance, female: Aretha Franklin, "Bridge over Troubled Water," Atlantic

Rhythm and blues performance by a duo or group (vocal or instrumental): Ike and Tina Turner, "Proud Mary," United Artists

Jazz performance by a soloist: Bill Evans, *The Bill Evans Album*, Columbia

Jazz performance by a group: Bill Evans, *The Bill Evans Album*, Columbia

Jazz performance by a big band: Duke Ellington, "New Orleans Suite," Atlantic

Country song (songwriter's award): "Help Me Make It through the Night," Kris Kristofferson

Country vocal performance, male: Jerry Reed, "When You're Hot, You're Hot," RCA

Country vocal performance, female: Sammi Smith, "Help Me Make It through the Night," Mega

Country vocal performance, duo or group: Conway Twitty, Loretta Lynn, "After the Fire Is Gone," Decca

Country instrumental: Chet Atkins, *Snowbird*, RCA

Ethnic or traditional recording (including traditional blues): *They Call Me Muddy Waters*, Muddy Waters, Chess

Instrumental composition (composer's award): Michel Legrand, "Theme from *Summer of '42*," Warner Bros.

Album, classical: *Horowitz Plays Rachmaninov* (études tableaux, piano music, sonatas) (solo: Vladimir Horowitz) Columbia

Classical performance, orchestra (conductor's award): Carlo Maria Giulini conducting the Chicago Symphony, *Mahler: Symphony No. 1 in D Major*, Angel

Opera recording: *Verdi: Aida*, Erich Leinsdorf conducting the London Symphony; John Alldis Choir (solos: Price, Domingo, Milnes, Bumbry, Raimondi) RCA

Classical performance, vocal soloist: Leontyne Price (Garvey accompanist) *Leontyne Price Sings Robert Schumann*, RCA

## 1972

Album: *The Concert for Bangla Desh*, George Harrison, Ravi Shankar, Bob Dylan, Leon Russell, Ringo Starr, Billy Preston, Eric Clapton, Klaus Voormann, and others, Apple

Record: "The First Time Ever I Saw Your Face," Roberta Flack, Atlantic

Song (songwriter's award): "The First Time Ever I Saw Your Face," Ewan MacColl

New artist: America

Pop vocal performance, male: Nilsson, "Without You," RCA

Pop vocal performance, female: Helen Reddy, "I Am a Woman," Capitol

Pop vocal performance by a duo, group or chorus: Roberta Flack, Donny Hathaway, "Where Is the Love?," Atlantic

Pop instrumental performance by an instrumental performer: Billy Preston, "Outa-Space," A&M

Pop instrumental performance with vocal coloring: Isaac Hayes, *Black Moses*, Enterprise

Rhythm and blues song (songwriter's award): "Papa Was a Rolling Stone," Barrett Strong, Norman Whitfield

Rhythm and blues vocal performance, male: Billy Paul, "Me and Mrs. Jones," Philadelphia International

Rhythm and blues vocal performance, female: Aretha Franklin, *Young, Gifted and Black*, Atlantic

Rhythm and blues vocal performance by a duo, group or chorus: Temptations, "Papa Was a Rolling Stone," Gordy/Motown

Rhythm and blues instrumental performance: Temptations, Paul Riser, "Papa Was a Rolling Stone," Gordy/Motown

Jazz performance by a soloist: Gary Burton, *Alone at Last*, Atlantic

Jazz performance by a group: Freddie Hubbard, *First Light*, CTI

Jazz performance by a big band: Duke Ellington, "Togo Brava Suite," United Artists

Country song (songwriter's award): "Kiss an Angel Good Mornin'," Ben Peters

Country vocal performance, male: Charley Pride, *Charley Pride Sings Heart Songs*, RCA

Country vocal performance, female: Donna Fargo, "Happiest Girl in the Whole U.S.A.," Dot

Country vocal performance by a duo or group: Statler Brothers, "Class of '57," Mercury

Country instrumental performance: Charlie McCoy, *The Real McCoy*, Monument

Instrumental composition (composer's award): Michel Legrand, "Brian's Song," Bell

Album, classical: *Mahler: Symphony No. 8 in E Flat Major* ("*Symphony of a Thousand*") Georg Solti conducting the Chicago Symphony, Vienna Boys' Choir, Vienna State Opera Chorus, Vienna Singverein Chorus and soloists, London

Classical performance, orchestra (conductor's award): Georg Solti conducting the Chicago Symphony, *Mahler: Symphony No. 7 in E Minor*, London

Opera recording: *Berlioz: Benvenuto Cellini*, Colin Davis

---

conducting the BBC Symphony; Chorus of Covent Garden (solos: Gedda, Eda-Pierre, Soyer, Berbie) Philips
Classical performance, vocal soloist: Dietrich Fischer-Dieskau (Richter, accompanist) *Brahms: Die Schone Magelone*, Angel

## 1973

Album: *Innervisions*, Stevie Wonder, Tamla/Motown
Record: "Killing Me Softly with His Song," Roberta Flack, Atlantic
Song (songwriter's award): "Killing Me Softly with His Song," Norman Gimbel, Charles Fox
New artist: Bette Midler
Pop vocal performance, male: Stevie Wonder, "You Are the Sunshine of My Life," Tamla/Motown
Pop vocal performance, female: Roberta Flack, "Killing Me Softly with His Song," Atlantic
Pop vocal performance by a duo, group or chorus: Gladys Knight and the Pips, "Neither One of Us (Wants to Be the First to Say Goodbye)," Soul/Motown
Pop instrumental performance: Eumir Deodato, "Also Sprach Zarathustra (*2001*)," CTI
Rhythm and blues vocal performance, male: Stevie Wonder, "Superstition," Tamla/Motown
Rhythm and blues vocal performance, female: Aretha Franklin, "Master of Eyes," Atlantic
Rhythm and blues vocal performance by a duo, group or chorus: Gladys Knight and the Pips, "Midnight Train to Georgia," Buddah
Rhythm and blues instrumental performance: Ramsey Lewis, "Hang on Sloopy," Columbia
Rhythm and blues song (songwriter's award): "Superstition," Stevie Wonder
Jazz performance by a soloist: Art Tatum, *God Is in the House*, Onyx
Jazz performance by a group: Supersax, *Supersax Plays Bird*, Capitol
Jazz performance by a big band: Woody Herman, *Giant Steps*, Fantasy
Country vocal performance, male: Charlie Rich, "Behind Closed Doors," Epic/Columbia
Country vocal performance, female: Olivia Newton-John, "Let Me Be There," MCA
Country vocal performance by a duo or group: Kris Kristofferson, Rita Coolidge, "From the Bottle to the Bottom," A&M
Country instrumental performance: Eric Weissberg, Steve Mandell, "Dueling Banjos," Warner Bros.
Country song (songwriter's award): "Behind Closed Doors," Kenny O'Dell
Instrumental composition (composer's award): Gato Barbieri, "Last Tango in Paris"
Album, classical: *Bartók: Concerto for Orchestra*, Pierre

Boulez conducting the New York Philharmonic, Columbia
Classical performance, orchestra (conductor's award): Pierre Boulez conducting the New York Philharmonic, *Bartók: Concerto for Orchestra*, Columbia
Opera recording: *Bizet: Carmen*, Leonard Bernstein conducting the Metropolitan Opera Orchestra and Manhattan Opera Chorus (solos: Horne, McCracken, Maliponte, Krause) Deutsche Grammophon
Classical performance, vocal soloist: Leontyne Price (Downes conducting the New Philharmonia), *Puccini: Heroines (La Bohème, La Rondine, Tosca, Manon Lescaut)*, RCA

## 1974

Album: *Fulfillingness' First Finale*, Stevie Wonder, Tamla/Motown
Record: "I Honestly Love You," Olivia Newton-John, MCA
Song (songwriter's award): "The Way We Were," Marilyn and Alan Bergman, Marvin Hamlisch
New artist: Marvin Hamlisch
Pop vocal performance, male: Stevie Wonder, *Fulfillingness' First Finale*, Tamla/Motown
Pop vocal performance, female: Olivia Newton-John, "I Honestly Love You," MCA
Pop vocal performance by a duo, group or chorus: Paul McCartney and Wings, "Band on the Run," Apple/Capitol
Pop instrumental performance: Marvin Hamlisch, "The Entertainer," MCA
Rhythm and blues song (songwriter's award): "Living for the City," Stevie Wonder
Rhythm and blues vocal performance, male: Stevie Wonder, "Boogie on Reggae Woman," Tamla/Motown
Rhythm and blues vocal performance, female: Aretha Franklin, "Ain't Nothing Like the Real Thing," Atlantic
Rhythm and blues vocal performance by a duo, group or chorus: Rufus, "Tell Me Something Good," ABC
Rhythm and blues instrumental performance: MFSB, "TSOP (The Sound of Philadelphia)," Philadelphia International/Epic
Jazz performance by a soloist: Charlie Parker, *First Recordings!* Onyx
Jazz performance by a group: Oscar Peterson, Joe Pass, Niels Pedersen, *The Trio*, Pablo
Jazz performance by a big band: Woody Herman, *Thundering Herd*, Fantasy
Country song (songwriter's award): "A Very Special Love Song," Norris Wilson, Billy Sherrill
Country vocal performance, male: Ronnie Milsap, "Please Don't Tell Me How the Story Ends," RCA
Country vocal performance, female: Anne Murray, "Love Song," Capitol
Country vocal performance by a duo or group: Pointer

---

Sisters, "Fairytale," Blue Thumb

Country instrumental performance: Chet Atkins, Merle Travis, *The Atkins-Travis Travelling Show*, RCA

Instrumental composition (composer's award): Mike Oldfield, "Tubular Bells" (Theme from *The Exorcist*)

Album, classical: *Berlioz: Symphonie Fantastique*, Georg Solti conducting the Chicago Symphony, London

Classical performance, orchestra (conductor's award): Georg Solti conducting the Chicago Symphony, *Berlioz: Symphonie Fantastique*, London

Opera recording: *Puccini: La Bohème*, Georg Solti conducting the London Philharmonic (solos: Caballé, Domingo, Nilnes, Blegen, Raimondi) RCA

Classical performance, vocal soloist: Leontyne Price, *Leontyne Price Sings Richard Strauss*, RCA

Producer: Thom Bell

## 1975

Album: *Still Crazy After All These Years*, Paul Simon, Columbia

Record: "Love Will Keep Us Together," Captain and Tennille, A&M

Song (songwriter's award): "Send in the Clowns," Stephen Sondheim

New artist: Natalie Cole

Pop vocal performance, male: Paul Simon, *Still Crazy After All These Years*, Columbia

Pop vocal performance, female: Janis Ian, "At Seventeen," Columbia

Pop vocal performance by a duo, group or chorus: The Eagles, "Lyin' Eyes," Asylum

Pop instrumental performance: Van McCoy and The Soul City Symphony, "The Hustle," Avco

Rhythm and blues song (songwriter's award): "Where Is the Love?," H.W. Casey

Rhythm and blues vocal performance, male: Ray Charles, "Living for the City," Crossover

Rhythm and blues vocal performance, female: Natalie Cole, "This Will Be," Capitol

Rhythm and blues vocal performance by a duo, group or chorus: Earth, Wind and Fire, "Shining Star," Columbia

Rhythm and blues instrumental performance: Silver Convention, "Fly, Robin, Fly," Midland/RCA

Jazz performance by a soloist: Dizzy Gillespie, *Oscar Peterson and Dizzy Gilespie*, Pablo

Jazz performance by a group: Return to Forever Featuring Chick Corea, *No Mystery*, Polydor

Jazz performance by a big band: Phil Woods with Michel Legrand and His Orchestra, *Images*

Country song (songwriter's award): "(Hey Won't You Play) Another Somebody Done Somebody Wrong Song," Chips Moman, Larry Butler

Country vocal performance, male: Willie Nelson, "Blue Eyes Crying in the Rain," Columbia

Country vocal performance, female: Linda Ronstadt, "I Can't Help It (If I'm Still in Love with You)," Capitol

Country vocal performance by a duo or group: Kris Kristofferson, Rita Coolidge, "Lover Please," Monument

Country instrumental performance: Chet Atkins, "The Entertainer," RCA

Instrumental composition (composer's award): Michel Legrand, *Images*

Album, classical: *Beethoven: Symphonies (9) Complete*, Sir Georg Solti conducting the Chicago Symphony, London

Classical performance, orchestra (conductor's award): Pierre Boulez conducting the New York Philharmonic, *Ravel: Daphnis et Chloé*, Columbia

Opera recording: *Mozart: Così fan tutte*, Colin Davis conducting the Chorus and Orchestra of the Royal Opera House, Covent Garden (solos: Caballé, Baker, Gedda, Ganzarolli, Van Allen, Cotrubas) Philips

Classical performance, vocal soloist: Janet Baker (Bernstein conducting the Israel Philharmonic), *Mahler: Kindertötenlieder*, Columbia

Producer: Arif Mardin

## 1976

Album: *Songs in the Key of Life*, Stevie Wonder, Tamla/Motown

Record: "This Masquerade," George Benson, Warner Bros.

Song (songwriter's award): "I Write the Songs," Bruce Johnston

New artist: Starland Vocal Band

Pop vocal performance, male: Stevie Wonder, *Songs in the Key of Life*, Tamla/Motown

Pop vocal performance, female: Linda Ronstadt, *Hasten Down the Wind*, Asylum

Pop vocal performance by a duo, group or chorus: Chicago, "If You Leave Me Now," Columbia

Pop instrumental performance: George Benson, *Breezin'*, Warner Bros.

Rhythm and blues song (songwriter's award): "Lowdown," Boz Scaggs, David Paich

Rhythm and blues vocal performance, male: Stevie Wonder, "I Wish," Tamla/Motown

Rhythm and blues vocal performance, female: Natalie Cole, "Sophisticated Lady (She's a Different Lady)," Capitol

Rhythm and blues vocal performance by a duo, group or chorus: Marilyn McCoo, Billy Davis, Jr., "You Don't Have to Be a Star (to Be in My Show)," ABC

Rhythm and blues instrumental performance: George Benson, "Theme from *Good King Bad*," CTI

Jazz vocal performance: Ella Fitzgerald, *Fitzgerald and Pass... Again*, Pablo

Jazz performance by a soloist: Count Basie, *Basie and*

**.. December 1 ...**
Casey Silver steps down at Universal after **Babe: Pig in the City** opens to a disastrous $8.5 million.

*Zoot*, Pablo

Jazz performance by a group: Chick Corea, *The Leprechaun*, Polydor

Jazz performance by a big band: Duke Ellington, *The Ellington Suites*, Pablo

Country song (songwriter's award): "Broken Lady," Larry Garlin

Country vocal performance, male: Ronnie Milsap, "(I'm a) Stand By My Woman Man," RCA

Country vocal performance, female: Emmylou Harris, *Elite Hotel*, Reprise

Country vocal performance by a duo or group: Amazing Rhythm Aces, "The End Is Not in Sight (The Cowboy Tune)," ABC

Country instrumental performance: Chet Atkins, Les Paul, *Chester and Lester*, RCA

Instrumental composition: *Bellavia*, Chuck Mangione

Album, classical: *Beethoven: The Five Piano Concertos*, Daniel Barenboim conducting the London Philharmonic (solo: Rubinstein), RCA

Classical performance, orchestral (conductor's award): Sir Georg Solti conducting the Chicago Symphony, *Strauss: Also Sprach Zarathustra*, London

Opera recording: *Gershwin: Porgy and Bess*, Lorin Maazel conducting the Cleveland Orchestra and Chorus (solos: Mitchell, White) London

Classical performance, vocal soloist: Beverly Sills (Kostelanetz conducting the London Symphony), *Music of Victor Herbert*, Angel

Producer: Stevie Wonder

## 1977

Album: *Rumours*, Fleetwood Mac, Warner Bros.

Record: "Hotel California," Eagles, Asylum

Song (songwriter's award): "Love Theme from *A Star Is Born* (Evergreen)," Barbra Streisand, Paul Williams

New artist: Debby Boone

Pop vocal performance, male: James Taylor, "Handy Man," Columbia

Pop vocal performance, female: Barbra Streisand, "Love Theme from *A Star Is Born* (Evergreen)," Columbia

Pop vocal performance by a duo, group or chorus: Bee Gees, "How Deep Is Your Love?," RSO

Pop instrumental performance: London Symphony, John Williams, conductor *Star Wars*, 20th Century

Rhythm and blues song (songwriter's award): "You Make Me Feel Like Dancing," Leo Sayer, Vini Poncia

Rhythm and blues vocal performance, male: Lou Rawls, *Unmistakably Lou*, Philadelphia International/Epic

Rhythm and blues vocal performance, female: Thelma Houston, "Don't Leave Me This Way," Motown

Rhythm and blues vocal performance by a duo, group or chorus: Emotions, "Best of My Love," track, Columbia

Rhythm and blues instrumental performance: Brothers Johnson, "Q," A&M

Jazz vocal performance: Al Jarreau, *Look to the Rainbow*, Warner Bros.

Jazz instrumental performance by a soloist: Oscar Peterson, *The Giants*, Pablo

Jazz instrumental performance by a group: *Phil Woods, The Phil Woods Six − Live from the Showboat*, RCA

Jazz performance by a big band: Count Basie and His Orchestra, *Prime Time*, Pablo

Country song (songwriter's award): "Don't It Make My Brown Eyes Blue," Richard Leigh

Country vocal performance, male: Kenny Rogers, "Lucille," United Artists

Country vocal performance, female: Crystal Gayle, "Don't It Make My Brown Eyes Blue," United Artists

Country vocal performance by a duo or group with vocal: Kendalls, "Heaven's Just a Sin Away," Ovation

Country instrumental performance: Hargus "Pig" Robbins, *Country Instrumentalist*, Elektra

Instrumental composition (composer's award): "Main Title from *Star Wars*," John Williams

Album, classical: *Concert of the Century* (recorded live at Carnegie Hall May 18, 1976) (solos: Leonard Bernstein, Vladimir Horowitz, Isaac Stern, Mstislav Rostropovich, Dietrich Fischer-Dieskau, Yehudi Menuhin, Lyndon Woodside) Columbia

Classical performance, orchestra (conductor's award): Carlo Maria Guilini conducting the Chicago Symphony, *Mahler: Symphony No. 9 in D Major*, Deutsche Grammophon

Opera recording: *Gershwin: Porgy and Bess*, John De Main conducting the Houston Grand Opera Production (solos: Albert, Dale, Smith, Shakesnider, Lane, Brice, Smalls) RCA

Classical performance, vocal soloist: Janet Baker (Marriner conducting the Academy of St. Martin-in-the-Fields) *Bach: Arias*, Angel

Producer: Peter Asher

## 1978

Album: *Saturday Night Fever* (soundtrack), Bee Gees, David Shire, Yvonne Elliman, Tavares, Kool and the Gang, K.C. and the Sunshine Band, MFSB, Trammps, Walter Murphy, Ralph MacDonald, RSO

Record: "Just the Way You Are," Billy Joel, Columbia

Song (songwriter's award): "Just the Way You Are," Billy Joel

New artist: A Taste of Honey

Pop vocal performance, male: Barry Manilow, "Copacabana (At the Copa)," Artista

Pop vocal performance, female: Anne Murray, "You Needed Me," Capitol

Pop vocal performance by a duo, group or chorus: Bee

---

Gees, *Saturday Night Fever*, RSO

Pop instrumental performance: Chuck Mangione, *Children of Sanchez*, A&M

Rhythm and blues song (songwriter's award): "Last Dance," Paul Jabara

Rhythm and blues vocal performance, male: George Benson, "On Broadway," Warner Bros.

Rhythm and blues vocal performance, female: Donna Summer, "Last Dance," Casablanca

Rhythm and blues vocal performance by a duo, group or chorus: Earth, Wind and Fire, *All 'n' All*, Columbia

Rhythm and blues instrumental performance: Earth, Wind and Fire, "Runnin'," Columbia

Jazz vocal performance: Al Jarreau, *All Fly Home*, Warner Bros.

Jazz instrumental performance by a soloist: Oscar Peterson, *Montreux '77, Oscar Peterson Jam*, Pablo

Jazz instrumental performance by a group: Chick Corea, *Friends*, Polydor

Jazz instrumental performance by a big band: Thad Jones, Mel Lewis, *Live in Munich*, Horizon/A&M

Country song (songwriter's award): "The Gambler," Don Schlitz

Country vocal performance, male: Willie Nelson, "Georgia on My Mind," Columbia

Country vocal performance, female: *Here You Come Again*, Dolly Parton, RCA

Country vocal performance by a duo or group: Waylon Jennings, Willie Nelson, "Mammas, Don't Let Your Babies Grow up to Be Cowboys," RCA

Country instrumental performance: Asleep at the Wheel, "One O'Clock Jump," Capitol

Instrumental composition: "Theme from *Close Encounters of the Third Kind*," John Williams

Album, classical: *Brahms: Concerto for Violin in D Major*, Carlo Maria Giulini conducting the Chicago Symphony (solo: Itzhak Perlman) Angel

Classical performance, orchestra (conductor's award): Herbert von Karajan, conducting the Berlin Philharmonic, *Beethoven: Symphonies (9) (Complete)* Deutsche Grammophon

Opera recording: *Lehár: The Merry Widow*, Julius Rudel conducting the New York City Opera Orchestra and Chorus (solos: Sills, Titus) Angel

Classical performance, vocal soloist: Luciano Pavarotti, *Luciano Pavarotti, Hits from Lincoln Center*, London

Producer: Bee Gees, Albhy Galuten, Karl Richardson

## 1979

Album: *52nd Street*, Billy Joel, Columbia

Record: "What a Fool Believes," Doobie Brothers, Warner Bros.

Song (songwriter's award): "What a Fool Believes," Kenny

Loggins, Michael McDonald

New artist: Rickie Lee Jones

Pop vocal performance, male: Billy Joel, *52nd Street*, Columbia

Pop vocal performance, female: Dionne Warwick, "I'll Never Love This Way Again," Artista

Pop vocal performance by a duo, group or chorus: Doobie Brothers, *Minute by Minute*, Warner Bros.

Pop instrumental performance: Herb Alpert, "Rise," A&M

Rock vocal performance, male: Bob Dylan, "Gotta Serve Somebody," Columbia

Rock vocal performance, female: Donna Summer, "Hot Stuff," Casablanca

Rock vocal performance by a duo or group with vocal: The Eagles, "Heartache Tonight," Asylum

Rock instrumental performance: Wings, "Rockestra Theme," Columbia

Rhythm and blues song (songwriter's award): "After the Love Has Gone," David Foster, Jay Graydon, Bill Champlin

Rhythm and blues vocal performance, male: Michael Jackson, "Don't Stop till You Get Enough," Epic

Rhythm and blues vocal performance, female: Dionne Warwick, "Déjà vu," Artista

Rhythm and blues vocal performance by a duo, group or chorus: Earth, Wind and Fire, "After the Love Has Gone," ARC/CBS

Rhythm and blues instrumental performance: Earth, Wind and Fire, "Boogie Wonderland," ARC/CBS

Disco recording: "I Will Survive," Gloria Gaynor, Polydor

Jazz fusion performance (vocal or instrumental): Weather Report, *8:30*, ARC/CBS

Jazz vocal performance: Ella Fitzgerald, *Fine & Mellow*, Pablo

Jazz instrumental performance by a soloist: Oscar Peterson, *Jousts*, Pablo

Jazz instrumental performance by a group: Gary Burton, Chick Corea, *Duet*, ECM/Warner Bros.

Jazz instrumental performance by a big band: Duke Ellington, *At Fargo, 1940 Live*, Book-of-the-Month

Country song (songwriter's award): "You Decorated My Life," Bob Morrison, Debbie Hupp

Country vocal performance, male: Kenny Rogers, "The Gambler," United Artists

Country vocal performance, female: Emmylou Harris, *Blue Kentucky Girl*, Warner Bros.

Country vocal performance by a duo or group: Charlie Daniels Band, "The Devil Went down to Georgia," Epic

Country instrumental performance: Doc and Merle Watson, "Big Sandy/Leather Britches," track, United Artists

Instrumental composition (composer's award): "Theme from *Superman (Main Title)*," John Williams

Classical album: *Brahms: Symphonies (4) (Complete)*, Sir

Georg Solti conducting the Chicago Symphony Orchestra, London

Classical orchestral recording (conductor's award): *Brahms: Symphonies (4) (Complete)*, Sir Georg Solti conducting the Chicago Symphony, London

Opera recording: *Britten: Peter Grimes*, Colin Davis conducting the Orchestra and Chorus of the Royal Opera House, Covent Garden (solos: Vickers, Harper, Summers) Philips

Classical performance, vocal soloist: Luciano Pavarotti (Bologna Orchestra) *O Sole Mio (Favorite Neapolitan Songs)* London

Classical producer: James Mallinson

Producer: Larry Butler

## 1980

Album: *Christopher Cross*, Christopher Cross, Warner Bros.

Record: "Sailing," Christopher Cross, Warner Bros.

Song (songwriter's award): "Sailing," Christopher Cross

New artist: Christopher Cross

Pop vocal performance, male: Kenny Loggins, "This Is It," Columbia

Pop vocal performance, female: Bette Midler, "The Rose," Atlantic

Pop vocal performance by a duo, group or chorus: Barbra Streisand, Barry Gibb, "Guilty," Columbia

Pop instrumental performance: Bob James, Earl Klugh, *One on One*, Columbia

Rock vocal performance, male: Billy Joel, *Glass Houses*, Columbia

Rock vocal performance, female: Pat Benatar, *Crimes of Passion*, Chrysalis

Rock performance by a duo, group with a vocal: Bob Seger and the Silver Bullet Band, *Against the Wind*, Capitol

Rock instrumental performance: The Police, "Regatta de Blanc," A&M

Rhythm and blues song (songwriter's award): "Never Knew Love Like This Before," Reggie Lucas, James Mtume

Rhythm and blues vocal performance, male: George Benson, *Give Me the Night*, Warner Bros./Qwest

Rhythm and blues vocal performance, female: Stephanie Mills, "Never Knew Love Like This Before," 20th Century

Rhythm and blues vocal performance by a duo or group: Manhattans, "Shining Star," Columbia

Rhythm and blues instrumental performance: George Benson, "On Broadway," Warner Bros./Qwest

Jazz fusion performance (vocal or insturmental): Manhattan Transfer, "Birdland," Atlantic

Jazz vocal performance, male: George Benson, "Moody's Mood," Warner Bros./Qwest

Jazz vocal performance, female: Ella Fitzgerald, *A Perfect Match/Ella and Basie*, Pablo

Jazz instrumental performance by a soloist: Bill Evans, *I Will Say Goodbye*, Fantasy

Jazz instrumental performance by a group: Bill Evans, *We Will Meet Again*, Warner Bros.

Instrumental jazz performance by a big band: Count Basie and His Orchestra, *On the Road*, Pablo

Country song (songwriter's award): "On the Road Again," Willie Nelson

Country vocal performance, male: George Jones, "He Stopped Loving Her Today," Epic

Country vocal performance, female: Anne Murray, "Could I Have This Dance," Capitol

Country performance by a duo or group with vocal: Roy Orbison, Emmylou Harris, "That Lovin' You Feelin' Again," Warner Bros.

Country instrumental performance: Gilley's Urban Cowboy Band, "Orange Blossom Special/Hoedown," Full Moon/Asylum

Instrumental composition: "The Empire Strikes Back," John Williams

Classical album: *Berg: Lulu (Complete)*, Pierre Boulez conducting the Orchestre de l'Opéra de Paris (solos: Teresa Stratus, Yvonne Minton, Franz Mazura, Toni Blankenheim) Deutsche Grammophon

Classical performance, orchestra (conductor's award): Bruckner: Symphony No. 6 in A Major, Sir Georg Solti conducting the Chicago Symphony, London

Opera recording: *Berg: Lulu (Complete)*, Pierre Boulez conducting the Orchestre de l'Opéra de Paris (solos: Teresa Stratus, Yvonne Minton, Franz Mazura, Toni Blankenheim) Deutsche Grammophon

Classical performance, vocal soloist: Leontyne Price (Henry Lewis conducting the Philharmonic Orchestra), *Prima Donna, Vol. 5, Great Soprano Arias from Handel to Britten*, RCA

Classical producer: Robert Woods

Producer: Phil Ramone

## 1981

Album: *Double Fantasy*, John Lennon, Yoko Ono, Geffen/Warner Bros.

Record: "Bette Davis Eyes," Kim Carnes, EMI-America

Song (songwriter's award): "Bette Davis Eyes," Donna Weiss, Jackie DeShannon

New artist: Sheena Easton

Pop vocal performance, male: Al Jarreau, *Breaking Away*, Warner Bros.

Pop vocal performance, female: Lena Horne, *Lena Horne: The Lady and Her Music Live on Broadway*, Qwest/Warner Bros.

Pop performance by a duo or group with vocal: Manhattan Transfer, "Boy from New York City," Atlantic

Pop instrumental performance: Mike Post Featuring

Larry Carlton, "Theme from *Hill Street Blues*," Elektra/Asylum

Rock vocal performance, male: Rick Springfield, "Jessie's Girl," RCA

Rock vocal performance, female: Pat Benatar, "Fire and Ice," Chrysalis

Rock performance by a duo or group with vocal: The Police, "Don't Stand So Close to Me," A&M

Rock instrumental performance: The Police, "Behind My Camel," A&M

Rhythm and blues song (songwriter's award): "Just the Two of Us," Bill Withers, William Salter, Ralph MacDonald

Rhythm and blues vocal performance, male: James Ingram, "One Hundred Ways," A&M

Rhythm and blues vocal performance, female: Aretha Franklin, "Hold on, I'm Comin'," track, Arista

Rhythm and blues vocal performance by a duo or group: Quincy Jones, *The Dude*, A&M

Rhythm and blues instrumental performance: David Sanborn, "All I Need Is You," Warner Bros.

Jazz fusion performance (vocal or instrumental): Grover Washington, Jr., *Winelight*, Elektra/Asylum

Jazz vocal performance, male: Al Jarreau, "Blue Rondo à la Turk," track, Warner Bros.

Jazz vocal performance, female: Ella Fitzgerald, *Digital III at Montreux*, Pablo Live

Jazz performance by a duo or group: Manhattan Transfer, "Until I Met You (Corner Pocket)," track, Atlantic

Jazz instrumental performance by a soloist: John Coltrane, *Bye Bye Blackbird*, Pablo

Jazz instrumental performance by a group: Chick Corea, Gary Burton, *Chick Corea and Gary Burton in Concert, Zurich, October 28, 1979*, ECM

Jazz instrumental performance by a big band: Gerry Mulligan and his Orchestra, *Walk on the Water*, DRG

Country song (songwriter's award): "9 to 5," Dolly Parton

Country vocal performance, male: Ronnie Milsap, "(There's) No Gettin' over Me," RCA

Country vocal performance, female: Dolly Parton, "9 to 5," RCA

Country performance by a duo or group with vocal: Oak Ridge Boys, "Elvira," MCA

Country instrumental performance: Chet Atkins, *Country after All These Years*, RCA

Instrumental composition (composer's award): "Theme from *Hill Street Blues*," Mike Post

Classical album: *Mahler: Symphony No. 2 in C Minor*, Sir Georg Solti conducting the Chicago Symphony Orchestra and Chorus (solos: Isobel Buchanan, Mira Zakai) London

Classical orchestral recording: *Mahler: Symphony No. 2 in C Minor*, Sir Georg Solti conducting the Chicago Symphony, London

Opera recording: *Janácek: From the House of the Dead*, Sir Charles Mackerras conducting the Vienna Philharmonic (solos: Jiri Zahradnicek, Vaclav Zidek, Ivo Zidek) London

Classical performance, vocal soloist: Joan Sutherland, Marilyn Horne, Luciano Pavarotti (Richard Bonynge conducting the New York City Opera Orchestra), *Live from Lincoln Center Sutherland, Horne, Pavarotti*, London

Classical producer: James Mallinson

Producer (other than classical): Quincy Jones

Music video: *Michael Nesmith in Elephant Parts*, Michael Nesmith, Pacific Arts Video

## 1982

Album: *Toto IV*, Toto, Columbia/CBS

Record: "Rosanna," Toto, Columbia

Song (songwriter's award): "Always on My Mind," Johnny Christopher, Mark James, Wayne Thompson

New artist: Men at Work

Pop vocal performance, male: Lionel Richie, "Truly," Motown

Pop vocal performance, female: Melissa Manchester, "You Should Hear How She Talks about You," Arista

Pop performance by a duo or group with vocal: Joe Cocker, Jennifer Warnes, "Up Where We Belong," Island

Pop instrumental performance: Ernie Watts, "Chariots of Fire" (theme, dance version), Qwest/Warner Bros.

Rock vocal performance, male: John Cougar, "Hurts so Good," Riva/Polygram

Rock vocal performance, female: Pat Benatar, "Shadows of the Night," Chrysalis

Rock performance by a duo or group with vocal: Survivor, "Eye of the Tiger," Scotti Brothers/CBS

Rock instrumental performance: A Flock of Seagulls, "D.N.A.," Jive/Arista

Rhythm and blues song (songwriter's award): "Turn Your Love Around," Jay Graydon, Steve Lukather, Bill Champli

Rhythm and blues vocal performance, male: Marvin Gaye, "Sexual Healing," Columbia/CBS

Rhythm and blues vocal performance, female: Jennifer Holliday, "And I Am Telling You I'm Not Going," Geffen/Warner Bros.

Rhythm and blues vocal performance by a duo or group (tie): Dazz Band, "Let It Whip," Motown; and Earth, Wind and Fire, "Wanna Be with You," ARC/CBS

Rhythm and blues instrumental performance: Marvin Gaye, "Sexual Healing," Columbia/CBS

Jazz fusion performance (vocal or instrumental): Pat Metheny Group, *Offramp*, ECM/Warner Bros.

Jazz vocal performance, male: Mel Tormé, *An Evening with George Shearing and Mel Tormé*, Concord Jazz

Jazz vocal performance, female: Sarah Vaughan, *Gershwin Live!* CBS

Jazz vocal performance by a duo or group: Manhattan Transfer, "Route 66," Atlantic

Jazz instrumental performance by a soloist: Miles Davis, *We Want Miles*, Columbia

Jazz instrumental performance by a group: Phil Woods Quartet, *"More" Live*, Adelphi

Jazz instrumental performance by a big band: Count Basie and His Orchestra, *Warm Breeze*, Pablo Today

Country song (songwriter's award): "Always on My Mind," Johnny Christopher, Mark James, Wayne Thompson

Country vocal performance, male: Willie Nelson, "Always on My Mind," Columbia/CBS

Country vocal performance, female: Juice Newton, "Break It to Me Gently," Capitol

Country performance by a duo or group with vocal: Alabama, *Mountain Music*, RCA

Country instrumental performance: Roy Clark, "Alabama Jubilee," Churchil

Instrumental composition: "Flying (Theme from *E.T. The Extra-Terrestrial*)," John Williams

Classical album: *Bach: The Goldberg Variations*, Glenn Gould, CBS

Classical orchestral recording (conductor's award): *Mahler: Symphony No. 7 in E Minor ("Song of the Night")* James Levine conducting the Chicago Symphony, RCA

Opera recording: *Wagner: Der Ring des Nibelungen*, Pierre Boulez conducting the Bayreuth Festival Orchestra (solos: Gwyneth Jones, Jeannine Altmeyer, Orton Wenkel, etc) Philips

Classical performance, vocal soloist: Leontyne Price (Zubin Mehta conducting the Israel Philharmonic), Verdi: Arias (*Leontyne Price Sings Verdi*) London

Classical producer: Robert Woods

Producer (other than classical): Toto

Music video: *Olivia Physical*, Olivia Newton-John, MCA Video

## 1983

Album: *Thriller*, Michael Jackson, Epic/CBS

Record: "Beat It," Michael Jackson, Epic/CBS

New song (songwriter's award): "Every Breath You Take," Sting

New artist: Culture Club

Pop vocal performance, male: Michael Jackson, *Thriller*, Epic/CBS

Pop vocal performance, female: Irene Cara, "Flashdance... What A Feeling," Casablanca/Polygram

Pop performance by a duo or group with vocal: Police, "Every Breath You Take," A&M

Pop instrumental performance: George Benson, "Being with You," Warner Bros.

Rock vocal performance, male: Michael Jackson, "Beat It," Epic/CBS

Rock vocal performance, female: Pat Benatar, "Love Is a Battlefield," Chrysalis

Rock performance by a duo or group with vocal: Police, *Synchronicity*, A&M

Rock instrumental performance: Sting, *Brimstone & Treacle*, A&M

New Rhythm and blues song (songwriter's award): "Billie Jean," Michael Jackson

Rhythm and blues vocal performance, male: Michael Jackson, "Billie Jean," Epic/CBS

Rhythm and blues vocal performance, female: Chaka Khan, *Chaka Khan*, Warner Bros.

Rhythm and blues vocal performance by a duo or group: Rufus and Chaka Khan, "Ain't Nobody," Warner Bros.

Rhythm and blues instrumental performance: Herbie Hancock, "Rockit," Columbia

Jazz fusion performance (vocal or instrumental): Pat Metheny Group, *Travels*, ECM/Warner Bros.

Jazz vocal performance, male: Mel Tormé, *Top Drawer*, Concord Jazz

Jazz vocal performance, female: Ella Fitzgerald, *The Best Is Yet to Come*, Pablo Today

Jazz vocal performance by a duo or group: Manhattan Transfer, "Why Not!" Atlantic

Jazz instrumental performance by a soloist: Wynton Marsalis, *Think of One*, Columbia

Jazz instrumental performance by a group: Phil Woods Quartet, *At the Vanguard*, Antilles/Island

Jazz instrumental performance by a big band: Rob McConnell and the Boss Brass, *All in Good Time*, Dark Orchid

New country song (songwriter's award): "Stranger in My House," Mike Reid

Country vocal performance, male: Lee Greenwood, "I.O.U." MCA

Country vocal performance, female: Anne Murray, "A Little Good News," Capitol

Country performance by a duo or group with vocal: Alabama, *The Closer You Get*, RCA

Country instrumental performance: New South, "Fireball," Sugar Hill

Instrumental composition: "Love Theme from *Flashdance*," Giorgio Moroder

Classical album: *Mahler: Symphony No. 9 in D Major*, Sir Georg Solti conducting the Chicago Symphony, London

Classical orchestral recording: *Mahler: Symphony No. 9 in D Major*, Sir Georg Solti conducting the Chicago Symphony, London

Opera recording (tie): *Verdi: La Traviata (Original Soundtrack)*, James Levine conducting the Metropolitan Opera Orchestra and Chorus (solos: Teresa Strates, Placido Domingo, Cornell MacNeil), Elektra; and *Mozart: Le Nozze di Figaro*, Sir Georg Solti conducting the London Philharmonic Orchestra (solos: Kiri Te Kanawa, Lucia

---

**. . . December 6 . . .**
On this day in 1942, producer Val Lewton released his first horror film, **Cat People**.

Popp, etc) London

Classical performance, vocal soloist: Leontyne Price, Marilyn Horne (Levine conducting the Metropolitan Opera Orchestra), *Leontyne Price and Marilyn Horne in Concert at the Met*. RCA

Classical producer: Marc J. Aubort, Joanna Nickrenz

Producer (other than classical): Quincy Jones, Michael Jackson

Music video, short film: *Girls on Film/Hungry Like the Wolf*, Duran Duran, EMI Music Video/Sony

Video album: *Duran Duran*, Duran Duran, Thorn EMI Video, Disc-Pioneer Artists

## 1984

Album: *Can't Slow down*, Lionel Richie, Motown

Record: "What's Love Got to Do with It?," Tina Turner, Capitol

Song (songwriter's award): "What's Love Got to Do with It?," Graham Lyle, Terry Britten

New artist: Cyndi Lauper

Pop vocal performance, male: Phil Collins, "Against All Odds (Take a Look at Me Now)," Atlantic

Pop vocal performance, female: Tina Turner, "What's Love Got to Do with It?," Capitol

Pop performance by a duo or group with vocal: Pointer Sisters, "Jump (for My Love)," Planet

Pop instrumental performance: Ray Parker, Jr., "Ghostbusters," Arista

Rock vocal performance, male: Bruce Springsteen, "Dancing in the Dark," Columbia/CBS

Rock vocal performance, female: Tina Turner, "Better Be Good to Me," Capitol

Rock performance by a duo or group with vocal: Prince and the Revolution, *Purple Rain*, Warner Bros.

Rock instrumental performance: Yes, "Cinema," Atco

New Rhythm and blues song (songwriter's award): "I Feel for You," Prince

Rhythm and blues vocal performance, male: Billy Ocean, "Caribbean Queen (No More Love on the Run)," Jive/Arista

Rhythm and blues vocal performance, female: Chaka Khan, "I Feel for You," Warner Bros.

Rhythm and blues vocal performance by a duo or group: James Ingram, Michael McDonald, "Yah Mo B There," Qwest

Rhythm and blues instrumental performance: Herbie Hancock, *Sound-System*, Columbia/CBS

Jazz fusion performance (vocal or instrumental): Pat Metheny Group, *First Circle*, ECM

Jazz vocal performance: Joe Williams, *Nothin' but the Blues*, Delos

Jazz instrumental performance by a soloist: Wynton Marsalis, *Hot House Flowers*, Columbia/CBS

Jazz instrumental performance by a group: Art Blakey and the Jazz Messengers, "New York Scene," Concord Jazz

Jazz instrumental performance by a big band: Count Basie and His Orchestra, *88 Basie Street*, Pablo

Country song (songwriter's award): "City of New Orleans," Steve Goodman

Country vocal performance, male: Merle Haggard, "That's the Way Love Goes," Epic

Country vocal performance, female: Emmylou Harris, "In My Dreams," Warner Bros.

Country performance by a duo or group with vocal: Judds (Wynnona and Naomi) "Mama He's Crazy," RCA

Country instrumental performance: Ricky Skaggs, "Wheel Hoss," Epic/CBS

Instrumental composition (composer's award) (tie): "The Natural," Randy Newman; and "Olympic Fanfare and Theme," track from *The Official Music of the XXIIIrd Olympiad at Los Angeles*, John Williams

Classical album: *Amadeus* (soundtrack), Neville Mariner conducting the Academy of St. Martin-in-the-Fields, Fantasy

Classical orchestral recording: *Prokofiev: Symphony No. 5 in B Flat, Op. 100*, Leonard Slatkin conducting the St. Louis Symphony, RCA

Opera recording: *Bizet: Carmen* (film soundtrack), Lorin Maazal conducting the Orchestre National de France, (solos: Julia Migenes-Johnson, Placido Domingo, etc), Erato

Classical performance, vocal soloist: Jessye Norman, José van Dam, Heather Harper (Pierre Boulez conducting the members of the Ensemble Intercontemporain and BBC Symphony), *Ravel: Songs of Maurice Ravel*, CBS

Classical producer: Steven Epstein

Producer (other than classical) (tie): David Foster; Lionel Richie, James Anthony Carmichael

Music video, short film: *David Bowie*, David Bowie, Sony/Picture Music

Video album: *Making Michael Jackson's "Thriller,"* Michael Jackson, Vestron Music Video

## 1985

Album: *No Jacket Required*, Phil Collins, Atlantic

Record: "We Are the World," USA for Africa, Columbia/CBS

Song (songwriter's award): "We Are the World," Michael Jackson, Lionel Richie

New artist: Sade

Pop vocal performance, male: Phil Collins, *No Jacket Required*, Atlantic

Pop vocal performance, female: Whitney Houston, "Saving All my Love for You," Arista

Pop performance by a duo or group with vocal: USA for Africa, "We Are the World," Columbia/CBS

Pop instrumental performance: Jan Hammer, "*Miami*

Vice Theme," MCA

Rock vocal performance, male: Don Henley, "The Boys of Summer," Geffen

Rock vocal performance, female: Tina Turner, "One of the Living," Capitol

Rock performance by a duo or group with vocal: Dire Straits, "Money for Nothing," Warner Bros.

Rock instrumental performance: Jeff Beck, "Escape," Epic/CBS

Rhythm and blues song (songwriter's award): "Freeway of Love," Narada Michael Walden, Jeffrey Cohen

Rhythm and blues vocal performance, male: Stevie Wonder, *In Square Circle*, Tamla/Motown

Rhythm and blues vocal performance, female: Aretha Franklin, "Freeway of Love," Arista

Rhythm and blues vocal performance by a duo or group: Commodores, "Nightshift," Gordy/Motown

Rhythm and blues instrumental performance: Ernie Watts, *Musican*, Qwest

Jazz vocal performance, male: Jon Hendricks, Bobby McFerrin, "Another Night in Tunisia," from *Vocalese* (Manhattan Transfer), Atlantic

Jazz vocal performance, female: Cleo Laine, *Cleo at Carnegie the 10th Anniversary Concert*, DRG

Jazz vocal performance by a duo or group: Manhattan Transfer, *Vocalese*, Atlantic

Jazz instrumental performance by a soloist: Wynton Marsalis, "Black Codes from the Underground," Columbia/CBS

Jazz instrumental performance by a group: Wynton Marsalis Group, *Black Codes from the Underground*, Columbia/CBS

Jazz instrumental performance by a big band: John Barry, Bob Wilber, *The Cotton Club* (film soundtrack), Geffen

Jazz fusion performance (vocal or instrumental): David Sanborn, *Straight to the Heart*, Warner Bros.

Country song (songwriter's award): "Highwayman," Jimmy L. Webb

Country vocal performance, male: Ronnie Milsap, "Lost in the Fifties Tonight (In the Still of the Night)," RCA

Country vocal performance, female: Rosanne Cash, "I Don't Know Why You Don't Want Me," CBS

Country performance by a duo or group with vocal: Judds, *Why Not Me*, RCA

Country instrumental performance: Chet Atkins, Mark Knopfler, "Cosmic Square Dance," Columbia/CBS

Instrumental composition: "*Miami Vice* Theme," Jan Hammer

Classical album: *Berlioz: Requiem*, Robert Shaw conducting the Atlanta Symphony Orchestra and Chorus (solo: John Aler), Telarc

Classical orchestral recording (conductor's award): *Fauré: Pelléas et Mélisande*, Robert Shaw conducting the Atlanta

Symphony Orchestra and Chorus, Telarc

New classical artist: Chicago Pro Musica

Opera recording: *Schoenberg: Moses und Aron*, Sir Georg Solti conducting the Chicago Symphony Orchestra and Chorus (solos: Franz Mazura, Philip Langridge), London

Classical performance, vocal soloist: John Aler (Shaw conducting the Atlanta Symphony Orchestra and Chorus) *Berlioz: Requiem*, Telarc

Classical producer: Robert E. Woods

Producer (other than classical): Phil Collins, Hugh Padgham

Music video, short form: *We Are the World, the Video Event*, USA for Africa, Tom Trbovich, director, RCA/Columbia Pictures Home Video

## 1986

Album: *Graceland*, Paul Simon, Warner Bros.

Record: "Higher Love," Steve Winwood, Island

Song (songwriter's award): "That's What Friends Are for," Burt Bacharach, Carole Bayer Sager

New artist: Bruce Hornsby and the Range

Pop vocal performance, male: Steve Winwood, "Higher Love," Island

Pop vocal performance, female: Barbra Streisand, *The Broadway Album*, Columbia/CBS

Pop vocal performance by a duo or group with vocal: Dionne Warwick, Elton John, Gladys Knight and Stevie Wonder, "That's What Friends Are for," Arista

Pop instrumental performance (orchestra, group or soloist): Harold Faltermeyer, Steve Stevens, "*Top Gun* Anthem," Columbia/CBS

Rock vocal performance, male: Robert Palmer, "Addicted to Love," Island

Rock vocal performance, female: Tina Turner, "Back Where You Started," Capitol

Rock performance by a duo or group with vocal: Eurythmics, "Missionary Man," RCA

Rock instrumental performance: Art of Noise Featuring Duane Eddy, "Peter Gunn," China/Chrysalis

Rhythm and blues song (songwriter's award): "Sweet Love," Anita Baker, Louis A. Johnson, Gary Bias

Rhythm and blues vocal performance, male: James Brown, "Living in America," Scotti Brothers/CBS

Rhythm and blues vocal performance, female: Anita Baker, *Rapture*, Elektra

Rhythm and blues vocal performance by a duo or group: Prince and the Revolution, "Kiss," Paisley Park

Rhythm and blues instrumental performance: Yellowjackets, "And You Know That," MCA

Jazz vocal performance, male: Bobby McFerrin, "Round Midnight," Columbia/CBS

Jazz vocal performance, female: Diane Schuur, *Timeless*, GRP

Jazz vocal performance by a duo or group: 2+2 Plus

(Clare Fischer and His Latin Jazz Sextet), *Free Fall*, Discovery

Jazz instrumental performance by a soloist: Miles Davis, *Tutu*, Warner Bros.

Jazz instrumental performance by a group: Wynton Marsalis, *J Mood*, Columbia/CBS

Jazz instrumental performance by a big band: Tonight Show Band with Doc Severinsen, *The Tonight Show Band with Doc Severinsen*, Amherst

Jazz fusion performance (vocal or instrumental): Bob James, David Sanborn, *Double Vision*, Warner Bros.

Country song (songwriter's award): "Grandpa (Tell Me 'bout the Good Old Days)," Jamie O'Hara

Country vocal performance, male: Ronnie Milsap, *Lost in the Fifties Tonight*, RCA

Country vocal performance, female: Reba McEntire, "Whoever's In New England," MCA

Country performance by a duo or group with vocal: Judds, "Grandpa (Tell Me 'bout the Good Old Days)," RCA

Country instrumental performance: Ricky Skaggs, "Raisin' the Dickens," Epic/CBS

Instrumental composition (composer's award): *Out of Africa* (film soundtrack), John Barry

Classical album: *Horowitz: The Studio Recordings, New York 1985*, Vladimir Horowitz, Deutsche Grammophon

Classical orchestral recording (conductor's award): *Liszt: A Faust Symphony*, Sir Georg Solti conducting the Chicago Symphony Orchestra, London

Opera recording: *Bernstein: Candide*, John Mauceri conducting the New York City Opera Orchestra and Chorus (solos: Erie Mills, Maris Clement, etc), New world

Classical performance, vocal soloist: Kathleen Battle (Previn conducting the Royal Philharmonic Orchestra), *Kathleen Battle Sings Mozart*, Angel

Classical producer: Thomas Frost

Producer (other than classical): Jimmy Jam, Terry Lewis

Music video, short form: *Dire Straits Brothers in Arms*, Dire Straits, various directors, Warner Reprise Video

# 1987

Album: *The Joshua Tree*, U2, Island

Record: "Graceland," Paul Simon, Warner Bros.

Song (songwriter's award): "Somewhere out There," James Horner, Barry Mann, Cynthia Weil

New artist: Jody Watley

Pop vocal performance, male: Sting, *Bring on the Night*, A&M

Pop vocal performance, female: Whitney Houston, "I Wanna Dance with Somebody (Who Loves Me)," Arista

Pop vocal performance by a duo or group with vocal: Bill Medley, Jennifer Warnes, "(I've Had) The Time of My Life," BMG Music/RCA

Pop instrumental performance: Larry Carlton, "Minute by Minute," MCA

Rock vocal performance, solo: Bruce Springsteen, *Tunnel of Love*, Columbia/CBS

Rock performance by a duo or group with vocal: U2, *The Joshua Tree*, Island

Rock instrumental performance: Frank Zappa, *Jazz from Hell*, Barking Pumpkin

Rhythm and blues song (songwriter's award): "Lean on Me," Bill Withers

Rhythm and blues vocal performance, male: Smokey Robinson, "Just to See Her," Motown

Rhythm and blues vocal performance, female: Aretha Franklin, *Aretha*, Arista

Rhythm and blues vocal performance by a duo or group: Aretha Franklin, George Michael, "I Knew You Were Waiting (for Me)," Arista

Rhythm and blues instrumental performance: David Sanborn, "Chicago Song," Warner Bros.

Jazz vocal performance, male: Bobby McFerrin, "What Is This Thing Called Love?," Blue Note

Jazz vocal performance, female: Diane Schuur, *Diane Schuur and the Count Basie Orchestra*, GRP

Jazz instrumental performance by a soloist: Dexter Gordon, *The Other Side of 'Round Midnight*, GRP

Jazz instrumental performance by a group: Wynton Marsalis, *Marsalis Standard Time, Vol 1*, Columbia/CBS

Jazz instrumental performance by a big band: Duke Ellington Orchestra conducted by Mercer Ellington, *Digital Duke*, GRP

Jazz fusion performance (vocal or instrumental): Pat Metheny Group, *Still Life (Talking)*, Geffen

Country song (songwriter's award): "Forever and Ever, Amen," Paul Overstreet, Don Schlitz

Country vocal performance, male: Randy Travis, *Always and Forever*, Warner Bros.

Country vocal performance, female: K.T. Oslin, "'80s Ladies," BMG Music/RCA

Country performance by a duo or group with vocal: Dolly Parton, Linda Ronstadt, Emmylou Harris, *Trio*, Warner Bros.

Country vocal performance, duet: Ronnie Milsap, Kenny Rogers, "Make No Mistake, She's Mine," BMG Music/RCA

Country instrumental performance: Asleep at the Wheel, "String of Pars," Epic

New age performance: Yusef Lateef, *Yusef Lateef's Little Symphony*, Atlantic

Instrumental composition: "Call Sheet Blues," Dexter Gordon, Wayne Shorter, Herbie Hancock, Ron Carter, Billy Higgins

Classical album: *Horowitz in Moscow*, Vladimir Horowitz, Deutsche Grammophon

Orchestral recording (conductor's award): *Beethoven:*

---

*Symphony No. 9 in D Minor ("Choral")* Sir Georg Solti conducting the Chicago Symphony Orchestra, London
Opera recording: *R. Strauss: Ariadne auf Naxos*, James Levine conducting the Vienna Philharmonic (solos: Anna Tomowa-Sintow, Kathleen Battle, etc), Deutsche Grammophon
Classical performance, vocal soloist: Kathleen Battle (James Levine, accompanist), *Kathleen Battle Salzburg Recital*, Deutsche Grammophon
Classical producer: Robert Woods
Producer (other than classical): Narada Michael Walden
Performance music video: *The Prince's Trust All-Star Rock Concert*, David C. Croft, director, MGM Home Video
Concept music video: *Land of Confusion*, Genesis, John Lloyd, Jim Yukich, directors, Atlantic Video

## 1988

Album: *Faith*, George Michael
Record: "Don't Worry, Be Happy," Bobby McFerrin, EMI/Manhattan
Song (songwriter's award): "Don't Worry, Be Happy," Bobby McFerrin
New artist: Tracy Chapman
Pop vocal performance, male: Bobby McFerrin, "Don't Worry, Be Happy," EMI/Manhattan
Pop vocal performance, female: Tracy Chapman, "Fast Car," Elektra
Pop vocal performance by a duo or group with vocal: Manhattan Transfer, *Brasil*, Atlantic
Pop instrumental performance: David Sanborn, *Close-Ups*, Reprise
Rock vocal performance, male: Robert Palmer, "Simply Irresistible," EMI/Manhattan
Rock vocal performance, female: Tina Turner, *Tina Live in Europe*, Capitol
Rock performance by a duo or group with vocal: U2, "Desire," Island
Rock instrumental performance: Carlos Santana, *Blues for Salvador*, Columbia/CBS
Rhythm and blues song (songwriter's award): "Giving You the Best That I Got," Anita Baker, Skip Scarborough, Randy Holland
Rhythm and blues vocal performance, male: Terence Trent D'Arby, *Introducing the Hardline According to Terence Trent D'Arby*, Columbia/CBS
Rhythm and blues vocal performance, female: Anita Baker, "Giving You the Best That I Got," Elektra
Rhythm and blues vocal performance by a duo or group: Gladys Knight and the Pips, "Love Overboard," MCA
Rhythm and blues instrumental performance: Chick Corea, "Light Years," GRP
Jazz vocal performance, male: Bobby McFerrin, "Brothers," MCA

Jazz vocal performance, female: Betty Carter, *Look What I Got!* Verve
Jazz vocal performance by a duo or group: Take 6, "Spread Love," Reprise
Jazz instrumental performance by a soloist: Michael Brecker, *Don't Try This at Home*, MCA-Impulse
Jazz instrumental performance by a group: McCoy Tyner, Pharoah Sanders, David Murray, Cecil McBee, Roy Haynes, *Blues for Coltrane: A Tribute to John Coltrane*, MCA-Impulse
Jazz instrumental performance by a big band: Gil Evans and the Monday Night Orchestra, *Bud and Bird*, Intersound
Jazz fusion performance: Yellowjackets, *Politics*, MCA
Country song (songwriter's award): *Hold Me*, K.T. Oslin, RCA
Country vocal performance, male: Randy Travis, *Old 8 x 10*, Warner Bros.
Country vocal performance, female: K.T. Oslin, "Hold Me," RCA
Country performance by a duo or group with vocal: Judds, "Give a Little Love," RCA
Country instrumental performance: Asleep at the Wheel, "Sugarfoot Rag," Epic
Instrumental composition: "The Theme from *L.A. Law*," Mike Post, Polydor
Classical album: *Verdi, Requiem and Operatic Choruses*, Robert Shaw conducting the Atlanta Symphony Orchestra and Chorus, Telarc
Orchestral recording (conductor's award): *Rorem: String Symphony*, Robert Shaw conducting the Atlanta Symphony Orchestra and Chorus; and *Sunday Morning, Eagles*, Louis Lane conducting the Atlanta Symphony, New World
Opera recording: *Wagner: Lohengrin*, Sir Georg Solti conducting the Vienna State Opera Choir and Vienna Philharmonic (solos: Placido Domingo, Dietrich Fischer-Dieskau, etc), London
Classical performance, vocal soloist: Luciano Pavarotti, tenor (Emerson Buckley conducting the Symphonic Orchestra of Amelia Romagna "Arturo Toscanini") *Luciano Pavarotti in Concert*, CBS Masterworks
Classical producer: Robert Woods
Producer (other than classical): Neil Dorfsman
Performance music video: *Where the Streets Have No Name*, U2, Meiert Avis, director, Island
Concept music video: *Fat*, Weird Al Yankovic, Jay Levey, director, Rock 'n' Roll/Epic

## 1989

Album: *Nick of Time*, Bonnie Raitt, Capitol
Record: "Wind beneath My Wings," Bette Midler, Atlantic
Song (songwriter's award): "Wind beneath My Wings,"

---

Larry Henley, Jeff Silbar
New artist: Milli Vanilli (award revoked)
Pop vocal performance, male: Michael Bolton, "How Am I Supposed to Live without You?," Columbia/CBS
Pop vocal performance, female: Bonnie Raitt, "Nick of Time," Capitol
Pop vocal performance by a duo or group with vocal: Linda Ronstadt, Aaron Neville, "Don't Know Much," Elektra
Pop instrumental performance: Neville Brothers, "Healing Chant," A&M
Rock vocal performance, male: Don Henley, *The End of the Innocence*, Geffen
Rock vocal performance, female: Bonnie Raitt, *Nick of Time*, Capitol
Rock performance by a duo or group with vocal: Travelling Wilburys, *Travelling Wilburys, Vol. 1*, Wilbury
Rock instrumental performance: Jeff Beck, Terry Bozzio, Tony Hymas, *Jeff Beck's Guitar Shop with Terry Bozzio and Tony Hymas*, Epic
Rhythm and blues song (songwriter's award): "If You Don't Know Me by Now," Kenny Gamble, Leon Huff
Rhythm and blues vocal performance, male: Bobby Brown, "Every Little Step," MCA
Rhythm and blues vocal performance, female: Anita Baker, *Giving You the Best That I Got*, Elektra
Rhythm and blues vocal performance by a duo or group: Soul II Soul, "Back to Life," Virgin
Rhythm and blues instrumental performance: Soul II Soul, "African Dance," Virgin
Jazz fusion performance: Pat Metheny Group, *Letter from Home*, Geffen
Jazz vocal performance, male: Harry Connick, Jr., *When Harry Met Sally*, Columbia/CBS
Jazz vocal performance, female: Ruth Brown, *Blues on Broadway*, Fantasy
Jazz vocal performance by a duo or group: Dr. John, Rickie Lee Jones, "Makin' Whoopee," Warner Bros.
Jazz instrumental performance by a soloist (on a jazz recording): Miles Davis, *Aura*, Columbia/CBS
Jazz instrumental performance by a group: Chick Corea Akoustic Band, *Chick Corea Akoustic Band*, GRP
Jazz instrumental performance by a big band: Miles Davis, *Aura*, Columbia/CBS
Country song (songwriter's award): "After All This Time," Rodney Crowell, Columbia
Country vocal performance, male: Lyle Lovett, *Lyle Lovett and His Large Band*, MCA
Country vocal performance, female: k.d. lang, *Absolute Torch and Twang*, Sire
Country performance by a duo or group with vocal: Nitty Gritty Dirt Band, *Will the Circle Be Unbroken?, Vol. 2*, Universal
Country instrumental performance: Randy Scruggs, Nitty Gritty Dirt Band, "Amazing Grace," Universal
Instrumental composition: "*The Batman* Theme," Danny Elfman (Sinfonia of London Orchestra), Warner Bros.
Classical album: *Bartók: 6 String Quartets*, Emerson String Quartet, Deutsche Grammophon
Orchestral performance (conductor's award): Leonard Bernstein conducting the New York Philharmonic, *Mahler: Symphony No. 3 in D Minor*, Deutsche Grammophon
Opera recording: *Wagner: Die Walküre*, James Levine conducting the Metropolitan Opera Orchestra (solos: Lakes, Moll, etc), Deutsche Grammophon
Classical performance, vocal soloist: Dawn Upshaw, soprano (David Zinman conducting the Orchestra of St. Luke's) *Knoxville: Summer of 1915*, Elektra/Nonesuch
Classical producer: Robert Woods
Producer (other than classical): Peter Asher
Music video, short form: *Leave Me Alone*, Michael Jackson, Jim Blashfield, director, Epic
Music video, long form: *Rhythm Nation*, Janet Jackson, Dominic Sena, Jonathan Dayton, Valerie Faris, directors, A&M

## 1990

Album: *Back on the Block*, Quincy Jones, Qwest
Record: "Another Day in Paradise," Phil Collins, Atlantic
Song (songwriter's award): "From a Distance," Julie Gold
New artist: Mariah Carey
Pop vocal performance, male: Roy Orbison, "Oh Pretty Woman," Virgin
Pop vocal performance, female: Mariah Carey, "Vision of Love," Columbia/CBS
Pop vocal performance by a duo or group with vocal: Linda Ronstadt, Aaron Neville, "All My Life," Electra
Pop instrumental performance: Angelo Badalementi, "*Twin Peaks* Theme," Warner Bros.
Rock vocal performance, male: Eric Clapton, "Bad Love," Reprise/Duck
Rock vocal performance, female: Alannah Myles, "Black Velvet," Atlantic
Rock performance by a duo or group with vocal: Aerosmith, "Janie's Got a Gun," Geffen
Rock instrumental performance: Vaughn Brothers, "D/FW," Epic Associated
Rhythm and blues song (songwriter's award): "U Can't Touch This," James Miller, M.C. Hammer
Rhythm and blues vocal performance, male: Luther Vandross, "Here and Now," Epic
Rhythm and blues vocal performance, female: Anita Baker, *Compositions*, Elektra
Rhythm and blues vocal performance by a duo or group: Ray Charles, Chaka Khan, "I'll Be Good to You," Qwest
Jazz vocal performance, male: Harry Connick, Jr., *We Are*

*in Love*, Columbia/CBS

Jazz vocal performance, female: Ella Fitzgerald, *All That Jazz*, Pablo

Jazz instrumental performance by a soloist: Oscar Peterson, *The Legendary Oscar Peterson Trio Live at the Blue Note*, Telarc

Jazz instrumental performance by a group: Oscar Peterson, *The Legendary Oscar Peterson Trio Live at the Blue Note*, Telarc

Jazz instrumental performance by a big band: Count Basie Orchestra, "Basie's Bag," Warner Bros.

Jazz fusion performance: Quincy Jones, various artists, "Birdland," Qwest/Warner Bros.

Country song (songwriter's award): "Where've You Been?," Jon Vezner, Don Henry

Country vocal performance, male: Vince Gill, "When I Call Your Name," MCA

Country vocal performance, female: Kathy Mattea, "Where've You Been?," Mercury

Country performance by a duo or group with vocal: Kentucky Headhunters, *Pickin' on Nashville*, Mercury

Country instrumental performance: Chet Atkins, Mark Knopfler, "So Soft Your Goodbye," Columbia/CBS

Instrumental composition: "Change of Heart," Pat Metheny

Classical album: *Ives; Symphony No.2; The Gong on the Hook and Ladder* (*Fireman's Parade on Main Street*); *Central Park in the Dark; The Unanswered Question*, Leonard Bernstein conducting the New York Philharmonic, Deutsche Grammophon

Orchestral performance (conductor's award): Leonard Bernstein conducting the Chicago Symphony Orchestra, *Shostakovich: Symphonies No.1, Op. 10, and No. 7* (*"Leningrad"*), *Op. 60*, Deutsche Grammophon

Opera recording: *Wagner: Das Rheingold*, James Levine conducting the Metropolitan Opera Orchestra (solos: Morris, Ludwig, etc), Deutsche Grammophon

Classical vocal performance: José Carreras, Placido Domingo, Luciano Pavarotti, tenors (Zubin Mehta conducting the Orchestra del Maggio Musicale Fiorentino and Orchestra del Teatro dell'Opera di Roma) *Carreras, Domingo, Pavarotti in Concert*, London

Classical producer: Adam Stern

Producer (other than classical): Quincy Jones

Music video, short form: *Opposites Attract*, Paula Abdul; Michael Patterson, Candice Reckinger, directors, Virgin

Music video, long form: *Please Hammer Don't Hurt 'Em, the Movie*, M.C. Hammer, Rupert Wainwright, director, Fragile Films

# 1991

Album: *Unforgettable*, Natalie Cole, Elektra Entertainment

Record: "Unforgettable," Natalie Cole (with Nat King Cole), Elektra

Song (songwriter's award): "Unforgettable," Irving Gordon

New artist: Marc Cohn

Pop vocal performance, male: Michael Bolton, "When a Man Loves a Woman," Columbia

Pop vocal performance, female: Bonnie Raitt, "Something to Talk about," Capitol

Pop performance by a duo or group with vocal: R.E.M., "Losing My Religion," Warner Bros.

Pop instrumental performance: Michael Kamen conducting the Greater Los Angeles Orchestra, *Robin Hood: Prince of Thieves*, Morgan Creek

Rock song (songwriter's award): "Soul Cages," Sting

Rock vocal performance, solo: Bonnie Raitt, *Luck of the Draw*, Capitol

Rock performance by a duo or group with vocal: Bonnie Raitt, Delbert McClinton, "Good Man, Good Woman," Capitol

Rock instrumental performance: Eric Johnson, "Cliffs of Dover," Capitol

Rhythm and blues song (songwriter's award): "Power of Love/Love Power," Luther Vandross, Marcus Miller, Teddy Vann

Rhythm and blues vocal performance, male: Luther Vandross, *Power of Love*, Epic

Rhythm and blues vocal performance, female (tie): Lisa Fischer, "How Can I Ease the Pain?," Electra; and Patti LaBelle, *Burnin'*, MCA

Rhythm and blues vocal performance by a duo or group: Boyz II Men, *Cooleyhighharmony*, Motown

Contemporary jazz performance (vocal or instrumental): Manhattan Transfer, "Sassy," Columbia

Jazz vocal performance: Take 6, *He Is Christmas*, Reprise

Jazz instrumental performance, solo: Stan Getz, "I Remember You," Emarcy

Jazz instrumental performance, group: Oscar Peterson Trio, *Saturday Night at the Blue Note*, Telarc

Large jazz ensemble performance: Dizzy Gillespie and the United Nation Orchestra, *Live at the Royal Festival Hall*, Enja

Country song (songwriter's award): "Love Can Build a Bridge," Naomi Judd, John Jarvis, Paul Overstreet

Country vocal performance, male: Garth Brooks, *Ropin' the Wind*, Capitol

Country vocal performance, female: Mary Chapin Carpenter, "Down at the Twist and Shout," Columbia

Country performance by a duo or group with vocal: Judds, "Love Can Build a Bridge," RCA

Country instrumental performance: Mark O'Connor, *The New Nashville Cats*, Warner Bros.

Instrumental composition: "Basque," (James Galway), Elton John

---

**. . . December 12 . . .**

**Saving Private Ryan** wins three honors from L.A. Film Critics Assn., including Best Pic.

Classical album: *Bernstein: Candide*, Leonard Bernstein conducting the London Symphony Orchestra (solos: Hadley, Anderson, etc), Deutsche Grammophon

Orchestral performance (conductor's award): Daniel Barenboim conducting the Chicago Symphony Orchestra, *Corigliano: Symphony No. 1*, Erato/Elektra International Classics

Opera recording: *Wagner: Götterdämmerung*, James Levine conducting the Metropolitan Opera Orchestra and Chorus (solos: Behrens, Studer, etc), Deutsche Grammophon

Classical vocal performance: Dawn Upshaw, soprano, *The Girl with Orange Lips*, Elektra/Nonesuch

Classical producer: James Mallinson

Producer (other than classical): David Foster

Music video, short form: *Losing My Religion*, R.E.M.; Tarsem, director, Warner Bros.

Music video, long form: *Madonna: Blonde Ambition World Tour Live*, Madonna; David Mallet, Mark "Aldo" Miceli, directors, Pioneer LDCA Inc.

## 1992

Album: *Unplugged*, Eric Clapton, Reprise

Record: "Tears in Heaven," Eric Clapton, Reprise

Song (songwriter's award): "Tears in Heaven," Eric Clapton, Will Jennings

New artist: Arrested Development

Pop vocal performance, male: Eric Clapton, "Tears in Heaven," Reprise

Pop vocal performance, female: k.d. lang, "Constant Craving," WB/Sire

Pop performance by a duo or group with vocal: Celine Dion, Peabo Bryson, "Beauty and the Beast," Epic

Pop instrumental performance: Richard Kaufman conducting the Nuremberg Symphony Orchestra, "Beauty and the Beast," Varèse Sarabande

Rock song (songwriter's award): "Layla," Eric Clapton, Jim Gordon

Rock vocal performance, male: Eric Clapton, *Unplugged*, Reprise

Rock vocal performance, female: Melissa Etheridge, "Ain't It Heavy," Island

Rock performance by a duo or group with vocal: U2, *Achtung Baby*, Island

Rock instrumental performance: Stevie Ray Vaughan, Double Trouble, "Little Wing," Epic

Rhythm and blues song (songwriter's award): "The End of the Road," L.A. Reid, Babyface, Daryl Simmons

Rhythm and blues vocal performance, male: Al Jarreau, *Heaven and Earth*, Reprise

Rhythm and blues vocal performance, female: Chaka Khan, *The Woman I Am*, Warner Bros.

Rhythm and blues vocal performance by a duo or group:

Boyz II Men, "The End of the Road," Motown

Rhythm and blues instrumental performance: Miles Davis, *Doo-Bop*, Warner Bros.

Contemporary jazz performance, instrumental: Pat Metheny, *Secret Story*, Geffen

Jazz vocal performance: Bobby McFerrin, "Round Midnight," Blue Note

Jazz instrumental solo: Joe Henderson, "Lush Life," Verve

Jazz instrumental performance (individual or group): Branford Marsalis, *I Heard You Twice the First Time*, Columbia

Large jazz ensemble performance: McCoy Tyner Big Band, *The Turning Point*, Verve

Country song (songwriter's award): "I Still Believe in You," Vince Gill, John Barlow Jarvis

Country vocal performance, male: Vince Gill, "I Still Believe in You," MCA

Country vocal performance, female: Mary Chapin Carpenter, "I Feel Lucky," Columbia

Country performance by a duo or group with vocal: Emmylou Harris, Nash Ramblers, *Emmylou Harris and the Nash Ramblers at the Ryman*, RCA

Country instrumental performance: Chet Atkins, Jerry Reed, *Sneakin' Around*, Columbia

Instrumental composition: "Harlem Renaissance Suite," Benny Carter

Classical album: *Mahler: Symphony No. 9*, Leonard Bernstein conducting the Berlin Philharmonic Orchestra, Deutsche Grammophon

Orchestral performance (conductor's award): Leonard Bernstein conducting the Berlin Philharmonic Orchestra, *Mahler: Symphony No. 9*, Deutsche Grammophon

Opera recording: *R. Strauss: Die Frau ohne Schatten*, Sir Georg Solti conducting the Vienna Philharmonic (solos: Domino, Varady, etc.), London

Vocal classical performance: Kathleen Battle, soprano (Margo Garett, accompanist), *Kathleen Battle at Carnegie Hall*, Deutsche Grammophon

Classical producer: Michael Fine

Producer (other than classical) (tie): Daniel Lanois, Brian Eno; and L.A. Reid, Babyface

Music video, short form: *Digging in the Dirt*, Peter Gabriel, John Downer, director, Geffen

Music video, long form: *Diva*, Annie Lennox; Sophie Muller, director, 6 West Home Video

## 1993

Album: *The Bodyguard* (soundtrack), Whitney Houston, Arista

Record: "I Will Always Love You," Whitney Houston, Arista

Song (songwriter's award): "A Whole New World (*Aladdin*'s Theme)," Alan Menken, Tim Rice

---

New artist: Toni Braxton

Pop vocal performance, male: Sting, "If I Ever Lose My Faith in You," A&M

Pop vocal performance, female: Whitney Houston, "I Will Always Love You," Arista

Pop performance by a duo or group with vocal: Peabo Bryson, Regina Belle, "A Whole New World (*Aladdin's* Theme)," Columbia and Walt Disney

Pop instrumental performance: Bruce Hornsby, Branford Marsalis, "Barcelona Mona," RCA

Rock song (songwriter's award): "Runaway Train," David Pirner

Rock vocal performance, solo: Meat Loaf, "I'd Do Anything for Love (but I Won't Do That)," MCA

Rock performance by a duo or group with vocal: Aerosmith, "Livin' on the Edge," Geffen

Rock instrumental performance: Zappa's Universe Rock Group Featuring Steve Vai, "Sofa," Verve

Rhythm and blues song (songwriter's award): "That's the Way Love Goes," Janet Jackson, James Harris III, Terry Lewis

Rhythm and blues vocal performance, male: Ray Charles, "A Song for You," Warner Bros.

Rhythm and blues vocal performance, female: Toni Braxton, "Another Sad Love Song," La Face

Rhythm and blues vocal performance by a duo or group: Sade, "No Ordinary Love," Epic

Contemporary jazz performance, instrumental: Pat Metheny Group, *The Road to You*, Geffen

Jazz vocal performance: Natalie Cole, *Take a Look*, Elektra

Jazz instrumental solo: Joe Henderson, "Miles Ahead," Verve

Jazz instrumental performance (individual or group): Joe Henderson, *So Near, So Far (Musing for Miles)*, Verve

Large jazz ensemble performance: Miles Davis, Quincy Jones, *Miles and Quincy Live at Montreux*, Warner Bros.

Country song (songwriter's award): "Passionate Kisses," Lucinda Williams

Country vocal performance, male: Dwight Yoakam, "Ain't That Lonely Yet," Reprise

Country vocal performance, female: Mary Chapin Carpenter, "Passionate Kisses," Columbia

Country performance by a duo or group with vocal: Brooks and Dunn, "Hard Workin' Man," Arista

Country instrumental performance: Asleep at the Wheel, "Red Wing," Liberty

Instrumental composition: "Forever in Love," Kenny G.

Classical album: *Bartók: The Wooden Prince and Cantata Profana*, Pierre Boulez conducting the Chicago Symphony Orchestra and Chorus (John Aler, tenor; John Tomlison, baritone), Deutsche Grammophon

Orchestral performance (conductor's award): Pierre Boulez conducting the Chicago Symphony, *Bartók: The*

*Wooden Prince*, Deutsche Grammophon

Opera recording: *Handel: Semele*, John Nelson conducting the English Chamber Orchestra and Ambrosian Opera Chorus (solos: Battle, Horne, etc), Philips Classics

Vocal classical performance: Arleen Auger, soprano (Joel Revzen accompanist), *The Art of Arleen Auger*, Koch International

Classical producer: Judith Sherman

Producer (other than classical): David Foster

Music video, short form: *Steam*, Peter Gabriel, Steven R. Johnson, director, Geffen

Music video, long form: *Ten Summoner's Tales*, Sting, Doug Nichol, director, A&M

## 1994

Album: *MTV Unplugged*, Tony Bennett, Columbia

Record: "All I Wanna Do," Sheryl Crow, A&M

Song (songwriter's award): "Streets of Philadelphia," Bruce Springsteen

New artist: Sheryl Crow

Pop vocal performance, male: Elton John, "Can You Feel the Love Tonight?," Hollywood

Pop vocal performance, female: Sheryl Crow "All I Wanna Do," A&M

Pop performance by a duo or group with vocal: All-4-One, "I Swear," Blitzz/Atlantic

Pop instrumental performance: Booker T and the MG's, *Cruisin'*, Columbia

Pop album: *Longing in Their Hearts*, Bonnie Raitt, Capitol

Rock song (songwriter's award): "Streets of Philadelphia," Bruce Springsteen

Rock vocal performance, male: Bruce Springsteen, "Streets of Philadelphia," Columbia/Epic

Rock vocal performance, female: Melissa Etheridge, "Come to My Window," Island

Rock performance by a duo or group with vocal: Aerosmith, *Crazy*, Geffen

Rock instrumental performance: Pink Floyd, "Marooned," Columbia

Rhythm and blues song (songwriter's award): "I'll Make Love to You," Babyface

Rhythm and blues vocal performance, male: Babyface, "When Can I See You?," Epic

Rhythm and blues vocal performance, female: Toni Braxton, "Breathe Again," LaFace Records

Rhythm and blues vocal performance by a duo or group: Boyz II Men, "I'll Make Love to You," Motown

Rhythm and blues album: *II*, Boyz II Men, Motown

Contemporary jazz performance: Brecker Brothers, "Out of the Loop," GRP

Jazz vocal performance: Etta James, *Mystery Lady (Songs of Billie Holiday)*, Private Music

Jazz instrumental solo: Benny Carter, "Prelude to a Kiss," MusicMasters Jazz

Jazz instrumental performance (individual or group): Ron Carter, Herbie Hancock, Wallace Roney, Wayne Shorter, Tony Williams, *A Tribute to Miles*, Reprise/Qwest

Large jazz ensemble performance: McCoy Tyner Big Band, *Journey*, Birdology/Verve

Country song (songwriter's award): "I Swear," Gary Baker, Frank J. Myers

Country album: *Stones in the Road*, Mary Chapin Carpenter, Columbia

Country vocal performance, male: Vince Gill, "When Love Finds You," MCA

Country vocal performance, female: Mary Chapin Carpenter, "Shut up and Kiss Me," Columbia

Country performance by a duo or group with vocal: Asleep at the Wheel, Lyle Lovett, "Blues for Dixie," Liberty

Country instrumental performance: Chet Atkins, "Young Thing," Columbia

Instrumental composition: "African Skies," Michael Brecker

Classical album: *Bartók: Concerto for Orchestra: 4 Orchestral Pieces, Op. 12*, Pierre Boulez conducting the Chicago Symphony Orchestra, Deutsche Grammophon

Orchestral performance (conductor's award): Pierre Boulez conducting the Chicago Symphony Orchestra, *Bartók: Concerto for Orchestra: 4 Orchestral Pieces, Op. 12*, Deutsche Grammophon

Opera recording: *Floyd: Susannah*, Kent Nagano conducting the Orchestra of the Opéra de Lyon (solos: Jerry Hadley, Samuel Ramey, etc), Virgin Classics

Classical vocal performance: Cecilia Bartoli, *The Impatient Lover*, London

Classical producer: Andrew Cornall

Producer (other than classical): Don Was

Music video, short form: *Love Is Strong*, Rolling Stones, David Fincher, director, Virgin

Music video, long form: *Zoo TV – Live from Sydney*, U2, David Mallet, director, Polygram Video

## 1995

Album: *Jagged Little Pill*, Alanis Morissette, Maverick/Reprise

Record: "Kiss from a Rose," Seal, ZTT/Sire/Warner Bros.

Song (songwriter's award): "Kiss from a Rose," Seal

New artist: Hootie and the Blowfish

Pop album: *Turbulent Indigo*, Joni Mitchell, Reprise

Pop vocal performance, male: Seal, "Kiss from a Rose," ZTT/Sire/Warner Bros.

Pop vocal performance, female: Annie Lennox, "No More 'I Love You's,'" Arista

Pop performance by a duo or group with vocal: Hootie and the Blowfish, "Let Her Cry," Atlantic

Pop instrumental performance: Los Lobos, "Mariachi Suite," Epic Soundtrax

Rock album: *Jagged Little Pill*, Alanis Morissette, Maverick/Reprise

Rock song (songwriter's award): "You Oughta Know," Glen Ballard, Alanis Morissette

Rock vocal performance, male: Tom Petty, "You Don't Know How It Feels," Warner Bros.

Rock vocal performance, female: Alanis Morissette, "You Oughta Know," Maverick/Reprise

Rock performance by a duo or group with vocal: Blues Traveller, "Run-Around," A&M

Rock instrumental performance: Allman Brothers Band, "Jessica," Epic

Rhythm and blues album: *Crazysexycool*, TLC, LaFace

Rhythm and blues song (songwriter's award): "For Your Love," Stevie Wonder

Rhythm and blues vocal performance, male: Stevie Wonder, "For Your Love," Motown

Rhythm and blues vocal performance, female: Anita Baker, "I Apologize," Elektra

Rhythm and blues vocal performance by a duo or group: TLC, "Creep," LaFace

Rhythm and blues instrumental performance: Miles Davis, *Doo-Bop*, Warner Bros.

Contemporary jazz performance: Pat Metheny Group, *We Live Here*, Geffen

Jazz vocal performance: Lena Horne, *An Evening with Lena Horne*, Blue Note

Jazz instrumental solo: Michael Brecker, "Impressions," Impulse!

Jazz instrumental performance (individual or group): McCoy Tyner Trio Featuring Michael Brecker, *Infinity*, Impulse!

Large jazz ensemble performance: GRP All-Stars Big Band, Tom Scott, *All Blues*, GRP

Country album: *The Woman in Me*, Shania Twain, Mercury Nashville

Country song (songwriter's award): "Go Rest High on That Mountain," Vince Gill

Country vocal performance, male: Vince Gill, "Go Rest High on That Mountain," MCA

Country vocal performance, female: Alison Krauss, "Baby, Now That I've found You," Rounder

Country performance by a duo or group with vocal: Mavericks, "Here Comes the Rain," MCA

Country instrumental performance: Asleep at the Wheel, "Hightower," Capitol Nashville

Instrumental composition: "A View from the Side," Bill Holman

Classical album: *Debussy: La Mer; Nocturnes; Jeux; etc.*, Pierre Boulez conducting the Cleveland Orchestra, Cleveland Orchestra Choir, Franklin Cohen, clarinet, Deutsche Grammophon

---

**. . . December 15 . . .**
Arnold Schwarzenegger and James Cameron announce they "will be back" in
**Terminator III.**

Orchestral performance (conductor's award): Pierre Boulez conducting the Cleveland Orchestra, *Debussy: La Mer*, Deutsche Grammophon

Opera recording: *Berlioz: Les Troyens*, Charles Dutoit conducting the Montreal Symphony Orchestra, (solos: Lakes, Pollet, etc) London

Classical vocal performance: Sylvia McNair, soprano (Christopher Hogwood conducting the Academy of Ancient Music), Philips Classics

Classical producer: Steven Epstein

Producer (other than classical): Babyface

Music video, short form: *Scream*, Michael Jackson, Janet Jackson, Mark Romanek, director, Epic

Music video, long form: *Secret World Live*, Peter Gabriel, François Girard, director, Geffen Home Video

## 1996

Album: *Falling into You*, Celine Dion, 550 Music/Epic

Record: "Change the World," Eric Clapton, Reprise

Song (songwriter's award): "Change the World," Gordon Kennedy, Wayne Kirkpatrick, Tommy Sims

New artist: LeAnn Rimes

Pop vocal performance, male: Eric Clapton, "Change the World," Reprise

Pop vocal performance, female: Toni Braxton, "Unbreak My Heart," LaFace

Pop performance by a duo or group with vocal: Beatles, "Free as a Bird," Capitol

Pop instrumental performance: Bela Fleck and the Fleckstones, "The Sinister Minister," Warner Bros.

Rock vocal performance, male: Beck, "Where It's At," DGC

Rock vocal performance, female: Sheryl Crow, "If It Makes You Happy," A&M

Rock performance by a duo or group with vocal: Dave Matthews Band, "So Much to Say," RCA

Rock instrumental performance: Jimmie Vaughan, Eric Clapton, Bonnie Raitt, Robert Cray, B.B. King, Buddy Guy, Dr. John and Art Neville, "SRV Shuffle," Epic

Rhythm and blues album: *Words*, Tony Rich Project, LaFace

Rhythm and blues song (songwriter's award): "Exhale (Shoop Shoop)," Babyface

Rhythm and blues vocal performance, male: Luther Vandross, "Your Secret Love," Epic/LV

Rhythm and blues vocal performance, female: Toni Braxton, "You're Makin' Me High," LaFace

Rhythm and blues performance by a duo or group with vocal: Fugees, "Killing Me Softly with His Song," Ruffhouse/Columbia

Contemporary jazz performance: Wayne Shorter, *High Life*, Verve

Jazz vocal performance: Cassandra Wilson, *New Moon Daughter*, Blue Note

Jazz instrumental solo: Michael Brecker, "Cabin Fever," Impulse

Jazz instrumental performance (individual or group): Michael Brecker, *Tales from the Hudson*, Impulse

Large jazz ensemble performance: Count Basie Orchestra, *Live at Manchester Craftsmen's Guild*, Jazz MCG

Country album: *The Road to Ensenada*, Lyle Lovett, Curb/MCA

Country song (songwriter's award): "Blue," Bill Mack

Country vocal performance, male: Vince Gill, "Worlds Apart," MCA

Country vocal performance, female: LeAnn Rimes, "Blue," MCG/Curb

Country performance by a duo or group with vocal: Brooks and Dunn, "My Maria," Arista/Nashville

Country instrumental performance: Chet Atkins C.G.P., "Jam Man," Columbia Records

Instrumental composition: "Manhattan (Island of Lights and Love)," Herbie Hancock, Jean Hancock

Classical album: *Corigliano: Of Rage and Remembrance (Symphony No. 1, etc.)*, Leonard Slatkin conducting the National Symphony Orchestra, Male Choir of the Oratorio Society of Washington, D.C., Male Chorus of the Choral Arts Society of Washington, RCA Victor Red Seal

Orchestral performance (conductor's award): Michael Tilson Thomas conducting the San Francisco Symphony, *Prokofiev: Romeo and Juliet (Scenes from the Ballet)*, RCA Victor Red Seal

Opera recording: *Britten: Peter Grimes*, Richard Hickox conducting the London Opera, London Symphony Chorus and City of London Sinfonia (solos: Langridge, Opie, Watson), Chandos

Classical vocal performance: Bryn Terfel, bass-baritone (James Levine conducting the Metropolitan Opera Orchestra) *Opera Arias*, Deutsche Grammophon

Classical producer: Joanna Nickrenz

Producer (other than classical): Babyface

Music video, short form: "Free as a Bird," Beatles, Kevin Godley, director, Capitol

Music video, long form: *The Beatles Anthology*, Beatles, Geoff Wonfor, director, Capitol Video/Turner Home Entertainment

## 1997

Album: *Time Out of Mind*, Bob Dylan, Columbia

Record: "Sunny Came Home," Shawn Colvin, Columbia

Song (songwriter's award): "Sunny Came Home," Shawn Colvin, John Leventhal

New artist: Paula Cole

Pop album: *Hourglass*, James Taylor, Columbia

Pop vocal performance, male: Elton John, "Candle in the Wind 1997," Rocket

Pop vocal performance, female: Sarah McLachlan, "Building a Mystery," Epic

Pop performance by a duo, or group with vocal: Jamiroquai "Virtual Insanity," Work Group

Pop collaboration with vocal: John Lee Hooker, Van Morrison, "Don't Look Back," Pointblank/Virgin

Traditional pop vocal performance: Tony Bennett, *Tony Bennett on Holiday*, Columbia

Pop instrumental performance: Sarah McLachlan, "Last Dance," Arista

Dance recording: "Carry on," Donna Summer, Giorgio Moroder, Interhit

Rock album: *Blue Moon Swamp*, John Fogerty, Warner Bros.

Rock song (songwriter's award): "One Headlight," Jacob Dylan

Rock vocal performance, male: Bob Dylan, "Cold Irons Bound," Columbia

Rock vocal performance, female: Fiona Apple, "Criminal," Work Group

Pop performance by a duo, or group with vocal: Wallflowers, "One Headlight," Interscope

Rock instrumental performance: Chemical Brothers, "Block Rockin' Beats," Astralwerks

Hard rock performance: Rage against the Machine, "People of the Sun," Epic

Metal performance: Tool, "Aenema," Zoo/Volcano

Alternative music performance: Radiohead, *OK Computer*, Capitol

Rhythm and blues album: *Baduizm*, Erykah Badu, Kedar/Universal

Rhythm and blues song (songwriter's award): "I Believe I Can Fly," R. Kelly

Rhythm and blues vocal performance, male: R. Kelly, "I Believe I Can Fly," Jive/Atlantic/Warner Sunset

Rhythm and blues vocal performance, female: Erykah Badu, "On and on," Kedar/Universal

Rhythm and blues performance by a duo or group with vocal: Blackstreet, "No Diggity," Interscope

Rap album: *No Way out*, Puff Daddy and the Family, Bad Boy

Rap solo performance: Will Smith, "Men in Black," Columbia/Sony

Rap performance by a duo or group: Puff Daddy and Faith Evans Featuring 112, "I'll be Missing You," Bad Boy

Contemporary jazz performance: Randy Brecker *Into the Sun*, Concord Vista

Jazz vocal performance: Dee Dee Bridgewater, *Dear Ella*, Verve

Jazz instrumental solo: Doc Cheatham, Nicholas Payton, "Stardust," Verve

Jazz instrumental performance (individual or group): Charlie Haden, Pat Metheny, *Beyond the Missouri Sky*, Verve

Large jazz ensemble performance: Joe Henderson Big Band, *Joe Henderson Big Band*, Verve

Latin jazz performance: Roy Hargrove's Crisol, *Habana*, Verve

Country album: *Unchained*, Johnny Cash, American

Country song (songwriter's award): "Butterfly Kisses," Bob Carlisle, Randy Thomas

Country vocal performance, male: Vince Gill, "Pretty Little Adriana," MCA Nashville

Country vocal performance, female: Trisha Yearwood, "How Do I Live?," MCA Nashville

Country performance by a duo or group with vocal: Alison Krauss and Union Station, "Looking in the Eyes of Love," Rounder

Country collaboration with vocal: Trisha Yearwood, Garth Brooks, "In Another's Eyes," MCA Nashville

Country instrumental performance: Alison Krauss and Union Station, "Little Liza Jane," Rounder

Rock gospel album: *Welcome to the Freak Show*, DC Talk, ForeFront

Pop/contemporary gospel album: *Much Afraid*, Jars of Clay, Silvertone/Essential

Southern, country or bluegrass gospel album: *Amazing Grace 2: A Country Salute to Gospel*, various artists, Sparrow

Traditional soul gospel album: *I Couldn't Hear Nobody Pray*, Fairfield Four, Warner Bros, Nashville

Contemporary soul gospel album: *Brothers*, Take 6, Warner-Alliance

Gospel album by a choir of chorus: *God's Property from Kirk Franklin's Nu Nation*, God's Property; Kirk Franklin, choir director, B-Rite

Traditional folk album: *L'Amour ou la folie*, BeauSoleil, Rhino

Contemporary folk album: *Time out of Mind*, Bob Dylan, Columbia

Traditional blues album: *Don't Look Back*, John Lee Hooker, Pointblank/Virgin

Contemporary blues album: *Señor Blues*, Taj Mahal, Private Music

Bluegrass album: *So Long So Wrong*, Alison Krauss and Union Station, Rounder

Latin pop performance: Luis Miguel, *Romance*, WEA Latina

Latin rock/alternative performance: Los Fabulosos Cadillacs, *Fabulosos Calavera*, BMG U.S. Latin

Tropical Latin performance: Ry Cooder, *Buena Vista Social Club*, World Circuit/Nonesuch

Mexican-American/Tejano music performance: La Mafia, *En tus Manos*, Sony Discos

Reggae album: *Fallen Is Babylon*, Ziggy Marley and the Melody Makers, Elektra/EEG

Polka album: *Living on Polka Time*, Jimmy Sturr, Rounder

New age album: *Oracle*, Michael Hedges, Windham Hill

World music album: *Nascimento*, Milton Nascimento, Warner Bros.

Instrumental arrangement: Bill Holman, "Straight, No

Chaser," (Bill Holman Band), JVC Music

Instrumental composition (composer's award): "Aung San Suu Kyi," Wayne Shorter

Musical show album: *Chicago, new Broadway cast*, Fred Ebb, lyricist, John Kander, composer, RCA Victor

Instrumental composition written for a motion picture or TV (composer's award): "The English Patient," Gabriel Yared

Song written specifically for a motion picture or TV: "I Believe I Can Fly," R. Kelly (*Space Jam*)

Instrumental arrangement accompanying vocal(s): Slide Hampton, "Cotton Tail," (Dee Dee Bridgewater), Verve

Classical album: *Premieres – Cello Concertos (Works of Danielpour, Kirchner, Rouse)*, Yo-Yo Ma, violoncello, David Zinman conducting the Philadelphia Orchestra, Sony Classical

Orchestral performance (conductor's award): Pierre Boulez conducting the Cleveland Orchestra and Chorus, *Berlioz: Symphonie Fantastique, Tristia*, Deutsche Grammophon

Chamber music performance: Emerson String Quartet, *Beethoven: The String Quartets*, Deutsche Grammophon

Small ensemble performance (with or without conductor): Claudio Abbado conducting members of the Berliner Philharmonic, "Hindemith: Kammermusik No. 1 with Finale 1921, Op. 24, No., 1," track from *Hindemith: Kammermusik Nos. 1,4 and 5*, EMI Classics

Classical performance, instrumental soloist(s) (with orchestra): Yo-Yo Ma, violoncello (David Zinman conducting the Philadelphia Orchestra) *Premieres – Cello Concertos, (Works of Danielpour, Kirchner, Rouse)*, Sony Classical

Classical performance, instrumental soloist(s) (without orchestra): Janos Starker, cello, *Bach: Suites for Solo Cello Nos. 1-6*, RCA Victor Red Seal

Opera recording: *Wagner: Die Meistersinger von Nürnberg*, Sir Georg Solti conducting the Chicago Symphony Orchestra and Chorus, (solos: Lippert, Mattila, etc), London

Choral performance: Robert Shaw conducting the Atlanta Symphony Orchestra and Chorus, *Adams: Harmonium; Rachmaninov: The Bells*, Telarc

Classical vocal performance: Cecilia Bartoli, mezzo-soprano (James Levine, piano), *An Italian Songbook (Works of Bellini, Donizetti, Rossini)*, London

Contemporary composition: "El Dorado," John Adams

Engineered recording, classical: Michael Bishop, Jack Renner, *Copland: The Music of America*, Telarc

Classical producer: Stephen Epstein

Spoken comedy album: *Roll with the New*, Chris Rock, DreamWorks

Spoken word or nonmusical album: *Charles Kuralt's Spring*, Charles Kuralt, Simon and Schuster Audioworks

Musical album for children: *All Aboard!* John Denver, Sony Wonder

Spoken word album for children: *Winnie the Pooh*, Charles Kuralt (A.A. Milne), Penguin Audiobooks

Engineered album (other than classical): Frank Filipetti, *Hourglass* (James Taylor), Columbia

Remixer: Frankie Knuckles

Recording package (art director's award): Hugh Brown, Al Q, Jeff Smith, *Titanic: Music as Heard on the Fateful Voyage* (various artists), Rhino

Recording package, boxed (art director's award): Hugh Brown, David Gorman, Rachel Gutek, *Beg, Scream and Shout! The Big Ol' Box of '60s Soul* (various artists), Rhino

Album notes (annotator's award): John Fahey, Luis Kemnitzer, Jon Pankake, Chuck Pirtle, Jeff Place, Neil V. Rosenberg, Luc Sante, Peter Stampfel, Eric Von Schmidt, *Anthology of American Folk Music (1997 Edition Expanded)*, Smithsonian Folkways

Historical album: *Anthology of American Folk Music (1997 Edition Expanded)* (various artists), Smithsonian Folkways

Producer (other than classical): Babyface

Music video, short form: *Got till It's Gone*, Janet Jackson, Mark Romanek, director, Virgin

Music video, long form: *Jagged Little Pill*, Alanis Morissette, Alanis Morissette, Steve Purcell, directors, Warner/Reprise Video/Maverick

## 1998

Record: "My Heart Will Go On," Celine Dion, 550 Music/Sony Classical

Album: *The Miseducation Of Lauryn Hill*, Lauryn Hill, Ruffhouse/Columbia Records

Song (songwriters' award): "My Heart Will Go On," James Horner and Will Jennings

New artist: Lauryn Hill

Pop vocal perfomance, male: Eric Clapton, "My Father's Eyes," Reprise Records

Pop vocal perfomance, female: Celine Dion, "My Heart Will Go On," 550 Music/Sony Classical

Pop performance by a duo or group with vocal:The Brian Setzer Orchestra, "Jump Jive An' Wail," Interscope Records

Pop collaboration with vocals: Elvis Costello and Burt Bacharach, "I Still Have That Other Girl," Mercury Records

Pop instrumental performance: The Brian Setzer Orchestra, "Sleepwalk," Interscope Records

Dance recording: "Ray Of Light," Madonna, Maverick/Warner Bros. Records

Pop album: *Ray Of Light*, Madonna, Maverick/Warner Bros. Records

Traditional pop vocal performance: Patti Page, "Live At

Carnegie Hall - The 50th Anniversary Concert," DRG Records

Female rock vocal performance: Alanis Morissette, "Uninvited," Warner Sun-set/Reprise Records

Male rock vocal performance: Lenny Kravitz, "Fly Away," Virgin Records America

Rock performance by a duo or group with vocal: Aerosmith, "Pink," Columbia

Hard rock performance: Jimmy Page and Robert Plant, "Most High, "Atlantic

Metal performance: Metallica, "Better Than You," Elektra/EEG

Rock instrumental performance: Pat Metheny Group, "The Roots Of Confidence," Warner Bros

Rock song (songwriter's award): "Uninvited," Alanis Morissette

Rock album: *The Globe Sessions*, Sheryl Crow, A&M

Alternative music performance: Beastie Boys, *Hello Nasty*, Grand Royal/Capitol

Rhythm and blues vocal performance, male: Stevie Wonder, "St. Louis Blues," Verve

Rhythm and blues vocal performance, female: Lauryn Hill, "Doo Wop (That Thing)," Ruffhouse/Columbia

Rhythm and blues performance by a duo or group with vocal: Brandy and Monica, "The Boy Is Mine," Atlantic and Arista

Rhythm and blues song (songwriter's award): "Doo Wop (That Thing)," Lauryn Hill

Rhythm and blues album: *The Miseducation Of Lauryn Hill*, Lauryn Hill, Ruffhouse/Columbia

Traditional rhythm and blues vocal performance (albums only): Patti LaBelle, Live! One Night Only, (MCA)

Rap solo performance: Will Smith, "Gettin' Jiggy Wit It," Columbia

Rap performance by a duo or group: Beastie Boys, "Intergalactic," Grand Royal

Rap album: *Vol. 2 Hard Knock Life*, Jay-Z; Joe Quinde, engineer/mixer, Roc-A-Fella/Def Jam

Country vocal performance, male: Vince Gill, "If You Ever Have Forever In Mind," MCA Nashville

Country vocal performance, female: Shania Twain, "You're Still the One," Mercury Records Nashville

Country performance by a duo or group with vocal: Dixie Chicks, "There's Your Trouble," Monument Records

Country collaboration with vocals: Clint Black, Joe Diffie, Merle Haggard, Emmylou Harris, Alison Krauss, Patty Loveless, Earl Scruggs, Ricky Skaggs, Marty Stuart, Pam Tillis, Randy Travis, Travis Tritt and Dwight Yoakam, "Same Old Train," Columbia Nashville

Country instrumental performance: Randy Scruggs and Vince Gill, "A Soldier's Joy," Reprise

Country song (songwriter's award): "You're Still the One," Shania Twain

Country album: *Wide Open Spaces*, Dixie Chicks, Monument Records

Bluegrass album of the year: *Bluegrass Rules!*, Ricky Skaggs and Kentucky Thunder, Rounder/Skaggs Family Records

New age album: *Landmarks*, Clannad, Atlantic Records

Contemporary jazz performance: Pat Metheny Group, "Imaginary Day," Warner Bros. Records

Jazz vocal performance: Shirley Horn, "I Remember Miles," Verve

Jazz instrumental solo: Chick Corea and Gary Burton, "Rhumbata," Stretch Records

Jazz instrumental instrumental performance (individual or group): Herbie Hancock, "Gershwin's World," Verve

Large jazz ensemble performance: Count Basie Orchestra, "Count Plays Duke," MAMA Records

Latin jazz performance: Arturo Sandoval, "Hot House," N2K Encoded Music

Rock gospel album: *You Are There*, Ashley Cleveland, Cadence/204 Records

Pop contemporary gospel album: *This Is My Song*, Deniece Williams, Harmony Records

Southern, country of bluegrass gospel album: *The Apostle - Music From and Inspired by the Motion Picture*, Various Artists: Peter Afterman, John Huie and Ken Levitan, MCA

Traditional soul gospel album: *He Leadeth Me*, Cissy Houston, House Of Blues Music

Contemporary soul gospel album: *The Nu Nation Project*, Kirk Franklin, Gospo Centric Records

Gospel album by a choir or chorus: *Reflections*, The Associates, Warner Alliance Records

Latin pop performance: Ricky Martin, "Vuelve," Sony Latin

Latin rock/alternative performance: Mana, "Suenos Liquidos," WEA Latina

Tropical Latin performance: Marc Anthony, "Contra La Corriente," RMM Records

Mexian-American music performance: Los Super Seven, "Los Super Seven," RCA Records Nashville

Tejano music performance: Flaco Jimenez, "Said And Done," Barb Wire Productions/Virgin Records America

Traditional blues album: *Any Place I'm Going*, Otis Rush, House Of Blues Records

Contemporary blues album: *Slow Down*, Keb' Mo', Okeh/550 Music

Traditional folk album: *Long Journey Home*, The Chieftains With Various Artists, Wicklow Records

Contemporary folk album: *Car Wheels On A Gravel Road*, Lucinda Williams, Mercury Records

Reggae album: Friends, Sly And Robbie, EastWest Records America/EEG

World music album: *Quanta Live*, Gilberto Gil, Atlantic/Mesa Records

---

**You've Got Mail,** starring Tom Hanks and Meg Ryan, tops pre-Christmas weekend at B.O., beating out **The Prince of Egypt.**

Polka album: *Dance With Me*, Jimmy Sturr And His Orchestra, Rounder Records
Musical album for children: *Elmopalooza!* The Sesame Street Muppets With Various Artists, Sony Wonder Records)
Spoken word album for children: *The Children's Shakespeare*, Various artists including Jim Belushi, Linda Hamilton, etc., Dove Audio
Spoken word album: *Still Me*, Christopher Reeve, Random House Audio Books
Spoken comedy album: *The 2000 Year Old Man In The Year 2000*, Mel Brooks and Carl Reiner, Rhino Records
Musical show album: *The Lion King*, Lebo M, Mark Mancina, Tim Rice, Jay Rifkin, Julie Taymor and Hans Zimmer, lyricists; Elton John, Lebo M, Mark Mancina, Jay Rifkin and Hans Zimmer, composers, Walt Disney Records
Instrumental composition (composer's award): "Almost 12," Bela Fleck, Future Man and Victor Lemonte Wooten, Warner Bros. Records
Instrumental composition written for a motion picture or for television (composer's award): "Saving Private Ryan," John Williams, DreamWorks Records
Song written for a motion picture or for television (songwriter's award): "My Heart Will Go On," (From Titanic) - James Horner and Will Jennings, 550 Music and Sony Classical
Instrumental arrangement: Don Sebesky, "Waltz for Debby," RCA Victor
Instrumental arrangement with accompanying vocal(s): Herbie Hancock, Robert Sadin and Stevie Wonder, "St. Louis Blues," Verve
Recording package: Kevin Reagan, art director, "Ray of Light" (Madonna) Maverick/Warner Bros. Records
Boxed recording package: Jim Kemp and Virginia Team, art directors, "The Complete Hank Williams" -(Hank Williams) Mercury Records Nashville
Album notes: Bob Belden, Todd Coolman and Michael Cuscuna, album notes writers, *Miles Davis Quintet 1965-1968*, (Miles Davis Quintet) Columbia/Legacy Records
Historical album: *The Complete Hank Williams*, Colin Escott and Kira Florita, compilation, Mercury Records Nashville
Engineered album, non-classical: Tchad Blake, Trina Shoemaker and Andy Wallace, engineers, *The Globe Sessions*, (Sheryl Crow) A&M
Producer of the year: Rob Cavallo
Remixer of the year, non-classical: David Morales
Engineered album, classical: "Barber: Prayers of Kierkegaard/Vaughan Williams: Dona Nobis Pacem/Bartok: Cantata Profana" - Jack Ren-ner, engineer (Robert Shaw, conductor) Telarc
Producer of the year, classical: Steven Epstein

Classical album: *Barber: Prayers of Kierkegaard/Vaughan Williams: Dona Nobis Pacem/Bartok: Cantata Profana*, - Robert Shaw, conductor; James Mallinson, producer, Richard Clement, tenor; Nathan Gunn, baritone; Carmen Pelton, soprano; Atlanta Sym. Orch. Cho.; Atlanta Sym. Orch., Telarc
Orchestral performance (award to conductor and orchestra): Pierre Boulez, conducting Chicago Sym. Orch, *Mahler: Sym. No. 9*, Deutsche Grammophon
Opera recording: *Bartok: Bluebeard's Castle*, Pierre Boulez conducting Chicago Sym.Orch., Deutsche Grammophon
Choral performance: Robert Shaw conducting Atlanta Sym. Orch. Cho., *Barber: Prayers of Kierkegaard/Vaughan Williams: Dona Nobis Pacem/Bartok: Cantata Profana*, Telarc
Instrumental soloist performance (with orchestra): Anne-Sophie Mutter, violin, Kryzysztof Penderecki conducting London Symphony Orchestra, *Prenderecki: Violin Con. No. 2 Metamorphosen*, Deutsche Grammophon
Instrumental soloist performance (without orchestra): Murray Perahia, piano, *Bach: English Suites Nos. 1, 3 & 6*, Sony Classical
Chamber music performance: Andre Previn, piano; Gil Shaham, violin, *American Scenes*, (Works of Copland, Previn, Barber, Gershwin), Deutsche Grammophon
Small ensemble performance (with or without conductor): Steve Reich and Musicians, "Reich: Music for 18 Musicians," Nonesuch
Classical vocal performance: Renee Fleming, soprano (Jeffrey Tate, conductor; English Cham. Orch.) *The Beautiful Voice*, (Works of Charpentier, Gounod, Massenet, Flotow, etc.) London
Classical contemporary composition: "Penderecki: Violin Con. No. 2 Metamorphosen," Krzysztof Penderecki
Classical crossover album: *Soul of the Tango - The Music of Astor Piazzolla*, Libertango; Mumuki; Milonga Del Angel, etc., Yo-Yo Ma, cello; Jorge Calandrelli, conductor, Sony Classical
Music video, short form: *Ray of Light*, Madonna; Jonas Akerlund, video director, Maverick/Warner Bros. Records
Music video, long form: *Rock and Roll Heart*, Lou Reed; Timothy Greenfield-Sanders, video director, Fox Lorber Associates, Inc./WinStar Home Entertainment

> *I have had five lifetimes.*
> *(Frank Sinatra)*

# Video

Variety's coverage of video cannot match that of its sister publication, *Video Business*, but since the technology's inception in the 1970s the paper has devoted numerous articles and news items to its fortunes. In a mere 20 years, the home-entertainment scene has undergone a revolution. The choice has expanded from cumbersome, horrendously expensive cassettes on three competing formats to the current buffet of DVDs, laser discs, and bargain cassettes. Rental remains the engine-room of the industry, but "sell-through" is catching up fast, with a release like *The Lion King* or *Titanic* capable of generating $200 million and more in a single week's sales across the U.S. And for an ill-reviewed, low-budget film, the modern equivalent of the old "supporting movie," the video shelves represent a last bid for survival if not for salvation.

## U.K. video rental: 1998

1. *Men in Black* — Columbia Tristar
2. *Face/Off* — Buena Vista
3. *Air Force One* — Buena Vista
4. *Starship Troopers* — Buena Vista
5. *The Fifth Element* — Fox Pathe
6. *The Full Monty* — Fox Pathe
7. *Lost World – Jurassic Park* — CIC
8. *Devil's Advocate* — Warner
9. *Austin Powers* — Fox Pathe
10. *The Jackal* — CIC

*Source: BVA/Rental Monitor*

## U.K. video sales: 1998

1. *Titanic* — Fox
2. *The Full Monty* — Fox
3. *Lady and the Tramp* — Buena Vista
4. *Men in Black* — Columbia Tristar
5. *Hercules* — Buena Vista
6. *Flubber* — Buena Vista
7. *Cats* — PolyGram
8. *Peter Pan* — Buena Vista
9. *Anastasia* — Fox
10. *Lost World – Jurassic Park* — CIC

*Source BVA/CIN*

## U.K. DVD sell-through: 1998

1. *Contact – Special Edition*
2. *Species*
3. *Mars Attacks!*
4. *Tomorrow Never Dies*
5. *Interview With the Vampire*
6. *Michael Collins*
7. *The Game*
8. *While you Were Sleeping*
9. *One Flew Over the Cuckoo's Nest*
10. *The Three Tenors*

*Source: Blockbuster*

1. *GoldenEye*
2. *L.A. Confidential*
3. *Face/Off*
4. *US Marshals*
5. *The Rock*
6. *Con Air*
7. *Tomorrow Never Dies*
8. *From Dusk Till Dawn*
9. *Contact – Special Edition*
10. *As Good As It Gets*

*Source: HMV*

**...December 21...**

Eyemark Entertainment inks big-bucks distrib deal with Tribune Broadcasting for syndie rights to **Everybody Loves Raymond**.

# U.K. DVD top 10: 1998

| Title | Distributor |
|---|---|
| 1. *Tomorrow Never Dies* | MGM/UA |
| 2. *Contact* | Warner |
| 3. *Mars Attacks!* | Warner |
| 4. *Sphere* | Warner |
| 5. *Batman & Robin* | Warner |
| 6. *GoldenEye* | MGM |
| 7. *Face/Off* | Buena Vista |
| 8. *Earthlight* | DVD International |
| 9. *Con Air* | Buena Vista |
| 10. *L.A. Confidential* | Warner |

*Source BVA/CIN*

# Top 10 U.S. non-theatrical sell-through videos: 1998

| Title | Distributor |
|---|---|
| 1. *Lion King II: Simba's Pride* | Disney |
| 2. *Pocahontas, Journey to a New World* | Disney |
| 3. *Cats* | Polygram |
| 4 *The Land Before Time 6* | Universal |
| 5. *Dr. Seuss's How the Grinch Stole Christmas...* | MGM |
| 6. *Cinderella (1997)* | Disney |
| 7. *Land Before Time 5* | Universal |
| 8. *Billboard Dad* | Warner |
| 9. *Blue's Clues: Story Time* | Paramount |
| 10. *Scooby-Doo on Zombie Island* | Turner/Warner |

*Source: Videoscan*

# U.S. video sales: 1998

| Title | Label |
|---|---|
| 1. *Titanic* | Paramount |
| 2. *The Little Mermaid* | Buena Vista |
| 3. *The Lion King II: Simba's Pride* | Buena Vista |
| 4. *Lady and the Tramp* | Buena Vista |
| 5. *Peter Pan* | Buena Vista |
| 6. *Hercules* | Buena Vista |
| 7. *Anastasia* | Fox |
| 8. *Austin Powers* | New Line |
| 9. *Armageddon* | Buena Vista |
| 10. *Flubber* | Buena Vista |
| 11. *Barney's Great Adventure* | PolyGram |
| 12. *Soul Food* | Fox |
| 13. *Air Force One* | Columbia |
| 14. *As Good as It Gets* | Columbia |
| 15. *Spice World* | Columbia |
| 16. *Dr. Dolittle* | Fox |
| 17. *Mouse Hunt* | DreamWorks |
| 18. *Pocahontas: Journey to a New World* | Buena Vista |
| 19. *Small Soldiers* | DreamWorks |
| 20. *Godzilla* | Columbia |

*Source: Videoscan Inc.*

# U.S. DVD sales: 1998

| Title | Label | Sales Index |
|---|---|---|
| 1. *Tomorrow Never Dies* | MGM | 100 |
| 2. *Air Force One* | Columbia | 92 |
| 3. *Godzilla* | Columbia | 84 |
| 4. *US Marshals* | Warner | 81 |
| 5. *Lost in Space* | New Line | 76 |
| 6. *Starship Troopers* | Columbia | 72 |
| 7. *L.A. Confidential* | Warner | 63 |
| 8. *Contact* | Warner | 59 |
| 9.= *As Good as It Gets* | Columbia | 53 |
| 9.= *The Fifth Element* | Columbia | 53 |
| 11.= *Gone With the Wind* | MGM | 50 |
| 11.= *Sphere* | Warner | 50 |
| 13. *Con Air* | Buena Vista | 49 |
| 14. *The Wedding Singer* | New Line | 45 |
| 14. = *Austin Powers* | New Line | 45 |
| 16. *Twister* | Warner | 44 |
| 17. *City of Angels* | Warner | 43 |
| 18. *The Rock* | Buena Vista | 41 |
| 19. *Top Gun* | Paramount | 36 |
| 20. *The Man in the Iron Mask* | MGM | 35 |

*Source: VideoScan Inc.*

# *Video Business* Video Hall of Fame honorees: 1998

*Titanic* filmmaker James Cameron (also *T2, The Abyss, Aliens, True Lies*)

Musicland Stores Corporation chairman and CEO Jack Eugster (America's largest chain of record and video sales outlets, with $2 billion in revenue and more than 200 million videos sold to date)

Barney the Dinosaur creator Sheryl Leach

---

**... December 22 ...**
Warner Bros. and Universal announce they will co-finance Castle Rock pics.

# Books

In 1998, book-selling weathered the tides of recession better than almost any other consumer sector. Superstores are opening in practically every main street and shopping mall, alongside the explosion of online bookstores on the internet, and each year literally hundreds of thousands of new titles appear in the Anglo-Saxon world. We include here some of the key literary awards on both sides of the Atlantic, along with the critical bestselling paperback lists for 1998.

## The Pulitzer Prize, fiction awards: 1965-98

1965: *The Keepers of the House*, Shirley Ann Grau
1966: *Collected Stories*, Katherine Anne Porter
1967: *The Fixer*, Bernard Malamud
1968: *The Confessions of Nat Turner*, William Styron
1969: *House Made of Dawn*, N. Scott Momaday
1970: *Collected Stories*, Jean Stafford
1971: No Award
1972: *Angle of Repose*, Wallace Stegner
1973: *The Optimist's Daughter*, Eudora Welty
1974: No Award
1975: *The Killer Angels*, Michael Shaara
1976: *Humboldt's Gift*, Saul Bellow
1977: No Award
1978: *Elbow Room*, James Alan McPherson
1979: *The Stories of John Cheever*, John Cheever
1980: *The Executioner's Song*, Norman Mailer
1981: *A Confederacy of Dunces*, John Kennedy Toole
1982: *Rabbit Is Rich*, John Updike
1983: *The Color Purple*, Alice Walker

1984: *Ironweed*, William Kennedy
1985: *Foreign Affairs*, Alison Lurie
1986: *Lonesome Dove*, Larry McMurtry
1987: *A Summons to Memphis*, Peter Taylor
1988: *Beloved*, Toni Morrison
1989: *Breathing Lessons*, Anne Tyler
1990: *The Mambo Kings Play Songs of Love*, Oscar Hijuelos
1991: *Rabbit at Rest*, John Updike
1992: *A Thousand Acres*, Jane Smiley
1993: *A Good Scent from a Strange Mountain*, Robert Olen Butler
1994: *The Shipping News*, E. Annie Proulx
1995: *The Stone Diaries*, Carol Shields
1996: *Independence Day*, Richard Ford
1997: *Martin Dressler: The Tale of an American Dreamer*, Steven Millhauser
1998: *American Pastoral*, Philip Roth

## National Book Awards, finalists and winners: 1998

**YOUNG PEOPLE'S LITERATURE**
**Finalists:** Ann Cameron, *The Secret Life of Amanda K. Woods* (Frances Foster Books/Farrar, Straus and Giroux); Jack Gantos, *Joey Pigza Swallowed the Key* (Farrar, Straus and Giroux); Anita Lobel, *No Pretty Pictures: A Child of War* (Greenwillow Books/ William Morrow & Company); Richard Peck, *A Long Way From Chicago* (Dial Books for Young Readers/Penguin Putnam Inc.)
**Winner: Louis Sachar**, *Holes* (Frances Foster Books/Farrar, Straus and Giroux)

**NON-FICTION**
**Finalists:** Harold Bloom, *Shakespeare: The Invention of the Human* (Riverhead Books/Penguin Putnam, Inc.); Yaffa Eliach, *There Once Was a World: A 900-Year Chronicle of the Shtetl of Eishyshok* (Little, Brown and Company Publishers); Beth Kephart, *A Slant of Sun: One Child's Courage* (W.W. Norton & Company); Henry Mayer, *All on Fire: William Lloyd Garrison and the Abolition of American Slavery* (St. Martin's Press)
**Winner: Edward Ball**, *Slaves in the Family* (Farrar, Straus and Giroux)

POETRY

**Finalists:** B.H. Fairchild, *The Art of the Lathe* (Alice James Books); Alicia Suskin Ostriker, *The Little Space: Poems Selected and New, 1968-1998* (University of Pittsburgh Press); Linda Pastan, *Carnival Evening: New and Selected Poems* 1968-1998 (W.W. Norton & Company); Carl Phillips, *From the Devotions* (Graywolf Press)

**Winner: Gerald Stern, *This Time: New and Selected Poems*** (W.W. Norton & Company)

FICTION

**Finalists:** Allegra Goodman, *Kaaterskill Falls* (The Dial Press); Gayl Jones, *The Healing* (Beacon Press); Robert Stone, *Damascus Gate* (Houghton Mifflin Company); Tom Wolfe, *A Man in Full* (Farrar, Straus and Giroux)

**Winner: Alice McDermott, *Charming Billy*** (Farrar, Straus and Giroux)

**1998 DISTINGUISHED CONTRIBUTION TO AMERICAN LETTERS**
**Winner: John Updike**

# Booker Prize: 1969-98

1969: *Something to Answer for,* P.H. Newby
1970: *The Elected Member,* Bernice Rubens
1971: *In a Free State,* V.S. Naipaul
1972: *G,* John Berger
1973: *The Siege of Krishnapur,* J.G. Farrell
1974: *The Conservationist,* Nadine Gordimer
1975: *Heat and Dust,* Ruth Prawer Jhabvala
1976: *Saville,* David Storey
1977: *Staying on,* Paul Scott
1978: *The Sea, The Sea,* Iris Murdoch
1979: *Offshore,* Penelope Fitzgerald
1980: *Rites of Passage,* William Golding
1981: *Midnight's Children,* Salman Rushdie
1982: *Schindler's Ark,* Thomas Keneally
1983: *Life & Times of Michael K,* J.M. Coetzee
1984: *Hotel du Lac,* Anita Brookner

1985: *The Bone People,* Keri Hulme
1986: *The Old Devils,* Kingsley Amis
1987: *Moon Tiger,* Penelope Lively
1988: *Oscar and Lucinda,* Peter Carey
1989: *The Remains of the Day,* Kazuo Ishiguro
1990: *Possession,* A.S. Byatt
1991: *The Famished Road,* Ben Okri
1992: *The English Patient,* Michael Ondaatje; *Sacred Hunger,* Barry Unsworth
1993: *Paddy Clarke, Ha Ha Ha,* Roddy Doyle
1994: *How Late It Was, How Late,* James Kelman
1995: *The Ghost Road,* Pat Barker
1996: *Last Orders,* Graham Swift
1997: *The God of Small Things,* Arundhati Roy
1998: *Amsterdam,* Ian McEwan

# U.K. fastselling paperbacks: 1998

The 100 titles on this list were published for the first time in paperback during 1998. Below this cut-off point, 29 other titles passed the 100,000 units mark, the largest number since the first time these records were kept in 1979. Only four authors have appeared every time since 1979: Dick Francis, Danielle Steel, Stephen King, and the late Catherine Cookson. Astrology, humour, and gardening, which all usually have a representation, have none this year. The fiction element is even more overwhelming than usual. The number of American authors is slightly, but not significantly, down. The percentage of women has very gradually increased (after being static at 25% through the 1980s) to its highest point so far, 43%.
**Alex Hamilton**

| Title, Author, Imprint | Total |
|---|---|
| 1 *The Partner,* John Grisham, Arrow | 1,018,428 |
| 2. *James Cameron's Titanic,* James Cameron, Boxtree | 628,425 |
| 3. *The God of Small Things,* Arundhati Roy, Flamingo | 598,386 |
| 4. *Unnatural Exposure,* Patricia Cornwell, Warner | 570,589 |
| 5. *Birds of Prey,* Wilbur Smith, Pan | 563,608 |
| 6. *The 10lb Penalty,* Dick Francis, Pan | 523,745 |
| 7. *The Ghost,* Danielle Steel, Corgi | 505,435 |
| 8. *Bondage of Love,* Catherine Cookson, Corgi | 490,793 |
| 9. *Hornet's Nest,* Patricia Cornwell, Warner | 479,111 |
| 10. *The Ranch,* Danielle Steel, Corgi | 473,177 |
| 11. *Best Laid Plans,* Sidney Sheldon, HarperCollins | 443,156 |
| 12. *Desert Crop,* Catherine Cookson, Corgi | 442,372 |
| 13. *Executive Orders,* Tom Clancy, HarperCollins | 441,523 |
| 14. *A Walk in the Woods,* Bill Bryson, Black Swan | 413,858 |
| 15. *Windfall,* Penny Vincenzi, Orion | 388,718 |

**. . . December 24 . . .**
Chicago star Bebe Neuwirth exits B'way's **Over & Over** over "creative differences."

16. *Special Delivery*, Danielle Steel, Corgi — 387,614
17. *Cold Mountain*, Charles Frazier, Sceptre — 383,152
18. *Falling Leaves*, Adeline Mah Yeng, Penguin — 373,351
19. *The Lady on My Left*, Catherine Cookson, Corgi — 366,522
20. *Jingo*, Terry Pratchett, Corgi — 365,821
21. *Cat and Mouse*, James Patterson, Feature — 325,122
22. *Wizard and Glass*, Stephen King, NEL — 322,948
23. *Memoirs of a Geisha*, Arthur Golden, Vintage — 315,828
24. *Tom Clancy's Net Force*, Tom Clancy, Feature — 315,256
25. *Remote Control*, Andy McNab, Corgi — 298,970
26. *A Dark Devotion*, Clare Francis, Pan — 295,709
27. *Rachel's Holiday*, Marian Keyes, Penguin — 295,676
28. *Ruthless.com*, Tom Clancy, Penguin — 290,666
29. *Thrill!*, Jackie Collins, Pan — 290,205
30. *Longitude*, Dava Sobel, Fourth Estate — 280,905
31. *Road Rage*, Ruth Rendell, Arrow — 275,271
32. *Deception on His Mind*, Elizabeth George, NEL — 268,021
33. *Enduring Love*, Ian McEwan, Vintage — 267,870
34. *Fear Nothing*, Dean Koontz, Feature — 267,772
35. *Déjà Dead*, Kathy Reichs, Arrow — 267,502
36. *Filth*, Irvin Welsh, Cape — 265,041
37. *Dickie Bird Autobiography*, Dickie Bird, Coronet — 263,865
38. *Part of the Furniture*, Mary Wesley, Black Swan — 263,691
39. *Miss You Forever*, Josephine Cox, Headline — 262,615
40. *Silent Witness*, Richard N. Patterson, Arrow — 256,390
41. *The Echo*, Minette Walters, Pan — 231,747
42. *London*, Edward Rutherfurd, Arrow — 231,235
43. *Love Me or Leave Me*, Josephine Cox, Headline — 227,275
44. *Blood Work*, Michael Connelly, Orion — 225,117
45. *Under the Tuscan Sun*, Frances Mayes, Bantam — 214,634
46. *Detective*, Arthur Hailey, Corgi — 212,729
47. *Point of Origin*, Patricia Cornwell, Little,Brown — 212,606
48. *Power of a Woman*, Barbara T. Bradford, HarperCollins — 210,686
49. *Does My Bum Look Big in This?*, Arabella Weir, Coronet — 210,565
50. *Human Croquet*, Kate Atkinson, Black Swan — 209,890
51. *Killing Ground*, Gerald Seymour, Corgi — 208,676
52. *Matarese Countdown*, Robert Ludlum, HarperCollins — 204,448
53. *Drink with the Devil*, Jack Higgins, Penguin — 200,707
54. *Sextet*, Sally Beauman, Bantam — 194,082
55. *Woman to Woman*, Cathy Kelly, Headline — 191,608
56. *Op Centre: Balance of Power*, Tom Clancy, HarperCollins — 189,173
57. *President's Daughter*, Jack Higgins, Penguin — 187,289
58. *The Diving Bell & the Butterfly*, J-D Bauby, Fourth Estate — 186,385
59. *Caught in the Light*, Robert Goddard, Corgi — 185,275
60. *Love Song*, Charlotte Bingham, Bantam — 177,963
61. *Survival of the Fittest*, Jonathan Kellerman, Warner — 175,767
62. *Chloe*, Freya North, Arrow — 172,914

63. *Floodtide*, Clive Cussler, Pocket Books — 172,392
64. *Eleventh Commandment*, Jeffrey Archer, HarperCollins — 171,728
65. *Question of Integrity*, Susan Howatch, Warner — 171,361
66. *Demon Seed*, Dean Koontz, Feature — 170,029
67. *The Runaway*, Martina Cole, Headline — 165,173
68. *Song of Stone*, Iain Banks, Abacus — 162,329
69. *Jemima J.*, Jane Green, Penguin — 157,205
70. *Plum Island*, Nelson DeMille, Warner — 156,796
71. *The Reader*, Bernhard Schlink, Phoenix — 155,636
72. *Trunk Music*, Michael Connelly, Orion — 154,915
73. *Excalibur*, Bernard Cornwell, Penguin — 154,601
74. *Larry's Party*, Carol Shields, Fourth Estate — 149,625
75. *Fugitive Pieces*, Anne Michaels, Bloomsbury — 146,680
76. *Tomorrow's Memories*, Audrey Howard, Coronet — 145,755
77. *Miracle Strain*, Michael Cordy, Corgi — 145,482
78. *Rosie*, Lesley Pearce, Penguin — 139,189
79. *Come Rain or Shine*, Susan Sallis, Corgi — 139,038
80. *Cold Heart*, Linda La Plante, Pan — 138,556
81. *The Street Lawyer*, John Grisham, Century — 137,577
82. *Instance of the Fingerpost*, Iain Pears, Vintage — 137,243
83. *Certain Justice*, P.D. James, Faber — 137,138
84. *Monstrum*, Donald James, Arrow — 136,476
85. *She's Leaving Home*, Edwina Currie, Warner — 135,339
86. *The Coffin Dancer*, Jeffery Deaver, Coronet — 134,468
87. *Zero Option*, Chris Ryan, Arrow — 132,151
88. *Big Picture*, Douglas Kennedy, Abacus — 131,976
89. *The Perfect Storm*, Sebastian Junger, Fourth Estate — 131,535
90. *Bible Code*, Michael Drosnin, Orion — 130,814
91. *Midnight Club*, James Patterson, HarperCollins — 129,836
92. *Black Market*, James Patterson, HarperCollins — 127,599
93. *Genesis Code*, John Case, Arrow — 125,777
94. *When Tomorrow Dawns*, Lyn Andrews, Headline — 125,038
95. *The Girl from Leam Lane*, Piers Dudgeon, Headline — 124,826
96. *Moab Is My Washpot*, Stephen Fry, Arrow — 121,546
97. *Superplonk 1998*, Malcolm Gluck, Coronet — 121,250
98. *The Craggy Island Parish Magazine*, Linehan & Matthews, Boxtree — 120,555
99. *Tall Poppies*, Louise Bagshawe, Orion — 120,470
100. *Fermat's Last Theorem*, Simon Singh, Fourth Estate — 120,241

> *Be nice to people on your way up, because you meet 'em on the way down. (Jimmy Durante)*

---

# *Publishers Weekly*'s U.S. hardcover bestsellers: 1998

| Title, Author, Publisher | Weeks On '98 List |
| --- | --- |
| **FICTION** | |
| *Memoirs of a Geisha*, Arthur Golden, Knopf (6) | 49 |
| * *Cold Mountain*, Charles Frazier, Atlantic Monthly (26) | 34 |
| * *The Street Lawyer*, John Grisham, Doubleday | 29 |
| *Message in a Bottle*, Nicholas Sparks, Warner | 28 |
| * *Summer Sisters*, Judy Blume, Delacorte | 24 |
| * *I Know This Much is True*, Wally Lamb, HarperCollins/Regan Books | 24 |
| * *A Widow for One Year*, John Irving, Random House | 21 |
| * *Black and Blue*, Anna Quindlen, Random House | 20 |
| * *Rainbow Six*, Tom Clancy, Putnam | 19 |
| * *Paradise*, Toni Morrison, Knopf | 18 |
| *Bridget Jones's Diary*, Helen Fielding, Viking | 16 |
| *A Night without Armor*, Jewel Kilcher, HarperCollins | 15 |
| **NON-FICTION** | |
| *Tuesdays with Morrie*, Mitch Albom, Doubleday | 51 |
| *Angela's Ashes*, Frank McCourt, Scribner (65) | 41 |
| *The 9 Steps to Financial Freedom*, Suze Orman, Crown | 39 |
| *In the Meantime*, Iyanla Vanzant, S & S | 36 |
| *The Millionaire Next Door*, Thomas J. Stanley and William D. Danko, Longstreet (25) | 35 |
| * *Sugar Busters!*, H. Leighton Steward, Morrison C. Bethea, Sam S. Andrews, and Luis A. Balart, Ballantine | 32 |
| * *Simple Abundance*, Sarah Ban Breathnach, Warner (90) | 32 |
| *Conversation with God*, Book 1, Naale Donald Walsch, Putnam (45) | 27 |
| *Talking to Heaven*, James Van Praagh, Dutton | 21 |
| * *Midnight in the Garden of Good and Evil*, John Berendt, Random House (150) | 21 |
| *A Walk in the Woods*, Bill Bryson, Broadway Books | 19 |
| *The Gift of the Jews*, Thomas A. Cahill, Doubleday/Talese | 19 |
| *The Man Who Listens to Horses*, Monty Roberts, Random House (19) | 18 |
| * *A Pirate Looks at Fifty*, Jimmy Buffett, Random House | 17 |
| *Into Thin Air*, Jon Krakauer, Villard (34) | 15 |
| *Citizen Soldiers*, Stephen E. Ambrose, S & S (6) | 15 |
| *Don't Worry, Make Money*, Dr. Richard Carlson, Hyperion (5) | 15 |

# *Publishers Weekly*'s U.S. paperback bestsellers: 1998

| Title, Author, Publisher | Weeks |
| --- | --- |
| **MASS MARKET** | |
| * *Dr. Atkins' New Diet Revolution*, Robert C. Atkins, M.D, Avon (48) | 51 |
| * *The Notebook*, Nicholas Sparks, Warner | 45 |
| *Into Thin Air*, Jon Krakauer, Doubleday/Anchor | 36 |
| *The Perfect Storm*, Sebastian Junger, Harper Paper | 28 |
| *Protein Power*, Drs. Michael R. Eades and Mary Dan Eades, Bantam | 25 |
| *She's Come Undone*, Wally Lamb, Pocket Books | 22 |
| * *The Partner*, John Grisham, Dell Island | 19 |
| * *The Horse Whisperer*, Nicholas Evans, Dell (25) | 17 |
| **TRADE** | |
| * *Don't Sweat the Small Stuff...*, Dr. Richard Carlson, Hyperion (37) | 51 |
| *Chicken Soup for the Teenage Soul*, J. Cangield, M.V. Hansen & K. Kirberger, Health Communications (29) | 49 |
| * *Divine Secrets of the Ya-Ya Sisterhood*, Rebecca Wells, Harper-Perennial | 45 |
| *Under the Tuscan Sun*, Frances Mayes, Broadway (13) | 41 |
| *A Child Called "It"*, Dave Pelzer, Health Communications | 33 |
| *The Beanie Baby Handbook*, Les and Sue Fox, West Highland | 30 |
| *The Color of Water*, James McBride, Riverhead (41) | 27 |
| *Don't Sweat the Small Stuff with Your Family*, Dr. Richard Carlson, Hyperion | 24 |
| *The God of Small Things*, Arundhati Roy, HarperPerennial | 24 |
| *Into the Wild*, Jon Krakauer, Doubleday/Anchor (34) | 21 |
| *James Cameron's Titanic*, Ed. W. Marsh, HarperPerennial | 18 |
| *Little Altars Everywhere*, Rebecca Wells, HarperPerennial | 18 |
| *Chicken Soup for the Pet Lover's Soul*, J. Canfield, M.V. Hansen, M. Becker & C. Kline, Health Communications | 17 |
| *Cold Mountain*, Charles Frazier, Vintage | 17 |
| *A Civil Action*, Jonathan Harr, Vintage (56) | 15 |
| * *Here on Earth*, Alice Hoffman, Berkley | 15 |

* *These titles achieved the number 1 spot during their 1998 presence on PW's bestseller list.*
*Numbers in parentheses show how many weeks the book was on PW's list prior to 1998.*

---

**. . . December 26 . . .**

Monica Lewinsky was the "It" girl of 1998, according to two studies that tracked TV news and newsmagazine coverage during the past year.

# *Announcements*

## Marriages

British model **Marianne Roy** (23), married Anak Agumg Raty Kumara Susila Panji Pandita (42), a cousin of the King of Bali in January.

**Will Smith** married Jada Pinkett, star of *Scream II*, in January.

**Sharon Stone** (40) married Phil Bronstein, executive editor at *The San Francisco Examiner* (47), on February 14.

**Tori Amos**, U.S. singer, married Mark Hawley, British sound engineer, in February.

**Tom Berenger** (47) married Trish Alvaran (23) in February. This is his third marriage.

**Vincent Lindon**, French actor, married Sandrine Kiberlain, actress, in February.

**David Carradine** (62) married Marina Anderson (37) in late February. This is his fourth marriage.

**Shane Lynch** (21), Boyzone star and Easther Bennett (25), Eternal singer, got married in March.

**Blythe Duff**, *Taggart* star married real-life police officer Tom Forrest in March.

**Molly Wayne Muñoz**, the granddaughter of John Wayne married Dillon in March.

**Yazz**, the flamboyant pop star married Spanish pianist Enrique Hernandez in April.

**Ronan Keating** (21), Boyzone star, married Yvonne Connolly, (24), model, on April 30.

**Alvaro Domingo**, the youngest son of Placido Domingo, married Rene Alvarez in May.

**Ian McCaskill** (59), legendary BBC weather forecaster, married Pat Cromack (53) in May.

**Tristan Oliver** (32), the grandson of Sir Laurence Olivier, a businessman, married Emma Gervois in May.

**Jim Belushi** (43), married Jennifer Sloanon in May. This is his third marriage.

**Henry Dent-Brocklehurst** (32), reportedly England's most eligible bachelor, married Hawaiian model Lili Maltese (24) on May 9.

**Sally Meen** (32), former weather girl on the U.K.'s GMTV, married GMTV vp Nick Chesworth (36) on May 9.

**Uma Thurman** married **Ethan Hawke** on May 1.

**Jane McDonald** (35), star of U.K. docu-soap *The Cruise* and subsequent U.K. chart-topping singer, married Henrik Brixen (31), a Danish marine engineer in May.

**Erika Eleniak** (28), former *Baywatch* beauty, married sports fitness and nutrition expert Philip Goglia (38) on May 22.

**Cindy Crawford**, supermodel (32) and Rande Gerber (36), multimillionaire nightclub owner, got married on May 29.

**Julie Walters**, British actress, and Grant Roffey got married in June.

**Tina Hobley** (26), ex *Coronation Street* star and Steve Wallington (32), a graphic designer, got married on June 20.

**Louise Nurding** (23), U.K. singer, married soccer pin-up **Jamie Redknapp** (25) on June 29.

**Macauly Culkin** (17) and Rachel Miner (17) wed in June.

**Barbra Streisand** and **James Brolin** married on July 1.

**Janet Dibley** (39), ex *Eastenders* star married Tyler Butterworth (39), (ex-*Darling Buds of May*) on July 4.

**Catherine Oxenburg** (35), former star of *Dynasty*, and veteran Hollywood player Robert Evans (67) married on July 12, then divorced after 12 days of marriage.

**David Seaman** (34), England goalkeeper, and Debbie Rodgers (36) got married on July 15.

**Martin Bell**, former BBC TV foreign correspondent turned independent MP, married Fiona Goddard in July.

**Nelson Mandela** (80) married Graca Machel (52), Mozambique's former first lady, on July 18 (Mandela's birthday).

**Douglas Kennedy**, son of Robert Kennedy, a reporter with Fox News and formerly with the *New York Post*, married Molly Starkin, schoolteacher, in August.

**Traci Bingham** (27), former *Baywatch* beauty, and musician Robb Vallier (27) married in August.

**Anna-Jane Casey** (27) and **Graham Macduff** (29), stars of the new West End production of *West Side Story*, married in August.

**Patsy Palmer** (25), Bianca from *Eastenders* married Nick Love (28), a TV producer on August 12.

**Mel B** (aka Melanie Brown, aka Scary Spice) (23), married dancer Jimmy Gulzar (23), on September 13.

**Mary McCartney** (eldest daughter of Paul and Linda McCartney) (27) married TV producer Alistair Donald on September 26.

**Tony Booth** (66), former actor and father-in-law of U.K. Prime Minister Tony Blair, married Stephanie Buckley (46) in October.

**Tony Curtis** (73) married lingerie model Jill Vanden Berg (28) in November. This is his fifth marriage.

**Kate Winslet** (23), star of *Titanic*, married assistant film director Jim Threapleton (25) on November 23.

**... December 27 ...**

Patch Adams earns more than $25 million in its first weekend at the box office.

**Jackie Stallone**, (reportedly 74), astrologer and mother of Sylvester Stallone, got married on November 13 to Dr. Stephen Levine, a prominent brain surgeon (55). This is her fourth marriage.

**Carmen Electra**, model and ex-*Baywatch* star, married flamboyant American basketball star and sometime actor **Dennis Rodman** in Las Vegas in November. The marriage lasted only nine days.

**Melinda Messenger** (27), ex-page-three girl and TV presenter married Wayne Roberts, her manager and personal assistant on 26 November.

**Chuck Norris** (59), actor and martial arts champion, married Gena O'Kelley (35) on November 28.

**Christian Moore** (25), Roger Moore's son, married Heidi Moore (30), a model, in early December.

**Adriana Sklernikova**, the Wonderbra model, married Christian Karembeau, French soccer star now playing for Real Madrid, in late December.

Other marriages of 1998: **Woody Harrelson** and Laura Louie; **Robert Carlyle**, *Full Monty* star, and make-up artist Anastasia Shirley; **William Hague**, leader of the British Conservative Party, and Ffion Jenkins; **Keith Duffy** of Boyzone and Lisa Smith; **Prince Naseem Hamed**, boxer, and Eleasha Elphinstone.

## Divorces

**Michael Douglas** divorced wife Diandra after 20 years in January.

**Pamela Sue Martin** (44), Fallon Carrington from the 1980s soap opera *Dynasty*, filed for divorce from her fourth husband Bruce Allen in February.

**Paula Abdul**, singer and choreographer, filed for divorce from her husband of 17 months, Brad Beckerman, in March.

**Steven Bochco**, *NYPD Blue* producer (54), filed for divorce in April from his wife of 28 years, actress **Barbara Bosson** (58).

**Kirstie Alley** divorced Parker Stevenson in May.

**Carol Channing** (77) divorced her husband Charles Lowe (86) after 41 years of marriage in June.

**Jennifer Lopez** divorced Ojani Noa in June.

**Eva Hercigova** (24), model, and Bon Jovi drummer **Tico Torres** (44), filed for divorce in June.

**Paloma Picasso** divorced playwright Rafael Lopez-Cambil in September.

Golfer **Nick Faldo** and his wife Gill divorced in October.

Actress **Gemma Craven** divorced husband David Beamish in November.

**Dudley Moore** (63) and fourth wife Nicole Rothschild (34) divorced in November after four years of marriage.

## Notable separations

**Grant Bovey** (36), video tycoon, left wife Della in January.

**Pamela Anderson** and **Tommy Lee** split in February.

**Geri Halliwell** (the Ginger Spice Girl) split with her boyfriend Jamie Morrison, a polo player, in March.

**Don Johnson** (48) split with his girlfriend Jodi O'Keefe (19) in March after two years.

**Rupert Murdoch**, media tycoon, and his wife Anna split in April after 30 years of marriage.

**Jennifer Aniston**, *Friends* star, and actor Tate Donovan split in April.

**James Cameron** left wife **Linda Hamilton** in April.

**Geri Halliwell** (Ginger Spice) left the Spice Girls in June.

**Bruce Willis** (43) and **Demi Moore** (36) separated after 11 years of marriage in June.

**Aneka Rice** (39), TV presenter, split from boyfriend Tom Gutteridge in July.

**Isla Fisher** (22), star of *Summer Holiday* broke up with Anthony de Rothschild, record producer in July.

**Calista Flockhart**, star of *Ally McBeal*, broke up with Jeffrey Kramer, a producer of the legal comedy, in July.

**Caroline Aherne**, aka Mrs. Merton, broke up with her boyfriend Alexis Denisof in July.

**Julian Lloyd Webber**, cellist brother of Andrew Lloyd Webber, and his second wife Zohra broke up after nine years of marriage in July.

**Sid Owen**, *Eastenders* actor and model Lucy Braybrook split in August.

**Lord Snowdon** and wife Lucy broke up after 20 years of marriage in August.

**Matt Dillon** and **Cameron Diaz** ended their longtime relationship in September.

**Anne Diamond**, U.K. TV presenter, and Mike Hollingsworth, manager of Venture Artists, separated in October. Anne Diamond filed for divorce in November.

**Felicity Kendall**, actress, and playwright **Tom Stoppard** separated after eight years in October.

After 21 years of marriage and numerous extra-marital affairs it seems that **Jerry Hall** finally decided to dump bad-boy-of-rock **Mick Jagger** in November.

---

**... December 28 ...**
NBC cancels its much-hyped sitcom, Conrad Bloom.

# Births

**Mark Knopfler**, Dire Straits star, and Kitty Aldridge, his actress wife, celebrated the birth of their first child, Isabella, in January.

Supermodel **Elle Macpherson** (32) gave birth to her first baby, a boy (Arpad Flynn Busson) on Valentine's Day. The father is banker Akie Busson (35).

**Edward Kennedy, Jr.**, son of Senator Edward Kennedy, and his wife Katherine, a psychiatrist, celebrated the birth of a son, Edward M. Kennedy III, in March.

**Anastasia Cooke** (30), British TV presenter and husband James Baker (34), head of programs at BSkyB, celebrated the birth of their first child, daughter Amelia Rose on March 8.

**Lesley Anne Down** (44), actress, and film director husband Don Fauntleroy (45), celebrated the birth of son George on March 11.

**Michael Jackson** and wife Debbie Rowe celebrated the birth of a daughter, Paris Michael Katherine, in March.

**Phil De Glanville**, former England rugby captain and wife yolanda celebrated the birth of their first child Jake Oliver in March.

**Damon Hill**, Formula One champion and his wife Georgie celebrated the birth of their fourth child, a daughter, in March.

**Robert De Niro** and Grace Hightower celebrated the birth of their son in March. This is DeNiro's fifth child.

**Tracy Austin**, tennis star turned sports commentator, and her husband, mortgage broker Scott Holt, celebrated the birth of their second child, son Brandon Scott, in April.

**Bill Wyman** and wife Suzanne celebrated the birth of their third daughter, Matilda, in April.

Actors **Dan Aykroyd** and Donna Dixon celebrated the birth of their third daughter, Stella Irene Augustus Aykroyd, in April.

**Corbin Bernsen**, star of *L.A. Law*, and Amanda Pays, his actress wife, celebrated the birth of a son in April.

**Annabel Croft**, British TV presenter and her husband Mel Coleman celebrated the birth of their third child, Lily, in May.

**Sally Gunnell** (31), Olympic gold medallist and her husband Jonathan Bigg celebrated the birth of their first child, a son, in May.

**Pierce Brosnan** became a grandfather – his late wife Cassandra's daughter Charlotte (26), a former actress, gave birth to a baby girl in August.

**Lisa Kudrow** (34), star of *Friends*, and husband Michael Stern, a French advertising executive, celebrated the birth of their first child, son Julian, in May.

**Tony Randall** (78) and his wife Heather (28)

celebrated the birth of their second child, son Jefferson Salvini, in June.

**Daniel Day-Lewis** and his wife Rebecca Miller celebrated the birth of their first son, Ronan, in June.

Actors **Lisa Rina** and Harry Hamlin celebrated the birth of a baby daughter on June 10.

**Sylvester Stallone** and wife Jennifer Flavin celebrated the birth of a girl, Sistine Rose, in June.

**Stephanie, Princess of Monaco**, gave birth to a girl Camille in July.

Actors **Uma Thurman** and husband **Ethan Hawke** celebrated the birth of their first child, daughter Maya Ray, in July.

**Sandra Bernhard** (42) gave birth to daughter Cicely Yasmin, on July 4.

**Jada Pinkett** gave birth to son Jaden Christopher Syre Smith, in July.

**Christy Brinkley** gave birth to daughter Sailor Lee in July.

**Jodie Foster** gave birth to son Charles in July.

**Ian Walker**, Spurs goalkeeper and wife Suzi celebrated the birth of their first child Sophie Jacqueline on 24 July.

Model **Stella Tennant** gave birth to son Marcel in August. The father is her boyfriend David Lasnet.

**Tara Newley** (daughter of Joan Collins and Anthony Newley) gave birth to a baby girl, Miel Celeste, on October 5.

**Greta Scacchi** (37) and Carlo Mantegazza (42), celebrated the birth of a baby boy in September.

**Helen Baxendale**, actress, and David Elliot, actor, celebrated the birth of daughter Nell in September.

**Melanie Blatt** (23) of All Saints gave birth to a baby daughter, Lilyella, in November.

**Melissa Etheridge**, singer and her partner Julie Cypher, ex-wife of actor Lou Diamond Phillips, celebrated the arrival of their second child, a baby boy, in November.

**Blair Underwood** (34), actor, and his wife Desiree, celebrated the birth of baby daughter Breille Nicole in late November.

**Nat Parker** (36), hot British TV actor and wife Anna Patrick, actress, celebrated the birth of their second daughter Raphaella on 13 November.

**Tania Bryer**, Sky TV presenter and Tim Mouffarige celebrated the birth of their first child, daughter Natasha Joy in late December.

> *You're not very smart, are you? I like that in a man. (Kathleen Turner, Body Heat)*

# *Obituaries*

From its earliest years, *Variety* has been tracking the quick and the dead, the latter often under the somewhat mordant banner of "Necrology" Shorn of sentiment and tightly compiled, these obituaries focus on the facts in the careers of everyone from superstars to the humblest journalist or technician. The important names appear in the weekly edition of *Variety*, while those lesser mortals whose reputation might be familiar only to Los Angelinos figure in *Daily Variety*.

*Variety* journalists are taught to be rigorous in their pursuit of accurate facts about the newly departed, and ascertaining the cause of death remains a priority. Indeed, our venerable gossip columnist, Army Archerd, has for decades been the first person to be entrusted with bad news – Rock Hudson's contracting AIDS, Henry Mancini's battle with cancer, or Jimmy Stewart's death in 1997. For the purposes of this *Almanac*, we list those who died during 1998 only by name, age, profession, and date of passing. The full-length "Obits." can be accessed through our website, at www.Variety.com.

## Obituaries for 1998

**Philip Abbott**, veteran character actor, who played FBI assistant director Arthur Ward in the TV series, *The FBI*, died February 23 in Los Angeles of cancer. He was 73.

**John Addison**, a prolific scorer of British films and Oscar-winning composer of *Tom Jones*, died December 7 of a stroke at the Southern Vermont Medical Center in Bennington, Vermont. He was 78.

**Robert (Tex) Allen**, a longtime film and stage actor who began his career during the 1930s co-starring in such films as *The Perils of Pauline*, died October 9 in Oyster Bay, N.Y., following a brief bout with cancer. He was 92.

**Bill Alton**, an early member of Chicago's Second City acting troupe, died of heart failure March 23 at the Actors' Fund Nursing Home in New Jersey. He was 73.

**Eric Ambler**, author of modern thrillers and an Oscar-nominated screenwriter, died at his London apartment on October 22 of unreported causes. He was 89.

**Fred Asparagus**, a comedian and character actor with numerous credits in film, TV, and stand-up comedy, died June 29 of a heart attack in Panorama City, California. He was 51.

**Arnold M. Auerbach**, a longtime comedy writer whose resume included Broadway, film, radio, TV, and writing gags for Al Jolson, Frank Sinatra, and Milton Berle, died October 19 of natural causes in New York. He was 86.

**Gene Autry**, the Texas-born crooner who parlayed a career as a singing cowboy in films and TV and as a bestselling recording artist into a diverse business empire, died October 2. He was 91.

**Dorothy Babbs**, a film and legit actress and one of the original dancers in the "Jivin' Jacks and Jills" during the 1940s, died May 13 in Thousand Oaks, California, of complications from heart surgery. She was 71.

**Ben Bagley**, who produced several hit Off Broadway revues and a series of recordings of obscure Broadway songs, died March 21 at his home in Queens, N.Y., of complications from emphysema. He was 64.

**Marcella Bannett Rabwin**, a longtime executive assistant to David O. Selznick, died December 25 from complications of a stroke. She was 90.

**Binnie Barnes**, British-born actress who appeared in dozens of Hollywood films during the 1930s and 1940s, died of natural causes July 27 at her home in Beverly Hills, California. She was 95.

**Philip Barry, Jr.**, a well-known stage, film, and television producer, died May 16 of cancer at Lenox Hill Hospital in New York City. He was 74.

**Eva Bartok**, a Hungarian-born film actress of the 1950s and 1960s, died August 1 at St.Charles' Hospital in London having been ill for some time. She was 69.

**John Bassett**, flamboyant Canadian newspaper publisher, sporting franchise owner, and broadcasting pioneer, died April 27 of heart failure in his Toronto home. He was 82.

**Lucio Battisti**, singer-songwriter, among the most

influential and enduringly popular figures in contemporary national pop music, died September 9 in Milan of undisclosed causes. He was 55.

**Laurie Beechman**, the longest-running Grizabella in Broadway's longest-running hit, *Cats*, died March 8 in her White Plains, N.Y., home of complications from ovarian cancer. She was 43.

**Ralph Bell**, a longtime voiceover artist who began his career as a radio performer during the 1940s, died August 2 after a heart attack in New York. He was 82.

**Richard H. Berger**, longtime theatrical producer and founder of the Starlight Theater in Kansas City, Mo., died October 8 of natural causes at his home in Los Angeles. He was 94.

**Svetlana Beriosova**, ballerina who danced across many stages in Britain, often in lead roles, died November 10 of cancer at St. Charles' Hospital in London at age 66.

**Jerome (Jay Lewis) Bixby**, a science-fiction writer whose screen work included one of the stories for *Twilight Zone – The Movie* and the original screenplay for the cult classic *It! The Terror From Beyond Space*, died April 28 in San Bernardino, California, of complications from quadruple bypass surgery. He was 75.

**Sonny Bono**, who achieved fame as half of the 1960s singing duo Sonny and Cher and parlayed that popularity into a successful career as a politician, was killed January 5 in a skiing accident in South Lake Tahoe. He was 62.

**Eve Boswell**, the glamorous Hungarian-born singing star who dominated British pop charts in the 1950s, died of a heart attack August 13 in Durban, South Africa. She was 76.

**Thomas F. Boutross**, director, producer, and editor of numerous network TV shows and low-budget films, died June 24 of heart failure in Kansas City, Mo. He was 69.

**Owen Bradley**, veteran country-music producer, who helped advance the careers of Loretta Lynn, Brenda Lee, Conway Twitty, and Patsy Cline, died January 8. He was 82.

**Carlo Ludovico Bragaglia**, the doyen of Italian filmmakers who worked in a number of genres during his long career but was best known as the director of several hits starring popular Neapolitan comic Toto, died January 4 in a Rome hospital after an operation for a broken hip. He was 103.

**Olive Brasno Wayne**, a midget actress who worked with a number of top entertainment luminaries during the 1930s, died January 25 of heart failure at a hospital in Lakeland, Fla. She was 80.

**Lloyd Bridges**, who had a long and successful acting career in films like *High Noon* and TV series such as

the popular *Sea Hunt*, and who spawned a small acting dynasty thanks to his sons Beau and Jeff Bridges, died of natural causes at his Los Angeles home March 10. He was 85.

**D. Tennant Bryan**, former chairman of Media General who led the company to become a major communications player in the Southeast, died December 9 at his home in Richmond, Virginia. He was 92.

**Beryl Bryden**, jazz singer, dubbed "Britain's queen of the blues" by Ella Fitzgerald, died July 14 of cancer of the lymph glands at St. Mary's hospital in London. She was 78.

**Henry Butler**, opera director and librettist, died of cancer August 1 at St. Vincent's Hospital in Manhattan. He was 79.

**Rolan Bykov**, a Russian actor who made his mark in more than 80 films ranging from tragic epics to adventures for children, died October 6 in Moscow of unreported causes. He was 68.

**Clara Calamai**, Italian actress, best remembered for her leading role as the sultry, adulterous housewife Giovanna in Luchino Visconti's 1942 debut feature, *Ossessione*, died September 21 in Rimini, Italy, after a brief illness. She was 89.

**Hope Cameron**, veteran actress who originated the role of Letta in Elia Kazan's Broadway production of Arthur Miller's *Death of a Salesman*, died November 20 of cancer at her home in New York City. She was 78.

**Harry Caray**, legendary hall of fame baseball announcer, who took millions of fans out to the ball game on radio and television, died February 18 in Palm Springs, four days after collapsing at a Valentine's Day dinner. He was believed to be 77.

**Betty Carter**, jazz vocalist, died September 26 at her home in Brooklyn, N.Y., from complications due to pancreatic cancer. She was 69.

**Helen Carter**, of the singing Carter family whose songs from the Appalachia region added to the rich heritage of country music, died June 2 at Vanderbilt University Medical Center in Nashville after a lengthy illness. She was 70.

**Randolph Carter**, author of several Broadway plays, died October 12 at St. Albans Naval Hospital in Queens, NY. He was 90.

**Joseph Cates**, television and broadway producer, father of actress Phoebe Cates, and the man who cast Art Carney in *The Honeymooners*, died October 10 in New York of leukemia complications. He was 74.

**Keith Christopher**, actor, singer, songwriter, and AIDS activist, died February 23 of complications from AIDS. He was 40.

**Dane Clark**, a popular character actor whose career on

stage, film, and television dated back to the early 1940s, died September 11 in Los Angeles after a lengthy illness. He was 85.

**Jerry Clower**, a comedian who regularly appeared on the Grand Ole Opry, died August 24 from cardiorespiratory arrest after heart surgery at Baptist Memorial Hospital in Jackson, Missouri. He was 71.

**Sally Cobb**, 1930s model and bestselling author of *The Brown Derby*, died of cancer September 22 at St. Johns Hospital in Santa Monica, California. She was 83.

**Donna Coe**, entertainment writer and reviewer, died at Mt. Sinai Hospital in Manhattan on June 13 after a lengthy illness. Coe married Jim Tatum in her hospital room on June 11. Coe, a resident of Manhattan, was 45.

**Shepard Coleman**, cellist and Tony Award-winning Broadway musical director, died May 12 in Ridgewood, N.J., after triple-bypass surgery. He was 74.

**Arlene Colston**, one half of the Colstons brother-sister comedy dance duo, died November 18 of lung cancer. She was 76.

**Roselle Como**, Perry Como's wife, died of a heart attack in August just days after they celebrated their 65th wedding anniversary. She was 84.

**Ruth Cornelius**, whose acting career extended from silent films to talkies including *Dante's Inferno* and *The Keys of the Kingdom*, died November 30 at age 98 at the hospital in Woodland Hills, California, after an extended illness.

**Luiz Jose Costa**, half of the hugely popular Brazilian country duo Leandro and Leonardo, died June 25 from complications of lung cancer at a hospital in São Paulo, Brazil. He was 36.

**Vittorio Cottafavi**, Italian film and TV director, died December 13 in Anzio, near Rome. He was 84.

**Peter Cotes**, celebrated English actor and director, remembered for staging the first theater production of Agatha Christie's venerable *Mousetrap* in 1952, died November 10 of natural causes at his home in the English village of Chipping Norton. He was 86.

**Kenneth Cowan**, associate producer for such PBS series as *This Old House*, *The Victory Garden*, and *The New Yankee Workshop*, was one of the casualties of the China Airlines Airbus crash in Taipei, Taiwan on February 16. He was 35.

**David Marshal Cox**, longtime comedy writer, died November 16 in Reno, Nevada, of a stroke-related illness. He was 79.

**Robert W. Cresse**, a former indie exploitation-film producer-distributor-exhibitor, died April 6 of a heart attack at his home in Miami. He was 61.

**Beverley Cross**, the playwright and screenwriter who helped launch Dame Maggie Smith on her illustrious acting career and later married her, died March 20 at his home in London. He was 66.

**Steve Currie**, former prexy of the National Assn. of Television Program Executives and a longtime TV executive for the CBS affiliate in Portland, Oregon, died October 2 of undisclosed causes at his Portland home. He was 52.

**Tom D'Andrea**, a character actor with a comedic flair who achieved a measure of popularity during the 1950s as William Bendix's chatty next-door neighbor in the popular 1950s TV series *The Life of Riley*, died May 14 in South Port Square, Fla. He was 88.

**Jean Dalrymple**, the dynamic producer of musicals and plays for City Center, the legendary Manhattan performing arts center, died November 15 at her home in Manhattan. She was 96.

**Anatole Dauman**, 73, creative and adventurous European producer who made landmark films with such directors as Alain Resnais, Jean-Luc Godard, Robert Bresson, Nagisa Oshima, Volker Schlöndorff, Andrei Tarkovsky, Chris Marker, and Wim Wenders, died April 8 of an apparent heart attack at his home in Paris.

**Donald Davis**, a Canadian actor who gained prominence on Broadway and founded theater companies in his native Ontario, died January 23 of emphysema at Wellesley Central Hospital in Toronto. He was 69.

**Barrett Deems**, drummer for Louis Armstrong and Benny Goodman among other jazz greats, died September 15 of natural causes in Chicago. He was 83.

**Duilio Del Prete**, Italian actor, who worked both on stage and screen – including roles in films by Peter Bogdanovich and Joseph Losey – and was a popular singer and television entertainer, died February 2 at Rome hospital after a long illness. He was 61.

**Jerome Dempsey**, legit, television, and film star, whose career spanned more than 40 years, died August 27 in New York of natural causes. He was 69.

**Richard Denning**, actor, who starred in the film *Creature From the Black Lagoon* and played the governor in the TV series *Hawaii Five-O*, died October 11 of cardiac arrest at Palomar Medical Center in Escondido, California. He was 85.

**John Derek**, the handsome leading-man-turned-filmmaker who propelled the careers of his wives Ursula Andress, Linda Evans, and Bo Derek, died May 22 in Santa Maria, California, after heart surgery. He was 71.

**Carl Desuze**, 83, a veteran journalist and radio personality for Boston's WBZ-AM for more than four decades, died April 30 in Concord, Mass. of undisclosed causes.

**Frank DeVaney**, longtime executive in the field of motion picture and television product placement, died June 13 of cancer near his home in Burbank. He was 58.

**Richard Dior**, Oscar-winning sound engineer for *Apollo 13* and more than 200 other features and TV shows, died October 26 of a heart attack in Freehold Township, N.J. He was 51.

**Joe Dixon**, a jazz musician who played with some of the genre's greatest bands during his 50-year career and with the CBS staff band and the NBC Orchestra, died May 28 of natural causes in Oceanside, California. He was 81.

**Robert E. Dore**, prize-winning editor and producer in a long career with NBC and National Public Radio, died January 7 at Holy Cross Hospital in Silver Spring, Maryland. He was 44.

**Jimmy Driftwood**, folk singer-songwriter, whose penning of *The Battle of New Orleans* vaulted him to fame 40 years ago, died July 12 in Fayetteville, Ark. He was 91.

**Todd Duncan**, opera star, who was hand-picked by George Gershwin to play the original role of Porgy in *Porgy and Bess*, died February 28 of a heart condition at his home in Washington, D.C. He was 95.

**Linwood Gale Dunn**, an Oscar-winning and Emmy-nominated visual-effects cinematographer and photographic-equipment designer who worked on nearly 200 films during a 70 year career, died May 20 of natural causes in Burbank, California. He was 93.

**Richard Dunn**, former chief executive of Thames TV and one of British broadcasting's most senior figures, died suddenly August 4 in London. He was 54.

**Ruth Easton**, former Broadway actress and St. Paul, Minn., benefactor, died March 16 of natural causes at her home in Beverly Hills. Her age was unreported.

**Penny Edwards**, a former film and TV actress groomed by Warner Bros. for stardom, who eventually made her mark in numerous Republic westerns, died August 26 of lung cancer in Friendswood, a suburb of Houston, Texas. She was 70.

**Edward Eliscu**, one of the last of the great lyricists from the golden age of Broadway and Hollywood, who wrote the words to *Without a Song* and *More Than You Know*, died June 18 of natural causes in Newton, Connecticut. He was 96.

**Gene Evans**, rugged character actor who appeared in more than 30 films including *Operation Petticoat* and *Walking Tall*, died April 1 in Jackson, Tennessee, of natural causes. He was 75.

**Falco**, a classical-music prodigy who turned to pop music and had a 1986 hit with *Rock Me Amadeus*, died

February 6 in a traffic accident in Santo Domingo. He was 40.

**Alice Faye**, perhaps the brightest musical comedy light at 20th Century Fox during the 1930s and 1940s, died May 9 of cancer. She was 83.

**Charlie Feathers**, rockabilly legend, who co-wrote *I Forgot to Remember to Forget* with Elvis Presley at Sun Records, died August 29 after suffering a stroke. Age unreported.

**Norman Fell**, ubiquitous character actor, who had a flair for both comedy and drama and is perhaps best known for portraying Mr. Roper in TV's *Three's Company* died December 14 of cancer. He was 74.

**Peter L. Feller**, theatrical production supervisor, who won two Tony Awards, including one for lifetime achievement, died of a heart-related illness March 13 in Melbourne, Florida. He was 78.

**Nino Ferrer**, a popular French singer for three decades, committed suicide August 13 in Cahors, France. He was 63.

**Sylvia Field Truex**, a longtime legit and feature actress who is perhaps most remembered as the kindly Mrs. Wilson in the early 1960s TV series *Dennis the Menace*, died July 31 in a nursing home in Fallbrook, a community north of San Diego. She was 97.

**Donald Flamm**, a radio pioneer who helped start the Voice of America, died February 15 in West Palm Beach, Florida. He was 98.

**Gene Fowler, Jr.**, an Oscar-nominated and Emmy-winning editor and director, perhaps best remembered for helming the 1957 cult classic *I Was a Teenage Werewolf*, died May 11 of natural causes at his Hollywood Hills home. He was 80.

**Douglas V. Fowley**, a character actor who enjoyed a five-decade career, died May 21 of natural causes in Woodland Hills, California. He was 86.

**Charlie Foxx**, 64, who wrote the duet *Mockingbird* that twice became a chart topper, once for himself in the 1960s and then again for James Taylor and Carly Simon in the 1970s, died September 18 of leukemia in Mobile, Alabama.

**Sandro Franchina**, Italian filmmaker, who played the doomed son of Ingrid Bergman in Roberto Rossellini's *The Greatest Love* and became known in recent years for his docuportraits of contemporary artists, died February 22 in Paris after a year-long battle with cancer. He was 58.

**Massimo Franciosa**, a screenwriter, novelist, and director who wrote or co-scripted nearly 70 features including such classics as Luchino Visconti's *The Leopard* and *Rocco and His Brothers*, died of a heart attack at his home in Rome on March 30. He was 73.

**Ricardo Franco**, Spanish film director, died May 20 in

Madrid from heart failure. He was 48.

**Gerold Frank**, an award-winning author and pioneer of the as-told-to celebrity biography, died September 17 in Philadelphia. He was 91.

**Kenneth Frankel**, whose theatrical career spanned 25 years, died of a brain tumor February 12 at his home in Los Angeles. He was 56.

**Mary Frann**, actress, who played Bob Newhart's television wife in the hit series *Newhart*, died in her sleep September 23 at her Los Angeles home. She was 55.

**Fred Friendly**, who put his stamp on a generation of news producers and correspondents as a hands-on executive during the glory days of CBS News, died at his New York home March 3 after a series of strokes. He was 82.

**Christopher Gable**, a British ballet star who also had a successful acting career on stage and film, died of cancer October 23 in London. He was 58.

**William P. Gallagher**, longtime entertainment executive, died November 14 of congestive heart failure in Scranton, Pennsylvania. He was 77.

**Martin Gang**, entertainment law pioneer, whose celebrity roster included some of the giants of the entertainment business, died January 26 in Santa Monica after a long illness. He was 96.

**Anne C. Gartenberg**, wife of Seymour L. Gartenberg, a retired executive VP of Sony Music, and mother of Mark Gartenberg, former A&R director for Epic Records, died February 3 of cancer at her home in Brooklyn. She was 62.

**John Gary**, a former RCA recording artist who also made film and TV appearances, died January 4 of cancer at Baylor Hospital in Dallas. He was 65.

**Frank Gillard**, veteran broadcaster and the BBC's war correspondent at the D-Day landings in Normandy, died aged 89.

**Sidney Ginsberg**, retired motion picture distribution and production executive, died of cancer June 18 in Sarasota, Florida. He was 78.

**Rumer Godden**, prolific author whose imagination was fired by living in India and whose writings inspired films, died of natural causes November 8, in a nursing home near her daughter's home in Thornhill, Scotland. She was 90.

**Fred Golden**, a theatrical ad exec for more than 60 years who was honored with a special Tony award in 1988, died July 3 at his home in New York. He was 83.

**Edmund Goldman**, a longtime foreign distribution manager who began his career with Columbia Pictures before World War II, died August 5 of natural causes in Los Angeles. He was 91.

**James Goldman**, an Academy Award-winning screenwriter who also penned the Sondheim musical *Follies*, died October 28 of a heart attack at Lenox hospital in Manhattan, N.Y. He was 71.

**Charles Goldsmith**, a longtime employee at MGM, died February 14 of heart failure at Good Samaritan Medical Center in Lake Worth, Florida. He was 90.

**Nelson Gonzalves**, one of Brazil's most popular crooners, died April 18 of heart failure at his daughter's Rio de Janeiro home. He was 78.

**Claudio Gora**, popular Italian film, theater, and television actor, who worked with many of the country's best-known filmmakers during the golden years of Italian commercial cinema and also directed nine features, died March 13 of heart failure at his home near Rome. He was 84.

**Marius Goring**, British stage and screen actor, star of *The Red Shoes*, died in October. He was 86.

**Lew Grade**, Britain's larger-than-life TV and film mogul, died December 13 in a London hospital. He was 91.

**Virginia Graham**, popular hostess of TV talk shows from the 1950s to 1970s, died December 22 of complications from a heart attack in New York. She was 86.

**Benny Green**, British saxophonist, journalist, and raconteur, died June 22 from cancer. He was 71.

**William E. Greenfield**, Emmy-winning lighting designer, died January 24 in Riverdale, N.Y. He was 68.

**James Gregory**, a musical theater coach for nearly 50 years, died February 4 at Roosevelt Hospital in New York. Gregory, who suffered from emphysema, was 77.

**Florence Griffith Joyner**, the triple gold medalist at the 1988 Olympics who captivated the world with her meteoric speed and flamboyant style, and became a media regular, died September 21 of an apparent heart seizure in Mission Viejo, California She was 38.

**Arthur Groman**, celebrated entertainment lawyer, died December 1 of natural causes in his Beverly Hills home. He was 84.

**Lee Gunther**, an Emmy-winning animation producer, died August 25 of a stroke at his home in Woodland Hills, California. He was 63.

**Henry Hampton**, who fostered *Eyes on the Prize*, the acclaimed TV series about the civil-rights movement, died November 22 of unreported causes at Brigham and Women's Hospital in Boston. He was 58.

**Mark Harrington**, an Emmy-winning producer who, as VP and general manager of MSNBC, helped launch the allnews cable network, died June 25 of cancer in New York. He was 51.

**Phil Hartman**, a regular on NBC's *News Radio*, who had risen to fame on *Saturday Night Live*, died May 28 at his Encino, California, home in what police called a murder-suicide. Hartman's wife, Brynn, also died as a result of a self-inflicted gun-shot wound. Phil Hartman was 49.

**Hurd Hatfield**, the American leading man known for his portrayal of the title character in the Oscar-winning *The Picture of Dorian Gray*, died December 25, at a friend's home in Ireland at age 80. Cause of death was not known.

**Joy Hatton Haynes**, singer and actress, and widow of actor and musician Tiger Haynes, died of cancer January 10 at her home in Manhattan. She was 64.

**Patricia Hayes**, British comic actress, a star of many popular television shows and best known for her portrayals of crotchety cockney characters, died September 19 in London. She was 88.

**Gianni Hecht Lucari**, veteran Italian film, documentary, and television producer, who worked with many of the country's foremost filmmakers and, with Arthur Cohn, produced Vittorio De Sica's 1970 Oscar winner *The Garden of the Finzi-Continis*, died August 27 in Rome of undisclosed causes. He was 76.

**James E. Henry**, a productions director at Showstar Prods., died of heart failure August 26 in Los Angeles. He was 49.

**Sue Herring**, an Emmy-nominated writer and producers' assistant for Charles/Burrows/Charles Prods, died June 17 of cancer at Tarzana Medical Center. She was 49.

**Irene Hervey**, the dimpled leading lady who appeared in dozens of 1930s and 1940s films, died of heart failure December 20 in Calabasas, California. She was 89.

**Joan Hickson**, British actress, best known for her TV portrayal of the shrewd amateur detective Miss Marple, died October 17 in a hospital in Colchester, England. The cause of death was not announced. She was 92.

**Leonardo K.C. Ho**, president and co-founder of Golden Harvest, died February 16 in Hong Kong of a heart attack. His age was not reported.

**Valerie Hobson**, an elegant English film star who remained loyal to her husband, British MP John Profumo, when his affair with call girl Christina Keeler caused a political scandal in 1963, died November 13, of a heart attack in a London hospital. She was 81.

**John Hopkins**, British playwright and screenwriter, whose long career included such notable films as the James Bond actioner *Thunderball* and the recent Showtime telepic *Hiroshima*, died July 23 of unreported causes in Woodland Hills, California. He was 67.

**Eric Horvitch**, a longtime and active member of the American Society of Cinematographers, died August 10 in Johannesburg, South Africa, after heart surgery.

He was 76.

**George Howard**, jazz saxophonist, died of cancer in Atlanta on March 29. He was 41.

**Jack R. Howard**, former president and general manager of E.W. Scripps Co., died March 22 at his New York home. He was 87.

**Josephine Hutchinson**, actress, who made her film debut as a child in Mary Pickford's 1917 *The Little Princess*, died June 4 in a New York City nursing home. She was 94.

**Megs Jenkins,** British actress, died in October. She was 81.

**Albert Johnson**, 74, former artistic director of the San Francisco Film Festival and popular lecturer on cinema at U.C. Berkeley and throughout the world, died October 17 of a heart attack while attending the Chicago Film Festival, where he was scheduled to present some programs.

**Dean X. Johnson**, composer, conductor, and a leading figure in the worldwide gay and lesbian choral movement, also a popular accompanist and musical director in the cabaret world, died January 4 in New York of complications from AIDS. He was 42.

**Grandpa Jones**, whose banjo playing, brightly colored suspenders, and mischievous grin made him a country music favorite and a *Hee Haw* regular for two decades, died February 19 in Nashville of complications resulting from a series of strokes he had suffered. He was 84.

**Jim Jordan**, the tall-tale teller from the 1930s and 1940s radio show *Fibber McGee and Molly*, died December 24 from a heart attack. He was 75.

**Irene Kampen**, whose humorous tale of her struggles as a divorced mother became the basis of TV's *The Lucy Show*, died February 1 of breast cancer at her home in Oceanside. She was 75.

**Bob Kane**, the comic book artist and writer who created the mythic hero "Batman" for DC Comics while still in his teens, died November 3 of natural causes at his home in Los Angeles. He was 83.

**Mike Kaplan**, reporter, critic, and editor for *Variety*, died August 23 of a heart attack at his home in Studio City, California. He was 80.

**MaryAnne Kasica-Scheff**, a television writer whose work included *Magnum P.I.* and *Murder She Wrote*, died September 5 in Los Angeles of a brain tumor. She was 58.

**Eleanor Norris Keaton**, widow of acclaimed silent screen comedian Buster Keaton, died October 19 of emphysema and lung cancer at the Motion Picture Relief Fund Hospital in Los Angeles. She was 80.

**Tim Kelly**, a prolific playwright whose works included *Terror by Gaslight* and *The Butler Did It*, died

December 7 of a cerebral hemorrhage. He was 67.

**Tina Marie Kernan**, associate director of research for Turner Network Television, died August 18 in Riverdale, Georgia, as a result of complications due to child birth. She was 31.

**Persis Khambatta**, a former Miss India who played a navigator in the film *Star Trek – The Motion Picture*, died of a heart attack August 18 in a Bombay hospital. She was 49.

**Edwin Kinley**, a former vaudeville performer who later worked as a comedian with some of the top performers in the 1940s and 1950s, died March 31 of heart failure in New York City. He was 82.

**Keisuke Kinoshita**, acclaimed Japanese director known for his intimate portrayals of human sorrow and joy, died of a stroke December 30 in Tokyo. He was 86.

**Leonid Kinskey**, a stylish Russian-born character actor of the 1930s and 1940s, who is perhaps best remembered as Sascha the bartender in *Casablanca*, died September 9 of complications from a stroke in Fountain Hills, Arizona. He was 95.

**Charles Korvin**, a handsome Hungarian-born actor who made a career out of playing cads, died June 18 at Lenox Hill Hospital in Manhattan. He was 90.

**Richard Paul Krawetz**, a former talent and literary agent, died March 6 of AIDS complications at his home in Los Angeles. He was 45.

**Kurt Kren**, Australian filmmaker, who spearheaded the underground and structuralist avant-garde movements in the 1960s and 1970s, died June 23 in Vienna of pneumonia. He was 69.

**John N. Krier**, a leading movie-industry analyst whose box-office reports were closely watched by Hollywood moguls and film fans alike, died June 13 of pneumonia in Los Angeles after a week of hospitalization. He was 89.

**Akira Kurosawa**, the internationally acclaimed Japanese film director, died September 6 in Tokyo of a stroke. He was 88.

**Sherman Labby**, a storyboard artist in the film industry for more than 30 years, who is perhaps best remembered for his work on *Blade Runner*, died May 31 of natural causes in Los Angeles. He was 68.

**Charles Lang**, the Academy Award-winning cinematographer who shot *The Magnificent Seven* and *Some Like It Hot* and whose innovative work lent glamor to some of the biggest names in Hollywood, died April 3 of pneumonia in Santa Monica, California. He was 96.

**Rex Lardner**, a writer who received an Emmy nomination for his work as head writer on *The Ernie Kovacs Show* in the 1950s, died July 27 from heart trouble while playing tennis in Great Neck, N.Y. He was 80.

**Sid Lawrence**, veteran British bandleader, died suddenly May 5 of unreported causes in London. He was 74.

**Buddy Lee**, CEO of Buddy Lee Attractions, died February 13 in Houston of respiratory failure. He was 65.

**Phil Leeds**, a longtime stage comedian and television actor, died of pneumonia August 16 at Cedars-Sinai Medical Center in Los Angeles. He was 82.

**Mike Levine**, a popular radio talkshow host from the 1960s to the 1980s, died August 18 of leukemia in Pittsburgh. He was 74.

**Shari Lewis**, puppeteer, the Emmy-winning children's entertainer who charmed youngsters for decades with her furry sidekicks Lamb Chop, Charlie Horse, and Hush Puppy, died August 2 of pneumonia at Cedars-Sinai Medical Center in Los Angeles after a battle with cancer. She was 65.

**Ned Liben**, musician, composer, producer, and studio engineer, died of a heart attack February 18 at his Manhattan home/studio. He was 44.

**Kevin Lloyd**, British actor best remembered as Tosh from the long-running TV cop show *The Bill*, died May 2, after a long battle with alcohol. He was 49.

**Jack Lord**, actor, who achieved TV stardom portraying a tough, steely-eyed detective on the hit series *Hawaii Five-O*, died of congestive heart failure January 21 at his beachfront home in Honolulu. He was 77.

**Roger Luard**, chief executive of British pay TV group Flextech, died August 15 in London from a rare neurological virus. He was 49.

**John T. Lyons**, a senior correspondent and former general manager of news operations who worked for ABC News Radio from 1980 to 1997, died of a pulmonary ailment July 16 at Inova Fairfax Hospital in Falls Church, Virginia. He was 54.

**Bryan Maclean**, co-leader of seminal 1960s musical group Love and uncle of country rock singer Maria McKee, died Christmas Day of an apparent heart attack at a Los Angeles restaurant. He was 52.

**Joseph Maher**, whose performances included a Tony-nominated role in Joe Orton's *Loot* and characters in the films *Heaven Can Wait* and *Sister Act* as well as TV's *Seinfeld* and *thirtysomething*, died July 17 of a brain tumor at his home in Los Angeles. He was 64.

**Barbara Mandel**, Britain's first national TV newsreader, died in September. She was 78.

**Wolf Mankowitz**, British playwright, screen writer, and novelist, died May 20 of cancer in County Cork, England. He was 73.

**David Manners**, handsome leading man of numerous

early 1930s films, died December 23 of natural causes at a retirement home in Santa Barbara, California. He was 97.

**Dorothy Manners Haskell**, a columnist who chronicled the lives of Hollywood celebrities, died August 24 at her Palm Springs, California, home. She was 95.

**Jean Marais**, the French film and stage actor whose body of work ranged from Jean Cocteau's classic *La belle et la bête* to a host of swashbucklers in the 1960s, died at a hospital in Cannes on November 8 of pulmonary disease. He was 84.

**Betty Marsden**, comedy actress, died in July. She was 79.

**E.G. Marshall**, two-time Emmy winner for the TV series *The Defenders*, died August 24 at his home in Mount Kisko, N.Y., after a short illness. He was 88.

**Rosemary Martin**, TV and stage actress, died in August. She was 61.

**Daniel Massey**, award-winning British stage actor and member of a distinguished theatrical family, died March 25 in a London hospital after a long illness. He was 64.

**George Masters**, renowned Hollywood hair stylist, makeup artist and author, whose clients ranged from Betsy Bloomingdale to Marilyn Monroe and Dustin Hoffman, died of heart failure March 6 in Los Angeles. He was 61.

**Hedley Mattingly**, British character actor, who appeared in numerous TV shows and a few films during the 1960s, died March 3 in Encino, California, of cancer. He was 83.

**Ferdinand Mayne**, German actor, who appeared in numerous international film and TV productions from the 1940s, died January 30 of Parkinson's disease in London. He was 81.

**Linda McCartney**, the American photographer, musician, and animal welfare activist, who dashed a generation of teenage girls' hopes when she married then-Beatle Paul McCartney in 1969, died April 17 of cancer, apparently at the McCartneys' ranch in Tucson, Arizona. She was 56.

**Roddy McDowall**, who began in the 1930s as a child thesp and became a Hollywood fixture over the next six decades as an actor, as well as folklorist, charity worker, photographer, raconteur, and memorabilia collector, not to mention President of the Academy Foundation's Board of Trustees, died of cancer October 3 in Studio City, California. He was 70.

**Terry McQueen**, daughter of legendary actor Steve McQueen, died of liver disease in March. She was 38.

**Richard Merrell**, actor and screenwriter, who formed an inseparable duo with actress Jan Miner, his wife of 35 years, died September 13 of unreported causes in Southbury, Connecticut. He was 75.

**Bob Merrill**, composer and lyricist, who garnered numerous nominations for his work as a Broadway lyricist, including an Oscar nomination in 1968 for the film *Funny Girl*, committed suicide February 17 in front of his Beverly Hills home, his publicist said. He was 77.

**Theresa Merritt**, stage, television, and film actress who starred in the TV series *That's My Mama*, died June 12 of skin cancer in Calvary Hospital in New York. She was 75.

**Charles Milhaupt**, former film producer, died March 13 of an AIDS-related illness at his home in Manhattan. He was 48.

**Mary Millar**, a British television star and veteran of the London musical stage, best known for her role as Rose in the BBC comedy *Keeping up Appearances*, died November 10 of cancer in London. She was 62.

**Sigmund Miller**, a playwright, screenwriter, and author who was blacklisted in the 1950s, died August 5 at Mt. Sinai Medical Center in New York City owing to complications from pneumonia. He was 87.

**John Paul (Jay) Monahan III**, an attorney and legal analyst for NBC News and husband of *Today* show co-anchor Katie Couric, died January 24 of an undisclosed form of cancer. He was 42.

**Johnny Moore**, the singer who replaced Clyde McPhatter in the Drifters and later sang lead on the smash hit *Under the Boardwalk*, died December 30 on the way to hospital in London. He was 64.

**Dermot Morgan**, the Irish comedian and satirist, famous for his role in the award-winning TV series *Father Ted*, collapsed and died of a suspected heart attack while hosting a dinner party on March 1. He was 45.

**Ed Mullinax**, a former broadcaster and state representative, died June 20 of Alzheimer's disease in LaGrange, Georgia. He was 80.

**Jim Murray**, the *Los Angeles Times* columnist who won a Pulitzer Prize and filled America's sports pages with heart and humor for nearly four decades, died of cardiac arrest August 16 at his Brentwood, California, home. He was 78.

**Janet Murrow**, a CBS and BBC journalist and widow of legendary CBS journalist Edward R. Murrow, died December 18 of heart failure in Needham, Massachusetts. She was 88.

**Gary Nardino**, former head of television production at Paramount and Orion, died January 31 at Cedars-Sinai Medical Center in Los Angeles after suffering a stroke on January 22. He was 62.

**Murray George Newey**, one of New Zealand cinema's most colorful characters and prolific talents, took his own life at his Auckland home on April 8. He was 45.

**Jeanette Nolan**, actress, who had a 70-year career in radio, stage, television, and film, died June 5 at Cedars-Sinai Medical Center after a stroke. She was 86.

**Joseph Norden**, retired actor, who appeared in films such as *Dillinger* and *The Felony Squad*, died March 30 at the Motion Picture & Television Hospital in Woodland Hills, California, after an extended illness. He was 84.

**Assia Noris**, one of the most popular Italian screen stars of the 1930s, who frequently starred opposite Vittorio De Sica and played shy, honest girls who chose love over riches, died January 27 after a brief illness at a hospital in San Remo. She was 85.

**Darcy O'Brien**, award-winning novelist and bestselling non-fiction author, died of a heart attack March 2 at his home in Tulsa, Oklahoma. He was 58.

**Kendall O'Connor**, a legendary Disney layout artist and art director who helped to pioneer the art of animation with his contributions to 13 animated features and nearly 100 shorts, died May 27 of natural causes at his home in Burbank, California. He was 90 years old.

**Dick O'Neill**, longtime character actor perhaps best remembered for his role as Charlie Cagney on the TV series *Cagney & Lacey*, died November 17 of heart failure at St. John's Hospital in Santa Monica. He was 70.

**Thomas F. O'Neil**, a longtime radio and TV executive who helped create the popular *Million Dollar Movie*, died March 14 at his home in Greenwich, Connecticut, of heart failure. He was 82.

**Maureen O'Sullivan**, the Irish-born beauty who starred as Jane in a string of Tarzan films, died June 22 of a heart attack at Scottsdale Memorial Hospital in suburban Phoenix. She was 87.

**Edith Oliver**, the distinguished drama critic at the *New Yorker* for more than 30 years, known for both her toughness and her love of theater, died February 23 at her home in Manhattan. She was 84.

**William Edward Olvis**, former tenor with the New York Metropolitan Opera and father of film composer William Patrick Olvis, died of throat cancer November 27, at his home near Redlands, California. He was 70.

**David Overbey**, critic and film programmer, died of an apparent heart attack December 16 in Toronto. He was 62.

**Jim Oyster**, a veteran actor of Broadway, national tour, and regional theater productions, died February 23 at his home in New York City of acute, late-stage alcoholism. He was 67.

**Gene Page**, whose music arrangements included the Righteous Brothers' *You've Lost That Lovin' Feeling* and Whitney Houston's *The Greatest Love of All*, died August 24 after a long illness at the UCLA Medical Center. He was 58.

**Ken Page**, a longtime TV maven who was much respected in the global TV distribution community, died April 6 of cancer in Toronto. He was 69.

**Alan J. Pakula**, who enjoyed acclaim as a producer (*To Kill a Mockingbird*, *Up the Down Staircase*) and director (*Klute*, *All the President's Men*, *Sophie's Choice*) died November 19 in a car accident on the Long Island Expressway in New York. He was 70.

**Alfred Palca**, whose film about the Harlem Globetrotters became a favorite of basketball fans even after a McCarthy-era blacklisting forced him to remove his name from the credits, died June 19 of cancer in New York. He was 78.

**Dominic Richard Palmieri Jr.**, a retired cinematographer who lensed the TV series *M*A*S*H* for nearly a decade, died February 2 of cancer at his home in central Florida. He was 58.

**Richard Paul**, actor, died December 25 of cancer in Studio City. He was 58.

**Zivojin Pavlović**, Yugoslav film director and writer, died November 29 after an operation. He was 65.

**Leo Penn**, an Emmy-winning television director and actor, died September 5 of cancer in Los Angeles. He was 77.

**Carl Perkins**, an industry pioneer, whose guitar playing influenced generations of musicians and who penned the classic *Blue Suede Shoes*, died January 19 of complications related to a recent series of strokes. He was 65.

**Louis Peterson**, playwright, best known for his groundbreaking play *Take a Giant Step*, about a young black man coming of age in a white neighborhood, died of lung cancer April 27 at his residence in Manhattan. He was 76.

**Norma Peterson**, whose 55-year acting career touched all facets of showbiz, died September 24 from injuries sustained in an auto accident in Pasadena, California. She was 83.

**Jack Petry**, retired network executive who spent 39 years at NBC and was father of Jerry Petry, an executive VP of NBC Enterprises, died November 28 of natural causes in Rancho Mirage, California. He was 82.

**Webster Phillips**, a celebrated makeup artist for film and television stars, died May 13 of cancer at Cedars-Sinai Medical Center in Los Angeles. He was 83.

**Rob Pilatus**, a former model whose career as half the pop music duo Milli Vanilli crashed in disgrace and drug addiction after it was revealed that the group lip-synched its songs, was found dead April 3 in a hotel room near Frankfurt, Germany, after consuming alcohol and pills, according to the *Bild am Sonntag* newspaper. He was 33.

**Cozy Powell**, British rock drummer, who played in Rainbow, Whitesnake and the Michael Schenker Group, was killed in a car crash near Bristol on April 5. He was 50.

**William Preston**, character actor, who gained popularity playing Carl "Oldy" Olsen on NBC's *Late Night with Conan O'Brien*, died July 10 in New York after a brief illness. He was 77.

**Eddie Rabbitt**, country-pop singer who topped the charts with bouncy hits like *I Love a Rainy Night*, died May 7 in Nashville, Tennessee. He was 53.

**Reuben Rabinovitch**, New York theatrical press agent, died July 12 at Montefiore Hospital in the Bronx of heart failure due to pneumonia. He was 94.

**Betty Rankin**, a major figure in New Orleans jazz music, died February 24 in New Orleans. She was 79.

**Gene Raymond**, a handsome blond film star of the 1930s, died of pneumonia May 3 at Cedars-Sinai Medical Center in Los Angeles. He was 89.

**Gigi Reder**, Italian character actor, who worked with such leading directors as Federico Fellini, Vittorio De Sica, and Alessandro Blasetti during his five-decade career but was best known for his role alongside popular comedy star Paolo Villaggio in the long-running *Fantozzi* series, died October 8 in a Rome hospital after a long illness. He was 70.

**Stuart Regen**, *Leaving Las Vegas* movie producer, who was also a prominent Southern Californian art dealer, died of cancer. He was 39.

**Jerome Robbins**, the brilliant director and choreographer who helped dissolve the boundaries between ballet and popular dance and who had a powerful and enduring influence on musical theater, died July 29, after a stroke a few days earlier. He was 79.

**Neil Roberts**, who founded New Zealand's biggest indie, Communicado, and a former director of television for pubcaster TVNZ, died November 6 of cancer. He was 50.

**Eleodoro Rodriguez Matte**, for the last 24 years executive director of leading Chilean broadcaster UCTV (Canal 13), died July 20 of a lung-related illness. He was 80.

**Adam Rogers**, specialized-film distribution exec, who was instrumental in turning Cinepix Film Properties into an important indie player in the U.S., died January 25 in New York of unreported causes. He was 36.

**Roy Rogers**, the amiable singing cowboy star of scores of motion pictures and early television shows, died July 6 of congestive heart failure. He was 86.

**Rita Roland**, a film editor who began her career in Europe before World War II, died of a stroke August 17 in Los Angeles. She was 84.

**Esther Rolle**, a character actress who played the feisty maid in the 1970s sitcom *Maude* and the iron-willed mother in the spinoff series *Good Times*, died November 27 at Brotman Memorial Hospital in Culver City, California. She suffered from diabetes. She was 78.

**Morton Rosenthal**, one of the founders of Warner Communications Inc., now Time Warner Inc., died May 15 in Chappaqua, N.Y., of congestive heart failure. He was 89.

**Sam Ross**, a novelist and television screenwriter for the 1950s series *The Naked City*, died of heart failure March 30 in Laguna Beach, California. He was 86.

**Lord Rothermere**, U.K. press baron and proprietor of the *Daily Mail*, *Mail on Sunday*, and *Evening Standard*, died September 1. He was 73.

**Roy Rowan**, a longtime radio and TV broadcaster best known as Lucille Ball's announcer for more than two decades, died May 10 of heart failure at his home in Encino, California. He was 78.

**Arthur Rowe**, 74, a longtime radio, TV, and occasional feature film writer, died August 6 at his home in Beverly Hills, California, after a lengthy illness.

**Tiny Rowland**, former owner of the U.K. *Observer* newspaper, died from skin cancer on July 24. He was 81.

**Bob Russell**, co-creator of the popular gameshow *Name that Tune* and one of the creators of the Miss America TV extravaganza, died January 24 at a hospital near his home in Sarasota, Florida. He was 90.

**Leonie Rysanek**, the celebrated soprano whose career spanned nearly 40 years and 2,100 performances, died in Vienna, the city of her birth, on March 7 after a battle with bone cancer. She was 71.

**Enrico Sabbatini**, Oscar-nominated film, theater, and television costume designer, who specialized in historical productions, died November 25 in a car accident in Morocco. He was 66.

**Michael Samuelson**, best remembered as the director of Samuelson Film Service, died August 26 at his home in London of a blood clot in the lung. He was 67.

**Lawrence Sanders**, whose debut thriller *The Anderson Tapes* launched his career as a bestselling suspense novelist, died February 14 at his home in Pompano Beach, Florida. He was 78.

**Steve Sanders**, who was part of the Oak Ridge Boys for nearly a decade and sang on some of the million-selling group's later hits, died June 10 at his Florida home. His wife told police he shot himself. He was 45.

**Henry G. Saperstein**, longtime owner of UPA Prods, died of cancer June 24 in Beverly Hills, California. He was 80.

**Ulrich Schamoni**, German director, influential member of the New German Film movement, and commercial media pioneer, died March 10 in Berlin of unreported causes. He was 58.

**Alfred Schnittke**, one of the great Russian composers of this century, died August 3 of a stroke in Hamburg. He was 63 and had suffered from persistent ill health for more than a decade.

**Aurelia Schwarzenegger**, mother of Arnold Schwarzenegger, died in July. She was 76.

**Jeannine Seawell**, veteran film sales executive, who did much to champion pictures from Australia and New Zealand during her 28-year career, died June 8 in Paris after a struggle with cancer. Age unreported.

**Tazio Secchiaroli**, the Italian celebrity photographer who arguably was the inventor of the paparazzi profession and partly inspired Federico Fellini's *La Dolce Vita*, died July 24 in Rome after a long illness. He was 73.

**Dennis Selinger**, British theatrical agent, who worked with Hollywood luminaries ranging from Laurel and Hardy and Charlie Chaplin to Marlon Brando and Dudley Moore, died of cancer February 2 in London. He was 77.

**Alejandro Sessa**, Argentine producer-director, died of heart failure July 10 in Buenos Aires. He was 60.

**Ray Shaw**, a former legit actor-producer, died March 24 of heart failure in Nashville, Tennessee. He was 71.

**George Shdanoff**, a prominent actor, director, writer, and teacher, died August 14 of natural causes at UCLA Medical Center in Los Angeles. He was 92.

**Robert M. Sheerin**, a lifelong theater and film aficionado and member of the Texas Film Commission, died December 24. He was 62.

**Louis K. Sher**, founder of the Art Theater Guild, a theater chain that specialized in showing foreign and independent films, died November 25 of natural causes in Phoenix. He was 84.

**Ed Simmons**, an Emmy-winning TV writer, died May 18 of cardiac arrest at Cedars-Sinai Medical Center in Los Angeles. He was 78.

**Frank Sinatra**, legendary singer and actor, died May 14 of a heart attack. He was 82.

**Emil Sitka**, a veteran character actor best known for his many roles with the Three Stooges, died January 16 in Camarillo, California, after a stroke he had suffered in July. He was 83.

**Robert E. Smith**, better known as "Buffalo Bob" Smith, the cowboy-suited host of *The Howdy Doody Show* who delighted the baby-boom generation in the early years of TV, died July 30 of lung cancer at a hospital near his home in Hendersonville, N.C. He was 80.

**Frank M. Smith, Jr.**, a senior CBS executive for more than 30 years, died April 2 at the Hospice of Palm Beach in Florida after a long illness. He was 70.

**Reg Smythe**, the creator of the comic strip character Andy Capp, died in June. He was 80.

**Johnny Speight**, British comedy writer, who created the character of Alf Garnett for the sitcom *Till Death us do Part*, died July 5. He was 78.

**Dorothy Squires**, singer, a star of the 1940s and 1950s who was left penniless after a string of misfortunes, died April 14 of cancer in Llwynypia, Wales. She was 83.

**Harry Stanley**, a vaudeville performer who perfected a routine of mixing scholarly sounding nonsense with complete and utter gibberish, died February 15 in Englewood, N.J. at the Actor's Fund Home, a retirement home for entertainers. He was 100.

**Barbie Stein**, a casting director for theater, TV, and film, died February 6 of heart failure in San Francisco. She was 40.

**Leslie Stevens**, screenwriter, director, and producer, who created, produced, and served as the writer-director of the popular 1960s TV series *Outer Limits*, died April 24 of a heart attack at UCLA Medical Center. He was 74.

**Roger L. Stevens**, Broadway producer, real estate tycoon, and the driving force behind the creation of Washington, D.C.'s John F. Kennedy Center, died February 2 in Washington of pneumonia. He was 87.

**Dorothy Stickney**, the beloved Broadway actress who originated the role of the mother in the long-running play *Life With Father*, died June 2 at her home in New York City. She was 101.

**Martin Stone**, a broadcasting pioneer and entertainment lawyer whose career ran the gamut from presidential adviser to producer of *Howdy Doody* to founder of a suburban radio network, died of a heart attack June 7 in Washington, D.C. He was 83.

**Don Stotter**, a talkshow host and critic who lived and worked in Florida, died of heart failure February 4 at his home in Hollywood, Florida. He was 69.

**Shinichi Suzuki**, the man who developed the "Suzuki method" of teaching violin and other instruments to young children, died January 26 of heart failure at his home in Tokyo. He was 99.

**Georgy Sviridov**, one of Russia's most prominent composers, died January 6 of a heart attack at Moscow's Central Clinical Hospital. He was 82.

**Helen Taini Nayfack**, a veteran of television and film production, died December 25 of leukemia. She was 73.

**Don Taylor**, actor-director-writer who played

Elizabeth Taylor's bridegroom in *Father of the Bride* and directed *Escape from the Planet of the Apes*, died December 29 of heart failure. He was 78.

**Adele Thane**, founder and artistic director of the Boston Children's Theater, died January 25 in the Bear Hill Nursing Center in Wakefield, Massachusetts. She was 94.

**Michelle Thomas**, actress, who had television roles in *The Young and the Restless*, *The Cosby Show*, and *Family Matters*, died December 22 of cancer in Manhattan. She was 29.

**Kay Thompson**, a popular vocal arranger who was the author of the *Eloise* children's books, died July 2 in New York City. She was believed to be between 92 and 95 years old.

**Harrel G. Tillman, Sr.**, a film and stage actor in the late 1940s who later became the first black judge in Texas, died of cancer June 19 in Houston. He was 73.

**Michael Tippett**, leading British composer, died January 9 of pneumonia at his south London home. He was 93.

**Emily Torchia**, legendary film publicist who worked at MGM during Hollywood's Golden Age and served as a publicist until her retirement in 1980, died October 7 of congestive heart failure in Marina del Rey, California. She was 91.

**Oliver E. Treyz**, the colorful former president of ABC Television who in the late 1950s brought ABC into a competitive standing with the much larger NBC and CBS, died June 14 after a long illness. He was 80.

**Sheldon Tromberg**, a major figure in showbiz circles in D.C. as well as a radio personality, entertainment reporter and film producer, died July 5 of a heart attack in Richmond, California. He was 68.

**Bob Trow**, who portrayed Robert Troll, Bob Dog, and himself for some 30 years on *Mister Rogers' Neighborhood*, died November 3 of a heart attack at his home in New Alexandria, Pennsylvania. He was 72.

**Catherine Turney**, who wrote major 1940s screenplays that featured Bette Davis, Joan Crawford and others in tough female roles, died September 9 in her sleep at her home in Sierra Madre, a suburb of Los Angeles. She was 92.

**Dorothy Tuttle Nitch**, a dancer who appeared in 1940s film musicals with Judy Garland, died of natural causes August 12 in Encino, California. She was believed to be 80.

**Jim Uebelhart**, who worked for nearly 40 years as a broadcaster, died October 3 of complications from a heart attack in Toledo, Ohio. He was 88.

**Robert A. Vanselow**, a longtime actor-singer who essayed Broadway roles and appeared in features and TV shows, died March 30 in Los Angeles after a

lengthy heart-related illness. He was 79.

**John Veitch**, president of worldwide production for Columbia Pictures from 1979 to 1983, died December 8 from pancreatic cancer. He was 78.

**Joseph (Wally) Walcott**, owner of one of America's legendary jazz clubs, died March 23 in Boston. He was 101.

**J.T. Walsh**, actor, who played Jack Nicholson's suicidal lieutenant colonel in *A Few Good Men* and more recently starred as the villain in *Breakdown*, died February 27 in La Mesa, California. He was 54.

**Arnot E. Walker**, veteran press representative for ABC News *World News Tonight* and anchor Peter Jennings, died September 28 in New York from pneumonia complications. He was 44.

**Norman D. Waters**, advertising executive, an advocate of television, and producer of the first fashion show broadcast on television, died June 23 at the Osborn Retirement Community in Rye, N.Y. He was 92.

**Gus Wayne**, one of the 124 midgets who graced the screen in *The Wizard of Oz* in 1939, died January 23 of heart failure at a nursing home in Lakeland, Florida. He was 77.

**Richard B. Weaver**, a longtime Broadway press agent, died May 17 in New York after a lengthy illness. He was 88.

**Nick Webb**, founding member of the contemporary jazz group Acoustic Alchemy, died February 6 in London of pancreatic cancer. He was 43.

**Davina Wells**, New York talent agent, died June 24 in Hospice House in Concord, New Hampshire, after a long battle with cancer. She was 58.

**Junior Wells,** Chicago blues singer and harmonica player died in January. He was 63.

**Robert Wells**, songwriter, Oscar nominee, and multiple-Emmy winner, perhaps best remembered for supplying the lyrics to *The Christmas Song* with friend and co-writer Mel Tormé, died of cancer September 23 in Santa Monica. He was 76.

**Paul West**, a television and radio writer whose credits include *Father Knows Best* and *My Three Sons*, died June 15 in his home in San Anselmo, California, after a bout with pneumonia. He was 86.

**Helen Westcott**, stage and screen actress, died March 17 at Stevens Hospital in Edmunds, Washington, of complications from cancer. She was 70.

**Ross Wetzsteon**, a writer and editor at the *Village Voice* for more than 30 years who helped establish the Obie Awards, died February 20 in Manhattan of complications after cardiac surgery. He was 65.

**Clifton White**, the guitarist who led Sam Cooke's band after launching his career with the Mills Brothers, died April 2 at Midway Hospital Medical

Center in Los Angeles from complications related to diabetes. He was 77.

**O.Z. Whitehead**, a film actor who appeared in *The Grapes of Wrath* and *A Song is Born*, died July 29 in Dublin, Ireland after a long bout with cancer. He was 87.

**Carey Wilber**, a television writer and member of the Writers Guild of America West since 1954, died of cancer May 2 in Seattle. He was 81.

**Tamara Wilcox-Smith**, improv teacher and director, died January 30 of heart failure in Los Angeles. She was 57.

**Mark Williams**, best remembered as a special-effects artist for features including *The Brain* and *Blue Monkey*, died May 27 of respiratory failure at Kaiser Hospital in Panorama City, California. He was 38.

**Wendy O. Williams**, a Grammy-nominated singer whose stage theatrics as lead singer of the 1980s punk-rock band the Plasmatics included blowing up equipment and chain-sawing guitars and appliances, committed suicide April 6 in the woods near her home in Stors, Connecticut. She was 48.

**Bruce Williamson**, film critic, who served as a contributing editor to *Playboy* magazine for 30 years, died October 6 of bladder cancer at New York Presbyterian Hospital. He was 71.

**Carl Wilson**, a founding member of the Beach Boys and lead guitarist for the band that helped define the California "surfing" sound, died February 6, from complications of lung cancer. He was 51.

**Flip Wilson**, comedian, the first African-American to host a successful weekly variety series for a network, died November 25 of liver cancer at his Malibu home. He was 64.

**Tony Witzel**, chief projectionist for the Academy of Motion Picture Arts and Sciences, died December 16 of brain cancer. He was 52.

**Davina J. Wollenberg**, a retired New York talent agent, died of cancer June 24 in New Hampshire, where she had lived for the past year. She was 58.

**Marvin Worth**, one of the entertainment industry's most accomplished and prolific writer-producers, died April 22 in Los Angeles of complications from bronchioloalveolar carcinoma. He was 72.

**Garland Wright**, the influential artistic director of Minneapolis' famed Guthrie Theater for a decade and one of America's leading theatrical directors, died of cancer July 24 in New York. He was 52.

**George Wright**, a renowned organist who served as staff organist at Radio City Music Hall and the Paramount Theater in New York and was perhaps the most recorded theater organist of all time, died May 10 of unreported causes in Southern California. He was 77.

**Tammy Wynette**, who rose from beautician to "the first lady of country music" with hits including *Stand by Your Man*, died April 6 at her home in Nashville of a blood clot in the lungs. She was 55.

**Frank Yankovic**, the Grammy-winning "polka king" whose songs wore out thousands of pairs of dancing shoes over six decades, died October 14 at his home in New Port Richey, a Gulf Coast town north of Tampa, Florida. He was 83.

**Nagaharu Yodogawa**, Japan's most famous movie critic, who interviewed stars ranging from Charlie Chaplin to Steven Seagal, died November 11 of heart failure. He was 89.

**Freddie Young**, the three-time Oscar-winning cinematographer of *Lawrence of Arabia*, *Doctor Zhivago*, and *Ryan's Daughter*, died December 1 in London of natural causes. He was 96.

**Robert Young**, actor, who epitomized the perfect patriarch in the 1950s TV series *Father Knows Best* and was later the wise medico in the long-running *Marcus Welby, M.D.*, died July 21 of respiratory failure at his home in Westlake Village, California. He was 91.

**Henny Youngman**, the undisputed king of the one-liners, whose quip, "Take my wife – please," defined a comedic style, died February 23 in New York. He was 92.

---

*Infamy! Infamy! They've all got it in for me. (Kenneth Williams as Julius Caesar in* Carry on Cleo*)*